RETRIEVAL & RENEWAL
IN CATHOLIC THOUGHT

The middle years of the twentieth century marked a particularly intense time of crisis and change in European society. During this period (1930-1950), a broad intellectual and spiritual movement arose within the European Catholic community, largely in response to the secularism that lay at the core of the crisis. The movement drew inspiration from earlier theologians and philosophers such as Möhler, Newman, Gardeil, Rousselot, and Blondel, as well as from men of letters like Charles Péguy and Paul Claudel.

The group of academic theologians included in the movement extended into Belgium and Germany, in the work of men like Emile Mersch, Dom Odo Casel, Romano Guardini, and Karl Adam. But above all the theological activity during this period centered in France. Led principally by the Jesuits at Fourvière and the Dominicans at Le Saulchoir, the French revival included many of the greatest names in twentieth-century Catholic thought: Henri de Lubac, Jean Daniélou, Yves Congar, Marie-Dominique Chenu, Louis Bouyer, and, in association, Hans Urs von Balthasar.

It is not true — as subsequent folklore has it — that those theologians represented any sort of self-conscious "school": indeed, the differences among them, for example, between Fourvière and Saulchoir, were important. At the same time, most of them were united in the double conviction that theology had to speak to the present situation, and that the condition for doing so faithfully lay in a recovery of the Church's past. In other words, they saw clearly that the first step in what later came to be known as *aggiornamento* had to be *ressourcement* — a rediscovery of the riches of the whole of the Church's two-thousand-year tradition. According to de Lubac, for example, all of his own works as well as the entire *Sources chrétiennes* collection are based on the presupposition that "the renewal of Christian vitality is linked at least partially to a renewed exploration of the periods and of the works where the Christian tradition is expressed with particular intensity."

In sum, for the *ressourcement* theologians theology involved a "return to the sources" of Christian faith, for the purpose of drawing out the meaning and significance of these sources for the critical questions of our time. What these theologians sought was a spiritual and intellectual communion with Christianity in its most vital moments as transmitted to us in its classic texts, a communion that would nourish, invigorate, and rejuvenate twentieth-century Catholicism.

The *ressourcement* movement bore great fruit in the documents of the Second Vatican Council and deeply influenced the work of Pope John Paul II.

The present series is rooted in this renewal of theology. The series thus understands *ressourcement* as revitalization: a return to the sources, for the purpose of developing a theology that will truly meet the challenges of our time. Some of the features of the series, then, are a return to classical (patristic-medieval) sources and a dialogue with contemporary Western culture, particularly in terms of problems associated with the Enlightenment, modernity, and liberalism.

The series publishes out-of-print or as yet untranslated studies by earlier authors associated with the *ressourcement* movement. The series also publishes works by contemporary authors sharing in the aim and spirit of this earlier movement. This will include any works in theology, philosophy, history, literature, and the arts that give renewed expression to Catholic sensibility.

The editor of the Ressourcement series, David L. Schindler, is Gagnon Professor of Fundamental Theology and dean at the John Paul II Institute in Washington, D.C., and editor of the North American edition of *Communio: International Catholic Review*, a federation of journals in thirteen countries founded in Europe in 1972 by Hans Urs von Balthasar, Jean Daniélou, Henri de Lubac, Joseph Ratzinger, and others.

RETRIEVAL & RENEWAL

IN CATHOLIC THOUGHT

volumes published

Mysterium Paschale
Hans Urs von Balthasar

The Heroic Face of Innocence: Three Stories
Georges Bernanos

The Letter on Apologetics **and History and Dogma**
Maurice Blondel

Prayer: The Mission of the Church
Jean Daniélou

On Pilgrimage
Dorothy Day

We, the Ordinary People of the Streets
Madeleine Delbrêl

The Discovery of God
Henri de Lubac

Medieval Exegesis, **volumes 1-3:**
The Four Senses of Scripture
Henri de Lubac

Letters from Lake Como:
Explorations in Technology and the Human Race
Romano Guardini

Divine Likeness:
Toward a Trinitarian Anthropology of the Family
Marc Cardinal Ouellet

The Portal of the Mystery of Hope
Charles Péguy

In the Beginning:
A Catholic Understanding of the Story of Creation and the Fall
Joseph Cardinal Ratzinger

In the Fire of the Burning Bush:
An Initiation to the Spiritual Life
Marko Ivan Rupnik

Love Alone Is Credible:
Hans Urs von Balthasar as Interpreter
of the Catholic Tradition, **volume 1**
David L. Schindler, ed.

Hans Urs von Balthasar: A Theological Style
Angelo Scola

The Nuptial Mystery
Angelo Scola

MEDIEVAL EXEGESIS

VOLUME 3

The Four Senses of Scripture

HENRI DE LUBAC, S.J.

Translated by
E. M. Macierowski

William B. Eerdmans Publishing Company
Grand Rapids, Michigan

Originally published as
Exégèse médiévale, 3: Les quatre sens de l'écriture
© 1961 Éditions Montaigne
English translation © 2009 Wm. B. Eerdmans Publishing Co.
All rights reserved

Published 2009 by
Wm. B. Eerdmans Publishing Co.
2140 Oak Industrial Drive N.E., Grand Rapids, Michigan 49505 /
P.O. Box 163, Cambridge CB3 9PU U.K.

Library of Congress Cataloging-in-Publication Data

Lubac, Henri de, 1896-
[Exégèse médiévale. English]
Medieval Exegesis / Henri de Lubac; translated by E. M. Macierowski.
  p.   cm.
Includes bibliographical references and index.
Contents: v. 3. The four senses of scripture.
ISBN 978-0-8028-4147-6 (pbk.: alk. paper)
1. Bible — Criticism, interpretation, etc. — History — Middle Ages, 600-1500.
I. Title.
BS500.L82513   1998
220.6'09'02 — dc21   97-32802
                                                              CIP

www.eerdmans.com

This volume is respectfully dedicated to the
Most Reverend James P. Keleher
Archbishop Emeritus of Kansas City in Kansas.

Nihil obstat
Imprimatur:
†Joseph F. Naumann
Archbishop of Kansas City in Kansas
January 16, 2007

Contents

Translator's Preface	xi
List of Principal Abbreviations	xii
1. Berno of Reichenau	1
2. Subjectivism and Spiritual Understanding	73
3. A Lineage Stemming from Jerome?	147
4. Hugh of Saint Victor	211
5. The Victorine School	269
6. Joachim of Flora	327
Notes	421
Index of Names	769

Translator's Preface

This third volume of the late Henri Cardinal de Lubac's Medieval Exegesis is dedicated to the Most Reverend James P. Keleher, Archbishop Emeritus of Kansas City in Kansas, who has provided important moral support when it was most needed.

I should like to thank Mr. William B. Eerdmans, Jr. for his patience and prayers when our five adoptive children Jacob, Jeremiah, Janea, David, and Hailey joined Carol and me in the midst of this project. Perhaps readers of this book may continue to pray for our expanded family.

Special thanks are due to Benedictine College for providing a semester's sabbatical leave in the spring of 2006, enabling me to resume focused work on this book, to Dr. Jean Rioux, Chair of the Department of Philosophy, Dr. Richard White, Chair of Theology and Head of the Division of Humanities (who also read all of volume 2 and a portion of volume 3), and Dr. Kimberly Shankman, Academic Dean of Benedictine College, for supporting my application for the sabbatical. Dr. Barbara Baumgartner, Professor Emerita of French, read through a draft of this volume, and my student Mr. Leven Harton provided a typed transcription of the Latin texts in volumes 3 and 4.

Finally, by happy accident, this volume is being completed just in time to contribute to the sesquicentennial celebration of the founding of St. Benedict's Abbey, which, along with Mount St. Scholastica Monastery, is the co-sponsoring institution of Benedictine College.

E. M. MACIEROWSKI
Atchison, KS

List of Principal Abbreviations

1. Journals

AHDLMA	Archives d'histoire doctrinale et littéraire du moyen âge
ASOC	Analecta sacra ordinis cisterciensis
BALC	Bulletin d'ancienne littérature chrétienne
BLE	Bulletin de littérature ecclésiastique
BTAM	Bulletin de théologie ancienne et médiévale
CCM	Cahiers de civilisation médiévale
COCR	Collectanea ordinis cisterciensis reformati
ETL	Ephemerides theologicae lovanienses
HTR	The Harvard Theological Review
JTS	The Journal of Theological Studies
Med. St.	Mediaeval Studies
NRT	Nouvelle revue théologique
RAM	Revue d'ascétique et de mystique
RB	Revue bénédictine
R. bibl.	Revue biblique
RDSR	Revue des sciences religieuses
REL	Revue des études latines
RHE	Revue d'histoire ecclésiastique
RHEF	Revue de l'histoire de l'Église de France
RHLR	Revue d'histoire et de littérature religieuse
RHPR	Revue d'histoire et de philosophie religieuse
R. Mab.	Revue Mabillon
RMAL	Revue du moyen âge latin

List of Principal Abbreviations

RQH	Revue des questions historiques
RSPT	Revue des sciences philosophiques et théologiques
RSR	Recherches de science religieuse
RTAM	Recherches de théologie ancienne et médiévale
S. Er.	Sacris erudiri
Vig. Chr.	Vigiliae christianae
ZFKT	Zeitschrift für katholische Theologie

2. Anthologies, Collections

An. mar.	Germain Morin, OSB, *Anecdota maredsolana*. 3 tomes (5 vols.). Maredsous, 1893-1903.
ASS	*Acta sanctorum* (Bollandistes).
CCL	*Corpus christianorum*, series latina. Turnholti.
DAFC	A. D'Ales, *Dictionnaire apologétique de la foi catholique*. Paris, 1911-1931.
DB	F. Vigouroux, *Dictionnaire de la Bible*. Paris, 1895-1912.
DBS	F. Pirot, A. Robert, H. Cazelle, *Dictionnaire de la Bible, supplément*. Paris, 1928 ff.
DHGE	A. Baudrillart, R. Aubert, E. Van Cauwenbergh, *Dictionnaire d'histoire et de géographie ecclésiastique*. Paris, 1912 ff.
D. Sp.	M. Viler, F. Cavallera, J. De Guibert, Ch. Baumgartner, M. Ophe-Gaillard . . . , *Dictionnaire de spiritualité, ascétique et mystique, doctrine et histoire*. Paris, 1937 ff.
DTC	A. Vacant, E. Mangenot, E. Amann, *Dictionnaire de théologie catholique*. Paris, 1909-1950.
HLF	*Histoire littéraire de la France*, ouvrage commencé par les Bénédictins et continué par les membres de l'Institut. 3 vols. Paris, 1865-1941.
L. de lite	MGH, *Libelli de lite Imperatorum et Pontificum saec. XI et XII*. 3 vols. Hanover, 1891-7.
Mai	Card. Angelo Mai, *Nova Patrum Bibliotheca*. 10 vols. Rome, 1852-1905.
MBVP	Margarin de la Bigne, *Maxima Bibliotheca veterum Patrum et antiquorum scriptorum ecclesiasticorum*. 27 vols. Lyon, 1677 (tome 13: Ambrose Autpert, *In Apoc.*; tome 17: Raoul of Saint Germer, *In Levit.*; tome 21: Potho of Prüm).

LIST OF PRINCIPAL ABBREVIATIONS

M.D.	Martène et Durand, OSB, *Thesaurus novus anecdotorum.* 5 vols. 1717; *Veterum scriptorum . . . amplissima collectio.* 9 vols., 1724-33.
MGH	*Monumenta Germaniae Historica.* Hanover-Leipzig.
M.W.	Misset and Weale, *Thesaurus hymnologicus.* Tome 1, 1888.
Pez	Bernhard Pez, OSB, *Thesaurus anecdotorum novissimus.* 6 tomes (16 vols.). Vienna, 1721-8.
PG	Migne, *Patrologia graeca.* Paris.
Pitra	Card. J. B. Pitra, *Spicilegium solesmense.* 4 vols. Paris, 1852-8.
PL	Migne, *Patrologia latina.* Paris.
SC	*Sources chrétiennes.* Paris, 1942 ff.
Sp. cas.	*Spicilegium casinense.*
St. ans.	*Studia anselmiana.* Rome, 1933 ff.
St. patr.	*Studia patristica.* Ed. Kurt Aland and F. L. Cross: *Papers presented to the Second International Conference: Patristic Studies held at Christ Church.* Oxford 1955. 2 vols. Berlin, 1957.
TU	*Texte und Untersuchungen zur Geschichte des altchristlichen Literatur.* Ed. O. von Gebhart and A. Harnack, *et al.* Leipzig, 1883 ff.

Clement and Origen (Or.) are cited for the most part according to the editions of the Leipzig-Berlin Corpus: *Die griechischen christlichen Schriftsteller der ersten drei Jahrhunderte;* they are indicated only by the page of the volume containing the work cited. The same is true for certain Latin authors cited according to the editions of the Vienna Corpus: *Corpus scriptorum ecclesiasticorum latinorum.*

3. Certain Frequently Cited Works

Aug., *Conf.*	Saint Augustine, *Confessions.* Ed. P. De Labriolle. 2 vols. Coll. des universités de France. Paris, 1925-6.
Bardenhewer	Otto Bardenhewer, *Geschichte des altkirklichen Literatur.* 5 vols. Freiburg-im-Breisgau. Tome 1 and 2. 2nd ed., 1913 and 1914.
Bardy, *Recherches*	Gustave Bardy, *Recherches sur l'histoire du texte et des versions latines du De Principiis d'Origène.* Paris, 1923.

List of Principal Abbreviations

Baron	Roger Baron, *Science et sagesse chez Hugues de Saint-Victor*. Paris, 1955.
S. Bernard th.	*Saint Bernard théologien, actes du congrès de Dijon* (15-19 Sept. 1953). ASOC, Rome, 1953.
Blumenkranz, *Juifs et chrétiens*	Bernhard Blumenkranz, *Juifs et chrétiens dans le monde occidental, 430-1096* (École pratique des hautes études, Études juives, 2, Paris, 1960).
E. de Bruyne	Edgar de Bruyne, *Études d'esthétique médiévale*. 3 vols.
Chenu	M.-D. Chenu, OP, *La théologie au XIIe siècle*. Paris, Études de philosophie médiévales, 1956.
Cillier	Remy Cillier, OSB., *Histoire générale des auteurs sacrés et ecclésiastiques*. 17 vols. Paris, 1865-9.
CM	Henri de Lubac, *Corpus mysticum*. 2nd ed. Paris, 1949.
Courcelle	Pierre Courcelle, *Les lettres grecques en Occident, de Macrobe à Cassiodore*. Paris, 1943.
Crocco	Antonio Crocco, *Gioacchino da Fiore, la più singolare ed affascinante Figura del Medioevo christani* (Napoli, 1960).
Curtius	Ernst-Robert Curtius, *La littérature européenne et le moyen âge latin*, tr. Jean Bréjoux. Paris, 1957.
Delhaye, ET	Philippe Delhaye, *Le microcosmus de Godefroy de Saint-Victor, étude théologique*. Lille, 1951.
Ebert	A. Ebert, *Histoire générale de la littérature du moyen âge en Occident*. Tr. J. Aymeric and J. Condamin. 3 vols. Paris, 1883-9.
Fontaine	Jacques Fontaine, *Isidore de Séville et la culture classique dans l'Espagne Wisigothique*. 2 vols. Paris, 1959.
Gautier	Léon Gautier, *Oeuvres poétiques d'Adam de Saint-Victor*. 3rd ed. 1894.
Gerhoh, *Op. in.*	*Gerhohi praepositi reichersbergensis Opera inedita*. I: Tractatus et libelli, cura et studio PP. Damiani ac Odulphi Van den Eynde et P. Angelini Rijmersdad, OFM. Rome, 1955.
Gerhoh, *In Ps.* (Van den Eynde)	*Gerhohi praepositi reichersbergensis Opera inedita*. II: Expositionis psalmorum pars tertia et pars nona (2 vols.), cura et studio PP. Damiani ac Odulphi Van den Eynde et P. Angelini Rijmaersdael, OFM.

	Spicilegium Pontificii Athenaei Antoniani, 9. Rome, 1956.
Ghellinck, *Mouvement*	Joseph de Ghellinck, *Le mouvement théologique du XIIe siècle*. 2nd ed. Museum lessianum. Bruges-Bruxelles-Paris, 1948.
———, *L'essor*	Id., *L'essor de la littérature latine au XIIe siècle*. 2 vols. Museum lessianum. Bruxelles-Paris, 1946.
———, *Litt. Lat.*	Id., *Littérature latine au moyen âge*. 2 vols. Paris, 1939.
Gorini	S. Gorini, *Défense de l'Église*, 9th ed., 4 vols. (1882).
Gr. D'Elv., Tr.	*Tractatus Origenis de libris SS. Scripturarum*. Ed. Batiffol. Paris, 1900.
HE	Henri de Lubac, *Histoire et Esprit*. Paris, 1950.
Hugo Métel	(Letters of Hugo Métel in) *Sacrae antiquitatis monumenta*. Tome 2 (1731).
Jerome, *Ep.*	(Ep. 1 to 120:) Saint Jérôme, *Lettres*. Ed. J. Labourt. 6 vols. Coll. des universités de France. Paris, 1949-58.
Keble	John Keble, *On the Mysticism attributed to the Early Fathers of the Church*. 2nd ed. Oxford, 1868.
Labriolle	Pierre de Labriolle, *Histoire de la littérature chrétienne*. 3rd ed., revised by G. Bardy. 2 vols. Paris, 1947.
Laistner	M. L. W. Laistner, *Thought and Letters in Western Europe A.D. 500-900*. New ed. London, 1957.
Leclercq, *L'amour des lettres*	Jean Leclercq, OSB., *L'amour des lettres et le désir de Dieu*. Paris, 1957.
———, *Études*	Id., *Études sur saint Bernard et le texte de ses écrits*. ASOC, Rome, 1953.
Lesne	E. Lesne, *Histoire de la propriété ecclésiastique en France*.
Manitius	Max Manitius, *Geschichte der lateinischen Literatur des Mittelalters*. 3 vols. Munich, 1911-31.
Martin-Fliche	*Histoire de l'Église*, publiée sous la direction de V. Martin et A. Fliche. Paris, 1938 sqq.
Al. Neckam	Alexander Neckam, *De naturis rerum libri duo, with the Poem of the same Author, De laudibus divinae sapientiae*. Ed. Thomas Wright . . . . London, 1863.

List of Principal Abbreviations

Or. vis.	*Oracional visgotico,* ed. D. Josáe Vivàes (Monumenta Hispaniae sacra, series liturgica, 1, Barcelona, 1946).
Ozanam	Frédéric Ozanam, *La civilisation au VIe siècle,* 2 vols., in *Œuvres complètes,* 2e éd. (Paris, 1862).
Paré	G. Paré, A. Brunay, P. Tremblay, *La renaissance du XIIe siècle: les écoles et l'enseignement.* Paris-Ottawa, 1933.
Petit, Prémontrés	François Petit, *La spiritualité des Prémontrés . . . aux XIIe et XIIIe siècles.* Paris, 1947.
Pontet	Maurice Pontet, *L'exégèse de saint Augustin prédicateur.* Théologie, 7. Paris, 1946.
Richesses	*Richesses et déficiences des ancients psautiers latins,* par Dom Pierre Salmon, etc. Collectanea biblica latina, XIII. Rome, 1959.
Roger	Maurice Roger, *L'enseignement des Lettres classiques d'Ausone à Alcuin, introduction à l'histoire carolingienne.* Paris, 1905.
Smalley	Beryl Smalley, *The Study of the Bible in the Middle Ages.* 2nd ed. Oxford, 1952.
Spicq, *Esquisse*	C. Spicq, O.P., *Esquisse d'une histoire de l'exégèse latine au moyen âge.* Paris, 1944.
Van den Eynde, *Essai*	Damien Van den Eynde, *Essai sur la succession de la date des écrits de Hugues de Saint-Victor.* Spicilegium Pont. Ath. Ant., 13. Rome, 1960.
V. G.	A. Viñayo-Gonzáles, *San Martín de León y su Apologética antijudía.* Madrid, 1948.
Zumthor	Paul Zumthor, *Histoire de la littérature latine du moyen âge.* Paris, 1957.

CHAPTER ONE

Berno of Reichenau

1. The Indignations of Berno

The pieces of evidence brought up toward the end of the preceding volume have surely not slipped past all historians of hermeneutics and exegesis. The Catholic historians are generally more attentive to them than the rest, and, if they were the only ones at issue, many pages of this work would be pointless. It is true that the undiscerning disrepute that the symbolic functions of thought have finally fallen into has not completely ceased to hide from us "the extent and the quality of the immense field in which, in the twelfth century, symbolism developed as an organic expression of earlier ages." Father Chenu has asserted it again just yesterday. It is equally true that certain "later blemishes," being added to certain original vices and certain ever-present faults, for many good minds compromise the intellectual value and even the "Christian value" of doctrines whose essence is badly disengaged.[1] Nevertheless, for some time, very great progress has been made in trying to understand as well as do justice to the ancient forms of Christian thought and especially to biblical exegesis. Day by day, the historical works of Dom Jean Leclercq, along with divers studies by Dom J. Gribomont, Father Jean Châtillon, J.-P. Bonnes, and many others, the vigorous syntheses by Father Louis Bouyer, the new interpretations of the evolution of medieval thought advanced by Father Chenu himself in writings where an open-minded receptivity often engenders an astonishing clarity of understanding, have happily begun to disturb the slumbers of our modern self-sufficiency. We are already a little bit less cocksure that the intellectual syntheses that have preceded our own could be merely childishness, as some would have us believe, particularly philosophers whose judgment spares none of the authentic forms of our faith. We are beginning to understand better that medieval symbolism is "the evidence and the effect of a sense of the sacred in full flower"[2] and that, in its application to Scripture, it manifests a deep understanding of the Christian mystery in continuity with the great patristic epoch. We are noticing that it is a complex affair and we are no longer tempted to reject it as something wholly irrational. We can from now on hope for this: that after sometimes allowing themselves to be annexed, in their judgments in sacred matter, by a narrowly secularist science, Christian scholars will succeed little by little at enlarging or setting this very science right. They will nevertheless have to resign themselves to the fact that not everything that touches on the history of their faith will ever be entirely grasped by historians whose mind has been shaped by an unbelieving society.

Today, in the history of exegesis as most scholars, even the most penetrating, usually reconstitute it, there is one point regarding which there seems to be at least some exaggerated emphasis. Something like two currents are generally distinguished among the numerous interpreters of the holy Books who lived between the seventh and the thirteenth centuries: the greater of these would display itself in broad daylight and flow in great torrents, whilst the other at first would be merely a thin trickle of water, hidden and almost subterranean. The first would be the river — or perhaps it might better be called the marsh — of common opinion; the second, the harbinger of promise, would just scarcely force its way along its bed in opposition to the spirit of the age.[3] Toward the beginning of the twelfth century, this second current increased in power and amplitude and came to initiate a general change of orientation in exegesis. Accordingly, for the historian it would become a question not only of locating a certain number of isolated writers, distant precursors of the critical and purely literal exegesis of modern times, but also of establishing in a precise manner a transvaluation that came about in the relations between *historia* and *allegoria*. This reversal of value would take place particularly with Hugh of Saint Victor and in his school.

In 1922, and then in 1935, Father Mandonnet observed the birth, starting in the eleventh century with Berengar of Tours, and then the strengthening, during the first decades of the following century with Peter Abelard, of an intellectual movement that tended to replace the then-dominant "symbolic theology" with a "theological science" at last worthy of the name. This "new movement" appeared to him a healthy reaction against "the unrestrained allegorism" in the exegesis of the age. Saint Anselm, Abelard, and Hugh of Saint Victor have, he said, made their protest be heard: thus were opened the paths to the new theology as well as to the new exegesis which would soon impose themselves in a single decisive step.[4] Taken in its generality, this historical epitome contains much truth. But instead of getting the additions and corrections that would have fine-tuned it, it seems itself to have been imposed to excess. The disputable parallelism between the developments of rational dialectic and the transformations of hermeneutics has been turned into a system. Some have tried to highlight the supposedly preponderant role of Hugh of Saint Victor, but without defining it exactly enough. A little after Father Mandonnet, Fathers Paré, Brunet, and Tremblay called attention to a detail which, though not entirely novel, at least deserves to be emphasized owing to its new importance: the fact that the founder of the Victorine school wanted us to begin by studying Scripture according to its letter.[5] Soon Father Joseph de Ghellinck also wrote, as if there were a question of some paradoxical contrast, that Hugh "bases his dogmatic synthesis upon the historical order of biblical history and the history of the world in depicting his strong tendencies toward symbolism."[6] For Father Hughes Vincent, who, to be sure, is speaking chiefly as a reporter, "it is Hugh of Saint Victor who will then more exactly define the attitude of the exegete toward Scripture: the literal sense lies at the base and is neatly distinguished from the spiritual, allegorical, or tropological sense."[7] At the conclusion of more detailed analyses, Father C. Spicq presents an enlarged picture of the evolution that has been accomplished. He judges that Hugh, in fact "much more precise" than the majority, "had made great progress toward this theory of the scriptural senses, which had been stagnant from the time of Rabanus Maurus," and he attributes this progress, of which the literal sense is the great beneficiary, to the fact that the Victorine master could deliberately commit himself no longer to the school of Saint Augustine or of Saint Gregory, as did almost all his predecessors, but rather to that of Saint Jerome. Such progress, he adds, was moreover being prepared for a long time. Little by little, since around the eighth century, the authority of Saint Jerome, patron of literal exegesis — Father Spicq seems to understand 'literalist' — had gained ground while that of Saint Gregory correspondingly fell back. One could follow in the trail of this line stemming from Jerome, a trail blazed with the names of Paschasius Radbertus, Christian of Stavelot, Berno of Reichenau, Bruno of Segni, Rupert of Deutz, making in-roads into the trend then most in favor. Finally, a bit before the middle of the twelfth century, "notably in the school of Saint-Victor," there would come to appear in broad daylight "that independence as regards the traditional method and that spirit of exegesis stemming from Jerome" which were ultimately to triumph in the following century with Saint Thomas Aquinas.[8] Such, too, in its large outlines, is the thesis of Miss Beryl Smalley, whose work is, in other respects, so valuable. In her less measured boldness, Miss Smalley does not even see the progress of "the study of Scripture" or of "biblical science" except in the abandonment of theological commentary and in the pure and simple rejection of the patristic distinction between the literal sense and the spiritual sense in favor of the literal sense alone.[9]

These judgments have made a sometimes excessive impression, it seems, even upon excellent specialists: Father R. E. Brown,[10] for example; so too, quite recently, Father Roger Baron.[11] Further, here as elsewhere, it comes about that the masters serve as a warning, despite themselves, to disciples less respectful of the complexity of things. In that way one ends up with astonishing schemes in works whose particular erudition is not in dispute. For example, up to the twelfth century, we are told, "allegory" would be attached "only to the words of the New Testament and to the properties of things; Hugh of Saint Victor was the first to advocate an allegory based upon the historical realities of the Old Testament as figures of those of the New"; and again: "The method inaugurated at Saint-Victor is characterized by solidly establishing the literal or historical sense before rising to the spiritual sense, and thus by a break with the purely spiritual explication of the ancient monastic commentaries."[12] Or else one alleges that the exegesis of the twelfth century differs *toto caelo* from that of the previous centuries, that it finally becomes purely literal in certain works of the Victorines Hugh and Richard, and, in the course of this century of transition, one even imagines a struggle between two "doctrines of interpretation," the one characterized by the admission of three senses in all, the other by the admission of four, until the second finally carried it off to rule alone.[13] We now find ourselves in a novel. Or again, after having spoken of a "degradation" and a "rottenness" of the symbolic exegesis in the times that precede Hugh of Saint Victor's entry on the scene, one shows him coming at last to warn the theologian "that he can propose an authentic explication of the divine mysteries only by respecting the historical sense of revelation."[14] We are on the way to pamphleteering, to boot.

A very informed historian of ideas, habituated to weighing the texts carefully, Father M.-D. Chenu, who has lately produced a multitude of extremely suggestive works on the change of attitudes and methods during the twelfth century, having collected what is essential in his magisterial work on *Theology in the Twelfth Century*, shows himself to be infinitely more circumspect. Nevertheless, he does not content himself with vigorously highlighting "the historicist reaction of Hugh of Saint-Victor against the premature allegorization of the scriptural texts," as well as "his major principle of founding historically all reflection on the biblical economy."[15] He also believes that he can discern in this reaction a completely new orientation impressed upon exegesis at its encounter with the till-then predominant authority, and, in the affirmation of this principle, a "requête," an "appeal" that might be appropriate to the "théologiens victorins." These latter, not without struggles, would have ended by carrying it off. We shall have to accept the conclusions of Father Chenu, as well as those of some of his predecessors, at least in part. But before following the fortunes of the fourfold sense through the scholastic period and up to modernity, we must first of all examine one after the other, in their totality, the two conjoined theses relating to the lineage stemming from Jerome and to the innovations of the school of Saint Victor. Such will be almost the only object of the first volume of this second part (Chapters One to Five). In a final chapter (Six), we shall ask ourselves whether the work of Joachim of Flora, at the very end of the twelfth century, represents the supreme (and unfortunate) effort of the traditional allegorism, or if it might not rather have traced out some new and aberrant path.

Among the isolated precursors of the Victorine movement such as he believes he can reconstruct it, Father Spicq attaches major importance to the one who would perhaps be the most isolated of all: Berno, monk of Prüm, subsequently twenty-ninth abbot of Reichenau from 1008 to 1048, at the time of the apogee of this famous abbey which Walafrid Strabo had long ago celebrated.[16] Hence we shall begin with him.

This Berno, who was in regular contact with the chief theologians of his age and who played an important role at the Council of Constance of 1043, has nevertheless not been judged worthy of the least notice in the *Dictionnaire de théologie catholique*, nor again in the *Dictionnaire de la Bible* or its *Supplément*. This is a grave and unpardonable omission, if Father Spicq is right. For, he tells us, Berno, addressing himself to the exegete in one of his opuscula, "formulates the prohibition (surprising for the epoch) against substituting one's own personal sentiment for the meaning of the sacred text." Is that not to manifest in almost revolutionary fashion "a more genuine concern with the literal sense" against then almost unanimous tendencies?[17] "One will be unusually surprised," writes

Berno's historian once again, "to hear, in the eleventh century, Berno of Reichenau expressing this principle, which, unfortunately, he did not have occasion to put into practice: '*O prudent reader, always beware of a superstitious understanding, so that you do not adjust the Scriptures to your own sense; join your sense to the Scriptures.*'"[18]

Ought not the brief writing in which this golden maxim is found serve to inaugurate the critical method in exegesis — or at least to reconnect the chain after the barbarian ages that had interrupted it? "No contemporary would have dreamed of prohibiting a reader to substitute his own personal sentiment for the sense of the sacred text." Father Spicq insists on it. Subsequently, ought we not then to regard this miraculous *De varia psalmorum atque cantuum modulatione* as "the unique work of criticism, properly speaking, of the Middle Ages"?[19]

Let us own up right away: I do not believe it. Neither in this opusculum in general nor in the two lines that have been cited from it do we discern such great originality. We scarcely find any "critique" in it, any more than we see all the other men of that time so smitten with their own "personal sentiment." Berno is evidently putting his reader on guard against a certain sort of subjectivism in the manner of treating the sacred text. But what, according to him, does this subjectivism consist in? Does it consist in the search for, or at least in an excessive practice of, the allegoric sense? To understand him in this way, perhaps it is necessary to begin by committing oneself to the belief that all "allegory" is, to a greater or lesser degree, subjective fantasy. Now whatever be the factual basis for such a belief, it would seem in fact quite "astonishing" in a Benedictine abbot of the eleventh century. So if one admits provisionally with Father Spicq that Berno did not have occasion to put his principle into practice and thereby to clarify for us its true significance, one might legitimately doubt whether this significance is indeed the one that has been proposed to us. But let us examine things a bit more closely.

First of all it is necessary to make it clear that this *De varia . . . modulatione* is not in fact one treatise, but a mere collection, "whose unique title ill befits its content." Someone acting under conditions that remain unknown has combined several of Berno's little disquisitions on neighboring but different topics. To make it into something that looks like one work, one had to make certain adjustments in the conclusions and the *incipits* of each disquisition. This is what appears from an unfortunately incomplete letter of Berno himself that was published by Dom P. Blanchard in 1912.[20] The abbot of Reichenau is sending, as was his custom, his latest productions to his friend the emperor Henry III.[21] He tells him:

> Here are a few series of accounts, which though they smack but little of the salt of wisdom, nevertheless I have put down, having been overcome by love of those who were anxious to ask about this matter, namely, on the dissonant interpretation of the Roman Psalter and the Gallican Psalter that we use; on some utterances of Isaiah the prophet; on verses less befitting their responses; on antiphons or responsories not regularly or fittingly corresponding to each other; on the alleluia intermission and the words of its chants. . . .[22]

Here we have five quite distinct titles. The first corresponds to Chapters I to V of the *De varia modulatione* as we actually have it. The second corresponds to Chapter VI; the third, to Chapters XII and XIII; the fourth, to Chapters IX and X; and finally, the fifth, to Chapter XI. There remain then Chapters VII and VIII, to which, at least at first sight, none of the five titles enumerated by Berno in his letter to Henry III would seem to belong. Perhaps they might complete the first of the five treatments. Perhaps, too, there might be a sixth little treatise that would be a little earlier or a little later than the five others. These two chapters might even have originally been independent of each other. For Chapter VII protests against the use of non-scriptural pieces in the liturgy or the use of the words of the Bible in a sense alien to them, whereas Chapter VIII is concerned with some corrections that some people wanted to bring to the sacred text under the pretext of "grammar." The long initial sentence of this Chapter VIII — the one that chiefly held our attention just now — is a transitional sentence, which might therefore not even be, as such, by Berno himself.[23] In any case it seems to us to sum up clearly, on the one hand, the second of the two complaints laid out in Chapter VII, and on the other hand, the new complaint which now becomes the object of all of Chapter VIII. As we shall see, then, he is speaking of two distinct things, and it is in this sense fitting to take the conjunctive particle 'et' which we are about to emphasize. Nevertheless what restores the unity is the fact that, in the judgment of our abbot, the same men become guilty of the two different abuses that he denounces, and in both cases it is the same motive that drives them, namely, a desire for worldly wisdom:

> And strangely, when certain men of this world want to seem and to be wise, they try to bend the words of sacred Scripture to their own sense, *and (et)* they chant the words that . . . the Wisdom of God itself brought forth through itself or that the Holy Spirit . . . foretold, in an-

other manner — by changing them so as to follow Donatus and Priscian.[24]

Let us now go back to the sentence that Father Spicq focuses on. It is found in the last paragraph of this same Chapter VIII. We note immediately that Berno had no desire to innovate or to express any bold opinion. Quite the contrary. Under the form of urgent advice, he recalls a principle that he does not at all regard as personal, a principle not of a new science, but rather of an ancient wisdom. For here is how he introduces it: "Attendentes quod quidam sapiens admonet dicens: Prudens lector, semper cave, etc." ["Paying close attention to what a certain wise man *(quidam sapiens)* reminds us of, saying 'O prudent reader, always beware, etc.'"]. We shall look further on to find out what sort of person this "quidam sapiens" might be. In our opinion, there is nothing in the text, as it is presented, to show or even to insinuate that Berno might want to react against the insufficiently critical hermeneutics of his age or against the excessively allegorical exegesis inherited from the Bedes, the Rabanus Mauruses, and their numerous emulators. The particular object of the chapter as well as the general context of the opusculum, if we take it as a whole, rules out such a hypothesis from the start. For the author himself explains to us the precise intention that governs the citation of the "quidam sapiens" as clearly as one could hope for. Under the hypothesis that he may not be telling us everything that he means in this sentence, at any event he most clearly designates the sort of adversaries he has in mind all through this chapter. These adversaries are not just any commentators, any more than in the neighboring chapters. Here they are people who permit themselves, he says, to modify the text of Scripture, not for reasons of science or doctrine, but for simple reasons of "grammar" or elegance. These are people who, having the weakness of wanting to appear wise in the eyes of the world, consequently submit to the school of Donatus and Priscian even in translating the Bible.

The authority that these two illustrious grammarians enjoyed is well known: the one, a pagan, a professor at Rome in the fourth century, and the other, a Christian, a professor of Latin at Byzantium toward the fifth-sixth centuries; the first more elementary and more practical, suitable for beginners,[25] the second, more erudite, fuller, a sort of Justinian of the grammatical code.[26] Their work was imposed upon everyone. Saint Jerome was proud of himself as a youth for having taken Donatus's courses.[27] Cassiodorus, who saw grammar as the "beautifier of the human race," had recommended these two authorities, and himself had written two commentaries on Donatus.[28] The *Ars major* [of Donatus] "forms the foundation of the theoretical grammar of Isidore."[29] Both Donatus and Priscian were held in honor in the Celtic churches. Bede had composed an elementary grammar following step by step that of the old Roman master.[30] In the same way Saint Julian of Toledo's *Ars grammatica* was entirely borrowed from Donatus and his disciples, notably from the commentary of Sergius.[31] Ambrose Autpert had cited Donatus and Priscian in the list of the principal sages according to whom the majority of the Fathers of the Church were formed prior to undertaking the explication of the Scriptures, while adding that he himself owed nothing of his own first formation to them: "Donatus brought me nothing; Priscian, nothing," any more than he did to Plato, Cicero, or Virgil. He was aware of the exceptional character of his own case, and he avowed it out of modesty.[32]

The Carolingian renaissance, which was a renaissance of "grammarians," i.e., of literary men and scholars, had increased the prestige of these two masters even more. The paganism of the one, the supposed apostasy of the other, did not shake this prestige. Sedulius Scotus had commented on both of them, associating Eutyches with them. Alcuin had particularly praised Priscian, the "truest teacher of the grammatical art,"[33] and the work of the one whom one could, along with Salomon of Constance, call "our Priscian,"[34] would remain justly famous; this work was even more esteemed than that of his rival, because it was more learned, perhaps also because it belonged to a more decadent period, an age more hospitable to the novelties of the "moderns,"[35] and finally because it was full of classical citations.[36] Meanwhile, Paul the Deacon had written an *Ars Donati*. Smaragdus, the learned abbot of Saint Mihiel, had composed a gloss on Donatus's treatise *De octo partibus orationis*, a long very widely known gloss which was "full of ingenious and sensitive remarks wherein a deep knowledge of the Latin language could be seen,"[37] and in which, following a practice inaugurated by Bede, all the rules were illustrated by examples taken from Scripture and the Fathers. Theodulf of Orléans used to congratulate himself in his verses for having extensively practiced Donatus.[38] Rabanus Maurus had made an *Excerptio de Arte grammatica Prisciani*.[39] His disciple Lupus of Ferrieres did not cease to refer to the two "distinguished" grammarians. A bit later, Remigius of Auxerre (†908) had even given a *Commentum* on the two *Artes* of Donatus.[40] Before teaching others to cross the whirlpools of this world, as an expert pilot, Odo of Cluny, who was a student of Remigius, had "traversed the immense sea of Priscian as a swimmer."[41] Guitmond of Aversa, a contemporary of Berno, referred to Priscian as "that most expert grammarian."[42] Soon

Thierry of Chartres would make a big place in his plan of studies, the famous *Heptateuchon,* for our two grammarians: of Donatus he will say: "he taught with marvelous brevity, compendious technique, an extremely clever arrangement of teaching."[43] To signify that the cycle of studies opens with grammar, Godfrey of Saint Victor will write:

> Donatus presides over the first bank of the river . . .
> Priscian sits on its opposite side.[44]

For Alan of Lille, Donatus will be not so much a "grammarian" as "grammar itself," and the *Anticlaudianus* will associate with him "our apostate," under which label we recognize Priscian.[45] Peter Helias's commentary on Priscian, ca. 1140, will prove an enduring achievement, and the Byzantine master will inspire the grammatical section of the *Doctrinale* of Alexander of Villedieu (1199). Let us add that for a long time the job of grammarian did not belong only to professional literati. Thus, the great apostle Saint Boniface himself, drawing upon the same sources (Donatus, Chaminius, and Diomedes), composed an *Ars grammatica;* he considered this sort of activity an essential part of his missionary apostolate and he loved to give himself the title "grammaticus germanicus."

Thus Priscian and Donatus reigned for a long time and were to reign still longer over the scholarship of the Middle Ages.[46] Their authority extended not only over grammar in the strict sense of the word, but also over rhetoric, i.e., at least nominally, even over dialectic, for, following the teaching of Isidore of Seville, all the arts depended upon the first: "the arts are the hand-maidens of grammar."[47] They were not without a role to play even in theology — a more contested role, whose limits we shall soon discuss — as can be seen in a reproach that Hincmar of Reims once threw in the face of the unfortunate Godescalc regarding the Trinity: "You have forgotten your Donatus!"[48] Indeed it was "the keenest reproach that was possible"[49] in that age of extraordinary grammatical enthusiasm, whereas the praise of the greats of the world and of the Church ritually involved titles like "grammaticae doctor" or "artis grammaticae summus sophista."[50] In short, the art of Priscian and Donatus was judged indispensable by everyone and no one could risk interpreting holy Scripture without being well versed in it. Donatus and Priscian occupied the lower floors of the palace of knowledge, dominated by the turret of "theology."[51]

Now the rules of language signified by these two prestigious names had awakened here or there a certain number of scruples of divers nature and quality touching the Church. Here we have to consider first the most superficial case of it. On comparing their beautiful classical Latin to the humble Latin of the Church, some clerics, benighted a bit in their fastidiousness, felt themselves embarrassed or ill at ease. They were bothered by a slight "inferiority complex," analogous to the more serious one experienced long ago by the Jeromes and the Augustines on their first contact with the Bible. Perhaps in some cases — literary history offers other examples[52] — they were simply looking for a bit more euphony for the singing of their office. In short, they had attempted to "correct some things in the usage" of the Church, wishing to improve the Latin of their liturgical books. The place where these temerarious souls lived was doubtless near enough to Reichenau for Berno to be able to dread a contagion. Thus we see him rise up against them with the cry "sacrilege."

So what sort of effronteries were they involved in? The abbot of Reichenau drew up a list of examples that leave no room for any serious ambiguity regarding the object of the conflict. In the text of the Gospel, these unfaithful clerics change "alio" into "alii," "defraudavi" into "defrudavi," "exiebat" into "exibat." In the same way, at the offertory of the Mass for the dead, they chant "de profundo lacu" though the biblical usage requires "laci." Taking up against them an ironic witticism employed long ago by Saint Ambrose against the Peripatetics,[53] then redelivered by Saint Jerome to Saint Hilary[54] — a witticism which had since then become proverbial[55] — Berno mocks their pretentiousness: "they sing wearing a mental buskin."[56] Moreover, he is indignant; he protests vehemently. What a hare-brained effort, blindly to follow profane rules when it is a question of divine truth! There are, then, Christians who dare to subject the text of their Scripture to a treatment that the admirers of Terence, Virgil or Cicero do not permit anyone to inflict upon the text of their authors! Should we let ourselves treat the Word of God with such little respect? Shall we be more attentive to Priscian than to the truth, which is God himself? Rather than bow to any grammarian who wants to make us write "lacus," ought we not instead to heed Isaiah who twice says "laci" — the self-same Isaiah whose lips had been purified by the heavenly fire?[57]

It is at that point that Berno adds, so as to introduce the proposal of the "sage" quoted above: "We ought therefore firmly to hold to the sequence of sacred Scripture and to observe its tenor in all things inviolably, attending carefully to what a certain wise man (*quidam sapiens*) reminds us of." And again, immediately after the citation that we are already familiar with:

> Therefore it is to be resolved that we should unchangingly keep, hold, guard . . . the sacred words of the gospels, the oracles of the patriarchs and prophets, the writings of the apostles, with complete fidelity and fitting devotion, just as they are found in the authentic books.[58]

As we see, it is always a question of *words,* not of their explanation; and it is a question of maintaining, not of correcting. As to the "authentic" books, they are quite simply the approved or official books, those that are, as a consequence, in use and have authority. Such at that time was the usual meaning of the epithet "authenticus," which was almost equivalent to "canonicus," and which is found in such expressions as "modus authenticus," designating a proof by authority, i.e., the "authentici doctores."[59] Then, to end with, after a citation from the Apocalypse which there will be occasion to examine in the following chapter, Berno returns to his unworthy grammarians in one final sentence:

> Therefore, if anyone should want to sharpen his wits through the rule of the grammatical art, let him practice in the schools; let him use Donatus and Priscian as his teachers, if he pleases, so long as he does not refuse to preserve due honor for the words, the integrity of the true interpretation being kept. But enough of this.[60]

There is in fact nothing like a principle of hermeneutics at stake here. Is there anything like criticism? Not up to this point, it seems. If Berno is so strongly opposed to taking the slightest liberty with the text of Scripture, it is not for any scientific motive; placing ourselves in his perspective, we can say it was motivated by faith. Again, it is not a question of the text, properly speaking, nor of a version universally accepted, but of the version in use at Reichenau. In his "scrupulous" respect, he considers that version as participating in the inspiration of the original text, or at least as so perfectly faithful that it is impossible to change anything in it without raising one's hand against that sacred original: "the oracles of the heavenly words ought to remain steadfast in their own rule."[61] It is doubtless this that, in a daring piece of reasoning, permits him to invoke the divine authority in questions where the Latin language alone would seem to be at issue. Those whom he blames do not sin in his eyes owing to any human ignorance or lack of critical spirit: they sin by lack of respect for the sacred, by lack of the spirit of faith. They touch the untouchable. Those people, says he, want to pass for sages in the eyes of the world and in their own. He treats them as severely and according to the same criteria as those who compose liturgical chants and whose twofold temerity he has just condemned in the preceding chapter, drawing support from a decision of an African council.[62] Against both groups he has no recourse to any scientific principle or human authority: what he puts forward is nothing less than the "rule of faith." It is the authority of Scripture itself.[63] If we take the text of these two chapters as it presents itself, it even seems that the memory of those who borrow expressions from Scripture so as to give them a sense which is not proper to it and so as to fabricate their chant from such phrases had in part inspired Berno to choose his citation from the "sage" or perhaps to accommodate what he did with it. For him, it is almost one and the same "sacrilege" to dare to praise God with entirely human words, or to use the sacred text offhandedly, or finally, to alter the least syllable of it under any pretext whatsoever. He manifestly intends to assimilate these last two cases to each other. And this is how the two words "sensus" and "verba" seem to become confused[64] under his pen in a manner that can seem surprising. The principal object throughout this eighth chapter of the opusculum nonetheless remains just this correction of syllables.

2. Berno and Exegesis

Nothing, to be sure, was less unheard of in this first part of the eleventh century than the theme of the "grammarians." A bit further on we shall gather abundant evidence about them. Berno takes it up in a very particular context, and for a rather flimsy quarrel, but he does oppose the authority of Scripture to that of Donatus in the most classic manner. Our polemicist consigns the latter to the schools: let it rule there as much as he likes, but let it not encroach upon the former. It ought rather to bow before her, since "all worldly philosophy and all secular science have taken their origin from the authority of holy Scripture."[65] In addition, this is an argument which puffs up the debate a little but is still a commonplace characteristic of a common enough habit of thought,[66] and does not call for ranking its author among "advanced" thinkers. In all this, Berno shows well enough that he belongs to his age. Let us not transform him into a distant precursor of modern times. Let us not attribute to him an exceptional turn of mind. If "textual criticism" truly did make its "appearance" with him — or its reappearance — it would have been quite "modest" indeed.[67] By the passionate interest that he brings to such a dispute as well as by the manner in which he comports himself in it, he would rather appear as a belated heir of that "renaissance" or of that attempt at restoration of the Carolingian era — so careful about textual fidelity in the wake of men like Cassiodorus, Isidore, and Bede, so attached to the "venerable senses of the Fathers"[68] and at the same time so fond of problems of words and grammatical debates;[69] where one was everywhere talking about "the order and rule of the art of grammar,"[70] where writings dealing with the highest subjects of theology or morals were interlarded with reflections on verbal or syntactic curiosities,[71] where men of action were often themselves determined grammarians, where one of the greatest praises that one could make of the great emperor consisted in saying:

"There stands a shining teacher of the grammatical art."[72]

Let us add that the Saints' Lives that Berno has left us show him to be rather less critical in hagiography than many of his contemporaries. He is neither more nor less credulous than the average amongst them.[73] He is doubtless neither more nor less so than the good Saint Gregory, whom he loves to cite and whose marvelous stories from the Dialogues he, like everyone at that time, savors.[74]

We find it hard to see in this little exercise — we might rather call it a diatribe — that constitutes Chapter VIII of the *De varia modulatione*, any concern of an exegetical order, despite the repeated use of the word "sensus," or indeed any critical, textual, or historical rigor.

Three things might cause such an illusion. We have already drawn attention to the first: that allusion to the complaints of Chapter VII, coming to color the new reproach. Berno denies "personal sentiment" the right to appear in the liturgy by an arbitrary borrowing of the words of Scripture: nothing could be truer; but such an "abuse," which he was not the first to denounce, had nothing to do with the traditional exegesis, that is to say, with the allegorical explication of the Scriptures; if this censor of ours denounces the abuses he speaks of as sacrilege, he would surely have denounced such assimilation as blasphemous. In the second place, one can be tempted to assign excessive importance to statements that, if we take them literally, manifestly surpass the actual — and scant — merits of the debate. Berno effects this transformation by the unique way in which he manages to transpose the themes of the doctrinal struggle with a view to magnifying the difference that, in other circumstances, would not have taken on such proportions. We shall discuss this in the following chapter.

Finally, perhaps there is, right at the end of his Chapter VIII, an ambiguous word: the expression "salva verae *interpretationis* integritate" ["the integrity of the true *interpretation* being kept." Cf. n. 60, above.] On a quick reading, one might believe that he spoke there about the interpretation of Scripture, in the sense of explication or commentary. Hence it would involve exegesis. But the context, as has just been specified, as well as Berno's own usage, are both opposed to adopting such a sense — which is, besides, neither the proper sense nor the then usual sense of *interpretatio*. Berno is simply repeating at the end of his chapter what he has not ceased saying from one end to the other: it is necessary to respect the integrity of the text, such as the tradition of the Church has handed down to us in its authorized version, without changing a jot in it.

To comment on a text, to clarify its sense through one's own explications, is to expound it, to explicate it, to explain it: "exponere, explicare, explanare." A commentary is an "expositio," an "explicatio," an "explanatio." A commentator is — and this is the usual word — an "expositor." Let's call up a few examples.

Saint Jerome designates the books of his commentaries as "libros explanationis,"[75] and he observes that "by many the work of the commentaries is denominated 'explanation.'"[76] Speaking of those, whether speakers or writers, who have commented on the Bible, Saint Gregory used to say: "Sacred Scripture is being explained to us by the mouths of mortals in the *expositions*";[77] he called his own commentary on the Book of Job "nostra expositio,"[78] and Saint Paterius said of Saint Gregory himself: "He was compelled by the need to explain things to expound the whole sequence of the Old and New Testament," or again: "and he strove to discuss that testimony by the additional explanation of an exposition."[79] This was the language of Origen, of Rufinus,[80] and of Cassiodorus.[81] It was also that of Isidore,[82] of Bede,[83] and others. It will be maintained as such after Berno's time, for example, in Saint Bruno, Saint Bernard,[84] Hugh of Saint Victor,[85] and Aelred of Rievaulx.[86] Godfrey of Saint Victor will make mention of certain "ancient expositors of sacred Scripture."[87] "Each of the Fathers, about to expound a book," John of Salisbury will write.[88] They readily spoke of the "expositions of the orthodox Fathers."[89] They sometimes even spoke, in the neuter, of an "expositum,"[90] or a "commentum": these are the two names that Paschasius Radbertus gives to the commentary he had undertaken on Saint Matthew.[91] Or again, one commentary on the Psalms that stems from an anonymous author of the twelfth century contains three parts for each Psalm, borrowed respectively from Cassiodorus, from Bede, and from Manegold: a short "argumentum" is followed by a longer "explanatio," which itself in turn is developed into a "commentarium."[92] When one explained Scripture to the people under the form of "tractatus" or homilies,[93] the commentator received the name "tractator": like Saint Augustine in his sermons on Saint John's Gospel, or his sermons on the Psalms, which the manuscripts designate by various names: "tractatus," or "expositiones," or "commenta," or "explanationes";[94] or again, according to the monk of Sankt Gall, like Gregory and Bede.[95] "Origen, the most expert treater of sacred Scriptures," said Sulpicius Severus;[96] "an explainer and treater of the prophecies," writes Aimo;[97] "Scripturarum tractatores," Rupert[98] will say; "sacrarum litterarum tractatores," Herbert of Bosham[99] will say, and others as well. "Catholici tractatores" is practically synonymous with "catholici doctores." The term "enarratio," a bit rarer, deriving from classical antiquity, also designated the explication of a text, along with its various phases.[100]

On the other hand, in the vast majority of cases, an "interpretatio" is a "translatio," i.e., a translation or version. According to the Vulgate, Saint Paul had written to the Corinthians: "Let him who speaks in a tongue pray that he may interpret."[101] Saint Hilary had spoken of the "Latin interpretation" of the Bible.[102] Saint Jerome had given his principles of translation in a little work entitled *De optimo genere interpretandi*;[103] he had noted that certain biblical words, such as *alleluia* and *amen* are simply transliterated from the Hebrew "without translation";[104] on the difficulty of translating from Greek into Latin, he had said in his preface to Eusebius's *Chronicle* "that if anyone does not think that the style of language is changed in translation (*interpretatione*), let him render Homer word for word into Latin";[105] on a passage from Isaiah, he had nicely distinguished the two phases of translation and explication, saying: "Let us first talk about the translation (de interpretatione), and afterwards we shall discuss what has been written (quae scripta sunt)."[106] Aquila, Symmachus, Theodotion for him were the "interpreters" of the Bible.[107] Having translated a *Paschal Epistle* of Theophilus of Antioch, he presented it in these terms: "in which I declare that I have labored to match the elegance of its words with the beauty of the translation (*interpretationis*)."[108] Rufinus kept the same language: when in a preface he was announcing that he was going to "interpret" the *Peri Archôn,* this was not a way of implying that his translation would be unfaithful; he was vouching for the fact that he could not compete with Jerome, who, even in translating the work of another, used a style so personal, "that he seemed to be the father rather than the translator *(interpres)* of the word."[109] In the *De doctrina christiana,* that charter of biblical studies, Saint Augustine had admired how "the divine Scripture ... was so well able to be disseminated throughout the world through the various languages of the translators," and he had indicated the translation that he preferred in these terms: "Among the translations, however, the *Itala* is preferred over the rest, for it sticks closer to the words while keeping the sense clear";[110] in the *Contra Faustum,* regarding passages that seem to be unintelligible, he had laid down this rule: "It is not permissible to say 'the author of this book did not hold to the truth'; but rather: 'either the manuscript is faulty, or the translator (interpres) went astray, or you yourself do not understand'";[111] he had written to Jerome on learning that he was setting about to translate the Bible into Latin according to the Hebrew: "I should much rather want you to translate (interpretari) for us the canonical Greek Scriptures";[112] as regards certain Psalms, he had noted the "diversitas interpretum" ["variety of translators"] from one manuscript to the other, coming from what each of the "latini interpretes" had rendered the same Greek word in his own fashion; the "interpretes," again he used to say, have followed rather the sense than the words of the original, etc.[113]

The first translators of the Bible into Greek were everywhere called "the Seventy translators" (interpretes): for example, by Jerome,[114] Augustine, Gregory, and likewise through the ages. "According to the translation of the Seventy interpreters," wrote Claude of Turin, for example.[115] "According to those ancient translators (interpretes), it is read in Job," William of Saint Thierry will write once again.[116] Saint Gregory the Great more than once compares the "translation of the Seventy translators" to the other "translationes";[117] he has in addition a few, like Origen and Jerome, his "interpreter," whom he consults not only on the sense but also on the exact tenor of the Hebrew text.[118] The same terminology is found in Eusebius of Emessa, where it is a question of an "expounded translation (interpretatio)";[119] in Isidore of Seville,[120] Ambrose Autpert,[121] and the others. When he speaks of Saint Jerome the translator of the Bible, Rabanus Maurus calls him "Jerome the translator (interpretes) of the divine Law"[122] — we have here a sort of stereotyped expression — though when he wants to designate his commentaries he writes: "in explanatione, in expositione."[123] "The noteworthy translator (interpres)," says another;[124] another says: "veridicus interpres";[125] still another: "fidelis interpres."[126] Hincmar of Reims speaks of "the men who translate from the Greek tongue" and of the effort that consists in "translating (interpretari) from Greek into Latin."[127] Paulus Alvarus of Cordova, who in more than one respect anticipates Berno and like him refuses to allow "the art of Donatus" to rule over Scripture, wants "to compare the editions of the individual translators."[128] Uttering in advance a thought analogous to that of Berno, Rabanus Maurus opposes a person who respects the biblical text to one who does not care about it in these terms: "The former is the devout hearer of the Word of God; the latter, a malicious interpreter of the Scriptures";[129] and in his *De laudibus sanctae crucis*, at the moment of translating his own verses into prose, he makes this remark: "For in this work I am in a way a translator (interpres), not of another language but of another manner of speaking, so that I may explain the truth of the self-same sense."[130] Just before this he cites these verses of Horace:

Nor will you, my faithful translator, care
to render anything word for word.[131]

"We think that . . . Jerome is the translator (interpres) of this word," says Paschasius Radbertus of the Latin translation of the word "Emmanuel."[132] "Whether translators (interpretes) or commentators (expositores) of the divine pronouncements," writes Agobard of Lyon.[133] "I believe that our rendering (interpretatio) is the true one," says Angelome of Luxeuil of a disputed translation.[134] Anastasius the Librarian writes in a letter to John VIII: "What is called 'hypostasis' in Greek some have rendered (interpretati sunt) 'person', others 'subsistence'";[135] elsewhere he passes in review the successive "interpretations" of the Bible in the Latin language.[136] "Both the Greek and the Latin translator (interpres)," Werner of Saint Blaise will write.[137] When Burgundio of Pisa will undertake to translate *de verbo ad verbum* Chrysostom's commentary on the Gospel of Saint John, he will justify this method, so different from the one that Saint Jerome had advocated, by saying: "The old translators (interpreters) both among the Greeks as well as the Latins are reported to have continually done the same thing."[138] For John of Cornwall, a principle of translation bears the name a "law of interpretation."[139] The distinction between the two expressions will once again be nicely made in this sentence of Hugh of Saint Victor: "Since we have above translated 'this throne' in two ways, we ought to adapt our explanation according to each of the two."[140]

Doubtless there are a number of exceptions or limiting cases. When Saint Jerome points out to Saint Augustine that he had perhaps committed some mistakes "in Scripturarum expositione," particularly in his commentary on the Psalms, "and if I wanted to disperse them . . . , I would show that they disagree with the *interpretations* of the old Greeks,"[141] is he speaking of translations or of exegeses? Undoubtedly, both at the same time. In another letter, replying to his advice to translate on the basis of the Greek instead, he turns Augustine's argument back in the following terms:

> Further, because you say that I ought not to interpret after the elders, and you use a novel syllogism: "What the LXX interpreted had either been obscure or clear; if obscure, one must believe that you also could err in those matters; if clear, it is obvious that they could not err in them," I answer you with your own speech. All the elder tractators who have preceded us in the Lord and who have interpreted the holy Scriptures have interpreted either obscure things or clear ones. If obscure, how have you dared after them to discuss what they could not explain? If clear, it is superfluous for you to want to discuss what was not hidden from them, especially in the explanation of the Psalms, which they had interpreted in many volumes, first among the Greeks, Origen and others; then, among the Latins, etc. Let your good judgment answer me: why would you after so many great interpretations detect various senses in the explanation of the Psalms?[142]

In this perfectly beastly trick, the two terms are scrambled. Furthermore, we see the reason for it. Augustine was speaking to Jerome of translations; Jerome serves him back the reproach about commentaries; by a somewhat forced parallelism, then, he makes use of the vocabulary of his correspondent, and in addition this serves as a way to make him understand that the shortcomings of his commentaries might well have their source in shortcomings of translation. At a pinch, Jerome could express himself in this manner. He does it again on other occasions, speaking for example of a "historical interpretation"[143] or of an "ecclesiastical interpretation."[144] For the two concepts were not totally unrelated, nor would they be: the border between the *interpretatio verborum* (interpretation of words) and the *explanatio rerum* (explanation of things) keeps shifting; it always remains undefined. A commentary always presupposes a translation, even if this translation is not from one language into another; it is itself a sort of translation or paraphrase. This is more especially true of that kind of commentary that is devoted to render the sense of the text, following the etymology given by Saint Isidore: "called 'com-mentary' as being with *(cum)* the mind *(mente)*";[145] and on the other hand a translation is always more or less already an explication; it is an attempt at deciphering, a beginning of commentary, especially the kind of translation *ad sensum*[146] or *ad intentionem*[147] which is not content with a barbarous and unintelligible word for word rendering. One can see this in the French word "interprétation," which signifies both things at once or successively. One can see it as well in Rabanus Maurus, for example, "interpreting" his own verses by translating them into prose; or in the "interpretatio sermonum" of 1 Cor. 12. Whence doubtless again arises the usage of contemporary scholastic Latin in the manuals where the history of exegesis and the principles of hermeneutics are taught under the heading *De interpretatione*.[148]

An extremely frequent intermediate case was to facilitate this semantic glide: the translation of proper names from the Bible. These proper names being enigmas, as it were, their translation, their *interpretatio* had to be above all an *explanatio*. This was the quest after an equivalent meant to convey comprehension: "Bethany, which is interpreted 'house of obedience,'" "Benjamin, i.e., son of the right hand."[149] Now the constant role that this interpretation of names plays in allegorical exegesis is well known, both by dint of literalism, so to speak, and of ingenuity: "'Noah', which is interpreted as 'rest', is Christ"; "'Abram', which is interpreted as 'exalted father'";[150] "'Balaam' is interpreted as 'fickle people'," "'Dagon' is translated as 'fish of sadness', signifying the ancient Enemy who was put into the sea of the whole world to devour fishermen";[151] "'Jesus' is translated 'savior' or 'saving'";[152] "'Boaz', who is interpreted as 'strength', signifies the Christ, of whom it is said: 'May the Lord come in strength'"[153] — and so on. The pattern is visible to anyone. The examples can scarcely be counted, and this is one of the things that go on to facilitate the formation of these two formulas: "spiritualis interpretatio"[154] and "allegorica interpretatio,"[155] though they remain rather rare. "Each thing indicates its true origin and its nature by its name": this principle, formulated by the enigmatic Ambrosiaster, was attributed to Saint Augustine.[156] Philo had already said that those "who established the names were among the wise."[157] Clement of Alexandria had practiced the "game of etymology, revived from the *Cratylus* — or ought it be said, presaging Heidegger?"[158] Saint Jerome had been keen on writing in Latin, in the fashion of Philo and Origen, a *Liber interpretationis hebraicorum nominum*. Saint Ambrose remarked: "The deeper sense of names is designated by translation (interpretatione)."[159] Cassiodorus in his turn remarks regarding the Patriarchs: "the interpretation of their name is in each case consistent with a great sacrament of some reality";[160] he wants one to give himself over "most zealously" to this quest for the sense of the Hebrew names,[161] because each of them contains an intention of the Spirit; that, he thinks, is a prerogative of the holy Books: the names one meets with elsewhere contain no such mysteries.[162]

Such a belief was common. It was a small point, if one will — there are others — of this great thing that is the traditional understanding of the Scriptures. Perhaps it is a manifestation of a philology still in its "infancy,"[163] and one that will remain so for a long time still. Or perhaps it is a partially filtered residue of a long distant past, Semitic even more than Greek. "But one ought to know," Rupert will say, "that in the Hebrew language literature echoes the manifest etymology or derivation of a name."[164] The biblical names were therefore full of "spiritual virtues."[165] After Origen,[166] Saint Jerome was persuaded of it as well. Saint Augustine, who seems not to have set such great store by them,[167] nonetheless readily used to tell his hearers: "First off, pay close attention to the names, how mystical they are," or: "Even if we attend to the name itself, it is not without a mystery."[168] The place that etymology has, whether profane or sacred, in the works of Saint Isidore is well known.[169] Alcuin stressed the privilege of biblical inspiration to draw many explanations of just the name 'Israel', following a generally established custom.[170] Saint Peter Damian will take up Cassiodorus's remark: "And the very interpretation of the names does not decline to understand this figure."[171] Rabanus Maurus consequently directs one to resolve the enigmas of the Scriptures: "if one can interpret them."[172] In a sermon Nicholas of Clairvaux will say: "binding moral together with mystical themes through . . . the interpretation of the names."[173] In fine, the *Allegoriae in universam Scripturam* will testify to the everywhere recognized importance of this "interpretation of names" in medieval exegesis.[174]

One will perhaps see even better the permanence of the original sense in these classic remarks, recalled by Hugh of Saint Victor in his *Grammar*: "Etymology is the origin of words, when the force of a verb or noun is gathered through interpretation. . . . The knowledge of every thing becomes plainer once the etymology of the name has been examined";[175] or in these words from a sermon of Lothaire of Segni: "'Cana' is translated from Hebrew into Latin as 'zeal', and 'Galilee' as 'migration'";[176] or again, in this beautiful reflection of Rupert upon the *Alleluia* of the Liturgy:

> The 'Alleluia' of the Latin language is a foreign name, whose mystery has fallen like a dripping of joy from the riches of the heavenly Jerusalem. . . . For this reason this Hebrew name stays (un)translated, so

that the word might betoken rather than express a foreign joy, which though glimpsed within this life is nevertheless foreign: for this reason, then, it is, as it were, a word that properly belongs to a future beatitude.[177]

This was an "interpretation," itself traditional, that Innocent III was to take up again.[178] Though invoking another reason for it, Rabanus Maurus had already said in the same sense: "These two Hebrew words, then, namely *Alleluia* and *Amen,* can be translated . . . nevertheless the authority of that original language is kept out of reverence for their holiness."[179]

Before the time of Berno, Claudius of Turin offers us a good example of these translations which immediately open into Christian allegorism, uniting within themselves the most "literal" *interpretatio* with the most "mystical" *explicatio*. It is concerned with the name 'Melchizedek': "'Melchi' is translated as 'king', 'sedek' as 'of justice'; and what else is the King of Justice unless it is our Lord Jesus Christ, of whom it has now been said: 'You have loved justice and hated iniquity'?"[180] Nonetheless, neither the most ordinary usage, nor, above all, that of Berno himself permits any doubt about the sense that the latter attaches to his expression "interpretationis integritas." The beginning of his opusculum is in fact devoted to the versions of the Bible. He wants, first off, he tells us, "to bring to mind something about the translation of the translators (interpretes)"; then, after having mentioned the "Septuaginta interpretes," he adds: "There were also other translators (interpretes), who translated the sacred eloquence from the Hebrew language into Greek, such as Aquila, Symmachus, Theodotion. There is also the Vulgate translation (interpretatio). . . ." Then he comes to the first Latin translations of it and finally to the best *interpretatio* of Saint Jerome, invoking in its favor the twofold authority of Saint Gregory and Saint Isidore.[181] In this same passage, he treats *interpretatio* and *translatio* as synonyms.[182] What's more, the title treatise that today forms the first five chapters of the *De varia modulatione*[183] in our edition had been, as we have seen, designated by Berno under the title: "De dissona psalterii romani ac gallicani qua nos utimur interpretatione" ["On the divergent translation (interpretatio) of the Roman Psalter and the Gallican one that we use"]. The "vera interpretatio" for him, then, is quite simply the Gallican interpretation, otherwise called the Gallican version.

However, on closely reading this work about liturgy that the *De varia modulatione* is, one perceives that it is not entirely silent on applied hermeneutics, that is to say, on exegesis. If the chapter that most closely interests us gives no example of it, this is, as we have just seen, because something else is at stake there. But in the rest of the work a few instances of it are met with. They suffice to assure us that our author's exegesis was in no way unique in his time. In the words of Isaiah, "Filiae tuae lac sugent" ["Your daughters suck milk"], Berno sees a figure of souls newly born in Christ, who suck in the apostolic teaching just as little children suck milk — unless, he adds, he should be misreading "Filiae tuae de latere surgent" ["Your daughters rise from the side"], which would be a presaging of the Church, which one day is to come forth from the side of Christ at Calvary. In these other utterances: "Sitientes venite ad aquas" ["Thirsting come to the waters"], he recognized an allusion to the Scripture; then, as the text runs next: "comedite cum laetitia" ["eat with joy"], he reproves the correction of those who chant "bibite" ["drink"], which obliges him to ask himself: "Sed quomodo possumus aquam comedere?" ["But how can we eat water?"]. His reply is that Scripture is in fact both solid nourishment and also drink: a classic theme since the time of Origen, Augustine, and Gregory, but which serves as a rather facile expedient.[184] Elsewhere, the sparrows of the Psalm appeared to him to be "Christ's true poor."[185] (We shall soon find other sparrows, those of the Gospel.) Writing the Life of Saint Uldaric (Ulrich), bishop of Augsburg, he composed this elogy of him: "He used to pluck the sweet fruits of contemplation every day, when he promptly turned the words that he was reading in the sacred books into deeds,"[186] which is a way of saying that his hero practiced allegory and that from it he subsequently drew the tropology, so as to live it himself. That he had no literalist prejudice — or, if you prefer, no literalist forwardness, no encroachment — we see again in his taste for the symbolism of numbers and musical instruments, a very pronounced taste, quite natural in the musicologist that he was, and one which is expressed in some very beautiful forms. Another indication is furnished by the regard in which he held Amalarius, one of the great liturgists of the earlier age, known everywhere for the richness of his allegorism; he eulogizes him for it in two of his other works: "Amalarius, a not-to-be-despised investigator of the divine offices"; "Amalarius, a most adroit tracker of the divine offices, one whose utterances shine forth fortified with the judgments of catholic men."[187] These are some facts, then, that seem to confirm nicely the historians, who, along with Mr. Edgar de Bruyne, assign Berno of Reichenau "to that enormous allegorical current whose principles are sketched by Othloh of Saint Emmerain in his little treatise *Quomodo legendum sit in rebus visibilibus.*"[188]

3. Traditionalism

It is a curious thing that at the same time that he calls up Amalarius, Berno of Reichenau is found to be following Agobard, who was predecessor and successor of Amalarius on the archiepiscopal throne of Lyon and who violently fought him.[189] Perhaps Berno had even wanted to imitate him. The analogies of the one to the other are in any case striking.

Already in his polemic against the abbot Fredegesius, Agobard reviewed the different versions of the Bible as Berno will later, to exalt, like him, the "faithful and magnificent" translation "from Hebrew into Latin" effected by Saint Jerome.[190] Already with a purism of his own more rigorous than Fathers of the Church such as Ambrose or Augustine ever had, Agobard declared that he could not endure "plebeian songs" or poetic compositions, that is, non-scriptural chants, in the liturgical office; he wanted this office expurgated of all "human artifices and lies"; he wanted it to be composed from one end of the liturgical year to the other exclusively of "divine utterances": let no one mingle anything in, he said, with the "most pure words" of holy Scripture![191] By exhibiting the same fussiness, the abbot of Reichenau will, it seems, be unfaithful to the practice of his father Saint Benedict, who "had enriched the monastic office with non-biblical texts in use in certain churches, like those hymns that he had called 'ambrosians.'"[192] Already, in the same way, Agobard was criticizing the arrangement of certain antiphons or other pieces that more or less turn the words of the holy Books from their normal sense — whether by changing their order in the sentence, or by constructing new sentences with them — which would necessarily lead, he thought, to "bunk" or to "ridiculous and fantastic" senses, and transform the Scripture of truth into a labyrinth of error.[193] Already he had branded such abuses with the same reproach: "he fits the words of sacred Scripture to the perversity of his own sense."[194] Already he inveighed against adversaries who did not always deserve so much invective, treating them not only as "frivolous" and "temerarious" men, but as liars, blasphemers, and false prophets.[195] Already he had addressed them with the precept, apparently drawn from Scripture itself, that we shall find again in Berno: add nothing to the words of God.[196] This was to proscribe in principle, as Berno was to do, a very widespread practice, which to be sure could degenerate into abuse, but a principle which someone like Rupert of Deutz will find nothing to carp at,[197] and the happy effects of which the severe Saint Bernard himself, basing himself on the fact that "the Church has the mind of the Spouse,"[198] will, not perhaps without some imprudence, even praise.[199] Berno is not so emphatic as Agobard to show, against a too clever or too well-disposed apologist, that neither the sacred authors nor their translators nor their commentators cared about the art of grammar, which may encroach upon Berno's diatribe by bending that traditional theme a bit;[200] he rejects with brilliance, and yet not without justice, all admiration of Scripture, of its "majesty," of its "nobility," which would furnish it with the sort of beauty that the rhetors or "philosophers" look for; in his eyes this is the prior question of "right faith" and of "catholic sense."[201] In fine, the situation presupposed by Agobard's three treatises, *Contra Fredegisius*, *On the Divine Psalmody*, and *On the Correction of the Antiphonary*, appear to be substantially the same as that which was a little later on to provoke the ardent pages of Berno's *De varia psalmorum atque cantuum modulatione*. The conflict that this intervention of Berno reveals to us had therefore had its own precedents. It constitutes merely a rather lively episode in the age-old rivalry between two versions of the Bible and two liturgical schools, whose zones of influence were trying to penetrate each other. Let us also note that by distinguishing on several occasions for himself in precise language the *interpretes* of the Bible and its *expositores*,[202] Agobard helps us to understand the text of his imitator.

Furthermore, the attitude of the first helps us to understand that of the second. They both, the archbishop-bishop and the Benedictine abbot, the man from Lyons and the German, belong to the tribe of traditionalists. Both are instinctively opposed to all change, in rites as well as in faith, in the received text as well as in the usages of their Church. Agobard, aided or led by his archdeacon Florus, the intellectual head of the School of Lyons, had not contented himself with energetically struggling against the abuses and superstitions of his time; he had reacted against the reforming spirit, judged to be revolutionary, brought in from outside of the venerable primatial community of the Gauls by the interloper Amalarius. For him, everything had to be immutable; everything had to go on being done "in the fashion of our Fathers"; nothing was to come to disturb "the ancient usage of the Church of God"; "the venerable structure of the holy Fathers," assimilated to "the truth of the divine law," had to be maintained in all things "with immovable and unshaken caution"; as far as the sacred text is concerned, he reproached the composers of the antiphons with acting "against the practice of duty."[203] His traditionalist conception of religion is expressed even in his theses on the antiquity of Christianity: pushing to the limit a traditional view that Saint Augustine and Saint Leo had magnificently illustrated, he saw it as being as old as the world itself — "coming down from the very origin of the world" — and all the novelty that Isaiah used to proclaim or that the Apocalypse celebrates is in him nothing more, to believe him on the matter, than the novelty of its diffusion in the time of the Apostles: "recently spread, not recently discovered."[204] Berno is less a theoretician than is the archbishop, but he does not, any more than does the archbishop, want to permit any adulteration of rites; like him, he thinks that everything should be regulated "according to the ancient custom":[205]

> As often as we are less in accord with the rite of the ecclesiastical order, we must go back to the advice of our teachers, through whom, as Scripture testifies, the divine Wisdom has searched the depths of the rivers and has brought what was hidden to light, as the Legislator prescribes: "Ask your father and he will proclaim it to you; your elders and they will tell you."[206]

Infidelity to the thought of the ancient Fathers, upon which rests the whole edifice of holy Church, is a transgression of the divine law itself.[207] They are the "catholic Fathers." The rules of cult that they have established are, in their most minute details, as inviolable as the rules of doctrine.[208] As Saint Augustine said, even in things about which Scripture has decided nothing certain, the usage of the people of God and what the ancients have promulgated ought to be held as law.[209]

It is this same traditionalism, assuredly in principle very praiseworthy in a man of the Church, it is this sacred respect for rite, a respect that could serve as a lesson for us, which laid down the parameters for the work of the abbot of Reichenau. Another liturgist, Hervaeus of Bourg Dieu, happening to examine the sacred texts chanted at the office, just as Berno had done, will declare that he prefers the truth to custom: Berno for his own part, without formulating the antithesis, sticks to custom. In his eyes there would be no value in correcting what exists. For him argument by stipulation is sovereign. The correctors whom he finds fault with were indeed concerned with grammar or elegant style; but one can believe that he would have blamed them no less if they had proposed their corrections from a concern for textual criticism; he would nonetheless have reproached them for wanting to appear wise in the eyes of the world. Their mistake is to violate the received text. Against them, Berno revives the formulas of the other great man from Lyons, Florus. Endowed with a bit more "critical awareness,"[210] Florus in fact blames no less the "temerarious presumption" of those who, he says, treated Scripture "according to their own peculiar sense."[211] In these matters — to borrow a word from Florus again and Agobard, which for them had no pejorative connotation, quite the contrary — Berno is a partisan of immobilism.[212] Not that he, reversing Hervaeus, prefers custom to the truth: but rather he knows a priori that he holds the truth in the very custom that he maintains. Thereby, admittedly, his traditionalism goes hand in hand with a certain particularism, and that renders him no less worthy to rank with our two men from Lyons, Agobard and Florus.[213] One even gets the feeling that if, like Agobard, he did recognize the legitimacy of divers customs and merely lays claim to liberty on behalf of the custom of Reichenau, he would not be upset if he were in the position to impose it everywhere. A "disparate order of singing the Psalter" in contrast with the "same order of believing" is as little pleasing to him as it was to the promoters of the great Carolingian reform; like them, he thinks that all those who read the same sacred books ought to celebrate the same offices.[214] He would therefore love a universal Church as unanimous in its tiniest rituals as in its dogmas of the faith — if only this unity were entirely to establish the usage of Reichenau. That at least is the tendency that comes to light in his setting. This tendency emerges indeed from an anecdote, perhaps apocryphal, but in any case illustrative of a not very tolerant cast of mind, that can be read at the end of his short treatise *De initio adventus*,[215] that deals with a dispute between canons of Orleans and the monks of Fleury-sur-Loire. It was concerned with determining the precise day on which Advent ought to begin; the narrator does not admit that there might be two equally legitimate customs about it: "If there is one Lord, one faith, one baptism, let there also be one unanimity of the Church"![216]

Be that as it may, the received text that he holds on to so tightly and that he wants to protect from every sacrilegious touch, is not just one version, but it is the particular version of one group — a considerable one, to be sure, but just one group of churches. Two versions of the Psalter (in these discussions, this was the book that was chiefly at issue) were concurrently in use at that time: they were called the "Gallican" and the "Roman." The latter, which reigned at Rome and throughout Italy, was likened to the first Latin translation made on the basis of the Septuagint; the former, which Ireland was apparently the first to have adopted for liturgical use, and whose success Alcuin and Charlemagne had assured over a vast region, passed for having been made by Saint Jerome directly from the Hebrew.[217] Berno canonizes the "Gallican" version against that which the Romans use. "The Romans chant . . . , but we . . ."; "Where they chant . . . , we . . ."; "They sing, but we . . ."; "Where the Roman edition has . . . , ours has . . . ," etc.:[218] these antitheses keep multiplying as he writes. In the very long fifth chapter of the *De varia modulatione*, he contents himself with noting in this fashion the divergences — often extremely minor[219] — that exist between the one version of the Psalter and the other.[220] To that end he conducts himself on the basis of the parallel edition that Saint Jerome had given of it. If, to justify the version that he prefers, he often calls upon the purport of the Hebrew: "It is written in the Hebrew — The Hebrew agrees with this judgment — It is not in the Hebrew,"[221] this is, of course, by placing confidence in "the pious and expert master Jerome."[222] When he says "the Hebrew text," we ought as a practical matter to understand "Jerome's Latin," that is to say, the "Gallican" version. On one occasion, however, he does copy out a Hebrew word, to note that the Latin translation supplies its etymological sense.[223] He copies an obelisk and points out four or five asterisks that he found marked in his own Psalter.[224] Here or there he adds some justificatory gloss or other — and that is all. There is no trace, then, of critical correction in this whole long chapter, which forms the whole substance of the first treatise, which Berno entitled quite exactly: "De dissona psalterii romani ac gallicani qua nos utimur interpretatione" ["On the discrepant translations of the Roman Psalter and the Gallican one that we use"].

Will it be necessary to form a different judgment about the following chapter, the sixth, comprising the treatment "De quibusdam Esaiae prophetae sermonibus" ["On certain sermons of Isaiah the prophet"]? Does Berno not propose "for the verses of a certain number of responses" corrections that "are almost all found in the current breviary"?[225] These would not do as far as corrections brought to the text of the Bible are concerned; following his principle, which was explained above, Berno would correct only certain texts of the office, so as to render them more rigorously biblical. In other words, his corrections would not be biblical at all, but liturgical. But it seems that even this is not entirely the case. In fact, properly speaking, Berno does not propose corrections; here and elsewhere he rightly protests against corrections made by others: "Some erroneously add"; "Certain manuscripts have a word in the masculine gender, though it is to be pronounced, according to the Hebrew, with the feminine gender"; "The antiphon that some sing: . . . is in the Hebrew. . . ."[226] So too for those who mistakenly divide sentences. These reprehensible correctors are not all illiterate or clumsy; some are very educated, "educated in the liberal arts," close relations of those whom Berno condemns in Chapter VIII, and it is these whom he is here in like fashion trying to call to order. He once even finds a fault within his own office. At Reichenau itself, the introit of the Christmas Mass departs from Scripture:

> In the introit that we chant on the Lord's birthday, "A boy has been born to us and a son has been given to us," our translation according to the truth of the Hebrew has: "A little one has been born to us, a son has been given to us"; and instead of what we chant: "whose rule is on his shoulder," the Hebrew truth has: "And his government is on his shoulder"; and instead of what we chant: "And His name shall be called Angel of great counsel," in the Hebrew there are six names: "Wonderful, Counselor, God, Strong One, Father of the Age to Come, Prince of Peace."[227]

"The chant of our introit," therefore ought to be corrected, according to "the Hebrew truth," that is to say, according to "our translation." In other words, the text of the liturgy ought to be lined up with that of the Bible. The Gallican version is therefore left unscathed, and if the "Hebrew custom" is cited,[228] it is always done with confidence; Jerome is its usual guarantor, just as he was for Agobard.[229] What is more, he was going to be so for centuries for everyone, or almost everyone, as we shall see further on.

When he compares two versions of the Bible, or when he "takes refuge in the Hebraic truth" and appeals to the "harmony of the Hebrew truth,"[230] Berno does as Saint Gregory had done many times,[231] the one whom he calls the "most wise Pope Gregory."[232] But he does it more simplistically, more obstinately even, and with a view to less disinterested ends. Gregory did not neglect to examine carefully ("sollicite perscrutantes") the text given by each of the ancient translators; he observed, moreover, that the Apostolic See admitted two Latin versions as well, the one more ancient, the other more recent, and, following perhaps debatable criteria, but "with a certain real critical care," he was simply looking for the best text in each case, i.e., "the truer one."[233] Berno sticks a priori to the text that he possesses without having had to choose it; he wants to prove against certain interlopers that his text is the good one. In fact, he is not wrong to value that Gallican version; his appealing to original purity, however, does not differ much from what others might call prejudice. As interesting as they are, his works demonstrate neither personal investigation, nor any real debate. Moreover, if he wants to impose silence on certain presumptuous recalcitrants (such is the goal of Chapter VIII), if he gets so intensely angry with them, it is liturgical texts that are at stake.

Only those passages of Scripture that are chanted in the Office really interest him: "The Hebraic version chants,"[234] "The Gallican Psalter, which we chant,"[235] "In that introit, where they chant . . . ,"[236] "They chant the words changing their order. . . ."[237] In his eyes, the sacrilege is twofold, since the verbal innovation entails a liturgical innovation. Agobard, likewise, did not pardon Amalarius for having brought the disturbance "into the customary service of the chants."[238] Once again, in this matter, Berno cares no more about science than Agobard does. As traditionalists often are, he is a lover of books, just as Agobard had been; he is extremely well-read, extremely cultivated;[239] but culture and scientific spirit are two distinct things, not necessarily found together. What he craves are not critical texts or literal commentaries, but rather "authentic antiphonaries."[240] The title under which his collection of little works is edited, even though it does not give a complete idea of the question that will be found to be dealt with in it, indicates well enough his major preoccupation: it is the *varia psalmorum atque cantuum modulatio*. The work is not so much a work of musicology, as the place that it occupies in the edition of Dom Martin Gerbert and that Migne has respected might lead one to believe; but neither is it — except for a few minute details — a work of criticism, hermeneutics, or exegesis. It is a work of liturgy.

Sigebert of Gembloux, who wrote less than fifty years after Berno's death, concerned himself with Berno on two occasions. Let's pick out two traits by which he characterizes his actions. Unbeknownst to Sigebert, they do not lack irony. The irony of the first strikes at the ever so traditionalist liturgist in Berno: "Berno's understanding went outside customary usage . . .";[241] this involved a dispute about fasting and the ember days. As to the second, the irony would rather strike at those moderns who would turn Berno into a critic reacting against the allegorism of his own epoch. Why, asks Sigebert, does the abbot of Reichenau brush aside the traditional usage? It is because he wanted to posit rules "in accord with *allegory*. . . ."[242]

If there truly is among the men of that time a "miracle of the age," this miracle is indeed, as reputation proclaims him, a monk of Reichenau: but this monk is rather Hermann the Cripple, a mathematician, astronomer, and historian, and not his abbot, Berno.

Berno's work — here we can take it as a whole — is surely not without good points. It contains more than one judicious reflection, for example, about the words of the antiphon "natures are being renewed,"[243] and recognizably solid qualities that render its author one of the strong personalities of his age, not a very great mind, but a vigorous and steady one. Still, Berno did not appear in it to best advantage. The pages that hold our attention here manifest a twofold narrowness as well as a twofold excess. On the one hand, Berno attributes to one simple version — whatever be its worth — a sacred authority and an irreformable character that it does not deserve. On the other, his zeal to hound down all "personal sentiment" (to speak in the fashion of his interpreter) in the manner of treating the Bible, is rather similar to the zeal of the so-called "integrist" of our own days. To brand confreres who, doubtless wrongfully, permit themselves certain liturgical liberties or who allow themselves to execute grammatical correction without sufficient reason, he borrows his reproaches from phrases long used in exegetical literature to brand the heretic or the obstinate Jew. The examination of this second excess will be dealt with in the following chapter. But first there remains one point for us to clear up. We have left unsettled the question of knowing the nature of the "sage" whose authority Berno invokes. Perhaps it will be useful to begin by broadening our scope a bit, by considering the use that had been made of this formula, "quidam sapiens," in ancient Christian literature to introduce the citation of a proverb or a maxim.

The phrase could designate a profane author. This is how it is used in Alcuin, who cites the remarks of "a certain Greek sage [sapiens]"[244] or the proverb of "a certain philosopher,"[245] and who reports the sayings of "the wise Seneca."[246] We read in the (anonymous) *Life* of Saint Aldric of Sens (†837): "Recalling, according to the saying of the wise (sapiens), that character is formed by living together,"[247] which might in a pinch pass as a citation of the proverb already cited by Saint Paul in the first Epistle to the Corinthians 15:33: "Evil communications corrupt good manners"["Corrumpunt mores bonos colloquia mala"]. In his *Vita sancti Udalrici* Berno himself writes: "As a certain wise man [quidam sapiens] says, there is weight in discourse and measure in words."[248] Abelard will mention "that proverb of the sage [sapiens] which children have learned: 'for to read and not to understand is not to read at all.'"[249] Saint Bernard will cite "a certain sage," who turns out to be Seneca.[250] Hugh of Saint Victor will, like Alcuin, speak of "a certain philosopher,"[251] and it is in this way that William of Saint Thierry will designate Plato[252] and Hugh of Pontigny (†1151), Juvenal. This same Hugh, who will cite Saint Augustine using the simple title "quidam," will while preaching invoke the authority of "a certain sage" who is a pagan writer.[253] Philip of Harvengt will allude to a certain "sapiens," who this time will turn out to be Solon.[254] The abbot Absalon too will present as a "quidam sapiens" the stranger of the *Timaeus* who described the Athenians as children.[255] Alexander Neckham will recount a little story in the form of a charade, whose hero is once again a "quidam sapiens."[256]

At other times, the author cited with such anonymity is a Christian, and then it is religious matters that are at stake. Criticizing those who invoke custom to keep texts of human origin in the liturgy, Agobard asks them to examine themselves to see if they might be tolerating an evil "which one of the ancient Fathers wisely and briefly warned to be watched out for [*cavendum*], saying . . .":[257] let us notice this "*cavendum*" in the passage, which Berno's "*cave*" seems to echo, but which perhaps is rather already itself a first echo. The same Agobard confronts Felix of Urgel with a text of Saint Augustine which he presents simply as attributed to "one of the Fathers."[258] On two occasions, the tenth of the *Celtic Catecheses* edited by Dom Wilmart cites a certain "sage," who is Saint Gregory the Great.[259] In the ninth of these *Catecheses*, the formula "ut sapiens dixit" introduces another citation which we have been as unsuccessful in identifying as the learned editor was.[260] Hugh of Saint Victor in his *Didascalicon*, will mention the sayings of a "certain sage" laying down the conditions necessary for the acquisition of wisdom,[261] and to discover his identity it is doubtless necessary to go no further than Bernard of Chartres. In this same work he does not hesitate to write once more: "A certain wise man argued that there were seven other rules pertaining to the utterances of the holy Scriptures," and there is nothing mysterious about the identity of these sages: they are Tyconius and Saint Augustine.[262] Thomas of Perseigne and Gilbert of Stanford report a few opinions of Saint Bernard, announcing them as follows: "as a certain wise man says," "as a certain wise man argued."[263] By means of the same formula Helinand of Froidmont designates a grammarian-biblicist, who is perhaps Saint Jerome,[264] and Saint Martin of Leon introduces, in a more unexpected manner, the citation of a liturgical hymn.[265]

But the "quidam sapiens" can equally be a sacred author. One immediately thinks of the five sapiential books. Are not the first three — Proverbs, Ecclesiastes, the Canticle of Canticles — due, according to common opinion, to the one whom people love to call the "most wise Solomon"?[266] "The wise man" is what Gerhoh calls the author of the Proverbs;[267] again, Peter Comestor[268] will speak of "Ecclesiastes, the wisest of men," following many others. Whether one refuses to assign the authorship of the Book of Wisdom to the great king, as Saint Augustine had done, or, with Cassiodorus,[269] does attribute it to him, such a book was no less evidently in exemplary fashion the work of a "sage." As for Ecclesiasticus, which was often cited, as was natural, under the name of the son of Sirach, and sometime also by custom, following the usage of the Septuagint and the old Latin version, under the name of Solomon,[270] it, along with the other four, could be designated as the work of a "sage." This is the straightforward manner in which Saint John Chrysostom regularly announced his citations of the five Solomonic books amongst the Greeks. Saint Ambrose at least once had introduced Ecclesiasticus in the same manner: "a certain wise man before us not unfittingly says."[271] The usage of Saint Gregory the Great, whose works were familiar to Berno, is particularly noteworthy. In the *Moralia*, although he usually designates Solomon as the author of Proverbs and Ecclesiastes,[272] Gregory, following Augustine in this respect, never does so for Wisdom or for Ecclesiasticus. To cite a passage drawn from one of these latter two books, each time that he is not satisfied with banal expressions like "it was written" ["scriptum est"] or "it is said" ["dicitur"] or "as Scripture attests" ["Scriptura attestante"] or again "Wisdom says" ["Sapientia dicit"], he, like Chrysostom, mentions a "quidam sapiens": eighteen times, if I am not mistaken, for Ecclesiasticus, and eight for Wisdom: "it is said through a certain sage," "a certain sage well points out," etc. He uses the same formula in the commentary on the Book of Kings.[273] God, writes Rabanus Maurus, "wanted to say through a certain sage . . . ," and thereby he introduces a text from the Proverbs and a text from Ecclesiasticus.[274] Hincmar, who cites the sapiential books as Saint Gregory did, albeit with less circumspection in his reserve,[275] at least once alludes to the "quidam sapiens."[276] The tenth *Celtic Catechesis* of Dom Wilmart, having cited "the Patriarch Job," immediately afterwards mentions "another sage," who is the author of Ecclesiasticus.[277] The "quidam sapiens" whom Angelome of Luxeuil[278] cites is again the same author. "A wise man" is the anonymous title that Saint Peter Damian gives to the son of Sirach.[279] Rupert of Deutz, without any originality in this respect, simply calls the author of Wisdom "sapiens."[280] Peter Cellensis does the same for the author of the Proverbs.[281] For Peter the Cantor, the "quidam sapiens" is sometimes sacred, sometimes profane.[282] Philip of Harvengt practices the same eclecticism, when he too mentions a "quidam sapiens" and an "alius sapiens," who are the authors of Ecclesiasticus and of *Wisdom*,[283] etc.

One might suppose that in his *De varia modulatione* Berno, who himself also speaks of the "sapientissimus Salomon,"[284] follows the usage of Saint Gregory, which would call for looking for the source of his "quidam sapiens" in Wisdom or in Ecclesiasticus. This path, however, is not promising. There is nothing in Wisdom like the advice given to the "prudens lector." In Ecclesiasticus 6:33, it is written: "My son, if thou shalt attend to me, thou shalt learn, and if thou wilt apply thy mind, thou shalt be wise" ["Fili, si attenderis mihi, disces, et si accommodaveris animam tuam, sapiens eris"]. One can detect a certain parallelism between the mind so invited to apply itself to wisdom and the "sense" that, in the sentence cited by Berno, would have to apply itself to the Scripture, a parallelism sufficiently marked that this biblical text could indeed have influenced the formation of that sentence; but even if one takes account of the great liberties permitted by the customs of that time, this parallelism is too vague for one to be able to speak of citation.

Indeed, the "quidam sapiens" of Berno is none other than Saint Jerome. Commenting on the apostolic discourse in Saint Matthew's Gospel and arriving at Matthew 10:29: "Are not two sparrows sold for a penny? and not one of them shall fall on the ground without your Father," Jerome said:

> The word of the Lord coheres with itself, and the things that follow are dependent on what is above. O prudent reader,[285] always watch out for a superstitious understanding, so that you do not accommodate the Scriptures to your own sense, but yoke your sense to the Scriptures and understand what follows. He had said above.... Now he is consequently saying...."[286]

Jerome's advice had been collected, perhaps through an intermediary, in the eighty-first and final chapter of the *Scintillae* of Defensor of Ligugé: *De lectionibus*.[287] This collection, composed at the end of the seventh century, was much used in the high Middle Ages, and it is there, as well as in the commentary on Saint Matthew, that Berno had been able to get hold of the sentence.[288] There he found an indication of its author's identity. Whatever the detail, there is no doubt about its origin with Jerome. A slight difference might be noted, however, between the two sentences, which somewhat affects its sense. Where Jerome had written: "... *sed* Scripturis *jungas* sensum tuum" ["*but yoke* your sense to the Scriptures"], we find in Berno: "... Scripturis sensum tuum *adjungas*" ["<to> *add* your sense *to* the Scriptures"]. By suppressing the conjunction *sed* and adding a prefix *ad* to the verb, the meaning of the words is turned around: instead of being a positive recommendation, following on the warning given at the beginning and contrasting with it, this second part of the sentence now becomes a doubling of the warning and a reinforcement of the complaint.[289] But in our editions, the text of Berno is not certain. In the absence of a critical edition, there is no place, in my view, to rely on such a difference, tiny as it is, and without special interest for us. Let us rather simply note that on each side, if this is indeed essentially the same form of warning, the construction of the sentence is not at all the same.

Saint Jerome in fact wanted to inculcate in his reader the necessity, too neglected by the then-current methods taught in the schools and naturally followed by the Christians who were commenting on the Bible, to pay attention to the context, so as to understand a given passage according to what precedes it and what follows it. This is what he repeated a little further on, in this same commentary on the first Gospel, in almost identical terms, once again setting aside "superstition," that is, arbitrary interpretation, and recommending that one always consider the "priora, media, et sequentia."[290] Now, in the *De varia modulatione*, this perspective will have entirely disappeared, and this will be enough to change the sense and bearing of the sentence in question.

Jerome criticizes an exegete who had believed that he could discern in the two sparrows mentioned by Jesus the body and soul of each human being. This, he says again a few lines later, is to interpret the text violently *(coacte)*; then, coming back to his starting point: "How that understanding is to be fitted to the whole body of evangelical discourse is a matter of no little difficulty."[291] The exegete in question here is Saint Hilary. The latter indeed already aspired to be guided in his explication by the sequence of ideas: "this passage," says he, "sets out from the thought given above"; at the same time he was inspired by a principle of "coherence" taken more broadly than it is here by his critic: instead of contenting himself with looking for the internal coherence of the "speech of the Lord" or the "speech of the gospel" in his manner of understanding the care that God brings to the two "sparrows" he wanted, in addition, to avoid opposing this statement with Saint Paul's: "God does not care about brutes."[292] This is, after all, a normal concern in a believing exegete. More severe than Jerome himself, Jean Daillé will exhibit the intensity of his bigotry when he will give this passage as an example of those "fictions that can not so much edify sagacious readers as stupefy them."[293] Hilary's care was to be shared by other exegetes, like Ambrose,[294] Augustine,[295] Julian of Toledo,[296] and again by a Rupert of Deutz. . . .[297] Such care was nonetheless excessive, at least on a first time through. Each author ought to be explicated first on his own terms. Jerome is completely right against Hilary. His principle is indispensable: "The Lord's speech is coherent with itself."[298] But his reproof is nonetheless another one of those spiteful remarks, or as Dom Paul Antin says, one of those "clawstrokes,"[299] that are so often met with in his writing. But he would never dream of criticizing — any more than Berno would — a general method of exegesis which is as much his own as Hilary's. Both are disciples, imitators — or "translators"[300] — of the great Origen. Both are also "allegorists." Jerome's warning has nothing to do with a "literalist" manifesto. Jerome just thinks that Hilary is mistaken in explaining a passage from the Gospel, because he has not sufficiently paid attention to the immediate context or sufficiently taken account of the sequence of ideas.

In the epoch in which Berno was living, though, the words that Saint Jerome had used to express his reproof were no longer just any words. They had a long history already. The "superstitious understanding," detached from its own context, had taken on a very general sense in contemporary discourse.[301] The whole of the sentence had long been used with a different intention from Jerome's; it had acquired new overtones. It is this history — begun well before Jerome — that we must learn at least in its main lines, for it touches on the heart of our subject; it is this meaning, the one that had become traditional, that we will have to determine if we want in addition to appreciate exactly the use that Berno made of these same words to express a quite different complaint. This will be the goal of the next chapter; it will furnish the opportunity to see the patristic and medieval doctrine of the spiritual sense asserted under a particularly instructive aspect. But from now on, we know enough to establish once again our author's traditionalism in his sticking to the letter of a formula the spirit of which he scarcely cares to rediscover. We are going to establish it once again with regard to another formula — borrowed this time not from Saint Jerome, but from Saint Gregory.

4. The "Barbarism" of Saint Gregory

In declaring his refusal to bend holy Scripture to the rules of Donatus, Berno called to mind not, to be sure, the customary sweetness of Saint Gregory the Great but at any event a thought of his, which he did not fail to attribute: "as Saint Gregory confirms."[302] At the end of the letter addressed to his friend Leander of Seville as prologue to his *Moralia in Job*, the sainted Pope had indeed declared:

> I do not flee the clashing of metacism; I do not shy away from the confusion of barbarism; I turn up my nose at preserving the restings

and movings and the associated case-endings governed by prepositions ablative and accusative, respectively, since I very much think it unfitting that the words of the heavenly oracle should be tied up under the rules of Donatus.[303]

If the verbal filiation from the one to the other is evident, the abbot of Reichenau has nonetheless diverted Gregory's remarks from their original sense, just as he had done with those of Jerome. How many others from that point on have understood them still more badly! They repeated them, without taking care to put them back into their context. They did not perceive the deliberate paradoxical tone, appropriate in its place at the end of an epistle dedicatory. Moreover, they had no regard for what is reflected in it from literary tradition, both profane[304] and sacred.[305] Nor was any effort made to evaluate its peculiar mixture of personal modesty and Christian pride.[306] Finally, they did not know how to tease out the doctrinal intention that is enfolded within it. They turned it into a manifesto in favor of obscurantism. Despite some protests, even today the complaint lingers on everywhere. Now the historians who keep rehashing it from generation to generation are not only victims of a failure of analysis or a lack of historical perspective: they depend, perhaps without knowing it, upon an old polemical tradition, which has ended up by imposing its own interpretation on them.

We find the expression of this tradition already well established at the beginning of the eighteenth century, in the indignant commentary of Jean Barbeyrac, the author of a copious *Treatise on the Morals of the Fathers of the Church*: "Thus it is that, according to Saint Gregory the Great, in order to teach men religion and their duties, it is necessary to put them off them with barbarous language and to speak to them in a manner not to be understood: for even a horrible negligence could not cast such great obscurity into the discourses."[307]

A moment's reflection might have permitted this refined but passionate mind to recall that the good Saint Gregory had many a time manifested anything but a "horrible negligence" in the edition of his *Moralia* as well as of his other works. On the contrary, he brought to bear a meticulous care for both style and composition, as can be seen both from his own remarks[308] and from the repeated declarations of John the Deacon[309] — a man who knew his author and knew that of which his author spoke. In matters of textual correction as well as of literary propriety Gregory manifested even an "extreme sensitivity."[310] One can well suppose, moreover, that if "the discourses" of the great pope had truly suffered from such a great "obscurity" and from such "barbarous language," they would not have found and kept such a large number of assiduous readers for so many centuries.[311] Nor would the Venerable Bede, no mediocre writer himself, have invoked the name of Gregory with a view to promoting good usage of the language.[312] The "stylus gregorianus" would not have been so diligently studied by the authors of the *Artes dictaminis*, and the Gregorian sentence structure, with its "most extraordinary" cadence, would not have been cited as a model by the humanists — such as Hugh of Bologna, Robert of Basevorn, John of Garland — who struggled against the invasion of a barbarous Latin in the first decades of the thirteenth century.[313] We would not have so many examples of that beautiful figured and rhymed prose that Bede admired so much in its principal instigator and that influenced the most artistic writers of the Middle Ages.[314] It is precisely concerning the *Moralia*, "that broad river of eloquence," that Saint Isidore of Seville already was saying: "No scholar [sapiens] will be able to unfold the multifarious ornaments of language that shine there."[315] Did not the finest man of letters of the Carolingian age, Lupus of Ferrières, write not only that Gregory was "learned to the highest degree" and "marvelously fluent," but also that his works would be a great help "to all good men capable of handling Latin"?[316]

A number of ancient elogies can be taken as pure rhetoric, like the one that a monk of Sankt Gall, an imitator of Isidore of Seville, pronounces of Gregorian eloquence, so perfect, he assures us, that "if Cicero were to hear the man, he would go off astounded."[317] One will suspect the Cluniac Bernard of Morval of just a bit of excess in singing of the "golden, fiery style" of his hero.[318] One would be remiss if he took the liturgical prose characterizing Gregory in comparison with three other great Latin doctors as more than conventional praise regarding the "grace of the words."[319] One will smile, perhaps, as if it were a sign of barbaric naïveté, on reading in Guibert of Nogent's autobiography the testimonial which his mother rendered to the great pope's reputation as she sent her son off to school:

> At last about to hand me over to school, she picked out the feast-day of Blessed Gregory. She had heard that your aforementioned servant, o Lord, had overflowed with marvelous sense, had blossomed with infinite wisdom; and so with many a heap of alms she quite often used to solicit the favors of your confessor, so that the one to whom you had furnished understanding would effect her heart's desire — my obtaining a bit of understanding.[320]

The "Barbarism" of Saint Gregory

But once such witnesses of ages past have been left aside, one will at least perhaps be able to sense the enthusiasm of, say, Paul Claudel, feeding his young genius on many "delicious" passages of the *Moralia* copied down in his Journal.[321] Perhaps one will listen to the authoritative opinion of Edward Kenner Rand, who, after having observed that the critics of Saint Gregory had condemned him on the basis of one sentence torn from its context, declares — albeit a trifle too optimistically — that he had searched in vain through his entire work for even a small grammatical error,[322] or that of Dom Robert Gillet, who, at the end of many long years devoted to the study of it, avows, regarding the "metacisms" whose "clashing" Gregory did not avoid, that he "had never been struck by a fault of this type" in reading him.[323] Doubtless one will also let himself be convinced by the competent judgments of L. W. Laistner, who recognizes in Gregory's writings a certain literary talent, pregnant sentences, a skillful handling of antithesis — qualities that he regards as quite superior to the preciousness of the literature in favor at that time;[324] of Dap Norberg, protesting against the negligence on the part of modern scholars to study so cultivated a writer, whose literary influence was immense and whose prose offers such a rich variety;[325] of Miss Christine Mohrmann, finding that Gregory was "endowed with a typically Roman sense of style,"[326] or of Jacques Fontaine, seeing in him an "eminent representative of artistic prose within the genre of homily."[327]

Nevertheless, Barbeyrac set a fashion. In a "Critical History of Philosophy," the first in its kind, Jakob Brücker a short time later bestowed the title "acutissimus" upon his French predecessor and in his own turn declared: Gregory "confesses that he had neglected every bit of humanistic culture in those books of his, so that he can be seen to have written them precisely to cut the throat of every more elegant teaching with a single stroke."[328] This was therefore more than merely a "horrible negligence," it was a horrible outrage! and even a premeditated assault! Such was the criminal origin of the "Night of the Middle Ages." It is necessary again to quote Brücker's own words: "For when so great a man, who was gathering together for himself the highest power and was engaging in *ex cathedra* determinations, having been seized by such great prejudices would rage against secular literature and particularly against philosophy, practically the whole flock had to follow the judgment, howsoever incompetent and pitiful, of its shepherd."[329] One marvels at this ponderous and pedantic style as though wittingly adopted to condemn the writer who, in Bacchantic frenzy, would have struck "all elegance of doctrine" in the throat. One will marvel no less at how, in his anti-Gregorian zeal, the historian forgets himself to such an extent as to retroject the affirmation of a universally recognized papal infallibility, right down to literary matters, into the sixth century! One will ask, however, how it comes about that, among the causes that provokes the abasement or the breakdown of culture in the first centuries of the Middle Ages, Jacob Brücker seems never to have thought to mention the Germanic invasions. No, the only possible cause is this wretched pope! To believe him, the monstrous power of a single man would have been enough to plunge a whole continent into an "inept and miserable" lack of culture. "The West," he concludes, "was darkened by a blind ignorance and corrupted by a sickening barbarism."[330]

But what is most astonishing of all is that texts as frenzied as those of Barbeyrac or Brücker should have become a sort of norm for a whole line of historians and critics. J.-G. Rosenmüller, in 1814, thought that Gregory, that "unlearned man," that "most superstitious human being," who in no way deserved his title "the Great," had been the "chief author and instigator of literary barbarism" through his letter to Leander; it was to him that one owed the "hatred of monks for languages and for all culture," the "barbarism of the Latin Church," and, in short, the "night" of the Middle Ages.[331] In his ardent imagination, Michelet saw Saint Gregory waging war against the Muses, and he compared him to Leo the Isaurian, the iconoclast emperor.[332] The dull V. Fèvre reproached him more prosaically for turning the "incorrectness" of his language and the "corruption" of his grammatical constructions into "a badge of piety."[333] Eugène Haag, in 1862, picked up a well-established tradition by showing the pope to be "full of contempt for profane literature, for grammar itself."[334] "Except for Ireland," wrote Reginald L. Poole again in 1884, "no region of Europe escaped this disastrous influence."[335] With more moderation, M. Roger in 1906 pointed to the Letter to Leander as proof at least of the "repugnance" of its author "to get involved in the shabby concern with words" and of the "disdain" he showed "for literary form."[336] In 1926, the Reverend W. H. Hutton wrote of Saint Gregory: "Literary elegance he never cared for, and he almost boasted of the barbarism of his style."[337] In 1927, F. J. E. Raby, who subsequently was to give a more favorable judgment,[338] thought that the "popularity of his writings accentuated the barbarization of the language" — an evaluation that scarcely accords, however, with the remark of the same author, that Gregory's Latin is much superior to that of the other writers of his time.[339] In 1941, Maurice Hélin declared that "it was the very fate of all culture that had been put in question"[340] by the letter dedicatory of the *Moralia*. In 1951, in a work on the classical tradition, Gilbert Highet broadened the traditional reproach, calling to witness Gregory's "bluntly" proposing to ensure that the Fathers of the Church took no care about grammar.[341] In 1958, Fr. B. Artz, as one will see further on, went one better still. The decree is so well established that the very scholars who are trying to react against the prejudice dare to do so only by halves, as if they were afraid of passing for shamefaced apologists.

In reality, let us note from the very start, the passage under indictment does not say what some seem to make it say. Gregory does not promise to produce any "solecism." Nor does he propose to commit "barbarisms" or "metacisms" on every occasion: he is merely letting us know in advance that he will not flee them, he will not avoid them, when he judges them necessary to his purpose. Saint Ambrose had spoken the same way: "If the Philosophers themselves have used words scarcely Latin and scarcely accepted so as to employ the proper terms in their discussions, how much more ought we to disregard the words to consider the mysteries!"[342] And Augustine did the same, in a work full of instructions about grammar: "I should prefer a barbarism to an ambiguous expression that might be better Latin."[343] More than one other writer has made analogous declarations since then, and the historians of literature are ordinarily inclined rather to recognize a praiseworthy boldness in this. In a note from the edition of the *Moralia* that he began to offer to the "Sources chrétiennes" series in collaboration with Dom André de Gaudemaris, Dom Robert Gillet cites as an example the following "nonconformist declarations" of Jean-Jacques Rousseau: "My first rule, for myself who care not a jot about what people will think of my style, is to make myself understood. Every time that I shall be able to express myself more forcefully or more clearly with the aid of ten solecisms, I shall never hesitate."[344] In addition to the concern "to make himself understood," Gregory, as an interpreter of holy Scripture, was concerned with not betraying it. For several centuries, all the translators had had the same concern as he did, forced as they were to aver that "the syntax of the great classical works that had been elaborated apart from all Semitic influence," was ill adapted "to calque the language of the Bible": they had found, on the other hand, first in "the plasticity of the koiné," then in that of "vulgar Latin," "abundant resources to stick close to the verbal image of the Hebrew," and their labor, scorned by the rhetors, had nonetheless contributed felicitously to "limbering up the language."[345] But again let us not exaggerate Gregory's thought in this matter. If he himself also judges that it is "supremely unfitting to subject the words of the heavenly oracle to the rules of Donatus," he does not pretend that these rules do not apply there at all. Far from it! As is easy for anyone to check for himself, the entire work of the *Moralia* sufficiently shows the contrary: "The exegete of the Book of Job does not always turn up his nose at grammatical attainments. He knows how to choose between two readings of one and the same verse, to point out the tropes of comparison and metonymy, the importance of the coordinating conjunction, the etymology of a word. In short . . . , he does not eliminate recourse to the methods of classical grammatical explication from his exegesis."[346]

Later on we shall see the deep significance that is found at least implied in the words referring to the relations between Scripture and "Donatus," a signification already intimated, I believe, by Saint Gregory himself, although it was not to be clearly perceived until much later. As to the relation of his own style to "Donatus," as to the barbarisms and the metacisms that he accuses himself or excuses himself of or glories in, one can find it astounding that a simple reading of that so much commented upon sentence does not immediately show any reader what D. Comparetti has clearly seen: by flaunting "an affected knowledge of grammatical technical terminology," the author of the letter to Leander is evidently taking care to "let it be understood that his not-wanting-to is not a not-knowing-how-to do so."[347] Still more, if one is willing to read the whole preceding page, a page whose universally cited words constitute the high-point, even without trying to focus minute attention on it, he will not fail to perceive that this alleged manifesto of barbarism could spring only from a refined writer, almost excessively concerned with literary form. A translation cannot convey its beauty; at least it will be enough to disengage its intention. It is above all a long apology presented to the reader for the imperfections of the work's form:

> I am sending this commentary to Your Beatitude for review, not because I thought it a worthy gift, but because I recall having promised it at your request. Your Holiness will quickly hold me excused for everything insipid and crude to be found in it: since you are not unaware that I am speaking while sick, you may forgive me all the more quickly. For when disease wears down the body, even efforts to speak grow feeble since the mind is affected. [Many years have run their course already, while I suffer from frequent intestinal pain; I grow weary at all the hours and minutes when my digestion has broken down; I breathe hard with low-grade but continuous fevers. And amidst all these infirmities, meditating upon the testimony of Scripture 'He scourgeth every son whom he receiveth', the more severely I

The "Barbarism" of Saint Gregory

am weighed down by present ills, the more surely I hope in the eternal plan.] And perhaps this was the design of divine providence, that having been struck down I might expound a Job who had been struck down, and that I might the better sense the mind of a man who had been whipped through whippings of my own.[348] But it is nonetheless clear for those who consider the matter rightly that bodily disease is no little obstacle to the pursuits of my work, in this, that when the strength of the body is hardly enough to let one talk, the mind cannot fittingly express what it feels. For what job does the body have except to be the instrument of the heart? And howsoever skilled a conductor may be, he cannot accomplish his art without concordant exterior aids; for rickety instruments obviously do not properly produce the song that the skillful hand directs nor does the blowing of air express art, if a pipe riddled with chinks is squealing on. How much the more heavily, then, is the quality of my exposition weighed down! The breakdown of the instrument scatters the style of speaking so much that no art will put it together again.[349]

This hardly looks like a profession of scorn for the art of writing, even in its subtler concerns; a fortiori, it scarcely could involve the rejection of its most basic features. Here, however, the excuse is going to turn into positive *apologia*. Gregory sketches out a sort of counter-attack against those who would be tempted to criticize the simplicity of his style. He is aiming at a whole decadent school, incurably superficial, incapable of freeing itself from a "frivolity of fruitless chatter," which was sacrificing the essential thing to a pretentious façade.[350] Without pronouncing any "anathema" against "the literary toil of expression"; without declining "to polish his own style or to strive to sort out terms," as his old French translator put it;[351] without affecting scorn, as Fleury believes, for "the art of speaking well,"[352] he thereby shows that, as far as he is concerned, he is abandoning the "farfetched style" of the letters of the low period, abandoning their preciousness that sometimes went as far as esotericism, abandoning their "puerile and pedantic games,"[353] abandoning their empty rhetoric.[354] He surely had better things to do, and the experienced historian, even the historian of literature, will be far from complaining about it. Assuredly more a stylist than Origen — his very profession of restraint is expressed in a learned and musical prose — he would not like, however, any more than he "those who busy themselves embellishing little bits of words."[355] He is going to tell them indirectly, using a biblical image to this end, just as Origen would have done:

I ask you, however, that in going through what is said in this work you not search for verbal trifles in them; for holy Scripture zealously enjoins her commentators to prune away the frivolity of fruitless chatter, when it is forbidden for a grove to be planted in the temple of God (Deuteronomy 16:21). And we all know well that whenever the stalks of the promising cornfield are over-abundant in leaves, the grains in the ears swell less plentifully.[356]

It is just at that point that a movement of Christian pride suddenly comes to reinforce both the excuse and the counter-attack: "I have therefore disdained to bind myself to that art of speaking well that the rules of an alien discipline introduce." To disdain to bind oneself to an art is not, let us observe, the same as to disdain to make use of it. An "alien discipline" should not exercise a "magisterium" over a Christian commenting upon the divine Word; it ought not to become his "mistress": it can only be his servant. There follows the sentence which was to rouse so many indignant controversies; we call attention to the same nuance here as before: it is not an issue of rejecting the rules of Donatus as some sort of barbarian; it is a question of not "restricting oneself to them" as a Christian. And Gregory, to conclude, uses one final stroke, a gracious image where modesty and pride, a writer's care and Christian conscience, unite and rely upon each other: "For none of the interpreters having been authorized by sacred Scripture to serve those rules; and as it is from this authority that our exposition is born, it is clearly fitting that the offspring brought forth should manifest the looks of its mother."[357]

Alluding to this page, Father Joseph de Ghellinck has written "one would perhaps have been wrong to take" certain of its "verdicts too literally."[358] More recently, Jacques Fontaine observed that sometimes Gregory is "an extremist with the pen," that he happens to express himself "rather provocatively," and that such "bits of virtuosity" ought to be taken *cum grano salis*.[359] Ozanam had already thought that "in this famous passage, which has too often been misused, it is necessary to see merely the disquiet of a mind that knows the barbarism of his age, who shrinks from feeling its after-effects, and who eloquently justifies himself, like Saint Paul, by trampling down eloquence."[360] And Renan, who doubtless had read Ozanam, has in turn declared: "Only a pedant could take this famous passage in a bad sense."[361] We shall surely not contradict what he has to say. We can, however, improve upon the timidity of the first arguments, as well as the trivial irony of the last. A more decisive defense can be presented on behalf of the noble defendant. If we want to be fully objective, we must do so. Has not Saint Gregory magnificently praised the profane culture of a Moses, of an Isaiah, of a Saint Paul?

> Moses, who has issued us the principles of the divine eloquence, did not become acquainted with the divine things beforehand, but he informed his uneducated soul with all the knowledge of the Egyptians, so that he could grasp or express the divine things.... Isaiah also was more eloquent than the other prophets, since . . . he was nobly educated and urbane. Paul, too, the vessel of election, was educated at the feet of Gamaliel before he was taken off into paradise or raised to the height of the third heaven, and so perhaps he excelled the other apostles in terms of doctrine, because he who was to be in the heavens zealously learned earthly matters beforehand.[362]

Doubtless it is not too much to think that in pronouncing this threefold elogy, the sainted pope, modest as he was, allowed himself to be guided by his own personal experience, as one who had received in his youth, thanks to the ephemeral renaissance of good studies stirred up at Rome through the conjoint action of Theodoric and Cassiodorus, the most careful education that could be had at that time. Just as Moses had first been educated in the science of the Egyptians, so had he in the first place received the rudiments of classical culture. Like Isaiah at Jerusalem, this scion of old Roman patricians had been "nobly educated and urbane."[363] Like Saint Paul, before being "converted" and raised to the summits of divine contemplation, he had learned much from his human masters; and like Paul, even more than him, he could say: "for a long time, indeed a very long time, I have put off the grace of conversion."[364] Undoubtedly the Rome of his youth was no longer that "of Cicero or of Virgil, nor even that which Saint Jerome and Saint Augustine had known";[365] it would not however be necessary to judge it in terms of what it was soon to become in the days of his pontificate. Paul the Deacon recalls it for us when, in a nostalgic tone — where we doubtless hear a distant echo of Peter the Deacon — he shows us the son of the noble Gordian so well educated in all the branches of knowledge "that, although the studies of literature were still flourishing at Rome at that time,[366] nevertheless in the city itself he was deemed to be second to none."[367] At any event, Maurice Roger tells us gratuitously, or at least too contemptuously for the tongue of someone like Jerome or Augustine, Ambrose or Leo: "After his leaving school(?), Gregory did nothing to maintain in himself the memory of the classical writers, or to secure the correctness of his own language against the inroads of rustic or ecclesiastical Latin."³⁶⁸ The first of these two remarks seems pertinent, but what follows makes legitimate sense only to the extent that it simply observes that toward the end of the sixth century in the Christian setting, Latin could no longer be exactly what it had been under Augustus and that Gregory, whose style "felt the effects of the worst taste of his age,"³⁶⁹ did not waste his time and energy trying to turn an archaizing dream into a reality; further than that, one can conclude nothing either against his taste in literary work or against his esteem for classical formation. The problem is not to know at what time that man lived, but what advantage he could draw from the conditions of his time. Besides, did he not himself declare that in order to study the divine science it was very important to unite a knowledge of secular books to that of the biblical text?

> For almighty God laid down this secular science at level ground in advance, so that he might furnish us who ought to rise to the height of the divine Scripture a step to climb.³⁷⁰

"There was no smith to be found in all the land of Israel," reports the first Book of Kings, "for the Philistines had taken this precaution, lest the Hebrews should make them swords or spears." On reading these lines Saint Gregory doubtless recalled the tactic employed not long ago against the Christians by Julian the Apostate. The memory of it was preserved in the Church, and it was kept alive by the account of the *Confessions,* in which Saint Augustine showed old Marius Victorinus stripped of his chair as rhetor, despite his renown, for having dared to declare himself a Christian; in virtue of the edict of 362, a Christian could no longer convey nor acquire education.³⁷¹ Was this not a situation such as the old biblical story described? Gregory saw in it an image of the trick of the demons, who want to prevent the disciples of Christ from forging the arms of culture:

> The demons obviously know that when we are instructed in the secular literature we are aided in the spiritual. Therefore, when they dissuade us from learning those things, are they doing anything else but trying to prevent us from making a lance or a sword?
>
> The evil spirits have eliminated the desire of learning from not a few hearts, so that they may both be ignorant of secular things and also not reach the sublimity of spiritual ones.³⁷²

These are obviously not the remarks of a "humanist" enthusiast of pagan literature; rather they represent the wise and thoughtful judgment of a man who knows the value of a "liberal" education, and who also knows from experience that such an education cannot in fact be acquired without frequenting pagan authors.[373] A hardly reasonable criticism has long set this evidence aside. It is true that in Gregory's commentary on the first Book of Kings some details can be discerned that seem rather to be the work of its redactor, the monk Claudius, future abbot of Classe (near Ravenna). But these "personal touches," which may be due to a slip of memory or perhaps to some tendentious inflexibility, would seem, all in all, to be "rare."[374] They would not be enough to cast any doubt on the substantial authenticity of the work. The reserve shown by Gregory himself as regards this commentary, in his letter to John of Ravenna,[375] is explained adequately by his usual scruples; it applies elsewhere as well, to the homilies on the Canticle, whose authenticity is certain. To speak of "interpolations" so serious that they would have "altered and denatured" the work, to lay the whole thing at the door of the fellow who was merely responsible for producing a "fair copy" of it and who was ever Gregory's dear and faithful disciple, is to fall into anti-criticism by way of hyper-criticism.[376] As for the passage that is of special concern to us here, one could hardly imagine that such a long and homogenous development whose sentences in addition bear Gregory's mark so tidily, should be totally, at its very foundation, an invention of Claude of Ravenna.[377] Dom Paul Chapman and Dom Bernard Capelle have been entirely right to assert, against an almost unanimous chorus of critics, the completely Gregorian character of the work, just as Denys of Sainte-Marthe had done long ago against Goussainville. Father Maurice de la Taille has been entirely right to protest against its "undeserved disfavor," even if the explanation he gives of it is insufficient and the correction that he proposes in the letter to John of Ravenna remains quite conjectural.[378] Rand has been entirely right to take it into account in the portrait he draws of Saint Gregory.[379] Laistner has been entirely right to denounce the dogmatism and question-begging that would deprive its author of this work, in the name of the very know-nothingism with which they want to charge him.[380] Through a minute analysis of the text, Dom P. Verbraken has recently confirmed what had long been assumed by those who had read the text without prejudice, and it is only by residual effect of this old prejudice that the arguments persist, to the point that his conclusions have encountered certain reservations.[381] Charles Thurot — whose vast erudition was not enough to protect him against the polemical judgments imposed by custom — asserted not long ago that Saint Gregory had been animated by a "fanatical aversion for profane literature": this would be to make him play precisely the role that he attributed to the devil.[382] Gregory's authentic followers long ago were better able to recognize the spirit of their model so as to draw inspiration from it: such as Edmer of Canterbury, a great devotee of Gregory;[383] such as Seifrid of Tegernsee, protesting to a friend who excessively under-valued or mistrusted the human preliminaries to divine science;[384] again, such as Angelome of Luxeuil, commenting on the same story from the Book of Kings, following Rabanus Maurus,[385] and in the same sense, and for whom alone the Philistines, servants of evil spirits, are no longer pagans, but heretics;[386] or Richard of Saint Victor, who, after an allusion to the measures of Julian the Apostate, does not hold back from making a pointed application to certain prelates of his own time.[387]

Another text again, it is true, came to engage the historians on the track of men like Barbeyrac, Brücker, and Rosenmüller, Thurot, Poole, and Highet. The saint pope had once written to Desiderius, bishop of Vienne in Gaul — the one who was to die a martyr in 608, murdered on the order of the queen Brunehaut — to blame him for "teaching grammar." "It is execrable for this to be said of a priest," he pronounced; "this," that is to say, "for the heart to be smirched with the blasphemous praises of unspeakable things," and again in terms used in imitation of Saint Jerome:[388] "the praises of Christ do not catch themselves in one and the same mouth along with the praises of Jove."[389] The harshness of the reprimand, however, calls into question whether the bishop had truly sinned, in the pope's mind, merely for cultivating literature a bit too much. In reality, as we will see, Gregory reproached him for something other than "his scholarly tastes."[390] He reproached him even more than for "spending his time teaching grammar,"[391] in the current sense of the French word.

"I don't know too well," Guizot will say, "what the praises of God or of Jupiter could have to do with grammar."[392] A candid admission, but hardly appropriate in a historian of civilization. The term "grammatica," a synonym for "litteratura,"[393] at that point covered a vast field, the very one, we would say today, covered by the "humanities": still such a word is very far from conjuring up for us what the word "grammatica" could conjure up in the mind of a man of the sixth century. Quintilian had defined grammar as "the knowledge of speaking correctly and the expounding of the poets"[394]; the second part of its definition was in fact so important, that it quickly took over first place: the "understanding of the poets," the "science of the things that are said by the poets," the "science of interpreting the poets," thus constituted the essence of the "art of grammar."[395] Thus, the "grammarians" had the job, as Rufinus of Aquileia says in one of his prefaces to the translation of the *Peri Archôn,* to explicate the "the poet's made-up songs and the ridiculous tales of the comedies."[396] In short and in practice, grammar was mythology.[397] It was not that literary fiction that was to come about in our classical literatures, nor that erudite dead science which today makes us yawn, but a still living and seductive science, mingled with manners, customs, rites, and habits of mind, a science that took imaginations captive. It was the old paganism, whose prestige was not by any means exhausted. No more than had the gods of stone or metal yet become simple statues had the myths become simple images for all. In Martianus Capella *Grammatica* presents herself as a very old woman, daughter of the god-king Osiris, having long ago come from Egypt to Greece and having subsequently been established at Rome. If she brought the Christians the "spoils" of these three cultures, these Christians need a serious exercise of discernment so as not to renew the adventure of the Idumean Ader by finding occasions of apostasy in them.[398] Something quite different was therefore at stake with grammar than merely correct or beautiful language! It was that "cup of gold," first described by Jeremiah, then by Saint John in the Apocalypse, a cup adorned on the outside by the poets, but within filled by them with the poisons of idolatry and turpitude as well as with false science and death-dealing doctrines.[399] It was the cup of Babylon, that tempting and deceptive cup, which, ever since Origen,[400] experienced believers did not cease to warn their brethren against. Saint Jerome had also denounced this cup in a more particular context, once again borrowing the language of Origen for the joy of criticizing Rufinus and, through him, of reaching Origen.[401] It will reappear often in medieval symbolism.[402] In the tenth century it will again seduce a Vilgard of Ravenna on Italian territory, if at least we believe Raoul Glaber.[403] It is always this cup with the bewitching aspect that Saint Odo, the future abbot of Cluny, will one day be contemplating in a dream as he is reading Virgil: at the very moment of putting his lips to it, he recoils in horror at seeing serpents escape from it and beginning to surround it; the serpents can not in fact bite him, however, and on his waking he will understand the reason for it: it is because he is walking in the path of Christ.[404] A beautiful dream, it seems to me, to include in the record of Christian humanism rather than that of obscurantism.[405] But in this sixth century, for a number of Christians, the "path of Christ" was not yet so firmly marked out. The perfidious cup once more came dangerously to inebriate the poet Ennodius, who ended up by repenting. And what in such cases was a loss for the Christian spirit was in no way, on the other hand, a serious gain for literature.[406]

Doubtless, under the circumstances, the bishop charged by Saint Gregory had been accused by him of deserting or at least of neglecting the duties of his charge — in a particularly troubled epoch which required a redoubling of zeal and vigilance — so as to abandon himself to a teaching completely impregnated with paganism. If we are looking for an analogy, let us imagine, for example, in times closer to our own, the reaction of a pope finding out that the pastor of a diocese in a critical pass, instead of watching over the faith of his flock, is going to give lectures in some institute of Masonic inspiration or to popularize the thought of that institute in the chair of his own cathedral; or again, that he is transforming a chair of his faculty of theology into a chair of "introduction to Marxism." Perhaps Gregory shows himself to be a bit too sharp — for he was not always mere sweetness itself — or perhaps he was a bit too quickly alarmed; nevertheless, if the expressions of his letter are harsh, one will note that he does not address them as a direct reproach to the bishop: he does not dismiss the possibility of erroneous information, but hopes on the contrary that more precise inquiries will permit him to give thanks to God.[407] His motive in any case is not doubtful. He had responsibility for the care of souls. No more than Saint Caesarius of Arles, no more than the three great Latin doctors from whom they were both heirs,[408] did he want to offer as food, instead of the dishes served by the Father of the family, the "husks of pigs": this pig-feed is all too often what the "secular scriptures" dispense, those writings, Caesarius used to say, "which wickedly bring this world tales of deception by assiduously offering praises with sweet vanity to various poems of idols or demons."[409]

Saint Gregory had a high notion of what a bishop ought to be.[410] He wanted a man of perfect purity.[411] On the other hand, in the face of pagan literature, with all the superstition and immortality it conveyed, his point of view as supreme pastor could not be simply that of a Cassiodorus, who did not have the same responsibilities, who had long been fed upon the culture and enjoyment of ideas that were scarcely Christian,[412] and who, in addition, sketches a program of studies without being preoccupied with contemporary life.[413] At that date and in that place, his point of view could no longer be that of someone like Bede — so inclined, however, to a certain ecclesiastical exclusivism — nor a fortiori that of an Alcuin or a Rabanus Maurus, whom an isolated situation, a foreign origin or the delay of centuries will protect against certain charms.[414] He could not share the usage of a Saint Columba, who permitted himself riotous sprees of mythological allusions, without scruple, and without danger. A fortiori, the situation that commanded his attention was not comparable to that of an educator of the French seventeenth century.[415] In his Rome, battered for two centuries by the barbarian flood, the continuity of traditions remained green. Though the political and religious situation there was quite different from what Saint John Chrystostom had known at Antioch in the time of Libanios, one immediately felt there the truth of what the great pagan orator had proclaimed: "Religion and letters are bound together by a close affinity; they are sisters."[416] In other words — one cannot insist upon this point too much if one wants to avoid a gross misinterpretation — pagan literature had not yet been devitalized; it had not become a purely "literary" matter. "Each renewal of the classical tradition," observes H.-I. Marrou, "was accompanied by an upsurge of neo-paganism": how much more did the danger threaten, when the tradition had not yet been broken! The Christian reaction to such a danger ought not be taken as a "hatred of profane Hellenism": it expressed something totally different — horror of an anti-Christian Hellenism.[417] Gregory, let us note, does not allude to the historians or to the orators, but only to the poets, to those who sing or celebrate the false gods. On the other hand, what the Christians were rejecting was not, as H.-I. Marrou again put so well, "the preparatory culture," useful for forming the mind and needed with a view to sacred studies; it was an "ideal" and a "mode of life" incompatible with their faith.[418] Gregory knew how to make such a sound distinction. He was not cursing profane literature, as Ferdinand Lot believed,[419] following so many others. It is just that his vigilance was aroused; he was afraid of "the stain of heart" to those of whom he was in charge, and Mr. Roger himself recognized that "if we put ourselves at his stand-point," i.e., the Christian point of view, "we would not blame him."[420] In addition, the beginning of his letter to Desiderius itself seems to confirm that he was in no way the enemy of sound studies.[421] The Middle Ages had generally understood this well, as the story from Guibert of Nogent cited above makes clear. He had clearly seen that the "simplicity" advocated by Saint Gregory was simplicity of heart and that it was not opposed to culture, but to duplicity.[422] One will not attach too much importance to an assertion of Saint Peter Damian, pleading for "sancta simplicitas" with his usual verbal exaggeration: "Blessed pope Gregory praises the discipline of the art of grammar in such a way as to say that it is not fitting for Christians."[423] Peter Damian is addressing some monks who are letting themselves be overtaken by the spirit of worldliness; he wants to deflate their pretensions, and he is not troubling himself with history. One will do better to rely on the common opinion expressed by the canonists, as it is found cited in two *Distinctiones* of Gratian's *Decretum:*

> Blessed Gregory took a certain bishop to task not because he had taught secular literature, but because contrary to the episcopal office he was expounding literature to the people instead of the gospel reading.
>
> In teaching, a bishop ought to prefer the authority of sacred Scripture, not to show off his skill at secular literature. For it is not the bishop's job to expound literature, lest praises of Jove should come out of the mouth of a pontiff.[424]

Synesius himself, the extremely learned bishop of Ptolemaïs, steeped in Hellenism as he was, had understood this earlier, a man who, to prove that he had conducted himself appropriately as a bishop, declared that he had never opened a school of literature.[425]

In modern times, many have understood this point less well. The letter to Desiderius has generally not been better interpreted than the letter to Leander. The two texts have been brought together as if they treated exactly the same object, in such fashion that they corroborate each other and make matters worse. That is what Frederick W. Farrar did, for example, in 1886, in his *History of Interpretation.*[426] Paul Renucci does likewise, though he does struggle for moderation.[427] L. W. Laistner could write with only too much reason:

> Every reader from time to time encounters assertions which by constant repetition have taken on the character of literary or historical commonplaces. A familiar example is that statement that Gregory the Great was uncompromisingly hostile to pagan literature.[428]

The power of the "commonplace" exerts itself even upon excellent historians, ordinarily quite detached from received opinions.[429] It leads to a forced interpretation of other facts, which in the same way combine to corroborate the commonplace itself. During his sojourn at Constantinople, Gregory did not learn Greek: for many, there it is: proof either of his hostility to culture or at least of his total unconcern in this regard; this is a flagrant crime of "barbarism."[430] But they fail to notice that, at that period, high culture at Byzantium itself was entirely Latin. It is in Latin that

The "Barbarism" of Saint Gregory

Justinian had published his Code. The language of the public law and of imperial administration was Latin. On the shores of the Bosphorus, high society spoke Latin; the poets composed Latin verses; the grammarians compiled their treatises in Latin. It is there that the *Institutiones* of Priscian had seen the light of day, at the beginning of the century, and Theodosius the Younger had undertaken to copy its eighteen books in his own hand.[431] All this was not enough to keep the apocrisarius, if he had wanted to, from learning Greek (and it is not certain that he had acquired none); but it all renders his abstention much less significant than some would like to believe.

For us to comprehend for ourselves the incomprehension of which Saint Gregory is sometimes the victim, we must note two inverse estimations, posited in some fashion a priori: the first by a certain number of modern historians, the second by the ancient Christian authors. For the former, it seems that the ancient paganism — under the names of culture, humanism, literature, or grammar — represents art, beauty, and, if not truth, at least, reason. For the ancient Christians, on the other hand, paganism was above all myth, superstition, intellectual poverty as well as moral corruption. Have we not seen already how insistently Saint Justin pities those who believe in vain fables, who cannot prove any claim that they advance, who think, just as they live, contrary to reason!ature[432] The apologists of the faith of Christ want to be the "good physicians," who struggle against the ravages produced in the human mind by absurdity and falsehood, "by treating it with the salutary methods of reasoning."[433] They proclaim that the truth triumphs over irrational custom. They know themselves to be the messengers of a luminous novelty, which is to free the world from its old prejudices and its old fears.[434] Facing so many venerated or dreaded powers that the imagination and the passions of men have forged so as to enslave themselves to them, they proclaim themselves to be "atheists of those pretended gods."[435] In the sixth century, this is once again the same conviction, calling for one and the same attitude. Though today many argue as though the whole ancient heritage was science and reason, Saint Gregory at Rome, Saint Caesarius in Gaul, Saint Martin of Braga in the Iberian Peninsula, were conscious, while struggling against the paganism of scholars and that of the masses, of struggling against the tenacious forces of superstitious immorality.[436]

The height of incomprehension seems to have been attained recently in a book on *The Mind of the Middle Ages*, which has appeared in successive editions. It is a worthy pendant of the judgments of Barbeyrac and Brücker. Through an audacious scissors-and-paste job, its author Fr.

B. Artz, is not afraid to stick a few words taken from the letter dedicatory of the *Moralia* to a few words taken from the letter to Desiderius, to such fine effect that, to judge by this travesty of Gregory, the mere fact of writing correctly is equivalent to singing the praises of Jupiter! Everything to be found in the poor pope is deemed despicable or odious: his "clumsy Latin," the "poor organization" as well as the lack of originality of his writings, his taste for "farfetched and unintelligible allegory," his "tendency to moralize everything," his "bad Latinity," his obsession with the fires of hell; he sinks Christianity into legends, superstition, sacramentary magic; even then — the ultimate disgrace! — he has "the mind of a mediaeval monk"; he is the creator of a "new religious syncretism, often removed from the spirit of the Gospel."[437] We have searched for some explanation for so many erroneous or excessive appraisals encountered in the past four centuries. But the final secret of all the negative points deplored by Fr. B. Artz comes down just to this: "More than any other man, Gregory is the founder of the mediaeval papacy."[438] Such is also, I believe, the final secret behind the animosity which, more than lack of imagination or critical acumen, lies at the origin of the judgments that we have seen passed on "this much calumniated pontiff."[439]

5. Stupet omnis regula! Every rule stands amazed!

It is to concede too much to such judgments, it seems to me, to plead, as A. Ebert does for example, that we see in the "incriminated" sentence, "simply a quite inexplicable exaggeration,"[440] or again, by saying with the old translator of the *Dialogues* that in the letter dedicatory of the *Moralia* Gregory "is joshing with his friend Leander."[441] Nor shall we say, with Father Schmitz: "If it is true that Gregory condemns classical studies in his letter to the bishop of Vienne, in another spot he explicitly asserts their necessity":[442] it is not necessary, in order to justify his conduct, to admit that he contradicts himself. Finally, we do not think it enough to observe, with A. G. Amatucci, that his "grandiose idea of the universality of the Church literally frees him from every grammatical bond that might obstruct the diffusion of the Christian truth."[443] However true it may be, such an explanation does not get to the root of the matter, that taproot which a still too literal analysis has not yet uncovered for us, but which we can perhaps now glimpse through a broader examination of the tradition in which the texts of Saint Gregory were written and which they in turn have helped to guide.

Stupet omnis regula! Every rule stands amazed!

Even now, a few preliminary indications will be useful to help us avoid a false trail. For Saint Gregory's talk about "Donatus" did not occur in isolation — any more than his talk about the opposed praises of Jupiter and Christ. It was already a commonplace. Now one may observe that it is often the most well-read authors, the ones most smitten with "grammar," or those most expert in the art of speaking well, i.e., the most ardent to promote liberal studies with a view to sacred studies, who turn out to be the propagators of this judgment. Well before Gregory, Saint Paulinus of Nola, a poet himself and a man of high classical culture,[444] had spoken severely of the "fable-filled literature," of "fabulous dreams" and of the "poets' falsehoods," so as to oppose to them the message of the "prophets of the truth."[445] To his master and friend Ausonius, too indulgent toward pagan imaginations, who, while writing to him, had ended his letter with a prayer to the Muses,[446] Paulinus, "shocked to the depths of his soul," had amiably but firmly replied:

> Why, father, do you bid me to return
>   To the renouncèd Muses?
> Christ-dedicated hearts deny those Songstresses
>   And are not open to Apollo. . . .
> Now a different power conducts the mind,
>   And the greater God calls for different morals.[447]

In other words, Paulinus rejected mythology under the name of the Muses as well as under the name of poetic falsehoods, just as Gregory was to do in speaking of "grammar"; and that did not keep him from emulating Ausonius, in the very piece under consideration, by intelligently using elegiac verses alternately composed of iambs and hexameters. Just as Paulinus altogether rejected both poets and philosophers, Jerome enveloped philosophers and grammarians in one and the same reprobation: "Where is the wise man?" he wrote, "where the grammarian, where the searcher after causes?" To fine literature he eloquently opposed the "foolishness of preaching."[448] A little later on, Saint Avitus, Desiderius's predecessor at the see of Vienne, kept denouncing the vanity of stylistic pursuits, of poetry, that "science of lying," and of "grammar," all the while himself publishing poems and defending himself at length before a rhetor for having committed an error of quantity in a word;[449] moreover, it is well known that this nephew of Sidonius Apollinaris was, just like his uncle, nourished on the classics and refined in his culture. In the ninth century, the layman Paul Alvarus of Cordoba, a great admirer of both

Jerome and Gregory, will, like those two, oppose on many occasions the simplicity of the apostolic word to the subtleties of "the art of Donatus":

> I have said that the holy apostolic men did not enslave themselves to the constructions of words, but rejoiced in the sense with its truth; and did not run through the art of Donatus, but through the simplicity of Christ. . . .
>
> Are you not ashamed, my dear fellow, to use the grammatical and liberal arts of Donatus that you keep beside you, that are so much weaker evidence for your side, and to join irrelevancies that belong in another work to this assertion of ours? . . . "God chose the foolish things of the world to confound the wise." What do we mean by the 'wise'? Do we mean our most holy Fathers or rather grammarians, philosophers, and orators? "I have not come through sublimity of speech . . .": For what is sublimity of speech but rules in terms of Donatus's metaplasm and tropes?[450]

These are, however, still merely literary generalities, and, if seriousness is not entirely absent, neither is rhetoric missing from these declamations against the rhetoricians.[451] Using somewhat staler language, Saint Isidore of Seville, in the wake of both Jerome and of Gregory, explained that the Christian who complacently gives himself over to the reading of the "fictions of the poets" risks falling into the "baleful opinions" that fill the books of the gentiles — in other words, of sacrificing to demons. Isidore mistrusted "the rouge of the grammatical art," which made the words to be loved more than the truth; he also could not stand the bragging that literary studies too often bring on; but this did not keep him from recognizing that, judiciously used, the "teaching of the grammarians" could "contribute to life."[452] To be sure, by reason of the difference in literary genres and the topics treated, perhaps also by reason of the difference in geographical situation — Seville was not Rome — classical culture seemed more secularized for Isidore than it did for Gregory; its paganism was more muted. Their doctrinal positions are nonetheless close, and the texts of Isidore help us to understand, at least in part, those of Gregory.[453] Bede, however, sticks more closely to the problem that lay beneath the epistle dedicatory of the *Moralia,* when he writes, speaking of the Christian poet Sedulius:

> He neglected ["neglexit"] a rule of grammatical disposition, so that he might sing the glory of the holy and individual Trinity with a

Stupet omnis regula! Every rule stands amazed!

clearer voice.... He laid aside ["postposuit"] the order of secular discipline, so that he might more openly commend the truth of the Sunday sermon.[454]

Now here is someone who is already preparing us to guess the most positive element, more hidden than apparent, in the letter to Leander. "Neglexit," "postposuit": these words of Bede are scarcely those of Gregory: "despexi," "contemno."[455] On the other hand, Bede's zeal as "grammarian" is well known, and under this apparent "negligence," this flaunted "scorn," it is not too hard to discern the positive and well-thought-out operative feature that is being affirmed.

There is hardly mere more-or-less-feigned modesty (which is, at any event, beside the point), in the following declaration by a representative of the School of Sankt Gall, recounting the life of the delightful Notker, "stammering in tongue but not in mind": "And so not having been fully imbued with the rules of Donatus, or practiced in Priscian's grammar or (still less) in the tricks of dialectic, nor exhilarated with the rhetorical flourishes of philosophical eloquence, we pursue the true judgments of reason, gathered under the direction of faithful humility, not in sublimity of discourse."[456] The hagiographical literature was to overindulge in this sort of declaration.[457] In the present case, such formulas notwithstanding, where pedantry is married with simplicity, it is well known that Sankt Gall was a lively center of culture and that "grammar" in the full extent of its meaning was much in honor there.[458] The *Versus de septem liberalibus artibus,* which had been attributed to Notker himself, would be enough to prove it; this rather labored school exercise little reflects his genius; it is nonetheless indicative of his cast of mind: in it one sees the ancient pagan "grammatica," that old woman long before described by Martianus Capella as a humble and valuable servant polishing the teeth of children "so that they may sound words in marvelous ways."[459] But a profession of faith from Smaragdus is more precise and closer to Gregory and Bede. The learned abbot of Saint Mihiel, too, knew how to appreciate Donatus, and if he composed his *Liber de partibus Donati,* it was precisely as an instrument to be of service for the study of the Bible; nonetheless he did say of him: "We are not following Donatus, since we hold a stronger authority in the divine Scriptures."[460] Nevertheless such a proposition does not take on a universal scope for him any more than it did for Gregory or Bede; as in both of them, however, it still had more than a vague signification: its scope is both limited and strong, if not yet very precise. In the eleventh century, Saint Peter Damian will give a new example of his extravagant genius by generalizing the antithesis, in the manner of Saint Jerome, so as to oppose the "rule of Benedict" to the "rules of Donatus"[461] and to conclude with a formula that smacks a bit of Tertullian, though the context limits its scope: "My grammar is Christ";[462] he was nonetheless a "consummate grammarian,"[463] almost too artistic in his style, and he himself admitted the charm long exercised over him by the "Sirens."[464] How could one reproach him for having preferred "wise inexperience" to "stupid wisdom," or the "simplicity of Christ" to the "sophistical railings" and "fabulous devices of mad poets"? At the same time as he was defending the dignity of Christian life, he likewise defended *bonae litterae*.[465] Peter Abelard, who was no more illiterate than Peter Damian, and who was not, like him, an anti-dialectician, nevertheless does not hesitate to cite the declaration of Saint Gregory with honor: this is because he discerns a certain deep sense in it.[466] It is cited in the same way by the author of the commentary on Nahum, whether that author be Richard of Saint Victor or someone else.[467] As for John of Salisbury, he also recalls Gregory, though less in his doctrinal intentions than in his capacity as a man of letters. He, the most humanistic of the humanists, the best writer of an era which counted many excellent ones, quite naturally takes up as his own, after so many others had done, the proposition of Jerome's dream, with the famous dilemma: Ciceronian or Christian;[468] he presents his *Polycraticus* to his friend Peter Cellensis by telling him: "I have published a book . . . ; it is uncultivated,"[469] and in his letter in verse, whose addressee, by a literary fiction copied from the classical poets and long in use since then, is the book itself,[470] he tells it, doing the letter dedicatory of the *Moralia* one better:

> Let your stride and clothes and bearing be those of a pilgrim,
> Let your barbarian tongue sound nothing but barbarism.[471]

Any of these texts show us this fact: from one end of the Christian Middle Ages to the other, and in the most diverse settings, as eager as one is for masters "of literature both divine and human,"[472] one carefully distinguishes the authorities presiding over the two of them. As Miss Christine Mohrmann writes, two *auctoritates* dominate Latin: "the *auctoritas divina* of the Bible and the *auctoritas humana* of Donatus."[473] But the domain that these two authorities divide is not only that of language; or at least, if it is the domain of language, its application extends to language considered as symbolizing the domain of thought. It is incumbent upon us to recognize the sense and the play of opposition that, in certain cases,

Stupet omnis regula! Every rule stands amazed!

is invoked. It is likewise necessary to eschew enlarging upon the meaning or stretching it excessively, but it is not obligatory to remain blind to the seriousness with which the wordplay is invested. The division proclaimed by the two *auctoritates* does not at all mean that the rules of grammar or of rhetoric summarized in the name of Donatus (or sometimes of Priscian) are of no use in the sacred science. Scripture, as is well known, abounds with "schemata," with "tropi," with still other forms of language, with all those "locutionum modi" that are indispensable to a good theoretical knowledge for interpreting it correctly.[474] With grammar as with other arts, and as with "secular letters," one borrows its principles as part of life; it constitutes as it were the first portal through which one is introduced "to the height of the divine Scriptures."[475] The case of someone like Saint Ambrose Autpert, who says he had owed nothing to Donatus or Priscian, any more than to Plato, to Virgil, or Cicero for his primary education, is the exception that confirms the rule, and he himself informs his readers that this is a "very rare" situation.[476] One of the most severe minds, the most scrupulous even, and the most purely "ecclesiastical," Peter Cellensis, will repeat the same thing after a hundred others: he had to have practiced "grammar" a lot in order to read the holy books "more zealously" and to understand them "more precisely."[477] From the time of Augustine and his *De doctrina christiana*, whatever the relative proportion of humanism or pragmatism that characterizes them, everyone kept repeating it.[478] But they also repeat, without any contradiction, that the sacred science, whether in small matters or in great, does not totally submit to these rules of human language. This is because it is the bearer of a principle that goes beyond them. Through the transcendence of its object, it shatters such conventions. Would not the Christians, with a view the better to respect the mysterious content of their faith, dare to do what the philosophers have customarily done, in view of rendering an original thought adequately?[479] At that time it was no longer a question of vulgar lack of corrections, accepted for the sake of comprehension by the vulgar: it is a question, one might say, of sublime lack of corrections, intended so as not to betray a sublime truth. "The divine utterance is not subject to the rules of the grammarians, and it cannot be compelled by necessity to follow the idiom of human speech."[480]

In that whole first period of the Middle Ages, the vocabulary is still insufficiently worked out. The analyses are sometimes clumsy: thus Godschalk, dealing at length with the uses of the preposition *in* in the sacred Books, concludes that "Donatus ought not be followed in everything."[481] Sometimes, too, the applications are petty: as is the case when

Smaragdus of Saint Mihiel in one passage of the Bible maintains the reading "scala" against a rule of Donatus that would have required "scalae."[482] The same is true again, as we have seen, in Berno of Reichenau. Or else, the applications remain extrinsic, as in the episode reported by the author of the *Life* of Lanfranc:

> One day, while he was reading at table, he said something during the reading as he ought to say it; but this did not please the presider, and he ordered him to say it differently, as if he had said 'teach' with a long e, and that fellow had ordered him to correct it with a short e: 'tetch', which does not exist. For the Prior in question was not competent at grammar. But the wise man, knowing that more obedience is owed to Christ than to the dictionary, abandoned what he had pronounced well, and said what he had been bidden to say incorrectly. For he knew that to prolong a short syllable or to shorten a long one is not a capital crime; but he was well aware that not to obey one who is giving orders on God's behalf is no light fault.[483]

Though without interest in themselves, such examples do have the advantage of showing us to what degree that classic opposition weighed upon their minds. But in other cases, when one refuses along with Saint Gregory to bend the oracles of Scripture to the prescriptions of Donatus, it is a question of something more serious, first appearances perhaps notwithstanding, where grammar and literature are not the only parties engaged. In those instances it is not merely the expression of a conflict between form and content, or between learned language and apparently barbarous language but of the divine reality of the Bible. From the earliest Christian era, have we not seen that the term "allegory," used as Saint Paul does in expressing the mystery of the two Testaments, finds no analogue in any other type of allegory, and that it is impossible to reduce it entirely to any one of the established definitions of the grammarians? The example is sufficient, and the testimonies cited above[484] prove that the ancient Christian exegetes were perfectly aware of it: the whole "art of Donatus" could not account for it. One could therefore not at all, like the barbarians, be well within the scope of this "art" — but one would find himself constrained sometimes to go beyond it. Everyone respected "the art of speaking without vice";[485] everyone, with more or less zeal or happiness, aspired to possess it; no one took up any "mystical anger" against it; many devoted an important part of their activity to it as writers or pedagogues. Nevertheless, certain cases presented themselves where one

Stupet omnis regula! Every rule stands amazed!

had to choose between what a spirit blind to the newness of Christianity had necessarily to reprove as a grammatical vice and what one faithful to Christ would have to denounce as a doctrinal vice.[486] As Saint Augustine had said of the word "salvator" ("savior"), a neologism that he himself had some difficulty accepting: "Let not the grammarians ask whether it is Latin, but the Christians whether it is true": this word, indeed, "was not Latin before the Savior came, but when the Savior came to the Latins, at that point it came about that this word was Latin."[487] Or again, as Saint Peter Damian will say, using that paradoxical and provocative tone that he loved to take up, in addressing a monk who wanted, in his view, to play the literary man a bit too much: "So, brother, do you want to learn grammar? Learn how to decline God in the plural."[488] Irrupting into the world, Christianity had to compose its language "from existing, rebellious elements"; it had therefore to "make" these elements "to endure a good bit of violence" so as to transform them.[489] If it were merely a question of some "Christian ideology" coming to substitute itself for other ideologies, of a new species within one and the same genus, then some innovation of vocabulary would have been enough. "Donatus" would have had no reason to take offence. But the transformation was far more radical! Through the power of the Spirit, it was at work in the very depths of the soul, whence it overturned intellectual paradigms and then took on the creations of syntax. The first words in which the faith expresses itself: "I believe *into God*" — or "in God" — were they not a solecism, as unbearable in Latin as in Greek? Yet how necessary a solecism! Linguistics, philology, "semasiology," semantics, or syntactics today can analyze well the process by which this or other forms have been produced and generalized, as well as the conditions that have opened the way for them:[490] they are not enough to explain them. "The revelation of the personal God, active within history," the recognition of the Word of God incarnated for the salvation of the world, "has produced an absolutely unique experience."[491] The appearance of new forms of language which resulted from it cannot be reduced to a banal fact of an evolution of vocabulary or syntax. Nor was it a late product of theological speculation: the latter, in its reflective movement, could only contribute to fixing its results, in struggling to render an account of it. This was the verbal repercussion of the much deeper spiritual revolution. All Christians had therefore said, each in his own fashion, prior to Saint Gregory: "I do not avoid the confusion of barbarism, nor that of *solecism*."[492]

In a fashion still more general, under a form inherited from an ancient time and traditionally transmitted, which will perpetuate itself right into the thirteenth century, one thought comes to light throughout the texts of Saint Gregory and of those who follow him:

> The sacred Page will not subject herself to the law
> Of grammar, nor does she will to be ruled by its art.[493]

This is the same, or almost the same, thought that is so often expressed, albeit less well packaged, among the great spirituals of the twelfth century, who were frightened, not always without just cause, by the intemperate uses of "dialectic" — for in certain cases it truly was a matter of the faith. The protest raised against the tyrannical invasion of sacred science by "grammar" is basically the same as the protest raised by these spirituals — and each of the two will be justified, backed up by the explanations that the best craftsmen of the later theological construction will bring to bear. "The art of Donatus," indeed, that "fundamental discipline," "the origin and foundation of the liberal arts,"[494] was more than a simple technique concerned with language, more too than that "explication of the poets" about which Saint Isidore of Seville was still talking. In the form of culture that prevailed in the first Middle Age, as a result of a process to which Christianity was otherwise alien, the whole life of the mind develops, so to speak, under its sign. "Grammar" here has become a "tool of intellectual research,"[495] comprising the totality of the rules that govern discourse and thereby those that govern thought. "It is necessary," says a capitulary of Charlemagne, whose influence was immense, "to know the figures of words and thoughts to comprehend the mysteries of holy Scripture."[496] The discussion instituted about the *modi significandi* therefore extended, in fact, albeit in a still indirect manner, implicit or ill-perceived, to the *modi intelligendi*. The "science of speaking correctly" was close to the "science of speaking truly."[497] Under grammar, "the most elaborated form of profane knowledge," logic was concealed,[498] and the latter was already heavy with metaphysics. Could one not have said, with enough truth, that several of the definitions of theology are "the grammar and syntax of belief"?[499] Thus, when Godschalk, for whom "grammatical speculation was a veritable passion," declared that the reference "according to the Lord" annuls all the others,[500] this affirmation of principle had more far-reaching consequences than the examples he immediately calls up might have let him believe: does it not frequently happen that a mind falls back into just average thoughts after having been elevated for an instant to an intuition that it has not yet got the power or the means to exploit? When Smaragdus decided to assign two distinct et-

Stupet omnis regula! Every rule stands amazed!

ymologies for the same word "verbum," this too was for him a way to designate as well as he could the distance that he had perceived between the ordinary grammatical acceptation of the word and its Christian acceptation. In the same way, again, when Agobard approved the translators and commentators of the Bible who were not afraid, under certain circumstances, of expressing themselves "against the grammarians," this was because such instances of incorrectness seemed to him, rightly or wrongly, necessary to save "the integrity of the sense" and to assure "agreement with the mystery."[501] The historians of the ancient Greek or Latin translations today make analogous observations.[502] And, when they are clear-sighted, so do the historians of thought.[503]

Under the name and along the slant of grammar, there were a certain number, then, of older habits of the human mind, bequeathed by classical antiquity, that were put into question. They were the terms of the common language, the concepts of the common philosophy that called for a recasting in order to be of service to the expression of revealed truth. The Christian revelation had sown the seed of a novelty which bore unforeseen upheavals along with it. Our writers did not want so much to ignore — let us use the same words as a Cistercian author from the end of the twelfth century — "what Priscian orders"; but they also measured "what a Christian owes to his God."[504] Grammar and logic were not at all neglected: they were, when it was necessary, transgressed, because they were transcended. "Sacred Scripture transcends all sciences and doctrines by the very manner even of its speech." This is how Saint Gregory explains himself through this text from the *Moralia*.[505] This is also the conviction of Saint Peter Damian: the revealed doctrines, such as the doctrine of the mystical Body, transcend, he thinks, every "literary discipline," every "earthly wisdom," and the arguments of the dialecticians ought not to be adapted lightly to matters of the faith.[506] Once again, Peter Abelard echoes them both:

> So is it any wonder that if, since God ineffably transcends all things, he should also exceed every discourse of human institution? . . . Is it any wonder also that God in himself should break the rules or models of the Philosophers, which he frequently nullifies in his deeds? . . . that . . . just as he transcends human thoughts, so too does he go beyond the traditions of the human disciplines?[507]

In his treatise on the *Hexameron*, Hugh of Rouen develops the same thought, with respect to the Being of God:

Our words and whatever expressions we use to indicate him who is to the highest and truest degree, do not posit any action or passion, nor any variety whatsoever, in the deity itself. You may prudently consider concerning this cause that the words and whatever expressions are taken to signify God, are now not among those eight parts of speech posited by the grammarians, but rather signify by the divine ritual, not in grammatical fashion, nor rhetorical, nor dialectical, etc.[508]

In the same way again, Raoul Ardent (Radulfus Ardens), in a language that already smacks of the new schools:

Therefore the expressions known by our natural faculty had to be transferred to theology, so that we might in some way or other advance through our expressions to a knowledge of a thing unknown. Yet let no one think that when natural names are said of God they keep the proper character of their discovery, but let him subtly inquire into the reason for the adaptation.[509]

With his customary clearsightedness, Father Chenu has drawn attention to the great importance of this sort of struggle. "A goodly number of theologians," he writes, "having a right judgment of the transcendence of the faith and its objects, do not resign themselves to let its expressions be subjected to the laws and procedures of human language. If God is speaking, they think, he ought to know his grammar better than Donatus and Quintilian; let us not read his words with the eyes and the grammar of those pagans."[510] Only, to understand the idea of those ancient theologians at base and to render them full justice, it is appropriate to add, I believe, that this "just sentiment" did not lead them all to misunderstand the autonomy of the disciplines of human wisdom or the need to use them and the rules that determine their exercise. It simply provoked them to think that, in the synthesis that had to operate when those disciplines were called upon to furnish a means to express the content of the Scripture, it was the divine content, not the human wisdom which had to furnish the active principle of the transformation. At their level, in the state of maturity of the problems in their epoch, these theologians of the high Middle Ages, continuing the work of the time of the Fathers, were already searching for what in their turn the great masters of the thirteenth century were searching for, namely — to borrow once more the same words of Father Chenu — to modify the ancient matter intrinsically, to transubstantiate it

Stupet omnis regula! Every rule stands amazed!

somehow, so as to put it at the service of the sacred science. Or, to take up again the word of Alan of Lille and of Raoul Ardent (Radulfus Ardens), they understood the prior necessity of a "transsumption." For to express mysteries such as the Trinity, the Incarnation, the Eucharist, etc., correctly, according to the perceived requirements of analysis, the most essential notions, such as those of 'nature', 'substance', or 'accident' had to be placed upon a new foundation; and what about the word 'person',[511] or 'love'? and the very idea of 'being' itself? Reason itself had to be enlarged, rendered supple, deepened, under the action of the faith, which could not go forward without long trials and errors and bitter struggles. Neither "Donatus" nor "Plato" nor "Aristotle" later on would hand over adequate "human language" as such.[512] If the humane studies were to be treated, within the very exposition of the mysteries of God, not as "captives" but as "noble daughters" of God, this could not always be without that first step of purification and superior ennobling whose program was outlined in Deuteronomy for the warriors of Israel.[513] The synthesis and harmony could come only at a later time. That is why, in one perhaps oversimplified view but one that was in general both fair and deep, the ancient theologians of the Church had for such a long time treated as a pair, not philosophy and heresy,[514] but the (pre-Christian) "philosophers" and the "heretics," and pointed to the latter as generated from the former: "the philosophers, patriarchs of the heretics."[515] In this respect, there was scarcely any difference between an Origen, for example, and a Tertullian, and the tradition has followed them both.[516] They did not want to use the captive-girl and treat her as a wife before having "converted" her.[517]

If, with a bit of elevation, we now let the individual differences, the scholastic oppositions, the diversity of tasks involving various points of view to fade away, if we let even the distance between the centuries get narrower, we shall see one basic idea emerge, common to all those who belong to the great Christian tradition. Whatever field of human knowing may be considered, and whatever the value one attributes to this knowing, everyone measures the abyss that separates it from the divine revelation. This is not contempt of nature or of its fruits, nor mistrust of reason. This is a "just sentiment" of the grandeur of the supernatural gift, of its paradoxical, unheard of character. "Speech is powerless to tell us the [divine] nature, and words do not explain the thing as it is."[518] God has become man, the Word has been made flesh:

| "In hac Verbi copula | In this linking of the Word/Verb |
| Stupet omnis regula": | Every rule is confounded. |

This refrain of Latin rhymed prose, well known but perhaps too little admired, on the seven liberal arts confronted with the Incarnation,[519] expresses the center of the Christian faith. In here noting the "stupefaction" that overtakes "every rule," Alan of Lille (1128-1203) indicates with the same stroke the origin of all the "barbarisms" and all the "solecisms" of "grammar" that were to follow if Christian thought were victoriously to resist the barbarisms and solecisms of faith that threatened it.[520] For the mystery of the Incarnation of the Word, that "marvel of marvels," that "paradox of paradoxes," by changing the relation of man to the divinity, has come to change many other things; and these other things do not always willingly accept being changed. The two little verses of the theologian-poet punctuate the first strophe of his piece, devoted to grammar; but they punctuate all the other strophes as well, each of which is devoted to one of the humanistic disciplines. Thus grammar still remains, so to speak, just as in the Gregorian tradition, the entry-gate of all knowledge:

Exceptivam actionem	An exceptional action
Verbum Patris excipit,	The Father's Word began,
Dum deludit rationem,	Whilst it deludes reason,
Dum naturam decipit:	Whilst it deceives nature:
Casualem dictionem	The Substantive takes on
Sustantivum recipit	A casual expression
Actioque passionem	And within this word Action
In hoc verbo concipit.	Conceives the Passion.

The same astonishment, the same "stupor," line after line, applies to Rhetoric, Arithmetic, Music, Dialectic, Astronomy. Here, for example, is what he has for Music:

Dum factoris et facturae Mira fit conjunctio . . . ,	While marvelous conjunction Is made of Maker and the made . . . ,
Stupet sui fracto jure	There stands amazed at its broken law
Musica proportio.	The musical proportion.

Dialectic is no less stupefied:

. . . Fit elinguis, obstupescit,	She turns tongueless, dumbfounded,

Stupet omnis regula! Every rule stands amazed!

Fallitur in propriis	She fails in her properties
Et de suis erubescit	And there blushes Lady Logic
Logica fallaciis.	At her own fallacies.
— In hac Verbi copula	— In this copula of the Word
Stupet omnis regula!	Every rule stands amazed!

This piece from the *Doctor Universalis* does not merely show in him a love of technical virtuosity. Perhaps one will feel all its evocative force only if he recalls by way of contrast that Alan was also the cantor of the natural order, that order so magnificently accorded to human reason. Nature appeared to him in her sovereign majesty. He had greeted that "daughter of God" not only as the "mother of all things," or as the very fecundity of the Word, as Bernardus Silvestris had expressed himself,[521] but again, more precisely, as the "universal Rule," the *Regula mundi*.[522] Now, the awestruck "stupor" that had overcome him before that apparently unbreakable plenitude makes way for a new stupor, before the unique Exception by which everything is put into question again.[523] But at the same time, through those verses on the Incarnation of the Word, Alan brilliantly puts into a nutshell a number of earlier attempts. Adam of Saint Victor, for example, had just chanted:

Super tali genitura	Over such a birth
Stupet usus et natura	Custom stands amazed, nature too —
Deficitque ratio . . .	And reason fails . . .
Potestate, non natura	By power, not by nature
Fit Creator creatura	Creator becomes creature

And again:

Mirabiles hae mixturae! . . .	These marvelous blendings! . . .
Harmonia diversorum	A harmony of diversities
Sed in unum redactorum	But of what's reduced to unity
Dulcis est connexio![524]	Sweet is the connection!

Like many others, Adam was again here blending two themes: the theme of the union of the Word with human nature called for the more developed theme of the *partus virginis* as accompaniment in his hymns:

Splendor Patris et figura	The Father's splendor and figure
Se conformans homini,	Conforming itself to man,
Potestate, non natura	By power, not by nature
Partum dedit virgini.	Gave the virgin offspring.

This was one theme that traditionally held its place, both in prose and verse, in the theological literature:

Virgo genuit: forsan quis	A virgin gave birth: perhaps one
quomodo quaerit.	will ask how.
Non est nosse meum:	It is not mine to know:
sed scio posse Deum.[525]	but I know that God is able.

Marius Victorinus, while still a pagan, had long ago come up with an application for the topos from Cicero's *De inventione*: "If she gave birth, she lay with a man."[526] This topos was seized upon in the controversy with the Jews,[527] and the Christian response had at that time tried to distinguish the *supra naturam* from the *contra naturam*: was not the Creator of nature able to act *supra naturam* in the formation of the second Adam, just as he had done in the formation of the first?[528] But while dismissing the scandal to reason, it did not allow wonder to be lost:

O mira atque nova genitura,	Oh marvelous new generation!
Fit virgo gravida, fideliter credula,	A virgin becomes pregnant, faithfully believing,
Naturam dum hominis induit deitas.[529]	Whilst Deity puts on the nature of a human being.

Godfrey of Saint Victor, too, came to proclaim his own astonishment; but if he bypassed the consideration of the miracle, it was only to pay more particular attention to the nature of the redemptive act itself than to the Being of the Redeemer:

Hujus ergo gratiae modum	Therefore as I got to know the
mox me ut novi,	mode of this grace
Multa mecum disputans,	Disputing many things with
totum commovi,	myself, I was totally shaken,
Stupefactus operis qualitate	Stupefied by the quality of this
novi:	new work:

Stupet omnis regula! Every rule stands amazed!

Pastor neci devovet se misertus ovi . . .	The shepherd having had pity on the sheep vows to let himself be killed . . .
Quam dum non admitteret in se forma Dei,	Whilst the form of God would not admit this into itself,
Res stupenda! fit homo par in paena mei.[530]	Stupendous thing! He becomes a man, equal in my punishment.

Alan leaves aside the miracle — which he does explain elsewhere — in the *Anticlaudianus*.[531] Neither does he face, in his little poem, the strange marvel of redemptive Love. He goes right to the metaphysical paradox — that is the very word he uses[532] — to that paradox that provokes and always will provoke scandal from every rationalist mind,[533] just as it provokes admiring stupor from every believer. Far from trying to reduce it, following an inclination that can be a temptation for an apologist or theologian, he on the contrary makes it stand out, knowing full well that if theology is to bring reason to bear within the faith, it would take a false path by trying more or less to rationalize the data of the faith.[534] In this he shows that he is the worthy successor of John Scotus, like him both a poet and a metaphysician, who had before him chanted this mystery of the Word incarnate:

Nulla quidem virtus potuit dinoscere pure,	No power could distinguish purely
Quem Pater occultum gremio velabat opaco:	The hidden One whom the Father veiled in a dark womb:
Sed caro nunc Verbum factum, mirabile dictu!	But the Word now made flesh, marvelous to tell!
Clare se cunctis hominemque Deumque revolvit . . .	Clearly unveils itself, both man and God, to all . . .
Quis modus est animo, dum talia cernere tentat,	What measure is there for a mind, while it tries to discern such things,
Quive valent sensus meditari famine vocum?[535]	Or what can senses meditate with lack of words?

He rediscovers — or perhaps he is intentionally taking it up again — Origen's exclamation in that beautiful chapter of the *Peri Archôn* that certain recent historians seem, along with so many other texts, to ignore when they say they have a hard time discerning in this Alexandrian a recognition of the unique marvel of the Incarnation: "We are astounded with the highest wonder"; "The narrowness of the human understanding hesitates and, having been struck with the perplexity of such great wonder, it knows not where to bend, what to hang on to, where to turn."[536] He casts it into a poetic mold whose abstract allegorism juxtaposes, or rather fuses together, "dialectical rigor" and "poetic force," into an amazing alloy.[537] In a sort of little drama, he comments on the principle that he expounds at length from another side, in another sort of language, in his *Theological Summa*, in the wake of Saint Hilary and Boethius,[538] and that he recalls again at the head of his *Theological Distinctions:* "In the sacred page ... a construction is not subject to Donatus's laws. ... Words wander from their proper significations and seem, thunderstruck, to crave new meanings."[539] He celebrates in grammatical terms the most baffling mystery, more disconcerting than the very mystery of the Divinity;[540] the mystery of which the Venerable Bede, being inspired once again by Saint Gregory,[541] used to refer to as "that sandal-strap" which John the Baptist declares that he is unworthy to untie, that is, that universal Knot which the human mind will never untie.[542] The strange verses of this disciple of the Porretanians, this man of universal knowledge,[543] who was "the most vigorous and novel thinker" of his generation,[544] one of the greatest among those who immediately prepared the age of high Scholasticism,[545] are, in their very strangeness (which can on first examination seem bizarre), of a suggestive power rarely attained.[546] The Jesuit Jean Buzelin was indeed inspired to publish them in the seventeenth century, in his great work *Galloflandria sacra et profana*.[547] It is naturally in poetry that this grammatical language, already archaic at that time, was to survive; but it is significant that it is found coming from the pen of one of the men who had most magnificently celebrated theology[548] and who had pushed furthest the requirements of the rational organization of revealed wisdom.

At least for the most part, then, it is a quite positive sentiment that underlies the appearance of certain negative propositions, starting with those of Saint Gregory, whether they explicitly envisage "grammar" or "dialectic" or even "reason." Across all the Christian centuries the awareness persists, sometimes a bit drowsy, but always ready for sudden awakenings, of the incomparable newness of Christianity — a newness which is not at all a matter of chronology but is, rather, essential — as well as an awareness of the comprehensiveness that this newness confers on human effort in its entirety. We shall end with the testimony of a writer who was among the best educated and most fruitful of his epoch. Almost a contemporary of Alan of Lille, Alexander Neckham (1157-1217), an encyclopedic mind and a great popularizer, is at once a "grammar-

Stupet omnis regula! Every rule stands amazed!

ian," a naturalist, and a poet. He is also a Churchman. Educated in Paris, like his compatriot John of Salisbury, at the celebrated school of the "Petit-Pont," he celebrates in his verses the capital of the intellectual world, where he taught for many years before being called back to his own country to govern an abbey. Author of a *Speculum speculationum*,[549] he is especially interested in Aristotle, and he is on the lookout for progress in every direction. He knows the importance of questions of grammar and logic in theology. He chants a loving description of the work of the ordering Wisdom in the marvels of Nature. Here is how he expresses himself on the "earth" of our own nature and that of the universe before it came to be inhabited by Christ:

> Therefore the earth was empty, since the Word has not yet become flesh. The earth was void, since the Godhead has not yet dwelt amongst us, i.e., having been united to it in our nature. Therefore the earth of our flesh was void, since the fullness of grace and truth did not yet inhabit it. It was empty, since it was not yet firm or stable through unions of divinity. It was void, since it had not yet been filled with the solidity of the divine fullness. The earth of our habitation was also void, because it was subject to laws out of laws of multiple error. For the Master had not yet come, who has eliminated the vain and erroneous traditions. The Truth that has annulled the empty assertions of the philosophers has not yet arisen from the earth. His inhabited world was void, since the fullness of time had not yet come. The hearts of the earth-born were void, since the Holy Spirit, who later was to be sent in fiery tongues to Christ's disciples, had yet to fill them up. And darkness was upon the face of the deep, since the true light had not yet come, the light that illuminates every human being coming into this world, the light which makes light to shine from the darkness.[550]

In this page, which speaks only of "void" and "darkness," one might denounce a manifesto of obscurantism, just as in the sentences of Saint Gregory on Donatus or many another. One might read into it a testimony of contempt regarding the cosmos as well as science, to accuse these authors of fideistic barbarism or of irrational supernaturalism. But in the majority of these cases, as diverse as they are, this would turn out to be merely a thick-headed misconstruction. Let us rather recognize in truth the corollaries of an acute awareness of the unique marvel, the Incarnation of the Word of God.[551]

CHAPTER TWO

Subjectivism and Spiritual Understanding

1. Where Is the "Proper Sense"?

Once again it is necessary for us to begin by reading Origen. After having explicated a passage from Leviticus, he remarks: "I shall prove this not by my own sense, but from the gospels."[1] If we listen to these simple words carefully, we shall have the key to all that follows. But let us allow the texts to clarify each other a little at a time. Origen says again, later in the same homily: "To construct and defend their dogmas, the heretics have gone madly hither and yon in the Scriptures, but they find nothing but perdition"; then in contrast to their behavior he opposes "the Catholic manner of treating the Word of God within the Church."[2] Elsewhere, taking issue with one of these heretics, he cries: "Ungrateful heretic, see how these new things fit together with the old from start to finish"; or else he denounces the "perverted senses of the letter of the Law";[3] or again, he warns the faithful against the heretical explications that would make them fall outside the mystery of the Church: "We owe it to ourselves to beware that we not be despoiled by the plausibility of a heretical doctrine, and fall away from the mystery of the Church."[4] Instead of letting themselves be guided by "the sense and the will of Scripture"[5] and welcoming the Holy Spirit who has spoken through the Apostles, the heretics in fact listen to "a sense of their own" and "a will of their own"; they "steal" the divine words from the Church and they denature their sense by a "perverted explication."[6] On the other hand, one who is able to discover "the sense of Christ" in Moses and in the Prophets does not speak "of his own heart," but "of the Holy Spirit";[7] he is not "heretical," but "ecclesiastical"; following Paul, he is "a servant of the New Testament, not through the letter, but through the spirit."[8]

The same idea was already found in the *Peri Archôn,* where Origen methodically expounded how many fall into error because they do not know how to understand the Scriptures spiritually: first off, there are the Jews, who, after the coming of the Christ, still obstinately read everything "secundum litteram"; there are also the heretics properly so called, who, victims of the same prejudice albeit on the flip side of the coin, reject that Old Testament to which the Jews adhere literally,[9] or explain it in accordance with philosophy, which thereby turns from serving-girl into mistress.[10] The later tradition will bear the mark established by this firmly drawn figure and indeed by the very words in which Origen had defined the Catholic reading of the Bible against those who, from right or left, would impose their own meaning upon the sacred text and thereby do it violence.[11] Thus Victorinus of Pettau is already opposing the heretics, on the one hand, "who do not use the prophetic testimony," and the Jews, on the other, "who do not accept the preaching of the New Testament," the only objective exegesis, the one that shows the Scriptures to be fulfilled in the Christ.[12] Thus Saint Hilary characterizes heresy as an interpretation imposed on the text "in favor of the sense of one's own will, not for the perfection of the truth itself,"[13] going against the grain of an understanding "according to the preaching of the gospel."[14] Thus Saint Ambrose, assimilates the heretics to so many Antichrists, "who seduce us with a perverse interpretation," and remarks that the Jews do not know how to read the holy Books, because "they want God to have written in ink instead of with the spirit."[15]

It is no surprise that Saint Jerome, who so often copies Origen, expresses himself here just like him, as clearly as clear can be, all the while sometimes mixing with his language a point of paradox that puts it in greater relief. Commenting upon the Epistle to the Galatians, he endeavors to show that the heretics, who cannot see the gospel of the Christ in all the Scriptures, are inspired by the devil:

> Marcion and Basilides and the rest of the plague of heretics do not have God's Gospel, since they do not have the Holy Spirit, without whom the gospel that is taught becomes merely human. Nor do we reckon the Gospel to be in the words, but in the sense, of the Scriptures; not on the surface, but in the marrow; not in the leaves of the

words, but in the root of reason. . . . Scripture is useful to its hearers exactly when it is not spoken without Christ, when it is not uttered without the Father, when he who preaches it does not slip anything into it without the Spirit. Otherwise, both the devil, who is always quoting the Scriptures, and all heresies, according to Ezekiel (13:18), are sewing cushions, which they put under everyone's elbow. If I myself who am speaking have Christ within me, I do not have the gospel of man. . . . There is a great danger to speak in Church, lest perchance, by reason of a perverse interpretation, a gospel of man — or what is worse, of the devil — should emerge from the Gospel of Christ.[16]

Marcion and Mani wrongly maintain that, through the allegorical interpretation, we take the Law in a sense that does not belong to it: it is rather they who do not understand that Moses has written of spiritual things.[17] Their mistake is always the same — "the carnal interpretation of the Scriptures";[18] there we have a Judaic interpretation, an occasion of multiple ills, doing violence to the interpretation of the Church and rejecting "the spiritual bread that has come down for us from heaven."[19] The same doctrine is taken up on several occasions in the commentary on Isaiah:

Heretics also corrupt the Gospel truth (of the Scriptures) with a crooked understanding, and are the very worst innkeepers, making water from wine, whilst our Lord in contrary fashion turned waters into wine, and such a wine that the head waiter is amazed at it: in which fashion also the queen of Sheba marveled at Solomon's banquet, praising with her own voice his butlers and the ministers of the wine (2 Chronicles 9). But Ecclesiastes (ch. 2) also describes in mystical language the ministries of the wine and of his banquet.[20]

Here Saint Jerome applies to the situation created by the preaching of the Gospel what Saint Irenaeus had said of the ancient situation, when the Jews mixed the water of their human traditions with the wine of the divine Law.[21] A bit later on he again reproaches the heretics for their earth-hugging exegesis that makes them look like animals devoid of reason; for them Zion is a valley, though for the faithful it is a mountain, because they fall "from the sublimity of the sense of the holy Scriptures" down "to things that belong to the ground," although the orthodox exegete rises "to the spiritual understanding."[22] From that time on we see the meaning of his exhortation: "let us kill the sons of heretics . . . with spiritual arrows,"²³ and we understand that he is addressing himself to the Judaizers to say to them: "Why do you want to build yourself a home in the letter that killeth, and to fix your tent, which has no foundation in the firmness of rock? It should be called not so much a tent and a home as a tomb and a memorial."²⁴

Jerome deals with the question again from the same point of view in his *Dialogue against the Luciferians*. The heretics to whom he is alluding are the Marcionists, the Valentinians, and the "Montenses sive Campitas," i.e., the Donatists: the devil himself, he observes, cites the Scriptures, and the heretics do as he does; but it is not enough to quote them, one must also understand them: that is to say, it is necessary to read them in the spirit; "otherwise, if we follow the letter, we ourselves can also fashion some new dogma."²⁵ In this passage Jerome is not inspired only by Origen, as in the preceding ones; he is also using Saint Hilary word for word,²⁶ of whom, however, he says ungenerously elsewhere on a couple of occasions that he [Hilary] gathers a few too many of the "flowers of Greece" in the garden of Alexandria. Perhaps, observes Dom Antin, he had "hoped for the monopoly" for the exploitation of a mine so rich as that.²⁷ We can note this in passing. But there is another remark that leads us to the heart of our subject. The irascible doctor transposes the reproach made against the heretics to use its terms against some of his colleagues (mei similes); this is in a letter to Saint Paulinus of Nola; passing in review the diverse sorts of people who unduly arrogate "the art of the Scriptures" for themselves, he mentions a certain number of them, who, he maintains:

> think that whatever they say is the Law of God, nor do they deign to know what the prophets or what the apostles meant, but they join unfitting testimonies to their own meaning, as if it is a grand and not a most vicious kind of speaking to distort the judgments of the prophets and the apostles and to drag them off to their own repugnant will.²⁸

This is the same kind of transposition that inspired the apostrophe addressed to Saint Hilary in Jerome's commentary on Saint Matthew. To this Jerome, in another circumstance, and this time without explicit polemic, opposes his own plan:

> The task set before me was not to drag the Scriptures to my own will, but to say what I understood the Scriptures to intend. The job of the

commentator is not to expound what he himself intends, but rather what he whom he is interpreting means.[29]

With Saint Augustine we again find the straight lineage of the tradition, that of Origen and that of Jerome commenting on Isaiah or the Epistle to the Galatians. Having to explicate the Psalm verse: "Rebuke the beasts of the reed," Saint Augustine asks himself what sort of things these curious ferocious beasts are: they are, he answers, the heretics; being without understanding, they are by that very fact harmful, and they are "beasts of the reed," because they so perverted the sense of the Scriptures by bending them to their own errors.[30] Let us always, like Origen and Jerome, understand the beings without understanding, comparable to beasts, and indeed ferocious beasts, as readers who refuse the spiritual understanding, so as to hang on to the letter which killeth. The same thought recurs in almost the same terms and with the same characteristic use of the word "understanding" in the letter to Consentius. Without that spiritual understanding, says Augustine to his correspondent, the Scriptures will be of no use to you; that understanding must also be correct:

> But love the understanding very much; since even the holy Scriptures themselves, which recommend faith prior to the understanding of great things, cannot be of any use to you unless you understand them rightly. For all the heretics, who accept the Scriptures as authoritative, seem in their own eyes to be following them, even though they are actually following their own errors; indeed, they are heretics not because they have contempt for the Scripture but because they do not understand them.[31]

If one stuck to the pure letter of Scripture, it would be useless: this thought, in its formulation, comes from Origen. But now Augustine's perspective is larger. At the beginning of the fifth century, the "heretics" are no longer merely men who reject the Old Testament through literalist prejudice; there are also among them some who accept it and pretend to comprehend it; nevertheless they draw no fruit from it, because the understanding that they have of it is still "carnal." Hence arise these counsels and these warnings, as in the explication of Psalm 48:

> All the divine utterances are helpful to those of good understanding, but dangerous for those who want to twist them to the perversity of

their own heart rather than to rectify their own heart to the rightness of the utterances. For this is a great and frequent perversity amongst men.[32]

Also in the *De genesi ad litteram,* through a transposition analogous to the one that Saint Jerome had performed, but without the same polemical intention, Augustine advises the Catholic reader himself to be wary not to substitute his own sense for the sense of the Scripture:

> And in matters dark and very far from our eyes, if we should read from thence any writings, even the divine, which can show up with various senses consistent with the faith with which we were imbued, let us not hurl ourselves head over heels into asserting any of these [senses] lest, if perchance under more diligent discussion the truth should rightly shake that [sense], we should fall; whilst struggling not on behalf of the sense of the divine Scriptures themselves but on behalf of our own, in such fashion that we may have wanted our sense to be the sense of the Scriptures, when we ought rather to want that of the Scriptures to be our own.[33]

This is exactly the same advice on the particular application, and it is the self-same phraseology as was in Jerome and will be later on in Berno. Saint Augustine says the same thing in the *De doctrina christiana* relating to the reader of the Bible who goes astray in his exegesis; it is doubtless possible for this reader to discover a thought true in and of itself; his situation is nonetheless dangerous:

> For by rashly claiming what he whom he is reading did not sense, he often runs into other items that he cannot fit together with the former sense: and if he consents that the latter are true and certain, that which he had sensed may not be able to be true; and it comes about in him, I know not how, that, by loving his own sense, he may begin to be more displeased with Scripture than with himself.[34]

Before leaving Saint Augustine, let us say once again that if he does not designate the carnal interpretation of the Scriptures, that of the Jews or that of the heretics, in so many words as a "superstitious understanding," he comes quite close to it. For in the same *De doctrina christiana* he denounces at length the "superstition of the gentiles" and the "superstitious inventions" as leading to pernicious errors in biblical exegesis, he also carefully endeavors to separate them off from the profane arts and sciences that are, in opposition to them, capable of promoting a correct understanding of Scripture[35]; in the *Contra Faustum*, likewise, he will once again treat the literalist interpretation of the Jews, as we shall see a bit later on, as "vain superstition."[36]

Eusebius of Emessa also characterizes the heretics by saying that they cut the Old Testament off from the New.[37] Again, a Psalm verse gives Cassiodorus the opportunity to express straight Origenian doctrine: "Guide me in the right path because of my enemies": this path is Scripture; it is a right path, when the understanding of it is right; the prophet is therefore praying to obtain a right understanding of the Old Testament, that is, in all its books to catch a glimpse of the Lord to come; in this way he will escape his enemies, that is to say, both the heretics and the unbelieving Jews, men of perverse intention and detestable will, who endeavor to denature its sense.[38] Saint Gregory in due course enters into the concert; but, like Saint Augustine in his explication of the "ferocious beasts," he has not more than the heretics in view. Just as Origen had said of the "Philistines" of his own time,[39] he sees them blocking up the wells of Scripture, drying them out by their earth-hugging explications, whereas the orthodox exegete keeps mining them out so as to discover the depth of the senses hidden within them.[40] He sees them once again figured in those men under discussion in the twenty-fourth chapter of Job, who, always in search of prey, reap in a field that does not belong to them and gather grapes in a vineyard not their own: they want "to ravage" everything "to their own peculiar sense" and in the vast field of the Scriptures "they carry away various sentences far from their proper meanings"; relying on their very own will, "they free themselves from every bond of faith and reason"; "serving their own desires," they harvest the clusters of biblical judgments "for the intention of their own understanding" and do not fear to lift a sacrilegious hand against the master of the vineyard, the Author of the Scripture, "since they strive violently to bend its sense into the words of sacred eloquence."[41] Gregory meditates again on the impious and the violent under discussion in chapter 27 and once more he recognizes in them the heretics:

> Not absurdly are those who are aliens to the knowledge of the truth through an error of perverse teaching called "impious heretics"; and he even calls them "violent" in the following word, since they try violently to bend the judgments containing the correct teachings of sacred Scripture to a perverse understanding.[42]

And for him those young mockers found in chapter 30 are always the heretics: in their pride, isolating themselves from the great Church, they no longer find anything to eat except grass and the bark of trees, i.e., despite all their pretensions they remain at "the surface of the Scriptures" and do not comprehend them; "deceived by the perversion of their senses," they entirely bypass the "spiritual understanding." Sometimes they believe, in their pride, that they have been raised up to "a sublime understanding" and brag about the "spiritual secrets" that they have penetrated, when in reality they have scarcely heard the exterior sound of the divine words.[43] In these various passages, except for one or two expressions peculiar to him, Saint Gregory is, right down to the words themselves, dependent upon Origen[44] and Jerome,[45] and the epithets that he receives from them to crush impious exegesis — *violens, pravus, perversus* — will be transmitted to posterity.[46]

But well before Gregory, the author of the tenth book of the *Clementine Recognitions*, whoever he may have been, as he is presented to us through Rufinus's Latin translation, had perhaps expressed the same thought already. It is the Apostle Peter who is supposed to be speaking:

> One must watch out when God's Law is read, that it be read not according to the understanding of one's own mind. For there are many words in the divine Scriptures that can be drawn to the sense that each one presumes for himself of his own accord; but this must not be done. For you ought not to look for an alien and extraneous sense that you have brought in from outside, which you confirm from the authority of the Scriptures, but rather you ought to grasp the sense of the truth from the Scriptures themselves; and so one must learn the understanding of the Scriptures from him who preserves it according to the truth handed down to him by our ancestors, so that he himself can also competently claim what he has rightly received.[47]

Some have recognized there a manifesto of "distrust regarding Christian allegory"; these sentences have even seemed to be "formal declarations of the wrongdoings of biblical allegory."[48] Following the analogous texts that have just been cited, one will have to admit at least that such an interpretation is by no means necessary. Furthermore, in that case it would be harder to explain the facts (a) that Origen had cited this same book of the *Recognitions* with praise;[49] (b) that Rufinus had taken the trouble to translate it; and (c) that this translation had enjoyed a great success in the Christian Middle Ages.[50] Did not the author, who has devoted himself to a long critique of the arbitrary allegorical system by which the pagan philosophers wanted to justify their myths, just now allude to the heretics who treat the Bible in the same way in order to justify their ideas? If one believes he can divine under this writing a critique of all Christian allegory, it might be because one is thinking of a doctrine which was doubtless that of the Clementines under an older form, and perhaps also because one has been led to define Christian allegory in terms of pagan allegorical method from the very start. But it will be enough, I believe, to read in sequence the chapters in which our author develops his critique to understand what to make of them. Those whom the pagans adore as gods, he thinks, were men; but their story is full of crimes and shameful actions; thus the ancient writers subsequently struggle to find another meaning for them:

> When prudent men saw that such disgraceful, such base superstition was common and yet they had not learned any method or science for correcting it, they tried, with whatever arguments and interpretations they could, to drape the dishonorable realities with an honorable account, and not, as they say, to hide the honest reasons with dishonest fables.[51]

In other words, it is not true that the ancients among the gentiles had hidden wise and deep ideas under fables invented to that end; it is the moderns who have tried to veil the scandal of those stories under ideas that came from elsewhere. Now such a procedure would be even more worthy of condemnation in the case of the divine Scriptures. One ought to draw an understanding of them from themselves, and following the norms received from the tradition;[52] not from an "alienus," "extraneus" sense; not from a sense dragged in from elsewhere, "extrinsecus": these words are found in the sequel. Do not all the exegetes of the Church at large, all the "Fathers" — whatever be the degree, the shading, or the absence of "allegorism" among them — all say basically the same thing?

Saint Isidore of Seville summarizes nicely the teaching of the principal Fathers when he writes that many "have fallen into heresy . . . by not understanding the Scriptures spiritually"; these heretics, he continues, "do not savor the Scriptures with a sound sense, but lead them to the error of a perverse understanding; nor do they subject themselves to the senses of the Scriptures, but perversely drag them off to their own error."[53] On the contrary, it is necessary to look for the "sound allegorical understanding," namely, the "sense of the interior understanding," which everywhere shows the unity of the two Testaments.[54] This is what the *Liber mozarabicus sacramentorum* calls the "open manifestation of the truth," or "the omni-dimensional fullness of the mystical understanding."[55] Saint Bede too finds fault with the "wandering, gentile sense" of the heretics,[56] with their "peculiar sense," from which only a "perverse" or "stupid understanding" can proceed.[57] Their "astuteness" has been conquered by the "spiritual sense" that "the holy preachers" expound.[58] To the narrow and false views to which anyone is condemned who relies on his own understanding to comprehend the prophetic Scripture, Bede again opposes the understanding obtained by the faithful from the "broader mysteries" with which it is full.[59] He promises a particular glory in the Kingdom to the one who will have received the Law in its spiritual sense. But to the promise there corresponds a threat:

> But if some doctor should have preferred his own sense to the words of Scripture and should have inflamed his hearers through dogmas that he has composed for himself rather than to [illuminate] spiritual things, . . . the fool will lose the kingdom.[60]

This topic will become a great spiritual preoccupation in Carolingian times, in those times of bitter doctrinal struggles, where the additional concern about the unity of the revived empire, piggy-backing upon the permanent concern about the unity of the faith, intensifies the aspiration "for the peace and unity of the holy Churches of God,"[61] and seems to promote among religious writers an obsession about the heretic.[62] Charlemagne assuredly does not envisage the traditional use of allegory when he instructs the "venerable pastors and rectors of the Churches of God" not to tolerate "that some, proceeding from their own sense and not according to the sacred Scriptures, should be making up novelties or non-canonical things and preaching them to the people."[63] Sedulius Scotus criticizes those who understand the Scripture "perversely" by interpreting merely according to the letter passages that in spirit contain prophecies of Christ.[64] Florus of Lyon, whom we have already seen, also rises up against this "sense of one's own" that attacks the immutable truth of the Scripture.[65] Alcuin is able to speak peacefully of "the venerable sense of the Fathers,"[66] but he also knows how to thunder against "the practice of all the heretics" who oppose a "foreign sense" to this "venerable sense" by using entirely subjective methods, "otherwise than the character of the truth holds."[67] These men, he says again, "are striving to interpret the judgments of divine speech through a perverse sense to prove their own error."⁶⁸ He does not always speak in general terms, using worn-out coin; on occasion he designates the one at fault: for example, the unhappy Felix of Urgel, who, searching everywhere through the vast field of the Scriptures for what might authorize the errors of his sect and not being able to find it, nevertheless does not stop interpreting the sacred words "in the sense of his own perversity."⁶⁹ Hincmar of Reims, thundering against another unfortunate, Godescalc of Orbais, opposes both the depraved commentaries of the heretics and the vanities of the grammarians to the "hidden mysteries" that the orthodox tradition discovers in "the heavenly documents."⁷⁰ To inveigh against John Scotus, Prudentius of Troyes takes up the same theme by invoking the authority of all the Catholic doctors, especially Saint Gregory.⁷¹ As regards Felix again, Saint Paulinus of Aquilaea contrasts, in the reading of the sacred text, the heretic with "most evil heart" and "twisted mind," and the Catholic with "devout mind" and "sound sense."⁷² He blames Felix for a "personal twist" and an "unbelieving sense" that make him corrupt rather than submit to the "apostolic sense": he does not agree simply to look at "the wheel within the wheel," that is to say, following the image that Saint Gregory had so brilliantly explicated, "each Testament working in gear with the other"!⁷³

> But what wonder if you stupidly err in these matters which are a thick forest of allegory, and, you do not know how with learned hand to pluck the spiritual fruits, wrapped with the trappings of shadowy enigmas, hanging from under the leaves of the letters, since, understanding it badly, you have depraved the orthodox teaching produced in public by the holy preachers.⁷⁴

Such is also the doctrine of Charlemagne, with the help of Alcuin, or more likely, it appears, of Theodulf of Orléans.⁷⁵ In the *Libri carolini*, he expounds it at length to struggle against the cult of sensible images.⁷⁶ To accommodate Scripture to each person's own sense, to turn its real signification "to strange understandings," is to reject its spirit. Christ, he explains, is the source of life, as he is the bread of heaven:

> Whoever receives his spiritual drinks and spiritual foods otherwise than he gives them, that is, strives to interpret the divine Scriptures in some other sense and not in the way they were handed over by the Holy Spirit, is convicted of being alien to his pastures. . . . Of such the Lord complains through the prophet as follows: "I have given them silver and gold, and they have made a Baal" (Hosea 2), i.e., they have

turned the dignity of spiritual understanding and beauty of speech to the savagery of the depraved senses and empty glory. For since the lawgiver says: "In the right hand of the Lord there is the fiery Law" (Deuteronomy 33:2, Vulg.), it is amazing how sluggish they are who are neither delighted by its beauty nor terrified by its heat.[77]

But those wretches, who were not willing here below to let themselves be enlightened by the flame, will in the world to come be burned by the fire.[78] Paschasius Radbertus is neither softer nor more original when he several times denounces the "perverse thoughts" and "depraved intentions" of the heretics in their explication of Scripture;[79] but on one occasion he broadens the reproach by accusing them of perverting even the writings of the ancient philosophers in the same way:

> Each one of the heretics bends God's Scriptures away from what is right and pours them out more broadly to the paths of their own perversity . . . , and I do not speak of the Scriptures only, for they have also corrupted the words of the philosophers.[80]

As to Rabanus Maurus, he plays his role of compiler in amplifying the voices of Origen, Jerome, and Gregory. There are numerous sacred texts in which he, like Gregory, sees a symbol of the heretics "imposing upon the Scriptures a sense unconcerned with the Lord,"[81] i.e., a sense which does not recognize the Lord announced under the letter. These men constantly "introduce a sense contrary to the truth," which is "a low sense";[82] they "corrupt the witnesses after their own sentiment," "teach erroneous dogmas thanks to false interpretations," "sully as much as in them lies the oracles of the Scriptures" and make of them "the matter of all sorts of their abominations."[83] Just like the unbelieving Jews, "they follow the letter of the Old Testament," attack "the true understanding of the spiritual circumcision" and thus do "violence" to the text.[84] Over against them there rise up "the doctors of the Catholic truth," "those who teach the faith within the Church and enlighten the people of God with the word of truth."[85] Like David fighting against Goliath, they fight against those who corrupt the true sense.[86] They dispel their errors by digging up the surface of the letter so as to reach the various senses that a true faith renders perceptible;[87] they correct both Jewish decrepitude and novel superstition through the spiritual grace of the twofold Testament; in deference to the Redeemer, they explain everything through the Gospel;[88] sustained by prayer, they discover the hidden mystery without surrendering to subjective opinions.[89] They distribute, as Remigius of Auxerre will soon say, the bread of the spiritual teaching, whereas the Scribes and Pharisees, like the heretics and the philosophers of the gentiles, squander or lose the brilliance of their eloquence "in the surface of the letter and in human knowledge," where one does not find the spiritual bread that satisfies the soul, namely, the Christian understanding which makes known the living Bread.[90] And, to go on, Remigius, addressing heretics opposed to the only correct understanding, which is spiritual, will invoke reproaches of "perverse understanding" or "perverse interpretation."[91] Apparently the vocabulary had varied no more than the thought.

2. *"Bovinus intellectus"*

In this intensely secular context, will the words of Berno of Reichenau, or rather the words cited by him — "non tuo sensui attemperes Scripturas" ["thou shalt not adjust the Scriptures to thine own sense"] — seem to render a novel sound again? Will anyone still be tempted to attribute to them, without any further indication, a significance exactly the opposite to the one that all such words took on among so many other ecclesiastical writers? It is true that even the most traditional formulations, while themselves still intact, can change meaning in the course of ages, sometimes to such an extent as to receive a signification just the reverse of what they had at first. Such is not at all the case here. For there are still indications following the eleventh century that will show that the theme is permanent.

Some years after Berno, Saint Bruno of Segni himself complained that when reading the Scripture, the heretics "turn it around to their own sense."[92] They do it, he says, "with an evil mind," and the understanding they arrive at is "prava et erronea."[93] But what precisely is vicious about them? Here is the reply, and it is always that of Origen and of Jerome, that of Augustine, Cassiodorus, and Gregory:

> In the thick forest of the sacred Scriptures . . . the heretics *violently* gnaw at and mangle what they cannot understand. . . . They are delighted at mere novelty, and, since *the spiritual understanding* has been *left out,* they explain almost everything literally. . . . When they find something novel that seems to agree with their errors, they are soon running around in all directions clamoring for joy, and sticking it into their own books and disputations.[94]

The same theme, though a bit less explicit, shows up in Manegold of Lautenbach,[95] who also takes up the Augustinian comparison of the "wild beasts."[96] It appears again in Guibert of Nogent: "Through false interpretations of the Scriptures . . . they expound the examples of the Scriptures as though they were uttered in a carnal sense."[97]

With the same end in view, Rupert of Deutz takes up the image of the wells of the Patriarchs from Origen and Gregory, as Bruno of Segni had just done:[98]

> The heretics . . . have stopped up these wells, i.e., the Scriptures, as much as they could, so that it might not be easy to find where the doctrine of the truth would be. . . . Thus indeed the heretics . . . have stopped up the sacred Scriptures with their own earthly senses.[99]

And here is Rupert once more taking up Gregory and Origen's term *violently*, by introducing another, more forceful image: "In this way the heretics . . . *violently* climbing up onto the bed of God the Father, i.e., the Scripture of the sacred Law, have corrupted the people with bad seed."[100] The heretics render themselves guilty of rape, and, instead of the spiritual understanding that would give God new children, they, like adulterers, are just hunting after their own gratification:

> "The eye of the adulterer," he says, "watches out for darkness" (Job 24:15), i.e., just as an adulterer seeks not offspring but pleasure in carnal intercourse in the dark; so does the heretic hypocritically adulterate God's Word, since he desires not to beget spiritual sons of God, but rather to show off by preaching his own knowledge and, as it were, carries off another man's wife, whilst he draws the faithful soul into his own error.[101]

The implicit reference to Saint Paul is remarkable.[102] The essential element of the image comes from Origen.[103] Rupert shows perhaps a bit more originality in another passage, where he applies the thought and the common expressions no longer merely to the Jews and the heretics, but to the gentile philosophers as well. Paschasius reproached the heretics for corrupting the sense of the ancient philosophers: Rupert, for his part, reproaches these philosophers themselves for having been the first to pervert the sense of the Scripture.[104] His originality does not, however, entail any real innovation in thought, since through this transposition of a traditional theme, he rediscovers a more ancient one, inherited from the Jews, the famous theme of theft. He introduces it in a quite unexpected way, while commenting on the story of Naaman the Syrian recounted in the fourth book of Kings [2 Kings 5]. Some brigands from Syria had captured a young Israelite, who had become the slave-girl of the wives of the leprous king:

> The girl is holy Scripture. Next, the brigands, Pythagoras, Socrates, Plato, and the rest were the philosophers, who had actually led this girl captive from the land of Israel by acting like brigands, by stealthily reading over and over and violently bending every little piece of holy Scripture to their own errors of sense, and they kept trying to force her to serve, like a wife of Naaman's, under fickle philosophy.[105]

Even in this last passage, as can be seen, there is nothing which might apply against the allegorical exegesis as it was practiced in the Church. Rupert is, on the contrary, one of its most illustrious representatives.[106] His biographer, the Canon A. Cauchie, who recognized this fact, expresses regret that he had thereby given "popularity to a system of interpretation that subjected not the mind of the interpreter to the text of the Bible, but the text of the Bible to the fancies of the interpreter."[107] Even more, he thinks that he sees in a passage from the *Dialogues* of Anselm of Havelberg (†1158) a reaction against the alleged allegorism of Rupert. Anselm, he tells us, justifies his reaction in terms full of good sense. But in my view there are, in fact, three misunderstandings here. In the first place, the terms cited by Canon Cauchie are put by Anselm not into his own mouth, but into that of the Greek interlocutor with whom he is debating. This detail, however, is of no importance, since Anselm himself holds entirely similar positions. However, in the second place, we do not see that there is the least allusion, howsoever distant or implicit, to the exegesis of Rupert. In the third place, allegorical exegesis is not at all, in fact, at issue between the two interlocutors, whether to favor it or to blame it.[108] The Bishop of Havelberg and the Archbishop of Nicomedia are arguing about the scriptural texts concerning the Holy Spirit; the question at issue is whether or not the Spirit proceeds from the Son as it proceeds from the Father. The subject is particularly delicate; so the Latin believes he ought to take certain preliminary precautions. He beseeches the Greek to avoid subtleties by which too often one tries to impugn troublesome texts:

> But if you want to try to turn the proposed authorities back to your own sense, and do not care rather to accommodate your own sense to the divine Scripture, I fear lest in this too you should be set against

the Holy Spirit and resist him, when you do not blush at temerariously turning away the things that have been written at the dictation of the Holy Spirit outside the understanding of the Holy Spirit, and twist it to your own sense; we have come together not to be victorious but to investigate the truth. . . .

At this the Greek, himself also good at fencing, replies to the Latin with his own "on guard":

Nechites, the Archbishop of Nicomedia, said: "How evil it is to twist the understanding of the Scripture, which deservedly has been called 'divine', to one's own sense, as it were, by violent exposition, and not rather humbly to deliver up and accommodate one's own sense entirely to the divine Scripture, is something that ought to be unknown to no one who is accustomed to devote his time to sacred readings, and so you have given a good warning. Hence do yourself what you have warned me to do; and if you want to propound the sacred authors, may you expound them in such a way that you not seem to want to prove your opinion with a twisted exposition: because it is yours, not because it is true."[109]

But the Latin, in his prologue, had given us notice: "He [the Greek bishop] seemed to affirm as right all the things in which the Greeks disagree with the Latins, once a few authoritative passages of the holy Scriptures had violently been twisted to his own sense."[110] The opponent has therefore been well targeted, without any hidden agenda. Rupert and allegorism are entirely irrelevant.

The misunderstanding could have been facilitated, however, by the fact that Anselm uses the same argument in the course of another polemic, or rather formulates the same critique in almost the same terms, in writing to Ecbert, abbot of Huisbourg, who was maintaining against him, the canon regular, the point of view of Benedictine monasticism. In this other controversy, what is at stake is to know whether the "cor unum et anima una" the ["one heart and one soul"] of the fourth chapter of Acts ought to be understood of the "society of the monks" or of that "of the Apostles and their disciples"; if the first interpretation were good, says the champion of the canons, Luke would have had to entitle his book the *Actus monachorum*. Anselm has just reread a letter that Ecbert had sent him; addressing him all the while as "frater dulcissime" ["O very sweet brother"], he sends him back a bittersweet reply:

"Bovinus intellectus"

> I have come upon some superstitious things that are useless to mention, which you, on the other hand, have striven to prove with a few rationalizations based on opinion and a few authoritative texts called back to your personal sense. But how wicked it is to alienate any sacred Scripture to one's own sense rather than to adapt one's own sense to the divine Scripture, ought not be unknown to anyone who has grown accustomed to devote himself to the sacred readings.[111]

Now, a few years earlier, Rupert had taken part in the quarrel, intransigently maintaining the "monastic" thesis. Anselm had argued with him about it in a conversation that had not brought them to agreement, and in this very letter to Ecbert he recalls that incident, in terms indicating contempt for Rupert.[112] Still, one could not apply to Rupert what Anselm himself applies, on the one side, to the archbishop Nechites and, on the other, to the abbot Ecbert, or mix allegorism in with a quarrel that, in each of the two cases, obviously bears upon something else. In fact, Cauchie's error of interpretation, like that which we have brought up about Berno, arises from a prejudice which attributes to the men of the Middle Ages a completely "modern" conception. Those men do indeed condemn subjectivism in exegesis, but they do not at all put it where more than one modern has, without distinction, attempted to put it.[113]

It is to the Jews that Peter the Venerable utters his reproach, in terms that recall Saint Jerome and Berno:

> How long then, o Jews, will this cow-like understanding [*bovinus intellectus*] occupy your hearts . . . ? If you decide to persist in your usual insanity, and set out more to apply the Scriptures to your sense than to bend your sense to the Scriptures, listen to them resisting you and displaying things contrary to your perverse understanding.[114]

Gerhoh of Reichersberg returns to the classic theme exploited by men like Bruno of Segni, Guibert of Nogent, and Rupert of Deutz. He does not, by citing the exact words of the text, convey all the details that his predecessors adduced in favor of the spiritual understanding upheld by the Church. Nonetheless his thought is the same. He too finds fault with the heretics as well as certain overbold "masters" who risk becoming heretics; that is indeed a feature of his reform-minded conservatism in a time when disquieting novelties are bursting out on all sides. Against these innovators, he employs the old comparison of the bow, which is put side-by-side with the sword in the account of spiritual struggles.[115] Suggested by the biblical texts that speak of Yahweh's bow, this comparison, developed by Saint Augustine[116] and Saint Gregory,[117] and found everywhere, served not only to show the relations between the two Testaments, of which the Old was the wood of the bow and the New, the string,[118] but also to designate the use that orthodoxy could make of Scripture in projecting the arrows of true doctrine with this bow;[119] some used it also sometimes in the reverse direction, to denounce the abuse that Judaism or heresy was making of it.[120] These last two uses are going to be those of Gerhoh. He is going to offer us in one and the same instance, in a few sentences, a whole series of traditional formulas that we are already well acquainted with:

> Now then let the learned masters pardon us if we join the words of the Psalms to the course of our own time in the same way that blessed Augustine always obliquely noted the course of his own time in his exposition of the Psalms. For if the heretics of all times were aiming their bow, i.e., holy Scripture, toward their own error, and those who are now heretics, Simoniacs and Nicolaitans, do not cease to twist their bow by distorting the Scriptures according to their own sense,[121] why is it not legitimate for us to use those self-same Scriptures to refute their distorted senses, not as a bow bent violently athwart, but as a double-headed, two-edged sword? For we are not trying to deflect the Scriptures from their proper sense, but rather what had been given to us is speaking unto the glory of its Giver. . . . We do not violently wrench out some foreign sense from the Psalms, but by saying things that are in harmony with the Fathers, while refuting heresies, we willingly keep the former sense current for our own times.[122]

Gerhoh is well aware that in his explication of the Psalter he is in some fashion or other extending the sense of the words, to adapt it to the situation of his own time. He has thus embarked on a slope that could become dangerous, and in the next chapter we shall see that in fact the slope was sometimes descended. Nevertheless, it is one thing to believe that such and such a historical event was predicted or prefigured in the sacred text, and quite another to apply to such and such a concrete situation this sacred text which gives the spiritual key to it. Gerhoh was to do this second thing, not the first. For he knows as well as anyone that the Scripture has been put into our hands to respond to all the new situations arising from age to age,[123] and he had the example of Saint Gregory and of Saint Augustine for doing so. Besides, is not the situation basically always the same? The Catholic is always finding himself confronted with Judaizers, heretics, and innovators who do not want to take account of "the will of the Scriptures." These are sometimes men "of powerful erudition in the letter and conspicuous for their knowledge," but at the same time they are "blinded by hatred of the truth." In one way or another, as Berno already repeated it and as Gerhoh says it again himself on many occasions, "they turn" or "bend the Scripture toward their own sense":

> Howsoever often the followers of the Jews, the false Christians, chase after earthly things while talking about the Scriptures, they are thought to be muttering from the soil, not in the Holy Spirit but rather in the spirit of a python, and consequently they, along with Saul consulting the oracle, are rightly rejected in every audience of the faithful.[124]

The explications that Gerhoh used against those men of earthly spirit,[125] "adapted" so that they might aim at a topical refutation of their errors, are nevertheless, he thinks, neither "violent," nor "outlandish," nor "deviant," in the way theirs are, because his always at least conform to the doctrine of the Fathers and to the rule of faith, drawn from Scripture itself. Thus one can draw apparently new things along with the old from this treasure, without fear of subjectivism, so as to face new requirements. This again is just what Saint Augustine had said: many explications of one and the same text can be legitimate, provided that whichever one is adopted "it must conform to the rule of faith."[126] That is what he had expounded at length in the pages of the *De Genesi ad litteram* and the *De doctrina christiana*, which warned precisely against "personal sentiment."

Such then was the first rule of hermeneutics: orthodoxy. The whole tradition held it in high regard, opposing it to the "distinctive" sense of the heretics or to their "curious desire."[127] It was, as it were, the obverse, of which the "distinctive sense" was the reverse,[128] or the armor of gold and silver against which its features are shattered.[129] Only one prejudicial question was put before a commentator on the Scripture: "are the things that he is writing true and Catholic or false and heretical?"[130] Following so many others, Saint Anselm formulates this rule of orthodoxy in his *De fide Trinitatis*;[131] still elsewhere he stresses it, saying: "If Scripture is indubitably at odds with our own sense . . . , our reason must be believed to be sustained by no truth."[132] Now, what did this rule command, except that one understand the Scripture as the Lord himself understood and explained it, that is to say, that in reading "the Law" one finds "the Gospel"? Outside of that, one was merely a "false prophet," one was speaking "according to one's own heart" and not according to the Holy Spirit. That is what the unanimous tradition repeats ever since Origen. "A superabundance of heresy," Irimbert of Admont is still saying, "by a presumption of carnal understanding."[133] In analogous terms Saint Bernard reproves the men who, he says, "struggle to pervert the saving writings" by bending them "to the sense of their own malice,"[134] and he fears what he might take as divine inspiration if the Spirit should not keep his heart and his understanding from going off in pursuit of his own sense.[135] But this does not dissuade him from looking for the spiritual understanding — quite the contrary. Hugh of Saint Victor has the same strictures as Bernard:

> But now, since they have put their own sense ahead of the faith in the sacraments of God, and have disdained to hold to the sound form of interpretation in the holy Scriptures, it comes about that the very word of truth may becloud them all the more, since the understanding mistakenly serves error instead of truth. This vice does not belong to Scripture, though, but to the blindness of those who read and do not understand.[136]

Werner of Saint Blaise, who aspires less to originality than anyone else, in his collection called the *Deflorationes sanctorum Patrum*, writes that the heretics "do not savor the Scriptures with a sound sense, but lead them to an error of a depraved understanding; they do not subject themselves to their senses, but perversely drag [the Scriptures] toward their own error."[137] Expressing himself more positively, Raoul Ardent clearly and explicitly wishes:

> So let the ministers of the New Testament read and understand the sacred Scriptures not from the sense that they make, but rather from the sense out of which they themselves are being made; attending to what things are said historically, which ones mystically, which tropologically, and which ones are said anagogically, so that they may merit to be, along with Paul, fitting ministers of the New Testament not in the letter, but by the spirit.[138]

In a sermon very much in line with Augustine and Gregory, Peter Comestor condemns those who "destroy the Scripture" by explicating it according to "the images of their heart."[139] Biblical doctrine, he says again, is a sort of honey; but they "adulterate" this honey, like the Ebionites, by mixing in the water of pagan interpretations.[140] Peter the Cantor makes the same judgment; he wants only a pure wine, that having the sense of the Church, and not a wine cut with insipid water and corrupted by "one's own sense."[141] Once again, the idea came from the Fathers. Saint Jerome had expounded it while commenting on the words of Isaiah: "Your innkeepers mix water with the wine," as has been seen above.[142] It had already been exploited in Jerome's sense by Remigius of Auxerre, saying of the heretic: "he violates the wine of holy Scriptures":[143] by Bruno of Segni, who also rejected that mixed, turbid, corrupted wine;[144] by Manegold, for whom Scripture was a chalice "containing the spiritual understanding like a pure wine";[145] by Hervaeus of Bourg Dieu, who did not want the mixed wine of the Jews, that "sense of the Scriptures softened by the admixture of the carnal understanding."[146] Another closely related biblical metaphor, going in the other direction, had already allowed one to express what the only acceptable interpretation was, aside from any peculiar 'proper' sense. The chalice of the Lord, said Cassiodorus commenting on a verse from Psalm 75, is full of a mixed drink, i.e., the two Testaments have to be united in order to be a healthful drink for us: yet unbelieving Jews and Manicheans both reject this mixed drink; the former, by denying the New Testament; the latter, by condemning the Old.[147] The explanation came from Augustine, who himself had borrowed it from the Manichean Faustus, turning it around.[148] It is also found in Gregory,[149] and then Manegold also picked it up:

> Or we can think of it in another way. The chalice, i.e., the Scripture of the Old Testament, is in the hand of the Lord; in this chalice there is unmixed wine, i.e., the simple letter or understanding such as pertains to the Jews, who insist on the carnal understanding alone; but to the extent that it pertains to us, who are ascending through the carnal to spiritual things, it is full of mixed wine.[150]

As we have seen, this was always the fundamental doctrine of understanding the Old Testament by means of the New — in other words, the doctrine of the spiritual understanding, which was found to be inculcated thereby. In this "mixed wine" as well as in this "pure wine," allegory is found to be canonized. As Bede along with his successor Rabanus Maurus[151] articulated, allegory amounts to the very doctrine of the Catholic Church, who "drinks both the historical and the allegorical knowledge in mixed wine as a toast to her hearers";[152] that is, as Peter Cellensis also articulated in a text entirely drawn from Origen, the "evangelical sense":

> Let the preacher in the Church not dogmatize according to the errors of the heretics or according to the seductions of the philosophers.... Let him use the sense of the gospel . . . so as not to bend God's Word to his own sense, but rather to inflect both word and sense to the Gospel.[153]

Peter Lombard says the same thing in his own eclectic and, as Father Chenu says, "flabby" manner, albeit close to Saint Augustine, keeping both the pure wine and the mixed wine at hand for orthodoxy:

> The 'cup' is the Law; 'mere wine', the heavenly mystery, i.e., the spiritual sense; 'full', since even if it is being drunk, it is never all poured out; 'mixed', i.e., with each of the two Testaments, since the Old and the New are together. Hence Ezekiel says: "I saw a wheel in the midst of a wheel." The Jews do not drink the mixed wine, since they accept the Old but not the New, nor do the Manicheans, who accept the New but not the Old.[154]

This is the tack that Anselm of Laon had taken in his commentary on the Psalms.[155] And here are two more witnesses. One is Alan of Lille, explaining why he composed his *Liber Distinctionum*:

> Lest the theologian affirm the false as true, lest the heretic be confirmed in his error from a false interpretation or the Jew arrested by the literal understanding, lest a proud man inflict his own understanding upon Scripture, we have led the one who is worthy to distinguish the meanings of theological words.[156]

The other, as clear as can be, is John of Salisbury, speaking in his *Polycraticus* about the disciples just before their eyes were opened on the way to Emmaus:

> The one who desires to lord it over the Scriptures by which he is supposed to be instructed — who strives to drag them kicking and screaming to his own understanding, with their own sense held captive — is inept. For to seek in them what they do not contain is to ob-

struct one's own sense, not to learn another sense. Were not the eyes even of the disciples, whose hearts burned within them, prevented from recognizing the Wisdom that was accompanying them? For they were slow to understand what the prophets were saying, seeking what was absent from the minds of the prophets, and not attending to the Christ who was hiding within the letter.... For whoever by powers of wit or study assails the integrity of the Scriptures for his own pleasure,[157] remains a stranger to the understanding of the truth, as if excluded from the shrine of philosophy.[158]

Once again, we shall have recognized the old expressions coming from Origen and Jerome always used to condemn literalist exegesis. It is in this way that we ought to understand also the words of Arnaud de Bonneval, when he says that Scripture contains "certain rules of faith, so that everyone is made firm not by his own sense but by the authority of the eternal truth,"[159] or the words of Innocent III criticizing the one who, whilst citing the sacred text, "perverted it to a strange sense, so that the spirit of error instructed his heretical perversity."[160] It is always thus that, on the threshold of the thirteenth century, Stephen Langton, regarding the "red cow" under discussion in Numbers 19, will — albeit with some small-mindedness — undertake a defense of allegories against the heretics, a defense still styled, as in the time of Bede, "Catholic explanations."[161] In the same way Philip the Chancellor, in a discourse at a synod held in Lyon in 1226, will once again fight against the literalist exegesis of "the Jew and the heretic" and will oppose to it the spiritual exegesis of the great doctors of the Church and their successors, so as to stand against the "Poor Ones of Lyon."[162] As additional evidence coming from the other direction, William of Saint Thierry corroborates our idea that the only non-subjective exegesis is in fact the allegorical or spiritual exegesis, when he confidently tells us that one of the principal temptations confronting the faith consists precisely in imagining — "so to speak at the provocation of human nature and its sense" — that the mysteries of the faith, i.e., the mysteries of holy Scripture, may be merely "figments of human invention."[163] Such a temptation persists today, perhaps, in more restricted limits and under a less "perverse" guise, for the humble exegete hypnotized by critical method. While leading one to misunderstand the permanent value of the principle that governed spiritual understanding long ago, it falls short of making one doubt the "mysteries of the faith." But in the Middle Ages, the temptation could be more radical, and it was regarded as coming from pride:

Illiterate cleric,
Fond of exalting himself
And disdaining the mysteries,
Is abject as a dumb beast.[164]

The "ferocious beast" that was the heretic is now no more than the "dumb beast," for here Saint Peter Damian rails merely against the "illiterate cleric." But how would that whose interpretation is entirely "carnal" in fact be a "beast"? Except for the mention of pride, this is the same idea that Richard of Saint Victor expresses, using the same image of the "beast," in the prologue of his commentary on the Song of Songs; for him, it is the devil himself who, when we are reading Scripture, tries to inject us with these "earthly thoughts" and this "carnal science."[165] Other verses, stemming from Othloh of Saint Emmeran, showed essentially the same conviction; we shall end with them as a sort of "argument from tradition":

Those who seek to weigh with merely carnal sense
The sayings of the former Law or the sacred Newness
Are misled in all directions, they prove to know nothing.[166]

Othloh leads us to his contemporary, Berno of Reichenau. To assign its true meaning to Berno's thought, we need accurately to understand his formulations: "they try to fit the words to their own sense through a superstitious understanding of holy Scripture" [Per superstitiosam intelligentiam sacrae Scripturae verba suo sensui applicare conantur]; "Do not adjust the Scriptures to your own sense" [Non tuo sensui attemperes Scripturas]. We shall now begin as best we can. All the numerous analogous formulas that are met with in earlier centuries, as well as in his own and in those following, offer us one and the same perfectly clear meaning. They do not, invoking the name of some objective science, condemn the pious for being arbitrary; rather, in the name of the Christian faith, they condemn the heretic or Jew for being arbitrary. Scripture turned aside from its objective signification, bent to the "will," or "pleasure," or "personal sentiment" of the reader, Scripture grasped in a "perverse" or "superstitious" manner, which is as such subjective, is never the result of a frank allegorism; on the contrary, at least most frequently — as in the way one understands the Old Testament or the New — it is the effect of a literalism that rejects allegory in the Christian sense.[167] Jesus Christ had wanted to lead the Jewish people into his house, i.e., into the true understanding of his law, which is spiritual; but they refused to enter; they did not want to have knowledge of any other understanding than that of the letter, which leads to death.[168]

This way of speaking might seem surprising to anyone who does not go back to the origins of the traditional hermeneutical vocabulary and does not see how the spiritual battle that was waged over the Scriptures took place in the first centuries. But it might still appear strange even to a well-informed historian, if he does not thoroughly enter into the point of view of the faith. This is the case with more than one historian, even though a believer, habituated as he is to treat the question of "allegory" from the outside, as if it were a question that was entirely about culture or frame of mind, without recognizing that at bottom it was also — and still remains essentially — a question of faith. On the other hand, the traditional vocabulary will appear quite logical in the eyes of anyone who thinks, along with our ancient authors, that at least in principle "allegory" is Christianity, and that Christianity is "the truth of the Scripture." Indeed, from that time on, whatever be the particular applications and procedures by which our ancients obtained them, it becomes clear that to understand Scripture not in an arbitrary, "violent" way or according to the sense peculiar to the commentator, but in its objectivity and in its "integrity," in short, to understand it "in a good and catholic manner," as Saint Bruno of Segni puts it, it is indispensable to go beyond its letter. One must understand it "first according to the letter, then according to the spiritual understanding."[169] Deliberately to confine oneself to the "pure letter," even granting that one might do so with exactitude, is exactly what would count as producing a work of "one's own peculiar sense"; that would be to plunge into a subjective interpretation, to "corrupt" the Scripture by undermining its integrity. By refusing to see that it everywhere bears testimony to Christ, such an approach would empty it of the Spirit that fills it, to lower it to the level of merely human books. If, *per impossibile*, some modern had broken through into these ancient ages, uttering the objection that arbitrariness or subjectivism is exactly what dwelt or at least ran the risk of dwelling in this so-called "spiritual understanding," and calling for some scientific criterion to ward off the danger, one would have had substantially nothing to tell him in reply other than what Saint Hilary or Saint Jerome, both following Origen, offered in answer to the unbelieving Jews before addressing any particular explication — the foundation being the teaching of Saint Paul.[170] The spiritual man sees Christ synoptically in the holy Books, because he has "the sense of Christ" within him. Such a man — who is not such or such an individual left to himself, but one who identifies himself with "the man of the Church" — judges everything and is answerable to no one.[171] Only his vision integrates the whole of reality. He is, as Rabanus Maurus ingeniously puts it, like an observer stationed behind the blinds of his window, who sees all that passes without himself being seen by any passer-by.[172] He "treats spiritual things spiritually" in security,[173] and he "understands everything spiritually."[174] He alone comprehends sacred history, and he comprehends that he comprehends it. In conclusion, if, as always *per impossibile,* the methods and results of criticism, such as we have them today, were suddenly to appear to these ancients, the ancients would doubtless not all have shown the same ability to assimilate them; but, those who would show up at our school most unfettered in criticisms and most versed in biblical science, remaining true to themselves, could only go on to say: "This new world of human knowledge is valuable to us; if it requires us to revise many things in our opinions and exegetical methods, our supple principles offer no obstacle against it, and we shall work with you to enlarge it still further. But, on your side, do understand that it changes essentially nothing for one essential problem, for the examination of which these new lights that you are bringing up can be of great help, but which is essentially of another order."

3. Christian Dialectic

There are still a few words in Berno's maxim that we have not yet taken into account: the four last ones: "ut non . . . Scripturis sensum tuum adjungas." By the suppression of the *sed* which was found in Jerome and by the addition of the prefix *ad* to the verb, the sense of this end of the sentence has been, as we have said, profoundly changed: the positive counsel Jerome gave in ending becomes a redoubled warning or a new particular in designating a crime: ["so that you do not . . . add your sense to the Scriptures"]. Perhaps, as we have said, it is not appropriate to make too much of this fact, which might be due to a copyist's error. Only Berno does go on to denounce the crime that consists in *adding* something to Scripture and to cite the Apocalypse on this topic. This, at least, he did not find in the page Jerome wrote against Hilary. But he found it elsewhere, as we will see.

But how can removing the spiritual sense so as to hold to its literal sense be denounced as adding something to the Scripture? A new paradox! An examination of it will end up bringing us to the point of Berno's thought, howsoever shabby it may be in relation to the traditional thought that it transposes.

This "non adjungas" in our author is an allusion to the text of the

Apocalypse, 22:18-19, which is found cited subsequently. As he was laying down his pen, the author of the Apocalypse was threatening anyone who would dare to add or take away anything from the prophetic words of the book. He was inspired by Deuteronomy 4:2: "You shall add nothing to what I order you and shall take nothing away." Berno himself solemnly proclaims:

> Therefore it is to be resolved that we should unchangeably preserve, hold, and keep the sacred words of the gospel, the oracles of the patriarchs and the prophets, the writings of the apostles, with complete faith and fitting devotion, as they are found in the authentic books — neither adding nor deleting nor changing anything, if we should wish to evade the threat which the Holy Spirit seems to extend at the end of the Apocalypse: "If anyone should add to these things. . . ."[175]

Here again, Berno heavy-handedly exploits a commonplace.[176] Here again, he is imitating Agobard in particular, and those whom Agobard was already imitating.[177] "To add nothing, to take nothing away": this was an ancient rule in Christianity, but it is not certain that its origin is first to be sought for in the Bible.[178] It already existed as a proverb among the Greeks as well as among the Jews. Some philosophers had based it on the very essence of things. Philo had applied it to considerations about divinity. Plutarch and Thucydides had recalled it with regard to legislative acts and treaties. The *Letter of Aristaeus* puts it into the mouth of the leaders of the people when the Septuagint was published. Saint Irenaeus, Tertullian, and Origen had invoked it on behalf of the totality of the Scriptures against the pretensions of the Gnostics. It had been used in the Montanist controversy. It appeared validated at least by the two texts from Deuteronomy and the Apocalypse.

It is not necessary to let the explications of these two texts up to the time of Berno pass in review. A few examples will suffice. Here is how Berengaud explicated the final threat of the Apocalypse:

> We ought to understand that this is said not of expositors but of heretics. For an expositor adds or subtracts nothing; but through his exposition he either explains obscurities of the history or demonstrates a moral or spiritual understanding. So he is cursing the heretics, who within the divine Scriptures add certain false things to confirm their heresy, and take out certain things that seemed to be contrary to their heresy.[179]

This was the common explication. The same text had been called up by Paulinus of Aquilaea against the temerarious speculations of Felix of Urgel. Paulinus too showed how exposition per se was not at all properly to "add" anything to the Scripture as much as to explain, albeit at length, its doctrine; otherwise it would be necessary to condemn all the holy doctors, all the "preachers of the Church," that one ought on the contrary to be praising for having explicated each of the chapters of the Bible; it would even be necessary for us to condemn Saint Paul, "qui legis aenigmata per multiplicia disputationum disseruit verba" ["who discussed the mysteries of the Law through many words of arguments"], and to condemn the Lord himself, for having opened the sense of the Scriptures to the disciples of Emmaus in a long discussion. The text of Saint John was applied to the heretics — to all those who followed the example of the unfortunate Arius: was it not to "add to the gospel" to explain the maxim "The Father is greater than I" in terms not just of the Savior's humanity but also of his divinity? Was it not to "take away from it" to reject the testimony of that other maxim, "The Father and I are one"? But, with "their impure sense and their impious mouth," the heretics finally did harm only to themselves, whereas "the holy and venerable mysteries of the gospel will endure inviolate for all ages."[180]

As for the prohibition cited in Deuteronomy, it had constituted the object of a public debate between the Manichean Faustus of Milevis, disciple of Adimantius, and Saint Augustine. Faustus[181] rejected the Old Testament and by that very fact understood the New badly; for him, as for the gnostics opposed by Saint Irenaeus, this New Testament was quite plainly "an opposition to and dissolution of the past" ["contrarietas et dissolutio praeteritorum"]. So, intending to put Augustine into perplexity, he asked him: Why do you not accept the Law and the Prophets as the Jews do, if it is true, as you believe, that the Christ has said that he did not come to destroy them but to fulfill them? That was the very question that, on their side, the Jews themselves put to the Christians.[182] But in reality, continued Faustus immediately, you must admit it, the very discourse in which Christ is thought to have pronounced this sentence is quite clear: could he have done anything further and more obvious to destroy the Law and the Prophets? If this is what one calls fulfilling the Law, what would one call destroying it? The author of this Law had prescribed its observance without adding or taking away anything of it, without deviating from it to the right or to the left. Hence, if Jesus adds anything to the Law to fulfill it, he falls to the right; if he takes anything away from it, he falls to the left: in any case, he offends the author of the Law. Conse-

Christian Dialectic

quently, he could not have pronounced the sentence that the actual text of the Gospel assigns to him.[183] To this Saint Augustine replied: We do not deny that, in the eyes of the Jews who did not comprehend, Christ appeared to be a destroyer of the Law; but you do not understand any more than they did what it is to accomplish the Law. Its fullness, as the Apostle says, is charity. Now, through Jesus Christ, the Law has become grace and truth, which is to say that it has finally received its fulfillment in charity.[184] He has then come indeed not to destroy it but to accomplish it, and this is no longer to say that he added to it.[185] Faustus then insisted: If Christ had truly proclaimed that he did not want to dissolve the Law, it would be necessary for us, in order to be faithful to him, still to practice the Sabbath, circumcision, fasts, etc.; but in fact, we have abandoned all these practices; we therefore, both of us, you and me, believe that he has indeed come to destroy it, and it is in this respect that we regard ourselves to be his disciples. Only you are illogical in accepting at the same time as authentic a text that openly proclaims the contrary; for Jesus has founded the New Testament, which is nothing else than the destruction of the Old. If then a Jew or anyone else should interrogate you on this subject, you would have no recourse except to give in to a vain superstition, or to proclaim that the Gospel text is apocryphal, or to reject Christ.[186] Without allowing himself to be discouraged by these points which did not take account of his initial response, the bishop then explained once again the provisional and figurative character of one part of the Jewish Law: those who were practicing it for so long did not come to comprehend it; but now we can render an account of it ourselves. Now that what these precepts signified beforehand has arrived, one can and one ought to say of them: "they are no longer ordered to be done, but what is to be understood by them is being read."[187] Jesus Christ, who purifies us through his own blood, is the truth of all these figures:[188] they have all been realized in him, and it is precisely this fact — by which the Law seemed to Faustus to have been destroyed — which allows us to grasp that, on the contrary, it has been accomplished.[189] For the Law and the Prophets are truly contained within the twofold law of charity, rendered efficacious by the grace of Christ: everything that the deeds, words, or rituals of the ancient Scripture announced is all found today once again, rendered sublime, in Christ and his Church, and thus we can at once be disciples of Christ and accept his declaration from the Sermon on the Mount, without contradicting ourselves and without succumbing, as Faustus puts it, to a vain superstition.[190]

Lastly, in addition to the two frequently cited texts from the Apocalypse and from Deuteronomy, another was also sometimes adduced, drawn from the Proverbs 30:5-6, which could be exploited in an analogous manner: "Every word of God is purified by fire: he is a buckler to them that hope in him. Add not any thing to his words, lest thou be reproved, and be found a liar."[191] These three texts were accordingly used to reinforce the doctrine of the spiritual understanding — the only one declared objective — in the face of various deformations, corruptions, "superstitious" additions, i.e., works of the "proper" sense, due to Judaism or to heresy. The explication that they furnished will itself reinforce the remarks made above on the objectivity of allegorism and the subjectivity of literalism in the thought of the tradition. But in order to understand exactly the warning of the "quidam sapiens" according to Berno's intention, as we have read it in the previous chapter, it should be added that he had a particular reason to allude to the prohibition borrowed from the Apocalypse, having already used the general idea of exegesis falsified by the "proper sense" against his adversaries. For — if indeed there is nothing askew in the text that has come down to us[192] — the cleric in question addressed his reproaches to some who permitted themselves, as we have seen, to add or to take something away. They added, for example, a letter to the Gospel, saying "lacus" instead of "laci"; or else, they took away a letter, saying "defrudavi" instead of "defraudavi." In a sense, one can therefore say that the application was topical. Still one might admit that the solemn reproof of Yahweh in the book of Deuteronomy had a more serious offense in mind! What proportion is there between the peccadillo of a few clerics a bit too smitten with grammar, or fearing the rod of the grammarians a bit too much[193] — how much less brazen than our modern revisionists of the Psalter or a number of their precursors — and the "falsifiers" traditionally denounced in the same terms? What did they have in common, those liturgists scarcely less rigid than their censor, with those various "Antichrists" who "superadded" to the sacred text "their perverse errors," or who on the other side "mutilated the prophecy," or again who, "like Arius," weakened the sense or even the words of the Gospel?[194] Berno had not been willing to listen to the benevolent and wise reflection that had been passed on from age to age by the commentators on the Apocalypse, however, in the instance where it was most essential: "John said this owing to the falsifiers, not on account of those who merely say what they mean, with the prophecy in no wise mutilated."[195] How much more still would the adversaries of such a clumsy or excessively "simple" exegete, have the right to receive the benefit of the doubt!

Christian Dialectic

In sum, Berno's "wise man" is not an isolated case, and neither is Berno. If the sentence that the abbot of Reichenau borrows from Saint Jerome, while modifying it and while spicing it up, had to be taken in its immediate natural sense, this sense would scarcely appear doubtful: the traditional context, full and solid as it is, unlocks its meaning, it seems to me, with clarity. Now it is the reverse of what people believed could be attributed to him. Only, in reality — and that appears no less clear to me — Berno takes the theme with which the tradition furnishes him in a completely accommodative sense. He uses a theme that was classical in relation to the interpretation of Scripture so as to apply it to a completely different case that he finds interesting. In this transposition, he lets himself go, as we might say, in an "integrist" direction. For there is no common measure nor even any real analogy between the fault that he is reproving and the infidelity or heresy that the doctors from whom he appropriates his expressions were reproving. He has nevertheless explained himself sufficiently in the whole eighth chapter of the *De varia modulatione* that has occupied us at some length; he has sufficiently displayed the precise object of his complaints for everyone to be able to frame a judgment about it, and in such a way that we do not have the right ourselves to be too hard on him. We should rather say that it is merely a question of excess, of an abuse of language, of which the history of controversies offers us many an example; we shall probably suppose that he himself is not to be taken completely "literally" when he raises his voice in this way; we shall likewise imagine that, after all, he had an illustrious predecessor in Saint Jerome, though the two cases are not at all parallel; we shall excuse him even in making his reaction too violent and even a bit ridiculous on account of a venerable respect for Scripture, a praiseworthy attachment to the traditional rites of his Church, and an ardent zeal for the perfection of liturgical chant. And finally we shall leave him to return to the fundamental subject to which the examination of his maxim had already brought us.

One will have noted that, in the discussion that took place between Saint Augustine and Faustus with regard to the twofold defense — "add nothing, take nothing away" — it was principally the second term that was at stake from start to finish. The spiritual understanding of the Mosaic Law seemed to Faustus to be its very destruction, pure and simple, and Saint Augustine applied himself to prove to him that it was nothing of the kind; the reproach of adding something came merely by abstract hypothesis, for symmetry, and Faustus did not dawdle over it. On the contrary, he criticized at length the lack of logic of the Catholics who pretended to preserve the Jewish "superstition" while in reality they were abandoning it. As to Saint Augustine, even while vindicating the logic of his own position, he readily granted that the exterior practice of the Law, founded now upon a carnal understanding devoid of its prophetic value, would be today in fact "superstition." Just as in the *De doctrina christiana* he speaks of a bad understanding of the Bible owing to pagan superstition, he speaks accordingly in the *Contra Faustum* of an equally bad understanding, owing this time to Jewish superstition. To each of these, designated by the same name, he opposes Christian allegory.

If we point out this fact, it is because it goes further than a peculiarity of language and it is not confined to Saint Augustine. There was a subtle dialectic amidst the controversy conducted by the Christians against the exegesis of heretics or Jews — a simple echo, in the believing understanding, of that real dialectic, at once historical and spiritual, which the Act of Christ had set in motion. The Jews naturally reproached the Christians for adding to the letter of Scripture, by giving it a sense that it did not bear and thus falling into pagan errors through their new dogmas: tritheism, the adoration of a man. This reproach was expressed once again by the Jew whom Rupert of Deutz made to dialogue with a Christian, almost in the terms that the Christians themselves used in protesting against the literalism of the heretics which had been imitated from that of the Jews:

> *Jew:* You are speaking on behalf of your will, you are leading the words of the Scriptures hither and thither according to your intention and you are dragging them wherever you want.
>
> You have grown accustomed to dragging the Scriptures around with your meaning, and you are, as I said, leading them hither and thither in whatever direction you want.[196]

Though fictional, the dialogue composed by Rupert of Deutz under the title the *Annulus* at the request of Raoul de Saint Trond gives us an echo of the disputes that the eddies stirred up in the Rhine valley by the first crusade had just revived.[197] The analogous *Disputatio* that Gilbert Crispin, abbot of Westminster, reported to his archbishop Saint Anselm,[198] really had taken place, between 1093 and 1097; Gilbert's partner was a Jew who had come from Mainz to London. The same reproach of arbitrariness shows up there:

> *Jew:* You do violence to Scripture and twist Scripture toward the assertion of your faith.... If it is right for Christians to read and inter-

pret the Scriptures in this way about Christ, you will find many more things that you will somehow be able to interpret in this way too.

Since you have laid down allegories and figures wherever you want, and wherever the letter is repugnant to your sense you say that the letter has been rolled up with allegories and figures, and since you explain the letter by expounding it to your whim, you can, I say, with that sort of consideration, accommodate the Scriptures to whatever you want. For you do not subject your sense to Scripture, but you subject Scripture to your sense.[199]

There you have it once again: that same exegetical subjectivism! The description has not changed. And this time it is indeed allegorical exegesis that is at stake. Only, the reproach is put into the mouth of a Jew; it constitutes the argument by which the Jew in question rejects the Christian faith;[200] — unless it be, as in another dialogue composed by the same Gilbert Crispin, the argument of a gentile who takes up against the Church the reproach of illogicality addressed long ago by Faustus to Saint Augustine.[201] In the twelfth century as in the eleventh and as already in the fifth, the Christians respond to the "invetera quaestio" that the faithful followers of Moses continue to put to them by saying that, since their solution is faithful to the Spirit who is the author of the letter, it is on the contrary the only logical one, the only fully objective one, the only one respectful of the Scriptures, which they preserve without corrupting them, which they keep without adding anything to them or taking anything away.[202] They do not, however, defend their interpretations one by one, nor by the examination of texts *alone*. They know quite well that in that case the Jew would be right to reject them as arbitrary. But one great Fact has supervened, which has illuminated everything, at the same time as it has changed everything. They appeal to that Fact, which dictates their exegesis. In the sacred books, they say, we read of profound mysteries; nevertheless, do not believe that we pretend to discover them there without a light that has come from elsewhere:

> For there the incarnation is contained, there the passion, there the death, there the resurrection, there the ascension (of Christ). But who would believe these things heard of us, unless he had known the deeds? All the things that have been written of him in the sacred discourse, he has fulfilled in deed, so that what could not be understood on hearing might be made plain once seen.[203]

They then show that the Bible itself announced the new understanding which one day was to arise from it. Ever since the Christ has done his work amongst us, they say, this announcement has been realized. Now one can see that it is everywhere in Scripture. It is not the Christian, therefore, who violates and destroys the Law of Moses; rather, it is he who rejects the Christ whom Moses was announcing.[204] The one who reads Scripture arbitrarily is the unbelieving Jew. "And they have not believed Moses, so long as they do not believe in Christ";[205] and it is necessary to say the same thing on the subject of the prophets. By turning down that which is made New in Christ, they proclaim themselves to misunderstand the ancient Books that foretold it and called it forth.[206] They blaspheme God, they dishonor the Patriarchs, they despise the Prophets.[207] They pretend to remain unendingly attached to objects which themselves bear witness to their transitory character.[208] In Christ and in his Church, the whole Law is fulfilled at the same time as it is transcended; indeed it is fulfilled because it is transcended. "For it is not only being fulfilled, but also transcended," says Saint Ambrose Autpert.[209] Far from "adding to" the Law, the Christian merely preserves its inner essence. He lets its whole literal superstructure fall, which, once its role has been fulfilled, has no further reason to exist.[210] The grain remains alone, separated from the straw;[211] the sacrificial victim has been stripped of its fat;[212] the fruit is taken from the tree; the veil has been drawn back;[213] the Truth no longer needs the envelope of figures and enigmas. All the same, nothing substantial has been cut away; but, in the fire of the Holy Spirit, all the impurities of the letter have melted.[214]

Pushing their advantage and going on to the counter-attack, the exegetes of the Church then show those of the Synagogue that their rejection of the spiritual sense only succeeds in making Scripture sterile. By continuing to attribute to the Law, in its entirely figurative part, a literal meaning that it no longer bears (except for the historian who is reconstituting a past that has been done away with), they impose upon it and lay upon themselves the weight of a superstitious interpretation, that is to say, following the current etymology transmitted by Isidore of Seville,[215] one that has been superadded or arbitrary as well as vain and superfluous: *a vain superstition, the vain superstition of the ceremonies of the Law.*[216] Likewise Jewish messianism is no more than an illusion, a chimerical expectation, a "fabulous fiction."[217] Even the historical facts — those facts whose reality no one would dream of denying nor whose past grandeur they would dream of diminishing — from the moment that they are found emptied of their true prophetic meaning as well as their preparatory

Christian Dialectic

function, often deserve to be called, as by Saint Jerome, "useless and vain stupidities of the Jews."[218] While the Christians nourish themselves on the pith that they have taken in due time from the shell, while they carefully gather, once the straw has been cast off, the grain that has come to maturity, the Jews, remaining blind to the transformations that were the work of God, are always banging against the hardness of the shell; rejecting the nourishing grain, they remain encumbered with that which, though verdant long ago, is now no more than straw.[219] "Always reading and always following merely the straw of Scripture by always reading."[220] They always have the books, but the Spirit of the Scriptures has left them.[221] Not willing at all to "allegorize," refusing "to grow through the Gospel to the size of a full-grown man,"[222] they retain only a "puerile" sense of the great divine Plan.[223] And one can say as much of the "heretics," by habitually referring to heretical types, those who were the first ones aimed at, and whose refutation marked out the language of orthodoxy for the future. Some were relatives of the Jews: such were the Ebionites, "even poorer in sense than in name,"[224] who, wishing to keep their letter within Christianity, fell into the same superstition as did the Jews. Moreover, Pseudo-Gnostics or Manicheans, though quite distant from the Jewish position, nonetheless often had the same literalist conception of the Bible, which made them deny that it was of God.[225]

Meanwhile, the very word "superstition," in the reproach made to the Jews, was itself to be taken literally. By refusing the spiritual understanding, they wanted at least to keep intact the purity of the Law: now they ended up with the opposite result. By laying upon themselves a burden which no longer had any acceptable purpose, since Christ had come to liberate all men from it, they added to the Law,[226] such that adherence to it involved practices that it no longer ordered, that it no longer approved. They laid upon themselves a carnal "yoke." Henceforth, through this fault, they themselves fell into the pit that they said they wanted to avoid. Those who pretended to represent fidelity to the ancient Law turn out to be the very ones who are sacrificing to a "new superstition,"[227] a superstition not only vain, but impious ["superstitionis impietas"].[228] Their cult is no more than "impiety."[229] They are, then, victims now of that very "superstition" that had been till then the hallmark of paganism, its very definition, so to speak — "pagana superstitio," "gentilis superstitio,"[230] "vana superstitio et error antiquus."[231] One can therefore speak in a sense twice true, though twice paradoxical, of "Jewish fables" and of "Jewish superstition"[232] ["Judaeorum carnales superstitiones,"[233] "Judaeorum fabulosa superstitio,"[234] "Pharisaica superstitio"].[235]

The texts that expound this dialectic, summarize it, or presuppose it are countless. If one does not grasp the train of thought, one risks taking a number of these texts as grossly excessive, or seeing them as self-contradictory — like the texts of Saint Paul already,[236] and the words of Jesus himself.[237] One frequently runs the risk of accusing our exegetes of misunderstanding the realities of history as well. One has expressed surprise that a Saint Augustine, who in other works shows evidence of an informed historical sense and refuses to judge the conduct of the Patriarchs according to our own norms, "in the *Contra Faustum* totally lacks historical perspective" and in it "misunderstands the progress of revelation." Our ancient authors would all acquiesce with this remark of Karl Barth: "The Old Testament, taken in itself, considered as a thing in itself, does not exist."[238] In its Law, in its Prophecy, in the unfolding of its facts, in the progress of his light, it has constituted an "introduction" to Christianity.[239] It was its "preparation"[240] and in a certain way "the long birth-pang."[241] Considered prior to the Christ, then, it is rich and fruitful; it is full of developments of promise, it is alive. After the Christ, "after the truth of the gospel,"[242] if one always wants to know nothing but it alone, if one obstinately says with the Synagogue: "Just as God is unique, his Testament, as it has been given to Moses, is unique, and nothing could be changed in it until the end of the world,"[243] then that Testament becomes wretched and sterile: in it, the living spirit of prophecy has been extinguished; it is a body one is bound to after its soul is extracted;[244] it is dead.[245] While contemplating this cadaver, one should say: "As much distance there is between the blackness of crows and the sleekness of milky doves, nay even more, is the distance between the letter that killeth and the spirit that giveth life!"[246]

There is therefore a real "foresaking" of that Testament which, in everything figurative that it contains, is henceforward no more than "an old by-way."[247] It is no more than a "banished shadow"[248] and its literal sense is no more than an "extinguished sense."[249] That is one of the meanings of the epithet "old," which designates not only "aged" but also "abrogated." "It has ceased with the coming of the Lord."[250] But for the Christian, who sees its fulfillment realized, the Old Testament in another sense remains completely whole. Because he is its "intellector," the Christian can remain its "venerator." He grasps that Jesus is its "perfecting," not its "eliminating end."[251] That Old Testament does not however remain as such: "not without change," says Saint Gregory;[252] but "while it is being changed, it is being fulfilled."[253] Its glory vanishes before the glory of the Gospel, or rather *within* that glory, as infancy disappears to make way for adulthood,[254] or as the seed gives way to the fruit in which it is found. In short, the Old Testament lives again, transfigured, in the New.[255] It merely constitutes a unity with it, meaning one and the same thing.[256] In a certain way, the New was already even in the Old — this being all the more true, so to speak, the more one acquires the vantage-point of God.

The Old Testament, says Barth again, did not know the true face of its Lord; it did not gauge the full scope of its incognito. And Saint Augustine: "Illa prophetia, quando in illa Christus non intelligebatur, aqua erat" ["When Christ was not understood within that Prophecy, it was water"]; but that water was nevertheless not just anything at all: "in aqua enim vinum quodammodo latet" ["for somehow wine lies concealed within the water"].[257] The incognito having once been lifted, the miracle of transformation once having been accomplished in Christ, the pretence of maintaining the earlier state of reality by maintaining the earlier reading of the Book is a desperate enterprise; in fact it can only be a regression, to wit, a corruption. Despite the appearances, the water one wants to drink again is no longer the water of long ago. No wine is hidden within it any longer. It is therefore a water without strength.[258] Further, it is no longer pure water; it has now been infected with parasites. Once potable in its historical sense, it now communicates the evils of heresy.[259] In the very measure that it has been emptied of the Spirit, the letter is found polluted with idolatrous stains and various superstitions.[260] If the water refuses to let itself be changed into wine, then it changes into blood, just as took place in the first plague of Egypt.[261] The vine of the Lord is drying out, the rod of Aaron is withering, the ancient paradise is being transformed into a desert, the springtime of the Law is giving way to a winter without hope. This is a veritable suicide.[262] *Judaica siccitas!* O deadly dryness from the north wind, which dissipates all the fecundating clouds, that is to say, all spiritual understanding of the Law and the Prophets![263] Without even having to change on the outside, under the deceptive appearance of continuity, the "veteranus usus" ["old usage"] has in this way become the "nova superstitio" ["new superstition"].[264] Long ago, in the middle of the desert, the cloud was obscure to the Egyptians, yet clear to the Hebrews; but the Hebrews have taken the place of the Egyptians.[265] For it is one thing to watch over the "veiled mystery" and quite another to hold in one's hands no more than the "veil of the mystery."[266] Emmanuel is no longer present under that letter to which the unbelieving Jew is always attached. He, fixed in a hostile immobility, even now unjustly holding back the truth of which he is the bearer, tends, in his worship of a dead letter, to join up with the position of the pagan. "The people of the

Jews, once the faith has been lost, has turned into the winding forest of paganism."[267]

All this argumentation rested, as we see, upon the consideration of the Time and of the Act, as the fifth chapter of this work has sketched it out. "The Lord's resurrection has utterly changed the times."[268] The Christian understanding of the Scriptures does not only take account of a historical evolution; nor does it come forth from a simple change of intellectual perspective. It supposes the accomplishment of a spiritual revolution and it results from a dialectical movement through which the signs are reversed. Hence come this perpetual passing from the continuity or the succession to the antithesis, then from the antithesis to harmony, "so that all contention may end with peaceful quiet";[269] hence too that change from one inclusion into another: at first mysteriously contained in the Old Testament, the New in its turn contains the Old, but in a different way. The Old Testament is not simply annulled by the proclamation of the New, as Faustus imagined;[270] nor does the New come to be added to the Old either, as certain Jews could be shown ready to agree[271] and as certain Jewish historians today have tended to maintain is an idea of Jesus.[272] To fulfill the Law is not to "complete" it by "superadding" to it a certain number of new precepts or new teachings, as even some theoreticians have attempted to do within Christianity who have grown less sensitive to one of the essential spurs of ancient Christian thought.[273] Each of these points of view doubtless has merit, but only on the surface. In the eyes of the Christian, sometimes the two Testaments seem to be opposed to each other in a contrast devoid of nuances as though without appeal, and sometimes they seem contrariwise to be identified with each other. Sometimes, it seems, Moses, the "Moses of the ancients," is nothing but an antithesis and his Law is nothing but a foil;[274] sometimes, through this same Mosaic Law, he hears God speaking to him in person "face to face."[275] The two affirmations are both quite real; there exists a central point of view that harmonizes them; but each, if one stops by taking either one alone, yields a deceptive appearance.

More than one historian, indeed, has been deceived in this matter. In the first affirmation, some have sometimes thought they sniff a stale odor of Manichaeism; in the second, an undue overestimation of the Old Testament, by a forgetting of the differences in favor of the similarities; in the one case as in the other, there is a tendency to "suppress history." From their coexistence in one and the same author, some have been tempted to conclude either that the author in question contradicted himself, or that he found himself led to make "concessions" to the thesis that he had been

Christian Dialectic

combating, and then one is astonished to find him so close to modern historical positions after having seen him so distant from them.[276] For some did not take account of the dialectical movement which engenders the one affirmation as well as the other from history, and which alone allows one to understand their interrelationship. Again, it is necessary to specify that this movement had been effected within the fabric of historical reality before being recorded in the mind of the believer. The perpetual recurrence of certain words in the language of the traditional exegesis should be noted: "prius, antea, tunc, olim" ["previously, before, then, once"] on the one hand, and "postea, modo, nunc, jam nunc" ["afterwards, yet, now, just now"] on the other, as well as conjunctions that express the distance or explain the passage from the first ones to the second: "quamdiu, donec" ["for as long as, until"]. Time, under the divine action, had done its work first. But on the decisive Day, the grain has not detached itself all alone from its shell; the pure essence of the victim has not been released without the steel of the performer of the sacrifice; neither did the faithful become unfaithful nor the religious person superstitious by the mere action of time or of reflection. Everything has been changed, everything has been made new, "since that new Man has come."[277] In a unique καιρός, the Act of Christ has brought the passage about. It has drawn the line demarcating the times. It has separated; it has united. The Cross of Christ has with its double bar changed the signs around. As such it is, if one can say so, the pivot of Christian dialectic.

As right and positive, as eminently real, as this principle [of the uniquely decisive Christ event] may be, it was in its current formulation, let's recognize it, strongly tainted with polemical spirit. So it was since Saint Paul. Moreover, it had been subtly, sometimes too subtly refined, but at the same time hardened, to the extent that it had become necessary to respond to the twofold reproach of being arbitrary and pagan that had been addressed by the Jews to the faithful of Christ by turning it around. But at the end of ten or twelve centuries, it remained combative. For it did not proceed merely from a peaceable and distantly retrospective reflection upon the crisis of the origins. The problem that it had to resolve was in a certain fashion permanent; each generation rediscovered it, and the risk of a controversy or a disciplinary incident could always reactivate it.[278] This was not only a problem *for* the Church: this was a problem *within* the Church. Christianity always had to define itself in relation to the faith of Israel, whose witnesses did not cease to compass it about and confront it. The Jewish objection resonated in the popular soul, and perhaps the Jewish mentality did no less in the mind of some theologians and churchmen,

SUBJECTIVISM AND SPIRITUAL UNDERSTANDING

whenever allegory lost some of its character among them as spiritual understanding in such a way that it shrank, became externalized, and hardened into pure typology. Then the prevailing concern to harmonize the two covenants rendered allegory less sensitive "to the unconditioned newness of events," the perception of the great metamorphosis dimmed before the establishment of a parallelism, and the "shadow" took on a prolonged consistency of its own which no longer entirely yielded before the "truth."[279] The books of Joshua and Judges ran the risk of turning into codes of holy war; kings were to be literally new Davids or new Josiahs; the priesthood itself was to use the sword, and so on. The spirit of the Old Testament was reborn. This was a permanent temptation, against which, however, it would be a mistake to believe that many minds were not on guard.[280] It was a temptation which, under various forms, remains at all times: its effect can be remarked, closer to ourselves, in more than one page of the *Politique tirée de l'Écriture sainte* [*Politics Derived from the Words of Holy Scripture*, by Jacques-Bénigne Bossuet (1709)] and perhaps, much closer still amongst many adepts of the recent "Biblical movement."[281] One must not be forgetful of the first truth: that if Christianity is a " fulfilled Judaism," it is because it is a "transfigured Judaism."[282]

Good historians have also noted, no doubt exaggerating it a little, "cette sort de nostalgie qui n'a jamais cessé d'habiter l'âme médiévale" ["that sort of homesickness that has never ceased to dwell in the medieval soul"]; they have studied that "occult influence of Judaism upon the Christian consciousness" and stress "the danger of Judaizing syncretism, traces of which can be found both in exegesis and theology as well as in liturgy and canon law."[283] To discuss these "traces" would take us outside the scope of our study. Let us merely recognize that during the Middle Ages Christianity was in fact rather often on the defensive in the face of its old ancestral religion.[284] The contagion that might come from an ill-oriented reading of the Bible or still more from frequenting Jewish circles was ever to be feared. For in the period under our consideration, if the situation of the Jews varied considerably according to times and places, it was nevertheless as a whole quite different from what it would become in the course of the following centuries.[285] For a long time there had been no ghetto, not even a voluntary one: Jews and Christians ordinarily dwelled in the same neighborhoods, even the same houses. They rubbed shoulders with each other and conversed freely among themselves. They often had not only business relations, but ties of friendship. The *Life* of Saint Nilus the Younger, a monk of Calabria, has transmitted for us the account of an admirable conversation of the saint with a Jew who used to question him about God.²⁸⁶ Rupert of Deutz recounts that Saint Heribert's father had a Jewish friend, whom he used to see "for customary companionship of conversation or family business," and that the two men one night had had the same dream, relating to the baby that was going to be born.²⁸⁷ From sympathetic curiosity, some Jews readily frequented the churches, and the Christians did not abstain from attending functions of the synagogues. It was not rare to see Jews as managers of dioceses or monasteries, which put them "into close contact with ecclesiastical dignitaries"; others exercised various functions for kings or lords. Those whose religious zeal was up to using the opportunity could thus exert some influence.

The Carolingian empire was especially favorable to them.²⁸⁸ At Lyon, if one is to believe an acerbic but likely critique from Florus about it, the bishop Amalarius, imbued with the spirit that was reigning at court, let himself be surrounded with Jews, even during liturgical ceremonies.²⁸⁹ Agobard and his successor Amolo would denounce the perils of the pro-Jewish policy of Louis the Pious, which was continued by Charles the Bald. They kept combating the Jewish pamphlets that were circulating against the Gospels. More than one prelate, at that time or subsequently, doubtless had to deplore such "familiaritas nimia" ["excessive familiarity"] and such "assidua cohabitatio" ["incessant cohabitation"] that Agobard was complaining about one day while writing to one of his colleagues, Nabridius, the old bishop of Narbonne. Indeed in some quarters there arose a practice of celebrating the sabbath; many preferred the sermons of the rabbis to those of their priests; some, too attentive to "Jewish fables," even lost at least "the simplicity" of their faith.²⁹⁰ If there were conversions of Jews, there were also sometimes resounding conversions to Judaism. There is the well-known story of a young man named Bodo, a deacon of the court of Louis the Pious, who, deceiving his companions, went and got himself circumcised in 838 in Muslim Spain, which tended to treat Jews rather more considerately than Christians. There he took the name Eleazar and, says Amolo, "superstitione et habitu totus Judaeus effectus" ["rendered a complete Jew in superstition and in dress"],²⁹¹ set about to write against his old co-religionists and even to rouse the authorities against them.²⁹² There were also renegade clerics, such as, in 1006, that fellow Vecelin of the diocese of Metz, who had fallen "into the maw of the faithless Jews," a copy of whose manifesto Albert of Saint Symphorien preserved for us;²⁹³ such men again as that Andrew, archbishop of Bari, who took refuge in Egypt around 1080, and that young priest of Oppido, John, who, having taken the name Obadiah in 1102, also fled into Muslim territory.[294] Raoul Glaber sketches the curious portrait of a certain Raynaud, count of Sens, who denigrated the Christian dogmas and who "used to love the prevaricating customs of the Jews so much that he commanded all his subjects to address him with the title as king of the Jews."[295] Peter Damian believes it necessary to furnish spiritual arms to Christians who are enduring the ascendancy of Jewish thought, which is why he addresses his *Antilogus* and his *Dialogus* to an "honest man."[296] Rupert thinks that his *Annulus* will help the inexperienced faithful, the *tirunculi*, to resist "the Jewish sense raising itself up against the knowledge of God,"[297] etc. Until the thirteenth century, with few exceptions, the times had not come for one-way proselytism and conversion-sermons that Jews were required to attend.[298]

Debates had taken place between scholars of the two religions almost everywhere and in every epoch. Gregory of Tours recounts one that was held in 582 by Chilperic in person, ex tempore, with his contractor the Jew Priscus; the king, who loved to surround himself with Jews, prided himself on his command of theology as well as grammar and poetry.[299] At Pavia between 750 and 760 the young Alcuin was present at a tournament, doubtless more serious, which opposed the Jew Julius and Peter of Pisa. At the end of the tenth century, a similar tournament in southern Italy has been noted by a Jewish source at Oria, between an archbishop and a rabbi.[300] In 1010, Audouin the bishop of Limoges set some of his priests to argue with Jewish scholars for a month — but there a measure of authority was chiefly at stake.[301] Waso, the future bishop of Liège, held a public debate around 1031 with one of the chief Jewish doctors, a physician of the emperor Conrad II.[302] Starting with the first crusade, these sorts of tournaments apparently became more frequent. One of them, noted by William of Malmesbury, was eventually to have the potential conversion of the king William Rufus to the Jewish faith at issue.[303] There were written disputes as well, like the regular exchange of letters between our Bodo-Eleazar and Paul Alvarus of Cordoba.[304] Some of these dialogues are entirely made-up; they form part of a genre illustrated since the fifth century by the *Altercatio Simonis judaei et Theophilo christiani* of Evagrius the Gaul.[305] A genre cultivated more often perhaps for the sake of Christians tempted to judaize than for Jews themselves is instanced by such works as the *Altercatio Ecclesiae contra Synagogam*, written very probably in England toward the middle of the tenth century and closely tracking some of the treatises of the Pseudo-Augustine.[306] Such again is the *Dialogus* of Saint Peter Damian, which is merely a series of questions and answers, and which, along with its complementary *Antilogus*, forms a sort of "Hand-

Christian Dialectic

book of the Perfect Controversialist."[307] Some simply intend to furnish a framework suitable for catechetical instruction: this is doubtless the case with that other *Altercatio,* composed around the end of the twelfth century, which we have already cited; its author has Gamaliel and Saint Paul argue with each other and claims to have been inspired, for the book's setting, by the dialogues of Boethius. As to the ardent demonstrations that Saint Martin of Leon addresses to the Jews, they were indeed actually uttered and they did indeed intend the conversion of Jews; they nevertheless seem to have had as their immediate hearers only the canons regular of the royal collegiate church of Saint Isidore,[308] although the preacher does not cease apostrophizing his adversaries, and his deacon Luke tells us (in a style too conventional to be convincing) that they "could not resist the wisdom and the Spirit that spoke within him."[309] All this literature lards itself with Tertullian's *Adversus Judaeos,* Saint Cyprian's *Testimonia,* the writings of the Psuedo-Augustine, Saint Isidore of Seville's *De fide catholica contra Judaeos,* etc. From a Pseudo-Augustinian homily dating from the fifth or sixth century, a liturgical drama will even emerge, the extremely popular *Ordo prophetarum,* part of the Christmas cycle; from the eleventh century forward presentations of this drama would multiply throughout all of western Europe.[310]

Other texts, however, preserve the memory of real debates: the *Annulus* of Rupert, for example, or the *Disputatio* of Odo of Cambrai (†1113),[311] or, in 1186, the *Discussio* of the Mallorcan Contendo.[312] The tone is generally moderate and courteous. Waso and the Jewish doctor are "adversaires pleins de bonhomie" ["adversaries full of geniality"].[313] The ardor of convictions and of zeal does not impede the spirit of tolerance, and some such disputes breathe the deep sincerity of a search conducted in common. The violent Paul Alvarus himself writes to his renegade adversary: "Do not start sharpening your mind in a battle for conquest, but in a search for improvement for us both; you know that the faith consists not in dialectical victory, but in the truth."[314] The celebrated *Disputatio* recorded by Gilbert Crispin (†1117), which was under discussion above, offers us a better example. The two interlocutors, each of them highly educated,[315] have prepared for it through a series of friendly conversations and in it they proclaim their desire to conduct their dispute while banishing the spirit of contention;[316] if, toward the end of the text as we can get it from Migne, politeness and sincerity give way "to crudeness and insult," that is because this ending is apocryphal.[317] In the same way, in the encounter of Peter of Cornwall with Simon the Jew, both declare their firm desire to search for the truth "with all peace and tranquility."[318]

It was not always the Christian who took the initiative in these debates. "So then that Jewish debater . . . rose and called me out," says Gilbert Crispin at the moment of undertaking his account.[319] Leon the Jew accosted the bishop Odo, asking him: "Tell me, bishop, what good did the coming of your Christ bring to the world?"[320] Peter Damian describes the soldier of Christ reduced to silence through his ignorance in the face of the "calumnies" of the Jews who attack his faith, and suffering for the honor of the Christian name.[321] The anonymous author of an incomplete *Tractatus adversus Judaeos* written in France in the year 1166, says that he has decided to write it "so that we may be educated to have something to say about the Scriptures against the faithlessness of the Jews, who are detracting the Christian faith"; that seemed indispensable to him, he explains, "lest we furnish the Jews, who so often insult us, occasion to laugh at our inexpertness and somehow like Goliath say: 'Pick one from amongst you who has it in him to engage in single combat with us.'"[322] There was, therefore, truly a sense of urgency, in face of the old Israel, and urgency arising from the sacred precept, so often recalled during the eleventh and twelfth centuries, "to render an account of the faith."

4. *Perfidi*

These few examples suffice to demonstrate the way Christian thought sought to protect itself at once from an internal temptation and an external threat by detailing the situation of Jewish infidelity and setting it side by side with pagan infidelity. Yet in itself, as was well known, Jewish infidelity was not the same thing as the pagan form, any more than it was exactly the same thing as the revolt of the heretic or the apostasy of the renegade Christian. From antiquity, one word frequently specified it, a word that cannot be understood precisely except within the dialectical perspective expounded in the preceding section. Jewish infidelity is *perfidia*.

Doubtless this word is encountered bearing quite differentiated uses or charged with various nuances. In general, *perfidia* is, like *infidelitas*, the contrary of *fides*. Thus, in this verse of Saint Paulinus of Nola comparing Ruth and Orpah:

> The one daughter-in-law exhibits faithlessness *(perfidiam)*; the other, faith *(fidem)*.[323]

"To build up the faith and to avoid faithlessness of heart," says Saint Bede; and again: the "house of faithlessness" is opposed to the "house of faith"; it is *fides* that saves and *perfidia* that destroys.[324] The latter, then, is less a simple absence of faith than an antithesis of faith or an opposition to the faith; it is a lack of faith in one who ought to believe, as among those ancient Hebrews who, "favoring their usual faithlessness," attributed to themselves successes that they owed to none but God.[325] Or again, it is a false faith, in contrast with the "true faith."[326] To the "right faith" are opposed the "errors of faithlessness."[327] A Mozarabic prayer for the feast of Saint Romanus implores the Lord "that our faith may achieve the crown through him by whom the faithlessness of unbelievers has been driven away."[328] "In the cause of faith or faithlessness," says Sedulius Scotus.[329] By Jesus, in the Gospel — as Gerhoh of Reichersberg observes[330] — "a little faith is blamed, a great faith is praised, and faithlessness is condemned." The prologue to the works of Saint Martin of Leon, composed by the deacon Luke, says that in the writings of the holy bishop "the faith of the Catholic Church is strengthened, the faithlessness of the Jews refuted," and Saint Martin himself on many occasions adjures the Jews to renounce the "faithlessness" of their ancient error and finally to accept the "true faith."[331] "Faithlessness of unbelief," "faithlessness of infidelity" are redundant expressions. The "perfidi" are opposed to the "fideles."[332] Thus, just as *infidelitas* is sometimes attributed to a Jew without further qualification — many texts say "infidelitas Judaeorum," "infidelitas Synagogae"[333] — so is *perfidia* often enough applied to the pagan or the heretic.

These three categories of adversaries of the Christian faith are simultaneously addressed in a doctrinal letter of Pope Saint Damasus: "All the heretics holding bad opinions about the Son of God and the Holy Spirit are found within the faithlessness of the Jews and the gentiles."[334] *Perfidia*, then, is unbelief, or false belief, or impiety. So it is with Apringius, who sees the perfidy of heretics, of schismatics, and of pagans leagued against the Church.[335] So too with Cardinal Humbert: "For faithlessness or the general character of impiety belongs to them all, namely, to pagans, Jews, and heretics."[336] For Saint Augustine, the Jewish sin is the "sin of infidelity,"[337] and the distance between the unbelieving Jews and the Apostles is that between infidelity and faith.[338] Chromatius of Aquilaca speaks of the "the faithlessness of Jewish infidelity."[339] "Turn back to your Redeemer with your infidelity laid aside," says Saint Leo, addressing the Jewish people.[340] Saint Gregory the Great in a homily refers to the "hearts of the unfaithful Jews"; he recounts the "unfaithfulness of the Jews."[341] Eventually he comes to use the two words ["perfidy" and "unfaithfulness"] indiscriminately,[342] a practice in which he would have many imitators.[343] For him "perfidia" occurs as much among the gentiles as in the Synagogue:

> The gentile tribe, however, which had over a long time become rigid in the chill of faithlessness, is figured by means of the north wind.... The Synagogue [by contrast], raging in persecution of our Redeemer, virtually erupted into unbelief.[344]

Furthermore, he mentions the *perfidia* of the gentiles and the *infidelitas* of the Jews in one and the same sentence.[345] Some of the debate writings bear titles like "An argument against the unbelief of the Jews,"[346] or "An attack against the faithlessness of the Jews."[347] Another *Altercatio* reproaches a Jew for his "infidelitas et falsitas."[348] In his *Chronicon*, Otto of Freising mentions the "faithless city of the Jews and pagans," confronting the City of God; he observes that Rome was already "the city of the world" when it found itself again "placed in faithlessness" and he poses the question that did not cease being posed for some eleven centuries in the following form: "Why did God permit the totality of the gentiles to perish in the error of faithlessness for so long, so many ages having gone by?"[349] This was already the language of Tertullian, calling upon the Christian to contemplate as a spectacle, instead of the pugilists of the circus, "faithlessness felled by the faith";[350] that of Augustine, opposing "fides" to "perfidia" without any particular allusion to the Jewish people;[351] that of Ambrose, saying that the believers ought not weep over their deaths in the manner of unbelievers, because "there ought to be a difference between the faithful and the faithless";[352] that of Vincent of Lerins;[353] that of Cassiodorus, saying "perfidi" instead of "infideles";[354] that of Bede, who even wrote while commenting on Samuel: "The faithlessness of the gentiles has raged against the Jews."[355] The first apostles of Spain have vanquished the "error perfidiae" of the infidels by the flaming arrows of their preaching; those infidels have "laid aside the blackness of their perfidy to clothe themselves in the whiteness of the Catholic faith":[356] it is the Mozarab liturgy that celebrates this triumph, and, in its usual language, the "perfidi" are the pagans.[357] The same language is picked up in, among others, John the Deacon, describing the nation of the Angles as "faithless in the worship of sticks and stones";[358] in Rabanus Maurus, laying down the conditions for the validity of baptism;[359] in Manegold, saying of believers who have been able to ravish the "Egyptians" of their spoils: "they have brought over the armor of the faithless into the worship of the faith";[360] in Guibert of Nogent;[361] in Honorius, showing in the "house not consecrated" the symbol of a "god's base gentile character shut up within the walls of faithlessness."[362] For Sedulius Scotus, the Jews who have not believed in Jesus have become unfaithful and faithless, i.e., "equal to the gentiles."[363] For Hrodswitha, the religious dramaturgist of Gandersheim, the Saracens are "the faithless tribe of Saracens."[364] Jean of Salisbury, who himself also opposes "fides" and "perfidia,"[365] introduces a citation of the pagan Plutarch with a warning, saying: "It is a speech lacking faith and worthy of all reprobation . . . , but perhaps. . . ."[366] Honorius characterizes the apostolate of Saint Paul by saying: "he beat out the darkness of faithlessness from the gentiles,"[367] and says that Christ has come to draw his Church "from the faithlessness of paganism."[368] Ever since the age of the Fathers the expressions *infidi, plebs infida, gens infida* have typically been used as much for Jews as for pagans.[369]

Even more than the infidel, and, in a sense more justified, as we shall see, the heretic is called "perfidus." Saint Hilary uses the word for every wound against the faith: "Wherever there are scandals, wherever there are schisms, wherever instances of faithlessness are to be found!"[370] The Arian peace, he says again, is a false peace; it is the "unity of faithlessness."[371] The heresiarchs, says Rufinus, are "authors of faithlessness":[372] "Let the heretics feel that you are hostile to their faithlessness," writes Saint Jerome to Pope Boniface;[373] and in his pamphlet against Rufinus he judges the work of Eusebius as follows: "for six volumes he does nothing else but to show Origen off to his own faith, namely, the Arian faithlessness."[374] That "ariana perfidia," having become the prototype of all the heresies,[375] will very often be alluded to,[376] right up to the threshold of the thirteenth century,[377] where we still find it being denounced by Joachim of Flora[378] and by Alexander Neckham.[379] John of Salisbury will say that Saint Hilary, in combating the Arians, "attacks faithlessness," for "he perceives that there is faithlessness beneath the Catholic words in the mouth of such men."[380] The second book of the *Chronicle* of Sulpicius Severus is full of the "perfidiae" of the heretics; he recounts that at the council of Rimini the emperor wanted to impose a faith "wrapped in deceptive words," a faith "that would utter Catholic teaching with hidden faithlessness."[381] The *Chronicle* of Marcellinus for the year 512 describes a Catholic population shouting down certain "faithless hawkers," who are heterodox preachers.[382] Saint Leo speaks of "the faithlessness of Photinus."[383] It is by way of allusion to his Arianism that Saint Gregory calls Totila, king of the Goths, "a faithless king."[384] The father of Saint Hermenegild was also "perfidus"; his son, on the other hand, faced up to an Arian bishop, "and repulsed his faithlessness with worthy rebukes."[385] Saint Columban does not fear to write to Boniface IV whom he thinks too soft on error "Come to the aid of your reputation . . . lest it be chalked up as faithlessness by your rivals."[386] Against Felix and Elipandus, Paulinus of Aquilaea went on a veritable spree with the word.[387] "Judaei et perfidi" is the Jews and the heretics for the *Liber mozarabicus ordinum* — unless it be the Jews and the pagans: the sound of bells ought to fill them with wholesome terror, so as to call them back to recognize their errors.[388] Heterius and Beatus, seeing the heretics or those whom they judge to be such to delight in the error of faithlessness, mock them in immodest terms.[389] In his commentary on the Apocalypse, Beatus uses another image, one more classic: the heretic "is slinking around whilst his faithlessness is hidden."[390] Ambrose Autpert censures the "perfidia" of the Donatist Tyconius, who, he says once again, in days gone by has mixed the honey of the spiritual senses "with the venom of *perfidia*"; he argues against the "inexperience and faithlessness" of those who deny the eternity of hell.[391] The metaphor of venom, which Saint Jerome was already acquainted with,[392] was found again in Saint Bede, writing about Pelagius in his *Ecclesiastical History*: "venena suae perfidiae longe lateque dispersit" ["he has spread the poisons of his faithlessness far and wide"];[393] it is found again in Rabanus Maurus, frightened by these "many sorts of venom,"[394] and in Prudentius of Troyes, who scents the "venoms of Pelagian faithlessness" in the work of John Scotus;[395] it will be found yet again in Guibert of Nogent, who will denounce the "venom of faithlessness" inherited from Arius and found in Mohammed.[396] The Saracens, for Liutprand of Cremona, are "no less cunning than faithless," and one will note that these two epithets are just the ones that belong to the tempter serpent.[397] Hincmar attacks the "faithlessness of Godschalk."[398] Saint John Gualbert struggles against "the faithlessness of simony"; Saint Wolfgang, bishop of Ratisbon (†994), overthrows Berengar's "perfidia";[399] Hugh of Fleury wants to unmask the "perfidia" of certain secret heretics.[400] Saint Anselm declares that Roscelin's "perfidia" is flagrant, for, in his thought, "he is not a Christian at all."[401] Ill-disposed minds will say of Gilbert de la Porrée, "that he used to hide faithlessness adroitly under the obscurity of his words."[402] Helinand of Froidmont will recount how Peter Abelard in his teaching was "faithlessly dogmatizing about the faith."[403] Writing in 1207 to Philip Augustus about the Albigensians, Innocent III will promise the same indulgence to "those who would take up arms to fight against the faithless" as to the crusaders of the Holy Land.[404] Some see the "sects of the heretics" on various sides engendering the "divisions of faithlessness."[405] "Heretical faithlessness"[406] or the "faithlessness of the heretics,"[407] their "lying faithlessness,"[408] is opposed to the "right faith,"[409] the "sound faith."[410] The "faithlessness of dogma" is opposed to the "scientia" of the orthodox doctor,[411] and the latter ought always be ready to combat all "perfidies," whether of the Jew, the pagan, or the heretic.[412] The faithful of Christ ought always to struggle, says Angelome of Luxeuil, "against any of the faithless of this world."[413] In the same sense also some speak of a "faithlessness of the blasphemers,"[414] and John Scotus, less "faithless" than Prudentius of Troyes said he was, contrasts the "faith of the just" with the "faithlessness of the impious."[415]

There is, nonetheless, in a more precise and very frequent language, a *perfidia*, "an evil of faithlessness,"[416] which is, if one can say it, particular to the Jews. Ambrose Autpert distinguishes this evil from the simple "pagan error"[417] and the fourth Lateran council will oppose it to the "Christian religion."[418] "Jewish faithlessness,"[419] "the faithlessness of the Jews,"[420] "the faithlessness of the Jewish tribe,"[421] "the faithlessness of the transgressing people":[422] these expressions or others analogous to them are routine. "The faithlessness of the Jews will be judged by the faith of the Apostles."[423] A canon from the Council of Agde in 506 — which, despite the contrary practice encouraged by Saint Gregory the Great, would be inserted into the *Decretum* of Burchard of Worms, then into the *Decretum* and the *Panormia* of Yvo of Chartres, and finally into the *Decretum* of Gratian — prescribes prudential delays for admitting the sons of Israel to baptism, "since their faithlessness frequently returns them to their vomit."[424] Saint Anselm exhorts a converted Jew to rejoice, having passed "from faithlessness to the true faith."[425] To recommend another converted Jew, Gilbert Foliot says that one is obliged to help those who forsake everything to embrace the faith of Christ, "once the faithlessness of the Jews has been rejected."[426] Jesus Christ, as Saint Avitus used to say, endured the "perfidia" of his own.[427] In those days there were faithful Jews: they became the first Christians, the Lord's preferred believers; but there were too many "disbelieving Jews" as well.[428] The "faithless tribe," i.e., the Jewish nation,[429] is "faithless and unbelieving,"[430] indeed "perfidissima." "Faithless Judaea,"[431] "faithless people,"[432] "faithless people of the Jews."[433] Again, some speak of the "perfidia Synagogae" ["faithlessness of the Synagogue"] or of the "faithless Synagogue."[434] Some say "perfidi Judaei,"[435] or "Judaei perfidentes,"[436] or "perfidiantes";[437] but also simply "perfidi."[438] Daniel, says Rabanus Maurus, predicted "that the Lord was to be killed by the faithless."[439] Alvarus of Cordoba writes in his poem on the cross:

> Behold our God Christ flowers forth from heaven. . . .
> Let the faithless mob, blackened with pain, depart.[440]

A hymn from the tenth century sings at Lauds for Palm Sunday:

> Having entered the noble courtyard
> With whips he hurls out the faithless
> From the halls of prayer.[441]

Guibert of Nogent depicts a cleric abashed by one of the "faithless,"[442] etc. The "arguments of faithlessness against the faith" are the Jewish interpretation of the Messianic prophecies.[443] "Perfidia," then, represents a particular species within the common genus of "infidelitas."[444] It is distinguished from "haeretica pravitas," from "superstitio gentilis," and from "schisma fraternum." These are the four sorts of "sins,"[445] constituting the four members of the "body of the devil";[446] one will not count among them the simple infidelity of ignorance, which is a mere absence of the true faith, as was the case with our forefathers to whom Jesus Christ had not yet been announced.[447] The description is classic. A late author, letting the category of schism drop out, will propose the following explication:

> Everyone unfaithful is a pagan, a Jew, or a heretic. The first through stupidity contemns hearing and recognizing the salvation received of faith. The second recognizes and understands something of it from his own Scriptures, but through envy casts it away in contempt of Christ. The third recognizes and accepts it, but later through pride breaks away from it once accepted. Hence the first is perverse and ungrateful; the second, envious and obstinate; the third, faithless and proud.[448]

Let us close our eyes for a moment to the slight twist that this explanatory text makes in ending with the most common terminology, and that we shall understand better in a moment. According to the occasion, the Jewish *perfidia* is sometimes set in contrast with idolatry,[449] sometimes with heresy,[450] sometimes with every other sort of error or impiety.[451] Remembering Saint Paul and the first Christian age, it happens that some

Perfidi

distinguish *perfidia* from the wisdom of the world once again, in order simply to condemn the pair of them at once:

> All faithlessness and worldly wisdom or philosophy is vanquished by the faith of the Trinity.[452]

How then is this "Judaic faithlessness," this "faithlessness of the Judaic superstition,"[453] characterized? To start with, it presupposes a faith: not just any faith, the true faith, whose substance is already the same as that of the Christian will be, though in other "sacraments." But this faith, because it refuses to go all the way to its very end, is going to change direction, so to speak; it is going to turn back into its contrary. In the days of the Messiah, the crisis has opened; the time has come for the decisive choice, and no one can avoid it. The Jew cannot rest with the status quo: he must either finish the edifice of his faith, or ruin it.[454] If he bucks against the internal logic of the revelation that he has received, if he closes himself off from the Truth the promise of which he possesses and which is now being made manifest to him, if — contrary to the testimony of his own Scriptures — he discards the spiritual understanding of it,[455] not only does he deserve to be called "carnal": by that very fact, from being faithful, he becomes "perfidus." Because he has not been willing to pass, as Saint Paul used to say, "out of faith into the faith," that is to say, "out of the faith of the Old Testament into the faith of the New Testament," or, what is the same thing, "out of the faith of words and hope into the faith of things and their manifestation,"[456] he falls "from faith into faithlessness."[457] He loses the reality of that beautiful name of Jew, which signifies "confessor" of the faith.[458] The good odor of the faith of Abraham is corrupted in his soul.[459] Through that "perfidia" he ceases to be the son of the Patriarch.[460] He falls away from the "nobility of our elders out of the faith."[461] A fatal "interruption" of the prophetic current is produced in him.[462] He has been seized with a deadly "languor."[463] This is a "torpor,"[464] at least a baneful "sleep," the cause of a fall.[465] It is a strange "madness."[466] Once again, it is a "frost,"[467] it is a "deafness," a "blindness,"[468] because it is already a "hardness,"[469] a "lack of discernment."[470] It is a night that swoops down upon his soul. It is the beginning of a turn to "obstinacy" in him, one that will quickly increase: "determined faithlessness,"[471] "longlasting blindness," "deadly obstinacy," "faithlessness of deadly obstinacy."[472] This is the refusal to follow and let the "basic elements of the faith"[473] blossom by turning to Christ. This is the rejection of the Savior: "as though they have forgotten the One whom they have

SUBJECTIVISM AND SPIRITUAL UNDERSTANDING

prophesied, while they would sing that he is to be incarnated in the words of the Law, they would deny that he has been incarnated with their words of faithlessness."[474] "Adamantine faithlessness!" Saint Martin of Leon will cry.[475]

He thus passes into *perfidia* under the appearance of literal and unchanged fidelity, as an element of "rebellion"[476] and apostasy: "apostate Jews."[477] For their part, the Jews say the same of those among their own who become Christian.[478] "Apostate faithlessness" is perhaps a natural epithet. Apostasy exists at the second degree if it is no longer just a question of a Jew who loses the true faith at the moment he rejects the Messiah whom he ought to accept, but of a Christian who becomes a Jew.[479] The most emphatic type of the "perfidus" is Lucifer, the "apostate angel": in the great heavenly combat, "the faithless apostate angel violently pursues the faithful servant of God."[480] The first man also "fell into the fault of faithlessness."[481] Another great example is that of Solomon, who, after having built a temple to the true God, " he was not afraid to build a temple to idols, paved with faithlessness"; a "continual nagging of the flesh" leads him to that "faithlessness of mind."[482] One can therefore be in "infidelitas" for a long time, but one falls into "perfidia" suddenly.[483] "The Jewish people slipped down to faithlessness."[484] This is a "shipwreck."[485]

Such was the case also with those Christians who had become *lapsi*, fallen from their faith during the persecutions, whom Saint Cyprian called "perfidi."[486] Lactantius used to speak as well of those excessively weak Christians who "have deserted the heavenly sacrament by fear of pain or death or by their own faithlessness."[487] Saint Ambrose knows that the just can fall "into the pit of faithlessness," i.e., lose their confidence in God so as to trust in their own powers.[488] Thus, in the strict sense, the "faithless" are always "fallen," whilst the latter are not always necessarily merely "unbelievers."[489] Their fall is the reverse of "conversio"; it is "perversio."[490] The first who fell in that way, the apostle Peter, "wept bitterly over his fall to faithlessness."[491] A Carolingian prayer asks the Holy Spirit: "Drive away from me the darkness of all iniquity and faithlessness."[492] When Saint John Gualbert said in his prayer: "Do thou lift my heart from faithless cogitations," he was begging the Lord to preserve him from temptations against the faith; this was the negative form of a prayer that he formulated in a positive form as well: "Preserve in me, O Lord, a spotless faith."[493] In his work in praise of the faith, Gerhoh of Reichersberg also asks "that the spirit of faithlessness not find entry into our heart."[494] Othloh of Saint Emmeran was once tempted by demons who incited him to despair and to "faithlessness."[495] One departs from the rule of faith, says Adam Scotus, through the error of "perfidia."[496] Richard of Saint Victor does not want anyone to be exposed, through an imprudent exegesis, to the risk of losing the faith: "to incur the danger of faithlessness," specifically, the risk of becoming a Jew.[497] Men are not heroes, says John of Salisbury — that is to say, of firm and stable character — since they are capable of "faithlessness";[498] but "the discipline of Christ" is not in itself affected by the fall and wanderings of the "faithless disciples of Christ."[499] The "perfidus," then, has rejected the faith, just as the "perversus" has rejected innocence, and as the "perjurus" or the "perjurans" has rejected his oath:[500] these three epithets are sometimes very close to each other.

The case of the Jews is similar. "The older Jews, by hoping that Christ the Redeemer was to come, were Christians, . . . therefore those who are guilty of having violated the Law, for so long as they do not accept Christ, should necessarily be regarded as apostates."[501] The incredulous Jew rejects the Savior "through the sacrilege of apostate faithlessness"[502] (one should note the association of these three terms); he therefore withdraws "from the whole virtue of faith," imitating his pre-Christian ancestors who turned aside to idols.[503] This is the point at which their case approaches that of the Christian falling into heresy: "They are the brothers of the Jews, with whom they are related by the bond of faithlessness," says Saint Ambrose of the heretics of his own time.[504] Jews and heretics, says Chromatius of Aquilaea, are also "faithless in preaching on behalf of the faith."[505] Though not properly heretics and deserving a certain indulgence, the "lapsi," whose case Cyprian studied, were "apostate and faithless."[506] The Pseudo-Cyprian used to say to the partisans of Novatian: "You have exchanged your first faith for your later faithlessness."[507] In the *Chronicon* of Idatius, dating from the 302nd Olympiad, one can read of Gaiseric, king of the Vandals in Betica: "Having become an apostate from the Catholic faith, he is said to have crossed over to the Arian faithlessness."[508] Saint Jerome, blinded by polemical spirit, holds that Rufinus and his like want "to defend the faithlessness of the men of former times so as to lose their own faith."[509] And here is Saint Paulinus of Aquilaea inveighing against Felix of Urgel: "He does not submit his own notion to the apostolic sense, but rather, following his own perversity, he has been softened up by his own faithless sense to corrupt the apostolic utterance."[510] We have read earlier several similar accusations: this text merely adds the aggravating feature of "faithlessness" to the mention of "one's own sense." "We were aghast at the usual faithlessness of your faith," writes Paul Avarus to an apostate.[511] Again, like the Jew, the heretic changes the sweetness of the true faith into bitterness;[512] that is why his doctrine is figured in Scripture as absinthe.[513] Like the Jew, he is obstinate: "The heretics . . . defend a faithless conception of novel error with persistent perversity."[514] Though in one way differing, the one and the other have both become "faithless starting from the faith."[515] Both the former and the latter, "concealing fictitious dogmas as with a covering of truth, persist in the faithlessness of night with an obstinate and closed heart."[516] It can be said of Jews as well as of heretics that it is not far from the "faithless man" to the "man of ill faith."[517] Whence arises the conjoint expression: "the faithlessness of the Jews and the heretics."[518] Thus the Synagogue and heresy are often put within the sphere of the same reprobation. The similarity is such that the Jews themselves are sometimes called "heretics": "so long as the Synagogue sticks to the carnal observance of the Law, the leprosy of heretical perversity will stick to her."[519] And by way of reciprocity, a Nestorius, whose error is equivalent to a rejection of the mystery of the Incarnation, is said to have "deviated as far as the unbelief of the Jews."[520] As to the Pseudo-Augustine who undertook to struggle "against the five heresies," he included under this common title, with less reason, the pagans, the Jews, the Manicheans, the Sabellians, and the Arians all at once.[521]

The impious, those who do not want to believe, are, as the book of Wisdom puts it, mad: "perfidiorum insanas"! Maddest of all are those who turn faith into unbelief: "O amentes, o perfidi!"[522] But there was not merely stupidity among them. The Christian Middles Ages, in the fervor of a usually untroubled faith, and perhaps in the familiarity of its secular doctrines as well, could sometimes scarcely comprehend that it had been possible not to interpret the prophets immediately in their Christian sense. Doubtless the ancient Scripture was at first a sealed book; but after the event, had not the testimonies of its prophecies become "lucidissima, evidentissima"? Do they not shine henceforward like the noon-day sun? Do they not constitute, as it were, so many radiant stars?[523] If, therefore, the Scribes and Pharisees, by some truly stupefying miracle, had not been able to recognize the Word incarnated within their race, when his arrival had been so clearly, so openly, so lucidly predicted in the Scriptures that they used to meditate upon from their infancy,[524] it is, in the estimation of the Christian Middle Ages, because they misunderstood the "ways of humility" by which he came to us so as to raise us up with himself.[525] This people, alas, is "readier at faithlessness."[526] Its "perfidia" is deep, as deep as the sea.[527] The obstinacy that it sinks into is moreover a sort of ingratitude.[528] Finally, it is pride which has produced in its leaders the refusal to believe:[529] "being puffed up with the observance of the Law, they were unwilling to understand the spiritual Law spiritually";[530] what keeps them in it is "the proud minds of the Hebrews remaining in faithlessness."[531] Pride modifies "perfidia" to such a point that the "perfidus" ends up by becoming in certain cases the direct antithesis of the "humilis," and this goes a long way in analogical applications where it is no longer a question of Judaism, as in the address of the popular chief William Long-Beard: "I shall separate the humble and faithful people from the proud and faithless people,"[532] or in this symbolic explication from the liturgist Sicardus of Cremona: "The Pontiff wears a ring since he must seal up the mysteries of Scripture and the sacraments of the Church from the faithless and reveal them to the humble";[533] or even in cases where it is no longer a question of religion at all, as in this piece of Carolinian verse predicting the submission of his proud enemies to the emperor:

> The proud and stiff-necked faithless will justly be bowed before you;
> The mind of the humble bends the faithless necks to you.[534]

"That proud Synagogue."[535] By an equivalence of the same order, the "faithlessness of the Jews" in the writing of Peter of Blois immediately becomes the "obstinacy of Judaic cheating";[536] and such obstinacy is not only a "vanity excelling all vanities"; it is, as the *Caroline Books* say, "a deceit more tenacious than all deceits."[537] In the same way again, after having spoken of "perfidia" as a sort of "lack of skill," a simple "error" that the mere evidence of demonstration ought to be able to correct, the author of the *Altercatio Ecclesiae contra Synagogam* edited by Mr. B. Blumenkranz ends up by declaring to his interlocutor that he would already believe in Christ if his "perfidia" had not hobbled the normal play of his understanding.[538] For the incredulous Jews cannot believe, as the Gospel of Saint John notes on several occasions, but this impossibility comes "from a vice of their own will"; they are, at bottom, "enemies of the truth."[539] Their "perfidia" is therefore a fault.[540] It is malice toward God: "judaica malitia."[541] It is an injustice against him: "iniquitatem, perfidiam intelligo."[542] Since it is implicitly a form of apostasy, it is a sort of treason. It is related to blasphemy.[543] How could it not be the object of a severe disapproval? For the "ministers of faithlessness" are "ministers of death."[544]

A large number of texts dealing with "perfidia" are too engaged in polemic not to cast upon this concept darker colors than it would have had in the calm and precision of purely dogmatic thought. On the other hand, let us remark that their application is more collective than individual, more concerned with the leaders of the people at the time of Jesus than with the whole of the Jewish nation, and defines a type more than real individuals. More fundamentally: the disapproval of which the *perfidus* constitutes the object is in principle limited to the mysterious order of the faith. The harsh terms that are not spared for Jewish *perfidia* concern only the relation to God, not human relations. They are not injuries at the social level. As severe and as grave as he was about the religious situation of the incredulous people, Saint Gregory the Great still never had a word against the Jews that might be wounding at a human level,[545] and his policy regarding them, habitually continued by his successors, has always been marked with humanity. The same must be said of Saint Isidore of Seville[546] and many others. Again in 1199, while constantly deploring the "faithlessness" of the Jews from the religious point of view and while disapproving of that "blindness" that keeps them from attaining the marrow of the Scriptures, Innocent III will promulgate a *Constitutio pro Judaeis* which is an edict "in favor of the Jews."[547] One Christian, for example, says that he has known a Jew who, in daily life and especially on the occasion of great Christian festivals, had a very humble bearing.[548] Another — and this testimony is more telling — recognized that "the men of that race are quite habitually honest in business or with respect to matters of earthly judgment"; it is therefore necessary, he thinks, to protect those among them who might be in need of it, all the while disapproving of the "perfidia" of their opinions.[549] It is also necessary, as Saint Augustine advised, to watch out lest one fall into pride himself, from the opposite direction.[550] A Spanish charter of 1178 coming from the abbot of Sahagun, recalls that all Jews — as well as the pagans — are our neighbors.[551] Finally, if it is true, as Saint Ambrose said, that "the pagan nations have been chosen by God to destroy the faithlessness of the Jews,"[552] that "destruction" is in no way of a material order: it can not include anything else than their conversion. Now it is well known that the latter ought not to be obtained by force, and we do not despair of leading the "perfidi" finally to find, in Christ and through Christ, the true sense of the Scriptures, the veritable "character of understanding."[553] Here one is forced to have recourse to the arms of the Spirit. The Jew is before the Christian in the same way that Goliath was, in ancient times, before David:

> If then you want fully to catch and to exterminate his tricks, let the library of the Spirit be put in the middle, so that he may neither flee

Perfidi

nor turn his back, but like Goliath he may have his throat slit with his own sword.[554]

This is just what Saint Stephen, the first of all the martyrs and of all the Christian apologists, did, of whom the Spanish liturgy says that he wanted to be stoned "with the stony blows of the faithless," so as to arrive "at the precious stone, Christ the Lord";[555] of whom it is also said in a prayer from Leo's sacramentary: "destroying Jewish faithlessness with constant voice by the power of thy word."[556] Saint Peter had already done the same, as a hymn sung at matins within the octave of Pentecost recalls:

But once the miracles are produced
Peter runs up and teaches
That the faithless are uttering a falsehood,
Proving it, with Joel as witness.[557]

But if, for the doctor, the spiritual defense is an argument based on Scripture, for the Church herself such defense cannot exist other than in the form of prayer and witness to her faith. It is without any hostility that the Church tells the Jew who comes to her to ask for baptism: "Quake at Jewish faithlessness; spit back Hebraic superstition."[558] It is without any connotation of mistrust that she implores the divine light on their behalf: "Let the blind in heart enjoy the light; the Hebrews, the Catholic faith."[559] On Good Friday, the sacred day of the Passion, she prays: "also for the faithless Jews," "so that the unbelief of the faithless should return to Christ."[560] She sets aside a special prayer for them, and the words she uses are exactly those that are necessary to characterize their separate religious situation. With all the more reason there is nothing in this solemn prayer which calls out "the atrocious hatred of the Jews," which with good faith some have recently believed they recognized in it.[561] Perhaps the omission of ritual genuflection for this prayer alone, or rather the false interpretation which has sometimes been given of it — following a marginal note found in an old sacramentary,[562] and doubtless badly understood[563] — has helped to reinforce the conviction of some moderns, who suspected a certain offensive intention in the liturgical epithet.[564] It is clear that this epithet has "a pejorative theological content" — without which the faith of the Church would no longer be the Christian faith, and the prayer for the conversion of the Jews would lose its point — but one would not be able to conclude that it "sounds like an outrage." In fact, "the Catholic Church has never allowed into her prayers a single word injurious or unkind to the Jews."⁵⁶⁵ The explanation that was given in the Middle Ages for the Good Friday ritual was simple. It is found already in Amalarius, together with that for the omission of the kiss of peace: "They were bending the knee . . . , they used to do this in mockery; but we, to show that we ought to avoid works that come about by simulation, avoid bending the knee in the prayer for the Jews."⁵⁶⁶ In the eleventh century, Berno of Reichenau, following Amalarius, assigns it to the analogous omission that characterizes one of the prayers of Lent:

> (At that time) we ought to show humility of mind by bending our knees. . . . Only in the prayer about the furnace of fire do we not bend our knees, when Nebuchadnezzar compelled the people to adore a statue that he had made, so that our prayer, which is to the one God, may be separated from the error of the gentiles.
>
> For like reason also on the Preparation Day we do not bend our knees for the faithless Jews, who used to bend their knees in mockery before God, lest we seem to imitate those who strove to do a good work badly; just as at that time we abstain from the kiss, owing to the example of the traitor Judas, who betrayed our Lord Jesus through a kiss of simulated peace.⁵⁶⁷

Without being substantially transformed, the explanation given by Amalarius and then by Berno will little by little take on a more hostile coloration, in proportion as the state of mind unfavorable to the Jews will grow. Already the Roman Pontifical of the twelfth century emphasizes more the horror inspired by the gesture of the Jews on the day of the Passion than the risk of seeming to imitate it:

> When the prayer for the Jews is being offered, the knees ought not to be bent. For, since on this day the Jews bent their knees in mockery, the Church, shuddering at their outrage, does not bend her knees in praying for them.⁵⁶⁸

In the thirteenth century, the thought will harden again — one might think so at least — by the suppression of two words. Instead of "she does not bend her knees in praying for them," the *Ordo* of Holy Week for the Roman curia has merely "let her not bend her knees for them."⁵⁶⁹ The prayer, however, remains; it remains unchanged, and one could not say that these deteriorations in the rubric's justification seriously alter its meaning. Still less will this be said for the introduction of the rite itself. In the age of Amalarius, and despite this new rite which omits the genuflection, "the prayer for the Jews keeps its original tone, without being burdened with any polemical intention." It is Mr. Bernhard Blumenkranz who, after others, recognized it. We do not see from that time on how anyone could affirm, by the mere fact of this rite or of the explanation that Amalarius gives of it, that "a prayer which, at its beginnings, had been the expression of a touching solicitude of the religious soul, lamenting the lot of those who did not yet have the light that she alone believed she enjoyed, had become a petty manifestation of resentment with regard to those who remained insensitive to all the invitations."[570] Everything here below wears out, and the primitive fervor from whence the prayer for Israel had sprung forth had doubtless cooled; nevertheless, with or without genuflection, there is truly not a trace of anti-semitism in this prayer of the Church "pro perfidis Judaeis."[571]

Nor, from their title alone, is there any more anti-semitism in the various treatises of the Christian doctors "contra Judaeos," which are advanced to demonstrate, in a purely religious argument, the messianic character and the divinity of Jesus Christ. Of this type is the treatise of Saint Isidore of Seville, *De fide catholica ex veteri et novo Testamento contra Judaeos*. It is nothing other than a work of apologetics, based on the Scriptures. Written, it seems, by Isidore at the request of his sister Florentine, who had been alarmed by objections from the Jews, "it is perhaps," says A. Lukyn Williams, the most logical and best worked out of all the ancient essays attempting to present Christ to the Jews."[572] No reproach is called for against its author, its translators, or its disseminators[573] any more than should be leveled at Saint Thomas Aquinas for having written a work *Contra Gentiles*. Perhaps it is also overly subtle to want to discover manifestations of violent anti-semitism in the works of art that represent the Synagogue with blindfolded eyes and broken scepter, scarcely keeping hold of the Book or letting it slip from her hands, as in the famous statue from the portal of Strasbourg. Some compare these with earlier works, in which, instead of that defeated and humiliated posture, the Synagogue showed a fiery attitude, affecting rather insult and disdain. But the evidence is scarcely convincing, since the change of attitude is not produced in representation of the same scene. In the ancient images that one is referred to, the Synagogue is at Calvary on Good Friday afternoon, as the incredulous Jews were depicted by the gospel accounts, whereas the Synagogue of the Strasbourg type describes, in the Christian optic, the situation that followed, as Saint Paul had set it out and as the Fathers of the Church had commented on it after him. There is nothing novel there in the history of Christian thought. There is nothing that assumes anything other than the constant givens of the faith. When the author of a *Disputatio Ecclesiae et Synagogae* that likely dates from the twelfth century writes of the Synagogue, "she has been stripped of the raiment of the faith and the crown of her kingdom," or when he has her say to herself, "I have been destroyed in my beauty and in my Law which God has given me through Moses," his work may be "the literary reflection" of certain works of art, as Mr. Blumenkranz has hypothesized about the matter;[574] much more certainly, however, the works of art were themselves already the reflection of a teaching that dates from the origins of Christianity, whether this had been by the mediation of dramatic representations or not. To suppose, with Paul Hildenfinger or with Mr. Max Haller, that the creator of the two magnificent statues of Strasbourg, or those of analogous figures that came a little before them, had "wanted to set in stone the memory of less ancient and more passionate conflicts,"[575] is, it seems to me, a gratuitous hypothesis. Doubtless the hostility which at that time was increasing with regard to the Jews was able to contribute, psychologically, to spread everything that could show the Synagogue in an abased condition; but treating them *per modum unius,* as Hildenfinger has done, is totally to confound a clearly theological representation and later images whose character is completely different.[576] The Book, the blindfold, the broken scepter: they express exactly the spiritual situation consequent upon the coming of Christ and the drama of Calvary.

The history sketched out here is not sociological, but theological. Now we are well aware that in no age do men let themselves be guided by theology alone! If it is legitimate and necessary to trace out the facts and to analyze the human feelings of an epoch, it is nevertheless no less legitimate — and it may be equally necessary — to study its doctrines in the expressions that have been created for it, so as to enter into the knowledge of that epoch. In the present case, one runs the risk of misunderstanding these expressions if one makes no effort to reconstitute, at least in the imagination, the view of faith which from age to age considered what Amalarius already used to call "the sacrament of the Synagogue"[577] in the light of the New Testament. No longer would it be necessary to take an expression like "populus carnalis," which sometimes doubles for "populus perfidus," in a vulgar and grossly hostile sense. The Jewish people is called "carnal" because it rejects the spiritual interpretation of its Scriptures; but this theme did not of itself lead "by a fatal progression" to that of the "people of the Beast, of the Antichrist, and of the devil."[578] In the centuries that we have under view, that would have been, on the

Perfidi

part of the medieval reader, a grave misunderstanding, and we have not encountered a single example of it.

Only, it must also be recognized, as an effect of controversy and still more of human frailty, through the narrowness or harshness of certain doctors as well as through popular prejudices, a degradation of the authentic sense of "perfidus," the serious but respectful sense kept by the liturgy and by the doctrinal texts, was practically fatal. This degradation was all the greater because, just like its correlative term *fides, perfidia* was not a word invented by theology for its own exclusive use, any more, for example, than the word "ecclesia" or the word "allegoria." It was a transposition onto the religious plane of a moral and social attribute which tended by its own natural weight to rediscover its primary signification. One who is willfully blind, an ingrate, obstinate, proud — could the *perfidus* once more merit esteem? Will not his "perfidia" — which, in making him prefer the bitterness of the letter to the sweetness of the spiritual understanding,[579] is typically accompanied by "perversitas"[580] — be, humanly speaking, "malice"?[581] Prefigured in the murder of Abel by Cain, a murder which likewise had been caused by envy,[582] had this "perfidia" not been cruel in the bloody drama of Calvary?[583] Among the Christians, not all recall, however, that in this drama every human being is required to play a part, every human being is culpable, and that even historically the responsibility had been shared, as Saint Gregory attempted to say again and again.[584] Not all recall that, as Origen had preached,[585] the Christian who sins against his God shows himself more culpable than the very ones who crucified Jesus. Very few are even, alas, truly aware of this culpability, though there is no lack of theologians or preachers to remind them of it, sometimes in strong terms: such men as Saint Bede, who sees around him many new Judasas, attempting to sell their master down the river;[586] Candidus of Fulda, for whom every sinner in the Church offers Christ wine mixed with gall, thus rendering himself even more culpable because he already knew his Lord;[587] Remigius of Auxerre, who applies the prophet Micah's curses to "perverse teachers and leaders or judges of the Church"[588] and for whom the predicted ruin of the "faithless city" is the loss of every wicked Christian as well;[589] Bruno of Würzburg, certifying that those wicked Christians are more malicious and more hostile to Christ than any Jew ever was;[590] Saint Bruno the Carthusian, who did his utmost to humble the pride of a converted gentile;[591] the Victorine Absalon, denouncing those who through their wicked conduct destroy the Body of Christ, thereby "exceeding Jewish faithlessness."[592] "Et hodie quoque" ["And today, too"], "et usque hodie" ["and right down to the present day"], "in ipsa quoque Ecclesia" ["in the Church herself also"]: these are, in species, expressions still used today. Despite all this, too often one is stuck with findings of a more palpable order, which party spirit does not fail to deform or render gross. Is that "faithlessness" of the Synagogue, asks one, not today still accompanied by envy, this time regarding the Church, whose faith makes her weep?[593] Does it not also signify, someone even adds, a sort of duplicity?[594] Are not the lips of the "perfidi" crafty? Have not the faithless on more than one occasion given proof of a "most faithless iniquity"?[595] Besides, the epithet will be applied to the tempter Serpent,[596] to *the* enemy in the highest degree.[597] In its popular use, it connotes something not merely impious,[598] but "dark," "black" — whence in days long ago Jerome's nasty pun on the name of Melanie[599] — something "disgraceful,"[600] a "traitor":[601] was not Judas especially "faithless"?[602] It is not only for his incredulity that king Herod was declared faithless:

> They evade faithless Herod
> By the warning of an angel.[603]

Profane *perfidia* figures in the list of vices that characterize a scoundrel.[604] Finally, in a certain number of texts, the word "perfidus" denotes exactly what the modern French word "perfide" or the modern English "perfidious" means. It is a false brother. "The watchful faithlessness of false brethren," as Arno of Reichersberg put it in the twelfth century, deploring the decadence of the canons regular.[605] Already, when Rufinus in his *Apologia* was denouncing the doings of Eusebius of Cremona, that shifty character and past master of intrigue and calumny,[606] he treated him as "perfidus,"[607] that is to say, as a man without good faith. Since *perfidia* is the opposite of *fides*, which in the classical language used to signify "good faith," such an acceptation is normal. The slave or the deceiving lover, the wife or secretly unfaithful girlfriend, are "perfidi";[608] every literate person used to be quite familiar with that word, which Dido, burning with anger, hurls at Aeneas who is getting ready to leave her. In the human order as well as in the divine order, the "perfidus" fails in his pledged word: he is a perjurer.[609] To express the horror of his epoch, Bernard of Cluny cries:

> O evil times! Faithless hearts are treated as high-born.[610]

And Marbodius, laying out the misdeeds of avarice with a copious supply of mythological recollections, says:

Perfidi

> Through gold was Polymnestor a perjurer, Danae an adulteress,
> Tarpeia faithless, and Eryphile savage.[611]

Like the sea under its surface tranquility, the world is a "faithless element."[612]

The two acceptations of the word, the human and the sacred, are often more or less mingled, for example when Jean of Avranches writes that Scribes and Pharisees have "faithlessly" slain the Lord,[613] or in this citation from the Universal Chronicle of Ekkehard of Aura for the year 795: "A king, not unmindful of the faithlessness of the Saxons...."[614] They are at once brought together and contradistinguished in this verse from the *Apotheosis* of Prudentius describing Julian the Apostate:

> Loving three hundred thousands of gods, is he
> Faithless to God, though not faithless to the world.[615]

The mingling became practically inevitable in a society whose religion was bond and, in addition, whose feudal character emphasized above all the bonds of fidelity. This mingling is well illustrated in a letter from Fulbert of Chartres addressed to William Duke of Aquitaine around 1020, in which neither religious faith, nor Jews, but only the relations between lord and vassal are in question. In it Fulbert treats *de forma fidelitatis*. The "fidelis" is he who has "sworn fidelity"; he ought "faithfully to serve" his lord, and the latter, in turn, ought to protect "his faithful" man: "whereby if he should not do it, he will deservedly be reckoned a man of bad faith, just as, if that man were caught either in engaging, or consenting, in any prevarication, he would be reckoned faithless and perjured."[616]

In such a form of society, it is clear that "the concepts of civic fidelity and of religious fidelity interpenetrate each other"; defection from the one therefore led easily, if not necessarily, to defection from the other.[617] Thus, in his famous *Gesta Dei per Francos*, when Guibert of Nogent comes to recount the story of the crusader leader Raynaud — who, not content to betray his cause by handing his army over to the Turks, actually abjures the Christian faith — the narrative provides a double justification for Guibert to denounce his *perfidia*.[618] An example of this kind makes it easy to see the bond between the two acceptations, which nonetheless remain distinct: as treason is a failure against sworn fidelity, the abandonment of the divine faith is of itself a betrayal. A bishop unfaithful to his charge is a "perfidus," but his "perfidia" does not keep the whole Church from preserving her integrity.[619] Finally, the mingling is complete when "perfidia" is attributed to the Jews collectively by men scarcely spiritual. One can suppose, for example, that the Merovingian king Gontran, had he wanted to be a theologian, would have excluded no moral judgment or temporal perspective when, according to Gregory of Tours, he cried out to the Jews coming to acclaim him at the time of his entry into his capital Orleans: "Woe to the Jewish tribe, wicked and faithless, and living with an ever underhanded sense!"[620] Such cases, however, are rather rare. The most precise medieval texts that we have gathered, in which "perfidus" has the vulgar sense of "perfidious," do not have Jews in their sights. They aim principally at heads of armies, kings,[621] tyrants,[622] enemy peoples[623] or warriors.[624] Thus, in the *Liber revelationum* of Andradus Modicus, God announces to Charles the Bald the death of count Vivian, that "faithless and unspeakable" man who was not afraid to have himself proclaimed abbot of several monasteries.[625] A charter accorded by the emperor Henry II to the Jewish community of Worms in 1090 offers another example; it contains this clause:

> If at some time a faithless man among them [the Jews] should want to hide the truth of something done among them, let him be compelled to utter the truth by the one who is their overseer.[626]

Raoul Glaber opposes the fear-induced honor that surrounds the "perfidious" powerful to the fear which reverence inspires toward one who is good.[627] And in the *Gesta Dei per Francos,* Guibert of Nogent is often indignant at a "perfidus imperator," some "faithless emperor" whose impostures are leading the crusade to ruin. This fellow is an "emperor of Babylon," a "faithless, perjuring, betrayer." "The faithless emperor of the Franks deludes the leaders," he writes.[628]

5. *Verbum abbreviatum*

If *perfidia* is so grave a matter, it is because the people who let themselves be blinded by it had received the mission to enlighten all the others: "they who used to seem to bring others to the faith themselves trickled away into faithlessness."[629] If this people had been able to say, with John the Baptist: "He must increase, and I decrease,"[630] if it had consented to believe, then it would have been the guide of all the nations.[631] The Jews did not at all need to come to the faith like the gentiles, but, being within this faith which had already been granted, merely to consent to grace.[632] But rejection of that grace engendered in them a zeal in the wrong direction: this is the "zeal of faithlessness" of the elder brother, jealous at seeing the younger brother, the gentiles, now taking over the baton in preaching the living God.[633] "Remaining in faithlessness, they are in conflict with the Church of God."[634] They want to win over the others to their own "perfidia": "once the messenger of faith and religion, but now of impiety and faithlessness."[635] Certain Jews are even so "faithless" that they prefer to wait for the Antichrist than to entrust themselves to the Christ.[636] One may not, however, forget: everything that concerns that "Jewish faithlessness" was definitively a "dispensation of the divine mercy."[637] It had been announced by the prophets;[638] it was the occasion, the condition, and, as it were, the price of admission of the gentiles to the faith;[639] "the rejection of the Jews is the occasion of our salvation."[640] Their fault has enriched the world.[641] As Rachel died in childbirth, so the Synagogue has died as soon as it brought Christ and his apostles into the world.[642] Even the Christian who meditates upon the theology of history mitigates his opinion regarding the incredulous Jews a great deal:

> It happens that, whilst they are unknowing and as it were sleeping . . . , the spirit of truth, who had usually been with them, would hide and absent himself from them.[643]

Even more than being "perfidi" ["faithless"], these people are unhappy.[644] Just as David had pitied Saul, we must also have compassion for their misfortune:[645] "O unhappy — no rather O most unhappy Jews! O wretched ones and to be pitied!"[646] It is not necessary to take them as so many Judases: their blindness, which Christ has used for his redemptive plan, was more stupidity than malice.[647] Their "apostasy" was in reality a sort of "negligence"; they neglected to open the eyes of their mind to the spiritual understanding.[648] Today too this is merely a "delay." "A time will come when the yoke on their neck will be broken."[649] When they finally will be converted, after at first having submitted to the service of the Antichrist,[650] they will not, properly speaking, accede to the faith, "to the knowledge of the truth"; they will return to it.[651] They "will return to the Christ" whom they failed to meet first time around.[652] It is in their own writings that they will finally recognize him.[653] Elijah will explain the Law to them in its spiritual sense, and they will comprehend it, just as Moses and the Prophets had comprehended it long ago.[654] They will be satisfied by the spiritual understanding of the [five books of the] Pentateuch, which at first they would not or could not accept, as by the five loaves that the gospel speaks of prophetically.[655] At that time they will be lifted up from their fall: *casus eorum est recuperabilis*.[656] At that time they will rediscover their first dignity,[657] that "Israelite dignity" to which every Christian is happy to accede. They will enter into possession of the gifts that they have lost[658] and "the seed of the Lord will be in magnificence and glory."[659] Their return to the faith, also prophesied by the Scripture, will be the sign of a great joy for all the Church, which from now on lives in the expectation of that "holy joy."[660] At that time the fathers will turn back to their children and will come to rejoin them. At that time the children will gather their parents to the family table,[661] for a magnificent banquet.[662] "Having returned to the faith, they will be received with joy."[663] Like the daughter of Jairus, the Synagogue, daughter of Moses, will rise from her bed: this will be the joy of a resurrection.[664] The "warmth of the Word of God" will reanimate her members; the sun of Justice will shed its light upon her; the life-blood of the Spirit will spread through her veins. The long winter will be over. The whole universe will at last see "the complete Gospel."[665] Even more, if the Jews finally embrace our faith, this will come about so that we ourselves will be able to share in theirs: the preaching of the truth, which pitched camp so to speak here and there amongst the gentiles, will dwell anew in its own people; the prophet will have come back home.[666] In a situation restored to normal, the wild olive of the gentiles will once again be grafted upon the beautiful olive of Israel. The Christians who dispute with the Jews in such sometimes harsh terms do not all believe that "that time of mercy and of consolation" is soon approaching, as a Joachim of Flora does,[667] but they all call for it from their deepest wishes. Constantly recalling that the Lord has wept over the ruin of the "faithless city," following Saint Gregory the Great — for whom it was a favorite theme — they appeal to the prospect of Israel's spiritual reconstruction.[668] The Church is already crying to the Synagogue and does so unrelentingly: "Turn back, turn back, o Sunamite. . . . Turn back to the recognition of your Redeemer."[669] Exegetes and preachers comment on this cry, inviting the whole Christian people to share the desire of the Church:

> Turn back, turn back, o Sunamite! Turn back, turn back, that we may look at you. Sunam is called 'captivity'; hence the Sunamite is called a captive, and the Synagogue is understood as captive to the devil in faithlessness. The Sunamite is also said to be redeemed by the scarlet blood of Christ. Hence it is said four times by the preachers of the Gospel: Turn back! namely, from the four snares of the world; convert from the error of faithlessness to the faith of Christ, or turn back to

your Redeemer who is calling you ... so that we may look at you, i.e., that we may imitate you. Or: turn back through the four gospels, turn back through the four virtues, so that seeing your conversion we may praise the Lord. For once having been converted at the end of the world, the Jews' conversion will be such that the Church will marvel and will use her as an example.[670]

The Church knows well then that she cannot "without peril lose sight of the Pauline promise of the global reintegration of Israel": she hopes for "the end of the fundamental split that implicitly contained all the rest, and that the hardening of Israel has caused for the whole people of election."[671] But until that time, *perfidia* continues to bear its fruit. We know it. It is an inexorable dialectic! The gold is growing dark.[672] Light is changing into darkness.[673] The inner eye is being covered with night,[674] just as the earth was covered with darkness on the night of Good Friday:

For faithless,
Most dark with the sins of the Jew,
This present moment has held in contempt
The lights of the heavenly kingdom.[675]

The Sun, which is the Christ, has set over this ungrateful earth.[676] The people has, along with the kingdom,[677] lost all its privileges." "The wandering, exiled Jewish people groans on the earth":[678] this is nothing but the sign of a more intimate, more essential unhappiness there. Because this people has not been able to pass "from faith into faith" in due time, because it has rejected the key which had been offered it, the understanding of the Scriptures has eluded it. All its ambitions have been ruined at a stroke.[679] In maintaining its ancient pretensions, it now constitutes the figure of a usurper.[680] Israel, having become a "faithless faction,"[681] has by that very fact become "Egypt and Babylon."[682] The very sight of the signs that ought to have led to its conversion drive it deeper into its perversion.[683] The veil of "perfidia" covers its leprous face.[684] It has fallen into misery.[685] Now emptied of its own spiritual sense by that people, the land of the Scriptures has become brazen.[686] It is always a lion — but now a dead lion.[687] God is abandoning it: he has left, he has withdrawn.[688] "Has not God's mercy been taken away from the one whom he has allowed to apostasize?"[689] The "faithless Jews" are therefore the "Judaei abjecti," that is to say, not "abject," but "rejected,"[690] rejected by him whom they have rejected first.[691] For "just as faith promotes slaves to the rank of friends, so *perfidia* reduces those who were sons to the penal condition of slavery"[692] — that slavery into which they have fallen for having chased Freedom from their city.[693] Their cult of the carnal Law is no more than the devil's slavery.[694] This fall is deeper than the first perfection was high.[695] In front of the bread of the Scriptures, which their obstinacy renders them incapable of breaking, they consume themselves in famine.[696] Not having wanted "the wheel within the wheel," the Synagogue has at her disposal only one of the two millstones: she can therefore no longer mill any flour, and she keeps turning around endlessly in "the circle of her *perfidia*."[697] Having "turned her face away, she is no longer recognized by her Author."[698] Thus she has been swallowed up in "spiritual desolation."[699] Having become "profane"[700] and superstitious, she has "fallen into the condition of the gentiles";[701] she has passed "among the incredulous tribes,"[702] even though the gentiles themselves in ever increasing number, are coming to the faith — to what used to be *her faith*.[703] The roles have been reversed. "How injurious is faithlessness!"[704]

In Jesus Christ, who is its end, the ancient Law found its unity in advance. From age to age, everything in this Law was converging toward him. It is he who, from the "totality of the Scriptures," was already making "the unique Word [Parole] of God."[705] The Word [Verbe] made flesh is the new Esdras who decisively rescues the sacred Books at the dispersion of Babylon, where they ran the risk of being lost, and who renews them while gathering them together.[706] In him, the "many words" of the biblical writers become "one Word" for ever.[707] Without him, on the other hand, the bond is undone: once again the Word [Parole] of God is fragmented into "human words"; words that are multiple, not merely numerous, but essentially multiple, and without any possible unity, for, as Hugh of Saint Victor puts it, "many are the utterances of man, since the heart of man is not one."[708] The incredulous Jew, whose *perfidia* is a faith turned backwards, consequently has in hand nothing but a Law that breaks apart, a dust composed of memories and superstitious rites. The Christian, by way of contrast, grasps its unity in its principle. The Word made flesh is, for him, the *Verbum abbreviatum*. He comprehends the marvel sung by the Prophet: "God made a shortened Word upon the earth."

In the Bible, under the figures and enigmas that announced it, the Word, which in itself is one, which is none other than the Son of God, still showed itself "diverse and varied." It found itself there once again "dilated" and, as it were, distended.[709] For human beings, "the word of the sacred page" could no longer be anything but a token or down-payment of the divine clemency in regards to them,[710] because it still resounded in a hundred ways, each incomplete, through the heart and mouth of many saints. It was indeed "preached by way of declamation, or signified figuratively, or dreamed through the imagination"; sometimes in word, sometimes in deed, its appearance was always transitory and piecemeal.[711] "Clearly the words disposed by the prophets' pen are many."[712] We ought, while thinking of that ancient epoch, also say: "God has spoken once, and many things are heard."[713] That was the epoch of the Old Testament. But new times have come: "Those words were spoken to a Jew, and a Christian heard" them.[714] The words of the revelation uncover their unity by accepting their final sense in the Spirit. By that very fact, they receive their final permanence. Indeed, just as the eternally uttered Word [Parole] is unique, so now is its human hearing, for time and eternity are joined in the Word [Verbe] made flesh.

Here he is, then, this unique Word. Here he is among us, "coming forth from Zion,"[715] having taken flesh in the Virgin's womb: "God has united all the totality of Scripture, his every word, within the womb of the virgin."[716] "Behold the great Word open before us. Behold the Word unfolded before us, and we can read within it at sight."[717] All the contents of the Law and the Prophets are substantially summarized in this Word, and in him for the first time acquire their whole sense. For this is indeed that self-same Word, born of the Virgin today, that the Prophets had given birth to of old. That was under another form, but it was already under the action of the same Spirit.[718] The Word of God had been truly sent to them, just as it was to be truly sent to Mary, and God has no other word [parole] than his Word [Verbe],[719] his only Son: "God's utterance is the Word of God; the Word of God is his Son."[720] This is so much the same Word [Parole] in the two cases that the exchange between the one and the other even enjoys what theological language calls 'communication of idioms'.[721] Under the one form as well as under the other, it is in reality entirely one and the same mysterious being, that very divine food which deserved the name "manna," "a name expressing a question or rather wonder," a name which designated its singular efficacy at the same time as its unheard of novelty.[722] Here it is now, total, unique, visible in its unity. The shortened Word, the "concentrated" Word, not only in the first sense that that which in itself is immense and incomprehensible, that which is infinite in the bosom of the Father shuts itself up within the womb of the Virgin, reduces itself to the proportions of a little infant in the stable of Bethlehem — as Saint Bernard[723] and his sons used to retell it,[724] as Mr. Olier retold it in a hymn for the Office of the interior life of Mary,[725] and again just yesterday, Father Teilhard de Chardin[726] — but also, at the same time, in that sense that the diverse content of the Scriptures disseminated along the ages of Waiting comes entirely together so as to be *accomplished,* i.e., to be unified, to be completed, to be illuminated, and to be transcended in this abbreviated Word. *Semel locutus est Deus: God has spoken once:* God pronounces only one word [parole], not only in himself, in his unchanging eternity, in the immovable act by which he engenders his Word [Verbe], as Saint Augustine recalled, but also, just as Saint Ambrose already taught, in time, and among human beings, in the act by which he sent his Word to dwell in our earth. "God has spoken once, when he spoke in the Son": for it is he who gives all the words that he announced their sense, everything is understood in him, and only in him "and even those things that had not been heard before by those to whom he had spoken through the prophets have now been heard."[727]

A twice shortened Word, therefore, since at the moment of his incarnation "He has recapitulated in himself the long unfolding of human history, bringing us salvation condensed in him."[728] A twofold shortening, of a Word which is thus neither mutilated nor diminished. A twofold shortening, that of time and that of eternity, which join together to become just one, as time and eternity join indissolubly together in this shortened Word. A twofold recapitulation, that of the Word [Parole] eternally pronounced in the breast of the Father and that of the Word addressed to men in the sequence of the ages, the first being there to permit the second, and the second also to reveal the first, so that we can and should say, in two crisscrossed senses: "We have heard the shortened Word from the shortened Word."[729] Twofold shortening, twofold recapitulation, but always of one unique Word [Verbe], since God has only one Word in his breast and he proffers only one single Word [Parole], which is never other than this Word [Verbe], this very incarnate Word — so that, again, we can and should say, in two conjoined senses: *God has spoken once, since he has begotten one Word.*[730] A twofold marvel, which for us then is always becoming merely one, made manifest in the mystery of Christmas:

> O brothers, if we piously and diligently attend to this Word which the Lord has made today, he shows us how many things and how easily we can be taught by him! If the Word has indeed been shortened, nevertheless this is so that every word that is unto salvation may be summed up in it, since doubtless it is the Word that sums up and shortens in equity. And this "shortened summary has poured forth justice" (Isaiah 10:23). But what wonder is that, if God's Word has shortened all his words for us, when he willed that he himself be

shortened and somehow diminished, so that he might somehow contract himself from his own incomprehensible immensity to the narrowness of a womb, and, containing the world, suffer himself to be contained in a manger?[731]

Yes, a shortened Word, "very much shortened" — "brevissimum"[732] — but in the highest degree substantial. A shortened Word, but greater than what it shortens. It is a unity of plenitude. A concentration of light. The incarnation of the Word is the opening of the Book, whose exterior multiplicity henceforward allows one to perceive the unique "marrow," that marrow upon which the faithful have come to nourish themselves.[733] Behold: the Word [Parole] which by Mary's *Fiat* in reply to the announcement of the angel, till then only "audible to the ears," has become "visible to the eyes, palpable to the hands, able to be carried on the shoulders."[734] Still more: it has become "edible."[735] None of the ancient truths, none of the ancient precepts has perished, but everything has passed into a better state.[736] All the Scriptures are gathered together in Jesus' hands like the eucharistic bread,[737] and in bearing them it is himself whom he bears in his hands: "so that in substance we may fashion a mere mouthful from the whole Bible."[738] "At many times and under many forms," God had distributed to men, page by page, a written book, in which one unique Word [Parole] was hidden under many words; today He opens up that book for them, so as to show them all those words united in the single Word. "The Incarnate Son," "The Word Incarnate," "The Greatest Book": the parchment of the Book henceforward is his flesh; what has been written down is his divinity.[739] Thus the New Testament succeeds the Old, the Old is rediscovered in the New, the one and the other make just one, and in the same way that in God Unity dilates into Trinity, then Trinity gathers itself in Unity, so the New Testament dilates into the Old and the Old is condensed into the New.[740]

Here then at last the highest wish has been realized! Here, at last, unity in all its richness! Behold: the unique Sacrifice, and the unique Priest, and the unique Victim. The great passage has been accomplished, "the crossing over from many sacrifices to the one victim":[741]

Designated by the Patriarchs in a multitudinous order,
He is honored in the Law, and sung by the Prophets.[742]

Here then is the perfect holocaust! Behold the holocaust that God will never disdain, the one who remains always before his Face. In the eucharistic mystery, it is he whom we hold, completely and entirely. Odo of Cluny explains it in his *Occupatio,* a poem both grand and poor, which we cite only for the doctrine:

> Far off he makes the Word, as he promised, shortened;
> Once many various gifts have been cast away,
> He offers this one grain and wine to all.
> He consecrates this, which undoubtedly becomes short, which was
>   too tall.
> Now moderate to eat, and so easy to prepare,
> But so sublime, by which it may have the whole godhead.[743]

In this shortened Word, which covers all the earth, behold the remedy for all our wounds,[744] behold the perfect healing:

> This alone is enough to purge the world's fault.[745]

Behold the purity of the Gospel![746] "The evangelical discourse has been shortened and perfected."[747] Moses had spoken well of things, and yet his Law had not at all led to perfection: by just one word of Jesus the ultimate perfection has been taught.[748] "The Word, shortened and shortening, is a healthful summary!"[749] The whole essence of the revelation fits within the precept of love: in this single utterance is contained "the whole Law and the Prophets."[750] But if this Gospel announced by Jesus, this utterance pronounced by him, contains everything, this is because it is no other than Jesus himself. His work, his teaching, his revelation, his word, is himself! The perfection that he teaches is the perfection that he provides. Christ is the fullness of the Law.[751] It is impossible to separate his message from his person, and those who tried to do so had long before been forced to betray the message itself: person and message ultimately constitute just one thing. The shortened Word is the Word all rolled into one: the condensed, unified, perfect Word! The living and life-giving Word.[752] Contrary to the laws of human language, which becomes clear as it unfolds, this Word which was obscure, in appearing under its abridged form now becomes manifest: the Word at first pronounced "in hiddenness" is now "made manifest in the flesh."[753] The abridged Word, the Word always ineffable in itself, and yet explaining everything![754] The final Word, summarizing everything, finalizing everything, concluding everything, sublimating everything, unifying everything:

Jesus, shortened yet summarizing Word, bringing the Law and the Prophets to a conclusion with the two-part precept of charity. O summarizing Word, o Word shortening in equity! Word of charity, Word of complete perfection.[755]

This does not involve — as some might have believed or as some have said particularly about Saint Bernard — any "depreciation of the divine Word [Parole] in favor of the divine Word [Verbe]," a depreciation which would happily have remained "completely speculative, and, if one can say so, oratorical."[756] This is a profound teaching, contained in principle in the prologue of the Gospel of Saint John,[757] corroborated by a long series of witnesses and by the liturgy itself. By making visible in the ancient Scripture the manner in which "the unique divine Word [Parole] was already approaching us,"[758] by affirming (in perhaps paradoxical-sounding terms) its ontological bond with that Word in which God reveals himself, this teaching on the contrary magnified it and extended its actuality to the whole duration of Christian time,[759] all the while refusing to canonize the *littera sola* within it. Luther had well understood this, in the best period of his biblical reflections, when, in his first commentary on the Psalms,[760] and then in that on the Epistle to the Romans,[761] he took up that old theme of the "Verbum consummans et abbrevians."[762] Saint Augustine had said it well in his response to Faustus, and all those who say it with him are right: the Christian neither adds anything to Scripture nor takes a bit of it away. He extracts the substance of it. He abridges it, he condenses it, he unifies it without letting any of it be lost, he holds it all in Jesus Christ: *for he is book enough for all.*[763] He accepts from the chosen people all the books of the Old Testament; he venerates them, he does not cease to explore them and to meditate upon them, he marvels at the ways of God within them — but this is always to culminate in Christ. All that he discovers in them — and his discoveries are endless — he sees finally transfigured in Christ. Always, in some manner, whatever the knowledge that he uncovers and whatever the processes of his exegesis over the centuries, after many detours perhaps, he recognizes Christ in them. A ray has come to him from the inner light with which the soul of Jesus was illuminated when, in the days of his mortal life, he took the Bible in hand:

> Jesus discovers himself, he recognizes himself in reading the Old Testament. He sees himself as the end-point of that whole History "of which the Law and the Prophets prophesied right up to the present moment." In it he sees the anticipation of his coming. From all the

scattered features mentioned by the prophecies — the Messianic Prince of Peace, Isaiah's Emmanuel, Daniel's Son of Man, the Servant, the Judge, the Shepherd — he does not through some constructive labor perform an induction of what he ought to be, he just recognizes himself.... He allows the 'wrapping' to fall into the shadow.... From all these features he divinely makes the synthesis: not from without, but from within. He casts his inner light upon the prophecies: then they are united, they lose any trace of the circumstances where they had been proclaimed, they harmonize and are fulfilled.

In uncovering the Bible, Jesus recognized the reflection of the Light that shines in him; he hears a feeble echo of the Word [Parole] that rings within his human consciousness.[764]

Rejoining the theologians and linking up the old tradition with them, some modern exegetes recognize it as well: in all that the apostles and the evangelists relate to us about Jesus, one rediscovers "the ore of the Old Testament melted down and purified," and "that entirely Christological orientation has not for good or ill been imposed" on the Old Testament, "but it is interior to it and penetrates all its parts."[765] The two forms of the Word, abridged and dilated, are inseparable. The Book remains, therefore, but at the same time it passes over entirely into Jesus,[766] and the believer's meditation upon it consists precisely in contemplating this passage. Mani and Mohammed have written books. For his part, Jesus has written nothing — it is Moses and the other prophets who "have written about him." The relation of the Book to its Person is therefore the reverse of the relation that one observes elsewhere. The evangelical Law is thus not at all a "lex scripta," a "written law." Christianity is properly speaking not a "religion of the Book" at all:[767] it is the religion of the Word [la Parole], but not only or principally of the Word under its written form. It is the religion of the Word [du Verbe], "not of a mute, written word, but of an incarnate, living Word."[768] The Word [Parole] of God is now present among us "in such a way that one can see it and touch it."[769] It is a "living and efficacious"[770] Word, unique and personal, unifying and sublimating all the words that give witness to it.[771] Christianity is not "the biblical religion": it is the religion of Jesus Christ.[772]

CHAPTER THREE

A Lineage Stemming from Jerome?

1. Paschasius Radbertus

With Berno of Reichenau, it seems to us that a central link stemming from the lineage of "Jerome" has snapped. For one to be able to speak of a lineage, this man must be the indispensable intermediary between the Carolingian group, composed, according to some historians, of Paschasius Radbertus and Christian of Stavelot, and the better provided group which, with Bruno of Segni in the lead, included especially Rupert of Deutz, Hugh of Saint Victor, Adam Scotus, and finally Richard of Saint Victor. Will these other links in the chain prove to be more resistant? Will they allow us truly to establish this "more and more preponderant influence of Saint Jerome at the expense of that of Saint Augustine and above all of Saint Gregory,"[1] who, from the eighth century to the twelfth, had slowly prepared the launching pad for the true exegesis?

We fear that there may be a myth here, commingled with many accurate observations, a myth inspired by an evolutionist and finalistic, even a bit Manichean, conception rather than by the patient examination of the texts. One scholar takes his destination — by placing it in the thirteenth century — to be an exegesis entirely oriented "toward the clarification of the literal sense" and finally "stripped of the swaddling-clothes of allegorism";[2] from that allegorism which, some think, could only be a "solution of last resort,"[3] or, to put things in a better light, merely a provisional expedient during those unfavored times when nothing was known of the true science of the Scriptures. Such being the case, one imagines that this true science — which paradoxically had begun to dawn in Christian antiquity at the very time when allegorism was getting formed — could never be altogether lost. On the surface, it was always declining: "the compilers of the Carolingian period were less scientific than Bede, their 'master'. They worked in a more mechanical, less critical way";[4] after them, for at least two centuries, it got still worse. Nevertheless, throughout those dark ages, thanks to certain exceptional personalities swimming against the current of their period, the torch would be handed on. Hidden at first under the bushel, the light would at last flash forth, its beam would grow wider, and at last in broad daylight one would see established that "exegetical spirit stemming from Jerome" which would little by little free all minds from "the traditional allegorical method."[5] This victorious ascent, they sometimes add, would go hand-in-hand with the slow rediscovery of Aristotelian philosophy and especially of his dialectic, and these two movements, once joined together in applying "the light of reason" to the sacred text, would assure the triumph of a sound exegesis in the following century.[6]

We are not challenging the value judgments that such language exhibits. But we do believe that this very language denotes at the start certain a priori elements that cannot fail to distort observation. There are, to be sure, many signs of some influence from Saint Jerome among the authors cited, or at least of the esteem in which these authors held him; but neither this influence nor this esteem involves anything unusual. They can be seen in a number of other authors as well. Moreover, among the latter as well as among the former, Saint Jerome is allied with Saint Augustine, Saint Ambrose, or Saint Gregory without any violent opposition. The opposition amongst these great Doctors, as perceived by certain moderns, does not exist in the hospitable mind of the medievals themselves. Even when they deal with them specifically, the medievals generally bring them together to be admired and exploited as a common resource. But let us say it again: it is to blind oneself to see in Saint Jerome an adversary, albeit an unconscious one, of all use of allegory, when one can read in his commentaries "hundreds of texts [that] oppose the excellence of the spiritual sense to the paltriness of the letter";[7] and it is an exaggeration to attribute anything that looks like any care about textual criticism, precise translation, or literal investigation to his influence alone. But let us look a bit more closely at the principal writers involved in the case.

Paschasius Radbertus (†ca. 865) is surely one "of the most original commentators" of the Carolingian period. He is "one of the greatest exegetes of the high Middle Ages both with reference to his learning and to his personal judgment."[8] This point will easily be granted to Father Spicq. The merits of Paschasius are generally recognized. Though in his "poverty of spirit" he modestly affects contenting himself with copying the Fathers, we can say of his exegetical work in general what Dom Blanchard wrote in 1911 of his treatise *De benedictionibus Patriarcharum*, that it "contrasts strongly with the works of centonization of the high Middle Ages."[9] This amounts to noting that in every epoch there are minds of various quality. Paschasius Radbertus is surely one of the best minds of his age; but this is not enough to set him in opposition to his age. His great *Expositio in evangelium Matthaei* is doubtless the masterpiece of Carolingian exegesis. But that does not mean that it is a manifesto against the principles or inclinations of this exegesis.

In what way will Paschasius be specifically "Jeromian," in the restrictive sense that this epithet seems to be taken? His method and his spirit are completely traditional. At the beginning of the *Expositio*, he tells us with his usual modesty what he intends to do and his statement conceals no hidden agenda, for it is in fact just what he does: "by the labor of my pen to bring together the eloquent readings of the holy Fathers."[10] How can one anyone attribute "literalist" tendencies to someone who speaks of "sacraments" and "mysteries" on every page; who constantly proclaims that nothing is said or done "without good reason," i.e., "without its mystery";[11] who is looking for "the science of the heavenly sacraments"[12] in everything; who ceaselessly invites us to approach "the things mystical";[13] who puts forth this principle of interpretation: "Wherever understanding is called for in the sacred Scriptures, the divine mystery is not communicated by the carnal sense, but in the totality of the spiritual sense";[14] who declares that to remain at the "surface" of the history, at this "most contemptible husk" is to show oneself to be "excessively foolish and stupid and a negligent idiot," and who says regarding the spiritual realities hidden under the letter: "Whoever reads without these, even if he seems to understand something, is in fact accomplishing nothing, since he is not at all understanding or reading as he ought";[15] who, reading the Lord's recommendations in his apocalyptic discourse, interprets them in the following terms:

> We ought to flee from Judea to the mountains, from which help comes to us. That is, once the letter has been dismissed as well as the Jewish depravity, we ought to approach the eternal mountains, from which the Lord will in marvelous fashion shed light upon us, and it is necessary to stay under the shelter and in the dwelling of the heav-

enly understanding, where the fiery arrows of the devil cannot reach.[16]

Paschasius assures us that even taken somehow in their materiality, certain syllables and letters which precede each lamentation of the Prophet are significant: "nor is it to be believed that so many letters are devoid of a mystery."[17] He is interested in number mysticism.[18] Again, not only regarding the texts of the Old Testament but also regarding the Gospel itself, he tells us: "Although the Gospel is no longer a shadow but rather the truth, nevertheless no diacritics, no letters, no syllables, no word, no names, no person, in themselves are devoid of divine figurations, owing to the mystic discourses of their doctrines."[19] Moreover, these last words are an imitation of Saint Jerome;[20] but it is not this imitation that we are discussing. Again, Paschasius Radbertus wants us to see "with the eye of the spirit" and to comprehend "the things that have been accomplished by the Lord, since they are very mystical and to be admired," and when the redactor of the apocalyptic discourse opens a parenthesis to invite his reader to comprehend, this is, he thinks, because "he wants to exercise us and call us forth to the sacraments of the mystical understanding."[21] "Everything has been shown to Moses on the mountain, i.e., in Christ."[22] "All the pages of the Old Testament" manifest the divine and human works of Christ. The two Testaments are, as it were, his two lips, which keep back or deliver his mysteries.[23] The Gospel itself is full of deep meanings that one must search to discover by scrutinizing the tiniest details of the text. Thus, regarding the words "on the evening of the sabbath," Paschasius observes, using a sentence quite characteristic of Gregory: "an admirable kind of speech, in which both the truth of the history is preserved and, if I may say so, the ineffable sacrament is construed." And on the words that follow, "Mary Magdalene came along with the other Mary," he notes with subtlety:

> The Evangelist does not say 'came' [in the plural] but 'came' [in the singular], since they two are coming under one name, in mystery, not by chance, since there were two Churches about to come to Christ: two, since composed of two peoples, since the Church is one, and one the dove of his mother chosen of God.[24]

Such then is the constantly expressed, constantly implemented deep conviction of our exegete. A poet of the time was therefore not wrong to celebrate:

Paschasius Radbertus

The often mystical discourse. . . of Radbertus.[25]

Miss Smalley brings Paschasius Radbertus's exegetical method together with his eucharistic doctrine. The preliminary findings made on this subject are correct; but the conclusion drawn from them does not seem to me necessarily to follow. Paschasius does indeed teach that the eucharist is at the same time both truth and figure; for, he explains, a figure is not necessarily something illusory and fallacious: thus the figures that fill the Old Testament were quite real persons and facts that, in their very reality, pre-signified the realities of the New Testament. In the Bible there is a primary sense, the literal sense, prior to the allegorical sense in which one finds the fullness of the Christian teaching.[26] Here Paschasius goes back to the comparison of the letters of the alphabet; we first teach them to children before explaining what each is the sign of; they are something in themselves; thus it is necessary for us first to get to know the literal sense of the text, so that we may subsequently rise to the spiritual sense, in which truth exists as a whole.[27] In these considerations Miss Smalley wants to see an exceptional evaluation of the letter, whereby Paschasius would stand a cut above his age. When he explains, she tells us, that the sacrifices offered by the Patriarchs were figurative, he does not deny their reality, but rather gives the word "'figurative' a wide and historical meaning." This is quite true. Of this, "nemo qui sanctas litteras legit, ambigit" [No one who reads the holy letters has any doubt]. How then can she conclude from this that "Paschasius, as an exegete, was quite exceptional in his grasp of the letter"?[28]

Would not the Commentary on Lamentations, at least, be probative? It is an explication at once literal and mystical; before applying the prophecy to Christ, the Church, and the individual soul, Paschasius recognizes in it Jeremiah's own sufferings as well as the ruin of Jerusalem foretold or mourned over: "According to the history, Jeremiah is shown to deplore no less the fall and ruin of his own people than the straits of his own tribulation"; "it is clear that enough has happened to Jerusalem"; "no one has any doubt that these laments apply to the Jews,"[29] etc. Once again, is there anything out of the ordinary here? Ought we to suppose the men of the ninth century so stupid as to be completely unaware of the tragic fate of Jerusalem or to find no echo of it in the writings of Jeremiah? Could they not all have read, if need be, what Cassiodorus said about it?[30] Miss Smalley observes that none of Paschasius's contemporaries had said anything of the sort.[31] That might be the case quite simply because Paschasius had been the only one to comment specifically on the Lamentations. But in fact, it is enough to open Rabanus Maurus's *Expositio in Jeremiam* and to read this at the beginning of the eighteenth book:

> the last part of Jeremiah the prophet, which is called Lamentations, for as much as the Lord, by the grace of his Spirit whereby the prophet himself has spoken, wanted to enlighten us according to the history and according to the mystical sense.

And this is not at all a misleading reference. A little further on, Rabanus Maurus clarifies his point:

> The Book of Daily Events shows that these lamentations were written not only about the devastation of the city of Jerusalem and the captivity of the Jewish people, but also about the fall of King Josiah. . . . Hence, we have first disclosed the history by way of explanation; then we have inserted the allegory at appropriate places, whether with reference to Josiah . . . or to the Jews. It is even more opportune for us now to lament than it was for the prophet of God then.

In these last words, he is exaggerating. But in what generation would one not exaggerate in the same manner? Are not the evils that we suffer always the worst ones? Here we do not see an excess of allegorism, to say nothing of an exclusive preoccupation with it. In the whole sequel, with Rabanus as well as Paschasius, a historical sense is regularly furnished; only then will the standard formula come up: "mystice autem," "spiritualiter vero," "sed etiam haec mystica," "juxta allegoriam vero," "juxta mysticos vero intellectus," "altiori sensu," or "sed et nunc pari modo," etc. The two following books are conceived in the same fashion. Arriving finally at Jeremiah's prayer, Rabanus explains once again:

> There follows the prophet's prayer, which in the historical sense mourns the devastation of the city of Jerusalem and the fall of the Jewish people, and which in the spiritual sense tearfully recalls the ruin of faithful souls and the devastation that they have suffered from their spiritual iniquities.[32]

[Turning back now to Paschasius], not one word permits the understanding that he wants to apply novel or careless principles to get some unexpected exegesis; several of his formulations suggest the opposite understanding: "it is obvious," says he, or "no one has any doubt."[33] Like

Rabanus, he does for the Lamentations what others, such as Smaragdus or Alcuin, did for other prophetic texts in their own time. Thus it is that Alcuin, commenting upon the benedictions of the Patriarchs, asks himself "are they to be understood historically or allegorically?" and answers: they express "them both, both the history and the allegory"; it is just in this connection that he brings up the need first to lay down "the foundation of the history."[34] And is this not precisely how Rufinus had already proceeded? Soon Angelome of Luxeuil, regarded as *the* allegorist of the highest water, will proceed in the same way again, on the occasion of the Lord's promise to Rebecca:

> Is what the Lord answers Rebecca ["There are two tribes in your womb, etc."] to be understood historically or allegorically? In both ways. Now it is customarily understood spiritually. . . . But it is also found to have been accomplished in the historical manner.[35]

Paschasius expounds the three senses in a completely classical fashion. From the start, he points out the general outline that he will follow in his commentary. The Prophet announces the ruin of the holy city: historically, this ruin had taken place first under the Chaldeans, then, more completely, under Titus and Vespasian; it took place spiritually — and this is much more to be lamented — each time that the Church, "our Jerusalem," is, by reason of her faults, separated from Christ, her spouse, deprived of the aid of the angels, devastated by enemies from within and without; finally, in the tropological sense, he goes on in the same vein with respect to each of our souls.[36] The exposition is personal, often beautiful in its expression, but it does not deviate from the received norms.[37] Moreover, it seems that the work did not raise the least controversy, nor the least wonder. It enjoyed, M. Henri Peltier the historian of Paschasius tells us, an "extraordinary success."[38] This was due, in part, to its intrinsic worth, in part also perhaps to the situation. For from the preface on, Paschasius exhibits his intention to be timely: the Lamentations of Jeremiah, says he, "deplore the overthrow of that earthly Jerusalem and people in such a way that they do not omit to bewail the injuries of the present Church."[39] The terrible time of the "ruin caused by the pillaging of the Northmen" was already at hand.[40] "From the fierce tribe of Northmania deliver us, o Lord!" says an antiphon of the ninth century.[41] Perhaps these brutal men had already appeared outside Corbie, where Paschasius had returned a bit earlier.[42] Paris itself was living under their constant threat for years; the neighboring regions had more than once suffered from their raiding and pillaging; in 845 they had advanced as far as the capital's walls, had burned the suburbs, and withdrew only on payment of ransom, carrying off a part of the population into captivity.[43] The same occurred in 852. At the end of 856 there was a new incursion.[44] Paschasius alluded to these misfortunes while commenting on Saint Matthew's Gospel. So many desolations, said he, so many murders, helped him to understand the dire predictions of the apocalyptic discourse: "With groaning every day we are merely awaiting our end."[45] He returns to this point a bit later, in the commentary on Lamentations which is undoubtedly his last work.[46] In a page full of feeling, he applies the words of the Prophet to the present circumstances: "the kings of the earth and all the inhabitants of the world did not believe that a hostile enemy would enter the gates of Jerusalem." Everyone sized up the situation the same way he did. They were not only thunderstruck and apprehensive; horror at the present and dread of the future were accompanied by confusion. They could not understand how Paris, "our Paris," the center of such a glorious realm, so vast and so populated, provided with such strong fortifications, could have been subjected to such an outrage. And how could a people so base have been able even to dare to tread on such soil? Here it was no less necessary to keep the mind from succumbing to scandal than it was in days of yore at the misfortune of the Holy City: "Who would ever believe or who could ever have imagined?"[47] In these tragic circumstances, Paschasius made himself the voice of all.[48] No more than the Prophet of old did Paschasius attempt to recount the facts in detail; but, meditating on the ruins already heaped up and on those still threatening, he raises a song of lamentation: "if it is not what I may expound, it is nevertheless what I may bewail and lament."[49] He took it upon himself to express the shock and anguish of all. He did not lock himself up in some ivory tower.

He knew a bit of Greek. Perhaps, like a number of his contemporaries, he had a few rudiments of Hebrew, but it is doubtful whether he had received them directly from a Jewish instructor. He was capable of comparing the various versions of the Bible with each other.[50] Neither this nor a knowledge of some of the classics sets him apart from the best-read scholars of his day; it does not at all mean that he stands out as a distinct type of mind. Besides, most of his remarks concerning the "veritas hebraica" are borrowings, and he does not conceal that fact.[51] More than others, and despite his own advice not to trust in them, he exploits some of the apocrypha,[52] which is not an indication of an exceptionally critical mentality. He is, however, able to recognize the "difficulties of the issues" raised by the accounts of the Lord's [post-Resurrection] appearances; in this connection he even goes so far as to write: "This is clearly a great topic for calumniators, and we are tied in knots by inextricable questions," and does not pretend to say more than what appears "more probable" to him.[53] There is no indication here either of prejudice or marked bias in his manner of citing, to say nothing of criticizing, as occasion warrants, Jerome, Augustine, Hilary, or others.[54] Further, it is not in exegesis that he uses Saint Jerome most heavily: he depends upon him chiefly in his work on the perpetual virginity of the Blessed Virgin Mary. He often cites Origen, whom he knew in a rather free Latin version, as well as the Commentary on Saint Matthew, as we have said before; more often still, he is inspired by him without naming him, e.g., regarding the scene of the transfiguration.[55] Like Origen, he is rather hard on the "philosophers," those teachers of error.[56] Like him, he turns away from their wells of dead water to dig into the wells of Scripture.[57] He loves to repose in contemplation "among the deep silences of the heart, among the lovely recesses of the holy Scriptures."[58] In the classic question about the use of pagan authors, he lines up at the side of the most severe. Less liberal than a Rabanus Maurus, he does, however, give some evidence of moderation. He formulates a wise rule of criticism, when he entreats the reader not to be too quick to correct a text that he does not understand.[59] Finally, let us cite from him the following beautiful principle of spiritual hermeneutics, one at least sketched out by Origen,[60] and one that would subsequently be recalled by others.[61] Paschasius formulates it to apply to the prophecies of the Passion contained in the Book of Lamentations:

> But since . . . in that place there are many things found in a higher sense concerning the Passion of Christ, a higher sense is called for, though I believe they cannot be found without tears.[62]

2. Christian of Stavelot, Bruno of Segni

Christian of Stavelot and Bruno of Segni, as different as they are from one another, are going to suggest analogous reflections. It would be difficult to put either of them in a separate and scientifically privileged lineage.

Christian, originally from Aquitaine or Burgundy, a monk of the Abbey of Saint Remacle at Stavelot in the Ardennes (†880), is a person of lesser stature than Paschasius.[63] His case is scarcely more 'singular' than that of Paschasius.[64] He is nicknamed "grammaticus": this attribute, far from distinguishing him from his period, shows rather that he belongs to it. Like many educated men of that time, he readily refers to Priscian, "that source of the first medieval humanism." He cites the classics often enough (though most of his citations come from Isidore and from a grammarian of the sixth century); he even seems to have a smattering of Homer.[65] To his credit, let us also mention that he has no love for airy hypotheses or groundless debates, as is shown by the following reflection he made about the star of the Magi: "Various men have said many things about this star, but since they do not have a source in the truth, I have preferred to omit them."[66] Nor, however, does he, any more than any other author around him, ever seem to have suspected that grammar and allegory might make a bad mixture. He rightly thinks that it would be "unreasonable" to search out the spiritual understanding while being entirely ignorant of the history, since "history is the foundation of all understanding" and without it one cannot perfectly possess any of the other senses of Scripture.[67] These truths are always good to recall; ultimately, rather than paradoxical, they were then, as Father René Wasselynck was able to write, a "slogan."[68] In this connection, if Christian is a bit more insistent than others, in him this is a mark of a "judicious" mind, and maybe even of a certain influence stemming from a few exegetes of the Irish school.[69] If his commentary on Matthew's Gospel, which uses Jerome, Pseudo-Bede, and Rabanus Maurus, devotes a large place to the historical sense, it is because this work is an echo of what is, properly speaking, instruction, and not, like so many other biblical works, an anthology of sermons or a menu of exegeses to be used by preachers. When writing in the last [nineteenth] century that Christian showed in that way "to what point the route that he claimed to follow had been little traveled," J.-J. Ampère allowed himself to exaggerate in at least two ways.[70]

This reflection from a not particularly competent writer would not need to detain us, if it did not reflect a tradition that still finds favor even today. It is to be feared, however, that the honor credited to the monk of Stavelot may stem from a suspicious root. Toward the end of the eighteenth century, the Protestant rationalist J. G. Rosenmüller, in his history of Christian exegesis, had only praise for him; but he could not hide the reason for giving it: a passage from Christian's commentary on Matthew seemed to him to be contrary to papal dogma and, still more, another "maxime memorabilis" passage on the dogma of transubstantiation; the work had been censured by Rome and anti-Catholic polemicists loved to use it from the sixteenth century on.[71] So there we have it: Paschasius and Christian are each placed in one and the same exceptional lineage, the one because he professed the reality of the Eucharist and did not regard the figures as "falsities," the other because he seemed to refuse to recognize it by suppressing the truth of the figure![72] It is true that these two opposed reasons are not simultaneously given by the same interpreters. Like Rosenmüller, Charles Schmidt in 1885 praised the treatise of the "monk Druthmar" for the concern it has for the literal sense; but he took care not to associate him with Paschasius Radbertus, author of a work on the Eucharist where one finds "along side of passages that seem favorable to a symbolic explanation, the whole doctrine that ends up prevailing in Catholic theology." He associated him with Claude of Turin, at first blush an astonishing choice: but Schmidt shut his eyes to his allegorism, on account of the fact that he "preached against any cult rendered to sensible objects and had the images removed from the churches of his diocese."[73] A fine example of ingenuously one-sided history! A marvelous sign of the blinding power of prejudice twice over! For not only did Claude of Turin *not* (any more than anyone else of his epoch) have any grounds to be regarded as having cultivated "the literal rather than the spiritual sense"; there was, in fact, a quite striking correlation between his strong allegorism and his hostility to the cult's excessively sensible elements.

More attentive to detail than Charles Schmidt was to be, Rosenmüller added this into the bargain: "We are dispatching the mystical interpretations that Druthmar occasionally connected with the grammatical and historical ones."[74] He really wanted to pass the sponge over these aberrations, which plunged him back into the common herd. In fact we see our Christian, from the very first chapter of his commentary, embarking upon a long symbolic explication of the four gospels, then of the three kinds of philosophy in their relation to holy Scripture, and concluding with the following resolution, which leaves no doubt as to his participation in the common understanding: "Wherever therefore those understandings may have existed, let us call them to notice, as much as the Lord may grant."[75]

Christian is, it is true, spiritually short-winded. In his abbey, he is an honest school-master. His commentary is rather dry, and his thought is a bit matter-of-fact. Richard Simon will judge him to be "sometimes too literal."[76] This does not mean that he wanted to compose a "purely historical" commentary.[77] He values the allegories and anagogies, and has no intention of depriving his reader of them.[78] But he is scarcely able to make the most of them. "His breasts have been tied off," as Origen would put it;[79] he has not received the "donum abundantis intelligentiae," as Saint Gregory would say.[80] The fact that one speaks less spiritually, however, is not of itself a guarantee of greater science. It is not enough, as Peguy says, for there to be less nature for there to be more grace — or vice versa. The merit attributed to our exegete, then, is real, but for all that it does not live up to his pretensions. If we are to believe him, he is going to make up for the defects of his greatest predecessors. He criticizes Jerome and Bede for having forgotten to tell us whether the dove that represented the Holy Spirit at the baptism of Jesus was a real, flesh-and-blood dove or not.[81] Against Jerome he raises the complaint of having too quickly bypassed many words of the text that needed explication.[82] As for Augustine, he wanted too much to act like Saint John himself: such an eagle, he gets lost in the clouds.[83] Is it reasonable, when commenting on a text, to speak in such a manner that it is necessary to look for someone else to comment on the commentary? Fie on such "gibberish"![84] Christian promises to do better. The essential point of these remarks is understandable, coming from a good pedagogue. Christian is right not to want anything left unexplained for the "parvuli sensus" ["those who are little ones in the sense"]. But the tone is a bit surprising. How much more modestly is the Venerable Bede able to comport himself in a similar circumstance![85] How much more respectful of the great Augustine is the author of the *De luminaribus Ecclesiae*, a contemporary of Christian's![86]

"An unambitious little work, addressed to beginners," writes Miss Smalley of this commentary on Saint Matthew.[87] Yes and no. The author is indeed concerned about beginners. One can only praise his patience in inculcating in them totally elementary notions (such as the correct spelling of the word "evangelium" and how to read it). But he is nevertheless not without ambition, although his ambition is middlebrow. His good sense has something aggressive about it. Despite his solid qualities, Christian is one of those small minds who appear proud at besting the "cloudy" great minds; he does not turn up his nose at having a little laugh at their expense. But he himself, as Father Charles Trochon has written, "affects more erudition than he really has." He records, as others did as well,[88] a number of geographical facts: but they are not the fruit of personal study. He sometimes cites Greek authors: "since he was able to consult a monk named Euphemius who was able to read these authors in their own tongue," and "the etymologies that he complacently shows off demonstrate either that this monk was not very bright," or that he himself "did not profit much from his lessons."[89] Richard Simon did not fail to notice as much.[90] This is a rather weak recommendation for an author who sets out "to complete Saint Jerome." In any case, that is indeed still a characteristic of the epoch, and our middle-brow exegete gets rather lost in the gloom of his age from which he did not emerge. It was not necessary for him to know much Hebrew to say, as everyone did in the wake of Isidore of Seville: "In Hebrew for 'Christ' they say 'Messiah'," or "The Hebrew word 'ieron' means a fortification," etc.[91] If Christian's commentary has been only infrequently recopied, if it seems scarcely ever to have been used, the reason for this is doubtless less its scientific character than its banality. How much better, among others, is "the philological equipment" of a John Scotus! How much better too is his linguistic equipment![92] On the other hand, John Scotus was interested more in "the metaphysical content of Scripture" than in "allegories and moralities,"[93] and his fine independence of mind made him frankly state the divergences that exist between the interpretations of the Fathers and to claim for reason the right to judge as last resort: here at least is a condition of scientific seriousness. Nevertheless, doubtless because John Scotus is also a thinker whose method "is more theological than exegetical" and because he was imbued with Greek and Augustinian ideas, it does not seem that he should be judged altogether worthy of entering, alongside a Christian of Stavelot, into the thin anticipatory lineage whose next relay-runner was to be Berno of Reichenau.

Berno having already occupied our attention, we come to Saint Bruno of Segni (1045-1123).

Aside from the importance of the role he played in the history of the Church, Bruno of Segni has acquired the reputation, as Father de Ghellinck says, "of being the best exegete of the Middle Ages."[94] The eulogy is perhaps excessive, but one can at least admit, along with Dom Philibert Schmitz, "as for exegesis, he has no rival in Italy, from the fifth to the twelfth century."[95] In the preface to his *Expositio in Apocalypsim*, Bruno celebrates the merits of Saint Jerome, "by whose authority and prudence holy Church is strengthened no little bit."[96] But what does he especially admire in him? The citation that he makes of Jerome in the passage in question tells it all: "The Apocalypse of John has as many mysteries as it has words; I've said too little: indeed all praise is inadequate to the value of the scroll; many layers of understanding lie hidden in every single word." Both in the explanation of the Gospels and in that of the Old Testament, Bruno himself never ceases to allegorize.[97] Like everyone, he thinks that if Scripture is full of mysteries, one cannot enter into an understanding of them unless a key is given, namely, the mystery of the cross.[98]

Might not his *Expositio in Pentateuchum*, at least, constitute an exception? Would it not be "a continuous explication of the text according to the literal sense, at least for Genesis and Exodus? The fact, supposing it to be a fact, would be more telling if one did not have to admit at the same time that his commentary on the book of Job, for example, is "allegorical":[99] this commentary, the whole substance of which is drawn from the *Moralia*, outdoes even the allegorism of Saint Gregory, constantly choosing the allegorical passages in preference to the other ones. Hence it could not be, on Bruno's part, a question of excluding allegorism in principle. His explications of the Psalms and of the "Strong Woman" [of Proverbs 31] are allegorical as well. Allegorical, too, is his commentary on Isaiah, in which, moreover, one can read the following: "The lion devours straw at the point when the powerful of this age, who are abstaining from the spiritual understanding, will be sated on the surface itself and the history."[100] We could also say the same of his many homilies or of his *Sentences*, the first book of which, entitled *De figuris Ecclesiae*, begins with these words: "in the divine scrolls there are many, indeed almost countless, things that signify the Church as the bride of Christ."[101]

But in reality the commentary on the Pentateuch itself is inspired by exactly this hermeneutic. In a short preface, Bruno of Segni tells his reader that he will explain the text to follow in a "continuous exposition," i.e., tracking the text up to and including the account of the building of the ark by Noah, by reason of the peculiar difficulty of these first pages; then, he will go faster, not tying himself down to comment on everything, and, "once the histories have briefly been sketched," he will give "the allegories with enough summary"; once he gets to Jacob's blessings, which are again a chewy morsel, he will resume the "continua expositio" for them.[102] The execution is faithful to the plan. From the very first page of the commentary on Genesis, Bruno writes: "Once these things pertaining to the letter have been laid out, let us see what they also signify allegorically," and in all the rest of the work, for each book of the Pentateuch, the allegories follow each other without stop.[103] He will search out the "deep mysteries of the Scriptures" everywhere, with a zeal inspired by love.[104] In the allegorical exposition of the flood and the ark, it is worth noting, no detail is neglected. We are told that "in his literal commentary on Genesis and on Exodus" Bruno closely follows "Saint Jerome, Saint Augustine, Saint Ambrose."[105] Indeed, the very page we are referred to, in fact the one that contains these three names, is quite entirely allegorical. It even lays claim to the traditional principle of Christian allegory against "the heretics and the philosophers." This is an explication, classic since Origen, of the wells dug in the desert by the servants of Abraham and blocked up by the Philistines; the three Fathers of the Church, at the end of the development, are cited together as a model for having been able to offer "not a carnal, but a spiritual understanding" of Scripture; and so they are to rank among the true servants of Abraham: "For as many wells as Jerome has dug, as many as Augustine, as many as Ambrose, the place in which those men dwell, namely the Church, may deservedly be called Beersheba, i.e., 'the well of abundance'."[106]

There are two passages of this same commentary on Genesis, however, that might at first glance offer some difficulty. The first of these may mislead a reader who is in too much of a hurry. When he arrives at the construction of Noah's ark, Bruno recapitulates the remark made in his preface. Now, says he, he will go more quickly, without tying himself down to explain everything:

> It is not necessary, however, to explain all the other things that follow. So let us lay out the allegories, explaining with a short summary only where it would be needed.

In other words, the commentator will limit himself to the essentials, whether that be for history or allegory. Moreover, it is sufficient to read the sentences immediately following to notice that an allegorical explanation is in fact added to each point of "history" quoted.[107] As for the second passage, which figures in the commentary on the book of Numbers, it might fool the reader who does not pay sufficient attention to the ambiguity, albeit so frequently denounced, of the ancient terminology. At issue are the twelve princes who offered the Lord six chariots and twelve oxen to carry the tabernacle and all its accessories:

> These were quite necessary, to be sure, and the Levites were hardly able to carry the burdens of his tabernacle and all the additional baggage. Concerning these things ["*in his*"] it does not seem necessary to search for an allegory. Allegory is necessarily to be sought for where the letter designates either something useless or utterly devoid of reason.[108]

On the one hand, we see the little sentence beginning with the words "in his" ["concerning these"] applies only to the episode recounted here in chapter 7 of the Book of Numbers, and not to the whole of the book; but on the other hand, the sentence that follows explains the sort of allegory at stake: it is the classical allegory, what we today refer to more generally using the expression "sens figuré." Here there is no point, says Bruno, in taking this passage figuratively, since it lacks neither coherence nor utility in its own right; consequently there is not the least doubt that it is historical. But does this fact mean, in his thought, that this history itself does not involve any allegorical sense? Surely not, since he immediately expounds this allegorical sense, and does so even with a certain fullness: "Every believer can be called a tabernacle.... As to the altar, it is dedicated when the man is converted to the faith and is consecrated to God by baptism." The vessels offered are rightly said to be of gold and silver, for they signify the book of the Law, which, full of the oil of the Holy Spirit and once grasped by the spiritual understanding, is all aglow from the light of wisdom and knowledge. The sacrificed animals prefigure the Passion of Christ, each one of which signifies more precisely a certain character, etc.[109]

Moreover, Bruno of Segni is perfectly aware of the Christian principle of his allegorism. He knows well that the text of the Old Testament, if *per impossibile* one could abstract it from the Event that has changed everything, would not require these secondary interpretations that the Christian tradition, founded upon that Event, confidently gives of it. The spiritual understanding of Scripture is a new understanding, "a new and spiritual understanding," and this newness is justified only by the One who can truly say:

> I am the end of the Law. The letter of the Law has been fulfilled in me. "Behold I make all things new." The things that till now were understood in terms of the letter are being understood spiritually.[110]

So there is nothing in Bruno of Segni to announce the coming of a more literalist exegesis. Full of zeal for the Gregorian reform and closely involved with the struggles of his time, he nonetheless remained a "man of the cloister"; "he loves the intellectual culture of the cloister and quite naturally moves within the ideas and the form of monastic literature"; he "envelops his teaching in the allegorical forms received, admitted, and included by everyone in the epoch when he was writing";[111] to this effect, he exploits the writings of Bede and Aimon, who transmitted to him the heritage of the Fathers. The author of the *De vita sancti Brunonis commentarius* tells us that he had appointed Saint Ambrose as his principal model:[112] this is not the mark of a tendency to literalism. The same author praises in him "a profound understanding of the divine Scriptures, a great knowledge of Hebrew and Greek and a treasurehouse of universal learning"; he recounts that in his youth Bruno learned "dialectic, ethics, history, chronology, the art of oratory, and poetry," and that in addition he was "expert in natural history" and that he had taken jurisprudence as mistress;[113] he recalls his memorable dispute in 1079 at Rome with Berengar, a "man full of trickery and sophisms, very practiced in the school of the Peripatetics."[114] In short, Saint Bruno had acquired all the knowledge that he was able to acquire. He was on good terms with Saint Anselm and showed he was a capable dialectician not only against Berengar, but also, it appears, against Roscelin, as is seen in some of his discourses.[115] This surely does not prevent him from "mistrusting dialectic,"[116] nor from being opposed, like many others before him, to what he calls "the stupid wisdom of the heretics and philosophers,"[117] or "heretical and philosophical depravity." He sees this doltishness and perversion of mind prefigured in the book of Genesis by the daughters of men seducing "the sons of God."[118] He compares those who "turn to dialectical questions" to a scorpion that strikes its victim with its tail.[119] All this establishes him as an eminent representative of his epoch, not a discordant exception. We cannot see how this would permit classing him among the rare medieval exegetes who would have professed an extraordinary and ill-appreciated esteem for the letter to the detriment of the allegory, and who would at least have begun to explain the sacred Books "by means of Aristotelian philosophy."

3. Rupert of Deutz

Closely following Saint Bruno of Segni, Rupert, the abbot of Deutz near Cologne from 1120, dying in 1135, stands like a giant at the threshold of the twelfth century. He is very well read and, for that age, extremely scholarly. His secular learning, obtained from his teacher Heribrand of Saint Laurent at Liège, is extensive in its own right.[120] Under his governance, the Abbey of Deutz enjoyed an exceptional brilliance.[121] But did he play a special part in paving the way for a new, more scientific, more sober and less allegorizing exegesis? That is the question to be examined.

He too praises Saint Jerome. There is nothing unique in that, however, and he praises Saint Augustine[122] and Saint Gregory no less. His praise of Jerome is at times somewhat more detailed than many of those written before him: he is grateful to the great Hebrew scholar for having successfully executed an enormous labor, from which henceforth everyone can only profit; thanks to his excellent translations, it is no longer necessary to go toilsomely oneself to look for water at the fountain of the Hebrews![123] Rather than being an encouragement to critical thought, if we commented on this passage a bit heavy-handedly, would we not say that Rupert has drawn from Jerome's work a pretext for laziness? In fact, like many another, he is quite able to go back to the "hebraica veritas," to point out the error of a translator or copyist, to note that the Septuagint has added a few words here or there to the original text, etc.[124] It would nevertheless be a bit paradoxical to find a "Jeromian" rather than an Augustinian in the man whose great work on the *Victory of the Word of God* was for the Middle Ages, as Father Spicq[125] and Dom Paul Séjourné[126] before him have said, what Saint Augustine's *City of God* had been in its own time and what one day Bossuet's *Discourse on Universal History* would be.

It has been written that with him "the quest of the literal sense is predominant."[127] Up to a point, this is true of one of his works, the one just mentioned: Rupert conceives it as an epic rather than as a symbolic poem.[128] But overall, his biographer A. Cauchie was not wrong to say that he inaugurated in the twelfth century "the mystical and allegorical trend in exegesis," provided that the word "inaugurate" simply indicates that Rupert was writing at the beginning of his century. It is to this trend that Cauchie attributes his "literary fortune."[129] Father E. de Moreau observes as well that "his allegorical system pervades his whole work."[130] The same goes for Father de Ghellinck: Rupert's exegesis, he says, is "overwhelmed by allegorism"; his liturgical writing is, "like his exegesis, allegorizing"; in short, his whole work "is stuffed with allegorism."[131]

As early as 1872 Hauréau was writing that in his commentaries "nothing is judged critically, everything is mystical; there is not a sentence of Scripture that does not provoke him to look for an allegory." To be sure, we would not conclude from this that Rupert has "a hatred for science."[132] Hauréau saw only a part of the truth; and he saw it badly. Rupert does not disdain the letter any more than the vast majority of his emulators do. He does not deny it any more than all the rest do. "Even in his excesses of allegory," as Dom Séjourné used to say, "he has not lost all habits of historical observation and textual analysis."[133] More than most and one of the first among them to do so, he loves the grand vistas of the theology of history or of theological history, and with him this tendency is easily allied with that of allegory: it is even predominant. From the fact that he observes that in the face of God's love for us, in the face of his depth, of his immensity, of his constancy, our carnal loves from which we draw our analogies to think about him are merely shadows and transitory images, one is hardly justified to conclude that he explicitly professed the functional unreality of the temporal and that his allegory can therefore have nothing in common with recognizing the spiritual dimensions of history.[134] In fact, Rupert is inspired at once by the Apocalypse, the Book of Daniel, and the Canticle of Canticles to imagine the unfolding of the centuries as a gigantic struggle between Satan, the ancient serpent, the dragon with seven heads, and the Holy Spirit: this is the struggle between *aquilo* the north wind and *auster* the south wind, the former breathing desolation and rendering the whole earth an arid desert, the latter transforming this desert into a marvelous garden through its halcyon breath.[135]

Again, as much as anyone else, he often traverses what he calls "the plain, familiar surface of the history."[136] He runs past the letter *cursim* so as to explore *diligenter* the mysteries that he knows are hidden within,[137] those mysteries which are "worthy of a delightful song."[138] The "silver feathers" of the dove are not enough for him; he wants to contemplate "the golden glints" that they conceal, to penetrate right to "the innermost beauty of the allegory."[139] For it belongs to those who "perceive the fullness of the Scriptures with sweetness and desire, and the treasures of subtle thoughts hidden in the depth of the letters."[140] Hence he is constantly inviting us to understand the sacred text "anagogically," "according to a higher sense."[141] He celebrates, sometimes even in lyric tones, the "spirit of understanding," whose activity opens us up to understanding the Scriptures so as to discover within them "the mystery of God's plan."[142] To him the "Judaic sense" appears "too dry and scanty."[143] Everywhere he is looking for "whatever mystery lies hidden within the deeds that have been done."[144] He rejoices at seeing "the dead letter" cast out by "the life-giving Spirit."[145] All sorts of textual peculiarities would seem superfluous or even ridiculous to him, and, like Origen, he thinks that the Holy Spirit would not have taken the trouble to call them to our attention if they did not support some mystery;[146] in addition, so that the letter itself might appear "more worthy," it was necessary to uncover "the mystic reasons" for it.[147] This is why he himself wants to peel away the "cortex litterae" so as to attain the meaty "medulla,"[148] to crush the shell of the letter so as to pull from it the grain of spiritual sense.[149]

In a word, throughout his work on the Spirit, Rupert is looking for the spirit [beneath the letter].[150] Not only does he experience the most lively joy in it, but he believes that in many cases it is the only way to save the letter itself.[151] "And in the history you may have an understanding of the spirit, and in the tropology the truth of the history": each of the two senses is necessary for the other, and if one of the two is missing, "one lacks perfect knowledge."[152] Moreover, this quest for the spirit is the essential task for the exegete, because only in this way can one treat Scripture "conformably to the custom of the Church"[153] and induce it to bear witness everywhere to the Christ.[154] Of the Jews who scrutinize the Law Rupert says: "How will those who are seeking God's Word find it while amazingly devoid of the Word of God, which is Christ?"[155] For him the "eyes of the knowledge of Scriptures" are the eyes of the spiritual understanding;[156] it is the resurrected Lord, says he, who opens them up for us, following the word of the Psalm: "The light of thy countenance has been marked upon us, o Lord."[157] There is no place in the "legal and prophetic" Scripture where he does not discern through these "eyes of faith" the presence of Christ, "like that of a fish in the water."[158] He especially delights in the vision of Ezekiel, where the wheel appears "within the wheel,"[159] as well as in the scene from the Apocalypse where the Lamb is breaking the seals of the Book.[160] He applies himself to "contemplate the mysteries of the eternal kingdom"[161] within the temporal matters that the Bible relates to him. One detects in him a tone of joy each time he can say: "Now let us pursue the allegorical sense."[162] In these and many other respects he resembles Saint Gregory, and it is not surprising that he for his part celebrates with a sort of tenderness the "sweetness of the grace that was so abundantly bestowed on him."[163] These features also bring him close to Origen, from whom he reproduces many an interpretation and whose hermeneutic — with its evident faults as well as the depths of its principles — is his own.

His personal symbolism is particularly rich. He does not disdain the most extremely detailed forms of it, forms that we would regard as highly arbitrary. Thus it is that on coming to comment on the Lamentations — which he understands in the manner of Paschasius Radbertus,[164] but also somewhat in the manner of Hugh of Saint Victor[165] or of an exegete as conservative as Gerhoh of Reichersberg[166] — he wants the exegete to stand before the letters that precede each strophe "just like a child before his alphabet," persuaded, as Saint Jerome had been,[167] "that these letters contain a science hidden to the wise and the prudent, so well hidden that the first elements escape them."[168] That the Psalmist is recounting the life of the Word Incarnate up to his resurrection and his exaltation, that he is chanting all the mysteries of Christ and the Church through past or present events, seems to him as to everyone "clearer than light itself."[169] Of many a personage of the Old Testament, Isaac for example, he says: "he accomplishes a mystery of the likeness of the Son of God."[170] The Books of Kings suggest to him this exhortation: "Let us contemplate the image of the kingdom of Christ the Son of God depicted in mystic figures."[171] It is in this same spirit that he contemplates Daniel, whose "admirable history" is so simple in its letter: "In that herald of Christ the Lord and King too we are looking upon his glory."[172] Of the "three books of Solomon" he candidly writes: "Who would not know to look into the mystery of the grace or glory of Christ?"[173] Even in the disappointed remarks of the man of the assembly, the Ecclesiastes — whom he does not hesitate to identify with Solomon[174] — he discovers a manifold mystical sense. This sense seems to him so sweet, and he is in such a hurry to taste its savor, that he expounds it even before having set out the "history." *The sun is rising and setting and returning to its place:* this sun, the Ecclesiast, will therefore be first of all a human being, in his natural life, and then in his life of faith; subsequently and above all this sun will be Jesus Christ, the Sun of Justice, the true Sun,[175] the Star that lights the Church until the day when he will have conferred upon her all his own brightness.[176] Indeed it is from Jesus Christ that all light flows, as well as all life-giving water; the light and the water which constitute the true understanding of the Scriptures.[177] The sea which engulfs the enemies of Israel is the sacrament of the blood and water, which, flowing from the side of the Savior, would engulf our sins.[178] All the victories of the chosen people, all the brilliant deeds recorded in the Bible, prefigure the spiritual victories of the Savior.[179] Everywhere in the beautiful heavens of the Scriptures the stars are sparkling, but they all look at Jesus Christ, they all go back to Jesus Christ, the unique source of their brightness.[180] The "brilliant face" of Moses is the "knowledge of the mysteries of Christ the Son of God."[181] Again, Jesus Christ is "the glorious harp, the sweet-sounding harp, in which the music of the Father has been introduced."[182] He is the candelabra whose light makes clear all the pages of the sacred books.[183] He is the man contemplated by Ezekiel, who stands holding the key of David on the threshold of the Temple of the two Testaments, as architect and surveyor of his building.[184] He is the true David, true king of the true Jerusalem, just as his adversary the devil is the true Nebuchadnezzar, king of this Babylon which is the world. He [Jesus] is also the true Joseph, the only one capable of interpreting the Father's plan, hidden under the veil of the letter as in a symbolic dream.[185] It is from him that every spiritual explanation proceeds,[186] and it is in him that all truth is brought to perfection,[187] just as it is for him that every being has been created.[188] His coming marks the pinnacle of history.[189] He is the "Holy of Holies," the "New Man," the starting-point of all renewal.[190] His whole earthly life is the portico through which one enters within the Temple of the Scripture, into the Temple of Divinity.[191] It is because he wanted "to follow Jesus Christ" that Rupert has devoted himself to the study of the

Scriptures.[192] Also, immediately on starting each book, Rupert is in search of the mystery it contains:

> Transeamus ad librum Judicum, et planam tritamque historiae superficiem transilientes, in his dumtaxat venerandum quaeramus mysterium, ubi pro re vel tempore se erexit Domini Verbum, ubi ad ejus [sic] dicitur vel agitur quid caeleste imperium.

> Let us cross over to the book of Judges and, skipping across the plain and well-trodden surface of the history, let us search for the venerable mystery as far as it is in these matters, the Word of the Lord.[193]

Thus, completely occupied with scrutinizing the Scriptures and, like the Fathers, commending himself to the example and authority of Saint Paul,[194] Rupert does not cease to look for, to contemplate, to celebrate Jesus Christ. In everything, he wants to belong to the "school of Christ."[195] He is trying to show the Jews that the "Scripture of the Law and the Prophets" that they have in their hands is nothing but "the tunic of the Christ."[196] He will not be satisfied that they ultimately recognize in it the One who is "alpha and omega."[197] For him "the two Testaments are two living beings, which respire, which breathe life, and between which stands the Lord."[198] The essence of Rupert's program of exegesis is summed up in the following words, at once completely Pauline and completely Origenian: "to find the sense of Christ in the Scriptures";[199] or again, "to seek the faith of Christ and the glory of his kingdom";[200] to conduct everyone "to the gospel Church, in which Christ is to be found."[201] As to the application of the program, it did not always lack convincing force, at least according to the testimony (perhaps to be taken with a grain of salt) of Hermann the Jew, who at first reproached the Christians for putting into the Scripture a bunch of things that are not there, and who admitted that he was finally overcome by Rupert's exegesis:

> Sicque Robertus omnibus objectionibus meis tam pulcherrimis rationibus, quam validis Scripturarum auctoritatibus, eas velut quamdam tetrae noctis caliginem clarissimis responsionum suarum radiis propellebat.

> And in this way, against all of my objections, Rupert, both with beautiful arguments and with powerful proofs of the Scriptures, kept dis-

persing them like a cloud of dark night by the brilliant rays of his responses.[202]

One ought, therefore, to give up trying to turn Rupert into one of the founders or precursors of literalism. But considering his work from another angle, ought one not at least to see in him, in his very exegesis, the precursor of a sort of new theology? He has been called "the founder of biblical theology."[203] It is a beautiful title and one that sets Rupert closer to Augustine than to Jerome; the latter, in fact, has never been regarded as the most theological of the Fathers. The idea rests upon a sound perception of the doctrinal character of Rupert's exegesis, which is at the same time augmented by its breadth. It does seem to me, however, that for quite a long time already — for about eleven centuries, since the letters of Saint Paul — biblical theology, no doubt called in the course of time to be clothed in many diverse forms, had no need of being founded. Further, Rupert has no need of such a title to enhance his own greatness. More sober is the eulogy which Gerhoh of Reichersberg, one of his students, made of him the day after his death, after having battled with him over some points but also having used him a good deal, and even having frequently copied him: "Rupert, abbot of Deutz, a man of blessed memory, most illustrious amongst those who treat holy Scriptures."[204] We may also bear in mind the eulogy that Renier of Liège made of him a bit later: "God's Wisdom opened the sense to him, so that he might understand the Scriptures."[205] Or consider what is expressed in one of his own sentences: "Having taken delight only in the sweetness of the divine Word."[206]

It has also been observed that in both his general bearing and in the detail of the solutions that he brings forward he exhibits a certain independence with regard to the ancient Fathers. The point is well taken,[207] and it earned him many disappointments. He had been reproached — as he tells us himself — for not placing the writings of blessed Augustine or those of other Fathers, "in the canon."[208] More than someone like Hugh of Saint Victor, for example, he in fact tended to set completely apart, like the unique living waters descended from Lebanon, "all the holy Scriptures that alone are called and are canonical."[209] Here again, we want only to respond to a certain excess in the interpretation of the fact. This attitude of Rupert's is marked off with original shading. It does not, however, bring him closer to Saint Jerome than to the other Fathers; nor does it move him further off from them all; it does not give him a true resemblance with the scholars of modernity. The reason for this is not that he approved less of patristic method or that he would have wanted to undertake reforming its foundations.[210] It is rather that he has so profoundly assimilated it that he proceeds with ease as though still being one of the ancients. Instead of slavishly copying their interpretations he freely participates in their spirit. He has the profound feeling that God has opened up for him, as he had for them, his own Book, and that in consequence it falls to him sometimes to read it better than they did.[211] It is delightful to him to find personal interpretations.[212] His great principle for the explication of the Scripture by means of the Scripture,[213] a principle which he is, however, not the only one to recall,[214] he owes to the Fathers. Naturally one finds in him an echo of the debates of his own time — doctrinal debates and ecclesiastical debates — an echo still more lively since he himself was of a combative disposition; one also finds in him many a precisely dated indication of some state of theology and discipline: by what absurd miracle would he be an exception to the universal rule? Still, he does show himself to be open to every sort of research, for he knows that the human arts are gifts from God, talents which he must love in order to make them bear fruit: in this he is a brother of a Rabanus Maurus as well as of a Hugh of Saint Victor.[215] He understands the exigencies involved in controversy with the infidel who does not recognize the authority of the Scriptures, and a page of this nature from his work, under the garment of its symbolic system, recalls Saint Anselm at the same time as it anticipates the *Summa contra Gentiles*.[216] With Saint Augustine and all those who are more or less happily inspired by him, he thinks that there is always something to search for beyond what he has found; in digging wells long ago the Patriarchs have given us an example that we should in our turn dig our wells in the same vast and inexhaustible field, so as to reach the same underground layer.[217] When stupidity or envy murmurs, "That fellow is writing what is unnecessary: the writings of the saints are enough, indeed more than enough," he is right to turn a deaf ear and go on his way.[218] To be sure, in terms of the details of his spiritual life, notably his emotional sensitivity and his visions[219] — though he puts them under the patronage of Saint Jerome[220] — he is more medieval than ancient. But this does not keep him from reviving the age of the Fathers more than all the makers of florilegia, the excerpters, the authors of *catenae* and collectors of "sentences" from previous centuries; more, too, than a goodly number of his contemporaries of less eminent reputation, some of whom seem always to dread the reproach of even verbal novelty.[221]

What is more, his freedom is not all that exceptional. It scarcely stands out over what, say, a Saint Peter Damian[222] would claim, or a Guibert of Nogent.[223] It scarcely exceeds that which authors with the humblest pretensions indulged in around the same epoch. Gerhoh of Reichersberg was one of that sort, who resembled him in ardor as well as in lavishness, and who burned with the same zeal for the glory of the incarnate Word;[224] he and his brother Arno found themselves at the side of Rupert in theology, though they were on opposite sides in the combat which at that time opposed monks of the Benedictine tradition and canons regular; despite the affectation of a few formulas,[225] they too did not disdain to dig a few new wells themselves.[226] For Gerhoh, to walk in the footsteps of the Fathers was not always to repeat them: it was merely not to advance anything injurious to their faith.[227] As for Arno, he based himself upon the great diversity of opinions to be found among the Fathers, choosing quite independently the opinion that appeared the best to him, "provided that respect for the Fathers be maintained."[228] William of Saint Thierry knew still better how to make an original work, all the while proclaiming: "walking in the footsteps of the Fathers, presuming nothing of ourselves."[229] And it is with declarations humbler still that Alan of Lille would soon undertake a work which would contribute to change the orientation of theology.[230]

The freedom that Rupert accords himself does not differ much from the freedom that most of the commentators accorded themselves: even a "compiler" like Rabanus Maurus, who knew how to put forward on occasion his personal contribution;[231] even a writer as violently traditionalist as Alvarus of Cordoba, who did not fail to rely on the "catholic doctrine" authorizing the multiple senses to set aside some of the interpretations of Saint Gregory when he wanted to.[232] If at one time or another Rupert disputes an opinion of Saint Augustine, this is not anything unheard of; while employing all manner of disclaimers, Aelred of Rievaulx will likewise dispute an opinion of Saint Gregory, whose authority was no less.[233] Rupert's freedom, then, is not the sign of an emancipation as regards an ancient mode of thinking: it is simply the liberty of a great mind. It is a free but deep reflection upon the most central themes of the most traditional thought. We see it, for example, in his exegesis of the Canticle of Canticles: he has given us the first of the "Marian" commentaries, as they are customarily called; one might say more precisely: the first coherent commentary which celebrates the marriage of Christ and the Church in their principle, in the mystery of the incarnation of the Word. Neither a rhapsode nor an innovator, in it he sings this "latest song," this "love-song," "whereby God descends into the blessed Virgin, so that from her he might beget the Son who is Christ Jesus, true man and God, blessed above all things."[234]

Ultimately this liberty never broke free of certain limits. For Rupert as for everyone, the first and immutable rule of hermeneutics is the rule of faith: "We have spoken following the opinion of the holy Fathers and the rule of the Catholic faith." After the invocation of the Holy Spirit, he says again, with vigilant eye and heart one must be guided by the holy Doctors, "who like the shining stars of never-setting Arcturus have stood ever fixed with stable faith, and pouring forth the light of faith they have not known the sundown of error."[235] He calls forth the "authority of our forefathers" — all the while rightly considering it not as imposing a boundary-stone, but as opening a path for the understanding.[236] In practice, he sometimes makes extensive use of the ancients, quite like a Rabanus Maurus or a Bruno of Segni: thus, by his own admission, he follows Saint Gregory[237] to comment on the Book of Job, and quite often one feels that he is completely suffused with the *Moralia*, even in his style.[238] Reminiscences of Origen are particularly frequent in him, and we have seen in a preceding chapter how it is to be accounted for. The Origenian themes are perfectly assimilated. This is perhaps one of the factors leading some to divine in his work — as in that of an Isaac of Stella or a William of Saint Thierry — beyond his Augustinism, "a whole archaic and oriental background whose content is hard to specify."[239] In this respect, he is comparable to his contemporary Saint Bernard. But he is less modern than Saint Bernard. In this age where so many things are changing, the Abbot of Saint Héribert of Deutz looks to me, in his finest enthusiasms and in some of his insufficiently knowledgeable reactions, like an eminently traditional author: not a traditionalist, not somebody caught up in the past; not a man anxious merely to preserve; but we should almost say, if it were possible to get rid of the artificiality of the word, an archaizer.[240]

Rupert did not in fact blaze new trails for the understanding, like Saint Anselm or Peter Abelard; nor, like Saint Bernard, for spirituality. He was not touched, like William of Saint Thierry, by the grace of Cîteaux, which at that time was rejuvenating the world. He did not anticipate the techniques of thought, as the deep and misunderstood dialectician Gilbert de la Porrée did.[241] He did not achieve, as did Hugh of Saint Victor, the balance of an original synthesis, a bit artificial and thereby fragile, but rich and measured. He even protested, without sufficient discernment, against irresistible forces whose nature he ill understood. In the theological firmament of that marvelous epoch[242] he nonetheless shone as the seventh "precious stone," seventh golden candelabra,[243] or seventh star of the Pleiades,[244] scarcely more distant from our eyes.[245] Among those great testimonies of the Spirit, he deserves to remain associated in our memory with those "spiritual men who are the luminaries of the world."[246] One understands that in the seventeenth century the Benedictines had considered him a doctor of the Church.[247] His genius was a blend of strength and dash: "the sails of faith are to be unfurled into the deep."[248] In terms of his most personal gifts, he is "the most perfect witness of the traditional monastic theology."[249] Above all, he is permeated with "the fullness" and "the majesty of the Scriptures,"[250] of that "veritable Land of Promise, where we begin to see God,"[251] and the idea that he conceived of the work of the exegete is great. It is the ascent of Mount Sinai.[252] It is, so to speak, the chaste conquest of a modest virgin, whose consent one receives little by little with respect, for all sound doctrine and the whole religion of the Gospel "walks modestly, and under the honorable and humble veil of the sacraments of Christ her lover she compliantly presents herself."[253] Again, it is a hunt for the truth through a thick forest.[254] It is conquest of the precious Pearl. It is the digging of wells where the charisms of the Holy Ghost are contained.[255] Above all it is a hand-to-hand combat with the Book, the book which is from cover to cover "the book of the combats of the Lord";[256] even more, which is nothing other than the Word of God, than Jesus, Son of Mary. *Sweet struggle, and more delightful than any peace!* A struggle at once sweet and harsh, strenuous and humble, for him to seize its secret. This inspired monk recommences the eternal struggle of Jacob with the angel, that angel "in whom, without any doubt, God was present"; as he explains it himself in an admirable address to the Virgin:

> For God is a spirit, and . . . he who wrestles must enter the struggle in spirit and truth. We have an example of this praiseworthy fortitude in our father Jacob. . . . According to that example, the man (who was wrestling with him) still allowed himself to be beaten by his opponent, as often happens as the studious and faithful mind keeps turning around the Word of God, until wresting from it the blessing of the Holy Spirit, which is the true and useful understanding of the mystery, or the Scripture that God with reason designed so that it cannot easily be apprehended . . . .
>
> Therefore, o Lady Mary bearer of God, and incorrupt mother of the eternal Word, God and man, Jesus Christ, armed not by merits of my own but yours, I crave to wrestle with that man, namely, with the Word of God, so that I may extort from the Canticle of Canticles a work that may not unfittingly be called "On the Incarnation of the Lord."[257]

A long and hard struggle, from whence one always emerges, though victorious, wounded, forever lame.[258] A struggle that comes to an end only in tears and prayer, as Origen had already said.[259] For all that, truly a most beautiful wrestling-match! The fusion of exegetical labor and contemplative ardor, as Saint Gregory,[260] again following Origen, had understood, and as a Saint Bernard and a Richard of Saint Victor would soon understand it again.[261] "A fever of holy zeal."[262] The huge books of Rupert are not merely the fruit of patient and laborious leisure hours; nor are they the pretext for scholarly expatiations. They are the work of a poet alive to the beauty of the Scriptures, to their "elegantia,"[263] to their "virginal beauty."[264] In his writing the word "beauty" keeps coming back again: beauty of the mystery, beauty of the allegory, "intimate, grand, and delectable" beauty;[265] beauty of that dove with wings of gold and silver;[266] beauty of the two Testaments which confront each other and harmonize with each other,[267] beauty of that image of Christ who is resplendent in his mirror.[268]

Here and there, the presence of a more secret element is given away, which gives us a glimpse of something more than a religious poet in Rupert. In a language that had none of the rigor of Scholasticism, he readily spoke of the inspiration of the Fathers in his century. He too is one of those inspired. Among his earliest readers some noticed it: "You have noticed that the things I have written or that I am writing are not without the Spirit of God."[269] Honorius has recognized as much in his own brief notice.[270] It has often been noticed, notably at a passage like the one in which Rupert calls up the visitations of the Word who made himself known to the soul by some sort of substantial contact, without the soul being able to explain how;[271] in another such passage in which he praises the science that comes from experience, that intimate knowledge of the "new name," received "not from outside like an alien document, but from within, as an effect of the Spirit of adoption";[272] in still another such passage in which — as his confrere Ambrose Autpert had almost done in days gone by[273] — following the example of Jeremiah, he three times asserts the imperious necessity that compelled him to speak of what he suffers, despite the reproaches of presumption and love of vainglory that he is going to bring upon himself.[274] One gets a detailed account of it by reading the amazing commentary on certain points of the Rule of Saint Benedict, the whole first book of which is an ardent personal apologia. While one treated Rupert as an innovator, another affected to have pity on the poor monk, even in his presence, for having been too late initiated into the mysteries of the new dialectic.[275] They tried to find fault with him from both these directions at once. Thus too Rabanus Maurus found himself long ago in a double crossfire.[276] "I am closed in on every side."[277] That is what always occurs when a witness of the tradition, not content passively to record its data and to preserve them as in a tomb, succeeds at making them really his own, i.e., to keep them alive; with a single movement that takes it on as a whole, almost instinctively he refuses sterile repetitions and innovations stemming from any impure source when he knows from experience (though perhaps saying it a bit too loudly) "that the rivers of living water gushing forth from the spring of Christ are better than the water held in human cisterns,"[278] and when without sufficient human prudence he proclaims (though well aware of his not lacking excellent teachers) that a single "visit from the Most High is worth more than the instruction of ten human teachers."[279] This contemplative has not gone off from town to town to look for famous schools: like Jacob, he has remained at home with his mother Rebecca; in addition, his adversaries look at him with contempt; they come together from the various directions of the theological horizon to point their finger at him and say: "Who is this?" And they stand around in ambush to extract something from his words to blame him for.[280] They reproach him for his abundant commentaries which are like a perfume poured over the head and feet of the Lord.[281] But in the face of his detractors he takes refuge, he says, on the breast of Jesus.[282] He was indeed exposed to the small-minded and to the envious.[283] Perhaps his attitude may have been on one occasion or another a bit provocative.[284] One sometimes senses that he is not far from seeing in the remarks of his adversaries at least one affluent of the river of the Apocalypse, the "diabolical river, the tangled river of heretical chattering, full of sophistical snares."[285]

In every sort of thought that does not seem to him immediately in conformity with biblical habits he is ready to denounce at least any traces of false wisdom inspired by "the impure spirit."[286] At any event he has no respect for the "fabled didacticism" of certain men who believe themselves to be the bearers of the progress of the spirit.[287] To defend his exalted idea of the monastic profession, he uses a rather high tone that might alienate him from more than one contemporary.[288] Nevertheless, at the end of his apologia, after meticulously defending each of the positions which had been impugned, he finally cries out in a transport which is of itself quite the best evidence of his being inspired:

> So let them now stop being opposed, saying of the man who has spoken: "Who is this, or what business is it of his to speak, since the holy

doctors of old have spoken enough?" And if they still do not stop, I shall still dare to speak and to say in the fashion of Isaiah: Since after all or under all the limits of the earth, i.e., the humble who have remembered the name of the Lord and have spoken in the name of the Lord, perhaps he comes into contact even with that pauper of yours: "Lord, they have sought after thee in distress, in the tribulation of murmuring thy instruction was with them. As a woman with child, when she draweth near the time of her delivery, is in pain, and crieth out in her pangs: so are we become in thy presence, o Lord. We have conceived and have been as it were in labor and have brought forth" (Isa. 26).

Who, I ask, is the sage, who may say to a woman, when she has reached the time of her delivery: "Why do you cry out, why are you not quiet, why do you not cover your mouth with silence?" Perhaps someone will tell me: "Are you like this? When or how have you conceived? How do you know that you conceived in the presence of the Lord, so that you would speak what you have written as though bringing forth?" To this I say: "My secret to myself, my secret to myself" (Isa. 24). But let them stop, because of what Isaiah says in like manner: "Woe to him that saith to his father, Why begettest thou?" and to the woman: "Why dost thou bring forth?" (Isa. 45). For he who envies the pregnant disparages the father; he who envies the one bringing forth disparages the offspring. The Father of mercies and the God of all consolation begets mercy and consoles the widow with his word [as to her] soul, and yet you say: "Why begettest thou?" She is seeking a voice, the word conceived by the mind, and you say: "Woman, why dost thou bring forth?" Tamar the daughter-in-law of Judah was vindicated by fitting evidence, answering, "By the man to whom these things belong I am with child: See whose ring, and bracelet, and staff this is" (Gen. 38). See then for yourself, if you will, whether there not be in my writings the ring of faith, the staff of hope, the bracelet of charity, and heed my soul saying: "By the man to whom these things belong I am with child." For I too am reworking something sensibly made in myself, so that without a doubt I may say that this "gift" (*datum* and *donum*) "is from above, coming down from the Father of lights" (James 1).[289]

4. The Hebrew, the Greek, and Saint Jerome

Let us not take the religious writers of the first Middle Ages (i.e., of any century occurring between the seventh and the twelfth) to be, as a whole, more ignorant, or less curious, or more devoid of "critical sense," or more exclusively "allegoristic" than they really were, so as then to set up against this herd some rare and privileged individuals who might miraculously stand in opposition to their times. Nowhere is so trenchant a duality to be found. It will often be worth recalling, as we have already done above, an elementary distinction of kinds to see how such apparent gulfs can be filled in. Paschasius and Christian, Berno, Bruno of Segni, and Rupert, were in any case not from the start the only ones to look for "the sense of the letter according to the tradition of the Hebrews." Many others, without enslaving themselves to it any longer, kept an ear open to this tradition. "The Hebrews hand it down"; "this is the tradition of the Hebrews"; "the Hebrews affirm"; "at this point the Hebrews explain"; "these points have been said following the tradition of the Hebrews": these expressions are regularly found.[290] Many others, following the example of Saint Augustine as well as Saint Jerome, also kept themselves informed of the writings of the gentiles,[291] or occupied themselves with aligning biblical history with the "secular histories," well aware of the difficulty of their task.[292] Still others used Josephus, who from the ninth century was appearing in all the libraries.[293] Had not Saint Jerome made a place for him in his catalogue of illustrious men? Had not a passage relating to Christ been cited from him by Eusebius? Cassiodorus, who called him a second Titus Livy, had remarked as particularly useful his seven books, already translated into Latin, on the *Captivity of the Jews,* and, putting into execution a project that Saint Jerome had abandoned long ago, he had arranged to have some friends make a translation "magno labore" of the twenty-two books of the *Jewish Antiquities,* as well as the *Contra Apion.*[294] Right at the end of his little Patrology, Notker the Stammerer likewise recommended reading Josephus.[295] Among others, Rupert would cite him often.[296] On every side, during the Carolingian age, Hebraic studies were exalted. Peter the grammarian could offer Paul the Deacon no better compliment than these verses:

> We believe that after the Greek canon, which you point out to many,
> You will hand down to those already learned the studies of the
> > Hebrews
> In which that doctor of the Law Gamaliel was famous.[297]

A LINEAGE STEMMING FROM JEROME?

To explicate Hebrew words, to note "the difference between the Hebrew manuscripts and our own" and to compare, as Saint Augustine had done, the chronologies of the Hebrew text with those of the Septuagint,[298] to verify carefully the citations of the Old Testament made by the authors of the New,[299] to confront the various Greek versions,[300] to weigh, as Saint Gregory[301] had done, the relative merits of Jerome's translations with those of the *vetus translatio*,[302] to debate various problems of language or spelling,[303] etc.: all this was common currency. They knew and endeavored to apply the rules sketched by the *Institutio divinarum litterarum*.[304] They knew that many manuscripts were defective and they generally took great pains to obtain the most correct ones.[305] They chased down "faulty manuscripts" and warned the reader to be wary of them. They did not hesitate to suppress one passage or another, remarking: "it is not contained in the Hebrew,"[306] or to restore some passage or other "as it is found in the exemplars that are in Hebrew."[307] Indeed they were unanimous in believing in the unqualifiedly normative value of the "Hebrew source," the "Hebrew truth,"[308] the "Hebraic truth,"[309] that "Hebraic truth bequeathed through Origen, published through Jerome, praised through Augustine, and confirmed through Josephus," as Bede puts it in a strongly stylized summary.[310] After centuries of resistance, fascination with [the Hebrew text] had at length become universal in the West.[311] Attention was perpetually being drawn to it. Its authority was beyond dispute. Thus scholars had no scruples about omitting passages attested only by the Septuagint version. Certain commentaries were studded with Hebrew words.[312] In the Saint Riquier Bible, the second Book of Chronicles is followed by this note: "If anyone wants to blame anything in this translation, let him ask the Hebrews."[313] A few more exacting good minds even tried really to take account of the "peculiar character of the Hebrew language,"[314] etc.

To be sure, in most instances, all this does not imply real intellectual mastery nor abundant philological resources. Even the best minds do not entirely escape the limits of their epoch. It is clear that none of our exegetes had yet been disturbed by the discoveries of Chinese chronicles, by those of Egyptology or Assyriology, by prehistoric discoveries, or the manuscripts from Qumrân. Furthermore, their scientific baggage, such as it was, does not always indicate a regard for criticism properly speaking nor even a genuine spirit of research. Often it is merely a question of data gathered here and there, principally from translations and commentaries by Saint Jerome, copied as such, and affirmed with confidence. Just as, for the controversialists of the Carolingian age, "the application of dialectic to

The Hebrew, the Greek, and Saint Jerome

theological problems" was often merely "an intention,"[315] so too, for the majority of our exegetes, the application of critical method to biblical problems is at most scarcely more than an intention. Indeed, they are chiefly concerned with recopying the "dialectical" passages, on the one hand, and the "critical" passages, on the other, from the Fathers. But still, they did recopy them. They were interested in them, often passionately so.

Furthermore, it was not rare — though it was extremely bad method — to practice a generous eclecticism of Platonic lineage in their explications. For they did not want anything to be lost. Some had no scruples about mixing or adding to etymologies. For example, here is Wigbode (born 780) expounding on the serpent in Genesis:

> You shall crawl on your chest and belly: for by the name "chest" is signified pride of mind; by "belly," on the other hand, as the Septuagint has translated it, the desires of the flesh are signified. For by these two things the devil slithers toward those whom he wants to deceive.[316]

The Venerable Bede had energetically protested against procedures of this sort. To hunt for a Hebrew etymology, said he, in a Greek or Latin noun, as some have done regarding the name of Peter, is to do violence to Scripture; it is merely an abuse and falsification.[317] He had even been on the point of correcting a passage from Saint Jerome, who had allowed himself to explicate another Greek name according to a Hebrew root.[318] In the twelfth century, Hervaeus of Bourg Dieu will extend the same protest in the opposite direction regarding the name Paul, a name of Hebrew origin, which many then wanted to explicate following the Latin or the Greek.[319] The Gloss on the Apocalypse would pass on a wise comment of the same type regarding the interpretation of numbers.[320] But the abuse would be tenacious. Gerhoh of Reichersberg will turn out to be an old hand at it. He will want to know how Ambrose and Jerome each interpret the Hebrew words, and, having noted that the latter was "more expert at the Hebraic truth," he will nonetheless keep both of their interpretations, saying for example: "which all converge and agree with each other," or: "but each of the two interpretations is fitting." He will even ingeniously combine them:

> *Mem* is translated "from them," as Jerome would have it; "entrails," as Ambrose would have it. Let us link each of the two interpretations so as to say "from the entrails themselves."[321]

A LINEAGE STEMMING FROM JEROME?

Still later, Joachim of Flora will proceed in almost the same way and, in such divergences as occur between the "Hebraic truth" and the text of the Septuagint, rather than think of a bad translation or some copyist's error, as others would, he will prefer to recognize the result of the "liberty of the Spirit," who would not have willed these divergences except "for the sake of some mystery."[322] This will turn out to harmonize well with opportunities arising in exegesis. It is true that this procedure, though condemned by Saint Jerome,[323] could, in a pinch, be authorized by his actual practice,[324] or by that of Saint Augustine,[325] and even, up to a certain point, by that of Origen.[326]

Even outside certain privileged circles, as the Spanish schools of Seville[327] were for some time and then those of Cordova,[328] thanks to their relations with the many Jews living in the region of old Baetica, Hebrew was not always completely unknown. At every available opportunity scholars followed the example given long ago by Origen, Eusebius of Caesarea, and Saint Jerome, who were tutored at the side of their rabbis. Saint Hildegard herself would frequent Jewish scholars, and it is believed that she was visited at Bingen by the celebrated Benjamin of Toledo. Perhaps, for some, mentioning that they were going to consult the Hebrew over a difficult textual or ritual problem was merely a literary device; this was doubtless the case of Werner of Saint Blaise.[329] Was it not also the case on several occasions with Saint Jerome?[330] With others, such as Rabanus Maurus, such mention [of consultation with Jews] corresponds to some reality.[331] Right up to the thirteenth century, the scientific or religious relations between Christians and Jews were, in many regions, normal practice, and it was not rare for Christians to take Hebrew lessons from a Jew. They readily admired the zeal of the Jews to study the letters and thence, in view of their intelligence, the language of the Scriptures, and many were stimulated by their example.[332] At the beginning of his treatise *De naturis rerum*, Alexander Neckham will devote several pages to explicate the first verse of Genesis in accordance with the Hebrew; indeed he rather thinks he will find a readership to appreciate his demonstrations: in his opinion, every reader ought to be able to follow it, "even one modestly trained in the language of the Hebrews."[333]

Nevertheless, this "veritas hebraica" or "auctoritas hebraica" that is unceasingly invoked often seems more like a dogma of faith than an established fact. This seems to be so for two reasons. To start with, it seems more like a dogma, because, if they do believe it, it is almost always at the word of Saint Jerome, a word that they take a bit too literally, however — for it sometimes occurred to the learned translator and learned commentator of Bethlehem "to read and to cite the Hebrew through the Greek of Origen."[334] "According to our translation, that is, the Hebraic truth," as Rupert expresses himself,[335] and as all concur: in other words, practically speaking, the "veritas hebraica" is quite simply the Latin text of Jerome.[336] Again, it is a sort of dogma, because the adoption of this text was reinforced by a mystical belief in the incomparable excellence of the Hebrew language. Saint Jerome had gloried in the labor, howsoever thankless, that he had endured to get used to the "harsh and breathy words" of this barbarous language, in tearing himself away from the charms of the great Latin writers; he had recalled how he started the task "like a slave who is attached to the millstone," and how he had plunged into the darkness of the text "like a miner in a tunnel"; he had ultimately thanked the Lord for such sweet fruits that he had drawn from such dry seeds.[337] His Latin was getting so rusty, he claimed, that a "certain un-Latin harshness grates"[338] even within his conversation. He had written on another occasion that "a harshness stemming from reading Hebrew aloud has sullied all elegance of my speech and the beauty of my Latin pronunciation."[339] This proud profession of faith, sign of a triumph ultimately gained over "humanist" prejudices, could be taken in several convergent senses. This "stridor quidam," this piercing, "strident" sound, this hoarse and wheezing pronunciation, which used to call to mind the grating of a saw — and the rage of the wicked and the fury of the damned[340] — also rang out like the shout of a warrior, the cry foretelling victory. The "stridor lectionis hebraicae," which long before had grated upon the ears and irritated the throat of the translator, was turning into a quality sublime. Now they attributed this quality not only to such and such a sacred author, considered in his individual talent, in his doctrine or his rhetoric: more radically, they saw it as a fact, as an inalienable property, of the language itself. Everyone in the Middle Ages then shared an admiration for Hebrew; both those like Alvarus of Cordova[341] and Agobard of Lyon who praise the Bible for disdaining all elegance, and those like the Venerable Bede,[342] Paschasius Radbertus,[343] Rupert,[344] or Peter Abelard[345] who, on the contrary, make much of the natural splendor of its eloquence, the depth of its symbolic powers, and the rich structure of its speech.

They therefore try to outdo each other in praising "the dignity of Hebrew."[346] It is the ultimate poetic language, since the "carmen heroicum," first of all the metric songs, was sung by Moses and Job before Pherecydes and Homer, whatever the profane grammarians may say about it;[347] since David was the first poet to make hymns, since Solomon created the epithalamion,[348] and Jeremiah composed the first Lamentations or threnodies.[349] Hebrew is "the perfect language,"[350] because it is the original language, the "mother-tongue."[351] If they do not look for subtler proofs of this claim amidst linguistic[352] or historical[353] facts, that is because they judge it to be already assured by the Bible. The first man had received it as a gift from God himself: how could this marvel of language that constructs such edifices of thought with the twenty-two letters of its alphabet be a human invention? How much more marvelous to have a language made for the express purpose of expressing divine things![354] From Adam up till the dispersion of peoples provoked by the prideful undertaking of the Tower of Babel, then, the human race spoke Hebrew.[355] Once the lamentable effect of the great "machina contradictionis"[356] had been produced, however, the primitive language was not utterly lost. It was kept pure in the house of Heber, who was to pass it on to Abraham.[357] It is from this house, as is generally thought, that the Hebrew people draw its name, which signifies "the part of the Lord."[358] Saint Isidore stood behind this etymology,[359] though it was contested by some, to the advantage of Abraham.[360] Hebrew also had the benefit of two great authorities, that of Saint Jerome,[361] and (albeit with some hesitations) of Saint Augustine.[362] A Carolingian poet puts the common opinion into verse:

> A man has been born into the world, a noble patriarch,
> Abraham the friend of God, a most faithful lad;
> He was to arise from the golden stem of Heber,
> From whom the people of the Hebrews began to be proclaimed.[363]

Without professing a superstitious devotion to Hebrew, without seeing in it a divine language with a nature set apart, and without assigning to the unity of the language itself an importance that belongs only to the unity of the faith, Saint Augustine in his *City of God* came forward to guarantee the essential point of these facts.[364] Later on, Otto of Freising confirmed them in his *Chronicon*.[365] For a long time afterward and well after the end of the Middle Ages, many will hold them to be indisputable.[366]

Following a tradition already recorded by Saint Hilary,[367] two other languages share with Hebrew to some extent its universal, sacred character: Greek and Latin, since they figured along with Hebrew on the placard over the cross; also, at the time of the consecration of the Popes, the Gospel is proclaimed in these three languages[368] — which is tantamount to "every tongue."[369] But if the Greek language is doubtless the clearest of the three, and if the Latin language is the most "imperial," the Hebrew language, as carrier of the Law of God, is surely the most noble.[370] It is through Hebrew that men were given "the first foundations of theology."[371] It is not only "the mother of all languages,"[372] but, as Rupert says, "the mother of holy Scripture."[373] Just as it was spoken in the Garden, so, according to common belief, will it be spoken in the heavenly Jerusalem: "once the Judgment has been executed, she herself will remain one"; at least "that is what certain doctors think."[374] These two words from the liturgy — *Amen* and *Alleluia* — as well as the word *Hosanna* — words charged with mystery, words that the translators of holy Scripture did not dare, "propter mysterium" or "propter sanctiorem auctoritatem,"[375] to render into Greek or Latin[376] constitute part of the song of the angels:[377] now these are Hebrew words. Hence the angels themselves speak this more than human language,[378] each letter of which includes in addition mysteries such as other alphabets do not.

Let not the modern reader cry out too quickly at how naive they seem. Once more, he might be trapped. Those who speak in this way do not understand all their affirmations literally. They know well that the unity met with in the first language is in fact the unity of hearts in praise of the one and only God, and that the vision of the concord and peace of Jerusalem is opposed to the confusion of Babel; they are well aware that God does not speak any language producing an audible word: "with God there is pure understanding without the din and diversity of tongues,"[379] and that neither the angels nor the elect praise him through a material repetition of the syllables "Amen, Alleluia"; they are well aware that these two words, in our mouths, "honorem habent sacramenti." Saint Gregory has reminded them that the heavenly contemplation is accomplished in silence, all the words of preaching as well as all those of praise vanishing before the unique Word of God.[380] Saint Augustine has instructed them about this at length: the angels speak Hebrew as they are the temple of God; the alleluia that we sing now "in hope" is nothing but the sensible and passing sign of that which one day we will sing with them "in reality."[381] The true Amen, the true Alleluia, none can know in themselves. They are not words of any earthly language, and no one here below knows how to provide an interpretation of them, a translation properly speaking.[382] They are a part of those things "that the eye has not seen, that the ear has not heard, which have not entered into the heart of man." We know only that after having too often regarded them as a burden upon our shoulders, they will be our food and our drink, at once our activity and our repose, the fullness of our joy.[383] But the two signs of this eternal fullness, kept untranslated in our liturgy, are nonetheless two Hebrew words.

These various arrays of reasons are sufficient for the Hebrew text of the Bible to have been quite generally regarded as superior to the Septuagint version, despite the esteem in which the latter was held owing both to its being regarded as miraculous in origin[384] and to the place it holds in the tradition of the Church and the services it renders on occasion in discussions with the Jews.[385] The "doctissimus Augustinus" served in vain as an apologist and panegyrist for the Septuagint; it was useless for him to recall that it owed its existence "more to a prophetic gift than to the task of translating": Bede himself was unimpressed.[386] Furthermore, the very use that the inspired writers of the New Testament have made of this text of the Septuagint did not induce our exegetes to canonize it. They readily "excuse" a Saint Luke, a Saint Paul, and the rest, because these first messengers of the Good News had to address themselves to the gentiles, among whom this version was already becoming widespread and with whom in certain cases it enjoyed great credit;[387] but the medievals do not think that apostolic authority is engaged in it or that it is fitting to follow the New Testament writers in this point.[388]

Besides, Greek does not have a very good reputation in the West. It is well known that, contrary to Saint Augustine, who used to praise its excellence,[389] Saint Jerome little appreciated it, that he found it, in comparison with the Hebrew, as poor as the Latin.[390] It is not entirely beyond the realm of possibility that they might notice that the genius of this language squares badly with that of the Latin. The group feeling of peoples who are aware of being a Johnny-come-lately to culture is a factor as well: "Thank God, I believe that our lateness has more than made up for their priority!"[391] Finally, Greek is somewhat a victim of the quarrels that divide Christendom. Do not most of the heresies come from the fatherland of the Greeks? The West, if it does not watch out, runs the risk of being overrun by these "inventors of perverse dogmas," this "brood of vipers" ceaselessly "swarming." They are unequaled at raising a thousand contemptible and useless questions that lead rather to things temporal than to things spiritual and proceeding less from a truly intellectual need than from an external and reprehensible sense.[392] "Greeks go positively mad over reason," as a less sophisticated Westerner puts it.[393] Is it not the case that that terrible pestilence, Islam, that dreadful "heresy," is the fruit, at least indirectly, of their theology?[394] The counter-example of Pelagius, who came from Brittany, raises a momentary embarrassment perhaps: but he is quickly recognized as the exception that confirms the rule.[395] "O unhappy Greece, which could never allow itself to live without heresies!"[396] In our own regions, those who feed on Greek doctrines ordinarily come thereby to construct suspicious systems; they lose themselves in "an ocean of dialectical subtlety" and get discussions all tangled up with their captious arguments.[397] Is it not the case of poor John Scotus who, in the judgment of some weighty theologians, got drunk, as he put it, on the "sacrum Graecorum nectar"[398] and who became a heretic by imitating "a certain Maximus"?[399]

Besides, why bother always to keep looking back? Saint Jerome had already cried out in his rhetorical extravagance: "Today it is in the West that the Sun of Justice is born; Lucifer is ruling in the East."[400] In 837, while dedicating his *Life of Saint Germain* to Charles the Bald, Heric of Auxerre declares that he hears the groans of a Greece now dismissed from her ancient privileges.[401] Notker the Stammerer, celebrating Bede's praises, asserts that God, "who on the fourth day of creation made the sun to rise in the East, made this poet to rise in the West on the sixth and last age of humanity as a new sun to illuminate the whole earthly universe."[402] This "western" sentiment will be found again in the following centuries. Chrétien de Troyes will express it in the wake of scholars and theologians. In a manner more or less toned down and conveyed in various ways, he will always let the persuasion of a superiority that has definitively been obtained for the West to show through.[403] This is the theme of the "transfer of scholarship" and the "transfer of wisdom," that runs parallel to and connects with the theme of the "transfer of power" or the "transfer of rulership"[404] — a conspicuous twofold role that was assigned to Charlemagne as founder of the Empire of the West and of the University of Paris.[405] It also takes on the form of a universal law; thus, as Otto of Freising writes in his great *Chronicle*: "All human wisdom or power beginning from the East has ended up in the West."[406] Or again, in Hugh of Saint Victor: "a development is running in a straight line from East to West."[407] In this final age of the world, therefore, it is in our West that God has caused his light to emerge; it is there that he has made the seeds of renewal to sprout. Then too, rivalries sowed mistrust. Recalling the regrettable conflicts that had brought him to oppose the emperor Maurice and the patriarch John the Faster, Saint Gregory scarcely appreciated the excessive refinement of the Greeks: it led them, he thought, into imposture,[408] and his biographer John the Deacon reproached them not only for their frivolity[409] but also for a certain "crafty perversity."[410] Liutprand of Cremona, who twice served on embassy to Constantinople, demonstrates a still more severe attitude.[411] Rathier of Verona sums up the opinion of more than one Latin in the cry: "Mendax Graecia!"[412]

A LINEAGE STEMMING FROM JEROME?

Doubtless there it was a question only of extreme cases, though frequent enough. Never, in these centuries of the first Middle Ages, did one take the thought of the Greeks as negligible a priori, as would often happen later on. The medievals were ordinarily curious about the thought of the Greek Fathers. Everybody loved and venerated them. Their authority was invoked by the very people who were not displeased with dealing "with the heresies of the Greeks."[413] Very rare indeed would be those, like Geoffrey of Clairvaux, who would dare to dismiss the testimony of a Father like Saint Athanasius with a few contemptuous reflections.[414] Nourished by many exchanges, the unity of the Christian world remains stronger than the schisms, and the feeling of universal Christendom, in principle at least, was not constricted.[415] The most modern Greek saints are venerated by the Latins. On the eve of the great schism of 1054, the two halves of the Church each bore testimony of a great respect for the other.[416] Nevertheless, distrust is tenacious. From ideas and men, it seems that it sometimes even went back to language. Such was the case, it seems, with Saint Isidore.[417] When John Scotus, a fine Hellenist, began to praise the precision and expressive power of Greek vocabulary,[418] when he appealed to the Greek origins of certain words to enter into theological subtleties and to discuss certain theses of Latin theology, when in fine he allowed himself to write: "The Greeks, however, customarily considering things more sharply and signifying them more distinctly . . . ,"[419] he provoked a vexation traces of which can be detected in the response of Prudentius of Troyes:

> What a truly most sagacious man, who drags us off to the Greek because it is missing in the Latin, and makes out Greek origins in Latin words! You keep bringing in Attic origins for us in Latin expressions![420]

One does not like hearing a language one understands badly be praised and see it occurring in a controversy.

There is a well-preserved dictionary composed by Martin of Ireland dating from the end of the ninth century called the "Glossary of Laon," which "for the letter A alone gives the translation of about 1200 [Greek] words relating to all sorts of uses."[421] It is nevertheless a fact that, despite the example that was given by Bede,[422] despite the influence exercised on the continent all through the eighth, the ninth and even still in the tenth century by numerous Irish scholars[423] as well as by a number of Greek monks,[424] the number of real experts in this language remained, right up to the twelfth century, quite few in number.[425] A John Scotus and a Martin of Ireland, capable of writing poems in Greek, a Paul the Deacon, a Sedulius Scotus, a Liuddo of Laon, a Walafrid Strabo, an Anastasis, a Heric of Auxerre (†876), are perhaps brilliant exceptions. The same also doubtless goes for a Notker the Stammerer,[426] a Regimbald of Eichstädt (†989), or a Bruno of Cologne (†965), who served both as interpreter and arbiter in the philosophical disputes between the Latins and Greeks;[427] then, in the eleventh century, an Ekkehard IV of Sankt Gall,[428] a Cardinal Humbert of Silva Candida, and, if one must believe his biographer on the matter, a John of Gorze.[429] A number of others, among whom are Sedulius Scotus still in the ninth century, Fridegod of Canterbury, an author from Auvergne who composed toasts in hexameters,[430] and the biographer of Saint Donatus of Ireland in the tenth century,[431] Thierry of Echternach in the eleventh, Sigebert of Gemblous near the beginning of the twelfth, like to cram their prose or verse with Greek words; but this fashion, which arises from time to time, like that of Greek titles, does not necessarily signify that one knows the language well.[432]

In the twelfth century, the situation will change. An Abelard, desiring to slake his thirst "in ipso ortu fontis,"[433] will understand, like Heloise, the importance of the study of Greek as well as of Hebrew. Even more will a John of Salisbury, under the influence of his correspondent John Sarrazin.[434] Relations with Byzantium will multiply, all the while becoming worse. The school of translators at Toledo, where they are interested in Greek as well as in Arabic, will be frequented by men the world over. Sicily and Italy will tell of excellent Hellenists, such as the three "wise men, skilled in both languages," who will assist the Latin Anselm of Havelberg in 1135 with his controversy with the Greek Nicetas: one of them will be Burgundio of Pisa, the most celebrated of the translators of Saint John Damscene.[435] Still, profane science will profit more from all this renewal, at least immediately, than will sacred science. The tearing apart of the Christian world will not find a remedy here. What is more, the pit will be opening up between the two halves of Christendom. The shocks created by the Crusades will enlarge this pit. A new invasion of Greek expressions portending "novelties" in certain intellectual circles will provoke lively protests from certain conservative theologians: a Robert of Melun will rise up against such a "prostitution of Catholic doctrine."[436] An Eberhard of Bamberg will set aside as "less authoritative" the testimony that Gerhoh of Reichersberg went to get in the writing of the Greeks and will not hide his "contempt" for this kind of argument.[437] Worthy ancestors of that "Trojan faction" that Blessed Thomas More will

A LINEAGE STEMMING FROM JEROME?

one day complain of. Gerhoh himself will criticize in passing "certain chatterers sharing opinions with heretics from among the Greeks."[438] The Porretanians, such as Alan of Lille, will have a good bit of trouble fighting against this ever renewed Latin provincialism,[439] and, in the new wave of disapproval that will rise against John Scotus up until his condemnation by the Fourth Lateran Council in 1215, it is once again the Greeks, those eternal sophists, that they will hold responsible for his "heresies."[440]

This persistent mindset makes them grateful to Saint Jerome for having somewhat desacralized the Septuagint: he sometimes treated it, as is well known, even off-handedly.[441] He is praised for having replaced the old Latin translation based on the Greek with this version which finally gives the Latin peoples "the truth of the Hebrew." Following him, they are content to observe that Saint Paul was more skillful in Hebrew than in Greek and that at the end of his Epistles he used to inscribe his name in Hebrew letters.[442] From the eighth and ninth century on, they study Jerome's prefaces closely, as is evidenced in particular by the *Explanationes in Praefationes sancti Hieronymi ad evangelia* composed by Sedulius Scotus.[443] Wigbode is constantly transcribing it to explicate Genesis. It seems to have pride of place in Claude of Turin,[444] and Rabanus Maurus uses it with particular frequency. "As blessed Jerome says": such is the refrain of Remi of Auxerre commenting on the Minor Prophets.[445] "As blessed Jerome witnesses": this formula of Cassiodorus's backing up his reflections on the Hebrew alphabet[446] was that of everyone else, too.[447] This is not an occurrence of a small school, or of a particular type of mind, or of a backward epoch. One does not remark that the influence of the great Doctor had had to grow, to expand, or to overcome the influence of others between the eighth and twelfth centuries, though naturally he, like the other doctors, was more copied, more cited, and, in accordance with the peculiar resources of each, more truly imitated in the periods of the most intense intellectual activity. In the first chapter of his *De interpretibus*, Notker the Stammerer accompanies the short list of commentators he recommends to read with the following remark: "though as regards all the prophets the most hardworking Jerome is enough for the studious reader."[448] At the end of the tenth century, Odilon of Cluny, who is an "unremitting reader of Jerome's books," calls him "that holy man, incomparable in divine and human wisdom, the venerable Jerome."[449] Toward 1100, Reginald of Canterbury — who will borrow from Jerome what he offers with little critical judgment as a paraphrase in verse of the Life of Saint Malchus[450] — will call him a "wonderful writer," "colleague in the priesthood of the whole Church," "chest of wisdom," etc.[451] Several years later, Geoffrey the Fat will bestow on him the title "lamp of the world."[452] But Cassian had long since spoken of "Jerome, the teacher of catholics, the one whose writings glow like divine torches through the whole world."[453] Sulpicius Severus has declared, all the while expressing reserve regarding his polemic excesses, that no one was comparable to him in knowledge.[454] Cassiodorus praised his work to the skies.[455] The so-called Mozarabic liturgy multiplied the saint's praises: it held up his knowledge of the biblical languages, his art of translation, his sense of the Catholic faith, his courage, and his ability to overwhelm heresy "through the javelin of evangelical diction."[456] Saint Isidore of Seville composed this inscription for his library's bookcase to hold Jerome's works:

> O Jerome, translator most learned in various tongues,
> Bethlehem celebrates you, the whole world declaims you,
> Our library too advances you with your books.[457]

In a difficult problem, Saint Julian of Toledo took as his guide "Jerome, the man of blessed memory, who translated the divine Scriptures from Hebrew into Latin."[458] Saint Aldhelm was himself also happy to celebrate in Jerome the translator "turning the Hebrew oracles into Roman words."[459]

Another poem, dedicated to Charles the Bald, exalts the beauty of his translations as well as the depth of his knowledge:

> Penetrating the Hebrew archive with the torch of his heart
> Jerome unlocks the sacred entrances and ivory temples
> For his disciples, he transmits what is to be had to Latium,
> And having entered the Judean grove, which till then had enclosed places inaccessible to our people,
> He surrounds the entries with sagacious light.[460]

The author of the *Caroline Books* declares himself his disciple: "as we have learned from the teaching of blessed Jerome, the most expert teacher of the Hebrew tongue,"[461] and he sends the reader off to the school of Jerome.[462] In the environment surrounding Alcuin, they called him the "most famous doctor of divine Scripture in holy Church."[463] Alcuin himself calls him "maximus doctor." Rabanus Maurus observes that he is the only one to have made Scripture pass directly from the original text into Latin; after the fashion of Isidore, he speaks highly of the unique value of his edition,[464] and it is again out of reverence for Jerome, who reckoned twenty-two books in the Old Testament, that he divides his own *De Universo* into twenty-two books.[465] Hincmar of Reims, who admires his mastery in the three languages, also says of him: "With the Lord's inspiration, he merited to penetrate into the marrow and innards of sacred Scripture by his investigation."[466] Jonas of Orléans greets him with the title "Librarian of Mother Church." The Psalter of King Lothair elogizes him in verse:

> Jerome stood out as the most celebrated man in the world. . . .
> He handed over the consonant Testaments of God and the twin
>   Laws
> And turned them transmuting them in Latin discourse.
> He also translated these most gracious songs of the Psalms
> And corrected them right down to the last touch.[467]

Three miniatures in the Bible of Charles the Bald represent the Doctor of Bethlehem learning Hebrew. In his important *Liber officialis*, Amalarius shows "a very great familiarity with the works of Saint Jerome"; he makes frequent use of his letters and cites almost all his commentaries.[468] Othloh of Saint Emmeran will want to copy for himself the collection of Jerome's letters.[469] A sequence from the Abbey of Sankt Gall celebrates in him both the scholar and the saint:

> He had Donatus as his instructor in the art of grammar,
> The sevenfold spirit purifying and preparing for him a vessel of
>   election.
> After he accomplished his study of all the headings of worldly
>   literature,
> He eagerly followed the approved habit of holy men,
> Continuously holding on to the things that are pleasing to you,
>   o true Wisdom.[470]

The commentaries of Jerome are known by everyone in the Carolingian age; the most popular at that time seem to be the commentaries on Isaiah, Saint Matthew, and the Epistle to the Galatians; but none is disdained.[471] When Notker the German undertakes to translate and comment on the Psalter in Old German, Saint Jerome is one of his principal sources. When, at the threshold of the thirteenth century, Helinand of Froidmont will speak of "our Jerome,"[472] he will be the echo of the voice of the ages.

The Hebrew, the Greek, and Saint Jerome

But the authority of Saint Jerome seems never to have been exclusive, even in biblical matters. He is always placed next to the other principal doctors. He is never invoked against them. The opposition imagined to exist by certain modern historians between his authority and that of Saint Gregory does not in fact exist, any more than that between the authority of Saint Gregory or Origen and that of Junilius.[473] Saint Jerome has not "dethroned" Saint Gregory in the twelfth century any more than he had dethroned him in the ninth, as C. H. Turner seemed to believe;[474] the two following chapters will put the finishing touches on the proof of this point. From one end of the Middle Ages to the other, the names of the two doctors [Jerome and Gregory] are peacefully juxtaposed. They are tightly associated when it comes to commenting on Ezekiel and the Apocalypse. Indeed, Bede's devotion to Gregory did not keep him from thoroughly exploiting the works of Jerome, almost all of which he had at his disposal. In one and the same sentence Ambrose Autpert based himself on the authority of Jerome "beatae recordationis" and of Gregory "tractatorum Ecclesiae egregius," and, in another passage, after having praised Gregory's ideas and style, he pronounces a no less warm eulogy of Jerome, "whose writings are of such authority that none dare to mutter against them."[475] Paul Alvarus, who is constantly citing "our Jerome," "the great Jerome," "this abyss of knowledge,"[476] who has pursued him so much as to reflect his very style,[477] and who composes a whole poem in praise of him,[478] often mingles the name of Gregory along with his, and if, for example, he refers to Jerome's commentary on Daniel, he refers at the same time to Gregory's commentary on Job.[479] Alcuin announces that he is going to follow Jerome to explicate *Ecclesiastes*, and on the following page he makes a beautiful elegy of Gregory, himself also a "doctor mirabilis."[480] He dedicates an inscription to each of them:

> Jerome, the marvelous doctor of the whole world. . . .
> Gregory, doctor, pastor, patriarch, priest. . . .[481]

He unites them once again in a unique dedication "to the altar of SS. Gregory and Jerome":

> Our patron Gregory and nourishing doctor Jerome,
>   The former was a father, the latter a teacher of the Church.
> May they bring our offerings along with their prayers to the
> Thundering One
>   That God may always and everywhere protect us.[482]

Jonas of Orléans appeals to the authority of each of them on one and the same page.[483] Godscalc cites Gregory more than seventy times and Jerome almost as often,[484] and although in each instance it was not a question of exegesis, nothing shows that he felt obliged to make a choice in principle in this domain. Lupus of Ferrières celebrates without taking sides these "two brightest lights among the doctors, Augustine and Jerome, and after them Gregory and Bede."[485] Angelome of Luxeuil, who is sometimes wrongly regarded as a pure allegorist, embraces both these doctors with the same admiration.[486] At least twice Aimo of Auxerre proposes two exegeses of one and the same text, the one from Jerome, the other from Gregory; he leaves the choice to the reader.[487] It is on the authority of Gregory that Berno of Reichenau praises the biblical version of Jerome.[488] Odo of Cluny, Gregory's abbreviator, constantly cites Jerome in his Conferences, which were nourished on life-giving sap stemming from Gregory.[489] Goscelin of Saint Bertin cites them both as well.[490] Paulinus of Aquileia invokes their conjoint testimony in the same way on several occasions.[491] At the head of his own commentary on Saint Matthew, Bruno of Segni copies over the preface of Jerome.[492] Saint Bernard himself sometimes follows rather closely the interpretations of Jerome, a score of whose works belonged to the library of Clairvaux.[493] Hervaeus of Bourg Dieu unhesitatingly helps himself both to Jerome and to Gregory. In a single short sermon, Serlon of Savigny calls on each of them.[494] Peter Cellensis, so much a follower of Gregory, has concerns about literal exactitude that lead him to consult Jerome.[495] John of Salisbury in a single letter has recourse to Jerome — of whom he shows a deep knowledge — to determine the human authors of the Bible and then to Gregory to explain that the question is, after all, secondary, considering that its true author is the Holy Spirit;[496] in his various works he cites them both with grand eulogies. Jerome and Gregory are as familiar to Peter of Blois as they are to the Abelardian commentator on Saint Paul. Saint Martin of Leon depends upon each of them. In the Preface to his critical revision of Peter Lombard's *Gloss* on the Psalms, Herbert of Bosham follows Saint Jerome closely, whom he calls "our doctor" and whose merits he celebrates; but at the same time he is inspired by a passage from the *Moralia in Job* to put forward a principle of method following Saint Gregory.[497] The canonists have recourse to Saint Jerome to establish the authority of all the Fathers in the explication of the Scriptures.[498] If, as is normal, people often recall his eminent merit as linguist and translator — "conspicuously distinguished in the various utterances of languages"[499] — they praise him no less on occasion, albeit associating him with others, for his teaching on the spiritual understanding, as well as for the sublime and reverential manner with which he himself praises the majesty of the divine Word.[500]

5. Criticism in the Middle Ages

The exegetes are not always content to swear by Saint Jerome, regardless of whether or not he is associated with other doctors, and this is so even for the matters of his own specialty. Here again a few summary indications will suffice for our purpose.

Braulio of Saragossa (†651) is not the most scholarly of the brilliant Spanish group. He produced no work similar to that of his master and friend Isidore of Seville in revising the Psalter.[501] He manifests nonetheless a serious taste for scientific labors: research about biblical chronology, a study of the properties of Hebrew, collecting manuscripts in various languages in view of collating them. He observes that more than one embarrassing problem disappears if one goes back to the original text. What increases our interest in these facts is that, naively refusing the dilemma in which they seem sometimes to want to trap our authors and tidily noting the succession and hierarchy of tasks, he goes on to say:

> Lo! I have responded in a pedestrian and peculiar discourse. . . . But I would prefer that, if God should grant what I have set down earlier on questions to be allegorized and understood mystically, our effort in the affirmation of the New should also be consistent with that of the Old Instrument, so that deep would truly cry unto deep in the voice of your cataracts, since the one preceded in time, the other in dignity; for the latter is baby-food for the Christian soul; for the soul is fed on the things it delights in. . . .[502]

The Englishman Saint Aldhelm had given an indication of a more refined critical spirit than Paschasius Radbertus, in rejecting with distrust the apocryphal scriptures, though the motives for his exclusion were chiefly of a spiritual order.[503] Thanks to systematic efforts, Saint Bede had acquired mastery of the Greek language; thus in his commentaries he is able to make a significant contribution to textual criticism for which he shows a lively interest; "he compares the reading of the manuscripts that are available to him," and even ventures a few comparisons with the Hebrew text. When in his explication of the *Hexaemeron* he notices discrepancies of chronology between the Hebrew and the Septuagint, or divergences of redaction between the "old translation" and the "Hebraic truth," or again when he observes a peculiarity of Hebrew syntax, one feels that, though all the while he is referring himself to Jerome, he has looked things over at first hand.[504] For the Acts of the Apostles, he has recourse to a bilingual manuscript of the sixth century. To explicate the Psalms, he uses the prologues of Theodore of Mopsuestia. Be it through the channel of the Irish exegetes, or again through Theodore of Tarsus, the easterner who became Archbishop of Canterbury in the seventh century, Bede was able to know a certain number of interpretations characteristic of the School of Antioch. He does not always follow them, as when we see him dealing with a text from the second Epistle to the Corinthians: "Nocte et die in profundo maris fui": "A night and a day I was in the depth of the sea." Theodore of Mopsuestia had maintained that this "profundum maris" referred to a deep pit, an instrument of torture that had been applied to the Apostle. In rejecting this exegesis, Bede assuredly evinces less repugnance for the marvelous and, if one wants to take it in this sense, a less "scientific" spirit, as well as a greater attachment to the tradition of the "venerable writings of the Fathers" — but, not the least, concern with the literal sense, since he wants, on the contrary, to hear in Paul's expression "nothing other than what it signifies."[505] On the other hand, his eminent qualities as an historian were well known. Richard Simon, who was able to praise his knowledge and "his great judgment," did not hesitate to count him "among the most able critics."[506]

Theodulf of Orléans is not only the bishop and the man of policy that is regularly admired, the poet composer of the magnificent processional chant *Gloria, laus et honor,* the grand seigneur artiste of Germigny, the bold theologian and the pedantic as well as brilliant and dashing polemicist of the Caroline Books: learned, judicious, he knows enough Hebrew to correct for himself, doubtless with the aid of the monks of Fleury-sur-Loire, several manuscripts of the Latin Bible by matching them up with the original text.[507] Sedulius Scotus has not only copied a collection of Pauline epistles in Greek in his own hand; he has also transcribed the entire Psalter, to correct the errors of the Latin texts that he had before him; his work shows evidence both of a very serious knowledge of the Greek language and of very serious critical abilities, which gives him the right to deal with incompetent correctors as "falsifiers."[508] But this was a work that always needs to be redone. The quadruple Psalter of Solomon III is, in the words of Samuel Berger, "a very beautiful work"; the "Gallican," "Roman," and "Hebrew" Psalters are there "finished off with the Greek text transliterated into Latin characters."[509] Endowed, like Sedulius, with "the most acute critical sense,"[510] Florus of Lyon, encouraged by Agobard, revises the Roman Psalter, having recourse to several Jewish luminaries of his city; for, as he explains, "the involved and falsifying variety of many manuscripts to me seemed extremely bothersome and burdensome, a variety that, having arisen through the vice of sleepy copyists, is daily nourished and propagated by the fecklessness of the incompetent." His ambition is therefore greater than that of Sedulius Scotus. He wants to consult the "volumen hebraicum" for himself, and he quite knowingly determines what the "veritas hebraica" requires.[511]

Florus's contemporary, Rabanus Maurus, does not pass as a genius at criticism. Nonetheless he has published an edition of the *Cena Cypriani,* a work then much in vogue, purged of everything that was taken from apocryphal books.[512] Also in his *Clericalis institutio,* he gives intelligent advice, accompanied with precise examples, about how to explicate the biblical text by means of the context. Many ambiguities that present themselves at first can, he thinks, be eliminated if one takes the trouble to do so: too often they remain merely because of the "reader's excessive carelessness."[513] Moreover, he does all he can, in the tradition of men like Origen and Jerome, to assure himself of a good text and a correct interpretation of the letter: "I have in several places inserted the opinion of a certain well educated Hebrew of modern times as to what he said . . . the tradition of the Hebrews holds, along with an indication of his name." It is in his commentary on the four Books of Kings that he expresses himself thus, in addressing Hilduin, Abbot of Saint Denis of Paris.[514] The details that he provides, the very character of this preface, in which Rabanus expatiates about himself and his work, rule out the hypothesis that these are merely conventional formulas,[515] as is doubtless once the case for Paschasius Radbertus.[516] Moreover, he does not speak of a man that he would go to consult in oral conversations, but of an author who, though "modern," was perhaps not a contemporary of his. Many of his readers would murmur against him. Rabanus does not allow himself to be intimidated: he shows up again to comment on the Paralipomena and he justifies his conduct in a new preface, in the form of a letter to Louis the Fair. For each of the two works, he says, "I have in several places inserted the opinions of a certain Hebrew flourishing in modern times in knowledge of the Law"; those who reproach him for it have failed to notice that he does not force the opinions of this Hebrew upon them; they have just been unable to make an elementary distinction: "our job is to bring the witnesses forth; theirs, to judge the reliability of the witnesses." But he is always finding himself amidst people who, instead of producing positive work, spend their time denigrating the works of others; let the king protect him against these envious characters![517]

The continuator of Sigebert (†1112) for the Chronicle of the abbots of Gemblout writes of his predecessor:

> He was very dear not only to the Christians, but also to the Jews dwelling with them in that city, for he was an expert at discerning the Hebraic truth from the other editions, and in the things that he used to say regarding the Hebraic truth, he was consistent with the assertions of the Jews.[518]

Such an elogy does not at all require us to think that Sigebert had been a master of criticism, nor even that he had known Hebrew very well. But it does suggest something a bit more than his intellectual good will in his relations with the Jews: a taste for the authentic text and literal exactitude, which were at that time sufficiently shared or at least sufficiently valued that they could be put into relief in the course of a brief notice in a chronicle of a completely religious and, as it were, official character.

Guibert of Nogent (†1124), though little inclined to cultivate the first of the four biblical senses for himself, nevertheless possesses some very sound historical principles that he applies to Scripture. Following Saint Jerome[519] and anticipating Father Lagrange, he makes a remark of great importance for the understanding of the sacred Books in their literal level: "But you should know that many things are included in Scripture not as indicating how they are in themselves, but as they are in opinion."[520] Elsewhere he gives many indications of his "critical abilities"; in calling attention to them recently, Abel Lefranc was merely wrong to believe them to be completely exceptional and to conclude from them that Guibert was a precursor of the Reform.[521] Let us add that Book IV of the *De pignoribus sanctorum*, neglected by Lefranc, is a sort of critique of religious consciousness that can serve as an initiation, in all that concerns transcendent realities, to a rational reading of the sacred Books.[522] It is a principle analogous to that of Guibert — a simple echo of a common knowledge, as Bede had seen already — which Honorius applies while commenting on the *Hexaemeron*: "They are called the great luminaries because they seem great to us; in fact, the moon is borne about as the smallest of the heavenly bodies."[523] John of Salisbury shows himself to be an experienced critic in calling attention to a certain "modus loquendi" frequent in the Bible, "such that something that cannot faithfully be understood without some sort of distinction is uttered without qualification."[524] Imitating the enterprise of the great Origen with his own limited equipment, Odo of Cambrai (†1113) recopied the whole Psalter into four columns, in Hebrew, in Greek, in "Roman," and in "Gallic."[525] Hervaeus of Bourg Dieu (†1149 or 1150) practiced, as is well known, the most traditional sort of exegesis; he regrets that Saint Gregory had not finished explicating Ezekiel's last vision, and he undertakes to make up for it in the same spirit; he declares while commenting on Saint Paul that God is with those who "take spiritual solace from the divine Scriptures through the spiritual understanding":[526] he also judges that if the people ordinarily are able to see only the "bare surface of the history," the proper task of priests and doctors is to hunt to "understand the mysteries."[527] Now this same Hervaeus again is himself a true scholar, the author of a remarkable treatise *De correctione quarumdam lectionum*; his intentions, like those of Berno in the preceeding century, are liturgical, but his criticism is more serious.[528] Moreover, monastic opinion was not affrighted by it; on the contrary, it saw matter for praise, as his mortuary roll attests.[529] And these are only a few examples.[530]

A critical work of considerable importance is due to another monk, Saint Stephen Harding. A reformer and legislator,[531] father of those Cistercians who were going to cultivate the most "allegorical" type of exegesis and in all respects the most "subjective" that ever was, Stephen toward 1100 undertakes to revise the whole text of the Vulgate, so that the monks may chant a suitable and uniform text at the divine office.[532] For this work of correction, he does not content himself with bringing together a number of Latin manuscripts; he compares them, for the books of the Old Testament, with the Hebrew and Aramaic originals that he arranged to procure, also getting the assistance of the luminaries among Jewish scholars whom he had gathered at Cîteaux for that very purpose. He began, he explains, by comparing several Latin exemplars amongst themselves, but this elementary method seemed to him quite insufficient:

> We have been not a little disturbed about the discordances of the histories. . . . Hence, marveling much about the discrepancy in our books which we get from one translator,[533] we have approached certain Jewish experts in their Scripture and have most carefully inquired in the Romance language about all those passages of the Scriptures, etc. . . . And they, unrolling their many books in our presence and explaining the Hebrew or Chaldean scripture in our Romance words, scarcely found any parts or verses corresponding to

what we were disturbed about in the passages where we were asking them.... For this reason, trusting in the Hebrew and Chaldean truth and the many Latin books that did not contain those things but did agree in all respects with those two tongues, we utterly scraped away all those superfluities.[534]

We see that for Saint Stephen, even more than for men like Theodulf and Florus long before, the "veritas hebraica" became a tangible reality, and that it required some forcible mutilations. "We utterly scraped away (*prorsus abrasimus*)": the work was finished in 1109. We can see the results in the four handsome codices that came from Cîteaux, which are today in the municipal library of Dijon.[535] This reality remains as a testament of the great, multifaceted intellectual progress of that age, of which Odericus Vitalis had just written: "An unexpected change is coming about in our time, with marvelous subjects being provided for our study."[536] Moreover we do not see any movement of protest or any sign of mistrust in such a project. This was some thirty or forty years before the *Suffraganeus Bibliothecae* or *Libellus de corruptione et correctione* of Nicholas Maniacoria, another Cistercian, who is sometimes presented as the first of the medieval experts in textual criticism. It was prior to the similar but much more limited works of a Gilbert de la Porré (who did not know Greek) and of a Peter Lombard; before the intellectual rumbling most brilliantly signaled by the manifestos of Peter Abelard. It was well before the publication of the *Decretum* of Gratian, which occurred between 1140 and 1150. Following an article by Msgr. Landgraf over thirty years ago,[537] we gladly repeat that the insertion of two texts into this famous *Decretum*, the one from Saint Augustine[538] and the other from Saint Jerome,[539] each drawn from their correspondence, was at the origins of the textual criticism in the Middle Ages.[540] These two texts do not, however, have the exceptional importance that one might be tempted to assign them. Their insertion in the work of Gratian does surely emphasize them; but, aside from the fact that by themselves they were not of such a nature as to reveal a whole new science, the preceding generations were doubtless not unaware of them. The first text, in particular, had already been picked up twice by Yvo of Chartres[541] — and he said nothing that had not also been said with greater detail in the *De doctrina christiana*, which had been universally exploited for centuries.[542] Furthermore, in the years that follow the publication of the *Decretum*, no trace is observed of any new facts that would suffice to mark a sort of birthday for textual criticism. What Msgr. Landgraf has shown very well is merely that in the second part of the twelfth century the two texts of Jerome and Augustine would be, under the influence of Gratian, cited together and brought into accord: a new example of that abundant *Sic et non* literature, which, after having had the texts of Scripture as its object, was, by a natural sequence, applied to the texts of the Fathers of the Church.

The critical work of Nicholas of Maniacoria does not manifest any particular dependence with regard to the two patristic texts inserted into Gratian, and in all likelihood, as we are going to see, it had been begun at least prior to the publication of the *Decretum*. This work is a corrected and annotated edition of the Bible, and, notably, with even greater care, of Saint Jerome's Psalter *juxta Hebraeos*. Its goal and principles were expounded in a "suffragatorium Bibliothecae opusculum": "little work in support of the Library," usually called the *Suffraganeus* for short; the full, exact title is "Libellus de corruptione et correptione psalmorum et quarumdam scripturarum" ["A Little Book on the Corruption and the Plundering of the Psalms and Certain Scriptures"]. The work was soon complemented by an analogous revision of the "Roman" Psalter, furnished with a new explanatory preface, then with the "Gallican" Psalter *(Libellus)*.[543] It is written in the lineage of the work accomplished by Saint Stephen Harding, starting from the same line of investigation as Origen, Jerome, Florus, and many others had practiced before them, and which was to be redone from time to time. In his turn then, Maniacoria remarks the discordances among the copies in use and the arbitrariness of the corrections that each "learned" man too easily permits himself to bring forward "by adding, taking away, and moving things around," thus adding to the corruption already due to the faults of the copyists, making "things utterly corrupt from those merely corrupt."[544] In his turn, he undertakes a methodical reform, restoring passages or words that certain presumptuous characters had suppressed as useless, suppressing the glosses that others had added.[545] A better knowledge of Hebrew lets him take a more personal part than his predecessor in a task for which, like so many others already before him, he in the meantime consults, at least in his writings, a learned rabbi.[546] If one is tempted to despise the text he establishes in this manner "owing to the dissonance of its style," let the despiser know, he says, that "it is much better to say true things in a country accent than to utter false ones eloquently." Less an innovator than one might believe, Maniacoria, "temere definire nil audens": "not daring to define anything temerariously," on the other hand wisely resists hypercriticism. He dismisses simple conjectures; he contents himself with following the Hebrew "littera vel sententia"; he abandons the Latin text

only when the Latin *codices* are in evident disagreement.[547] However —
and this is what above all else interests us — if he devotes himself to a
work of textual criticism that appears to him to be necessary, this does not
at all come about with the thought or hidden motive of instituting a new
type of commentary or of battering down the traditional principles of
Christian exegesis, whose fruit he admires in the arrangements of the liturgy.[548] On this point again, a worthy continuator of Saint Stephen,
Baronius, had indicated the neighborhood of 1144 as the date of his
works; toward the end of the last century, the critics thought that it was
necessary to push the date up by fifty years to after 1200; but Dom
Wilmart then came along to prove that our author, after having been deacon of Saint Laurence in Damaso, lived at the monastery of Tre Fontane
near Rome at the time when Bernard, the future Eugene III, was abbot
there, i.e., between 1140 and 1145; he must have died shortly afterwards.[549] The prejudice against the "pre-critical" ages had doubtless itself
not been entirely devoid of error in criticism. Less isolated, then, and less
modern than has been believed, Nicolas Maniacoria has merely to apply
in his own turn with fine vigor the principle that Sedulius Scotus had formulated regarding the Gospels from as early as the ninth century: "It is a
work of piety to vindicate the words of the Gospel by seeing to it that all
errors have been weeded out."[550] It is testimony for a certain continuity in
critical effort in the Middle Ages. Would that it had pleased heaven that
this continuity should have been extended to more recent periods!

When one says, with A.-D. White, that "Nicolas" corrected the Bible
"in accord with the orthodox faith,"[551] it would be fitting to make it explicit that this was not without a real concern for science, either. When
someone affirms, with Pierre Imbart de la Tour, that Lorenzo Valla was
"the first" who "put his finger on the faults of the Vulgate,"[552] it would be
fitting to fix a bit more closely the starting date from which the history of
criticism is being observed. When one shows, with Mr. Max Haller, "the
Reformers of the sixteenth century" having recourse to the text of the Bible as it was established through the labors of Jewish scholars, one ought
to refrain from adding that, in so doing, they saw themselves in radical
opposition with the Church of the Middle Ages, which was willing to recognize only the Septuagint.[553] But if the scientific effort of the monks that
we have just cited is noteworthy, no less noteworthy is the peaceful atmosphere within which an Odo of Cambrai, a Hervaeus of Bourg Dieu, a
Stephen Harding, a Nicolas Maniacoria are working and publishing the
fruit of their labors. What a difference, what a contrast with the mentality
which was to reign in the theological world at the end of the Middle

Ages, and later on still! "The new translations of the Bible that are being made from Greek or Hebrew into Latin are not useful to the Church, but pernicious . . . , and so in no way to be permitted or tolerated, but rather in every way to be eliminated from the Church through the prelates of the Church": such is the judgment pronounced on Saturday 22 August 1523 as the official conclusion of the doctors of the Sorbonne by the Dean, Boussart.[554] More than a simple mistrust regarding the projects of Lefèvre d'Étaples and of Erasmus, which at that time were directly at issue, it reflects a distrust, indeed a refusal in principle in the face of any serious correction of the "received text." Indeed, when one of the doctors present at the deliberations, the Dominican de Novimagio, expressed the opinion that the text of the New Testament then in use was incorrect and quite far off from the text that Saint Jerome had worked on, the chairman demanded an immediate retraction from him, under threat of a judicial inquest into his own case; seeing this, the minutes of the meeting add, the frightened holder of the opinion backed down, "saying that he did not want to assert it but had said it as a point of discussion, and that he did not want to stick with such a claim."[555]

Already thirty years earlier, when John Reuchlin had published his *De verbo mirifico* (1494), the doctors of Cologne, worthy emulators of those at Paris, had maintained against him that "all Jewish literature ought to be rejected from the field of sacred studies as being harmful."[556] In 1508, having noted that the Latin version of the Gospels was not, as was commonly believed, the work of Saint Jerome, and that, besides, it was often faulty, Guillaume Budé wrote: "I am not unaware that loud cries will be hurled forth everywhere; this translator, who is wrongly believed to be Saint Jerome, enjoys an unshakable influence; the version used with us is considered sacrosanct, and many cry out that one cannot even touch it without committing a sacrilege. For my part, I take Luke's narrative as sacrosanct, the one he has written in Greek; as to our version, I could easily show that in many places it departs from the original text, but would our readers even be capable of hearing the truth?"[557] In 1511, while editing the Epistles of Saint Paul, Jacques Lefèvre d'Étaples clashed in a similar manner with the prejudices of the learned; desiring to supply the Latin text with a few corrections, he began by convincing himself and by declaring that Saint Jerome was not their author, so scandalous would it have appeared to dare to touch a translation attributed to a Father of the Church. A Maniacoria, fully aware of his own audacity, and indeed suspecting that it would frighten the timid, nevertheless had no need to resort to any such precaution.[558]

A LINEAGE STEMMING FROM JEROME?

In 1514, Martin Van Dorp, mouthpiece of the theologians of Louvain, wrote to Erasmus, who had been permitted to touch up the Vulgate as well in his recent edition of the New Testament: "It is inadmissible to think that the Catholic Church had erred for so many centuries, she who has always made use of this text and approves it and uses it still today; and it is not likely that so many holy Fathers and so many accomplished men should have been deceived."[559] A bit later, in 1525, in a violent book, *De tralatione Bibliae et novarum reprobatione interpretationum*, the Carthusian Pierre Couturier (Petrus Sutor), coming to the rescue, explained that "the knowledge of Greek or Hebrew is not more useful for studying the Bible that that of Italian or Spanish"; wanting to translate the holy Books anew was to undertake a "vain, impious, temerarious, and scandalous" work; to pretend to amend the Vulgate was an "abomination," it was "to blaspheme against Saint Jerome and against the Holy Spirit who had inspired him"; even simply to call attention to the faults of a copyist was "to insult God": indeed, if the least part of the Bible were suspected of falsification, the whole Bible became entirely suspect: "madness worthy of blows rather than reasonable objections, meriting the whip rather than discussion"![560] On 30 April 1530, there came a new intervention from the Sorbonne, which censured as "temerarious, scandalous, and rendering its authors strongly suspect of Lutheranism" the following proposition: "Holy Scripture cannot be well understood without the Greek, Hebrew, and other like languages." The censure can take on an acceptable strict interpretation when put in these terms; in fact, however, it was aimed at the teaching by the first "royal lecturers" of Greek and Hebrew, and three years later, in 1533, the public announcement of their courses provokes a response from these censors of ours, who called on royal justice for immediate prosecutions.[561] A very well informed personage, Jerome Alexander, then Apostolic Nuncio at the court of Charles V, remarked in 1531 in a letter to Sanga, the secretary of Clement VII, that if Lefèvre had been accused of such grave errors, it was in fact because the pretension "of changing the least syllable and even of establishing an alternate textual reading owing to the fault of copyists in the ancient version then in use within the Church" was regarded as "unheard of."[562] Notwithstanding the much broader encouraging and even stimulating attitude adopted by the majority of the Roman Pontiffs,[563] this opposition, headed by the great university centers, could endure. When Luiz of Leon along with two of his colleagues from Salamanca would want to have recourse to the Hebrew text of the Bible and would modestly maintain that it is permitted to bring up certain original interpretations without contradicting those of the "saints," he would seem to have been hauled up before the Spanish Inquisition as a rebel against the decisions of the Council of Trent.[564] Though there have always been the "envious" around so as to treat every critical effort as "periculosa praesumptio,"[565] how much more liberal and less superstitious were the Middle Ages before their decline! There are still so many strange ideas in circulation about the Middle Ages!

Harding and Maniacoria are two Cistercian monks. Across their whole century, far from being the refuge for intellectual routine that other environments had just begun to shake off, the Cistercian school offers, from various standpoints, the spectacle of intense ferment. An authentic and powerful spiritual life is brilliantly manifest in the prodigious progress of the Order, as well as in the writings of its most eminent members. Now such a life cannot easily be accommodated to monastic routine; there are sacrifices that require separation from the world and the abandonment of "curiosity" — for life is indivisible. No more than other human beings are monks always intellectuals, but mediocrity and habitual lack of fervor among those who are dedicated to intellectual tasks would nonetheless be a sign of a mediocrity, of a lack of zeal for the monastic life itself. Turned away as they are by vocation from the "scientia saecularis" in all the ambitions and worldly rewards that it involves, their pursuit of the truth is all the purer for it, even in humanistic and scientific matters. Indeed, what fruitful advances are due to these "white monks"! Some have wanted to see indications of a mistrust of culture in two decrees issued by the chapters of the Order. A decree of 1137 forbids composing books without the authorization of the general chapter; another, from 1198, condemns the practice of producing "rhythms." But the first, which has its analogue in other religious orders and which is to be found routinely in the canonical texts, is merely a call back to the good order of obedience.[566] As to the second, it aimed at a kind of rather loose poetry, whose trendiness was invading the cloisters, and concerning which one might well, along with Hauréau, be surprised that it had been tolerated for so long.[567] Furthermore, some take into account another decree of 1198 concerning the case of a certain monk who took Hebrew lessons from a Jew without permission: the chapter of Catalonia entrusted the inquiry to the abbot of Clairvaux.[568] Concerning this affair of extremely small moment, reported from time to time inexactly, some have been ready to conclude that all serious study of Scripture had been forbidden within the Order. The incident would rather prove, it seems to me, something quite different: not the rigidity of alleged principles of know-nothing-ism[569] but, on the contrary, a zeal that might need to be regulated or channeled in conformity with the spirit of the Order. Harding and Maniacordia were not monks going out of bounds! At the very end of the century, Hebrew was held in honor within the order of Cîteaux. Garnier de Rochefort, who was abbot of Clairvaux, in the course of a sermon lays out the corrections that the Hebrew suggests to him to explain his text more precisely.[570] Another Cistercian abbot, Helinand of Froidmont, introduces learned parentheses into his preaching, reconstituting the Hebrew text to obtain a better sense, calling to witness some "experts from among the Hebrews," etc.[571]

Some have a tendency today to minimize the role of the monastic centers in what is called, perhaps equivocally or by too strictly delimiting its scope, the 'renaissance of the twelfth century'.[572] In particular, the Cistercians, owing to old-fashioned ideas that had governed at their foundation, and then under the determining influence of Saint Bernard, would remain outside the intellectual currents of the epoch. Did not one good historian recently go so far as to hold that Saint Bernard "had no real culture" — the very Saint Bernard who provoked the admiration of Petrarch?[573] In the meantime, whatever one thinks of the controversies in which he was engaged, or of the passion that he displayed, one must recognize that, in terms of his positive contribution, this great man is not only a "spiritual author" and a "monastic theologian": he is, in the most universal sense of the words, one of the great writers of universal literature and one of the great theologians of the Catholic tradition.[574] It is one of his spiritual sons, who became pope under the name Eugene III, who induced Burgundio of Pisa to translate Saint John Damascene and Saint John Chrysostom into Latin.[575] It is his intimate friend who, like himself, had become a Cistercian, William of Saint Thierry, who extols "the light of the east,"[576] and if under this expression he had nothing else directly in mind than the teachings of the ancient oriental monks, we also know all that his thought owes to the Greek Fathers, principally to the most philosophical among them, Saint Gregory of Nyssa, and what a principle of further thought could discover in him. The Cistercian libraries are generally well provided; one might say of them what Guibert of Nogent observed concerning those of the Chartreux, whose great priors are also craftsmen of this renaissance:

> Though they subjected themselves to all manner of poverty, they nevertheless collected an extremely rich library: for the less they overflow with abundance of this material bread, so much the more

do they laboriously sweat for the one that does not perish but lasts forever.[577]

In these libraries, the works of the Fathers abound, and masterpieces of classical antiquity are not wanting. It is at Clairvaux, for example, that the works of Tertullian and Eusebius of Emessa, missing elsewhere it seems at this period, are to be found.[578] John Scotus and Pseudo-Dionysius, whose boldness disquieted the minds of many outside, nourish the thought of an Isaac of Stella, of a Garnier of Rochefort, and a Helinand of Froidmont; that of an Alan of Lille as well, who died himself converted to Cîteaux in 1202, just like that of an Honorius or a Hugh or a Richard of Saint Victor, and once again it is a Cistercian, Alberic of Three Fountains (†1241), who, in 1225, will defend the cause of John Scotus, after the condemnation by Honorius IIII.[579] Isaac of Stella is one of the deepest metaphysicians of his age, just as Aelred of Rievaulx is one of its most sensitive humanists. The greatest historian of this century so impassioned with history is once again a Cistercian, Otto of Freising, and the *City of God* was without a doubt never so much read and meditated upon (and not without careful adaptation to the new situations that might appear as so many inflections)[580] as it was in the Cistercian cloisters of that time. Alcher of Clairvaux, who keeps in regular contact with Isaac, is not only an eclectic philosopher; he is a respected expert in natural history and in anatomy.[581] Helinand of Froidmont, a poet with "a very beautiful mind," takes his artistic imagination for a walk "amidst the graces of pagan literature" as well as among "the splendors of the Bible"; he frequently gives evidence of a refined taste or of a felicitous imagination, as well as of truly critical thought,[582] without departing from the rigorous idea of his Order;[583] his sermons are full of spontaneous strokes that break with the conventionality wherein Latin preaching was then getting bogged down; his *Vers de la Mort (Verses on Death)*, in the French language (ca. 1195), are a masterpiece, a model both in substance and in form.[584] Thomas the Cistercian, who does not have the creative genius of Helinand, like him does have an admirable knowledge of the ancient poets, and offers many citations of them in his own work; by a bold transposition of three kinds of disciplines recognized traditionally in the three principal works attributed to Solomon, he lays down a threefold epithalamion: between the "historical" epithalamion and the "theological" epithalamion, he makes room for the "philosophical" epithalamion or the "conjunction of the eloquence of the *trivium* with the wisdom of the *quadrivium*," which can be understood as the union of the literary and scientific disciplines, all summoned to come together in the free development of their respective methods into a spiritual synthesis.585 The "urban intellectuals" are therefore not the only ones at this moment to keep up or to renew the life of the mind. So much for "the mystics of forest and desert" producing nothing except "mirages."586 Nicolas Maniacoria does not seem like an isolated phenomenon any more with regard to his religious milieu than with regard to what was happening in biblical studies.

These facts and others like them are perfectly well known by the scholars one or another of whose assertions we have had the chance to discuss. Only, by exalting certain authors who did not always have such fine qualifications in science, they sometimes might appear to forget. For our part, we would not want to push too far. But perhaps, too, we are insufficiently cognizant that where the means of acquiring science are missing and even just of imagining with some precision what it might be, nevertheless esteem for science can exist, calling for approaches whose results can be disappointing, but whose momentum is admirable and will ultimately prove fruitful. In the centuries of the high Middle Ages, where it was difficult for a true expert in biblical matters to develop, many had nevertheless nourished a most fervent, albeit naive or clumsy, esteem for science. The majority, however, experts or not, shared in one and the same idea of Scripture, which was in their eyes consubstantial with their faith.

We shall end this chapter with two further examples, taken this time within the first generation of the Carolingian renaissance: those of Smaragdus and of Alcuin.

Smaragdus is abbot of Saint Mihiel in the first years of the ninth century (†c. 820). His *Collectiones in epistolas et evangelia* are scarcely more than a *catena,* and in addition, in this work he has neither a point nor scientific pretension. Quite simply, he is gathering "the flowers from the allegories," so as to extract from them "a deifying and vivifying drink for the soul."587 Now he nevertheless appreciates from among the ancient commentaries on the Pauline Epistles the learned commentary of Pelagius, whom he cites under the name Jerome, but whom he, like Sedulius Scotus, has read in a pure text, free of interpolation.588 Besides, for his own private use, he sprinkles his text with more Greek and Hebrew than all our "precursors" together, and they are not merely scattered words, but sometimes whole lines. He controls his Latin translation on the basis of the Septuagint; he proposes two Latin words to render a Greek word more fully; on another occasion he provides up to four Greek words to explain the various nuances of a Latin word.589 To be sure, in large measure all this is taken from his authors, among others, from Saint Jerome. At least he does not disregard him. He thus shows not only a vast reading but also a vigilant philological interest, and we are quite ready to admire such an intelligent curiosity in this monk with such solid spirituality sketching out his meditative canvas for the course of the liturgical year. Smaragdus, as has been recollected above, is a grammarian, that is to say, a man of letters; he does not absolutely mistrust the scientific disciplines; he approves and practices as much as he can the behavior of the ancient Israelites, carrying off with them the spoils of Egypt; a reforming monk with bold ideas, open to the intellectual problems as well as to the social problems of his time,[590] he counts as one of the principal restorers of studies and of culture in the West. Still, no more than Alvarus of Cordova or Berno of Reichenau does he want the tyranny of Donatus the grammarian over the sacred domain of Scripture. But in exegesis, if his goal is allegory, he distinguishes it very well from the history, as well as Paschasius and indeed everyone did.[591] Finally, again like Paschasius or Rabanus, he interprets prophecy very reasonably: he does not proceed immediately to its ultimate signification so readily that he cannot often recognize a primary, more proximate sense, a bearer of the *truth of the history*.[592]

The example of Smaragdus was taken among the most humble instances. If one wanted to meet with a genius of more stature in the same ninth century, who was a real precursor of textual criticism or literal exegesis, why would one not hang on to the name of Alcuin, who was truly "the head of the intellectual movement of his epoch,"[593] rather than that of the mediocre Christian of Stavelot?

One of Alcuin's works is a collection of *280 Interrogationes* on Genesis, etc., which deal only with the historical sense. He himself says of it: "they are mostly histories"; and again, after having by way of exception called attention to a spiritual sense that should allow an answer to a difficulty: "but even this response is found with historical propriety." For the entire history of Lot he does not offer a single allegorical feature.[594] If he had never composed anything except this work, would he still be regarded as one of the ancestors of modern exegesis? Like the majority in his time, he knew little Greek; he is at least curious about it, he got some instruction in it with certain Scots, he culled the elements that he found of it in the explications of the Fathers, in liturgical Psalters, or with the old grammarians,[595] and he uses it on occasion, not without some relevance, as one of his letters to Angelbert (addressed by his classical nickname, "Homer") shows.[596] He knows still less Hebrew; more than once, however, like everyone, he alludes to the Hebrew manuscripts, to the "Hebraic truth," or

A LINEAGE STEMMING FROM JEROME?

to the "Hebraic traditions."[597] His writings contain more than one critical remark.[598] To be sure, he too has recourse to the one whom he calls "Father Jerome"[599] and whose praise, as we have seen, he loves to utter. He seriously works hard at imitating him, and sometimes "not without luck" he is successful at it.[600] He declares that he is above all helping himself to Jerome to comment on *Ecclesiastes*.[601] He follows him for the Epistles to Titus and to Philemon as well. Following his example and like his compatriot Aldhelm, he mistrusts the apocrypha, those writings of unknown authors, full of frivolities and blunders.[602] It was he who was charged by Joseph Scotus to make an abridgment of Jerome's commentary on Isaiah, and to this end he recommended that he set aside "the uncertain and confused traces of both the Septuagint and other translators and commentators."[603] As Paschasius did for the Lamentations and as Smaragdus did for the Psalms, he lays down from the start that the prophecy of the blessing of Jacob, announcing "the things that are to come in the final days," nevertheless bears a twofold meaning, historical to start with, and then merely allegorical: "the history of the land of promise, portions of which were to be divided for their descendants; again, the allegory, about Christ and the Church, what is to be in the last times."[604] But if it is necessary to admire Christian of Stavelot for having wanted to put "the foundation of the history" in first place, there is no less reason to admire Alcuin, who, before him, says again in another passage: "But the foundations of the history are to be laid down first, so that the gable of the allegory may be more fittingly laid upon the prior structure."[605] Moreover, we know that the one did not have to copy the other and that neither of them had to discover for himself that old metaphor of Origen, which Jerome and Gregory, once again at one, and in company with Augustine and Isidore, offered them. The selfsame Alcuin, so sensitive to the "sweetness of understanding holy Scripture,"[606] nonetheless also says, regarding the allegorical explication of one text: "Though the mystery of Christ is great, still according to the letter it signifies, etc."[607] Would this not be the place to remark, as we have of another exegete, that, exactly in granting a "concession" to the allegorism of the time, he lets a clear tendency to "literalism" be seen? But in reality, the comment would be no more valid for the one than for the other.

In this great man we feel everywhere, aside from "a sort of pedagogical genius and the gift of grasping the needs of his own time,"[608] the most characteristic traits of the Carolingian renaissance: "joyful intoxication with knowledge, extraordinary confidence in the eternal wisdom, desire to renew, after the centuries of barbarism, the relations between the

Greek miracle and Christian civilization."[609] There is "a moving grandeur" in his efforts "to raise himself once again to the heights attempted by Augustine and Boethius."[610] Whatever may result from it, one cannot without injustice say that with him we are always "at most at the level of primary education." In his earliest youth he had accompanied his master Aelbert, who was traveling, "led by the love of wisdom," to Italy, everywhere inquiring:

> If he might find in those lands any new
> Book or study that he might take with him.[611]

This eagerness of mind, this craving for culture, was his. In him such dispositions are naturally allied with a beautiful spiritual elevation.[612] Alcuin did not turn only to the Latins, but also to the Greeks. At the side of his emperor-disciple he then dreamed of a marvelous Paris, of a learned and evangelical Paris, founded upon their common work. The seven arts would flourish there. It would be a new Athens,"but our Athens would be more beautiful than the ancient one, having been endowed also with the septiform fullness of the Spirit."[613] Some have denigrated this resolution; some have scoffed at the cheeky naïveté of this half-barbarian, who bravely used to compare the Paris of his own epoch to the city of Minerva.[614] That is because they were misreading it, confusing his resolution with the admiring judgment conveyed about his work after his death by the Chronicle of Saint Gall,[615] or following later and less measured formulations of like mind. Besides, howsoever bold it was, has his dream not been realized in some degree?

But these vast conceptions did not entirely occupy him. He knew how to set his hand to the most modest and most precise jobs, which require long, methodical effort. Alcuin, as is well known, is the author or at least the animator of a revision of the text of the Latin Bible then in use. That was a considerable undertaking. Charlemagne, the enemy of "uncorrected books," had wanted it right away.[616] He had entrusted the execution of this task to his minister.[617] Indeed Alcuin's high culture singled him out to carry the task through successfully. He devoted several years to it. In the collective effort that he organized, his part was preponderant. He used many manuscripts gathered from England and the continent, to end in a text of decisive influence.

Doubtless the way had been paved or at least the trail was blazed for the new Bible by the Bible of Maurdramnus, executed at Corbie prior to 778, and by still other attempts undertaken at Saint Germain, at Metz, and Saint Gall; and the analogous effort of Theodulf at Orléans is not to be forgotten. Doubtless, too, the idea that led to its completion was aesthetic, liturgical,[618] and political as much as (and even more than) scientific. To start with, there was no question of making a strict recension of all the manuscripts, but only of cleaning up the received text, correcting its spelling, and eliminating inconsistencies. Nevertheless the fact remains that the work undertaken did turn out to be a veritable recension, whose scientific value is by no means negligible. Charlemagne wanted in all things correctness of language, of script, and of thought. He wanted unity of faith and of worship throughout his domains. Alcuin seconded him in this plan, which he deepened. Remarkable from every point of view, the "Bibliotheca" that a messenger solemnly came to offer to his master at the palace of Aix-la-Chapelle, on the first anniversary of the Christmas coronation, is a beautiful volume, well copied, well spelled, well illustrated, well bound, and, in addition, containing a much improved text. This was the prototype exemplar which, starting from the workshop of Tours, was reproduced everywhere in western Europe. As for the books which Saint Jerome had revised, it contributed to the final triumph of the "Vulgate" over the other Latin versions.[619] This text of Alcuin's, let us remark in passing, is that which Christian of Stavelot will soon follow.[620] Though soon altered by the copyists at Tours themselves, it will exercise a sort of dictatorship during the whole Middle Ages. In the thirteenth century the Bible of the University of Paris will reproduce it still, but "amended, interpolated, and, finally, corrupted."[621]

If the epithet "exceptional" were applied to a work of this epoch, it would perhaps be to this one. The term might be a bit too strong, however. With Father Spicq, we recognize merely that, in spite of unavoidable faults, such a work was valuable. It is true that the *Interpretations of Hebrew Names* made by Alcuin are "often fantastic"; that his *Questions and Answers* constitute merely a recapitulation of "a very old formula" and are "pure compilation"; that if he gives a literal sense to Ecclesiastes, this is because he found this sense "elaborated in his source stemming from Jerome."[622] This judgment is exactly on the mark.[623] In every respect, Alcuin's knowledge is strictly circumscribed. In none is it creative. But what would be left of a Christian of Stavelot or a Berno of Reichenau, if the same yardstick were applied to them?

CHAPTER FOUR

Hugh of Saint Victor

1. Warnings to the *Litterati*

Hugh of Saint Victor is generally regarded as the principal figure in the constitution of the new exegesis. Indeed his work is of major importance. Yet we do not believe that the significance attributed to it entirely corresponds to the reality. That is what the present chapter aims to establish.

All the historians repeat the same thing: for Hugh, the principle of sacred doctrine, its foundation, is history. Samuel Berger was already writing in 1879: "He makes history the foundation of the three-fold sense."[1] Surely nothing is more evident. But in expressing himself in this way, Samuel Berger thought he was defining the characteristic originality of the Victorine. This means to close his eyes to another piece of evidence, namely, that no principle was more traditional. Hugh himself emphasizes this fact: the matter is still beyond dispute. For a theoretician who expounds the methods of work and of teaching at leisure in a didactic work, these issues may seem naturally, even necessarily, out of place or at least unexpected in other genres of writing. Thus, in days gone by, while composing a work *De artibus ac disciplinis liberalium litterarum,* Cassiodorus had emphasized the fundamental need for grammar: "The first item to be discussed is grammar, which is the source and foundation of independent literature."[2] Grammar, the foundation of literary studies; history, the foundation of biblical studies: many have recognized such principles and have been compelled, more or less happily, to apply them, without ever having had to make an explicit profession out of them. But what is more, in our subject, we have seen that the very word "foundation" to designate the history is trite. Father Mignon[3] and Father Spicq[4] have rightly recollected that it came from Saint Jerome. Jerome himself had gotten it from Origen and, ever since, it had been repeated as a commonplace. How could the author of the *Didascalicon* have avoided taking it up again?

We shall therefore rather say, with Father Chenu, whose opinion here too is carefully nuanced, that Hugh has merely conferred "a conscious methodological force" to this traditional theme.[5] He has done so to the very extent that he has done methodological work; and this is by no means negligible. Nevertheless, that he had intended thereby to substitute one method for another is a matter that appears rather less certain. Like any superior mind, Hugh stands a cut above the majority of his contemporaries. In this sense he was a restorer both of exegesis and of theology. Does this mean that while claiming "the primary necessity of the 'foundation'" he has conducted a "great, not merely exegetical, but also theological action"?[6] We shall have to retain something of this sort of judgment. Nevertheless, the operation was not to consist either in a very noticeable scientific advance, nor particularly in the abandonment of the ancient heritage. Hugh had rather reemphasized that heritage as much as he could. Both his deliberate thought and his actual practice are in large part quite simply traditional. Such is the conclusion that an attentive reading of his writings seems to require, and especially of those great methodological texts, the *Didascalicon* and the *De scripturis et scriptoribus sacris*.[7]

Hugh, according to one writer, "literally revolts against the pretension of certain allegorists who want to jump over the literal sense and see nothing but the figurative one."[8] Once again, there is nothing truer. Against these too hurried allegorists, the theoretician of Saint Victor, usually so calm, reacts vigorously. He does so on two occasions: in the fifth chapter of the *De scripturis* and the sixth book of the *Didascalicon*. The characterizations that he fires off at them are harsh:

> Since, then, the mystical understanding may only be gathered from what the letter proposes in the first place, I am amazed at the effrontery which some teachers of allegories display, particularly those who are still ignorant of the very first signification of the literal level.[9]
>
> I know that there are some who want to philosophize right away; they say that fables are to be left to false apostles. Their "knowledge" is asinine. Do not imitate such people.[10]

In the *De scripturis* he institutes a whole dialogue with these people. When we read Scripture, they say, we do not care about the letter, we are teaching the allegory. How, he asks them then, can you read Scripture without reading its literal level? Without that letter, what is left of it? He leads them to explain their thought a bit at a time, so as finally to show them the absurdity of it, and the questions that he opposes to their solicitations are a means for him to explain his own thought. He always keeps coming back to say: "So read the Scripture, and first off study carefully what it says corporeally."[11] Is there any sign of a decisive turn in exegesis in this? By such a manifesto is Hugh creating "a new period," that of "the scientific study" of the Bible?[12] That would doubtless be saying a lot. If our author shows any outburst of temper, it is because there were certain abuses around him, either particularly serious or particularly irritating. What exactly were they? That is not easy to determine. Perhaps the adversaries targeted in the *De scripturis* are not exactly the same as those in the *Didascalicon*. In the first case, one could take them to be merely slightly blustery intellectual light-weights too much in a rush to allegorize without the necessary preparation, and who confuse the spiritual sense of the history with verbal allegory. Such a practice is doubly erroneous, but above all it is ridiculous: it robs all importance from the exegesis of those who surrender themselves to it. Hugh does not treat these callow scatter-brains as masters of error: he is content to lower their pretensions; he merely warns them that with such lack of method, they will never arrive at real understanding; they want to "leap": it is a perilous leap; they will fall flat on their back.[13] In the second case, the same warnings are given, the same advice about sound conduct:

> Once you've got the small things down you can safely try the big ones.[14]

However, one can divine something more. These people who want to "philosophize" immediately, who pretend to have "science," who treat the common explanations as "fables" and whom Hugh in return calls "block-heads" and against whom he puts his disciple on guard, could hardly be, as some assure us, pious allegorizers, impervious to progress, stuck in their harmless ruts. These folks are perhaps even further off than those of the *De scripturis*. The latter did not get as far as understanding: the former positively fall into error, or at least seriously risk doing so. In criticizing both sides, Hugh is not shaking off a deep-rooted neglect; he is not trying to pull his age from a long dogmatic slumber: he is blocking the route to certain ambitious youths whose arrogance he judges severely. He does not forget the first mistake, which is found at all times: thoughtless precipitation; but the second, which aggravates the first, is proper to the new generation, or at least it is raging there more and more. This is what increases his apprehension. Besides, Hugh will have been able to observe these mistakes in the same individuals, whatever slight difference of tone we thought we discerned between the *De scripturis* and the *Didascalicon*.[15] Against the one mistake and the other, Hugh recalls the traditional doctrine with his customary balance, using the old metaphor of a building and its foundation.[16] Then, toward the end, he turns more specifically towards the "philosophers." He wanted to warn them against the presumption of the autodidact or the self-sufficiency of the intellectual, who run the risk of misleading them. Instead of pretending to judge right away by themselves, as only the saints can do, let them begin by relying on the "universal faith." Let them give up that intemperance which keeps them from stopping their quest in time and from humbly venerating the mystery. Let them agree to allow themselves to be instructed and formed; let them not imagine that they can get into sacred science all by themselves, but let them ask for enlightenment from those who are capable of initiating them into the knowledge of the holy Fathers and of Scripture itself.[17] Then, changing the application of the metaphor that he just developed, Hugh declares to them that at this cost alone will they have a chance to build on "the foundation of the truth"; only in this way will they be able "to build as it were a basis of unshakable truth on which the whole building rests." Otherwise, they will constantly disagree in their exegesis, incapable of settled understanding, condemned to fall into one error after another.[18]

Finally, it is less under the rubric of a scientific exigency, as can be seen, than under a religious one that Hugh of Saint Victor institutes his critique. One final detail confirms this again. Those mistaken exegetes seem so dangerous to him and so irritate him that he cannot keep himself from firing off a new, more stinging arrow. This occurs at the end of a paragraph in which he has just explained that, if allegory ought to be preceded by the letter, nevertheless the letter is not enough. The word *littera* then, in his writing, recalls the word *litteratus*. But in the context, the latter term signifies something more and other than a friend of the letter alone, hanging on to "the letter which killeth," as in Hervaeus of Bourg Dieu for example,[19] or like the word *litterator* in someone like Saint Bernard speaking of "the Jewish litterateurs,"[20] in the Abelardian commentary on the Epistle to the Romans,[21] or, a bit later on, in a Herbert of

Bosham.[22] It is not the simple correlative of "litteratura Judaeorum" about which Saint Augustine had spoken[23] and which the twelfth century used to know as well.[24] Here it no longer has the eulogistic meaning that generally belonged to it in language settled long ago;[25] a meaning that it would soon have again in Arnoul of Lisieux enticing after him "cultivated, honorable men,"[26] in Luke of Leon recounting his master Saint Martin's healing of a certain Peter, a "rather cultivated and honorable man,"[27] in Geoffrey of Auxerre pointing to Saint Bernard as "a cultivated man even in scholarly circles,"[28] or in John of Salisbury speaking of "the more educated and better sort of men."[29] Richard of Saint Victor will marvel in the same way at the scholarly Saint Jerome "being literate in three languages,"[30] and Peter Cellensis will see "experience in literature" as an attribute essential to the cleric.[31] Saint Bernard himself recognizes all the advantage that the Church gets from her "litterati."[32] Hugh of Fleury gives "literary skill" a completely eulogistic meaning,[33] whilst Abelard[34] and Peter the Venerable[35] admire the "litteratoria scientia," the "doctrina litteratoria," the "litteratoria disciplina" to be found in Heloïse. Taking this as the common usage, Hugh wants to mark a contrast here. To be sure he is far from despising the "litteratus"; he would not at all be opposed to so many biographies of holy monks or holy bishops praising their heroes for having been "quite, fittingly, very, appropriately, conspicuously, marvelously literate,"[36] "vir sanctus litteratusque," "divinis humanisque litteris imbutus," etc. But as to sacred matter, just as William of Saint Thierry at about the same period puts "litteratura" in its place,[37] Hugh does the same for "litteratus." By this word he designates precisely the one whom he said wanted to "philosophize" too soon and to rise too quickly beyond the letter. In other words, the "litteratus" is in his eyes someone who despises both the lowly letter and traditional allegory. To this innovator Hugh replies: "It is not the grammarian but the spiritual person that judges all things."[38] The "science" of Scripture is a spiritual science. And this whole long chapter of the *Didascalicon* finally seems like an advocate's plea for the spirit and for tradition, indissolubly united.

There is therefore, it seems, in the aggressive stroke launched by Hugh, a bit more than the commonplace recently uttered once again by Othloh of Saint Emmeran: "He who is intent upon secular literature cannot grasp the mysteries of sacred Scripture."[39] A sort of paradoxical kinship has subtly been established, by a sort of play on words, between the reader of the Bible who, like the Jew or the "Judaizer," is attached to the letter alone — to the "letter that killeth" — and the doctor, too sure of it, who embarks on risky speculations in the opposite direction by immediately philosophizing on the text. Both sides are unfaithful to the Christian interpretation of Scriptures. They are far from its spirit as well. The *litteratus*, the lettered, the educated, cultivated man, just like the *litterator*, the school master and, by extension, the scholar — but the two words have become nearly synonymous — is here contrasted to the *spiritualis* and to the *ecclesiasticus*. Hugh is not, however, the first to have emphasized this. Though a bit less explicit, the contrast could already be read in a text of Saint Jerome,[40] and the commentary on the first Gospel falsely attributed to the Venerable Bede used to say of the scribe who did not understand the call of Jesus: "He was a literalist, and not a spiritual hearer."[41] The same turn of phrase, in service of the same idea, is found half a century before Hugh as well, in the writing of a man of the Church quite different in temperament, Saint Peter Damian. Criticizing those who misuse dialectic and philosophy to explicate matters of faith, Peter Damian wrote:

> Hence, let it be enough for us to defend the faith with the brief summary that we hold; but we grant to the wise of this world the things that are their own. Let those who want it have the letter that killeth; whilst, through God's mercy, the life-giving Spirit does not depart from us.[42]

More recently again, Rupert says in analogous manner that in many passages of Scripture, whoever has eyes to see "beholds the jewel of spiritual understanding above the cheap literal level."[43] And in the following generation Philip of Harvengt will say, addressing his disciple: "I want you to be educated not so much in the letter as in the spirit."[44]

The moralists will naturally continue, as they did for a long time, to warn the "litteratus" to be on guard against pride,[45] or to remind him that to be lettered is one thing, to be "wise,"[46] another. The men of the Church also sometimes had to remind him that his title does not confer on him privileges in the order of ecclesiastical discipline.[47] Toward the end of the century, the Carthusian author of the *Life* of Adam Scot will again speak of "litteratura" as the "litteralis intelligentiae scientia" and he will oppose the "litteralis eruditio" to the "theoricae disciplinae," i.e., contemplation.[48] In each of these cases, however, this will occur without giving any pejorative connotation to this term, and the particular meaning that Hugh gives in passing to "litteratus" will not continue, even within the precise context which was that of the *Didascalicon*. The "lettered and wise" will be invited along with the "little and humble folk," by Godfrey of Admont to the same school of the Holy Spirit.⁴⁹ Hugh himself, putting himself at another point of view in the *De arca Noe morali,* is indignant at certain "litterati" who say they are Christians while they are thinking more of the gods and of pagan authors than of Christ and his saints.⁵⁰ The text of the *Didascalicon* accordingly looks almost like a *hapax legomenon.* It is merely the more instructive.

But for the moment let us abstract from this new aspect of the controversy, which shows still better that Hugh is just the opposite of an innovator. In the generality of his critique as well as in the counsels he offers and the doctrine he expounds, moreover, he is by no means the first to say it when he writes: "He advances most rightly who advances in order";⁵¹ he coins an almost Cartesian maxim, but one whose pedagogical intention was that of a number of others before him: such as Saint Hilary, amongst the ancients;⁵² such as Seigfrid, in the previous century, the abbot of Tegernsee, who reminded an excessively "supernaturalistic" correspondent: "one does not arrive at higher things unless one ascends through the lower levels; nor does a wall stand firm above ground unless it be supported from below by a firm-footed foundation";⁵³ such as Othloh of Saint Emmeran, who used an analogous metaphor borrowed from the art of building;⁵⁴ such as Guibert of Nogent: "For unless you patiently get to know the letter, you will struggle in vain in trying to search out the allegory or the morality."⁵⁵ As for the warning of the need to take account of the traditional interpretations, it is clear that it was neither novel,⁵⁶ nor, in that century, unusual.⁵⁷ The same goes for the more precise counsel first to have to listen modestly to the "lectores divinitatis" or the "magistros in Scripturis," instead of pretending to discover everything for oneself. Saint Augustine had given it more than once, whether in the *De utilitate credendi,*⁵⁸ or in the *De doctrina christiana:*⁵⁹ neither intellectual gifts nor any pretended infused knowledge provides a dispensation from such an apprenticeship. Saint Gregory had said it again.⁶⁰ In the school and in the cloister, one said it again and again. Did not Abelard tell us that he was reproached "because I had presumed to accede to teaching the divine reading without a teacher"?⁶¹ And soon Philip of Harvengt will shoot the shafts of his irony upon those men who "since they seem to themselves, in their little way, to be sharp at understanding, and are perhaps, in their little way, ready to speak, they disdain to subject themselves to learn from their betters, and, impatient with the nest, they fly off to dissertate before they have even started to grow feathers."⁶² In the same way again, well before Hugh, others had reacted in like fashion to the misuses of allegorism. They had done it sometimes in the very same terms. In his pleading on behalf of the history, Hugh develops the comparison of the body, through which he must necessarily pass in order to attain the spirit, and he follows out the comparison by alluding to the flesh and the divinity of the Savior.[63] These comparisons are as traditional as the metaphor of the foundation. Thus already in the eighth century, for example, after having recalled that the spirit of the Scripture is in its letter as the soul is in the body, the two Spaniards, Heterius and Beatus, hasten to add that no one can penetrate right up to that spirit, if he does not first consider the letter;[64] they charge with homicide those who outrageously neglect the body, namely, the letter of the holy Books, by wanting too quickly to be interested in the soul;[65] they compare such men to the Circumcellions, those African heretics who, through an unregulated love of martyrdom, went so far as to kill themselves.[66] Thus from century to century, ever since the distant time of Origen, one still speaks of the humility of the Word of God hiding or filtering his own divinity, which the gaze of our mind would not be able to stand, within the reality of his flesh.[67]

Hugh of Saint Victor is a methodical, studious mind. He readily splits up the operations of the understanding. He wants us to proceed step by step: to study the signs first, before trying to find out what they signify. He cannot stand imprudent acrobatics at the edge of a cliff. He is ever a wise, modest, essentially well-balanced mind, as a canon of Saint-Augustine ought to be.[68] In exegesis as in everything else, he loves that "discretion" which Saint Gregory admired above all in the Benedictine Rule,[69] that "temperance" which Peter Cellensis calls "the queen of the virtues."[70] He knows that one does not acquire wisdom by throwing himself unprepared upon every object of knowledge or by mixing up the disciplines, but by observing "due measure."[71] He recommends measure everywhere, the "temperatum exercitium": "If virtue has not measure, it is turned into vice."[72] His entire work is a search for balance.[73] He does not like us to wolf down solid food before having chewed it well. He does not like the bow to be stretched too far.[74] He has no taste for excess in any direction; he wants one to be "subtle," but not "temerarious." Thus, along with haste, which prevents good assimilation, he criticizes intemperance in the use of allegory. Only his measure is not our measure. And in his thought this twofold failure does not always depend only upon neglecting the letter: it seems still more dreadful to him when it leads to neglecting the moral dimension. Now it is not only this particular abuse that one can call by the name allegorism, but also the abuse that constitutes every biblical study guided by excessively speculative methods; today we would say: every *theology*, whatever its method exactly may be, which intends to be a mere study undertaken and conducted apart from the requisite moral and spiritual conditions.

A "Christian philosopher," declares Hugh, would not be able to take such an attitude: "a Christian philosopher requires reading and exhortation, not siegecraft or busyness."[75] He explains it in the preceding book of the *Didascalicon*. There, he opposes the "disciplina virtutum" to the "disciplina litteraturae"; he affirms that, despite his pretensions, one who gives himself over to an indiscreet study of the Scripture, in reality "is not philosophizing, but haggling."[76] To illustrate his thought, he recalls at length the history of a man who, after first having read the holy Books for his own edification, allowed himself to be carried away by his taste for the study to the point of turning into error; turned back by a revelation from the Lord, he finally repented, and merited once again to taste the consolation of the Scriptures.[77] Some have believed they could see there an allusion to Andrew of Saint Victor, whose literalism in the explication of certain prophecies had created a scandal.[78] It was rather a question of some doctor over-bold in his speculations, of a "dialectician," a "philosopher," whose imprudent reason was not able, in the judgment of Hugh, "to use the moderation of discretion"; having spurned the humbler aspects of Scripture, he had been crushed by the "weight" of the mystery that he examined instead of venerating it.[79] This passage is all the more remarkable in that it occurs in an academic treatise, not in a treatise on spiritual life. We shall see nothing in the passage, then, that is hostile to science, but it will completely dissuade us from believing that its author had wanted to promote a scientific movement even slightly breaking with traditional usage.

It will also perhaps permit us to advance a more precise hypothesis, touching the danger against which the master of Saint Victor intends to protect his disciple. The *Didascalicon* would seem to betoken a pedagogical experience as well as an intellectual maturity that would require assigning it a relatively late date. It was at any event drafted prior to the completion of the *De sacramentis*, which preceded the death of its author (11 February 1141) by several years.[80] From that time one might with sufficient likelihood situate it in the neighborhood of 1135. Now, at that date, Peter Abelard had long before finished the first part of his tumultuous career. After his amorous adventure, his conversion had been sincere and profound. After the condemnation directed at his doctrine at the Council of Soissons (1121), anyone might believe that, "having been drawn back from the tumultuous life of the world," he had finally arrived in the cloister, as he himself says nostalgically, "to a port of tranquility."[81] He had not yet shown himself again on Mount Sainte Geneviève for new successes, new scandals, and a new condemnation. Saint Bernard had just met him at the abbey of Morigny (1131), and their uneventful interview permitted no preview of the ferocious duel of 1140. Still more recently, the *Historia calamitatum* had just appeared, "between the end of 1132 and the year 1134."[82] In it Abelard confessed his fault and in it rendered testimony to the divine grace that had released him. Hugh had doubtless been intensely impressed by it. Is it entirely too bold to suppose that, in this chapter of his fifth book where he says "how to study Scripture with a view to the correction of morals," he is schematically recalling the unfortunate Abelard's story?

If one believes, with Father Damien Van den Eynde, that he ought to assign a later date to the *Didascalicon,* the hypothesis can also be sustained. Abelard had retired to the Paraclete as long before as 1123. Hugh can speak of it as he did, around 1124. He is therefore upset not by the memory of the drama that the *Historia calamitatum* has just recalled, but by the drama itself, which dates from the more recent past. This "Christian philosopher" who so impetuously embarked upon audacities of thought, is not just anyone. He resembles the "ambitious young man of genius,"[83] who, according to his own admission, thought himself to be the first, nay, the only philosopher of his time,[84] who published a little later (1124) a *Christian Theology,* who wants to become "God's philosopher," so as to draw his readers to the "true philosophy," as Origen, "the greatest of the Christian philosophers,"[85] had done long ago; the one of whom Peter the Venerable would one day vouch that he had in fact become "truly Christ's philosopher."[86] As a matter of fact this man is seen to have reproached himself long ago for "the audacity of having acceded to the theological teaching office without a master."[87] His ill-considered thirst for knowledge, his individualism, and his pride made him fall. The practice of virtue nonetheless failed him. Hugh could note it without impropriety; everyone had heard him speak of Heloïse and her lover; even before the publication of the *Historia calamitatum,* did not Roscelin write that the story was known "from Dan to Beersheba"?[88] He was not able to stand the "weight" of the mystery, and his thought itself had begun to fail. But God, in his mercy, had relieved him. Did he not come to recognize this himself? Regarding this topic, it was not too much to speak of a sort of revelation: "at last admonished through a revelation by the divine wisdom," says Hugh, as Bernard will soon say, commenting on the second catastrophe followed by the second and definitive withdrawal of the lightning-blasted hero: "warned by us, but more, as we believe, inspired by God."[89]

Is it not again this same disquieting thinker who appears in the background for the following book of the *Didascalicon,* when the master, as we have seen, deters his disciple from wanting to "philosophize" too quickly, after the fashion of those who pretend "to leave fables to the false apostles"?[90] When he entreats him to allow himself to be taught first, reminds him to respect the ancient commentators, and finally makes clear to him that in order to comprehend Scripture it is necessary to deal with it less as someone "lettered," i.e., as a scholar, than as a spiritual man? The tragic destiny of Peter Abelard thus would haunt our author from one book to the other of his work, just as it was to haunt the mind of a number of his contemporaries.[91] And would we not have a confirmation of this fact in still another passage, which occurs in the third book? It is a particularly eloquent passage, which deals precisely with humility as a necessary precondition for acquiring knowledge. It encroaches upon the chapter from the sixth book that we have already analyzed, containing almost word for word certain of its expressions from the corresponding passage of the *De scripturis,*[92] which would tend to show that there existed at least a kinship between the individuals referred to in each of the two instances. In these reflections that finish on a criticism of certain arrogant masters, Hauréau believed that he could recognize the portrait of Abelard.[93] The allusion seemed no less clear to Father Auguste Humbert.[94] Let the reader judge the matter for himself:

> When you start to know something, do not spurn others. This arrogance is noteworthy in certain masters who consider their own knowledge with a bit too much smugness and who, persuaded that they are something, think that other masters whom they do not know cannot be such as themselves. . . . From this vicious ferment these hawkers of twaddle have just arisen who, vainglorious for no known reason, tax the ancient Fathers with puerile joviality and believe that wisdom, created along with them, ought not to survive them either. The style of the Scriptures, they say, is so simple that they have no need of masters to teach them how to understand them; it is enough for each individual to use his own intelligence to penetrate the hidden mysteries of the truth.[95]

A timeless description of a bad habit this is not, but a painting taken from life. Its lines are already close to those that the pen of John of Salisbury will take when he finds fault with the "Cornificians," as we shall see in the next chapter. However it is less Abelard who is portrayed for us here — Hugh admired his repentance, and was doubtless not insensitive to his culture and the nobility of his inspiration[96] — than the caricatures of him that he had created in his lectures, and which Hugh can observe at present. With this reservation, it seems clear that Hauréau had seen aright. Hence one would be within his rights to think that, in the similar passages from the *Didascalicon* and the *De scripturis*, it is a question of that same category of minds, or nearly so. Does it not become evident from then on, that, far from revolutionizing the principles of exegesis by attacking the old allegorizing routine, Hugh of Saint Victor is merely trying to consolidate the imperiled tradition?

2. The Over-Squeezed Udders

In his moderation, Hugh of Saint Victor dreads, as we have seen, both precipitancy and excess in allegorical explications. On both these points more than one author has echoed him. In particular, against precipitancy, the anonymous Victorine who wrote around 1175 puts one of his friends on guard by explaining to him "by what steps" he might rise "to a full understanding of the sacred page": that he should begin by reading completely through the Old and the New Testament three or four times "secundum historiam," before grappling with the reading "secundum allegoriam," and then "secundum moralem instructionem"; then his "tripartita lectio" will be sure; he will be able to render himself "intrepid" in searching out the second and the third senses; he will even be able joyfully to attend "to pursuing new allegories and meditating new points of moral instruction."[97] Here is a good example of that step-by-step march, *"ordinate,"* dear to the founder of the School, and which has nothing, as we have seen, of timid literalism about it. In one of his sermons, Peter the Eater will protest against the excessive and the arbitrary exegete; he is one of those people, he will say, "who destroy Scripture" while pretending to explicate it:

> There are these fellows who grow vain in their own thoughts; who paint the images of their own heart on the pages of sacred Scripture; who accommodate the sparkling letter to their own devices and squeeze the understanding of Scripture to the point of bleeding.[98]

These last words allude to a text from Proverbs 30:33. The same allusion is found in Peter Lombard commenting on Psalm 77:

The Over-Squeezed Udders

> For just as elsewhere water is changed into wine, whereby is signified the people's change for the better, so here it is changed into blood, whereby flesh is taken, since they take spiritual things in a fleshly sense.[99]

It is also found in Arnaud of Bonneval criticizing certain exegetical excesses of Origen, who, he says, "labors at squeezing blood out of certain passages of the Scriptures."[100]

In these texts as well as in other, analogous ones we can recognize a sign of the Victorine's influence. But to put this influence in proper perspective, it is important not to forget that, at bottom, these were classic, even ancient, criticisms or recommendations. The image of the over-squeezed udders is developed twice by Hugh Metel, that brilliant lover of commonplaces, who uses it once, let us note, against Abelard.[101] Thus he shows us, as did Hugh of Saint Victor already, dialectical intemperance and allegorical intemperance judged at the same level, or rather the first judged in terms of the second; which will not be surprising, if one recalls that *allegoria*, defined as the application which "builds up the faith," defines the work of the theologian by that very fact, whatever precisely his method may be. And here is what Rupert of Deutz wrote a little earlier:

> [Job] begins to relate more subtly the good things he has done, which are in great part to be held according to the text of the history alone, lest if they be investigated more than is necessary, from the udders of its words blood should answer for milk, according to the saying of Solomon: 'He who squeezes the udders too hard draws forth blood'. For in the sequence of sacred Scripture, in part the understanding of the letter alone is to be maintained, as reason requires; in part, the brilliance of allegory is to be sought for. Just as is mystically figured in the deed of Jacob, who, about to set the rods before the eyes of the sheep . . . , pealed part of them, and once the bark had been removed . . . the brilliance appeared; but those that were untouched stayed green . . . (Gen. 30). So, I say, as often as we fix an understanding of the letter, we are, as it were, taking away the bark, and as often as we follow the understanding of the letter, we are, as it were, keeping the bark.[102]

The same image of the too forcefully squeezed udders was already used for the same purpose by Paschasius Radbertus:

Though he should want to raise them up higher, to allegorize, than the Catholic faith permits; since, as Scripture attests, "He who squeezes the udders too strongly draws forth not milk, but blood."[103]

Will one say that precisely Paschasius and Rupert are among the rare precursors of the literalist tendency that was to be affirmed in Hugh? Will one recognize in the agreement of these three exegetes a new confirmation of that line stemming from Jerome that used to struggle against the spirit of Saint Gregory? In fact all three of them did nothing but repeat what Bede had expressly written in his commentary on the Proverbs:

> We press the udders forcibly when we weigh the words of sacred eloquence with a subtle understanding; by means of this pressure, whilst we are seeking milk, we find cream, since while we are seeking to be nourished even with a thin understanding, we are anointed with the richness of the inner fat; but this ought not to be done too much or all the time, lest whilst milk is being sought from the udders, blood should follow; since, when the words of sacred eloquence are discussed more than they ought, they fall into a carnal understanding.... The sense that arises from excessive discussion of the spirit is rendered carnal.[104]

This is not the only time that Bede gives this sage counsel. Using still another image that two other texts from Proverbs furnish him under two slightly different forms, he writes in the same work:

> "Thou hast found honey; eat what is enough for thee etc." You have found the sweetness of heavenly understanding, which by the office of the spiritual Fathers has been prepared for you as though by the labor of most prudent bees. So see to it that you do not crave to taste in it more than one ought to taste, lest whilst you are seeking to understand the highest things beyond your powers, you lose even those that you have already understood well.
> "Just as he who eats much honey etc." For if more of the sweetness of honey is taken than is necessary, then the life of the eater is destroyed by the very source whereby his mouth is gratified. A quest for majesty is sweet; but the very glory of him who desires to scrutinize it more than the recognition of humanity allows, presses him, since it, just like honey consumed immoderately, destroys the sense of the investigator when it is not grasped. Moreover, any wise man

ought to pay attention not only not to seek things too high for him and not to scrutinize things too powerful, but also not to render things that he could rightly and usefully know less useful to himself by immoderate utterances.[105]

As we see, there is no moderation more Victorine than this; nor, indeed, a sobriety more like Bernard's. For, along with excess in allegory, temerity in speculation concerning divine things was condemned by Bede, just as it will be strongly condemned by Saint Bernard. The two excesses might be correlated. As to the advice of the anonymous Victorine on a first "historical" reading of the Bible, it was already almost that of Rabanus Maurus in his *Clericalis institutio*:

> Therefore the most skillful researcher into the divine Scriptures will be the one who first would have read them all and got acquainted with them, and if not yet by means of his understanding, at least by reading. . . . The first point to be observed in his work and his labor is, as we have said, to get acquainted with those books, even if not yet with respect to his understanding, still, by reading either to commit them to memory or at least not to have them completely unknown. Next . . .[106]

Rabanus did not specify precisely that it would be necessary first to read it "three or four times"; but he advised entrusting this first sort of reading to the memory: was this to ask for much less? However, as much as "diligent investigation" he also recommended a "sober understanding,"[107] and demanded a "sober reader"[108] for the Bible. In the same spirit, he reproduced word for word the passage that we just read in Bede about the udders that under too much squeezing make blood come out,[109] as well as the other two about the immoderate use of honey.[110]

To get a good understanding of all these warnings, it will be a good idea to refer to the principal texts of Scripture through which they are expressed, so as to see how the one was called for by the other and how they complemented each other. There are three texts from Proverbs and one from Ecclesiasticus. In Proverbs 30:33, our authors read this: "And he that strongly squeezeth the paps to bring out milk, straineth out butter; and he that violently bloweth his nose, bringeth out blood." It was natural to comment on the analogous image in the same sense, the image that was found a bit earlier, at Proverbs 25:16: "Thou hast found honey, eat what is sufficient for thee, lest being glutted therewith thou vomit it up."

But this second text itself led inevitably to a third one, quite near, which contained both the image of honey and its application. For one reads in Proverbs 25:27: "As it is not good for a man to eat much honey, so he that is a searcher of majesty, shall be overwhelmed by glory."[111] Finally, the juxtaposition of this third text with a fourth was no less inevitable; for the latter, this time unmetaphorically, gave the same advice and contained the same word "scrutinize"; this text was Ecclesiasticus 3:22: "Seek not the things that are too high for thee, and search not into things above thy ability."[112] Whence arises the question of Rupert, who, in connection with the third text, put the problem very well, recalling the apparently opposite advice or rather the command given by Jesus to "scrutinize the Scriptures": "But is not 'scrutinizing the Scriptures' the same as 'being a searcher of majesty'?"[113]

Bede had already answered that sort of question, though in summary fashion: "It is not eating honey that he forbids but eating a lot of it, since we are not totally prohibited from scrutinizing the majesty of God . . . , but we are called back from attempting the ones that exceed our measure."[114] Herbert of Bosham was to answer in like manner: "even if the scrutinizers of so great a mystery be moved perchance from causes of the faith and with regard to the faith itself to be more temerarious and even more curious than necessary."[115] Rupert himself made his answer in another passage, saying: "lest we be too scrutinizing of majesty," "by not excessively scrutinizing God's majesty."[116] A response of this kind, however, was rather vague. A question of measure could not be the only point at issue. In one sense, the Scriptures could never be too much scrutinized: no restriction weakened Jesus' command; no exception limited it. One could not bring too much eagerness to execute it. Neither before the "ways of God" in guiding the world, nor before his innermost Being, did any research have to be halted. As Origen had said in a homily that frequently served to inspire the medievals, those who try to understand the Scriptures or strive to subordinate all their powers to God's Law are truly "kings rooting up the depths of a pit and scrutinizing the hidden and mystical points of God's word."[117] In still another passage, then, Rupert replied even more appropriately to the question that he had set for himself. God's judgment, he explained, struck the Bethsamites who had gone too far into the sanctuary so as to contemplate the ark there:

> He made them err, because they had seen the ark of the Lord; because they had dared unworthily, not with a zeal born of love but with the vice of presumption and curiosity, to scrutinize the secrets of the di-

vinity in the Scriptures; and they became heresiarchs, God judging that the proud are not to be admitted to the sight of divinity and truth.[118]

The abbot Abraham would soon advance the same clarifying distinction:

> Concerning the third honey, which is the spiritual understanding of the Scriptures, Solomon says: . . . "Eat what is sufficient for thee, lest being glutted therewith thou vomit it up"; "eat," he says, "what is sufficient," i.e., for building up, do not scrutinize hidden things for curiosity; for as Solomon says elsewhere: "he that is a searcher of majesty shall be overwhelmed by glory."[119]

So there are two opposed ways of "scrutinizing." No limit was set for the spiritual drive — for the Christian has received the Spirit of God, the Spirit who scrutinizes everything, even the depths of God.[120] Only such a drive was to take place truly "in spiritu," and not "in sensu proprio"; it was to be not the proud effort of "the wise and the prudent," but the humble quest of the "little ones" and the "poor in spirit" — which did not mean, as Rabanus Maurus judiciously put it, spirits that are stupid and lazy: Jesus had condemned spiritual bloatedness, not spiritual acuity: "tumorem, non acumen."[121] Even Saint Bernard, who is so hard on the "temerarius scrutator majestatis," whom he denounces as a sacrilegious "housebreaker" and "burglar,"[122] did not fail to encourage such a drive unreservedly: "Let him not be annoyed at scrutinizing things still secret . . . , if perchance something spiritual should lay hidden within them, which might be able to come to light in public!" That is what he judged to conform to the nobility of human nature, that "sublime creature" destined to receive the gift of God: "celsa creatura in capacitate majestatis."[123] For him then, the desire to know, when applied to divine things, was good, if it was truly a desire for "understanding" and not for comprehending them; in other words, if it was not an ambition to get both hands around the object of its knowing, that divine object "whose immensity the receptive power of human sense cannot reach,"[124] but to contemplate it with respect. In that case, as Saint Bernard used to say again, "Do not fear what Scripture threatens against the scrutinizers of majesty; just bring forward a pure and simple eye."[125] His friend William of Saint Thierry did not cut the believer off from the path of research either. Provided that, truly "poor in spirit" ("pauper spiritu"), one clearly understood that there are two ways of searching and apprehending and that in divine things he does not proceed in the same way as he does in the human ones, William did not consider him a "scrutator majestatis" but rather authorized him to penetrate into the "maze of divine revelation."[126]

The defense of Ecclesiasticus remained no less protective of the sacred mystery, and each time rationalistic audacity became menacing, voices were raised in the Church to repel it.[127] Without ceasing to exalt the understanding and to encourage — with more or less warmth and more or less competence — the right research, these voices reproved such "audacity" and showed "how terrible and dangerous it is" "to argue inappropriately about God with careless speech."[128] In a word, in this sense they cursed "curiosity."[129] Taking up again the old objurgations of the Fathers, they most often glossed the warning of Ecclesiasticus by means of the two images from Proverbs.[130] In the same sense we shall rather quote a beautiful passage which is found in Rabanus Maurus and in Angelome of Luxeuil (ca. 855), in their commentary on the third Book of Kings [19:9ff]. Angelome is meditating upon the scene in which we see the prophet Elijah, on the approach of a light breeze that announced the passing of the Lord, cover his face with his mantle:

> The Prophet covered his face with a cloak, since he recognizes with how much ignorance man is covered in the very subtle contemplation of the truth. For veiling the face lest the mind should dare to seek things too high is to veil this consideration of one's own infirmity, and let him in no way rashly open the eyes of the understanding beyond himself, but let him reverently shut them to what he is not able to apprehend.[131]

Here one recognizes the twofold instruction that Hugh was to formulate nearly three centuries later: no precipitate interpretation! no intemperance, either! These extreme "allegorists" speak just like one who is deemed to represent the opposite tendency — and just as Saint Bernard too will speak.[132] We do not conclude from this that their trends of thought overlap, but such occasions do invite us not to oppose them too quickly. Angelome and Rabanus are already raising the cry that the eleventh and twelfth centuries are going to ring out in addressing the new schools: "Altiora te ne quaesieris!" "Seek not things that are too high for thee!" Allegory then formed, albeit in a somewhat conventional fashion, the ordinary framework of theological speculation; the counsel of doctrinal sobriety accordingly, as we have seen just now in Bede and Hugh Metel, naturally amounts to a counsel of sobriety in the use of allegory.

That is what is produced most especially in Hugh, considering that, more than anyone else, Hugh occupies himself with systematizing that old framework. But in him again, what such counsel chiefly aims at is much less a somewhat luxuriant traditional allegory than an indiscreet theological speculation, a rationalistic tendency, or something judged to be such. It is always that "curiositas," which, ceaselessly reborn in various new forms, is as it were *the* sin of the spirit.

Still, so as not to betray the thought of our authors, let's learn how to distinguish several sorts of curiosity. Amongst all of them, the blameworthy curiosity is evidently not "studium," which comes from love and which tends to "edification," but rather a curiosity that comes from presumption and which tends to disintegration. This is the "curious craving" that the Tempter had already kindled in the spirit of his victim at the very origin of our race.[133] This is the curiosity that turns to blasphemy. Evidently it is not at all that "healthy curiosity" that man naturally applies to the objects of this world to get a solid knowledge of them,[134] that interior spring defined by Hugh as "a certain curious and sagacious power of mind, striving to investigate obscurities and unravel perplexities";[135] nor is it that "pious curiosity" that Saint Bernard himself, so relished by the Victorines, praises in the "pius scrutator,"[136] just as he praises, whatever legend says of him, its application to the profane disciplines.[137] This is a reality quite different again from that "base curiosity," the vulgar vice of one who aspires to sell his knowledge for money or honors.[138] This is no longer that feverish taste for novelty, of the unheard-of bauble, of the rare or the original, that engenders all sorts of aestheticism and which not only spirituals like Saint Bernard criticize but also all minds seriously devoted to the sciences of nature; a taste especially disapproved of in art, because it involves dissipation and superfluity.[139] This is also something quite other and something much more serious than the "superstitious" curiosity that lets loose a torrent of all sorts of "stupid and inept questions" from which many disputes arise;[140] something other than the muddle-headed curiosity of inexperienced minds, which Saint Peter Damian accused of disturbing ecclesiastical discipline,[141] or that of the gyrovague students that Helinand and his like see roaming the world "so as to be made mad from much literature."[142] In fine, one ought not to confuse it with simple "vana curiositas" or "curiosa vanitas," a universally distributed disposition, which had so often deceived philosophers of old, and of which the chancellor Gerson will say that it is again deceiving the theologians of his own time;[143] with that "vain and curious craving, soothingly called 'knowledge' and 'science,'" the source of all the dispersions and divagations of the spirit, whose scope Saint Augustine in his own critique had tended to extend too far, at the risk of discouraging efforts at sound research;[144] or with that "anxious, agitated curiosity" that Gregory, following Scripture, associated with the "will of the flesh" and the "surging of ambition."[145] Hugh of Saint Victor in turn mentioned that "hollowness of curiosity or craving" and he analyzes it admirably: he points out in it the first origin of the multiform vanity in which the human being is dissolved; if it is perverse and culpable, he explains, that is because it is opposed not only to grace but also to the true nature of the spirit. When that "appetite for emptiness" takes over a man's heart, far from driving him to serious research, it extinguishes the "desire for truth"; the shadow that spreads within him hides from that man both what is in him and what is above him. Thus, meditating upon the "vanitas vanitatum" of Ecclesiastes according to the tradition of Christian Socraticism and the Augustinian critique interpreted in its better sense, Hugh ends by crying out, before the ravages of that "distraction," with an almost Pascalian tone:

> O most evil occupation! O pernicious distension! Whither dost thou draw the mind? How much you promise, and how much you take away! You promise man all that he is not, and you take away all that he is.[146]

But the cursed curiosity is rather worse. It is not the deed of the common run of men. It is that other sort of curiosity that Saint Augustine repudiated, declaring it to be "impious";[147] that sly curiosity of men who want to measure God, which inspired Saint Gregory Nazianzen with horror.[148] This is paradigmatically the "curiositas illicita," the "curiositas pestilens," which is always paradigmatically "noxia curiositas."[149] Augustine said it with full knowledge of the cause, the very one who, recalling the memory of his Manichean years, used to write: "I sought curiously."[150] "Temerarious" curiosity is associated with all whose enterprises, Saint Bernard says, are not questions posed by the faith, but rather wounds inflicted on the faith; curiosity without respect, by which, again following a forceful expression of Saint Bernard, "the mysteries of God are being gutted."[151] It is therefore essentially a curiosity in sacred matter, but not proceeding from that "soul caring after God," which does not cease to enquire after that which it loves.[152] It is not the taste for the essential truth, this taste which causes one to be "always searching,"[153] but the perversion of this taste; it is its very opposite. In explicating, it wants to possess and to dominate. It

The Over-Squeezed Udders

wants to turn the infinite Truth into its own tool. Hugh protests against such an outrage. He tracks down the warning signs of that sacrilegious fever. With more moderation than William of Saint Thierry had recently shown against Peter Abelard, but in a spirit quite akin to his, Hugh picks up the old complaint again, directed against certain new theologians of his own time. As Richard will do after him, he begs them not to forget, in the midst of their research, that they are human beings.[154] Like the *Gloss*, he cries out to them: "By seeking beyond your powers you lose what you have understood."[155] As Rabanus Maurus and Angelome of Luxueil did long ago, as John of Fécamp[156] did recently, as Bernard is doing today, as Gerhoh of Reichersberg[157] soon would do, as Honorius and Salonius of Geneva do (citing another text from Proverbs),[158] Hugh recalls them to prudence, to the humility of reason, to respect for the supernatural mystery.[159]

If, by analogy, one wants to get an idea of what obsesses the thought of all these believers when they so forcefully oppose themselves to "impious curiosity," it is not just any old favorite sin of the understanding that can be imagined. Nor again let anyone suppose something like those enterprises of rational theology that were soon to see the light of day — that, for example, of a Saint Thomas, who was on the contrary so sober and so reserved. Still less, if possible, let him think of the enterprise of a Descartes, who will think that "it is temerarious to want to discover the ends that God has proposed in the construction of the world,"[160] will beg off all "high theological metaphysics," will critique our faculties of knowing by carefully limiting the scope of their competence,[161] and will dismiss the mysteries of holy Scripture from the field of the activity of reason. Descartes was never tempted to "disembowel the secrets of God"! At the beginning of the twelfth century, the most clairvoyant mind could never even have dreamed that such forms of thought would arise. Let us rather consider, *mutatis mutandis*, what would be the ambition of a Rimbaud, or that of a René Guénon. Ever since the first days of Christianity, particularly ever since Saint Irenaeus, one sees periodically reappearing, in new ways in new circumstances, the opposition between the "believer" and the "gnostic" — or the "pseudo-gnostic" — a close relative, in the strong sense of the word, of the magician.[162] We see the old idea of the heretic as someone eager for the secret knowledge that would give him power, treating Scripture as if it were the tree of knowledge. We see him struggle: against that "elevation of heart" which forms a perfect contrast with the spirit of the Gospel; against that idolatry of one's own thought which is incompatible with the recognition of the Creator;[163] against that "infinite evil of human desire," which can corrupt the desire to know as well as the desire for pleasure, possession, or power;[164] against that ambition — which is, properly speaking, Luciferian in the heresiarch, and Adamic in those whom it sweeps away — to become "like a god."[165] Intellectual pursuit, whatever the method that it brings into play, is for the believer always a struggle where he knows from the start that he will ultimately be overcome by the mystery, and where, at the very start, he accepts this defeat with joy.[166] As sincere and as ardent as he may be in such research, one sees him issue many curses against the "craving mind" which "delights at knowing hidden things through curiosity,"[167] warnings against a temptation "much more perilous" than the concupiscence of the flesh[168] — the temptation of "eternal gnosis"[169] — or warnings directed to those "whom heretics deceive with the false promise of reason and knowledge."[170] It often occurs to the believer to exaggerate; sometimes, to apply his principle badly or to deceive himself in his diagnosis. But the opposition he perceives is not a chimaera.

Peter Lombard, Peter the Cantor, Hugh, Rupert, Angelome, Paschasius, Paulinus of Aquilaea, Rabanus Maurus, and Bede: that is quite a fine lineup. It is necessary, however, for us to go back further still. In reality, all of those authors, when they preach sobriety, are doing nothing but repeating what Saint Gregory dictated to them in texts that each generation kept rereading and which had found a place as well in a number of anthologies or summaries, ever since those of Paterius and of Taio of Saragossa. The biblical image of the over-squeezed udders, that of honey taken in too large a quantity, as well as that of the pealed branches of Jacob — which one still reads about in Claude of Turin[171] — all come from that vast reservoir from which the Middle Ages never stopped drawing: the *Moralia*. The application that Saint Gregory made of these images to exegesis is already exactly what all the authors that we have just mentioned will make. His balance, his moderation, his sense of Christian humility, his restraint from leaping ahead, his dread of "precipitancy," his respect of mystery, the very words in which these dispositions are expressed, are sometimes exactly those that we shall find particularly in Hugh. The story that the latter recounts of the scholar led astray by an intemperate and too purely theoretical study seems made to illustrate this paragraph of Gregory:

> Whilst all heretics desire to scrutinize the secrets of God in sacred Scripture more than they can grasp, they become fruitless in their hunger. For they do not even seek the things whereby they may edu-

cate themselves to humility . . . , but only those that show them to be learned prattlers . . . since the wretches do not know themselves. . . . For what they scrutinize are things beyond themselves, and whilst they reach for what they cannot grasp, they neglect to learn the things from which they could be educated.[172]

Gregory then goes on to quote Saint Paul: "not to be more wise than it behooveth to be wise, but to be wise unto sobriety," and then the Book of Proverbs:

> Hence Solomon says: "set bounds to thy prudence" [Prov. 23:4]. Hence again he says: "Thou hast found honey, eat what is sufficient for thee, lest being glutted therewith thou vomit it up" [Prov. 25:16]. For he who desires to eat the sweetness of spiritual understanding beyond his capability vomits forth even what he had eaten, since while he is seeking to understand the highest things beyond his powers, he loses even what he had well understood. Hence again he says: "As it is not good for a man to eat much honey, so he that is a searcher of majesty shall be overwhelmed by glory" [Prov. 25:27]. For the glory of the invisible creator, which, sought for in moderation, raises these men up, crushes them when scrutinized beyond their powers.[173]

In this passage Gregory had the "heretics" in view. But at the very interior of the great Church he denounces an analogous kind of abuse. The heretics do violence to Scripture.[174] Now they have "sons" who follow them in their errors; they also have "grandsons," who, without going quite so far as they do, are starting on the same slope:

> Whilst they seek more sense in the food of the sacred Word than they are capable of, they are always fasting from knowledge of the truth; and the categories of teaching that they strive to search in quest of, they are not able to have for refreshment.[175]

These are the very men, too sure of themselves, too smitten with profound knowledge, in short too "curious," that a homily on Ezekiel criticizes again:

> When some readers of the sacred eloquence penetrate its more sublime senses, they customarily look down with a swollen sense upon

the lesser mandates that have been given to weaker folk, and want to change them into another understanding. But, if they rightly understood the deep things in it, they would not regard even the smallest mandates as to be looked down upon, since in certain matters the divine precepts speak in this way to the great, but yet so as to be congenial in certain matters to little ones, who keep growing by increments of understanding, as though with the foot-steps of the mind, and come to understand greater things.[176]

One will have noticed this characteristically Gregorian balancing, through which equilibrium of thought is expressed. One will also notice that "want to change the lesser mandates into another understanding" ("minora mandata velle in alium intellectum permutare"): this is exactly the allegorism that jumps "over the literal sense at a single bound", as Father Mandonnet used to say with regard to the criticism formulated by Hugh in the *De scripturis*, and as Hugh himself used to say.[177] One will have noticed at the same time the qualification, "if they rightly understood the deep things" ("si recte alta intelligerent"), which shows clearly that Saint Gregory did not reject every flight of thought. One will also have noticed those "increments of understanding," the "incrementa intelligentiae," that are a major theme of Gregory's hermeneutical doctrine, a theme that he develops particularly when commenting on Ezekiel's vision of the chariot and the living beings, and that we shall also soon rediscover in Hugh.

It does not go as far as the explication offered by Angelome and Rabanus Maurus regarding the Prophet Elijah's covering his eyes at the threshold of his cave, which again had its source in a homily of Saint Gregory:

> But now it is necessary for the one who stands at the mouth of the cave and perceives God's words in the ear of his heart to veil his face, since, whilst we are led to understand higher things through heavenly grace, the more sublimely[178] we are lifted, the more we ought always through humility to press ourselves down in our own understanding so as to be wise to a sober limit, lest we try to be wiser than one ought; lest we stray whilst we crack open invisible things too much; lest we seek something of corporeal light in that incorporeal nature.[179]

Here one sees the perfect harmony between the two texts, that of Gregory and that of our compilers from the Carolingian age, though the expression is different in the two cases. But there is another passage still from the pope and doctor which it will not be necessary to quote at full length, because we have already read it reproduced almost verbatim, in Bede, Rabanus Maurus, and Rupert. In it Gregory proposes the two images of the over-squeezed udders and of the peeled branches.[180] Let us merely note that these two images do not come to illustrate in some incidental way a brief and inconsequential reflection. They are presented in the course of a very sustained exposition, whose beginning is yet again a eulogy about due measure and balance in exegesis:

> The understanding of sacred speech is to be weighed with such great balance betwixt text and mystery, that, once the balance-pan of each side has settled, at that point neither should the weight of excessive discussion push it down, nor again the torpor of carelessness leave it empty. Indeed, many of its sentences are heavy with so great a conception of the allegories, that anyone who tries to hold them to the history alone would through his own lack of care be deprived of an awareness of them. On the other hand, some [sentences] are so devoted to the exterior precepts that he who desires to penetrate them more subtly would find nothing inside, but even what they say openly escapes him.[181]

And, once the lesson has been administered to the self-styled "spirituals" that their excessive haste or their intemperate speculation makes them fall to the level of the "carnal," the pope concludes with the obligation to scrutinize carefully — *perscrutemur* — the biblical words from the very start *juxta pondus historiae*.[182] One will find no stronger expression in Hugh, and the presence of that same word, *perscrutari*, in the same context, to translate the same advice, written by the anonymous Victorine, is a further indication, among many others, of Gregory's influence at Saint Victor.[183]

But Gregory was not alone. If one can challenge Miss Smalley's assertion that "Hugh is criticizing the Gregorian tradition,"[184] there is nevertheless no reason to set the contrary idea, which would also be quite false, of an exclusive "lineage stemming from Gregory," in opposition to the idea of a lineage stemming from Jerome and at odds with Gregory, the result of which would have been Hugh. For here again we shall find Gregory entering into partnership with Jerome, who had written in his own commentary on Isaiah:

> I know that I have read an extremely wide and inextricable tropology in these books.... And if when they want to attain some deeper wis-

dom and to find something mystical concerning holy Scriptures, while sweating with excessive toil, nevertheless they will not carry off the fruits of doctrine, but will be filled with the briars and thorns that arise in the hands of a drunk.[185]

What is more, the meeting is not accidental, any more than in other cases. The two Latins express a common thought. Gregory did not necessarily get it from Jerome. Both of them — as when they speak of the "foundation of the building" — are identically echoing Origen. In a homily on the Book of Numbers, the Alexandrine gave this sage advice — where, let us note, the word "pertransire," one of the two verbs used by the anonymous Victorine,[186] already figures: "Let him who reads the divine literature observe the words of Scripture diligently and not go beyond (*pertranseat*) them as he pleases."[187] Beyond Gregory and beyond Jerome — we shall see other examples in the sequel — if one wants to know one of the most ancient "sources" of Hugh, he must go back to Origen, to that Origen whose practice did not always appear to conform to the wisdom of his counsel.[188] Indeed, it is precisely of him that Paschasius Radbertus was thinking, him whom he expressly named, both to praise him and to criticize him, on the page where he was commenting in the manner of Saint Gregory on the text of Proverbs about the over-squeezed udders.[189]

3. Noah's Ark

Hugh of Saint Victor, again writes Miss Smalley, "had taught exegetes to distinguish carefully between the literal and spiritual exposition, not to begin on the second until they had considered the first. Neither expositors nor glossators had been as alive to the distinction between letter and spirit as Hugh."[190] No one had distinguished them so methodically in fact, because no one had yet organized a complete program of sacred studies on their basis. In the thought of Master Hugh, however, this meant much less the abandonment or the loosening of the traditional doctrine of the senses of Scripture than its consolidation and, if one can say so, its promotion. Moreover, for Hugh, the distinction between the first two senses is neither cleaner nor more emphatic nor of any other nature than it had been for his predecessors: he understood it just as anyone before him had understood it; he merely began to exploit it more. We have already quoted many texts of earlier writers in which the distinction appeared as clear as anyone could want. Let us quote once more, amidst so many others that are available, these words of Rupert commenting on Exodus: "Now at last let us return from the start again with the historical demonstration; and let us follow up with the topic of the spiritual understanding."[191] Hugh applies, among others, one of the rules of Tyconius as well, which he places prominently, following Saint Augustine, in his *Didascalicon:* "that the law should be treated not only in its historical sense but also spiritually."[192] He would without difficulty have subscribed to the assertion of Saint Isidore, saying that one becomes a heretic "to the extent that the difference between the historical truth and the spiritual sense is not considered."[193] Let us again gather those formulations of the so often despised allegorist, i.e., Angelome of Luxueil:

> For by continuing the history a little here we have decided to touch on it first, so that by hunting it down we may divulge later what it contains mystically.
>
> For we have already inculcated what those things signify with respect to the history. However, inasmuch as it pertains to a higher understanding. . . .
>
> Behold, we have touched upon the history, but let us hunt down what it signifies spiritually.[194]
>
> Inasmuch as it pertains to the simple history. . . . Inasmuch as it pertains to the typic understandings. . . .[195]

Angelome, however, did nothing but repeat classic formulas, principally coming from Saint Gregory and encountered everywhere. In his *Life* of the holy pope, had not John the Deacon been able fittingly to write regarding the *Moralia in Job:* "The book of blessed Job . . . how is it to be understood according to the letter? How is it to be related to the sacraments of Christ and the Church? In what sense is it to be fitted to each of the faithful? [This] he explained with a marvelous account through three species of understanding."[196] Did not Pseudo-Isidore's *Liber de variis quaestionibus* explicitly recall "the difference between the historical truth and its spiritual sense"?[197] And most recently, had not Anselm of Laon filled his commentaries with subtitles: "historia, moralitas, allegoria"? Could one "distinguish carefully" any better than this? In Hugh, the distinction will be better supported, however, in its methodological consequences, and in this respect Miss Smalley had a sound view of the matter.

In another place, Miss Smalley speaks more particularly about that distinction of the two senses in the prophetic texts. "Hugh," she explains, "had read Paschasius on Lamentations. He makes an open demand for the literal exegesis of which Paschasius had quietly set the example. Both men were objective."[198] But, as has been seen in the previous chapter, if Paschasius had so "quietly" attributed a primary sense, the literal one, to prophecy, he had done so less by providing the example than by following the example already given. The same goes for Hugh. When he explicates the text of the prophecy first "to the extent that it looks to the letter," then "according to the sense of allegory," and finally "according to the moral understanding," Hugh does not at all separate himself off from his predecessors as a whole.[199] Again, let us call as a witness a contemporary of his, Gerhoh of Reichersberg, commenting on Isaiah's Canticle:

> The prophecy preceding that canticle having been carefully examined — understood not only historically, but also spiritually — reveals the matter and sense of this whole canticle.[200]

"Primo historialiter, deinde mystice," he says again a bit further on.[201] He likewise distinguishes two senses, or two successive realizations, in the prophecy of the Canticle of Hezekiah. No more than Paschasius or Hugh does he give the allegorical sense immediately; no more than they does he directly apply the text to the realities of the New Testament: "but these things have been fulfilled even more magnificently in Christ."[202] In the same way again, regarding the phrase of the Psalm: "et invitatos destruxisti," he observes that it has been realized many times *ad litteram* before being accomplished *spiritualiter* within us, in the struggle between the "armed strong man" and the one who is stronger than him.[203]

Would not Hugh nevertheless be an innovator through the devotion that he showed for the letter and through a hitherto unknown care to enter into the tiniest details of the history? In his two works, the *De arca Noe morali* and the *De arca Noe mystica*, he provides in fact — at least what can at first appear as — a minute description of the form of the ark; he calculates its measurements; he explicates its interior arrangement. In the course of his description, in the *De arca morali*, he recounts the opinion of Origen, who imagined an ark "rectangular at its base and making its sides converge little by little until the top, where it had no more than a cubit."[204] This opinion did not satisfy him: "but this interpretation," he says after having expounded it, "seems to involve many difficulties." Among other objections, such a shape seemed to him impossible.[205] After having spoken in that way as an architect and a geometer, he will do his best, in the *De arca mystica*, to give a concrete figuration of the ark, where even the colors would not be left out.[206] On this point, Miss Smalley says again:

Noah's Ark

O yes! We think of the Kindergarten. We smile when Hugh, with the gravity of one in the forefront of a scientific movement, rejects Origen's figure of the ark as top-heavy, and when he proposes "little compartments," round the outside, for the amphibious beasts. Our smile is mistaken: a scientific movement is really afoot. Hugh is doing, for biblical history, what Saint Anselm of Bec and Master Anselm had done for theology in their different ways. He is making the letter a proper subject for study, as they had made the content of the Christian faith. He wants to understand the literal meaning of Scripture exactly, so as to visualize the scene. He had that curiosity which set explorers in quest of El Dorado and led to the discovery of a continent.[207]

Perhaps it is our turn to smile. Is this new smile of ours a mistake? Let's look further.

Hugh is not content with the form that Origen imagined for Noah's ark. But at the end, both the one and the other give the ark an equally material and "historically" precise form.[208] In this respect, each of the two manifest a "scientific" care of the same order. This obtains within one and the same literal meaning, to which each of them attaches the same importance or accords the same credence, and on the mere question of the "form" and not that of the "quantity," which the discussion circumscribes; this discussion is, if one can say so, nautical even more than exegetical in character: the arrangement in a truncate pyramid, as conceived by Origen, would render flotation impossible.[209] After having described the ark, Hugh carefully measures its dimensions: Origen had done so before him. He is interested in its interior arrangement, in its various compartments: Origen was interested in it first; he had admired "the structure of such a ship, like a large town."[210] There is nothing there to mark or even foreshadow the least change in the principles or methods of exegesis, certainly nothing like the birth of some new "scientific movement." The curiosity exhibited by the Victorine is not that of an explorer of virgin continents. With him, biblical history is not engaged in any path of discovery here. Furthermore, thanks to the translation of Rufinus, Origen's explications had been well known for centuries. Starting with Saint Augustine,[211] many had copied or summarized them. Exegetes and historians were wont to recall them. This is what "the Irish Augustine" did with the *De mirabilibus sacrae Scripturae*.[212] This is what Bede did in his *Hexaemeron* when he cited the famous homily of Origen only for its details of a material order. So too did Beatus, Alcuin, Claudius of Turin,

Freculph of Lisieux, Rabanus Maurus, Remigius of Auxerre, Angelome of Luxueil.[213] Its essentials were unanimously retained and would be transmitted through the *Glossa ordinaria*.[214] When he sided with it, Hugh speaks of the "solution of the doctors."[215] Opinions were divided regarding certain details of arrangement: again it is Hugh himself who tells us.[216] This kind of exegesis therefore contained nothing unheard of, and the explications at which the author of the *De arca* stopped do not all even seem to be of his own invention.

One would say that at least the details that he furnishes are fuller than usual. Ought we to be surprised, seeing that he writes neither a universal chronicle, like Freculphe, nor a coherent commentary on the whole of Genesis, like Claudius and the others, but devotes two whole works just to the ark — one of them in four books? What is more important to observe is the relative length of his two explications, the literal and the spiritual. Now as early as the *De arca morali,* in comparison to the spiritual portion, the part accorded to the literal is infinitesimal, a single chapter in the first book alone — and in fact a mere trifle in that chapter itself. He himself warns his reader about it: many subtle details might be added from geometry regarding the letter, but it would be tedious to do so;[217] besides, he wants to be brief, so as to be able to expand upon "the ark of wisdom," which is his principal topic of discussion.[218] And indeed, even from a critical standpoint, so many "literal" curiosities more vivid than his own had to generate fruitless disquisitions later on,[219] that one can only be grateful to him for his restraint.

Well aware of where he wants to arrive, immediately after this "literal" chapter, Hugh surrenders himself to conjectures. In his own construal, it is enough for him not to advance anything formally at odds with the biblical text.[220] Once again he takes his liberties rather generously. His ark will have five stages, though others distinguish only three: this is because in the following chapter he wants to distinguish five successive states in the advancement of the spiritual life.[221] The three lower stages will have vertical walls, because in the first three states, which are those that pertain to the earth, "we climb through merit, but are not inclined to [God] himself through the presence of contemplation"; the walls of the two last stages, however, which are above the water, converge towards the single cubit at the summit, symbol of the divinity in whose bosom we are to be joined together.[222] This last symbolism was already present in Origen.[223] Hugh knows the height of each stage as well: they are of four, five, six, seven, and eight cubits, respectively, because the five states that they symbolize are respectively in relation with the four elements, the five senses, the perfection of virtues (which the number six signifies), the rest on the seventh day, and finally the octave of resurrected life.[224]

But that is not all. We ought to remark further that, in the *De arca Noe mystica*, the features of the so-called literal explication that provoke Miss Smalley's admiration, themselves constitute in reality a "mystical description." This time too Hugh warns us of that fact, from the very first words of his treatise, and from them one easily realizes what follows:

> First, as to the mystical description of Noah's ark, I am looking for the central point in the surface where I want to depict the ark, and there at the point fixed I describe *(circumduco)* around it a small square in the likeness of the cubit in which the ark was finished.... And again around that square I describe another one a little larger.... Within the inner square I paint *(pingo)* a cross.... Then I invest *(investio)* with color the spaces that remain on the surface of the square between the four angles of the cross and the square, [coloring] the upper two fiery-red and the lower two sapphire-blue.... Then I clothe *(induo)* the surrounding space of the fringe with purple and green coloration, the outside in purple, and the inside green, and in the middle of the golden cross that I had made, I paint a yearling lamb standing, etc.[225]

"Circumduco, circumscribo, superduco, pingo"; and again: "scribo, facio, pono, induo, includo, signo, divido, traho...." These are not the words of a man who is trying to reproduce an object that impresses itself upon him, but those of a man who determines and executes a plan. To be sure he has his eyes set upon a model, but that model is more within his own imagination than in the text of Moses. What he has undertaken is not so much to offer a material description of the historical ark, even as a point of departure, as to make a mystical ark materialize before our eyes. After the scale model of the whole comes the detail of the façade. Hugh tackles it with the same willful tone: "In the very front of the ark I make a small square, to represent the four directions of the world." At each angle he inscribes one of the four letters of the symbolic name of Adam; then a series of tripartite divisions allow him to recount universal history in inscriptions and images, whilst an ingenious combination of three dwellings, four angles, and twelve ladders allows him to speak again of all sorts of other things.[226] He explains a little later on that he paints the three dwellings of the ark in three different colors, which signify the three successive laws: natural law, written law, and the law of grace, at the same time as the three senses of Scripture: green will call forth the history; red, the tropology; blue, the allegory...."[227] This unassuming great pedagogue does not forget that at that time "coloring" is a current practice in the schools, and he gets happy results using it.[228]

Doubtless, in all this, besides colors, besides images and inscriptions, it does occur to Hugh to meet with Moses. But obviously that is not his principal concern. Forms, dispositions, ornaments, measurements — if he does not invent them all, he always is at least recombining them in view of some symbolism soon to be exploited. Such and such a measurement gets in his way: he cuts it down.[229] This or that numerical detail is not furnished: he settles it as he pleases.[230] He is primarily visual. He loves to see and to speak to the eyes.[231] He is thrilled at the beauty of visible things and especially that which comes from their color-scheme: in another of his works a chapter of this sort entitled *De rerum variis coloribus* is just one long cry of admiration.[232] Besides, for his symbolic purpose what is needed is a painting that speaks, as he calls it;[233] or, using another expression which also comes from him, he needs "visibiles figurationes."[234] They are not in his view, however, merely necessary for knowledge: they are generative sources of joy.[235] He also brings a punctilious care to bear upon his painting. But this care is not employed to describe the historical ark with any scientific intent: let us say it again, from beginning to end, the *De arca Noe mystica* is a vast symbolic tableau. We too admire its author; but we admire him for the art he devotes to composing such a tableau, not for the new trails he would blaze for science.

A little later, just as he was about to write his copious treatise *De tripartito tabernaculo*, whose construction owes much to Hugh of Saint Victor, Adam Scot will warn his reader in the following terms: "Now regarding these steps, pictures, and variety of colors, the reader ought to very clearly informed that it was not in fact at all to be found in Moses' visible tabernacle."[236] Hugh could have said this of his own description of the ark just as Adam did of his description of the tabernacle. If he did not make a completely explicit declaration of it, nevertheless it was not hidden and he could legitimately suppose that no one would be deceived on that point.

Furthermore, in both of his two Arks, the moral as well as the mystical, Hugh breaks away from any continuous commentary. Unlike his predecessors, he is no longer interested at all in Noah or in the flood.[237] His treatises are composed with full knowledge, like the ark itself. Everything, absolutely everything, in them is governed by the symbolic intention. According to the old catalogues[238] and according to Hugh himself,[239] the true title of the *De arca morali* was "On the ark [or: the threefold ark] of Noah, standing for the ark of wisdom, along with the ark of the Church and the ark of the Mother of Grace." From its very first line Hugh treats of the love of God. It is, he declares, a spiritual edifice that he intends to depict:

> From this, and to this, and because of this all of Scripture was made. Because of it, the Word was made flesh, God became lowly and man exalted. If you have this, then, you have the whole thing; if you have the whole, there is nothing more to wait for, and your heart comes to rest.
>
> As exemplar of this spiritual edifice I shall give you Noah's ark, which your eye will see on the outside, so that your mind may be built up within according to its likeness. There you will see certain colors, forms, and figures that delight the vision. But you ought to know that they have been set down so that in them you may learn wisdom, discipline, and virtue that might adorn your mind. And since this ark signifies the Church, and the Church is the body of Christ, in order that the exemplar may become more evident to you, I have depicted the whole person of Christ, i.e., the head along with the members, in visible form, etc.[240]

And the work ends with a sort of hymn to the ark, whose lyricism we find admirable:

> What then is this ark about which so many things are said and in which so many paths of the sciences are contained? Do you think it is a labyrinth? It is not a labyrinth: there is no labor in't, but there is rest in it. How do I know this? Since he who used to say: 'Come to me, all you who labor and are burdened, and I will refresh you, and you will find rest for your souls' dwells within it. . . . What sort of thing, then, is this ark? . . . It is like a storeroom stocked with a variety of all delicacies. There is nothing you could ever seek in it that you won't find, and when you have found one item, you will see many laid open for you. There all the works of our restoration from the beginning of the world to its end are most fully contained. . . . There is made manifest what we ought to believe, to do, to hope for. There the form of man's life and the sum of perfection is contained. . . . There something like the body of the universe is brought to shape, and the harmony of all

the details is unfolded. ... There things present do not give way to the past, etc.[241]

From that subtle and complicated but perfectly balanced masterpiece of allegory, to the divers stages ordered like those of the first ark; from that commentary which redoubles the three senses of Scripture so as to count six of them, in imitation of Isaiah's seraphim each bearing six wings,[242] to want to make (on an equal footing with that other masterpiece, the entirely mystical one, which is the other *De arca*) a sort of historical-critical manifesto, inaugurating a scientific movement in exegesis analogous to what the movement of rational reflection inaugurated by Saint Anselm was in theology: this is a paradox a bit too hard to bear. To suppose, moreover, that what our Victorine says about history and allegory should be nothing but a "concession" to tradition or to sheer habit,[243] is not only gratuitous: but also, Hugh's extensive practice, wherein he shows himself to be evidently at home, is consistent with the doctrinal statements he makes. He had, one can say, in the most general sense of the word, a genius for allegory. Even in his *Grammatica*, when he ventures to offer a few personal explications, these explications, as Dom Jean Leclercq remarks, "belong to allegory more than to philology."[244] One would be rather hard pressed to show in what respect his distinction of the three senses would, by itself, have "enormously increased the dignity of the historical sense" and "the importance of the letter."[245] He distinguishes these three senses just as they were distinguished before him, and neither is the letter found to be more valued nor allegory "devalued." Hugh sets store on them both. He partakes in no way — is it necessary to say it again? — in the modern prejudice which lies at the foundation of so many historical failures at comprehension, that prejudice which believes itself bound always to oppose letter and allegory, that is, always to choose between them as two incompatible alternatives.[246] "Great are the depths of the spiritual senses in sacred Scriptures";[247] "Many mysteries lie hidden in them all";[248] "Whereby there are many other things that ... can be called 'mystical'":[249] such is his constant conviction. The abbé Jean Châtillon saw aright when he said that the most traditional allegorical method is handled by Hugh "with particular fervor,"[250] and Ford Lewis Battles was justified in saying that, along with Saint Bernard, the Master of Saint Victor was one of the two great allegorists of his age.[251] If the Victorine methodology does indeed imply a certain novelty (time will tell), it is not always appropriate to look for it in the two *Arks*.

We can conclude with Father de Ghellinck, prescinding from the pejorative connotation of the epithet, that Hugh exhibits an "exaggerated predilection for allegory."[252] He no doubt imposes a certain sobriety upon himself as he does upon his disciple; at least he imposes it on himself from time to time. In exegesis, like Rabanus Maurus long ago, who was himself in this respect a disciple of Saint Gregory, Hugh dreads "the stupidity involved in lack of discernment."[253] This is a result of a natural balance and a prudence that sometimes almost borders on scrupulosity, not of a restricted or shaky conviction. He has left us a beautiful testimonial of his conviction as well as of his prudence in the prologue to his explication of the *Magnificat*:

> I find this to be the greatest difficulty in the divine Scriptures: that, where a circumstantial cause compels us sometimes to look for some sort of great and sublime things, the letter would seem to offer nothing there except for what is customary and not difficult to say. For I do not even think it so laborious that the mind of the reader should be able to reach for things that are proposed as new and marvelous, however strong and clouded over with figurative speech they may be, than that it should promote to a sublime understanding those that on first approach it finds to be modest and humble.
>
> For consider the Canticle of Mary, which Holy Church repeats throughout the world with such frequent and assiduous, indeed with daily, recitation: who could fail to be aware that it contains very great mysteries of spiritual understanding? Who could entertain the doubt that blessed Mary, recently filled with so much of fullness and grace of the Holy Spirit coming over and within her, would not have been able to offer a small something that would not exceed the capacity of earthly minds, for the praise of her Savior?
>
> And nevertheless while running through the sequence and text of that Canticle, we find certain things proposed on the surface of the narrative in such fashion as to seem to call for nothing more to explain them: nevertheless, though these things too may be true, since it can be doubted whether they be sufficient for so many mysteries and sacraments, I am therefore all the more afraid in expounding it, lest I bring in foreign matters, or leave out those that properly belong to it; and so, standing accused either of negligence or of temerity, I run the risk of causing you offense instead of gratitude.[254]

The following section will let us see the Victorine master's contribution to exegesis under still other aspects.

4. Hugh and Saint Gregory

Some again have thought they could detect certain other signs of literalist tendencies in Hugh. Samuel Berger said that Hugh "excludes anagogy" from his list of the scriptural senses.[255] C. E. Boeren says that he "takes no account" of it.[256] Would not that be something like a first step toward excluding or at least neglecting every spiritual sense, every "allegory"? That conclusion would be risky; but even the fact itself is not quite right. The only thing that is true is that in the chief instance of his enumerations, Hugh does not assign an explicitly distinct place to anagogy. There is nothing symptomatic in that. Indeed we know that for centuries the tripartite scheme was as frequent, if not more so, than the quadripartite scheme. It was one of the two schemes inherited from Bede. Hugh was able to prefer it for reasons of symbolism: B. Geyer has noted the importance of the number three in the philosophy of the Victorines.[257] In it, just as there are three heavens, so there are also three books of life and three trees of life, three faculties of the soul, three kinds of contemplation, and, within contemplation itself, three degrees, which penetrate into three successive places, etc.[258] The first two books of the *Miscellanea*, which must be restored integrally to Hugh,[259] are full of these sorts of triads: at least thirty or so can be enumerated, as against nine or ten tetrads. Hugh distinguishes three spirits, three times, three exercises of life, three tyrants, three pharaohs struggling against three gods, three sojourns of the children of Israel, three kinds of eyes, three kinds of prayer, three elements of penitence, three wills in Christ, three ways that God touches the heart; he distinguishes a threefold peace, a threefold erudition, a threefold compassion, a threefold punishment of sin, a threefold fruit of reading, a threefold reflection of the soul, a threefold operation of philosophy. There are, he says again, three ways to read, or to meditate, three sorts of music, three modes of "spiritual speculation."[260] In the philosophy of the Victorines there are three fundamental divine attributes, corresponding to the three Persons, three tokens of love given by God to the soul, three kinds of lovers, three ways of subsisting. The whole universe manifests itself to him under the sign of trinity, by means of the three sorts of beings that compose it. A number of triads are themselves subdivided into three, and three biblical personages symbolize them; or rather they generate each other, so to speak, as in a certain passage from the *Miscellanea*.[261] The homilies on Ecclesiastes lay out three kinds of vanity, the second of which comprises three species.[262] Hence in our author one should also expect to find a preference for the threefold sense of Scripture.

Moreover, let us call attention to the fact that one ought to expect to find it in a reasonable curriculum of studies, where it was much more advisable to join anagogy to allegory, so as to complete the exposition of doctrine, before passing on to tropology. In this case Hugh puts it very well: "allegory is subdivided into simple allegory and anagogy."[263] But in reality, as has been seen in a previous chapter, it is two sorts of anagogy: the first, the one that he has just talked about, which is more the consideration of the ultimate ends; the second, which is more the summit of contemplation. The one is under the jurisdiction of doctrine; the other, spiritual life. Hence the one can find its place before tropology, at the end of allegory; the other, the supreme crowning-piece, breaking loose from all didacticism besides, is normally the fruit of allegory and tropology combined, and can therefore come only in the ultimate place. Now Hugh neither excludes nor neglects the second any more than the first. He gives due place to this second anagogy, for example, albeit without naming it, when he writes, after having listed history, allegory and tropology: "Above these, prior to them all, is that divine [point] toward which the divine Scripture leads whether in allegoria or in tropology"; allegory gives knowledge of the truth, tropology gives love of virtue, both the one and the other together thus cooperate toward the reparation of man: the way from then on is open to that "divinum" which consists no longer merely in the knowledge of ends and in the use of means, but, at the very depth of the "repaired" soul, in the anticipation of the end itself; in other words, in anagogical contemplation.[264] Finally one can point out that the *Speculum de mysteriis Ecclesiae*, which is closely dependent upon the *Didascalicon* and the *De sacramentis*,[265] explicitly counts four senses and spells out anagogy in full.[266] The same thing goes on in the *De contemplatione* — even though stuck on tripartite divisions — whose relation with Hugh is doubtless still closer, albeit difficult to clarify.[267] So it goes also in the *Fons Philosophiae* of Godfrey, his faithful disciple.[268]

Nevertheless, let us add: not only does Hugh not speak about anagogy all the time; he does not allegorize all the time, either. From this quite simple remark, there is no need to draw any unwarranted conclusions. Miss Smalley marvels that, alone among his contemporaries, our Victorine does not discover a figure of the Eucharist in the episode with Melchizedek. To us this does not appear so marvelous in either of the two meanings of the word "marvel." In the first place, the fact of neglecting or suppressing a spiritual explication consecrated by tradition does not by itself entail any deepening of the literal explication: the latter remains just what it is, whether or not it be followed by the former. In the second place, there is nothing surprising in the fact that one does not meet with such a spiritual explication in a very short writing that was never intended to offer anything about it. The passage that Miss Smalley alludes to was part of the *Notulae in Genesim*.[269] Now, Hugh warns his reader precisely that the stories of Genesis indeed have an allegorical signification: "we are carried forth through that historical account to an understanding of higher things," but that in his *Notulae* he is concerned only with two things: "namely, the truth of things accomplished and the form of the words";[270] in other words, his *Notulae* ought not to be taken as a complete commentary. No author of this period, Hugh no more than anyone else, had ever tried to speak or ever to write merely so as to develop allegories! Hugh says nothing more, two pages earlier, of the symbolism of Noah's ark, a symbolism of which he offers sufficient evidence on the other side that he does not hold it to be negligible! He knows very well, and says as much, that in all these *Notulae* he touches merely upon the *superficies litterae*.[271] He knows very well that under this surface, from one end to the other of the Scriptures, there are hidden depths which wait for the opportunity to call to light elsewhere: "by expounding . . . the whole sequence of the divine Scriptures, to call forth the mysteries of its profundity into the light."[272] This is what he has done for the ark in particular. In another work, having just called up Melchizedek, he does not fail to point out in him a prefiguration of the Christ.[273]

Let us now return to the sixth book of the *Didascalicon*, so as to complete a reading of those chapters that have already long held our attention: [namely,] the third and fourth, *De historia* and *De allegoria*. We shall thus finish off with an elucidation of Hugh of Saint Victor's hermeneutical doctrine.

History is the indispensable foundation. So we have seen. But has this indispensable foundation been called up to the detriment, howsoever slight it may be, of allegory? Quite the contrary. If it is indispensable, it is precisely as a foundation: it is necessary to be assured of a "good foundation" so as to be able subsequently to "build over" it.[274] In other words — Hugh pursues the metaphor once again in a completely traditional manner — it is essentially in view of this edifice that allegory is entrusted with building, which ought to be the very edifice of the faith. For everything ought to be done in order. One does not start a house with the roof! One does not paint the walls before raising them! "Indeed the primary foundation is laid, thence the structure is built over it; at last . . . the house is clothed with a good coating of color." In itself

Hugh and Saint Gregory

again the letter is nothing much; nevertheless one would be wrong to despise it: one can compare it to the letters of the alphabet, which he who wants to become a literary man cannot be unaware of.[275] This is also an old comparison, which one finds already in Origen's writings.[276] This letter, Bede used to say, is "the milk of primary education":[277] the expression was typically Victorine, by way of anticipation. Or rather, as Hugh says it once again, what the history procures is the shadow, the figure, and it is through this shadow and through this figure that one reaches the "body" and the "truth." The body of the doctrine, or the truth of the allegory, is here the nutritious and delicious honey that must be extracted from the wax:

> begin in order: through the shadow one comes to the body; study the figure, and you will find the truth. . . .[278] Just as you see that every building that lacks a foundation cannot be stable, so is it also in doctrine. Now the foundation and starting-point of sacred doctrine is the history, from which the truth of allegory is squeezed out like honey from the comb. So when you are going to build, set down the foundation of the history first; then, through the typic meaning raise up the building of the mind into the citadel of the faith: then at the end through the grace of morality paint the building with, as it were, a most beautiful color laid on top. In the history you have the wherewithal to marvel at God's deeds; in the allegory, the wherewithal to believe his mysteries; in the morality, the wherewithal to imitate his perfection.[279]

Everything that Hugh says in favor of the history, his whole warning against misusing allegory, we have found in the long, previous — completely Gregorian — tradition.[280] Now, by a movement in the opposite direction, we find in Hugh everything that this long tradition said in praise of allegory. Shadow and body, figure and truth: the very words are identical. The image of the honey in the comb that Hugh had already used in the preceding book[281] is no less traditional than the rest, as we know already, and once more we have to go back at least as far as Origen to catch it at its source.[282]

By insisting upon the need for the first foundation, Hugh intends to spare the exegete the subjectivism that would consist in a superficial or ill-understood allegorism. But it is another subjectivism that he rejects with no less vigor. The latter consists in an obstinate literalism, which would be deadly:

"The letter killeth, but the spirit giveth life" (2 Cor. 3): since obviously the reader of divine things must be solidly grounded in the truth of the spiritual understanding, so that the flourishes of the letters, which sometimes can be understood perversely, should not incline him to any diversions. Why has that ancient people who had accepted the Law of life, been rendered reprobate, if not because it followed the mere letter that killeth, in such fashion that it did not have the life-giving spirit? I say this not to offer occasion to any to interpret the Scriptures at their own whim; but to show that he who follows the letter alone cannot advance without error for long.[283]

Yes, Hugh of Saint Victor was an "objective" spirit. Only his objectivism strongly resembled what many today consider subjectivism. It was the objectivism of men like Origen, Augustine, Jerome, and Gregory. As it was for all of them, his objectivism consists in "constructing a spiritual building on the foundation of the history."[284] He pursues the construction of this edifice with an abundance and precision of details that are rather more characteristic of a mason than of an architect in the chapter on *allegoria* that immediately follows the chapter on *historia* and is much longer.[285] Hugh even pushes the "allegoristic" impulse to its extreme limit, borrowing from Saint Gregory the image of Ezekiel's chariot. Does he not ask his reader to observe that, in the Prophet's vision, as elsewhere in the nature of things, it is the wheels of the chariot that follow the movement of the animals both in their walking or in their flight, and not the other way around: the wheels follow the animal, the animals do not follow the wheels"? What does this mean? This means that the depths of Scripture, inaccessible to any profane science which would be a profaning science, do disclose themselves to the spirit of the exegete in the measure that he himself goes deep into himself: "these wheels follow the animals, and they follow the spirit." Advice and warnings ultimately have as their end merely to keep this going-into-the-depths or this spiritual drive on the right course. But in that case spirit answers unto spirit, and, in an order opposite to what occurred at first, the Spirit that is within the Scripture answers to the Spirit — the self-same Spirit that is within the man, within the believer, within the contemplative. "The divine utterances grow with the reader."[286]

This is, as can be seen, pure Gregorian doctrine.[287] Hugh, let us say it again, owes much to Saint Jerome. But, whatever his debt to him may be, whatever his admiration for him or the authority that he recognizes in him might be,[288] it is not Jerome whom he takes to be the great master. He would not call him, as Jean of Salisbury will, "the teacher of teachers."[289] As the majority did, after Gregory, Isidore and Rabanus, after Berno of Reichenau, he esteems above all the translator in him, whose version, so faithful to the Hebrew, is preferable to every other one[290] and has been imposed in the Church "throughout the whole Latin world."[291] As for breadth of mind as well as knowledge and the fecundity of wit, to him Augustine seems to surpass all the others.[292] But in tropology, it is Saint Gregory who carries off the palm. Now the whole of Scripture is directed to that end:[293] this is a thesis dear to Hugh, and it is indeed tropology, as the worker of the "education of morals," which is by preference practiced at Saint Victor. Thus Hugh embraces with singular delight the writings of blessed Gregory, who was filled by the Spirit; for him, he says, they are sweeter than all others ("mihi prae caeteris dulcia") because he finds them full of the love of life eternal.[294]

If the work of the great Victorine does not properly mark a "return" to Saint Gregory, who had never truly been abandoned, it does confer on it a new currency. As the abbé René Wasselynck has shown at the end of a patient inquiry, Hugh often closely follows the thought of Gregory, in his didactic works as well as in the others. For his explications concerning the letter, for his exposition of the threefold sense, he copies from it even down to the expressions. "Even in the detail," his teaching "on the sense of Scripture flows in a straight line from the *Moralia*"; "with the *Didascalicon*, with the *De scripturis*, the Gregorian method actually becomes" for a limited time "the medieval hermeneutics."[295] In composing the *Gregorianum*, then, Garnier of Saint Victor was going exactly in the line of his master, and Dom Pitra was perhaps wrong not to assign to Hugh an explicit place in his *Legio gregoriana*.[296] In this first half of the twelfth century, one does not perceive any "Victorine reform" that would be directed against "the allegorical idealism" of Saint Gregory. Hugh has not conducted any "major operation" against Gregorian *moralisatio*. Where one had wanted to see in him a sign of an innovating spirit, opposing that of Saint Gregory, we discern — without prejudice regarding many individual differences and despite a scholarly organization all of whose consequences Hugh had not foreseen — completely the contrary: the authentic Gregorian spirit.

Much more objectively than this or that other historian, Father Chenu has remarked that the "renaissance" of the twelfth century, of which Hugh of Saint Victor is one of the principal craftsmen, was more "historical" in its spirit than that of the ninth had been.[297] Nevertheless, the simple comparison of the *Didascalicon* — to which one ought to join the third chapter of the *De scripturis*[298] — with the *Clericalis institutio* of Rabanus Maurus is not perhaps very significant in this regard. Indeed, on both sides, the didactic apparatus appears equally logical and atemporal; nor is there any more appreciable difference in the manner in which the two masters, almost three centuries apart, appeal to the seven liberal arts, i.e., to all the profane sciences, particularly to "physics," for the study of Scripture;[299] each of the two equally want us to study history and geography to clarify the sacred text.[300] Besides, their two works are a bit too closely inspired by the Augustinian program — at the same time as by certain Gregorian views[301] — not to resemble each other in many points. Finally, let us note that if, while speaking of *historia* and *allegoria* in the preface of his *De universo*, Rabanus Maurus understands by "historia" practically the "nature of things" and the "normal use of words," and by "allegoria" their "mystical meaning,"[302] then these acceptations in this place were governed by the object of the work: they in no way prejudge what can or cannot be its historical sense in the exposition of sacred history.

One ought no less to recognize, with Father Chenu, that the *De sacramentis* evinces a broad historical spirit the like of which is not found, at least not completely, in Rabanus Maurus. Only it will be good to recall also that the scholarly and encyclopedic effort of the great Carolingian monk does not sum up the whole exegetical tradition from the time of the first Fathers up to that of the Victorines. The literary genres and the methods of thought that are observed in the course of that long history overflow the pedagogical categories and the teaching techniques of certain theoreticians. The twelfth century sees the blossoming of the great theologies of history: but neither that of an Otto of Freising,[303] nor even that of an Anselm of Havelberg seems to owe anything to Hugh; and without having produced any work analogous to the *De sacramentis*, the *Chronicon*, or the *Dialogi*, Saint Bernard himself seems to have quite a lively sentiment of sacred history in its totality, though his immediate intention is not to emphasize the latter, when he says that the Bible is "one, continuous, perpetual discourse."[304] We shall not force any further the contrast between a symbolic cosmos, nourished by the liturgy, which would have been that of the monks and consequently of almost all pre-Victorine exegesis, and a symbolism based upon history, which Saint Victor would have inaugurated. Not only had the historicity of the facts of salvation, which was always affirmed most categorically at all times, always furnished the basis for biblical allegory, but also the vast development of these facts had not always been neglected: witness the recent work of someone like Rupert; and if it is true that, in the monasteries where the ancient traditions were kept up, liturgical prayer encouraged spiritual understanding to take flight,[305] nevertheless the reading of the Bible was not so bound to the liturgy there as to preclude many coherent commentaries on the holy Books from being made. As to Hugh himself, indeed, he has searched out the allegory of such objects as the ark, rather than the interpretation of broad historical sequences; he enters many cosmic elements in his own symbolism, just as he enters many historical elements in the liturgy; finally, frequenting Dionysius was done not to turn his imagination onto the history alone: it would doubtless have emphasized his bent for the "exemplarist symbolism whose roots simultaneously sink deep into the spirit of Platonism and into an authentic biblical tradition,"[306] that symbolism whose theory Origen also had constituted in his commentary on the Canticle,[307] and with which the whole Middle Ages remained impregnated. If, in his commentary on the *Celestial Hierarchy*, Hugh has augustinianized Dionysius, this is not done by historicizing him but by substituting for his cosmic objectivism a psychological and moral atmosphere, as the abbé René Roques has well shown.[308] It is therefore not without reason that he has sometimes been placed in the same symbolist school as a Honorius[309] or a Saint Hildegard,[310] or that H. O. Taylor, studying "medieval thought," spoke of him in his chapter on "the symbolic universe."[311] Let us add that the *Distinctiones* literature, which proceeds in part from him, does not manifest any change over the previous epoch with regard to the proportion of "naturalistic" elements that are mixed in with the symbols drawn from sacred history.[312] Thus, we think, always with Father Chenu,[313] that it is advisable not "to exaggerate the change of perspective proposed by Saint Victor." We even believe, to tell the truth, that there was no change of perspective intended. Once more again, the principal abuse against which Hugh protested was not that which would have been able to be claimed in some measure from certain old texts of Rabanus Maurus or Bede; it did not come from an old "routine" and it was not passively kept alive by the weight of a traditionalist mind: it was rather more the seduction of a novelty, as has just been related. Against this seduction, Hugh of Saint Victor was driven, in his work of reorganization, to maintain the spirit of past centuries.

It was necessary for us to get to see this in this chapter, before getting to know in the next chapter the genuine novelty that the methodology of the Victorine master nevertheless did possess.

5. History of the Revelation

As traditional as it may appear to us till now, might not the work of Hugh of Saint Victor still be, in some respect at least, the effect of an "awakening" to the "sense of history," an awakening at that time fostered by "a civilization taking flight" which sensitized it "to the time of an economy on the march"? If one understands thereby only that this work has played its role in a magnificent renaissance whose intellectual dimensions are not unrelated to its social dimensions, the matter is indisputable. It is no less certain that one of its characteristics was to emphasize history, either by the first operations of theological labor in quest of the literal sense of the Bible, or by the syntheses of thought considering the divine economy of salvation. And these results were not acquired without struggle. Yet, if the master of Saint Victor had to fight against a tendency toward "the evacuation of history," or even "the elimination of time,"[314] this was less by running into rear-guard resistance than by himself resisting currents which were forming around him. If then it is true that "it is through a vigorous reaction in favor of the *historia* and its irreplaceable value that characterizes Hugh's vocation,"[315] this vocation was in reality more defensive than offensive; it was essentially conservative. Nothing appears to us to show that he is specifically trying to liberate the mind from Carolingian techniques or pseudo-techniques, expressing the aspirations of a rising generation that is trying to liberate itself from the old "feudal" constraints. He was rather part of the "resisting Augustinian environment," once again to accept Father Chenu's expression.[316]

Now the resistance had to be made on more than one front. There was in fact, for some time, the somewhat insolent rush of the new dialecticians, of the "philosophers," such as Peter Abelard, unmindful of the concrete history and reversing the traditional methods to build their idea-palaces on new plans. There were also resurgences of the platonic ideal, not particularly well-disposed to "becoming." In the wake of the enthusiastic discovery of Nature by such men as Adelard of Bath, Bernardus Silvestris and William of Conches,[317] there was once again, and would soon be still more, an effort of cosmologists to discover the "properties of natural things" beneath the letter of Scripture: under their curious gaze, the worth of *historia* vanished even more than it had long ago in someone like Rabanus Maurus, in favor of *physis*, which amounts to saying that they perverted *allegoria* by turning Scripture away from its proper end. The movement that carried them along had to contribute subsequently, along with Abelard's enterprise, to the grandiose flight of metaphysics as well as to the constitution of a new equilibrium in theology; but in the meantime it was hardly propitious for a sound development of exegesis. Finally, drawing its strength from those more general causes, there was the insidious influence of a "nominalist" logic, which was in danger of ending up "somehow de-existentializing the chief facts of the *dispensatio* under the pretext of assuring the unity of faith and salvation through time."[318] This logic was at work again in Abelard, and especially in Bernard of Chartres.[319] Peter Lombard himself, not very consistent in his rather shallow Augustinianism, was soon to undergo its influence while treating of the divine foreknowledge, but without subsequently drawing its consequences for salvation history, or rather not seeming to draw them at the very first except to come back to more nuanced solutions later on.[320]

Now Hugh of Saint Victor does not participate in this fourfold drunkenness. He does not give way to any of these "spiritual pressures." The vertigo of timelessness does not trouble him for an instant. Notwithstanding certain other features that we have pointed out in his exegesis, in him allegory remains frankly "historical," in contrast to a naturalistic allegory which breaks through here and there in his century and which will be affirmed in the following century, for example, in a Roger Bacon — scarcely a traditional traditionalist — or in a Bartholomew the Englishman.[321] The seven rules of Tyconius, assimilated by Saint Augustine and transmitted from then on from generation to generation, are for him a sure guide for the direction to impress upon "spiritual" exegesis.[322] Consorting with Dionysius does not turn him any the more from the spirit of Augustine. Our Victorine opposes the grandiose view of the *De vera religione* to the diverse thoughts that are sketched in the contrary direction, just as the Benedictine Rupert of Deutz did a bit earlier, as the Premonstratensian Anselm of Havelberg in the same epoch, as the Cistercian Henri of Marcy (†1189) a bit later, each one doing it in accordance with his own point of view and with his own nuances: "The head of this pursuit of religion is the history and the temporal dispensation of divine providence to secure reforming and repairing the human race unto eternal life."[323] Through his own "favorite expression" *series narrationis* he provokes the revival of Augustinian expressions such as "the order of things"[324] or "the ordered sequence"[325] — as well as Origenian expressions that passed into Latin from Rufinus, such as "the order of the history,"[326] "the historical order of reporting," "the sequence of historical understanding,"[327] which did not, however, habitually have such a vast import.[328] Thereby he fixes "the characteristic feature of a history as opposed to the logical connection of the theoretical disciplines."[329] Always in the wake of Saint Augustine,[330] with many others besides,[331] he lays stress upon the three great steps of the economy of salvation: "before the Law, under the Law, under Grace — in peace."[332] Also in his wake,[333] and that of many others again,[334] he enumerates the six ages of the world, figured in terms of the six days of creation, which traditionally furnished their framework to the universal chronicles. Through a Christian adaptation of the ancient doctrine of the macrocosm and the microcosm, these six ages made a development analogous to that of individual existence out of the whole sequence of history; they are, says Hugh, recapitulating an old comparison that Saint Julian of Toledo had exploited long ago, "to the likeness of the age of a man" and they are distinguished "not according to equal intervals of time, but according to the common new stages of things."[335] In the measure that *allegoria* in him is organized into an already systematic theology, it is organized also according to the order of the history: this is what the summary program contained precisely within the chapter of the *Didascalicon* devoted to *allegoria*,[336] in addition to the *De sacramentis*, clearly shows. By recalling as well[337] so many passages where the great Doctor used to show such a lively feeling for what belongs to each epoch according to the providential laws of development,[338] he precludes the temptation of a sort of timeless Christianity which might turn toward abstraction or gnosis.[339]

This was a real temptation, truly current in that twelfth century, though as yet unconscious, just as that rationalist temptation implied in a too under-disciplined use of dialectic was at once unconscious and yet current among several people. The tendency to eliminate time inevitably involved the tendency to eliminate the Act. The debates that were begun in that epoch regarding the faith of the "ancient Fathers" in comparison to the faith of the Christians are a good illustration of this point. Besides, the grammatical theory that nourished these debates and sometimes apparently even provoked them matters little to our point of view: this was merely one of the subtle expedients whereby a temptation not unique to that age insinuated itself, one of the disguises under which it made its way into people's minds. A thinker as little adventurous as Peter Lombard let himself be caught up in it. This was one of the forms that this always open "curious dialectic" took, a dialectic "of a faith that, in quest of the eternal, stabilizes time, and of a reason that, bound to time and place, gives way to an eternalism of abstraction."[340] It was therefore a question of knowing whether the change of times and circumstances, from the one Testament to the other, had involved a change in faith. This was not the first time that this was debated. Let it suffice to recall how, in the ninth century, Fredegesius had maintained that it was absurd to believe that there were any Christians under the Old Law, and how Agobard had answered back to him that his double formula — "there were no Christians" and "there was no Christ" — was a double blasphemy.[341] But now, in the context of thought of which we have just spoken, the problem took on a new pointedness. The opinions were quite diverse, and sometimes, even amongst friends, the tone of the discussion began to rise.[342] In the chapter of the *De sacramentis* where he deals with the object of the controversy in his own turn, after having grappled with it several times in the course of the previous years,[343] Hugh of Saint Victor begins by observing that it is going to be necessary for him to put into play "some serious thought," in so delicate a question, where "the thoughts and opinions of men are so many, and dispute about orthodoxy is conducted with such diversity of faith."[344] Let us overlook the fine points for the moment. The new School of the *Nominales*, whose protagonist was Peter Abelard, claimed to be the only one to respect the thought of Saint Augustine — just as Agobard had already claimed — by positing a complete identity between the faith of the Old Testament in the Christ to come and the faith of the New Testament in the Christ already come. For had Augustine not observed that when Saint Paul shows God justifying the circumcised "ex fide" and the uncircumcised "per fidem," he does not intend to posit the least difference between the two cases, but expresses himself thus merely "for linguistic variety"?[345] And had he not said over and over: "Tempora mutata sunt, non fides" ("The times have changed, not the faith")?

In reality, however, the Augustinian axiom was far from carrying so absolute a meaning. The self-same Augustine also said: "the signs have been changed, but not the faith," and immediately explained his thought, showing clearly that for him these changes of "signs" or "sacraments" from one economy of salvation to the other were much more than changes in rites:

> [Israel] was awaiting from God, according to the Old Testament, not knowing that signs of things to come were there; so they were awaiting from God a happiness of the present life, and they were seeking on the earth what God was keeping for his people in heaven.[346]

A hundred other texts took up the same idea,[347] showing to what extent, for Saint Augustine, the change that took place in the *signa* or the *sacramenta*, or more precisely the cause of this change, affected, if not the deepest essence of the faith, at least its mental expression and its behavior.[348] Doubtless the two Testaments both have the same God as their author, and so they cannot contradict each other, but their harmony involved a prefiguration of the truth. Undoubtedly Israel was already "that selfsame people of God which is now the Christian people";[349] without doubt, the holy society which today is called the Catholic Church existed, albeit under another form, from the time of the first just man, Abel; and since Jesus Christ is the unique Mediator, it was necessarily through faith in Jesus Christ, that, under the Old Law itself, men could be saved.[350] What is more, did not the Apostle intentionally write: "habentes eumdem Spiritum fidei" ["having the same Spirit of faith"]? Augustine loved to recall this text.[351] But in his eyes it did not at all follow that those men would have had the same sources of enlightenment as we do with regard to Jesus Christ and the salvation of which he is the Author. If they participated in the same faith, they did not have the same understanding of it;[352] they praised God, without grasping the reality of what God was signifying to them; they could not yet perceive the true object of the divine promises: "for not only are the signs (*sacramenta*) different, but also the promises; temporal things seem to be presented there, by which the spiritual reward is signified in a hidden way."[353] Depending on the occasion, Saint Augustine found himself led to emphasize the one or the other of these two aspects of the truth; but he never denied nor even completely eclipsed the complementary aspect. Against the Pelagians, for example, he insisted upon everyone's needing the unique liberating grace.[354] Elsewhere, against the Manicheans, or again against the Jews, he explained how what has become obvious today was hidden long ago. The just of the old covenant had a faith that was still obscure: "at that time the faith that was later revealed had been hidden";[355] though they sincerely sought to please God, they took the signs as the things themselves and did not know what to relate them to.[356] For the times had not yet obtained their fullness. "Indeed the sacrament of the kingdom of the heavens, which in the fullness of time would be revealed in the New Testament, was veiled in the Old."[357]

The explication was that of Origen already, for whom the words of Moses to the people had within them, as did those of the other prophets, "the appearance, albeit hidden, of knowledge."[358] In this way and by many other distinctions too, Origen tempered the abruptness that some of his own formulations had as well.[359] Nevertheless, like Origen again, who admitted that "under the reign of the spirit of slavery some already received the spirit of adoption,"[360] and also just like Irenaeus,[361] Augustine thought that at all times certain great friends of God — the holy Patriarchs, Moses, the Prophets — had received, through Christ and in his Spirit, certain more abundant sources of light, a veritable anticipation of messianic times; these sources of light permitted them to comprehend that portion of the salvific Plan that still remained "hidden within the figure"[362] for the Israelites as a whole. Although some among them served the Lord with a view to his apparently earthly promises, these latter loved him gratuitously.[363] They were among the "the righteous in spirit," that the "letter that commands" did not kill, but that the "helping spirit" vivified.[364] Thus one has the right to say of them, in terms that at the same time show clearly the exceptional character of their situation: "Though during the dispensation of the time they ministered to the figures of the Old Testament, nevertheless, they belonged through God's grace to the New Testament even though it had not yet been revealed."[365] Might not such a conviction also be authorized by Jesus' saying: "Abraham has seen my day and rejoiced"?[366] Following in the footsteps of Irenaeus and Origen, Augustine thought so too. As to the revelation of the mystery of God in his Trinity, however, he exhibited more reserve. What is more, he added, those privileged by the Lord have ever been merely an extremely small number: "paucissimi pii," and that which was given them to foresee of the whole revelation, they received "not from a manifestation of things present, but from a revelation of those to come."[367] Thus the essential difference between the times and the "economies" was always maintained. Thus what belonged to each stage would be found marked off. All things appeared to be disposed "fittingly," "with fitting times,"[368] the "custom" of one time was not that of another, and Saint Augustine could still say: "This grace, veiled within the Old Testament, used to lie hidden, a grace that has been revealed in the Gospel of Christ with the most orderly dispensing of the times, as God knows how to dispose all things."[369]

The *Nominales* of that epoch thus misunderstood one whole side of Augustine's thought — as some historians of theology still seem to do so today when they speak of a "certain devaluation of the properly historical character of God's work" — transmitted by Saint Augustine to Latin theology. Without doubt, like all the ancients, our Doctor had received "a decidedly anti-historical philosophical culture"; what is surprising is precisely that, under the pressure of his own Christian reflection, he more than anyone else had nonetheless sketched a "theology of history" which was to act powerfully to integrate history within philosophical thought. Again, just as in our own day a Péguy had to be aware of it, so too Augustine was doubtless quite aware of that "proper effect of time," namely the "senescence" that nothing here below can escape: but this all-too-indisputable recognition of one of the aspects of reality did not, it seems to me, entail an alienation from the historical process itself; it did not "disqualify" all becoming and did not "evacuate" man's historicity.[370] Now, the very real historical orientation of Augustine has as a whole remained part of the later tradition.

As in Augustine himself, a certain number of texts simply point out or emphasize the analogy between the situation of Christ's faithful and that of the righteous members of ancient Israel. In each of the two cases, it is, they aver, "the same faith,"[371] it is "the same spirit,"[372] namely, "the same love of the Trinity."[373] That is because they are very eager to show in that way the unity of the path that leads to salvation,[374] the oneness of the Redeemer and his grace, and the identity of the single Church across the ages:[375] "For the Church is one both in the preceding and the later Fathers,""The Church, which began at the origin of the world and will last until the end of the age."[376] Such will be the point of view of Saint Thomas Aquinas, forcefully affirmed once again in the *Summa theologiae*.[377] The Church of the New Testament, says Gerhoh of Reichersberg, is the daughter of Sion: she is nourished with her milk; her faith is like unto that of her mother.[378] And has not this unity of faith under both covenants been proclaimed by the Apostle Peter the day he cried out: "We believe ourselves to be saved just as they were — by the grace of the Lord Jesus"? Consequently, comments Aimon, "we believe that what they foretold has already come about."[379] Nevertheless, it is only when one compares the situation of the just "before the Law" and that of the just "under the Law," to wit, the two principal periods out of which the Old Testament itself is composed, that one affirms an identity without reservations or qualifications: "one faith, one expectation or hope."[380] On the other hand, when it is a question of comparing the common situation of all those ancient just men to the situation of the Christians, as was done of old in Origen or Augustine, qualifications abound everywhere. Everywhere, in formulations that scarcely vary, one affirms the diversity of the modes and signs. Everywhere there recurs the explanation of the single faith in terms of *sacramenta* or of *mysteria* that are dissimilar *pro temporum ratione*.[381] Everywhere the various ages of the world mark off a series of levels in the development of revelation and, at the last level, a deeper change of governance or "state."[382] At each step, says Lethbert of Saint-Ruf (†1100), with a happy feel for nuances, "the manner of speaking varies, and the ancient reality is renewed by the very manner of speaking."[383]

Within one and the same faith which alone brings salvation,[384] one everywhere likewise detects differences of "awareness,"[385] or of "knowledge."[386] One finds that, before Jesus Christ, nothing could be brought to its proper perfection;[387] the perception of the figure is opposed to that of its spiritual signification once the thing itself has arrived,[388] and the expectation of temporal goods is opposed to that of eternal goods,[389] and one concludes: "there is a big difference between us and them."[390] Finally one everywhere sets aside the privileged case of the "prophets" illuminated by the Spirit, who were "in occulto" aware of the realities of the Testament to come:[391] "Saint Abraham," "Saint Jacob," "Saint Moses," and the rest, who, without seeing the Messiah with eyes of flesh, have so much desired him, and perhaps — this is an ancient conviction, authorized by some of the Fathers — along with them, the small group of priests and doctors that they had initiated in secret.[392] Concerning them one takes up once more Augustine's terms: they are "few,"[393] "only a few," "very few," "rare and obscure," "a very few perfect ones"; one even says: "none, or at any rate few."[394] They were stars shining in the night.[395] These "saints" and "Fathers" who were by special favor "foreknowing of things to come"[396] are not confounded with the mass of the "carnal people," who were attached only to the letter of earthly promises.[397] With Augustine again, one repeats the claim that, living under the Old Testament, they already mysteriously belonged to the New, just as today there are some men who in reality belong to the Old; they were of the spiritual offspring of Sarah and Isaac, just as the spiritual offspring of Hagar and Ishmael is perpetuated among us.[398] The former were therefore already living "in the liberty of sons"[399] — "not outside the mystery, but outside its time."[400] They alone comprehended, "by revelation from God, the mysteries of Christ and the Church," which for all the others, even the just, remained secretly "wrapped" within the Law.[401] Sometimes again the point is made that they understood them only "partially."[402] For them alone was the door that gives access to knowledge of the great Mystery left half-open.[403] Once again, it was only half-open: they themselves did not comprehend the redemptive Plan to the foundation, "to the full."[404] Each of them, Helinand tells us, catches a glimpse only of one of the numerous aspects of the mystery of salvation, with the result that John the Baptist himself, who was nevertheless more than a prophet, was unable unhesitatingly to recognize the expected Messiah in Jesus.[405] What Hugh of Rouen said of Moses can be said of each of them: "Nor yet did Moses know everything in them that the Holy Spirit who taught him knew within them."[406] Thus, though they may have taught many things, "the simple symbol of the faith taught by the holy Apostles" is more important, richer and more necessary for the salvation of men.[407] Until Christ, only one voice was resounding; since the Incarnation of the Word [le Verbe: verbum], it is the Word [la Parole: vox] which is ringing back.[408] Even an extreme traditionalist like Agobard, who, as we have seen, exploits by predilection the line of unchanged unity, and who wants there to have been nothing else new in the Christian faith than a larger diffusion of the old Faith,[409] has not been able to keep himself from attenuating his thesis somewhat.[410]

To express the common teaching, Rupert draws a symbol from the luminous cloud that guides the Hebrews of old at their departure from Egypt:

> We know the mysteries of this pillar that at night, i.e., not yet revealed by the light of grace, was fire, and small, i.e., was shining for very few unto the grace of prophecy. . . . [Today] the whole source of fire, the true Sun, and the whole source of light has come with the cloud of his flesh; though he is the Sun in a cloud, he nevertheless shines more brightly than fire ever did in the night.[411]

Another symbol is taken from the description of the new temple in Ezekiel. There the question concerns a door and two doorsills: the door is Christ; the Fathers of the Old Testament are the outer doorsill, not only because they have preceded those of the New Testament, but also because only the latter, who are the inner threshold, grasp the divine teachings from within. This explication, which was developed by Saint Gregory[412] and reached the *Glossa ordinaria,* was taken up again by Saint Martin of Leon.[413] Aelred of Rievaulx compares the knowledge that one has of Christ under the old Law to the meager provision of bread and oil that was with the widow of Sarepta:

> At that time, while the reputation of God's word was weak, a widow, i.e., the Jewish people, had a bit of flour and a little oil; but thence a little bit of baked bread is made, i.e., an awareness of Christ.[414]

Gerhoh of Reichersberg distinguishes a whole series of stages in the progress of revelation, comparing them either to the various levels of human growth, or to those of the preparation of a marriage.[415] Absalon will say that in ancient times the Spirit of God showed itself "rather sparing, not to say stingy," and he will compare the Church before Christ to a still-sealed spring.[416] Garnier of Rochefort will develop the image of a plant: its root was the natural law, it grew and flowered in the prophets, it bore its fruit in the faith of the apostles.[417] Along with this image, Saint Hildegard will take up the no less classic image of passing from infancy to maturity:

> [Before the incarnation of the Word] prophecy was like the words of infants whose words cannot be understood, but after they have become more mature, then their words are understood; so too prophecy was neither known nor understood prior to the incarnate Son of God; but it was laid open in Christ, since he stands forth as the root of all good branches.[418]

More often, a "very well-known allegory,"[419] already generally worked out in the patristic age,[420] allows everyone to express the whole doctrine, always basically the same, albeit with a variety of subtle differences. It is the allegory of the grape-cluster carried from Canaan, hefted on a long pole, into the camp of the Israelites by the two scouts. Let us set aside the exegeses that apply it, in the present state of history, to the respective situations of the enlightened Christian people and the now blinded Jewish people,[421] or that envisage the latter in its past history while yet giving thought to its future blindness.[422] For a number of interpreters, who also see in the grape-cluster a symbol of Christ borne on his cross, the first of the two bearers is ancient Israel, which precedes him and consequently, even while believing in him, does not see him; the second, the one in the rear, is the Christian people: in bearing Christ, it also contemplates him. Here again, some authors are content with the general idea that both the one and the other are bearing Christ:[423] thus, the symbol of the grape-cluster is for them what the symbol of the two groups of children preceding and following the Lord on his entrance into Jerusalem was for others: it serves to tell them one more time about the concord of the two Testaments, as of two "choirs," or the unity of testimony rendered to the Redeemer by the "order of the prophets and that of the apostles,"[424] without closing in on the problem that is of concern to us.[425] But many others observe the difference of position of the two bearers:

> The grape-cluster placed on the pole is the Lord lifted up on the cross. . . . Now two men are carrying the grape-cluster on the pole, through which they furnish the people with the fruitfulness of the Land of promise, since the preachers of both Testaments, who have

learned of the glory of the heavenly fatherland at the Lord's revelation, do not cease to intimate the same mystery of his passion to the people. . . . But the fact that though the two bearers were able to carry it in the same way they could not look at it the same way, clearly signified what the Savior himself says: "Blessed the eyes that see what you see," etc. Hence it is said here that, once the signs of his incarnation had been accomplished, the Lord opened up to the disciples the sense so that they would understand the Scriptures.[426]

That is how Saint Bede expresses himself. Saint Ambrose Autpert does so as well.[427] In his great poem, the *Occupatio*, Odo of Cluny puts the parable into verse:

> [As to] that pole carrying the grape-cluster from the land of the giants:
> The front man does not see this cluster and the second man carries it with vision;
> The Jew, who is first in time, offers it his back,
> The gentile people, having followed last, offers their face. . . .[428]

The same symbolism is found in Saint Peter Damian[429] and in Rupert, who knows that for the ancient Jews everything concerning Christ was "under seal":[430] "They kept reading, but they did not understand, and to those who were the best, who were wont to see with prophetic eyes, it was said in such wise as not to be divulged."[431] The same symbolism persists in Richard of Saint Victor,[432] as well as in Arno of Reichersberg, who strives to explain how the prophets can nevertheless be called "seers."[433] This was also already the symbolism of Saint Gregory.[434]

Gregory's historicality manifests itself still better in the passages where he explains that if as yet "rude" Hebrew people already had the same faith as we do — "one hope, one faith, belongs to both the peoples preceding and following" — nevertheless it did not have the same "perfection of faith," to wit, the same knowledge of the mysteries: "that rude people of the Hebrews . . . was not educated with the knowledge of the holy Trinity"; it did not know "the subtlety of the faith."[435] This historicality manifested itself again in the passages where Gregory compared the time of the Law and the time of the Prophets,[436] or, as has been said, the Fathers of the two Testaments to the two doorsills of the Temple of Ezekiel.[437] The holy pope had, however, quite clearly formulated the principle of the development of the revelation: "The knowledge of the Fathers increased with the times,"[438] and he had applied his principle in distinguishing the "tiny" Church under the Old Testament and the "adult" Church under the New.[439] Now, once again, it is exactly this teaching, stemming from Gregory as well as from Augustine, that we rediscover in Hugh of Saint Victor, along with his explicit reference. In the manner of Gregory and Augustine, Hugh affirms the diversity of the three economies which mark the succession of the times and which distinguish three classes of men, all the while recognizing that under each of these three economies men are found belonging to each of these three classes.[440] Hugh draws support from Gregory to comment upon Augustine and to avoid the dangerous theses of the "intemporal" theologians. "Yes," says he, "under the Old Law it was indeed the same Savior, it was the same faith, the same grace, but of a Savior who was expected, not already arrived; it was the same salvation; but at that time the signs of that salvation had to be obscure, and little by little, to the extent that the time of the Savior approached, the faith had to increase and grace had to manifest itself more clearly."[441] The believers of Israel were waiting for a redemption, and it was the same redemption as ours, but they could not at that time know how it would come about. And again, not without a certain irony: If the conscious content of the faith of the ancients was already, as some would have it, the same as the content of our own, then let us praise God and his gifts! But in that case, we no longer see what could be left for the time of grace:

> But, as Saint Gregory also says, even the knowledge of the spiritual Fathers grew with the growing times, and by as much as they stood closer to the advent of the Savior, by so much did they more fully grasp the mystery of salvation. There is no doubt that even to those who were present, the exhibition of those things, as well as the presence of the Exhibitor, contributed much more.[442]

Hence Hugh also himself distinguishes the *fides* or "faith," which remains the same, and the *cognitio* or *agnitio fidei*, the "awareness of the faith,"[443] which changes and increases. This is a distinction of capital importance and very strongly emphasized: "much more" ["multo amplius"], "the presence of the Exhibitor" ["praesentia exhibentis"]. This is the way, he thinks, Augustine also understood it before Gregory and Bede after him, and it is indeed just what the allegory of the grape-cluster suggests: those who have gone before have carried but have not seen."[444]

Hugh of Saint Victor was indeed, then, in the twelfth century, "the master" or at least one of the masters "of this traditional perception" of a historical *dispensatio salutis*.[445] His merit is not so much that he had, as some have said, "introduced a sense of time into theology," but of having maintained it. It was not for having emphasized the historicity of the Bible or for having turned it in some new direction, but rather for having defended it — as Saint Gregory in particular had formulated it, and especially as Saint Augustine had exploited it — against rising theories that would compromise it or risk even to empty it of all content.[446] He speaks about this as Cassiodorus had spoken.[447] He speaks in the same way the Pseudo-Isidore had spoken, "For the people of God have been ordered in this way through the passings of the times, and have always been changed toward better things, until the perfection, etc."[448] He speaks as Rabanus Maurus had spoken in commenting upon Exodus: "By as much as the coming of the truth itself approached in the flesh, by so much were the mysteries more clearly revealed to the Fathers."[449] He speaks as Hugh of Fleury spoke a little earlier when laying out the program that he was establishing for his *Ecclesiastical History*:

> I shall now take care to explain to readers according to the text of the history how the correct education of the faith proceeded in the world through certain steps and divisions of ages and times, and how the Old Testament served the principles of the Gospel in prefiguring the divine mysteries, just as the age of boyhood is wont to precede the age of manhood.[450]

Hugh speaks as Rupert did, the one who carefully distinguished among the "faith," the "knowledge of the faith," or the "knowledge of the faith or of its profession,"[451] and who, not content with taking over the old parallelism between the six ages of the world and the six ages of human life,[452] commented on it in detail, showing that the biblical revelation had something new to offer to each age, from the time of earliest infancy, before the flood, when man had still been "left to himself"[453] before the Word of God had begun to instruct him.[454] He speaks as Bodo of Prüfning had in his own generation, who closely recapitulates the words of Saint Gregory;[455] just as soon a Werner of Saint Blaise would speak, who recalls the Gregorian principle of development in these terms: "It is necessary, however, that the signs of spiritual graces should be rendered more and more evident with the passage of time and calling ever more for being declared, so that an awareness of the truth should increase along with the effectiveness of salvation."[456] Garnier de Rochefort would soon repeat this in his own more personal language: "By as much as the fullness of time approached more closely, by so much did the crown of this year of benignity stand out more perfectly and, if I may say so, more roundly."[457] This will also be once again the solution of Saint Thomas Aquinas.[458] More precisely, and the matter is worth noting, Hugh here is speaking just as Saint Bernard did: the passage of the *De sacramentis* that we have just commented on is in fact taken, word for word, from a long letter that the abbot of Clairvaux had written him in response to his questions.[459]

On so essential a question, which commands several others, the unity of Hugh and Bernard seems to be telling. It is not, however, surprising. Indeed one can speak of a historicality permeating the whole "allegorical" tradition. It was the very same as Saint Paul's. According to Paul, as Msgr. Lucien Cerfaux has written, "the prophets of the Old Testament were aware of the mystery, but could reveal it only under certain symbols; we today penetrate their symbols"; the people as a whole, then, did not penetrate them, "but to the extent that they were aware of the mystery, the prophets were precursors in the ancient world, and their prophecies were an anticipation; they were Christians ahead of time."[460] Origen, Augustine, Gregory, and all who follow them in the Latin West, in substance said nothing different. It is a completely modern prejudice, it must be repeated still again, to oppose symbol and reality as contradictories, or to think that history and allegory are incompatible in one and the same mind. It is this prejudice that leads one to attribute Augustine's esteem for the spiritual sense of Scripture, for example, to his Neoplatonism, while his Christian faith was making him perceive the value of the letter, and which saw him torn (quite unconsciously, one ought at least to admit!) between these two incompatible inclinations; it is this prejudice that prevents one from recognizing that, quite to the contrary, "his philosophy of history, based on the Incarnation," supposes them both equally.[461] For with him, as with every Christian nourished on the same tradition, it is the very movement of the faith which, from the simple "narrative," leads right to the "mystery"; and faith is well aware that the fact is not extenuated nor the uniqueness of the event compromised thereby. Quite the contrary! More particularly, as regards the Old Testament, let us recall that it is the self-same Epistle to the Galatians which laid the basis for the Christian philosophy of history as well as for the Christian allegory of the Scriptures.[462] Ever since, then, as we have already had occasion to point out, the idea of the historical development of the revelation and the allegorical interpretation of sacred history have essentially gone hand in hand.[463]

That "new Augustine," Hugh of Saint Victor, is a new witness for us of this fact.

CHAPTER FIVE

The Victorine School

1. Canons of Saint Victor

Hugh of Saint Victor is a genius "rich and variegated." So too was his posterity numerous and varied.[1] The men who, for various reasons, have generally been regarded as his disciples are very different from each other. They often even seem to be opposed to each other. Indeed, for the most part, one hesitates to give them the name "disciples," since they also differ so much from their master, though having retained this or that from his teachings, this or that orientation from among the many that only when taken together characterize him. We shall select a few of these disciples, to start with, more or less arbitrarily, in two groups. The first group will consist of certain Victorine writers: Richard, Andrew, Godfrey, Gautier, Garnier, Absalon. The second will include personalities as diverse as John of Salisbury, Peter the Eater, Peter the Chanter, Stephen Langton, Adam Scotus.

Richard, the greatest of them all, will occupy us in a little while. Andrew (†1175?) is a learned exegete, whose importance has been uncovered in the works of Miss Beryl Smalley.[2] Contrary to so many others, he appeals to the *hebraica veritas* with a knowledge of the facts. He received his scientific drive from the head of the school, but did not inherit from him either his spirit of synthesis, his sense of symbol, or his traditional vigor. With him, "the Bible becomes the object of scientific study," and, it seems, an exclusively scientific one. Now this is completely new. To be sure, Hugh already spoke of "science" regarding holy Scripture. He said, for example: "The seven liberal arts subserve this science."[3] But it would be an error to believe that this "science" according to Hugh really paved the way for "science" according to Andrew. The word *scientia* did not yet have the specific signification that it was soon to obtain in scholasticism or the quite distinct sense that it has in our language now. It was not yet, as it were, a "magic word" evoking the ideal of a body of doctrine technically organized according to the "Aristotelian canon of demonstration," which was to become an enthusiasm of theologians in the following century.[4] Nor did it designate that "experimental science" envisaged and celebrated already by Roger Bacon, that strictly specialized "positive" discipline, based upon an analytic method, whose success we find so intoxicating today. It was the whole order of knowledge in general.[5] It was often applied to the totality of teaching, human and divine; sometimes, more precisely, it was the "spiritual science," the "gift of true science," one of the seven gifts of the Holy Spirit:[6] *the light of knowledge, the erudition of the Holy Spirit.*[7] One spoke of it then by calling up the text of Exodus [35:31], slightly modified: "The Lord hath filled them with the spirit of wisdom and understanding and knowledge and all learning."[8] Such, in its essential character, was the science of Scripture, that science which all clerics were to acquire with diligence, which engendered pure and robust minds, and which Saint Gregory had praised.[9] It was, next to the science of God itself that had long ago been communicated to Moses and the other sacred writers,[10] a participation in that divine science, in that "universal knowledge which profits unto salvation" in which the whole content of holy Scripture consists or is summarized.[11] Hence it was the science "which penetrates the depths" of Scripture;[12] in short, it was its spiritual or mystic understanding, its understanding according to the threefold sense: "rich in all knowledge, i.e., literal, moral, and allegorical."[13] A science which an attention fixed upon external things could not grasp. An eminent science, which God himself entrusted to us "through his most faithful instrument."[14] A science that made one see Jesus Christ in Moses and in the Prophets.[15] A science enlightening the mysteries of the kingdom of God,[16] which could shine forth only within Catholic unity.[17] An alluring science within the soul of one who devotes himself to the divine presence there.[18] The "science of the Apostles and the Prophets," the science of the twofold Testament.[19] A holy science, to which Christ alone had the key;[20] a science consequently reserved for those who, like Saint Paul, having received "the sense of Christ," have been enlightened by the Spirit of Christ.[21] The Jews, lacking the faith, could not possess this science, because they were "wandering in spirit."[22]

Carnal men might have been scandalized at such a "science."[23] But, as Richard will say, "borne aloft by this science of Scriptures as by wings, we leave the things of earth to climb to those of heaven."[24] So it was indeed a question of science in the highest sense, that which was symbolized by the cherubim, of whom it was constantly repeated from the time of the Fathers that their name signified "the fullness of knowledge."[25] One humbly begged for it and received it from God.[26] It was the mystical water drawn from the wells of Jacob.[27] It communicated a spiritual drunkenness.[28] While pointing out that this science is served by the natural disciplines, the "natural arts,"[29] Hugh did not keep the knowledge of faith apart from them; on the contrary, he included it among them. Indeed he called it "a divine knowledge," and, without any intention to change his thought or to modify its object, he also used to say: "All the arts are in service to the divine wisdom."[30] He did not proceed in the same manner as Andrew, however. The latter is a technician of exegesis; he practices exegetical science already in the modern senses of these two words. He is a specialist. Father Chenu's remark regarding "the innovative character of exegesis at Saint Victor" applies to him with complete truth.[31]

Hugh contributed to making Andrew's works possible. These works naturally find their place in the general framework of biblical studies as it was then structured. But Hugh did not anticipate those works either in their precise tenor or in their spirit. He would not have condemned them in principle, but he would surely not have approved of their exclusivism — if that were in fact what it seemed. Thus we do not believe that we could maintain with Miss Smalley, if it is true that Andrew is "merely a scholar," that "Hugh's promise is fulfilled in Andrew."[32] Hugh's ideal is not to be "merely a scholar." Whatever the terminology, Andrew innovates by making a separate science of exegesis. From then on exegesis becomes a specialty, constraining doctrine or "theology," by way of reaction, to become something else. It is still unheard of that anyone should understand it badly. Perhaps he himself did not understand it quite right either. Rarely does a founder reflect upon his own invention sufficiently to define its nature exactly and to calculate all its consequences. He is thus not entirely capable of justifying his own initiative, even in what it offers to make better. The inevitable and therefore legitimate limits of a technical specialization necessary for the advance of knowledge run the risk of leading it to doctrinal poverty. Even more, when badly grasped, they risk awakening a crisis of faith among those who follow it.

Master Andrew of Saint Victor has left a reputation for being a man both religious and also able and eloquent, a "diligent examiner of the

Word of God."[33] His intellectual position, to the extent that it can be reconstructed — his principal commentaries have not always been edited — was no less ambiguous. It is so easy to pass, almost without perceiving it, from methodological abstraction, which is an indispensable instrument of progress in science as well as of rigorous debate, to fideistic isolation, or even to the denial of a higher order of truth! The scholar and the believer then are so well divided that the second sees himself completely robbed of his object. One fact is certain: that Victorine student of the Jewish rabbis[34] came to be treated as a "Judaizer" by his brethren — this expression was not new — because, in his literalism, he rejected or wished to ignore the Christian explication of certain prophecies.[35] He gave the impression of reestablishing what Saint Paul had called "the letter that killeth," which was then also called, by Rupert, "the letter of the Synagogue."[36] He declared that as a believer he admits that interpretation, but then went on to make no further allusion to it in his exegesis. Others, he said, have already answered the objections that the Jews have made to us on this subject; but he added: "sed an sufficienter responsum sit, ipsi qui responderunt viderint" ["but those who have answered will have seen whether their response is enough"]; as for him, he left to others stronger than himself the task of attempting a definitively victorious response, out of fear lest his own weakness in such a difficult fight should do harm to the cause he was incompetently attempting to defend.[37]

Such language was disquieting. One can easily imagine the situation. In a context of thought and expression that is obviously different, the problem that is posed here is already basically the same problem that would exercise all the minds in the Church at the beginning of the twentieth century, in the storm raised "about a little book." It is the problem of how history as science is related to history as reality, and it is at the same time the problem of history in relation to dogma, or, as once upon a time we used to say (in certain cases the meaning would be almost the same), of history in relation to allegory. This problem is not reducible to the question of knowing which literal sense one ought to recognize in such and such a text, as it might sometimes seem. It is much more general and much more fundamental; one rediscovers it as well with regard to the Gospel as with regard to prophecy, as with regard to all spiritual history. How ought one to understand the critic's silences? Does he really deny and in that case does he have the right to deny everything that the scientific examination of texts does not permit him to affirm? Do there exist other methods permitting him, under certain conditions, to affirm something extra? Does the prejudice of adhering to what is called scientific objectivity allow one to comprehend the object he is studying?[38] Does not such an exegesis, being dogmatic in the wrong way, allow for serious "philosophical gaps"? These and other questions like them pose not only a critical problem: they pose a prior problem, *the problem of criticism itself,* its role, the place to be assigned to it in thought as a whole, and the limits of its competence.[39] It is quite normal for the exegete in the modern, specialized sense of the word to be attentive, as such, only to the first of these two problems; but the historian of theology who considers "the study of the Bible" in all its dimensions, cannot neglect the second. In terms of scientific accomplishment, the bottom line of Andrew of Saint Victor's ledger is clearly in the black: the esteem in which he was immediately held by such men as Peter the Eater, Peter the Cantor, Adam Scotus, Herbert of Bosham, and Stephen Langton, as well as the use that they made of his writings[40] are sufficient proof for us. The oppositions that he aroused cannot surprise us, however — if his sayings have been correctly reported by Richard — and we should not be tempted to see in them merely the result of personal rivalries[41] or of a mechanical exegesis opposed to a critical one.

Of the whole Victorine group, Godfrey (†1194) is the one who best exemplified the ideal of a disciple, to the extent that it involves both intelligent fidelity and a degree of self-effacement. Like his master, Godfrey is didactic, and he made his master's conception of science and of sacred studies entirely his own; like him, he is moderate, traditional, and prudently open-minded; like him, he loves synthesis and balance. He is perhaps a bit more optimistic than his master: there are "secret sympathies between his work and the new philosophy,"[42] and, though he is also a fervent admirer of Saint Augustine — he devotes ten strophes to praising him in the *Fons Philosophiae* — it would not be too hard to make him a precursor of Thomism a century in advance. Like Abelard, he admires the Seneca of the *Letters to Lucilius*. If he ever gets his dander up, it is occasioned by thinking about the excessively somber and strict doctrine of some of his confreres, and to oppose them with his own elogy of noble human nature.[43] If he comments on the phrase from the Psalm "the sharp arrows of the powerful," it is, in opposition to a firmly established tradition, devoid of any polemical spirit: he wishes to shoot his arrows with the bow of Scripture only with a view to "saving souls."[44] Still, in his irenic manner and in his somewhat scholarly thought, this bashful character is a bit behind the times; this is doubtless what accounts for there being little said of him of yore and for his having been neglected by the moderns, until the fine publications that have been devoted to him in our own day by Philippe Delhaye and Pierre Michaud-Quentin. Previously [e.g., Vol. 1, intro.; Vol. 2, ch. 9] we have cited some of the verses of the *Fons Philosophiae* in which Godfrey describes the pedagogical methods of Saint Victor: it is a classic treatment of the fourfold sense. Substantially the same treatment is found in his other great work, the *Microcosmus*, which itself in its entirety is nothing but "a vast moralizing allegory."[45] In it Godfrey develops the "threefold expository method of Gregory," and Saint Gregory is, after Saint Augustine and Saint Isidore, his most cited ancient authority.[46] In both works, he urges the reader to study the *Moralia*,[47] and, in the *Fons Philosophiae*, he intentionally mentions the author of the *Moralia* before Ambrose and Jerome.[48]

Gautier, on the other hand, is narrow-minded and closed. The prior of Saint Victor of Paris, as head of the School, wants to be conservative and is indignant at novelties from any source, which seem to him the potential ruination of untouchable doctrine. This "blustering" and "angry" man does not even spare Saint John of Damascus, recently imported from the East, nor his own confrere Godfrey, guilty, in his eyes, of having mixed the water of human wisdom with the wine of theology, forsooth the cup of demons with that of Christ;[49] and, if he can do nothing against the person of Damascene, his persecutions drive the unfortunate Godfrey into exile.[50] He sees nothing but "cheeky" people everywhere, who vex our minds with "all sorts of ridiculous questions," who have merely a false science, and whose faith is a shipwreck.[51] With his vows he calls down the Roman thunder which will silence these "rotten frog-croakings." What in fact prevails in him is integrist violence, with its stigmas of stubborn "incomprehension" and "bad faith," at the service of a traditionalist reply. Every doctrine that does not agree with him is a "new heresy compounded from an old one."[52] He uses the procedure — unfortunately still too widespread today — of speaking indeterminately in the plural to fabricate Frankenstein monsters, enlarging the errors of some by those of others, and shaping those errors in turn with enlargements and false comparisons: thus all whom he takes as adversaries jointly "vomit" a thousand "heresies."[53] He is not, as someone has written somewhere, an "exaggerated mystic." There is nothing mystical in his attitude. On the contrary, it is a cramped fundamentalism. It would do him too much credit to compare his bile to the fiery passions of a Saint Bernard, even when excessive or occasionally unjust. To him, every effort at thought is suspect. If he rejects the application of the "rules of the dialecticians" to the mysteries, this is not because he has some peculiar feeling, like Alan of Lille for example, for the transcendence of the revealed truth: he just wants to say that the *dialectici*, these adepts of a "diabolical art," arbitrarily undertake to defend both the affirmative and the negative: "If you believe them . . . , you don't know whether or not God is God."[54] The Spirit does not dwell in him. His work, being completely negative, is sterile. He cites Saint Gregory very rarely, but Saint Jerome, whose polemical and rhetorical extravagances attract him, he cites a lot.[55] When he alludes to "pig fodder" or the "chalice of evil spirits," it is not to Origen or to Gregory that he is referring, as well he might: it is to Jerome,[56] whose quarrel against Origen he naturally drives home.[57] Again, he borrows the diatribe against Aristotle, the "prince of dialecticians," from Jerome.[58] What a distance from Hugh to Gautier! What an abyss! A marvel of accelerated decadence, of which the history of theological schools offers other examples.[59]

At his side, his confrere Garnier was patiently engaged in a completely peaceful construction project. He brought forth nothing original, but his substantial *Gregorianum,* which must have been finished around 1170, is the best and most complete of the many analogous collections composed using the writings of Saint Gregory for six centuries.[60] However massive the work, it belongs to a relatively minor literary genre; and, as is always the case with works of this kind, it came too late. It could only nourish an over-familiar exegetical style whose life was already waning. Paradoxically, he himself became connected with a relatively new literary genre: those *Allegoriae,* those *Distinctiones* which go on being multiplied and becoming complicated, the purpose of which is to assist an allegorical explication more conscious of its resources, more knowledgeably constituted, and the result of which would be to hasten its decline.[61] Besides, Garnier is neither an exegete nor a thinker. Still, in his modest place, he is still in the line — or rather in one of the lines — of the master. He picks up with new disbursements and on a new level the blueprint of a work begun at the time of Hugh and probably by Hugh himself, unless it was already done by William of Champeaux, the founder of Saint Victor.[62] In systematizing it, he completes a part of what was sketched out in the collection of the *Miscellanea,* which is, as is well known, full of texts from Gregory. Like the liturgical feast of Saint Gregory that was solemnly celebrated there each year,[63] the *Gregorianum* of Garnier indicates to us the permanent influence of the great pope upon Saint Victor. Without polemics, without apology, by its mere existence, this massive dictionary, a work of loving diligence, stands as a challenge against the legend of a Victorine center all lined up against the principles of Gregorian exegesis.

The brilliance of the Victorine Order was shortlived. Some of its most beautiful rays shine in the poetic work of Adam (†1192), "the most magical wordsmith to have made the Latin psalms resound" (Remy de Gourmont); a poet more artistic than spiritual, but one whose verses "were nourished on the same doctrinal, mystical, and symbolic sap" as the prose of Hugh and Richard.[64] In the first part of the thirteenth century, he will again cast a belated glow, along with Thomas of Verceil, who exploits deeply but one-sidedly the dionysianism of the founder.[65] Less brilliant and less abundant is the work of Absalon, who was abbot of Sprinkirsbach in the diocese of Trèves (†1203). Still, Absalon has left us a few specimens of his preaching that have true merit. He admires Aristotle's wisdom, his search for the supreme cause, and his high ideal of contemplation.[66] As the celebrated Psellos did a century earlier at Byzantium, he enjoyed seeing Christian truths figured through the most ingenious literary inventions due to the wise men of old: the tree with the golden branch at the gate of the underworld, the golden chain descending from heaven to earth.[67] He is not afraid to appeal more directly on occasion to the thoughts of the "philosophers of this world."[68] He knows nevertheless that there exists only one true wisdom: higher wisdom, holy wisdom, given from on high, which teaches nothing about how to resolve the problems of Donatus or those of Aristotle or Plato; which confers neither the art of Euclid nor that of Cicero nor that of Boethius, nor any other human discipline; but just how to live following God.[69] Without [this wisdom] one would be — as Gautier wrongly reproached Godfrey — mixing the water of secular wisdom with the fine, pure wine drawn from the cellar of holy Scripture.[70] Thus, Absalon is far from condemning the use of the profane sciences. He wants those who are to pour the people the drink of the divine Word to prepare themselves for the task with solid studies.[71] He does not blame those who celebrate "the marriage of Mercury and Philology" but wishes them to occupy themselves a bit more with the marriage of Christ and the faithful soul.[72] He makes the classic interpretation of the beautiful captive his own.[73] And why, he asks, stop at meditating upon the Ideas of Plato, or again to render Gratian's *Decretals* concordant, to weigh the laws of Justinian, etc., in short, always to be studying but without making up one's mind to take the last step, which consists in searching for God and finding him?[74] Finally, transposing at once the exclamation of the old sage of Egypt and those of the Apostle Paul, he cries out to address his contemporaries: "O Greeks, will you always be children, then? Will you never reach true knowledge? When will you finally get weaned from this milk? Do you not know that God has rendered foolish the wisdom of this world?"[75]

Absalon hearkens back to Hugh, whose "singularis auctoritas" he extols.[76] He himself is not a creator. But he is a mind much superior to that of Gautier or Garnier. His careful balance and his taste for symbolism as well as his preoccupation with the moral dimension in the "investigation" of Scripture[77] make him an authentic Victorine. He effortlessly unites "allegorical mysticism with deep thought," which he expresses with the elegance of a humanist. This combination is highlighted by Father de Ghellinck. Every time he meets with it, it amazes him and even scandalizes him: How can men "of such obvious intellectual soundness," men who are "educated," "level-headed," even profound, give in to such "eccentricities" and surrender to such "outrageous taste"? By what aberration did they believe that they see all these *mystica sacramenta* in the Old Testament?[78] Our own astonishment will be rather less, and, we will simply salute this good disciple of Hugh and Saint Gregory[79] — who was given to ruminating upon Scripture,[80] a bit timid in the face of the new science, and already more withdrawn than the best representatives of Cistercian thought at that time[81] — as a good witness of the common tradition.

2. Parisian Masters

The authors that remain to be mentioned before we go on to Richard were not formed at Saint Victor. They in no way form a homogenous group. But, by reason of this or that feature of their intellectual physiognomy, they are customarily looked at, as Father Chenu says of one of them, "in the wake of the Victorines."[82] This is why we are examining their position in exegesis here.

John of Salisbury (†1180), who was later to be bishop of Chartres, one of the two cities of his student days,[83] is a complex personality. Longtime secretary of Thibaut, and then of Thomas Becket, Archbishops of Canterbury, in this office he bore "responsibility for all of Britain"; though experienced in political and ecclesiastical affairs, for which he traveled to Rome ten times in a dozen years, he considered such things trifles — "the nonsense of court,"[84] a sort of slavery, a lie,[85] the destroyer of all virtue, an adversary of all philosophy.[86] But he came to overcome the dilemma by following the example of the "great Aristippus," who, he says, "accommodated himself equably in every circumstance, exhibiting amiability to all and philosophizing amidst the vanity of affairs."[87] For all that, he is not the "light-hearted, winsome, sceptical spirit" that Michelet thought he was.[88] Open to all knowledge, an ardent inquirer, solidly based upon the principles that are the object of "living reason," nevertheless, following Cicero, he thinks that the wise man often ought to be content with the probable and that one of his virtues is even to know how not to know.[89] For him prudence and truth are two sisters that require equal praise.[90] Seeing that everything vanishes in smoke under the gaze of the philosophers,[91] he might be tempted to let the world go, but human feeling blocks this retreat: "He is not enough a man whom [the misfortunes of] others do not move," and the thought of Christ's teaching and example rouses him into action: "Clearly a disciple who fails to rejoice with the truth and does not burn against the enemies of the public weal is unworthy of so great a Teacher."[92]

This moderate, conciliatory man of experience accords equal praise to the various mutually quarreling religious communities.[93] He refuses to apply the title 'wise man' to anyone who does not strive for peace every time peace can be obtained without loss of honor.[94] Tactfully complaining to the misguided sovereign who is responsible for his exile,[95] he seems more like an early Thomas More than his own boss Thomas Becket, whose ardor he would have wanted to temper:[96] but nonetheless he upheld the cause of the archbishop martyr, after having contributed more than anyone else to his conversion. "At first, upon reading his work," observes one of his readers, "one gets the impression of being at school among the pagans,"[97] while another thinks his teaching strongly influenced by Jewish theocracy: the *Polycraticus* combines Deuteronomy and Plutarch.[98] This biographer of Saint Anselm, this intimate friend of Peter Cellensis and Pope Adrian IV, is at any event not only a sincere believer, a veritable man of the Church, close to the political thought of a Bernard or a Hugh, but still a profoundly spiritual man, living the Pauline motto that he loves to recall: "Wherever the Spirit of God is, there is freedom,"[99] and some of his expressions, while recalling those of Saint Gregory, anticipate those of Thomas à Kempis.[100] He shows great boldness in his criticism of the rapacious and bullying Roman Curia,[101] of episcopal ambitions and tyrannical behavior,[102] of the ecclesiastical vice of flattery;[103] but at the same time his loyalty is total: when the heretic or schismatic raises his head, he says, "it is pious to stand by the truth and most devotedly to wait upon the Roman pontiff."[104] He even goes so far as to proclaim in oracular tone: "The whole creative Trinity is turned against one who lacks the grace of the Church,"[105] and he pronounces an absolute elogy on obedience:

> Christ promulgated this [obedience] by command and by example, having become obedient unto death, teaching to what extent the vir-

tue of obedience ought to be limited. For obedience is required not merely up to the loss of one's temporal goods or the sufferings of the body, but unto the event of death.[106]

In its capacity to embrace two extremes, the *Polycraticus* of John of Salisbury (1159) more than once reminds one of Saint Bernard's *De consideratione*.[107]

Very erudite, enamored of history and poetry, a friend of the classics, our author might be thought to cling to the past: yet he himself declares that he prefers the moderns to the ancients. He is extremely well-read, a humanist in the most aristocratic sense of the word. Like the spirituals of the preceding generation and the best pioneers of the new learning, he is hard on the sort of innovators "who show off of their knowledge, to dazzle their hearers but not to make themselves understood by them."[108] These intemperate "scholars" disdain lowly "grammar," blaspheme against the "eloquentiae studia," are proudly oblivious of the great authors, treat the best teachers like blockheads, "hardly sparing master Hugh"; they play at being philosophers and "cast leaves of words to the winds without allowing the fruit of meaning to ripen." *Trifling jugglers!*[109] Sophists, jeered at already by Abelard himself, by Bernard and Thierry of Chartres, by William of Conches, jeered at now by a Godfrey of Saint Victor[110] and a Peter of Blois,[111] and soon to be jeered at again by a Peter the Cantor. They could well be the cousins or nephews of those whom Hugh criticized for their attitude regarding the Bible.[112] They are, says John, "Cornificians," worthy heirs of that Cornificius who had been Virgil's detractor, the one whose portrait Donatus had sketched long ago.[113] That crew despises even Cicero, indeed every great writer "and whatever captured Greece has given to the Latins."[114]

He who was recently an ardent disciple of Abelard and Guibert and who frequented the very subtle Adam of Petit Pont is surely no enemy of logic! On the contrary, he is undertaking to defend it![115] It is, he says, a science "agreeable and fruitful" ["jocunda et fructuosa"]. Only, "they all yearn for logic, but they don't all reach it" ["omnes logicam appetunt, sed non omnes assequuntur"].[116] He is no dupe of a totalitarian dialectic which, in the mouth of these neo-barbarians, turns to logomachy. To it he opposes "the sweet and fruitful mating of thought and speech" ["dulcis et fructuosa conjugatio rationis et verbi"], the only integral logic, a humane and fruitful force, mother of all civilization.[117] There is sometimes a moment of indulgence toward these pretentious young men, as though they lacked good teachers: indeed, how many professors might not be asked, as the apostle Philip asked the eunuch of the queen of Ethiopia: "Do you think you understand what you are reading?"[118] Nevertheless, he warns them that, without this "grammar" that they no longer want, they will never be "litterati."[119] He raises against them an ideal of culture then in decline, with a little too abundant luxuriance of citations and allusions, a bit in the manner in which a fifth- or sixth-century Roman struggled against the rising tide of barbarism. It is a hopeless struggle already: the trends that he is trying to restrain are the very ones at play in the schools of Paris, those of the great new university.[120] Thus, in this regard, John of Salisbury looked like a defeated figure, as he, along with his archbishop, was defeated in public life. The Cornifician carries him off, spreading his own jargon like a leprosy.[121]

Still, along with his taste for philosophy, "without which anything is devoid of spice and without taste, and completely erroneous, and displeasing to good morals,"[122] John of Salisbury received from his masters at Chartres, whose memory he loved to recall, a taste for the sciences of nature, and his lively understanding led him to anticipate in momentary sallies the great movement of independent thought that from then on would spread everywhere. Not only is he alive to "the goad of questions" and "keen on the seven ways," but he takes the side of Gilbert de la Porré, from whom he was able to profit, against Saint Bernard, whom he venerates and to whom he is bound by a debt of gratitude;[123] the chapters of the *Historia pontificalis* that he has devoted to these two illustrious adversaries, both of them "the very best men of letters and extremely eloquent, but in dissimilar pursuits," are remarkable for their psychology, intelligence, and nobility of soul.[124] He wants to have a collection of Bernard's letters, a florilegium of his sayings;[125] but he also enters into relations with Jean Sarrazin, the specialist on Dionysius, whom he presses to send him the results of his work. At Benevento, he is also associated with a "Greek translator and grammarian," namely Henricus Aristippus, who acquainted him with the *Meno* and the *Phaedo*,[126] and he studies the translations of Aristotle with the same curiosity. He would prefer them to be a bit more exact, he complains in the original text of the explanatory notes.[127] He was the first of anyone in his century to analyze the *Organon* of the Philosopher as revealed to him by Thierry of Chartres and Burgundio of Pisa; he professes that without knowledge of the *Analytics* "whoever professes logic is laughable";[128] in their author he discovers more "subtlety" than one ordinarily praises in him, a "marvelous sweetness of expression" which almost rivals the art of Plato[129] and his very name seems symbolic:

> Great Aristotle possesses the arts of speech
> And has a name derived from the apex of the virtues.[130]

In the *Polycraticus* he incidentally projects the idea of a mathematical logic and, in the *Metalogicon*, that of a universal system, which makes one think of Leibniz.[131] In many a passage of his work one urges "the development that, in the thirteenth century, will announce the autonomy of the forms of nature, of intellectual methods, of the laws of society."[132] At the same time, he foreshadows Petrarch and the humanism of the Italian fourteenth century.[133] Finally, if there is a "modern" of the twelfth century, he is it.

At the same time, however, he forcefully maintains, as did Hugh, that all knowledge is vain, all philosophy deceptive, which causes one's love of God to diminish,[134] or which does not offer some aid to practical life by urging one on to virtue.[135] He also knows that by leaving the tomb alive Christ overturned the false doctrines of Aristotle and the other philosophers. He thinks that it is permissible for a Christian to cite a pagan author, but not without taking precautions against his errors and not without nicely distinguishing nature and grace.[136] Like Hugh again, in all things he requires a certain Christian modesty without which the highest gifts of the spirit do more harm than good.[137] Like him, every time that he speaks of the "books of the divine page," he does so in the most traditional terms. If he deals with exegesis, it is to recall *ex professo* the doctrine of the four senses: only it, in his view, permits one to enter with the necessary "seriousness" within that treasury of the Holy Spirit, where one finds nothing which is not filled with mysteries.[138] In his own commenting upon Scripture he readily refers to Saint Gregory, whom he admires, whom he even regards as an organ of the Holy Spirit,[139] but that does not keep him from having a veneration for Saint Jerome, "a distinguished doctor of the Church, a man accomplished in practically all things literary."[140] John of Salisbury was not a pupil of Hugh: he calls him "master," but not "my master"; more critical-minded, more free-spirited, more versatile and less artificial, he is not his disciple any longer, in the strict or exclusive sense of the term; but he has been nourished on his thought, from which he has retained less the didacticism than the spirit.[141]

Peter the Eater, Peter the Cantor, and Stephen Langton share the common distinction of being teachers. In them the flesh-and-blood human dimension is less richly developed than in John of Salisbury. All three belong to that new species denominated "masters in the sacred page" ["magistri in sacra pagina"]. All three happily rely upon the works of Andrew of Saint Victor for the literal sense.[142] All three taught at Paris, which from then on begins to become the intellectual center of Christendom. They have the common characteristics of their age and their office. It can be said that the three of them formed a sort of school. Exactly what the connection of this school with that of Saint Victor and what its force or nature is are matters for further discussion.

The *Historia scolastica* (ca. 1170) of Peter the Eater (who was to die a canon of Saint Victor in 1178) immediately knew a prodigious success, which was not to fade before the sixteenth century. It was soon glossed by Nigellus of Longchamp.[143] It is known to have been translated into French in 1297 by Guyart des Mouslins under the title *Bible historiale*.[144] There were only two other books that enjoyed a comparable reputation: the *Sentences* of Peter Lombard and the *Decretum* of Gratian. As its title indicates, it is essentially a scholarly work. It answered to the needs of a society where the schools were taking a novel status, first place.[145] Again, as its title indicates, this summary of the Bible sticks only to the first of its four senses, namely, the *historia,* whose whole sequence it summarizes. Peter the Eater is by no means the herald of literalism: in his Preface, he lays out the classical theory of the four senses, and there is nothing to allow us to think that this theory lost any of its value in his eyes. Well, ought we at least to say that his book results from a decision of high import, "the decision taken . . . to restore sacred *historia* within its very letter"? There is no sign to show it. Nor have we been able to discern in him that "novel curiosity toward the texts of Scripture" that the generosity of one historian attributes to him. What he does exhibit that is relatively new is rather the phenomenon of specialization. Previously there had been many "chronicles," many more or less universal histories, one whole part of which was devoted to summarizing biblical history. But we did not yet have a separate work for the Bible, systematically confining itself to the "foundation" of history. The work was provoked by new instructional needs; but the conception itself for such a work had already been facilitated, nay even called for, by the methodological distinctions of the *Didascalicon*.

Such, then, in essence was the influence of Hugh upon Peter the Eater. But the fact that he had taken recourse, here or there, to pagan histories, or that his continuous recital contrasts with the piece-meal method of the gloss are not novel or symptomatic facts.[146] Many others before Peter have used extra-biblical sources, and the exegetical literature of the past was not composed only of glosses: whether in the chronicles, or again in the great frescoes of a Rupert, there was a sense of historical con-

Parisian Masters

tinuity and development, received from the ancient Augustinian tradition, rather superior to that which one could draw from this book, also very scholarly in this regard, namely the *Historia scolastica*. For our Peter, history is a genus subdivided into three species: "annalis, kalendaria, ephimera,"[147] a distinction itself classic, inspired by Isidore of Seville;[148] one will with difficulty say that it supposes an effort of profound reflection upon the meaning of history. Nor shall we at all agree with Father Chenu, for whom this History "establishes and spreads the historico-literal method of Saint Victor within current practice in teaching and preaching";[149] in the first place, because the method of Saint Victor — or at least that of Hugh and his continuators — does not appear to us to be "historico-literal," except in its initial period, which was never supposed to be sufficient; additionally, because the preaching at the end of the twelfth century, which is known in sufficiently numerous examples, convinces us that it was in no way traced from the *Historia scolastica*. Peter the Eater is the first to tell us as much: a "most eloquent man,"[150] he preached a lot; further, in his own sermons he shows himself to be the most allegorical of preachers.[151] He unceasingly exhorts his audience, usually composed of students,[152] to pass beyond the *litterae superficies*, just as Saint Gregory long ago exhorted his to look further than the *superficies historica*; he invites them to peel away the surface so as to reach the core of spiritual understanding,[153] to bore a well to where the living water may spring up.[154]

Only he preaches in a new way, quite different from that which had long been dominant, rather far from the monastic sermon, whose simpler and more flexible structure provided a better continuation of that from the time of the Fathers.[155] He made great use of the *Distinctiones*. This kind of lexicon was doubtless "aussi ancien que l'étude de l'Écriture": "as old as the study of Scripture"; however, at that time one threw himself into cultivating it with fervor and, let us admit it, a level of pedantry never attained before.[156] If the content of Peter the Eater's sermons is traditional, their artificial and complicated structure presupposes a theory of *allegoria* conceived as a strictly codified discipline. He can be called a scholastic allegorizer. "Allegory," he tells us, is "sometimes taken in terms of a person, sometimes a thing, sometimes a place, sometimes a time, and sometimes a deed."[157] There too one can discern, if not a direct product, at least a belated effect of Victorine didacticism. The spirit, however, is no longer truly that of the initiator.

Two features of vocabulary will enable one to grasp the difference clearly. One may recall that epigram fired off by Hugh in his *Didascalicon*, at the pretentious exegete who "was philosophizing" in his own way about a quite insufficiently meditated text: "It's not the erudite but the spiritual person who judges all things" ["Non litteratus, sed spiritualis omnia dijudicat"]. But it is the litterati that are more and more in honor.[158] This is what takes place: their promotion to the chairs of the young University of Paris. For there are now more "professors" than "litterati." Peter the Eater is one of the first among them: "first of the Parisian Masters," as Robert of Auxerre calls him.[159] Like all those of his generation, he is puffed up with enthusiasm for this new form of biblical knowledge. Charging for rights to grant teaching licenses, he "sells" them without suffering any longer the repugnance that such a sort of trafficking inspired a short while earlier in Saint Bernard.[160] Pope Alexander III, himself full of admiration for the "men of letters," granted him the privilege by way of exemption.[161] He conceives his teaching as a high mission. For him this is not mere bluster. He knows that more than one *litteratus* is unequal to his task, and that there are many ways to betray; he takes the requirements, which are not of a merely scientific order, seriously. But at the end of the day, if he is what he ought to be, the *litteratus*, formed by the schools, is above all others: he is, according to an expression that Peter borrows from John Scotus, *deividus*, which is to say "he who sees God through understanding the Scriptures."[162] This seer discerns what is hidden under the "puerilis verborum superficies." It is given to him to know the mysteries of the kingdom of God, which others know only in parables.[163] It is he who "dwells in" the Bible; it is to him that it is delivered as nourishment:

> Blessed, therefore, are the men of letters, to whom holy Scripture is present, who have ready the authorities of each of the two Testaments, by which they can extinguish the fiery weapons of the enemy! If this is so, blessed indeed! But . . . not all men of letters dwell "in the aid of the Most High." For there are some who fear holy Scripture; others even mock it; others destroy it; others disdain it; others travel through it cursorily; others dwell in it.
>
> Those who fear it are slothful; those who mock it are proud; those who destroy, heretics; those who disdain, false brethren; those who pass through it, strangers; those who dwell within it are citizens.[164]

> But the food of the lofty is spiritual and intellectual. Such is holy Scripture, which serves as many courses to the man of letters as there are lessons of instruction.

For we say that the men of letters, of whom the Apostle says "You who are great, instruct such a one" (Gal. 6), are lofty in the Church.[165]

One also recalls the biblical trio: Noah, Daniel, and Job, the trio in which Daniel enfigured the contemplatives. The contemplatives were able to be subdivided, for example, into "cloistered" and hermits; or opposed to each other, as the more perfect to the simple "continent." Further, Peter the Eater imagines, or makes his own, an additional subdivision. Contemplatives, he explains, are of two sorts: there are the "cloistered" and the "scholars." The first, who live in common, pray in this way: "Lord, teach us to pray"; the second, in their poor and laborious life, superior to every other, pray: "Lord, teach us to be open to the reading, since wisdom is sweet."[166]

Here we have a new beatitude: "Blessed are the learned!" A new hierarchy: "Great in the Church are the learned!" Here is a unique privilege preeminently belonging to the *litterati*, the "scholares," the "magistri": the mysteries of the kingdom have been revealed to these "sages"; their intellectuality makes them the true spirituals of the new times. In this lyricism there is more naïveté than pride; that is just the price to be paid for a totally new, beautiful enthusiasm, and we would be wrong to be scandalized over it. Our professor in no way forgets that literary erudition can be "a knowledge that puffs one up," and by which one is enticed by the Tempter; he puts his hearers on guard against it.[167] But how far we have come from "Master Hugh"!

Just as Peter the Eater is the author both of the *Historia scolastica* and of ultra-allegorical sermons, so Peter the Cantor (†1197), author of the *Verbum abbreviatum* (1191-92), a work in which the letter is dominant, has also composed the enormous *Summa quae dicitur Abel*, or *Vocum obscurarum explicatio,* one of the fullest collections of allegories, supplemented still further by the *Distinctiones super Psalterium*. These were the biblical and theological dictionaries of the epoch, for the use of preachers. This second Peter of ours is also convinced that the first obligation incumbent upon a "master" is to preach; he cannot conceive of biblical studies that would not add to *lectio,* considered as the foundation of the edifice, a *disputatio* that constitutes its walls and that would not end with a *praedicatio,* which forms its roof.[168] Connected with the school of Laon, doubtless through the intermediary of Alberic of Reims, he wants this preaching to be essentially practical.[169] Himself the inspirer of the "rough, simple, and pure" language of the celebrated Foulques de Neuilly, he can intervene vigorously against flatterers, the ambitious, slanderers, the slothful, the avaricious, and usurers.[170] Though extremely well-read and keen to appear such, he loves simplicity in everything, in lifestyle as well as thought; he loves it especially in the theologian: "Simplicity is most becoming a theologian, since holy Scripture is a friend to simplicity." He too protests in strong terms, as did Hugh, against the intemperances of the new school, against the invasion of "novel questions" and the dust of quibbling which can, he says, only blind the spirit.[171]

This important personage, canon of Saint Omer, who had become cantor of the Church of Paris, who had influence with popes and the king of France, and whose word was much heeded — Etienne of Tournai went so far as to compare him to Origen[172] — is therefore intellectually not an innovator; this does not, however, keep him from showing himself open to the needs of his own time. He strongly senses certain apostolic pressures and he wants to lift the burden of pseudo-traditions that trammel the freedom of the Gospel. Cultivated, wise, eclectic — to the point of reconciling Saint Bernard and Gilbert of Porrée — he is nevertheless more traditional in intention than in spirit. A bit more boldness, combined with deeper reflection, would have been more valuable. His exegesis, like that of the Eater, carries us off, not to a sphere of novel thought that might already be called scientific, but into a quite different climate though one which is still bathed in Hugh's exegesis. Even more than the Eater, the Cantor exhibits for us the dislocation that ended up being produced, in a fateful progression, in the train of more and more hardened distinctions between the letter and allegory. Though on the one hand he multiplies his "distinctions," he abandons himself on the other, in the *Verbum abbreviatum*, to a literalism that does not always avoid being flat-footedly moralistic. The lifeblood of the Fathers is drying out. Victorine symbolism has disappeared just as much as the spiritual verve of Cîteaux. This new "word" [*Verbum*] has indeed been "abridged" [*abbreviatum*], since it has been cut off from doctrine and from mysticism. It has been reduced, but not concentrated. It is merely a "summary of pastoral theology,"[173] solid, to be sure, and lacking neither psychology nor evangelical spirit, but the excessively curt moralism of which reminds one of Bourdaloue, just as another recently edited work of Peter the Eater makes one think of the casuists.[174] Following Saint Jerome, the author makes a profession of avoiding useless complications and glosses in exegesis: he is right to do so; but his simplicity is sometimes simplistic;[175] the "spiritual understanding," which he opposes not only to the "letter that killeth," but also to the "overflow of glossing," and whose beauty he admires, is orientated under his pen not toward a deepening of the mystery but to a rather small-scale "moralitas."[176] When he rose up against "curious and restless men," against the "suspicious scrutinizers of God's secrets," when he cried out: "O man, thou who dost turn over such questions! Stop pounding so on the heights of the Creator's majesty!," Rupert of Deutz even in his excess had a quite different tone.[177] One is grateful to the wise Peter, who also does not fail to enumerate the four senses faithfully, for not having superimposed his own prefabricated allegories upon the explication of the letter, so little capable does he show himself of securing a living spiritual relation between them.

The same zeal and an analogous deficiency characterize the third of our great *magistri*. Stephen Langton, who will die as Archbishop of Canterbury in 1228, is also one of the glories of intellectual Paris: "once the ornament and rector of the Paris school."[178] In this he was a disciple of Peter the Cantor. Like his predecessor Peter the Eater, like the contemporaries the Victorine Absalon,[179] the Cistercian Nicholas of Clairvaux,[180] and another anonymous "clarevallensis,"[181] he set a high value on the ideal of the *litterati*, whom he sees figured in the "nobles" that Isaiah spoke of. He bemoans seeing them so often handing themselves over to the law and to the other money-making disciplines instead of searching out "the simple understanding of the Scripture" so as by means of it to nourish the Christian people, who are dying of hunger and thirst.[182] This complaint echoes the one Alexander III made,[183] that Saint Martin of Leon[184] is uttering at the very same time, and that Dante will make to be heard again:[185] isn't this sort of abuse something eternal?

More than the two Peters, Stephen Langton is himself a scholar of profound merit. Like the other two, however, he remains a partisan of an essentially practical approach to sacred knowledge; in this respect, he like them is attached to the Victorine school, and through it to the Gregorian current flowing from the *Moralia*, as can, for example, be recognized in the little Victorine writing on "the seven chords and their harmony."[186] Like the Peters and perhaps more, he rightly insists — in allegorical language — upon a serious and patient study of the letter.[187] It would not occur to him, however, to compose purely literal commentaries: the "literal" expositions by him that survive — as well as his "moralitates" — are in fact merely *Extractiones* taken from more complete works.[188] He is always faithful to the doctrine and the practice of the four senses — often, moreover, in practice treating anagogy *per modum unius* along with allegory, following the usage of the majority. He values tropology to a higher degree, regretfully seeing it neglected by so many "scholares" embarked upon the pursuit of "curious questions." Like the two Peters again, he unites the old "love of the Word" with concern to practice the new techniques — those two things that disturb (perhaps excessively) many spirituals in the monasteries, even at Saint Victor itself, who see them now dissociated, to the detriment of the first.[189] His sermons, in the "casual style," are animated with a "lively movement"[190] indicating that he feels the presence of the divine Word. In his work as a professor he has not lost a bit of the secret of that intimate movement which alone could validate the deployment of the four senses by assuring their union. Finally, though he composes a large part of his work in the course of a long exile,[191] among his friends the Cistercians of Pontigny, he often merely ends up with a "bad biblical scholasticism."[192]

3. The Temple of Ezekiel

Richard, who was prior of Saint Victor beginning from 1162 (†1173), ought to detain us a bit longer, both because of his intrinsic importance, and because of some of the interpretations that have recently been given of his hermeneutics. For, in the judgment of Miss Smalley, this second Hugh would be characterized by "his master's criticism of Gregorian method," and through him the literal, scientific exegesis inaugurated by Hugh and intrepidly pursued by Andrew would have advanced a giant step. This more than anything would justify pausing to situate his biblical work and evaluate its import.

A single example is brought forward of his insurrection against Saint Gregory; but this example is taken as "typical": it involves the commentary that Richard makes on Ezekiel's vision concerning the future temple of the reconstructed Jerusalem. "St. Gregory," writes Miss Smalley, "commenting on the vision of Ezekiel, says that the literal or fleshly sense would be absurd, the measurements of the building being physically inconceivable as the doors were bigger than the walls" in which they were supposed to open. From this he concludes that "the survey in all its detail has no meaning except as a series of phrases which can be explained allegorically and morally. He does not ask how Ezekiel pictures the building, but goes straight to the spiritual sense." In contrast, Richard undertakes his whole work to present a purely literal explication of the temple of Ezekiel, with elaborate formulas, sketches, plans, and diagrams. In so doing, he is well aware that he is contradicting Gregory. But precisely in this typical case he wants to criticize a whole long traditional method, whose yoke his master Hugh began to shake off. In an interesting prologue he justifies his daring, by arguing that times have changed since Gregory and that one's attitude toward the letter can no longer be what it was long ago.[193]

To be sure, there is much literal truth in such a summary. But in order to understand the significance of Richard's opusculum better, let's first see exactly what Gregory said. In that famous homily that opens the second book of the homilies on Ezekiel, which is devoted entirely to the vision of the eschatological temple, he did not put any fact, properly speaking, in doubt, not a single historical datum. He only said that the vision of the prophet, in its well-molded figure, could not be realized *ad litteram*. One can think that he had not tried very hard to exercise his imagination, but it would be going too far to say that he did not try to understand how the prophet conceived of the building; on the contrary, it is precisely through his investigation that he came to conclude that no architect could realize it as such. He explains why: the various measurements given in the text don't harmonize with each other. Moreover, he is anxious to recall, as Origen had done in other circumstance, that such passages in the Bible are rare; most of the time one can rely upon "the truth of the history," and in such cases one would wrong to neglect it, for it is starting from there that one rises to the spiritual understanding. But, in the present case, he himself has informed us that he had been "taken by the hand of the Lord," and that on the mountain he saw, not "an edifice," but something "as an edifice" [*quasi aedificium*]: did this not mean that he wanted us to understand, at the literal level, the unreal character of his vision?[194] One can say, therefore, that it is upon a literal analysis and a historical exegesis of the sacred narrative that Gregory based his opinion about the nature of the edifice contemplated by the prophet in his vision.

The opinion of Saint Gregory had become authoritative. It was soon followed by the Irish author of the *De ordine creaturarum,* for whom the beginning and the end of the Book of Ezekiel had to be understood "according to the figurative understanding without any reference to things."[195] Rabanus Maurus,[196] and then Aimon[197] had adopted it, too. From then on, certain variations in detail notwithstanding, it was apparently transmitted without discussion.[198] That is why Richard, when sustaining an opposed opinion, drafts a prologue which is a very studied, very cautious piece, a veritable personal defense; he will insert an analogous development again within the body of the work, to render his thought quite precise. As he said elsewhere, it was not his custom, especially in important matters, to affirm or settle anything by appealing to his own views;[199] all that he pours out for his readers to drink he has drawn, for the most part, "from the fullness of the holy Doctors."[200] But here is the decisive element in his choice: the Scriptures are sweeter to us when we can find a prime meaning for them in their very letter, and the construction of the spiritual understanding is more secure when it is based upon firm historical ground. Moreover, we are living at a time when certain minds are scandalized when they find a passage in the Bible of which it is said that the letter does not hold. The Fathers judged matters otherwise; they went so far as to rejoice at certain literal impossibilities, because they had to face many people who, in principle, rejected allegory: here they hoped to find a reason to force them to admit it. Whence it comes about that they somewhat neglected certain obscure texts: for, if they had wanted to, they would doubtless have clarified them better than any modern.[201] So rich had been their harvest that they have left us much to glean. Today, many flaunt their authority so as to dispense themselves from searching further; they jeer at zeal, which they regard as indiscreet: in reality, it is sloth on their part. There is more to do than to copy glosses indefinitely. It is necessary to take from the Fathers all they have to offer, and to fill in what they have omitted. That an opinion is new is of little importance if it is true; it is of little import that it is different if it does not advance anything perverse.[202]

Richard then gets to the point. Blessed Gregory, he observes, explains the vision of the four living things that opens the prophecy of Ezekiel in a mystic sense; but he does not begin by showing how it "holds" to its literal level. As to the final vision of the temple, he positively says that it does not hold. In the explanation that he gives of it, this is true; but is there no way to represent things differently by scrutinizing the text better? Doesn't he himself teach that in its providential obscurity, Scripture can, in several passages, be explicated in many ways?[203] It is in this way already, as we recall, that an Alvarus of Cordoba used the authority of this doctrine of the holy pope to set aside his interpretations.[204] So Richard goes on to try. First he devotes a few pages to the first of the two visions, "describing the animals so graphically that one sees them, the eagle, 'having a longer neck than the others', dominating the group."[205] Then he passes on to the second vision, which comes to occupy him for the whole length of twenty chapters.

A man with the appearance of brass, says the Prophet, stood before the porch, with a flaxen cord and a measuring rod in his hands. Is this man not a silent invitation? So Richard takes up the rod and the cord. We must give up following him in the exhausting detail of his surveying and

The Temple of Ezekiel

his measuring. Never has an architect so well gauged, planned, adjusted everything. He enters into all the minutiae. He capably resolves problems of clearance and lighting. He even arranges the relative placement of the beds and windows. To make sure that nothing slips past the reader, he affixes plans, sketches, even a geometric figure, to his text. He is not afraid, he says, to be prolix in a matter so obscure, so ambiguous, where everything needs to be established "by the authority of Scripture or by the testimony of reason."[206] For, as he recognizes, one is banging into more than one apparent impossibility; one is sometimes engaged on paths that lead to the absurd; it is necessary to retrace one's steps, to study the hints of the Prophet more closely, to scrutinize his vocabulary, to see, for example, that he can use the simple word "port" to designate a portico; it is also necessary to fill in certain of his silences, to understand that such and such an astonishing measurement is given only in length, to reason by way of analogy from other edifices, etc.[207] That one single measurement should be really off, and the whole subtle scaffolding come down; that such and such a datum be taken too — we dare to say it — "literally," and "the truth and authority of the whole description is voided."[208] At certain moments, then, Richard is perplexed. He then draws himself out of the business by means of an ingenious hypothesis. When two measures are definitely not in harmony with each other, then one of the two concerns the whole of the edifice, and the other, only a part:

> Is it not much more correct and much more fitting to refer to the part than by referring to the whole to void the whole thing? Does it not seem more suitable and consistent with reason to believe that in this passage Scripture is describing the measurements of a building, which was next to or above a gate . . . ? Since Scripture has named the whole edifice, could it not or ought it not then to use this word to designate a part? Did it not likewise name the whole house, and yet subsequently not fear to refer this name to a part, when it says: "and there was an inner house within the sides of the house"? If we find the name "edifice" where it has been put, why can't it be completely referred to the whole?[209]

In the heat of argument, one senses a bit of impatience in Richard's tone. His ingenuity has worked wonders; his puzzle has almost been finished. One embarrassing measure has called everything into question again. Will the edifice collapse? Is he himself going to be shipwrecked in sight of port? If one refuses the explanation that he offers, he will have to despair. Thus he condescends a bit to the objector whom he expects to come along:

> This alone ought to engender faith in us regarding this matter; since if we want to relate this name "building" to the whole, we shall be convicted of nullifying the faith of all that is being said here. Still, I think that no one is so reprobate, that no one can be found so wanton that he would not be ashamed to go against us in this part in so obvious an argument, who would not blush at blaming us for this opinion, when he would have seen that everything else stands consistent with the letter according to our exposition, if he should not mock sound understanding in so clear a truth.[210]

It would no doubt not be impossible to disclose some begging of the question in such reasoning. The hypothesis being advanced is exactly adjusted to what is needed. As always in such cases, need dictates the law so as to obtain the desired result. Richard's opusculum is nonetheless, let us repeat, a masterpiece of ingenuity. It reminds us a good deal of the homily in which Origen strove to demonstrate against Apelles the perfect constructibility of Noah's ark, while also turning himself into a surveyor and geometrician. Instead of varying the object to which the measure is applied, which was Richard's procedure, Origen understood the self-same measure (the cubit) in varied fashion; the cubits at stake in the biblical description of the ark were, he thought, "geometrical cubits," worth six ordinary cubits: Moses did not study wisdom in vain among the Egyptians, who were especially versed in geometry. The difficulty that Origen had to resolve was quite similar to that which Richard was to meet with; the explanatory procedure by which he escaped it was also analogous. "This is just what we had to say," he concluded, "as to the historicity of the fact, against those who try to attack the Scriptures of the Old Testament under the pretext that they contain impossible and unreasonable things."[211] It is known that his explanation was taken up again twice by Saint Augustine, who admired its "elegance" and who remarked: "in this case there is no longer any question."[212] Quodvultdeus made it his own.[213] It has become classic in the West from the time that Bede had cited it at length[214] and that Claude of Turin, Rabanus Maurus, Remigius of Auxerre, and others had reproduced it.[215] It was admitted into the *Glossa ordinaria*. The analogous solution proposed so imperiously by our Richard was therefore not a thing totally unheard of. However, is it a masterpiece of criticism? Is it the manifesto of an emerging historical

School? Is it, in the intention of Richard and in the things themselves, the dissolution of the Gregorian School? In fine, is it the fruit of a literalist spirit?

We think not. Richard might be right against Saint Gregory, just as Origen might well have been right against Apelles. We have not redone their calculations, either for the Temple or for the ark, and the excessive subtlety or too obvious expediency of their arguments is not itself a positive argument against their thesis. It is certain that Apelles was moved to disparagement by obstinate prejudice, and it may well be that Gregory was too quickly discouraged or that he too easily resigned himself to certain apparent contradictions. In the case of the ark, history in the proper sense of the word was involved. In the case of the Temple of Ezekiel, the situation is not the same, since it is a question of a vision, indeed a vision of the future.

If we now ask the moderns, what do they tell us? First let us open the *Monographie du Temple de Salomon,* a grand in-folio of 412 pages, full of numerous plans and drawings, a magnificent monument of exegesis in the last days of its pre-critical age (1885). In it, the author, Father Xavier Pailloux, SJ, offers "to the learned world" a complete reconstitution of the ancient Temple. His sketch will be "guided only by the Prophet-Architect," whose vision "allows us to fill in all the gaps that the historical account of the Bible naturally allowed itself." He himself is heir to numerous precursors, at the head of which he places the Spanish Jesuit Villalpand (†1608), "the Champollion of the Temple," who "has been able, under the pressure of his logic, to make the mysterious descriptions of Ezekiel yield a magnificent, finished, complete temple," and thus, "without neglecting even a stone designated by the prophetic vision, without permitting any gap or breach, to rebuild the edifice of Solomon in its entirety."[216] The historian ought to distrust Josephus, "who wrote a historical novel"; the rabbis, who had "no notion of the art of building"; and certain modern archeologists, who are infatuated with Egyptian origins. To reconstitute the work of Solomon (and of Zerubbabel), one ought to scrutinize Ezekiel; the identity among these temples is perfect. As a matter of fact, it is "impossible to point out any difference among them." As a matter of law, to one who would ask: "Would it be heterodox to suppose diffidently that through Ezekiel God had slightly amended and considerably embellished the plans of Solomon?" it is necessary to respond: "What's there to amend? What's there to embellish? Not being subject to surprises and not needing to profit from experience, God has endowed his Temple with all the accoutrements that he judged to be suitable"; having destined it "to be unique and eternal, within it the totality of symbolic, liturgical, utilitarian treasures that it was agreeable for him to attribute to his Temple was exhausted, literally *exhausted*."[217] Saint Gregory was no doubt opposed to such an exegesis; against it, "he goes so far as using the weapons of irony": but he was neither an architect nor a Hebraist. "Le bon Richard" of Saint Victor, even if he commits more than one mistake in detail, and though he is "completely devoid of a feeling for the arts," had a sounder view. Ezekiel's vision is a true "prophetic bid"; by following it to the letter one can "establish a system of finished and completed plans." Just like Solomon, Ezekiel "was inspired as an architect." "It is indisputable that his plans were made on Mount Moriah and adapted to the local conditions. This can be the only reason why the Prophet had been transported to Jerusalem on a high mountain." The principal difficulties of his text come from the fact that he wanted to be obscure by reason "of the dangers to which his perilous mission exposed him."[218]

But the monument of Père Pailloux had scarcely been erected when another chorus began to make itself heard. For contemporary exegetes, the vision of Ezekiel seems to involve at least some features that cannot be realized literally. Many writers, to be sure, think more of the organization of the territory than of the material construction of the building.[219] Others, however, explicitly state that "the temple whose blueprint Ezekiel draws up is not an architectural project: its significance is prophetic"; calling up that "ideal temple" would herald "the messianic instantiation of a domain of purity, which will be that of God's dwelling-place, surpassing the material existence of Israel and the Mosaic institutions."[220] They also point out the entirely symbolic character of those "waters that flow from the southern wall of the temple" without undermining it, which become an enormous torrent, fertilizing its banks in marvelous fashion. They consequently think that all this vision of the temple to come "belongs to Utopian literature."[221] One of them even attempts to establish a distinction, on the one hand, between the two great visions that frame the Book of Ezekiel, the latter being as precise as the former is vague, and, on the other hand, between the vision of the Temple properly speaking and the paradisal landscape called up in the sequel, the prophet seeing the Temple for himself and only hearing the description that God then gives him of the landscape.[222] But it is merely to express astonishment at such distinctions and to assert that the prophet is speaking symbolically everywhere.[223] One of the more recent writers, after having noted in these chapters "the strange union of a hallucinatory and visionary reality with a geometric and juridical style," thinks that their literary genre is the same as that of the vision of the [dry] bones; he too is astonished that anyone could have treated that temple "like a real building" and draw up "precise plans" for it, when it is manifestly only an "abstract architecture" which "is worked out in an ideal world," "a castle in the clouds," a "dream-house."[224] If Richard of Saint Victor can be considered as the patron of the modern lineage which leads to Père Pailloux, the precursor of the second group of exegetes is good old Saint Gregory. But what exegete today would want to give Pailloux's name as a reference?

Gregory and Richard can, however, be at the same time both right and wrong. Richard is doubtless right to think that the prophet believed or could have believed in a certain future material realization of his prophecy. Gregory, for whom this psychological issue is secondary, is perhaps right to think that the building could not have full consistency outside the imagination of the prophet and that, to convey its truth, it is necessary to take it according to the intention of the Holy Spirit, as the symbol of a reality of a different order, a reality which is, for the Christian, "a building of holy Church, a building of the heavenly city."[225] But if we reduce the problem to its immediate data, we would confess that Gregory is perhaps wrong to credit his own thought to the Prophet, or rather scarcely to care about the thought of the prophet, which might well not have been perceived, even if the incoherences of his vision really do exist in accordance with his text. Only, on his own side, Richard is nonetheless wrong when, at the start, he lets himself be guided by his desire to find an explanation dearer to his own heart or more conformed to what is expected in his circle, and then, during the trip, by the need to succeed at any price; he is also wrong to posit as an indisputable a priori the perfect coherence of an imaginative vision down to the last detail. At any event, this is not at all such a critical attitude. Besides, neither the historical value of the Old Testament accounts, nor the interest brought to the history of the people of God, nor the principles of historical criticism in general seem to be seriously compromised by Gregory's scruples, any more than "the realistic import of the prophetic hopes of the heavenly City." On the other hand, neither does Richard seem to have advanced the cause of the history by upholding the perfectly molded coherence either of the "four heavenly living things,"[226] or of the eschatological Temple seen by Ezekiel in spirit. One no longer sees that there was any more critical sense in the opinion of Richard that the future Jerusalem is materially achievable — if not, in fact, destined to be achieved materially — according to the letter of the biblical text, than in the contrary opinion of Gregory declaring that such a city "can in no way be taken literally," and saying why.²²⁷ One might even without too much paradox sustain the view that here the true critic is Gregory. Undoubtedly he uses an excessively loose principle, which, since the time of Origen, had been too often invoked for many centuries. Doubtless, too, in his preaching on the temple of Ezekiel, he cares about anything except critique. But his spiritual zeal transports him instantaneously to a position that, in its negativity, among other elements, seems to require of him a critical response.

We will no doubt render a better account by opening Books XII and XIII of the commentary on Ezekiel belonging to the most critical of the exegetes of old. These two books are entirely devoted to the vision of the Temple. They would pack a surprise for anyone who might suppose that, if Richard is here against Saint Gregory, he is by that very fact to be found on the side of Saint Jerome.

Toward the beginning of Book XII one can read a famous passage in which Jerome calls up his former visits to the catacombs of Rome. It is often cited for its quite romantic, picturesque quality. That it has as its object to introduce the exegesis of the Temple is usually forgotten: "Let me say this so that the prudent reader will understand how I may have an opinion about the explanation of the temple of God in Ezekiel, of whom it is said: 'Clouds and darkness are under his feet' (Ps. 97:2), and, earlier: 'Darkness his cover' (Ps. 18:11)."²²⁸ In the same way, at the very end, a few verses from Virgil will serve him for a conclusion:²²⁹

> Here is that labor of a house and inescapable wandering.
>
> As once in high Crete the Labyrinth is said
> To have held a route woven of blind walls,
> And an intricate trick of a thousand passage-ways,
> Where the unsolvable and unretraceable wandering
> Belied any blazes of a trail.²³⁰

Jerome acknowledges as much: he is lost in the labyrinth; he was not able to recognize himself in the "obscure night" of the catacombs. To speak without images, he has not succeeded in "realizing" at their literal level the numerous and complicated details furnished by the Prophet. With his usual knowledge, he made many an observation on the text throughout these two books, on the liberties that the Septuagint took regarding the Hebrew, etc. In short, as elsewhere, he did his work of criticism. But he did not spend a moment's effort to justify the coherence of the vision itself. He does not for any instant attempt, as Richard did, to explicate that dream-architecture in the strict sense of the letter. Falsely modest, he declares: "Overlook the difficulty, dear reader, and grant pardon to one who is poor in understanding."[231] He even emphasizes certain material impossibilities in the passage: for example, the altar, which is entirely made of wood, and yet suffers no damage from the fire that is kindled on it.[232] Rather than imagining some clever system to reconcile all the measurements among themselves, he observes that the numbers are symbolic, and he explains them accordingly: one ought, he says, to pay serious attention to the perfect numbers, as well as to the ratios of the various numbers among themselves.[233] In this vast description, for him everything is "hidden" language, figured language, and without lingering to contemplate the building through some effort of sensible imagination, he wants us to contemplate it immediately "in spirit" in a sort of purifying leap.[234] After having invoked the Holy Spirit — "Come thou, O Spirit, from the four winds" — he himself immediately explains each of the features of the text one after the other "according to the mystic senses."[235] The man with the reed, for example, is Jesus Christ, the true Architect; the two cubits of the vestibule are the letter and the spirit, or, what comes down to the same thing, the two Testaments; if there are three rooms arrayed on one side and the other, that is just the two senses, historical and spiritual, equally being related to the mystery of the Trinity; if the gate on the north has seven steps and the gate on the south eight, that is to mark the difference from the Law to the Gospel or from the Synagogue to the Church; the four tables of the holocaust are the four evangelists; the wood with which the walls of the temple are lined is the wood of the tree of life, i.e., wisdom.[236] The treasure-rooms are the humble souls; the fifty cubits of the upper stories give the number of the remission of sins, etc.[237]

These are only a few examples, taken amidst the simplest ones. From time to time Jerome engages in subtler symbolic explications — but always, as he says, "with the mind more of a diviner than an explainer." In the manner of Origen — or perhaps, more simply, by copying Origen[238] — he avows that he himself is little satisfied with his discoveries: he feels that he is pounding on a closed door, he can only slip a glance, the glance of the heart, through the slanted windows to the interior of the building, perceiving merely in shadow and in image.[239] He knows only, as the Prophet indicates "in hidden fashion," that "in the temple of the Lord he finds nothing that lacks reason, measure, and wisdom."[240] Here Jerome seems to be playing on the word "measures." In short, to his mind, the temple of Ezekiel is a "mystic temple,"[241] a "spiritual temple," and everything that is related to it ought "to be understood spiritually"[242] — or, as we would say today, taken in a figurative sense. As for the sensible vision, he keeps returning to its paradoxes again and again: that house, built on a mountain top, is at the same time a whole city; it encloses a "holy of holies," and is itself in all its parts this holy of holies.[243] So let's not be astonished any longer at the incumbustible altar: like the burning bush, it burns and is not consumed, because it is made of the wood of paradise.[244]

This agreement of the two doctors of old, Jerome and Gregory, can be explained very simply: Gregory knew Jerome's work; from his preface onward, he started in unison with his predecessor: "We are making a night journey, so we've got to feel our way as we go."[245] Without forcing himself to follow him in every detail, he adopted Jerome's vision of the whole.[246] Thus, when Rabanus Maurus, careful as always to exploit the treasures of patristic thought exhaustively, came to deal with the chapters concerning the vision of the temple in his own copious commentary on Ezekiel, he made no great effort to harmonize his two illustrious predecessors' opinions: their harmony was pre-established. Juxtaposed in large sections, they harmonize and complement each other very well, and, were it not for the difference of styles, the reader would pass over the manifold passages that Rabanus incorporated without perceiving any shift: the compiler's guileless amalgam holds together better than the learned construction of the commented text.[247] Their twofold authority, associated henceforth, seems to have fixed for ever the great lines of the traditional interpretation. Conscious of his own audacity, Richard of Saint Victor has just broken, or striven to break, the prescription.[248] Is it certain, however, that the new way he is embarking upon holds the promise for the future?

In Scripture another vision resembles the vision of Ezekiel and is inspired by it: that of the City of the Apocalypse, the heavenly Jerusalem.[249] Richard has commented on it, too, at length, and this time in a completely spiritual sense right from the start: "About to enter upon the elucidation of the marvelous structure of so great a city according to the spiritual understanding."[250] That city is "the immense assembly of the just"; the throne which occupies its center is the group of the holy doctors, "in which God reigns"; its twelve gates are the twelve Apostles; its wall, its precious stones, its light, is the Christ; the golden reed measuring rod is the holy Scripture, which is "a reed-pipe through the sound of preaching, and golden through the flash of divine cognition"; its different measurements are the different merits of the saints who make up the city; its

The Temple of Ezekiel

"square arrangement" signifies the perfection that reigns there, etc.[251] The intention of the sacred author has appeared too obvious to Richard for him even to trouble himself to examine the question whether or not his description first off involved a sensible literality: "What man in his senses would be willing to take this literally?"[252] But lo and behold, in our own age, the long ago initiated discussion about the temple has come to life again with regard to that city. Reincarnated in Father Bernard Allo we see Richard, the Richard of the commentary on Ezekiel, being counterattacked by Saint Gregory resuscitated in the person of Paul Claudel. Father Allo assuredly has more critical acumen than Richard, and if Paul Claudel does not have much less of it than Gregory, he is perhaps less excusable than Gregory for not having more. The relative situation of the two parties is nonetheless almost the same in a debate that is substantially the same. Is it necessary to attempt, as it was long ago for the Temple of Ezekiel, to achieve a well-molded model, pursuing its every last detail, in a coherent perspective, that Jerusalem which has just been put upon the earth, or instead ought not what the Seer tells us about it be taken as a series of suggestions appropriate to awaken some higher understanding in us directly? We neither sooner nor later mean to arbitrate the debate — though the "realist" interpretation appears here even more paradoxical than for the vision of Ezekiel,[253] and though the authority of the historical Richard, as we have just seen, does not favor the Richard *redivivus*. We shall note only that if the position held by Father Allo, who is trying to combine all the features of the text with each other to the maximum, aims to be more "historical," the position of Paul Claudel, right or wrong, aims to be not only more spiritual, but also more critical. It is in the name of a tighter meaning of "intelligence" in the examination of this same text, that he stands up against what he calls "the literalist prejudice."[254] Are Richard of Saint Victor and, above all, Father Allo truly victims of such a prejudice? In any case, let us observe that they do not, in the manner of the millennarians, transport either the temple seen by Ezekiel or the city contemplated by Saint John as such into the future and into facts. They do not hold that this temple or this city is, in its letter, more than a vision, and on the other hand they do not doubt that this vision is symbolic. Their exegetical literalism is, therefore, provisional; it does not extend into a doctrinal literalism, nor even, as a matter of fact, into a historical literalism.[255] When he attaches himself, as we have seen, in the most material and most minute fashion to the letter of the Prophet's vision, Richard was at bottom scarcely doing more than laying claim to a certain quality of imagination, analogous to his own, without prejudice to the action of the Holy Spirit. Let us recognize that he was also showing by this, in a certain sense, his estimation of the historical sense of Scripture and of his own exact interpretation, an estimation of which he gives other indications elsewhere as well,[256] and which we will thank him for. Let us recognize, moreover, that by his declaration of healthy independence regarding the ancients — a moderate independence, which is blended with gratitude, as well as with deep respect for the tradition[257] — and by his very practice, he gave a wholesome example to others as well, one that was favorable for intellectual research.[258] But he did not contribute by that very fact to the progress of critical exegesis, and the little work that we have just analyzed is not at all sufficient to make of him "the best biblicist" of his age.

At least, however, let this episode of his career not make us forget that the prior of Saint Victor was a warm partisan of the "fourfold exposition";[259] that like Origen and Saint Bernard, he celebrated with a personal emphasis the "inner sparring of the amorous soul with God who hides himself,"[260] and that he was also not only a bold dialectician, but also a great mystical thinker, whose doctrine integrally derives from the paths of allegorical exegesis:

> For what else do we call holy Scripture but Rachel's bedchamber, in which we do not doubt that divine wisdom hides beneath the decorous veil of allegories?[261]

4. Arks and Tabernacles

Richard of Saint Victor was not, as we know, the first to claim a certain freedom in his own interpretations as compared with those of the Fathers. Among others, Rupert did it before him, sometimes in a rather brusquer tone. Once he did it notably with regard to an opinion of "the blessed Pope Gregory":

> There is no canonical Scripture to support that opinion; rather the prophetic truth in Ezekiel stands in complete opposition. . . . So with greater truth and reason we say. . . .[262]

Nevertheless, in commenting on the vision of the temple, Rupert did not believe that he ought to abandon a traditional interpretation that would have seemed necessary to him. In his turn he avowed its obscurity,[263] he emphasized certain difficulties of the literal sense,[264] expressed the idea that the given measurements were "mystical,"[265] and, without worrying further whether Jerome or Gregory was [the source] of [its] material realization, he launched, as was his wont (like Saint Gregory but more systematically) into a beautiful Christological exegesis.[266] Richard's innovation was not universally well received. If Peter the Eater seems still to be unaware of it,[267] a reproach formulated by Peter the Cantor would seem at least to have it, along with a few others, in mind. What a waste of time, groans the austere moralist, to combine these "mechanical dispositions in the buildings and in the disposition of the imaginary temple." They are just "vana et superflua." Rather a sorry thought, which, if generalized, would ruin every research effort; still, in the present case, can we believe it entirely unjustified?[268] Another contemporary, Robert of Crickade, the author of still unedited homilies on Ezekiel, also raises a protest, but from another point of view. What he reproaches Richard and his partisans for is not for paying too much attention to the letter of the text in general, but more precisely for the idea that the temple of the vision could be materially constructed or depicted. Such a pretence, says he, is a "foolish raving"; his argument is the same as that of Saint Gregory: "that it is not only a building but also a city."[269] On the basis of this sentence alone, we cannot judge regarding the Robert in question. At least it is not at all enough to assure us that he drifted into all the excesses of allegorism. Except for the prologue, wherein the broadmindedness of men like John Scotus, Rupert, and all those for whom the tradition was neither a fetish nor routine, lives again, Richard's opusculum does not constitute his best contribution to exegesis. It is scarcely more than a curiosity. It does not seem to have exercised appreciable influence. The two conjoint great authorities, Jerome and Gregory, continued to dominate the explication of Ezekiel's temple; their natural association, brought about by Rabanus Maurus in the ninth century, consecrated by the Gloss, maintained itself for a long time.[270]

Along with his architect's taste, we ought to assign credit to Richard, "so sensitive to the order and the beauty of the world,"[271] for his astonishingly acute visual imagination. As Dom Jean Leclercq as written, the imagination of the men of the Middle Ages "was vigorous and active.... It permitted beings to be represented, to be made 'present', to see them along with all the details that the texts report: colors and dimensions of things, articles of clothing, attitudes, what people do, the complex framework in which they move.... They used to love to describe them and, so to speak, to create them by giving a very lively emphasis to images and feelings."[272] Let anyone read just a few of the visions of Saint Hildegard.[273] Without pushing spontaneous invention so far, the head of the Victorine school was particularly well endowed in this respect. The previous chapter acquainted us with the two arks constructed by Hugh. We have cited a few features of his mystical ark, with its geometrical figures, its colors, its symbolic letters, the emblem of the lamb. . . .[274] Here is how the *De arca morali* presented the reader with the historical ark, that of Noah, itself already half-mystical:

> An example of this spiritual building I shall give you as Noah's ark, which your eye will see on the outside, so that your mind may be built up on the inside according to its likeness. There you will see certain colors, shapes, and figures that delight your vision. But you ought to know that they are put there so that within them you may learn wisdom, discipline, and virtue, which adorn your mind. And since this ark signifies the Church, and the Church is the body of Christ, I have depicted the whole person of Christ, so that the example might become clearer to you, i.e., the head along with the members in visible form, so that when you see the whole, you can then more easily understand the things that are said of the part.[275]

We find the same kind of imagination, the same readiness to draw, to paint, to measure as well, that we find in a contemporary of Richard's, Peter Cellensis. Peter does not describe the temple of Ezekiel, as Richard did, nor Noah's ark, as did Hugh, but rather the tabernacle of Moses. The object can change, but the procedures are the same:

> He tries to make the structure reappear, he calculates the dimensions that Exodus gave it, verifies them against each other, tries to find the immediate, practical reason for it; he refers to the commentary that the Venerable Bede had already advanced regarding this text so as to complete his own; he gives the vernacular equivalent for one of the precious stones that the inspired author mentions so that one might properly grasp what it corresponds to. With a view to clarifying the description of the complicated structure where the forest can get lost in the trees, he sometimes modifies the plan followed by Exodus itself: his reader must have the structure before his eyes that he might look at it; he wants first off that one should comprehend the letter and, to this end, he evidences a care for precision which is rare at all times, but which one would expect perhaps to find less in a mystical author than in anyone else.[276]

Indeed Peter Cellensis passes for one of the principal representatives of this old monastic school, benumbed in its allegorical musings, which disdains, when not combating, the new historical school centered at Saint Victor. In reality, the spirit in which he explains the tabernacle is completely analogous to that in which Hugh explains the ark. His procedures are completely comparable to those of Hugh and Richard. One must even say that he is more preoccupied than the former with historical exactness in his descriptions, and that the preoccupation that he shares with the latter aims at a historically more secure target. Like Richard, he is very interested in the question of measures.[277] Like Hugh, he separates the literal description and the mystical explanations into two quite distinct parts; the first part of his *De tabernaculo Moysi*, edited by Dom Leclercq, is much longer, proportionally, than the corresponding first part of the *De arca morali*: six pages are devoted to the letter, and fourteen to the mysteries.

The abbot of Cella did not devote just one treatise to the tabernacle of Moses, but several.[278] The literary genre, long ago begun by Bede in conformity with a tradition that went back to the earliest times of the Church, was then regaining favor. A whole book of commentary on Exodus by Rupert also formed a treatise on the tabernacle.[279] There exists another, attributed to Achard of Saint Victor, who was abbot immediately after Hugh (1141-61) before becoming bishop of Avranches (1161-71). Richard himself composed one, or rather two or even three such treatises.[280] The same goes for Peter of Poitiers. In two sermons for the Day of the Dedication, Serlon of Savigny explains at length the symbolism of the tabernacle and that of the temple.[281] Aelred of Rievaulx preaches a panegyric of Saint Benedict on the theme of the construction of the tabernacle, and drafts another sermon on "the disposition of the troops of the children of Israel around the tabernacle," closely connected with this group of writings.[282] Garnier of Rochefort comments on chapter 6 of the first Book of Kings in a sermon *De arca spirituali*.[283] Saint Martin of Leon preaches on the temple of Solomon and is particularly interested on several occasions in the curtains of the tabernacle and in their rings.[284] Absalon the Victorine pronounces a long ceremonial discourse, at the time of a general chapter meeting, on the tabernacle of Moses, and four of his sermons for the feast of the Dedication also partake of the same literary genre.[285] An explication of Genesis and another of Exodus by Stephen Langton each begin with a description of the tabernacle, regarded each time as a symbol of the Church.[286] But the most voluminous treatise, the most elaborate, the one most characteristic of the methods of that age, is that of Adam of Dryburgh (Adam Scotus).

Adam Scotus, who died only in 1212, is close to the Victorine circle. He was a Premonstratensian, an Englishman in origin, who lived in a Scottish convent until he became a Carthusian at Witham in 1189. Toward 1176, urged by John of Kelso, the abbot of a nearby monastery, he undertook a long-term project on the tabernacle of Moses, which was studied according to the classical method of the three or the four senses (as we saw in Vol. 1, chapter 2, Adam shifts back and forth from the one formula to the other). This is the *On the Tripartite Tabernacle*. A laborious work! Nevertheless Adam was not lacking guides. Naturally he uses the Venerable Bede's treatise, which he says he wants to follow "diligenter et sollicite," without ever expressing an opinion that might be contrary to it.[287] As for his reading, to complete this work, he appeals to the *Jewish History* of Josephus, which Bede had already used, as well as contemporary writings: Master Andrew's commentary on the Pentateuch, the *Scholastic History*, a little treatise about the royal genealogies attributable to Aelred of Rievaulx.[288] He explicitly advises one to consult Hugh of Saint Victor regarding the fourfold sense which he calls up when beginning his study,[289] and his whole work offers a great structural analogy with the *De arca Noe morali*. His principles of interpretation are generous; he does not scruple to juxtapose two dissimilar explications, provided that the unity of the faith be unscathed.[290] Regarding the desire expressed by his correspondent, far from neglecting "the historical foundation," he first expounds it with care. He is keen on getting precisely informed by experts. Nevertheless, he was himself — as a Carthusian, his biographer, tells us — "but moderately imbued with knowledge of the literal understanding."[291] Besides, like the abbot of Kelso, he thinks that the Scriptures, though they may seem clear to heretical sects, are full of deeply hidden mysteries, accessible only to those who rise, by the vigor of contemplation, "to the height of the Scriptures."[292] If he wants to secure a solid foundation for "the house of his work," it is with a view to the construction of the walls and the roof, following the traditional method. Just as much as the tabernacle, however, he knows that everything that is recounted in the Bible, Old and New Testament, is to be understood "recte et catholice" according to the four senses.[293] One feels that he shares John of Kelso's enthusiasm, marveling at "how good it would be to understand all the Scriptures in the threefold manner." All the "savor" of the feast served by the sacred histories comes to them, he thinks, from their spiritual sense.[294]

As has been written, Adam does not notice that his precursors "have left the historical sense" of the temple "in the shade." But he keeps trying to elucidate two material details which constituted the object of a classic dispute and about which no agreement was ever reached; the one concerned the exact position of the sixth tapestry and the other that of the brass grating.[295] Moreover, this has but a small place in a work which is voluminous and whose scope extends well beyond this controversy.[296] On the whole, like Hugh, Adam too dallies less with the *historia* than a Peter Cellensis did. That he should be so interested in the material form of the tabernacle, however, is nothing unheard of. That sort of curiosity belongs to every age. If he supplements his text with a colored picture — "pictura quaedam"[297] — that is exactly what John of Kelso, if one dare say it, expressly commanded him to do.[298] He did not create it from whole cloth, however; what is essential seems to come to him from Bede, who himself got it from Cassiodorus, and Cassiodorus in turn had executed his plan according to the description contained in the *Antiquities* of Josephus, supplemented by observations from a certain Eusebius.[299] According to Father Chenu, Adam's title reflects only "the part adopted: [it allows him] to hang on to the historical tabernacle prior to any allegorical transposition . . . , then to consent to the efflorescence of a polyvalent symbolism — cosmic, moral, ritual, eschatological."[300] We shall not contradict him. Only, we believe that in this our Premonstratensian did not show a really audacious determination, even in the wake of Master Hugh; for if it is true that few [writers of] sermons or the briefer essays over-insisted on a literal description that each found, with as much detail as he could hope for, in the Bible itself, nevertheless no one doubted even for a second the historical reality of the Jewish tabernacle, in that century any more than in the previous ones. As a good student, as a good popularizer, and to answer the expectation that was offered him, Adam applies himself to the *historia* more than Hugh ever did on like occasion;[301] but that part of his task "has scarcely any attraction for him."[302] As to the "consent" that he subsequently gives to symbolism, it is surely the sort that moralists call "full consent"; it asserts itself in an "efflorescence" and exuberance that leave no doubt regarding its fullness![303]

Adam Scotus is really a true disciple of Hugh of Saint Victor. He cites him readily.[304] He got his didacticism from him. He also got from him a taste for vast collections of symbols, a taste that in execution does not exclude minuteness of detail. With a much more considerable richness of detail he applies to the tabernacle of Moses the formula adopted by the Victorine Master for Noah's ark, so well that it is the whole of biblical history, the whole history of the Church, even the whole history of England which — by means of a daring extension little conforming to the spirit of great exegesis — is found depicted along with the aid of figures, inscriptions, and colors, within the "allegorical tabernacle," without prejudice to analogous figures in the "moral tabernacle."[305] From Hugh he still has the firm will to advance always within the "royal road" of the tradition.[306] Hence he is a faithful disciple, only a bit behind the times, more than one would expect from a canon regular at this period (it is true that Adam would soon become a Carthusian), in the peace of his distant monastery, or in the peaceful discussions of an already rather closed monastic world. "Master Adam is scientifically quite old school."[307] What a contrast with that other canon regular, Anselm of Havelberg, so aware of the illusions that cover themselves with the veil of the contemplative life, so sensitive to the dangers that "quies et securitas"[308] engender for the monk, so ready even with satire against the lazy and garrulous inhabitants of the cloister who favor themselves over the apostolic laborers![309] Our Adam's optimism is no longer the same as the optimism of a Godefroy of Saint Victor, who was open to the future. He makes a still further contrast with the obsessions of a reformer like Gerhoh of Reichersberg, who always sees the barque of the Church about to founder,[310] or even with the gloomy descriptions of a mystic moralist like Saint Bernard. Good Adam does not seem to perceive any of those alternations of prosperity and adversity that foist themselves upon the attention of Gilbert of Hoyland; he does not, like Gilbert, sense the blast of Aquilo which continues periodically to ravage the garden of the Spouse.[311] He does not even seem to have any qualms for the Church having a too easy and too respectable prosperity, which makes it so different from the one in the earliest days; he does not ask himself, as Otto of Freising did not so long before, whether this might not perhaps be the sign of an infidelity to her Spouse.[312] Tranquilly seated in his mystical Jerusalem, where he occupies himself with commenting on Scripture "in sublimis verbis," he gives thanks to the Lord for having guided his Church to this "third state" in which his ancient enemies have become believers and the kings of the earth have been won over to his authority.[313] The situation that he enjoys does not any longer really offer anything in common with that of his ancient predecessor and model, who lived amidst trials and perils, saw himself in his monastery like Saint John on the Isle of Patmos, and devoted himself to writing his commentary on the temple and the tabernacle whilst hoping: "that we may have hope through patience and the consolation of the Scriptures."[314] Adam himself cries out ecstatically: "O stabilitas! O tranquillitas!" He lives in his little cell like a fish in water. He marvels at seeing "the placid repose of the saints" so often prefigured and encouraged in Scripture.[315] He himself, as a monk who visited him in his Charter-house tells us, "was resting under the most happy slumber of contemplation."[316] Moreover, Adam is persuaded that this "third state to which the world has presently arrived and within which he himself finds his flourishing," will scarcely cease except on the day of entering into the beatific vision, when we shall pass "de pace in pacem."[317] As was already the case for Honorius in the preceding generation, "the age of monks" seemed to him still to mark the apogee of the earthly history of the Kingdom, after which formidable but transient time no more could come but "the age of the Antichrist." Like his compatriot Aelred of Rievaulx, he thinks that henceforth there is nothing more than to "live well in the peace of the Church," in that happy "time of consolation" which ought to endure until the "very last persecution."[318] The latter will come, since it has been foretold; it makes for the arrival of the age to come; but nothing indicates it as threatening yet.

Ought we to see there an insular feeling of security? Whatever it might be, Adam Scotus's thought seems to carry us back to a slightly earlier epoch. Adam, who is not combative, does not play the part of a reactionary, but rather — to use with Dom Wilmart "a rather crude term" — of someone "a bit backward."[319] He does not perceive the advance signs around him of the impending temporal reversals, any more than he is aware of the profound transformations that are being prepared in the life of the spirit. For him, within his peaceful retreat, time has suspended its flight. With him, thought too perhaps is beginning to fall asleep. He is nonetheless able deftly to criticize exegetes more learned than himself, but who, without internal experience, are often content with a verbal understanding.[320] On the other hand, if the *Allegoriae in universam Scripturam* are by him, as seems to be the case, it would draw him closer to someone like Peter Cantor and the other authors of *Distinctiones,* and would emphasize the fatal gap which has already been produced between the first generation of Saint Victor and his own. At least the Preface to these *Allegoriae,* of which no one can doubt that he is the author,[321] reflects, like the *De tripartito tabernaculo,* the thought of the head of the School. The Preface is faithful to his method; it reproduces his very terms. It will not at all contradict but merely add, with Father François Petit, the observation that it also reflects the thought of a Saint Gregory the Great.[322] If it took a "critical realization" to dismiss Saint Gregory, the dutiful Adam Scotus has not accomplished that realization. He is, like Hugh and like Richard, though without the reservation of Richard, a fervent admirer of Gregory: "Blessed Gregory spoke no less clearly than he perceived deeply."[323] He does not constitute an exception amongst the chorus so full of the writers and preachers of his age who love to base their authority on the holy pope's exegeses and even to borrow from him some of his "honied words."[324]

Let us return to our Richard and to his imagination. Linked to a remarkable sense of beauty,[325] his imagination is no less lively or less precise than that of a Hugh, a Peter Cellensis, or an Adam Scotus. Perhaps it is even superior in that, instead of creating its object more or less at whim, as with Hugh, or on the other hand instead of reconstituting a real object, as with Peter of Cella or Adam Scotus, on occasion Richard's conjures up a precise, total, and credible vision from a text whose apparently irreconcilable data would seem to discourage any such effort in advance. Richard's imagination somehow produced the miracle that a Robert of Crickade could not believe in. On this score, the opusculum *In visionem Ezechielis* is not as unimportant as one might believe.[326] The only thing that remains hard to admit is that the discussion undertaken by its author had all the symbolic value attributed to it by Miss Smalley. That discussion is not aimed at a "typical case," bringing into play a whole method and a whole concept of exegesis. It is rather a question of a very particular case, and, while recognizing that Richard rightly wants to make himself look more restrained than the "ancient Fathers" regarding the so-called shortcomings of the letter, one must not forget that neither did Gregory regularly deny the literal sense, nor does Richard always try to preserve it. Consequently, the present discussion cannot, except in a very limited degree, be taken as a sign of a conflict between the ancient allegorism, of which Saint Gregory would be both guarantor and symbol, and the new literal, even literalistic, tendencies, whose banner the Victorines would be raising. The manner in which Richard himself, who did not fear a fight, opposed his confrere Andrew, is well adapted to turn us decisively away from such an interpretation.

Richard pointed out certain passages in a treatise by Andrew on Isaiah that he thinks are "not expressed with due caution, argued in a none too catholic manner." In particular, the Jewish explanation of "the virgin who will give birth" is given in it as worthy of credence; or at least it is complacently presented, without any refutation or even a comment. Against anyone responsible for such an "error," which is revealed to be "contagious,"[327] Richard invokes the testimony of Saint Jerome;[328] and, pirating a famous remark from Saint Gregory, he compares Master Andrew, ponderous from all his science, to an elephant: "Behold, where the lamb gambols, an elephant is floating — but it does not swim off."[329]

Where "christiana simplicitas" has no trouble clearing the way, his critical method encumbers him and makes him trip up.[330] This "Judaizer,"[331] who wants only a reasonable sense for prophecy, is unable to see that the Holy Spirit is wont to conceal "the profundity of so great a mystery under a foolishness of the letter."[332] What is more, against him, Richard clearly knows, even at the most literal level, how to safeguard the Christian interpretation of the essential utterances of prophecy. This was the classic exegesis, received from Christian antiquity and, so to speak, canonized by Saint Jerome. Gilbert Crispin had defended it in his famous London disputation as indispensable for avoiding "a totally puerile and vain sense."[333] Godefroy of Saint Victor took it up again in his *Microcosmus*[334] and it was soon to show up yet again in an *Altercatio Synagogae et Ecclesiae* which depends upon the Victorines.[335]

No more than in his detailed descriptions of Ezekiel's temple shall we follow Richard in the very lively discussions of *De Emmanuele*. One simple remark is sufficient for our purpose. It concerns the proposed explication regarding the two kings who figure in that prophecy. The "Judaizers" such as Andrew wish to see in it only the kings of the earth. In it Richard recognizes demons. Over and above the analogy with other texts of Scripture, here is his reasoning: in speaking of these kings, the prophet says nothing "that cannot be understood of kings of spiritual injustice in the heavens; but clearly Scripture is taken to speak of certain kings in such fashion as to be able to be applied both to spiritual and to fleshly kings."[336] Whereas his interlocutor, misled by Master Andrew, declares that he understands these kings "secundum historiam," Richard therefore chooses the "spiritual" understanding. He chooses it, but he does not invent it: he throws in his lot with a tradition that dates back to Origen[337] and that Saint Jerome's hesitations and criticisms could not succeed in discrediting.[338] Rupert made the same choice regarding the "king of Tyre."[339] But here his adversary soon, under the blows of Richard's argumentation, yields, as is obligatory. Then, like a good prince, taking advantage of his half-victory and with a view to obtaining agreement to what is essential, Richard here offers a concession. He declares that he himself is ready to admit that "according to the history" the text can designate the kings of the earth, provided that his interlocutor grant that "according to the allegory" it designates "spiritual kings" as well.[340] All's well that ends well. Once Richard has finished his explications regarding "the mystical understanding," the former disciple of Andrew, fully convinced, avows that he "was astonished to discover such a depth of mysteries hidden within the prophetic words."[341]

Though the essential object of the discussion scarcely exceeds the limits of the literal sense, a text like this keeps us from supposing that the prior of Saint Victor would share the new spirit that his confrere Andrew seems to have just called forth; and all the more, from thinking that he took Andrew as his own "master." Against the "falsos christicolas judaizantes" — "false Christian Judaizers," who permit themselves to be led about by the Jews so as to deemphasize the prophets and to deny the figurative character of sacred history, Richard rather shares in the indignation of several of his contemporaries, like Gilbert Foliot for example, or Godefroy of Admont,[342] or Gerhoh of Reichersberg.[343] We see this again in his short treatise *Quomodo Christus ponitur in signum populorum*, which seems almost contemporary to the *De Emmanuele*[344] and which, with the fire of the latter text, proposes the same Christian exegesis. With regard to another prophecy of Isaiah's, that of the standard raised above the nations that gathers the scattered Israelites from the four corners of the earth, he cries out, with some impatience, as if he had a few recalcitrant characters near by:

> Would that the Jews, would that our Judaizers should pay attention and understand, should re-examine and consider what sort of sign this must be, how sublime, how outstanding, if the possibility of gathering together the exiles of Israel and the dispersed of Judah from the four corners of the earth is included within it.[345]

The historians agree, moreover, in recognizing that Richard had little interest in scientific research. One can see indications of this in the fact that he rather quickly rejects those whom he contemptuously calls the "contentiosos christianos";[346] also in the fact that, contrary to the majority of those around him, he never refers to the "Hebrew" text.[347] It is true that he is not scandalized at seeing Andrew frequenting Jewish scholars: but this practice has always been accepted, and no one would dream of taking scandal at it;[348] he himself did not hesitate to appeal to Jews to consult about the "Judaeorum scripta," to get information he needed to remove the apparent contradictions that he noticed in the chronology of the kings of Israel and Judah.[349] It is also true that in his treatise on the tabernacle of the covenant he shows both that he knows Josephus and that he is able to criticize him;[350] but such use of Josephus, as we have seen, which was also secular, was very frequent at that date: to the examples of Adam Scotus and Peter Cellensis, one can join those of Abelard, Peter the Eater, Philip of Harvengt, Peter of Blois, Sicard of Cremona, etc. These features, then, are not characteristic of any school and do not indicate that Richard follows properly in the line of Andrew, even with some discretion. If the treatise on the tabernacle, which was in part constructed on the model of that of the temple of Ezekiel,[351] is concerned only with the letter, it is because its author was being asked about that letter, which itself was accompanied by certain "difficulties."[352] Besides, Richard explained "the allegory" of it twice elsewhere: in an appendix to the *Benjamin minor*[353] and in the *Allegoriae in vetus Testamentum*.[354] In such a partition one will see only one effect, perhaps, of the didactic hardening brought about by the Victorine school in its manner of treating each of the diverse senses separately.[355]

As to the tabernacle, Richard has one point against Bede that one can compare to the criticism begun by Saint Gregory regarding the temple of Ezekiel. The two cases are, however, dissimilar. What Richard holds against Bede (without naming him) is not suppressing the "letter" or the "history" in any way: it is merely not being able to form a firm opinion regarding some point or other of historical explication. The uncertainty, he notes, redounds forcefully upon the allegorical explication.[356] Between the two exegetes, therefore, it is not a question of a general divergence of interpretation. Quite the contrary, apart from a few particular points where Bede and his disciples dared to raise a certain "ambiguity" of the text, one might better compare Richard's description — as well as those of Adam Scotus — only with those of Bede. In the description of Moses' tabernacle as well as of Solomon's temple, Bede already gathered all the possible details. He was already studying the measurements of the temple closely, for which he used to consult Josephus;[357] he used, for the future benefit of Adam Scotus, the table prepared by Cassiodorus, who made it possible to understand clearly the respective positions of the two altars and their accessories; he also consulted with Jewish scholars whom he had been able to meet; as to the temple, not content to study its construction and structure, he had wanted to get acquainted with its various materials, etc.[358] We have recalled above the care that he also devoted to the physical description of the ark. It is clearly not possible to find a "literal" exegesis in our Victorines, Hugh or even Richard, nor in Adam Scotus who is so like them, as a generalized reaction against the "allegorism" of bygone ages.

5. Explosion of the Three Disciplines

This glance that has just been cast upon "the Victorine School" should allow us better to grasp the historical significance of the work of its founder. After having had to deviate at several points from the interpretations that have been recently proposed about it, we will be in a much better position to formulate an overall judgment about it, if one agrees that this judgment goes beyond not only some of the available facts but also beyond fully conscious ideas and intentions.

All through his exposition of the classic thesis, formulated more or less skillfully from age to age from the Fathers of the Church down to the theologians of his own generation, Hugh of Saint Victor manifests in the *Didascalicon* the most explicit and most methodical effort to "to articulate theology in two pieces: the historical reading and the construction of the allegory." Father Chenu has shown this very well.[359] Before Hugh, the fourfold sense used to furnish already, in a broad way, a habitual framework for Christian reflection. This habitual framework was not catch-as-catch-can; it was truly organic. Only, despite the Carolingian effort of Rabanus Maurus, the resources that he could offer were not systematically exploited for regular theological studies that were themselves integrated within the complete cycle of learning. The *Didascalicon* undertook this effort, or at least codified it. One might believe that it was there to consolidate the tradition, assuring it the most stable triumph of all. Such was indeed Master Hugh's intention. But, in reality, his enterprise was a bit inconsistent. In any case, it would not take very long before these studies, in the course of getting organized, abandon the framework of the fourfold sense. The *Didascalicon* scarcely marked more than a link in the evolution which, in the epoch itself, was to result in the first Summas. Well, the result was opposite to what was intended. "The Victorine's effort was not to be established and successful, at least in its original plan."[360] Perhaps he put a lot more than he had intended into the simple formula that could have passed for a little tip from a schoolmaster: "The method of reading consists in dividing."[361] As Miss Smalley put it so well, the program elaborated by Hugh was "both too conservative and too modern."[362] Again, Hugh had said: "The same order of books is not to be kept in the historical as in the allegorical reading: the *history* follows the temporal order, whereas the order of cognition more pertains to the *allegory*."[363] But this passage from one "order" to another was to open the door to many unexpected novelties. It was impossible to constitute even a slightly systematized body of doctrine without an enlargement broader than the legislator of studies at Saint Victor would in principle have allowed, in relation to the form of a biblical exegesis. In practice, he himself already had to broaden his scope more than he would seem to admit: he could not dispense with effecting what Father Chenu called "a theological order."³⁶⁴ Is not his principal work, the *De sacramentis*, in his own opinion, something like a great parenthesis between *historia* and *allegoria*?

Thus, the very idea of *allegoria* was being transformed, though, for some time still, the word was preserved. In Hugh himself, this word designated, in practice, two quite different things; or, if one prefers, the *allegoria* that he theorizes about in the classic terms, tends to be realized in two divergent ways. This will become clear if we compare the brief but precise program that was sketched out in one chapter of the *Didascalicon*, which is itself devoted to *allegoria*, to the presentation in the two *De arca* treatises. We have already alluded to it. This program is that of a complete treatise; the "spiritual building" whose scaffolding he is erecting is coextensive with "divinity as a whole," namely, with what we today call the body of dogmatic theology. Its arrangement unfolds in eight "orders" starting with the "sacramentum Trinitatis" and ending with the "resurrectio."³⁶⁵ Here is what puts us quite far already, with Hugh himself, from the construction of the ark. Yet it was only a beginning. Perforce, what was foreseen as *allegoria* had to develop more and more separately, freeing itself more and more, in its method and structure, from the *historia* — that is, practically speaking, from exegesis — until finally it had to abandon a heading that had become just too inadequate.³⁶⁶ As a natural consequence, this is not what in exegesis would continue to be put under that term *allegoria*, which would from now on continue as the living part of sacred science.

Just as those who act are not always aware of the exact range of their initiatives, so too the history of ideas is never simple. In retrospect, it lends itself to various, sometimes inconsistent models, which, in any event, even when true and as objective as possible, are always merely models. Here at least is one of those that we might map out, it seems to me, to take account of the Victorine reform, without deforming too much any of the aspects of reality.

History and allegory, those two "main parts" of the unique construction more dreamed of than realized by Hugh of Saint Victor, are, to start with, two detached pieces. They are two consecutive disciplines, strictly linked in principle, but destined to become, in fact, quite independent of each other. Each is going soon to tend to be self-sufficient and each will evolve according to its own proper laws. The first will become historical and literal exegesis, free, when the time comes, to change into a veritable "positive" scholarship; to this end it will need many advances of varied order, but from now on the field is opening up before it: one day it will be "criticism"; it will even become, for many, religiously neutral, the exegete leaving to the theologian the burden of doctrinal commitments. At the same time, because of this separation, the second discipline will be free to organize itself more and more as an autonomous system. It will progress in rationality and in abstraction, to become the majestic edifice of the Summas of the great epoch, quite different from the style of what was to be the edifice foreseen by the "fourfold sense." In step with the future development of theological reasoning, in fact if not in law, theology will distance itself from its scriptural data. Will this emancipated daughter of the traditional *allegoria* be more "historical" so as to be less "allegorical"? It does not seem so. She will not content herself with the course pointed out by Hugh, which was that of salvation history. In the new structure, the realities of Christianity will each find their place "as the elements of a *work* of divine Wisdom rather than as a *plan* being brought into reality."[367] Under the weight of habit, however, for a long time, more or less backward exegetes were still producing allegorical commentaries of the holy Books. But their allegories will no longer really be taken seriously: they will be neglected by the best theologians, who will declare that they prove nothing and that consequently theologians should have nothing to do with them; who expect them likewise to be rejected by serious exegetes, who will also see in them mere fantasy, unworthy of their science. If then by similar dissociation biblical history seems to be winning — although still other conditions, which will not be realized until much later, are missing — this will not be with a view to informing theological thought; and if, on its side, theology is indisputably the gainer in more than one regard, this will nevertheless not be with a view to inspiring the work of the exegetes. Between the latter and the theologians, communication is weakening, and in consequence one will sometimes get the impression that it has been broken. In their "scholastic disputations," the masters of theology will be interested "less and less in the Bible, so as to be carried toward problems of a philosophical order."[368] More and more the exegetes themselves separate from their horizon the grand visions that alone render history intelligible, so as scarcely to envisage anything more than the multiform detail and the immediate significance of texts within their analytical science. Hence arise the incessant misunderstandings between them in the course of the modern centuries. Hence the mutual reproaches that they will happily utter. Was this not the big issue at the beginning of our age?

For his own part, Hugh of Saint Victor remained faithful to the old interpretation of the holy Books. He wanted to preserve that interpretation in its spirit, so to speak, as well as in its letter. He wanted to renew, not to

Explosion of the Three Disciplines

innovate. His method, in the exterior sense of the word, was nonetheless partly new. It was quickly abandoned. His initiative would therefore have ended — the experience is frequent — in a result contrary to what he desired. He had planned to found a veritable scriptural theology, which would be the whole of sacred science, and firmly to maintain its historical character, in opposition to the new trends that were disturbing him. Now it is here that, [in a manner] prepared by him, "scholasticism will become detached from sacred history."[369] Such detachment will not, however, remain merely exterior and methodological. It is undeniable that the "historical dimension of revelation," still so actively perceived by the Augustinians, "if not behind the times, at least conservative,"[370] will be much less so in the following epochs. There are some Thomists who say, sometimes even with a bit of exaggeration that the "Thomistic wisdom" itself seems to them a bit too filled, in its living parts, with the "sense of history" or the "sentiment of the irreversible historical process"[371] — though this may in no way be proper to Thomism *per se* but rather, within the School founded by Saint Thomas, reflect primarily a late "Thomism," little faithful to its founder;[372] for the history of salvation still holds a large place, too little noticed, perhaps a bit under-developed, in the *Summa Theologiae*. A time will even come — but it will no longer be that of high scholasticism — "where Scripture will be," for the theologian, "less the sacred memorial of sacred History, than an arsenal of texts arrayed according to purely ideological categories."[373]

Such a shortcoming, as is easy to imagine, was bound to have an impact upon exegesis: it would impede its normal development for a long time.[374] The separation of the two great disciplines, which, from a certain point of intellectual maturation needed to be accomplished, and which was the indispensable condition of the progress of each, could only be achieved with serious inconveniences both for the one and for the other. That is how all things here below come about.

As for the third of the "parts" of the ancient exegesis, represented by tropology (and anagogy), it was for the same reason to be detached from the first two parts, so as to be constituted as a body of spiritual doctrine rather remote both from its biblical foundations and from the newly constructed theology. We have quite often pointed out this sort of split that intervenes between a theology, once it has become purely "speculative," and a spirituality where feeling and imagination are dominant[375] — and which may secretly draw its principles from some non-Christian source. What may perhaps be less noticed, is that this split comes about as a consequence of the practical rupture of each of these two with exegesis, i.e., "the historical foundation," unless the unity of faith which serves as the foundation for them both should be attained in some other fashion. In fact it is from one and the same movement that, at least in its literary expression, spirituality becomes less scriptural and less theological. Thence a more immediately individual character is stressed, more purely interior in the strict sense of the word, leaving in the shade of implicit presuppositions what might be called its ecclesial dimension. Let us observe, for example, the evolution undergone by the theme of "spiritual marriage": to the extent that it is detached from the explication of the Canticle of Canticles, it also gives less prominence to the fundamental doctrine of the relations between Christ and his Church. In the same way, the "sapientia anagogica" which authors like Hugh of Balma[376] define especially according to Dionysius, will no longer be presented as the last moment of an exegesis; it will rather be the high point of a contemplation arising from the "plane of history," the "planities historiae": he will allow it to be opposed to "any speculative wisdom," as that which comes from God and not men. Many spirituals in the modern age seem to have followed less the example given by men like Origen or Saint Bernard than to have taken some of their advice, though out of context and understood rather one-sidedly: to describe their experience, if not to live it, they "drink at their own fountains," without appearing to care much about the original source that nourishes them. Such a tendency to autarchy could not fail here too to engender a number of misunderstandings and to provoke mutual reproaches, analogous to those that we noted between the exegetes and the theologians. Let us recall, for example, a certain famous chapter from the *Imitation*, or again the struggles between the "mystics" and the "scholastics" with which our French seventeenth century reverberates from one end to the other.

But, let us hasten to repeat, there it is merely a question of a very partial view, insufficient to warrant a judgment. The aforementioned disadvantages of a fragmentation that has become necessary can indeed summon us to new efforts of integration: they ought not to raise in us a romantic regret about past confusions. The old formula had seen its day — or rather, what had been thought has become a formula. Allegory was becoming sclerotic. Tropology was losing its savor. The harvested fruits did not have to be lost, provided that a renewal took place. Exegesis, theology, and spirituality did not fail to profit from a liberation that favored their development. The conquest of their autonomy — which was in part a re-conquest — ought to have allowed each to come up with more suitable tools. The most serious damage was not inevitable till much later, in the wake of more radical dissociations, and as a result of quite varied causes. Let us not forget, in particular, that at its apogee — which unfortunately lasted only a short while — high Scholasticism in its own way achieved a veritable synthesis of the three disciplines. The masters of doctrine then were at the same time masters in holy Scripture, and their work was also bursting with spiritual vigor. If there was more history in the *Summa* of Saint Thomas than there was in so many later theologians, that is because there was more Scripture in it. And the *Breviloquium* of Saint Bonaventure, in its harmonious density, exhibits an overall synthetic power that was perhaps never equaled. Moreover, when one considers the breadth of the results obtained, first in theology and later in exegesis, as well as the treasures of psychology resulting from centuries of spiritual analysis, it becomes impossible to dispute the fact that the dismemberment of sacred science involved immense advantages. As has been said of an analogous differentiation, that of the "theology of pastors" and the "theology of professors," it was surely "to run a great risk, but it was of the nature of things and in accordance to the laws of the progress of the mind."[377]

Furthermore, these are movements which, when they do take place, for the most part elude our freedom of choice. It is possible to impress a certain aspect and a certain orientation to new directions of thought: it is not possible to stop them. And in the present case, whatever judgment one has on the matter, one would be wrong to exaggerate the role played by Hugh of Saint Victor, one way or the other, upon the course of this ambivalent evolution. One man on his own could not rein in or turn aside the movement of his age, nor supply new vigor to an exhausted form of thought, nor permanently weld together two types of theological reflection, whose unity can only exist in individual successes which are imperfect and precarious. Hugh would never have dreamed of wanting to do away with time. Nor would he have founded some scientific, symbolic doctrine. At very least, he would have, along with others and in an important way, securely maintained a correct orientation and traditional fidelity in a theological activity using profoundly renewed methods.

Would he have wavered in his undertaking had he clearly perceived all the consequences? That is surely a useless question. But what we can be sure of is that he would trust in the urgings of the Spirit. His inclination for compromise[378] was not that of those mediocre minds that have nothing positive to offer of themselves. The conservative force that existed in his character was a living force. This willing "exile," who wanted the whole world to be an exile to him,[379] was not tempted to lock himself up within the wisdom of this world: nonetheless, he was open to all knowledge, and consequently to all progress. This "harp of the Lord," this "organ of the Holy Spirit," as Jacques of Vitry calls him,[380] this man imbued with the gift of heavenly wisdom, as the necrologist of Saint Victor expresses it,[381] knew that every human work is not only useless but even harmful if it leads to a neglect of the search for God.[382] But he also knew that every study can contribute to this search, and the more so to the extent that it is more disinterested. "Ignorance involves weakness; renouncing knowledge indicates a deficient will"; "Learn everything, and you'll see later that nothing is superfluous; a narrow knowledge is not a happy knowledge":[383] these two maxims from the *Didascalicon* lead us, beyond the forms, the particular methods and contents of thought, to the very spirit of that generation. An immense drive is rousing everyone of note, even when they are struggling against each other. This is the epoch in which Saint Anselm, already so free from allegorical methods and yet "no less unhurt by the desire for complete systematization" that is characteristic "of scholarly centers,"[384] has just assigned to the understanding the law of continuous transcendence, in an effort to conceive the Being which is always greater than what one can conceive. The signal role that goes back to the adventuresome genius of Peter Abelard is well known: one of his contemporaries compared him to Prometheus,[385] in the impulse of a movement of thought that will still be flourishing more than a century after him. No less influential is that which goes back to Gilbert de la Porrée, an austere thinker, perhaps even more daring in his more concentrated reflection. Their adversary, William of Saint Thierry, with equal audacity blazes the trails of the highest mysticism. Saint Bernard, the last of the Fathers, was not without reason called the first of the great moderns, and if it is true that he did not always "understand his time" and that he "made it a duty," sometimes an excessive duty, "to fight against the new trends,"[386] this fact ought not be interpreted in a petty way; in reality, like others who stand head and shoulders above the run of mankind, Bernard was very much ahead of his time, and ever since all sorts of revivals continue to claim him. Even Rupert himself, that giant of another age, that burgrave of the Holy Roman Empire, who seems to turn his back upon the world being born around him, shares in this same creative genius. He re-creates the spiritual drive of Origen's exegesis while impressing his own mark on it, and, in its massive proportions, his work communicates forcefully even to us today the feeling for what is a living tradition. Each in his own way, they all tell us: "Coarctata scientia jucunda non est" ["A narrow knowledge is not a happy knowledge"].

No, the spirit of that great epoch had nothing narrow, nothing skimpy, nothing anxious about it. Nor would what was best in it have been explicable merely in terms of what was to come after it. The notion that "the whole material susceptible of entering into future constructions" should "appear" in it by "recourse to geology"[387] is not a good way to understand it. Without doubt it was more a springtime than an autumn. It was a time of promise. Not all of the promises were kept. There were elements of progress and of consolidation in it; there were also aberrations and low points. There were other renewals, not all of whose promises were kept either. But never are all promises kept. Can the Christian in this world hope for more than a springtime?

After having gauged the role that belongs to Hugh of Saint Victor in the new constitution of these three disciplines, or, as he used to say, of these three "eruditions" — theology, exegesis and spirituality — one might, always from a formal point of view, try to indicate his contribution to each. As for theology, the matter is well enough recognized: the historical role of the *De sacramentis christianae fidei* is well known. In spirituality, the combined influence of his commentary on Dionysius and of the literary genre of his two *De arca* treatises is observed in two of his Victorine successors, Richard and Thomas of Verceil. We have previously spoken about the character of the *De arca* treatises. Though they get support from traditional interpretations, the biblical text scarcely offers more than a framework for treatises of a methodological character, and it is precisely the will to construct them methodically that has guided the choice for such a symbol to serve as their framework: the structure of the ark offered a fitting pretext for the construction of treatises that seem to be traced out on it.[388] Richard immediately exploits the formula that he so boldly sketches out. Already in the explication of certain Psalms, he distinguishes himself from the older commentators by the larger place he accords to psychological considerations.[389] His *De exterminatione mali et promotione boni* develops in logical order the symbols of Egypt, the Red Sea, the desert, the Dead Sea, and the Jordan;[390] nevertheless, if the title itself foreshadows its construction, the biblical data also everywhere rise to the same level. Thus, the reader sees clearly enough that the *Benjamin minor* presents itself as a commentary on Psalm [68:27]: "There is Benjamin, a youth, in ecstasy of mind" and expounding the traditional symbolism of Leah, Rachel, and certain other figures from the time of the Patriarchs.[391] But who then spontaneously recalls that the whole *Benjamin major*, that copious treatise on contemplation in five books, is itself also in theory a work of exegesis, explicating the ark of the covenant? Richard himself clearly thought that one would forget it; thus he followed the work with an appendix which is a sort of reminder; and the title itself already contains the acknowledgment that the biblical description of the ark is no more than a pretext or an "occasion."[392] But in addition, though the ark commented on by Hugh still bore the various sorts of classically enumerated senses, Richard chose his own as a purely tropological symbol, an unobtrusive support for a writing of pure spirituality:

> It is pleasant to unlock the mystical ark of Moses even to some degree, if it be permitted from the gift of inspiration of him who has the key of science through the exposition of our nocturnal study, and if anything deposited in this secret-box of the divine mysteries and in the hiding-place of the sciences still lies hidden, that could be extracted for the use of any others by our small talent, it will not grieve us to lay it out in public. . . . Many things have already usefully been said about this matter. . . . What this ark signifies mystically according to the allegorical sense, or how it signifies Christ, has already been said prior to us by the doctors. . . . Yet we do not for that reason suspect that we are guilty of reckless temerity, if we too should address the same matter in the moral sense.
> By the tabernacle of the covenant, understand the state of perfection.[393]

Likewise, in the *Benjamin minor*, a small number of facts from the time of the Patriarchs is enough to furnish a symbolic framework for an ample exposition of the contemplative life:

> In the death of Rachel contemplation ascends above reason; at Benjamin's entry into Egypt contemplation descends to the imagination; in the kiss of Benjamin and Joseph human reason applauds at divine revelation.[394]

Thus a genre of spiritual literature begins to be established, which has its own proper armature, which soon will live with its own proper life, and which will finally no longer have any visible organic attachment, as has been said before, either with exegesis or with theology properly so called.[395] What gains and what losses result from this is not something to be evaluated here. Richard of Saint Victor is still at the beginning of such a development. He remains quite attached to the "mystica lectio" ["mystical reading"].[396] He continues in principle to tie the explication of Scrip-

Explosion of the Three Disciplines

ture to contemplative process, and his mysticism is always chock full of doctrine.[397] On the other hand, if we take his work as a whole, we recognize that the influence of Pseudo-Dionysius in him, as in Hugh, is allied with that of Saint Gregory, which remains very strong. Gregory is one of the favorite authors of Richard,[398] who shows himself as a Gregorian not only in his method of exegesis or his ideas, but right down to his style. But after him, the evolution rushes headlong. To an extent never previously attained, Saint Gregory gives way to "divine Dionysius,"[399] whose anagogy was, as we have seen, not very scriptural. Origen and Saint Augustine alike back away before him.

Dionysius never entirely stopped being read since the time of his translation by John Scotus.[400] In the tenth century he was known at Cluny: the monk Syrus recounts that abbot Maieul spent some of his nights reading him, and someone recopied the *Expositio* that John Scotus had made of the *Celestial Hierarchy*.[401] The adversary of Cluny, Adalbéron of Laon (†1030), certainly never dreamed of disturbing the bases of thought, nor those of society, when he recommended the same reading to King Robert to introduce him to the problems of the order of the universe:

> Ask Dionysius who is called the Areopagite:
> He labored to write two books about this.[402]

Those at Chartres studied Dionysius. Honorius nourishes himself on him. Toward the same time as Hugh of Saint Victor, whose commentary dates from around 1124, it seems that Hervaeus of Bourg Dieu himself had commented on the first *Hierarchy*.[403] Dionysius is cited more than anyone else by Anselm of Laon. In the middle of the century, Bodo of Prüfning develops several Dionysian themes[404] and, toward the end, Adam Scotus, an author no less soberly traditional, will do the same in his little cell at the charter-house.[405] However, in the second part of the century, a new phenomenon arises. In part under the influence of the labors of John Sarrazin, the Eriugenian and Dionysian wave swells up; it affects many minds and affects them deeply. The passages from the *Divine Names* and the *Mystical Theology* cited in John Scotus's *De divisione naturae* heighten the shock effect. It constituted a veritable "spiritual trauma," as Father Chenu nicely put it, "whose glamorous and controversial effects will seize hold of the masters of the thirteenth century."[406] Just as the march of the mind had passed through Aristotle, so will it pass through Dionysius. It is notable from that point on. Dionysius left his mark upon the Porretainian school: on an Alan of Lille, whose *Summa* from the preface stands under the sign of the "magnus Dionysius Areopagita,"[407] on a Raoul Ardent, a Master Martin, a Simon of Tournai.[408] It exists no less among the Cistercians: the "thunder of Dionysius,"[409] which had scarcely touched Saint Bernard,[410] nor, despite a few traces, William of Saint Thierry, Arnaud of Bonneval, Otto of Freising, Aelred of Rievaulx, or Gilbert of Hoyland, now commands the attention of men like Isaac of Stella, Helinand of Froidmont, and Garnier of Rochefort.[411] We find it once again amongst the Victorines, with Thomas of Verceil (Thomas Gallus), whose work, quite forgotten in these last centuries until the works that Father Gustave Théry has devoted to it,[412] was to exercise a decisive influence from the thirteenth to the fifteenth century. Dating from the time he spent at Saint Victor of Paris, i.e., from before 1220 — stimulated by the example of Hugh commenting on the *Celestial Hierarchy* (ca. 1140), by the spiritual treatises of "Prior Richard" to which he refers several times,[413] and by the new translation of Dionysius by John Sarrazin[414] — Thomas Gallus works out his mystical doctrine: commenting on Isaiah by means of Dionysius, before apparently commenting on Dionysius by means of Scripture, thanks to a whole series of "concordances" in which he endeavors to demonstrate "that there is complete harmony between the first of the theologians and the inspired books."[415] A prolific writer, Thomas composed three commentaries on the Canticle of Canticles. The first, composed around 1224, is a work of spirituality *ad mentem Dionysii*:[416] its content is no longer either biblical or ecclesial: it is purely "mystical," in the modern sense. According to what Father Théry and Mlle. M.-Th. d'Alverny[417] tell us, we will also have to speak, it seems, of a second and a third version, which are similar. The slightly later commentary by the Dominican Bartholomaus of Vicenza (†1270), who "shatters the alabaster of the harshness of the letter so as to pour out the mellifluous sweetness of salvific wisdom," is also a treatise "on the deification of the mind," of a completely Dionysian aspect.[418] The new genre is now well established.

What made the transition from mystical understanding to speculative mysticism — to wit, from Scripture to Dionysius — so easy was the dominant opinion that Dionysius, the "beatus Pater Dionysius,"[419] had been the privileged disciple of Saint Paul. In his rapture to the third heaven, Paul had contemplated the secrets of the divinity, the supreme object of the whole biblical teaching, and the ancient tradition was much more interested in this rapture than people commonly are today.[420] Now, by a noteworthy miracle, the Apostle had then transmitted these secrets to Dionysius. Here is how Scholasticism, notably with the Franciscan Francis of Meyronnes, who depends directly on Thomas's Dionysian commentaries, will explain it:

> Since, once the face of the Lord had been revealed, by beholding his glory the doctor of the gentiles having been transformed into the self-same image by light into light as by the spirit of the Lord, for that reason he to whom the heavenly secrets have been revealed, Paul the Apostle, introduces the height of the heavenly wisdom that had been inspired in him in the word proposed. And since that salvific teaching which blessed Dionysius the Areopagite described had been radically derived from the supernal revelation that had been made to the Apostle, when the Apostle himself had been carried off unto the third heaven, for that reason that word is fittingly taken to introduce this teaching.[421]

Dionysius therefore allowed one to rise with a single bound, by a transcendent anagogy, right up to the sublime truths of "mystical theology," the summit of revelation, whose first steps the various senses of Scripture, apart from his influence, climbed pedagogically. The condemnation of John Scotus could cast into the shade the principal introducer of the Areopagite in the Latin West; the new interpretations of Thomas Gallus could be disputed.[422] But the reign of Dionysius would not be shaken. From that point on, for some centuries, high spirituality would be almost entirely under his sign.

The influence of the two great Victorines, Hugh and Richard, also made itself felt in a more modest sphere, that of literary genres. The biblical story or description was scarcely more than an ingenious prop for their spiritual constructions, and, the fuller and subtler their commentary became, the more it distanced itself from everything that the word exegesis might suggest. If they did not open a new path in that way, they at least enlarged and consolidated it. Others got involved after them. Rather later on, the *Spiritual Tabernacle* of John Ruysbroeck would also follow in their wake — a work which, by its structure, very closely recalls the treatises *De tabernaculo* or *De arca* from the twelfth century, but which no library cataloguer today would ever dream of placing among the works of exegesis any more than among the treatises of dogmatic theology, even though it also shares somewhat in both these genres. On the other hand, Adam Scotus's *Tabernacle* does not usually show up in the bibliographical listings of spirituality, either.

If, in fine, one wants to appreciate not so much the influence exercised by the Victorine school in general as the particular originality of its head in exegesis, it would be, I believe, fitting to recall, more than his didactic teaching or his mystical explanations of the ark, a page of his first homily on Ecclesiates like the one cited below. Compared to Rupert's commentary, for example, these homilies utter a new tone. Not that their method is more critical. But Hugh claims that a "new kind of exposition" is needed in order to understand this book well. A fertile remark, this, which could be generalized. By this "new genre of explanation," as Hugh understands it, one tries to burrow into the text, without having recourse to the classical procedures of allegory or tropology, by an effort of slow maturation. One attaches himself to the thought of the human author himself, not, however, for the purpose of historical reconstitution, but so as the more effectively to penetrate to the heart of his thought. One engages in a sort of dialogue with him, with a view to draw from him not some easily assimilated meaning but the very marrow of his thought. In this way one is little by little impregnated with the profound experience that the Holy Spirit has charged him to pass on:

> In this work I do not deem it necessary to concern myself with searching out the tropological or mystical senses of the allegories through the whole series of the narration at least.... It is to be known that this book requires a new kind of exposition; since, though it aims as a whole to move the affections of the human heart, it must more often form the discourse in conversational, as it were, rather than expository style. Hence it is sometimes necessary, even in matters that seem plain and obvious, to linger longer over the words, so that the very inculcation of the expression may more powerfully touch and more effectively penetrate the heart of the listener. Whoso wishes to treat this Scripture otherwise, even if he does fittingly contribute to the understanding of his hearers, nevertheless may edify them less, by not holding on to its force and proper character.[423]

This is not the leap from history to allegory, either, so as to attain the realities of the faith. If the "surface of the narrative" is also surpassed, if one is always searching for a "spiritual understanding," this comes about through a progressive deepening, "according to an increase of contemplation." Thanks to this method, he who meditates on the sacred text "attains spiritual things more and more and is removed from visible ones."[424] Then more than one passage becomes a parable for him.[425] The disillusioned utterances of the Ecclesiast become sweet for him to hear.[426] His bitter wisdom changes into mystical wisdom. Hugh himself is persuaded that [the author] ought to be considered a contemplative. How would he have penetrated the vanity of everything so well, if he had not been raised "super hominem," right up to that "truth," from whence one casts a sublime gaze over everything.[427] No doubt he was not a "veritable Hebrew," i.e., otherwise he would not have passed to contemplation of the divine wisdom. He was not merely disillusioned; rather, he was "converted."[428]

This was certainly not the starting point of a scientific exegesis. Nor did it represent Christian exegesis as a whole. It was, moreover, something other than one of those delirious "dreams" that Luther labeled all the commentaries on Ecclesiastes that were composed before him.[429] At any event, there is dreaming and there is dreaming. One type can open the way to a better understanding of the Old Testament taken in itself. Hugh is doubtless not the only one of the great commentators on Scripture who had, when the text calls for it, practiced such an exegesis from time to time. One could not deny, however, that an excessively forced research into allegory — quite like a certain literalist shortsightedness in the sequel — often made it atrophy. Better than a Rupert, who transformed Qôheleth into an announcer of the Christ at the very start, more soberly than Saint Jerome, who refrained from allegorizing less than he,[430] or than Alcuin, who closely followed Jerome,[431] Hugh of Saint Victor, toward the end of his life,[432] was able to say how to disengage the teaching of the old sage whilst extending it and transposing it. As interpreted by him, the song of the Qôheleth is no longer that "poem of decrepitude" or that "flower with petals of ashes" that Father Jean Steinmann so rightly recognized in it. His critique has lost that power to harbor "deadly poison." Hugh, however, does not betray him. He has merely exploited his discovery, which is "the sense of eternity at the heart of man," and without having recourse to a violently allegorical transformation, but rather by casting the light of the Christian law upon it, he better emphasized "the profound truth," that truth which Father Steinmann expresses again using Pascal's words: "man's poverty in the presence of God, if it is not the God of Jesus Christ."[433]

In that way, Hugh shows himself to us in still another light, which lets us catch a glimpse of the unobtrusive richness of his personality. The homilies that he devoted to Ecclesiastes are not the only proof that he had it in him to apply his method and to profit from his secret conversations with the Ecclesiast. Already in his *Didascalicon,* his fervent desire to know is fulfilled and comes to rest in a higher search: "the highest consolation in life is the pursuit of wisdom."[434] The *De vanitate mundi* is a true book of wisdom. The word of "Solomon" is preserved in it, his experience is assimilated in it; but this time it is Hugh himself who finally sets the tone. The voice we hear in it is that of a Christian and Victorine Ecclesiast. Not that of an "ageless mystic," as Ch.-V. Langois used to say;[435] on the contrary, it is that of a man who was strongly marked by his time and who strongly made his mark on it but who was not lost in time; of a man who has felt the attraction of the world's beauty, but disengaged himself from it: "O impure world, why do we love you so?"[436] The last lesson of this Christian Ecclesiast is also serene, but more positive than that of his precursor:

> So nothing is to be discarded in its time, and nothing is to be accepted apart from its time; but let the mind be prepared to use time, yet in such a way that it not be left to the mutability of time.[437]

CHAPTER SIX

Joachim of Flora

1. The Concord of the Three Ages

Two deviations threaten spiritual understanding at its peak. Spiritual understanding can forget that Christianity is eschatological and, effectively, suppress hope — at least the specifically Christian hope. On the other hand, by an inverse dissociation of the *invisibilia* and the *futura*, it can also conceive an eschatology upon earth and thereby transform hope — at least a primary phase of hope — into utopia. Some signs of the first tendency, due in part to the influence of Pseudo-Dionysius, had appeared for us with respect to anagogy and we have just picked up its trail once again. It remains to explore the second in its most illustrious instance: that of Joachim of Flora (ca. 1132-1202).[1]

If one confines oneself to certain general declarations, one might believe that Joachim simply partakes in what everybody thinks about the spiritual understanding of Scripture. But the detailed explications that he frequently offers show, beyond any doubt, that he has his own peculiar way of understanding it.

Scripture, says he, contains "mystic expressions"; it is possible to explicate them at first on the surface, merely pointing out the *history*; but then it is necessary to open them up, so as to point out the *spirit* that is found hidden within them.[2] While commenting on the history of the Magi, he compares this spiritual understanding to the star that guides them: "that glittering star without a knowledge of which reading the Scriptures is more like bumping about in the dark than coming to know the way of truth."[3] One ought not to be surprised that the spiritual understanding should be "multiform," since the Spirit, though one in itself, is multiple in its gifts. Thus, there exists a great diversity of mysteries in the holy Books, and one will need to take a good many precautions if one wants "easily to cross the seas of so many mysteries." The ways that lead to God are not like the routes found on our earth: they are rather comparable, as the Psalmist says, to those trackless routes of the sea. On embarking, each navigator — each new reader of the Scriptures — must therefore run the risk of choosing his own path, "according as the spirit of the winds should drive him." Nevertheless diversity constitutes neither opposition nor contradiction: it can be a sign of the depth and subtlety of the mystery. And all the mysteries agree in the service of the truth, which is one.[4] Similarly, if the navigators know how to consult the stars, they will all arrive at one and the same port.[5]

So whatever the itinerary that one may follow under the unforeseeable impulse of the Spirit, there exist certain fixed stars, certain objective rules, that hold good for everyone. Joachim exposes them methodically. If his thought about them remains obscure, it is not because the lines of the theory he constructs are hard to follow: on the contrary, they have a complex precision, like the mechanism of a finely adjusted time-piece. The essential texts are contained in four large works, which are of more or less the same date: the *Concordia novi et veteris Testamenti* and the *Expositio in Apocalypsim*, a double of his *Liber introductorius*, had been composed almost simultaneously around 1184; the *Psalterium decem chordarum* followed almost immediately[6] and the treatise *Super quatuor evangelia*, still incomplete, came a bit later. There is therefore no room to look for an evolution of any importance in his thought, which is systematically expressed in all four texts and which is found almost identically in the little treatise *De articulis fidei* and also in the treatise *On the life of Saint Benedict and the divine office according to his doctrine*.[7] A few differences of terminology[8] or presentation do not undermine their coherence.

Understanding flows entirely from one unique source: the letter. This letter in turn is either twofold, since it comprises the two Testaments,[9] or even threefold, since it may also add "what the holy Fathers have instituted" to the divine Scriptures.[10] Though one in its final objective — the "mystery of the Church," which comprehends everything — this understanding is not only manifold in the approaches of those who research it: it is objectively differentiated in its structure. It unfolds into a large fan comprising a dozen senses,[11] which can be reduced to four, or even to two, according as one counts them all or groups a certain number of them under more fundamental genera.

The Concord of the Three Ages

On the one hand, there is the spiritual understanding proper, and, on the other, the typic understanding. This is the essential distinction that commands the whole system.

The first of these two understandings is itself of three sorts: it can be either historical, or moral, or allegorical — and this last in its turn is subdivided into three, for it is at first tropological, then contemplative, and finally anagogical. This makes five sorts of spiritual or mystical understanding in all.[12] Joachim sees them symbolized by the five apostles who had been sent to announce the Gospel to the Greeks: Peter, Andrew, Paul, Barnabas, and John.[13] The first of the five, or the historical understanding, is not to be confused, as some believe, with the letter or history itself, though it is very close to it: "quite close to it and in accordance with it";[14] it presents individual or collective analogous situations to serve as an example to and as a consolation for the Christian.[15] The second, or the moral understanding, treats of the virtues and the vices.[16] The third, or the allegorical understanding, is related to spiritual doctrine and life,[17] "allegorically converting what is animal into the spiritual."[18] As Joachim understands them, these first three sorts of understanding are not in continuity, as are the three or four senses of the common theory; they neither engender nor do they even presuppose each other; each proceeds directly from the "spring of the letter," as an independent stream, by a movement which goes "from the visible to the invisible," seen each time under a peculiar angle.[19] If there is any order or relation among them, it is merely an order of dignity. The first two are inferior, because, though very necessary for conduct and capable of producing abundant fruit, they nevertheless do not yet introduce us into the sphere of the knowledge of God and His great works.[20] Allegory, however, which is superior to them, involves a true gradation among its three subdivisions. It necessarily begins by tropology, so named from [Gk.] *tropos* ([Lat.] modus) and *logos* (sermo), because "it embraces and discerns the ways (modos) of God's speeches (sermonum)";[21] it then passes through contemplation before blossoming into anagogy. Tropology is the specialty of the doctors and it corresponds to faith.[22] Contemplation, which comes next, is proper to those who have leisure for prayer and the singing of the Psalms; through contemplation one begins to rise to the "invisible things of God"; it is especially concerned with the gifts of the Holy Spirit, and corresponds to hope.[23] Finally, anagogy is proper to those who have already laid aside the burden of the flesh and are resting in the Jerusalem on high; it is concerned with the things belonging to that happy homeland and with God himself; it corresponds to charity.[24]

Just as there is no perfection above charity, nor any being above God, "there is no other understanding" above anagogy. The very name "anagogy" itself indicates as much.[25] The summit of contemplation is like oil, which is always floating on the surface of the vessel, whatever liquid be found contained therein.[26] It therefore marks the end-point of an ascent. What Joachim of Flora understands by "typic understanding" does not just constitute a new degree, superior to those of allegory. It is another kind of understanding, whose exercise belongs quite particularly to pastors.[27] In face of the cycle of spiritual understanding, it forms a new cycle, which itself unfolds in seven species, or according to seven special modes, "performed by the seven spirits sent from heaven upon the earth."[28] Each of these modes is relative to one of several divers "states" which are met with among men in the heart of the Church, i.e., to one of the divers holy functions or one of the divers moments of salvation history. Joachim's overall objective is essentially to manifest the "concord" between the two Testaments, or two sacred histories, that before and that after Christ; thus, for short, one can call it "concord": "that understanding which is called 'concord'" ["intelligentia illa, quae concordia dicitur"]. One will recall, however, that for there to be true concord, it is not necessary that the two terms should correspond at every point: "concord is not required with respect to the whole, but only with respect to what is clearer and more evident; not over the run of history, but only according to some aspect."[29] For example, one will recognize seven successive significations for the group constituted by Abraham and his two wives Hagar and Sarah:

> In the first species of typic understanding, Abraham signifies the high priests of the Jews; Hagar signifies the people of Israel; Sarah, the tribe of Levi. In the second species Abraham signifies the bishops; Hagar, the church of the laity; Sarah the church of the clerics. In the third understanding, Abraham signifies the prelates of the cenobites; Hagar, the church of the converted; and Sarah that of the monks. In the fourth species, Abraham signifies the high priests of the Jews and the bishops of the Latins; Hagar signifies the synagogue, as above, and Sarah the church of the Latins. In the sixth understanding, Abraham signifies the prelates of the second and third status; Hagar, the church of those at labor, which is the present church, and Sarah the church of those at rest, which is to come in the third status, when the eternal Sabbath will be given to the people of God.[30]

At the same time one will have to say that each of these seven species of typic understanding is in relation with the divine Trinity under some particular aspect: the first is relative to the Father, the second to the Son, the third to the Holy Spirit; the fourth is relative to both the Father and the Son at once; the fifth, to the Father and the Spirit; the sixth, to the Son and the Spirit; and as to the seventh, it is relative to the entire Trinity together.[31]

Or again, more simply, Abraham designates the order of the Patriarchs, i.e., the first age, which lasts up until the Christ; Isaac, with his two sons, designates the order of the Apostles instituted by Christ, i.e., the second age, with its duality of Greeks and Latins. From amidst them all arises the chaste Saint Joseph, who ends up by ruling over all the rest: he is the figuration of the order of monks initiated by Saint Benedict, whose life corresponds to that of Saint Joseph. After having been like the light under the bushel basket, or like Christ in the tomb, after having passed for a savage beast in the eyes of men, this order will light up the whole earth; through it men will finally become truly men, knowing "how good it is for brothers to live together."[32]

We shall not undertake a detailed exegesis of such passages. Certain points will become clearer in the sequel. Taken in their totality they suffice to show Joachim's predilection for weaving together symbols; they also give us some indication of his favorite themes and offer us an example of those recapitulating tabulations in which his precise and calculating imagination took such pleasure. Let us hold on to the idea of the continuity of the typic understanding in the succession of its species. This understanding, Joachim tells us, is like a long trail that starts from the desert and leads to a magnificent city; it traverses mountains and valleys; at the bottom of each valley the traveler hesitates and believes himself to be lost; but on each height he can turn around and contemplate the stages he has already crossed, while he recognizes before him at very least the direction he must take to reach his goal.[33]

Seven and five make twelve. There are, then, twelve understandings in all: a perfect number, the number of universality. If we leave aside the two first types of understanding — the historical and the moral — which are simple preparations of a lower order, we will have the ten chords of the *psalterion*.[34] Other combinations will get into the "fullness of understanding" under the numbers three, five, six, or seven.[35] Again, by new calculations one will obtain, always together with the psalterion, the number fifteen — for there are fifteen divers ways of speaking within Holy Scripture[36] — starting with what will set the understanding of Scripture in correspondence with the one hundred fifty Psalms that constitute the Psalter.[37] But if one reduces the seven species of the typic understanding to one and keeps the three degrees of allegorical understanding, one will obtain the most fundamental and usual schema, often recalled by Joachim, in a variable order: "the four principal understandings, which contain all the rest under them."[38] These are the historic, moral, and allegoric (or contemplative, or anagogic) understandings and the typic understanding. They correspond to the four directions; the four winds in the heaven that battle in the great sea (Daniel 7); the four rivers of paradise;[39] the four living creatures of Ezekiel and the Apocalypse;[40] the four sorts of nourishment appropriate to each of these living beings;[41] the four evangelists;[42] the four great mysteries of Christ; the four principal founders of monasticism; the four orders of martyrs, doctors, virgins, and apostles.[43] Finally, one can sum it all up in the two fundamental kinds: the spiritual understanding, sometimes also called allegory, "whose species are numerous," and the typic understanding, or concord.[44]

It is nevertheless clear that in these divers calculations and groupings, whatever their eventual number or order should turn out to be, Joachim of Flora adds in things that cannot go together. His distinctions are not adequate. There is no formal relation between the three degrees of allegoric understanding, on the one hand, and the seven species of typic understanding, on the other. The latter, moreover, is of a different nature than history, morality, and allegory. It is not, let us say it again, a "spiritual" understanding.[45] It is essentially the perception of a relation between two literal levels: the letter of the Old Testament and that of the New; or more precisely, between two histories: the history of ancient Israel and the history of the Church.[46] It does not make us pass "from the visible to the invisible," as did the moral understanding and the three allegorical sorts of understanding, each in its own way; but from one end to the other — if one leaves the seventh species out of account — it keeps us within exterior facts; each of its six first species concerns one of the six conditions of the Church or one of the six successive stages of her history.[47] Joachim is conscious of this fundamental difference.[48] He himself calls attention to it on several occasions. He attaches a special importance to it and does not want there to be any equivocation on this subject:

> Since there are some who think that concord is the same thing as the spiritual understanding, which properly is called allegory, it is first necessary for us to show what difference there is between concord and allegory.[49]

So allegory is one thing, namely a *spiritual* understanding, and concord something else, namely, as he precisely designates it, *concordia litterae*, i.e., "a concord of the letter." This is why, he explains again, the first four parts of his *Concordia,* which were devoted to the historical parallel between the two Testaments, contain so little of anything "according to the spirit."[50] Now it is this parallel, this "concordia litterae," which constitutes Joachim's proper contribution in the interpretation of Scripture. This is also what he most fully develops and what essentially dominates his vision. Hence it is this that ought to hold our attention. But to understand this "concord" properly, it is important to situate it within the larger framework wherein Joachim inserts it: that of the ages or states of the world.[51]

The Augustinian division into four ages was already classic. Joachim took it over, but added one unit to it. Thus he counted five ages, which determine five divers situations of the human race: "before the Law"; "under the Law"; "under the Gospel" (or "under the letter of the Gospel" or "under the letter of the New Testament"); "under the spiritual understanding"; and finally, "in the fatherland" (or "in the manifest vision of God").[52] From one age to the other, the work of the Trinity goes on getting clearer and clearer.[53] Only the first four ages, truly speaking, belong to time; the last "is called time not properly, but by misuse of language": it succeeds at the end of time, and consequently escapes us.[54] As to the first two, they can conveniently be united to form just a single one. In practice, then, we shall rather speak merely of three states, three ages, or three times: the time "before grace," the time "under grace," and the time "which we soon expect, under a fuller grace."[55] After the time of "the natural and Mosaic law" ["lex naturalis et mosaica"] there succeeds the time of the "evangelical law under the letter of the Gospel" ["lex evangelica sub littera evangelii"], which itself in turn is soon to be replaced by the "time under the spiritual understanding" ["tempus sub spirituali intellectu"]. The first was in the science of the spirit; the second is in its wisdom; the third will be in the fullness of the spirit.[56] Just as in the second period the people of God, freed from the "slavery of the Law," had to live following "the truth of the Gospel," so, in the third period, they will be freed "from the labor of passion" and be able to devote themselves fully to the praise of God.[57]

These three times are symbolized in many ways. They are symbolized by various trios of biblical personages, notably Saul, David, and Solomon.[58] They are betokened by the three periods of Elizabeth's sterility, her fruitfulness, and her giving birth.[59] They are marked by the three heavens spoken of by Saint Paul: "in the first, little children are trained; in the second, young adults are educated; in the third, friends are initiated";[60] these same three heavens correspond to the three orders of successive control: "the order of those who bring forth, the order of those who preach, the order of those who contemplate," themselves comparable to bronze, silver, and gold. Again, the three times are related among themselves as water, wine, and oil, or as the bud, the stalk, and the grain, or as nettles, roses, and lilies.[61] One can even say that the first time flows forth in fear and slavish servitude, the second in faith and filial servitude, the third in charity and freedom. The first is the time of the old; the second, that of young men; the third, that of children.[62] The first is that of the stars in the night; the second, that of the dawn; the third, that of broad daylight,[63] etc. Freed from metaphor, the first is the age of the laymen, the second is the age of the clerics, and the third is the age of the monks.[64]

Finally, if we want to synchronize this division of the three states with that of the seven days of creation or the seven periods of the world, we shall say that the first of the three states, that of the Old Testament, covers the first five periods; the second covers the sixth period; and the third will cover the seventh.[65]

Taking up the symbol of the four living creatures and the four evangelists that we saw him applying a moment ago to the four principal types of understanding, Joachim now uses it with subtlety to unite the three terrestrial ages with the eternal world at which they end:

> If we are up to examining the principles and aspects of the Gospels more subtly, it seems that with some propriety Matthew's Gospel touches on the time of the earlier Testament; Luke's on that from the rise of the early Church up to the coming of Elijah; Mark's from the coming of Elijah to the end of the world, when God's elect will be taken up into heaven; and John's Gospel deals with that happy age which will never ever be closed off by any end.[66]

Nevertheless, it is not all so simple as might have appeared up till now. For each of these three terrestrial ages has, as it were, a double date of origin: that of its anticipated inauguration, or, as Joachim says, its "initiation" or its "germination," and that of its complete foundation, its confirmation, "clarification" or "fructification," while awaiting the date of its "term" or its "passing away." The first age, inaugurated by Adam, was confirmed by the Patriarchs and by Moses; the second, inaugurated by the king Ozias [or Uzziah], bears fruits beginning with Jesus Christ and his apostles; as to the third, inaugurated already by blessed Benedict, whose monastic institution is figured in its present state by the Virgin

Mary prior to her giving birth, it will bear fruit only "at the end-time," beginning with the return of Elijah "according to the spirit."[67] However, already, at the present moment, "we have been constituted between the second state and the third."[68] As the different manner in which Saint John speaks of the number of martyrs and the number of virgins in the Apocalypse indicates, the third age, which is that of the virgins, commences during the course of the second, which is that of the martyrs.[69] Or yet again, between the second age, symbolized in the life of Saint Benedict by his predecessor Saint Germain, and the third age, which is symbolized by Benedict himself, there is the mediation of Saint Scholastica: she, like the Benedictine Order of today renewed by Cîteaux, is placed between the two, so as to prepare the way from Leah to Rachel or from the second age to the third; in like fashion, in days of yore, the Virgin Mary, symbol of the *Ecclesia primitiva*, stood as mediatrix between the first age and the second, which were symbolized by the old Simeon and John the Evangelist standing on either side of her.[70]

Thus the ages dovetail into each other: the one that follows is beginning to "germinate" while the one that precedes is, toward its mid-point, still "fructifying."[71] It is necessary to say the same about the periods into which these ages are subdivided; and still other complications arise, requiring still subtler divisions.[72] Let us add that certain of the symbols supplied by sacred history are susceptible of two sorts of interpretation, "general" or "special"; or even of three sorts, "broad," "strict," or "still stricter."[73] Finally the second age offers the peculiar characteristic of being entirely "twofold and twin-born," i.e., divided down its whole length into two parallel series, concerning two distinct peoples: for on the one side there is the Church of the East, with Saint John the Evangelist and the Virgin Mary, and on the other side the Church of the West, with Saint Peter and Saint John the Baptist:[74] God so willed it so as to establish both the sacerdotal order and the monastic order, the active life and the contemplative life, a *magisterium* of preaching doctrine and a virginal and chaste "religion." Nonetheless, what is essential here is the concatenation of the three ages, which Joachim usually symbolizes using an image that comes to him from the Jew Moses Sephardi, who was converted under the name Peter Alphonse:[75] three circles or three rings taken one within the other.[76]

The first and the second of these three ages correspond to what Joachim, along with everyone else, names the Old and New Testaments. But, as follows from what we have just seen, the relation of these two Testaments for him is no longer that of the letter and the spirit: it is rather the relation of one letter to another letter, the "littera novi Testamenti" ["letter of the New Testament"]. A dissociation has been effected between two ideas that, in the earlier tradition, had always been welded together to the point of constituting a simple unity: the idea of a spiritual understanding of Scripture and the idea of the perfect harmony of the two Testaments. Though the dignity of the New Testament is superior to that of the Old, the perfect "concord" that exists between the two is no longer equivalent to the "harmony" drawn out by the Fathers. It does not rest upon an "allegorical" signification but rather upon a "likeness of equal proportion" ["similitudo aequae proportionis"]. Joachim takes up anew the traditional symbols of the "wheel within the wheel" contemplated by Ezekiel and the two cherubim facing each other atop the ark: now it is a correspondence of two external histories, one old and the other new.[77] One order and another, one war and another, one person and another, people versus people, persecution versus persecution, and so on — face each other, so to speak, as things of the same nature and equal in number. Adam pairs up with Ozias [Uzziah] (who already, as has been seen, marks the beginning of the New Testament), Abraham with Zachariah, Sarah with Elizabeth, Isaac with John the Baptist, Jacob with Jesus the man, the twelve Patriarchs with the twelve Apostles, and so on in each subdivision of the twofold history.[78] The trio Abraham-Sarah-Isaac, according to other symbolic traits, corresponds to the trio Simeon-Mary-Elizabeth; to each of these trios in turn there answers a third, which is formed from Saint Germain, Saint Scholastica, and Saint Benedict.[79] The four "special histories" of Job, Tobias, Judith, and Esther announce the four gospels of Matthew, Luke, Mark, and John.[80] David is paralleled with Pope Sylvester, Hezekiah with Pope Zachary, Zadok with Gregory VII,[81] etc. To the Assyrians there correspond the Arabs; to the Chaldeans, the Alemanni; the new Babylon will be struck down just like the old, etc., everywhere "the new answering to the old point for point."[82] *O marvelous concord!*[83] All these things, Joachim says again and again quite clearly, ought to be taken as literal concord and not as spiritual or allegorical signification.

The correspondence — which Joachim tabulates slightly differently from one work to another — between the two letters, that of the time of the Law and that of the time of the Gospel, i.e., between the history of Israel and the history of the Church, is indicated by the book of the Apocalypse. This expresses the unique importance of this book. It contains all the secrets of history. It is, as it were, the inner key to the cycle of the books of the Old Testament; in the same way, it is also the key of the New: "the key to

The Concord of the Three Ages

things old, an acquaintance with things to come, the opening of things sealed, an uncovering of secrets."[84] By opening the seven seals in succession, he brings to light the seven periods whose parallel succession constitutes each of these two time periods.[85] For example, just as there had been seven persecutions in the first period, so are there seven in the second.[86] They each correspond to the three beasts of Daniel that were evoked in the *Vita Benedicti*, the third of which had four heads,[87] and the seven heads of the dragon of the Apocalypse that were represented in the *Liber Figurarum* are also on each side seven persecutor kings.[88] Just as the Israelites who had gone into schism had been punished for it by the invasion of the Assyrians, so were the Greeks, by being invaded by the Saracens.[89] And just as of old God destroyed the army of Sennacherib in the days of Hezekiah king of Judah, so for some time he made the army of the Saracens fall into the hands of the king of the Franks.[90] The tribulations that the king of the Turks is currently inflicting upon the Church correspond to those that Nebuchadnezzar, king of the Assyrians, had foisted on the Jews according to the Book of Judith.[91] Just as in the sixth epoch of the history of Israel one sees Cyrus and Darius appear, so must a new Darius soon arise in our Christian West, to strike down a new Chaldean people, enemy of our holy mother the Church, as well as a new Cyrus, to exalt the royal priesthood.[92] Then it will be necessary for a king worse than them all to come next, the head of a "new race of Saracens,"[93] just as the terrible king Antiochus came toward the end of the first state: "the last has not yet come."[94] But from then on concrete detail eludes us. While we clearly see the historic "concords" between the past of Israel and that portion of the history of the Church that also has already happened or that concerns a sufficiently proximate future event, what is to follow can scarcely give rise to anything but conjectures.[95] Regarding the third time period, "as yet we are up to exhibiting only the beginnings that are at hand." Will this third time, like the other two, also be divided into seven periods? Yes, of course.[96] Nevertheless it is too soon to be able to affirm it with certitude or at least for anyone to be able to distinguish these periods clearly.[97] We can only schematically determine the "concords" to come: "Though, with respect to things past, the truth is now already clear to Christians, nevertheless, with respect to the future, the perfection of the truth is still hidden."[98] Cautionary formulas are called for: "quantum datur intelligi" [literally, "to the extent that it is given to be understood"]. The Scripture, then, is not totally clear to us — and this is why so many heretics still arise in the bosom of the Church, "breaking the net of the Gospel, eluding the grasp of the men of the Church."[99] The last period to come, that of the seventh concord, beginning with the return of Elijah, rises from the third state:[100] thus it will not be able to be entirely clarified by a simple literal concord; from now on it is necessary to extract the "spiritual forms of understanding" starting from the "historical words."[101]

The divine pedagogy is progressive. God guides his elect by stages "from virtue unto virtue" and "from clarity unto clarity."[102] It was necessary for the Hebrew people, being a little child in the faith, first to be nourished on milk; then, when the Church became adult, she received the food of the higher sacraments, before she would be permitted one day to pass beyond the teaching of Christ, to attain the perfection of the third state.[103] Doubtless there had been certain exceptions at all times, certain particular anticipations: long ago certain persons privileged by the Spirit received spiritual understanding from that Old Testament under which they were living; in the same way today there are some who comprehend the letter of the New Testament in spirit, and it is still the same understanding. But one ought to consider the situation as a whole and, without stopping at special cases, to define the "general mysteries" for each time period.[104] Now, the Gospel of Christ, as it still prevails, taken literally, is merely an "inchoative discourse": it leads no one to perfection. Perfection becomes accessible only once "the discourse of the beginning of Christ's precepts has been left behind" ["relicto praeceptorum Christi inchoationis sermone"]. Those who preach the Gospel according to the surface of the letter are surely preferable to the Jewish doctors who preach the Law of Moses — for between the doctrine of Moses and that of Christ, there is the difference between the moon and the sun[105] — but they are nevertheless much inferior to those who taste the Gospel spiritually, and "no longer walk at all according to the flesh."[106] For the Church as a whole, the four books of the gospels are themselves still "closed and wound up within their scrolls."[107] Therefore it is necessary for the third age to come, the "tertius status," wherein the eternal Gospel, which is the Gospel of the Spirit, will be promulgated for all: not some new book that would again be bearing some new letter — the spiritual doctrine itself cannot be circumscribed so as to be shut up within some big scroll[108] — but the spiritual understanding of the books of both of the two Testaments.[109] Then what had till then remained hidden within these four Gospels will come to light for all.[110] Only then will the kerchief that covers the head of Jesus be removed.[111] Then what had appeared new in the time of John the Baptist will have to be thought old, in comparison with the new things that the Lord will be accomplishing upon the earth. Then, as in the third day at Cana, this third period will be the time for wedding: the

The Concord of the Three Ages

Church, made new again, will be joined to her heavenly Spouse;[112] prefigured by Jesus' first miracle, the greater miracle of the Spirit will change the letter into spiritual understanding;[113] and "the water of the Gospel will be changed into wine."[114] Then one shall see the heavens opened; i.e., once the gate of the letter has been penetrated, the gaze of the Spirit will without impediment plunge into the two Testaments.[115] A sort of new "religion," one that is entirely free and spiritual, will be started.[116] The institutional Church such as it exists from the time of Christ, the Church of the clerics and doctors, the one signified by Elizabeth or John the Baptist, will be succeeded by a humble and silent, "chaste and virginal" Church destined to last until the end of time, a Church signified by the Virgin Mary or by Jesus Christ Himself;[117] a Church not of scholars or doctors, but of contemplatives; a Church of charity, "which will repose in the silence of the desert,"[118] "in leisure and repose."[119] The "pious priests" and the "pious pastors," of whom Saint Peter was the head, will give place to the "good who are encloistered" or "the good hermits," who perpetuate the spirit of Saint John.[120]

Happy the men who will no longer have any desire for worldly things! Happy the Church in this third state! A Church completely free at last![121] A Church of the seventh age of the world, prefigured by the Sabbath,[122] "where there will no longer be labor and groaning, but repose and leisure and abundance of peace"![123] O universal joy! O fulfillment of our perfection! Here is the Lord's Dominion "from sea to sea"! O kingdom of truth over the whole earth![124] O third heaven! O happy time of Rachel![125] O time of the effusion of the Spirit! To sum up: O time of spiritual understanding, that is to say, of "the beginning of the anagogic understanding" which ought to be that of eternity![126]

This theology of history is not only trinary, following a number for which Joachim has special affection;[127] it is properly trinitarian. This does not mean simply that the divine Trinity has revealed itself little by little, step by step, in the course of time.[128] As we have just seen, moreover, Joachim sets up correspondences everywhere between the temporal unfolding and the action of the divine persons. *There are three states of the world, because of the three persons of the divinity.* It can assuredly only be a question of "attributions," since the three Persons of the Trinity do not act separately.[129] But these attributions are extremely significant. The first age pertained to the Father; the second pertains to the Son. In the image of the Father, the Old Testament is the first source of "science"; in the image of the Son, the New Testament is "scientia de scientia, littera de littera" ["science from science, letter from letter" — in phrasing that

339

seems to echo the Nicene Creed: "Deum de Deo, lumen de lumine"]. The third age will be that of the Holy Spirit, and that is why it will be the age of spiritual understanding, which proceeds from each of the two Testaments, from each of the two letters, in the image of the Holy Spirit proceeding from the Father and from the Son. It will be the age of the great contemplatives, whose "order" will be distributed among various species, because the graces of the Spirit are numerous and diverse.[130] In the same way as each of these three ages is subdivided into seven periods, so are all together divided in a single great septenary, and thus it is that, each corresponding to one of the three equal persons of the Trinity, together they all equally correspond to the divine unity.[131] The two Testaments are in perfect concord, because the Son wills all that the Father wills.[132] In the end, they both have but one single signification — "two signifying [marks, but only] one [object] signified" ["duo significantia, unum significatum"] — because just as there is but one single Father and one single Son, there is, proceeding from them, but one single Spirit.[133] That is a constant theme in Joachim of Flora: "it has often been said and is often to be said."[134] In his thought, it is a question of much more than an analogy. For if it is true that his dominant preoccupation, as some have written, is not "theological," but rather moral and eschatological; if it is true that "his theology is conditioned by his anthropology and his philosophy of history,"[135] it is no less true that the connection between these two poles of his thought is fundamental for him.

Though, following the letter, the promise to send the Spirit that was made by the Son after his resurrection had been accomplished on the day of the Pentecost, today one can still say in truth that the Spirit has not yet been given, because the Lord is not yet fully glorified: he will be only when, by the ministry of Elijah and his companions, the till-then rebellious people will at last turn to him.[136] In a sense, we are already in Jerusalem, we have penetrated to the interior of the Temple; but in a truer sense we are always on the outside, for we have not entered into the glory that we hope for.[137] But it is exactly at this point that the time of Elijah is at hand. *The time is near! Behold, the hour is approaching! It is near; indeed, it is at hand!* The firstfruits of the Spirit have fertilized the Order of the Cistercians, which is about to give birth.[138] That third state that Saint Benedict and, "secundum aliam rationem" ["following another rationale"], the prophet Elisha had "initiated" long ago is being prepared and indeed is already beginning within that order.[139] To be sure, only the Lord knows the day and the hour; but, according to the correspondences or "coaptations" of the "concord," we can at least calculate the year.[140] The beginning of the forty-first generation since the Lord's incarnation will be marked by the year 1201; this will be the next to the last generation of the second age: for that age, that "secundus status," must total sixty-three generations in all; now there have been twenty-one from Ozias [or Uzziah] to Christ, and forty generations can be counted from Christ to the end of this age. The calculation is easy, for if the ancient generations, like the moon which waxes and wanes, were not all of the same duration, each generation of the New Testament totals exactly thirty years, since it is at the age of thirty that Jesus Christ, the Sun of Justice, begat his spiritual sons.[141] So everything is going to dash headlong. The critical period will extend right into 1260. Then, once the inevitable tribulations have passed, the "monastic religion," a new virgin mother, will send the world the people to which the power will be granted, as Daniel had prophesied.[142] So we are situated between two ages, "at the end of the second state,"[143] at the vigil of that other time "which will be like a paschal feast."[144] Many of its features can already be observed. Its beginnings, its "initialia," are already there: "praesto sunt." Just as at the beginning of the forty-two generations Christ has been born, so in the near future, "once generations of the same number have been completed, the manifest truth will appear, proceeding from the womb of the letter and from the house of the New Testament, wherein it lay somewhat hidden up to the present day."[145] The opening of the sixth seal is completed.[146] The sixth period of that crumbling age is coming to an end. The seventh day is beginning to dawn. We are reaching the end of our labors.[147] Soon the light will be upon the candlestand.[148] The Church has just passed from the condition of Leah to that of Rachel. "The labor of teaching will pass, and the freedom of loving will remain!" The Spirit has just manifested itself anew under the form of a miraculous dove, but this time, this will be "not so much in a single person as in an assembly of the just."[149] Her fecundity has just spread upon the Sons of the Kingdom, and the faithful people has just passed immediately through the narrow gate of sorrow to enter into the Sabbath of their felicity.[150]

2. Joachim's Novelty

Even taken none too seriously, it is necessary to admit that one could hardly imagine a stronger contrast with the traditional doctrine. Ernesto Buonaiuti, an admirer of Joachim, has recognized this: there is "a substantial difference" between the abbot of Flora and all his predecessors in exegesis, near or far, in their use of biblical revelation. All the others, whether ancient or medieval, use symbolism with a chiefly theological or moral intent; Joachim himself, however, draws from it a method of argumentation to bring about his prophetic views on the future of the Church in history and on the end of time.[151] But we can determine the principle of this difference more precisely. It resides in the fact that Joachim spurns the idea of the relation between the two Testaments as it had been affirmed from the beginning and as the tradition, notwithstanding many individual weaknesses in application, had always maintained it. He quite self-consciously and bluntly substitutes a new idea for it, an idea which he will systematically apply in his works.

Surely, the "spiritual understanding of the Old Testament and the New Testament was not anything new," as Msgr. Tondelli reminds us; but was the originality of Joachim simply, as he adds, to lead the spiritual understanding to a point to which it had never yet been brought? The sequel of Msgr. Tondelli's explanation itself shows that that is not at all the case: Joachim "thought that this understanding ought to signify a profound spiritual transfiguration of the New Testament itself, analogous to that of the Gospel in which the Old Testament had been transfigured."[152] As to the relation of our two Testaments, as he explained at length, Msgr. Tondelli recognizes that it is not expressed precisely in the concept of spiritual understanding, but in the "fundamental concept" of "concord." "That too was not a new concept," either, says he: "the idea of the Old Testament as figure or type of the New was traditional; Joachim only extended its field immeasurably, seeing everywhere a constant recurrence of figures, events, ciphers; so much so that his idea of a concordance between the history before Christ and the history after Christ descends right down to the details and becomes a sort of arithmetic."[153] But once more, this explanation itself shows that Joachim has not merely pressed further but rather has radically changed the traditional idea. To become this field of "concordances," the field of spiritual understanding had to be not only "extended" but, even more, transformed. What is more, Joachim himself constantly says it again and again: his "typic understanding" means something quite else than allegorical, or mystical, or spiritual understanding. The concord that he sings is not the same as the one that was sung before him. Even if it did not descend as far the details, it would still be something else. It is no longer the correspondence of the history to the mystery, of the figure to the deep reality, or of the letter to the spirit. Even when it uses the classical figurative procedure, it rather consists only in the parallelism of two letters, two histories, two series of facts. Whence the primary interest that he accords to questions of chronology. Whence the diptych tabulations, the calculations, the constant reckonings of dates.[154] Whence the idea of discovering a secret or deciphering a riddle is substituted for the idea of going deeper into a mystery. Whence, in places, the appeal to "certain and necessary arguments" and the quasi-scientific, i.e., mathematical pretension of this exegesis.[155]

So the commission held in July 1255 at Anagni on the order of Alexander IV to judge Joachim's doctrine[156] had sagaciously called attention to the passage of the *Concordia* that opens its fifth book. In it Joachim of Flora explains that in the first four books he had chiefly spoken of "the concord of the two Testaments according to the letter" and that in this fifth and final book he was going to unveil the "ends of things,"[157] having recourse to the spiritual sense. In fact, to his eyes the "new testament" given by Christ to his apostles is still merely a "second testament," the letter of which is bearer of the same spiritual sense as the letter of the first testament. How many times does not Joachim, obsessed as he is by his trinary and trinitarian formula, declare: "the letter of the second Testament has been engendered in a wondrous manner from the letter of the first, and from both there proceeds a single and multiple spiritual or mystical understanding."[158] It is this understanding, reserved in its fullness for the third age, which for him constitutes the eternal Gospel. By a fatal consequence, however, in dissociating the Gospel of Christ as it had been preached in the Church for twelve centuries from that eternal Gospel, which will be the gospel to come, he dissociates Christ himself from his Spirit.[159] He strangely weakens the work of Christ: in the historical construction that he imagines, Jesus merely fosters the development of a seed deposited in Israel at the time of King Ozias [=Uzziah], and, on the other side, the fruit of that seed must be exhausted shortly before the consummation of the age.

This whole exegesis proceeds from an extreme literalism — upon which an extreme prophetic spiritualism has just been superimposed — and this spiritualism, in wanting to be realized from the beginning of this earth and within time, transforms itself once again into its contrary.[160] It is not at all, as has sometimes been said, a question of trying to revive primitive Christianity.[161] Neither does Joachimism in the least way foretell the spirit of the future "renaissance," as Michelet had imagined,[162] nor is it among those movements which the protestant Reform would have any right to recognize among its ancestors.[163] There is nothing more deceptive than the second title given by the publishers of the 1527 edition of the *Expositio in Apocalypsin:* "On the carnal church soon to be reformed and brought back to its primeval age."[164] The Reformers of the sixteenth century will be turning toward the most ancient past. Joachim himself, however, had turned toward the future. The period that he holds as idyllic is not what is behind him, but the one that lies ahead. His doctrine is an "anti-primitivism";[165] it is a doctrine of progress, albeit quite different from all those that are based upon the development of the natural sciences. *Science is multiplied through the various ages of the world.*[166] Naturally, he criticizes the present condition of the Church, especially that of the religious orders. The "modern religion" seems to him to have fallen from the "primitive form of the Church": then, by their spirit of unity, everyone truly formed one single body; now the members are no longer interested in the body; they separate themselves from each other, for "individual things are anxious for themselves, not for others." He is hard on the abbeys which are letting themselves little by little fall into the love of worldly goods and in which the fire of contemplation is being extinguished.[167] He is indignant at seeing the whole Church "become a house of commerce," as did the Temple of Jerusalem of old. He has no tolerance for so many clerics "who have been fattened and expanded from the substance of the Crucified One," as well as for so many others "who are being influenced by scholasticism."[168] But this criticism is entirely of a moral order; it is not a comparative judgment from a religious point of view on the regimes that follow. Joachim hurls anathemas at the world and foretells "the wrath of heaven" upon it.[169] He foresees terrible evils; he predicts their imminent arrival. But these evils will be merely a passing crisis, coming after other such, and in each of these crises their author, Satan, loses a bit more of his original power. In each of the six time-periods into which the second age is divided, the Dragon gets one head amputated: when no more than the seventh is left to him, he will only fight the more desperately.[170] These crises that periodically go through humanity are the pangs of birth, and when the woman has given birth, she forgets her pain and rejoices.[171] If Joachim's imagination had been shaken by the threats of Islam, the horror of that menace was for him merely the messenger of a radiant hope. The first age was a dark sky; the second unfolded by the light of the moon; soon the heaven of spiritual understanding will shine on the third.[172] Joachim also loves to recall that the young will hold sway over the old. His third age, as we have seen, will be "the age of children."[173] His religion of the spirit, in a qualified sense, will be a "new religion" ["nova religio"].

For though he, like every reformer and moralist, complains that the Christians of his time no longer had the fervor that the report of the Acts of the Apostles attests to, this does not mean a return to the Gospel is being sketched out in his work: it is a new millenarianism that is taking form. This is what infinitely transcends any exegetical singularities. It has often been remarked that the interpretations of Scripture given by the abbot of Flora were fantastic. But that he had recognized, for example, in Saladin the sixth Beast of the Apocalypse[174] and a hundred other remarks of the sort, would not be all that bad, provided that all these "phantasmagoria" did not flow from principles that ruin the whole economy of Christian revelation. Thus, Saint Thomas Aquinas in the following century would not be content in his Commentary on the *Sentences* to apply to Joachim a remark made long ago by Saint Augustine in the *City of God* regarding similar musings concerning the calculation of times: "not in the spirit of prophecy but through the conjecture of the human mind," and placidly to add that he was sometimes right in his conjectures and sometimes wrong.[175] Attacking at the essential point, he would direct, although without naming him, a whole question of the *Summa* against him, "Is the new law to last until the end of the world?":

> No status of the present life can be more perfect than the status of the new law. . . . One ought not to expect that there should be any future state in which the grace of the Holy Spirit would be held more perfectly than the one that had been held up till now, and most especially by the Apostles. . . . The new law belongs not only to Christ, but also to the Holy Spirit.[176]

As regards another problem he will come back to it in the *De Potentia*.[177] And in one of his sermons on the *Hexaemeron* Saint Bonaventure will speak to the same effect: "After the New Testament there will not be another one, nor can a single seed of the new law be taken away: and so it is an eternal testament."[178]

M. Étienne Gilson has characterized the gravity of the crisis opened up by Joachim of Flora rather well: "to preach a gospel of the Holy Spirit was completely to reverse the economy of the ages of the world."[179] From a more restricted point of view, Paul Fournier had also remarked that thereby "the essential organs of Christian society had been gravely threatened and its constitution undermined down to its foundations."[180] Not to mention certain panegyrists, such as Abbot Gervaise[181] in the eighteenth century, a certain number of historians have shown themselves to be more indulgent. Thus there is Renan, maintaining that "Joachim is content to compare the Old and the New Testaments and casts his eyes only very timidly upon the future,"[182] which lets us understand either that Renan had not read his author very attentively, or that the notion of timidity is extremely relative. Thus too there is Henri Delacroix, whom one can suspect of having put a bit too much confidence in Renan.[183] Thus, closer to us, there is Émile Jordan, who concludes a conscientious study by saying that "Joachim's eternal Gospel was merely the spiritual sense and the full understanding of the Gospel of Christ,"[184] a judgment exact in rigor but quite minimalist in intention, for one could as well say that that eternal Gospel was merely the full understanding of the Law of Moses. Joachim's modern apologists doubtless have the authority of Papebroch on their side. The celebrated Bollandist was compelled to explain why Saint Thomas never approved the spirit of the *Concordia* by all sorts of extrinsic considerations, such as an incompatibility between the two men arising from spiritual temperament.[185] But for once at least, his critique was off the mark: impressed by recent apologies[186] and by a recent beatification of Joachim,[187] he had inserted a doubtful biography into the *Acta sanctorum* and had not devoted himself to a thorough examination of the doctrine.[188] How could he have blamed in its very principle a sacred hermeneutics celebrated in these terms within the liturgical prayer of the newly beatified: "God, who hast manifested thy glory to the three apostles on Mount Tabor, and hast manifested the truth of the Scriptures to blessed Joachim in that same place"? How could he have been sparing in his admiration for one of whom the antiphon to the Magnificat proclaims: "Endowed with the spirit of prophecy, embellished with understanding, he told of future things as present, but without any heretical error"?[189]

New interpretations favorable to the orthodoxy of Joachim of Flora have been proposed in our own days,[190] following upon the publication of two little works, the *Liber figurarum* and the *Liber de septem sigillis*, which their respective editors, Msgr. Leone Tondelli and Miss E. Reeves, attribute to our Calabrian friend.

On several occasions the *Chronicle* of Salimbene draws attention to a *Liber figurarum*.[191] It is doubtless concerned with that collection of twenty-three tables, images, schemata or graphics (circles, triangles), known till quite recently through an incomplete copy preserved in a manuscript at Dresden. Msgr. Tondelli in 1937 had discovered a complete copy, which he edited under the name *Liber figurarum* in 1940. Joachim's whole system is in some fashion contained within it. There one sees the Church under the form of Noah's ark: an ancient symbol, a bit renewed since then, as has been seen, by Hugh of Saint Victor. In it one sees the ten-stringed psalterion and the seven-headed dragon of the Apocalypse.¹⁹² Each image is explained in the margins by means of a brief legend. The most important figure seems to be the twelfth, which bears the title: "The disposition of the new order, pertaining to the third state as regards the heavenly Jerusalem."¹⁹³ The text explaining it is more developed, but without ceasing to be enigmatic. One can believe that it carries the central idea of Joachim, that it establishes his dearest dream. According to Msgr. Tondelli, this dream would be none other than that of a finally purified Roman Church, freed of all temporal vicissitudes; soon the Holy Spirit, who has dwelt in it from its foundation, would take a more complete possession of it, using for this end a new religious order, which would be a source of regeneration for it.¹⁹⁴ So one need not let oneself be misled by certain hyperboles due to the Abbot of Flora's idealism: his third state is not radically different from the two states that precede it. The Church of the Spirit will not be of a radically different structure from the Church of Christ.¹⁹⁵

The idea of Msgr. Tondelli is also that of Father Francesco Russo and that of Antonio Crocco. The former advances in favor of the perfect orthodoxy of Joachim the fact that he is not waiting for a new Scripture and always speaks only of two Testaments — but from that he draws the conclusion a bit quickly that Joachim's third state would not be a new economy.¹⁹⁶ As to the latter, he also thinks that by the boldest of Joachim's expressions, e.g., the announcement of a triumph of the Church of John over that of Peter, or the affirmation of the provisional character of the "significatum Petri" [i.e., what is signified by Peter], Joachim would mean nothing except a future predominance of the contemplative life over the active one.¹⁹⁷ Miss Reeves wanted to examine the complex symbolism of the *Liber figurarum* more deeply. She has compared that text with a small document, the *De septem sigillis,* which she had published in 1954 with the collaboration of B. Hirsch-Reich.¹⁹⁸ She believes that from it one could deduce that Joachim had never really divided the history of salvation except into two time periods. His third age should be understood in an entirely "mystical" manner, without any notion of separate realization in history. He would never have envisaged a contemplative order destined in future to supplant the clergy; he would never have supposed that the present hierarchical Church should not last until the end of the world. In his work there would be two intermingled systems to be distinguished: the one, historical, in two terms, the other, mystical, in three terms.¹⁹⁹ His thought was not confused; it was only that, endowed with a powerful visual imagination, despite himself, he misled both his disciples and his detractors, who were inclined to take his descriptions too literally.

In its positive side, Msgr. Tondelli's idea can be admitted. However, if the purification of the Church were to consist in its emancipation from every temporal vicissitude, would it not thereby end up by suppressing its institutional character, or at least by profoundly transforming that character? Would it still be the Roman Church? The fact is that the twelfth Table of the *Liber figurarum* as well as its legend (which is quite explicit, by the way) no longer seem to leave any room for the present hierarchy: under the sign of the eagle and the dove, a certain number of monasteries associate the divers categories of the faithful, then the pure contemplatives, the summit of the new hierarchy, as far as the married laity, each [group] living under the authority of "priors" or "masters" who themselves all depend upon the principal "spiritual father who will be in charge of them all."[200] As to Miss Reeves' explanations, which are oriented in the opposite direction to those of Msgr. Tondelli, they are newer and bolder. If some day they should gain credence, their import would be considerable. Though the authenticity of the *Liber figurarum* has been disputed by many[201] and though not all the arguments by which that authenticity is upheld are equally solid,[202] in my opinion it can be admitted that if, in the form we know it, this text were not by Joachim himself, it would at least very likely be by an immediate and faithful disciple.[203] Only it is perhaps temerarious to want to rely more on Joachim's images than upon his texts to determine their exact signification, even if it is a question of texts serving as legends for the images.[204] Moreover, for the general interpretation of Joachim's thought proposed by Miss Reeves to be sustained, it would be necessary for this interpretation to be able to take account not only of the *Liber figurarum* and the *De septem sigillis* — which are merely a late collection and a short opusculum — but also of the other definitively authentic works, which are much more important and more explicit.

At any event, so as not to push the most formal texts too far, one might assert that Joachim does not always express himself so boldly. His thought is not only complicated: it is, in a certain degree, "fluctuating and variable."[205] Thus, in a sermon on Luke 1:13, in the course of an enumeration, he seems to treat "letter and spirit," on the one hand, and "Old Testament and New," on the other, as more or less equivalent.[206] Once in his *Treatise on the Four Gospels*, he even writes: "Since the Holy Spirit wanted to show what difference there was between Law and grace, the sons of the flesh and the sons of adoption, the doctrine of the letter and the doctrine of the spirit, and the Old Testament and the New, he wanted to designate these two points in John and in Christ."[207] But do these adventitious abridgments suffice to weaken long and insistent explanations whose significance does not appear to be in doubt? In the very same treatise, beside passages that affirm the duality of the Greek and Latin Churches and their equally provisional character, Joachim has others in which the unicity of the Church of Christ is well avowed.[208] But is that a sufficient guarantee of its unchanged permanence in the future? In spite of certain ways of speaking, one might also maintain that he even includes the third age within the New Testament,[209] since he identifies it with the seventh and last period of the history of the Church; but one could as well say, inversely, that the whole second age for him is nothing but the sixth period of the history of the world. It is still true that he rejects the idea of a "diversity of faith" from one age to the other and does not want to distinguish between the second and the third ages except in terms of their religious constitution, by the "proprietas religionis"; but, though in fact close to formulas that one can read, for example, in a Ratramnus,[210] or in a Saint Anselm,[211] or even more in an Anselm of Havelberg,[212] were these formulas not also precisely those that were then currently in use to distinguish between the two first ages?[213] It is also certain that the coming of an age of the Spirit does not constitute Joachim's whole eschatology; that age, he says, would not itself have a time; corresponding to the persecution of Antiochus, which marks the end of the first age, and then corresponding to the concordant persecution of another king, still unknown, which will soon mark the end of the second, there ought to be in a more distant future the persecution of Gog, "the ultimate tyrant and the ultimate antichrist," which will mark the end both of the third age and of all times:[214] then "the Lord will return in majesty to judge the living and the dead."[215] But is not even this of a piece with the idea of a temporal age of the Spirit?

Miss Reeves invites us to consider something else, which she regards as more decisive. If the *De septem sigillis* is truly from the hand of Joachim himself, it might represent "his final thought on a subject that he had declared to be the most difficult and the most crucial." But this thought is expressed there "quite unequivocally and precisely."[216] Indeed, in that entirely "limited and pedestrian" opusculum, it is no longer a question of a soon-to-come persecuting king, who would be intermediate between Antiochus and Gog; nor even, to speak properly, of a third age which would be that of the Spirit. The explanation offered of the "seventh seal" reports the "observance of the Sabbath" ["sabbatismus"] by the people of God at the extreme end of time, just before the days of God and the resurrection of the dead.[217] From that time on, what was said in explication of the sixth seal: "it began to pass over in the spirit of the spiritual Jerusalem," or: "many of the faithful will be crowned with martyrdom and the holy city which is the Church of the elect will be built again," can be understood in the sense of a quite classic orthodoxy.[218]

Would not the great works themselves offer a basis for that last interpretation? Indeed, they contain certain formulations which, re-read in the light of the *De septem sigillis*, would seem to signify that the age of the Spirit ought not be anything other than the goal toward which God is leading us, the last rolling up of the kingdom of the heavens. Thus, the *Liber introductorius* promises to show that "the sufferings of the end are near and that the kingdom is at our gates,"[219] for "the third state, no longer under the veil of the letter but in the full freedom of the spirit, will be established toward the end of the age."[220] In the same way, according to the *Explication of the Four Gospels*, at the sixth epoch, already begun at the hour when Joachim is writing, a virginal Church is going soon to conceive: she will nourish in her womb that saintly people to whom the kingdom has been promised, according to the prophecy of Daniel. Now it does not seem that she ought to present the fruit of her womb to the world for a seventh epoch which would be still unfolding upon the earth, for we have been told that her birthing would take place "at the consummation of the age,"[221] and the commentary on the Apocalypse likewise is precise in stating that the coming of the "third state" would take place "at the latest time."[222]

Yet, is there anything there to make us certain that the "Age of Monks" [*aetas monachorum*] envisaged in her "fructification" would no longer belong to time but already to eternity? Joachim himself does not forbid us to think it. Certain persons, he says, imagine that after the fall of the next antichrist the "worldly times" will have passed: this is because they take expressions like "the most recent day" or "the end of the world" too literally. These expressions do not, or at least do not always, designate the end itself, the "last moment of the end," the cessation of the "worldly times," but rather "the end-time," the period that has to unfold "round about the end," or "the last age of the world."[223] For the term "end" in Scripture is taken sometimes in a strict sense and sometimes in a broad, indeed a very broad sense.[224] It is true that he avows that he is uncertain about the duration of this last age: "I do not know whether the times of the third state . . . be shorter than those of the second"; "Who knows how short the Sabbath itself may be? . . . Once the battle has been finished, there will be a great peace, such as did not exist from the beginning of the age, and whose end will be in the will of God." Hence this age could be shorter than the second, which has already been shorter than the first, and one might perhaps apply to it in particular the word of Scripture: "The Lord will make a short speech upon the earth."[225] Perhaps. But as to its temporal and earthly character, Joachim manifests no hesitation. How is one to brush off a hundred passages as clear and explicit as anyone could hope for, which form the framework of the system, as can be read in the previous paragraph? Still other completely "unequivocal" texts state precisely that the kingdom of the Spirit will indeed be a temporal kingdom.[226] That Sabbath, a "happy time," a "time that will be like a Paschal solemnity," a time in the course of which "the earth will be filled with the knowledge of the Lord," will nevertheless still see the incredulity of many peoples, kept in reserve by the devil with a view to his last assaults, and the last tyrant of this earth together with the last antichrist will still be to come.[227] So once again one will be within the "secular times."[228] While he pointed out that the whole last state, that of eternity, ought no longer be called a "time," Joachim on several occasions writes of the third: "the time of the third state."[229] He also explains that many mysteries that are hidden within the letter of the two Testaments, will have to be opened "in the sixth time"; in other words, "the mysteries will be bare in the third state."[230] He says again, in his treatise on the Life of Saint Benedict, while developing the symbolism of the four Gospels:

> The three Gospels correspond to the three states that are conducted in the times of this age; but the fourth mysteriously touches on the life that is to come after the third state, the life in which we must know all the truth much more solemnly and gloriously than in the third state, which will serve as a Sabbath, just as the Lord's Day is even more solemn and blessed than the Sabbath.[231]

He frequently cites the words of Saint Paul: "Now we see through a mirror in a riddle," "we know in part";[232] but this is not, most often at least, to contrast the knowledge of time and that of eternity, as did the Apostle: it is to establish a difference between two states of knowledge here below, that of our age and that of the age to come, though the contrast of the one to the other is not so great, in its proper sense, that one could not pass by degrees from the one to the other: "little by little the riddle is for a time cut apart."[233] Finally, several tables from the *Liber figurarum* seem no less telling; notably Table XI, where three interlocking circles symbolize the three successive time-periods of the Father, the Son and the Spirit, or of the Law, the Gospel and the "typic understanding," whilst one reads, just outside the circles, on the left: ADAM, and on the right: FINIS MUNDI.[234]

Hence one cannot, it seems to me, reduce the Joachimite doctrine to some paradoxical insistence upon the eschatological signification of the monastic state and upon the anticipation of the heavenly realm since the time of Saint Benedict. One cannot avoid classing it among the so-called "millenarist" utopias. To be sure, Joachim regards the number of a thousand years as "mystic"; he thinks that the "thousand years," or some duration that ought to be the "fullness of years" that they designate, have begun from the day on which the Savior was resurrected,[235] and on the other hand he recoils in horror from the crude daydream of a time of earthly pleasures after the resurrection of the body. But he imagines an indeterminate period of already supra-terrestrial peace and contemplative happiness, a period that nevertheless ought to unfold upon the earth, after a first crisis and before the last upheavals which will precede the last resurrection, within the duration of our world. In a sense, it is quite true, as one of his interpreters has said, that "those who are going to enjoy the felicity of the Sabbath will not be mere mortals";[236] nevertheless, as another interpreter has put it, the third age is yet again "a sublime chapter of earthly history."[237] It is precisely the announcement of this marvel, this paradox, or this contradiction, which constitutes the principal originality of that doctrine, an originality which it shares with all the great "utopias." So perhaps the treatise *Super Hieremiam,* in summarizing Joachim's thought, hardens it, but it does not betray it, since while commenting on the words of Ezekiel, "The end is coming," he explains precisely what he means: "The end of the aging Church of the clerics . . . and not for all that the end of the world, since celebrating the Sabbath still remains for the people of God."[238] In the *Concord* he himself affirms that the third time-period ought to last "up to the end of the world."[239] And the judges of the Commission of Anagni were not wrong to affirm at the beginning of their report, relying on the analyses of the bishop of Saint John of Acre, that the whole basis of Joachimism consists in the doctrine of the "three states of the whole world-age," and then to conclude, after having made an exposition of it: "This doctrine tends finally to the subversion of the clergy, i.e., of the Roman church and those obedient to her."[240]

There is nothing in this to have put in doubt Joachim of Flora's love of Jesus Christ, nor his will to be orthodox, nor his Catholic sentiment. If one sees in the new Jerusalem a stream of living water springing from the throne of God, this is because, he thought, "outside the Catholic Church the gift of the Holy Spirit is not given."[241] Having arrived at the end of his commentary on the Apocalypse, he made this declaration: "The Roman Church, to whom universal teaching authority has been given and by

Joachim's Novelty

whose command and permission I have written these things."[242] On the last page of the *Concordia* he appeals to his readers, asking them to pray to God for him so that:

> If any article of those days about which we are speaking should find me still remaining in the flesh, may it allow me to fight the good fight for the faith of Christ and to arrive at the heavenly kingdom along with Christ's confessors who will then be there. Amen! Amen! Amen![243]

He himself was indulgent neither to schism nor to heresy. This is clearly visible in his attitude with regard to the Greek Church: separated from the Roman Church just as the tribes of Israel had been separated from Judah, that Church, which gave such magnificent promise, could only be destroyed in its faith just as the tribes of Israel had been destroyed by the enemy armies, "since what does not adhere to the Roman Church is to be banished outside the body of the Church"; by her own fault she had lost the grace of understanding, so much so that she can only err, misunderstanding "the Scripture according to the spirit."[244] It is also clearly visible in his attitude with regard to the Cathars and the Vaudois,[245] or even in regard to Peter Lombard. It is to compound the error to write, with Renan: "in his frequent relations with the Greek Church ... and perhaps with some branch of the Cathar Church" Joachim "conceived a great aversion for the organization of the Latin Church."[246] He praises Saint Bernard for having taken up the mission to fight against the heretics of his time.[247] He never treated the Roman Church as a "Babylon" or the "great prostitute," nor the pope as "antichrist." The truth is quite the reverse. The sympathies that a number of anti-Papist writers since the time of some of the first Reformers have accorded him rest on a legend nourished on pure misunderstanding, whose origin goes back to the Commission of Anagni,[248] and which endures down to the present day.[249]

In reality, in Joachim's imagery, which is not so particular to him, Jerusalem is primarily the throng of the good Christians or the "elect," whilst Babylon, the "church of the malignant," is that of the bad or false Christians, "who say they are faithful while they are not."[250] The city of God and the city of Satan, the one guarded by the four living creatures of Ezekiel or the Apocalypse, the other by the four beasts of Daniel; and between these two antagonistic cities, that of the just and that of the impious, there is Egypt, homeland of simply earthly men.[251] Jerusalem, Egypt, Babylon, then, are not three particular peoples with contrasting properties: they are three varieties of spiritual situation of the single great human population before God, whether before or after Christ. There were wicked people at Jerusalem, and there were just men at Babylon.[252] As to "Rome," for Joachim, it is sometimes identified with "Babylon," as in the Epistle of Peter, and then it is the idolatrous Rome of old;[253] or else it is the symbolic name of the whole body of the Church in her earthly state: at that point she holds in her breast, still mingled together in manner indiscernible, both the "assembly of the just" and "the multitude of the reprobate." It is this last, the "universal Babylon,"[254] which constitutes "the famous prostitute," the "whore Babylon," the "Babylonian prostitute."[255] Nor, then, is it necessary to look for its seat immediately within a realm, in a country, in a city, or in an ecclesiastical power; but the chaff of the reprobate, like the wheat of the elect, is scattered all over the threshing-floor of the Christian empire. The "kings of the earth," that is to say, the prelates, fornicate with that Babylon, while, to please men, they spurn and neglect the law of God.[256]

In all this Joachim was merely making explicit the most common teaching.[257] He was inspired, as he says, by the "Patres catholici," particularly Saint Augustine. He has sometimes, however, expressed his views more precisely, following his habitual "historical" bent, but always in a sense quite far from the anti-Roman spirit which was to be laid at his door. For him, then, "Jerusalem" became the Roman Church, the true "city of the sun";[258] and just as "Babylon" was the ancient Rome of the Caesars, a persecutor of the Christian name, so the "new Babylon" designated either, depending on the occasion, Islam, whose power was making new conquests by the day on Christian land,[259] or the schismatic empire of Constantinople,[260] or, most frequently, the current Empire of the West, each time that, in the hands of the Germans, it was to be opposed to or to dominate pontifical Rome. Indeed, just as the kings of Babylon had long ago struggled against Jerusalem and had enslaved it, so now were the "Roman" emperors too often menacing the freedom of the Church.[261] But just as ancient Babylon was finally beaten to death by the Persians and as the Jews, freed by Cyrus, returned to Jerusalem, so too the armies of the Empire will be vanquished by the kings who will come from the East, the whole empire will be entirely desolate, this will be the time of the great tribulation. But the Church will finally be freed from the yoke that the new Babylon had laid upon her, that yoke which even now allows us neither to breathe nor to sing the *Alleluia* in peace.[262] As we see it, Joachim did not allow only the voice of a Latin, or of a southern Italian, hostile to the barbarian from the north as well as to Byzantine oppression,

Joachim's Novelty

to speak in him:[263] he also remembered that he was a monk, and that his monastic profession created in him an obligation to serve the cause of the Papacy with ardent fidelity even while awaiting the days that would follow the expected reversals: "the very religion of monks most diligently cleaves to the doctrine of the Roman pontiffs."[264]

The Roman Church, in the person of her leaders, could only encourage her valiant defender. Joachim's relations with the popes seem always to have been excellent. It is Lucius III who had asked him to comment on the Apocalypse and to write his *Concordia*. Urban III, who had received him at Verona in 1186, had continued to encourage him in the task.[265] Clement III would show himself no less favorable, though there are reasons, despite the opinion of good critics, for doubting the authenticity of the letter that he had addressed to Joachim on his accession to the apostolic chair, in 1188, to urge him to complete his work.[266] Finally, Celestine III in 1196 confirmed the Order of Flora which the Cisterican ex-abbot had just founded (in 1190), without allowing himself to be dissuaded by the decision of the chapter-general of the Cistercians, who, in 1192, declared him a "fugitive."[267] When his works came to be known after his death, reading them did not at first change the popes' disposition in his regard. Had he not declared, for example: "The Church of Peter is on rock, outside of which the Holy Spirit cannot be obtained"? Had he not recognized in the archangel Saint Michael "the Roman pontiff, head of the Lord's people"?[268] Innocent III pronounces Joachim's eulogy everywhere even while condemning his now-lost treatise against Peter Lombard for an error about the Trinity,[269] the only one that he was reproached for. They were grateful to him, it seems, for having declared beforehand, in the quasi-testament constituted by the *Epistola prologalis* printed since then at the head of the *Expositio in Apocalypsim* and the *Concordia*, in which he submitted all his writings to the examination and judgment of the apostolic See.[270] In 1220 Honorius III would declare that he held him as a "follower of the holy orthodox faith,"[271] and Gregory IX would designate the order that he had founded as one of the four pillars of the Church.[272]

The Joachimite hermeneutic was nonetheless aberrant, and the sequel was to show that it was more than an excess or singularity of language. If the "spirituals" who claimed the abbot of Flora also often deformed his thought, it is still within that thought that they found the animating force of their movement.[273] One sees it even in the *Chronicle* of Salimbene (v. 1283-1288), which is an apologia for the abbot directed both against his enemies and against his over-eager disciples.[274] This "new, contemplative, completely free and spiritual religion," which was to "succeed the order of the bishops" and "the aging Roman pontiff," "as Christ had succeeded John the Baptist, or as Solomon the Peaceful had succeeded the warrior David," was indeed announced by Joachim himself.[275] He himself had designated the "barque of Peter," or the "Church of Christ," as characterizing the second age. He had pointed out the letter of the New Testament entrusted to the "Roman people," as the letter of the Old to the "Jewish people," while awaiting the time of spiritual understanding.[276] The most formal texts seem to me to set aside the explication offered by Msgr. Tondelli and later again adopted by M. W. Bloomfield, namely that "probably the Church would continue to be presided over by a purified Bishop of Rome,"[277] unless perhaps one would want to understand the "purification" in a very drastic sense, or the "presiding" as something extraordinarily pallid. Indeed, in the *Concordia*, Joachim says that after having first presided over the "church of those who labor" or "of those who sweat in the active life," the Roman pontiffs preside over the "church of those at rest" or "of those exultant in the contemplative life": but this text does not contain any prediction of the future. It does not signify anything but the current equal submission of the clerics and the monks to the Roman Church, starting from the time when the order of the latter was founded, so long as the second state endures: like Bathsheba, the wife of Uriah, the Benedictine institution, and most especially under the most beautiful form that she had worn in the Cistercian branch, ought to wash herself in prayer and compunction so as to please the great David and to follow him henceforth, that is to say, so as to embrace the cause of the Roman pontiffs in everything: for they, who hold the place of Christ, have desired her beauty.[278] The long and subtle developments in which Joachim thus applies what the Bible says of David, Uriah, and Bathsheba to the history of the Church and the institution of monasticism do not concern the third state.

The *Liber figurarum* itself scarcely appears to me to support the thesis of Msgr. Tondelli and Mr. Bloomfield. Substantially in agreement with the *Concordia*, the large table of the *Mysterium Ecclesiae* shows the first of the three states, that of the carnal people, in the period of the reign of Saul; the second state, that of the Christian people toiling and struggling under the direction of Peter, in the reign of David; finally, the third state to come, in which, according to the word of the Apostle, "there remains the celebration of the Sabbath for the people of God," in the reign of "peaceful and quiet" Solomon. This third state will cover the whole seventh age of the world: "thus, once that order which is signified in Peter and David has been consummated, in its stead there will remain that order which is signified in John, the disciple whom Jesus loved, and in the boy Solomon, who was said to be beloved of the Lord."[279] The following, moreover, is what the *Concordia* was saying, comparing the last Roman pontiffs of the second age to King David overtaken by the ice of age:

> David's . . . old age, in the letter of the Gospel designates the old age of this second state and order of the Church Militant. The Shunammite woman, who was joined with him but did not conceive from him, will be a new religion, which will be utterly free and spiritual. . . . But since in preserving its ancient order the Roman pontiff will begin to grow cold owing to old age, some of them are still being extolled who will seem to be ready for a fight, so as to stand in the kingdom of the Church . . . ; but they will not prevail, since it will not still be necessary to pursue the order of war in a day of peace; but it will rather be necessary for the religious to transfer into the order which is designated in Solomon.[280]

Is the "Roman pontiff" here, like the old David, merely a symbol, the symbol of the "letter" of the Scriptures, as Mr. Antonio Crocco would have it? I find it hard to believe. It is still true that in this passage from David to Solomon, or from Peter to John, Joachim writes in the *Liber figurarum*: "not by making a transfer but by granting a renewal,"[281] and in the *Concordia*: "So the church of Peter, which is the throne of Christ, will — far be it from that! — not be missing, but, having been changed into a greater glory, she will remain stable for ever."[282] But the context does not permit, in my view, any mistake about the depth of this "renewal" or this "change" by which the passage from the second state to the third is defined, i.e., from the Church of Peter to that of John, from the reign of Christ to the reign of the Spirit. What is true is that, by eliminating the papacy from his sabbatic Church, Joachim does not believe he is saying anything against the authority of the pope. He was considering how to interpret the predictions of the Gospel, of which the pope himself is the guardian. In the *Liber figurarum*, he attaches himself to the final scene of the fourth Gospel and his interpretation does not proceed without a certain crudeness:

> While that life that pertains to Peter is passing, the sixth age will be consummated. . . . So now Peter is to be bound and led whither he doth not will, so as to accomplish his course as quickly as possible, so

that what pertains to the age of labor may pass away and what pertains to rest may remain.... Let those who are signified in Peter hear this!²⁸³

In the *Treatise on the Four Gospels*, his manner is gentler. The pope, he thinks in his candor, "would not be able to suffer from the dissolution of his own power, once he sees that the substance of it persists better later":

> Can he who sees such fruit coming after him be pained that the particular perfection in himself ceases to be when the universal one follows? Far be this from the successors of Peter! Far be it that he should pine away with envy over the perfection of the spiritual order that he will see is one spirit with his God!²⁸⁴

If the last prelates of the second age are spirituals themselves, they will feel neither regret nor envy. They could not fail to marvel, contemplating the effusion of the Holy Spirit upon the new order of the just, the marvelous change due to the Right Hand of the Most High.²⁸⁵ And behold our abbot himself already contemplating the last pope receiving in his arms — "in the arms of his faith and affection" — this new spiritual order, like Simeon receiving the infant Jesus, and like him chanting his own "nunc dimittis."²⁸⁶

These sorts of solidly organized dreams did not escape everyone. It is very much exaggerated to say with Renan — who is inspired by Papebroch — that "the whole Latin world recognized Joachim as a prophet."²⁸⁷ After having recalled in a couple of words how Joachim understands the Apocalypse, the *Chronologia* of the Premonstratensian Robert Abolant of Auxerre will say, under the year 1186: "Let anyone say what he thinks: for our part, we adjudge it safer not to discuss than to argue about what we do not know."²⁸⁸ If that is not a condemnation, neither is it a declaration of adherence. But from 1195 on, Adam of Perseigne, who was charged with examining Joachim's doctrine at Rome, had judged it severely: now this Adam was "a wise man, a counselor of repute."²⁸⁹ The former secretary of Saint Bernard, Geoffrey of Auxerre, in a sermon on the Ascension of which only an undated fragment survives, had violently taken issue with that "new kind of prophetizing" and those "blasphemous novelties."²⁹⁰ The Cistercian resentment regarding a deserter who had, while he was still a member "of the Cistercian order," already shown himself to be "in no way subject to the Cistercians,"²⁹¹ can well explain the violence of tone in Geoffrey,²⁹² as well as a certain stalling in Adam: it would not have deceived but rather sharpened the clear-sightedness of the judgment.[293] Godfrey of Saint Victor was himself not a Cistercian; nor was he a hunter of heretics; one would have expected his ever-present moderation to be reinforced by great age: now he seems certainly to be the first to have had our Joachim in mind when he described in the second book of his *Microcosmus* a heresy which, he says, the Holy Spirit had foreseen:

> If indeed the Holy Spirit . . . , foreseeing future heretics who were saying that Christ would reign for a time, that the Church would cease in time, and that the catholic faith and the other gifts of grace would go to destruction. . . .[294]

3. Presumed Antecedents

How then had the abbot of Flora conceived such a system? He himself knew well that he was introducing a "new kind of explication" of the Scriptures. He had been the first to spurn the assertion of some of his admirers, who attribute to him, except for a slight modification here or there, "the traditional division" of the four senses.[295] On his part, however, there was not, he said, any "presumption of pride"; no more was it the fruit of a simple movement of piety; his unprecedented exegesis, he was convinced, was given to him "through a dispensation from on high,"[296] in view of the mission that he had to fulfill of announcing the imminent coming of the new time and to drag his contemporaries from their lethargy.[297] For a long time he had applied himself to reading and to study, without arriving at knowledge of the truth; quite the contrary, the truth seemed to escape him, and his anxiety only increased. One day, taken with a completely new fervor, abandoning his search, he gave himself with all his heart to the singing of the Psalms, through the love of God, and it is at that point that, in secret, the Word of God began to open itself up to him.[298] Like unto that resplendent star that had been put above the abode of the Infant-God to light the path of the Magi, the "grace of the Holy Spirit" visited him.[299] To speak the truth, he was not entirely inexperienced with these sorts of things.[300] The holy oil had already flowed upon him. From the time of his youth he had been visited with grace.[301] It was also following an ardent prayer, tormented as he was by the apparent antinomies of dogma, that he suddenly understood, through the image of the ten-stringed lyre, the mystery of the Trinity, in which all truth is encompassed.³⁰² He was among those "to whom it was granted to know and to taste," according to his own expressions, "the secret and free jubilation that the Holy Spirit pours forth." Nevertheless, he thought of himself as no more than a man of profane knowledge, not as a prophet. Adam of Perseigne had asked him at the time of their 1195 Roman discussion, whence he had gotten all those things that he was announcing: "from prophecy, or conjecture, or revelation?" ["ex prophetia, an conjectura, seu revelatione?"]. To which, according to the report of the Cistercian historian Raoul of Coggeshall (†1228), he had replied that in his case it was a question neither of prophecy, nor of conjecture, nor of revelation. But God, who had of old given certain men the spirit of prophecy, had given him the spirit of understanding, so that in the Spirit of God he grasped very clearly all the mysteries of holy Scripture.³⁰³

In what concerns the basic idea of Joachimite exegesis, one page of the *Enchiridion super Apocalypsim* — a sort of summary-in-advance as it were of the great *Expositio in Apocalypsim* or of his *Liber introductorius*³⁰⁴ — brings in a supplementary precision. If he does not believe that he had received a revelation in the proper sense of the word, Joachim has the quite distinct feeling that his essential doctrine has not been formed in him a little at a time after examining the biblical texts nor after reflecting upon the teaching of the Fathers. The gift of understanding that he prides himself on had not only assisted him in his labor; nor had it consisted in a light cast upon the traditional hermeneutics. It had made him understand immediately and a priori that the two successive histories, that of Israel and that of the Church, had to become tied to each other in their very letter, from one end to the other, by the principle of *concord*. Was not the life of Christ announced in the Old Testament? Was not the Church the body of Christ? From that time forth how could what was true of the Head not be true of the whole body? Before noticing anything definite, moved by a mysterious impulse, then, Joachim knows what he ought to find:

> When I had begun to read this book [the Apocalypse], and did not yet know the sacraments of the concords, I do not know by what original impulse I was led thither, God knows, whence I know that I was not led to the knowledge of the concord by any experience of the histories; but driven on by the mere comparison of past deeds, i.e., of the Old Testament, believing that what I found shared in the head could not be discordant in the body and that what I considered to be concordant in the Patriarchs and the Apostles would not be idle in

the other saints: I set to work in this matter so that, to the extent that God should grant me, I would compile a concord of testimonies; but I do not know whether I would satisfy the minds of the scrupulous.[305]

Here our "scruples" as to the results matter little. Only the question of principle is of interest to us. Whatever be the portion of personal inspiration that made Joachim conceive the idea of the concord of the two Testaments, then of their common spiritual understanding in a later age, we have the right to ask ourselves, without putting his own declarations in doubt, if any antecedent theories had set him on his way. But first it would be necessary for us to set aside certain quite ill-founded suggestions.

Some have said that the abbot of Flora "was inspired by a habit of mind that was widespread in the Middle Ages, namely, seeing symbols and figures everywhere, as well as by a universally accepted exegetical principle that made of the Old Testament the figure of the New."[306] This is an objective observation, but much too general, which renders no account of the features that characterize it. The opinion has been expressed that there was perhaps no point to look for a particular origin for his thought, considering that "the idea of three dispensations is natural, indeed inevitable, in one form or another, for all thought that moves in the framework of the Christian religion,"[307] [but this is] a lazy opinion likely to generate confusion, declaring beforehand that the theories that can "under one form or another" hearken back to Christianity are all practically identical, provided that they slip into a trinitarian framework. It has been said that "the mental inclination to see symbols in all things and the habit of searching for the allegorical sense" was one of the causes that "was to confer an incomparable sheen upon Joachim's doctrine":[308] a judicious enough observation, but one that remains insufficient in the measure that one recognizes any truth in it. It has also been said that, certain rather personal ways of expressing himself notwithstanding, "Joachim returns to the traditional division" of the four senses of Scripture.[309] Some have even assured us that his doctrine constituted "the culmination of the Patristic tradition";[310] and again, in an analogous sense, that it was "the final fruit," yet the legitimate fruit, of the exegesis of the first Middle Ages and that its bad habits "had to be the inevitable result of the allegoric method"; only "the application of the rules of reason and therefore the exegesis of thirteenth-century theology" would have been necessary to "keep Christian exegesis from turning into heresy and illuminism."[311] Recently another historian was still saying regarding "the whole method of allegory" that had reigned up until the twelfth century and was still common: "Joachim carried it to its final fruition."[312] If Joachim had been raving, then everyone or almost everyone in the Church till then had been raving! The tradition of the Church, considered at its very center in its legitimate inheritance from the Fathers and during a period of at least six centuries, would then have been found to be fatally engaged on the path of illuminism and heresy! Such indictments are severe. But at least in what concerns Joachim's situation, the one from which the argument is being drawn, they are weakened by what we have seen up till now. M. W. Bloomfield himself gets halfway to admitting as much by giving them a paradoxical formulation: "By the principle of opposites passing into each other, the extreme application of the allegorical and symbolic method gives rise to the literal and the old to the new."[313] This paradoxical form shows that up to a certain point the difficulty of sustaining the thesis has been perceived, but it does not, for all that, render it more acceptable.

Other historians have sided with the Greek monasteries of Calabria, of which the abbot of Flora was the spiritual heir; did not Saint Nilus the Younger (910-1004), for example, practice a moral and symbolic interpretation of the Scriptures?[314] Without a doubt he did, but the Latins did so just as much as he. Some have again tried to explain what was original in Joachim by the fact that, the spiritual interpretation being more and more systematized, "Gregory, Bernard and the Paris masters had left little for others to say" for one who followed the classic path; now a monk like him, however, was constrained to draw everything from the *lectio divina*; so he found himself "drawn, irresistibly, to the only sphere that his predecessors had neglected"; his trinitarian concepts, influenced by Byzantium, naturally furnished him "a new idea for the allegorical sense. Why should it express a simple relation of promise and fulfillment between Old and New Testaments? Why should not the Old and the New Testament prefigure some third period?"[315] Indeed, why not? But that amounts to an explication by way of contrast, which sheds very little if any light, and a rather strange psychology, which turns Joachim of Flora into a hack writer of no real originality.

In the last century, Xavier Rousselot believed that he had discovered the "source" of Joachim. It was Origen. Were they not both of them "spiritual" or "perfect" men as opposed to "carnal men" or "carnal philosophers"? Were they not both like Saint John? Did one not see in them both "the same religious and mystical enthusiasm, the same tendency for contemplation"? Perceiving himself that such similarities would remain rather vague, Rousselot thought he had put his finger on a more probative piece of evidence: it is in Origen, he explained, that Joachim "had been able to see the name *Eternal Gospel* which became the object of all his thoughts."[316] What a rare find! Adolphe Franck, a good publicist, soon popularized it — though it was in the very serious-minded *Journal des savants* that he did so.[317] To which Charles Denis had no trouble rejoining, in 1884, that "the name 'Eternal Gospel' belongs not to Origen, but rather stems from Joachim's favorite writer, the author of the Apocalypse." Besides, added Denis, for Origen the Eternal Gospel is "Christian philosophy or, to put it better, heavenly wisdom glimpsed under the veil and through the shadows of history; it is something quite different for Joachim, obsessed with social preoccupations completely foreign to Origen."[318] One might add further precisions, as we will see; but the rejoinder was a good one. Denis, however, thought that he ought to concede that there was "something of Origen's spirit" in Joachim, albeit "without Origen's ideas": an excessive concession dictated to this independent-minded philosopher by the conviction that one and the "same freedom of mind" characterized those two men in relation to the authority of the faith[319] — which was true neither of the one nor of the other, and which perhaps in addition supposed an insufficiently exact notion of "the authority of the faith." In fact, and even on the terrain of hermeneutics, we are in the presence of two profoundly dissimilar types of thought. By recalling that "it is not necessary to believe that the historical facts are the figure of historical facts," Origen had refuted in advance the idea that inspires the Concordia, that of a literal relation between the two Testaments. He had no less refuted the idea of the third age, when he had said, for example, in one of his homilies on Leviticus:

> If, however, there should be something else that divine Scripture does not settle . . . that no other third scripture ought to be accepted as authoritative for science; since this is called "the third day"; but let us hand over to the fire, i.e., let us entrust to God, whatever else there is. For God did not want us to know everything in the present life.[320]

What he said of the impossibility of a third Scripture evidently held good for him with regard to another interpretation of the Scripture, which, in the course of the time to come, would have been like a third revelation, a sort of third testament. He did not recognize and did not want to recognize any other way than "the great way of the Gospel," such as it had been paved from of old, and everyone who would pretend to extend it or sublimate it would only, according to him, make us deviate from it.[321]

Meanwhile, some have recently wanted to give a new lease on life to the inadvertency of Xavier Rousselot. Only an apologetic bias in favor of Origen, thinks M. W. Bloomfield, would lead anyone to resist the proposed assimilation of the two Eternal Gospels, that of the Calabrian and that of the Alexandrian. In both cases that expression would symbolize the idea, the very same idea, of a new revelation to come.[322] Four passages from Origen, whose references he cites, appear probative to Mr. Bloomfield. Perhaps, had he taken the trouble to transcribe them, he might have been surprised to discover that they were indeed probative — but for the thesis that he intended to combat. Of the four texts, let us begin by citing the one that is found in the commentary on the Epistle to the Romans; he crisply poses the question: can one believe or in what sense can one say that there were two successive Gospels?

> You who are reading this must consider whether the Gospel promised by God through the prophetic Scriptures ought to be accepted without qualification, or [with reference] to the distinction of the other Gospel that John in the Apocalypse calls "eternal," which is to be revealed when the shadow passes and the truth has come, and when death is swallowed up and eternity restored.[323]

The question thus raised through the very expression of the Apocalypse will receive two responses, which are mutually complementary without contradicting each other, and which Origen adopts in turn. The one was given in book IV of the *De principiis*:

> But one ought to see, lest perchance it seem to point it out the more, that just as a more evident and manifest legislation is expressed in Deuteronomy than in the [books] that were written first: so too that second coming in the glory of his Father may seem brighter and more glorious than that coming of the Savior which he fulfilled in humility, when he took on the form of a servant, and in it the form of Deuteronomy may be fulfilled, when all the saints in the kingdom of heaven live by the laws of his Gospel, and just as on his coming now he fulfilled that law which holds the shadow of future goods, so too the shadow of his coming will be fulfilled and brought to perfection through that glorious coming.[324]

But the commentary on Saint John in the passage Mr. Bloomfield refers to[325] takes things from a different slant. It no longer considers the disparity which exists between the earthly condition of the Christian following the Lord's coming in humility and the condition that ought to be his "in the realm of the heavens," "in the glory of the Father," after the second, glorious coming. It envisages the simultaneous disparity which exists, even today, between the still-carnal Christian and the spiritual Christian, i.e., between one who scarcely goes beyond the exterior data of the Gospel account and one who penetrates its sense in depth:

> Here is what is still necessary for us to know: just as the Old Law contains the shadow of future goods — those goods that have been clearly announced by this Law when it is itself announced according to the truth — so too the Gospel, which is thought to be understood by all comers, teaches the shadow of the mysteries of Christ. On the other hand, the Gospel that John calls "eternal" and which could properly be called "spiritual," openly sets before the eyes of the heart, for those who comprehend, everything that concerns the Son of God himself, whether the mysteries that constituted the object of his discourses, or the realities of which his actions formed enigmatic figures.[326]

In other words, if one wants to find a distinct signification for it, the "Eternal Gospel" that the Apocalypse speaks of can be understood in two ways: either (in the text of the commentary on Saint John) as the understanding in depth that each Christian is called to obtain of the "mysteries of Christ" starting from the letter of the Gospel, or as the recognition of the "Son of God" through the words and deeds of his flesh — or (in the text of the *De principiis*) as the new way of knowing, clearer, more manifest, and more complete, that we are to receive at the end of time, at the time of the glorious coming of the Savior, leading us in his trail into the Kingdom. These two perspectives are quite different. One will note that Origen, who has perfect mastery over his own thought, has recourse to the analogy from Deuteronomy or the "second Law" only in the second instance, where it is not a question of a difference within time, but of time giving way to eternity.[327] In the first of these two perspectives, however, the very name "Eternal Gospel" does not seem to him adequate, and he proposes to change it to "Spiritual Gospel." This "Spiritual Gospel," then, is the very substance of the Gospel, as opposed to its sensible or "corporeal" exterior which is first discovered by an imperfect faith and perceivable even by the unbeliever; this is the knowledge of the Savior that the Paraclete, the Spirit of Truth, pours forth within our hearts from the effusion of the Pentecost on.³²⁸ If one maintains at that point, with the Apocalypse, the name and the idea of an "Eternal Gospel," then this will rather be to distinguish the perfect knowledge that has been reserved for us on the last day from the imperfect knowledge of the type that must always remain ours here below: when "the figure of this world" shall already have been destroyed, when the second veil, that of the sanctuary itself, shall have been torn asunder, after the ultimate destruction of Death.³²⁹ For "in this present life," we have received the baptism of water which has buried us with Christ, but not the baptism of fire which is to configure us to the body of his glory; living unto the shadow of Christ and no longer of the Law, we live unto the shadow of Life, but not yet in Life itself; "we do not yet see God as he is, but as he has become for us by reason of our economy."³³⁰

So this is how, using a Johannine expression, Origen comments on the Pauline doctrine of the twofold knowledge: "Today I understand in an imperfect manner, but then I shall understand perfectly."³³¹ Thereby he comments upon the paradox of the twofold Coming, which is at the heart of the Christian faith. Thereby he expresses the third term of the triad that Ambrose will use after him, as he himself had done following the Epistle to the Hebrews,³³² using the three words: shadow, image, and truth.³³³ With or without mentioning the "Eternal Gospel," these views will not cease to inspire the entire tradition, right down to the time of Joachim of Flora. So if one places himself with Origen in either one of the two perspectives that he adopts in turn,³³⁴ whether one attaches himself to the thought of the *De principiis* or to that of the commentary on Saint John, under either hypothesis the Joachimite idea of a new understanding, the idea of some "Eternal Gospel" coming to succeed the Gospel of Christ on earth, is set aside at its very roots.³³⁵

There remains, however, the fourth text cited by Mr. Bloomfield. It is a passage from the thirteenth homily on Leviticus. Origen is addressing himself to certain Christians who, as always, risk misusing the light they have received. Be on guard! he tells them. The unbelieving Jews once had a light, too, and they have lost it; their lamp has been extinguished, because they did not want to recognize the Christ. The same misfortune can happen to us. Each of us can lose the light, if, though in other circumstances yet through a fundamentally similar act, we come to reject Christ; the lamp of faith runs the risk of being extinguished, if we allow charity to be extinguished in us. Whence arises this interrogative sentence, alluding to the lot of the Jews: "But what shall we say — that these things happened to them, but do not apply to us?"³³⁶ To draw from thence the idea that in the thought of Origen, just as the kingdom of the Jewish Law has given way to the kingdom of the Gospel, the kingdom of the Gospel could make way for a third kingdom is to misconstrue the text. Moreover, in his passionate development, the preacher precisely and formally excludes the coming of any new light superior to the course of history until the consummation of the age: "this lamp is burning for each of us unto the consummation of the age, and until the new day of the future age and of the new law should shine."[337] If one day through our own fault this "lamp" came to be missing for us, that would not be to make way for another stronger light: it would rather plunge us into the night.

There we are, then, far from Joachim, and we should not be surprised, seeing that, contrary to so many others among his contemporaries or predecessors, the abbot of Flora shows no tenderness with regard to Origen, one of those Greeks with adulterated doctrine, "who in doctrine often fade."[338] Nor do we see just what that "neo-gnosticism" might consist in that, according to M. C. Ottaviano, Joachim "indubitably" owed to Origen.[339] Emmanuel Aegerter was less far from the truth for once, when he saw the abbot of Flora rather joining up with "the first commentators on the Apocalypse, Saint Irenaeus and Saint Justin,"[340] for there is always some element of likeness amongst all those who give any credence to the millenarist idea. At any event, that likeness alone, which, as has been seen, is paired with strong points of opposition, is not at all sufficient to establish parentage.

According to Miss Beryl Smalley, the one who was soon to ruin the Joachimite method was Aristotle.[341] Yet there was really no need for Aristotle! The tradition of the Church was enough to do the job. Precisely in deference to Origen and despite many partial resurgences, the Church had rejected every sort of millenarianism. Her very hermeneutics were to guarantee it. Against "the Jews and the Judaizers" she affirmed the two fundamental principles that Joachim misunderstood: on the one hand, the exterior facts of the Old Testament are realized in the New in spiritual fashion, to such an extent that one can say in summary that the spiritual sense of the Old Testament is the New Testament; on the other hand, and by that very fact, one could not conceive that the New Testament, or the Gospel of Christ, would one day have to be relieved in history, or as Origen used to say, "within this passing world" by something beyond itself. One passage of Rabanus Maurus taken from a hundred others will remind us of the first of these two principles. It concerns one of Ezekiel's prophecies:

The Jews confirm [that] all these things had unfolded either under Zerubbabel, when there was a great commotion and the kingdom of the Chaldeans was transferred to the Medes and Persians, or in the presence of their Christ, whom they think is about to come. We, on the other hand, recall [that those things] completed spiritually after the cross of the Lord Savior are also being performed daily among them, most especially those who, like Lazarus, bound with the winding-bands of their own sins, are raised at the voice of the Lord.[342]

The second principle will be recalled to us by, among others, Bruno of Segni, Hervaeus of Bourg Dieu, and Irimbert of Admont. "By the Eternal Gospel," says Bruno commenting on the Apocalypse, "we understand the preaching of Christ."[343] The New Testament, says Hervaeus commenting on the Epistle to the Galatians, is called the Eternal Gospel by the Scripture itself, "since it will never be changed, as the Old Testament was changed, but will remain just as it was given by Christ."[344] Without change in interpretation, says Irimbert commenting on the Book of Judges, "holy Scripture, in which Christ is ever sought for and faithfully found, is being presented to the eyes of believers until the day of eternity."[345] To be sure, each of them is well aware that the present mode of knowing is still imperfect; each hopes for a better sort of knowledge; but the essential progress toward realization is not from one step to another on the same path: it is from the path to the goal. Hence if one reserves the name Eternal Gospel, as Origen did in the *De principiis,* for perfect knowledge, one does not await its revelation for a third age immanent to this world; one hopes for it beyond time, for eternity: "when, by the mercy of the Lord, we shall have received the pristine glory, or rather when we have received the everlasting compact of the Gospel."[346] And in each of these two states of knowledge, whatever name we give it, for all our authors the Gospel is always the Gospel of Christ. Not only is no surpassing it to be expected — notwithstanding the doctrinal developments of analytic order, developments that the Middle Ages were in no way blind to — but one admits rather that the time of fullness is to be located in the past. In each generation since the time of Christ and the Apostles, the doctors were always being compelled to clarify the obscurities of Scripture better; but, as Richard of Saint Victor explains, that would not entail any real progress in understanding in relation to the first disciples: "though the holy evangelists were earlier than those doctors, they are nevertheless not to be believed to have had less understanding than they,

Presumed Antecedents

inasmuch as the sacred authority testifies of them that Jesus himself opened their heart so that they might understand the Scriptures."[347]

In other words again, ever since "the truth of the Gospel" was announced to it, our world has from the religious point of view entered into its "perfect age";[348] but, on the other hand, to the extent that "we are on pilgrimage far from the Lord," we "walk in faith, not by sight," and between the one and the other there is no intermediary condition here below in any epoch to come.[349]

In short, for every theologian, for every Christian who cares about the traditional doctrine, the idea that a third Testament lived on this earth ought to be rejected out of hand in any form that could possibly be presented. The expression itself was repugnant, and to be able to accuse someone of wanting to introduce it was enough to discredit him. That is what Saint Wolfhelm had done in the previous century in his Epistle against the errors of Berengar:

> Behold, we prove these things by the authority of the Old and New Testament; to which Berengar adds a third, which we reject no less than that a third Cato should have come down from heaven. So then, after the two Testaments, he adds this third; and he adds the third, because he is alienated from the other two.[350]

The Augustinian division of the four ages or four states which, in the age of Joachim itself, enjoyed a return to favor,[351] was therefore not susceptible of being opened up to accommodate a would-be age of spiritual understanding intermediate between the last two, the age of "grace" and that of "peace" or of the "fatherland." This spiritual understanding, in the measure in which it is realizable here below, was already illuminating the age of grace; in the measure in which it pretended to go beyond the age of grace, it could only be saved up for the fatherland. Saint Hildegard recalls the common doctrine when she enumerates the "three times of the world: namely, before the Law, in the Law, and in the Gospel."[352] One of the holy monks of Calabria who lived prior to Joachim, namely Saint Vitalis, had recalled it as well: "He used to point out God's precepts, those that are before the Law, those in the Law, and those in grace," according to the author of his biography.[353] If we cite this text, it is not because it is distinguished in any way from a number of others: it is rather because some have believed that an expression of Joachim's doctrine could be seen anticipated in it;[354] just as in the trilogy of Ambrose cited above,[355] taken up again and commented on in 1152 by Bodo of Prüfning in the second book of his treatise *De statu domus Dei:* "one house exists in shadow, another in image, the other in truth";[356] or again in the threefold priesthood expounded by John Scotus Erigena:[357] the Jewish priesthood, full of still obscure riddles; the Christian priesthood, which "partly shines with the brightest knowledge of the truth, and partly is obscured in symbols"; and finally the priesthood that will be celebrated in the heavenly Jerusalem, "in which there are no symbols, no obscurity of figures, but the brightest truth will appear as a whole."[358] In each of these cases the mistake made by historians devoted to the study of the "sources" of Joachimism is the same. All these ways of speaking are similar; whatever the number or the name of their subdivisions, they always make "grace" the only intermediate between the "Law" and "glory," or the New Testament as it is known and lived on earth the only intermediary between the Old Testament and eternal life. So it is again with Honorius, who, after many others, divides time into "four vigils": from Adam to Noah, from Noah to Moses, from Moses to Christ, and from Christ to the end;[359] so is it with Saint Martin of Leon, who sticks to the three Augustinian ages and concludes: "Hence from the birth of Christ till now, and whatever remains until the end of the world, is the third day of grace."[360] These various nomenclatures agree in rendering the most common Christian truth as the most fundamental. In not a single one of them could anyone see a foreshadowing of the third age of Joachim. That third age could not be inserted into any of these frameworks without breaking it.[361]

There are, however, two authors in the twelfth century whom one might with a bit more plausibility have believed to be precursors of Joachim. They are Hugh of Saint Victor and Rupert of Deutz. Indeed, both of them use a ternary division, each member of which they put into relation with one of the persons of the Trinity. In a curious chapter of the *Didascalicon,* Hugh speaks of the "three days of invisible light":

> Therefore there are three days of invisible light, within which the course of spiritual life is distinguished. The first is fear, the second is truth, the third is charity. The first day has its sun, power . . . ; the second . . . , wisdom; the third . . . , benevolence. Power pertains to the Father, wisdom to the Son, and benevolence to the Holy Spirit.[362]

Only, these interior days are not like those on the outside, which pass and succeed each other; the coming of a subsequent day does not drive out the preceding one; these "mystical days" compenetrate each other,

Presumed Antecedents

though there is an order among them; all three remain. At every age since the incarnation of the Word, they are all three present in the human race; at every age, "they are to be completed in us."[363] They are the effect, the repercussion and, in a way, the prolongation of the three days of the death, burial, and resurrection of Christ, the mystery of which is indivisible, and that is why they have been really accomplished before even being achieved in each of the faithful. How can one discern there, as H. Bett[364] struggles to do, "a very strict parallel" with the three ages of Joachim of Flora? For Hugh, it is a matter of a completely spiritual rhythm, entirely dependent upon the mystery of Christ and already realized right now within his Church.[365]

As for Rupert, some historians believe they have found a decisive text in the prologue of his great work on the Trinity and its activities. From it they have concluded that Joachim was "strictly" dependent upon him[366] and merely had to push his "trinitarian conception of history" "up to its ultimate exaggerations."[367] Rather too hasty a conclusion! It is indeed true that, in this prologue, Rupert distinguishes, if not three reigns, at least God's "three" successive "works" in the unfolding of the universal history of salvation, and that he attributes each of them more particularly to one of the three Persons. But the analogy with Joachim goes no further. In that spot there is not even a vague "anticipation" of his three ages.[368] Nor could one speak of "ambiguities"[369] that might in some measure justify anything like a necessary assimilation. There can be no mistake about the thought of Rupert. For him the Old Testament is not the age of the Father; the age of the Son has not begun with the mortal life of Christ so as to continue in the history of the Church and give way in the future to some other age, still to come, which would be that of the Spirit. All that is needed is to read him:

> There is however a tripartite work of the Trinity, from the founding of the world to its end. The first is from the origin of the first light to the fall of the first man. The second, from the fall of the first man until the passion of the second man, Jesus Christ the Son of God. The third, from his resurrection to the consummation of the age, i.e., the general resurrection of the dead. And the first work is that proper to the Father; the second is that of the Son; the third, proper to the Holy Spirit.[370]

Nothing could be clearer, nothing simpler, nothing more traditional. It is the very sequence and the original structure of the *Credo*. Rupert does not, however, set these attributions in stone; he immediately proclaims: "The plainly inseparable Trinity is inseparably acting as the one God."[371] One can still speak of an action proper to each Person. Creation is the work of the Father; redemption, promised since the Fall, preached in Israel, accomplished on Calvary, is the work of the Son; sanctification or renewal, the resurrection of the soul which at the end of time is to be followed by the resurrection of the body, is the work of the Spirit. This sanctifying Spirit is the Spirit who succeeds to Christ and his Gospel: it is the Spirit of Christ, who bears witness to him all through the New Testament and who acts in his church:

> The day or the hour a man believes in Christ and takes up the sacrament of his baptism, God sends forth his Spirit, and he is created so as to be a new creature with respect to his soul, once all the hoariness of sin has been abolished, and in addition to this the 'face of the earth', i.e., the earthly body ... will be renewed on the last day of resurrection.[372]

Thus the trinitarian scheme of Rupert of Deutz is no more a precursor to that of Joachim of Flora than is the trinitarian scheme of Hugh of Saint Victor. On the contrary, it positively excludes it.[373] One will not at all be surprised, if one recalls that nothing is less like the abbot of Flora's ecclesial prophetism than the inspired conservatism of that other fellow, the abbot of Deutz, who is in principle as hostile to any sort of mystical anti-Caesarism[374] as he is to the new forms of religious orders. And if, on the other hand, in the preface of his commentary on Saint John, Rupert speaks several times of the Eternal Gospel, it is quite simply to qualify the fourth Gospel by that term.[375]

Furthermore, at least up to a point, Joachim himself is well aware of the novelty that he is introducing. Not only has he himself discovered in Scripture the announcement of the next upheavals that he predicts down to the date, but even the hermeneutics under which it is based is peculiar to him. He recognizes it. He knows that he is proceeding "at least with a new kind of exposition,"[376] which signifies not only a new style of presentation, but of explication as well. Without seeing it perhaps or without saying it so clearly, Joachim also knows that his third age, taken as a third terrestrial state, has no traditional connections. How then is one to make him admit that the promise made by Jesus to the Apostles to send them the Spirit of truth in reality concerned, beyond the Pentecost, the distant date that would mark the arrival of that third state? And how can one make him also admit the very idea of a state that would no longer be that of the Church militant, without yet being that of the Church triumphant? Ought not the transition from the one to the other be abrupt and without an intermediate? Finally, could there really be, in the future, that time different from our own, when one would already begin to "see face to face"?[377] that time when the new Jerusalem announced by Saint John would have begun to descend from on high, without its glory yet made manifest?[378] Could there be a time when one would already have departed from the Egypt of the present age, without yet having entered into the ultimate Fatherland; when the veil that still covers the mysteries contemplated by the Apostle in the third heaven, the heaven of spiritual understanding, would be lifted in the Holy Spirit just as the veil that of old used to cover the face of Moses was lifted in Christ?[379] The tradition knows nothing of the sort, aside from the old millenarianism long since excluded, and from which the abbot of Flora himself is as distant as possible. At the end, for the Church, "all things will be rendered peaceful and quiet"; but while waiting, "it is a mark of great virtue to struggle joyfully."[380] That is what anyone, along with Hervaeus of Bourg Dieu, can object to in Joachim. So he takes the trouble to justify his doctrine, in a rather sophisticated way. His subtle argumentation develops, so to speak, in three steps.

Joachim in fact finds the distinction of a sixth and a seventh age in the tradition. The sixth age — after the five first ages, which divide the whole history of the world up to Jesus Christ — is the time of the Church here below, which lasts until the Judgment: "the sixth age, which is going on now, will last until the world is ended"; the seventh is the eternal life inaugurated for men on the Day of Judgment: "the age of the highest peace and repose, in the other life," "the saints' rest, which has no dusk."[381] These last two ages, like the preceding ones, are consequently successive. All the same, in a certain sense, one can regard them as simultaneous, because, from now on, those who have died in the Lord enjoy that eternal rest that we in our turn must enter upon; that is the "Sabbath of the faithful souls resting in paradise."[382] One can therefore, even before the Last Day, speak of a seventh age that has commenced, which one will say is coextensive with the whole sixth age or even with all the six first ages, according as one will judge those who are just from the time that preceded the Incarnation, who have entered into the blessed Sabbath beginning with the descent of Christ to the underworld,[383] or each one beginning with his own death, from the time of Abel the first among them.[384] From the first consideration, Joachim retains the view that the two last ages are successive; from the second, at the same time, without more ado, he maintains that the seventh age precedes the Judgment. This is what authorizes him, he thinks, to distinguish the sixth and the seventh age as two time-periods, two successive earthly states. Moreover he agrees to attribute to them a certain simultaneity, since the Pentecost, which followed a little later than Christ's resurrection, partially inaugurated that kingdom of the Spirit in which the seventh age consists; the contemplative life already holds a certain place in the Church of Christ, whilst awaiting to take over the whole thing in the Church of the Spirit. Peter and John at first run together, but once Peter has disappeared, John will remain.[385]

However, is it not said again and again in peremptory fashion that the sixth age, to which Joachim's second stage corresponds, ought, for humanity living upon the earth, to last until the "last day," or up to the "end of time"? Now does this idea of the last day or the end of time not exclude all possibility of a third state that might extend itself upon the earth? The abbot from Flora cannot fail to see that the texts of Scripture that he explains regarding his third state are in fact those that should define the final state in the bosom of the heavenly Jerusalem. But we already know the essentials of his reply. There is no difficulty in distinguishing the one end from the other, one last day from another last day according to the holy Books themselves.[386] As to those who would contradict him on that point, he puts them to shame for their ignorance of the Scripture:

> Yet the general opinion, especially of those who are ignorant of scriptural usage, holds that the terms "last day" and "day of judgment" ought to apply only to the day on which good are to be separated from the evil, as sheep are sorted from goats, i.e., in the general last judgment of the dead, when the Son of Man is to sit in the seat of his majesty. . . . But still one ought to discuss in what ways one may say "the last day" and "the end of the world"; lest everything that is said to have to be done on the last day be assigned to that last day — to hold and believe which involves great error and not a little danger.[387]

He puts them no less to shame for their ignorance of tradition, especially the Augustinian tradition: "as Saint Augustine taught long before us in his book on the *City of God*," the whole sixth age, i.e., all the time that unfolds since the first coming of Christ, "is to be called the 'end of the world'"; "it pertains as a whole to the day of judgment."[388]

Such is the incontestable fact, a fact of language, itself resting upon the dogmatic fact of the entire sufficiency and fullness of the work accomplished by Christ, upon which Joachim constructs his reasoning: "If the whole sixth age is called 'the end of the world', how much more can one generation, or two, or three, be called the end either of the first state, or the second, or the third!"[389] And, from then on, why should not the whole "third state" be called "the last day" or "the end of the world," without, however, being in the strict sense of the word "the last moment of the end"?[390] What a magnificent *a fortiori* argument! But Joachim does not see that if, in the traditional New Testament language, the end-time is opened from the first coming of Christ, this is because every revelation has been given by Christ and every work of salvation has been accomplished in him. In declaring the sixth age the "end-time," one does not authorize the conception of a seventh age, which, coming later in duration, would be *a fortiori* the end-time: quite the contrary, by that very fact one disallows any idea of a further step, of a new time and a new state, which would come to add or change anything in the definitive Gift, the Gift of Jesus Christ, who is also the Gift of his Spirit. With Saint Gregory one does not cease to say it again: "The Father has willed that the God who is before the ages should become man at the end of the ages."[391] From the first Christian generation on, humanity is at the end-time, because "the Word has made the flowers to burst forth in abundance, i.e., he has sown the Holy Spirit upon the earth, just as at the end he has promised through the prophets to pour forth the Spirit upon the face of the earth."[392]

However — and this is the third step of his demonstration — to distinguish his "third state" from the second, no more remains for the abbot of Flora than to apply to it the texts of Scripture which in reality concern the totally final end, i.e., eternal life, by declaring that that seventh age, though quite earthly as it still must be, will nonetheless see the beginning of what must blossom in heaven, in the eighth age:

> All things will be naked and obvious to the saints who are to come at that time. . . . For they will then begin to see face to face what our ancient Fathers saw through a glass darkly; since at that time the iniquity will be removed in the people of God and everlasting justice will be established; since the saints of God will then be reigning. . . . In that time also it will truly be said by the elect: "This is the day the Lord has made, let us be glad and rejoice." And although this was properly said of the eighth day or time, nevertheless it can also not

unfittingly be said of the seventh, since it is written: "He blessed the seventh day and sanctified it."[393]

Thus does Joachim believe that he has a foundation in Scripture and the tradition for that "Sabbath," that "paschal time," that "third state," that "kingdom of the Spirit," which his imagination has conceived and projected into the future.

4. The Time of the Church

The interpretation of the Apocalypse in Joachim of Flora is commanded by his idea of a literal concord between the two Testaments, as well as by his expectation of an age of the Spirit. Or, if one will — for here the causality is reciprocal — the Apocalypse is the privileged book in which Joachim discovers or verifies both the principle of the *concordia secundum coaptationem*[394] and the detailed announcement of the passage from one age to the other. The result of the long struggle that he would wage in an initial period of his solitary meditations to wrest their secret from the Scriptures turned out to be an intuitive grasp of the permanent timeliness of the Apocalypse in the course of history. It took the twelve years that follow to give this illumination a systematic form in his great works. For him, the opening of the first six seals of which Saint John speaks reveals one after the other the corresponding periods of the old history and the new; as to the opening of the seventh seal, it more particularly explains the passage from the first state to the second and that from the second to the third: from the time of Nehemiah or king Antiochus on the one hand, and from the return of Elijah and the persecution of the new Antiochus on the other. At the approach of the great reversals that caused the passage to the third state, the seven thunderings of the Spirit redouble in intensity; the Apocalypse shines with a new light, and if every letter of the Scripture, that of the Old Testament as well as that of the New, remains useful to examine so as to determine the future, this is especially true of every letter of the last Book, which must now hold our attention.[395]

Joachim's "unprecedented method"[396] was fatally to divert him from traditional approaches in the explanation of the Apocalypse as well as elsewhere. Despite many divergences, and despite certain innovations that we shall soon examine, the commentators on the last Book for the most part remained dependent upon the "firm and just" principles already established long ago by Tyconius and Saint Augustine, then ex-

The Time of the Church

ploited by Primasius, Ambrose Autpert, Berengaud, Alcuin, and Aimo (or Remigius) of Auxerre. As controversial as they were in themselves, the idea of the "recapitulation"[397] and that of the analogy with the Canticle of Canticles,[398] as they were then employed, at least generally discouraged people from searching into the symbols of that Book — which was the most meditated on of all, the most active upon people's imaginations,[399] the "more fruitful part of holy Scripture"[400] — for a batch of some sort of literal prophecies. Among its many commentators, some were more attached to the old phase of the history of salvation, others to its Christian phase; some devoted more space to the struggles of the primitive Church, others to those of the end-time; the treatment adopted by some had a somewhat more historical character, whilst amongst others the problems of the inner life were more dominant; but generally all were in agreement in thinking that the seven seals had essentially been broken once and for all by Christ, in a definitive revelation:

> The same Lion of the tribe of Judah opened . . . that book enclosed in mystery by seven seals; and this book of the whole of holy Scripture has been opened, since the understanding of it has been revealed to men by Christ.[401]

That is how Saint Ildefonse of Toledo, or perhaps Justinian of Valencia puts it in the eighth century. And here is Beatus of Liebana: "The Church has unfastened these seven seals."[402] Pseudo-Alcuin and the mysterious Hemmo express themselves in almost the same way:

> Then the Lamb opened the book, when he fulfilled the work of his voluntary passion.[403]

> What else is meant by this book than holy Scripture, which our Redeemer alone has opened, who, having become man, has by his dying, rising, and ascending laid open all the mysteries that had been shut up within it?[404]

In the eleventh century, Saint Bruno of Segni repeats the affirmation and moreover insists on the solidarity of the seven seals and the objects that at first they hold concealed:

> Neither those who are in heaven (the men of the Church) nor those on earth (the philosophers and the wise) nor those under the earth

> (the wicked spirits) were able to see or understand this book until Christ opened it and gave it up to his disciples that they should understand the Scriptures. . . . The Lion of the tribe of Judah conquered so as to open the book and break the seven seals. . . . After they understood the Scriptures, all the holy apostles and doctors gave thanks to our Lord the Christ, who gave them the sense of understanding through the Holy Spirit.
>
> And the seven seals fit together so that he who knows one has no doubt about the others; hence nothing is closed to him to whom one seal is opened, and on the other hand nothing is opened for him to whom one is closed. For he who does not believe Christ's birth understands nothing of his passion, resurrection, and ascension, and so on for the others. Hence the seven seals are the seven mysteries in which our faith is principally contained.[405]

Hence everything is revealed at once, because the object of faith is indivisible and because it cannot be surpassed. The "new song" that the elect sing before the throne of the Lamb will still be the song of the Church, her unique song, the chant that unendingly celebrates and expounds the harmony of the two Testaments, the renewal of the Old Testament by means of the New.[406] Now let us consult Saint Bernard in the twelfth century:

> He broke the seven seals of that same book when he unlocked the understanding of sacred eloquence for the minds of the faithful; and whatever the Law and the prophets had preached about his mysteries allegorically, i.e., the things that he accomplished through man temporally, he preaches about himself and he has pointed them out more clearly in and through himself in broad daylight.[407]

At about the same time, Godfrey of Admont says the same thing:

> The shadow of ancient death has crossed over into the light of truth, in such wise that now we look upon the work of our redemption with our own eyes, a work that previously used to be foretold in the hidden, obscure words of the prophets and prefigured with riddles.[408]

Soon again, the Victorine Absalon would say: "For that book was once sealed and was once closed, but now it has been opened."[409] In his imagined manner, Rupert used to say that since the Lord has died, been resurrected, climbed to the heavens, "the splendor of the seven lamps" has been set to shine on the world and all seven have been placed together on the same lampstand, because they are "the seven spirits" sent by the one and only Christ.[410] Further on, however, Rupert made an exception for the seventh seal, which would be opened only at the end of the world, when the One who sits at the right hand of God would return to judge the living and the dead;[411] but then that seventh seal in his mind designated a different object: it was equivalent to the book that Saint John in another chapter calls "another book": no longer the book of the revelation of the salvation offered to all, but the book of the revelation of hearts[412] — in other words, the book of Judgment. After the book of creation and the book of the Scriptures, there is the book of the "divine secrets," the "eternal pages" or the "page of heaven."[413] Using the same image, Honorius commented in favor of the same doctrine on the verse of the Proverbs: "The meadows have been opened and green grasses have appeared" as follows:

> By "the meadows" is meant the heavenly mysteries, which are called meadows *(prata)* because they are the pasture *(pascua)* of the faithful; for these meadows, i.e., the divine mysteries, had long been enclosed under the signs and figures of the Law.... The meadows have indeed been opened, since the heavenly sacraments have been revealed through the grace of the Savior Lord, when he "opened for his disciples their sense, that they might understand the Scriptures" (Luke 24:45).[414]

At the end of the century, Saint Martin of Leon said it again: "By 'the seven seals'... is meant the fullness of the hidden mysteries, which, prior to the coming of the Lord, used to lie hidden."[415]

Why should not all the seals be pulled from the book, if the whole book were already understood? Besides, does not the very name "Apocalypse" signify that all the secrets had already been revealed?[416] Consequently, as has been seen in the preceding paragraph, was not that whole time that unfolded "from the Lord's passion till the end of the age," that unique hour of which Saint John himself had said: "Children, the hour is now very late"?[417] Was not the "day of life and of resurrection" a great day, qualitatively unique, which had begun with the resurrection of Christ and was to end — or to blossom out — with the resurrection of the whole human race?[418] It was doubtless necessary that for each generation the Catholic commentators should continue to use the key of David to open up to the faithful the mysteries of Christ contained within the Scripture, because each generation needs to be instructed in turn and to apply itself in its own proper situation to the lesson of these mysteries; but there it was a sort of perpetual recommencement, an ever renewed investigation, not a progressive opening-up.[419] As it is, the lampstand has been placed outside the veil; the truth of the Holy Spirit was already shining for all.[420] The steps of salvation are those of the progress of revelation: now, once the one and only Word and the one and only Savior has come, everything has been accomplished. At that point everything was revealed: "the secrets of all the mysteries have been made clear."[421] Thus, in her different computations, tradition never recognized any more than one single time from Christ up to the end, namely, the time of Christ.[422]

But Joachim, as we have seen, cared but little for tradition. To be sure, he was far from being totally ignorant of it. What has been recounted a bit after his death on the late illumination that had suddenly filled him with a divine wisdom when he was still almost illiterate, based on a deformation of his own testimonies,[423] is pure legend.[424] On occasion he appeals to the Fathers and the Doctors; one encounters such formulas as: "Tradunt sancti doctores" ["the holy doctors hand down"]; "sicut dicunt sancti" ["as the saints say"]; "una est dicentium sanctorum Patrum sententia" ["the sense of the holy Fathers is one in their saying"]. He cites Augustine, Gregory and Jerome. He speaks highly of the Cistercian Bernard.[425] At one time or another he even tries to show that his boldest thoughts contain no aberration: "But on the paths of the holy Fathers let us. . . ."[426] Nevertheless, he follows his own ideas above all, and what always interests him is to explain or to foresee the sequence of events. Has he undergone profound influence from Greek theology in the elaboration of his Trinitarian doctrine, which is itself tied to his conception of salvation history? It would appear rather less probable than many have believed.[427] If it is true that he emphasizes the plurality of Persons, so did Saint Anselm.[428] On the other hand, let us recall his repeated affirmation of the procession *ab utroque,* essential to his theory of the three ages. At any event, a Greek influence would not explain that constant "historical" curiosity, that paradoxically literal symbolism. If it is not mistaken to believe Geoffrey of Auxerre, whose formal testimony has unfortunately come down to us mutilated, Joachim was of Jewish origin; he would have been converted to the Christian faith only rather late[429] and he would have kept, along with his Jewish name, something of the Jewish mindset.[430] Is that an imaginary legend to explain this unusual name, Joachim? Or perhaps an invention stemming from Cistercian hostility toward a turncoat?[431] If the fact proved true, one would understand better that, when all is said and done, our exegete had judaized the Christianity of history — by making of the New Testament a letter analogous to the letter of the Old. One would also understand better that, in his treatise *Adversus Judaeos,* contrary to the custom then most widely held, he had systematically eliminated all "allegorical understanding," so as to argue only following the letter in the strictest sense.[432] Geoffrey of Auxerre, who was abbot of Fossanuova from 1170 to 1176, might have been sufficiently well informed; but he is perhaps not a very reliable witness, and no other datum has confirmed his assertion, so it is more prudent not to rely upon it. Let us merely observe, along with H. Grudmann[433] and Father Congar,[434] that Joachim looks rather like an isolated individual, an individualist, not only in relation to his own epoch but generally in relation to the tradition of the Church.

Nevertheless, in this tradition itself, or at least at the margin of this tradition, several lines of thought are perceivable whose point of convergence is the system imagined by Joachim.

The first of these lines, if one can speak about his "thought," is that of popular curiosity. Man is naturally curious, with a curiosity secretly guided by fear or by desire. We know the place held in the ancient cults of Greece and the Orient by oracles, astrology, methods of divination of all kinds. Though these practices had been reproved in Israel and subsequently in the Church, large numbers of Jews and Christians had always had a tendency to look into their sacred Books either for the figure or announcement of events that had just struck their imagination, or for the revelation of secrets concerning the future and particularly the end of history. Precisely in order to illustrate the kind of exegesis which characterizes one of the writings discovered at Qumrân, namely the commentary on Habakkuk, Mr. Millar Burrows cites a recent book in which the "vessels of Kittîm" of the Book of Daniel become the English ships sent from Cyprus during World War I to attack the coasts of Syria and Palestine.[435] This is almost the same as what Arnobius had seen long ago in the Psalm verse: "with a violent wind thou shalt shatter the ships of Tarshish" — a prophetic allusion to the vessels of Tarshish that Herod had ordered destroyed to take revenge for the fact that they had permitted the secret return of the Magi to their own country.[436] We know that after having criticized "the indiscreet study of times," a Saint Hippolytus still had not believed he could "refuse to supply clarifications for human curiosity"; he had calculated the duration of the world and had looked into the two books of Daniel and the Apocalypse for many a hint about its end.[437] However covered over by the sort of explication that Origen made dominant, the tradition represented by Hippolytus was never completely extinguished. We also know that Lactantius had described the last reversals at length, almost uniquely according to the pagan oracles. In the sequel, starting with certain passages from the two Testaments, with which certain legends of different origin were mixed up, divers systems of messianism were thought up, in the West as well as in the East.[438] Political intentions were not always absent from them. When the holy Books were not enough, apocryphal ones or later revelations were always presenting themselves. The fortune of some of these was great: for example, to cite certain of those writings that circulated under divers forms in the Latin world, the "Visions of Daniel" also called the "Sibylline Books,"[439] the "Revelations of Methodius," the "Prophecy of the monk Sergius,"[440] or again, later on, the prophecies of Merlin,[441] till the prophecies attributed to Saint Malachy or Joachim of Flora himself.[442] A whole "popular apocryphal library" of this sort was circulating in the margin of the official ecclesiastical literature.[443]

Joachim must have had knowledge of this sort of literature, which gratified his own inclinations. Did he borrow any elements from it? There is no decisive evidence to settle the matter.[444] He was at any event much impressed, as were all his contemporaries, by the repeated assaults of the "Saracens" against Christianity, whilst a Roman council already felt itself obliged to prohibit Christians from selling them arms![445] "They had come at some point to gobble down the Church!"[446] The great event was the recapture of Jerusalem by Saladin on 28 October 1187.[447] As the fateful day approached, Pope Urban III died of sorrow. It was a terrible awakening, after the long chant of "Jerusalem, exsulta!" The holy City, symbol of all the aspirations of the Christian soul and of Christian society, whose deliverance had been celebrated on the spot each year by a triumphal liturgy,[448] was once again reduced to servitude by the "gens erroris" ["tribe of error"]. Perhaps it is at that point that Joachim finally cried out: "Tempus praefinitum est!" ["The end of time is at hand!"] In that year, 1187, he had scarcely begun writing his exegetical work. Before getting his renown as a prophet, thanks to the commotion aroused in the whole Christian world, one can believe that this fact served as a central nucleus for him, around which his system of interpretation is organized.[449]

But for the very form of his thought, he was able to find a certain number of priming-devices in the theological literature of his age.

More than once, ever since the beginning in fact,[450] interpreters have departed from the principle of allegory or spiritual interpretation, so as to apply literally some prophecy or figure of the Bible that does not lend itself to that kind of application. This was perhaps not so much to depart from it, as we shall see better in the following paragraph, as to recognize, with Paul Alvarus, in the Behemoth and the Leviathan of the Book of Job, symbols of Mohammed.[451] On the contrary, Eusebius of Caesarea had made a strong appeal to the authority of Scripture when he had wanted to see the realization of the prophecies about universal peace in the reign of Constantine; for him, the "saints of the Most High" who were, again according to Daniel, "to receive the kingdom," were the emperor and his children.[452] Aiming at a considerably smaller target, certain monks of slight spirituality, forcefully reproved by Hugh of Fouilloy, claimed the right to wear long robes of expensive material, because the young Joseph had received a beautiful ankle-length tunic ["tunica talaris"] from his mother.[453] Aside from these sporadic interpretations, the idea came to light here or there in the twelfth century, especially perhaps in certain sermons to the laity, of a certain literal concord between the two Testaments, i.e., of a parallelism more or less followed between the history of Israel and that of the Church. In the *Gemma animae* of Honorius, a series of little chapters "de concordia officiorum": "on the concord of offices," grouped two by two, describes the facts that took place "sub lege" ["under the Law"] and the ones corresponding to them "sub gratia" ["under Grace"].[454] This may be nothing but mnemotechnical playfulness, a taste for methodical classifications and subtle arrangements on the part of an author who, on the other hand, expounds the traditional doctrine of the relation of the two Testaments with precision. It is nonetheless, in spite of the modest proportions, a genuine precedent.

In the *De investigatione Antichristi* (1162), Gerhoh of Reichersberg exhibits an analogous thought when he writes:

> The truth of the new things is in agreement with the type of antiquity in such fashion that the concessions piously made to God's Church by Prince Constantine, correspond fittingly with the concessions made by Cyrus, Artaxerxes, and Darius with regard to the rebuilding of the Temple.[455]

He entitles another chapter of the same work: "On the state of the Church in the times of Henry IV: how it accords with the times and actions of Antiochus."[456] In his work on the *Order of the Gifts of the Holy Spirit*, he establishes a parallel between Pope Nicholas and the Emperor Charles the Young on the one hand, and Joshua and the high priest Eleazar on the other.[457] Such agreements had to be tempting to a polemicist in writings of religious policy, just as they had to be tempting to popular preachers. They were merely episodic, however; they did not stem from any generalized hermeneutics. Gerhoh wanted less to show current events prefigured in their precise materiality than to explain them in the light of Scripture. Elsewhere, most of the time, in the exterior fact that he borrows from the history of ancient Israel, he recognizes the figure of a spiritual situation. Thus already in his first work, the *De aedificio Dei* (1127), where the Temple of Jerusalem and its re-builder symbolize the "verax Faber" ["true Builder"] and his Church:

> In the rebuilding of Jerusalem certain principal gates were called by mystical names: by means of them things that are to be done in the Church now were signified in advance by prophetic figures. For all those historical events that took place in those rebuildings of the earthly Jerusalem were prophetic signs of the things we see now.[458]

In the same way, in his long explication of Psalm 64, or the *Liber de corrupto Ecclesiae statu ad Eugenium III papam* (1148), he declares that he wishes to do nothing in it more than to gather the various senses of the Fathers ["Patrum sensus"].[459] So he does not pretend to have discovered any new manner of interpretation, which would be of a historic order, as that of Joachim will be. In the preceding century, Saint Bruno of Segni pretended to no more, when he commented on the Apocalypse, as a good pastor ought to do, in function of his epoch, taking the opportunity to discuss the role of the bishops, the morals of the clergy, the errors and the abuses then current.[460] Rupert did no more, when he interpreted the last phase of the combat between the Woman and the Dragon as the victory of the Church over heresy at the Council of Nicea; he did not say that this Council — in its particular reality of externally dated fact, in the divers incidents that marked its convocation, its conduct or its consequences, in the persons that took part in it — had been predicted by Saint John; he applied the same symbol, without changing a single feature in it, to the following Councils of Constantinople, Ephesus, and Chalcedon; he had been able to apply it to others as well: on each occasion, in fact, substantially the same spiritual process unfolded: by the triumph of the right belief in Jesus Christ the demon was vanquished in one of the heresies that he had awakened, and these victories across the whole history of the Church — of time past as well as that to come — were all really just one and the same thing.[461]

The pattern of these last commentators, if not the detail of their exegeses, was justified. If in fact, as Saint Gregory has taught, we have in Scripture, at least under the form of general schemata, the answer to all the problems that our soul can put to itself, in whatever situation it finds itself,[462] why should it not be the same as regards collective situations, i.e., as regards the life of the Church, since the Church and the soul are in mutual symbolic relation with each other? Does not the whole Church have an equal need for God to enlighten it? Is not Scripture always, for all and sundry, "the light of life"?[463] Does not each Christian generation always have in this Scripture "the presence of the Spirit who speaks to the Churches"?[464] And do not those who grasp Scripture and use it in this way still stay within the line of a spiritual interpretation? Besides, Saint Gregory himself, remarking specifically the complaints of Job, had applied Job's doctrine to the life of the Church:

> While he is telling of his own affairs he is foretelling ours, and whilst he is telling his own griefs explicitly in speech, through tacit understanding he trumpets the trials of holy Church.[465]

These explanations of the great pope, distinguishing our "special" questions and the "common" response that the divine Word always brings to it, whether it be a question of "our affairs" in particular or those of the whole Church, were quite close to one of the rules of Tyconius, the rule called "de genere et specie." In the sacred texts, Tyconius distinguished, aside from their special sense, that of the letter, another more general sense; the first *(species)* was the figure *(typus)* of the second *(genus)*; the object of the first sense prefigured less a second particular fact than it clarified in advance, in general, a whole possible series of analogous situations.[466] Such a principle had its antecedents in the most classic conception of history, as well as in the Jewish and Philonian hermeneutics. It is in virtue of this principle that already in the Bible itself, as Saint Jerome had recalled, "frequently the history itself is woven metaphorically, and, under the image of a woman or a single man, something is predicated of the whole people."[467] The rule of Tyconius had been in a certain fashion canonized by Saint Augustine. Beatus of Liebana, among others, did not miss an opportunity to recall it and explicate it.[468] He applied it in the spirit of Saint Gregory, saying: "That which *then* will have been done *by way of appearance (specialiter)* is *now* to be understood *spiritually.*"[469] It was by that rule that Paschasius Radbertus, for example, was so inspired as to apply, as we have seen, the Lamentations of the Prophet to the misfortunes of a Christendom devastated by the Normans.[470] The

Pseudo-Alcuin had applied it more methodically and precisely to comment on the Apocalypse; he had pointed out examples of how "God's word passes from species to genus."[471] To be sure, neither that rule of Tyconius nor the explication of Saint Gregory constituted a contribution to the development of a scientific exegesis. They were nevertheless valuable. In its simplicity the second, in particular, bears the mark of Gregory's balance. As great an invitation as it was to run back to the Word of God at every juncture, it was also a warning against having to look in it for some sort of details and anticipations that it does not contain. It maintained an ever-open exegesis,[472] and at the same time it avoided in advance the curiosities which are an aberration of exegesis only because they are a perversion of the Christian sense from the start. It supposed an idea of divine revelation both total and pure. Only, in practice, everything is not always so tidy. The boundary from the one level to the other is not always clear-cut: it must be admitted that the passage from the design of a Gerhoh, for example, or even of a Rupert or a Bruno of Segni, to that of a Joachim of Flora was sometimes easy.

Moreover, as the time since the foundation of the Church grew longer, the development of its history naturally became more interesting as well. Thus a greater and greater need was felt to put order into it by distinguishing it into a certain number of periods, as had first been done for the history of the Patriarchs and for that of ancient Israel. This is what the *Historiae* of Ademar do, for example. After having run through the principal stages of history prior to Christ, following the twofold chronology of the Septuagint and the Hebrew, these *Historiae* expound the sequence of events that have unfolded since the birth of Christ, first "up to the passing of Saint Martin," then "up to the passing of Clovis, King of the Franks," and then "up to the first year of the reign of Charles," etc.[473] Nothing was more legitimate, or even, truth to tell, more indispensable. Elementary pedagogy required it. No doctrinal principle was involved. They did not attribute to these successive periods of Christian history the same character as to those that had marked each single distinct step in the history of salvation prior to the coming of Christ. For, as they knew, the "fullness of time" was no longer something to wait for or to prepare for.

Through this new angle, we once more find, attested by a constant tradition, the fundamental belief which was soon to present itself as a dike against the rising tides of the Joachimite dream. The Gospel, they knew, had inaugurated the final age of the earth. Following the most generally accepted system, such as after some hesitations Augustine had established,[474] once the five ages had passed that had marked off the wait for the Redeemer,[475] it was now the sixth age, at which the repose of the seventh day was immediately to follow, "that eternal repose," the "true Sabbath," the "Sabbath of perpetual contemplation," a day which would never know night.[476] "The sixth age was from John the Baptist up to the coming of Elijah,"[477] "until that world should be ended."[478] One could no longer add a seventh earthly age — or, following another manner of reckoning, an eighth — unless one could introduce a fourth state upon earth to follow upon the three states of nature, the Law, and then grace. Between the time of the Savior and the end of all times, he who would have wanted to conceive any intermediate time would have been brought into collision, not only with the symbolism of the number six or seven,[479] but more radically, with the consciousness of the whole Church of the definitively fulfilling character of the work accomplished by Jesus Christ: *the disclosure of the signs, the complete redemption of the human race.*[480] That was one of the great leitmotifs of the controversy with Judaism.[481] In the history of salvation, there could no longer be any appreciable delay between the two advents of the Savior in the midst of a homogeneous duration: "The whole time of the Church is to be related to that continued Day of Resurrection."[482] It was therefore more just a question of sketching in summary fashion, according to Scripture, the whole state of the Church "from the coming of the Savior up to the end of the age."[483] A few strokes would suffice. No more levels, no more stages, no more substantial advances, no further new revelations — except, as we have seen, the revelation of hearts, till the Judgment. Everything has been given. The end has truly come. "Behold, now is the acceptable time; now is the time of salvation."[484] All generations of Christians would therefore say it again in the wake of the Apostle: "We, who have come at the end of time," or "for whom the end of time has come";[485] after us, whatever might be the number of the generations that this "we" encompasses[486] and whatever the variety of their human history ought to be, there would be no more time until the last day, because there is no other "law" nor any other "testament" nor any other principle of "understanding" to wait for. There *can* not be anything more.

Only, why should this ever-so-long "end of time," which was always getting longer, and why should this sixth and final age, which was always extending further in duration, not be able to be subdivided?

It came about principally following two systems, each of which found a basis or symbolic illustration in the Bible and more specifically in Daniel and in the Apocalypse. More than one saw, along with Saint Bernard,[487] in the four horses (sometimes brought together with the four beasts of Daniel), the four great temptations that the Church had to face in the course of her history: first the persecutions of the pagan empire, then the heresies, subsequently the hypocrisy of her wicked children, while awaiting the final coming of the Antichrist.[488] Or else one enumerated the era of the apostles, that of the martyrs, that of the doctors, finally that of the bad Christians,[489] the last Antichrist before leading this last age to its paroxysm. Transposing the symbol of the four watches of the night that Honorius applied to the four ages of the world,[490] Gerhoh saw in those four watches the four principal defenders of the Church, who had to struggle perilously in their turn against idolatry, heresy, luxury, and finally, avarice, the last and worst of evils, which at the end of the night shook the barque of Peter most violently.[491] As for the historians, they more readily refer to the "mutatio regnorum" ["change of kingdoms"] announced by Daniel and they maintain the classic interpretation of it, acquired from the beginning of the Christian era: the fourth and last of the four realms was that of Rome. This is what Otto of Freising did, announcing at the beginning of his *Chronicle* his plan to distribute the whole history of the world among the four great kingdoms — a history which ran through the history of the Church and kept its time homogeneous.[492] But on the other hand Otto also took up in the course of the fourth kingdom Bernard's schema of four persecutions, four successive assaults undergone from without and from within by the "City of Christ."[493] A disciple of Saint Bernard, Gébouin de Troyes, systematized a schema of the fourfold tribulation ["tribulatio quadrifaria"] borrowed from Psalm 90, and illustrated it with a whole series of correspondences.[494]

Others, for a long time, appealed to the seven seals, lined with seven trumpets, the number of which from that time on signified no longer just the mysterious plenitude hidden of old within the ancient Scripture;[495] rather than signifying aspects or phases of the unique mystery of Christ, it now referred to slices of history starting from the first advent. This was a secondary usage, which for all that did not eliminate the primary, more dogmatic, deeper symbolism. There were certain intermediate forms. Thus it was for Ambrose Autpert in the eighth century, and then for Berengaud in the ninth. For Berengaud, the opening of the first four seals explained the four parts of the history of Israel up until Christ; the opening of the last three seals explained the New Testament, for, though the latter is the explanation of the Old Testament, there are some things in it that themselves call for explanation. The opening of the fifth seal therefore rendered an account of the era of the martyrs; that of the sixth, the rejection of the Jews and the calling of the Gentiles; that of the seventh, fi-

The Time of the Church

nally, coming up at the end, concerned the birth of Christ: for God rested on the seventh day and "what is our rest, except the Christ?"[496] The system is a bit complicated, obviously; it is a compromise, a transitional form, which did not yet in fact introduce well-marked divisions into the time-periods of the Church, which was quite entirely under the sign of the contrasted destiny of the Jews and the Gentiles. Yet Saint Bede, with his mind-set as a historian, had already proceeded more resolutely in the partitioning process:

> In the first seal, therefore, he takes up the beauty of the primitive Church; in the next three, the threefold war against her; in the fifth, the glory of those who triumph in this war; in the sixth, the things that are to come in the time of the Antichrist . . . ; in the seventh, the starting-point of eternal rest.[497]

The system was completed and organized during the twelfth century, a fertile epoch for attempts at the theology of history. The "seven-formed Church" ["septiformis Ecclesia"][498] at that point becomes generally the Church passing through seven successive situations in the course of her earthly pilgrimage, starting with the first preaching of the Gospel. Rupert, however, in commenting on the Apocalypse remarkably confines himself to the seven mysteries of Christ;[499] in his commentary on the Canticle, he distinguishes seven great persecutions, the last of the seven being before the one that will unchain the Antichrist, the first five all concerning the period of the Old Testament; as to the sixth, it is identified with all the trials that the Church of Christ endures during the course of her history: it is therefore, in fact, none other than the traditional sixth day, the sixth act of the great drama which, from the beginning of the world, sets at odds *Aquilo* and the *Auster*, the spirit of the devil and the Spirit of God.[500] But Honorius, yielding to the tendency that we have already noted in him, established a numerical parallel between the two Testaments: the Bride and the Groom of the Canticle are, he says, to lead twelve successive fights against divers sorts of adversaries: six before the advent of Christ, and six afterwards.[501] The same goes for Anselm of Havelberg (†1158), who takes up the views of Bede more systematically. He subdivides the long sixth day, casting the categories of Bernard into the sevenfold mold of the Apocalypse:

> The seven seals that John saw . . . are the seven successive states of the Church from the advent of Christ until all things will be consummated in the last one, and God will be all in all.[502]

Anselm, at that point, goes on to describe each of these six "states." After the marvelous novelty of the nascent Church, the persecutions soon come; then there was the epoch of the heresies; once they were vanquished one saw, in the fourth epoch, the false brethren, the Christian hypocrites, but also the development of the religious orders; the miseries of the Church will grow in a manner still indefinable during the following epoch; they will finally culminate, at the time of the sixth, in the great persecution raised by the Antichrist; after which, once the Judgment has supervened, there will be the Peace, the silence of contemplation, the jubilee year which will have no end.[503]

Richard of Saint Victor, faithful to the seven visions of Bede, is still clearer, if that is possible. For him, the seven seals are opened in due course, revealing their role a little bit at a time, "the manifold tribulations of holy Church from the beginning of grace up to the very end, and the followers of the beatitude of retribution";[504] but he does not hesitate to render more precise what Saint John had said to start with in global fashion about the mystery of redemption properly speaking, a mystery which is unique and which had been revealed as it had been realized — in a single stroke; in the successive opening of the seven seals, it will therefore be no more than a question of seeing such effects unfold from it, as are recorded the whole length of the time that follows:

> The things that are made distinct by the opening of the seals ... are related to the order of the sequence of time. In those following events, the virtues of the elect and persecutions of the reprobate against the elect and the tribulations of the suffering are described from the beginning of the nascent Church right down to the end of the world, and not all at once, once and for all, but following the disposition and opening of the seals and the advance of times they show in many ways that the aforesaid things are being completed a little at a time and in due course and that the hidden things are made plain.[505]

Moreover, for Richard, the seven heads, like the seven mountains and the seven kings, continue to designate the universality of the times or the states through which the human race passes: five prior to Christ, just one from Christ to the Antichrist, the seventh being that of the Antichrist, just at the end.[506] As to the seven sections, he sees them grow empty at the beginning of the Christian era, as a chastisement upon those who are opposed to the preaching of salvation; but each of them determines much less a fraction of the history than a spiritual category of the reprobates:

The Time of the Church

But the outpouring of the vessels betokens the bringing in of the divine wrath against a diversity of men. The first outpouring is against the land, namely the Judea first reproved by the faith. . . . The second is against the sea, i.e., the gentiles, the slaughterers of the faithful. The third is against the rivers and mountains, i.e., the heretics that corrupt what flows from the Sacred Page. The fourth is against the sun, namely, the Antichrist, who says that he enlightens the world. The fifth is against the seat of the Beast, i.e., the princes of the peoples among whom the Antichrist himself will preside. The sixth is against the river Euphrates, i.e., the reprobate among the baptized. . . . The seventh is against the air, namely, the demons.[507]

Not only for Richard, but also for Honorius and for Anselm of Havelberg, and soon for Gerhoh, as well as for Anselm of Laon[508] and for the others in that twelfth century, in these divers subdivisions and symbolic correspondences it would therefore be less a question of history, even specifically religious history, than of spirituality. Here it is not the exterior aspect of the facts that rivets our attention, but the life of the Church considered in its relation to God. If one still wants an example drawn from the previous century, let him read the developments of Saint Bruno of Segni on the six periods revealed by the successive opening of the seven seals; just one single word defines them all: "praedicatio" [preaching]; only an ordinal numeral distinguishes them: "prima, secunda, tertia, etc."; only regarding the sixth is any precision made, but without any further detail: "which last preaching we think will be the one in which Enoch and Elijah are to come."[509] Bruno had begun by saying: "I looked and I saw the whole fabric of the Church, and whatever was to come unto the consummation of the age"; but no mention of any event corresponds to this announcement; there is no report, no prediction: what Bruno is contemplating is merely the great spiritual fact of the Church, of the resistance that it continually opposes through her preaching to the enemies of God.[510] One could hardly be more sober and less curious. Saint Bernard, faithful to the great principle of the mystic identity reigning between the Church and the soul, used to say that he wanted to expound the "four general temptations in the Church and the four special ones in each soul."[511] We have seen above what the third temptation consisted in: that "hypocrisy," that attitude of the "false brethren," the "false Christians," the "false Catholics," of the merely "nominal faithful,"[512] already denounced by Bede,[513] by Beatus,[514] by the Pseudo-Alcuin,[515] and which in the twelfth century constituted the object of constant concern for the spirituals. Preachers used to cry out one after the other: "What false brethren! Behold this is the time of the false brethren!" It was, they used to say, the "disease in the shadows" ["negotium in tenebris"], a graver evil than the "night terror" ["timor nocturnus"] of the persecutors and the "flying arrow" ["sagitta volans"] of the heretics, because it was more deeply interior and more hidden: "the internal, incurable plague of the Church" ["intestina et insanabilis plaga Ecclesiae"]. Isaiah had announced it when he said: "Ecce in pace amaritudo mea amarissima" [Behold! My bitterest bitterness is found in peace]. Godfrey of Admont even wanted to see in it the only temptation of the time of the Church between the end of the era of the martyrs at the beginning of the fourth century and the persecution of the last Antichrist; he used to symbolize it by the second temptation of Jesus, when the devil had transported him atop the parapet of the Temple:

> Since the painful enemy had been ringed within the patience and perseverance of the martyrs, he took another tack and introduced the incurable plague of hypocrisy which today winds its way through the whole body of the Church. By 'the pinnacle', i.e., the professor's chair, we take the prelates who, whilst they show themselves in the garb of Christ's humble ministers, hurl themselves down through hypocrisy at the devil's persuasion and more serve the Antichrist; they all seek things of their own kind, they all rush upon avarice and advancing in honor they do not pay it back to him to whom they owe honor.[516]

In virtue of the same principle as Saint Bernard, Richard of Saint Victor took it upon himself chiefly to show how God, the author of all the goods that adorn the rational creature, "distributes the grace of spiritual wisdom upon his own in many forms in variety and in the course of time so as to gather them together to one state of eternity."[517] His commentary on the Apocalypse abounds in methodical divisions and subdivisions of the time of the Church: now there is always a question of preaching, of conversions, persecutions, heresies, temptations, tribulations, graces, etc., without there ever being any allusion to any fact of history except for those facts that are mentioned in Scripture itself. Commenting on the Divine Office, Rupert also confines himself to a completely spiritual history: in the liturgical readings of the summer months, he wanted to see prefigurations of four periods that marked successively the triumph of the martyrs over idolatry, the schisms aroused by heresy, the doctrine fixed by the doctors, the internal trials of the Church at the time of external peace and prosperity; then, in the readings from the following months, there were the four cardinal virtues; then the struggle against the vices; and finally, the approach of the end times announced by the prophets.[518] As to Honorius, who, like Richard of Saint Victor, liked to multiply divisions when he applied himself in his *Epitome Psalterii* to a partition of the history of the Church into fifteen "decades," he too sketched merely a quite spiritual schema, without any more reference to a specific date or fact than is to be found in Bruno of Segni, Rupert, or Richard.[519] And when Saint Hildegard, in a symbolic vision whose details are not scriptural, sees in the regions of the North five ferocious beasts that correspond to the whole historical course of the temporal realms, she has no intention of designating some determinate realm corresponding to each of these beasts.[520]

What is essential among these characteristics is found again in the thought of Saint Martin of Leon, who is exactly contemporary with Joachim of Flora. He, like Joachim, died in 1203. Like him, he too composed his principal works only at a rather advanced age, after his entry into the monastery of Saint Isidore in 1185. Like him, at almost the same date or a bit later, he commented on the Apocalypse; finally, he brought his writings together in two large volumes which got the title *Concordia*, so as to feature its dominant idea, that of a "concord between the authorities of the two Testaments."[521]

As had been done since antiquity, Martin of Leon divides the history of salvation into a certain number of ages; he reckons on six of them: from Adam to Noah, from Noah to Abraham, from Abraham to Moses, from Moses to David, from David to Christ, and finally from Christ to the time of the return of Enoch and Elijah.[522] As was currently being done in his century, he also distinguished a certain number of successive states or situations in the time of the Church which develops starting from Christ. To him, the four first states show up in relation with the four horses of the Apocalypse: the preachers of the Gospel are designated by the white horse; the persecutors, by the red horse; the Jews and Gentiles, by the black horse; and the heretics, by the pale horse. We have entered the fifth state, where the rage of heresy has become less furious, but where hypocrisy reigns. A new situation will have been created by the coming of the Antichrist, and then there will be the seventh and last situation, that of the Judgment.[523] There, however, it is not a question, however, of clear-cut successions, but rather of dominant features: thus, the first state was not said to be that of the first apostles or the first preachers; thus again, the Jews and the Gentiles that the Church had to convert confronted her from the very first day; in the situation where the heretics dominated, it is again a question of persecution and already of hypocrisy, etc. But more precisely, Martin of Leon carefully distinguished the states and the ages. The seven states that we have just seen were all contained within the sixth age, the one "in which our reparation has been made," the one which lasts from the coming of the Lord "up to the day of judgment."[524] The succession of the ages of the world marks an advance in divine revelation: now, at the beginning of the sixth age, the revelation is complete; through the death and resurrection of the Savior, the mysteries of Christ and the Church have been both accomplished and revealed. The seven seals of the Apocalypse have been removed. If there had been seven of them, that was for two quite simple reasons, recalled once again: "since the universe is figured in terms of seven, or since it is enlightened by the seven-formed Spirit."[525] The symbolic book was "the divine plan for the reparation of the human race," that disposition hidden within the Old Testament, manifested in the New; the opening of the Book and the redemption of the human race are one and the same.[526] At one point, however, Saint Martin of Leon says, a bit more restrictively, that the mysteries at that time had been "in large part fulfilled,"[527] but this was not with a view to saving a new stage for the future; he is merely, like Rupert, thinking of the supreme day of Judgment, which will reveal the secret of hearts and which will mark the entry into the seventh age, that age which will no longer be an age of the world, properly speaking, but eternity itself. "For there are only six ages of the world."[528]

The thought of Joachim of Flora and the climate of Joachimism are evidently of a completely different character.

5. The Antichrist

Up till now, research into the elements that could in any respect have prepared the way for the Joachimite doctrine has revealed to us more contrasts than analogies. Nevertheless, let us pursue our inquiry.

Joachim of Flora believes that he perceives the signs that are precursors of the Antichrist. But did not the whole twelfth century before him believe that it perceived them as well? Such was already the view of Saint Norbert on his deathbed, according to a report made by Saint Bernard.[529] Saint Bernard himself believed as much, howsoever little disposed he might have been to the letter of Norbert's prognostications. Does he not conclude the somber depictions he draws of the present world with these observations: "The Angel of Satan is already working the mysteries of iniquity,"[530] or again: "It now remains for the man of sin, the son of perdition, to be revealed"?[531] Such too was the view of the author of a discourse attributed to him before the congregation at Reims: "Behold these plainly filthy times.... The Church's affliction is in her guts and incurable.... All that is left is for the noonday devil to arise from her midst.... For he is Antichrist."[532] In the middle of the century, Bernard of Cluny felt the same, singing in his bewitching rhythm:

> This latest hour, let's be on watch, the times are very bad ...
> What holds us back? A wild, a threatening Antichrist is there ...
> This foretells he's near at hand or shows the Antichrist is
>   here....[533]

So, too, much closer to Joachim, was Saint Hildegard, in one of her visions: "The son of perdition is coming in a very short time, since the day is already receding, the sun setting into the west, namely when the last time is already falling and the world is losing its hold."[534] Citations of this kind could well be multiplied.[535] Here again, however, so as not to exaggerate their import, it will be good to recall a few facts.

First of all, one will recall that it was a commonplace, transmitted from century to century. A Saint Cyprian, a Saint Hilary, a Saint Jerome, or a Saint Ambrose had spoken of the aging of the world, in a language not entirely devoid of a whiff of classical antiquity. "Behold the world totters and slips, and attests its downfall no longer by the oldness of things but by their end."[536] And again: "The ultimate age of the world has been crammed full with evils, like old age with sicknesses.... That day is driving us on, no longer merely our day, but that of the epoch as well."[537] Or, as a fifth-century bishop from Aquitaine, a real poet, put it:

> All things, weary, look down upon their aging end
>   And the hour is already turning with the last-most day.
> Note how death is suddenly to squeeze the whole world.[538]

In the time of Saint Gregory, the agony of Rome had seemed to presage the agony of the world, or even to be confused with it: "We ought to ponder that nothing that we have loved was left for the destruction of all things."[539] It might seem that the horror of the barbarous times that followed had heightened this feeling of the end: "The world is growing old!" "The end of the world is approaching!"⁵⁴⁰ But what age does not judge itself miserable? In the time of the Carolingian renaissance, Paschasius Radbertus saw evils increasing around him of such a sort that, he thought, "Next is that the ultimate evil should come, worse than this one."⁵⁴¹ And, from generation to generation, the litany continues. What keeps us from taking these formulas completely at face value is, for one, their literary, conventional character — almost out of an etiquette book.⁵⁴² This is also why, after having bewailed their situation, many have second thoughts: "But not yet right away. . . ."⁵⁴³ Thus they immediately add: "Our forefathers have passed away, we shall go away, our posterity will follow."⁵⁴⁴ After having announced the last hour, they still point to the means of postponing the day of reckoning.⁵⁴⁵

Among so many evocations of an imminent end, there are some, however, that expressed merely an indisputable human wisdom.⁵⁴⁶ Others rendered a fundamental Christian truth better by using contrasting aspects of it. Saint Eucher put one of these two aspects in sharp relief in his dissertation addressed to Valerian on the contempt of the world:

> All the painted glitter falls to the ground. The world now scarcely has the wherewithal to deceive. . . . Every intention of the mind is to be directed to the hope of what is to come.⁵⁴⁷

In the same way, following Saint Gregory,⁵⁴⁸ Saint Ambrose Autpert, in some happy formulations of a more theological character says:

> God's Son says, however, that he will come quickly, since, though all the time of the present life be prolonged by long periods of delays, it nevertheless shows by its very course — since it does not stand but passes — that it is quickly ending. Because of its very quick course, John defines its quantity by the period of a single hour, when he says, "My son, it is the last hour."⁵⁴⁹

But the other aspect of the question was no less considered by the eyes of faith. Some years after Ambrose Autpert, Claudius of Turin put it in these terms:

> But if someone should ask me how long a time or how many years the present mortal age ought to last, I profess that I do not know, since I do not recall ever having read it; and yet I do not blush at my inexperience, since I am not taught by reading; nor do I fear any dan-

ger, since I also do not presume upon what I do not read, lest I be found to be a transgressor against the divine oracle who answers the apostles questioning him about it as follows: 'No one knows the day and the hour'.[550]

And soon Paschasius Radbertus united both aspects so as to draw the same lesson from them:

> [The Lord] works the day of his coming every day among the wakeful, while he comes within the souls of those who are enlightened by the light of truth, . . . and he completely sums up why he concealed the day and the hour of his coming when he says: "Be wakeful, since you do not know the day and the hour" — as if to say: I wanted you not to know, so that you should always be wakeful and always be ready when your Lord is about to come, lest the darkness of night or the drowsiness of sleep should steal you away.[551]

Doubtless it was in the spirit of Gregory and of Autpert, and without any idea of calculated chronology, that Otto of Freising, who does not seem to have doubted the solidity of the empire, on seeing the end approach, which would at the same stroke be the end of time, nevertheless said:

> For we are experiencing what has been foretold about the end of what has been laid down, and we are awaiting in fear what is to come in what remains next. . . .
>
> And notice that these times of ours — which are especially believed to be the last, as being about to put an end to past crimes and as threatening the end of the world for its shamelessness and, contrary-wise, foreseeing the approaching kingdom of Christ — just as these times have some most criminal and eager lovers of the world, as I have said, so do they have others ablaze with God's zeal and brimming with heavenly desire; so that, just as the spirit of iniquity, still having a bit of time, consequently inflames the former still more toward their vices, so too the sweetness of the heavenly kingdom, as though already at the gates, attracts the latter to love it still more.[552]

More than any particular, reliable forecast, such texts express the tension within the Christian consciousness, an awareness of both the precariousness of earthly existence and the incessant urgency of the final end. Other considerations, however, intervened as well. The best, just as much as the worst, predicted the final fall. Toward the beginning of the twelfth century, the twofold scepter of power and knowledge seems to have reached the westernmost extreme or limit. In virtue of a law of spatio-temporal harmony, many concluded from this twofold *translatio*, that the life of the age had to be at its final phase. Hugh of Saint Victor echoed this conviction in his *De arca Noe morali*:

> Through divine providence it seems to have been so arranged that the things that were being done at the beginning of the world were subsequently also done up to the end, until the high-point began to settle toward the sunset of things, so that we might know that the end of the age is approaching, precisely because the course of things is already touching the end of the world. . . . The first man was in the East. . . . Again, after the flood, the chief of the kingdoms and the head of the world was in Assyria and among the Chaldeans and Medes in eastern regions. Then it came to the Greeks. Finally, around the end of the epoch it came to the Romans in the west, as to those dwelling at the end-point of the world. Afterwards the high-point descended.[553]

Does it follow that "in the higher circles of the Church" at that time "the anxious expectation of the last judgment" was dominant? Should "the intellectuals" around the years 1080-1120, "ceasing to live, as did so many previous generations, with their eyes fixed upon an exemplary but over-turned golden age," be supposed to "be anxiously on the lookout for the signs that were precursors of the end of time"?[554] We do not think so. One could well believe in the sunset of the age, all the while hoping that this majestic sunset would still last a long time. The historians of the Middle Ages put our submissiveness to the test: first they have spoken to us of the terrors of a millennial year, the obvious signs of which they enumerated; then they have tried to make us notice that "the true day of reckoning" had been "the millennium of the redemption," which obliged us to antedate the fateful terrors by thirty or forty years. Lo and behold, now we are invited to a new leap forward.[555] But in fact the men living around the year 1100 express themselves rather like their predecessors, an Odo of Cludy,[556] an Arnoul of Orleans[557] and many others. *Tempus Antichristi jam instat [The Time of the Antichrist is Already Nigh]*. Doubtless, in the course of the twelfth century — and still more after 1120 — the allusions to the forthcoming arrival of the Antichrist are numerous. But one would deceive himself about their precise import if he did not see that, except perhaps among certain hermits, they constitute then, more than ever, a veritable literary genre, which was adopted by moralists, reformers, and polemicists, who are apt to dramatize the situation.[558] "Charity is growing cold," the barque of the Church capsizes, the world is falling to ruin, we have entered into the "last watch of the night."[559] Each and every public misfortune, each abuse, each plague of the Church is a premonition of the ultimate catastrophe. It is a demonstration of hostility on the part of "the ancient enemy" against Christ and his Church, a new act of the great battle whose decisive phase stands in profile at the horizon. The Antichrist has always been at work here below in his "members": Was not Cain already, in the dictum of Saint Gregory, one of them?[560] Just as every sinner is a member of the "body of the devil," each heretic, each proud or scandalous prelate, each antipope[561] is Antichrist, because he is member or minister or preacher[562] or precursor of the last Antichrist.[563] So too is anyone who is separated from the unity [of the Church].[564] The same goes for every monk, every canon, every layman — every man who does not live according to justice, or who attacks the rule of his state in life, or who blasphemes what is good.[565] Of each of them one can say: "He is already going before the face of the Antichrist to prepare his ways." Alas, in each generation, numerous are the "new and modern Antichrists," who are heirs of those of the past.[566] "There are already many Antichrists within the Church."[567] Every spiritually miserable situation indicates the presence of him who is in all things the adversary and antithesis of Christ: "The Antichrist is, unless I am mistaken, he who both precedes and accompanies the fruitless craving of the good as a whole."[568] For that name does not come to him, as certain "simple" people imagine, from the fact that in the future he ought to precede the return of Christ, but rather from the fact that he does not cease to be opposed to him.[569] One recognizes him most particularly in the persecutor kings: not only in those great persecutors of times gone by — an Antiochus, a Nero, a Domitian — but also in those today who pretend to be Christians, like that Henry II Plantagenet, who was responsible for the murder of Thomas Becket, who has a prominent place in the poem by Gautier de Châtillon *De adventu Antichristi*:

> So why do you seek any other precursor
> Than that twisted ruler of Britain
> Who against law and custom with three swords
> Impudently mowed down the flower of priests?[570]

These ways of speaking, if not their abuse, could be justified by Saint John, who had in his first Epistle announced the coming of many antichrists. They could also be justified by Saint Paul, teaching that the "mystery of iniquity" was at work in this world, before manifesting itself in its fullness.[571] Isidore of Seville had recalled it, and the canonists had codified his utterances; thus the *Decretum* of Burchard of Worms says: "Everyone who either does not live according to the norm of his profession or teaches at variance with it is Antichrist."[572] In short, no name was more common; none was imposed more often than that one. Every "pseudo-Christian" was a "pseudo-Christ" and an "anti-Christ," just as he was a "son of Cain." "There are many pseudo-Christs and very many antichrists."[573]

In a sense, there is something reassuring in that. For if the Antichrist has come so often in the past, even if he should be pullulating at this moment, he would still be able to come back without the universe collapsing or the structure of the Church being subverted thereby. Many who will not always be the *novissimus Antichristus,* "the very last Antichrist," will still be able to play havoc. In this rhetoric, there is no trace of coldly objective calculation. If it is true that for the whole length of the Middle Ages — and the modern age, if not more, can also be said to be included — "an undiscerning curiosity had closed its eyes to this evidence" that the Day of the Lord is unknown, if it is true that here or there "someone has taken pleasure in vain calculations to attempt to determine the duration of the world,"[574] this is not altogether true of the theological tradition in the centuries that we are studying. Rather than follow Saint Jerome, who had taken too literally, like Saint Hippolytus, the equivalence of a thousand years and one day,[575] that tradition generally followed Saint Augustine, condemning along with him "the audacity of those men who dare to presume knowledge of the time," with him scoffing or complaining against the "misguided vanity" of those who gave credence to their "contrived divination."[576] To each generation of the faithful, that tradition used to say again and again that it is useful for us both to know that the last day is to come, and not to know when it will come.[577] Along with Paschasius Radbertus, it used to say: "Human frailty ought to be content, lest it crave to know too curiously what can doubtless be most advantageous even not to know."[578] It did not cease to proclaim and to preach: "The time remaining in the sixth age is known but to God";[579] "We dare not reckon the times. . . . When the end will be is doubtless hidden";[580] "The Lord wanted the time or day of judgment to be unknown to us";[581] "What is left for you, O man, is not to be known, but is within the Father's secret."[582] All Christians, it used to say again, live within the "thousand years" that separate the second coming from the first,[583] but this number of a thousand, which one utters of years, of generations or of centuries, is, like ten and like a hundred, a symbolic number.[584] It designates a collection, a plenitude; it is the number of universality. Scripture posits it as "something determinate used to stand for something indeterminate." Hence one must be on guard against believing those who would wish, using it, to calculate, in one fashion or another, the duration of our world.[585] That real duration can be longer — or shorter. "The sixth age, which is in progress now, with no specified length of years": in repeating this point, Hugh of Saint Victor expressed a common wisdom.[586] And now, at the end of the twelfth century, at the very moment when Joachim of Flora is prophesying, Saint Martin of Leon says once again: "Owing to its perfection, this number signifies all time present from the passion of our Lord up to the end of the age."[587]

No more than it is necessary to try to estimate and combine digits is it necessary to rely on the order of words and events in reading the Apocalypse. "Since the Holy Spirit often returns again to the self-same times where he has already run his course to the end of the latest time":[588] this is the so-called principle of "recapitulation" that was at issue previously. Moreover, within the very interior of each section of the book, in what John recounts as the events of a drama it is necessary to know how to recognize spiritual facts, which are surely not "timeless" truths, but which form, as it were, the tissue of the militant life of the Church and which take place each day:

> "And there was a great battle in heaven," etc. Far be it from the hearts of the faithful that they should believe that this battle was waged just when the ancient foe fell from heaven through pride along with his minions. Rather it is to be maintained that without any doubt it is being waged from the very beginning of the Christian faith right up to the end of the present life.
>
> The dragon falls from heaven to earth every day.[589]

Even those among our theologians who make the most copious use of apocalyptic imagery show clearly through their explications that they know what to hang on to: they are looking for the "truth" signified by these "images."[590] They are able to put it quite tidily: "Nothing in this Apocalypse is easy to understand literally." So, for example, let no one believe that on the great awaited Day the Lord is going to descend on a white cloud![591] The Antichrist, the beast with seven horns and ten heads, the mystery of iniquity, are expressions whose spiritual significance is to be discovered — not, however, exclusive of every historical[592] or eschatological[593] reference. Even the return of Enoch and Elijah at the very end might well turn out not to be a literal fact:[594] such is the opinion, from the time of the Fathers, of most, perhaps even all, of the doctors;[595] in any case, under the name of those two illustrious "witnesses," "many other preachers are also understood."[596] A fortiori, one ought not really to imagine, as is done in certain legendary or poetic writings,[597] the single combat in which the archangel Saint Michael will exterminate the Antichrist: it is doubtless a highly symbolic idea which causes the great Adversary to perish on the very spot of the Ascension, where he had pitched his tent, but here the archangel is merely the invisible minister of the invisible "power of the Lord Jesus."[598] The abyss, the key of which another angel holds in his hand, is, if not the devil himself, the shadowy heart of the impious; the smoke that rises from the depths of the abyss is the wicked doctrine of the heretics.[599] The angel seizes the dragon: this dramatization signifies that Jesus Christ is unveiling the sin of the devil; he chains him up for the duration of a thousand years: that is to say, the demonic power is, from the time of Christ's passion till the coming of the last Antichrist, (relatively) bound; he plunges him into the abyss: that is, through a judgment that still remains hidden, the Lord hands the heart of hardened infidels over to Satan.[600] Or yet again, that abyss from which the beast must one day be drawn, is perhaps the abyss of God's judgments, according to the expression in the Psalm: "The Lord's judgments are a manifold abyss."[601]

It would nonetheless be "frivolous" to want to fix geographical and historical coordinates for the two henchmen of the devil, Gog and Magog, as "the Jews and certain Judaizers among us" would do. Long ago Josephus had believed that he could recognize them in the Scythians, those peoples naturally "devoid of charity" who had left a terrible memory behind them.[602] Later on, they were just as surely identified with the Getes and Massagetes, or else the Goths, sometimes identified with them and sometimes distinguished from them. Then, once the Scyths, Getes and Goths had been taken by Isidore as a single people long ago domesticated in the countries of the West,[603] Gog and Magog then turned into the Huns, the new redoubtable barbarians. Others wanted to recognize them in those factious tribes further off than the ancient "Scythian races" whom Alexander the Great, after having called upon the God of Israel, had at last shut up behind high mountains and who had since then prolif-

The Antichrist

erated into an immense and savage multitude.[604] Finally, in recent times, they had become the Hungarians (Ungri, Hungares, Ungari), they too having come from Scythia. Their more recent invasion stupefied the imagination: "Cursed race! Monstrous nation! Barbarous and wild in language and customs! Race of Hungarians, crueler than any beast."[605] But our theologians protest. Such assimilations, they say, proceed from a false principle. In reality, Gog and Magog are two peoples sui generis, peoples not "corporeal," but rather "mystical,"[606] and their mustering will be done "not in a place but in thought"; it is the mob of sinners, unfortunately always numerous, of impure spirits, or of vices. Or else, if following Saint Jerome one observes that Gog signifies "covert" and Magog "overt," one will understand that these two names, which are to be taken "ad allegoriam," designate all the persecutors, hidden or open, of the Church. The war that the saints ought to wage against them is therefore "a spiritual war," and the city that these persecutors besiege now is no other than the soul of those saints; it is the city of which it is said in the Gospel: "A city placed on a hill cannot be hidden."[607] Who could reasonably doubt that everything in that book ought so to be understood since it is a "completely mystical" book? There is "nothing true" in suppositions of a "historical" order that many, in their curiosity, let themselves indulge in. Let us set aside these "Jewish fables."[608] They are deceptive exegeses, "human opinions, not divine."[609] They are explorations condemned in advance at their very starting-point, because they proceed from a carnal mind-set.

Thus the theological tradition, from age to age, engages in an unabated struggle against popular superstition, which belongs no more to that time than to any other. It has taken care to avoid not only such or such legendary features that were not based upon the letter of Scripture,[610] but also everything that might smack of anthropomorphism or mythology in the interpretation of that letter.[611] It was tenaciously opposed to the materialization of revealed doctrine. Already for Isidore of Seville, "Mosoch and Tubal" as well as "Gog and Magog" were merely figures, along with others, of the great persecution that was to assail the Church of God.[612] After him, the Ambrose Autperts and Aimons of Auxerre issued the same sort of spiritual and rational explanations. Adson of Montier-en-Der and Abbo of Fleury, each in his own way, rejected the ever-renewed efforts to calculate and predict the end of time.[613] The commentators of the eleventh and twelfth centuries, men like Bruno of Segni,[614] or Rupert, or Gerhoh, or Martin of Leon[615] repeat the same age-old lesson. The "mystery of iniquity" does not cease to act, they say, *hic et nunc.* The time of the Antichrist has arrived, from of old, from forever and aye, since all the persecutions, all the "temptations," all the setbacks of religion, all the audacities of impiety, whatever their nature or manner, proceed from the Antichrist and manifest the "mystery of iniquity."[616] Thus each of our commentators, in denouncing the kind of evil that he sees the Church infested with, essentially takes up the teaching of Saint Gregory; many, the pope used to say, hope that they will be spared the pain of living in the time of the Antichrist, and do not perceive that they already bear it within themselves; "Cain did not live in the epoch of the Antichrist and yet, through his sinful deed, he was himself a member of the Antichrist."[617]

Gerhoh of Reichersberg, as we have said, is one of the writers who at that time most appeared to systematize the somber prognostications and to venture further upon the terrain of exterior facts. Nevertheless, he too at times puts a stop to it all. He discusses at length the scriptural passages that some had believed they could call on to confirm the career of the Antichrist as they represented it: his origin from the tribe of Dan, his coming from Babylon, his installation in the Temple of Jerusalem, his victory over the three kings mentioned by Daniel, etc. But none of all this, he concludes, has a serious basis; in particular, the temple of God at issue in the sacred texts is not a temple made by human hands.[618] Above all, Gerhoh absolutely does not want to be considered "a curious inquirer into secrets"; he says as much in the preface to his treatise *De investigatione Antichristi,* the title of which may be a bit misleading:

> Let no one think, however, that I intend through speech or writing to frighten human beings, as though the day of the Lord is impending; since all my speech is quite free of prejudgment regarding the future, and I know by whom it was said that "it is not our business to know the times or moments. . . ." Rather my whole speech aims to demonstrate that the past events of the Church and the deeds of her enemies against her are adequate for fulfilling the Scriptures that speak of the Antichrist, even though he may not come in a form of the beast such as the vulgar think the Antichrist will come in.[619]

There is always, as we see, the same care in matters of this sort not to admit anything but, as Saint Peter Damian used to recommend, "sober thinking,"[620] to base nothing upon the imaginations of the "vulgar," to avoid all "historical" curiosities and all illusory calculations contrary to the very spirit of Christianity. This last reservation was sometimes

The Antichrist

pushed so far that it had led some to declare it impossible to foretell even the duration of the delay granted for repentance between the fall of the Antichrist and the very last day, namely the day of the Judgment: "otherwise, human beings could know the time of the judgment of that age."[621]

That general attitude, evidenced in serried ranks from century to century until the time of Joachim of Flora, to us seems to manifest anything but "a most pitiable confusion between history and figure, between poetic imagery and speculative elaborations." The use of "allegory" in the explanation of the Apocalypse and of other sacred texts, whether of the Old or of the New Testament, which are concerned with ultimate ends, did not come "to vitiate twice over chronologies emptied of their historical relativity." Quite the contrary. When medieval exegetes so insistently warned their reader that he had to scrutinize such texts "subtly," where "there resounds nothing historical,"[622] "nothing is to be taken as historical,"[623] and "nothing is reported as historical fact,"[624] this warning was evidently not to deter him from studying the historical circumstances of their redaction or of examining "the traditions and legends of Jewish origin that Saint John used for his draft," tasks where no stone should be left unturned if one wants to undertake scientific work, though, for the explication of the Book itself, they can, as one recent exegete put it, constitute "merely a starting-point."[625] They wanted to guard precisely against those risks that one sometimes a bit too hastily believes that they were habitually a prey to. If their allegorical "moralism," inherited especially from Saint Gregory,[626] had its risks also for him, at least in such a subject it would have tended to obviate rather than to provoke "anthropomorphic divagations."[627] Their Christological and ecclesial exegesis — which, according to the normal rhythm of allegory and tropology, becomes anthropological and "spiritual" only at a subsequent time — baffles our current habits of mind when taken in its detailed applications and corollaries; their incessant research into the "mystica sacramenta" hidden "under the figures of names or images"[628] often appears arbitrary to us. The idea that some of them (not all, for if some followed Saint Jerome here, others rallied behind the more moderate opinion of Saint Augustine[629]) contrive of Johannine symbolism — an idea that would use sensible images to translate an intuition of the contemplated mystery directly into some sort of entirely "intellectual" vision, "through pure understanding, all imagination having been eliminated"[630] — can be regarded as just too sublime. It is at least certain that they had thereby been kept from taking so many formulas of apocalyptic style, so many predictions of cosmic prodigies, so many scenes of strange persons or marvels, for anything other than just what each of them is in reality; they were not totally unaware of certain contemporary allusions, they in fact meant to take account of,[631] but this scarcely held them back from using figures that are indefinitely able to be exploited for the good of the Church, from the deepest dogmatic substance, or from the great spiritual drama that plays itself out in the Church for the salvation of the world. The temple of the Lord in heaven: Christ in the Church;[632] a third part of the moon having been struck: those who have perished by heresy;[633] the hand of an angel: the dispensation of human redemption;[634] the sound of hail: the lash of persecution;[635] the earth assists the woman: Christ has given his Church powers of endurance;[636] etc. They also thought that many symbols could designate one and the same reality: e.g., "the open temple, the tabernacle, and heaven — this is all the one Church," etc.[637] They knew that it was possible to frighten simple people or to delude them with chimerical hopes by taking certain descriptions, certain predictions, in their material sense, but they did not regard it as right to do so:

> All these things taken literally also strike great fear in their hearers; words of figurative expression are not, for that reason, to be bent violently to the literal sense.[638]

In fact, in this book which is "full of parabolical obscurities,"[639] Saint John speaks like all the prophets, and that which has so often been put forward against the unbelieving Jews by explaining the messianic prophecies of the Old Testament, could not be forgotten or repudiated now. The author of the Apocalypse does not speak directly "with the truth"; he speaks "in signs and figures," and moreover, his terrifying visions, the likenesses by which he upholds and lifts up our hope, are not to be taken literally. His realism is grounded quite otherwise! Through these beautiful images, he wants to suggest to us something of the invisible splendors. The heaven that he half-opens to our eyes, that heaven where the Lamb is reigning, has nothing in common with our cosmic heaven, the one we look at when lifting our head; there is nothing local about it; it admits of neither up nor down; its inhabitants are not carrying palms in their hands nor wearing crowns on their heads. Everything that he has told, or rather sung, to us about the future state of the holy Church is "foreshadowed in colorful speeches."[640] In short, if one wants to understand anything about the Apocalypse, he must read it in a state of mind analogous as much as possible to that of Saint John taken up in ecstasy at Patmos:

"And I was turned around, so that I would see the voice that was speaking with me." For, having been turned to the spiritual understanding, blessed John saw and understood that Word which was speaking with him. So too you who desire to understand this prophecy will turn around, so that you taste no fleshly wisdom but are wholly taken to the spiritual understanding.[641]

Thus, without suppressing the eschatology, but rather purifying it, the doctrine of *intelligentia spiritualis* or spiritual understanding permitted our ancient exegetes to hold in check a historical curiosity and an apocalyptic mindset that are, let us say it again, present more or less at all times, and that were always rising again among them. The spiritual understanding also contributed to inhibit certain forms of temporal messianism that were being encouraged in royal or imperial circles, which were then exploiting the little treatise on the Antichrist composed in the tenth century by Adson of Montier-en-Der and interpolated toward the year 1000 by the hermit Albuin.[642] It modified the spirit of temporal messianism. The commonly received doctrine of the transfer of imperial power ["translatio imperii"] that these circles came to exploit at the service of their policy, was soon to become a means for the theologians periodically to reassure the faithful in the face of the dreaded imminence of the end.[643] It allowed an unruffled vision of the future, echoing the words that Virgil attributed to Jupiter regarding the Romans:

For them I fix neither goalposts nor time limits:
I have given them unending command.[644]

In fact, that which should have been recognized in the Christian empire of the West,[645] or in the very city of Rome, or, increasingly, in the pontifical power, "the priesthood and the See of Rome"[646] — the mysterious "obstacle" mentioned by Saint Paul, that obstacle which the fevered rhetoric of Saint Jerome had already shown to have been overthrown long ago[647] — was now looked upon as solid. Its disappearance could well be the sign of the end of the world.[648] But the fourth kingdom predicted by Daniel, once metamorphosed, was not close to collapsing. One could build upon the "romana diuturnitas," Roman durability, more than in the past.[649] The serried Christians gathered around the new Rome could well put up with disorders, endure scandals, without believing that that last day had come, the thought of which still remained essential to their faith.

In its general outlines, such was the eschatology of our authors.

Those among them whom some have suggested to be taken as a separate group under the name of the German school[650] — Rupert, Honorius, Gerhoh, Anselm of Havelberg — do not really constitute an exception. Despite certain features that we have mentioned above, their doctrine is fundamentally the same as that of people like Bruno of Segni, Martin of Leon or Richard of Saint Victor. For both the one group and the other, the manner of understanding the Apocalypse is shared, because they all use the same principle of interpretation. It is precisely that doctrine, that principle of interpretation, sometimes inexactly described as "idealist," which turns out to be missing in Joachim.[651]

The eschatology of the Abbot of Flora is extremely complicated. It is methodically constructed through a system of concordance established between the texts of the Apocalypse and those of the other sacred books, notably Daniel, Ezekiel, and the first Epistle to the Thessalonians. There can be no question of summarizing it here. Besides, he himself cautions us that we cannot now know these things as those who will see them will know them,[652] and his various explanations from one work to another are perhaps difficult to reconcile perfectly with each other. We shall retain merely their essential character: the care of representation in some historical and chronological way which is at their base, as it was at the base of the whole concord of the two Testaments; thus there is one capital feature: the distribution of the eschatological facts predicted by Scripture into two separate and distinct phases, a transposition of the old millenarian schema, which placed the reign of a thousand years between the first and the second resurrection. In this way Joachim can introduce his "time of the Spirit" between the end of the time of the Gospel of Christ and the entry into life eternal. Hence, in the course of a first phase, which is situated immediately after the end of the sixth age, the devil will deliver a great attack. It is at that point that the first Antichrist properly speaking will arise, the one that is designated in Daniel by the eleventh king, the one who in the Apocalypse is the seventh king, or the seventh head of the dragon.[653] That Antichrist will be vanquished; the devil "for a time will lose the power to persecute the Church";[654] the dragon, with all its heads smashed, will be cast into the abyss and enchained. This will be, as it were, the first Judgment. Then the era of the "Sabbath of rest"[655] will open, inaugurated by the conversion of the Jews as well as of many Gentiles.[656] Under the reign of the Spirit, the human race will live in peace of a contemplative sort. But, after an indeterminate duration, that of the "third state," there will come the supreme test, in the form of the second Antichrist. Awakened like the first one by Sa-

The Antichrist

tan escaped from his prison, the second Antichrist will, like the first, be "similar and no less in malice."[657] Only his coming will be more obvious; it is he whom the personage Gog and the dragon's tail designate; he will recruit his troops from the four corners of the world, then he will surge from the East upon the West, and his power, like his pretensions, will burst forth in broad daylight.[658] Nevertheless, his army will finally be vanquished, and he himself, like the devil, will be forever engulfed in a pool of fire and brimstone.[659] After that final Judgment the eternal age will open up.[660]

This duplication of the last Antichrist, however, does not keep Joachim from recognizing a certain number of historical precursors for each of the two, basing himself, as did the authors whom we have cited above, on the affirmation of Saint John. But though, for most of the authorities of the tradition, the name Antichrist became even a common noun, which one could apply more or less truthfully to all sorts of persons, for Joachim it was above all a question of certain specific persons that Saint John had predicted under the figure of the dragon with seven heads. The list is found in Table XIV of the *Liber Figurarum;* it is also reproduced in identical form in the *Chronicle* of Roger of Hoveden.[661] They are: Herod, Nero, Constantius, Mohammed, Mesmot,[662] Saladin; still awaited is the seventh, "who is properly called the Antichrist," and then the eighth, the "the last and biggest Antichrist."[663] The contrast with the traditional conception is striking. It appears obvious, if one considers the exegetes themselves who are looking for a single historical sequence in the seven crushed heads of the dragon, for, once again, it is only in the course of the old covenant that they distinguish certain steps in this sequence: such is Rupert, who scans it through seven victories of the Word incarnate, the first victory being that which he wins over the Egyptians through Joseph and Moses, the sixth, that of Calvary, and the seventh, that of the Judgment;[664] for him, however, from all the evidence, it is a question merely of a symbolic schema judged to be fitting; for in the sequel of the same work he uses the same schema to expound the life of Christ.[665] What is more, the contrast breaks out even in the comparison that some have been able to try to establish with a lay writer like Paul Alvarus of Cordoba, who, like the abbot from Flora, was inclined to take things by external appearances and, like him, but three centuries earlier, was struck by the prodigious success of Islam.[666]

In 854 Paul Alvarus published the *Indiculus luminosus,* a vigorous and brilliant pamphlet, to awaken the courage of his coreligionists in the face of a dominant Islam. Just as Domitian, Nero, Antiochus and others had been the precursors of the Beast long ago, so, says he, in our times, it is that man amongst the damned, Mohammed. Rising as the eleventh, he had subjugated three realms, just as Daniel had foretold: the realm of the Greeks, that of the Franks or the Romans, and that of the Goths of the West. Perhaps one could even push the literal application of prophecy still further, showing by means of ingenious calculations that the delays foretold by Daniel have been completed. But Paul Alvarus soon catches himself: "But we leave this to God's understanding alone."[667] He wants to stay within the surer tracks of the traditional exegesis. (Future historians are free to think that they are ruts.) Another verse of Daniel [12:4] will keep him there: "Pertransibunt plurimi, et multiplex erit scientia" ["Many shall pass over and knowledge shall be manifold"]. What does that mean except that one can without error find divers applications for one and the same prophecy, because the circumstances of divers times have been revealed in a single expression? More precisely, is it not one and the same thing that is repeated a number of times? Thanks to an understanding of this sort, one can with a sure touch affirm that such and such a divine oracle, for example the oracle of Habakkuk directed against Nebuchadnezzar, is verified not only on a first determinate occasion, but also all through the ages. Is not such a way of looking at it more congenial to the divine wisdom, and consequently to the catholic dogma that we profess?

> And this ought to be understood in all the works of prophecy, I think, and it ought to signify the causes underlying the changing aspect of repetition throughout the whole of time by one book of prophecy.
>
> It betokens one thing by one text of speech in such fashion that it does not dismiss another; prophetic speech stamps the prior text in such fashion that the divine spirit does not leave the latest one untouched.[668]

And Paul Alvarus at that point is calling upon his twofold authority: Saint Gregory and Saint Jerome, who both have distinguished the general schema of the prophets and the special applications that one has a right to make of them. Hence every prophecy concerning the Antichrist ought to hold good both for the head and for the members; what Daniel had written about the last adversary to come ought to enlighten us as to each of his precursors or his henchmen. For what does "Antichrist" signify if not "contrary to Christ"? And who deserves this appellation better than Mohammed?

Since he rose up against Christ, the master of humility, and used contumacy, the scourge, and the sword against his mild and gentle precepts, he has rightly been called Antichrist, who has been found to be the most open defamer and subtlest subverter of the Christian religion.[669]

Here we recognize the hermeneutics of Tychonius, as well as of Gregory or Jerome; at the same date it was that of Paschasius Radbertus, and it will, as we have seen in the preceding paragraph, again be that of Bruno of Segni, and then of Rupert and Gerhoh; and in its very allusion to the Saracens, it will be that of Martin of Leon.[670] This hermeneutics, as Alvarus says, consists in "transplanting" the images of Scripture by finding a new point of application for them. Let us say that it consists quite simply in "actualizing" Scripture, or rather in showing it to be always at work, shedding light and bearing fruit.[671] Joachim himself did not understand it that way. In his eyes, the founder of Islam was seen through a particular prophecy, at its own precise chronological setting, in the line of the six precursors of the Antichrist. Mohammed is the horseman who rides the pale horse of the Apocalypse and who has the name "Death"; when his reign comes to an end, the reign of the next horseman will come, the one who has the name "Underworld," the Antichrist of the first end of time.[672]

Hence, everywhere that, at first blush, the doctrine of Joachim of Flora seems to have unexceptionable antecedents, a more precise examination requires us to recognize fundamental differences. It is true only that the idea of six epochs of the Church since Christ that was at that point beginning to gain ground and to fuse together with the search for symbolic antecedents in Israel, might suggest the Joachimite idea of a one-to-one correspondence between the history of the Old Testament and that of the New, feature for feature and epoch for epoch. The seven seals of the Apocalypse would then be thought to cover the parallel secrets of a twofold historical process.[673] While always saying "we are in the last age,"[674] little by little one got used to thinking that the Incarnation of the Savior had not quite strictly inaugurated those "fines saeculorum" that Saint Paul had spoken of.[675] Instead of the vision that had dominated the first six Christian centuries, another vision was slowly being substituted. Though without conceiving it to be less unique or less transcendent, for some time one liked to contemplate the great fact of the Incarnation, that unique Fact, transcending every other, less as fulfilling supernatural history than as dominating it and dividing it in its own historical setting. One more and more got used to it. Christ, the end of history, would come to be considered more and more as the center of history. Nevertheless, the second representation did not contradict the first. For one did not, as we have seen, go so far as to give an analogous structure to those two halves of history or to those two times of the single Church;[676] and besides one used to think rather of two slopes, the one rising and the other descending, symmetrically arranged on each side of the central summit. Rupert did so, for example, showing the seven gifts of the Spirit at work in succession, from fear to wisdom right up to Christ, then from wisdom to fear right up to the day of Judgment.[677] One can link the long-persistent idea of a certain fatal decadence in the very heart of Christianity to such a schema, an idea somewhat analogous to the progress of revelation under ancient Israel.[678] The parallelism of the seven epochs, as Joachim of Flora was wont to put it, not only protected him against such a pessimism; on the contrary, by an excess in the opposite direction, it furnished him with a new framework that permitted him to conceive a development of revelation at the heart of present history, analogous to that which had marked out the rising history of the Old Testament; even more, analogous to that which had led the human race to pass from the Old Testament to the New.

One final question arises. Whence could this dream of a Church of the Spirit have come to Joachim, a Church that would be an assembly of contemplatives, a dream at the service of which he imagined his whole system of exegesis? The most erroneous ideas, even when they are conceived in the womb of a strictly traditional society, are never the fruit of a totally spontaneous generation. Here too, two lines of thought originally independent of each other have, it seems, converged in a monastery of Calabria. The first, whose Greek origin was perhaps able to mislead the abbot of Flora, exploited the idea of a slow divine pedagogy in the advance of revelation; it started, for some, with the framework of the Old Testament, to be applied, without very clear distinctions, to the doctrinal developments that are recorded in the New Testament itself. The Spirit was at once the author and the principal object of these developments. It is in this way that Abelard took a passage from the Rule of Saint Benedict, saying that God sometimes reveals to a younger person what he did not to an older one, so as to conclude: "It could happen that something uncertain that lay hidden in Jerome's time might later become manifest with the revelation of the Spirit."[679] Just as the idea of inspiration admits of analogous uses without very precisely defined frontiers, the two concepts of revelation and of the aid of the Holy Spirit within the Church were often not well distinguished from each other, at least verbally. Was not the Spirit the "author" of conciliar decisions? Was it not he who "dictated" the laws of the Church, just as he had "dictated" the Gospel? Was he not then enlightening the whole Church by degrees, "teaching her the whole truth little by little"?[680] Following Saint Gregory Nazianzen, whose texts were known to the Latins,[681] Anselm of Haverberg applied those views precisely to the revelation of the Holy Spirit:

> The Old Testament preached God the Father manifestly, but God the Son . . . obscurely. The New Testament rendered God the Son manifest, but barely pointed out and hinted at the divinity of the Holy Spirit. Later on, the Holy Spirit is preached, giving us a more open manifestation of his divinity.[682]

It is true that Anselm added a qualification: "Nevertheless everywhere in the Gospel the Holy Spirit himself is also being compared to the Son" and also that in his own general exposition of progressive revelation, he had spoken out unequivocally in the most classic manner; after the "passing" or the "change" or the "transposition" from idolatry to the Law, and then the passing from the Law to the Gospel, he pointed out no more than just one passing: that from the present age to the future age.[683] The divers "states" through which the Church passed and which indicated a power of perpetual renewal within her, were for him like so many "superstructures" built upon an immutable foundation: "the foundation of faith in the Holy Trinity always having been preserved."[684] But nonetheless he conceived the "increase" of the light, at the heart of the New Testament, rather on the model of what had taken place in the course of the Old.[685] Someone like Werner of Saint Blaise, summarizing the great patristic law of "economy," showed himself rather more reserved.[686] Soon a Helindand of Froidmond, explaining in his turn the progress of the trinitarian revelation, was to be equally circumspect.[687] Finally, let us remark that neither for Gregory of Nazianzen nor for any of the Latins who, like Anselm of Havelberg, followed him, was the idea of a progress in the knowledge of the Spirit that Joachim took up in his turn[688] equivalent to the idea of a reign of that Holy Spirit before establishing himself after a crisis where the reign of the Son foundered along with the sixth age.

The second line of thought to consider is one that we have noted some signs of in a previous chapter. It is a question of the tendency of certain monastic circles to present their "religion" as realizing a new age, superior to the one that constituted the common Christianity. Might one not discern a distant anticipation of it in Pseudo-Dionysius's commentaries on the Gospel of Saint John and his *Ecclesiastical Hierarchy*, where John Scotus, not content with distinguishing, as in the passage cited above, three successive "hierarchies" — that of the Law, that of the New Testament, that of eternity — pointed to this last "now partially begun in the firstfruits of contemplation"?[689] For in this schema there is indeed something more than there was in the simple trilogy of the priesthood, a trilogy that, as we have seen, did not at all correspond to the Joachimite trilogy. Nevertheless, such an "inchoatio" of eternity in John Scotus does not harden into a determinate period or institution, and its natural interpretation is perfectly orthodox. One therefore cannot say with Émile Gebhart that "a whole religious evolution was contained in these views," a whole "historical vision," a vision that Joachim alone could have achieved;[690] nor, with J. A. MacCulloch, that in magnifying the contemplative life in that way, John Scotus and his like manifested, as Joachim was to do, an impatience with the yoke of the Roman Church, the desire for a future state, for a religious society whey they would be liberated "from priest and sacrament."[691] The Joachimite theory has really not "appeared with John Scotus."[692] Quite often some will subsequently present "contemplation" in the same way, as a foretaste of the beatific vision, as the "novitiate" or as the "suburb of eternity."[693] This is what is done by the Cistercian Henry of Marcy (v. 1140-1189), who is contemporary with Joachim of Flora and, like him, a theologian of history. Henry distinguishes three sorts of "spiritual clouds": the dark cloud of the Old Testament, the lighter cloud of the time of the Church, and finally the cloud already luminous with divine contemplation, produced within the soul by a certain anticipation of the divine presence.[694] But no more for Henry of Marcy than for John Scotus is this the privilege of a time to come, a getting ahead of the time of Christ's Church: it is, within that time, a series of comparatively bright periods, though still from a distance, till the broad daylight of eternal life. Only in that broad daylight will the New Testament be achieved, not however in the sense of putting an end to it, but rather, as Saint Gregory had said, in that of leading it to its perfection and its consummation:

> The New Testament will therefore be brought to an end, since it will be brought to perfection; for when he of whom it speaks has been seen, the words of this Testament will cease. This is why the expression uttered through the voice of the Bridegroom, namely: "Arise, hasten, my beloved" is also addressed to Holy Church awaiting the day of the true Light as if it were springtime. . . . Just as he fulfilled

the Law through the mystery of his Incarnation and perfect humanity, so will he fulfill the promises of the New Testament through the glory shown forth of his brilliance.[695]

Joachim's tendency to announce things appears more typically in one of the *Distinctiones super Cantica* due to another Cistercian, William of Ramsey, who wrote to him probably in the second half of the twelfth century as follows:

> Some precepts pertain to the Law, others to the Gospel, still others to the Monastery.... The first precepts start, the second advance, the third bring to perfection.... To the ancients keeping the precepts of the Old [Law], earthly goods were promised; to believers under grace ... a promise of things eternal has been made; but a deservedly fuller blessing is owed to the religious, walking a narrower path.[696]

In remarks of this kind, one can recognize, if one wishes, an effect of that intoxication that E. Benz used to speak of, an intoxication provoked or accentuated by the overwhelming success of the Cistercian reform. However, they no more constitute a system of exegesis than they suffice to constitute a theology of history. Moreover, William of Ramsey quickly dissuades us from taking his trilogy in an excessively rigorous sense, adding these qualifications:

> The precepts of the Law are not profitable without those of the Gospel; those of the Gospel do not exist without those of the Law; yet each of them can both exist and be profitable without the precepts of the Monastery, whereas the converse is not true.[697]

A stronger tone distinguishes a letter that Odo of Canterbury addressed, a little before 1175, *ad Adam novitium ignaciensem*. In it Odo enumerates four "testamenta salvationis" in the history of salvation: "natural law," "circumcision," "baptism," and finally, "the cowl."[698] Again, in a sermon on Saint Benedict, he said:

> When the testament of God, beginning from the natural law and ascending through the law of Moses, had arrived at the law of Christ, which has been consummated, he nevertheless wanted the law of consummation — i.e., the "law of faith," the "law of grace," the "law of the spirit of life in Christ Jesus" — to be confirmed through the

Rule of blessed Benedict, by adding a fourth level (albeit not a fourth law), so that no one would need to seek a level above that higher one [namely, the state of] religion, since along with its establishment he could find the end of all consummation.[699]

Perhaps there is little more there than "pious fantasies" and, without magnifying the import of such texts, still one does think of Joachim of Flora attributing the three ages of the world respectively to "the order of the married," which was figured through Abraham and Isaac, to "the order of preachers or clerics," figured by Moses and Aaron, and finally to the "order of monks," figured by Elijah and Elisha.[700] This deployment and this progression along the duration of the three traditionally distinguished "orders" were therefore not without some preparation that was "in the air at the time."

A chapter from Adam Scotus offers an analogous set of juxtapositions. In the course of the allegorical explication of the Tabernacle there is an explication which constitutes a sort of treatise *De Ecclesia*. Adam is not content with formulating the general principle in it according to which the five steps of the history of ancient Israel can be related "to the five states of holy Church which was called to the faith after the coming of Christ"; he goes on to apply it in the sequel in the following terms:

> The first state was at the persecution of the martyrs; the second, at the conversion of princes; the third, in the multiplication of Christians; the fourth, in the community of cenobites; the fifth, in the isolation of the anchorites. The first was like a field; the second, a garden; the third, like an atrium; the fourth, similar to a house; the fifth, like the bed-chamber.[701]

This is an optimistic theology of history, tied to an exaltation of the two forms of religious life successively known by Adam, and whose final feature is already entirely Joachimite. Nevertheless, one would be wrong to emphasize it more than Adam does himself. As to Odo of Canterbury, without repudiating all excess, he, like all those who at that time were magnifying the institution of monasticism, avoided in advance the most temerarious audacity, in saying of the Rule of Saint Benedict: "it is nothing but a confirmation of the Gospel."[702]

In his *Paradise*, Dante puts Joachim of Flora beside Saint Bonaventure, just as he puts Siger of Brabant beside Saint Thomas Aquinas. Neither for Joachim nor for Siger is this a complete canonization. But it is at least an invitation for us to become reconciled with him.[703] Have we perhaps been too hard on him? Have we perhaps taken him too literally? In any case, we might take into view all aspects of his thought, to say nothing of his action. Even if our interpretations of the texts are correct, our study is still incomplete, and we have not done full justice to the man.

This man was great. In variety of thoughts and attitudes, he is comparable to another great contemplative, Rupert of Deutz. He is related to him by impetuosity of style and the grandiose oddness of certain expressions. Like him, perhaps even more, he had received outstanding spiritual gifts. Doubtless he lacked the high human culture that Rupert had acquired at the time of his formation at Saint Laurent de Liège, as well as a more stable and prolonged contact with the great tradition that would have enabled him to exploit those gifts better. There is something abrupt, solitary, and almost savage in the prophetic activity of the monk from Calabria. He himself felt that he was not in control of his genius, when he said to his readers: "I don't want that anybody should think he should demand from me, a mere country boy, anything that was not right to demand of the prophets before their times."[704] He used to declare that his language was "rude and crude,"[705] and if, in a sense, the evaluation is excessive, in another sense it is profoundly true and it applies to more than the language. He nonetheless believed seriously that he would see, at least "ex parte," the city of his dreams, as one who is already "at the gates." Now he felt obliged to shout out what he saw: "Woe is me! How frightened I become if I keep silent."[706] What he was supposed to announce to the world did not come to him of his own thinking.[707] He only half denied being a prophet,[708] though he wanted to employ the ways of a "learned"[709] and "convincing" exegesis. But in truth, as with Rupert, so with him it was a need even more than a mission: cost what it would, he had to deliver the message that he was carrying within him.[710] The times have changed! The horizon is aglow! The kingdom of life is at hand! To awaken those who slumber, he provides thunder rolls and lightning-flashes.[711] He wants to awaken hope rather than fear. Everyone must understand that the Lord is going to do something new on the earth.[712]

Yet not all of these grandiose dreams were chimerical. In the tumultuous mind of the prophet a high truth was being sought for, without successfully being found. That is why the figure of Joachim of Flora exercises a fascinating attraction. Haunted by the thought of the schism, he passionately desired the unity of the Church. He wanted for her, more than any moral reform, a regeneration in spirit. He believed in that regeneration. His very prophetic activity, inasmuch as it concerns the entire

Church, in its historical and social existence as well as its mystical reality, and in the fullness of his destiny, relays a tradition that showed itself to be alive just yesterday in Saint Bernard and that came to be affirmed once again, under forms stranger for us than for contemporaries, in Saint Hildegard.[713] That tradition had been able to spread into the withdrawn meditation of the cloisters or into the new science of the university chairs. By an instinct as powerful as it was confused, Joachim reacted against an inclination toward psychologism and subtlety, which were harbingers of a draining away of substance. With equal and more conscious rigor, he struggled against the deadly desiccation that seemed to menace the Church, both in her pastors and in her doctors. For her as well as for himself, he thirsted for the Spirit.[714] "Scarcely able to be conceptualized in his theological expression and rather crude in his ecclesiology," his "internal dynamism" was consequently not an entirely aberrant force.[715] If in explicating the Scriptures he rather annoyingly replaces the traditional form with his search for "concord," it is not that he was unaware of the price to be paid. He is aiming for the day when one would have decidedly passed "from the eloquence of the word to spiritual understanding."[716] Moreover, it is in this very passing from the letter to the spirit that from now on, "each day," he discerns the mark of the divine veracity.[717] While commenting on the words of Jesus to the woman from Samaria, he understands that the reader who sticks to the letter of the Old Testament will never have his thirst quenched, but that he who drinks from the doctrine poured out "by the Spirit of the Lord" will never more be thirsty: his own heart will become a spring of spurting water, and, by rising step by step from history to anagogy, he will always find a new source of nourishment for his meditation, so as finally to arrive at the contemplation of Him Whom man cannot comprehend.[718] Reading in Genesis that "darkness covered the deep," he immediately thinks of the obscurity of Scripture, that fundamental obscurity that all the clarities of the "concord" cannot eliminate; but the words that follow restore his confidence: "the Spirit of the Lord was carried over the waters." This is the promise that, from the obscure depths of the letter, there will arise the flame of the spirit and that it will rise up to the heavens to illuminate the stars.[719]

Shall we absolutely refuse to listen to him? If we set aside the words where he goes astray, where perhaps at least at times he is aware of going astray, shall we remain entirely insensible to his action? Are we forbidden to hope, to ask for new effusions of the Spirit? In his explication Joachim has compromised — without intending to, it seems — the full sufficiency of Jesus Christ. But one can also compromise it by measuring it through narrow-minded perspectives. The sufficiency of Jesus Christ does not shut us up within some sort of rigid order, as in every epoch so many adversaries of so many "spirituals" would have it. To recognize Christ's sufficiency is not to maintain the cult of a past that would have merely to survive into dotage, without welcoming anything else, without discoveries, without progress. It is not necessary to oppose a search for a purely human security to the breath of an adventurous prophetic activity. Christ is capable of embracing everything and his Spirit is capable of renewing everything. The sap of Christianity can still always bear unexpected fruits that astonish the Christians themselves. If chimeras are pernicious, so is the refusal of the Spirit. There are two equally deadly ways of separating Christ and his Spirit: dreaming of a kingdom of the Spirit that would march off way ahead of Christ, and imagining a Christ who would always be tugging back this side of the Spirit.[720]

Yet one does not find merely aberrant and chimerical prophecy in this prophet. Absent critical reflection as well as a certain spiritual interiority, he has projected in space and time the symbols that the meditation of Scripture caused to spring up in his heart. There are symbols alternatively terrible and radiant, which are not all lacking in beauty. One such is that vision of the two brother orders that he perceives in the future, the order of hermits and the order of monks. They are in the image of his own soul: the one, "wilder and more passionate," walking "in the spirit of Elijah"; the other, "meeker and gentler," walking "in the spirit of Moses."[721] It is that twofold spirit that dwells in him, and though for him the first was guaranteed by the angels, he does not intend to sacrifice the second to it, the second that he sees incarnated in the life of Christ and his Apostles. The sweetness of Moses finally prevails in his esteem over the asperity of Elijah. At that point he is dreaming — and it is indeed always a dream, but not one of those that deserve to be called chimeras — of a fire, a fire from heaven, which is no longer the lightning drawn down by Elijah in his anger, but the flame brought to bear by Jesus and which is to set everything ablaze: "for as a small fire is made large in a woodpile, so does universal love grow within the unity of souls and hearts."[722]

Notes

Notes to Chapter One

1. "l'étendue et la qualité du champ immense dans lequel, au XIIe siècle, en expression organique des siècles antérieures, se développa le symbolisme"; "tares ultérieures": 162; with regard to scholasticism: "The later blemishes will compromise neither its Christian value nor its scientific truth" — "Les tares ultérieures ne pourront compromettre sa valeur chrétienne ni sa vérité scientifique."

2. "le témoin et l'effet d'un sens du sacré en pleine fécondité": 179.

3. Is this not a bit like the way in which others strive to find a line of precursors of the Reformation, or to discern across the centuries of belief "the chain of free spirits" ("la chaîne des libres esprits"), which for them forms "the essential element of history" ("l'élément essentiel de l'histoire")? Cf. H. Berr, preface to L. Febvre, *Le problème de l'incroyance au XVIe s.* (1942), xxi-xxiii.

4. "théologie symbolique"; "science théologique"; "nouveau mouvement"; "l'allégorisme sans frein": *Theologus Dantes, Bulletin du Jubilé*, 5 (1922), 479; *Dante le théologien* (1935), 168-9.

5. *La renaissance du XIIe s.*, 223-4.

6. "met à la base de sa synthèse dogmatique, en dépit de ses fortes tendances au symbolisme, l'ordre historique de l'histoire biblique et de l'histoire du monde": *L'essor*, 1, 52.

7. "c'est Hughes de Saint-Victor, qui définera le plus exactement alors l'attitude de l'exégète vis-à-vis de l'Écriture: le sens littéral est à la base et se distingue avec netteté du sens spirituel, allégorique ou tropologique": *R. bibl.*, 1946, 288.

8. "beaucoup plus précis" — "fait faire un grand progrès à cette théorie des sens scripturaires, stagnante depuis Raban Maur" — "notamment dans l'école de Saint-Victor" — "cette indépendance vis-à-vis de la méthode traditionnelle et cet esprit de l'exégèse hiéronymienne": "Pourquoi le moyen âge n'a-t-il pas davantage pratiqué l'exégèse littérale?" (*Les sc. philos. et théol.*, 1, 1941-2, 169-70). *Esquisse*, 100-1, etc.; 59: "in these four centuries one can discern a more and more

preponderant influence of St. Jerome, at the expense of that of St. Augustine and especially that of St. Gregory. . . . At first . . . , with Bede, Alcuin and Rabanus Maurus, there was an exclusively allegorical exegesis; but then, little by little, with Paschasius Radbertus, and particularly Christian of Stavelot and Berno, the authority of St. Jerome is established; from him they borrow literally this or that thing from his prefaces, his translations from the Hebrew; what they call the *truth of the Hebrew,* numerous philological remarks, and especially a more genuine concern with the literal sense" — "dans ces quatre siècles, on peut discerner une influence de plus en plus prépondérante de S. Jérôme, au détriment de celle de S. Augustin et surtout de S. Grégoire. Au debout . . . , chez Bède, Alcuin et Raban Maur, une exégèse exclusivement allégorique; mais peu à peu chez Paschase Radbert, et surtout Christian de Stavelot et Bernon, l'autorité de S. Jérôme s'affirme; on lui emprunte littéralement telle ou telle de ses préfaces, ses traductions de l'hébreu; ce qu'on appelle l'*hebraica veritas,* de nombreuses remarques philologiques, et surtout un souci plus réel du sens littéral." See the long review of this work by J. Leclercq, *B. thomiste,* 7 (1943-6).

9. *The Study,* 41: "The initial step in the progress of biblical science was to work out the patristic distinction between letter and spirit"; 76-7, etc. — In RB, 68 (1958), J.-B. R. observes that an "orientation trop exclusive vers la scolastique" led to a neglect of monastic exegesis on the part of Father Spicq and Miss Smalley. It has also, in our opinion, somewhat distorted their general perspective. Nevertheless, as the reader will see, we have made many of their judgments our own.

10. *The Sensus Plenior of Sacred Scripture* (1955), 58, following Spicq, on Hugh: "He attacks the tradition of Gregory and Bede with its disregard for the letter."

11. 101, etc.

12. "l'allégorie" — "uniquement aux mots du Nouveau Testament et aux propriétés des choses; Huges de Saint-Victor préconisa le premier une allégorie basée sur les réalités historiques de l'Ancien Testament, figures de celles du Nouveau" — "La méthode inaugurée à Saint-Victor se caractérise par l'établissement solide du sens littéral ou historique avant de s'élever au sens spirituel et, partant, par la rupture avec l'explication purement spirituelle des anciens commentateurs monastiques": P. C. Boeren, *La vie et les œuvres de Guiard de Laon* (1956), 166-7. In this work described as "very elaborate": "très fouillée" it has been noted that the conclusions were of a "somewhat conjectural character": "caractère quelque peu conjectural": RSPT, 1957, 144-5.

13. Gr. Calandra, *De historica Andreae Victorini exp. in Eccl.* (1948), xc-xciii.

14. "qu'il ne peut proposer des mystères divins une explication authentique qu'en respectant le sens historique de la révélation": J. J. de Santo-Tomas, *Revue thomiste,* 58 (1958), 730.

15. "la réaction historiciste d'Hugues de Saint-Victor contre l'allégorisation prématurée des textes scripturaires"; "son principe majeur du fondement historique de toute réflexion sur l'économie biblique": "L'homme de la nature, perspectives sur la renaiss. du XIIe s." (AHDLMA, 1953, 54). *Introd. à l'ét. de S. Th. d'Aquin* (1950), 204. "Théol. symbolique et exégèse scolast. aux XIIe-XIIIe s." (*Mél. J. de Ghellinck,* 1951, 513). *Th. au XIIe s.,* 29. *La théol. c. science au XIIIe s.* (3e éd., 1957).

16. Walafrid Strabo has sung of the "insula felix": "happy island" in his poem

De cultura hortorum. On Reichenau and its site, see J. De Ghellinck, *Misc. Fr. Ehrle*, 5, 362-3. On Berno, Manitius, 2 (1923), 61-71.

17. "formule cette interdiction, étonnante pour l'époque, de substituer son sentiment personnel à la signification du texte sacré"; "un souci plus réel du sens littéral": "Pourquoi le m. âge . . . ," 170.

18. "On sera singulièrement surpris"; "d'entendre, au XIe siècle, Bernon de Reichenau émettre ce principe qu'il n'a malheureusement pas eu l'occasion de mettre en pratique: *Prudens lector, semper cave superstitiosam intelligentiam, ut non tuo sensui attemperes Scripturas, Scripturis sensum tuum adjungas*": *De varia psalmorum atque cantuum modulatione* (M. Gerbert, *Scriptores ecclesiastici de musica*, 2, 1784, 93-101; PL, CXLII, 1131-54); c. 8 (1146 C). Spicq, *Esquisse*, 22.

19. "Aucun contemporain n'aurait songé à interdire au lecteur de substituer son sentiment personnel au sens du text sacré"; "l'unique ouvrage de critique proprement dite du moyen âge": *Esquisse*, 55.

20. "dont le titre unique répond mal au contenu": "Notes sur les œuvres attribuées à B. de Reichenau," RB, 29, 98-107. "If the beginning of the letter is missing, that is . . . because the copyist thought it useless to preserve everything that was not related to the treatise" — "Si le début de la lettre fait défaut, c'est . . . parce que le copiste a jugé inutile de conserver tout ce qui ne se rapportait pas au traité."

21. On the relations of the abbot and the emperor: Bernard de Vregille, "Fragment d'un traité de la prière dédié par Bernon de R. à Henri III, roi de Germanie," RMAL, 2 (1946), 2612-8.

22. "Subjeci series narrationum aliquas, etsi minus sapientiae sale conditas, eorum tamen victus amore qui me super hac re studuerunt rogare, vid., de dissona psalterii romani ac gallicani qua nos utimur interpretatione; — de quibusdam Esaiae prophetae sermonibus; — de versibus minus cum responsoriis convenientibus; — de antiphonis vel responsoriis non regulariter nec convenienter se habentibus; — de intermissione alleluia et ejus cantuum verbis . . .": RB, 29, 100. The letter subsequently makes mention "d'un opuscule sur la nature de l'âme du Christ et de deux sermons pour Noël et pour l'Assomption inconnus des bibliographes."

23. Blanchard, art. cit., insists on the numerous adaptations which the work of Berno had undergone.

24. "Et mirum in modum, dum quidam hujus mundi sapientes videri et esse volunt, . . . sacrae Scripturae verba suo sensui applicare conantur — *et* verba quae ipsa . . . Dei Sapientia per se protulit, vel Spiritus sanctus . . . praedixit, aliter secundum Donatum et Priscianum permutando canunt . . .": *De varia modulatione*, c. 8, init. (PL, CXLII, 1145 D). Cf. c. 6: "Some distinguish it in this way . . . , but blessed Jerome posits another sense" — "Quidam ita distinguunt . . . , sed b. Hieronymus alium sensum ponit" (1143 D); but here the subject is different: it is a question of a version (defective according to Berno) of certain texts from Isaiah figuring in the office. V. *infra*, iii, p. 43.

25. Cassiodorus, *Inst.*, c. 2, n. 1: "Yet we have decided to put Donatus in the center, him who is proven to be both especially fitting for boys and suitable for beginners" — "Nobis tamen placet in medium Donatum deducere, qui et pueris specialiter aptus et tyronibus probatur accommodus" (PL, LXX, 1152 C). Rupert,

In Jo.: "just as we were taken to Donatus as boys" — "sicut apud Donatum pueri accepimus" (CLXIX, 207 B). Ozanam, 1, 271: "The grammar of Donatus ... has become the framework, the prototype of all modern grammars; through his clarity and brevity it subjugated the whole Middle Ages" — "La grammaire de Donat ... est devenue le cadre, le type de toutes les grammaires modernes; par sa clarté et sa brièveté elle a subjugué tout le moyen âge."

26. P. Cahier's expression. Fontaine, 188, compares in the same way the authority of Donatus to that of the Theodosian Code.

27. *Chronicle,* a. 354. *Apol. adv. Ruf.,* l. I, c. 16 (PL, XXIII, 410 A).

28. "ornatrix generis humani": *Variae,* l. 9, c. 21 (letter of Athalaric; LXIX, 787 C). *De artibus,* c. I (LXX, 1152 BC).

29. Donatus "forme le substrat de la grammaire théorique d'Isidore": Fontaine, 188.

30. *Cunabula grammaticae artis Donati a Beda restituta* (PL, XC, 613-32).

31. H. Keil, *Grammatici lat.,* 4. intr., 37. Ch.-H. Beeson, "The *Ars gr.* of Julian of Toledo" (*Misc. Fr. Ehrle,* 1, 50-70).

32. "nihil mihi Donatus, nihil Priscianus contulit": *In Ap.,* l. 8 (836-7).

33. "veracissimus grammaticae artis doctor": *ep.* 27 (PL, C, 181-4). On Priscian: Courcelle, 307-11; E. de Bruyne, 1, 218.

34. "noster Priscianus": Salomon III: "He built such a grammar that Donatus, Nicomachus, Dositheus and our Priscian would seem to be nothing in comparison" — "Ille (Albinus) talem grammaticam condidit, ut Donatus, Nicomachus, Dositheus et noster Priscianus in ejus comparatione nihil esse videantur" (Manitius, 1, 281).

35. Jean Cotton, *De musica:* "The Moderns, ... as Priscian says, by as much as they are more recent by so much are they the more insightful" — "Moderni, ... ut ait Priscianus, quanto juniores tanto perspicaciores" (PL, CL, 1396 C).

36. Notker, *De interp.,* c. 12: "If you want to know the authors of the pagans, too, read Priscian" — "Si et gentilium auctores nosse desideras, Priscianum lege" (CXXXI, 1004 A).

37. "pleine d'observations ingénieuses, délicates, où l'on voit une connaissance profonde de la langue latine": B. Hauréau, *Singularités hist. et litt.* (1861), 104. J. Leclercq, "Smaragde et la grammaire," RMAL, 4, 15-22.

38. *Carmina,* 45, *De libris quos legere solebam: On the books that I used to read* (P. Lat., I, 543). An elogy of grammar: *De septem liberalibus art. in quadam pictura depictis* (544-5).

39. PL, CXI, 613-78.

40. Comm. on the *Ars minor,* ed. W. Fox (1892).

41. Joannes mon., *Vita S. Odonis,* l. I, n. 12: "Further, in these days, our most expert sailor, who under his leadership taught us to cross the whirlpools of this world, went across the vast sea of Priscian by swimming" — "His praeterea diebus nauta noster peritissimus, qui nos suo ductu docuit transmeare gurgites istius mundi, immensum Prisciani transiit transnatando pelagus" (PL, CXXXIII, 49 A).

42. "ille peritissimus grammaticus": PL, CXLIX, 1463 D. Cf. Fulbert of Chartres, sending a volume of Priscian to the archbishop Bonipertus (*Recueil des hist. des Gaules,* ed. Delisle, 10, 443).

43. "docuit mira brevitate, compendioso artificio, subtilissimo doctrinae schemate": Clerval, 284.

44. "Primi ripae fluminis praesidet Donatus . . .
Hujus ex opposito sedet Priscianus":

Fons philosophiae, v. 129 and 133 (P. Michaud-Quantin, 39); v. 129-40: *De antiquis magistris grammaticae.*

45. "grammaticus"; "ipsa grammatica"; "apostata noster": L. 2, c. 8 (PL, CCX, 508 BC).

46. Hugh, *De grammatica* (Leclercq, AHDLMA, 14, 263-322). John of Salisbury, *Polycr.*, l. I, c. 19 (PL, CXCIX, 850 A); etc. Cf. Lesne, 587-93. E. Dekkers, *Clavis P. Lat. (S. Er.,* 3), 258-62.

47. "artes, ancillae grammaticae": On this "pan-grammatical" character of the work of Isidore: Fontaine, 29-31, 330, 869-70.

48. *De una deit.,* 8: "Forgotten . . . the rudiments of the grammatical art, i.e., the teaching of Donatus" — "Oblitus . . . rudimenta artis grammaticae, i.e., Donati doctrinam"; "with Donatus teaching" — "Donate [sic] docente" (PL, CXXV, 540 D).

49. "le reproche le plus cuisant qui pût être": J. Jolivet, *Godescalc d'Orbais* (1958), 18.

50. Angilbert, *Carmen de Carolo magno,* l. 3 (MGH, *Scr.,* 2, 394). Ermenric of Elwangen (†874) writing to the abbot Grimald (MGH, *Ep.,* 5, 568):

> Artis grammaticae et summus sophista vocaris,
> Undique doctus suis artibus omnigenis . . .
> You are called even the highest professor of the grammatical art,
> Learned everywhere in the arts of all kinds. . . .

51. An anonymous grammarian cited by Ch. Thurot, *Notices et extraits des mss. de la Bibl. imp.,* 22, 2 (1868), 61-2: "You would have been able to search through the sacred pages more clearly than that, since expertise in the grammatical art is thought to be extremely useful to those who labor in the holy search to the subtler understanding that is frequently inserted in the holy Scriptures. . . ." — "Eo liquidius potueris sacras perscrutari paginas, quia peritia grammaticae artis in sacrosancto scrutinio laborantibus ad subtiliorem intellectum qui frequenter in sacris Scripturis inseritur, valde utilis esse dinoscitur, eo quod lector hujus expers artis in multis Scripturarum locis usurpare sibi illa quae non habet, et ignotus sibi ipsi esse comprobatur." For several analogous texts, in the wake of Cassiodorus, Aldhelm, Bede, Alcuin, Rabanus, etc., V. *supra,* I, ch. I, ii. Certain details in Roger, 328-39. The frontispiece of the *Philosophica margarita,* a small scholarly encyclopedia by Gregory Reisch printed at Strasbourg in 1504, will show Grammar inviting the scholar to enter into the palace; Donatus and Priscian are seen at the windows; at the top, Theology. Ch. Cahier, *Nouveaux mél. d'archéologie, curiosités mystérieuses* (1874), 295.

52. Cf. Dom Pierre Blanchard, *Le psautier dans la liturgie (Richesses,* 236).

53. *De Abr.,* l. 2, c. 10, n. 70: "Aristotle and the Peripatetics utter with great tragic buskin things that sacred Scripture expresses in simple words" — "Haec

quae simplicibus verbis sacra Scriptura exprimit, magno quodam cothurno Aristoteles et Peripatetici personant" (PL, XIV, 490 C).

54. *Ep.* 58, c. 10: "St. Hilary grows taller by wearing a French buskin" — "Sanctus Hilarius gallicano cothurno attollitur" (3, 84). Philip of Harvengt, *ep.* 7, will not want to see any malice in this remark: [Jerome] "obviously thinks that both flowery beauty of words and a seriousness worthy of the reverence of the hidden senses are present in his words" — "Manifeste judicat scriptis ejus inesse et verborum floridam venustatem et dignam reverentia occultorum sensuum gravitatem" (PL, CCIII, 61 AB). Indeed the word was not always ironic; cf. Ermenric, *Ad Grim.*: "But he wanted to celebrate the most blessed Gaul's deeds with poetic buskin" — "Voluit vero ille (b. Walafredus) poetico coturno gesta beatissimi Galli canere" (MGH, *Ep.*, 5, 566).

55. Cf. Odo of Cluny, *Epit. Mor.*, praef. metrica (PL, CXXXIII, 110 C):

Hoc opus exiguum caepi non corde cothurno. . . .
I have not undertaken this little work with a heart be-buskined. . . .

56. "cum quodam mentis cothurno canunt": In an analogous context, Agobard of Lyon, *L. de corr. antiph.*, c. 7: "contra morem . . . ab eminentiori loco purpatice concrepabat" (CIV, 332 A).

57. C. 8, sequel: "Quae enim est consequentia, ut Priscianus audiatur et veritas quae Deus est contemnatur? Sic (Si?) enim Terentius, Virgilius, Tullius caeterique liberalium litterarum sequaces in suis scripturis hoc meruerunt, ut eorum dicta permanerent inconvulsa . . . , quanto magis caelestium verborum oracula in sua perseverare debent regula. . . . Jure igitur censemus illius auctoritatem magis sequi, cujus labia mundata sunt igne caelesti, quam magisterium alicujus auctoris grammatici" (CXLII, 1145-6). — Cf. *Traditiones Frisigenses*, a. 902-3: "in summitate laci."

58. "Debemus igitur sacrae Scripturae seriem firmiter tenere ac ejus tenorem in omnibus inviolabiliter observare, attendentes quod quidam sapiens admonet etc."; "Igitur constituendum est ut sacra evangelii verba, patriarcharum ac prophetarum oracula, apostolorum scripta, fide integra, devotione congrua, ut in authenticis libris reperiuntur, incommutabiliter servemus, teneamus, custodiamus . . .": *Ib.* (1146 CD).

59. The expression "libri authentici" had often designated the books contained in the canon of the Scriptures. In his *Ars lectoria* (1086), Aimeric puts the books of the Bible and the canon of the Mass in the first class of works (authentica). St. Bernard will a little later write in the same sense, *Tr. de cantu*, n. 2: "We have, however, removed a few postcommunions, replacing them with currently authentic responsories" — "Postcommuniones autem quasdam removimus, usitata et authentica pro eis responsoria apponentes" (CLXXXII, 1123 A).

60. "Ergo, si quis per grammaticae artis regulam ingenium suum acuere voluerit, exerceat se in scholis; utatur, si libet, Donato et Prisciano magistris, dummodo salva verae interpretationis integritate non renuat debitum honorem eloquiis conservare. — Sed de his satis": C. 8 (1146-7).

61. "caelestium verborum oracula in sua perseverare debent regula": *Ib.* (1146 A).

62. This council had proscribed nonscriptural chants "except those that had

been discussed and approved in the synod, lest perchance anything be composed against the faith, whether through ignorance or through zeal. So that, in short, one should consider that not only those things that had been composed against the rule of faith by zeal of faithlessness but also those [composed] by simplicity of ignorance are with equal attention to be repudiated" — "nisi quae a prudentioribus tractata et comprobata fuerint in synodo, ne forte aliquid contra fidem vel per ignorantiam vel per studium sit compositum. Ubi breviter considerandum, quod non solum ea quae studio perfidiae, sed etiam illa quae simplicitate ignorantiae contra fidei regulam fuerint composita, pari animadversione sunt repudianda" (1145 B).

63. Cassiodorus had said, in almost the same language: "Let the expression that is recognized to have pleased God remain everywhere uncorrupted, so that it may shine forth in its splendor, not to be seized so as to be subject to human desire" — "Maneat ubique incorrupta locutio, quae Deo placuisse cognoscitur, ita ut fulgore suo niteat, non humano desiderio carpenda subjaceat"; but this was only against the arbitrary corrections: "but where you are won over by the authority of ancient manuscripts" — "ubi tamen priscorum codicum auctoritate convinceris...." At the same time he criticized the "copyists learned in the art of grammar" — "librarii grammaticae artis expertes" and said: "the blemishes introduced by copyists are to be corrected" — "sunt librariorum vitia corrigenda." *Inst.*, c. 15 (PL, LXX, 1028 AD).

64. "When by modifying ... we change either the words or sense into another" — "Cum modulando ... aut verba aut sensum in alienum intellectum mutamus" (c. 7, 1145 C). "They are trying to bend the words of Scripture to their own sense, and altering their connotation by changing the [sacred] words" — "Scripturae verba suo sensui applicare conantur, et verba (sacra) permutando canunt" (c. 8, 1145 D). "So as not to distort the sense of Scripture we make every effort to preserve the sacred words of the gospel" — "Ut non suo sensui attemperes Scripturas ... Igitur constituendum est ut sacra evangelii verba ... servamus" (c. 8, 1146 CD).

65. "dum omnis philosophia mundana et saecularis scientiae doctrina originem a sacrae Scripturae auctoritate sumpserint": *De varia mod.*, c. 8 (PL, CXLII, 1146 D).

66. *Supra*, I, ch. I, iii.

67. "critique textuelle"; "apparition"; "modeste": C. Spicq, *Esquisse*, 17.

68. Alcuin, *ep.* 22 (PL, C, 175 C), and a hundred other texts.

69. This taste will reassert itself again, a bit after Bernon, for example in Guibert de Nogent: *Gesta Dei per Fr.*, praef. (CLXI, 681 D); etc.

70. "ordo et regula artis grammaticae": Alcuin, *ep.* 101 (C, 314 A).

71. Cf. the letter of Ermenric to Grimald (MGH, *Ep.*, 5).

72. "Grammaticae doctor constat praelucidus artis": Angilbert (†814), *Carmen de Car. magno*, l. 3, v. 67 (MGH, *Scr.*, 2, 394).

73. *Vita s. Udalrici episc. Augustensis* (1083-1104), c. 8-9 (CXLII, 1191 A, 1192 A and C).

74. *Ib.*, c. 21-2 (1201 AC). The immense success of these stories is well known. Cf. Alcuin, *ep.* 140 (C, 380 C).

75. "books of explanation": *In Is.*, prol. (PL, XXIV, 22 A); "in simplici explanatione" (ib.); "explanationem in Isaiam" (313 D).

76. "a plerisque commentariorum opus explanatio nominatur": *In Gal.*, l. 3 (XXV, 400 C).

77. "Per ora mortalium Scriptura sacra nobis in expositionibus explicatur": *In Ez.*, l. 2, h. 5, n. 4 (LXXVI, 987 A).

78. PL, LXXVI, 174 B, etc.

79. "Per totam veteris ac novi Testamenti seriem rerum explanandarum necessitate est coactus exponere"; "idque testimonium studuit addita expositionis explanatione disserere": *L. de expositione V. ac N.T. de div. libris S. Gregorii magni concinnatus* (PL, LXXIX, 683 A); "the obscurity of the thing to be explained" — "obscuritas rei explanandae" (684 A). On the work of Paterius and its importance for the text of Gregory: R. Etaix, "Le *Liber testimoniorum* de Paterius," RDSR, 32 (1958), 66-78.

80. *In Lev.*, h. 4, n. 7; h. 7, n. 1 (PG, XII, 442 CD, 475 B), etc.

81. *Inst. div. litt.* (PL, LXX, 1112-47).

82. Cf. Fontaine, 251.

83. H. 8: "It is very well known by the exposition of the Fathers" — "Patrum expositione notissimum est"; h. 24: "let us run over this part of the gospel reading ... by explaining" — "haec de lectione evangelica ... explanando transcurrimus" (CCL, 122, 233, 363).

84. *Sup. missus est excusatio:* "I have expounded the gospel reading.... The Fathers have expounded.... A recent commentator ... not by a necessary explanation ... not so much to have intended to expound the gospel" — "Lectionem evangelicam exposui.... Patres exposuerunt.... Novus expositor ... non necessaria explanatione ... non tam intendisse exponere evangelium" (PL, CLXXXIII, 86 CD). In the commentaries of St. Bruno on St. Paul, each chapter of an epistle is followed by its own "expositio" (CLIII).

85. *De sacram.*, l. 2, P. 17, c. 6: "So when he should have come by explaining the Law spiritually" — "Cum ergo venerit [Elias] exponendo legem spiritualiter" (PL, CLXXVI, 598 C). Ps.-Hugh, *Q. in Paul.*: "the commentator says" — "dicit expositor" (CLXXV, 617 A, 623 B, 626 BD, 632 D ...).

86. PL, CLXXXIV, 870 A, etc.

87. "antiqui sacrae Scripturae expositores": *Microc.*, l. 3, c. 149 (Delhaye, 165).

88. "Singuli Patrum, librum aliquem exposituri ...": *ep.* 143 (PL, CXCIX, 127 B; cf. 130 A).

89. "orthodoxorum Patrum expositiones": Thus Peter of Cella (CCII, 960 A).

90. Theodemir to Claudius: "I have not sought to expound [those questions] for you, since they are available to us in the same text along with the exposition of Solomon's temple as ... it has been expounded by Bede" — "Non petivi [illas quaestiones] exponendas vobis, quia uno in corpore cum exposito de templo Salomnis sicut ... a Beda expositum est apud nos habentur" (CIV, 624 AB).

91. *Ep.* 7: "The exposition on Matthew that I had once begun" — "Expositum in Matthaeo quod olim inchoaveram ..." (MGH, Ep., 6, 144); ib.: "in an explanation of the gospel" — "evangelii in explanatione."

92. PL, XCIII.

93. Aug., *ep.* 224, n. 2: "the popular treatments that the Greeks call 'homilies' "

— "tractatus populares quos Graeci homilias dicunt" (PL, XXXIII, 1001). John of Salisbury, *ep.* 143: "The Holy Fathers ... in their treatments" — "Sancti Patres ... in tractatibus suis" (CXCIX, 127 B).

94. Bardy, RSR, 33, 230.

95. *Gesta Caroli*, 1. c. 2 (MGH, *Scr.*, 2, 731).

96. "Origenes tractator sacrarum Scripturarum peritissimus": *Dial.*, l. 1, c. 6 (Halm, 157).

97. "explanator et tractator prophetiarum": *In II Thess.*, ii (PL, CXVII, 779 C).

98. *In Ap.* (CLXIX, 1130 C). *In Ex.* (CLXVII, 696 C).

99. *Ep.* 1 (Giles, 2, 207). Odilo of Cluny, *s.* 15 (PL, CXLII, 1033 B). "Omnes tractatores S. Scripturarum" (authors of the 12th century: F. Stegmüller, *Mél. de Ghellinck*, 732, 736).

100. Cf. H.-I. Marrou, *Hist. de l'éducation dans l'antiquité*, 369-70, 416-8.

101. "Qui loquitur lingua, oret ut interpretetur": 1 Cor. 14:13.

102. "interpretatio latina": PL, IX, 532 C.

103. *Ep.* 57, *Ad Pammachium* (3, 55-73). *Ad Aug.* (*ep.* 112, c. 20: 6, 20).

104. "sine interpretatione": *ep.* 26, c. 1-4 (2, 15-6); cf. *ep.* 19, Damasus to Jerome (1, 78).

105. "Quod si uni non videtur linguae gratiam interpretatione mutari, Homerum ad verbum exponat latinum": PL, XXVII, 36; "fluent men ignorant that [the Scriptures] have been translated from Hebrew" — "diserti homines interpretatas esse [Scripturas] de Hebraeo nescientes."

106. "Primum de interpretatione dicamus, et postea de his quae scripta sunt disseremus": *In Is.*, l. 5, c. 19 (PL, XXIV, 184 A). "A different translation needs to have a different sense, as well" — "Diversa interpretatio necesse est ut diversum habeat et sensum" (302 A). *Praef. in Esdram* (XXVIII, 1405). *Ep.* 18, c. 6 (1, 60); etc.

107. *Ep.* 49, c. 19 (2, 147).

108. "in qua laborasse me fateor, ut verborum elegantiam pari interpretationis venustate servarem": *ep.* 97, c. 3 (5, 34).

109. "ut pater verbi sit potius quam interpres": *De Princ., praef. Ruf.* (4-5).

110. "Scriptura divina ... opportune potuit per orbem terrarum disseminari, per varias interpretum linguas"; "In ipsis autem interpretationibus, Itala caeteris praeferatur, nam est verborum tenacior cum perspicuitate sententiae": L. 2, c. 5, n. 6 (244); c. 12-6 (260-74); c. 39, n. 59 (328). Cf. Combès-Farges, 574-5. (Perhaps, following a conjecture of Father Alberto Vaccari, *Scritti di erudizione e di filologia*, 2, 1958, 240-2, it might be necessary to read: "... Aquila caeteris praeferatur.") *In ps.* lxi, n. 1: "it says in Latin based on the translation of the Hebrew tongue as it has come down to us" — "ex interpretatione enim hebraeae linguae ut ad nos pervenit latine dicitur" (CCL, 39, 772).

111. "Non licet dicere, auctor hujus libri non tenuit veritatem; sed: aut codex mendosus est, aut interpres erravit, aut tu non intelligis": L. 11, c. 5 (PL, XLII, 249); cf. c. 6. *Ep.* 82, c. 1, n. 3 (XXXIIII, 277).

112. "Ego sane te mallem graecas potius canonicas nobis interpretari Scripturas": Ep. 71, c. 2, n. 4 (XXXIII, 242); n. 3: "Job translated by you from the Hebrew, though we already had a translation.... In this later translation, which has been made from the Hebrew, there is not the same verbal fidelity" — "Job ex Hebraeo a te interpretatum, cum jam quamdam haberemus interpretationem....

In hac posteriore interpretatione, quae versa est ex Hebraeo, non eadem verborum fides occurrit"; c. 3, n. 5 (*ib.*). Cf. G. Jouassard, "Réflexions sur la position de S. Aug. relativement aux Septante dans sa discussion avec Jérôme," *R. des ét. august.*, 1956, 93-9.

113. *In ps.* lxx, s. 1, n. 19 (CCL, 39, 956). *In ps.* lvxii, n. 24 (39, 887). *In ps.* lxxxii, n. 5, 1142. Cf. *In ps.* ix, n. 7; xxxviii, n. 1; xlvi, n. 2 (CCL, 38, 61, 401, 529). *In Hept.*, l. 5, q. 19: "interpretes latini" (PL, XXXIV, 757); etc.

114. "Septuaginta interpretes": *ep.* 18, c. 15 and 19 (1, 72, 76), etc. Cf. Or., *In Ez.*, h. 6, n. 4 (PG, XIII, 713 B).

115. "Juxta Septuaginta interpretum translationem": *In Reg.* (PL, L, 1064 D), etc.

116. "Juxta antiquos illos interpretes legitur in Job": *Ad fratres de M. Dei*, l. 2, c. 3, n. 20 (CLXXXIV, 351 B).

117. "translationem Septuaginta interpretum": *In Ez.*, l. 1, h. 7, n. 23 (LXXVI, 852 BC). Philip of Harvengt: "all the translations of the interpreters" — "omnes translationes interpretum" (CCIII, 653 B).

118. L. 2, h. 1, n. 10: "as we learn through our translator, the history of the Hebrews does not have 'of stone-cutters' but a 'linen cord' in his hand" — "ut per interpretem nostrum didicimus, Hebraeorum historia non habet 'caementariorum' sed 'funiculus lineus' in manu ejus" (LXXVI, 943 A).

119. "interpretatio exposita": *Disc.* 12, n. 15: "This translation, gathered from many texts, seems to be expounded as . . ." — "Haec interpretatio, ex multis collecta scripturis, exposita videtur ut" (Buytaert, 1953, 287).

120. *Etym.*, l. 6, c. 4 (PL, LXXXII, 236 BC).

121. *In Ap.*, l. 10 (649 H).

122. "divinae legis interpres Hieronymus": *In Sap.*, prol. (PL, CIX, 671 C).

123. *In Eccli.*, praef. (763 A). *Ep. Gislae atque Rectudae ad Alb.:* "Open your mouth confidently for the exposition of John's Gospel" — "Aperi confidenter os tuum in . . . Joannis ev. expositionem" (C, 739 C).

124. "Nobilis interpres": *P. latini aevi car.*, 3, 243.

125. Cassiodorus, *In ps.* lxxvii, v. 69: "Blessed Jerome, a reliable translator amongst the others, put 'fortis' [strong] instead of 'potens' [powerful]" — "B. Hieronymus, inter alios veridicus, pro potente fortis posuit" (PL, LXX, 571 A).

126. Philip of Harvengt (CCIII, 652 CD).

127. "viri graecae linguae interpretes"; "de graeca in latinam linguam interpretari": *De una . . . deitate*, 6 (CXXV, 536 D).

128. "singulorum interpretum editiones conferre": *ep.* 16, n. 2 (CXXI, 484 C); etc.

129. "Ille devotus verbi Dei est auditor, iste maliciosus Scripturarum est interpretator": *In Eccli.*, l. 7, c. 9 (CIX, 996 D). *Cl. inst.*, l. 3, c. 8, after Aug. (CVII, 585 AB).

130. "Interpres enim ego quodammodo in hoc opere sum, non alterius linguae, sed alterius locutionis, ut ejusdem sensus veritatem explanem": L. 2, praef. (CVII, 265 B).

131. "Nec verbum verbo curabis reddere, fidus
    Interpres":

Ib., "Horace . . . gives the learned translator the same advice, saying . . ." — "Hoc idem Horatius . . . erudito interpreti praecepit dicens. . . ."

132. "Arbitramur . . . Hieronymum hujus verbi esse interpretem": *In Matt.*, l. 2, c. 1 (CXX, 117 B).

133. "Sive interpretes, sive expositores divinorum eloquiorum": *Adv. Fredeg.*, c. 8 (CIV, 164 A).

134. "Nostram interpretationem veram credo": *In Reg.*, l. 2, c. 5 (CXV, 348 A).

135. "Quod graece hypostasis dicitur, hoc nonnulli personam, nonnulli vero subsistentiam interpretati sunt": *ep.* 6 (MGH, *Ep. aevi car.*, 5, 417).

136. *Ep.* 2: "Is it really the case that since some have already translated sacred Scripture, later translators have translated it to a lesser degree? If this were true, would not the Latin drawn from the original Hebrew by blessed Jerome . . . have exhausted the same holy Scripture?" — "Num quidnam quia Scripturam sacram quidam interpretati sunt, idcirco posteriores interpretes hanc minus interpretati sunt ? Si hoc esset, eamdam sanctam Scripturam latinitas ex Hebraico fonte per B. Hieronymum . . . non hausisset" (399-400).

137. "Tam graecum quam latinum interpretem": *Defl.*, l. 2 (PL, CLVII, 1055 D). Cf. Abelard (CLXXVIII, 334 BC).

138. "Veteres tam Graecorum quam et Latinorum interpretes haec eadem continue egisse perhibentur": *Praef. ms.* (Haskins, 151).

139. "lex interpretationis": Greith, *Spicil. vatic.*, 98.

140. "Quia superius duobus modis hoc solium interpretati sumus, secundum utrumque modum expositionem adaptare debemus": *De arca Noe mor.*, l. 1, c. 2 (PL, CLXXVI, 624 A); cf. *Didasc.*, l. 4, c. 5; *De interpretibus* (780-1); but *In Eccl.*, praef.: "All Scripture explained according to its proper translation" — "Omnis scriptura secundum propriam interpretationem exposita" (CLXXV, 114 C). Cassiodorus, *In ps.* clx, v. 8: "This is the word that the translator Jerome set down and the commentator Father Augustine has followed him" — "Quod verbum Hieronymus translator posuit et expositor Pater Aug. secutus est" (LXX, 1002 B).

141. "quos, si vellem discutere . . . , a veterum Graecorum docerem interpretationibus discrepare": *ep.* 105, c. 5 (5, 103).

142. "Porro quod dicis non debuisse me interpretari post veteres, et novo uteris syllogismo: "Aut obscura fuerunt quae interpretati sunt Septuaginta, aut manifesta; si obscura, te quoque in eis falli potuisse credendum est; si manifesta, illos in eis falli non potuisse perspicuum est," tuo tibi sermone respondeo. Omnes veteres tractatores qui nos in Domino praecesserunt et qui Scripturas sanctas interpretati sunt, aut obscura interpretati sunt, aut manifesta. Si obscura, quomodo tu post eos ausus es disserere, quod illi explanare non potuerunt? Si manifesta, superfluum est te voluisse disserere quod illos latere non potuit, maxime in explanatione psalmorum quos apud Graecos interpretati sunt multis voluminibus, primus Origenes, etc.: apud Latinos autem, etc. Respondeat mihi prudentia tua: quare tu post tantos et tales interpretes in explanatione psalmorum diversa senseris?": *ep.* 112, c. 20 (6, 39-40).

143. "historica interpretatio": *In Matt.*, prol.: "I have briefly . . . composed a historical interpretation" — "Historicam interpretationem . . . digessi breviter" (XXVI, 20).

144. "ecclesiastica interpretatio": *In Matt.*, 1.3, c. 19 (133 B). Cf. Ambrose: "a

deeper interpretation" — "profundior interpretatio" (XVII, 375 B; 344 B: "a deeper understanding" — "profundior intellectus").

145. "commentaria dicta, quasi cum mente": *Etym.*, l. 6, c. 8, n. 5; "for there are interpretations such as comments about juridical matters, comments on the gospel" — "sunt enim interpretationes, ut commenta juris, commenta evangelii" (PL, LXXXII, 238 B). Cf. R. Simon, *Difficultés proposées au P. Bouhours*, 98: "You are putting . . . the commentary into the translation" — "Vous mettez . . . le commentaire dans la version" (J. Steinmann, *Richard Simon*, 1960, 317).

146. Florus, *De tenenda Script. ver.*, c. 6: "where the Latin translator was bringing over the gist of the original" — "ubi Latinus interpres ad sensum transferens" (CXXI, 1096 B). Aelfric, pref. to his *Sermones catholici*, translated into English: "Nor have we everywhere translated word for word, but rather thought for thought" — "Nec ubique transtulimus verbum ex verbo, sed sensum ex sensu"; etc.

147. [Translator's note: De Lubac gives two marks indicating footnote 4, one corresponding to our note 145, and the other, to our 147. The latter note has apparently dropped out and does not appear in the French text.]

148. *Inst. biblicae*, I (1927), and 6th ed. (1951), 510: "exegeseos sive interpretationis." — Cf. Or., *Sel. in Ez.*, vii: οὐχ ἑρμηνευσάντων. . . . = "non redditum a Septuaginta interpretibus," i.e., not rendered by the LXX translators (PG, XIII, 795-6 A).

149. "Bethania, quae interpretatur domus obedientiae," "Benjamin, id est filius dexterae": *In Matt. ser.*, 77 (178). Alcuin, *In Ap.*, l. 2 (PL, C, 1132 A), etc. The ancient *De montibus Sina et Sion*, c. 1-2 speaks of the "interpretatio de hebraica lingua in latinam" of these two names, and of their "hebraica interpretatio" (IV, 909 C).

150. "Noe, quod interpretatur requies, est Christus"; "Abram, quod interpretatur pater excelsus": Rupert (PL, CLXVIII, 247 A; 167, 367 D), etc.

151. "Balaam interpretatur populus varius," "Dagon interpretatur piscis tristitiae, significans hostem antiquum qui in mare totius mundi positus devorat piscatores": Alcuin, *In Ap.* (C, 1105 a). Rabanus (CIX, 28 A, following Jerome).

152. "Jesus salvator sive salutaris interpretatur": Odilon of Cluny (CXLII, 999 B), etc.

153. "Booz, qui fortitudo interpretatur, significat Christum, de quo dicitur: Dominus in fortitudine veniat": Anselm of Laon, *In Matt.*, c. 1 (CLXII, 1241 CD).

154. Or., *In Lev.*, h. 4, n. 8 (328). Jerome (PL, XXVI, 100 C).

155. Aug., *In ps.* lxxviii, n. 26 (CCL, 39, 1086).

156. *Quaest. V. et N. T.*, q. 108 (Souter, 251). Cf. Aulus Gellius, *Noctes atticae*, l. 10, c. 4 (C. Hosias, 1, 345), following Nigidius.

157. *Life of Moses*, 1, 23. Cf. *Q. in Gen.*, etc. — P. Boyancé, *Le culte des Muses* . . . , 295: "In the exegesis of myths, etymological word-play has been able to serve as a particularly fruitful principle of method. . . . And this use of etymology itself rests upon a certain conception of the origins of language" — "Le jeu de mots étymologique a pu être dans l'exégèse des mythes une sorte de principe de méthode particulièrement fécond. . . . Et cet usage de l'étymologie repose luimême sur une certaine conception des origines du langage." We may smile at many of these fantastic etymologies; but "we have no idea what wisdom and la-

bor is hidden in disentangling the chaos of the ancient tongues" — "nous n'imaginons pas ce qui se cachait de savoir et de travail dans le débrouillement du chaos des anciennes langues": Ozanam, 1, 268.

158. "jeu de l'étymologie, renouvelé de *Cratyle* — ou faut-il dire annonçant Heidegger?": H.-I. Marrou, in *Recherches sur la trad. platonicienne* (1947), 188.

159. "Altior autem sensus nominum interpretatione signatur": *De Noe et arca*, c. 28, n. 105 (PL, XIV, 409 A). *De Cain*, l. 1, c. 1, n. 3: "which is grasped more fully by a translation of the names" — "quod nominum interpretatione plenius deprehenditur" (317 A).

160. "Interpretationem nominis sui unumquodque eorum magno sacramento rei alicujus constat appositum": *Inst.*, c. 15 (LXX, 1127 B).

161. "studiosissime": *In ps.* lxxix, v. 2 (580 B).

162. *In ps.* lxxxvii, v. 72: "For it ought to be remembered that holy Scripture often shows us hidden causes through the Hebrew names. This type of speech is doubtless characteristic of sacred literature, while anything of this sort is by no means contained in worldly literature" — "Memoria quippe condendum est, quod per Hebraea nomina Scriptura sancta causas nobis saepius declarat occultas. Quod genus locutionis sacrarum litterarum proprium esse non dubium est, quando tale aliquid mundanis litteris minime continetur" (571 BC). Cf. Ps.-Max of Turin (Maximinus, Arian bishop?), *C. Judaeos qui sunt sec. litteram Judaei*, c. 1, regarding the names Cain and Abel (C. H. Turner, JTS 20, 293); etc.

163. "période d'enfance": Spicq, 239.

164. "Sciendum autem quod in Hebraea quidem lingua manifestam nominis aetymologiam sive derivationem litteratura resonat": *In Gen.*, l. 2, c. 38 (PL, CLXVII, 285 C). Cf. *In Jos.*, h. 15, n. 6, on the name of Satan: "the very interpretation of his name, as the scholars of the Hebrews hand it down" — "Ipsa nominis ejus interpretatio, sicut studiosi Hebraeorum tradunt" (A. Jaubert, SC, 71, 352).

165. Wicbold, *Sup. librum Gen.* (XCVI, 1147 B).

166. *In Num.*, h. 2, n. 2 (11); *De oratione*, c. 24, n. 2 (353-4); etc. Cf. Wutz, *Onomastica sacra* (TU, 41, 11, 764-71).

167. F. Cavallera, in *Miscell. Agost.* (1931), 362. Cf. B. Altaner, "Augustinus und die biblischen Onomastica" (*Festg. f. Fr. X. Seppelt*, 1953, 34-6). M. Pontet, 276-8.

168. "Primo nomina ipsa attendite, quam mystica sint"; "Etiam nomen ipsum si attendamus, non est sine mysterio": *In ps.* li, n. 2 and 4 (CCL, 39, 624, 625).

169. Cf. Fontaine, 40-4, 50.

170. "Various renderings of this name are held in esteem" — "Varia hujus nominis interpretatio aestimatur" (PL, C, 552 A). V. *infra*, ch. XIII, iv.

171. "Et ipsa interpretatio nominum, hujus figurae non refugit intellectum": *Collect. in V. T.* (CXLV, 1007 C).

172. "si quis ea possit interpretari": *Cl. inst.*, l. 3, c. 10 (CVII, 386 B).

173. "per . . . nominum interpretationem moralia mysticis internectens": *In nat. Dom.*, s. 2, n. 8 (CLXXXIV, 838 C).

174. "interpretatio nominum": PL, CXII, 860-1.

175. "Etymologia est origo vocabulorum, cum vis verbi vel nominis per interpretationem colligitur. . . . Omnis autem rei cognitio etymologia nominis

perspecta planior fit": *De grammatica* (Leclercq, AHDLMA, 14, 299). John of Salisbury, *Metal.*, l. 1, c. 14: "The very imposition of names and of other words, though it proceed by human choice, is in a way beholden to nature, which it imitates as best it can" — "Ipsa quoque nominum impositio aliorumque dictionum, etsi arbitrio humano processerit, naturae quodammodo obnoxia est, quam pro modulo suo probabiliter imitatur" (CXCIX, 841 A).

176. "Cana quoque zelus et Galilaea transmigratio interpretatur ex Hebraico in Latinum": S. 8 (CCXVII, 346 C). Adam Scot, *s.* 39, c. 12: "Those who know the translation of the Hebrew names say. . . ." — "Dicunt qui interpretationem norunt nominum hebraicorum" (CXCVIII, 360 A).

177. "Alleluia latinae linguae peregrinum nomen est, cujus mysterium, velut quoddam gaudi stillicidium, de divitiis supernae Hierusalem delapsum est. . . . Quapropter (non) interpretatum hoc hebraicum nomen remansit, ut peregrinum in hac vita gaudium, peregrinum nihilominus signaret potius quam exprimeret vocabulum: quoniam igitur futurae beatitudinis quasi proprium est vocabulum": *Div. off.*, l. 1, c. 35 (CLXX, 30 BC).

178. *S.* 31 (CCXVII, 818 C).

179. "Haec ergo duo verba Hebraica, id est, Alleluia et Amen, cum interpretari queant, . . . propter reverentiam tamen sanctitatis, primae illius linguae servetur auctoritas": *De laud. s. crucis*, l. 1, fig. 25 (CVII, 250 A). Cf. Jerome, above, note 104.

180. "Melchi, rex; sedech vero, justitiae interpretatur; et quid aliud est, rex justitiae, nisi Dominus noster Jesus Christus, de quo jam dictum est: Dilexisti justitiam et odisti iniquitatem?": Ps.-Atto, *In Hebr.* (CXXXIV, 764 B).

181. Cf. Isidore, *Etym.*, l. 6, c. 4, n. 5 (LXXXII, 236 C). One will note that he says of Jerome's version just what Aug. said of the *Itala;* above, note 110.

182. "aliquam de interpretum translatione memoriam facere"; "Fuerunt et alii interpretes, qui ex Hebraea lingua in Graecam sacra eloquia transtulerunt, sicut Aquila, Symmachus, Theodotion. Est etiam et Vulgata interpretatio . . .": *De varia*, c. 1 and 3 (CXLII, 1131 A, 1132 B). "Blessed Jerome translated the whole Scripture of the Old Testament from Hebrew into the Latin language; and his *translation* is deservedly preferred to the others, as Isidore says: for it is both more literal and clearer. But Pope St. Gregory also asserts that his *translation* is more reliable than the others" — "B. Hieronymus . . . omnem Scripturam veteris testamenti ex Hebraeo in Latinum vertit eloquium; cujus *interpretatio* merito caeteris antefertur, ut Isidorus ait: est enim et verborum tenacior et perspicuitate sententiae clarior. Sed et S. Gregorius papa ipsius *translationem* caeteris asserit esse veraciorem" (1132 D). [Translator's italics.]

183. *De varia*, c. 6 (1143-4).

184. Greg., *Mor.*, l. 1, c. 21, n. 29 (LXXV, 540-1), etc.

185. *Ep.* 1 (CXLII, 1159 A).

186. "Dulces theoriae carpebat quotidie fructus, cum verba, quae in sacris codicibus legebat, mox in opera vertebat": *Vita S. Udalr.*, c. 2 (1186 B). The expression came from Jerome, *ep.* 58, c. 2: "you turn words into deeds" — "verba vertis in opera" (3, 75), doubtless through Defensor, *L. scintill.*, c. 81, n. 12 (Rochais, CCL, 117, 231). It is also found in Alcuin, *L. de virt. et vitiis*, c. 5 (PL, CI, 617 A). Cf. B. De Vregille, *Dict. Sp.* 4, 177.

187. "Amalarius, divinorum officiorum scrutator non contemnendus"; "Amalarius, divinorum officiorum indagator solertissimus, cujus dicta catholicorum virorum sententiis fulgent munita": *De quibusd. rebus ad missae off. pert.*, c. 4 (1064 C); cf. c. 7 (1076 B). *Qualiter adventus Dom. celebretur*, c. 2 (1081 C). "As a liturgist, he belongs to the school of Amalarius, whom he often copies" — "Comme liturgist, il se rattache à l'école d'Amalaire, qu'il copie souvent": A. Gatard, DACL, 2, 1, 822.

188. "à cet énorme courant allégoriste dont Othloh de Saint-Emmeran trace les principes dans son petit traité *Quomodo legendum sit in rebus visibilibus*": T. 2, 5.

189. C. *Libros 4 Amalarii abb.* (PL, CIV, 339-50); *L. de div. psalmodia* (325-30). The true author, as is known, is Florus: Wilmart, RB, 36, 317-29. Cf. CM, 297-300.

190. "de Hebraico in Latinum": *Adv. Fredeg. abb.*, c. 9 (CIV, 154-5).

191. "plebeios psalmos"; "humana figmenta et mendacia"; "divini sermones"; "purissima verba": *Div. psalm.* (327 A, 328 A). *De correct. antiph.*, c. 9 (333); c. 19: "We have an antiphonary purged of all human artifices and lies and most sufficiently ordered through the whole cycle of the year out of the purest words of holy Scripture" — "Antiphonarium habemus omnibus humanis figmentis et mendaciis expurgatum et per totum anni circulum ex purissimis sanctae Scripturae verbis sufficentissime ordinatum" (338 C); c. 2: "Just as no one may ask in godly fashion unless he inspire it, so none may worthily praise God unless he do the training. Therefore the divine majesty is to be praised not by just anyone's artifices, but with the utterances of the Holy Spirit" — "Sicut nemo nisi ipso inspirante secundum Deum postulat, ita nullus nisi eo erudiente Deum digne collaudat. Non ergo cujuscumque figmentis, sed Spiritus sancti eloquiis majestas divina laudanda est" (330 B).

192. "avait enrichi l'office monastique de textes non bibliques en usage dans certaines églises, comme ces hymnes qu'il avait appelés ambrosiens": Leclercq, *L'amour des lettres*, 220; cf. 222. Berno, *De varia*, c. 7 (CXLII, 1145 AC). Amalarius, *De regula S. Benedicti*, n. 6: "Certum autem esse probatur quoniam ipse sanctus Benedictus consuetum morem sancti Ambrosii in nonnullis ecclesiasticis elegisse, v. d. de hymnis quos ambrosianos appellat" (J. M. Hanssens, 3, 274).

193. *Corr. antiph.*, c. 3-9 (CIV, 331-3); c. 5: "Everywhere the greatest care is to be observed lest the order of the divine words be changed and a maze of error be woven from the Scripture of truth" — "summopere utique cavendum est ne divinorum verborum ordo mutetur et de Scriptura veritatis labyrinthus texatur erroris" (331 C); c. 8: "Still another responsory [composed] of the words of the gospel, but not in gospel order" — "Aliud quoque responsorium de verbis evangelii, sed non ordine evangelico" (332 CD).

194. "Sacrae Scripturae verba sui sensus perversitati coaptat": *Ib.*, c. 5 (331 C).

195. C. 10 (334 A); c. 5 (331 C); c. 3 (330 C); c. 9 (333 BC).

196. C. 2 (29 B). V. *infra*, ch. XII, iii.

197. *Div. off.*, l. 5, c. 1, on the chants "that have been composed of the authentic Scriptures of the Old and New Testament" — "quae de authenticis veteris ac novi Testamenti Scripturis congesta sunt" (PL CLXX, 123 B). Abelard as well will be less rigorous; *ep.* 8: "Let nothing be read or chanted in the Church except what has been taken from the authentic scripture, especially the new or the old Testament" — "Nihil in Ecclesia legatur aut cantetur nisi de authentica sumptum

scriptura, maxime autem de novo vel veteri T." (LCXXVIII, 281 C). Cf. already Tertullian, *Apol.*, c. 39, n. 18 (G. P. Waltzing–A. Severyns, 85).

198. *In f. Petri et Pauli*, s. 2, n. 5 (PL, CLXXXIII, 410 D).

199. *In vig. nat.*, s. 3, n. 1: "When she alters or alternates words in the divine Scriptures, that composition is stronger than was the first location of the words" — "Cum ipsa (Ecclesia) in Scripturis divinis verba vel alterat vel alternat, fortior est illa compositio quam positio prima verborum" (CLXXXIII, 94 D). Cf. *In dom. palm.*, s. 1, n. 1 (253 D). *In Cant.*, s. 51, n. 4 (1027 AB). Bernard nonetheless pursued the abuses of it relentlessly: *Tr. de cantu*, n. 2 (CLXXXII, 1123 AB).

200. *L. c. objectiones Fred.*, c. 7: "You also say that you are defending divine Scripture with your whole intention along with its editors, translators, and commentators from the calumnies of our incompetence.... For who of us has ever calumniated any editor or translator of the divine Scriptures?... The translators or commentators do not at all worry about indeclinably hanging on to a rule of grammar; they did this neither from incompetence nor malice but by reason of condescension.... For its interpreters, in following it, strove to the utmost to bring across that whereby they might furnish readers with the rather plain sense, even if it were ungrammatical, so that it might be in accord with the mystery signified" — "Dicitis etiam tota vos intentione divinam Scripturam cum editoribus, interpretibus atque expositoribus suis ab imperitiae nostrae calumniis defendere.... Quis enim de nobis calumniatus est unquam editorem aut interpretem aliquem divinarum Scripturarum?... Interpretes divinorum voluminum vel expositores non curarunt omnino tenere indeclinabiliter regulam grammaticae artis; quod utique neque imperitia neque malitia fecerunt sed ratione condescensionis.... Interpretes enim ejus eam sequendo illud studuerunt summopere transferre, unde manifestiorem sensum legentibus praeberent etiam si contra grammaticam esset eatenus, ut sacramento rei concordaret" (CIV, 162-3). C. 8: "Neither the translators nor the commentators of the divine eloquence were afraid to speak ungrammatically so as to exhibit the integrity of the sense, and we not only do not take them to task but, through their example, we want to be defended from rebuke as well" — "Sive interpretes sive expositores divinorum eloquiorum ut integritatem sensus ostenderent contra grammaticam loqui non timuerunt, quos non solum non reprehendimus, verum etiam per eos a reprehensione defendi cupimus . . ." (163-4).

201. C. 7: "In this way everybody ought completely to spare us, who, even if we want to say everything grammatically, cannot do so, provided that we hang on to the true faith and the catholic sense" — "Ita nobis omnino debet (quisque) parcere, qui etiamsi velimus omnia secundum grammaticam loqui, non possumus, si tamen fidem rectam et sensum catholicum tenemus" (163 B).

202. Above, note 200; c. 9: "The translators of the whole of divine Scripture along with its catholic commentators can be reasonably defended from the calumny of incompetence" — "Totius divinae Scripturae interpretes cum catholicis ejus expositoribus ab imperitae calumnia rationabiliter defendi queunt" (164 BC); "those infamous judaizing and heretical translators, to wit, Aquila, Theodotion, and Symmachus" — "illi famosissimi interpretes judaizantes et haeretici, Aquila sc., et Theodotio, ac Symmachus" (164-5); c. 10: "So much for the translators...."

The commentators, too. . . ." — "Haec de interpretibus. . . . De expositoribus quoque" (165 AB).

203. "more paterno"; "sanctorum Patrum constitutio veneranda"; "divinae legis veritas"; "immobili atque inconvulsa observatione"; "contra morem officii": *Div. psalm.*; "faithfully to keep the custom of the Fathers that the statutes of the Church declare, and thereby in no way to depart from the ancient use of the Church of God" — "paternum morem, quem statuta ecclesiastica declarant, fideliter custodire ac per hoc ab antiquo Ecclesiae Dei usu nullatenus discrepare" (326 C). *De cav. convictu et soc. Jud.* (112 B). *De corr. antiph.*, c. 7 (331-2).

204. "ab ipsa mundi origine descendens"; "nuper dispersum, non nuper inventum": *Adv. Fred.*, c. 21-2 (173-4); c. 22: "But if anyone should think that what is called a 'new name' in Isaiah or in the Apocalypse, doubtless understanding the name 'Christian', is to count as an objection against this: let him know that the holy doctors have understood in such a way that it is called 'new' because it was recently spread, not because it was recently discovered; and hence the religion of the Christians is not some Johnnie-come-lately that has arisen recently, but coming down from the very origin of the world, with the self-same Christ as its teacher and founder" — "Si quis autem ad haec objiciendum putaverit illud, quod in Isaia vel in Apoc. nomen novum dicitur, quod procul dubio christianum intelligitur: sciat sanctos doctores ita intellexisse, ut novum dicatur propterea quia nuper dispersum, non quia nuper inventum; ac per hoc non novella vel nuper exorta est christianorum religio, sed ab ipsa mundi origine descendens, eodem Christo doctore et institutore" (174). But elsewhere, against Fredegisius, Agobard, following St. Augustine, laid claim to a just freedom in respect to the various commentators of the holy Books: c. 10 (165 B).

205. "secundum consuetudinem antiquam": *De quibusd. rebus ad missae off. pert.*, c. 7 (PL, CXLII, 1078 B). Cf. Deut. 32.

206. "Quoties in ecclesiastici ordinis ritu minus concordamus, oportet ut ad consilium magistrorum recurramus, per quos, ut Scriptura testatur, Sapientia divina profunda fluviorum scrutata est, et abscondita produxit in lucem, legislatore id etiam praecipiente: 'Interroga patrem tuum, et annuntiabit tibi; majores, et dicent tibi'": *Qualiter adv. Dom. celebretur*, init. (1079 B).

207. *Ib.*, c. 3: "We have accepted the rite by which we celebrate the Lord's coming unhesitatingly from the holy Fathers Gelasius, Gregory, Jerome, and Hilary, which stand as bases at the foundations of the holy Church; to be unwilling to acquiesce to their judgments is to break the divine law" — "Ritum quo adventum Domini celebramus, a sanctis Patribus Gelasio, Gregorio, Hieronymo atque Hilario indubitanter accepimus, quae velut bases consistunt in sanctae Ecclesiae fundamentis, quorum sententiis nolle acquiescere transgressio est legis divinae" (1084-5).

208. *Dial. de jejuniis*, c. 2 (1089-90). Compare Paschasius, *Vitae Walae*, l. 2, c. 3: "Alas! . . . At that point all, most especially the men of the Church, began asking and wrangling how else the dignity and honor of the churches could stand, as if they had not read the decisions of the holy Fathers" — "Proh dolor! . . . Tunc omnes caeperunt maxime ecclesiastici viri quaerere et contradicere, quomodo aliter dignitas et honor ecclesiarum stare potuisset, ac si decreta sanctorum Patrum non legissent" (MGH, *Scr.*, 2, 549).

209. *De quibusd. rebus,* c. 7: "The catholic Fathers have set the limits for the right faith and holy doctrine from the beginning, and it is utterly wrong to violate them. But there many church customs are also found constituted by the holy Fathers below the level of the limits of canonical rule, such as the Lord's Advent, Septuagesima [Sunday], rogation days, vigils of certain saints, as well as this fasting of four times . . . , and many other things, all of which we are to observe by longstanding right without any transgression and to take as law, as Augustine says . . . of the sabbath fast: For in matters about which divine Scripture has established nothing certain, the custom of the people of God or the institutions of our ancestors is to be taken as law" — "Terminos rectae fidei sanctaeque doctrinae posuerunt ab initio Patres catholici, quae omnino nefas est transgredi. Sed et multae consuetudines ecclesiasticae inveniuntur a sanctis Patribus infra canonicae regulae terminos constitutae, sicut sunt adventus Domini, Septuagesima . . . , dies rogationum . . . , vigiliae quorumdam sanctorum, necnon et haec ipsa quatuor temporum jejunia . . . , aliaque perplura quae omnia jure perpetuo absque ulla trangsressione nobis sunt observanda ac pro lege tenenda, dicente Augustino . . . de jejunio sabbati: In his enim rebus, de quibus nihil certi statuit Scriptura divina, mos populi Dei vel instituta majorum pro lege tenenda sunt" (CXLII, 1073 CD).

210. "flair critique": On this "flair" of Florus: C. Charlier, "Alcuin, Florus, et le 'Cogitis me'," *St. patr.* 1, 75-76.

211. *Libellus de tenenda immobiliter Scripturae veritate et SS. orthodoxorum Patrum auctoritate fideliter servanda;* c. 1: "ex proprio sensu temeraria praesumptione" (PL, CXXI, 1083 D).

212. *Ib.* (1083). *L. de tribus epist.*: "The answer of the faith, not based on our own sense but on the immobile truth of the Scriptures" — "Responsionem fidei, non ex nostro sensu sed ex Scripturarum immobili veritate" (987 D). *Adv. J. Scotum* (CXIX, 103 B, 116 D). Agobard (CIV, 112 BC).

213. Agobard, *Div. psalm.*: "nor to condemn anyone's variant custom, if it is determined that it can be approved" — "nec contemnere alicujus diversum morem, si constat esse probabilem" (CIV, 326 C).

214. "dispar ordo psallendi"; "compar ordo credendi": *L. Carolini,* 1, c. 6: "so that there were not a disparate order of singing the Psalter for those to whom there is the same order of believing; and those that had been united by the sacred reading of one holy law should also have been united by the venerable tradition of one modulation; nor should a varying celebration of the offices separate what pious devotion had joined to the single faith" — "ut non esset dispar ordo psallendi, quibus erat compar ordo credendi; et quae unitae erant unius sanctae legis sacra lectione, essent etiam unitae unius modulationis veneranda traditione; nec sejungerit officiorum varia celebratio, quae conjunxerat unicae fidei pia devotio" (XCVIII, 1021 CD). Charlemagne did not however look for total uniformity: *to Alcuin* (Alcuin, ep. 144; MGH, ep. 4, 230).

215. This *De initio adventus Domini sec auctoritatem Hilarii episcopi,* preserved without the author's name amongst the works of Berno, is, according to Dom Blanchard, "très différant de ton"; on the other hand, Berno had never studied at Fleury nor attended the Council of Orléans (in 1935 Volk adopts this thesis of

Blanchard, but Van de Vyver rejects it), which would render the account reported here impossible.

216. "Si est unus Dominus, una fides, unum baptisma, sit et una Ecclesiae unanimitas!": "Indeed we at Fleury were there, armed with the authority of the Fathers and well equipped without swords, and we were victorious speaking against them all in such wise as to impose eternal silence on them concernng this business. From that day forth there was not to be found amongst Gauls or Germans anyone reckless enough to be willing to go against so sound a determination. For if there is one Lord, one faith, one baptism, let there also be one unanimity of the Church!" — "Nos quippe Floriacenses, Patrum auctoritate armati et ingladiabiliter perarmati adfuimus, et ita contradicentes in omnibus convicimus, ut in aeternum eis silentium super hoc negotio imponeremus. Ex illo die et deinceps non est apud Gallos vel Germanos praesumptor inventus, qui huic tam sanae diffinitioni vellet contraire. Quapropter si est unus etc." (CXLII, 1088 AB). *Dial. de jejuniis*, c. 1 (1089 B). Cf. Affo of Fleury, *Apologeticus* (CXXXIX, 472 A).

217. On the rather more complex historical reality: *Collectanea biblica latina*, x, *Le psautier romain et les autres anciens psautiers latins*, crit. ed., by Dom Robert Weber (1953), intr., viii-ix, xi; *S. Hieronymi Psalterium juxta Hebraeos*, crit. ed., by Dom Henri de Sainte-Marie (1954), intr., v; xiii, *Richesses*; B. Botte, DBS, 5, 337-9; Id., "Les anc. versions de la Bible," in *la Maison-Dieu*, 53 (1958). J. Gribomont, "L'Église et les versions bibliques," *la Maison-Dieu*, 62 (1960), 59-60.

218. "Romani canunt . . . , nos vero . . ."; "Ubi illi canunt . . . , nos . . ."; "Illi modulantur, nos autem . . ."; "Ubi Romana editio habet . . . , nostra habet . . .": *De varia*, c. 5 (PL, CXLII, 1133-42). *De quibusd. rebus*, c. 2 (1058-61).

219. Thus, "in tremore" instead of "cum tremore"; "tibi derelictus" instead of "tibi enim derelictus"; "custodi me" instead of "custodi me Domine"; "intende mihi" instead of "intende in me," etc.

220. On these two versions, as they were seen at that time: Ps.-Bede, *In psalmorum liber exegesis*, praef. alt. (PL, XCIII, 481 AB). The author knows, however, that Jerome had made a less felicitous first translation completely "ad litteram"; he also knows that there were other Latin translations, "none of which is in use" — "quarum nulla in usu est." On Jerome and the Three Psalters: *Sigeberti chronica*, a. 382 (MGH, Scr., 6, 302).

221. "In Hebraeo scriptum est — Hebraicum huic sententiae congruit — in Hebraeo non habetur": *De varia*, c. 5, passim (1135 C, 1137 B, 1138 C . . .).

222. "pius ac peritus magister Hieronymus": *Ib.*, c. 4 (1133 C).

223. C. 5: "In the eighth Psalm 'I see your heavens' is not in the Greek, but *Samech* is found in the Hebrew, which means 'your heavens'" — "In octavo psalmo 'video caelos tuos', non habetur in graeco, sed in hebraeo legitur Samecha, quod interpretatur caelos tuos" (1134 C).

224. C. 5: "Where they chant, 'My soul has thirsted for the living God', under the asterisk we have 'for the mighty God'" — "Ubi illi canunt: 'Sitivit anima mea ad Deum vivum', nos habemus sub asterico: 'ad Deum fortem'" (1135 D).

225. "pour les versets d'un certain nombre de répons"; "se trouvent presque toutes au bréviaire actuel": A. Gatard, DACL, 2, 822.

226. "Quidam vitiose adjungunt"; "Quidam codices in masculino genere habent, cum juxta Hebraicum feminine genere pronuntiandum sit"; "Illam

antiphonam quam quidam modulantur: . . . , in Hebraeo habetur . . .": C. 6 (1142 BC, 1143 AB). "In the Hebrew" always means "in our version that was made by Jerome on the basis of the Hebrew." The expression comes from Jerome himself. Cf. Abelard's remark, PL, CLXXVIII, 334 BC.

227. "liberalibus artibus eruditi"; "In illo introitu quem canimus in die natalis Domini, 'Puer natus est nobis et filius datus est nobis', nostra translatio secundum Hebraicam veritatem habet: "Parvulus natus est nobis, filius datus est nobis"; et pro eo quod canimus: 'cujus imperium super humerum ejus', Hebraica veritas habet: 'Et factus est principatus super humerum ejus'; et pro eo quod canimus: 'Et vocabitur nomen ejus magni consilii angelus', in Hebraeo sex nomina habentur: 'Admirabilis, Consiliarius, Deus, Fortis, Pater futuri saeculi, Princeps pacis'": C. 6 (1142-3).

228. "hebraica consuetudo": C. 6 (1144 D, etc.; 1143 CD, 1144 AB).

229. Agobard: "this" is the reading "according to the Hebrew; but the older translation" has . . . — "haec juxta hebraicum; antiquior autem translatio . . ." (CIV, 190 C); "but according to the Hebraic translation" — "secundum hebraicam tamen translationem" (280 D).

230. "consonantia hebraicae veritatis": *De varia,* c. 3 (CXLII, 1133 A); etc. V. *infra,* ch. III, iv.

231. *Mor.,* l. 20, c. 32, n. 62: "The old translation is far off track from this notion. . . . But yet, since this new translation from the Hebrew and Arabic [sic] languages is regarded as having rendered everything more truly for us, whatever is said in it is to be believed" — "Longe ab hac sententia vetus translatio dissonat. . . . Sed tamen, quia haec nova translatio ex Hebraeo nobis Arabicoque eloquio cuncta verius transfudisse perhibetur, credendum est quidquid in ea dicitur" (PL, LXXVI, 174 B); l. 4, c. 9, n. 15 (LXXV, 645 A). *In Ez.,* l. 1, h. 7, n. 23: "But what is given below . . . is not in the old translation. . . . Carefully rereading the translation of the Septuagint translators, however, viz. Aquila, Theodotion, and Symmachus, we have found none of these words; but rereading blessed Jerome's writings, we have recognized that he has found this thought put in this way in the Hebrew truth, not to be sure following the word but rather according to the sense" — "Hoc autem quod subditur . . . in translatione veteri non habetur. . . . Translationem autem Septuaginta interpretum, Aquilae, Theodotionis et Symmachi, sollicite perscrutatentes, nihil ex his verbis invenimus; sed beati Hieronymi scripta relegentes, agnovimus quia hanc sententiam in Hebraea veritate ita positam, non quidem juxta verbum sed juxta sensum invenerit" (LXXVI, 832 BC,); l. 1, h. 10, n. 6: "In the old translation 'your belly has eaten' is not found, but rather 'your mouth may eat'; in the later translation, however, which we also believe to be closer to the truth, it does stand written" — "In translatione veteri non habetur 'venter tuus comedit', sed 'os tuum comedat'; in posteriori autem translatione, quam et veraciorem credimus, scriptum est . . ." (887-8). Cf. l. 2, h. 1, n. 10 (943 A).

232. "sapientissimus papa Gregorius": PL, CXLII, 1058 C.

233. *Mor.,* ep. miss., c. 5: "But I am discussing the new translation: still, when the situation requires it, I take up at one time the new, at another the old, for evidence; so that, since the apostolic See . . . relies on them both, the labor of my study may be upheld from them both" — "Novam vero translationem dissero:

sed cum probationis causa exigit, nunc novam, nunc veterem per testimonia assumo; ut, quia sedes apostolica . . . utraque nititur, mei quoque labor studii ex utraque fulciatur" (LXXV, 516 C); "avec un souci de critique réel"; "le plus véridique": Details can be found in P. Salmon, OSB, "Le texte de Job utilisé par S. Grég. dans les *Moralia*" (*Miscell. biblica et orient., St. ans.*, 27-8), 187-94.

234. "Hebraica canit": *De varia*, c. 5 (1137 D).

235. "Gallicanum psalterium, quod nos canimus": C. 4 (1133 C).

236. "In illo introitu, ubi illi cantant . . .": C. 5 (1141 C).

237. "Verba permutando canunt . . .": C. 8 (1145 D).

238. *Div. psalm.*: "Solito cantorum ministerio" (CIV, 325 C).

239. "It was doubtless he whom Notker had in mind when he wrote to the bishop of Sion that the abbot of Reichenau requests the loan of Cicero's *Philippics* and his commentaries on the *Topics*, offering him as security Cicero's *Rhetoric* and the commentary of Victorinus" — "C'est de lui sans doute qu'il s'agit quand Notker écrit à l'évêque de Sion que l'abbé de Reichenau lui demande le prêt des Philippiques de Cicéron et les commentaries des Topiques du même auteur, en remettant de gage la Rhétorique de Cicéron et le commentarie de Victorinus": Lesne, 5, 393-4; cf. 4, 432-3. On the library of Reichenau: Laistner, 234-5. It is Agobard, as is well known, who had the works of Tertullian copied.

240. *De quib. rebus*, c. 7: "in authenticis antiphonariis" (1078 C).

241. "extra usum sensit Berno . . .": *Ep. de quat. temp.* (PL, CLX, 824 AB). Cf. *De script. eccl.*, c. 156: "against the usual treatment of the major authors [on music, like Boethius] he usefully inserted a synemmenon within the tetrachordihypaton" — "contra usum majorum in ipso tetrachordihypaton inseruit utiliter synemmenon" (583 B).

242. "secundum allegoriam . . .": *De scr. eccl.*, c. 171: "Concerning the fast of four times [see note 209] I have answered those at Trèves who observe the rules of a certain Berno that are well-fitted according to allegory as it seems to him and they are out of harmony with the custom of those at Liège" — "Respondi Trenerensibus [sic] de jejunio quatuor temporum, qui regulas cujusdam Bernonis secundum allegoriam ut sibi videtur bene concinnatas observant et a consuetudine Leodiensium discordant" (587-8; cf. 823-30). Berno, *Dial. de jejuniis*, c. 4-5 (CXLII, 1092-5).

243. "innovantur naturae": C. 10 (CXLII, 1149-50).

244. "quidam sapiens graecus": *ep.* 165 (C, 431 B).

245. "quidam philosophus": *ep.* 183 (454 C); proverb "it is ridiculous to look for praise in vanity" — "ridiculum est in vanitate laudem quaerere."

246. "Senecae sapientis": *ep.* 367 (567 B). Cf. Paschasius, *In Lam.*, l. 1, citing Prudentius: "quidam poeta" (CXX, 1071 B).

247. "Recolens juxta illud verbum sapientis: mores ex convictu formari": PL, CV, 800 C.

248. "Ut quidam sapiens dicit, in sermone pondus atque in verbis modus": C. 6 (CXLII, 1184 B).

249. "illud sapientis proverbium quod pueri didicerunt: legere enim et non intelligere, negligere est": *Intr. ad theol.*, l. 2, c. 3 (CLXXVIII, 1054 B).

250. "sapientem quemdam": *ep.* 256, n. 1 (CLXXXI, 463 D).

251. "philosophus quidam": *Didasc.*, l. 3, c. 5: "Quidam philosopho cuidam referebat dicens" (CLXXVI, 775 C).

252. *De nat. amoris*, c. 14, n. 42 (CLXXXIV, 405 B).

253. "a certain someone"; "sapiens quidam": G. H. Talbot, *The Sermons of Hugh of Pontigny* (1956), 12-3 (extract from *Cîteaux in de Nederlanden*, 7).

254. *Ep.* 21 (PL, CCIII, 169 D).

255. *S.* 15: "Those who suck that milk [of philosophy] are called little children by a certain sage, who says, 'O Greeks, you are always children'" — "Illi qui lac istud (philosophiae) sugunt, parvuli a quodam sapiente vocantur, qui dicit: Graeci, semper pueri estis" (CCXI, 93 D).

256. *De nat. rer.*, c. 157, de carne (255). Cf. *Annalista saxo*, a. 973 (MGH, Scr., 6, 625).

257. "quem quidam antiquorum Patrum sapienter et breviter cavendum admonuit, dicens . . .": *De div. psalm.*, in fine (CIV, 330 A).

258. "quidam Patrum": *Adv. Fel.*, c. 4 (CIV, 35 C), text from the *De doct. christiana*.

259. *Anal. Regin.* (1933), 85, 93.

260. *Ib.*, 85 (85).

261. L. 3, c. 13: "A certain sage, when he was being asked about the method and form of learning, replied, 'a humble mind. . . .'" — "Sapiens quidam cum de modo et forma discendi interrogaretur: mens, respondit, humilis, etc." (PL, CLXXVI, 773 B).

262. "Septem esse inter caeteras regulas locutionum sanctarum Scripturarum, quidam sapiens disseruit": L. 5, c. 4 (791 B). Cf. Aug., *Doct. chr.*, l. 3, c. 30-7 (395-423).

263. "sicut ait quidam sapiens," "ut quidam sapiens disseruit": Leclercq, *Études*, 49, 108. Cf. the MS cited by Manitius, 1, 185: "Here begins a treatise of a certain sage and it is, as is reported, of blessed Columban" — "Incipit libellus cujusdam sapientis et est ut fertur b. Columbani."

264. *S.* 21 (PL, CCXII, 567 A).

265. *S.* 4, *In nat. Dom.*, c. 27 (CCVIII, 385 BC).

266. "sapientissimus Salomon": Thus Alcuin (C, 343 B; CI, 159 A); etc.

267. "Sapiens vir": PL, CXCIV, 1543 A. Cf. *V. s. Aldrici*, n. 3: "Recalling according to the word of the sage . . ." — "Recolens juxta illud verbum sapientis . . ." (CV, 880 C).

268. "Ecclesiastes, sapientissimus hominum": *S.* 30 (CXCVIII, 1788 D).

269. *Inst.*, c. 14: "The five books of Solomon" — "Salomonis libros quinque" (LXX, 1125 B); c. 13, on Aug. (1124 B).

270. Alcuin, *In Eccl.*, on Ecclesiasticus 27:29 (C, 708 C). Smaragdus (CII, 825 D); etc.

271. "non immerito ait sapiens ante nos quidam": *De Elia et jej.*, c. 18, n. 67 (XIV, 712 A).

272. "Salomon dicit — per Sal. dicitur — Sal. attestante — apud Sal. — Sal. insinuat."

273. "per quendam sapientem dicitur," "bene quidam sapiens indicat": *In I Reg.*, l. 5, c. 4, n. 2 (LXXIX, 360 A). The intention seems clear. Cf. Aug., *Speculum*, etc. Solomon of Geneva will be not more critical, *In Prov. et Eccl.*, praef.: "How

many books did Solomon publish? Only three" — "Quot libros edidit Salomon? Tres tantum" (CLXXII, 312). From Gregory's manner of speaking some have wanted sometimes to conclude that he regarded *Eccli.* as apocryphal: Basnage, *Hist. de l'Église* (1699), 445. On the canonical authority of the Solomonian books according to the Fathers: G. Bardy, in Aug., *Cité de Dieu*, 4, 740-2.

274. "per quendam sapientem voluit dicere . . .": *ep.* 10 (MGH, *Ep.*, 397)

275. An affected formula, *De praed.* 2: "it has been said by whomsoever it has been said" — "dictum est a quocumque est dictum" (PL, CXXV, 127 B).

276. *De cav. vitiis*, c. 4: "Hence it is said through a certain wise man" — "Hinc per quemdam sapientem dicitur" (891 A).

277. *Anal. reg.*, 91.

278. *In Reg.*, l. 2, c. 8; *Eccli.*, iii, 27 (PL, CXV, 358-9).

279. "Vir sapiens": PL, CXLIV, 415 AB, etc.

280. *In Is.* (CLXVII, 1298 B). For him the Ecclesiast is Solomon (CLXVIII, 1197 A). Hugh will be more circumspect (CLXXV, 153-4).

281. *L. de panibus*, c. 1 (CCII, 932 A).

282. *Verb. abbr.*, c. 18 and 20 (CCV, 70 D, 73 D); c. 118 (308 A).

283. *De scientia cler.*, c. 19 (CCIII, 702 C). Cf. Marbodius (CLXXI, 1466 A). Isidore constantly used to announce the most diverse citations using the formula: "ait quidam" — "somebody says."

284. *V. s. Udalr.*, c. 20: "a sapientissimo Salomone dicitur" (Prov. 20-1); PL, CXLII, 1199 D).

285. Jerome was an old hand at the formula: *In Matt.* (PL, XXVI, 74 C, 116 A, 203 B). It was often taken up again: Heter. (XCVI, 1018 B). Angelome (CXV, 478 C). Henr. Pompos. (CL, 1358 D). Gilbert of Nogent (CLVI, 339 B). Rupert (CLXVII, 1307 B; CLXVIII, 1486 D). William of S. Th. (CLXXX, 360 B, 361 D). Hervaeus (CLXXXI, 842 D). Gerhoh (CXCIV, 1108 D). Philip of Harvengt (CCIII, 18 C, 70 C, 167 B, cf. 623 A). Joachim of Flora, *Sup. 4 ev.* (Buon., 6, 7, 32, 173, 186); etc.

286. "Nonne duos passeres asse veneunt, et unus ex illis non cadet super terram sine Patre vestro": "Haeret sibi sermo Dominicus, et sequentia pendent ex superioribus. Prudens lector, cave semper superstitiosam intelligentiam, ut non tuo sensui attemperes Scripturas, sed Scripturis jungas sensum tuum et intelligas quid sequatur. Supra dixerat . . . Nunc loquitur consequenter . . .": *In Matt.*, l. 1, c. 10 (PL, XXVI, 66 D). Cf. *In Dan.:* "a doctrine contrary to the truth, which takes the words of the prophets and misuses the testimonies of the divine Scriptures for his own sense" — "doctrina contraria veritati quae assumit verba prophetarum et testimoniis divinae Scripturae abutitur ad sensum suum" (XXV, 519 BC).

287. C. 81, n. 10 (Rochais, CCL, 117, 231). We owe this double reference to our very learned friend Father Bernard de Vregille. Defensor did not always have recourse to the sources directly: "he knew most of the sentences taken from Jerome by way of a florilegium" — "c'est le cas pour la majorité des sentences prises à Jérôme, qu'il a connu par un florilège": Rochais, *R. Mab.*, 1951, 81, note 10.

288. In the text reproduced by Migne (PL, LXXXVIII, 715 C) the sentence was in the third person: "The prudent reader watches out for" — "Prudens lector cavet etc." But this text was extremely defective: Rochais, RB, 63, 275. The variant would not, however, have been enough to eliminate the *Scintillae* as Berno's possible source.

289. Defensor follows and sharpens Jerome: "you may yoke your sense to Scripture, so that you may understand what follows" — "Scripturae jungas sensum tuum, ut intelligas quod sequatur."

290. *In Matt.*, xxv, 13: "I always warn the prudent reader not to rest content with the interpretations of superstition, and [those] that are said piecemeal for the benefit of the judgment of falsifiers, but let him consider what is earlier, in the middle, and later, and connect up all the things said" — "Prudentem semper admoneo lectorem, ut non superstitionis acquiescat interpretationibus, et quae commatice pro fingentium dicuntur arbitrio, sed consideret priora, media et sequentia, et nectat sibi universa quae dicta sunt" (XXVI, 186 AB).

291. "Quomodo illa intelligentia toto evangelici sermonis corpori coaptetur, non parvae difficultatis est": *In Matt.*, l. 1, c. 10 (67 B).

292. "locus iste," said he, "ex sensu superiore proficiscitur"; "sermo dominicus"; "evangelicus sermo"; "Non est pecudum Deo cura": *In Matt.*, c. 10, nn. 18-20 (IX, 973-4).

293. "figmenta quae lectores cordatos non tam aedificare quam in stuporem dare possunt": Daillé at the same time used to say of Jerome: "He himself is often immeasurably wrong here" — "Ipse saepe et sine modo hic peccat": *De usu Patrum* . . . (Geneva, 1656), 248-50.

294. *In Luc.*, l. 7, n. 112 and 116 (Tissot, SC, 52, 47-8).

295. *In ps.* cxlv, nn. 13-4, citing 1 Cor. 11:9 and Deut. 25 (CCL, 40, 2114-5).

296. *Antikeim.*, l. 1, interr. 70: how to harmonize Ps. 36:6: "Thou wilt preserve men and beasts" — "Homines et jumenta salvos facies" with 1 Cor. 9:9: "Numquid de bobus cura est Deo?" — "Doth God take care for oxen?" He looks back to Aug. and cites Matt. 10:29, and Luke 12:6 (XCVI, 626-7).

297. *In Matt.*, 1, 8: "'Are not two sparrows . . . ?' It is truly known to all, that two sparrows are sold cheap, and are far cheaper than the body and soul, from which one rational man is constituted, 'and one of those shall not fall. . . .' But perhaps you falter and say: 'How does one sparrow not fall to earth without our Father, whilst God does not care about a cow, which is bigger than a sparrow?' . . . To this I shall say: The Apostle was talking about the written Law, and his point is that God did not care to have a Law written concerning irrational cattle" — "Nonne duo passeres . . . ? Vere omnibus notum est, quia duo passeres pro vili dantur pretio, et longe viliores sunt corpore et anima, quibus ex duobus subsistit unus rationalis homo, 'et unus ex illis, non cadet. . . .' Sed forte titubas et dicis: Quomodo unus passer sine Patre nostro in terra non cadit, cum nec de bove, qui utique major est passere, Deo cura sit? . . . Ad haec inquam: Apostolus de lege scripta loquebatur, et hic ejus sensus, quia non fuisset Deo cura, ut de bobus irrationalibus lex scriberetur . . ." (CLXVIII, 1499 BD).

298. "Haeret sibi sermo dominicus": *In Matt.*, l. 3, c. 18 (XXVI, 132 B). Same requirement in Aug., *C. Adim.*, c. 14, n. 2 (XLII, 149).

299. "coups de griffe": "Hilary is rendered taller by the Gallic buskin" — "Hilarius gallicano cothurno attollitur," RB, 57, 82-8. V. *supra*, I, ch. III, iv. Arno of Reichersberg will say of Hilary: "whilst uttering grand things, he also made fitting use of grandiloquent style" — "grandia quidem loquens, grandiloquo etiam stylo congrue usus est," *Apologeticus* (Weichert, 81).

300. Cf. Jerome on Hilary, *De viris ill.*, c. 100 (XXIII, 699-710). One could often

say almost the same thing of him as of Jerome and of his own commentary on Matthew: "this commentary, composed very quickly at the request of Eusebius of Cremona, was full of unacknowledged citations" — "ce commentaire, rédigé très rapidement à la demande d'Eusèbe de Crémone, est rempli de citations inavouées" (Bardy, RB, 46, 159).

301. "superstitiosa intelligentia": Cf. Hugh Metel, *ep.* 28: "Watch out, brother, watch out for a superstitious understanding . . . , watch out for stupid questions" — "Cave, frater, cave superstitiosam intelligentiam . . . , cave stultas quaestiones" (368).

302. "sancto Gregorio attestante": *De varia,* c. 5: "since, as St. Gregory confirms, the words of the heavenly oracle are not to be bent beneath the rules of Donatus; as the Prophet, unafraid of the grammarians' rod, asserted the same" — "cum, sancto Gregorio testante, verba caelestis oraculi non sint inflectenda sub regulis Donati; sicut idem Propheta, non veritus ferulam grammaticorum, posuit" (PL, CXLII, 1137 A).

303. "Non metacismi collisionem fugio, non barbarismi confusionem devito, situs motusque et praepositionum casus servare contemno, quia indignum vehementer existimo ut verba caelestis oraculi restringam sub regulis Donati": *Ep. miss.,* c. 5 (PL, LXXV, 516 B).

304. Tacitus used to call himself "rough, unadorned, uncultivated, unpolished, plain" — "rudis, incomptus, incultus, impolitus, simplex"; his style was "filthy" — "sordidus"; he blamed his "indigence, meagerness, barrenness" — "egestas, exilitas, sterilitas," etc. Symmachus does likewise. For examples: E. R. Curtius, 104, 509.

305. Chapter iv of the *Philocalia* was entitled: *De solecismo et tenui dictione Scripturae* (Or., *In Jo.,* l. 4; J. A. Robinson, 41-2).

306. On this modesty of Gregory's: *V. s. Gregorii,* l. 4, c. 77 (PL, LXXV, 223-4). But there is anything but an "exagération d'humilité" (Montalambert, *Les Moines d'Occident,* 2, 3ᵉ éd., 1868, 167).

307. *Traité de la morale des Pères de l'Église:* "C'est ainsi que, selon saint Grégoire le Grand, pour enseigner aux hommes la religion et leurs devoirs, il faut les rebuter par un langage barbare, et leur parler d'une manière à n'être pas entendu: car enfin il n'est pas possible qu'une si horrible négligence ne jette souvent dans les discours une grande obscurité": Ch. 17, n. 16 (Amsterdam, 1728, 333).

308. *Dial.,* l. 1, praef.: "If I had specifically wanted to keep the words themselves about all the persons, the stylus of the scribe would not fittingly pick up this stuff cited in casual fashion" — "Si de personis omnibus ipsa specialiter verba tenere voluissem, haec rusticano usu prolata stylus scribentis non apte susciperet" (PL, LXXVII, 153 B). *Mor.,* ep. miss., c. 2: ". . . The notes that I had taken when I was commenting on first reading, I have corrected so as to produce a well-written work. . . . Through an attentive revision of my oral commentary, I was then compelled to give it the more careful air of a written commentary, etc." (From the tr. by R. Gillet, SC, 32, 117).

309. *V. s. Gregorii,* l. 4, c. 70, 72, 78 (LXXV, 222-6).

310. "extrême susceptibilité": P. Verbraken, "Le texte du com. sur les Rois

attribué à S. Grég.," RB, 66 (1956), 159. Cf. PL, LXXVI, 1078 A; LXXVII, 1213 AC, etc.

311. To the contrary, Dom Besse praises the "clear language" of the *Moralia* in *Les mystiques bénédictins* (1922), 110.

312. *De orthographia* (Keil, VII, 267, 271, 286). Cf. M. Roger, 326.

313. "inter omnes rarissima": Cf. Ghellinck, *L'essor*, 2, 56-65. E. de Bruyne, 2, 677 (and 1, 158).

314. St. Augustine and St. Fulgentius had preceded him, but [this sort of prose really] took off with him and it is chiefly from him that so many medieval writers proceed, notably the Spanish group of the 7th century and a considerable number of 10th-, 11th-, and 12th-century writers.

315. "Quanta clareant (in eis) ornamenta verborum, nemo sapiens explicare valebit": *De script. eccl.*, c. 40, n. 54 (PL, LXXXIII, 1102 B).

316. "summe doctus"; "mire facundus"; "bonis omnibus Latini sermonis capacibus": *De trib. quaest.* (CXIX, 658 B, 662 C). Cf. Adam Scot, *L. de quadripertito exercitio cellae*, c. 27 (CLIII, 849 A).

317. "Tullius si audiret hominem, confusus abiret": Ekkehart IV, *Confutatio rhetoricae in facie Ecclesiae et sanctorum* (Dümmler, *Zeitschrift f. deutsche Alterthum*, 1869, 2, 22). Cf. 67:

> Ructat corde bonum sine lege Donatia verbum ...
> He heartily belches a fine ungrammatical word. ...

318. "stylus aureus et igneus": *De contemptu mundi*, l. 3, v. 313 (Hoskier, 81).

319. "venustas verborum": Prose de Lausanne, *De 4 doct. Eccl.*, strophe 6 (Missal of 1493; MW, 2, 456).

320. "Tandem scholae me traditura, diem Beati Gregorii festivitatis elegit. Audierat praefatum tuum famulum, Domine, mirabili superemicuisse sensu, infinita floruisse sapientia; et ideo multa eleemosynarum congerie confessoris tui instabat saepius sollicitare suffragia, ut, cui praebueras intellectum, intellectualitatis mihi consequendae impetraret affectum": *De vita sua*, l. 1, c. 4 (PL, CLVI, 844 A). Robert Gaguin, a "lover of beautiful style" and one of our first great humanists, similarly chose Gregory, along with Prudentius and Paulinus of Nola, as an originator of Latin poetics: *De arte metrificandi*: cf. P. Imbart de la Tour, *Les origines de la Réforme*, 2, 349, 581.

321. The perception of the poet will prevail over the opinion of a historian who declares the *Moralia* to be "indigestible" (E. Caspar, *Gesch. des Papsttums*, 2, 1933, 357) and over that of another who sees in his allegorism nothing but "platitudes," "insipid" ideas, or even "stupidities" (J. Haller, *Das Papsttum*, 1934, 1). In the wake of Mommsen, Haller is severe and scornful of Gregory; Caspar at least recognizes the greatness of his Christian character.

322. *Founders of the Middle Ages* (1928), 27-8.

323. "collision"; "n'avoir jamais été frappé d'un défaut de ce genre": Grégoire le Grand, *Morales sur Job*, SC, 32, 122-3, note; cf. 103-4. The author is willing to write once again on this subject: Gregory "is so conscious of a *clausula* based no longer upon quantity but upon stress, and of all the techniques of Asiatic rhetoric, parallelisms, assonances that make the final members of sentences rhyme with each other, alliterations, etc., which is at play whenever he is stylisti-

cally self-conscious and which, even where he is more relaxed, an exquisite natural delicacy makes him express admirably and in very fine fashion what a translation will always be powerless to render. Regarding what he says and how he says it, Pascal would surely conclude that he is an 'honnête homme'. Still, when he gets stilted in his prefaces and official correspondence, one can wonder a bit at his taste. In some letters, in whole passages of the second book of the *Moralia* . . . the looseness of expression betrays hasty dictation or weariness" — "est si conscient de la clausule fondée non plus sur la quantité mais sur les accents, et de tous les artifices de la rhétorique asiatique, parallélismes, consonances qui font rimer entre elles les finales des membres de phrases, allitérations, etc., qu'il en use partout où il surveille son style, et que, même là où il se relâche, une exquise délicatesse naturelle lui fait exprimer admirablement et très finement ce qu'une traduction sera toujours impuissante à rendre. De ce qu'il dit et de la manière dont il le dit, Pascal aurait sûrement conclu qu'il est 'honnête homme'. Cependant, quand il se guinde, dans les préfaces et la correspondance officielle, on peut douter de la justesse de son goût. Dans quelques lettres, dans des passages entiers du second livre des *Morales* . . . le lâché de l'expression trahit la dictée hâtive, ou la lassitude."

324. "The Christian Attitude to Pagan Literature," *History*, 20 (1936), 53.

325. *In Registrum Greg. magni studia critica* (Upsala universitets Arsskrift, 1937, 4, 1-4).

326. *Missa, Vig. chr.*, 14 (1960), 92. Cf. *Le latin médiéval*, CCM, 1 (1958), 284.

327. *Vig. chr.*, 14 (1960), 81.

328. "Adeo (Gregorius) omnem humanitatis cultum se neglexisse in istis libris fatetur, ut videri queat eos ideo scripsisse, ut omnis elegantioris doctrinae jugulum uno ictu peteret": *Hist. critica philosophiae*, 3 (Lipsiae, 1743), 563.

329. "Cum enim tantus vir, qui summam sibi auctoritatem conciliabat, et ex cathedra definiebat, tantis praejudiciis occupatus in litteras saeculares et inter eas in philosophiam debaccharetur, gregem sane totum judicium pastoris, quamvis ineptum et miserandum, sequi oportuit": *Op. cit.*, 562, 572: Gregory had again greatly increased barbarism by the care he brought to the chant of the Church: for centuries, those who would have been able to cultivate literature or philosophy had through his fault wasted their time chanting!

330. 560-4: "what severe wounds Pope Gregory would have inflicted upon humane letters and philosophy. . . . He would burn with an extraordinary hatred against philosophy. . . . Could it turn out otherwise, I ask you, than that blind ignorance should darken the whole West instead of literature and philosophy, and that foul barbarism should corrupt men of genius?" — "quam gravia vulnera litteris humanioribus et philosophiae inflixerit papa Gregorius. . . . Is cum insigni in philosophiam odio arderet. . . . An fieri, quaeso, aliter potuit, quam ut omnem occidentem litterarum et philosophiae loco caeca obumbraret ignorantia, et ingenia faeda corrumperet barbaries?" Citing this page of Brücker, "that critic otherwise so wise and competent" — "ce critique d'ailleurs si sage et si habile," M. Emery sees in it an example of the aberration "of enlightened and naturally just men, when they allow themselves to be dominated by a party spirit" — "des hommes éclairés et naturellement justes, quand ils se laissent dominer par l'esprit de parti": *Le christianisme de Bacon, chancelier d'Angleterre*, 2 (an VII), app.:

Eclaircissements sur l'accusation d'avoir voulu anéantir tous les auteurs et tous les monuments de l'antiquité payenne, intentée contre S. Grégoire; 367-70.

331. "vir indoctus"; "homo superstitiosissimus"; "magnus"; "praecipuus auctor et suasor barbariei literariae": *Hist. interpr. librorum sacrorum,* P. 5, p. 3-6, 53, 77.

332. *La Renaissance,* intr. (H. de Fr., n. éd., 9, 1876, 52).

333. "incorrection"; "vice"; "un mérite de piété": *Étude des Morales de S. Gr le Grand sur Job* (1858), 126-7. In 1878 S. Berger says simply: Gregory "made no secret of writing a not quite classical Latin" — "ne se cachait pas d'écrir un latin peu classique" (*Enc. des sc. rel.,* 5, 697). Through a double mistake, J.-J. Ampère, *H. litt. de la Fr. avant le XIIIe s.,* 183, attributes a "solecismum non refugio" to Gregory of Tours; the fact is picked up by Gorini, 2, 423.

334. "plein de mépris pour la littérature profane, pour la grammaire elle-même": *Hist. des dogmes,* I, 257 (following Margraff and Lau); cf. 2, 226, 342.

335. *Illustrations of the History of Medieval Thought in the Departments of Theology and Ecclesiastical Politics,* 9.

336. *Op. cit.,* 188.

337. *Gregory the Great,* in *The Cambridge Med. Hist.,* 2 (1926), 236.

338. *A History of Secular Poetry in the Middle Ages* (1934), 1, 126-7; the "noble and melancholic figure" of Gregory after that takes on more stature in his eyes.

339. *A Hist. of Christian-Latin Poetry from the Beginnings to the Close of the Middle Ages* (1927), 11-3.

340. "c'était le sort même de toute culture qui était mis en question": *Lit. latine, le moyen âge,* 13.

341. "sans détour": *The Classical Tradition,* 2^d ed., 7 and 558.

342. Gabriele Pepe has seen this, *Le m. âge barbare en Italie* (tr. J. Gonnet, 1956, 105): "What strikes him as unworthy is not the fact of obeying the rules of grammar (in this regard he too is a man of discipline), but the rhetoric that turns the whim of the schoolmaster into a theory opposed to the freedom of the original expression" — "Ce qui lui paraît indigne, ce n'est pas le fait d'obéir aux règles de la grammaire (en cela aussi il est homme de discipline), mais la rhétorique, qui transforme en théorie, contre la liberté de l'expression originale, le caprice du maître."

343. *Doct. chr.,* l. 3, c. 3, n. 7 (349). Cf. Ambrose, *In Luc.,* l. 2, c. 42 (SC, 45, 92). Jerome (PL, XXV, 141, 585, 1058). (Gillet, loc. cit., 122).

344. "Ma première règle, à moi qui ne me soucie nullement de ce qu'on pensera de mon style, est de me faire entendre. Toutes les fois qu'à l'aide de dix solécismes je pourrai m'exprimer plus fortement ou plus clairement, je ne balancerai jamais": *Lettre sur une nouv. réfutation du Discours sur les sc. et les arts par un académicien de Dijon (Œuvres,* 1, 1817, 154, note). Gillet, 122-3. Chateaubriand, *Litt. angl.,* avert.: "Milton . . . treats the language like a tyrant, violates and scorns the rules . . ." — "Milton . . . traite la langue en tyran, viole et méprise les règles. . . ."

345. "la syntaxe des grandes œuvres classiques, élaborées en dehors de toute influence sémitique"; "à calquer la langue de la Bible"; "la plasticité de la koiné"; "latin vulgaire"; "des ressources abondantes pour serrer de près l'image verbale

hébraïque"; "l'assouplissement de la langue": J. Gribomont and A. Thibaut, *Richesses*, 91.

346. "L'exégète du livre de Job n'y fait pas toujours fi des connaissances grammaticales. Il sait choisir entre deux leçons d'un même verset, indiquer les tropes de comparaison et de métonymie, la valeur de la conjonction de coordination, l'étymologie d'un mot. Bref . . . , il n'exclut pas de son exégèse le recours aux méthodes de l'explication grammaticale classique": Fontaine, 1, 35-6.

347. "une connaissance affectée de la technologie grammaticale"; "de faire entendre que son non-vouloir n'est pas un non-savoir": *Virgilio nel medio evo* (ed. G. Pasquali, 1, 1943), 109, note 1.

348. "Et fortasse hoc divinae providentiae consilium fuit, ut percussum Iob percussus exponerem, et flagellati mentem melius per flagella sentirem."

349. *Ep. miss.*, c. 5, tr. A. de Gaudemaris (121-2). Compare Jerome, *In Zach*, l. 3, praef., excusing himself for delivering "rudes libros" that he had not had the time to polish (PL, XXV, 1497). [Translator's note: de Lubac prints Gaudemaris's French version in the body of his text; I translate the Latin text facing Gaudemaris's French. I have put the portions ellipsized by Lubac into square brackets; for the second of these bracketed passages, see note 356 below where the text is continued.] "Quam videlicet expositionem recensendam tuae beatitudini, non quia velut dignam debui, sed quia te petente memini promisisse, transmisi. In qua quicquid tua sanctitas tepidum incultumque reppererit, tanto mihi celerrime indulgeat, quanto hoc me aegrum dicere non ignorat. Nam dum molestia corpus atteritur, affecta mente etiam dicendi studia languescunt. [Multa quippe annorum iam curricula devolvuntur, quod crebris viscerum doloris crucior, horis momentisque omnibus fracta stomachi virtute lassesco, lentis quidem, sed tamen continuis febribus anhelo. Interque haec dum sollicitus penso, quia scriptura teste: *Omnis filius, qui a Deo recipitur, flagellatur* (Heb. 12:6), quo malis praesentibus durius deprimor, eo de aeterna certius praesumptione respiro.] Et fortasse hoc divinae providentiae consilium fuit, ut percussum Iob percussus exponerem, et flagellati mentem melius per flagella sentirem. Sed tamen recte considerantibus liquet, quia adversitate non modica laboris mei studiis in hoc molestia corporalis obsistit, quod carnis virtus cum locutionis ministerium exhibere vix sufficit, mens digne non potest intimare quod sentit. Quid namque est officium corporis nisi organum cordis? Et quamlibet peritus sit cantandi artifex, explere artem non valet, nisi ad hanc sibi et ministeria exteriora concordent, quia nimirum canticum, quod docta manus imperat, quassata organa proprie non resultant nec artem flatus exprimit, si scissa rimis fistula stridet. Quanto itaque gravius expositionis meae qualitas premitur, in qua dicendi gratiam sic fractura organi dissipat, ut hanc peritiae ars nulla componat? [Quaeso autem, ut huius operis dicta percurrens in his verborum folia non requiras, quia per sacra eloquia ab eorum tractatoribus infructuosae loquacitatis levitas studiose compescitur, dum in templo Dei nemus plantari prohibetur. Et cuncti procul dubio scimus quia, quotiens in foliis male laetae segetis culmi proficiunt, minori plenitudine spicarum grana turgescunt. Unde et ipsam loquendi artem, quam magisteria disciplinae exterioris insinuant, servare despexi. Nam sicut huius quoque epistolae tenor enuntiat, non metacismi collisionem fugio, non barbarismi confusionem devito, situs modosque et praepositionum casus servare

contemno, quia indignum vehementer existimo, ut verba caelestis oraculi restringam sub regulis Donati. Neque enim haec ab ullis interpretibus in scripturae sacrae auctoritate servata sunt. Ex qua nimirum quia nostra expositio oritur, dignum profecto est, ut quasi edita suboles speciem suae matris imitetur. Novam vero translationem dissero; sed cum probationis causa exigit, nunc novam nunc veterem per testimonia adsumo, ut, quia sedes apostolica cui Deo auctore praesideo utraque utitur, mei quoque labor studii ex utraque fulciatur.]"

350. "infructuosae loquacitatis levitas": Cf. Laistner, art. cited, 52-3: "When Gregory spoke with contempt of literary form, it is reasonable to suppose that he was thinking of the many works, not a few of them written by clerics, in which an elaborate and often tortured rhetorical manner was considered a fine style and the subject-matter was treated as of quite subordinate interest. But in holy Writ the content was the essential thing."

351. "de polir son style ni de rechercher le triage des termes": Étienne Moreau, *Les œuvres morales de S. Gr. le Grand sur le livre de Job* (1642), preface; "Il ne m'appartient pas d'en dire autant de moi; j'ai travaillé autant que j'ai pu à bien parler Français" — "It is not my job to say so much about myself; I have just tried as much as I could to speak French well."

352. "l'art de bien parler": *Hist. eccl.*, 8 (1701), 236.

353. "style recherché"; "jeux puériles et pédants": expressions from J. Gonsette, *S. Pierre Damien et la culture profane*, 39. An analogous remark of Remy de Gourmont, *Le latin mystique* (1930 ed.), 17: The Christian poets created an original style; "ne furent-ils pas bien plutôt les décadents, les Italiens qui, alors, ou un peu plus tard, ovidifiaient de mythologiques lamentations?" — "were they not indeed rather the decadents, the Italians, who at that point or a little later, Ovidified mythological laments?"

354. Cf. H.-I. Marrou, *Hist. de l'éducation dans l'Antiquité*, 445: "Ce ne sont pas les valeurs éternelles de l'humanisme qu'ils (Césaire, Grégoire) refuse, mais les jeux d'une puérilité monstrueuse où se complaisent les derniers lettrés de leur temps" — "The eternal values of humanism are not what they reject, but the games of a monstrous childishness that the last literary men of their age were satisfied with": such as Virgil of Toulouse with his "mystifications pédantes."

355. "ceux qui s'appliquent à enjoliver de petits bouts de mots": Or., *In I Cor.*, viii (JTS, 9, 237). Cf. Greg. Thaum., *Disc. paneg.* (PG, X, 1052).

356. *Ep. miss.*, c. 5 (A. de Gaudemaris, 122). [Translator's note: This text continues that cited in note 349; compare the Latin in the square brackets with note 303.] "Quaeso autem, ut huius operis dicta percurrens in his verborum folia non requiras, quia per sacra eloquia ab eorum tractatoribus infructuosae loquacitatis levitas studiose compescitur, dum in templo Dei nemus plantari prohibetur. Et cuncti procul dubio scimus quia, quotiens in foliis male laetae segetis culmi proficiunt, minori plenitudine spicarum grana turgescunt. [Unde et ipsam loquendi artem, quam magisteria disciplinae exterioris insinuant, servare despexi. Nam sicut huius quoque epistolae tenor enuntiat, non metacismi collisionem fugio, non barbarismi confusionem devito, situs modosque et praepositionum casus servare contemno, quia indignum vehementer existimo, ut verba caelestis oraculi restringam sub regulis Donati. Neque enim haec ab ullis interpretibus in scripturae sacrae auctoritate servata sunt. Ex qua nimirum quia

nostra expositio oritur, dignum profecto est, ut quasi edita suboles speciem suae matris imitetur. Novam vero translationem dissero; sed cum probationis causa exigit, nunc novam nunc veterem per testimonia adsumo, ut, quia sedes apostolica cui Deo auctore praesideo utraque utitur, mei quoque labor studii ex utraque fulciatur.]"

357. "J'ai donc dédaigné de m'astreindre à cet art de bien dire qu'enseignent les règles d'une discipline étrangère . . ."; "Ces règles, aucun des interprètes s'autorisant de l'Écriture sainte ne s'y est asservi; et comme c'est d'elle que notre commentarie prend naissance, il est bien juste que l'enfant mis au monde garde cette ressemblance avec sa mère": *Ib.:* "Hence I have also disdained to bind myself to the art of speech as such, an art that teaching authorities of an alien discipline introduce" — "Unde et ipsam loquendi artem, quam magisteria disciplinae exterioris insinuant, servare despexi." A. de Gaudemaris has nicely translated "servare" by "m'astreindre à" — "to bind myself to"; one might also say "m'y asservir" — "to enslave myself to it." There is something of a play on words with "servire." Compare the theme, which has become classical from the time of Clement and Origen, of the profane disciplines as servants of theology, combined with the theme of the alien captive (see above, vol. 1, ch. 1.3 and ch. 4.5). "For none of, etc." — "Neque enim haec ab ullis interpretibus in scripturae sacrae auctoritate servata sunt. Ex qua nimirum quia nostra expositio oritur, dignum profecto est, ut quasi edita soboles speciem suae matris imitetur" (SC, 32, 123). Cf. Agobard.

358. "qu'on a eu tort peut-être de prendre trop au pied de la lettre": *Lit. lat.*, 1, 76.

359. "un extrémiste de la plume"; "comme par défi"; "morceaux de bravoure": *op. cit.*, 1, 36, 206.

360. "dans ce passage célèbre, dont on a trop souvent abusé, il ne faut voir que l'inquiétude d'un esprit qui connaît la barbarie de son siècle, qui craint de s'en ressentir, et qui se justifie éloquemment, comme saint Paul, en foulant aux pieds l'éloquence": 359.

361. "Il n'y a que le pédantisme qui puisse prendre en mauvaise part ce passage célèbre": *Mél. religieux et hist.*, 334.

362. "Moyses, qui nobis divinorum eloquiorum principia edidit, non prius divina didicit, sed, ut capere vel exprimere divina posset, in omni Aegyptiorum scientia rudem animam informavit. Isaias etiam prophetis aliis eloquentior exstitit, quia . . . nobiliter instructus atque urbanus fuit. Paulus quoque vas electionis, ante ad Gamalielis pedes instruitur, quam rapiatur in paradisum, vel ad caeli tertii altitudinem sublevetur; et ideo fortasse per doctrinam aliis apostolis excelluit, quia futurus in caelestibus, terrena prius studiosus didicit": *In I Reg.*, l. 5, n. 30 (PL, LXXIX, 356 BC). Cf. Origen, *In Luc.*, h. 31: "And so Paul received words even from outside sources, so as to sanctify them" — "Ideo assumit Paulus verba etiam de his quae foris sunt, ut sanctificet ea" (Rauer, 188). Rufinus, *H. eccl.*, l. 1, c. 31, on Hilary: "he published . . . nobly written books" — "libros . . . nobiliter scriptos edidit" (PL, XXI, 501 B).

363. "nobiliter instructus atque urbanus": Cf. Martin of Leon, *S. 4, de nativ.:* "He was offspring of a noble clan, endowed with urbane taste" — "Ipse quippe (Isaias) nobili genere extitit progenitus, urbanae elegantiae praeditus . . ." (CCVIII, 274 B).

364. "diu longeque conversionis gratiam distuli": *Ep. miss.*, c. 1 (SC, 32, 114).

365. "de Cicéron ou de Virgile, ni même celle qu'avaient connue saint Jérôme et saint Augustin": R. Gillet, *op. cit.*, 8.

366. "ut, quamvis eo tempore florerent adhuc Romae studia litterarum": In this phrase "eo tempore florerent adhuc," one perceives a vivid feeling regarding the abrupt decline that followed. Paul the Deacon, who was writing around 775, was able to gather Peter's impressions through his first-hand interlocutors.

367. "tamen nulli in urbe ipsa secundus esse putaretur": *Vita S. Gregorii*, c. 2 (PL, LXXV, 42 A). Gregory of Tours, quite knowledgeable, also vaunted even his profane knowledge: *Hist. Francorum*, l. 10, c. 1 (LXXI, 527 C), and this is a characteristic retained by the tradition. Hymn of the saint's feast day, 2nd noct., MS of the 12th century. (G. M. Dreves, *Analecta hymnica m. aevi*, 5, 184):

Studiis liberalibus
Nulli secundus habitus.
"In liberal studies
Regarded as second to none."

John the Deacon, l. 2, c. 13, produced a literary exercise on the same topic: "Septemplicibus artibus veluti columnis nobilissimorum totidem lapidum Apostolicae sedis atrium fulciebat" (PL, LXXV, 92 C). By way of notable exception, Basnage will recognize that Gregory "avait une vaste littérature": *Hist. de l'Église*, 1 (Rotterdam, 1699), 387.

368. "Après sa sortie de l'école(?), Grégoire ne fit rien pour entretenir en lui le souvenir des écrivains classiques, ni pour garantir la correction de son langage contre les atteintes du latin rustique ou de latin ecclésiastique": *op. cit.*, 188.

369. "se sent du mauvais goût de son siècle": Fleury, *loc. cit.*

370. "Hanc quippe saecularem scientiam omnipotens Deus in plano anteposuit, ut nobis ascendendi gradum faceret, qui nos ad divinae Scripturae altitudinem levare debuisset": *In I Reg.*, 1, 5, n. 30 (PL, LXXIX, 356 B).

371. *Conf.*, l. 8, c. 5, n. 10 (1, 184). Cf. Rabanus, *In Judith* (PL, CIX, 557 C).

372. "Aperte quidem daemones sciunt quia dum saecularibus litteris instruimur, in spiritualibus adjuvamur. Cum ergo nos ea discere dissuadent, quid aliud quam ne lanceam aut gladium faciamus praecavent?

"A nonnullorum cordibus discendi desiderium maligni spiritus tolunt, ut et saecularia nescient, et ad sublimitatem spiritalium non pertingant": *In I Reg.*, ib. (355-6). Cf. *I Reg.*, xiii, 20-1. Rupert will give a different interpretation of this passage: *In Reg.* (CLXVII, 1152 AC); the Pseudo-Eucher had already done likewise (L, 1061 AB).

373. Cf. Laistner, *loc. cit.*, 53.

374. Verbraken, art. cit., 217.

375. *Epist.*, l. 12, ep. 24 (PL, LXXVII, 1234 AB).

376. Mgr. Batiffol writes, *S. Grég. le Grand* (1928), 48: "Rien d'authentique ne nous est resté de ces commentaires" — "nothing authentic from these commentaries is left to us" and says of Claude that he was "traité par Grégoire de *carissimus quondam filius*" — "treated by Gregory as *once* a very dear son," as if to insinuate a sort of disavowal on the part of the pope; it deals with a posthumous elogy. (The note: "Claude doit être mort quand Grég. écrit cette lettre" — "Claude

had to be dead when Gregory writes this letter" only half-corrects this impression; it is quite certain, however, that Claude was dead.)

377. Laistner, *loc. cit.*, 54: "Yet the chorus of those who would deny the authenticity of the commentary is far less formidable than a mere list of names might suggest, the truth being that nearly all content themselves with denial without adding to the arguments, pro and contra already marshalled by the 17th- and 18th-century editors. Krüger, indeed, cites the passage quoted above as one proof that the commentary cannot be by Gregory, thus treating as a fact what is merely his pre-conceived theory about the pope's attitude to the liberal arts."

378. "défaveur imméritée": RSR, 6 (1916), 473. "Quite uselessly changed" — "Valde inutilius permutatum" would have to be read "changed into something rather more useful" — "valde in utilius permutatum"; "Gregory would then be saying: my little commentary has been changed into something much better. He was so satisfied with this review that he declared it superior to his own work. This was mock-modesty, designed to excuse the eagerness and harshness that he invests to recover this unique exemplar. In these circumstances, Claude's text is therefore entirely approved by St. Gregory" — "Grégoire dirait donc: mon modeste commentaire a été changé en quelque chose de beaucoup meilleur. Il fut tellement satisfait de cette recension, qu'il la déclara supérieure à son propre travail. C'est une feinte de sa modestie, destinée à excuser l'empressement et la rigueur qu'il met à récupérer cet exemplaire unique. Dans ces conditions, le texte de Claude est donc entièrement approuvé par S. Grégoire." Compare note 308, above.

379. *Founders*, 26.

380. *Loc. cit.*: "so many dogmatic negations." Manitius, 1, 96-7, does not list the commentary on *I Reg.* among Gregory's works; p. 106, he will even say that its authenticity has been dismissed. He nonetheless cites a sentence aimed at reinforcing the thesis of a Gregory holding human letters in contempt: "The liberal arts are to be learned only to the extent that the divine words may be more subtly understood through instruction in them" — "Ad hoc quidem tantum liberales artes discendae sunt, ut per instructionem illarum divina eloquia subtilius intelligantur" (l. 5, c. 3, n. 30; PL, LXXIX, 355 D).

381. In *St. ans.*, 42 (1957), K. Hallinger expresses some doubts. He sees the evidence of a late elaboration in the passage concerning secular studies as not agreeing with other declarations of Greg. (241, note). The argument will convince only those who adopted the polemical interpretation under dispute here for these passages.

382. *Notices et extraits de la Bibl. imp.*, 22, 2 (1868).

383. *Ep.* 13, n. 2: "For I strive to embrace truth as a shining crystal, wherever I find it, reading divine Scripture studiously and secular opinions, on the other hand, with a glance or a sort of skimming; and if any dust of error is found about, I brush it off the targets of reason and take up for fitting uses whatever has usefully been said" — "Studii enim mihi est ut divinam Scripturam studiose, saecularia vero dogmata raptim et quasi per transitum legens, ubicumque veritatem invenero, velut lucidam crystallum amplectar, et si quid de erroris pulvere in circuitu reperitur, scopis rationis excutiam et quod utiliter dictum est in congruos usus assumam" (Leclercq; *St. ans.*, 31, 105).

384. *Ep.* 5: "Quamvis saepe incautos decipiat (mundana philosophia), secumque maeroris foveam trahat, via tamen ac quasi praeludium consultis cautioribusque esse cognoscitur, per quod exercitati ad altiora et vera saltant" (Pez 6, 1, 242). This doctrine of Edmer and Seifrid (and so many others) will be that of Erasmus at the beginning of the *Enchiridion*, right down to the verbal expression.

385. *In I Reg.*, c. 13 (PL, CIX, 42 AC). *In Judith*, c. 7 (556-7). This last passage was reproduced by the *Gloss* (CXIII, 734 D).

386. *In I Reg.*, c. 13 (CXV, 299 C).

387. *Lib. except.*, P. 2, l. 5, c. 14: "For the pagans forebade Christians to be instructed in the liberal arts.... Even now the Ancient Enemy discourages prelates from attending to education, so that he can more easily deceive both them and their charges" — "Pagani enim prohibuerunt ne christiani liberalibus imbuerentur artibus.... Nunc quoque antiquus hostis ab instantia eruditionis praelatos abvertit, ut et ipsos et subditos facilius decipere possit" (J. Châtillon, 290). One is reminded of the abbot whom Erasmus scoffs at in his *Colloquia:* "I don't want my monks to be getting involved in books" — "Nollem meos monachos frequentes esse in libris."

388. "Exsecrabile est hoc de sacerdote enarrari"; "hoc"; "cor maculari blasphemis nefandorum laudibus": Jerome, *ep.* 21, c. 13: "Far be it that an 'omnipotent Jupiter' should escape from the mouth of a Christian" — "Absit ut de ore christiana sonet Jupiter omnipotens" (1, 94). Cf. Bernard de Morval, *De cont. mundi*, l. 3, v. 318 (Hoskier):

> Dant sibi turpiter oscula Jupiter et schola Christi.
> Jupiter and the school of Christ are scandalously kissing each other.

389. "In uno se ore cum Jovis laudibus Christi laudes non capiunt": *Ep.*, l. 1, ep. 54 (June 601): "and how grave and unspeakable it is for bishops to sing what is not fitting even for a lay religious" — "et quam grave nefandumque sit episcopis canere quod nec laico religioso conveniat" (PL, LXXVII, 1171-2). Gregory was not writing "to a Christian teacher of grammar" — "ad grammaticae doctorem quemdam christianum," as Brücker says, *op. cit.*, 561. Responding to the pamphlet of Jerome Balbi (*Rhetor gloriosus*, 1494), Guillaume Tardif will write, *Anti-Balbica* (1495): "Absit ... ut de ore christiano sonet Jupiter etc." Balbi (= Acellini, 1454-1535) had been the student of the paganizing Pomponio Leto at Rome.

390. "ses goûts de lettré": P. Batiffol, *op. cit.*, 48-9, note.

391. "passer son temps à enseigner la grammaire": L. Duchesne, *L'Église au VIe s.*, 53. H. O. Taylor, *The Medieval Mind*, 1, 98, understands: "to teach grammar and poetry is not the proper function of a bishop." The formula of Reto R. Bezzola, *Les origines et la formation de la litt. courtoise en Occident*, 1 (1944), 78: Gregory's reproof to Desiderius "for spending too much time teaching his priests grammar" — "de trop enseigner la grammaire à ses prêtres," does not seem to take sufficient account of the reality at stake either.

392. "Je ne sais trop ce que les louanges de Dieu ou de Jupiter pouvaient avoir à démêler avec la grammaire": Cited by Gorini, 2, 426, note.

393. Aug., *C. Cresc.*, l. 1, c. 14, n. 17: "grammaticam litteraturam latine,

linguae utriusque doctissimi appellarunt" (PL, 43, 456). Gramma = littera. *De ordine*, l. 2, c. 12, n. 37 (R. Jolivet, 428). Marrou, in *Rech. sur la tradit. plat.* (1957), 188: "For all the ancients, grammar was, above all, familiarity with the classics" — "Pour tous les anciens, la grammaire, c'était avant tout la fréquentation des classiques."

394. "recte loquendi scientia et poetarum enarratio": *Inst. orat.*, l. 1, c. 4, n. 2. Cf. Seneca, *ep.* 88, c. 3: "Grammar is concerned with speech, and, if one wants to go off more widely, with histories, and now to extend its limits to the widest extent, with poems" — "Grammatica circa curam sermonis versatur, et, si latius evagari vult circa historias, jam ut longissime fines suos proferat, circa carmina."

395. "intellectus poetarum"; "scientia eorum quae a poetis dicuntur"; "scientia interpretandi poetas"; "ars grammatica": Marius Vict., *Ars grammatica*, l. 1: "Now what is the art of grammar? — "The one that considers the speech and the poem. — In how many ways? — Three. — Which ones? — Understanding the poets, and explaining how to speak and write correctly. . . . According to Varro, the art of grammar that we call literature is for the most part the science of the things said by poets, historians, and orators": "Grammatica autem ars quae est? — Spectativa orationis et poematos. — Haec quot modis discernitur? — Tribus. — Quibus? — Intellectu poetarum et recte loquendi scribendique ratione. . . . Ut Varroni placet, ars grammatica quae a nobis litteratura dicitur, scientia est eorum quae a poetis, historicis, oratoribusque dicuntur ex parte majore." Idem, *De arte grammatica:* "Grammar [is] the science of interpreting the poets and historians, and an account of writing and speaking correctly" — "Grammatica (est) scientia interpretandi poetas atque historicos, et recte scribendi loquendique ratio." (H. Keil, *Grammatici lat.*, 6, 3-4 and 188.)

396. "poetarum ficta carmina et comoediarum ridiculas fabulas": Pref. to the transl. of the *Peri Archôn*, l. 3 (194). Donatus again was a "grammarian" when he was commenting on the comedies of Terence.

397. Cf. Justin, *2 Apol*, c. 5, n. 5: "les poètes et les mythologues" (Pautigny, 159).

398. Origen, letter to Gregory Thaumaturgus, n. 2 (PG, XI, 90 BD).

399. Origen, *In Jer.*, h. 29, n. 7: they pour "in calicem aureum venenum idolatriae, et venenum turpiloquii, venenum eorum quae animam hominis interimunt dogmatum, venenum falsi nominis scientiae" (PG, XIII, 539 AB). Cf. *In Jos.*, h. 7, n. 7, the analogous image of the golden ingot or the "golden tongue" (334).

400. *Sel. in Jer.*, li, 7: "The golden chalice is Babylon. Nebuchadnezzar's chalice is golden to deceive men, so that on taking it they may drink, when they see the gold, beautiful both to look at and to think on, but they do not pay attention to the fact that it contains condemnation. For its reprobate dogmas have been embellished with elegance of words, and its deceptiveness with beauty of speech and contrived method. For every poet, too, prepares a golden chalice, blending in the venom of idolatry, base discourse, and all the evils of the soul. But Jesus . . ." — "Calix aureus Babylon. Aureus est Nabuchodonosoris calix ad fallendos homines, ut accipientes bibant, dum vident aurum et visu pulchrum et cogitatu speciosum, sed quod in eo judicium est non animadvertunt. Improba enim ejus dogmata, vocum elegantia ornata sunt, decipientia elocutionis

venustate et methodo artificiosa. Nam et omnis poeta excellens calicem aureum comparavit, venenum immiscens idololatriae, turpiloquii et omnium animae malorum. At Jesus etc." (XIII, 599-600 CD). Cf. Caesarius, s. 54, n. 6 (Morin, 1, 230); etc.

401. *Ep.* 133, c. 3 (Hilberg, 3, 246-7). This applies to Rufinus's translation of the Sentences of Sextus, which had been cited by Origen. Cf. H. Chadwick, *The Sentences of Sextus* (1959), 119-21.

402. Beatus, *In Ap.*, l. 2, probl. (121). Card. Humbert, *De s. Romana Eccl.*; "Babylon ... has drunk of the wine of idolatry and inebriated all the nations with the golden chalice, viz., secular eloquence and power" — "Babylon ... de vino idololatriae potavit et inebriavit omnes gentes calice aureo, eloquentia sc. saeculari atque potentia" (P. E. Schramm, *Kaiser* ... , 2, 131). Rupert, *De vict. Verbi Dei*, l. 6, c. 15: "Rightly, then, is the golden chalice called Babylon through the prophet, inebriating every land. . . . By the chalice or cup of Babylon we understand sweet deception . . ." — "Recte ergo calix aureus Babylon dicitur per prophetam, inebrians omnem terram (*Ap.*, xvii). . . . Calicem sive poculum Babylonis, dulcem intelligimus deceptionem etc." (PL, CLXIX, 1348 CD).

403. *Hist.*, l. 2, c. 12 (CXLII, 644 AB).

404. John a Monk, *Vita s. Odonis*, c. 12: "When he had wanted to read Virgil's poems, a certain vessel was shown him in a vision, outside very beautiful, but inside full of serpents, by which he soon saw himself to be surrounded but yet not bitten; and on waking he understood the serpents to be the teaching of the poets; the vessel in which they were hiding, Virgil's book; and the path along which he was very thirstily marching, Christ" — "Virgilii cum voluisset legere carmina, ostensum fuit ei per visum vas quoddam, deforis quidem pulcherrimum, intus vero plenum serpentibus, a quibus se subito circumvallari conspicit, nec tamen morderi: et evigilans serpentes doctrinam poetarum, vas in quo latitabant librum Virgilii, viam vero per quam incedebat valde sitiens Christum intellexit." If in the sequel Odo does not read the poets any more, this is not a rejection on his part, it is normal progress; c. 13: "Then, the poets' songs having been left behind, he, having been taught by the deep spirit of counsel, turned entirely to the expositors of the gospels and the prophets" — "Deinde, relictis carminibus poetarum, alti edoctus spiritu consilii, ad evangeliorum prophetarumque expositores se totum convertit" (PL, CXXXIII, 49 AB). The Middle Ages offer more than one analogous dream, but they do not all have the same signification or manifest the same tendency. Cf. Ermenric, *Ep. ad Grim.*, c. 24 (MGH, *Ep.*, 5, 561-2); Everhelmus, *Vita Popponis abb. Stabulensis*, c. 32 (MGH, *Scr.*, 11, 314; ASS, 25 Jan., 651, n. 66).

405. B. Hauréau, who has translated the story of Odo's dream with a paraphrase, has let some of its words drop out: "but yet not bitten" — "nec tamen morderi" and: "he understood ... the path along which he was marching ... to be Christ" — "viam per quam incedebat ... Christum intellexit": *Singularités hist. et litt.* (1861), 140 and 144. The venom of the serpents is the "doctrina," which Origen's translator called the "judicium."

406. Arnoul de Lisieux will rightly say, *ep.* 26: "For his highest intention is to have said everything differently from others, and so he complicates and 'innodates' or 'puts knots into' everything he says, so that he ought to be called

more correctly Innodius than Ennodius" — "Summa enim ejus intentio est aliter omnia dixisse quam caeteri, ideoque totum quod loquitur exquisita quadam intricatione complicat et innodat, ut rectius Innodius quam Ennodius debeat appellari" (J. A. Giles, 132). Expression of his remorse, after a serious illness: MGH, *A. Ant.*, 7, 301. On Ennodius: Manitius, *Gesch. der Christ.-lat. Poesie* (1891), 360-6. A. Ebert, 1, 46-9. P. de Labriolle, 752-4. G. Bardy, *L'Églises et les derniers Romains*, 174-188.

407. "Although our most beloved son the priest Candidus, coming later and having been carefully asked about this affair, denied it and tried to make excuses, it has still not gone from my mind, since by as much as it is execrable for this to be reported of a priest, by so much ought it to be learned with strict and true satisfaction whether or not it be so. Hence, if after this they should make it evidently clear that the reports brought to me are false . . . , we shall give thanks to our God, who has not allowed your heart to be spotted with blasphemous praises of unspeakable things" — "Quamvis dilectissimus filius noster Candidus presbyter postmodum veniens hac de re subtiliter requisitus negaverit atque conatus fuerit excusare, de nostris tamen adhuc animis non recessit quia, quanto exsecrabile est hoc de sacerdote enarrari, tanto utrum ita necne sit districta et veraci oportet satisfactione cognosci. Unde si post hoc evidenter ea quae ad nos prolata sunt falsa esse claruerint . . . , Deo nostro gratias agimus, qui cor vestrum maculari blasphemis nefandorum laudibus non permisit . . ." (June 601; *Registr.*, 2, 303). Cf. *ep.* l. 3, 3 (1, 160): Gregory is writing to the bishop Paul to console him for having been calumniated, and prescribing an inquest.

408. The image is found in Ambrose, Augustine, and Jerome (*ep.* 21, c. 13; 1, 93). It also doubtless comes from Origen: B. Blumenkranz, "*Siliquae porcorum*, l'exégèse méd. et les sc. profanes," in *Mél. Louis Halphen* (1951), 11-7. In Paschasius, who seems harsh, however, the "siliquae porcorum saecularium litterarum" will turn out at the same time to be the food of the "pueri": *In Matt.*, l. 5, prol. (PL, CXX, 338 C).

409. "siliquae porcorum"; "quae male dulci vanitate diversis carminibus idolorum vel daemonum laudes assidue proferendo, mundo huic deceptionis fabulas intulerunt": Caesarius, s. 163 (Morin, 2, 632-3). Cf. Jerome, *ep.* 52, c. 3: "incentiva vitiorum" (2, 174). Aug., *De cat. rudibus*, c. 6, n. 10: "fictas poetarum fabulas et ad voluptatem excogitatas animorum quorum cibus nugae sunt" (C.-F., 40). Cf. Justin, *1 Apol.*, c. 4, n. 9: "The poets come and recount the impurities of Zeus and his children, and you impose silence on those who expose these teachings!" (L. Pautigny, 9). The *Liber de unitate Ecclesiae conservanda*, an anti-Gregorian pamplet (ca. 1092), c. 42, criticizes certain monks who, worse than the ancient pagans, prefer the "siliquae daemoniorum" to Scripture (*L. de lite*, 2, 274-5). Combining the two metaphors that we have just seen, Luther will say regarding Erasmus's *De libero arbitrio*, in the preface of his own *De servo arbitrio*: "as if pieces of garbage or shit were being carried in golden or silver vessels" — "tanquam si quisquiliae vel stercora aureis argenteisque vasis portarentur."

410. John the Deacon, *Vita*, l. 3, c. 13: "Prudently recognizing that the whole body of the Church as such happily stands through good bishops or unhappily falls through bad ones" — "Prudenter cognoscens totum corpus Ecclesiae tam

per bonos episcopos feliciter stare, quam per malos infeliciter cadere" (PL, LXXV, 138 B).

411. *Ep.* l. 5, ep. 15, to John of Ravenna: "See that whatever is on the tongue or in a deed should befit a bishop; let him be completely pure to your brothers" — "Vide quid in lingua, quid in actu episcopum deceat; esto totus purus fratribus tuis" (Nov. 594; *Reg.*, 1, 296).

412. *Varia*, l. 2, c. 40 (MGH, *A. ant.*, 12, 71). Cf. P. Courcelle, in *Rech. sur la trad. plat.*, 106.

413. Greg. is nevertheless perhaps less distant from Cassiodorus than some have said. Cassiodorus also "pursues explicitly utilitarian ends in the *Human Institutions:* he wants to filter the profane culture indispensable for the exercise of religious life for the use of his monks" — "poursuit dans les *Institutions humaines* des fins utilitaires et précises: il veut filtrer à l'usage de ses moines la culture profane indispensable à l'exercice de la vie religieuse": Fontaine, 805. Isidore gave a more generous reception to antiquity; this did not keep a recent historian from speaking of his "grande hostilité à la culture séculière": P. Pascal, cited by Fontaine, 806, note 2. For Laistner, Isidore's attitude "recalls that of Gregory rather than the broader outlook of Cassiodorus" (121).

414. In the 9th century, "the national culture and the literary tradition which was imposed upon that culture do not constitute a unity" — "la culture nationale et la tradition littéraire qui s'est imposée à cette culture ne constituent pas une unité" (C. Mohrmann, CCM, 1, 271) as was the case in the time of the Fathers.

415. This is what the old Jesuit Maimbourg, who had taught the humanities at Rouen, did not see; *Hist. du Pontificat de S. Gr.* (1686), 260: "I frankly avow that the judgment of the great St. Gregory makes me groan as I reflect upon the past and makes me regret in my old age the time that I wasted in the best days of my youth, where it was necessary for me to fill my mind with fables, with chimeras, with a thousand thoughts of false divinities" — "J'avoue de bonne foi que le sentiment du grand S. Gr. . . . m'a fait gémir en faisant un peu de réflexion sur le passé, et me fait regretter en ma vieillesse le temps que j'ai perdu dans les plus beaux jours de ma jeunesse, où il m'a fallu remplir mon esprit de fables, de folies, de chimères, de mille idées profanes de fausses divinités."

416. "La religion et les lettres se tiennent par une étroite parenté, elles sont sœurs": *Orat.* 62, c. 8 (Förster, 4, 350). Cf. A. J. Festugière, *Antioche païenne et chrétienne* (1959), 240.

417. "Chaque renouveau de la tradition classique s'est accompagné d'une poussée de néo-paganisme"; "haine de l'hellénisme profane": cf. Courcelle, 131.

418. "la culture préparatoire"; "idéal"; "mode de vie": Marrou, *op. cit.*, 423-5. It therefore seems hardly right to say, with G. Duby, in *Hist. de la civilisation française* (1958), 31, that "the ancient school" was "condemned because built upon the study of profane writers." Cf. Boccaccio, cited by J. Burckhardt, *The Civilization of the Renaissance in Italy*, P. 3, c. 4: "The situation was quite different, when the primitive Church still had to defend itself against the pagans. Today — praise Christ — the true religion is strong and powerful, paganism has been destroyed, the victorious Church is mistress of the enemy camp; today one can study and try to revive paganism without danger." We of course leave the responsibility of his judgments at the door of Boccaccio.

419. "quelle époque a-t-on cessé de parler latin?" ALAM, 6 (1931), 110.

420. "la souillure du cœur"; "si nous nous plaçons à son point de vue, nous ne saurions lui donner tort": op cit., 188-9: "It is difficult for us to account for the disturbance that the reading of all those masterpieces of antiquity could produce in the imagination of those young clerics and monks about whom Gregory was ceaselessly preoccupied; for them they were not the monuments of a world gone by, but the still warm and still quivering expression of a civilization, of a society full of life just yesterday and an object of admiration by the human race."

421. "When many good things had been reported to us about your studies, joy so filled our heart" — "Cum multa nobis bona de vestris fuissent studiis nuntiata, ita cordi nostro nata est laetitia, etc." It would be hard to maintain that he wanted to speak only of sacred studies to the exclusion of all human culture.

422. *In 5^m ps. paenit.*, n. 4 (PL, LXXIX, 605 A). *Ep.*, 5, 15 (1, 296).

423. "Beatus papa Gregorius artis grammaticae disciplinam eatenus in suis laudat epistolis, ut eam congruere deneget christianis": *De s. simplicitate*, c. 8 (PL, CXLV, 703 A). At least Peter Damian had the merit of citing Jerome as well, and this comparison is instructive. On the other hand, as a connoisseur he appreciates the "accuratus et limatus" style, the "flores eloquentiae," the "urbanitas dictionis": *Ep.*, l. 2, 8 (CXLIV, 273 B). Johannes Trithemius was able to call it "sweet and ornate, after the fashion of Gregorian eloquence" — "Gregorianae eloquentiae instar, dulcis et ornatus" (186 A). At Cluny, they admired "his eloquence, worthy of St. Gregory": J. Leclercq, *S. Pierre Damien* (1960), 119.

424. "Beatus Gregorius quemdam episcopum non reprehendit quia (saeculares) litteras didicerat, sed quia contra episcopale officium pro lectione evangelia grammaticam populo exponebat. . . ."

"In doctrina vero sacrae Scripturae auctoritatem debet episcopus praeferre, non saecularium litterarum peritiam ostentare. Non enim episcopalis officii est grammaticam exponere, ne laudes Jovis personent ore pontificis": *Decretum*, P. I, d. 37, c. 8; d. 86, c. 4 (Friedberg, 138, 298).

425. *Ep.* 57, *Adv. Andronicum*: "nor did I open a school" — "nec ludum aperui, οὐδὲ διδασκαλεῖον ἤνοιξα" (PG, LXVI, 1397 B). On Christian Synesius: *R. des ét. grecques*, 65 (1952), 474-84.

426. *Bampton Lectures*, 246.

427. *L'aventure de l'humanisme européen au moyen âge* (1953), 41-2.

428. *Illustrations . . .* , 7-8, Likewise E. Caspar, *Gesch. des Papsttums*, 2 (1933), 547.

429. H.-I. Marrou himself at first believed he was sure, "knowing the attitude of St. Gregory regarding classical literature," that he had to clear out the library inherited from Agapitus "before giving it to his own monastery" — "connaissant l'attitude de saint Grégoire à l'égard des lettres classiques," "qu'il a dû vider la bibliothèque"; "avant de la donner à son monastère" on the Caelian Hill: "Autour de la bibliothèque du pape Agapit," in the *Mél. d'arch. et d'hist.*, Ecole fr. de Rome, 48 (1931), 166-8.

430. So it is for W. H. Hutton, *loc. cit.*, 236.

431. Cf. L. Hahn, "Zum Gebrauch der lateinischen Sprache in Konstantinopel," *Festgabe f. M. von Schanz* (Würzburg, 1912), 173. Krumbacher, *Gesch. der*

byzantinischen Literatur, 2ᵈ ed. (1897), 605, 613, 941-1136. I owe these remarks and references to my friend Father Hasso Jaeger.

432. 1 *Apol.*, c. 25, n. 3; c. 53, n. 1; c. 57, n. 1; c. 58, nn. 2-3 (Pautigny, 51, 109-11, 121, 123); *Dial.*, c. 9, n. 1 (Archambault, 1, 44); etc.

433. Methodius of Olympus, *Symposium*, n. 205.

434. This thought will be expressed again, very much later, by Gerhoh of Reichersberg, *In ps.* xx, in these two verses (PL, CXCIII, 986 B):

> Cedant bestiolae quae currunt, nocte nocente,
>   Ambulet in luce lux homo, luce duce!
> Let the beasts that run whilst the night works harm give way,
>   Let the Light walk [as] Man in the light, light leading the way!

435. Justin, 1 *Apol.*, c. 6, n. 1 (Pautigny, 10). Lactantius, *Div. Inst.*, l. 1, c. 21, n. 18 (S. Brandt, 81).

436. Cf. *L. moz. sacram.*, regarding the law of the Magi: "the old superstition having been trodden under foot" — "vetusta superstitione calcata" (89).

437. "latin grossier"; "pauvre organisation"; "l'allégorie forcée et inintelligible"; "tendance à tout moraliser"; "basse latinité"; "la mentalité d'un moine du moyen âge"; "nouveau syncrétisme religieux, souvent éloigné de l'esprit de l'Évangile . . .": *The Mind of the Middle Ages*, 3ᵈ ed., 67, 191-2.

438. *Ib.* Already R. L. Poole, *Illustrations* . . . , 8: "This then was the policy, if we may so call, of the Church with regard to education, declared by him who has an undisputed title to be called the father of the medieval papacy and whose example was law to his successors, as indeed it was to the whole of Latin Christendom for many ages" (2ᵈ ed., 1920). And already Farrar, who introduced his own judgment on the letters to Leander and Desiderius with these words: "The papal system had established a secure despotism over the minds of men." And already Brücker.

439. "ce pontife si calomnié": Ozanam, 282.

440. "simplement une exagération assez inexplicable": Ebert, 1, 588.

441. "plaisante avec son ami Léandre": E. Carlier, pref. to the transl. of the *Dialogues* (1675).

442. "S'il est vrai que Grégoire, dans sa lettre à l'évêque de Vienne, condamne les études classiques, dans un autre endroit il affirme explicitement leur nécessité": *Hist. de l'Ordre de S. Benoît*, French tr., 2, 79.

443. *Storia della Letteratura latina cristiana* (1929), 355. Cf. Ozanam, 283: "One can believe that this great mind had understood the need to break with the obsolete methods of the grammarians and to save literature by putting them at the service of the new doctrine which was saving the world" — "On peut croire que ce grand esprit avait compris la nécessité de rompre avec les méthodes surannées des grammairiens et de sauver les lettres en les attachant au service de la doctrine nouvelle qui sauvait le monde." Leonhard Weber, *Hauptfragen der Moraltheologie Greg. des Grossen* (Paradosis, 1, 1947), 38-40, presents a sage defense of Gregory.

444. He knew how to distinguish content and form, Christian inspiration and classical workmanship: *ep.* 16, n. 11 (PL, LXI, 234 AB). Cf. Nora K. Chadwick, *Poetry and Letters in Early Christian Gaul* (1955), 88: "Paulinus, the Christian devotee,

Notes to Pages 55-56

with his background of classical culture, is typical of all that is best in the early Church in the West."

445. "littérature fabuleuse"; "songes fauleux"; "mensonges des poètes"; "prophètes de la vérité": *ep.* 13, n. 25: "For we are not gathering what is to come from human opinions or the fabulous dreams of poets or imaginings of the philosophers. . . . Let them flatter themselves with the lies of the poets, who do not have the prophets of truth. Let them be blinded by the wandering opinions of the philosophers, who are not illuminated by the testimonies of the apostles" — "Non enim ab humanis opinionibus nec a fabulosis poetarum somniis aut philosophorum phantasmatis post hominem futura colligimus. . . . Blandiantur sibi mendaciis poetarum, qui non habent veritatis prophetas. Caecentur opinionibus erraticis philosophorum, qui non illuminantur testimoniis apostolorum" (PL, LXI, 221 C). Cf. Peter Damian, *op.* 32, c. 9: "poetas et philosophos" (CXLV, 560 C).

446. That they should restore his disciple to poetry. Cf. Pierre Fabre, *S. Paulin de Nole et l'amitié chrét.* (1949), 160-3. On the nevertheless genuine Christianity of Ausonius: Gorini, 1, 185-209.

447. *Poem* 10, vv. 20-23 and 30-1 (year 393):

Quid abdicatas in meam curam, pater,
    Redire Musas praecipis?
Negant camaenis, nec patent Apollini
    Dicata Christo pectora . . .
Nunc alia mentem vis agit, major Deus
    Aliosque mores postulat.

448. "Ubi sapiens"; "ubi grammaticus, ubi causarum scrutator?"; "stultitia praedicationis": *In Gal.*, l. 3 (PL, XXVI, 399-400); on 1 Cor. 1:26-28. *Ep.* 22, c. 29 (1, 144). *Adv. Pelagianos*, l. 1, c. 14 (XXIII, 506 CD).

449. *Prol. poem.* and *ep.* 57 (Peiper, 20, 85). Cf. G. Bardy, *L'Église et les derniers Romains*, 156-9. Perrat and A. Audin, "A. E. Aviti homilia . . . ," in *Studi di Papirologia e di Antichità orientali* (1957), 445.

450. "Dixi sanctos et apostolicos viros non verborum compositionibus deservire, sed sensum veritate gaudere; nec per artem Donati, sed per simplicitatem currere Christi . . ."; "Grammaticam et liberalem artem juxta te Donati, non te pudet, dilecte, tam infirmiora parti tuae testimonia uti, tamque alio opere congruentia huic nostrae assertioni aptare? . . . 'Quae stulta sunt mundi elegit Deus ut confundat sapientes.' — Quid utique sapientes? Numquid nostros sanctissimos Patres, et non potius grammaticos, philosophos et rhetores? — 'Non veni per sublimitatem sermonis . . .': Quae est enim sublimitas sermonis, nisi regulae per metaplasmum et tropos Donati?": *ep.* 1, n. 2 (PL, CXXI, 413 C); *ep.* 4, nn. 6-7 (429-30). Cf. *Ep.* 5, n. 4 (451 BC). Regarding the captive that it is necessary to pluck, *ep.* 4, n. 8: "Quod si aliquid ex eadem seris, jam non perfecte grammaticus eris" (432 A); n. 10: "Prophecy instilled in him by God, not discovered from the art of Donatus" — "Prophetia a Deo illi inspirata, non ab arte Donati inventa" (433 C). In the same lineage: Othloh, *De eo quod legitur in psalmis* (XCIII, 1114 A; but also, 1196 AB). The commonplace on the simplicity of the Scriptures as opposed to the brilliant deceptiveness of the poets or philosophers

is found again in Hugh, *Didasc.*, l. 4, c. 1 (CLXXVI, 777 D). Cf. Helinand, *s.* 15, on Ovid: "the poetic-maker-of-deception deceptively renders them as happy" — "hos fallaciter beatificat poeta fallaciae . . ." (CCXII, 602 B), which does not prevent him from constantly citing the poets.

451. It has, as is well known, a great part to play in Jerome. In the opposite direction, he cited in *In Tit.*, the example of Paul to authorize the use of the poets. Sedulius Scotus (CIII, 159 D), Abelard (CLXXVIII, 1166 D) and others cite him on this subject. On Jerome's "inconsistent" attitude on this point, the gap between his declarations and his practice: Harald Hagendahl, *Latin Fathers and the Classics* (1958), 91-328; Gerard L. Ellspermann, *The Attitude of the Early Christian Latin Writers toward Pagan Literature and Learning* (1949).

452. "figmenta poetarum"; "perniciosa dogmata"; "fucus grammaticae artis"; "proficere ad vitam": *Sent.*, l. 3, c. 13, n. 6 and 10-11 (LXXXIII, 687-8); l. 2, c. 29, n. 12 (630 A).

453. If one takes account of these differences, the distance between Isidore and Gregory will appear smaller. We shall not dare to adopt the ingenious hypothesis of Fontaine, thinking that at Seville "the first readers of the *Moralia* . . . were legitimately able to interpret Gregory's points as discrete warnings for the use of Isidore" — "les premiers lecteurs des Moralia . . . ont pu légitimement interpréter les pointes de Grégoire comme de discrets avertissements ad usum Isidori" (34; cf. 390, 793-4).

454. "Ut gloriam sanctae et individuae Trinitatis clara voce decantaret, neglexit regulam grammaticae dispositionis. . . . Ut veritatem dominici sermonis apertius commendaret, postposuit ordinem disciplinae saecularis": Keil, *Grammat. lat.*, 7, 1 (1878), 252.

455. PL, LXXV, 516 B. [See note 349, above.]

456. "Nos itaque nec Donati regulis ad plene imbuti, vel grammatica Prisciani, minusve Dialecticis versutiis exercitati, nec Rhetoricis floribus Philosophicae eloquentiae exhilarati, non in sublimitate sermonis ea quae collegimus vera, fideli humilitate dictante, rationis judicia exsequimur": Ekkehart min. decanus S. Galli, *L. de vita b. Notk.*, prol. (Gold. — Senk., 1, 2, 226). A little later, the monk John will say, while composing the *Life* of St. Odo of Cluny: "that not even talk of grammar would embellish my words" — "quod nec grammaticae artis locutio mea decoraret verba" (PL, CXXXIII, 44 C), a formula no less suitable, but perhaps a bit more truthful.

457. Cf. *Miracula S. Agili* (ASS, Aug., 6, 587); etc.

458. Lesne, t. 5, 394-413.

459. "sut possint miris verba sonare modis": *Prol.* (W. von den Steinen, 152).

460. "Donatum non sequimur, quia fortiorem in divinis Scripturis auctoritatem tenemus": Thurot, *loc. cit.*, 81. The phrase "expressing the entire exegesis of the high Middle Ages" — "expressive de toute l'exégèse du haut moyen âge": Spicq, *Esquisse*, 46.

461. *Opusc.* 13, c. 11, against the monks "who go up to the mob of grammarians, who, spiritual studies having been abandoned, crave to learn the earthly trifles of an art, lightly regarding whether they in fact are rejoicing that the rule of Benedict should be forsaken in favor of the rules of Donatus" — "qui grammaticorum vulgus adeunt, qui, relictis spiritualibus studiis, addiscere

terrenae artis ineptias concupiscunt, parvipendentes siquidem regulam Benedicti regulis gaudent vacare Donati" (PL, CXLV, 306 C). *De s. simplicitate:* "before you have flown off to the desert ... to sweat over — let me not call them the 'studies', but — the 'stupidities' of the liberal arts" — "ante ad eremum pervolasti ... quam liberalium artium non dicam studiis sed stultitiis insudares" (695 A).

462. "Mea grammatica, Christus est": *Ep.*, l. 8, 8 (CXLIV, 476 C). *Op.* 11 (CXLV, 232-3); etc.

463. Gonsette, op. cit., 22-6. He himself was there not one of those "pure orientals" of whom A. Renaudet speaks, *Humanisme et Renaiss.* (1958), 48. Renaudet rightly observes, however, that "the masters of the great medieval schools had always been aware of watching over the deposit of a culture whose value they were unwilling to diminish" — "les maîtres des grandes écoles médiévales ont toujours eu conscience de garder le dépôt d'une culture dont ils ne voulaient pas abaisser le prix."

464. "Cicero once used to be sweet to me, the songs of the poets used to caress me, the philosophers used to shine with golden words, and the sweet Sirens used to sing enchantingly to the point of my destruction" — "Olim mihi Tullius dulcescebat, blandiebantur carmina poetarum, philosophi verbis aureis splendebant, et Sirenes usque in exitium dulces meum incantaverunt intellectum." Cf. *Ep.*, l. 6, 10 (CXLIV, 391 D).

465. "sapiens imperitia"; "stulta sapientia"; "Christi simplicitas"; "sophisticae cavillationes"; "insanientium poetarum fabulosa commenta": *Op.* 11, c. 1 (CXLV, 232-3); *Vita S. Romualdi*, prol. (CXLIV, 144 A). On the fitness of such an attitude: J. Leclercq, *S. Pierre Damien*, 193-4 and 197-200. One astonishing thing, J. Brücker, *op. cit.*, 3, 668, praises Peter Damian and his "love of philosophy" — "philosophiae amor."

466. *Intr. ad th.*, l. 2, c. 10: "Quod recte Gregorius attendens ... ait: Indignum est etc." (CLXXVIII, 1062 C).

467. *In Nahum*, n. 59 (XCVI, 733 D). Van den Eynde, *Franc. Studies*, 17 (1958).

468. *Polycr.*, l. 2, c. 17 (CXCIX, 435 CD).

469. "Edidi librum ..., incultus est": PL, CXCIX, 68 D. Alcuin, *ep.* 2 (C, 141 A); etc. Peter Damian (CXLIV, 336 D, 925 B; CXLV, 66 D, 154-5). Or Paul Alvarus, a brilliant disciple of Jerome, *Indic. lum.*, c. 20: "And rusticity which, as a slave of uncultured tongue, sticks to me, rightly had to impose silence ..., but yet an uneducated tongue does not keep my lips from defending justice" — "Et recte rusticitas, quae mihi vernula haeret incultae linguae, imponere silentium debuit ..., nec ad defensionem justitiae labia mea inerudita lingua prohibuit" (CXXI, 534 B). Or Gontier, *De oratione*, prol. (CCXII, 104 BC).

470. Thus Heric of Auxerre, *Allocutio ad librum*, in the preface to the *Vita S. Germani* (MGH, *P. lat. aevi kar.*, 3, 437). Gautier de Chatillon, *Alexandride:* "O mea Alexandreis etc." (PL, CCIX, 463-4).

471. "Sit gradus et cultus, habitus peregrinus cunti,
    Nonnisi barbariem barbara lingua sonet":

Entheticus in Pol., c. 13-4 (CXCIX, 379 A). The work was imitated by Nigel of Longchamp, in the poem put as preface to his treatise *Contra curiales.*

472. "tam divinae quam humanae litteraturae": Decree of the councils of Valence (853) and Savonnières (859); cited by B. Hauréau, *H. de la phil. scol.*, 1, 149.

473. "l'*auctoritas divina* de la Bible et l'*auctoritas humanae* de Donat": *Latin vulgaire, latin des chrétiens, latin médiéval* (1955), 49.

474. Bede, *De schemat.* (Halm, 607). Charlemagne, *De litt. colendis* (MGH, *Leges, Cap.*, 1, 79). *L. carolini.* Rupert, etc. See note 496, below.

475. "ad divinarum altitudinem Scripturarum": Hildebert, *Vita S. Hugonis*, c. 1, n. 2 (PL, CLIX, 861 AB), etc.

476. *In Ap.*, l. 8 (586-7). Peter Damian, *De s. simplicitate*, c. 7, cites an analogous case (CXLV, 701 AD).

477. "studiosius"; "acutius": *Dis. claustr.*, c. 6 (CCII, 1109 BC).

478. Already Aponius, *In Cant.*, ii, 15. On the interest borne by Augustine for grammar: Bardy, in Aug., *Cité de Dieu* (Bibl. august.), 3, 517-9.

479. Cf. Ambrose, *In Luc.*, l. 2, c. 42: "If the philosophers themselves ... have used fewer Latin utterances so that they might use the proper ones, how much more ought we to neglect the words and to behold the mysteries!" — "Si ipsi philosophi ... minus latinis usi sunt sermonibus, ut propriis uterentur, quanto magis nos verba negligere debeamus, et spectare mysteria!" (SC, 45, 92). *Ep.* 63: "since, then, philosophy would renounce the former, does not the Church exclude the latter?" — "cum igitur illos abdicaverit philosophia, hos non excludit Ecclesia?" (PL, XVI, 1195).

480. "Divina locutio grammaticorum regulis subjecta non est, et humanae loquacitatis idioma sequi ex necessitate cogi non potest": William of Rouen, at the council of Rouen, 1108. Ordoricus Vitalis, *H. eccl.*, P. 3, l. 8, c. 19 (PL, CLXXXVIII, 618 D). Cf. Ps.-Bede, *De sex dierum creatione:* "The authority of this Scripture is greater than all the capacity of the human mind" — "Major est Scripturae hujus auctoritas, quam omnis humani ingenii capacitas" (following Aug., XCIII, 210 D).

481. *De "in" prepositione explanatio* (Lambot, 359-72). Cf. J. Jolivet, *Godescalc d'Orbais et la Trinité* (1958), 26-7.

482. Gilson, *La Philosophie au m. âge*, 2ᵉ éd. (1925), 224.

483. "Quadam die, dum ad mensam legeret, dixit quiddam inter legendum sicut dicere debuit; quod non placuit praesidenti, et aliter dicere jussit; velut si ille dixisset "docere," media producta, ut est, et iste eadem media correpta emendasse "docere," quod non est. Non enim Prior ille literatus erat. At vir sapiens, sciens magis obedientiam Christo deberi quam Donato, dimisit quod bene pronuntiaverat, et dixit quod non recte dicere jubebatur. Nam producere brevem, vel longam corripere syllabam, non capitale noverat crimen; verum jubenti ex parte Dei non parere, culpam non levem esse sciebat": *Vita b. Lanfranci Cantuar. archiep.*, c. 2, n. 4 (PL, CL, 32 CD).

484. See above, vol. 2, ch. 6.2.

485. Hugh, *Did.*, l. 2, c. 31: "Grammatica est scientia loquendi sine vitio" (CLXXVI, 765-6).

486. "Nec quaerant grammatici quam sit latinum, sed christiani quam verum": Cf. in the opposite direction the reproach addressed by Alan of Lille against Priscian, whom he believed to have been an apostate: *Anticlaudianus*, l. 2, c. 8 (210, 508 BC):

Claudicat ille fide, ne fama claudicet ejus
Tractatus . . .
"That fellow wavers in his faith, lest the reputation of his
Treatise should waver. . . ."

487. Aug., *s*. 299, n. 6 (XXXVIII, 1371). Cf. C. Mohrmann, "Comment S. Aug. s'est familiarisé avec le latin des chrétiens," in *Études sur le latin des chrét.*, 383-9. For *salutare,* which becomes a substantive: J. Gribomont and A. Thibaut, "Méthode et esprit des traducteurs du psautier grec," in *Richesses,* 73-4.

488. "Ecce, frater, vis grammaticam discere? Disce Deum pluraliter declinare": *De sancta simpl.,* c. 1 (CXLV, 698 D).

489. "d'éléments existants et rebelles"; "faire subir bien des violences": Ozanam, 2, 118 and 134; 149: "how the Bible, having entered by main force into the old idiom of Cicero, enlarged it" — "comment la Bible, entré de vive force dans le vieil idiome de Cicéron, l'élargit. . . ." Cf. Hasso Jaeger, SJ, in *Iura, rivista internaz. di Diretto romano e antico,* 10 (1959), 301-2: "The long works on the manner of speaking proper to the Christian language that developed in the course of the patristic era . . . show well what a strong culture . . . is required to grasp the new linguistic contributions proper to Christianity within the texts" — "Les longues études sur l'idiomatique propre à la langue chrétienne qui se développe au cours de l'ère patristique . . . montrent bien quelle forte culture . . . est exigée pour saisir dans les textes les nouveaux apports linguistiques propres au christianisme."

490. "Credo *in Deum*" — or "in Deo": This is just what Miss C. Mohrmann did, with her universally recognized competence, *Latin vulgaire . . . ,* 98, 132-3, 203 (cf. 59-60); *Ét. sur le latin des chrétiens* (1958). Cf. Paul, in Acts 20:21: "fidem in Dom. nostrum J. Christum." The Credo of Aquileia had the ablative: "Credo in Deo Patre . . . in Jesu Christo . . . in Spiritu sancto"; Rufinus, *A Commentary on the Apostle's Creed,* tr. J. N. D. Kelly (1955). The contrast is even more apparent with the other articles.

491. "La révélation du Dieu personnel, actif dans l'histoire, avait produit une expérience absolument unique": Gribomont and Thibot, *op. cit.,* 52.

492. "Non barbarismi, non *solecismi* confusionem devito": Cf. Jerome, cited by Agobard, *Adv. Fred.,* c. 13: "Howsoever often as we annotate solecisms and suchlike, we are not insulting the Apostle . . . but we are rather the Apostle's defenders " — "Nos quotiescumque solecismos aut tale quid adnotamus, non Apostolum pulsamus . . . sed magis Apostoli assertores sumus" (PL, CIV, 166-7). Emery will say it again, *loc. cit.,* 363: "If it is necessary to choose between the necessity of setting aside ordinary rules of grammar and the necessity of mutilating or rendering more imperfectly the sense of the divine oracles, it would be a veritable indignity to accord the preference to the rules of grammar" — "S'il faut opter entre la nécessité de s'écarter des règles ordinaires de la grammaire et la nécessité de mutiler ou de rendre plus imparfaitement le sens des oracles divins, ce serait une véritable indignité d'accorder la préférence aux règles de la grammaire." In the opposite direction, apostasy or lack of understanding of dogmas and Christian sentiments is quite frequently expressed by balking at the non-classical terms used within Christian Latin. Cf. Étienne Dolet, cited by

L. Febvre, *Le problème de l'incroyance au XVIe s.* (1942), 56-7; or Christophorus Cellarius Smalcaldiensis, *De latinitate mediae et infimae aetatis liber, sive Antibarbarus* (2^d ed., Jena, 1682), at the words "supernaturalis," "cor," "humilis," "persona," etc. (92, 150, 166, 206-7).

493. "Pagina sacra non vult se subdere legi
    Grammaticae, nec vult illius arte regi":

John of Garland (Thurot, 526). Alexander of Villedieu, *Doctrinale:* "Since I am a cultivator of Christ, I do not care to make what the pagans have laid down a norm for what is proper" — "Cum sim christiocola, normam non est mihi cura de propriis facere quae gentiles posuere" (Mohrmann, CCM, 1, 279).

494. "origo et fundamentum liberalium artium": Quintilian, followed by Isidore, *Etym.*, l. 1, c. 5, n. 1 (PL, LXXXII, 81 BC). William of Conches, *De philosophia mundi:* "Since grammar goes first in every teaching " — "Quoniam in omni doctrina grammatica praecedit" (Thurot, 17). Rabanus, *Cl. inst.*, l. 3, c. 18 (CVII, 395-6). Dante, *Paradiso*, 12, 138: "La prima arte." On grammar in the Middle Ages: Heinrich Roos, SJ, *Die Modi significandi des Martinus de Dacia* (1952), 84-99.

495. "instrument de recherche intellectuelle": Fontaine, 29-30, analyzing in Macrobius, and then Isidore "the gradual absorption of all the domains of knowledge into a single grammatical erudition with unbounded ambitions" — "l'absorption graduelle de tous les domaines du savoir dans une érudition grammaticale aux ambitions démesurées." El. Elorduy, "S. Isidoro, Unidad orgánica de su educación reflejada en sus escritos, la gramática ciencia totalitaria" (*Misc. Isidor.*, 1936, 293).

496. *Capitul. de scholis* (MGH, *Cap.*, 1, 79). An argument of this sort seemed "singular" and "puerile" to Hauréau. Someone may ask, "Why?"

497. "scientia recte loquendi"; "scientia vere loquendi": Isidore, *loc cit.* William of Shyreswood: "The science of speech . . . has three parts: grammar, which teaches speaking correctly; rhetoric, which teaches speaking with embellishment; and logic, which teaches speaking truly" — "Sermocinalis scientia . . . tres habet partes: grammaticam, quae docet recte loqui; et rhetoricam, quae docet ornate loqui; et logicam, quae docet vere loqui" (Roos, 109).

498. P. Vignaux, *Philosophie au m. âge* (1958), 7: "Grammar and logic, closely kindred disciplines" — "La grammaire et la logique, disciplines assez proches l'une et l'autre"; cf. 22. John Scotus, *De div. nat.*, l. 5, c. 4: grammar, like rhetoric, is a "member of dialectic" (PL, CXXII, 869-70). That is again the case, despite the disdainful opposition affected by the grand prelate Adalberon of Laon in his *Carmen ad Robertum*, v. 315:

Grammatica simplex, nedum Dialecticus illex.
Simple grammar, to say nothing of dishonest dialectic.

Hugh, *Did.*, l. 2, c. 29, criticizes those for whom grammar did not constitute part of philosophy (CLXXVI, 763 BC).

499. "la grammaire et la syntaxe de la croyance": Robert Speaight, *Nat. et grâce dans les tragédies de Shakespeare*, tr. fr. (1957), 9.

500. "la spéculation grammaticale était une véritable passion"; "juxta Dominum": J. Jolivet, *op. cit.*, 23, 25, 29.

501. "contra grammaticos": *Grammatica*, fol. 28: "Since I understand 'verbum' in two ways, I want to present the etymology of 'verbum' in two ways" — "Quia duobus modis intelligo verbum, ideo duobus modis aethymologiam volo ponere verbi" (Leclercq, 20).

502. Cf. P. Salmon, etc., *Richesses*. In an analogous manner, Erasmus drew attention to certain words that did not have the same sense in the biblical language as they did in the classical: *Ratio verae theol.* (*Opera*, Leyden, 5, 123-4).

503. Thus Pierre Hadot, "La philosophie comme hérésie trinitaire," RHPR, 1957, 250: There needs to be "a Trinitarian history of philosophy that would study the role of the dogma of the Trinity in the evolution of philosophy. This last study would reveal that the Trinity has offered the philosopher, believer or not, during the whole history of philosophy from the beginning of Christianity, the model of an absolutely unique and paradoxical structural reality that has required thought to conceive an overstepping of classical logic" — "une histoire trinitaire de la philosophie, qui étudierait le rôle du dogme de la Trinité dans l'évolution de la philosophie. Cette dernière étude révélerait que la Trinité a offert au philosophe, croyant ou non, pendant toute l'histoire de la philosophie depuis le christianisme, le modèle d'une réalité de structure absolument unique et paradoxale, qui a obligé la pensée à concevoir un dépassement de la logique classique...."

504. "quid jubeat Priscianus"; "quid Deo suo debeat christianus": Gontier the Cistercian, *De oratione*, l. 1, c. 1 (PL, CCXII, 106 B).

505. "Scientias omnes atque doctrinas ipso etiam locutionis suae more Scriptura sacra transcendit": L. 20, n. 1 (LXXVI, 135 C).

506. "litteratoria disciplina"; "sapientia terrena": *Op.* 11 (CXLV, 231-7); *op.* 36, c. 5 (601 BD). Cf. J. Leclercq, *S. Pierre Damien*, 222.

507. "Quid itaque mirum si, cum omnia ineffabiliter transcendat Deus, omnem quoque institutionis humanae sermonem excedat? ... Quid etiam mirum si in seipso Deus Philosophorum infringat regulas aut exempla, quae in factis suis frequenter cassat? ... si ... sicut humanas cogitationes, ita et humanarum disciplinarum transcendet traditiones?": *Intr. ad theol.*, l. 2, c. 11 (CLXXVIII, 1062-3). Thereby it is clear that the suspicions of William of Saint Thierry and of St. Bernard as to Abelard's rationalism were at least exaggerated.

508. "Verba nostra et quaelibet vocalia, ad indicandum eum qui summe et vere est praesumpta, non actionem vel passionem, non quamlibet varietatem ponunt in ipsam deitatem. Hac de causa prudenter agnoscas, quia verba et quaecumque vocalia ad significandum Deum assumpta, jam non sunt de octo partibus illis, quas ponunt grammatici, sed significant ritu divino, non more grammatico, non rhetorico, non dialectico etc. ...": *In Hexaem.*, l. 1 (Fr. Lecomte, AHDLMA, 25, 240).

509. "Oportuit igitur a naturali facultate nota vocabula transferri ad theologiam, ut per nota vocabula proficeremus qualitercumque ad rei incognitae cognitionem. Nemo tamen aestimet naturalia nomina, cum de Deo dicuntur, inventionis suae retinere proprietatem at subtiliter perquirat transsumptionis rationem": Cited by M. Grabmann, 1 (1909), 256. This last word was that of Alan of Lille, "Somme 'Quoniam Homines,'" l. 1, P. 1, 12 (P. Glorieux, AHDLMA, 20,

146, 152). Alan's *Summa* has been dated by Msgr. Grabmann and by Dom O. Lottin in the neighborhood of 1160; the *Speculum* of Raoul would not be earlier than 1193.

510. "Bien des théologiens ne se résignèrent pas, dans le juste sentiment de la transcendance de la foi et de ses objects, à laisser ses expressions soumises aux lois et procédés du langage humain. Si Dieu parle, pensaient-ils, il doit mieux savoir sa grammaire que Donat et Quintilien; ne lisons pas ses paroles avec les yeux et la grammaire de ces païens": 90, 14-7, 380. Cf. *Théol c. science au XIIIe s.* (3e éd., 1957). Perhaps Father Chenu tends too much to oppose the two attitudes that can be complementary and characterize the same authors. On these "theologians" he observes, moreover: "They do not explain that it is precisely the economy of revelation to express itself, to be incarnated within the language of man, be it that of Moses, Paul, or Donatus, just as it will be accomplished within the authentically human incarnation of the Son of God" — "Ils ne se rendaient pas compte que c'est précisément l'économie de la révélation de s'exprimer, de s'incarner dans la langue de l'homme, que ce soit celle de Moïse, de Paul, ou de Donat, tout comme elle s'accomplira dans l'incarnation authentiquement humaine du Fils de Dieu." But is that to do them full justice? Those theologians would doubtless not have disputed that revelation is expressed in human language. But the economy of revelation has not "incarnated" it "in the language of man" without making it undergo certain fundamental modifications. Because the work has been accomplished (up to a certain point) by the earlier ages, we are led to forget it and to believe that our theological language is always the natural human language. It is nothing of the kind, and the historian ought to recall that fact.

511. I have still not been able to read: L. Minio-Paaluelo, "'Person', from Theology and Grammar to Logic," Oxford Patristic Conference, 1959.

512. Cf. Chenu, 20; *Lumière et Vie*, 11 (1953), regarding the Apocalypse: "In the 13th century the scholastic masters would concern themselves with discerning the characteristics of prophecy in certain texts irreducible to the then-standard laws of grammar and reasoning" — "Au XIIIe s. les maîtres de l'École s'emploieront à discerner les traits de la prophétie, dans des textes irréductibles aux lois courantes de la grammaire et du raisonnement." For the transformation of Aristotle by St. Thomas, reference will be made to the numerous analyses of Gilson, notably AHDLMA, 22 (1956), "Cajetan et l'humanisme théologique."

513. Before the 13th century, the "approaches and methods proper to each discipline" — "démarches et les méthods propres de chaque discipline" — were not always treated as "captives" as much as Father J. J de Santo-Tomas, *R. Thomiste*, 58, 729, seems to believe.

514. Thus Gerhoh, *In ps.* xxxv, all the while condemning the "mundani philosophi," distinguishes a "pagana philosophia" and a "christiana philosophia," of which he says: "But the fountainhead of each of the two sorts of philosophy is that true light which illuminates every human being" — "Utriusque autem philosophia[e] fons est illa lux vera quae illuminat omnem hominem" (Van den Eynde, 431).

515. "Philosophi, patriarchae haereticorum": Tertullian, *Adv. Hermog.*, c. 8 (Aem. Kroymann, 135); approved by Jerome, *ep.* 133, c. 2: "One of our [Christians] puts it beautifully" — "Pulchre quidam nostrorum ait" (PL, XXII, 1148).

516. Angelome (CXV, 499 BC). Gerhoh, *In ps.* cxxxvi (CXCIV, 906 D); etc. Still in the 13th century, "as a general rule, ... with just regard for nuances, the "philosopher" was reserved for pagans and infidels" — "en règle générale, ... avec un juste sentiment des nuances, on réservait le nom de 'philosophe' au païens et aux infidèles": Gilson, *Le philosophe et la théologie* (1960), 211.

517. It is precisely in his chapter *De arte grammatica* that Rabanus treats of the captive. The same goes for Alvarus: see above, note 450.

518. "Naturae sermo succumbit, et rem ut est verba non explicant": Hilary, *De Trin.*, l. 2 (PL, X, 56 B), cited by Alan, *Summa*, prol. (Glorieux, 119).

519. PL, CCX, 577-80.

520. Helinand, *s.* 16, will speak of "barbarismus doctrinae" in a slightly different sense, by an analogous application (CCXII, 611 B).

521. "Tu natura, uteri mei fecunditas": "Thou o nature, fruitfulness of my womb." Cf. Gilson, "La cosmogonie de B. S.," ADHLMA, 3, 22.

522. This is the celebrated hymn, one of the gems of medieval poesy, from the *Liber de planctu naturae* (CCX, 447-8):

O Dei proles, genitrixque rerum ...	O offspring of God, and mother of things. ...

523. *De planctu naturae,* account of the appearance of Nature: "... admirationis impotens hebetudo, frequensque stuporis concussio" — "impotent dullness of admiration"; "Ignorantia tenebrari, et stupore percuti, et admiratione saepe solet vulnerari" — "one is accustomed often to be darkened with ignorance, and struck by stupor, and wounded with admiration" (447 A). Dom Lottin has noted that the words "regula" and "regulare" were dear to Alan: *Psychol. et morale*, 6. 102.

524. Christmas hymn (Gautier, 4, 10, and 11).

525. Hildebert. Under another form, Adam (Gautier, 6):

Hujusmodi sacramenti	Of such a mystery
Non subtilis argumenti	Inquiry of subtle argument
Solvit inquisitio.	Offers no solution.
Modum nosse non est meum,	Mine is not to know how
Scio tamen posse Deum	But I do know that God can do
Quod non capit ratio.	What reason does not grasp.

526. "Si peperit, cum viro concubuit": Ghellinck, *Mouvement*, 289-93. Cf. Alcuin, *In Ap.*, l. 3, c. 5 (C, 1121 A).

527. Guibert de Nogent, *Tr. de incarn. c. Judaeos*, l. 1, c. 2: "The Jew's question. He could not be born against the laws of nature" — "Quaestio Judaei. Contra leges naturae nasci non potuit" (CLVI, 492 AB). John of Cornwall, *Eulogium ad Alex.* III, c. 9 (CXCIX, 1064 C). Cf. The *Altercatio* of Evagrius (XX, 1171 D). Hugh Métel, *ep.* 1: "Let the Greeks go mad with reason and say: 'if she gave birth, she lay with a man'; let them say and go mad: 'If he is God, he is not man'" — "Insaniant Graeci cum ratione et dicant: si peperit, cum viro concubuit; dicant et insaniant: si Deus est, homo non est" (314). Again Erasmus, to J. Colet, 1499: "it was very famous and very ancient amongst rhetoricians and dialecticians" —

"apud rhetoricos et dialecticos notissimum est et perantiquum" (*ep.* 109; Allen, 1, 258-9).

528. Rupert, *De vict. Verbi*, l. 11, c. 26: "A virgin, says the Jew, could not give birth contrary to nature. But we believe . . . that a virgin could give birth to such a Son above nature, etc." — "Contra naturam, Judaeus inquit, virgo parere non potuit. Nos autem credimus . . . quia talem filium supra naturam virgo parere potuit, etc." (CLXIX, 1460 AC). Already, for example, Ambrose, *In Luc.*, l. 2, n. 30 (SC, 45, 85). Garnier, *s.* 21: according to, aside from, contrary to nature and reason — secundum, praeter, contra naturam et rationem (CCV, 706 CD).

529. Anc. sequence (Blume-Bannister, 34). Cf. Leo, *s.* 27, c. 1: "But when we advance to understand the mystery of Christ's nativity, from what virgin mother he arose, let the darkness of earthly reasons be driven far away, and let the smoke of worldly wisdom be separated from the eyes of illuminated faith" — "Cum vero ad intelligendum sacramentum nativitatis Christi, qua de matre virgine ortus est, accedimus, abigatur procul terrenarum caligo rationum, et ab illuminatae fidei oculis mundanae sapientiae fumus abscindat" [*sic;* translator reads "abscindatur"] (LIV, 216 CD).

530. *Fons phil.*, v. 817-22 (P. Michaud-Quantin, 63).

531. L. 5, v. 471-9 (R. Bossuat, 137).

532. *Regula de sacra theol.:* "The necessity of the greatest theological [rules] is absolute and unbreakable. . . . Hence owing to their unchangeable necessity and their glorious subtlety they are called 'paradoxes' by philosophy, as being glorious, correct [rules]" — "Necessitas theologicarum maximarum absoluta est et irrefragabilis. . . . Unde propter sui immutabilem necessitatem et gloriosam sui subtilitatem a philosophia paradoxae dicuntur, quasi gloriosae rectae," etc. (PL, CCX, 621-2).

533. Cf. the celebrated letter from Spinoza to Oldenburg (*ep.* 21).

534. Cf. Gilson, *Introd. à la phil. chrét.* (1960), 50-1: "The theologian does not think for a moment that his work could consist in changing the revealed truth into philosophical truth. That thought would fill him with horror. The *faith seeking understanding* is a faith that remains irreducibly faith, so much that it is not eliminated before the beatific vision. The *understanding of the faith* is an intellection of something intelligible proposed by revelation, but what the intellect comprehends, as valuable as it may be, does not in any way attack the supernatural reality whose substance is the very object that the faith possesses in obscurity." — "Le théologien ne pense pas un instant que son œuvre puisse consister à changer la vérité révelée en vérité philosophique. Cette pensée lui ferait horreur. La *fides quaerens intellectum* est une foi qui reste irréductiblement foi, tant qu'elle ne s'est pas effacée devant la vision béatifique. L'*intellectus fidei* est une intellection d'un intelligible proposé par la révélation, mais ce que comprend l'intellect, si précieux que ce soit, n'entame aucunement la réalité surnaturelle dont la substance est l'objet même que la foi possède dans l'obscurité."

535. *De Verbo inc.*, v. 46-7 and 58-9 (PL, CXXII, 1231-2). Cf. *De cruce*, v. 44 (1244 C):

Laudibus amplificat tunc paradoxa Dei.	Then with praises he amplifies the paradoxes of God.

536. "Cum summa admiratione obstupescimus" — "Haeret humani intellectus angustia et, tantae admirationis stupore perculsa, quo declinet, quid teneat, quo se convertat, ignorat": *De prin.*, l. 2, c. 6 (140-1); "That utterly goes beyond the admiration of the human mind" — "Illud penitus admirationem humanae mentis excedit." Cf. Adam Scot, s. 23, *in die nat. Dom.*, c. 3: "Certainly three considerations about this sacrosanct nativity induce amazement in me" — "Certe mihi triplex in hac nativitate sacrosancta consideratio ingerit stuporem" (PL, CXCVIII, 220 C). On Origen, speaking of *"his* Lord Jesus" — *"son* Seigneur Jésus"*:* Irénée Hanskerr, SJ, "Noms du Christ et voies d'oraison" (*Orientalis christ. analaecta*, 157, 1960, 43-9).

537. "la rigueur dialectique"; "l'élan poétique": Ghellinck, *L'essor*, a, 84.

538. Glorieux, 119, 146, 152, etc. But the work is incomplete and stops before reaching the incarnation.

539. "In sacra pagina . . . constructio non subjacet legibus Donati. . . . Vocabula a propriis significationibus peregrinantur et novas admirari videntur": *Prol.* (CCX, 687 B). *De planctu nat.:* "And when natural reason languishes from all these things, we venerate the mystery of so great a thing with the mere firmness of faith" — "Et cum his omnibus naturalis ratio languet, sola fidei firmitate tantae rei veneramur arcanum" (446 A). An anonymous *Summa* of the same school: "While they stand amazed at the miraculous significations of the divine words in theological matters, they fabricate monstrous [words] in them. . . . For when terms are transferred from natural to theological things, people wonder at the new significations and seem to beg for the old ones" — "Qui dum in theologicis divinorum verborum miraculosas significationes obstupescunt, in eis monstruosa confingunt. . . . Cum enim termini a naturalibus ad theologica transferuntur, novas significationes admirantur et antiquas exposcere videntur" (J.-M. Parent, *Beiträge Bäumker*, 1935, 3, 306).

540. Cf. *Médit. sur l'Église*, ch. 1 (34-6).

541. *In ev.*, h. 20, n. 4: "Not only does he answer that he is not the Christ, but also that he held that he is not worthy to untie the strap of his sandal, i.e., to investigate the mystery of his incarnation" — "Non solum Christum non esse se respondit, sed etiam corrigiam calceamenti ejus solvere, id est incarnationis ejus mysterium perscrutari non se dignum esse perhibuit" (PL, LXXVI, 1162 B); cf. h. 22, n. 8 (1179 CD).

542. *In Luc.*, l. 1, c. 3 (XCII, 355-6). Garnier, s. 1 (CCV, 562 C).

543. "He who knew the two [i.e., the trivium and quadrivium], who knew the seven [liberal arts], who knew the whole of what is knowable" — "Qui duo, qui septem, qui totum scibile scivit" (Epitaph).

544. "le penseur le plus vigoureux et le plus neuf": E. Faral, *R. des ét. lat.*, 1 (1923).

545. J.-M. Parent, *Doctrine de la création dans l'École de Chartres* (1938), 110: "he summarizes the renaissance of the 12th century through his theological effort no less than through his concentrated and refined culture" — "il résume la renaissance du XIIe s., par son labeur théologique non moins que par sa culture réduite et raffinée." H. Vicaire, "Les Porrétains et l'avicennisme avant 1215," RSPT, 1937, 475: he is among those who "en contact étroit avec les disciplines des arts," "lisent les philosophes" and have perhaps "hérité d'Abélard . . . leur faculté d'accueil à

l'égard des païens": "in close contact with the studies of the arts," "read the philosophers" and have perhaps "inherited from Abelard . . . their receptive power with regard to the pagans." Cf. Raby, *Secular Poetry*, 2, 15: "Like so many of the Platonists, he had a strong humanistic and literary bent, and he turned to poetry for the expression of his speculative fancies and the deep things which moved his spirit." M. Grabmann, 2 (1911), 452-71.

546. One will not confuse their strangeness with the oddness of the developments on "the Verb which conjugates itself" — "le Verbe qui se conjugue" — of which Father L. Bourgain gives a specimen from Etienne de Tournai, *sermo in nat. Dom.*, in *La Chaire chrétienne au XIIIe s. d'après les manuscrits* (1889), 257-9. V. Cilento, *Alano de Lilla poeta e teologo del s. XII* (Napoli, 1958), cites the poem *De septem artibus* without commenting.

547. Douai, 1625; l. 1, c. 7: *De septem artibus generalibus quomodo subserviant theologiae seu de incarnatione Christi*. Buzelin published at the same time a second prose text of Alan, on the symbolism of the world ("Omnis mundi creatura"). Re-edition by Bulaeus (du Boulay), *Hist. universitatis parisiensis*, 2, 722, and by C. de Visch, *Alani opera* (1654).

548. Cf. the *Anticlaudianus*, l. 5, v. 114-23 (Bossuat, 126), where it is no longer a question of the Incarnation but of God:

Incircumscriptum describit, visibus offert	He describes the uncircumscribed, to sight he offers
Invisum; quod lingua nequit pictura fatetur:	The unseen; what the tongue cannot, a picture utters:
Quomodo naturae subjectus sermo stupescit,	How a subjected discourse comes to astound nature,
Dum tentat divina loqui, viresque loquendi	While he tries to utter things divine, and loses
Perdit et ad veterem cupit ille recurrere sensum,	The powers of speaking and he strives to run back to the old sense,
Mutescuntque soni, vix barbutire valentes,	And the sounds grow mute, scarcely able to babble,
Deque suo sensu deponunt verba querelam. . . .	And the words lay down the quarrel about their sense.

On grammar: l. 2, c. 8. Cf. *Summa*, prol. (Glorieux, 119).

549. Lottin, *Psych. et morale aux XIIe et XIIIe s.*, 2, 119-22.

550. "Terra igitur erat inanis, quia nondum Verbum caro factum est. Terra vacua erat, quia nondum Deitas habitavit in nobis, hoc est, in natura nostra ei unita. Terra igitur carnis nostrae vacua fuit, quia nondum eam inhabitavit plenitudo gratiae et veritatis. Inanis erat, quia nondum firma erat vel stabilis per uniones divinitatis. Vacua erat, quia nondum repleta fuit soliditate divinae plenitudinis. Terra etiam habitationis nostrae erat inanis, quia erroris multiplicis legibus ex legibus erat obnoxia. Nondum enim venerat Magister ille qui vanas et erroneas traditiones exterminavit. Nondum de terra orta est Veritas, quae inanes philosophorum assertiones cassavit. Vacua erat terra incolatus istius, quia nondum venerat plenitudo temporis. Vacua erant corda terrigenarum, quia

nondum repleverat ea Spiritus sanctus, qui postea in igneis linguis mittendus in Christi discipulos erat. Et tenebrae erant super faciem abyssi, quia nondum venerat Lux vera, quae illuminat omnem hominem venientem in hunc mundum, quae de tenebris facit lucem splendescere": *De naturis rer.*, l. 1, c. 1 (Th. Wright, 1863, 12-3).

551. In an unedited commentary *Super Cantica cant.*, Nickham offers an analogous passage. Cited by E. Faye Wilson, *Speculum*, 23 (1948), 45-6: "On the mystery of the Lord's incarnation and his miracles along with an interpretation of the same. In the beginning God created the heaven and the earth. And if sometimes the heavenly scripture is called 'heaven', when it deals with the deity of the Savior, and on the other hand the same is often called 'earth', when it deals with the Redeemer's human nature. . . . It was therefore pleasing to the divine disposition from eternity that in its time a law of spiritual understanding, which had lain concealed under the veil of the letter for a long time prior to the time of revelation, should come forth into the light, like a nut in the shell, like honey in wax, like gold in the earth" — "De mysterio incarnationis Domini et spectaculis cum eorumdem interpretatione. In principio creavit Deus caelum et terram. Et si caelum quandoque dicatur caelestis scriptura, cum agit de deitate Salvatoris, eadem vero dicatur plerumque terra, cum agit de humana natura Redemptoris. . . . Placuit igitur divinae dispositioni ab aeterno ut in tempore suo lex spiritalis intelligentiae in lucem prodiret, quae diu ante tempus revelationis sub velamine litterae latuerat, sicut nucleus in testa, sicut mel in cera, sicut aurum in terra."

Notes to Chapter Two

1. "Non meo sensu haec, sed de evangeliis approbabo": *In Lev.*, h. 4, n. 1 (316).

2. *Ib.*, n. 5: "The heretics, to construct and defend their own dogmas do much hunting in the Scriptures, to find perdition. . . . But if perchance any of them, hearing that the Word of God is being treated in a catholic manner in the Church. . . ." — "Haeretici ad construenda et defendenda dogmata sua multum perquirunt et discutiunt in Scripturis divinis ut inveniant perditionem. . . . Sed si forte aliquis horum, audiens in Ecclesia verbum Dei catholice tractari . . ." (321).

3. *In Jos.*, h. 12, n. 1: "Et vide, ingrate haeretice quomodo ex integro veteribus nova concordant" (A. Jaubert, SC, 71, 294); "legalis litterae sensus perversos": *Sel. in Thren.* (PG, XIII, 651-2 C); etc.

4. "Cavere nobis ipsis debemus, ne haereticae doctrinae sermonis probabilitate spoliemur, et Ecclesiae mysterio excidamus": *Sel. in Job* (PG, XII, 1035-6 A).

5. *In Jer.*, h. 7, n. 3, 5: "For he who quotes the words of God not in accordance with the will of the Scriptures nor according to the truth of the faith, sows wheat and reaps thorns; this is what the heretics do, who read the Scriptures and reap thorns not from the sacred books but from their own private interpretations. . . . And lest anyone take upon himself the understanding of this passage according to the will of his own mind. . . ." — "Qui enim neque juxta voluntatem

Scripturarum neque juxta fidei veritatem profert eloquia Dei, seminat triticum et metit spinas; hoc haeretici faciunt, qui legunt Scripturas et spinas non de libris sanctis sed de propriis sensibus metunt.... Et ne quis juxta voluntatem animi sui de hoc loco sibi praesumeret intellectum..." (PL, XXV, 638 B, 640 C).

6. *In Rom.*, l. 2, n. 11 (PG, XIV, 897-8; 898 AB); *In Ez.*, h. 4, n. 8: "the foolishness of some, who claim that the sense of their own mind is the truth of God" — "nonnullorum insipientiam, qui sensum animi sui Dei esse aderunt veritatem" (368).

7. *In Ez.*, h. 2, n. 2: "But if anyone reading the gospel fits his own sense to the gospel, not understanding it as the Lord has spoken, he is a false prophet, speaking of his own heart in the gospel.... So if I find in Moses and in the prophets the sense of Christ, I am speaking not of my own heart but of the Holy Spirit" — "vero legens evangelium proprium sensum aptat evangelio non ita intelligens ut Dominus locutus est, iste falsus propheta est, loquens de corde proprio in evangelio.... Si itaque invenio in Moyse et in prophetis sensum Christi, non de corde proprio sed de Spiritu sancto loquor" (342). N. 5: "Very many Churches, deceived by heretical perversity" — "Plurimae Ecclesiae, haeretica pravitate deceptae" (347).

8. *In Rom.*, l. 3, n. 1: "ministers of the New Testament not by the letter but the spirit: we find its sense much more exalted than the character of human art is believed to have" — "ministros novi Testamenti non littera sed spiritu: sensum ejus multo celsiorem quam humanae artis ratio habere creditur invenimus" (PG, XIV, 922 D); n. 2: "we ought to observe this, so that when we teach we utter not our own judgments but those of the Holy Spirit" — "hoc observare debemus, ut non nostras cum docemus, sed sancti Spiritus sententias proferamus" (929 B); cf. n. 7 (941 D).

9. L. 4, c. 2: "because many, not understanding the Scriptures spiritually may, by also understanding them badly, have fallen into heresies" — "Quod multi spiritualiter non intellegentes Scripturas et male intelligendo, in haereses declinaverint" (305-8).

10. *In Jer.*, h. 16, n. 9 (PG, XIII, 450 C). *To Gr. Thaum.* (*Philoc.*, c. 13; Robinson, 66).

11. One will note also that it is in opposition to the wisdom of this world, following 1 Cor. 2, that Origen expounds his doctrine of the spiritual understanding: *Peri Arch.*, l. 4, c. 1-2 (304-12).

12. "qui testimonio prophetico non utuntur" — "qui non accipiunt Novi Testamenti praedicationem": *In Ap.*, c. 4 (Haussleiter, 55-6).

13. "pro voluntatis suae sensu, non pro veritatis ipsius absolutione": *De Trin.*, l. 2, c. 3 (PL, X, 51 B): "There have existed many who have undertaken to interpret the simplicity of the heavenly words in favor of the sense of their own will, not for the perfection of the truth itself, [but] otherwise than what the force of the words demanded" — "Extiterunt plures qui caelestium verborum simplicitatem pro voluntatis suae sensu, non pro veritatis ipsius absolutione, susceperint aliter interpretandam quam dictorum virtus postularet etc."

14. "secundum evangelicam praedicationem": *In ps., instr. psalmorum*, n. 5 (6).

15. "qui prava nos interpretatione seducunt": *In Luc.*, l. 10, n. 21 (Tissot, SC,

52, 164); "volunt Deum atramento scripsisse, non spiritu": *De Noe et arca*, n. 45 (PL, XIV, 382).

16. *In Gal.*, l. 1, c. 1, 11-2 (XXVI, 322 BC): "Marcion et Basilides et caeterae haereticorum pestes, non habent Dei Evangelium, quia non habent Spiritum Sanctum, sine quo humanum fit evangelium quod docetur. Nec putamus in verbis Scripturarum esse Evangelium, sed in sensu; non in superficie, sed in medulla; non in sermonum foliis, sed in radice rationis. . . . Tunc Scriptura utilis est audientibus, cum absque Christo non dicitur, cum absque Patre non profertur, cum sine Spiritu non eam insinuat ille qui praedicat. Alioquin, et diabolus qui loquitur de Scripturis, et omnes haereses, secundum Ezechielem (c. xiii), inde sibi consuunt cervicalia, quae ponant sub cubito universae aetatis. Ego quoque ipse qui loquor, si Christum in me habeo, non habeo evangelium hominis. . . . Grande periculum est in Ecclesia loqui, ne forte, interpretatione perversa, de Evangelio Christi hominis fiat evangelium; aut, quod pejus est, diaboli."

17. *Ib.*, l. 2, c. 4, 24 (391 BC).

18. L. 3, c. 5, 13 (407 BD). This whole passage comes from Origen.

19. L. 3, c. 5, 9 (402 D). Cf. *ep.* 84, c. 3: "the dogmas of Origen do violence to the Scriptures" (4, 128).

20. *In Is.*, l. 1, c. 2, 22 (PL, XXIV, 38-9): "Haeretici quoque evangelicam veritatem (Scripturarum) corrumpunt prava intelligentia, et sunt caupones pessimi, facientes de vino aquam, cum e contrario Dominus noster aquas in vinum verterit, et tale vinum quod miretur architriclinus: quali et regina Saba in Salomonis est mirata convivio, pincernas ejus et ministros vini sua voce laudans (II *Par.*, ix). Sed et Ecclesiastes ministeria vini atque conviviii sui, mystico sermone describit (Eccles. 2)."

21. *Adv. Haer.*, l. 1, c. 22, n. 1 (trans. based on the Armenian version, Bayan-Froidevaux, *Rev. de l'Orient ch.*, 1933-4, 375-6). Jerome takes up the very words of Irenaeus on the "austerity" of the Scripture having been corrupted by one who mixes in impure water with its wine.

22. "de sublimitate sensus sanctarum Scripturarum" — "ad humilia" — "ad intelligentiam spiritualem": *In Is.*, l. 7, c. 22, 1 (XXIV, 267, AB).

23. "Filios haereticorum . . . interficiamus sagittis spiritualibus": *ib.*, l. 6, c. 13 (214 B).

24. "Cur tibi vis aedificare domum in occidente littera, et tabernaculum tuum, quod non habet fundamentum, in petrae figere firmitate? quod non tam tabernaculum et domus, quam sepulcrum et memoria appellandum est": *ib.*, l. 7, c. 22, 15 ss. (273 CD). *In Jer.*, l. 5, c. 29, 9: "With respect to tropology we ought to regard those who take the words of the Scriptures otherwise than as the Holy Spirit utters them as pseudo-prophets" — "Secundum tropologiam pseudoprophetas eos debemus accipere, qui aliter Scripturarum verba accipiunt quam Spiritus sanctus sonat" (859 C).

25. *Dial. adv. Lucif.*, c. 28: "Nor let them flatter themselves if they seem to themselves to affirm what they say from the headings of the Scriptures, since even the devil has said things from the Scriptures, and the Scriptures consist not in the reading but in the understanding. Otherwise if we follow the letter, we too can fabricate a new dogma for ourselves as well" — "Nec sibi blandiantur, si de Scripturarum capitulis videntur sibi affirmare quod dicunt, cum et diabolus de

Scripturis aliqua sit locutus, et Scripturae non in legendo consistant sed in intelligendo. Alioqui si litteram sequimur, possumus et nos quoque novum nobis dogma componere" (XXIII, 182 A). One must admit that the example brought up by Jerome is far from illustrating the whole doctrine: "so that we may assert that those who wear sandals and have two tunics ought not to be received into the Church" — "ut asseramus in Ecclesiam non recipiendos qui calceati sint et duas tunicas habeant." Cf. PL, XXVI, 67 C, which opposes a material understanding of the resurrection, which leads one to deny it, to the "intelligentia ecclesiastica."

26. Hil., *Ad Const.*, l. 2, n. 9: "For the Scriptures are not in reading but in understanding; for they are not in collusion but in charity" — "Scripturae enim non in legendo sunt sed in intellegendo; neque enim in praevaricatione sunt sed in caritate" (PL, X, 570 A). The expression is found again in Augustine.

27. "souhaité le monopole": RB, 57, 87, note 3. Jerome, *De vir. ill.*, c. 100 (XXIII, 699 B); *ep.* 58, c. 10 (3, 84).

28. "quicquid dixerint, hoc legem Dei putant, nec scire dignantur quid prophetae, quid apostoli senserint, sed ad sensum suum incongrua aptant testimonia, quasi grande sit et non vitiosissimum dicendi genus depravare sententias, et ad voluntatem suam trahere repugnantem": *ep.* 53, c. 7 (3, 15-6). Cf. Irenaeus and Tertullian (see below, note 52). Another transposition, directed against those who try to please by means of agreeable interpretations, *In Is.*, l. 1, c. 1, v. 22: "And every teacher who turns the austerity of the Scriptures, through which he can reproach his hearers, into graciousness and speaks in such fashion as not to correct but to please his hearers, does violence to the wine of the sacred Scriptures and contaminates it with his own sense" — "Omnisque doctor qui austeritatem Scripturarum per quam potest audientes corripere, vertit ad gratiam et ita loquitur ut non corrigat, sed delectet audientes, vinum sanctarum Scripturarum violat atque corrumpit sensu suo" (PL, XXIV, 38 C).

29. "Propositum mihi erat, non ad meam voluntatem Scripturas trahere, sed id dicere, quod Scripturas velle intelligebam. Commentatoris officium est, non quid ipse velit, sed quid sentiat ille quem interpretatur exponere": *ep.* 49, c. 17 (2, 144).

30. "Increpa feras calami" — "ferae calami": *In ps.* lxvii, n. 38: "Nam et ferae sunt, quoniam non intelligendo nocent, et ferae calami sunt, quoniam Scripturarum sensum pro suo errore pervertunt" (CCL, 39, 896). Jerome, citing Ps. 67: "increpa feras calami," sees in this verse the demons (PL, XXVI, 515 C).

31. *Ep.* 120, c. 3, n. 13: "Intellectum vero valde ama; quia et ipsae Scripturae sanctae, quae magnarum rerum ante intelligentiam suadent fidem, nisi eas recte intelligas, utiles tibi esse non possunt. Omnes enim haeretici, qui eas in auctoritate recipiunt, ipsas sibi videntur sectari, cum suos potius sectentur errores; ac per hoc non quod eas contemnant, sed quod eas non intelligant, haeretici sunt." N. 14: "But, my very dear brother, pray you bravely and faithfully that the Lord give you understanding and thus those things that the diligence of a teacher or doctor applies on the outside might be fruitful" — "Tu autem, carissime, ora fortiter et fideliter ut det tibi Dominus intellectum ac sic ea quae forinsecus adhibet diligentia praeceptoris sive doctoris, possint esse fructuosa." The type of carnal understanding that Augustine subsequently denounces and that he likens to the pretension of materially touching the body of Christ seated at

the right hand of the Father is the heresy of Photinus, who was able to see in Christ only the man (n. 14-5, *ib.*).

32. *In ps.* xlviii, s. 1, n. 1 (CCL, 38, 550): "Omnia divina eloquia salubria sunt bene intellegentibus, periculosa vero his qui ea volunt ad sui cordis perversitatem detorquere, potius quam suum cor ad eorum rectitudinem corrigere. Haec est enim in hominibus magna et usitata perversitas." *C. Adim.*, c. 14, n. 2: "the deceit of those who pick out certain fragments from the Scriptures with which to deceive the inexperienced, not connecting what was written above and below, from which the writer's will and intention might be understood" — "istorum fraus qui particulas quasdam e Scripturis eligunt, quibus decipiant imperitos, non connectentes quae supra et infra scripta sunt, ex quibus voluntas et intentio scriptoris possit intelligi" (PL, XLII, 149). Cf. Origen, *In Ez.*, h. 7, n. 2: "When we therefore twist the sense of the Scriptures into another sense which is contrary to the truth" — "Quando ergo torquemus sensum Scripturae in alterum sensum qui est contrarius veritati" (PG, XIII, 720 C).

33. L. 1, c. 18, n. 37 (PL, XXXIV, 260): "Et in rebus obscuris atque a nostris oculis remotissimis, si qua inde scripta etiam divina legerimus, quae possint salva fide qua imbuimur, alias atque alias parere sententia; in nullam earum nos praecipiti affirmatione ita projiciamus, ut si forte diligentius discussa veritas eam recte labefactaverit, corruamus; non pro sententia divinarum Scripturarum, sed pro nostra ita dimicantes, ut eam velimus Scripturarum esse, quae nostra est, cum potius eam quae Scripturarum est, nostram esse velle debeamus." This last sentence is reproduced by Hugh, *Didasc.*, l. 6, c. 11, to conclude a development which is an implicit citation of the same *Gen. lit.*, l. 1, c. 21, n. 41: "When we are reading the divine books, amidst such a multitude of true understandings. . . ." — "Cum divinos libros legimus, in tanta multitudine verorum intellectuum etc." (XXXIV, 262 = CLXXVI, 809 A).

34. L. 1, c. 37, n. 41 (XXXIV, 35): "Asserendo enim temere quod ille non sensit quem legit, plerumque incurrit in alia quae illi sententiae contexere nequeat: quae si vera et certa esse consentit, illud non possit verum esse quod senserat; fitque in eo, nescio quomodo, ut amando sententiam suam, Scripturae incipiat offensior esse quam sibi." Analogous thought but less characteristic expressions, l. 3, c. 27-8, n. 38-9 (80); passage reproduced by Rabanus, *Cl. inst.*, l. 3, c. 15 (CVII, 391-2).

35. "intelligentia superstitiosa" — "superstitio gentilium" — "superstitiosa figmenta": L. 2, c. 17-42 (XXXIV, 49-66), summarized in Rabanus, *ib.*, c. 16 (*Cl. inst.*, l. 3, c. 15 (CVII, 391-2).

36. "vana superstitio": L. 18, c. 7 (XLII, 348). See below, section 3.

37. *Disc.*, 12, n. 19 (Buytaert, 337).

38. "Dirige me in semita recta propter inimicos meos": *In ps.* xxxvi, 6: "We have already said that the 'path' pertains to the understanding of the Scriptures. Hence the prophet prays that he may understand the books of the Old Testament 'rightly', and recognize that the Lord is coming in them. He says 'because of my enemies', however, namely, the heretics or unbelieving Jews, who try to subvert them with their perverse intention" — "'Semitam' vero jam diximus ad Scripturarum intelligentiam pertinere. Precatur ergo propheta ut veteris Testamenti 'recte' libros intelligat, et venturum in eis Dominum esse cognoscat. 'Propter inimicos' autem dicit, id est haereticos, sive incredulos Judaeos, qui eos

nitebantur prava intentione subvertere" (PL, LXX, 191 CD). *In ps.* c, 6: "Whilst some of them seem to take up the Old and New Testament along with us, they nevertheless condemn understanding the divine Scriptures rightly through their detestable willfulness" — "Dum quidam eorum nobiscum vetus ac novum Testamentum suscipere videantur, recte tamen intelligere Scripturas divinas detestabili voluntate contemnunt" (702 C).

39. *In Gen.*, h. 13, n. 1-3 (SC, 7, 214-23).

40. *Mor.*, l. 16, c. 18, n. 23 (PL, LXXV, 1131-2). Pater. (LXXIX, 711 BC).

41. "sententias longe a suis sensibus diversas tollunt" — "pro suae intelligentiae intentione" — "quia ejus sensum in verba sacri eloquii inflectere violenter conantur": *Mor.*, l. 16, c. 47-9, n. 60-2 (1149-50). Garnier, *Greg.*, n. 631 (CXCIII, 341-2). *Reg. past.*, l. 3, c. 24: "those who do not understand the words of the sacred law rightly ... turn a most healthful drink of wine into a cup of poison for themselves" — "qui sacrae legis verba non recte intelligunt ... saluberrimum vini potum in veneni sibi poculum vertunt" (LXXVII, 93 D).

42. "Non absurde impii vocantur haeretici, qui per errorem pravi dogmatis a cognitione sunt veritatis alieni; quos sequenti verbo etiam violentos appellat, quippe qui Scripturae sacrae sententias recta dogmata continentes ad intellectum pravum conantur violenter inflectere": *Mor.*, l. 18, c. 13, n. 20 (LXXVI, 48 CD).

43. *Mor.*, l. 20, c. 6-13, n. 15-24 (145-52); n. 20: "They also chew bits of bark off trees, since ... they venerate only the surface of the letter in the sacred volumes, and keep nothing of the spiritual understanding. ... All the same, a craving for empty glory makes them persist in all their errors" — "Arborum quoque cortices mandunt, quia ... in sacris voluminibus solam litterae superficiem venerantur, nec quidquam de spiritali intellectu custodiunt. ... Quos tamen in cunctis erroribus suis inanis gloriae appetitus possidet" (149 C).

44. *In Lev.*, h. 7, n. 4: "Let no one think that I am forcing the divine Scriptures" — "Ne quis putet quod ego vim faciam Scripturis divinis" (382), etc. *Sel. in Jer.*, 3, 7: "of those who have a twisted sense in the faith": "perverse in fide sentientium" (translating the Greek expression: *tôn heterodoxôn*, PG, XIII, 545-6 D).

45. *Ep.* 64, c. 7: "But lest anyone think I am doing violence to Scripture and love Christ in such wise as to eliminate the truth of the history, I shall interpret in the members what is related to the Head" — "Sed ne quis me vim facere Scripturae putet et sic amare Christum ut historiae auferam veritatem, interpretabor in membris quod referatur in caput" (3, 124). *Ep.* 129, c. 6 (PL, XXII, 1105). *In Eph.*, l. 3, c. 5: "Were we seeming to do violence to Scripture" — "Videremur vim facere Scripturae" (XXVI, 520 C). *In Matt.*, l. 3, c. 16 (118 C).

46. *Brev. in ps.* (XXVI, 1045 B). Rabanus, *In Ez.*, l. 16: "But let no one think that I am bending the words of the Holy Spirit violently toward my own understanding" — "Sed ne quis me verba sancti Spiritus aestimet ad intellectum meum violenter inflectere" (CX, 958 C; copying Greg., *In Ez.*, l. 2, h. 10, n. 3: LXXVI, 1059 D); etc. Abelard, *Intr. ad th.*, l. 1, c. 20, will borrow these expressions while speaking in his own way to explicate the philosophers so as to put them at the service of the faith (CLXXVIII, 1028 A).

47. "Diligenter observandum est, ut lex Dei cum legitur, non secundum proprii ingenii intelligentiam legatur. Sunt enim multa verba in Scripturis divinis, quae possunt trahi ad eum sensum, quem sibi unusquisque sponte praesumpsit;

quod fieri non oportet. Non enim sensum quem extrinsecus attuleris alienum et extraneum debes quaerere, quem ex Scripturarum auctoritate confirmes, sed ex ipsis Scripturis sensum capere veritatis; et ideo oportet ab eo intelligentiam discere Scripturarum, qui eam a majoribus secundum veritatem sibi traditam servat, ut et ipse possit ea quae recte suscepit, competenter asserere": L. 10, c. 42 (PG, I, 1441 CD). On this translation of Rufinus: O. Cullmann, *Le problème litt. et hist. du roman pseudo-clémentine* (1930), 11-2, 161-5.

48. "défiance à l'égard de l'allégorie chrétienne" — "déclarations formelles sur les méfaits de l'allégorie biblique": Thus J. Pépin, *Mythe et alléq.*, 443, 445. There one might have an indication of a state of mind frequently to be found in the "various non-allegoristic Christian circles" — "divers milieux chrétiens non allégoristes" (444-5). That was the explication of J. G. Rosenmüller, *H. interpr.*, 1, 80-4, and of J. Jahn, *Enchiridion hermeneuticae generalis* (1812), n. 60. On which F. X. Patrizi, *Institutio de interp. Bibliorum* (n. ed., 1876, 247), justly observed: "What would you, who are able to assail the spiritual sense of the Scriptures, twist out of them?" "Quid ex his extorqueas, qui spiritualem Scripturarum sensum impetere possis?"

49. *In Matt.*, ser. 77 (PG, XIII, 1725-6); *In Gen.*, t. 3 (XIII, 85; *Philoc.*, c. 23; Rob., 210). Cf. R. Cadiou, "Origen et les 'Reconnaissances clémentines,'" RSR, 20 (1930), 506-28; Cullmann, 32-4, 156. The text known by Origen was perhaps not completely the one that Rufinus read subsequently.

50. Cullmann, 165-6.

51. "Prudentes viri, cum viderent communem superstitionem tam probrosam esse, tam turpem, nec tamen corrigendi modum aliquem vel scientiam didicissent, quibus potuerunt argumentis et interpretationibus conati sunt res inhonestas honesto sermone velare, et non ut dicunt, honestas rationes inhonestis fabulis occultare": L. 10, c. 36 (PG, I, 1439 B).

52. The author adds, c. 42: "For when one picks up the whole and firm rule of the truth from the divine Scriptures" — "Cum enim ex divinis Scripturis integram quis susceperit et firmam regulam veritatis, etc." (1441 C). Cf. Irenaeus, *Adv. Haer.*, l. 1, c. 8, n. 1; c. 9, n. 4 (VII, 521-4, 544-8). Tertullian, *De praescr.*, c. 37 (SC, 46, 139-43).

53. "non intelligendo spiritualiter Scripturas . . . in haeresim devoluti sunt" — "Scripturas sanu sensu non sapiunt, sed eas ad errorem pravae intelligentiae ducunt; neque semetipsos earum sensibus subdunt, sed eas perverse ad errorem proprium pertrahunt": *Sent.*, l. 3, c. 12, n. 2 and 4 (PL, LXXXIII, 683-4); n. 1: "He who runs through the words of the law in a carnal sense in no way understands the law, but only he who looks through it with the sense of its inner understanding" — "Nequaquam legem intelligit qui carnaliter verba legis percurrit, sed is qui eam sensu interioris intelligentiae perspicit." *L. de var. q.*, c. 76, n. 3 (216). This last writing, which we, along with its editors A. C. Vega and A. E. Anspach (1940), have attributed to Isidore, would be, according to J. Madoz and R. E. McNally, the work of Justus of Urgel (†818). Cf. Robert E. McNally, SJ, "*Isidoriana*," *Theological Studies*, 20 (1959), 437-8.

54. "sanum et allegoricum intellectum" — "sensum interioris intelligentiae": *De var. q.*, c. 61, n. 3 (195). Aside from an unhealthy curiosity, two things make a heretic: "either when the figured mysteries of sacred Scripture are less under-

stood, or when the difference between the historical truth and the spiritual sense is not considered" — "aut dum Scripturae sacrae figurata minus intelliguntur mysteria, aut dum historicae veritatis et spiritalis sensus non consideratur differentia" (26).

55. "aperta veritatis manifestatio" — "mysticae intelligentiae omnimoda plenitudo": Férotin, 350, 343.

56. "sensus erraticus et gentilis": *In Esdram*, l. 3: "The heretics ... turning the holy Scriptures over in their mouth, but interpreting them in a wandering, gentile sense" — "Haeretici ... Scripturas sanctas ore volventes, sed has erratico et gentili sensu interpretantes" (PL, XCI, 923-4).

57. *Sup. Par. Sal.*, l. 3, c. 15: "And the mouth of the heretics bubbles up with stupidity.... By understanding the sayings of sacred Scripture perversely and putting their own senses ahead of its authority" — "Et os haereticorum ebullit stultitiam.... Dicta sacrae Scripturae perverse intelligendo suosque sensus ejus auctoritati praeponendo" (XCI, 984 A).

58. *In Cant.*, l. 2, c. 1: "the sacred preachers ... by whose spiritual sense the sacred Scripture was completed, which cannot be corrupted by any astuteness of heretics nor consumed by the lifetime of a tottering age" — "praedicatoribus sanctis ... quorum sensu spirituali Scriptura sancta confecta est, quae nulla haereticorum astutia corrumpi, nulla potest saeculi labentis aetate consumi" (XCI, 1101 A). Cf. Aug., *In Job.* 4 (XXXIV, 857).

59. "latiora mysteria": *In Sam.*, l. 1, c. 12 (XCI, 645 C).

60. "At si doctor aliquis suum sensum Scripturae verbis praetulerit et per ea quae ipse sibi composuit dogmata, suos auditores, quam ad spiritualia accenderit..., perdet stultus imperium": *In Sam.*, l. 2, c. 7 (579 A). Autpert, *In Ap.*, l. 3, on Prov. 7: "If we should violently bend them toward the letter.... But come on, let us follow ... the life-giving spirit" — "Quae utique si ad litteram violenter inflectamus.... Age vero sequamur ... vivificantem spiritum" (456 E). Cf. Beatus, *In Ap.*, l. 8, c. 16: "But the heretics, the hypocrites, schismatics, and the superstitious and carnal priests are seeking not the thoughts, but are rather following the letter" — "Haeretici vero et hypocritae et schismatici et superstitiosi et carnales sacerdotes non sententias quaerunt, sed magis litteram sequuntur" (Florez, 468-9).

61. "à la paix et à l'unité des saintes Églises de Dieu": John VIII, a. 875. "Starting from 817, the word 'unity' is constantly flowing from the pen of the emperor's partisans and his opponents" — "A partir de 817 le mot d''unité' revient sans cesse sous la plume des partisans ou des adversaires de l'empereur": L. Halphen, *Charlemagne et l'empire carolingien* (1947), 241.

62. Angelome, *In Reg.*: "There is no doubt that the Philistines, whose number is said to be huge, have figured the masters of all the heretics" — "Philistim, quorum ingens numerus esse perhibetur, omnium haereticorum magistros figurasse non dubium est" (PL, CXV, 297 C). The influence of St. Jerome is also involved to some extent. A modern historian marvels at "the boldness with which this recently illiterate Church hurled itself into the most difficult theological controversies under a head who did not know how to write": "la hardiesse avec laquelle cette Église, hier analphabète, se lança, sous un chef qui ne savait pas écrire, dans les plus difficiles controverses théologiques" (E. Delaruelle, RHEF, 39, 1953, 187).

Still, it will be worth adding that if Charlemagne did not himself write, he was nonetheless very cultured, that he spoke Latin fluently, understood at least a little Greek, and that "his curiosity regarding all intellectual matters must have been extraordinary": "sa curiosité pour toutes les choses de l'esprit doit avoir été extraordinaire" (R. Bezzola).

63. "nova vel non canonica aliquos ex suo sensu et non secundum Scripturas sacras fingere et praedicare populo": *Capitularia ab Angesimo coll.*, 76 (PL, XCVII, 519 C).

64. *In Rom.*: "when they perversely interpret only in the literal sense things that have been prophesied of Christ" — "quando ea quae de Christo prophetata sunt, nonnisi ad litteram perverse interpretantur" (CIII, 102 D).

65. *De ten. Scr. ver.* (CXXI, 1083 D, 1088 A, 1131 D, etc.). See above, vol. 1, ch. 1.3.

66. "venerandus Patrum sensus": *ep.* 22 (C, 175 C).

67. "secus quam veritatis ratio habet": *Adv. Elip.*, l. 4, n. 1: "while the wisdom of the heavenly teachers . . . is judged not according to its proper sense, but is diverted into foreign senses at the whim and will of the reader otherwise than the character of the truth holds" — "dum caelestium doctorum sapientia . . . non secundum sui sensus proprietatem perpenditur, sed in alienos sensus pro arbitrio and voluntate legentis, secus quam veritatis ratio habet, derivatur. Et hoc ex omnium haereticorum commentis cuique . . . deprehendere facile est" (CI, 285 CD).

68. "divini eloquii sententias ad sui probationem erroris pravo sensu interpretari nituntur": *Adv. Fel.*, l. 2, c. 1 (CI, 146-7).

69. "pravitatis suae sensu": L. 5, c. 4 (190 D).

70. *De una . . . deit.*, n. 11 (CXXV, 565 A).

71. *De praed. c. J. Sc.*, c. 16 (CXV, 1260 A).

72. "cor pessimum" — "mens perversa" vs. "devota mens" — "sanus sensus": Letter of dispatch to Charlem. (MGH, *ep.*, 4. 523).

73. "propria pravitas" — "sensus perfidus" — "sensus apostolicus" — "utrumque Testamentum sibimet conglutinatum": *C. Fel.*: "according to the badly enough and obscurely depraved sense of your unbelief" — "secundum perfidiae tuae sensum satis male et obscure depravatum" (PL, XCIX, 381 D). "Why don't you . . . look into the wheel within the wheel, i.e., both Testaments combined to themselves" — "Cur non . . . inspicis rotam in rota hoc est utrumque Testamentum sibimet conglutinatum?" (407 A). "The heretic does not . . . submit his own to the apostolic sense but following a personal twist has labored to corrupt the holy apostolic sense with his own unbelieving sense" — "Haereticus non . . . sensui apostolico suum subdit sed secundum propriam pravitatem suo perfido sensu sanctum molitus est corrumpere apostolicum sensum" (451 C).

74. "Sed quid mirum, si stulti in his erratis, quae allegorica sunt silva condensa, et, umbrosis phalerarum aenigmatibus obvoluta, carpere nescitis docta manu de sub foliis litterarum pendentia spiritualium fructuum poma, cum in propatulo per sanctos praedicatores eductam male intelligentes orthodoxam depravatis doctrinam": *Libellus sacrosyll. c. Elip.*, c. 7 (XCIX, 158 A).

75. M. L. W. Laistner, 290: "For the so-called Libri carolini, though no doubt a work of collaboration, seem to have been compiled under Alcuin's editorship." Cf. Luitpold Wallach, "Charlemagne and Alcuin," *Traditio*, 9 (1953), 127-54, espe-

cially 143. Dom de Bruyne, "La composition des Libri car.," RB, 44 (1932), 227-34. But A. Freeman, "Theodulf of Orléans and the Libri carolini," *Speculum,* 32 (1957), 663-705, has well established, it seems to me, that the author is Theodulf.

76. *L. Carol.*, 1. 1, c. 16: "So all these things are filled with allegorical senses" — "Quae igitur omnia cum allegoricis plena sint sensibus" (PL, XCVIII, 1042 C); 1. 2, c. 4: "or because he may have striven to bend the words uttered by the Holy Spirit and filled with the secrets of the mysteries toward human affairs" — "sive quia verba mysteriorum arcanis plena ab Spiritu sancto prolata ad res humanas inflectere nisus sit" (1070 D).

77. "ad peregrinas intelligentias"; "Quisquis ejus spiritales potus et spiritales escas aliter quam ille dat percipit, divinas sc. Scripturas alio sensu, et non eo quo a sancto Spiritu traditae sunt interpretari nititur, ab ejus pascuis alienus esse convincitur. . . . De talibus Dominus ita queritur per prophetam: "Dedi eis argentum et aurum, et illi fecerunt Baal" (Hosea 2), id est, spiritalis intelligentiae dignitatem et eloquii venustatem ad pravorum sensuum et inanis gloriae verterunt immanitatem. Nam cum legislator dicat: "In dextera Domini ignea lex" (Deut. 33), mirandum est quantas sint hebetudinis qui nec ejus mulcentur candore, nec ejus terrentur ardore": L. 1, c. 5 (1018 BC, 1019 BC); c. 9 (1029 C).

78. L. 1, c. 5: "illi vero qui eam petrunt cum extraneis et temerariis sensibus aeterni ignis cremantur adustione" (1018 D). In l. 4, c. 11, comparing the sacred texts to pieces of gold, Charlemagne writes: "Therefore in the coin of each scripture it is asked whether it is finest gold, whereby the ark of the Lord can be adorned, or the work of the whole sanctuary may also glisten, so that the brightness of the spiritual understanding may stand out in it, whereby the divine law may be understood and the beauty of the whole church may sparkle" — "Quaeritur ergo in uniuscujusque scripturae nummo, utrum aurum probatissimum sit, unde arca Domini valeat exornari, vel etiam totius sanctuarii opus resplendeat, ut vid. in ea spiritalis intelligentiae nitor emineat, quo divina lex intelligatur et totius ecclesiae pulchritudo coruscet" (1204 D). *Ib.:* "since the testimonies of the divine eloquence . . . can not even by violence be usurped . . . to foreign senses" — "cum nec divinorum eloquiorum testimonia ad peregrinos sensus violenter nec valeant . . . usurpari" (1204 B). "Alienus," "peregrinus," "extranseus": one will note the affinity of the terms of the *Caroline Books* with those of the Pseudo-Clementinian romance translated by Rufinus.

79. *In Lam.*, l. 5: "Whilst heretics wickedly convert these understandings following the discovery of their depravity" — "Quas (intelligentias) dum haeretici male secundum suae pravitatis inventionem convertunt"; "who by perverse thoughts insert false depravities within the words of the divine Scriptures" — "qui perversis cogitationibus divinarum Scripturarum sermonibus falsas inserunt pravitates" (PL, CXX, 1339 B). Cf. RB, 1911, 427.

80. "Unusquisque eorum (=haereticorum) Scripturas Dei a recto deflectere, et ad suae perversitatis vias latius diffundere . . . , et non dico Scripturarum (tantum), verum etiam philosophorum corruperunt eloquia": *In Lam.*, l. 4 (CXX, 1228 AB; cf. l. 5, 1239 B). Cf. Abelard (note 46, above).

81. *In Num.*, l. 2, c. 18, l. 1, c. 6 (CVIII, 683 A, 653 A).

82. *In Ez.*, l. 12, c. 32 (CX, 823 A).

83. *In Jos.*, l. 2, c. 5 (CVIII, 1054 B). *In Ez.* (CX, 616 D, 678 A, 845 A). *In Prov.*

Sal., l. 2, c. 15: "by perversely understanding the sayings of sacred Scripture and setting two senses ahead of its authority" — "dicta sacrae Scripturae perverse intelligendo duosque sensus ejus auctoritati praeponendo" (CXI, 729 D). Analogous expressions: Berngaud, *In Ap.* (XVII, 858 C, 859 AD, etc.). Othloh, *Dial. de trib. q.*, c. 14, commenting on Isa. 5:20: "He puts the light into the dark who, perversely understanding the words of sacred Scripture, takes to filling it in with his own error, as many heretics are read to have been" doing — "Lucem in tenebras ponit, qui sacrae Scripturae verba perverse intelligens, in erroris sui supplementum sumit, sicut haeretici multi fuisse leguntur" (CXXXIII, 78 B).

84. *In Mach.*, l. 1, c. 5 (CIX, 1168 A, 1169 D, 1170 A). *In Ez.*, l. 11: "The Hebrews are accustomed . . . to understand these sayings among their other fables. . . . But the prudent reader judges how violent an interpretation this is without our judgment" — "Solent Hebraei, inter caeteras fabulas suas . . . haec dicta intelligere. . . . Verum haec quam violenta sit interpretatio, absque nostro judicio prudens lector intelligit" (CX, 793 AB).

85. *In Num.* (CVIII, 683 A, 653 A). *In Jos.* (1054 B). *In Ez.* (CX, 845 A).

86. *In Reg.*, l. 1, c. 17 (CIX, 53 BC); cf. Greg., *Mor.*, l. 18, c. 16, n. 24 (LXXVI, 50 BC). *In Ez.*, from Origen (CX, 652 A). Rupert, *In Reg.*, l. 2, c. 7 (CLXVII, 1103 D).

87. *In I Mach.*, l. 1: "so that if we want to be the possessors of the law of the Lord and to seize its spoils, i.e., the various understandings according to the correct faith, let us strive first to grind up the surface of the Letter and to condemn all the errors of the heretics" — "ut si legis Domini velimus esse possessores et ejus spolia, hoc est diversos intellectus secundum fidem rectam percipere, studeamus primum conterere superficiem Litterae et condemnare omnes haereticorum errores" (CIX, 1170 D). At that point the sun of justice will rise within us, "who illuminates the darkness . . . and reveals the secrets of the mysteries to those who are searching for him . . . in truth" — "qui illuminat tenebras . . . et revelat occulta mysteriorum his qui eum . . . fidei requirunt veritate" (1171 A).

88. *In Mach.*, l. 1: "But in the Jews and heretics, partly olden usage and partly new superstition had to be corrected through the spiritual knowledge of the two Testaments" — "In Judaeis vero et haereticis partim veteranus usus, partim nova superstitio, per duorum Testamentorum spiritalem scientiam corrigenda fuerunt" (CIX, 1165 D). "By the word of the Gospel through his doctors our Redeemer calls those who have been captured by heretics back to the Catholic faith" — "Redemptor noster per doctores suos verbo Evangelii eos qui ab haereticis capti sunt ad catholicam fidem revocat" (1169 A).

89. *In Jos.*, l. 1, c. 10: "In this passage a mystery is hidden, escaping the notice of as many as can be; but to you who are praying we shall attempt to disclose all these things, not by our own opinions but by the testimonies of the divine Scripture" — "Hoc in loco mysterium tegitur quam plurimos latens; sed orantibus vobis tentabimus haec omnia non nostris opinionibus sed Scripturae divinae testimoniis aperire" (CVIII, 1030-1). Once more, this is from Origen. Cf. Liutprand, *Antapodosis*, l. 4, c. 7: "For the devil does know the Scriptures, and yet, being perverse, he interprets them perversely" — "Diabolus quippe Scripturas novit et tamen, ut perversus perverse eas interpretatur" (Scr. rer. germ. in us. schol., *Liutpr. opera*, 106).

90. "in superficie litterae et in humana scientia": *In Is.*, c. 55 (PL, CXVI, 1001

BC). Whoever wants his interpretation of the Scripture to be considered should take care to recall that it comes not from his own 'proper sense'; thus around the year 1000, the hermit Albuin says: "All the things that I have written in this little book I have not made up using my proper sense" — "Omnia quae in hoc libello scripta habeo, non proprio sensu fingo, etc." (CXXXVIII, 185 A).

91. "perversus intellectus," "interpretatio perversa": *In Os.* (CXVII, 58 D, 64 C).

92. "ad suum sensum eam convertunt": *In Ex.*, c. 16 (PL, CLXIV, 269 A).

93. "malo ingenio": *In Ap.* (CLXV, 736 A).

94. "Haeretici . . . in densa silva sanctarum Scripturarum ea quae intelligere non possunt, *violenter* rodunt et lacerant. . . . Et novitate delectantur, et, *omissa spirituali intelligentia*, pene omnia ad litteram exponunt. . . . Dum aliquid novi, et quod eorum erroribus convenire videatur, inveniunt, mox undique cum clamore et laetitita ruunt, et suis libris et disputationibus illud inserunt": *In Job* (CLXIV, 647 AC).

95. *In ps.* vii: "The heretics, whom God permitted both to understand and to expound [Scriptures] in a depraved manner unto their own death and the death of many, since they have approached the divine Scriptures with depraved intention and for the sake of arrogance, can also be called a 'vessel of death'" — "Possunt etiam vasa mortis haeretici vocari, quos, quia prava vota et causa arrogantiae ad divinas Scripturas accedunt, Deus permittit eos et prave intelligere et prave ad suam et multorum mortem exponere" (PL, XCIII, 521 C). *In ps.* x: "You most wicked heretics . . . have corrupted holy Scripture with your depraved interpretations" — "Pessimi haeretici . . . pravis interpretationibus vestris Scripturam sanctam depravistis" (545 A). Cf. P. Lombard, *In ps.* lxii (CXCI, 566 D).

96. *In ps.* lxvii: "Rebuke *the wild beasts of the cane* or pen. . . . The heretics work their ferocity into the cane, that is, the sacred Scripture, which they destroy by interpreting corruptly" — "Increpa *feras arundinis*. . . . Haeretici feritatem exercent in arundinem, id est in Scripturam sacram, quam prave interpretando dissipant" (xciii, 840 cd). Again, there is a long allusion to the *"bestiae calami"*: the *"beasts of the reed* or the pen" in Herbert of Bosham, *In ps.*, ep. dedic., but without specific application to the heretic (Smalley, RTAM, 1951, 31-2). [Translator's emphases.]

97. "Per falsas Scripturarum interpretationes . . . quasi carnaliter dicta Scripturarum exempla exponunt": *Tropol. in Amos* (PL, CLVI, 443 CD).

98. *In Gen.*, c. 26 (CLXIV, 204-5). V. See below, ch. 3.2.

99. "Hos puteos, id est has Scripturas, quantum in ipsis fuit, haeretici . . . obturaverunt, ut non facile inveniri posset ubinam esset doctrina veritatis. . . . Sic profecto haeretici sacras Scripturas . . . terrenis sensibus suis obturaverunt": *In Gen.*, l. 7, c. 10-1 (CLXVII, 455 B, 456 AB).

100. "Sic haeretici . . . thorum Dei Patris, id est sanctae legis Scripturam, violenter ascendentes, plebem ejus iniquo semine corruperunt": *In Gen.*, l. 9, c. 26 (550 C). There is an image just as strong in H. Metel, *ep.* 5, to Abelard (around 1140: "You have deflowered holy Scripture and violated her to the very top" — "Scripturam sacram devirginasti et usque ad verticem violasti," 333).

101. "'Oculus, inquit, adulteri observat caliginem' (Job, xxiv, 15), id est sicut adulter per tenebras in carnali coïtu non prolem quaerit, sed voluptatem; sic haereticus in hypocrisi adulterat Dei verbum, quia vid. non spirituales Dei filios

gignere sed suam scientiam praedicando desiderat ostentare, et quasi alienam conjugem tollit, dum fidelem animam in suum errorem allicit": *In Job* (CLXVIII, 1066 BC).

102. 2 Cor. 4:2: "neque adulterantes verbum Dei." Cf. Ambrosiaster, *in loc.*: "Now adulterating is wanting to exclude the true sense through a false one" — "Adulterare est autem verum sensum per falsum velle excludere" (XVII, 289 AB).

103. *In Rom.*, l. 2, n. 11 (PG, XIV, 898 A).

104. There is an idea approaching this, but somewhat different, in the *Glossa* on Prov. 15:2: "He bubbles forth stupidity by perverting the Scripture, putting his own senses ahead of the author's, just like the silly philosophers" — "Ebullit stultitiam Scripturam pervertendo, suos sensus auctoritati praeponendo, velut fatui philosophi" (PL, CXIII, 1097 D).

105. "Puella ista, sancta Scriptura est. Porro latrunculi, Pythagoras, Socrates, Plato, caeterique fuere philosophi, qui revera, quasi latrocinando, captivam de terra Israël duxerant puellam hanc, furtim lectitando et ad suos errores sensus violenter inflectendo quamlibet sanctae Scripturae particulam, eamque variae philosophiae quasi uxori Naaman subservire cogebant": *In Reg.*, l. 5 (CLXVII, 1263-4).

106. *In Is.*, l. 1, c. 34: "For the prudent reader does not here receive the darkness of the letter, but the brightness of the spirit" — "Non enim obscuritatem litterae sed claritatem spiritus prudens lector hic recipit" (CLXVII, 1307 B), etc. See below, ch. 3.3.

107. "de la vogue à un système d'interprétation qui assujettit non pas l'esprit de l'interprète au text de la Bible, mais le texte de la Bible aux fantaisies de l'interprète": *Bibliogr. nat. de Belg.*, 11, 457 (art. *Rupert*). This judgment was reproduced by Dom Philibert Schmitz, *H. de l'ordre de S. Benoît*, 2 (1942), 121.

108. The same goes for these words addressed by Gerard of Cambrai to Adalbero of Laon (in 1030): "neither should you submit Scripture to yourselves, but rather yourselves to Scripture" — "neve Scripturam vobis, sed vos Scripturae submittatis" (*Recueil des hist. des Gaules*, ed. Delisle, 10, 511).

109. [In the exchange Anselm said:] "Si autem propositas auctoritates ad tuum sensum retorquere niti volueris, et non potius tuum sensum divinae Scripturae accommodare curaveris, timeo ne forte in hoc quoque Spiritui sancto adverseris et resistas, dum ea quae dictante Spiritu sancto scripta sunt, extra intellectum Spiritus sancti temere evertere, et ad tuum sensum retorquere non erubescis; et nos non ad vincendum, sed ad investigandum quid verum sit, convenimus. . . ." [In reply,] "Nechites archiepiscopus Nicomediae dixit: 'Quantum malum sit intellectum Scripturae, quae divina meruit appellari, ad proprium sensum quasi violenta expositione distorquere, ac non potius proprium sensum omnino divinae Scripturae humiliter mancipare et accommodare, nulli debet esse incognitum qui sacris lectionibus vacare consuevit, et ideo bene monuisti. Fac ergo et tu quod tu in me monuisti; et si vis proponere sacras auctoritates, ita eas exponas, ne videaris tuam sententiam, quia tua est, non quia vera est, extorta expositione velle probare'": *Dial.*, l. 2, c. 14 (PL, CLXXXVIII, 1183-4). Cauchie cites the first sentence of the Greek's reply (435).

110. "Ipse quidem (episcopus Graecorum), nonnullis auctoribus sanctarum Scripturarum ad suum sensum violenter retortis, universa in quibus Graeci a

Latinis discordant tanquam recta visus est affirmare": *Dial.*, prol. (1139 C); l. 2 (1187 A). The dispute had taken place in Constantinople in 1136. Anselm composed his *Dialogi* at the request, in 1149, of Eugene III.

111. "Inveni quaedam superstitiosa, et dictu inutilia, quae tu tamen quibusdam ratiunculis ex opinione adductis et quibusdam auctoritatibus ad tuum sensum revocatis nisus es approbare. Quantum vero malum sit, quemvis sacram Scripturam suo sensui emancipare, et non potius divinae Scripturae suum sensum adaptare, nulli incognitum esse debet, qui sacris lectionibus vacare consuevit . . .": *Ep. apol. pro ordine canon. reg.* (CLXXXVIII, 1119 BC; 1121 A; between 1138 and 1152).

112. *Ib.:* "You tie in the teaching of some Robert or other that I've never heard of, whose authority, since it is unknown in the Church, is as easily rejected as approved" — "Nescio cujusdam Roberti doctrinam adnectis, cujus auctoritas, quia in Ecclesia ignoratur, ea facilitate contemnitur qua probatur," and the sequel, which is in rather bad taste.

113. Cf. A. Dupont-Sommer, *Aperçus préliminaires sur les manuscrits de la Mer Morte* (1950), 75, note: "Subtlety, violence against the texts, is the very law of all allegorical exegesis" — "Subtilité, violence faite aux textes, c'est la loi même de toute exégèse allégorique" (regarding a commentary on Habakkuk found at Qumrân).

114. "Quamdiu igitur, o Judaei, hic bovinus intellectus cordibus vestris insederit . . . ? Si . . . in insania solita permanere decernitis, et magis Scripturas sensui vestro applicare quam sensum vestrum Scripturis inclinare disponitis, audite eas vobis resistentes et perverso intellectui vestro contraria proponentes": *Tr. c. Judaeos,* c. 3 (PL, CLXXXIX, 539 D).

115. Cf. Yvo of Chartres, *letter* 60, in 1097 (Leclercq, 1, 238).

116. *In ps.* vii, n. 14 (CCL, 38, 45-6); *in ps.* x, n. 2 (75).

117. *Mor.*, l. 19, c. 20, n. 55 (PL, LXXVI, 134 AB). Garnier (CCV, 324 D, 342 A).

118. Walafrid Strabo, *In ps.* vii, 13-4: "But he calls the sacred Scriptures a 'bow', where the hardness of the Old Testament has been bent and tamed by the strength of the New as by a sort of cord" — "Arcum autem Scripturas sacras appellat, ubi fortitudine novi T. quasi nervo quodam duritia veteris flexa et adomita est" (CXIV, 765-6). Manegold, *In ps.* vii (XCIII, 521 B). Anselm of Laon, *In Ap.:* "By 'wood', which is of itself useless, the Old Testament is signified; by the 'string', which tempers the wood and makes [the arrow] sail, is signified the New Testament, through which the old Law becomes effective" — "Per lignum, quod per se est inutile, significatur vetus T.; per chordam, quae temperat et facit velere lignum, significatur novum T., per quod valet vetus Lex" (CLXII, 152 CD). Innocent III, *s.* 13 (CCXVII, 516 BD); etc. See above, vol. 1, ch. 5.4.

119. Paulinus, *L. sacros c. Elip.*, c. 2: "boldly to pierce through the breasts of the enemy with spiritual darts to be hurled from the bow of the Scriptures" — "hostium pectora spiritalibus jaculis ex arcu intorquendis Scripturarum intrepide perforare" (PL, XCIX, 154 A). *Glossa in ps. VII* (CXIII, 855 A, following Aug.); *in Reg.*, xiii, 14 (619 D, following Rabanus). Anselm of Laon, *In Ap.* (CLXII, 1522 CD). Hervaeus, *In Is.* (CLXXXI, 82 S). Peter of Cella, *s.* 83 (CCII, 890 D). Bruno of Segni, *In Is.* (*Sp. cas.*, 3, 44); etc. Each word of Scripture is an arrow: Alcuin, *In Ap.*, l. 4 (C, 1123 C). Peter Damian, *op.* 3: "While I laid before you almost bare examples of the

Scriptures, as though I put a bunch of arrows into a quiver" — "Dum nuda pene tibi Scripturarum exempla proposui, velut sagittarum fasciculum in pharetram misi" (CXLV, 67 A).

120. Walafrid Strabo, *In ps.* x, 3-4: "'They have stretched the bow', i.e., the Scriptures, which ... the heretics or Jews have sent off as poisoned opinions by interpreting them carnally" — "'Tetenderunt arcum', Scripturas vid., quas carnaliter interpretando venenatas sententias inde emittunt ... haeretici aut Judaei" (CXIV, 774 BC). Richard, *In Cant.*, c. 39: "For 'they aim' something, the 'bow' of Scripture, and 'prepare their arrows in their quiver so that' with their arrows 'they may pierce the upright of heart in the dark', and they destroy and bend to their own error what the Lord has perfected, i.e., done perfectly and expounded through the doctors" — "'Intendunt' quippe aliquid 'arcum' Scripturae et 'parant sagittas suas in pharetra sua ut' sagittis suis 'sagittent in obscuro rectos corde', et quae Dominus perfecit, id est perfecte fecit et super doctores exposuit destruunt et ad suum errorem inflectunt" (CXCVI, 515 B). Bede, *In Luc.*, story of the temptation: "He breaks the false arrows of the devil drawn from the Scriptures with the true shields of the Scriptures themselves" — "Falsas de Scripturis diaboli sagittas veris Scripturarum frangit clypeis" (XCII, 369 BC). *Or. vis.*, prayer of Lent: "Preserve your Church undefiled from every arrow of heretical corruption" — "Ecclesiam tuam ab omni haereticae pravitatis sagitta intemeratam conserva" (190). Garnier, *s.* 4 (CCV, 597 CV).

121. "Jam nunc ignoscant nobis magistri litterati, si nos verba psalmorum ita coaptamus nostri temporis cursui, sicut beatus Augustinus ex latere semper notavit in expositionem psalmorum sui temporis cursum. Si enim omnium temporum haeretici arcum suum, id est, sanctam Scripturam, ad suum errorem intenderunt, et illi, qui nunc sunt haeretici, Simoniaci et Nicolaïtae, non desinunt arcum suum secundum suum sensum detorquere Scripturas depravando": cf. Manegold, *In ps.* x: "Arcum, id est divinam Scripturam intenderunt, id est valde pravis tentationibus suis coarctaverunt etc." (PL, XCIII, 544-5). P. Lombard (CXCI, 118 A, 148 B). Letbert of St. Rufus (XXI, 687 C); etc.

122. "quare non licet nobis uti eisdem Scripturis ad eorum prava sensa confutanda, non quasi arcu violenter in transversum curvato, sed quasi gladio ancipiti et bis acuto? Neque enim conamur Scripturas a suo sensu deflectere, sed quod datum nobis fuerit, in gloriam dantis loquitur. . . . Non extorquemus de psalmis violenter alienum sensum, sed consona Patribus dicendo et nostris temporibus haereses interdum refellendo ultraneum et sponte concurrentem sensum tenemus": *In ps.* x (*L. de lite*, 3, 416; PL, CXCIII, 792-3). Cf. *In ps.* vii (735 B, 736 D).

123. Cf. *P. Claudel interroge l'Apoc.*, 48.

124. "voluntas Scripturarum"; "valenter litterati et per scientiam oculati"; "per odium veritatis caecati"; "ad suum sensum Scripturam convertunt" or "inflectunt": "Sequaces Judaeorum, falsi christiani, quotiescumque de Scripturis loquentes terrena sectantur, non in Sancto Spiritu, sed quasi in spiritu pythonico de humo mussitantes reputantur, et ideo juste, in omni auditorio fidelium cum Saule pythonissam consulente repudiantur": *In ps.* xxxiv and xxxv (Van den Eynde, 322, 416).

125. Again *Dial. de cler. can. et rel.*: "I know well enough that certain masters

in the schools are occupied with this in such wise that they bend the Scriptures to their own sense, rather than align themselves to the rectitude of the Scripture" — "Satis scio magistros quosdam in scholis circa haec occupari ut Scripturas ad suum sensum inflectant, potius quam se ad rectitudinem Scripturae dirigant" (PL, CXCIV, 1417 B); etc.

126. "opus est ut regulae fidei congruat": *In ps.* lxxiv, n. 12 (CCL, 39, 1033).

127. "curiosa cupiditas": Heterius and Beatus, *Ad Elip.*, l. 2, c. 28 (PL, XCVI, 993 C).

128. Cf. Alcuin, *V. s. Vedasti*, dispatch to Rado, n. 3: "Exhort the brothers also that they read the sacred Scriptures most diligently. Let them not trust in knowledge of the language, but in the understanding of the truth, that they may be able to stand fast against those who contradict the truth" — "Fratres quoque hortare, ut sanctas diligentissime legant Scripturas. Non confidant in linguae notitia, sed in veritatis intelligentia, ut possint contradicentibus veritati resistere etc." (CI, 666 AB). Ps.-Remigius, *In ps.* cxix: to know Scripture to confirm the faith against "the faithlessness of blasphemers and the attack of heretics" — "perfidiam blasphemorum et impugnationem haereticorum" (CXXXI, 768 B).

129. Notker, *De int. div. Script.*, c. 8: "For if you should want to call this the helmet or breastplate of the Old and New Testament, you will find this name less suitable for it, when you ... have learned that that brazen shield had been put together with golden nails and coated with purest silver against heretics and all idolators, but also false brothers, or super-heated over dry wood": "Quod si enim galeam vel thoracem veteris ac novi T. nuncupare volueris, hoc nomen ipsi minus idoneum reperies, cum eum contra haereticos et omnes idolatras, sed et falsos fratres clypeum aereum clavis aureis compactum et argento purissimo vestitum esse, seu nimium ignitum contra ligna arida ... didiceris" (CXXXI, 1001 A).

130. "utrumne vera et catholica an falsa et haeretica sint quae scribit": Claudius, *In Reg.*, praef. (CIV, 634 B).

131. C. 2, commenting on Isa. 7:5: "unless you believe, you will not understand" — "nisi credideritis non intelligetis" (CLVIII, 263-5).

132. "Si ipsa (Scriptura) nostro sensui indubitanter repugnat ..., nulla tamen veritate fulciri (ratio nostra) credenda est": *De concordia praesc. Dei*, q. 3, a. 6 (CLVIII, 528).

133. "Superabundantiam haereseos"; "carnalis intelligentiae praesumptione": *In Jud.*, l. 2 (Pez, 4, 383). Cf. *Glossa, in Prov.*, xv, 2: "By perverting Scripture he boasts stupidity, by preferring his own senses over authority" — "Ebullit stultitiam Scripturam pervertendo, suos sensus auctoritati praeponendo" (PL, CXIII, 1097 D); *In Ap.*, viii, 10: "the two senses of the faithful [are] the historical and the allegorical; the third belongs to the heretics, since they confirm their own heresies by depraved explanations of the Scriptures" — "duo sensus fidelium, historialis et allegoricus; tertius est haereticorum, cum haereses suas confirmant pravis expositionibus Scripturarum" (CXIV, 726 A).

134. *In ps.* xc, praef. (CLXXXIII, 186 B).

135. *In Cant.*, s. 17, n. 1: "Let the Spirit guard our hearts and our understandings lest perchance we think he is present when he is not, and we follow our own sense, going off track" — "Spiritus custodiat corda nostra et intelligentias nostras

ne forte, cum non aderit, adesse putemus nostrumque pro ipso sequamur sensum, deviantes" (CLXXXIII, 853 C).

136. *Sup. Hier. cael.*, l. 2, c. 1 (CLXXV, 951 C): "Nunc autem, quia in sacramentis Dei sensum suum fidei praeferunt, et in Scripturis sacris sanam interpretationis formam tenere contemnunt, fit ut ipse sermo veritatis amplius eos caligare faciat, dum non recte intellectus errorem pro veritate ministrat. Quod tamen Scripturae vitium non est, sed legentium et non intelligentium caecitas."

137. *Defl.*, l. 2 (CLVII, 1078 A): "Scripturas non sano sensu sapiunt, sed eas ad errorem pravae intelligentiae ducunt, neque semetipsos earum sensibus subdunt, sed eas perverse ad errorem proprium trahunt"; "heretics . . . corrupting the rivers of Holy Scripture" — "haereticos . . . sanctae Scripturae flumina corrumpentes" (1079 A; cf. 1050 D).

138. *H. in dom. 12 post. Trin.* (CVL, 2035 D): "Legant ergo et intelligant ministri novi Testamenti sacras Scripturas, non ex sensu quem faciunt, sed ex sensu ex quo fiunt; attendentes quae historialiter, quae mystice, quae tropologice, et quae anagogice dicantur, ut mereantur esse cum Paulo idonei ministri novi Testamenti non littera, sed spiritu."

139. *S.* 12: "There are others who destroy it: these are the ones who have vanished within their own thoughts, who paint images of their own heart within the pages of holy Scripture, who fit the flashing letter to their own devices and squeeze the understanding of Scripture to the point of bleeding": "Sunt alii qui destruunt eam: hi sunt qui evanuerunt in cogitationibus suis, qui imagines cordis sui in paginis sacrae Scripturae depingunt, qui litteram renitentem suis adinventionibus accommodant et intellectum Scripturae usque ad sanguinem emungunt" (CXCVIII, 1755D). Cf. Greg., *Mor.* (below, ch. 4.2).

140. *S.* 31 (1793 AC). Agobard, *Ep. ad cler. et monachos lugd.*, c. 11: "Not only do the heretics adulterate the Word of God by mixing in their own fallacies": "Non soli haeretici adulterant verbum Dei miscendo fallacias suas" (CIV, 195 B). See above, vol. 2, ch. 10.5.

141. *Is.*, 1. *Verb. abbr.*, c. 40, citing Jerome: "He who softens the precepts of holy Scripture toward the will of his hearers, when he ought to be correcting them, corrupts the wine with his own sense mixed in. . . . Its wine, namely the pure and sincere truth . . . has been mixed with water, with a depraved explanation that corrupts and softens the rigor of holy Scripture by means of its own blandness": "Qui praecepta sacrae Scripturae, quibus debet auditores corrigere, ad eorum voluntatem emollit, suo sensu immisto, vinum corrumpit. . . . Vinum suum, id est pura et sincera veritas . . . mistum est aqua, prava expositione corrumpente et molliente rigorem sacrae Scripturae insipiditate sua."

142. "Caupones tui miscent aquam vino": *In Is.*, 1, 22 (PL, XXIV, 38).

143. "vinum sanctarum Scripturarum violat": *In Is.*: "since the precepts of the Law . . . have been corrupted and softened by the false traditions of the Scribes and Pharisees": "quia legalia praecepta . . . corrupta sunt et mollita falsis Scribarum et Pharisaeorum traditionibus, etc." (CXVI, 726 B).

144. *In Ap.*, l. 4, c. 14: "The chalice of unadulterated wine in the hand of the Lord is full of mixture; whereby we understand holy Scripture, which in itself is indeed unmixed and pure, but tainted, clouded, and depraved by heretics; hence the Lord is said to be angry not at the chalice, but at the wine of the heretics, be-

cause it has been mixed with the unadulterated wine of sound understanding": "Calix in manu Domini vini meri plenus est mixto (Ps. lxxiv, 9 [ed.: Ps. 75:8]); per quem sacram Scripturam intelligimus, quae quidem secundum se mera est et pura, sed ab haereticis inficitur, turbatur et depravatur; unde non calici, sed vino haereticorum quod mero vino et sanae intelligentiae mistum est, iratus Dominus esse dicitur" (CLXV, 683 C).

145. *In Ps.* (XCIII, 884 C).

146. "sensus Scripturarum emollitus admistione carnalis intelligentiae": *In Is.*, l. 1 (CLXXXI, 38 BC; cf. 42 A).

147. *In Ps.:* "The chalice of the Lord is indeed full of mixed [wine]. . . . The term 'mixed' signifies the New Testament and the Old, and once these both have been mixed together, they constitute the most healthful drink of minds. For the Jews drank wine, but not the one that was mixed; since they were unwilling to receive the deliverance of the New Testament. Again the Manichaeans did not drink the mixed wine, since, though on their part receiving the New Testament, they spat out the sacraments of the Law with temerarious boldness": "Plenus est mixto utique Domini calix. . . . Quod autem dixit, mixto, novum vetusque significat Testamentum, quae utraque permixta, animorum efficiunt saluberrimam potionem. Judaei enim vinum biberunt, sed non mixtum; quia novi T. noluerunt recipere sospitatem. Itemque Manichaei non biberunt mixtum vinum, quia, novum T. ex parte recipientes, veteris legis sacramenta ausu temerario respuerunt" (LXX, 5639 AB). Gerhoh, *In Ps.* (CXCIV, 388 A).

148. *In ps.* lxxiv, n. 12: "the chalice of unmixed wine, i.e., of the sincere law, is full of mixed [wine], i.e., along with the dregs of bodily sacraments": "calix vini meri, id est legis sincerae, plenus est mixto, id est cum faece corporalium sacramentorum" (CCL, 39, 1033). *C. Faust.*, l. 15, c. 1-2 (PL, XLII, 301-4).

149. *Mor.*, l. 17, c. 29, n. 43: "He mixed the wine, blending a drink of his instructors out of the historical narrative and the spiritual understanding": "Miscuit vinum, praeceptorum suorum poculum ex narratione historica et intelligentia spirituali contemperans" (LXXVI, 31 A).

150. "Vel aliter. Calix, id est Scriptura veteris Testamenti, est in manu Domini; in quo calice est vinum merum, id est simplex littera vel intellectus, quantum ad Judaeos, qui sola carnalia insistunt; plenus vero misto est quantum ad nos, qui per carnalia ascendimus ad spiritualia": *In Ps.* (XCIII, 884 D).

151. *In Prov.*, l. 1, c. 9 (CXI, 712 AB).

152. "In vino mixto historicam simul et allegoricam auditoribus suis (catholica Ecclesia) scientiam propinat": *Sup. Parab. Sal.*, l. 1, c. 9 (XCI, 968 B).

153. "Non dogmatizet in Ecclesia praedicator secundum errores haereticorum vel secundum seductiones philosophorum. . . . Sensu utatur evangelico . . . , ut non ad sensum suum inclinet Dei verbum, sed ad Evangelium inflectat et sermonem et sensum": *Mos. tab. myst. et mor. exp.*, l. 1 (CCII, 1059 AB).

154. "Calix est lex; vinum merum, caeleste mysterium, id est spiritualis sensus; plenus, quia et si semper bibitur, nunquam expenditur; musto, id est utroque testamento, quia vetus et novum simul sunt. Unde Exechiel: vidi rotam in medio rotae. Judaei non mixtum bibunt, quia vetus sine novo recipiunt; neque Manichaei, qui novum recipiunt sine veteri": *In ps.* (CXCI, 702 C).

155. Ps.-Aimon, *In Ps.:* "The chalice of unmixed wine, I say, i.e., of the pure

sense, i.e., the spiritual understanding; the chalice full of mixed [wine], i.e., a mixture, since it contains both the New and the Old Testament": "Calix dico meri vini, id est puri sensus, id est spiritualis intellectus: calix plenus misto, id est mistura, quia continet et novum et vetus T." (CXVI, 448-9).

156. "Ne falsum pro vero affirmet theologus, ne ex falsa interpretatione errorem confirmet haereticus, ut a litterali intelligentia arceatur Judaeus, ne suum intellectum sacrae Scripturae ingerat superbus, dignum duximus theologicorum verborum significationes distinguere": 2nd prol. (CCX, 687-8).

157. [Commenting on the manuscript variant *voluptatem* (pleasure) in the text quoted in the next note:] *Sic* (1595 ed., 390). The variant might be intentional. Cf. Hildemar, *In reg. s. Bened.*: "There are many who distinguish the will in terms of holding on to God, and the will *(voluntatem* with an *n)* to hold on to man, and pleasure *(voluptatem* with a *p)* to hold on to the devil": "Sunt multi qui distinguunt voluntatem per attinere ad Deum, et voluntatem per *m.* attinere ad hominem, voluptatem vero per *p.* ad diabolum" (Mittermüller, 1880; cited by D. Comparetti, *Virgilio nel med. Evo,* ed. G. Pasquali, I, 157).

158. "Ineptus enim est, qui Scripturis, a quibus instruendus est, appetit dominari et captivato sensu earum ad intellectum suum eas nititur trahere repugnantes. Nam in his quaerere quod non habent, proprium sensum obstruere est, non addiscere alienum. Nonne et discipulorum oculi tenebantur, ne Sapientiam, quae eos comitabatur, ex ardore agnoscerent? Quia tardi erant ad intelligendum quae prophetae loquebantur, quaerentes quod aberat a mentibus prophetarum, et non attendentes Christum qui latebat in littera.... Quisquis enim ad voluptatem suam ingenii aut studii viribus, Scripturarum integritatem attentat, quasi a sacrario philosophiae exclusus, ab intelligentia veri alienus exstat": *Polycr.*, l. 7, c. 13 (PL, CXCIX, 667 BC).

159. "certas fidei regulas, ut non quisque suo sensu, sed veritatis aeternae auctoritate firmetur": *De op. sex dier.* (CLXXXIX, 1519 B).

160. "illud ad alienum sensum pervertit, ut spiritus erroris haereticam instrueret pravitatem": *S.* 13 (CCXVII, 376 B). Garnier de Rochemont, *s.* 2: "they have brought a sense to the words rather than drawing the sense from the words": "sensum attulerunt verbis, potius quam retulerunt ex verbis" (CCV, 576 D).

161. Commenting on Hosea 7:14: "they have thought upon wheat and wine" — "super triticum et vinum ruminabant." "To think upon wheat is taken in a bad sense..., i.e., they were mocking the Catholic expositions of holy Scripture, and diminishing them with the teeth of destruction; thus, he who, hearing that the cow from which the ashes of lustration were made was red, since it signified Christ's flesh about to be made red by the blood of his passion, said in detraction: it would not take away from the mystery if it were black, as if to say: that allegory is not worth much, since of whatever color the cow should be, some fabulous allegory can be drawn" — "Triticum ruminare in malo accipitur..., id est catholicas expositiones Scripturae sacrae deridebant, et dentibus destructionis comminuebant; ut ille qui, audiens quod vitula de qua fiebant cineres lustrationis erat rufer, quia signabat carnem Christi sanguine passionis rubricandam, detrahendo ait: non vacaret a mysterio si nigra esset; tanquam si diceret: nil valet ista allegoria, quia cujusque coloris esset vitula, inde potest fabulosa allegoria trahi" (Smalley,

Speculum, 6, 67). Cf. Honorius, *Spec. Ecclesiae*, Dom. de passione Domini: "The red cow is Christ's flesh made red by his blood" — "Rufa vitula (Lev. 16) est caro Christi sanguine rubricata" (PL, CLXXII, 912 A). The symbolic explication went back to the *Ep. of Barnabas*, viii, 1-2, and even to Heb. 9:13-14; it will engender a whole literature, notably in Protestant exegesis.

162. Text in Ch. H. Haskins, *St. in Med. Culture* (1929), 251.

163. "quasi suggerente natura humana et sensu ejus"; "figmenta humanarum adinventionum": *Spec. fidei* (PL, CLXXX, 372 C; J.-M. Déchanet, *Le miroir de la foi*, c. 3, 76).

164. Peter Damian (PL, CXLV, 974-5):

Illiteratus clericus,
Elationi deditus,
Despiciens mysteria,
Ut stulta jacet bestia.

165. "For the beast touches the mountain when, having been given over to irrational motions, they approach the height of holy Scripture, and do not understand it as they should, but irrationally bend it to an understanding of their own pleasure" — "Bestia enim tangit montem quando irrationalibus motibus dediti Scripturae sacrae celsitudini propinquant, et non eam secundum quod debent intelligunt, sed irrationabiliter ad suae voluptatis intelligentia flectunt" (CXCVI, 407 B); c. 21, on the devil: "The enemy tries to impede us in the understanding of the Scripture lest we advance in being educated by it; [he does this] by sullying and obfuscating the purity of the spiritual understanding by means of earthly thoughts or carnal science" — "Ipse inimicus in Scripturae intelligentia nos impedire conatur, ne in ejus eruditione proficiamus, terrenis cogitationibus vel carnali scientia puritatem spiritualis intelligentiae maculans et offuscans" (470 BC).

166. Undique falluntur, etiam nil scire probantur
Qui priscae legis vel dicta sacrae novitatis
Carnali tantum sensu perpendere quaerunt:

De doctr. sp., c. 12, *De spir. Scr. sacrae intelligentia* (CXXXIII, 271 A).

167. Again, Jean du Transtévère, *De vera pace* (1171), l. 2, c. 24: "Quod nonnulli haeretici, quia male more judaizantium ad litteram intellexere mandatum, animos simplicium pervertentes, salvandi colebant salvare facultatem; quibus Spiritus sanctus per Ecclesiae doctrinam opponitur, et nos non tam ad correctionem litterae quam ad ejus intelligibilis medulae hortatur. Unde, dicente Domino, 'beati pauperes spiritu', non commendat exterior[e]m renuntiationem substantiae, sed interiorem concupiscentiae paupertate" (Wilmart, 91). Similar expressions are found in the *Liber c. Manichaeos* (Fr. Stegmüller, *Mél. Gilson*, 1959, 586, 591-2), but without precise allusion to the spiritual sense.

168. Anselm of Laon, *In Matt.*, c. 1 (PL, CLXII, 1244 BC).

169. "bene et catholice" — "prius secundum litteram, postea secundum spiritualem intelligentiam": Bruno of Segni (Pseudo-Eusebius of Emessa, MBVP, 6, 710 F). Martin of Leon, *In Ap.*: There are "two senses of the faithful, namely the historical and the allegorical; the third belongs to the heretics": "duo sensus

fidelium, historialis vid. et allegoricus; tertius est haereticorum" (PL, CCIX, 348 A). One may compare Hervaeus (Ps. Anselm, 4. 1): "Those who explain Scriptures to soundly make Christ known bring wisdom to light": "Elucidant sapientiam, qui ob salubriter declarandam Christi notitiam Scripturas explanant" (CLVIII, 595 A).

170. 1 Cor. 2:15, etc.

171. Jerome, *In Gal.*, iv, 24: "We call him a true spiritual because he judges all things and is himself judged by no one: a person who, knowing all the mysteries of the the Scriptures, understands them in the sublime fashion, and, seeing Christ in the divine books, admits nothing of the Jewish tradition within them": "Nos spiritalem, quia omnia judicat et ipse a nemine judicatur, eum verum dicimus, qui universa Scripturarum sacramenta cognoscens, sublimiter ea intelligat et Christum in divinis libris videns, nihil in eis Judaicae traditionis admittat" (PL, XXV, 390 B); etc. See below, ch. 4.1 (on Hugh).

172. *In Prov.*, l. 1, c. 7 (CXI, 701-6).

173. Hilary, *Tr. Myst.*, l. 1, c. 4: "But comparing spiritual things with spiritual things in safety": "Sed tuto spiritalibus spiritalia comparantes" (SC, 19, 80); etc. Garnier, s. 10: "comparing the signs of things with the things of the signs": "signa rerum rebus comparantes signorum" (PL, CCV, 634 A).

174. Luke of Mont Cornillon (PL, CCIII, 566 C). Anselm of Havelberg, *Dial.*, l. 2: "Indeed what else is comparing spiritual with bodily things or adapting divine things to human ones than to seek the living amongst the dead?" — "Sane spiritualia corporalibus comparare, aut divina humanis adaptare, quid aliud est, quam viventem inter mortuos exquirere?" (CLXXXVIII, 1187 A); etc.

175. "Igitur constituendum est ut sacra evangelii verba, patriarcharum et prophetarum oracula, apostolorum scripta, fide integra, devotione congrua, ut in authenticis libris reperiuntur, incommutabiliter servemus, teneamus, custodiamus, nec aliquid addentes, nec delentes, nec mutantes, si velimus illam comminationem evadere quam Spiritus sanctus juxta finem Apocalypsis videtur intentare: 'Si quis adposuerit ad haec'": *De varia mod.*, c. 8 (PL, CXLII, 1146 D).

176. Philip of Harvengt will write, praising the fidelity of Jerome's translations [reading 'traductions' instead of 'traducteurs': translators]: "so that, as he himself says many times, he would neither add nor subtract nor change anything in the divine Scriptures" — "ut, sicut ipse multoties fatetur, nihil in divinis Scripturis vel addiderit vel subtraxerit vel mutaverit": *Resp. de damn. Sal.* (CCIII, 652 C). Hildegarde will take up the threat of the Apocalypse against those who would add or take away from her own work: *Liber div. operum*, l. 3, vis. 10, c. 38 (CXCVII, 1038 C).

177. Agobard, *De corr. antiph.*, c. 2: "So, adding nothing to the word of God" — "Nihil itaque Dei verbo addentes" (CIV, 330 B).

178. W. C. Van Unnik, "De la règle μήτε προσθεῖναι μήτε ἀφελεῖν dans l'hist. du Canon," *Vig. chr.*, 3 (1949), 1-31. Cf. Tertullian, *De praescr.*, c. 38, 8 (Refoulé, SC, 46, 142). Origen, *In Matt. ser.*, 47 (98).

179. "Non de expositores, sed de haereticis hoc dictum esse intelligere debemus. Expositor namque nihil addit aut minuit; sed aut obscuritates historiae exponendo manifestat, aut moralem aut spiritalem intelligentiam demonstrat. Haereticos ergo maledicit, qui in Scripturis divinis ad confirmandam haeresim

suam quaedam falsa apponebant, et quaedam detrahebant, quae eorum haeresi videbantur esse contraria": *In Ap.*, vis. 7 (PL, XVII, 968 B). Apringius: "Not because he denied that the words he had said were set forth, but because at that time . . . an error of the opinionated and of heretics had begun to emerge and to advance" — "Non quia exponi negaverit verba quae dixerat, sed quia eo tempore . . . dogmaticorum et haereticorum error emergere ceperat ac prodire" (Vega, 77). Beatus: "He said this because of the falsifiers themselves, not because of those who are saying simply what they think" — "Haec propter ipsos infalsatores dixit, non propter eos qui simpliciter quod sentiunt dicunt" (Florez, 574-5). Autpert (405 AB, 655-5). Bruno of Segni, *In Ap.:* "lest anyone . . . assert that vain dreams exist, or, wanting to bend things to his own understanding, try to expound [the Scriptures] in a depraved manner and contrary to the faith" — "ne quis . . . vana somnia esse dicat, vel, ad suum volens flectere intellectum, prave et contra fidem exponere conetur" (PL, CLXV, 735 B). Rupert, *In Ap.:* "This punishment of damnation doubtless belongs to the heretics" — "Haec paena damnationis sine dubio haereticorum est" (CLXIX, 1213 B). Cf. Ambrose, *ep.* 8, n., 37, against the Arians (XVI, 927 B).

180. "sancta autem et veneranda evangelii sacramenta cunctis inviolata saeculis permanebunt": *Conc. For.,* c. 8-10 (XCIX, 291-2).

181. Cf. Paul Monceaux, "Le Manichéen Faustus de Milève, restitution de ses Capitula" (*Mém. de l'Ac. des inscr.*, 43, 1924). The order proposed by Monceaux is not beyond dispute; it presents some difficulties; perhaps there might not even be any order to look for: Aug. had made a sort of anthology of Faustus's oratorical works, citing mutually independent tracts that more or less repeated themselves: Paul Cantaloup, *L'harmonie des deux Testaments dans le C. Faustum* (Toulouse, thèse polycopiée, 1955, 200-16).

182. Aug., *Adv. Jud.,* c. 5, n. 6: "They think that they are saying something significant when they ask us how we accept the authority of the Law and the Prophets, when we do not observe the precepts commanded there" — "Aliquid se dicere existimant, cum requirunt a nobis quomodo accipimus auctoritatem legis et prophetarum, cum sacramenta non observemus quae ibi praecepta sunt" (PL, XLII, 54); c. 2, n. 3 (52). Again, Peter Damian, *Dialogus* (CXLV, 57-68); cf. *L. qui dicitur Dom. vobiscum,* c. 4 (234 D).

183. Aug., *C. Faust.,* l. 17, c. 1-2: "Faustus dixit: Cur legem non accipitis et prophetas, cum Christus eos non se venisse solvere dixerit sed adimplere? . . . Quid quod etiam ex ipso sermone, quo praecipit non putare quia venerit legem solvere, magis intelligi detur quia solverit? . . . Et quid amplius, quidve manifestius fieri potuit in destructionem legis ac prophetarum? Aut si hoc adimplere est legem, quid erit solvere? . . . Quapropter, sive adimplendi causa Jesus legi aliquid et prophetis adjecit, in dexteram videtur lapsus; sive dempsit ut destrueret, in sinistram; utrumque certe offendit legis auctorem; idcircoque aut aliud aliquid significet istud, aut falsum est" (XLII, 339-41: Monceau, c. 22). [The explicit conclusion just quoted can be translated "Consequently, it either means something else, or it is false."]

184. Cf. *In ps.* lxxiii, n. 2: "What was ordered through the letter is being fulfilled through charity" — "Impletur per caritatem, quod per litteram jubebatur" (CCL, 39, 1006).

185. *Ib.*, c. 5: "As if we should say to the uncomprehending Jews that Christ could not be seen as a destroyer of the Law and the Prophets" — "Quasi nos negemus Judaeis non intelligentibus videri potuisse Christum destructorem legis et prophetarum" (XLII, 343). C. 6: "Nor does Faustus understand, or perhaps he pretends not to understand, what it is to fulfill the Law, when he thinks that the text 'let not anything be added to or taken away from the Scripture of God' should be taken as referring to the addition of words.... Hence they do not know how it is that those who live as the Law prescribes fulfill the Law: for the fullness of the Law is charity.... When the Law itself has been fulfilled, it has been made grace and truth. Grace pertains to the fullness of charity; truth to the fulfillment of the prophecies. And since each of the two comes about through Christ, he comes not to remove the Law or the Prophets but to fulfill them; not that things that were missing should be added to the Law, but rather that those that had been written down might come into being" — "Nec intelligit Faustus, aut forte se fingit non intelligere quid sit implere legem; cum hoc de verborum adjectione putat accipiendum, quia scriptum est: ne quid addatur Scripturae Dei vel detrahatur.... Nesciunt ergo isti quomodo adimpleat legem, qui sic vivit ut lex praecipit: plenitudo enim legis caritas.... Ipsa lex cum impleta est, gratia et veritas facta est. Gratia pertinet ad caritatis plenitudinem, veritas ad prophetiarum impletionem. Et quia utrumque per Christum, ideo non venit solvere legem aut prophetas, sed adimplere; non ut legi adderentur quae deerant, sed ut fierent quae scripta erant" (344). Cf. Leo, *s.* 63, c. 5: "And he himself is the end of the Law, not by emptying it of its meanings, but by fulfilling them" — "Et ipse est finis legis, non evacuando significationes ipsius, sed implendo" (LIV, 356 B).

186. L. 18, c. 1-3: "Faustus said: 'I have not come to destroy but to fulfill the Law' but ... unless this perhaps means something else, you know that to believe this saying by Christ is less contrary to you than to me. For under this opinion each of us two is a Christian, since we have thought Christ to have come for the destruction of the Law and the prophets.... For hence it is that you yourself also contemn the precepts of the Law and the prophets; hence it is that we say that Jesus established the New Testament: whereby what else are we saying than the destruction of the Old Testament?" — "Faustus dixit: non veni legem solvere sed adimplere; sed ... hoc, nisi aliud forte significat, a Christo dictum credere non minus tibi contrarium scias esse quam mihi. Uterque enim nostrum sub hac opinione christianus est, quia Christum in destructionem legis ac prophetarum venisse putavimus.... Inde enim est quod legis ac prophetarum praecepta et ipse contemnis; inde quod novum T. Jesum condidisse utrique fatemur: quo quid aliud quam destructionem fatemur veteris T.?" (343). "When a Jew or anyone else aware of this utterance will ask you, 'why do you not keep the precepts of the Law and the prophets, though Christ says that he came not to destroy but to fulfill them?' Doubtless you will be compelled to succumb to vain superstition, or to avow the text to be false, or to deny that you are a disciple of Christ" — "Cum te Judaeus, seu quis alter sermonis istius non inscius interpellabit, quid ita legis ac prophetarum praecepta non serves, cum Christus eadem non se venisse solvere dicat sed adimplere? Nempe cogeris aut vanae superstitioni succumbere, aut capitulum profiteri falsum, aut te Christi negare discipulum" (345; Monceaux, c. 23).

187. L. 18, c. 4: "For they were figures of things to come, which [figures] had to be removed by the things themselves that had been revealed and made present through Christ, so that by as much as these have been removed, the Law and the prophets would be fulfilled. . . . Then they were celebrated by those who do not understand. But when . . . what was signified by them arrived, those things are no longer ordered to be done but what is to be understood by them is being read. . . . Hence, since this too had been foretold, all the more if those things were not removed from our celebration, the Law and the prophets would not be fulfilled; since what they had foretold would not have come about; but since this is indeed coming about, they are understood to be being fulfilled the more powerfully from the very fact that they do not seem to be fulfilled to you" — "Illae quippe erant figurae futurorum, quas rebus ipsis per Christum revelatis et praesentatis auferri oportebat, ut eo quoque haec ablata sunt, lex et prophetae implerentur. . . . Tunc a non intelligentibus celebrabantur. Cum autem venerunt . . . quae illis significabantur, non jam illa jubentur facienda, sed leguntur intelligenda. . . . Quia ergo et hoc praedictum erat, magis si ista de nostra celebratione non auferrentur, non implerentur lex et prophetae; quia non fieret quod praedixerant; cum vero et hoc fit, inde potius intelliguntur adimpleri, unde vobis videntur non adimpleri" (XLII, 345-6). Cf. *Adv. Jud.*, c. 1, n. 2; c. 5, n. 6 (51, 54); *In ps.* lvii, s. 2, n. 7 (XXXVI, 710). Leo, s. 69, c. 2: "The figures have gone ahead, so that the effects might follow, and the duties of the announcers have been brought to an end by the arrival of the things announced": "Praecesserunt figurae, ut sequerentur effectus, et adventu rerum nuntiatarum finita sunt officia nuntiorum" (XLIV, 376 C).

188. L. 18, c. 6: "But the truth of those figures is Christ, by whose blood we have been redeemed and made clean": "Sed illarum figurarum veritas Christus est, cujus sanguine redempti et mundati sumus" (346). Cf. Gilbert Crispin, *Disp. Judaei et christiani:* "The very truth of the figure is now present at hand" — "Ipsa figurae veritas jam praesens adest" (Blumenkranz, 35).

189. Cf. *Adv. Jud.*, c. 3, n. 4: "He did not empty those old signs of things by arguing against them, but rather changed them by fulfilling them": "Illa vetera signa rerum non evacuavit arguendo, sed implendo mutavit" (PL, XLII, 53).

190. C. 7: "Catholic Christians . . . also by the grace of Christ have a legitimate love of God and neighbor, on which two precepts the whole Law and the prophets depend; and they know that whatever things have been prophesied there figuratively either by deeds done, or the celebrations of the sacraments, or in the ways of the utterances, are fulfilled in Christ and the Church. Hence we neither succumb to vain superstition, nor do we say that the text of the gospel is false, nor do we deny that we are disciples of Christ" — "Christiani catholici . . . et ex gratia Christi habent legitimam caritatem Dei et promixi, in quibus duobus praeceptis tota lex pendet et prophetae; et quaecumque ibi vel rebus gestis, vel sacramentorum celebrationibus, vel locutionum modis figurate prophetata sunt, in Christo et Ecclesia impleri cognoscunt. Unde nec vanae superstitioni succumbimus, nec illud evangelicum capitulum falsum esse dicimus, nec Christi discipulos nos negamus" (347-8). C. 9: "The Christian does not observe it precisely because Christ has already fulfilled what was being prophesied by that figure" — "Id propterea non observat christianus, quia quod ea figura pro-

phetabatur, jam Christus implevit" (353). Cf. Paschasius, *In Matt.*, l. 3, c. 5 (CXX, 236-7).

191. "Omnis sermo Dei ignitus clypeus est sperantibus in se; ne addas quidquam verbis illius, ne arguaris invenierisque mendax" (Prov. [30: 5-6]): Cf. Rabanus, *In Prov.*, l. 3, c. 30: "Do not corrupt the eloquence of the holy Scriptures, because certain heretics are known to have done so lest they be won over by them" — "Ne corrumpas eloquia sanctarum Scripturarum, quod quidam haeretici ne his convincerentur fecisse noscuntur" (CXI, 775 A). Agobard (CIV, 330 B). Notker (CXXXI, 1001 A).

192. One can indeed ask himself whether Berno's reproach might not fall better (or less badly) upon those who take liberties with Scripture in the redaction of liturgical texts, and whom he criticizes in ch. 7.

193. *De varia*, c. 4: "A Prophet unafraid of the grammarians' rod" — "Propheta non veritus ferulam grammaticorum" (PL, CXLII, 1137 A).

194. Caesarius of Arles, *In Ap.*, h. 19 (XXXV, 245). Bede, *Expl. Ap.*, l. 3 (CXIII, 206 C). Aimon, *In Ap.* (CXVII, 1219-20).

195. "Hoc propter falsatores [Joannes] dixit, non propter eos qui simpliciter quod sentiunt dicunt, in nullo prophetia mutilata": Bede, *loc. cit.;* etc.

196. *"Jud.:* Pro velle tuo loqueris, secundum intentionem tuam Scripturarum voces ducis ac reducis et trahis quo vis"; "Tu Scripturas tuo sensu tractare consuevisti, et ducis ad reducis, ut jam dixi, qualem in partem vis": *Annulus, seu Dial. inter christ. et Jud. de fidei sacramentis*, l. 1, and 3 (CLXX, 573 C, 397 C).

197. Cf. André Boutemy, *Carmina Trudonensia, Mél. de Ghellinck*, 2, 583-601. Ghellinck, *L'essor*, 1, 166.

198. Cf. R. W. Southern, "St. Anselm and Gilbert Crispin, abbot of Westminster," *Med. and Renaissance Studies*, 3 (1954), 78-115.

199. *"Jud.:* Violentiam Scripturae infers et ad fidei vestrae assertionem Scripturam intorques. . . . Si fas est christianis hoc modo Scripturas de Christo legere et interpretari, multo plura invenietis, quae ita quoquo modo poteritis interpretari.

Quia ubicumque vultis, allegorias et figuras posuisitis, et ubicumque littera sensui vestro repugnat, allegoriis et figuris litteram obvolutam esse dicitis, et ad libitum vestrum exponendo explicatis, ista, inquam, consideratione Scripturas potestis accommodare ad quaecumque vultis. Non enim sensum vestrum Scripturae subditis, sed sensui vestro Scripturam subponitis": *Disp. Judaei et christ.* (B. Blumenkranz, 51, 54, 72).

200. The same thing occurs again in Martin of Léon (†1203): *s.* 4, *in Nativ.*, c. 25 (PL, CCVIII, 351 B, 354 BC).

201. Clement C. J. Webb, "Gilbert Crispin . . . Dispute of a Christian with a Heathen Touching the Faith of Christ," *Med. and Ren. Studies*, 3, 55-77. "Gentile: What Christ said is written in those gospels, 'I have not come to destroy the Law.' He promised that no things would be left undone, but he established that all things are being done. You Christians, however, disciples of Christ, do not keep the Law which Christ kept, etc." — "Gentilis: In evangeliis illis est scriptum quod Christus dixit, Non veni solvere legem. . . . Nulla non fieri promisit, sed omnia fieri instituit. Vos vero christiani, Christi discipuli, legem quam Christus servavit non servatis, etc." (61). "Christian: When the Truth of the things existing under a

mystery has come, the previously announced figure of the Truth to come would now be kept in vain" — "Christianus: Ubi rerum sub aenigmate existentium veritas venit, supervacue jam servaretur figura venturae veritatis praenuntia" (65).

202. Peter the Venerable, *Tract. c. Judaeos*, c. 4 (PL, CLXXXIX, 571 BC): "Following the author of the letter, the Spirit, as I have said, I add nothing to your Law, I take nothing off" — "Auctorem litterae Spiritum magis sequens, nihil, ut dixi, ad verbum legis tuae adjicio, nihil demo" (582 B). "We keep the books intact, we keep them uncorrupted.... Nothing is added to them, nothing is lessened" — "Servamus libros intactos, servamus incorruptos. . . . Nihil eis additur, nihil imminuitur" (581 A).

203. Greg., *In Ez.*, l. 2, h. 4, n. 19 (LXXVI, 983 D): "Ibi quippe incarnatio, ibi passio, ibi mors, ibi resurrectio, ibi ascensio (Christi) continetur. Sed quis nostrum haec audita crederet, nisi facta cognovisset? Cuncta quae de eo in sacro eloquio scripta sunt, opere implevit, ut quae intelligi audita non poterant, visa panderentur."

204. Origen, *In Rom.*, l. 3, n. 11: "The Savior in the gospels says, 'Moses wrote about me'; therefore, he who does not believe in the Christ, about whom Moses wrote in the Law, has broken the Law" — "Salvator in evangeliis dicit: Moyses de me scripsit; qui ergo non credit Christo, de quo Moyses scripsit in lege, destruit legem" (PG, XIV, 957 C; cf. 896 D). Sed. Sc., *In Rom.* (PL, CIII, 32 C, 46 A). Martin of Leon, *s.* 4, *in Nativ.*: "After the institution of the New Testament, whoever observes [the Law] in ceremonial fashion is no longer a doer of the Law but a prevaricator" — "Post Novi T. institutionem, quicumque caeremonilaiter observat, jam non est legis factor sed praevaricator," etc. (CCVIII, 292-3, 297-8, 308 D, 312 B, etc.). Paul Alvarus to Bodo-Eleazar, *ep.* 18, c. 4: "Your whole Law — no, it's even more mine — announces Christ" — "Omnis lex tua, imo plus mea, Christum annuntiat" (Madoz, 247).

205. "Nec Moysi crediderunt, dum in Christo non credunt": Or., *In Jer.*, h. 6 (PL, XXV, 634 A). Jerome, *In Marc.*, viii: "I read the Law and the prophets so that I do not abide in the Law and the prophets but rather arrive at Christ through the Law and the prophets" — "Sic lego legem et prophetas, ut non permaneam in lege et prophetis, sed per legem et prophetas ad Christum perveniam" (*An. mar.*, 3, 2, 353). Tertullian, *Adv. Jud.*, c. 3 (PL, II, 642). Chrys., *In II Cor.*, h. 7, n. 3 (PG, LXI, 445-6).

206. Ildefonse of Toledo, *L. de virg. perpetua S. M.*, c. 6: "But what shall I say? That you are unwilling to accept the new [books] because you have spurned the old?" — "Quid vero dicam? Ideo te nolle recipere novos, quia sprevisti vetustos, etc." (PL, XCVI, 77 A). The work is indeed authentic: H. Barré, "Les premières pièces mariales de l'occident," *Marialia*, 21 (1959; off-print, p. 15).

207. Irenaeus, *Adv. Haer.*, l. 4, c. 26, n. 5 (PG, VII, 1056 B).

208. Aug., *In ps.* cx, n. 8 (CCL, 40, 1624). Alvarus, *ep.* 18, n. 4-5 (Madoz, 247-9).

209. "Non solum impletur, verum etiam transcenditur": *In Ap.*, l. 2 (447 AC).

210. Heterius and Beatus, *Ad Elip.*, l. 2, c. 102: "And we having divested our foot of the letter, climbing Mount Sinai barefoot with Moses" — "Et discalceati nos pedem litterae, nudis pedibus cum Moyse ascendentes montem Sina" (PL, XCVI, 1029 A). J. Scot, *In Jo.*, fr. 3: "What is seen is perishing, since it is sensible and temporal; what is not seen remains, since it is spiritual and eternal" — "Perit

quod videtur, quia sensibile est et temporale; manet quod non videtur, quia spirituale est et aeternale" (CXXII, 348 A).

211. Aelred, *s. ined.* (Talbot, 120). Rupert (PL, CLXVII, 946 C), etc. Sed. Scot.: "The letter of the Law is cast out and the spiritual sense remains in the body of the Church as food for the soul" — "Littera legis ejicitur et sensus spiritualis ad cibum animae in corpore Ecclesiae remanet" (CIII, 215 D).

212. Peter Lombard, *In ps.* xvi, 11: The Jews "have blocked in their fat, i.e., they have kept the thick and carnal sense" — "Adipem suum concluserunt (Judaei), id est pinguem et carnalem sensum retinuerunt" (CXCI, 182 A), etc.

213. Or., *De princ.*, l. 4, c. 1, n. 1 (302). Bede, *In Sam.*, l. 1, c. 9 (PL, XCI, 525 C); *Hexaem.*, l. 4 (188-9); etc.

214. Luke of Mont Cornillon: "What then does the 'mass covered with rust and filth' signify, if not the Scripture of the prophets, which was extremely obscure and wrapped in riddles and figures; which it is necessary for us to cook with the fire of the Holy Spirit as long as it takes until once it has been freed from the letter that killeth we arrive at wisdom and spiritual understanding" — "Quid igitur significat massa auri rubigine et sordibus cooperta, nisi Scripturam prophetarum, quae valde est obscura et diversis aenigmatibus et figuris involuta; quam necesse est ut tam diu igne Spiritus sancti decoquamus, donec abjecta litterae occidentis, ad sapientiam et spiritualem intelligentiam perveniamus" (CCIII. Cf. 361 D). Rabanus (CVIII, 160 BC, 218 A, 654 A, 839 B, 966 B).

215. *Etym.*, l. 8, c. 3, n. 6 (LXXXII, 297 A). Rabanus, *Cl. inst.*, l. 2, c. 58 (CVII, 371 C).

216. *superstitia vana, legalium vana caeremoniarum superstitio*: Godfrey of Admont, *In Scr.*, h. 5 (CLXXIV, 1080 D). Martin of Leon, *In Nat.*, c. 29: "O Jews . . . , we are evidently proving you superstitious in your opposition" — "O Judaei . . . , vos in vestra oppositione superstitiosos evidenter comprobamus" (CCVIII, 418 A). Walafrid Strabo, *De exord.*, c. 19: "an error of certain simple people, [an error] born from the seedbed of Jewish superstitions" — "quorumdam simplicium error, de judaicarum superstitionum seminario natus" (MGH, *Capit.*, 491). Charlemagne to Alcuin (Alcuin, *ep.* 144; MGH, *Ep.*, 4, 230).

217. Leo, *s.* 29, c. 2: "O Jews, you have blocked the path of understanding for yourselves, and whilst you look at the mere nature of flesh, you have deprived yourselves of the whole light of truth. For awaiting, according to the fabulous figments of your opinion, David's son from mere bodily stock," etc. — "Intercludistis vobis, o Judaei, intelligentiae viam, et dum solam naturam carnis aspicitis, tota vos veritatis luce privastis. Exspectantes enim, secundum vestrae persuasionis fabulosa figmenta, David filium de sola stirpe corporea, etc." (LIX, 228 B).

218. "Judaeorum stultitias, inutiles et vanas": *In Tit.* (XX, 596 B). Rupert, *In Mal.* (CLXVIII, 827 D).

219. Jerome, *In Is.:* "In this place let us question the Jews and all those who, under the name 'Christian', are still eating the straws of Scriptures, which, once separated from the grain by the winnowing-fan of the Lord, will be handed over to the wind and the flames" — "Interrogemus in hoc loco Judaeos, et omnes qui sub nomine christiano adhuc paleas comedunt Scripturarum, quae, ventilabro

Domini a tritico separatae, vento tradentur et flammis" (XXIV, 651 BC). Heterius and Beatus, l. 1, c. 98 (XCVI, 955 B).

220. "Semper legentes semperque legendo solam Scripturae paleam sectantes": Rupert (PL, CLXVII, 528 B).

221. Or., *In Jer.*, h. 14, n. 12 (PG, XIII, 417). Cf. *In Matt.*, xvi, 3 (470).

222. Greg., *In Reg.*, l. 2, c. 2, n. 4: "so long as he preferred literally to hang onto the weak points of the Law, he refused to grow into a perfect man through the Gospel" — "dum infirma legis ad litteram tenere maluit, in virum perfectum crescere per evangelium recusavit" (PL, LXXIX, 92 B).

223. Julian of Vézelay (middle of the 12th cent.), *s*. 18: "Libet intueri stultitiam Judaeorum qui, Scripturarum superficie contenti, dum ad litteram cuncta suscipiunt, allegorizare nihil volunt. . . . Nos autem, Judaeis puerilem sensum litterae relinquentes . . . , verba sublimius indagemus" (MM. Lebreton, St. ans., 37, 120). Rupert, *In Amos*, l. 4: "Sic denique Judaei, quoniam sunt sensu puerili, nescientes quid ferant, panem ferunt verbi Dei mente jejuni" (CLXVIII, 3632 C).

224. Helinand, *s*. 4 (CCXII, 516 D).

225. Aug., *De haer.*, 21: "Cerdon . . . spernens etiam Testamentum vetus" — "C. . . . spurning even the Old Testament" (XLII, 29); etc. The Ps.-Abelard, *L. adv. Haer.*, c. 3, gives the old notion of the heretic again: "Dicunt haeretici legem Moysi, quam veterem dicimus, ab omnipotenti Deo non datam" — "The heretics say that the Law of Moses, which we call the Old, was not given by Almighty God" (CLXXVIII, 1824 B). Gerhoh, *In ps.* xxi, 19: "Diviserunt sibi Scripturas, vel sacramenta, quibus ego vestior. Nam ego Dei Patris Verbum, Scripturis et sacramentorum figuris vestior, quae ab haereticis dividuntur; v.g. cum impii Manichaei solum novum T. recipiunt et vetus rejiciunt; Judaei vero e contra vetus recipiunt in littera, sed novum non recipiunt in spiritu" — "They have divided up the Scriptures or sacraments with which I am clothed. For I, the Word of God the Father, am clothed with the Scriptures and figures of the sacraments that are divided up by the heretics; e.g., while the impious Manichees accept only the New Testament and reject the Old, the Jews on the other hand accept the Old literally, but do not accept the New in the spirit" (CXCIII, 1024-5). Cf. Or., *In Lev.*, h. 13, n. 4, h. 14, n. 3 (473, 480); *Peri Arch.*, l. 4, c. 2 (305-10).

226. Here we are not speaking about the mutual accusations of material alterations or interpolations.

227. Agobard, *De judaicis superst.*, c. 10 (PL, CIV, 87 B); c. 1 (77 A). In the *De cavendo convictu* he applies to the Jews the harshest passages of the Bible that were directed against the pagans.

228. Avit., h. 1, fr. 2 (MGH, *A. ant.*, 6, 104). Cf. Aug., *ep.* 36, c. 10, n. 23-4: the Sabbath is no more than a "superstitiosa vacatio," a "vacatio temporalis jam superstitiosa" (PL, XXXIII, 147). Fulbert, *Tr. c. Judaeos* (CXLI, 309 D).

229. *Glossa, In Rom.*, xi, 26 (CXIV, 508 D).

230. Gerhoh, *In ps.* xxiii (CXCIII, 1063 B). Aug., *Doct. chr.*, l. 2, c. 17, n. 27: "errores gentilium superstitionum" (282); *In ps.* viii, n. 6; *in ps.* lxxi, n. 16 (CCL, 38, 51; 39, 982). Rabanus, *Cl. inst.*, l. 3, c. 26 (PL, CVII, 404 B). Walafrid Strabo, *In ps.* viii (CXIV, 767 B). The Theodosian Code recognized three categories of "supersti-

tions": pagana (idolorum), judaica, haeretica; only, the word "superstitio" designates what we denominate paganism.

231. Rufinus, *H. eccl.*, l. 2, c. 23 (XXI, 532 A).

232. Jerome, *In Is.*, l. 1 (XXIV, 27 A). Julian of Toledo, *Antik.*, l. 1, on the two tunics of the high priest (XCVI, 610 AB). Alcuin, *In Ap.*, x, 3 (C, 1144 C). Walafrid Strabo, *In Lev.* (CXIV, 806 D). Guibert of Nogent, *De vita sua*, l. 2, c. 5 (CLVI, 903 B). Martin of Leon (CCVIII, 135 D, 1330 C). Luke of Mont Cornillon (CCIII, 531 A); etc.

233. Isidore, *De var. quaest.*, c. 56, n. 8 (172).

234. Rabanus, *De laud.*, l. 2, c. 10 (PL, CVII, 275 B); *In Ez.*, l. 19: "quod stulta Judaeorum credit superstitio" — "which the stupid superstition of the Jews believes" (CX, 1058 A).

235. Angelome, *In Reg.* (CXV, 498 D).

236. "Inutile de dire que Paul n'était pas toujours cohérent": "Needless to say, Paul was not always consistent," says a recent historian. Sedulius Scotus said more justly, *In Rom.*, c. 3: "Non est praetereundum quod contraria sibi scribere videtur Apostolus etc." — "It is not to be neglected that the Apostle does seem to write opposite things" (CIII, 46 AC).

237. In fact, the Gospel presents "deux traits apparemment antinomiques: un immense respect de Jésus pour le Temple; au-delà même d'une critique très vive des abus et du formalisme, l'affirmation constante d'un dépassement, voire d'une caducité et d'une condamnation" — "two apparently antinomic characteristics: Jesus' immense respect for the Temple; even more, a lively criticism of abuses and formalism, the constant assertion of an excess, to wit, of a decay, and a condemnation": Congar, *Le mystère du Temple* (1958), 139.

238. "L'Ancien Testament pris en lui-même, considéré comme une chose en soi, n'existe pas": *Dogmatique*, tr. fr., l. 2, 1, 85.

239. Or., *C. Cels.*, l. 2, c. 4 (1, 130).

240. Primasius, *Super Ap.*, l. 2 (PL, LXVIII, 835 A); etc.

241. Bede, *In Sam.*, l. 3, c. 4: "post longam quasi parturitionem tempore congruo nobis (Christum) intuendum protulit" — "after a long birthing, as it were, it brought him forth to be beheld at the fitting time" (XCI, 632 A).

242. "post evangelii veritatem": Jerome, *In Is.* (XXIV, 624 A); etc. A number of texts insist upon this point: thus Rabanus (CVIII, 160 B, 899 B); etc.

243. Martin of Leon, *s.* 4, c. 20 (CCVIII, 284 D); *s.* 2 *de Nativ.* (548 A).

244. Aug., *s.* 10, n. 3: "cum ipsi, ex operibus legis excluso intellectu spirituali, tanquam de corpore operis sui animam ejecerunt, et exstinguentes prophetiae spiritum vivum, ad carnalia opera sine vita, hoc est sine intellectu spirituali remanserunt" — "when, once the spiritual understanding had been shut out of the works of the Law, they cast out the soul, as it were, from the body of its work, and, extinguishing the living spirit of prophecy, they stayed stuck to the carnal works without life, i.e., without the spiritual understanding" (PL, XXXVIII, 94).

245. Cf. Jerome, *In Gal.*, l. 2, c. 4 (XXVI, 376 C). Gilbert Foliot, *In Cant.*, c. 4: "vetus interiit " — "the old perished" (CCII, 1258 D).

246. "Quantum distat inter nigredinem corvorum nitoremque columbarum lactearum, imo et amplius, distat inter occidentem litteram et vivificantem spiritum": Rupert, *In Cant.*, l. 5 (CLXVIII, 923 B).

247. "destitutio"; "vetusta via": Peter Cellensis, *s.* 36 (CCII, 742 C); *s.* 20 (699 B). This "foresaking" or "destitutio" has been accomplished at the Last Supper. Cf. Heb. 8:13.

248. "umbra depulsa": Rupert, *In Cant.*, l. 1: "Ne hoc tempore gratiae, quando, figura jam praeterita, res illuxit; umbra depulsa, sol veritatis ascendit" — "so that in this time of grace, once the figure has gone past, the reality has shed its light; once the shadow has been banished, the sun of truth arises" (PL, CLXVIII, 851 C).

249. Gilbert of Hoiland, *In Cant.*, *s.* 16, n. 7 (CLXXXIV, 85 D).

250. "Veniente Domino, cessavit": Alcuin, *Disp. puer.*, c. 7 (CI, 1120 D); etc. Cf. Heb. 7:18.

251. "finis perficiens, non interficiens": Aug. C. Adim., c. 15, n. 1 (XLII, 152). *In Jo.*, tr. 55, n. 2 (CCL, 36, 464). Cf. C. H. Dodd, *Morale de l'Evangile* (tr. J.-H. Marrou, 1958, 118): The term of fulfillment implies "dénonciation sur le plan ancien mais totale réaffirmation sur un nouveau": "negation on the old level but total reaffirmation on a new one."

252. "non sine immutatione": *In Ez.*, l. 1, h. 6, n. 17 (LXXVI, 836 D). Peter the Venerable, *Tr. c. Jud.*, c. 4 (CLXXI, XIX, 575 D); etc.

253. "dum mutatur, impletur": Leo, *s.* 58, c. 1 (LIV, 333 A). Cf. Odo of Cluny, *Occupatio*, l. 6, v. 7: the time has come "quo nova lex veterem mutet et adimpleat illam" — "at which the new law changes the old and fulfills it" (A. Swoboda, 119). Samuel mon., *L. de Messiae adventu praeterito*, c. 19 (PL, CXLIX, 357 D).

254. Sedulius Scotus, *In II Cor.*, c. 3: "Quia gloria legis per gloriam evangelii evacuatur, sed ita evacuatur ut perficiat, sicut infantiam ipse dixit evacuari in viri perfecti aetatem, semen quippe evacuatur in fructum" (CIII, 166 B).

255. Or., *In Rom.*, iii, 11: Christ destroys the Law as perfect glory destroys partial glory (PG, XIV, 957 B), as he absorbs within his own glory that of Moses and Elijah. Compare William of St. Thierry, *Spec. fidei*, c. 1: "Nec tamen fides et spes peribunt, sed in res suas transibunt" — "Nor yet will faith and hope perish, but they will cross over into their very realities" (Déchanet, 50).

256. Bruno of Segni, *In Ap.*, l. 2, c. 4: "Quia vetus et novum T. idem sunt et idem significant" — "Since the Old and New Testaments are the same and signify the same thing" (PL, CLXV, 628 C).

257. *In Jo.*, tr. 9, n. 3 (CCL, 36, 91-2). Beatus, *In Ap.*: "In lege ignis Spiritus sancti latet" — "The fire of the Holy Spirit lies concealed in the Law" (194).

258. Jerome, *In Is.*, l. 2, c. 3, n. 1 (PL, XXIV, 58 AB).

259. Bruno of Segni, *In Ap.*, l. 5, c. 16: "Et prius quidem isti fontes, secundum historiam intellecti, potabiles erant; nunc autem nisi spiritualiter intelligantur haereticos faciunt" — "Those springs, when understood according to the history, were previously drinkable; but now, unless they be understood spiritually, they produce heretics" (CLXV, 692 CD).

260. John Scotus, *In Jo.*, fr. 1: "Judaea quippe in desertum reducta est, omni divino cultu evacuata, idololatriaeque sordibus contaminata, legalem litteram solummodo, omni spirituali sensu evacuatam, diversis superstitionibus pollutam sequens" — "For Judea has been reduced to a desert, emptied of every divine cult and contaminated with the filth of idolatry, following merely the letter of the Law emptied of all spiritual sense, polluted with various superstitions" (CXXII, 304 B).

261. Heterius and Beatus, *Ad Elip.*, l. 1, c. 51 (XCVI, 924 C).

262. Hildegarde, *L. div. operum simplicis hominis*, P. 3, vis. 10, c. 18: "Floriditas autem vineae Sabaoth, quae de flore virgae Aaron processit, quae per spumam serpentis non incaluit, quando Filius meus in cruce passus est, exaruit; quia oculi Judaeorum in umbra mortis gravati fuerunt, ubi, verba prophetiae audientes, ea cum vero flore abjecerunt, quam tota terra cognovit, cum in cruce exspiravit. Et ideo, etiam seipsos occiderunt, ac sic tam in veteri quam in novo T. exaruerunt, quoniam vetus T. est sicut hiems, quae omnem viriditatem in se abscondit; novum vero quasi aestas, quae gramina et flores producit" (CXCVII, 1021 BC). Gerhoh, *De invest. Antich.*, c. 35: "Quando adhuc gens illa Judaica velut arbor ex qua fructus vitae sperabatur" — "When that Judaic tribe like a tree from which the fruit of life was hoped for" (*L. de lite*, 3, 344). Cf. Jerome, *In Is.*, l. 1, c. 2 (XXIV, 42 A).

263. *Judaic dryness!:* Rupert, *In Is.*, l. 2, cx. 19 (PL, CLXVII, 1336 D); cf. *In Jer.*, c. 9 (1374 A). Berengaud, *In Ap.*, vis. 3: "siccatus est torrens" — "the torrent has been dried" (XVII, 835 B). Absalon, *s.* 36 (CCX, 209 D).

264. Cf. Rabanus, *In I Mach.*, l. 1 (CIX, 1165 D). Agobard, *De jud. sup.* (CIV, 87 B). Joachim of Flora, *Sup. 4 ev.*, 105: "Noluerunt ipsi Judaei mutari cum tempore" — "The Jews themselves did not want to be changed with the time"; also the spirit of truth has been withdrawn from them.

265. *Glossa in Ex.*, xiv, 20 (PL, CXIII, 226 B). Gilbert, *In Cant.*, *s.* 5, n. 2: "Vides quomodo aridas fecit fides Christi Judaeorum traditiones et dogmata philosophorum; quomodo arefecit flumina Aegypti" — "You see how the faith of Christ has rendered the traditions of the Jews arid as well as the dogmas of the philosophers; how it has dried up the rivers of Egypt" (CLXXXIV, 32 D).

266. "mysterium velatum"; "mysterii velamen": Bernard, *In Cant.*, *s.* 73, n. 2 (PL, CLXXXIII, 1134 D).

267. "Populus Judaeorum, amissa fide, in tortuosam silvam gentilitatis est versus": Greg., *Mor.*, l. 27, c. 28, n. 52 (LXXVI, 430-1). Hervaeus, *In Is.*, l. 4 (CLXXXI, 279 D); "Tales enim nunc sunt Hebraei, quales temporibus erant Tharae, et deteriores" (279-80). Cf. Gaston Fessard, SJ, *Libre méditation sur un message de Pie XII* (1957), 71-3. [Trans.: on the last page of ch. 2, de Lubac adds the following sequel to this note:] In this sense there is a dialectic immanent to history itself. Our Middle Ages were aware of this dialectic, as so many texts show. There was no need to borrow the idea from some "Hegelian" philosophy: it was an old Christian idea. It was the Pauline and patristic idea, and the tradition never disavowed it, although in the modern epoch we have excessively ignored its fecundity while the Hegelian philosophy was pirating it. Once again, as our ancients used to say, the Christian truth ought to be taken back from its "unjust possessors" after having been purified. Cf. *Sur les chemins de Dieu*, pp. 210-1.

268. *Domini resurrectio tempora permutavit:* Hugo of Rouen, *Tr. in Hexaem.*, l. 1 (Fr. Lecomte, AHDLMA, 25, 19). Cf. Paschasius, *In Matt.*, l. 12, c. 27: "Scinditur ergo velum, et profanatur Synagoga, et destruitur legis littera" — "Hence the veil is being torn, and the Synagogue is being profaned, and the letter of the Law is being destroyed" (PL, CXX, 964 B).

269. "ut omnis contentio pacifica quiete finiatur": Aug., *In ps.* xvii, n. 17 (CCL, 39, 880-1). Or., *In Matt.*, t. 2 (*Philocalia*, c. 6; Robinson).

270. *C. Faust.*, l. 15, c. 1: "Et omne vas plenum superfusa non recipit, sed effundit, et stomachus saturus rejicit ingesta. . . . Nos ex Christi praeventione novo referti [Testamento] respuimus vetus etc." — "And every full vessel does not accept but rather pours out excesses, and a glutted stomach casts up the things it has ingested. . . . We, stuffed with the New [Testament] from the anticipation of Christ, spit out the Old" (PL, XLII, 301; Monceaux, c. 21, 1).

271. Cf. Gilbert Crispin, *Disp. Jud. et chr.*: Judaeus: "Christus caerimonias legis omnes observavit, et evangelium addendo legem adimplevit. Jungemus dextras, legem non solvamus, et spirituales sancti evangelii justificationes addendo, legem impleamus" — The Jew says, "Christ observed all the ceremonies of the Law, and he fulfilled the Law by adding the gospel. Let's shake hands, let's not destroy the Law, let us fulfill the Law by adding the spiritual justifications of the holy gospel" (Bl., 18; cf. 32-3). He invoked 1 Tim. 1:8: "Bona est lex" — "the Law is good."

272. S. W. Baron, *Hist. d'Israël*, 2 (tr. fr., 1957), 681: "La formulation, probalement originale, en araméen, qui est conservée dans le Talmud: Je sui venu non pour retrancher à la loi de Moïse mais pour y ajouter, a un accent encore plus authentique" — "The formulation, probably original, in Aramaic, that is preserved in the Talmud 'I have come not to cut back the Law of Moses but to add to it' sounds rather more authentic."

273. Thus Abelard, promoter of a different logic, *Problemata Heloissae*, pr. 15, sol.: "Ad moralia itaque tantum legis praecepta referendum est quod Dominus ait . . ." (PL, CLXXVIII, 703 AC), a passage characteristic of a change in the modes of thinking. The Abelardian commentary *In Hebr.*: "(Lex) ut Apostolus dicit nihil ad perfectum perduxit; cui quod deerat doctrina Christi perfecta et praedicatio superaddidit" (Landgraf, 661). In the same way, *Dial. inter Philosophuym, Judaeum et Christianum*: "Christianus: Jesus dixit, Nisi abundaverit justitia vestra, etc; et statim per singula novae legis abundantiam prosecutus, quae morali deerant perfectioni diligenter expressit et veram ethicam consummavit etc." (CCV, 241 C). Compare Aug., above, note 185.

274. St. Avitius, *s.* 20: "Why does the Ancient one praise his Moses to me?" — "Quid mihi laudet antiquus Moysen suum etc." (MGH, *A. ant.*, 6, 134).

275. "os ad os": Or., *In Num.*, h. 7, n. 2: "For God is now speaking through the Law face to face" — "Nunc enim os ad os loquitur per legem Deus" (39).

276. Thus R. P. C. Hanson, *Allegory and Event* (1959), regarding Origen: 202: "the reader is constantly tempted to conclude that for him there is no fundamental distinction between the revelation given in the Old Testament and that given in the New"; 204: "Origen did a little modify his extreme doctrine of the relation between the Old Testament and the New"; 210-1: "On several occasions Origen makes a distinction between the gospel and the law"; 212-3: "The consequence of these concessions is that Origen occasionally speaks of the Bible in terms not very different from those which a modern exegete etc." And on Aug., Paul Cantaloup, *L'harmonie des deux T. dans le C. Faustum* (1955), 125-6: "The idea of Revelation is cut in two: the Old Testament and the New Testament" — "L'idée de Révélation est scindée en deux, l'A.T. et le N.T."; and p. 177: "To his mind, the message of the Old Testament already contained the perfections introduced by Christ" — "A son

sens, le message de l'A.T. contenait déjà les perfectionnements introduits par le Christ."

277. *quia ille Homo novus venit:* Aug., *In Jo.,* tr. 30, n. 7 (CCL, 36, 293). Or., *In Lev.,* h. 10, n. 2: "The old things have passed away; behold: all things have been made new through our Lord the Christ" — "Vetera transierunt, ecce facta sunt omnia nova per Christum Dominum nostrum"; h. 16, n. 7: "The new gospels have come" — "Venerunt evangelia nova" (445, 506).

278. Greg., *Ep.,* l. 13, 1 (PL, LXXVII, 1253-4); etc. Cf. H. Lietzmann, *Geschichte der alten Kirche,* 1, 219.

279. "à la nouveauté inconditionée des évéments survenus"; "l'ombre"; "vérité": Chenu, 219, 213.

280. Thus Gerhoh, *De invest. Antichristi,* c. 39: "I do not think that what was not only blameless but even praiseworthy in the character of that time among the priests of the Lord, namely, to smite with the sword, is devoid of murderous blame particularly of the priesthood in the priesthood of Christendom" — "Quod pro illius temporis ratione in sacerdotibus Domini non solum inculpabile, sed et laudabile fuit, vid. in gladio percutere, in christianismi sacerdotio culpa etiam sacerdotii peremptoria carere non arbitror" (*L. de lite,* 3, 347). Cf. Bonizon, *Ad amicum,* l. 9: "If it be permitted for a Christian to fight for the truth using arms" — "Si licet christano armis pro veritate certare" (Jaffé, 2, 686), and the protest of Anselm of Liège († after 1056), *Gesta episc. leod.,* l. 2, c. 7 and 64 (MGH, *Scr.,* 7, 194, 228).

281. For the 11th cent., cf. E. Delaruelle, "Charlemagne et l'Eglise," RHEF, 39 (1953), 165-99, which seems, however, to distort things a bit; for the 11th to 12th cent., G. Funkestein, *Das Alte T. im Kampf von regnum und sacerdotium* (1928; cf. BTAM, 4, no. 728).

282. "judaïsme accompli"; "judaïsme transfiguré": Cf. Stanislas Fumet, "Devant la question juive" (*Le retour d'Israël,* 15 May 1928, 10-1). Newman, *Grammar of Assent,* 437.

283. "influence occulte du judaïsme sur la conscience chrétienne"; "le danger de syncrétisme judaïsant dont on aperçoit tant de traces aussi bien dans l'exégèse et la théologie que dans la liturgie et le droit canon": B. Blumenkranz and J. Chatillon, "De la polémique anti-juive à la catéchèse chrétienne," RTAM, 23 (1956), 40, 1. Cf. A. C. Vega, "Una herejia judaizante de principios del siglo 8 en España" (*Ciudad Dios,* 153, 1941, 57-100). A. E. Haydon, *The Influence of Med. Judaism on Christianity,* 232-51 (cf. BTAM, 6, no. 117). A. L. Williams, "The Jews and the Christian Apologists in Early Spain," *Church Quarterly Review,* 100 (1925-6), 267-87.

284. Th. Reinach, *Hist. des Israélites,* 109-9. Isidore Loeb, "La controverse relig. entre les chrétiens et les Juifs au m. âge en Fr. et en Esp." (RHR, 17 and 18, 1888), 375: "One sees quite well through the accounts of Agobard and Amolo that the Jews, as religious ancesters, inspired them with a sort of veneration" — "On voit très bien, par les récits d'Agobard et d'Amolo, que les Juifs, en qualité d'ancêtres religieux, leur inspiraient une sorte de vénération." Cf. Mgr. Bressolles, RHEF, 28 (1942), 51-64. James Parkes, *The Jew in the Med. Community* (1938), 53-7: "The religious influence of the Jews."

285. Bernhard Blumenkranz, *Juifs et chrétiens dans le monde occidental, 430-1096* (1960).

286. C. 7, n. 51 (PG, CXX, 94 AB). It seems that at that time in southern Italy conversations among Jews, Christians, and Muslims were not a rare thing.

287. "pro consuetudine colloquii sive negotii familiaris": *Vita S. Hereb.*, c. 1 (PL, CLXX, 39 D).

288. The reign of Louis the Pious, under the influence of his second wife Judith, marked the apogee of their favor. On the Jews in the 9th to 10th cent.: E. Amann, in Fliche-Martin, 7, 463.

289. Florus, *Notes against Amalarius:* "Why do you admit . . . Jews to . . . the Lord's altar, in such wise that so great a mob of Jews surrounds you with me present in the presbytery, that touching the altar with their backs they almost knock it over?" — "Quare admittis . . . Judaeos ad . . . altare Domini, ita ut me praesente in presbyterio turba Judaeorum tanta tibi circumdet, ut altare dorsis suis tegentes ita pene impellant?" (Wilmare, RB, 36, 328-9). Cf. Parkes, *The Jew in the Med. Community*, 35, 50-2.

290. Agobard, *De cavendo convictu* (PL, CIV, 111 A, 112 A). Cf. Jean Régné, *Étude sur la condition des Juifs de Narbonne du Ve au XIVe s.* (1912), 35-6. A. Lukyn Williams, *Adversus Judaeos, A Bird's Eye View of Christian Apologiae until the Renaissance* (1935), 348-65.

291. *L. c. Judaeos*, c. 42 (CXVI, 170-1). *Chronicon Suevicum universale*, a. 838: "Bodo, a deacon of the palace, has fallen into Judaism" — "Poto diaconus palatii in Judaismum lapsus est" (MGH, *Scr.*, 13, 64). Prudentius of Toyes, *Annals of St. Bertin[us]* (PL, CXV, 1348).

292. B. Blumenkranz, "Du nouveau sur Bodo-Eléazar?" REJ, 112 (1953), 35-42; "Un pamphlet juif médio-latin de polémique antichrétienne," RHPR, 34 (1954), 401-13; *Juifs et chrétiens*, 11 and 177.

293. "in perfidiorum voraginem Judaeorum": *De diversitate temporum*, l. 2, c. 22-4 (MGH, *Scr.*, 4, 720-3).

294. Blumenkranz, *Juifs et chrétiens*, 161-2 and 169.

295. "Judaeorum in tantum praevaricatorias diligebat consuetudines, ut se regem ipsorum suo prenomine . . . suis omnibus imperaret": *Hist.*, l. 3, c. 6 (M. Prou, 69). Cf. Blumenkranz, RMAL, 8 (1952), 54.

296. "honestus vir": PL, CXLV, 41-2 and 57 B. Cf. Williams, 366-74.

297. "sensus judaicus extollens se adversus scientiam Dei": *Annulus*, prol. (CLXX, 561-2).

298. Jewish proselytism would slacken but not be stopped by the Crusades: Blumenkranz, *Juifs et chrétiens*, 211. The 13th century inaugurated for the Jews the most unhappy period of their history: Salomon Graysel, *The Church and the Jews in the Thirteenth Century* (1933).

299. *H. Franc.*, l. 6, c. 5 (PL, LXXI, 373-5).

300. Blumenkranz, *Juifs et chrétiens*, 68-9; "even if the fact is not authentic, our document nevertheless gives witness to the frequency of such encounters" — "même si le fait n'est pas authentique, notre document atteste pourtant la fréquence de telles rencontres."

301. Adhemar of Chabannes, *Hist.*, l. 3, c. 47: "Bishop Alduin forced the Jews of Limoges to baptism, a law having been promulgated that they should either be

Christians or leave the city, and for one month he ordered the divine doctors to argue with the Jews to drive them to the faith" — "Alduinus episcopus Judaeos Lemovicae ad baptismum compulit, lege prolata ut aut christiani essent, aut de civitate recederent, et per unum mensem doctores divinos jussit disputare cum Judaeis ut eos ad fidem cogerent" (MGH, Scr., 4, 136).

302. Anselm of Liège, *Gesta episc. Leodiensium*, l. 2, c. 44 (MGH, Scr., 7, 216).

303. *Gesta regum Angl.*, l. 4 (Stubbs, 2, 371).

304. There remain four letters of Alvarus in a unique manuscript, of which an ancient owner has torn out or scraped off the pages containing Eleazar's replies. Blumenkranz, *Juifs et chrétiens*, 76-7. Madoz, 211-81. Williams, 224-7.

305. PL, XX, 1165-82.

306. Blumenkranz, *Hist. judaica*, 12 (1950), 21-32. Cf. BTAM, 7, no. 67-8; RMAL, 10, 10.

307. *Antilogus:* "Often . . . lack of experience and an excessive simplicity not only encouraged the audacity of the unbeliever, but even beget error and doubt in the hearts of believers" — "Saepe . . . imperitia et cavenda simplicitas non solum audaciam incredulis suggerit, sed etiam errorem et dubietatem in cordibus fidelium gignit" (PL, XLV, 41 B). Blumenkranz, *Juifs et chrétiens*, 75.

308. V. G., 96.

309. *Vita S. Martini*, c. 1 (*ib.*, 219). Cf. Acts 6:10.

310. Paul Weber, *Geistliches Schauspiel und kirchliche Kunst in ihrem Verhältnis erläutert an einer Ikonographie der Kirche und Synagogue* (1894). Williams, 338. Zumthor, 140. Blumenkranz, RMAL, 5, 195; RSDR, 29 (1955), 242; *Juifs et chrétiens*, 78-84.

311. *Disp. c. Judaeum Leonem de adventu Christi* (PL, CLX, 1103-12).

312. *C. Judaeos disc.* (Fr. Carbone, *Flagellum Hebraeorum*, 1672). Cf. Ghellinck, *L'essor*, 1, 163-4.

313. Blumenkranz, *Juifs et chrétiens*, 46-7 and 221.

314. *Ep.* 14, c. 3 (Madoz, 214).

315. The Jew knows the New Testament well, he knows the thought of St. Anselm, etc. "He has a skill practised in Scriptures and debates against us" — "Exercitatum in scripturis atque disputationibus contra nos habebat ingenium" (Bl., 27, 43).

316. *Prol.*: "As often as we got together, we held our discussion with a friendly spirit in a manner befitting the Scriptures and our faith" — "Quociens conveniebamus, more de Scripturis et de fide nostra sermonem amico animo habebamus" (27). The Jew says to him: "I want to devote our leisure in these matters rather to reason than to contention" — "in his rebus rationi potius vacare volo quam contentioni" (28).

317. PL, CLIX, 1034-6. Cf. Blum., REJ, 1958, 49-58.

318. "It is fitting that between ourselves we should meet together not contentiously nor clamorously nor with a mind to winning, but with all peace and tranquillity and such great desire for searching out the truth" — "Convenit inter nos ut non contentiose nec clamose nec animo vincendi, sed cum omni pace et tranquillitate et tanto desiderio veritatem inquirendi simul tractaremus" (R. V. Hunt, 155). See above, vol. 2, ch. 8.4.

319. "Sic ergo Judaeus ille disputator . . . me provocando adorsus est": Bl., 28.

320. "Dic, o episcope, adventus Christi vestri quid utilitatis contulit mundo?": PL, CLX, 1103 B.

321. *Antilogus:* "For it is dishonorable that a man of the church should be silent through ignorance before public calumniators, and that a Christian, not knowing how to render an account of Christ, should go off defeated and confused by insolent opponents" — "Inhonestum quippe est, ut ecclesiasticus vir his qui foris sunt calumniantibus per ignorantiam conticescat, et christianus de Christo reddere rationem nesciens, inimicis insultantibus victus et confusus abscedat" (CXLV, 41 B).

322. "ut de Scripturis contra perfidiam Judaeorum, qui detrahunt fidei christianae, aliqua respondere simus instructi"; "ne Judaeis risum nostrae imperitae praebeamus, qui toties nobis insultant et quodammodo cum Golia dicunt: 'Eligite ex vobis unum qui inest nobiscum singulare certamen'": PL, CCXIII, 749 AB. For Greg., Goliath was the heretic (LXXVI, 50 BC).

323. "Perfidiam nurus una, fidem nurus altera monstrat": *Poema* 27, v. 535 (PL, LXI, 660 B). Nicetas of Remesiana, *De psalmodiae bono*, c. 6: "God is pointed to, ... the faith is sown, faithlessness is repudiated" — "Deus ostenditur, ... fides adseritur, perfidia repudiatur" (Burn., 73).

324. "Propter aedificandam fidem et fugandam de corde perfidiam"; "domus perfidiae"; "domus fidei": *Hexaem.*, l. 2 (PL, XCI, 87 A); *In Luc.* (XCII, 629 B, 544 C). Ps.-Bede, *In Jo.* (662 C).

325. "pro solita perfidia": Sulpicius Severus, *Chron.*, l. 1, c. 25 (C. Halm, 28); c. 42: "Asab picked up the tracks of the faithlessness of his fathers" — "Asab vestigia paternae perfidiae sustulit" (44).

326. "vera fides": Martin of Leon, *s.* 2 *de nat.* (PL, CCVIII, 119, etc.). Cf. Cyprian, *De cath. Eccl. unitate* (IV, 498).

327. "recta fides"; "errores perfidiae": Peter Damian, *op.* 6, c. 30 (CXLV, 145 A).

328. "ut per quem incredulorum est repulsa perfidia, per eum fides nostra perveniat ad coronam": *Or. vis.*, 15; *ib.*, 258.

329. "In causa fidei vel perfidiae": *In Rom.* (PL, CIII, 86 C).

330. "modica fides arguitur, magna laudatur, perfidia damnatur": *De quarta vig. noctis*, c. 21 (L. de lite, 3, 524).

331. "catholicae Ecclesiae fides roboratur, Judaeorum perfidia redarguitur"; "perfidia"; "vera fides": PL, CXCVIII, 11 B, 122 C, 247 A.

332. "Incredulitatis perfidia"; "infidelitatis perfidia": Martin of Leon, *s.* 4 *in nat.*, c. 10 and 15 (CCVIII, 211 A, 246 A). Guibert of Nogent, *De incarn. c. Judaeos*, l. 3, c. 10 (CLVI, 527 B).

333. Or., *In Rom.*, l. 2, n. 14 (PG, XIV, 918 B). Aug., *C. Faust.*, l. 31, c. 4 (PL, XLII, 497). *L. moz. sacram.*, n. 1233 (Férotin, 556); n. 753: "the incredulous people of the Jewish multitude" — "incredula plebs Judaicae multitudinis" (327). Isidore, *De var. q.*, c. 33, *De infidelitate Jud.* (105). Martin of Leon (PL, CCVIII, 195 BC, 211 D, 547 B). Gerhoh (L. de lite, 3, 506); etc.

334. "Omnes haeretici de Filio Dei et Spiritu sancto male sentientes, in perfidia Judaeorum et gentilium inveniuntur": *ep.* 4, c. 23 (PL, XIII, 363-4). Arnobius the Younger, *Conflict.*, l. 2, c. 32 (LIII, 322 A). Bruno of Segni, *In Ap.*: "Judaeus, paganus, haereticus" (CLXV, 681 D). Cf. Garnier, *s.* 4 (CCV, 592 AB); etc.

Notes to Pages 117-18

335. *In Ap.*, c. 20 (Vega, 62). Guibert of Nogent, *De vita sua*, l. 3, c. 16: "Judaeorum et haereticorum perfidiam" (PL, CLVI, 949-50).

336. "Perfidia enim sive impietas generalis caracter est illis omnibus, paganis sc., Judaeis, haereticis": *Adv. Simoniacos* (*L. de lite*, 1, 191).

337. "peccatum infidelitatis": *In ps.* cxviii, s. 3, n. 3 (CCL, 40, 1673).

338. *In Jo.*, tr. 38, n. 5 (36, 340); cf. tr. 51, n. 9 (442).

339. "judaicae infidelitatis perfidia": *In Matt.*, tr. 10, c. 2, n. 5 (CCL, 9, 421).

340. "Ad Redemptorem tuum deposita infidelitate convertere": s. 35, c. 2 (PL, LIV, 251 A).

341. "infidelium Judaeorum corda"; "infidelitatem Judaeorum": *In Ez.*, l. 1, h. 8, n. 31 (LXXVI, 868-9), etc. Agobard, *ep.* 6 (MGH, *ep.* 5, 181). Alan of Farfa: "Judaeis infidelibus" (Hosp, *Eph. lit.*, 51, 1937, 225); etc. On the idea of *infidelitas*: H. Schmek, "*Infidelitas*, ein Beitrag zur Wortgesch.," *Vig. chr.*, 5 (1951), 129-47.

342. *In Ev.*, h. 10, n. 2 (PL, LXXVI, 1111 B).

343. *De var. q.*, praef. (2), etc. Julian of Tol. (PL, XCVI, 766 B). *Insultatio vili storici* (XCVI, 797-8). Honorius (CLXXII, 346 C). Hervaeus (CLXXXI, 47 D, 95 C, 106 A, 114 C, 118 B, 138 C, 177 C, 491 D, 512 A). Adam. Scot. (CXCVIII, 137 C). Garnier (CCV, 652 B). Joachim of Flora, *Sup. 4 ev.*; etc. Angelome: "Jewish faithlessness . . . , the malice of infidelity" — "Judaica perfidia . . . , malitia infidelitatis" (CXV, 264 A). Richard: "Jewish faithlessness abandoned in infidelity" — "Perfidia Judaea in infidelitate derelicta" (CXCVI, 824 A). Martin of Leon (CCVIII, 870-1). Gautier of Lille, *C. Judaeos*, prol. (CCIX, 424 B); etc.

344. "Per Aquilonem vero gentilitas figuratur, quae diu in perfidiae suae frigore torpuit. . . . Synagoga, in persecutione Redemptoris nostri saeviens, ad torporem perfidiae prorupit": *In Ez.*, l. 2, h. 6, n. 20; h. 9, n. 7 (LXXVI, 1009 A, 1046 D). *Mor.*, l. 27, c. 43, n. 71: "Ab Aquilone ergo aurum venire dicitur, quia per respectum gratiae Redemptoris a gentilitate dudum perfidiae torpore frigida inter sanctam Ecclesiam pretiosa Deo vita fidelium multiplicatur" (440 C). On Gregory and the Jews: Blumenkranz, REJ, 1948-9, 66-7.

345. *Mor.*, l. 29, c. 29, n. 56 (LXXVI, 509 A).

346. "Disputatio contra incredulitatem Judaeorum": Anonymous 12th cent. (Hunt, 146).

347. "Invectiva contra perfidiam Judaeorum": Peter of Blois (PL, CCVII, 825-72).

348. RMAL, 10, 92 (Blum.).

349. "perfida Judaeorum et gentilium civitas"; "in perfidia posita"; "Cur universitatem gentium tamdiu, tot retroactis saeculis, in errore perfidiae perire permisit?": l. 5, prol., l. 3, prol. (MGH, *Scr.*, 20, 214, 143, 169).

350. "perfidiam caesam a fide": *De spect.*, c. 29 (PL, I, 660 B).

351. *In ps.* cxxxix, n. 1 (CCI, 40, 2012).

352. "debet aliquid inter fidos et perfidos interesse": *De exc. fr. sui*, l. 1, c. 70 (PL, XVI, 1312 A). *De Jacob et vita beata*, l. 2, c. 7, n. 33 (XIV, 627 B and C).

353. *Common.*, c. 26: "The faithless are speaking . . . to the faithful" — "Loquuntur . . . perfidi fidelibus" (Rauschen, 57).

354. PL, LXX, 377 B, 702 C, 815 B, etc.

355. "Furit gentium perfidia contra Judaeos": *In Sam.*, l. 4, c. 8 (XCI, 702 D; cf. 561 B).

356. *L. moz. sacr.* (F., 314), *L. moz. ord.* (F., 163)

357. *L. moz. sacr.* (44, 87, 316).

358. "in cultu lignorum ac lapidum perfida": *Vita s. Greg.*, l. 2, c. 39 (LXXV, 102 CD).

359. *In Matt.*, l. 1, c. 2: "Unless one departs from infidelity and, leaving the company of the faithless . . . , renounces the pomp of the devil, he will not be able to achieve a wholesome baptism" — "Nisi quis ab infidelitate recedat et a perfidorum consortio egrediens pompae diaboli . . . abrenuntiet, baptismum salubrem consequi non poterit" (CVII, 769 C).

360. "armaturam perfidiae in cultu fidei transtulerunt": *C. Wolfelm.*, c. 10 (CLV, 158).

361. *Gesta Dei*, l. 8, c. 4: The Lord "establishes the earth when he permits the faithlessness of gentiles to grow hard of heart" — "Fundat terram (Dominus) cum permittit gentilium praecordialiter obdurari perfidiam" (CLVI, 806 A).

362. "domus non consecrata"; "gentilitas Dei ignara et perfidiae repagulis inclusa": *Gemma*, l. 1, c. 1512 (CLXXII, 590-1).

363. "gentilibus aequales": *In Rom.* (CIII, 107-8); *In I Cor.* (166 D).

364. "perfida Saracenorum gens": *Passio S. Pelagii* (CXXXVII, 1095 B).

365. *Ep.* 208: "de fide aut perfidia" (CXCIX, 232 D).

366. "Sermo quidem perfidus est et omni reprobatione dignus . . . , sed forte . . .": *Polycr.*, l. 5, c. 4 (546 C; cf. 541 C).

367. "tenebras perfidiae de gentibus excussit": *Spec. Ecclesiae, In s. Pauli die* (CLXXII, 860 C).

368. "de perfidia gentilitatis": *s.* 7 (CCXI, 52 A).

369. Ambrose, *In Luc.*, l. 4, c. 57: "infidiae plebis corda demulcet" (Tissot, SC, 45, 174). Prudentius, *Apoth.*, 2, 550. Julian of Toledo, *L. de hist. Galliae* (PL, XCVI, 796 B). Peter Lombard, *In Ps.* (CXCI, 701-2). Paschasius, *Vita Walae*, c. 4: "that the unfaithful accept the faith" — "ut infidi fidem recipiant" (MGH, *Script.*, 2, 534). The "diffidentia" of which Hilary speaks, *C. Constantium imp.*, c. 1, which is perhaps simply timidity or cowardice, could also signify "lack of faith" (Rocher, Mémoire de Poitiers, 1959). Cf. Hélinand, *s.* 18, commenting on Apoc. 3:15: "Would that you should be fervent in Christianity or else be unfaithful!" — "Utinam aut christianitate ferveres, aut infidus esses!" (PL, CCXII, 627 B).

370. "Ubique scandala, ubique schismata, ubique perfidiae sunt!": De synodo, c. 63 (PL, X, 523 A); cf. c. 39 (513 A).

371. "unitas perfidiae": *Ad Constant.*, l. 2, c. 6 (X, 577 A). Ambrose, *In ps. cxviii, s.* 11, c. 20: "So let faithlessness go silent" — "Conticescat igitur perfidia" (XV, 1356 C); *De incarn. dom. sacramento*, c. 4, n. 30: "but it is the job of the faithless to preach faithlessness" — "opus autem est perfidorum perfidiam praedicare" (XVI, 826 B).

372. "auctores perfidiae."

373. "Sentiant haeretici inimicum te esse perfidiae": *ep.* 153 (Hilberg. 3, 366). *In Is.*, l. 17 (PL, XXIV, 595 C); *In Jer.*, l. 5 (829 D); *In Job* (XXVI, 680 C).

374. "per sex volumina nihil aliud agit, nisi ut Origenem suae ostentat fidei, id est, Arianae perfidiae": *Adv. l. Rufini*, l. 2, c. 6 (XXIII, 438 C). Ambrose, *De fide*, l. 3, c. 16, n. 129 (XVI, 615 B); *ep.* 8, n. 59 (934 B). Rufinus, *H. eccl.*, l. 1, c. 13 (XXI, 486

A, 486 B); c. 38: "a storm of heretics and whirlwinds of faithlessness" — "haereticorum procella et perfidiae turbines" (498 A).

375. Cf. Bonizon, *Ad amicum*, l. 2: "The greatest devastator of the Church, Arius, from whom arose the Arian heresy and a thousand novelties of heresy" — "Arrius, maximus Ecclesiae devastator, a quo arriana haeresis exorta est, et ab eo mille haereseos novitates" (Jaffé, 2, 606-7).

376. Numerous examples for the patristic age in Erik Peterson, "Perfidia Judaica," *Eph. lit.*, 10 (1936), 296-311. Greg., *Dial.*, l. 3, c. 32 (PL, LXXVII, 293 B); etc.

377. The expression at that time often designates neo-Manichaeism: M. J. Congar, RSPT, 43 (1959), 449-61.

378. *De 7 sigillis*, 2 (RTAM, 21, 241).

379. *De nat. rer.*: "The faithlessness of Arius" — "Arii perfidia" (189).

380. "occurrit perfidiae"; "verbis catholicis in ore talium sentit subesse perfidiam": *Hist. pontif.*, c. 14 (Chibnall, 40, 41).

381. "verbis fallacibus involutam quae catholicam disciplinam perfidia latente loqueretur": l., 2, c. 37, 38, 40, 41, 45, 46, 48 (Halm); *Vita S. Martini*, c. 6 (*ib.*, 11)

382. "perfidos praecones": "and scolding the faithless hawkers with their shouts" — "perfidosque praecones clamoribus objurgantes" (PL, LI, 937 C). John the Deacon, *V. s. Greg.*, l. 4, c. 71: "with the mad faithlessness of the Lombards" — "Langobardorum perfidia saviente" (LXXV, 223 A).

383. "Photini perfidia": *s.* 96, c. 2 (LIV, 467 A).

384. "perfidus rex": *Dial.*, l. 3, c. 13 (LXXVII, 241 B).

385. "ejusque a se perfidiam dignis increpationibus repulit": *Ib.*, c. 31 (292 A).

386. "Subvenite famae vestrae ... ne perfidiae vestrae reputetur ab aemulis": *ep.* 5, n. 9 (Walker, 1957, 46).

387. *C. Elip.; C. Fel. Urg.* (PL, XCIX, 153-4, 157 C, 159 A; 358 A, 369 A, 381 D, 387 D, 400 A, 416 A, 451 C, 454 A, 465 C, 467 B).

388. 56 (F., 160).

389. "in perfidiae errore": *Ad Elip.*, l. 2, c. 95-6: "Sometimes by as much the heretics are more agreeable in the error of faithlessness, by so much do they more simulate holiness.... They are the testicles of the Antichrist, from whose seed is born a perverse offspring, which copulates in the mouth of the Antichrist" — "Aliquando haeretici, quanto magis in perfidiae errore blandiuntur, tanto magis sanctitatem simulant.... Hi testiculi Antichristi sunt, de quorem semine perversa proles gignitur, quae in Antichristi ore copulatur ..." (XCVI, 1025 C).

390. "Serpit (haereticus) dum latet ejus perfidia": l. 6, c. 13 (430). Cf. Council of Orleans of 1022, c. 6-7 (*Recueil des hist. des Gaules*, éd. Delisle, 10, 539).

391. "imperitia atque perfidia": *In Ap.*, l. 7 (573 D); l. 10 (644-5).

392. *In Job:* "These (heretics) are hastening to offer a venomous toast to their faithlessness" — "Hi (haeretici) perfidiae suae venenum propinare festinant" (PL, XXVI, 683 B).

393. *H. eccl.*, l. 1, c. 10 (Holder, 17).

394. "multiplicia venena": *In i Mac.*: "They stir up new wars against the Church and pour out the manifold venoms of their faithlessness" — "Nova adversus Ecclesiam excitant bella ac perfidiae suae multiplicia effundunt venena" (PL, CIX, 1168 B).

395. "Pelagianae venena perfidiae": To Wenilo of Sens (MGH, *Ep.*, 3, 632).

396. "perfidiae venenum": *Gesta Dei*, l. 1, c. 3 (PL, CLVI, 690 A).

397. "non minus callidi quam perfidi": *Antapodosis*, l. 1, n. 4 (CXXXVI, 792 BC; cf. 800 C, 870 C).

398. "Gotescalci perfidiam": *De una . . . deit.*, 13 (CXXV, 576 D).

399. "simoniaca perfidia": Atto, *Vita*, c. 45 (CXLVI, 686 B). *Vita S. Wolkangi*, c. 11 (CLIV, 414 C).

400. *H. eccl.*, l. 3, prol. (CLXIII, 833 A; cf. 836 D). Peter Damian, *De sancta simplicitate*, c. 8: "haeretica perfidia" (CXLV, 703 B). Gerhoh, *De quarta vig. noctis*, c. 17 (*L. de lite*, 3, 519).

401. "omnino christianus non est": *Ep.*, l. 2, 41 (CLVIII, 1193 B).

402. "quod astu et obscuritate verborum occultabat perfidiam": John of Salisbury, *H. pontif.*, c. 12 (ch. 26).

403. "de fide perfide dogmatizans": *Chronicon*, a. 1142 (PL, CCXII, 1034 D).

404. "qui contra perfidos arma susceperint expugnandos": a. 1207, *ep.* 149 (CCXV, 1247 D). Cf. *ep.* 38: "the faithlessness of the pagans" — "paganorum perfidia" (1132 B).

405. "haereticorum sectae"; "perfidiae divisiones": *Consult. Zacch. et Apoll.*, c. 2, c. 2 (Morin, 72).

406. "haeretica perfidia": Counc. of Frankfort, letter to the Spaniards (PL, 101, 1344 CD). Rupert, *In Ap.* (CLXIX, 883 C).

407. "haereticorum perfidia": Cassiodorus, *In Ps.* (PL, LXX, 1002 B). Autpert, *In Ap.*, praef. (404 G). Alcuin, *In Ap.* (PL, C, 1101 D, 1138 B, 1154 D). Ps.-Bede, *In Job* (XCII, 773 A). Rabanus, *h.* 21 (XCIV, 247 A). Bruno of Segni, *In Ap.* (CLXV, 619 AB). Rupert (CLXIX, 1121 D; 170, 314 D). Honorius (CLXXII, 317 D). St. Martin I, *ep.* 1 (LXXXVII, 124 B); etc.

408. "mendax perfidia": Martin of Leon, *s.* 4 *in nat.*, c. 30 (CCVIII, 439 B).

409. "recta fides": Paulinus to Charlem. (MGH, *Ep.*, 4, 523).

410. "sana fides": Rabanus (PL, CXI, 963 D).

411. "perfida dogmatis": Rabanus: "The heart of heretics . . . takes faithlessness for knowledge" — "Cor haereticorum . . . perfidiam pro scientia concipit"; "to any heretic trusting in the faithlessness of his dogma" — "haeretico cuilibet confidenti in sui perfidia dogmatis" (CXI, 730 B, 736 D).

412. Rabanus, *In Mac.* (CIX, 1197-8).

413. "contra perfidos quosque istius saeculi": *In Reg.* (CXV, 380 A).

414. "perfidia blasphemorum": Ps.-Remigius, *In Ps.* (CXXXI, 768 B).

415. "justorum fides"; "perfidia impiorum": *In Jo.*, fr. 3: "There are indeed two sorts of temptation: the one tests the faith of the just; the other disproves the faithlessness of the impious" — "Tentationis siquidem duae species sunt, quarum una justorum probat fidem, altera impiorum reprobat perfidiam" (CXXII, 340 C).

416. "malum perfidae": Bede (XCI, 686 A).

417. "error gentilis": *In Ap.*, l. 3 (457 C).

418. "christiana religio": c. 67, *De usuris judaeorum* (Mansi, 22, 1054 E).

419. "Perfidia judaica": Ambrose, *In Luc.* (SC, 52, 46). Leo (PL, LIV, 462 D). Peter Chrysologus, *s.* 50 (LII, 339; cf. 57, 506 A). Greg. (LXXIX, 157 B). Ps.-Ildefonsus, *s.* 13 (XCVI, 281 D). Agobard (CIV, 77-8). Rabanus (CIX, 58 C).

Godfrey of Admont (CLXXIV, 1083 C). Bernard (CLXXXIII, 1149 B). Richard (CXCVI, 605 D). John of Salis., *Polycr.* (CXCIX, 426 D); etc.

420. "perfidia Judaeorum": Ambrose (PL, XIV, 899 A). Jerome (XXIV, 874 D). Leo (LIV, 381 B). Cassiodorus (LXX, 948 D). Greg. (LXXVI, 537 C, 1173 C; LXXIX, 97 B, 100 D). Isidore (LXXXIII, 450 B, 460 A, 640 A). Sed. Scot. (CIII, 11 D). Angelome (CXV, 342 A). Paschasius (CXX, 1197 C, 1210 B). Othloh (CXLVI, 93 D). Hugh of Fleury (CLXIII, 834 B). Hervaeus (CLXXXI, 106 A, 114 C, 491 D). Gerhoh (CXCIII, 1170 C; *Op. in.*, 1, 231). Aelred (*S. in.*, Talbot, 130). John of Salis. (CXCIX, 418 CD). Philip of Harvengt (CCIII, 574 A). Peter of Blois (CCVII, 825-6). Martin of Leon (CCVIII, 31 C). Sicardus of Cremona (CCXIII, 318 C). Joachim of Flora, *Sup.* 4 *ev.* (39, 71, 99, 101). Herbert Losinga (G.-S., 2, 118); etc.

421. "perfidia Judaeae gentis": Bede (PL, XCI, 597 D). Godfrey of Admont (CLXXIV, 34 B). Greg.: the "faithlessness of the Jewish people" — "judaicae plebis perfidia" (LXXV, 883 B).

422. "perfidia populi praevaricantis": Ambrose, *De Cain*, l. 1, c. 2, n. 5 (XIV, 318 A).

423. "Perfidia Judaeorum judicabitur fide apostolorum": Rabanus, *In Rom.*, ii, 2 (CXI, 1320 D).

424. "quorum perfidia frequenter ad vomitum redit": P. 3, d, 4, c. 93 (Aem. Friedberg, 1392).

425. "de perfidia ad veram fidem": *Ep.*, l. 3, 117 (PL, CLIX, 154 B).

426. "Judaeorum spreta perfidia": *ep.* 309 (Giles, 2, 43).

427. *Ep.* 2 (MGH, *A. ant.*, 6, 2, 19).

428. "Judaei diffidentes": Rabanus, *In Rom.*, l. 1 (PL, CXI, 1319-20).

429. "gens perfida": Ps.-Cyprian, *Ad Vigil.* (Hartel, 127). Bede, *Sup. Cant. Hab.* (PL, XCI, 1252 D). Martin of Leon (CCVIII, 119 D, 246 C, 339 BC, 870 D). *Altercatio* (RMAL, 10, 115). Ps.-Cyprian: "perfidus populus" (H., 120, 123, 124).

430. "perfida et incredula": Quiricius, *Ep. ad Ildef.*, n. 1: "unbelieving and faithless in mind" — "incredulus ac mente perfidus" (PL, XCVI, 193 C). Godfrey of Admont (CLXXIV, 281 C).

431. "Perfida Judaea": Bede, *In Marc.* (XCII, 166 D).

432. "perfida plebs": Greg. (LXXVI, 541 B). Alcuin, *In Ap.* (C, 1132 C).

433. "perfidus Judaeorum populus": Autpert, *In Ap.* (412 D). Hervaeus (PL, CLXXXI, 95 C); etc.

434. "perfida Synagoga": Maximus of Turin, *s.* 94 (LVII, 721 B). Rupert (CLXIX, 1176 A). Godfrey of Admont: "The Synagogue, worthy of the title faithlessness" — "Synagoga, merito perfidiae" (CLXXIV, 34 B). Irimbert, *In Jud.* (Pez, 4, 205, 288).

435. Bede (PL, XCII, 172 A, 433 C). *L. carol.* (XCVIII, 1060 D, 1061 AB). Rabanus (CIX, 679 D). Bruno of Würzburg (CXLII, 67 C). Rupert (CLXX, 69 D). Bruno of Segni, *In Is.* (*Sp. ca.*, 3, 174). Godfrey of Admont (PL, CLXXIV, 268 D, 327 C). Hervaeus (CLXXXI, 572 A). John of Salisbury, *ep.* 150 (CXCIX, 144 D). Garnier, *s.* 11 (CCV, 636 C). Herbert Losinga (2, 122); etc.

436. Rabanus (PL, CX, 534 A; CXI, 1320 C).

437. Greg., *In Ez.*, l. 1, h. 7; n. 13 (LXXVI, 847 A).

438. Greg., *Mor.* (LXXVI, 499 D); *In Ez.* (1066 B); *In I Reg.* (LXXIX, 108 C). Bede (XCI, 686 B). Sed. Scot., *In Rom.* (CIII, 53 A). Hincmar citing "Gelasius" (CXXV,

394 C, 497 C); etc. Ambrose, *De Sp. sancto*, l. 2, n. 46: "from the variety of the Latin manuscripts, some of which the faithless have falsified" — "de latinorum codicum varietate, quorum aliquos perfidi falsverunt" (XVI, 752 B).

439. "Dominum a perfidis occidendum": *De laud. s. crucis*, v. 41-3 (CVII, 291 C).

440. Ecce Deus noster Christus ex aethere floret . . .
    Perfida discedat turba fuscata dolore.

In crucis laudem, v. 41-2 (*P. lat. aevi car.*, 3, 138).

441. Ingressus aulam nobilem
    Flagris rejecit perfidos
    Orationis aedibus.

P. Gall-Morel, 20.

442. "And when the cleric could not hold firm against the faithless fellow's windiness" — "Cumque clericus perfidi illius resistere ventositati non posset" (PL, CLVI, 528 A).

443. "perfidiae argumenta contra fidem": Richard, *De Emm.*, l. 1, c. 7 (CXCVI, 613 D).

444. Bede, *In Luc.* (XCII, 542 D). Smaragdus (CII, 454 A). Hincmar (CXXV, 414 AB).

445. Geoffrey, *Ep.*, l. 5, 16: "Those four sins, namely, pagan error, brotherly schism, heretical crookedness, and Jewish faithlessness" — "Illa utique quatuor peccata, error vid. gentilis, schisma fraternum, haeretica pravitas et Judaica perfidia" (CLVII, 199 C). Agobard, *De jud. superst.*, c. 9 (CIV, 86 C). Cf. *Glossa* (CXIII, 615 B, 1212 A).

446. "diaboli corpus": Alcuin, *In Ap.*, l. 4 (C, 1125 D, 1136 D).

447. Cf. Aimon, *In Ap.*, l. 7 (CXVII, 1199 D).

448. "Omnis autem infidelis, aut gentilis, aut Judaeus, aut haereticus est. Primus, oblatam fidei salutem per stultitiam audire et agnoscere contemnit. Secundus autem agnoscit quidem, et de Scripturis suis intelligit, sed in Christi contemptum per invidiam repellit. Tertius et agnoscit et suscipit, sed ab illa jam suscepta se postmodum per superbiam abrumpit. Primus ergo improbus est et ingratus; secundus invidus et obstinatus; tertius, perfidus et elatus": Guntherus, *De orat. et jej.*, l. 2, c. 1 (CCXII, 116 BC). Cf. Rupert, *In Ex.* (CLXVII, 579 D); *In ev.* (1539 D).

449. Bede, *In Tob.*: "he who would redeem both the Jewish people from the darkness of faithlessness and paganism from the slavery of idolatry" — "qui et populum Judaicum a tenebris perfidiae et gentilitatem idololatriae servitute redimeret" (XCI, 926 D).

450. Paulinus: "(The) uninjured (Church) is being shaken . . . by the hostile winds of heretics, the violent storms of the faithless" — "adversis haereticorum flatibus, violentis perfidorum procellis . . . , illaesa concutitur (Ecclesia)" (XCIX, 154 A).

451. Ps.-Alcuin, *Div. off.*, c. 56, on the Nicene creed: "for it tramples down all the blasphemies of error, of impieties, and of faithlessness" — "omnes enim erroris, impietatum, perfidaeque blasphemias calcat" (CI, 1284 C).

Notes to Page 123

452. "Omnis perfidia, et mundana sapientia, vel philosophia, fide Trinitatis vincitur": *Glossa in Ex.* (According to Walafrid Strabo: PL, CXIII, 207).

453. "perfidia judaica"; "judaicae superstitionis perfidia": Martin of Leon, *s.* 4 *in nat.*, c. 5 (CCVIII, 135 D).

454. Cassiodorus, *In Ps.*: "The Jews, however, have by no means brought the building of their faith to perfection" — "Judaei vero fidei suae fabricam minime perfecerunt" (LXX, 832 B).

455. John Scotus, *In Jo.*, fr. 2: "He has abandoned the carnal and faithless Jews . . . unwilling to accede to the spirit of the letter, which is Christ" — "Reliquit carnales perfidosque Judaeos . . . ad spiritum litterae, qui est Christus, accedere nolentes" (CXXII, 331 B). Rabanus, *In Esther:* "They reject understanding the Law of God spiritually through the grace of the sevenformed grace of the Holy Spirit, a grace full of spiritual dogma and perfect" — "Legem Dei per septiformem Spiritus sancti gratiam, spirituali dogmate plenam atque perfectam, spiritualiter intelligere respuunt" (CIX, 667 A). *Adv. Jud.* (Anon., 12th cent.), n. 6 and 9 (CCXIII, 753 D, 756 A). Garnier, *s.* 11: the "perfidi" find the "intelligentiae rationem" in the Lord (CCV, 636 C).

456. "ex fide in fidem"; "ex fide veteris Testamenti in fidem novi Testamenti"; "ex fide verborum et spei in fidem rerum et speciei": Martin of Leon, *s.* 4 *in nat.*, c. 29 (CCVIII, 410 BD).

457. "a fide in perfidiam": Paschasius, *In Lam.* (CXX, 1197 C).

458. Alcuin, *In Ap.* (C, 1103 D). Cf. Martin of Leon (CCVIII, 135).

459. Cf. Maximus the Arian, *C. Judaeos:* "Would that you had the odor of the faith of Abraham and not of your own faithlessness" — "Utinam haberetis odorem fidei Abrahae et non perfidiae vestrae" (LVII, 797 B).

460. Rabanus, *In Matt.* (CVII, 771 B).

461. "majorum nobilitas ex fide": *Alterc.* (10th cent., Blum., RMAL, 10, 56).

462. Greg., *Mor.*, l. 14, c. 47, n. 55: "Though the very ones who seemed to be doctors of the Law, who used to assert that he was to be incarnated along with the prophetic words, have seen the incarnate one and yet have been separated from him by the interruption of their faithlessness" — "Cum ipsi quoque qui legis doctores esse videbantur, qui cum verbis propheticis incarnandum esse perhibebant, et incarnatum viderunt, et ab eo tamen perfidiae interruptione divisi sunt" (PL, LXXV, 1067 B).

463. Paschasius, *In Matt.*, l. 5, c. 9: "Having been turned to Christ, . . . she is being made whole; but soon she dies by the languor of her faithlessness" — "Illa . . . conversa sanatur ad Christum; illa mox perfidiae suae languore moritur" (CXX, 382 C).

464. Greg.: "cold with the torpor of faithlessness" — "perfidiae torpore frigidi" (LXXVI, 508 C, 509 B). Rabanus, *In Ez.* (CX, 953 A). Hervaeus, *In Rom.* (CLXXXI, 760 A).

465. Autpert, *S. de lect. ev.*, n. 10: "In the disciples having fallen in the sleep of faithlessness" — "In discipulis somno perfidiae lapsis" (LXXIX, 1300 B).

466. Ps.-Bede, *In Jo.*: "the extraordinary insanity of faithlessness" — "mira perfidorum dementia" (XCII, 692 D).

467. Rupert, *Div. off.*, l. 6, c. 27: at Easter, "once the frost of faithlessness has been driven away, . . . the world flowers again with the beauty of the faith" —

"pulso perfidiae gelu . . . , fidei pulchritudine refloruit mundus" (CLXX, 170 C). Cf. Greg., *Mor.* (LXXVI, 508 B). Godfrey of Admont (CLXXIV, 54 B); etc.

468. Or., *In Gen.*, h. 15, n. 7 (135). Ambrose (PL, XVI, 1389 C). Leo, *s.* 29 (LIV, 228 C). Greg. (LXXV, 585 D): "the night of their faithlessness" — "noctem suae perfidiae" (863 C); "in the blindness of their faithlessness" — "in perfidiae suae caecitate" (LXXIX, 146 B). Julian of Toledo: "Seized by the blind night of unfaithfulness, they fell in a pit of detestable faithlessness" — "Caeca infidelitatis nocte possessi, barathro detestabilis perfidiae concidunt" (XCVI, 540 D; cf. 548 B). Rupert, *De vict. Verbi:* "the clouds, i.e., the blindness of the Jews" — "nubes, sc. caecitas Judaeorum" (CLXIX, 1438 D). Anselm of Laon: "blinded by faithlessness" — "caecati perfidia" (CLXII, 1478 A). Peter the Venerable, *C. Judaeos*, c. 4: "O pitiable deafness of the faithless! O abominable blindness of the impious" — "O miseranda perfidorum surditas! O detestanda impiorum caecitas!" (CLXXXIX, 566 B). Martin of Leon (CCVIII, 43 D, 115 A). Hymn for the feast of the three kings (G. M. Dreves, *Hymni ined. m. aevi*, 4, 17):

> Magi et reges inclyti
> Noctem pellunt perfidiae.
> The celebrated Magi and kings
> Drive away the night of faithlessness.

469. Greg. (PL, LXXVI, 65 A, 764 A). Honorius, *Sp. Eccl.:* "Jews hard in faithlessness" — "Judaeos in perfidia duros" (CLXXII, 853 A). Martin of Leon (CCVIII, 805 D). Cf. Joachim of Flora writing "against the age-old hardness of the Jews" — "contra vetustissimam duritiam Judaeorum" (Miquel Batllori, *Anal. sacra Tarrac.*, 28, 1955, 11). Helinand, *s.* 4 (212, 513 A). Not every hardened unfaithfulness is Jewish: William of St. Thierry, *Spec. fidei*, c. 2 (Déchanet, 68).

470. Chromatius, *In Matt.*, tr. 17 (CCL, 9, 440). Rabanus, *In Jer.*, l. 7: "He appeared manifestly in the flesh and yet Judea, crushed under the darkness of its faithlessness, did not know him" — "Manifestus in carne apparuit et tamen hunc pressa perfidiae suae tenebris Judaea minime cognovit" (PL, CXI, 928 A); etc.

471. "obstinata perfidia": Greg. (LXXVI, 506 C, 508 C; LXXIX, 154 D). Avitius, *Ep. ad div.*, 42: "those who, even though frequently warned, persist in the obstinacy of faithlessness" — "qui et moniti totiens, in perfidiae obstinatione persistunt" (MGH, *A. ant.*, 6, 72). Autpert, *In Ap.*, l. 3 (457 C). John of Salisbury, *Polycr.*, l. 2, c. 4: "to blunt the obstinate faithlessness of the Jews" — "ad retundendam obstinatam Judaeorum perfidiam" (CCXCIX, 418 D). Cf. *L. carol.*, 1, c. 26 (XCVIII, 1059-60). Alvarus, *ep.* 18 (Madoz, 242). *Or.* 252: "perdurantes in perfidia."

472. "diuturna obcaecatio"; "mortifera obstinatio"; "mortiferae obstinationis perfidia": Martin of Leon (PL, CCVIII, 122 C, 335 BC, 338 D, 352 C, 1341 CD).

473. "primordia fidei": Greg., *Mor.*, l. 4, c. 4: "at the coming of the Redeemer, for the most part remaining in faithlessness, they were unwilling to follow the basic elements of the faith" — "in redemptoris adventu, ex maxima parte in perfidia remanentes, primordia fidei sequi noluerunt" (LXXV, 636 C).

474. "Quasi obliti sunt quem prophetaverunt, dum eum et incarnandum verbis Legis canerent, et incarnatum verbis perfidiae negarent": Greg., *Mor.*, l. 14, c. 39, n. 47 (LXXV, 1064 BC). John Scotus, *In Jo.*, fr. 1: "His own did not accept him:

Notes to Page 124

this was said of the faithless Jews and all the impious who did not want to accept the Word of God, i.e., willed neither to believe in it nor to understand it" — "Sui eum non receperunt; hoc dictum est de perfidis Judaeis et omnibus impiis, qui noluerunt Dei Verbum recipere, hoc est, neque in eum credere neque eum intelligere voluerunt" (CXXII, 297 A).

475. "Adamantina perfidia!": s. 4 in nat., c. 5 (CCVIII, 138 A); s. in festo Trin. (1343 D).

476. Martin of Leon, s. 4 in nat., c. 28: "O rebelles et perfidi" (404 B).

477. "Judaei apostatae": Hervaeus (CLXXXI, 179 A).

478. Hermann of Cologne, De sua convers., c. 14: "for they took me as faithless and an apostate" — "tu sc. me tanquam perfidum et apostatam comprehenderunt" (CLXX, 827 B).

479. "Apostatica perfidia": Julian of Toledo, Insultatio vili storici, c. 2 (MGH, S. rer. merov., 5, 526). Albert of St. Symphorian, De div. temp., l. 2, c. 22-4 (MGH, Scr., 4, 720-3).

480. "angelus apostata"; "perfidus apostaticusque angelus fidelem Dei famulum insectatur": Quodvultdeus, De prom. (LI, 750 C). Cf. John of Salisbury, Polycr., l. 7, c. 21 (CXCIX, 692 B). Angelome (CXV, 374 B). L. moz. sacr. (447, 449). Gregory V (H. des Gaules, 10, 430).

481. "in perfidiae culpam ruit": Berno, De varia, c. 13 (CXLII, 1154 D).

482. "perfidiae substratus, idolis construere templum non timuit"; "assidua carnis petulantia"; "mentis perfidiae": Greg., Mor., l. 12, c. 18, n. 23 (LXXV, 998 BC).

483. Othloh: "they will have fallen into such great blindness or faithlessness" — "in tantam caecitatem vel perfidiam inciderint" (CXLVI, 94 A).

484. "Judaicus populus ad perfidiam declinavit": Greg., Mor. (LXXVI, 166 C).

485. Richard, In Joel (CLXXV, 339 C). Joachim of Flora, Sup. Ev.: "who have suffered shipwreck concerning the faith from whence they ought to have advanced in spiritual doctrine" — "qui, unde debuerunt proficere in spiritali doctrina, inde naufragaverunt circa fidem" (B., 324).

486. Ep., 74, c. 8: "Let the Church yield to heretics, light to darkness, faith to faithlessness" — "Cedat Ecclesia haereticis, lux tenebris, fides perfidiae" (Bayard, 285). Other texts in Peterson, loc. cit.

487. "doloris vel mortis metu, vel sua perfidia, caeleste sacramentum deseruer(unt)": Div. inst., l. 5, c. 9 (PL, VI, 577 A).

488. "in perfidiae foveam": Apol. David, c. 2, n. 8 (XIV, 855 A).

489. "perfidi"; "lapsi"; "increduli": Cyprian, De lapsis, c. 1: "which, though difficult, would seem impossible to those who were recently unbelievers and faithless" — "quod difficile nuper incredulis ac perfidis impossibile videbatur" (4, 465 B). Cf. Glossa, In Eccli., XXII, 17 (CXIII, 1206 C).

490. Cf. Hugh of Barzelle: "of the perverted, not the converted" — "perversorum, non conversorum" (J. Morson, St. ans., 41, 129).

491. "casum perfidiae flevit amare": Beatus, In Ap., l. 3, c. 4 (255).

492. "Repelle a me tenebras totius iniquitatis et perfidiae": Libellus turonensis; and to the Trinity: "to divest me from the night of faithlessness and error" — "me exutum nocte perfidiae et erroris, etc." (Wilmart, Precum libellis aevi karol., 1940, 139).

493. "Abstollas cor meum de perfidis cogitationibus"; "Custodi, Domine, in me immaculatam fidem": PL, CXLVI, 973 C, 978 A.

494. *L. de laude fidei:* "ut neque spiritus perfidiae inveniat illic introitum" (*Op. in.*, 1, 174).

495. *Liber visionum* (PL, CXLVI, 353 D).

496. *Ad viros rel.*, s. 8: "si vel a fidei regula exorbites per errorem perfidiae" (Petit, 194). Cf. Or., *In Cant.*, l. 3: "So at first all heretics come to credulity, and after this they turn aside from the path of the faith" — "Omnes ergo haeretici primo ad credulitatem veniunt, et post hoc ab itinere fidei declinant" (179).

497. "perfidiae periculum incurrere": *De Emm.*, l. 1, c. 7 (PL, CXCVI, 614 A).

498. "perfidia": *Metal.*, l. 4, c. 34 (Webb, 202).

499. "discipuli Christi perfidi": John of Sal., *Polycr.*, l. 7, c. 2 (PL, CXCIX, 692 B).

500. Othloh: "perjurors may deserve to be burned" — "Quanta perjuri poena mereantur aduri" (CXLVI, 368 A; the Jews are not under consideration here). Quodvultdeus, *De prom.*: "so every foreswearing heretic" — "omnis itaque haereticus perjurans" (LI, 762 A).

501. "Judaei veteres, sperando futurum Christum redemptorem, christiani erant, . . . igitur apostatae habeantur necesse est, qui, dum Christum non recipiunt, rei sunt violatae legis": Ambrosiaster, *In Rom.*, IX (XVII, 137 C, 139 D).

502. "per apostaticae perfidiae sacrilegium": Peter Damian, *op.* 45, c. 8, on Jerome: "Devotatur ille hac se prorsus ultione plectendum, si saeculares libros ulterius legeret, ac si Christus per apostaticae perfidiae sacrilegium denegaret" (CXLV, 703). Honorius, *In ps.* i: "'Blessed is the man who walks not in the sight of the impious', i.e., has not apostasized from God in any faithlessness by the counsel of demons or impious men" — "Beatus vir qui non abiit in conspectu impiorum, id est in nulla perfidia a Deo apostatavit consilio daemonum vel hominum impiorum" (CLXXII, 279 B).

503. "ab omni fidei virtute": Robert of Tombelaine, *Sup. Cant.* (LXXIX, 542 B). Sulp. Sev., *Chron.*, l. 1, c. 27: "Having again turned back to idols, the Israelites . . . have paid the penalty for faithlessness" — "Rursus Israeliticae ad idola conversi . . . paenas perfidiae pependerunt" (Halm, 30).

504. "Fratres sunt Judaeorum, quibus perfidiae germanitate nectuntur": *In Luc.*, l. 8, c. 13 (SC, 52, 106).

505. "pro fide perfidi in praedicando": *In Matt.*, tr. 5, c. 4, n. 2 (CCL, 9, 407). Cf. Joachim of Flora, *Concordia*, l. 4, c. 26 (f. 54, 3-4).

506. "apostatae ac perfidi": *De lapsis*, c. 33 (Hartel, 1, 261).

507. "Primam fidem vestra perfidia posteriore mutastis": *Adv. Novat.*, c. 8 (Hartel, 3, 59).

508. "Effectus apostata de fide catholica, in arianam dictus est transiisse perfidiam": PL, LI, 879 C.

509. "sic veterum defendere perfidiam, ut perdant fidem suam": *ep.* 119, c. 11 (6, 119).

510. "Non sensui apostolico suum subdit, sed secundum propriam pravitatem suo perfido sensu molitus est corrumpere apostolicum sermonem": *C. Fel.* (PL, XCIX, 451 C). Alcuin, *Adv. Fel.*, l. 1, c. 13: "Who is so contentious and so faithless so as not to believe the testimony of God the Father about his own Son?"

Notes to Pages 126-27

— "Quis est tam contentiosus et tam perfidus, qui testimonio Dei Patris non credat de Filio suo?" (CI, 138 B); *Adv. Elip.* (234 B, 236 A).

511. "Solitam fidei tuae perfidiam horruimus": *ep.* 18 (ca. 840; Madoz, 241).

512. Jerome, *In Jer.*, l. 5: "one of whom shows the sweetness of right faith, and the other the bitterness of the faithlessness of heretics" — "quorum alter rectae fidei dulcedinem, alter haereticorum perfidiae amaritudinem demonstrabit" (PL, XXIV, 829 D).

513. Martin of Leon, *In Ap.* (CCIX, 348 B).

514. "Haeretici . . . conceptam novi erroris perfidiam pertinaci pravitate defendunt": Isidore, *De haeres.* (Vega, 25).

515. "ex fide perfidi": Cf. Optatus, *De schismate Donat.*, l. 6, c. 8 (155).

516. "ficta dogmata quasi veritatis velamine operientes, in noctis perfidia obstinato et obturato corde persistunt": Jerome, *In Job* (PL, XXVI, 735 B).

517. "perfidus"; "malefidus": Abbo of Fleury, *ep.* 3: "it often has happened that the purity of the integral faith wavers with the opinion of the interpreter of ill faith" — "saepius contigit ut puritas integrae veritatis sententia vacillet malefidi interpretis" (*Rec. des hist.*, 60, 435).

518. "Judaeorum et haereticorum perfidia": Guibert of Nogent, *De vita sua*, l. 3, c. 16 (CLXVI, 949-50). Angelome (CXV, 397-8). Bruno of Segni (CLXV, 72 B); etc. Mohammed's "perfidia": Ps.-Hildebert, *De Mahumete* (CLXXI, 1345-8).

519. "haeretici"; "Quamdiu Synagoga carnali legis observantiae inhaeret, lepra haereticae pravitatis ei adhaeret": Irimbert, *In Jud.*, l. 2 (Pez, 4, 396). Gregory of Tours, *Hist. Franc.*, l. 8, c. 1, the words of Clotarius (LXXI, 449 B).

520. "usque ad Judaicam perfidiam erupit": John the Deacon, *S. Greg. vita*, l. 3, c. 53 (LXXV, 163 B).

521. *adversus quinque haereses:* PL, XLII, 1101-16.

522. Paschasius, *V. s. Adalhardi*, n. 1 (PL, CXX, 1508 D). Ambrose, *In Luc.*, l. 10, c. 65 (SC, 52, 178). *Consult. Zacch. et Apoll.*, c. 3, n. 8: "the devotion of the faithful . . . and the faithlessness of the impious" — "devotio fidelium et perfidia . . . impiorum" (Morin, 113). Cf. *Sap.*, ii, 1.

523. Peter Damian, *op.* 2, allowing himself to be carried away by rhetoric (PL, CXLV, 41 A, 53 B, 56 A, 57 A).

524. Bruno of Segni, *In Is.:* "Extremely amazing is the miracle that the scribes and Pharisees, having the key to knowledge, meditating upon the sacred Scriptures from their very cradles, do not find the Christ so openly prophesied within them, who so manifestly occurs to us whenever we read them" — "Valde stupendum est miraculum, quod Scribae et Pharisaeai scientiae clavem habentes, et ab ipsis cunabulis sacras Scripturas meditantes, Christum tam aperte in eis prophetatum non inveniunt, qui nobis utique legentibus tam manifestus occurit" (*Sp. cas.*, 3, 85). Martin of Leon (PL, CCVIII, 352 B).

525. Greg., *Moral.;* in Garnier, *Gregor.*, l. 2, c. 1: "Whose paths the faithless people of the Jews did not know, since they were unwilling to consider the ways of his humility by which he lifted us on high" — "Cujus semitas perfidus Judaeorum populus ignoravit, quia humilitatis ejus vias quibus nos ad alta sublevavit considerare noluit" (CXCIII, 66 D).

526. "perfidiae promptior": Ambrose, *ep.* 74, n. 3 (XVI, 1255 A).

527. Aimo, *In Ap.*, iv, 13: The "beast rising from the sea" = "from the deep

faithlessness of the Jews" — "Bestia ascendens de mare" = "de profunda perfidia Judaeorum" (CXVII, 1092 C).

528. *Glossa in Deut.*, xxxi, 30: "Israelitis largitori Deo ingratis exprobrat perfidiam" (CXIII, 487 D).

529. Hugh of Fleury: "the faithlessness of the reprobate . . . does not will to believe" — "perfidia reproborum . . . non vult credere" (CLXIII, 824 A). Cf. Greg., *In ev.*, h. 40, n. 2 (LXXVI, 1304 BC).

530. "de observantia legis tumentes, spiritalem legem spiritualiter intelligere noluerunt": Autpert, *In Ap.*, 1. 7 (586 D).

531. "superbae Hebraeorum mentes, in perfidia remanentes": Richard, *L. except.*, P. 2, l. 6, c. 14 (J. Châtillon, 302-3).

532. William of Newburgh (*Chronicles* . . . , R. Howlett, 2, 1885, 466).

533. "Pontifex annulum portat quoniam Scripturae mysteria et Ecclesiae sacramenta perfidis sigillare debet et humilibus revelare": *Mitr.*, l. 2, c. 5 (PL, CCXII, 79 B). Paul of Santa Maria, *Addit. ad Postillas Nicol. de Lira:* "I began . . . to inquire into the truth no longer faithlessly but humbly" — "Caepi . . . jam non perfide sed humiliter veritatem inquirere" (CXIII, 35 B).

534. Perfidum colla tibi flectentur jure superbi
  Mens humilis sub[j]et perfida colla tibi.
Lotharii versus (P. lat. aevi kar., 3, 235).

535. *Superba illa Synagoga* . . . : Godfrey of Admont, *In Script. s.* 5 (PL, CLXXIV, 1079 A); h. 6 (1082 D). Joachim of Flora, *Sup. 4 ev.:* "the pride of that people remaining in the faithlessness of their incredulity" — "superbia illius populi manentis in perfidia incredulitatis suae" (304). Greg., *Mor.*, l. 4, c. 4: "By the 'mountains of Gilboa' are signified the proud hearts of the Jews" — "Per Gelboae montes superba Judaeorum corda signantur" (LXXV, 636 B; cf. LXXVI, 4514 B, 1304 B).

536. "perfidia Judaeorum"; "judaicae fraudis obstinacia": *C. perf. Jud.*, c. 1 (CCVII, 827 D).

537. "vanitas omnes vanitates excellens"; "dolus omnibus dolis tenacior": l. 1, c. 26 (XCVIII, 1060 B).

538. "imperitia": Blum., RMAL, 10, 73, 84, 93-5. Cf. Greg., *In ev.*, h. 21, n. 6: "Therefore all the arguments of faithlessness have been done away with" — "Ablata ergo sunt omnia argumenta perfidiae" (PL, LXXVI, 1172 D). Again, Petrus Gallatinus, *Opus de arcanis cath. veritatis* (1550), 1: "to defeat the faithlessness of the Jews through their Talmudic writings" — "ad Judaeorum perfidiam per Talmudicas eorum scripturas convincendam."

539. "ex vitio propriae voluntatis": Ps.-Hugh, *In Rom.*, q. 264 (CLXXV, 496 D). Martin of Leon, *s.* 4 *in nat.*, c. 23 (CCVIII, 329 A).

540. Bede, *In Cant.:* "The Synagogue, because of the fault of faithlessness" — "Synagoga, ob culpam perfidiae" (XCI, 1187 B).

541. [correcting de Lubac] Petrus Chrysologus, *Sermo* 84 (PL, LII, 437 A).

542. Aug., *In ps.* liv, n. 10 (CCL, 39, 664).

543. Cf. Cyprian, *ep.* 73, c. 14: "perfidios et blasphemos" (Bayard, 271). Chromatius, *In Matt.*, tr. 9 (CCL, 9, 418). Maximus of Turin, *h.* 87: "perfidia et blasphemia" (PL, LVII, 451 D).

544. "ministri perfidiae"; "ministri mortis": Paschasius, *In Matt.*, l. 12, c. 28 (CXX, 980 D).

545. The remark is from B. Blumenkranz, REJ, 1948-9, 66.

546. *Hist. Gothorum,* on King Sisebut (†621): "At the beginning of his reign, moving the Jews to the Christian faith, he had zeal, but did not employ it with knowledge: for by force he compelled those whom he ought to have called to the faith by reason" — "In initio regni Judaeos ad fidem christianam permovens, aemulationem quidem habuit, sed non secundum scientiam: potestate enim compulit, quos provocare fidei ratione oportuit" (MGH, *Chr. min.*, 2, 291).

547. "perfidia"; "caecitas": S. Graysel, *The Church and the Jew,* 92-6.

548. Guibert of Nogent, *De vita sua,* l. 3, c. 16: "He presented himself so humbly that we scarcely thought him faithless" — "Tam humilem se praebebat ut vix perfidum putaremus" (PL, CLVI, 950 A).

549. Sidonius Apoll., *Ep.*, l. 6, 11 (LVIII, 559-60); to the functionary Felix, to recommend to him Gozolas the Jew (ca. 480). Cf. his recommendation for a converted Jew: l. 8, 13 (611 BC).

550. *Adv. Jud.*, c. 15: "nor let us proudly boast against the broken branches" — "nec superbe gloriemur adversus ramos fractos" (XLII, 63). Gerhoh, *In ps.* xxxvi (V. den Eynde, 470).

551. V. G., 74.

552. *In ps.* xliii: "Electae sunt gentium nationes ut destruatur perfidia Judaeorum" (PL, XIV, 1104 C).

553. "intelligentiae rationem": Garnier, *s.* 11 (CCV, 626 C).

554. "Si ergo vis ad plenum deprehendere et exterminare versutias ejus, *bibliotheca spiritus* in medio proponatur, ut ei fugere aut tergiversari non liceat, sed ut Goliath ense proprio juguletur": Peter of Blois, *C. perf. Jud.*, concl. (CCVII, 870 D). Isidore, *De fide cath.:* "To refute faithlessness, we have gathered a few passages from the Old Testament" — "Ad ... refellendam perfidiam quaedam ex V.T. aggregavimus testimonia" (LXXXIII, 450 B); *Hist. Goth.,* on Sisebut (MGH, *Chr. min.*, 2, 291), etc. Anon., *Tr. adv. Jud.* (see above, note 322).

555. "saxeis ictibus perfidorum"; "ad lapidem pretiosum, Christum Dominum": *L. moz. sacram.* (558).

556. "Verbi tui potentia Judaicam destruens constanti voce perfidiam": Feltoe (1896), 88. Martin of Leon, *in nat.*, c. 3: "To overcome your faithlessness we shall introduce other witnesses from your own tribe" — "Ad vestram perfidiam superandam alios ex gente vestra testes introducemus" (PL, CCVIII, 115 A; cf. 115 D).

557. Sed editis miraculis
    currit et docet Petrus,
    Falsum profari perfidos,
    Joele teste, comprobans.

Preceding strophe: "Judea being incredulous at that time" — "Judaea tunc incredula."

558. "Horresce Judaicam perfidiam, respue Hebraicam superstitionem": *Rituale romanum,* ordo baptismi adultorum.

559. "Perfruantur caeci corde lucem, Hebraei catholicam fidem": *L. moz. sacr.* (114).

560. "et pro perfidis Judaeis"; "ut ad Christum redeat infidelitas perfidorum": *Sacr. gelas.*, n. 41 (Wilson, 77). *Sacr. greg.* (PL, LXXVIII, 80). P. Bruylants, *Les oraisons du missel romain*, 2, 220. Cf. Robert Anchel, "La prière 'Pro Judaeis,'" *l'Univers israélite*, 21-28 août 1936, 741-2. *Missale mixtum* (PL, LXXV, 588 A). *L. moz. sacr.*, Mass of St. Vincent: "By your intercession let the blind of heart enjoy the light of faith; the Hebrews, the Catholic faith" — "Tuo suffragio perfruantur caeci corde fidei lucem, Hebraei catholicam fidem" (n. 77; Férotin, 41).

561. "la haine atroce des Juifs": Thus Alexandre Hérenger, "Renan et les Juifs," *Rev. juive de Genève*, cited by R. Anchel.

562. *Sacram. de S. Vast de Corbie:* "No one of ours ought to bend his body now, owing to the offense along with the fury of the people" — "Hic nostrum nullus debet modo flectere corpus, ob populi noxam ac pariter rabiem." Cf. H. Nitzer, *L'introd. de la messe romaine en Fr. sous le Carolingiens* (1910), 257.

563. Louis Canet, "Diverses pratiques populaires anti-juive le vendredi saint," REJ, 61 (1911), 213-21, thinks that the clergy and the Christian people were involved in the 9th century, an explanation rejected by G. Morin but kept by H. Leclercq; discussed by J. M. Oesterreicher, "Pro perfidis Judaeis," *Theol. St.*, 8 (1947), 80-96 (Tr. fr., *Cahiers sioniens*, 1947, 85-101).

564. Cf. Oesterreicher, 80: "The Liturgy does not pass moral judgments, nor would it label the Jews 'treacherous' or 'wicked'. In saying *perfidia Judaica*, the Church mourns Israel's disbelief in Christ, holding that from Abraham's children, least of all, would one expect such refusal of faith." R. Anchel, accepting Canet's explanation, did not conclude from it anything against the words of the liturgy: "The Christian people did not delay manifesting an extreme repugnance to pray for the Jews. It did not allow one to kneel for them. The Church was therefore led, in order to restrict popular irritation, to pass over the prayer *For the Jews* as quickly as possible. She suppressed the invitation to kneel and the silent meditation during which minds, far from rising to charitable thoughts, would have merely been incited to violence. Today, and from the end of the 16th century, one passes without transition from the instruction to the summary recited by the officiator" — "Le peuple chrétien ne tarda pas à manifester une extrême répugnance à prier pour les Juifs. Il ne permettait pas qu'on se mît à genoux pour eux. L'Église fut donc amenée, pour ménager l'irritation populaire, à passer le plus vite possible sur l'oraison *Pro Judais*. Elle supprima l'invitation à s'agenouiller et la méditation silencieuse pendant laquelle les esprits, loin de s'élever à pensées charitables, n'auraient fait que s'exciter à la violence. Aujourd'hui et depuis la fin du xvie siècle, on passe sans transition de la monition au résumé récité par l'officant."

565. "un contenu théologique péjoratif"; "sonne comme un outrage"; "l'Église catholique n'a jamais admis dans ses prières aucun mot injurieux ou désobligeant pour les Juifs": R. Anchel, *loc. cit.*

566. "Genu flectebant . . . , illudendo hoc faciebant; nos, ad demonstrandum quod fugere debeamus opera quae simulando fiunt, vitamus genu flectionem in oratione pro Judaeis": *Liber officialis*, l. 1, c. 13, n. 17 (J. H. Hanssens, 2, 98). Histori-

cal explanation of the same kind regarding the Gospel in the *De ordine romano*, c. 16 (3, 245).

567. "(Tunc) debemus mentis humilitatem per genuum flexionem ostendere. . . . In sola oratione de camino ignis non flectimus genua, quando Nabuchodonosor compellebat populum adorare statuam quam fecerat, ut separata sit nostra oratio, quae est ad unum Deum, ab errore gentium."
"Similem ob causam etiam in Parasceve genua non flectimus pro perfidis Judaeis, qui illudendo genua flectebant coram Deo, ne videamur illos imitari qui opus bonum studebant male operari; quemadmodum tunc ab osculo abstinemus, propter Judae traditoris exemplum, qui per simulatae pacis osculum tradidit Dominum Jesum": *De off. missae*, c. 7 (142, 1078-9). *Dial. de jejuniis* 4 *temp.*, c. 7 (1096 CD). E. Peterson, *loc. cit.* (1936), reconnects this interpretation: the "people" of the text of St. Vastus would be the Jewish people on the day of the Passion. The same goes for Jules Isaac, *Genèse de l'antisémitisme* (1956), 298-305.

568. "Quando oratio datur pro Judaeis, non debent flecti genua. Nam, quia Judaei die hac Dominum irridendo genua flectebant, Ecclesia, illorum perhorrescens facinus, non flectit genua in orando pro ipsis": M. Andrieu, *Le Pontifical romain au moyen âge*, 1 (1938), 235.

569. "non flectit genua in orando pro ipsis"; "genua pro ipsis non flectat": *ib.*, 2, 558-9. An analogous indication, 561: "In some churches, however, today pure wine is offered, so that the cruelty of the Jews may be represented and the harshness of Christ's passion" — "In quibusdam vero ecclesiis purum hodie sine aqua vinum offertur, ut in puro et forti vino crudelitas Judaeorum repraesentetur et asperitas passionis Christi."

570. "la prière pour les Juifs conserve son accent primitif, sans être chargé d'intention polémique"; "une prière qui, à ses débuts, avait été l'expression d'une sollicitude touchante de l'âme religieuse, pleurant le sort de ceux qui n'avaient pas encore la lumière dont elle seule croyait jouir, était devenue une mesquine manifestation de dépit à l'égard de ceux qui restaient insensibles à toutes les invites": *Juifs et chrétiens*, 92, note 109, and 90-1. It is possible, however, that if the omission of the genuflection had been rather more ancient, it would be explained more naturally; Amalarius (or someone else already prior to him) would, after the event, have imagined his explanation of a fact which was surprising as an anomaly because its origin would have been lost from view. This is what Mr. Blumenkranz suggests, following Erik Peterson: "Perhaps that suppression dates from a period when the prayer for the Jews was found at the end of the series of three prayers (pagans, heretics, and Jews) and at that time was quite normal" — "Peut-être que cette suppression date d'une époque où la prière pour les Juifs se trouvait à la fin de la série des trois prières (païens, hérétiques et Juifs) et n'était alors que normale" (92). Even if the imagined explanation for the rite did denote some ill will, the content and spirit of the liturgical prayer are not at all affected by it.

571. Some rather recent theologians, however, have been disposed to understand the expression in an odious sense and to want to justify it in that sense. To cut short every wicked interpretation, wherever it might come from, a decision of the Congregation of Rites suppressed the word "perfidis" in 1959.

572. "il est peut-être . . . le plus logique et le mieux réussi de tous les anciens essais tentés pour présenter le Christ aux Juifs": *Adversus Judaeos* (1935), 217.

573. Some have seen in the fact that Alcuin encouraged the translation of this treatise into Old German a sign that "Charlemagne's intellectual and ecclesiastical entourage does not at all appear to have shared the emperor's sympathetic and tolerant attitude toward the Jews" — "l'entourage intellectuel et ecclésiastique de Charlemagne ne semble aucunement avoir partagé l'esprit de sympathie et de tolérance de l'empereur à l'égard des Juifs": Max Haller, "La question juive pendant le premier millénnaire chrétien," RHPR, 15 (1935), 326.

574. "Expoliata est vestimenti fidei et diademae sui regni"; "Destructa sum in ornatu meo et in lege mea quam Deus mihi dedit per Moysen": "Un vitrail ou un bas-relief historié de l'abbaye de la Colombe?" RDSR, 29 (1955), 239-49.

575. "voulu fixer sur la pierre le souvenir de conflits moins anciens et plus passionnants": O. Hildenfinger, "La figure de la Synagogue dans l'art du moyen âge," REJ, 47 (1903), 187-96. Haller, *loc. cit.*, 322-4: "Did the artist, like St. Paul, intend simply to herald the ancient victory of the New covenant over the Old? But then why were the two figures not called the Old and the New Testament?" — "L'artiste entendait-il, comme saint Paul, chanter simplement l'antique victoire de la nouvelle sur l'ancienne alliance? Mais alors pourquoi les deux figures ne furent-elles pas dénommés l'Ancient et le Nouveau Testament?" Simply because, for the Christian, the Old Testament and the reading of that Old Testament by the Synagogue or by the Israel that rejects Christ, are two quite different things. See also the two statues of the façade of Notre Dame of Paris.

576. Hildenfinger, *loc. cit.*, puts the images of the Synagogue and those of the sow suckling Jewish children together so as to draw the same conclusions: David Kaufmann, "La Truie de Wittenberg," REJ, 20 (1890), 269-74.

577. "sacramentum Synagogae": *Liber officialis*, l. 1, c. 19, n. 9 (J. H. Hanssens, 117). One sees that it is not only starting from the 10th century that Synagoga comes to replace Judea (which is, however, not its equivalent), as Hildenfinger says, 192. Cf. above, note 424.

578. "par une progression fatale"; "peuple de la Bête, de l'Antéchrist et du démon": as Mr. Jules Isaac fears, 290.

579. Bruno of Segni, *In Is.*: "they delight in the bitterness of the letter and loathe the sweetness of the spiritual understanding" — "in litterae amaritudine delectantur et spiritualis intelligentiae dulcedinem abominantur" (*Sp. cas.*, 3, 18).

580. Greg., *In Ez.*, l. 1, h. 7, n. 15: "the perversity of faithlessness" — "perversitas perfidiae" (PL, LXXVI, 847 C).

581. *Glossa in Deut.*, xxxiii, 2: "of the Jews most harsh by reason of the thornhedge of malice and faithlessness" — "de Judaeis malitiae et perfidiae spineto asperrimis" (CXIII, 493 C).

582. Long parallel in Bede, *Hexaem.*, l. 2 (XCI, 69-72). Ps.-Bede, *In Jo.*: "The envious brother slays Abel the just. . . . If they should have understood Cain's homicide to be the faithlessness of the Jews" — "Abel justum frater invidens occidit. . . . Si intellexerint Cain homicidium Judaeorum esse perfidiam" (XCII, 659 A). Martin of Leon (CCVIII, 217 C, 352 C, 384-5). St. Bruno, *Confessio* (CLIII, 571 A).

583. Ps.-Cyprian, *Adv. Jud.*: "Oh new hardness, oh unique audacity, oh bloody faithlessness!" — "O duritia nova, o audacia singularis, o perfidia cruenta!" (Hartel, 137). Candidus of Fulda, *De pass. Dom.*: "O cruel faithlessness

and fierce malice!" — "O perfidia crudelis et saeva malitia!" (PL, CVI, 89 C). Bede, *In Luc.:* "What great cruelty of the faithless" — "Quanta perfidorum crudelitas" (XCII, 612 C).

584. *Mor.*, l. 3, c. 19, n. 35; l. 6, c. 20, n. 44 (LXXV, 617 D, 748 D, 883 A); l. 27, c. 26, n. 50 (LXXVI, 430 A). The Protestant Basnage, *Hist. des Juifs*, l. 6, c. 21 (t. 4, 1706, pp. 1403-7) does Gregory justice on this point.

585. *In Ez.*, h. 5, n. 3 (374).

586. *In Marc.*, l. 4 (PL, XCII, 271 CD).

587. *De passione Domini*, c. 16 (CVI, 91-2).

588. "perversis doctoribus et principibus seu judicibus Ecclesiae": *In Mich.*, c. 3 (CXVII, 152-3).

589. "civitas perfida": h. 5 (CXXXI, 894 B). The claims of Remigius are less isolated than J. Parkes believes, *op. cit.*, 31.

590. *In ps.* xxx (CXLII, 134 D; 135 D).

591. *In Rom.* (CLIII, 95 A). It has not been proved that the commentaries of Bruno are inauthentic.

592. "judaicam superantes perfidiam": *s.* 23 (CCXI, 140 AB).

593. "perfidia": Rabanus, *In ev.*, h. 87: "The Synagogue immediately was destroyed by the death of faithlessness and envy together: of faithlessness, since she was unwilling to believe in Christ; of envy, because she grieved that the Church had believed" — "Continuo Synagoga perfidiae simul invidiaeque letho soluta est: perfid[i]ae quidem, quia in Christo credere noluit; invidiae vero, quia Ecclesiam credidisse doluit" (PL, CX, 314 C). Bede, *In Marc.* (XCII, 162 CD, 182 A). Greg. (LXXVI, 65 B). Gerhoh, *In ps.* xxxvi and lxxviii (V. den Eynde, 474, 479, 674).

594. Ambrose, *In Luc.*, l. 7, c. 109 (SC, 52, 46).

595. "iniquitas perfidiosissima": *L. carol.*, 1, c. 27: "from the deceitful lips of the faithless Jews" — "de perfidorum J. labiis dolosis" (PL, XCVIII, 1060 D); "For they had the jealousy of spite and most faithless iniquity.... Hence the most faithless crew of Jews had deceitful lips and boastful tongue" — "Habuerunt zelum livoris et perfidiosissimae iniquitatis. . . . Labia ergo dolosa et linguam magniloquam perfidiosissima Judaeorum cohors habebat" (1061 AB). Cf. Jerome, *In Ez.*: "whose faithlessness and mendacity we witness" — "quorum perfidiam et mendacia detestamur" (XXV, 242 C).

596. Hymn for the Annunciation, in A. Dechevrens, SJ, *Du rythme dans l'hymnographie latine* (1895), 162:

Deus qui mundum crimine jacentem	God, who hast by the flesh of thy Son
Filii tui carne relevasti	Raised up a world lying dead in sin
Et veternosi perfidi serpentis Noxam delesti.	And has removed the harm Of the age-old faithless serpent.

597. Rabanus, *De laud.*, l. 2, c. 10: "For the potent virtue of the holy cross shatters and dooms all the faithlessness of the Enemy" — "Causat enim et damnat omnem perfidiam Inimici potens virtus sanctae crucis" (PL, CVII, 275 C). Prose of St. Martial of Limoges (L. Gautier, *H. de la prose liturg. au m. âge, les tropes*, 1886, 168):

Hostis perfidiam	This little lad has broken
Non per injuriam	The faithlessness of the enemy
Hic fregit parvulus.	Not through injury.

598. Conrad of Hirschau, *Dial.*: "Quicquid in homine licet perfido et impio veritatis unquam inveniri poterit, ejus fuit qui hominem creavit" (39).

599. *Ep.* 133, c. 3: "her whose name 'blackness' bears witness to the darkness of faithlessness" — "eam cujus nomen nigredinis testatur perfidiae tenebras" (Hilberg, 3, 246).

600. Aelred, *s. in.*, 1: "Quaecumque perfide et turpiter operatur injusti" (Talbot, 34). John of Salis., *ep.* 190: "faithlessness or even some mark of turpitude" — "perfidia aut etiam quaecumque nota turpitudinis" (PL, CXCIX, 202 B).

601. John of Sal., *ep.* 175: "the faithlessness of betrayers" — "proditorum perfidiam" (166 D).

602. "perfidus": Greg., *Mor.*, l. 2, c. 2: "Judas is said to have gone out by night for the faithlessness of betrayal" — "ad traditionis perfidiam nocte Judas exiisse perhibetur" (LXXV, 555 C). Bede, *In Luc.*: "de perfidia proditoris" (XCII, 436 C).

603. Herodem vitant perfidum
  Angelico admonitu.

"Feast of the Three Kings," hymn at vespers (Breviary of the 16th cent; Dreves, *Hymni ined.; Analecta hymn. in.*, 4, 1888, 17).

604. Hugh of Fleury, *De regia pot.*, c. 1: "with pride, robberies, faithlessness, murders, and finally almost all manner of crimes" — "superbia, rapinis, perfidia, homicidiis, et postremo universis pene sceleribus" (PL, CLXIII, 941 B).

605. "Falsorum fratrum vigilante perfidia": *Scutum canonicorum* (CXCIV, 1495 A). Saxo grammaticus: "Grimalda's faithlessness toward the brothers" — "Grimaldae erga fratres perfidiam": Landulf of Mailand: "the tribulations which ... he has suffered at the hands of the faithless citizens" — "tribulationes quas ... a perfidis civibus passus est" (Manitius, 3, 506, 509).

606. H. Leclercq, *S. Jérôme*, 130-1: "He was one of those types that are entirely devoid of moral sense and whose name is always turning up again in shady dealings" — "Il était de ces gens qui sont entièrement privés de sens moral et dont le nom reparaît toujours dans les tripotages." G. Bardy, "Faux et fraudes dans l'antiquité chr.," RHE, 32 (1936), 297 ff.

607. *Apol.*, l. 1, c. 19: "to provoke discords rather than harmony; to be faithless in return for faith; a counterfeiter in return for the truth" — "pro concordia movere dissidia; perfidus esse pro fide; pro veritate falsarius" (PL, XXI, 556-7).

608. Hilarius Anglicus, 12th cent.: "The tongue of a slave is a tongue of faithlessness" — "Lingua servi, lingua perfidiae." A poem of the 10th cent.: "In this way the S. had deluded his faithless wife" — "Sic perfidam — Suevus conjugem — deluserat." Hildebert: *De perfida amica* (Raby, *Sec. lat. Poetry*, 2, 115; 1, 297, 323). Cf. *Aeneid*, l. 4, v. 366. Cicero: "Avoid faithless friends" — "Perfidos amicos devita."

609. *Judicium in tyrannorum perfidia promulgatum* (PL, XCVI, 801-8). Perfidare = perfide agere, a fide promissa deficere, fidem fallere (cf. du Cange).

610. "O mala tempora! Perfida pectora nobilitantur": *De cont. mundi*, l. 3, v. 7 (Hoskier, 71). Cf. Gerbert, *ep.* 15 (*Hist. des Gaules*, 10, 391).

611. Auro perjurus Polimnestor, adultera Dane,
Perfida Tarpeia, trux Eriphile fuit.

De trib. inimicis, c. 3 (PL, CLXXI, 1493 A).

612. Hugh, *De vanit. mundi*, l. 1: "Why have you not held the sea's tranquillity to be suspect? Why were you not afraid to entrust your life to the faithless element?" — "Quare tranquillitatem aequoris suspectam non habuistis? Quare perfido elemento vitam vestram committere non timuistis?" (CLXXVI, 706 A). Cf. Arator (an. 544): "I am deserting the faithless sails of the worldly sea" — "Perfida mundani desero vela freti" (LXVIII, l 77).

613. "perfide": *De off. eccl.*: "who on that day invited the scribes and Pharisees so that our lord Jesus Christ, who was under investigation by them, might faithlessly be killed" — "qui ea die ob hoc Scribarum et Pharisaeorum fecit invitationem, ut dom. noster J. Christus ab eisdem investigatus perfide necaretur" (R. Delamare, 23).

614. "Rex, perfidiae Saxonum non immemor": MGH, *Scr.*, 6, 168.

615. Amans tercentum millia divum,
Perfidus ille Deo, quamvis non perfidus orbi.

vv. 453-4 (Lavarenne, 2, 19).

616. "quo si non fecerit, merito censebitur malefidus, sicut ille, si in eorum praevaricatione vel faciendo vel consentiendo deprehensus fuerit, perfidus et perjurus": *ep*. 38 (*Recueil des hist. des Gaules*, ed. L. Delisle, 10, 1874, 463). Cf. Robert of Monte, *Chronica*, a. 1135 and 1163 (MGH, *Scr.*, 6, 492, 513).

617. "les concepts de fidélité civique et de fidélité religieuse s'interpénétraient": B. Blumenkranz, "Du nouveau sur Bodo-Eleazar?" REJ, 11 (1953), 37. C. Mohrmann, *Le latin médiéval* (CCM, 1, 279). Cf. Amolon, *C. Judaeos*, c. 42 (PL, CXVI, 171 AC).

618. L. 2, c. 5: "Rainaldus, abjecta fide . . . , tradit exercitum. . . . Machinantur sibimet ii qui duces exstiterant praesidium perfidia. Rainaldus enim, qui eis in prosperitate praefuerat, clam sibi Turcos faeda conciliat, etc." (CLVI, 707 C).

619. Gerhoh, *De novitatibus hujus temporis*, c. 13 (*L. de lite*, 3, 298); cf. *De aedificio Dei*, prol: "contempto judicio perfidorum" (37). Alvarus, *Ind. lum.*, c. 7 (PL, CXXI, 522 A). Ekkehard, *Chron. Wirzib.*, a. 903 (MGH, *Scr.*, 6, 28).

620. "Vae genti Judaicae, malae et perfidae, ac subdolo semper sensu viventi!": *Hist. Francorum*, l. 8, c. 1 (PL, LXXI, 449 B). Gontran concludes, however, simply that he will not get a synagogue rebuilt.

621. Cf. Didier of Cahors, *Ep.*, l. 1, 3: "when faithless kings are condemned along with the unjust" — "quando perfidi reges cum iniquis damnantur" (CCL, 117, 313). Pope Hadrian to Charlemagne: "Nefa perfidi regis calcabis Desiderii colla" (*P. lat. m. aevi*, 1, 91).

622. *Judicium* (PL, XCVI, 801).

623. Salvianus, *De gubern. Dei*, l. 4, c. 14 (LIII, 87 A). Paschasius (CXX, 803 B).

624. "The faithless enemy is retiring out of our territory" — "Perfidus e nostris abscedit finibus hostis" (MGH, *Ep. sel.*, 3, 58; Poem 20 of Tegernsee, ed. K. Strecker). Gerbert, *ep.* 45; Ditmar, *Chronicon*, a. 1012 (*H. des Gaules*, 10, 399 and 134). Annalista Saxo, a. 811 (MGH, *Scr.*, 6, 568).

625. "perfidus et nefandus": S. Berger, *Hist. de la Vulgate*, 217-8. Cf. *L. moz. sacr.* (40).

626. "Si aliquando inter eos (Judaeos) perfidus alicujus rei inter eos gestae occultare voluerit veritatem, ab eo qui est episcopus eorum veritatem fateri cogatur": n. 14 (Parkes, *The Jew* . . . , 393).

627. *Hist.*, 1.3, pref. (M. Prou, 51).

628. "perfidus, perjurus, proditor"; "Perfidus imperator Francorum duces deludit": *Gesta Dei*, l. 2, c. 5 (PL, CLVI, 709 B); l. 8, c. 6, n. 23 (813 B); where the Greek emperor is in question. Cf. Martin of Leon, *s. de Act. Ap.*: "just as the innocent Gedaliah was slain by the faithless Ishmael" — "sicut Godolias innocens a perfido Ismaele occisus est" (CCIX, 156 B).

629. "ipsi ad perfidiam defluunt, qui ad fidem alios tenere videbantur": Greg., *Mor.*, l. 20, c. 28, n. 57 (PL, LXXVI, 171 D). Garnier, *s.* 1 (CCIII, 564 A).

630. Cf. Or., *In Rom.*, fr. 13 (Schérer, 178); *In Rom.*, iii, 11 (PG, XIV, 960 A).

631. Bruno of Segni, *In Is.*: "and if the Jews believed in him, they would prevail over all the nations" — "cui si Judaei crederent, cunctis gentibus praevalerent" (*Sp. cas.*, 3, 25).

632. Cf. Joach. of Flora, *Sup. 4 ev.*: "The crossing-over has now been accomplished, be it from Judaism to grace or from paganism to the faith" — "Jam facta est transmigratio sive de judaismo ad gratiam, sive de paganismo ad fidem" (128).

633. "zelus perfidiae": Greg., *In I Reg.* (PL, LXXIX, 147 A). *In ev.*, h. 33, n. 6 (LXXVI, 1243 A).

634. "Manens in perfidia, contrarius est Ecclesiae Dei": Joach. of Flora, *op. cit.*, 322. Hesychius, *In Lev.*, l. 7: "The adversaries of those who believe in Christ, because they have produced opponents through their infidelity and envy" — "Adversarii eorum qui in Christo credunt, quod ipsi per infidelitatem et invidiam contrarios fecerunt" (PG, XCIII, 1146 C). Bede: "the faithless are persecuting the Church" — "persequentibus Ecclesiam perfidis" (PL, XCI, 668 C).

635. "quondam fidei et religionis, nunc autem impietatis et perfidiae nuntius": Autpert, *In Ap.*, l. 4: "Whilst the faithless drag others to faithlessness, whilst the iniquitous lead many to iniquity" — "Dum perfidi ad perfidiam alios pertrahunt, dum iniqui ad iniquitatem multos perducunt" (506 B). Aimo, *In Cant.*: "The Synagogue was rivaling the gentiles and used to envy their salvation" — "Synagoga gentes emulabatur et invidebat saluti eorum" (PL, CXVII, 354 B). Bede (XCI, 637 D).

636. "perfidi": Bede, *In Act.* (XCII, 979 B).

637. "judaica perfidia"; "divinae pietatis dispensatio": Alcuin, *ep.* 307 (= 165; MGH, *Ep.*, 4, 470).

638. Aug., *De cons. evang.*, l. 1, c. 26, n. 40 (PL, XXXIV, 1060). Rabanus, *In Ez.* (CX, 548 B). Honorius (CLXXII, 962 A); etc.

639. Bede, *In Marc.*: "Judea dissenting, the gentiles poured to Christ" — "Differente Judaea, gentilitas confluxit ad Christum" (XCII, 165 D); etc. Cf. Leo, *s.* 68, c. 4 (LIV, 375 AB). St. Bruno, *In Rom.* (CLIII, 95 A). Cf. *L. moz. sacr.* (595).

640. "reprobatio Judaeorum, nostrae salutis occasio": Jerome, *In Jer.*, l. 6, c. 30 (24, 871 C). *Glossa, In III Reg.*, vii, 25 (CXIII, 595 D). Cf. *L. moz. sacr.* (595).

641. Lanfranc, *In Rom.*, xi, 5 (CL, 141 B). Cf., regarding Judas, Aimo, *h.* 62 (CXVIII, 353 A).

642. Rupert, *In Gen.*, l. 8, c. 19 (CLXVII, 505 C).

643. "Accidit ut, eis nescientibus et quasi dormientibus . . . spiritus veritatis, qui esse consueverat cum illis, occultaret se et absentaret ab eis . . .": Joach. of Flora, *Sup. 4 ev.* (105).

644. Alexander Neckham, *De nat. rer.*, c. 189 (338). Rufinus, *H. eccle.*, l. 1, c. 37: "infelices Judaeos" (PL, XXI, 505 A). Martin of Leon (CCVIII, 115, 126, 140, 176, etc.

645. Martin of Leon, *s. 4 in nat.* (CCVIII, 122 B).

646. "O infelices, immo infelicissimi Judaei! O miseri et miserandi!": *Ib.* (127 B, 165, 246-7, 338 A, 377 D, 546-7); *s.* 34 (1335 B, 1342 C).

647. Leo, *s.* 67, c. 3: "In this way he somehow used the insanity of the blinded people and the faithlessness of the betrayer" — "Sic usus est (Christus) obcaecatae plebis insania quomodo et perfidia traditoris" (LIV, 370 C).

648. Greg., *Mor.* (LXXV, 585 A).

649. Greg., *Mor.*, l. 11, c. 15, n. 24 (964-5). Cf. Ambrosiaster, *In Rom.*, xi (XVII, 149 D, 153 A, 153 D).

650. Burchard, *Decretum*, l. 20, c. 93 (XCL, 1052 D; following Isidore); etc.

651. Greg., *In Ez.*, l. 1, h. 12, n. 9: "the Jews . . . returning to the faith . . . by the preaching of Enoch and Elijah" — "In praedicatione Enoch et Eliae . . . Judaei ad fidem redeuntibus" (LXXVI, 922 A); n. 6 (920 D); n. 8: "they are returning to knowledge of the truth" — "ad cognitionem veritatis redeunt" (921 D). Autpert, *In Ap.*, l. 5 (528 CD). Joach. of Flora: "he was both faithful among the predecessors and is to be called back to the faith at the end of ages" — "et in praedecessoribus fidelis fuit et in fine saeculorum revocandus est ad fidem" (34). Bruno of Würzb., *In ps.* xx (PL, CXLII, 106 C).

652. Aimo, *In Ap.*, l. 3 (PL, CXVII, 1073 D).

653. *Glossa*, *In l. Tobiae*, xi, 3, following Bede (CXIII, 730 D); *In III Reg.*, xvii, 19, following Rabanus (607 A).

654. Aug., *Civ. Dei*, l. 20, c. 29 (XLI, 704); cf. *In Hept.*, l. 6, qu. 22 (XXXIV, 788).

655. Sicardus, *Mitrale*, l. 8, c. 25 (CCXIII, 403 D). Absalon, *s.* 37 (CCXI, 217 D); etc. Cf. Greg., *In Ez.* (LXXVI, 814 C).

656. St. Bruno, *In Rom.*, xi (153, 95 AC).

657. Robert of Tombelaine, *In Cant.*: "At the end of the world the faith will be offered to the Synagogue by the Church, so that she may get back the pristine dignity which is held captive by the yoke of infidelity imposed by the demons" — "Synagogae in fine mundi fides ab Ecclesia offeretur, ut dignitatem pristinam recipiat quae ab infidelitatis jugo a daemonibus captivatur" (LXXIX, 533 A). Cf. Joach of Flora: "And something has been found . . . among the Hebrews, once they have returned to God, which may be venerable in the presence of all" — "Et inventum est aliquid . . . in Hebraeis cum conversi fuerint ad Deum, quod sit prae omnibus venerabile" (291).

658. Greg., *In Ez.*, l. 1, h. 12, n. 6 (LXXVI, 921 A).

659. Martin of Leon, *In nat.*, c. 3 (CCVIII, 121 A).

660. Adam Scot., *s.* 7, c. 14: "Concerning the holy spiritual joy which the Church now has in her sons, and also concerning the return of the Jews to the

faith, which will exist at the end, we have explained these prophetic words for the glory of God" — "De sancta ac spirituali laetitia, quam nunc in filiis suis Ecclesia de gentibus habet, de reversione quoque Judaeorum ad fidem, quae in fine erit, haec verba prophetica ad laudem Dei exposuimus" (CXCVIII, 140 D).

661. Greg., *Mor.*, l. 35, c. 14, n. 26: "So let the parents come to the banquet" — "Veniant ergo parentes ad convivium" (LXXVI, 764 A).

662. Burchard, *Decretum*, l. 20, c. 97 (following Greg.; CXL, 1054 C). Cf. Aimo, *In Ap.* (CXVII, 1179 AB).

663. "Regressi ad fidem, suscipientur cum laetitia": Cf. Ambrosiaster, *In Rom.* (XVII, 142-56).

664. Peter Cellensis, *s.* 12: "Adhuc apud Moysen hospitatur Dominus, tanquam apud archisynagogum cujus filia, id est Synagoga, infidelis, licet mortua, si crediderit, ab eo ressuscitatur" (CCII, 670 D). Cf. Rom. 11:15.

665. Paschasius, *In Matt.*, l. 11, c. 24 (CXX, 823 D).

666. Leo, *s.* 70, c. 2: "And so we bear witness to the faithlessnes" of the Jews; "if they should convert, we embrace their faith" — Judaeorum "itaque perfidiam detestamur; eorum fidem, si convertantur, amplectimur" (LIV, 381 B); "we wish that that people should obtain mercy, and we have accepted the grace of reconciliation for the sake of its offense" — "ut ille populus misericordiam consequatur optamus, ob cujus offensionem gratiam reconciliationis accepimus." Greg., *In Ez.*, l. 1, h. 12, n. 6: "When the Jews come back to the faith, as though the prophet is led back home, so that preaching may dwell once again amidst his own people, a preaching that now is glittering in various tribes like campfires" — "Dum Judaei ad fidem redeunt, quasi ad domum propheta reducitur, ut in suo populo rursus praedicatio inhabitet, quae modo velut in campo ita diversis gentibus fulget" (LXXVI, 920 D).

667. *Adv. Jud.:* "but also because I sense that the time of having mercy upon them is at hand, the time of their consolation and conversion" — "Mihi autem propter istud non modo . . . eorum contentioni et perfidiae obviare pro viribus voti est, verum etiam quia adesse sentio tempus miserendi eis, tempus consolationis et conversionis eorum" (A. Frugoni, 3).

668. "perfida civitas": Greg., PL, LXXV, 528 A, 585 B, 863-4; LXXVI, 108 CD, 166 CD, 541-2, 763-4. 769 A, 831 B, 920 D. Cf. *In ev.*, h. 39, n. 1 (LXXVI, 1294 C). Philip of Harvengt, *In Cant.*, l. 6, c. 32: "since he loves it that the Jews are turning back to the faith once lost, or rather, interrupted" — "cum ad fidem jam amissam vel potius intermissam Judaeos diligit sic reverti" (CCIII, 474 C).

669. "Revertere, revertere, Sunamitis . . . Revertere ad agnitionem tui Redemptoris."

670. "Revertere, revertere, Sunamitis! Revertere, revertere, ut intueamur te. Sunam dicitur captivitas; inde dicitur Sunamitis captiva, et intelligitur Synagoga a diabolo in perfidia captiva. Dicitur etiam Sunamitis coccinea sanguine Christi redempta. Hinc dicitur a praedicatoribus Evangelii quater: Revertere! scilicet, a quatuor plagis mundi; ab errore perfidiae ad fidem Christi convertere, vel revertere ad Redemptorem tuum te vocantem . . . ut intueamur te: id est ut imitemur te. Vel: revertere per quatuor evangelia, revertere per quatuor virtutes, ut conversationem tuam intuentes laudemus Dominum. Judaei namque in fine

mundi conversi, tantae conversationis erunt, quod Ecclesia admirabitur, et ejus exemplo utetur." Honorius, *In Cant.* (CLXXII, 455 BC).

671. "perdre de vue sans péril la promesse paulinienne de la réintégration globale d'Israël"; "la fin de la déchirure fondamentale qui contenait en germe toutes les autres, et que l'endurcissement d'Israël a provoqué au sein de l'ensemble du peuple de l'élection": F. Lovsky, "Comment l'Église du Christ doit-elle annoncer aujourd'hui l'Évangile au peuple d'Israël?" *Foi et vie*, 58, 6 (1959), 40-1.

672. Paschasius, *In Lam.*, l. 4: "How has gold been darkened, has the best color been changed? (Aleph.) For through the darkened gold the prophet is lamenting the faithlessness of the Jews, since, as the faithlessness of malice breaks in, the ancient vigor of the faith and the splendor of innocence has blackened itself in them with night" — "Quomodo obscuratum est aurum, immutatus est color optimus? (Aleph.) Per aurum namque obscuratum propheta Judaeorum plangit perfidiam, quia in eis antiquus ille fidei vigor atque innocentiae splendor, ingruente perfidia malitiae se nocte fuscavit" (PL, CXX, 1197 C; cf. 1210 B).

673. Leo, *s.* 68, c. 4 (LIV, 375 A); etc.

674. Bede: "crushed down by the night of their own faithlessness" — "suae perfidiae nocte depressis" (91, 635 D); "as the evening of faithlessness presses down" — "incumbente perfidiae vespera" (522 C). Cf. Or., *In Matt.*, xvi, 3: they have become "blind and deaf of spirit" (467).

675. Judaei enim perfida,
   Peccatis obscurissima,
   Contempsit haec praesentia,
   Caelestis regni lumina.

Hymn of Sankt Gall (LXXXVII, 53 B). Rupert, *Div. off.*, l. 5, c. 26: "of the Jewish tribe, which has been cast forth in the darkness of faithlessness and its face has been bereft of light. . . . [He] has left them the profound darkness of error and faithlessness " — "Judaicae gentis, quae in tenebris perfidiae projecta et a lumine vultus derelicta est. . . . Profundas illis erroris et perfidiae tenebras reliquit" (CLXX, 148 BD). Ps.-Leo, *s.* 9, cc. 2 and 3 (LIV, 497-8).

676. Rupert, *In Amos*, l. 4 (CLXVIII, 362 A).

677. Bede: "Judea . . . has lost . . . the kingdom . . . for the sin of faithlessness" — "Judaeam, pro culpa perfidiae . . . regnum . . . amisse" (XCI, 689 D). Or., *In Rom.*, l. 2, c. 14: "I think that he would have called the sense of the Law the kingdom of God" — "puto quod sensum legis regnum Dei dixerit" (PG, XIV, 917 B).

678. "Vagus et profugus gemit in terra judaicus populus": Martin of Leon, *s.* 4 *in nat. Dom.*, c. 11 (PL, CCVIII, 216 AC).

679. "ex fide in fidem": Or., *De princ.*, l. 4, c. 2, n. 3 (311); cf. Luke 11:52. *Ib.*, c. 1, n. 3: "But even all those Jewish ambitions . . . have all been destroyed together" — "Sed et omnes illae ambitiones judaicae . . . simul universa destructa sunt" (296-7).

680. Hilarius, *In ps.* lxvii, n. 31: "whilst carnal Israel usurps God's mercy as peculiar to herself alone" — "carnalis Israel, dum sibi tantum peculiarem Dei misericordiam usurpat" (306).

681. "perfida factio": Bede (PL, XCI, 700 B).

682. Rupert, *In Amos*, l. 4 (CLXVIII, 361-3). Beatus, *In Ap.* (161).
683. Greg., *Mor.*, l. 18, c. 32, n. 51 (LXXVI, 65 C).
684. Rupert, *In Ex.*, l. 1, c. 17 (CLXVII, 585 C). Cf. Lev. 13.
685. Angelome, *In Reg.*, l. 2, c. 3 (CXV, 342 A).
686. Rabanus, *In Lev.*, l. 7, c. 13 (CVIII, 560 C).
687. Honorius, *In Eccl.*, ix, 4 (CLXXII, 343 B).

688. Aug., *In ps.* cxiii, s. 1, n. 2: "which has justly been condemned for faithlessness" — "quae merito perfidiae reprobata est" (CCL, 40, 1636). Cassiodorus, *In ps.* lxxii, 10: "the Jewish people emptied out by its faithlessness" — "Judaicum populum perfidia sua vacuatum" (LXX, 518 D). Rupert, *Div. off.*, l. 4, c. 15: "that he is about to depart from them owing to their faithlessness" — "se ab illis propter perfidiam ipsorum recessurum" (CLXX, 105 D). *Glossa in Ex.*, xxxiii, 22: "But God is said even to 'cross over', when from the hearts of certain human beings by whom he was previously believed through faith, he later departs from them and goes over to others, when faithlessness or some crime steals in" — "Sed et transire dicitur Deus cum de cordibus quorumdam hominum, sed quibus ante per fidem credebatur, postea, surrepente perfidia vel quolibet delicto, ab eis recedit et ad alios transit" (CXIII, 290 BC).

689. "Nonne ablata est ab eo misericordia Dei, quem apostatare permisit?": Peter of Blois, *C. perf. Jud.*, c. 8 (CCVII, 837 A).

690. "Judaei perfidi": Ps.-Cyrian, *Adv. Jud.*, c. 7 (PL, IV, 924 A). Peter Lombard, *In Ps.*: "so that the worship of the one God may be taken up once superstition has been rejected" — "ut superstitione abjecta unius Dei cultus suscipiatur" (CXCI, 159 B; cf. 762 C).

691. Hugh, *In Thren.*: "For because he had been disapproved by the faithless Jews" — "Per hoc namque quod a perfidis Judaeis reprobatus est" (CLXXV, 279 A). Martin of Leon: "cast out from communion of the sacraments of the Church" — "ejecti a communione sacramentorum Ecclesiae" (CCVIII, 226 B).

692. "Sicut fides servos promovet in amicos, ita perfidia filios in paenalem redigit servitutem": Peter Chrysologus, *s.* 102 (LII, 485 C).

693. Neckham, *De nat. rer.*, c. 189: "They have thrown Liberty out of their city, and so they were later made slaves" — "Extra civitatem suam Libertatem ejecerunt, unde et postea servi effecti sunt" (338).

694. Berengaud, *In Ap.*: "After the Gospel has been given, keeping the Law according to the letter is nothing but the devil's servitude" — "Post evangelium datum custodia legis secundum litteram nihil est aliud quam servitus diaboli" (PL, XVII, 784 B).

695. Greg., *Mor.*, l. 18, c. 33, n. 52 (LXXVI, 65 D).
696. Rupert, *In Jer.*, c. 83 (CLXVII, 1414 C).

697. Maximus of Turin, *h.* 3 (LVII, 230 BC). Galland of Rigny, *Lib. Prov.*, 75: "It belongs not to the Synagogue but to the Church to know the Scriptures" — "Ecclesiae est, non Synagogae, Scripturas nosse" (J. Châtillon, 67).

698. Greg., *Mor.*, l. 9, c. 33, n. 49: "Plebs quippe judaica ... commutata facie, dolore torquetur. ... Quasi enim commutata facie ab auctore non cognoscitur, quae perdita bonae conscientiae fide reprobatur" (LXXV, 885 C).

699. Fulbert of Chartres, *Tr. c. Judaeos* (CXLI, 310 C, 315 A, 318 A).

Notes to Page 140

700. Paschasius, *In Matt.*, l. 12, c. 27: "The Synagogue is being profaned" — "Profanatur Synagoga" (CXX, 964 A).

701. Sicardus, *Mitr.*, l. 1, c. 6: "The left corner of the east is Judea, in which Christ . . . owing to faithlessness, is regarded as belonging with the sinister. The right corner of the west is the gentiles, in which faithlessness has fallen" — "Sinister angulus orientis est Judaea, in qua Christus . . . cum sinistris ob perfidiam reputatur. Dexter angulus occidentis est gentilitas, in qua perfidia cecidit" (CCXII, 30 CD). Cf. John Scotus, *In Jo.*, fr. 1 (CXXII, 304 B).

702. "ad numerum incredularum gentium": Autpert, *In Ap.*, l. 5 (521 F).

703. Hugh, *In Thren.*: "The faithless people of the Jews does not accept the Savior sent to it. . . . Hence his faith has gone over to the gentiles, because Judea, remaining in faithlessness, has disapproved of it" — "Perfidus Judaeorum populus Salvatorem ad se missum non recipit. . . . Per hoc fides ejus ad gentes transit, quod Judaea illam in perfidia manens reprobavit" (PL, CLXXV, 279 A).

704. "Quam damnosa perfidia est!": Ambrose, *Exhort. virg.*, c. 10, n. 66 (XVI, 356 B); "mercenaria esse desiderat, quae sibi vindicabat ante dominatum."

705. Rupert, *De S. Spiritu*, l. 1, c. 6: "Now what do we believe holy Scripture to be, if not the Word of God? . . . The totality of the Scriptures is the one Word of God. . . . Hence, when we read holy Scripture, we are dealing with God's Word, we hold the Son of God before our eyes through a mirror and in a riddle" — "Quid autem Scripturam sanctam, nisi Verbum Dei esse credimus? . . . Unum est Dei Verbum universitas Scripturarum. . . . Cum igitur Scripturam sanctam legimus, Verbum Dei tractamus, Filium Dei per speculum et in aenigmate prae oculis habemus" (PL, CLXVII, 1575-6). *In Reg.*, l. 3, c. 14: "What . . . was it for Moses and the prophets to weave together holy Scripture which is the Word of God, if not to conceive Christ in the heart through the prophetic spirit and to give birth to him through the mouth?" — "Quid . . . fuit Moysi et prophetis sanctam Scripturam quae Verbum Dei est contexere, nisi Christum et corde per spiritum propheticum concipere et ore parere?" (1157 C).

706. Rupert, *De vict. Verbi*, l. 7, c. 32 (CLXIX, 1380 A).

707. "verba multa"; "Verbum unum": Rupert, *In Jo.*, l. 7: "The many words which he has spoken are one Word; one, I say, because it even itself became flesh. He spoke that one Word with many words, i.e., with many elementary articulate sounds; he put it into the mouths of our souls with the many mysteries of his incarnation, passion, resurrection, and ascension" — "Verba quae multa locutus est, unum Verbum sunt; unum, inquam, quod et ipse caro factum est. Illud unum Verbum multis verbis, id est multis elementaribus et articulatis sonis locutus est, multis mysteriis incarnationis, passionis, resurrectionis et ascensionis suae in ora nostrarum animarum immisit" (CLXIX, 494 D). Jerome, *In Eccl.*, xii, 16-17 (XXIII, 1113-5). Cf. Aug., *In Jo.*, tr. 28, n. 9 (CCL, 36, 282-3).

708. "multi sunt sermones hominis, quia cor hominis unum non est": *In Eccl.*, h. 13 (PL, CLXXV, 204 D); h. 17: "Since [man] has been divided and rendered other, so that he is not one whole" — "Quoniam (homo) divisus est, et alius factus, ut non sit unus totus" (237 D). [Trans. note: de Lubac gives no source for the citation "Verbum abbreviatum fecit Deus super terram." The Vulgate of Rom. 9:28 has "Verbum enim consummans, et abbrevians in aequitate: quia verbum breviatum faciet Dominus super terram," alluding to Isa. 10:22-23: "Si enim fuerit

populus tuus, Israel, quasi arena maris, reliquiae convertentur ex eo; consummatio abbreviata inundabit iustitiam. Consummationem enim et abbreviationem Dominus Deus exercituum faciet in medio omnis terrae." The Douai version of Rom. 9:27-28 reads: "And Isaiah crieth out concerning Israel: 'If the number of the children of Israel be as the sand of the sea, a remnant shall be saved. For he shall finish his word, and cut it short in justice; because a short word shall the Lord make upon the earth.'"]

709. Or., *In Gen.*, h. 14, n. 1: "Though our Lord Jesus Christ is one through his substance and nothing but the Son of God, nevertheless he is shown as various and diverse in the figures and forms of the Scriptures" — "Cum unus sit Dominus noster Jesus Christus per substantiam suam, et nihil aliud Filius Dei sit, in figuris tamen et formis Scripturarum varius ac diversus ostenditur" (121). Aug., *In ps.* ciii, s. 4, n. 1: "Though one utterance of God having been dilated in all the Scriptures, still one Word sounds through the many mouths of the saints" — "Cum sit unus sermo Dei in Scripturis omnibus dilatatus, et per multa ora sanctorum unum Verbum sonet" (CCL 40, 1521).

710. "verbum sacrae paginae": Peter the Cantor, *Verb. abbr.*, c. 1; and the School of Peter the Cantor: "The word of the sacred page that he left us as earnest money and pledge of his sweetness and love" — "Verbum sacrae paginae quod nobis in arrham et pignus suae dulcedinis et dilectionis reliquit" (Landgraf, *Gregorianum*, 1940, 50-1).

711. "aut declamatorie praedicatum, aut figuraliter significatum, aut imaginarie somniatum": Bernard, *Sup. missus est*, h. 4, n. 11 (PL, CLXXXIII, 86 BC).

712. "Plane multa sunt, verba digesta calamo prophetarum": Rupert, *De S. Sp.*, l. 1, c. 6 (CLXVII, 1575 D).

713. "Semel locutus est Deus, et plura audita sunt": Ambrose, *In ps.* lxi, n. 33-4 (XIV, 1180 BC).

714. "Judaeo ista dicta sunt, et christianus audivit": *Id., In ps.* cxviii, s. 13, n. 6 (XV, 1382).

715. Prayer for Advent, *Or. vis.*, 21: "Your Law and Word, O God the Father, coming forth from Zion" — "Lex tua verbumque, Deus Pater, de Sion prodiens, etc."

716. "Omnem Scripturae universitatem, omne verbum suum Deus in utero virginis coadunavit"; *Sacramentary of Lyon,* 11th cent., feast of the Annunciation: "O God, who hast willed to unite thy Word to the womb of the blessed virgin Mary on this very day" — "Deus qui hodierna die Verbum tuum beatae Mariae virginis alvo coadunare voluisti." Rupert, *In Is.*, l. 2, c. 31: "In this way all the Scripture pertaining to the Law and the prophets had been established before God united the totality of Scripture — all his Word — in the virgin's womb. The virgin herself conceived in mind before she did in flesh; she brought forth by prophesying with her mouth prior to laboring in the womb. Therefore it is false [to say] that Christ did not exist before Mary. For before she bore his flesh, blessed Zion gave birth by the mouth of the prophets to one and the same Christ, one and the same Word" — "Sic omnis Scriptura legalis et prophetica condita est antequam omnem Scripturae universitatem, omne Verbum suum Deus in utero virginis coadunaret. Ipsa virgo prius mente quam carne concepit, prius ore

prophetando quam ventre parturiendo peperit. Igitur falsum est ante Mariam non extisisse Christum. Nam antequam carnem ejus parturiret, peperit ore prophetarum beata Sion unum eumdemque Christum, unum eumdemque Verbum" (PL, CLXVII, 1362 BD).

717. "Voici le Verbe grand ouvert devant nous. Voici le Verbe devant nous déployé, et nous pouvons lire dedans à livre ouvert": P. Claudel, *Un poète regarde la croix*, 61.

718. Rupert, *De S. Sp.*, l. 1, c. 8: "The Father had proposed before all ages that his Word, which. . . . he had made vocal through the hearts and mouths of the prophets, should become flesh through the womb of this blessed virgin" — "Verbum suum, quod . . . per corda et ora prophetarum vocale fecerat, per hujus beatae virginis uterum carnem fieri ante omnia saecula Pater proposuerat" (CLXVII, 1577 CD). Arno of Reichersberg, *Apol.*: "so that the same Word that the virgin generated bodily, might previously have been generated by the eloquent mouth of the holy Prophet" — "ut idem Verbum, quod virgo corporaliter genuit, prius sancti prophetae ore facundo generaretur" (Weichert, 90). Cf. Bernard, *De circumc.*, s. 1, n. 3: "And the very one that was shortened in the Prophet is read more clearly in the Gospel, having been made flesh" — "Et ipsum quod in propheta abbreviatum, manifestius in evangelio legitur caro factum" (PL, CLXXXIII, 133 D), etc.

719. Or., *In Jo.*, 52; *In Jo.* fr. 2, 486; *In Jer.*, . h. 9, n. 1, 64. Aimon, *In Os.*: "Verbum Domini, quod factum est ad Osee . . . . Verbum Domini illud debemus intelligere, de quo Joannes in exordio evangelii sui dicit: In principio erat Verbum" (PL, CXVII, 11 A).

720."Eloquium Dei, Verbum Dei; Verbum Dei, Filius Dei": Adam of Perseigne, *Fragmenta mariana* (CCXI, 750 D).

721. Helinand, s. 4: "For the Jews still find the boy Jesus wrapped in swaddling clothes and lying in a manger, i.e., they read him in the Old Testament wrapped with the simple country words of the prophets and the ragged mysteries of the figures" — "Adhuc enim Judaei inveniunt puerum Jesum pannis involutum, et positum in praesepio, id est, legunt eum in V.T. verbis simplicibus et rusticanis prophetarum et pannosis figurarum mysteriis involutum" (CCXII, 513 A); etc. Cf. Rabanus (CVIII, 248).

722. Helinand, s. 3 (CCXII, 502 BC).

723. Bernard, *In vig. nat.*, s. 1, n. 1 (CLXXXIII, 87 B). *In nat. Dom.*, s. 1, n. 1 (115 B). *In circ.*, s. 1, n. 1 (131 D). *In annunt.*, s. 3, n. 8: "excelsus, humiliatus; immensus, abbreviatus" (396 D). V. Lossky, "Études sur la terminologie de S. Bernard, *B. du Cange*, 17 (1943), 87-90, nicely expounds this sense of "abbreviare, abbreviatus" in Bernard; but it is not, as he believes, "a new sense" there.

724. Guerric, *De nat.*, s. 5, n. 1 (CLXXXV, 43 BD); etc. Already Heterius and Beatus, *Ad Elip.*, l. 1, c. 37: "The Jews and heretics who do not believe that the shortened Word, i.e., the one made man, is the Son of God" — "Judaei et haeretici, qui Verbum abbreviatum id est hominem factum non credunt esse Filium Dei" (XCVI, 914 D). Absalon, *s.* 15 (CCXI, 94 B).

725. "Christ's Mother, the Father's Word — Makes flesh for the Word — And the Word becomes shortened — And if sense fails, — To form the Son in this way — The Mother's faith is enough" — "Christi Mater, Patris Verbum — Verbo

carnem efficit — Fitque Verbum breviatum — Et si sensus deficit, — Ad Filium sic formandum — Matris fides sufficit": *Vie intérieure* . . . (Rome, 1866), 23, 430.

726. *Le Milieu divin* (1957), 168: "Quand le moment fut venu où Dieu avait résolu de réaliser à nos yeux son Incarnation, il lui fallut susciter au préalable, dans le monde, une vertue capable de l'attirer jusqu'à nous. Il avait besoin d'une Mère qui l'engendrât dans les sphères humaines. Que fit-Il alors? Il créa la Vierge Marie, c'est-à-dire Il fit apparaître sur terre une pureté si grande que, dans cette transsparence, Il se concentrera jusqua'à apparaître Petit-Enfant."

727. "Semel locutus est Deus, quando locutus in Filio est"; "et audita sunt etiam illa quae ante audita non erant ab iis quibus locutus fuerat per prophetas": Aug., *In ps.* lxi, n. 18 (CCL, 39, 786). Ambrose, *In ps.* lxi, n. 33 (PL, XIV, 1180 C). Rupert (note 84). For the contrast with an apparently analogous theme in Buddhism: H. de Lubac, *Aspects du bouddhisme*, 1 (1951), 132-4 and 187.

728. Irenaeus, *Adv. Haer.*, l. 2, c. 18, n. 1: "Quando incarnatus est . . . longam hominum expositionem in se ipso recapitulavit, in compendio nobis salutem portans" (PG, VII, 832 B).

729. "Verbum abbreviatum de Verbo abbreviato audivimus": Garnier, *s.* 5, *de nat. Dom.* (PL, CCV, 599 C).

730. *Semel locutus est Deus, quia unum genuit Verbum:* Bernard, *De div.*, s. 73 (183, 695 B). Cf. *In Cant.*, s. 5, n. 1 (554 BC). Bede, *In Cant.* (XCI, 1119 C).

731. "O fratres, si pie ac diligenter intendamus huic Verbo quod Dominus fecit hodie, et ostendit nobis, quanta quamque facile possemus ab ipso perdoceri! Verbum siquidem breviatum est, ita tamen ut in eo consummatum sit omne verbum quod ad salutem est, quia nimirum verbum consummans et abbrevians in aequitate ipsum est. Et haec 'consummatio abbreviata inundavit justitiam' (Isa. 10:23). . . . Sed quid mirum, si omnia verba sua nobis Verbum Dei breviavit, quando et se ipsum breviari et quodammodo minui voluit, adeo ut de incomprehensibili immensitate sui ad angustias uteri quodammodo se contraxerit et, continens mundum, in praesepi se passum sit contineri?": Guerric, *In nat. Dom.*, s. 3, n. 3 (CLXXXV, 44 CD). Cf. *In Purif.*, s. 2, n. 5 (70 D).

732. Absalon, s. 22: "Ipsum est illud Verbum abbreviatum, quod fecit Dominus super terram, imo vere brevissimum. Nam licet in natura suae divinitatis incomprehensibile sit et infinitum" (CCXI, 130 C). As with Heterius and Bernard, here Jesus is the Word shortened — with reference no longer to the Scriptures but to his state as eternal Word.

733. Rupert, *In Jo.*, l. 6: "The five untainted loaves of the Mosaic Law, i.e., as many books, and two fish, i.e., the prophets and Psalms, bearing witness at once to the Law and the Gospel. . . . He bears the burden of those loaves and fishes of the Scriptures and does not eat of them; he sweats under the weight of the letter and does not touch with hand or tooth the marrow of the spiritual understanding" — "Integros quinque mosaicae legis panes, id est totidem libros, duos quosque pisces, id est prophetas et psalmos, legem simul et evangelium testificantes. . . . Illos Scrpturarum panes ac pisces, collo servili bajulat nec manducat, sudat sub onere litterae nec attingit manu vel dente medullam spiritualis intelligentiae" (CLXIX, 441 D; cf. 444 CD).

734. Bernard, *Sup. Missus est*, h. 4, n. 11 (CLXXXIII, 86 B).

735. Helinand, s. 3 (CCXII, 503 B).

736. Hildegarde, *Scivias*, l. 1, vis. 5: "hence the ancient precepts do not perish, since they have been brought over into a better state" — "unde antiqua praecepta non periunt, quia in meliorem statum translata sunt" (CXCVII, 435 D).

737. Rupert, *ib.*: "He took the book and opened the book, i.e., the whole of holy Scripture. . . . He received of the divine power to fulfill it in himself, that is, the whole dispensation of which, having been taken up within human nature for our salvation, the opening up of that book is the fulfillment of the holy Scriptures. . . . Hence the Lord took the loaves of the Scriptures in his hands at the moment when, having been incarnated according to the Scriptures, he suffered and rose again" — "Accepit librum et aperuit librum (Apoc. 5), id est universam Scripturam sanctam . . . de divina potentia suscepit in semetipso complendam, cujus vid. tota circa salutem nostram in natura hominis assumpta, dispensatio, praedicti libri apertio, id est sanctarum Scripturarum adimpletio est. . . . Tunc ergo Scripturarum panes in manibus suis accepit Dominus Jesus, quando secundum Scripturas incarnatus, passus est et resurrexit" (CLXIX, 443 CD).

738. P. Claudel, *Apocalypse*, 50, has renewed this traditional theme in his own manner: "Behold: this word, dilated to the measure of Infinity, shrunk down, still in contact with itself, in the hand of the Angel, to the dimensions of a little book, a *bibliorídion*, is no longer the formidable Roller it was just now; it is a tiny pastry of pages and verses, the whole Bible in substance so that we may make a mere mouthful of it. . . . Let us say that this shortening consists in just this sentence that the same St. John gives us in his Epistle: God is love. And so you, too, should love" — "Ce verbe dilaté à la mesure de l'Infini, le voici rétréci, en contact avec lui-même, dans la main de l'Ange, jusqu'aux dimensions d'un petit livre, βιβλιαρίδιον, ce n'est plus le formidable Rouleau de tout à l'heure, c'est un mince feuilletage de pages et de versets, toute la Bible en substance pour que nous n'en fassions qu'une bouchée . . . . Cette abbréviation, disons qu'elle consiste en ce seul mot que dans son Épître nous donne le même S. Jean: Dieu est Amour. Et toi aussi tu amieras" (Cf. Apoc. 10:9-10). This is the interprepration of Jerome and of Sedulius Scotus.

739. *Filius incarnatus, Verbum incarnatum, Liber maximus:* Garnier, s. 6 de nat. Dom.: "God once wrote us a book in which he grasped one thing under many words; today he has opened a book for us, in which he shuts together many things under one word" — "Olim librum scripsit nobis Deus, in quo sub multis verbis unum comprehendit; hodie librum nobis aperuit, in quo multa sub uno verbo conclusit" (PL, CCV, 609 D); "For he himself is the book which had flesh for parchment and the Father's Word for writing. . . . The Greatest Book is the Incarnate Son, since just as the word is united to the parchment through writing, so has the Father's Word been united to flesh through the assumption of humanity" — "Ipse enim liber est, qui pro pelle carnem habuit et pro scriptura Verbum Patris. . . . Liber maximus est Filius incarnatur, quia sicut per scripturam verbum unitur pelli, ita per assumptionem hominis Verbum Patris unitum est carni" (610 A, C). Absalon, s. 25: "The book that has been mentioned, therefore, is Christ" — "Liber ergo cujus habita est mentio (Apoc., Ezek.), Christus est" (CCXI, 148 D). Gerhoh, *In ps.* xxi (CXCIII, 1015-6); etc. Cf. Hebr. 1:1.

740. Jerome, *In Ez.*, l. 4, c. 48: "and it will come about both that the Old Testament is narrowed in the New, and the New is dilated in the Old" — "atque ita fiet

ut et vetus Testamentum constringatur in novo, et novum in vetere dilatetur" (PL, XXV, 482 C). Rabanus, *In Ez.*, l. 20 (CX, 1072 D).

741. "a multis sacrificiis ad unam hostiam translatio": Leo, *s.* 68, c. 3 (LIV, 374 D). Cf. *s.* 50, c. 7 (341 C). Or., *In Lev.*, h. 4, n. 8; h. 5, n. 3 (327, 338). Cf. G. Salet, SJ, "La Croix du Christ, unité du monde," in *Le Christ notre vie* (3e éd., 1958), 47-100.

742. Ordine multiplici signatus Patribus olim
    Mactatur legi, vatibus et canitur.

John Scotus Erigena, *De Christi resurrectione*, vv. 23-4 (PL, CXXII, 1228 C).

743. Porro facit Verbum, promisit ut, abbreviatum;
    Muneribus variis et pluribus inde rejectis,
    Frumentum et vinum, cunctis hoc praetulit unum.
    Hoc sacrat, hoc nimirum quod fit breve, quod nimis altum.
    Tam modicum sumptu, tam perfacile atque paratu,
    Tam sublime tamen, quo totam habeat deitatem.

l. 6, c. 27-32 (A. Swoboda, 120). The "pathetic style" of this poem is still, in the judgment of Zumthor, 73, not devoid of beauty. Cf. Aug., *In ps.* xlix, n. 15 (CCL, 38, 588). Helinand, *s.* 3 (CCXII, 498 D).

744. Evagrius, *Alterc. Sim. et Theoph.*: "God will make a shortened word in all the earth. This is the Word which has healed our lashings" — "Verbum breviatum faciet Deus in omni terra. Hoc est Verbum, quod verbera nostra sanavit" (Bratke, 10). Bodo of Prüfning, *De st. domus Dei*, l. 2 (494 A).

745. "Sufficit hoc solum mundi purgare piaclum": Odo, *ib.*, v. 33.

746. Jerome, *In Is.*, l. 1, c. 1, v. 11: "Henceforward according to the Hebrew, God shows that he never wanted the sacrificial victims of the Jews; which we read even in the forty-ninth psalm.... And when he rejected the ceremonies of the Old Law, he crosses over to the purity of the Gospel, and he shows what he wants instead of these things.... He rejected the sacrifices of victims, and teaches that the obedience of the Gospel is superior to sacrifice" — "Porro juxta Hebraicum, nunquam se Deus hostias Judaeorum voluisse demonstrat; quod et in quadragesimo nono psalmo legimus.... Cumque veteris Legis caeremonias respuisset, transit ad evangelii puritatem, et quid pro his cupiat ostendit.... Respuit sacrificia victimarum, et evangelii obedientiam docet esse super sacrificium" (PL, XXIV, 33-4).

747. "Abbreviatus atque perfectus sermo evangelicus est": Jerome, *In Is.*, l. 4, c. 10: "The discourse of the Gospel has been shortened and perfected, and for all the ceremonies of the Law it has given the very short precept of love and faith, so that we should not have done to another what we would be unwilling to have done [to us]. This is also why the Lord says in the Gospel: 'In these two commandments, etc.'" — "Abbreviatus autem atque perfectus sermo evangelicus est, qui pro cunctis laciniosae legis caeremoniis dedit praeceptum brevissimum dilectionis et fidei, ut quod fieri noluerimus ne fecerimus alteri. Unde et Dominus in evangelio: 'In his, inquit, duobus mandatis etc.'" (140 A). John Béleth, *Rationale*, c. 40: "Once the creed has been recited, at the end of it the sign of the cross should be made, since the word of the Gospel is not separate from the Gospel itself, except that it is a shortened word" — "Pronuntiato symbolo, sub finem ipsius debet fieri signum crucis, quoniam verbum est evangelicum non secus

Notes to Page 144

atque ipsum evangelium, nisi quod sit verbum abbreviatum" (CCII, 49 D). Peter Comestor expresses himself in the opposite sense, *In f. Trin.*: "Through Moses the Lord made ... a shortened word upon the earth, i.e., as far as the surface of the letter is concerned; but it is heavy with fruit with respect to the marrow of the judgment sensed" — "Per Moysen fecit Dominus ... verbum abbreviatum super terram, id est quantum ad litterae superficiem; sed grave est et fecundum quantum ad sententiae medullam" (CLXXI, 595 D).

748. Abelard, *ep.* 8: "Let him who lays down a law watch out lest he multiply transgressions along with a multiplication of precepts. The coming Word of God made a shortened word upon the earth. Moses spoke many things and yet, as the Apostle says, the Law brought forth nothing to perfection. With few words Christ instructed the apostles about the upbuilding of morals and holiness of life, and he taught perfection" — "Qui legem imponit, provideat ne multiplicatis praeceptis transgressiones multiplicet. Verbum Dei veniens, verbum abbreviatum fecit super terram. Multa Moyses locutus est et tamen, ut ait Apostolus, nihil ad perfectum adduxit lex. Paucis Christus de aedificatione morum et sanctitate vitae apostolos instruxit, et perfectionem docuit" (CLXXVIII, 294 BC). Cf. Rupert, *In Ap.*, l. 1, c. 1 (CLXIX, 858 AB).

749. "Verbum abbreviatum et abbrevians, salubre compendium!": Bernard, *De dilig. Deo*, c. 7, n. 21 (CLXXXII, 986-7). *Glossa in Rom.*, ix, 28-29 (CXIV, 502 D).

750. Sedulius Scotus, *In Rom.*: "For 'the word that sums up and shortens in equity.' Historically, the sense amounts to this: just as I shorten and quickly define a word, so God will effect this very quickly. In prophecy, however, the shortened word is taken as the New Testament, since all things are grasped and enclosed in it briefly ... 'For Moses wrote of Me.' Or it is a shortened word of the doctrine as a whole, so that what the previous law and prophets contained in wide-ranging precepts the Lord on his coming ... would say: 'You shall love, etc.' (Matt. 22), in which he evidently shortened the prophets and the law with these two utterances" — "Verbum enim consummans et brevians in aequitate. Historice habet hoc sensus: sicut ego verbum abbrevio, et cito diffinio, ita Deus hoc omni velocitate perficiet. In prophetia autem, breviatum verbum novum Testamentum accipitur, quia in eo omnia breviter comprehensa sunt et clausa ... 'De me enim scripsit Moyses.' Sive verbum breviatum est totius doctrinae, ut quod prior lex et prophetae continebant in latitudine praeceptorum, veniens Dominus ... diceret: Diliges etc. (Matt. 22), in quo evidenter prophetas et legem duobus his sermonibus breviavit" (CIII, 93 CD). Gilbert Crispin, *Disputatio* (Blum., 39).

751. *Christus, plenitudo legis: L. moz. sacram.* (517, 622).

752. *Verbum abbreviatum, Verbum coadunatum:* Bernard, *In Cant.*, s. 59, n. 9: "O Verbum abbreviatum, attamen vivum et efficax!" (PL, CLXXXIII, 1065 D).

753. "in abscondito"; "manifestum in carne": *Or. vis.*, Oration for Advent (32).

754. Garnier, *s.* 5, *de nat. Dom.*: "The Word has become flesh. We have heard the shortened Word about the shortened Word. But,

> Whilst I struggle to be brief,
> I become obscure (Hor., *Art. poet.*, 25-6), since we are talking about the shortened and obscure word through the shorted and obscure word. My

word, since it is short, is obscure. That word, however, since it is obscure, is short. For it was obscure before it had been shortened, and it has been shortened so that it might be made manifest. Before it had been shortened, it could not be seen by the eyes of the mind; but, once shortened, it could be seen with eyes of flesh. The word had not been shortened, nor could it be spoken; the word having been shortened could be spoken. Perhaps not what it was but that it was could be spoken; but what it was could not be spoken, only what it was not.... O ineffable Word, and fabulous infant! O Word ineffable with the Father, and infant fabulous with the mother!...." [Translator's note: the untranslatable pun on the infant *(infans)* 'that does not speak', and the infant 'able to speak' *(fabilis)* is almost 'unspeakable' *(ineffabilis)* in English.]

"Verbum caro factum est. Verbum abbreviatum de Verbo abbreviato audivimus. Sed,

Dum brevis esse laboro,
obscurus fio (Hor., *Art. poet.*, 25-6),

quippe quia per verbum abbreviatum et obscurum de verbo abbreviato et obscuro loquimur. Sed verbum meum, quia abbreviatum, obscurum. Verbum vero illud, quia obscurum, abbreviatum. Obscurum enim erat, antequam esset abbreviatum, et abbreviatum est ut esset manifestum. Antequam esset abbreviatum, videri non poterat oculis mentis; abbreviatum vero, videri potuit oculis carnis. Verbum erat non breviatum, nec dici poterat; verbum abbreviatum fuit, et dici potuit. Dici forte potuit, non quid erat, sed quod erat; sed dici non potuit quid erat, sed quid non erat.... O Verbum ineffabile, et infans fabilis! O Verbum ineffabile apud Patrem, et infans fabilis apud matrem!..." (PL, CCV, 599 CD). *Ib.*: "Therefore the Wisdom of the Father took out of many words (a knowledge of which was prolix and incomprehensible) a shortened Word, whose teaching is wholesome and compendious" — "Ex multis igitur verbis, quorum scientia prolixa et incomprehensibilis erat, excepit Sapientia Patris Verbum abbreviatum, cujus doctrina salubris est et compendiosa" (605 D). In his sermons 5 and 6 Garnier develops the theme of the "verbum abbreviatum" with his customary subtlety.

755. "Jesus, Verbum abbreviatum, sed consummans, legem et prophetas bipartito caritatis praecepto concludens.... O Verbum consummans et abbrevians in aequitate! Verbum caritatis, Verbum totius perfectionis": Aelred, *De Jesu duod.*, n. 13 (SC, 60, 76); *Spec. carit.*, l. 1, c. 16 (PL, CXCV, 520 A). For the sense of St. Paul and that of Isa. 10:22-3 cited by Paul, cf. Huby-Lyonnet, *Ep. aux Romains* (1957), 354-5.

756. "dépréciation de la Parole divine au profit du Verbe divine"; "toute spéculative et, si l'on peut dire, oratoire": A. Humbert, *Les origines de la th. mod.*, 1 (1911), 52.

757. Cf. C. H. Dodd, *Morale de l'Evangile* (tr. J.-H. Marrou, 1958), 139-41.

758. "l'unique Parole divine s'approchaît déjà de nous": L. Bouyer, *Le sens de la vie monast.* (1950), 260.

759. H. Urs von Balthasar, *Théol. de l'hist.* (tr. R. Givord, 1955), 104-5.

760. *In Ps.* (W. A., 3, 262).

761. *In Rom.*, xi, 28 (Ficker, 232).

762. The origin of this theme is in Origen: *In Rom.*, l. 7, c. 19 (PG, XIV, 1153-4); cf. *In Luc.*, h. 34 (199-200). Cf. H. H. Crehan, SJ, JTS, n. ser., 6 (1955), 87-90.

763. *liber quippe sufficiens omnibus:* Absalon, *s.* 25 (PL, CCXI, 149 A).

764. "Jésus se découvre lui-même, il se reconnaît en lisant l'Ancien Testament. Il se voit le terme de toute cette Histoire 'dont la Loi et les Prophètes prophétisent jusqu'à maintenant'. Il y voit l'attente de sa venue. De tous les traits épars des prophéties: du Messie roi de paix, de l'Emmanuel d'Isaïe, du Fils de l'Homme de Daniel, du Serviteur, du Juge, du Pasteur, il n'induit pas ce qu'il doit être, par un travail constructif; tout simplement, il se reconnaît. . . . Il laisse retomber dans l'ombre l'enveloppe. . . . De tous ces traits il fait divinement la synthèse: non pas du dehors, mais du dedans. Il projette sur les prophéties sa lumière intérieure: alors elles se réunissent, elles perdent la trace des circonstances où elles furent proclamées, elles s'harmonisent et s'achèvent"; "En découvrant la Bible, Jésus reconnaît le reflet de la Lumière qui brille en Lui, il entend un écho affaibli de la Parole qui retentit dans sa conscience humaine": Louis Richard, PSS. Cf. K. Rahner, SJ, "Réflexions théol. sur l'Incarnation" (tr. G. Daoust, *Sciences ecclés.*, 12, 1960, 19): in the Word made flesh "God's Word expressing itself and its being heard make merely one thing" — "la Parole de Dieu s'exprimant elle-même et son audition ne font qu'un."

765. "fondu et purifié, le minerai de l'Ancien Testament"; "cette orientation entièrement christologique n'est pas imposée tant bien que mal"; "mais elle lui est intérieure et elle en pénètre toutes les parties": Hoskyns, *Mysterium Christi*, cited by Hebert, 118.

766. Absalon, *s.* 25: "Therefore the Book that has been mentioned is Christ" — "Liber ergo cujus habita mentio Christus est" (PL, CCXI, 148 D).

767. "Christianity, religion of the sacred Book" — "Christianisme, religion du Livre sacré," writes Curtius (378), who devotes scarcely any pages to the Bible, however.

768. "non d'un verbe écrit et muet, mais d'un verbe incarné et vivant": Bernard, *Sup. Missus est*, h. 4, n. 11, making Mary say: "let it not be for me a written, mute word, but one incarnate and alive" — "nec fiat mihi verbum scriptum et mutum, sed incarnatum et vivum" (PL, CLXXXIII, 86 B).

769. "de telle manière qu'on la voit et qu'on la touche": John 1; 1 John 1:1-3. Georges Auzou, *La Parole de Dieu*, nouv. éd. (1960), 426.

770. Martin of Leon, *s. de Jo. Bapt.*: "Truly the efficacious and living utterance of God, i.e., the Son of God" — "Vere sermo Dei efficax et vivus, id est Dei Filius" (PL, CCIX, 18 B).

771. Cf. Gerhoh, *In ps.* xix (CXCIII, 961 D), picking up once again Origen's symbol of the Transfiguration.

772. One can readily speak of biblical religion today, of biblical thought, of biblical metaphysics; but howsoever legitimate the use of such expressions may be, one ought not forget that they are not at all enough to define the Christian faith. "Verbum abbreviatum" sometimes has simply the sense of a creedal statement: Or., *In Rom.*, l. 7, c. 19, on Rom. 9:27-33 (PG, XIV, 1154 A: gloss of Rufinus.

Cf. Rufinus, *Exp. in symb.*, i; PL, XXI, 336 B). Bernard, *In Cant.*, s. 79, n. 2 (CLXXXIII, 1163 D).

Notes to Chapter Three

1. "influence de plus en plus prépondérante de saint Jérôme au détriment de celle de saint Augustin et surtout de saint Grégoire": C. Spicq, *Esquisse*, 59.
2. "vers l'élucidation du sens littéral"; "dépouillé des langes de l'allégorisme": *op. cit.*, 173. We are challenging merely certain passages that are in our opinion a bit exaggerated, from a book whose merit in other respects I am glad to recognize.
3. "solution de détresse": an expression of J. A. Jungmann, who rightly applies it to the late, contrived allegorisms of certain liturgists.
4. B. Smalley, *The Study*, 38.
5. "l'esprit de l'exégèse hiéronymienne . . . la méthode allégorique traditionnelle": Spicq, *Esquisse*, 171.
6. Father A. Vaccari, *Inst. biblicae*, 1 (1927), cites Anselm of Laon, Bruno of Asti, Rupert of Deutz, Hugh of Saint Victor, Honorius, Peter Comester, as having prepared the renaissance of exegesis, "in such wise . . . that they applied the light of reason, exercised through Aristotelian philosophy, especially dialectic, to shed light on the divine pages" — "ita . . . ut lumen rationis per aristotelicam philosophiam, in primis dialecticam, exercitatum ad illustrandas divinas paginas admoverint" (267).
7. "des centaines de textes (qui) oppose l'excellence du sens spirituel à la *vilitas litterae*": F. Cavallera, "Jérôme (St.)," *D. Bibl.*, suppl. (1948), 896: "the literal sense does not long detain him; he is eager to escape from it so as to rise to the typic meaning" — "le sens littéral ne le retient pas longtemps, il lui tarde de s'en évader pour s'élever au sens typique."
8. "des commentateurs les plus originaux" — "l'un des meilleurs exégètes du haut moyen âge tant par son érudition que par son jugement personnel": Spicq, 46.
9. Elle "tranche fortement avec les œuvres de centonisation du haut moyen âge": Dom P. Blanchard, "Un traité *De Benedictionibus Patriarcharum* de Paschase Radbert?" RB, 1911, 425-432.
10. "mei laboris stylo, sanctorum Patrum sensus unitatis eloquio legentibus coaptare": PL, CXX, 31; cf. 33 D. One will recall that the work owes much to Origen.
11. "absque ratione"; "absque mysterio." Other frequent expressions: "it is not devoid of mystery" — "non vacat a mysterio"; "nothing devoid of mystery, nothing superfluous" — "nihil vacuum a mysterio, nihil superfluum" (CXX, 796 A); "they are said not without a great mystery" — "non absque magno mysterio dicuntur" (823 A); etc.
12. *Exp. in ps.* xliv, l. 3: "having an awareness of God's testament, the science of the prophets and the heavenly sacraments" — "habentes notitiam testamenti Dei, scientiam prophetarum et sacramentorum caelestium" (CXX, 1049 A).
13. "ad ea quae sunt mystica": *Ib.*, l. 1 (1012 C).

14. "ubicumque in Scripturis sacris intelligentia requiritur, non carnale aliquid, sed spirituale totum atque arcanum divinitus commendatur": *Ib.*, l. 1 (1002 D). *In Matt.*, l. 6, c. 12: No one can discover all the mysteries hidden within the Scripture; but no one ought to think that there was anything in it "without a mystery" — "absque sacramento" (477 A). Blanchard, 430, rightly notes in Paschasius the habitual opposition between "the two terms spiritualis et carnalis, spiritualiter et carnaliter."

15. "vilissimus cortex"; "nimis insipiens et stultus atque negligens idiota"; "Quicumque sine his legit, quamvis videatur aliquid intelligere, nihil est quod agit, quia omnino prout oportet non intelligit nec legit": *De bened. Patr.*, prol. (RB, 1911, 426-7).

16. "Debemus de Judaea fugere ad montes, ex quibus veniat auxilium nobis. Hoc est, dimissa littera et Judaica pravitate, et appropinquare montibus aeternis, de quibus nos illuminet mirabiliter Dominus, et manere oportet in tecto atque in domate caelestis intelligentiae, quo non possint ignita diaboli jacula pervenire": *In Matt.*, l. 11, c. 24 (PL, CXX, 809 AB); c. 25 (851 D).

17. "neque credendum est quod tot litterae vacent a mysterio": *Exp. in Lam. Jer.*, praef. (CXX, 1064 A; cf. 1103 C). *In Matt.*, l. 2, c. 2: "Indeed there is clearly nothing empty in the divine letters, but, by a marvelous distinction of words, they are all referred to mysteries and by marvelous beauty varied in their senses" — "Profecto patet in divinis litteris nihil supervacuum, sed, mira distinctione verborum, sunt omnia mysteriis referta et mirabili decore sensibus variata" (136 A); l. 3, c. 5: "The things that are regarded as smallest in it [the Law] are all full of mysteries" — "Quae minima putantur in ea (lege), sacramentis plena (sunt) omnia" (237 C); l. 12: "Nothing is devoid of mystery — not a time, not a place, not an order, not any story of the holy Gospel" — "Nihil vacat a mysterio, non tempus, non locus, non ordo, non ulla sancti evangelii narratio" (899 C).

18. *In Matt.*, l. 8 (641-2), etc.

19. "Quamvis evangelium non sit jam umbra sed veritas, propter mystica tamen doctrinarum eloquia non apices, non litterae, non syllabae, non verbum, non nomina, non persona in se divinis vacua sunt figuris": *In Matt.*, l. 2, c. 1 (103 CD); l. 11, prol.: "Not only is the history woven within them . . . , but the divine mysteries of things are ordered in their places as if the Holy Spirit determined the interpositioning of gems here or there to adorn the very clothing of Christ" — "In quibus non historia tantum texitur . . . , sed divina rerum mysteria suis in locis ordinantur, ac si gemmarum interpositiones, ubi vel ubi Spiritus sanctus eamdem vestem Christi exornare decrevit" (796 AB); l. 12 (898 A).

20. *In Eph.*: "since . . . in the divine Scriptures the words, syllables, diacritics, punctuation are each full of senses" — "quia . . . singuli sermones, syllabae, apices, puncta, in divinis Scripturis plena sunt sensibus" (XXVI, 481 A). *Ep.* 18 A, c. 12: "There are not, as some think, simple words in the Scriptures; most of what is in them is hidden" — "Non sunt ut quidam putant in Scripturis verba simplicia, plurimum in his absconditum est" (1, 66).

21. "quae gesta sunt a Domino, quia valde mystica sunt et admiranda"; "exercere nos vult et provocare ad mysticae intelligentiae sacramenta": *In Matt.*, l. 11, c. 26, regarding Bethany (CXX, 876 B); l. 5, c. 24 (806 A). Cf. Gerhoh, *De invest. Antichristi*, c. 43 (*L. de Lite*, 3, 350).

22. *In Matt.*, l. 12, c. 27 (963-4).

23. *In ps.* xliv, l. 2 (1016 B, 1024 D).

24. "vespere sabbati"; "Admirabile loquendi genus, in quo et historiae servatur veritas, et ineffabile, ut ita dicam, construitur sacramentum"; "Venit Maria Magdalena et altera Maria"; "Non ait evangelista: "venerunt," sed "venit." "Quia sub uno nomine veniunt duae, mysterio, non casu, quia duae ad Christum venturae erant Ecclesiae: duae quidem, quia ex duobus populis, quia una est Ecclesia, unaque columba Dei electa genetricis suae": *In Matt.*, l. 12, c. 28 (978 AC).

25. "Radberti... saepe mysticum sermonem": *P. lat. aevi car.*, 3 (L. Traube), 42.

26. *L. de corp. et sang. Dom.*, c. 4: "Utrum sub figura an in veritate hoc mysticum calicis fiat sacramentum" (CXX, 1277-9); "nam figuras veteris testamenti umbras fuisse, nemo qui sacras litteras legit, ambigit" (1278 a); "non enim omnis figura umbra vel falsitas" (1287 C). It is interesting to compare this passage with the *Commentum de narratione caenae Domini,* a Celtic text of the same century, published by A. Wilmart, *Anal. Reginensia* (1933), 36: "Primo in hoc quaeritur, utrum figura an historia an sensus esse credi oportet haec oblatio. Id est: figura est, sed non est in tantum figura, quoniam veteris legis figurae fiebant, id est proprior est haec oblatio ad similitudinem Christi. Historia est, sed non in ea solum finitur, quia spiritualiter accipitur, id est quia tanquam pars de carne et sanguine Christi acciperetur. Sensus est, sed non solus quia historialiter perficitur."

27. *Ib.:* "Just as our childhood first attains reading step by step through the shapes or figures of the letters, then the spiritual senses and understanding of the scriptures" — "Sicut per characteres vel figuras litterarum infantia nostra prius pertingit gradatim ad lectionem, deinde ad spiritales scripturarum sensus et intelligentiam" (1278-9); "falsity consists neither in the shapes of the letters nor anything but the letters themselves" — "neque characteres litterarum falsitas, neque aliud quam litterae" (1279 A); "the figure or shape, however, is what is sensed externally; but the whole truth with no shadow is what is perceived internally" — "est autem figura vel character hoc quod exterius sentitur; sed totum veritas et nulla adumbratio, quod intrinsecus percipitur" (1279 B). Cf. Origen, *In Jo.*, t. 1, 18 (22); Hugh, below, ch. 4.1.

28. *The Study*, 90-1.

29. "Juxta historiam, ostenditur Jeremias non minus deplorare populi sui casus et ruinam, quam tribulationis suae angustias"; "quod satis Hierusalem accidisse manifestum est"; "nulli dubium quod haec lamenta Judaeis congruant": *In Lam.*, l. 3 (1148 B, 1157 B); l. 4 (1227 A).

30. Cassiodorus, *Inst.*, c. 3: "in forty-five sermons in Attic Greek Origen expounded Jeremiah, who bewailed the ruins of his own city in fourfold alphabetical order" — "Jeremiam vero, qui civitatis suae ruinas quadruplici, flevit alphabeto, quadraginta quinque homiliis attico sermone Origines exposuit" (LXX, 1114 C). Rupert, *In Jer.*, c. 12: "the Babylonian captivity of God's people, which he had seen with his own eyes" — "populi Dei captivitas Babylonica, quam sub oculis suis viderat" (CLXVII, 1379 A).

31. *The Study*, 91-2; cf. 42.

32. "Ultimam partem Jeremiae prophetae, quae appellatur Lamentationes,

prout Dominus Spiritus sui gratia, quo ipse propheta locutus est, nos illustrare voluerit, secundum historiam et secundum mysticum sensum exposituri . . ."; "Quod lamentationes praedictae non solum super urbis Hierusalem vastatione et Judaici populi captivitate, sed etiam super Josiae regis occasu conscriptae sint, Liber verborum Dierum demonstrat. . . . Unde, primum historiam in explanatione retexemus; deinde allegoriam per congrua loca, sive ad Josiam . . . sive ad Judaeos . . . pertinentem inseremus. Opportunius ergo multo nunc a nobis quam tunc a propheta Dei lamentatur"; "Sequitur oratio prophetae, quae vastationem urbis Jerusalem et casum populi Judaeorum historialiter deplorat, et spiritualiter ruinem animarum fidelium et vastitatem quam passae sunt a nequitiis spiritualibus flebiliter commemorat": PL, CXI, 1181 CD, 1184 AB, 1262 B. Rabanus observes an analogous distinction and exhibits the same sobriety, *In Ez.*, l. 1: "But, keeping silence about what the human race will have from the crafty enemy at the end to come, we turn the words to Judea alone, in which the Prophet was and whose perdition he saw in prophesying" — "Sed nos ista reticentes, quae humano generi erunt ab hoste callido in fine ventura, ad solam Judaeam in qua Propheta fuit et cujus perditionem prophetando conspicit, verba vertamus" (CX, 502 D); and l. 13, announcing the prophecies and promises of ch. 35: "All these things can be applied not merely historically to the earlier people and the times of the Law, but also even more allegorically to the time of the New Testament and to the Christian people" — "Quae omnia, non tantum juxta historiam ad plebem priorem et legis tempora, sed etiam multo magis secundum allegoriam ad tempus novi Testamenti et ad populum christianum transferri possunt" (847 BC). Compare Jerome, *In Jer.*, l. 6, c. 31 (XXIV, 881 BC).

33. "manifestum est"; "nulli dubium est": PL, CXX, 1157 B, 1246 D.

34. "an historice vel allegorice intelligendae sunt"; "Utrumque (sonant), et historiam et allegoriam": *Quaest. et resp. in Gen.*, q. 281 (C, 558-9). In the previous century, Julian of Toledo understood Jacob's blessing by Isaac as applying to Christ, but without excluding a primary sense: *De comprobatione aet. sectae*, l. 1, n. 18 (XCVI, 551-2; on Gen. 27:28-9). On the earliest Christian tradition (Justin, Irenaeus) regarding the twofold realization of the prophets: Dom Pierre Salmon, *Les "Tituli Psalmorum" des MSS Latins* (1959), 13-14.

35. "An secundum historiam vel etiam allegoriam intelligendum est, quod Dominus respondit Rebeccae: "Duae gentes in utero tuo sunt, etc."? Secundum utrumque modum. Spiritaliter vero solet intelligi etc. Sed etiam historica proprietate invenitur esse completum . . . .": *In Gen.*, xxv (CXV, 206 C; cf. 232 C).

36. *In Lam.*, l. 1, Aleph: "Here [the Prophet] plainly insinuates that the overthrow of the wretched city and the ruin of its wicked people occurred not just under the Chaldeans, but would all be more fully completed under Titus and Vespasian. . . . Further, spiritually, more sadly, as often as the Church is widowed, as her faults require, from Christ, she is mourned by the prophet or holy men: 'How is the city sitting alone?' She is rightly required to sit alone, since, having been rendered desolate of the assistance of God and the holy angels, she has been ravaged by the enemy within and without. . . . So too, our Jerusalem, as often as she comes into the confusion of her sins, has neither chair nor throne nor any other heavenly dignity, but is rightly compelled to sit in the dust of the earth. . . . Tropologically, however, the soul. . . ." — "In qua patenter (propheta) insinuat

subversionem miserae civitatis et ruinam scelesti populi, non solum sub Chaldaeis accidisse, verum sub Tito et Vespasiano plenius omnia completa fore.... Caeterum, spiritualiter lacrymosius, quoties Ecclesia, culpis exigentibus, sponso Christo viduatur, a propheta vel sanctis viris plangitur: Quomodo sedet sola civitas? Sola quippe sedere jure queritur, cum Dei et sanctorum desolata angelorum auxilio, intus forisque ab hostibus vastatur.... Ita et Jerusalem nostra, quoties in confusionem peccatorum venerit, non est ei solium neque thronus neque ulla dignitas celsitudinis, sed in terrae pulvere sedere perhibetur jure.... Tropologice autem, anima . . ." (CXX, 1063-5).

37. Thus again l. 5: "They have humiliated the women of Zion and the virgins in the cities of Judah: which no one doubts has literally occurred to the Jews" — "Mulieres in Sion humiliaverunt, et virgines in civitatibus Judae: quod ad litteram Judaeis accidisse nulli dubium est"; then he passes to the mystic and moral application: the humiliations of the Church and of the soul (1246-7).

38. *Paschase Radbert* (1938), 117.

39. "sic terrenae illius Hierusalem et populi excidia deplorant, ut praesentis Ecclesiae damna deflere non praetermittant": CXX, 1062 D.

40. "infectatio Northemannicae depopulationis": Hucbald, de S. Amand, *V. s. Ritruidis*, c. 1 (ASS, May 2, 81 E); cf. c. 2 (81 F). Hucbald is writing in 907.

41. "De gente fera Normanniae libera nos, Domine!": L. Delisle, *Litt. latine et histoire du moyen âge* (1890), 17. Sequence: "From the fierce tribe — deliver us — the Norman tribe — which is ravaging our possessions — rule, oh God!" — "De gente fera — nos libera — normanica — quae nostra vastat — Deus regna!" (Zumthor, 181). Cf. Lupus of Ferrières in Hilduin in 854 (L. Levillain, 2, 90-2). In a poem (v. 859), John Scotus asks Christ to protect the emperor against the Normans: *P. latini*, 3, 527. After a period of victorious defense, Sedulius Scotus composed an ode: "On the overthrow of the Northmen" — "De strage Normannorum."

42. The Northmen were threatening Corbie in 858 or 859; they would take and destroy the abbey in 881. After a sojourn of a few years at Saint Riquier (851ff.), Paschasius returned to Corbie as a simple monk. In *In Matt.*, l. 9, prol. (643 CD), he is already speaking of his old age.

43. On the Norman raids from 845 to 885: Edouard Favre, *Études comte de Paris et roi de France* (1893), 22-6; R. Dion, *Paris dans les récits histor. et légendaires du IXe au XIIe s.* (1949). P. Zumthor, *Charles le Chauve* (1957), 125. Pierre Héliot, *L'abbaye de Corbie* (1957), 31, 36. The siege of 885-96 has been recounted in detail in verse by Abdon of S.-Germain-des-Prés, *De bello Parisiaco*, l. 1-2 (MGH, Scr., 2, 776-805; cf. *ib.*, 532-6: *Chronicon de gestis Normannorum in Francia*); l. 2, v. 380-1:

> Urbs age Parisius, sub quid defensa fuisti.
> Principibus? . . .
> Come on, o city of Paris, under what had you been defended.
> Princes? . . .

44. It is of this latter that Paschasius is speaking, *In Lam.*, cf. Peltier, 82-3.

45. "Nihil aliud quotidie quam finem nostrum cum gemitu exspectamus!": *In Matt.*, l. 11 (801 BC, 802 D).

46. Cf. the prologue *Ad Odilmanum Severum*: "Exhausted by the long weari-

ness of life, encumbered by my ills, old age, unsummoned, has unexpectedly arrived" — "Longo confectus vitae taedio, meis praegravata malis, inopinate senectus non vocata venit"; "made harsher by long habit" — "usu longiori durior effectus"; "amidst the decisive moments at end of life" — inter discrimina ultimae vitae"; "I have entered the house of mourning" — "domum luctus intravi" (1059-61).

47. "non crediderunt reges terrae et universi habitatores orbis, quod ingrederetur hostis et inimicus portas Jerusalem"; "Quis unquam crederet, vel quis unquam cogitare potuisset . . . ?": This is reminiscent of Jerome, *ep.* 123, c. 17: "Who would believe it? What histories could recount it in fitting words? That Rome in her very heart is to fight not for glory but for survival, nay, not even to fight, but . . . to ransom her life for gold?" — "Quis hoc credet? Quae digno sermone historiae comprehendent? Romam in gremio suo non pro gloria sed pro salute pugnare, imo ne pugnare quidem sed auro . . . vitam redimere?" (XXII, 1058).

48. *In Lam.*, l. 4: "Who ever would believe or who in our parts could ever have imagined what in the course of time we have all seen, grieved and wept for and much feared? From that moment till this very day we grow no less fearful lest pirates gathered together helter-skelter from various families, should reach the city-limits of Paris and here and there burn down Christ's churches along the shore. Who ever, I ask, would believe that thieves of mongrel race would ever dare such things? Or who could imagine that so glorious, such a well-fortified and extensive kingdom, so populous and stable, was to be humiliated and soiled with the filth of such men? And I am not saying that these fellows [were] to carry away vast inventory and to seize prey or lead their captives off, but who could even believe that men so utterly vile would dare to approach our borders? For, though I do not reckon back a long time, I own that none of the kings of the land would have thought of those things, nor could any inhabitant of the world have heard that an enemy would be entering our Paris" — "Quis unquam crederet vel quis unquam cogitare potuisset in nostris partibus, quod transcurso tempore omnes accidisse conspeximus, doluimus ac deflevimus et valde pertimuimus? Unde et adhuc hodie non minus pertimescimus, ut piratae diversis admodum collecti ex familiis, Parisiorum attingerent fines ecclesiasque Christi hinc inde igne cremarent circa litus. Quis unquam, quaeso, crederet quod latrones promiscuae gentis unquam talia auderent? Vel quis aestimare potuisset quot tam gloriosum regnum tamque munitum et latissimum, tam populosum et firmissimum, talium hominum humiliari vel faedari sordibus deberet? Et non dico hi[c] quod censum plurimum asportare et praedas diripere vel captivos transducere, verum quis credere posset quod tam vilissimi nostros adire fines auderent? Fateor enim, ut ne aestimo non longe retro, quod nullus ex regibus terrae ista cogitaret, neque ullus habitator nostri orbis audire potuisset, quod Parisium nostrum hostis intraret" (1220 BD).

49. "si non est quod exponam, est tamen quod defleam et plangam": *ib.*, (1220 D).

50. Peltier, 123-31. See, for example, PL, CXX, 116 D, 722 C, 966 B, 999 A, 1027 C, 1029 A, 1031 B, 1035 D, 1041 B, 1045 AB, 1046 B, 1050 D.

51. *In Matt.*: "considering the Hebraic truth with blessed Jerome" —

"hebraicam veritatem considerans, juxta b. Hieronymum" (966 B); "following the Hebraic truth" — "secundum hebraicam veritatem" (1175 A), etc.

52. *In Matt.*, l. 5, c. 24: "within certain of the Scriptures, do not trust the secret or apocryphal [works], since they are dubious or false" — "Intra quaedam Scripturarum secreta vel apocrypha, quia dubia vel falsa sunt, nolite credere" (813 C). He also rejected two writings that Hincmar attributed to Jerome: Ebert, 2, 271.

53. "difficultates rerum"; "Magnus calumniantium patet locus, et multis involvimur inextricabilium quaestionum nodis"; "probabilius": *In Matt.*, l. 12, c. 28 (984 CD; cf. 987 AB).

54. *In Matt.* (585 B, 629 D, 786 BD, 837 A, 877 D, 930 B, 955 C). He does say, however, *De partu virg.*, c. 2: "Augustine, whom it is not right to contradict" — "Augustinum quem contradicere fas non est" (d'Achery, *Spicil.*, 1, 1723, 51 A).

55. L. 8, c. 17 (577-89). The Scripture is an ocean of mysteries: L. 12, prol. (875-6); etc.

56. *In ps.* xliv, l. 3: "the philosophers, namely Plato and Aristotle, as well as other... teachers of various opinions or errors" — "philosophos, Platonem sc. et Aristotelem, necnon et reliquos ... diversorum dogmatum vel errorum magistros" (1053 D). Along with Paul Alvarus, he is perhaps the greatest "rigorist" of the 9th century (Laistner, 211).

57. *De fide, spe et car.*, l. 3, prol. (1457-8); "since indeed even the philosophers wanted to dig the same wells, which they called 'physics', 'ethics', 'logic'; but since they find water without Christ, not a living water" — "siquidem et philosophi eosdem voluerunt fodere puteos, quos physicam, ethicam, logicam appellaverunt; sed quia sine Christo aquam inveniunt sed non vivam etc." (1458 C).

58. "inter alta cordis silentia, inter amoenos Scripturarum sanctarum recessus": *In ps.* xliv, l. 1 (993-4).

59. *In Matt.*, l. 12, c. 27 (957 CD).

60. *In Gen.*, h. 7, n. 6: "Incessant tears and prayers are needed to get the Lord to open our eyes" — "Il faut des larmes et des prières incessantes pour obtenir que le Seigneur nous ouvre les yeux" (SC, 7, 160). *In Jo.*, x, 13: "The flesh of the Lamb" ought to be cooked "with the heat of the Spirit"; but it is often necessary, "for such research to lead to any good, that our own flesh should endure the cooking" — "Les chairs de l'Agneau" doivent être cuites "à la chaleur de l'Esprit"; but it is often necessary, "pour mener à bien une telle recherche, que notre propre chair subisse la cuisson" (188-9). Cf. Aug., *C. ep. Manichaei*, c. 2: "Let those who are ignorant of the sighs and groans whereby it may come about that God may to an ever so tiny extent be able to be understood keep raging against you" — "Illi in vos saeviant, qui nesciunt quibus a suspiriis et gemitibus fiat ut ex quantulacumque parte possit intelligi Deus" (PL, CXII, 174).

61. Rupert, *In Cant.*, prol.; *In Matt.*, l. 12 (CLXVIII, 840 A, 1397-8). Philip de Harvengt, *De scientia cler.*, c. 32: it is necessary to pray with tears so that the "shadowy surface of the Scriptures" — "obscura superficies Scripturarum" — might be dissipated (CCIII, 705 BD).

62. "Sed quia ... sunt multa ibi quae de passione Christi altius reperiuntur,

altior est sensus requirendus, licet non inveniri posse credam sine fletibus": *In Lam.*, l. 3, prol. (CXX, 1142 A). On the various kinds of tears: *praef.* (1061-3).

63. Cf. François Baix, *Étude sur l'abbaye de Stavelot-Malmédy* (1924), 173-85. The name Druthmar which is currently used to designate him has no justification.

64. "singulier": Cf. Spicq, *Esquisse*, 16 and 80.

65. H. Focillon, *L'an Mil* (1952), 81. Laistner, HTR, 20 (1927), 142-5; *The Intellectual Heritage* (1957), 216-36, and *op. cit.*, 244-5 and 305.

66. "Multa dicunt aliqui de stella hac, quae, quia non habent fontem veritatis, praetermittere malui": *In Matt.* (PL, CVI, 1282 A).

67. *In Matt.*, prol.: "I have taken pains more about the historical than the spiritual sense, however, since it seems unreasonable to me to search for the spiritual understanding in a book and to have utterly no knowledge of the historical; since the history is the foundation of every understanding, its stability is to be sought and embraced, and without it one cannot perfectly go over to the other understanding" — "Studui autem plus historicum sensum quam spiritalem, quia irrationabile mihi videtur spiritalem intelligentiam in libro aliquo quaerere et historicam penitus ignorare; cum historia fundamentum omnis intelligentiae sit, et ipsa frimitus [sic] quaerenda et amplexanda, et sine ipsa perfecte ad aliam non possit transiri" (CVI, 1262-3). [Trans. is reading "firmitas" for "frimitus."]

68. *L'influence des Moralia*, 79, note 45, citing Gregory, "fundamenta historiae"; "This golden rule was destined to remain the slogan of exegetes for several centuries" — "Cette règle d'or était destinée à rester pendant plusieurs siècles le slogan des exégètes." Among others, Berengaud, *In Ap.*, vis. 7: "For whoever desires the moral and spiritual understanding in the divine Scriptures must first possess an understanding of the history" — "Quisquis enim moralem et spiritalem intelligentiam in divinis Scripturis investigare desiderat, necesse est ut historiae intelligentiam prius possideat" (XVII, 960 D). See above, vol. 2, ch. vii.

69. B. Bischoff, *S. Er.*, 6, 219. Laistner, 146.

70. "à quel point la route qu'il prétendait suivre était peu fréquentée": *H. litt. de la Fr. avant le XIIe s.*, 3 (1840), 100.

71. This text, commenting on Matt. 26:26, had frequently been disputed at length. Rosenmüller, *Hist. interpr.*, 5 (1814), 167-74. Cf. Richard Simon, *Critique de M. du Pin*, 1, 300 ff. Christian's *Expositio*, writes Father Spicq, *Esquisse*, 49, "would long enjoy a justly merited influence, since in the 17th century it would provide a topic for a long controversy between Catholics and Protestants" — "jouira longtemps d'un crédit justement mérité, puisqu'au XVIIe siècle il donnera lieu à un longue controverse entre catholiques et protestants."

72. In fact Christian here depends strictly upon Augustine through the intermediary of Bede.

73. "à côté de passages qui semblent favorables à une explication symbolique, toute la doctrine qui finit par prévaloir dans la théologie catholique"; "prêcha contre tout culte rendu à des objets sensibles et fit enlever les images des églises de son diocèse"; *Précis d'hist. de l'Église d'Occident pendant le moyen âge*, 56-7, 60, 63.

74. "Interpretationes mysticas, quas Druthmarus interdum grammaticis et historicis adjunxit, missas facimus": *Hist. interpretationis librorum sacr. in Ecclesia christ.*, 5 (1814), 160.

75. "Ubicumque ergo fuerint istae intelligentiae, prout Dominus dederit, deducemus ad notitiam": *Exp. in Matt. ev.* (PL, CVI, 1264-7).

76. "quelquefois trop littéral": *Critique de la Bibl. des auteurs ecclés.* (1730), 305-6.

77. Cf. Smalley, *The Study*, 43: "Christian of Stavelot wrote a commentary on St. Matthew which, he tells us, was intended to be mainly historical."

78. C. 2: "Since we have run across the historical understanding as best we could, let us now take a look at the spiritual" — "Quia ut potuimus historicum intellectum transcurrimus, nunc spiritalem videamus" (1284 D); "if again we inquire anagogically" — si secundum anagogen requiramus" (1285 D).

79. *In Ez.*, h. 6, n. 4 (PG, XIII, 713 B); or: he suffers from "poverty of the senses" — "inopia sensuum," *In Matt. ser.*, 38 (72).

80. *Mor.*, l. 22, c. 5, n. 8 (PL, LXXVI, 217 A).

81. C. 5 (CVI, 1295 B).

82. "And if anyone should ask why I would have dared to do this after St. Jerome, I answer that I have seen that St. Jerome had passed over many words as though they were easy and given difficult ones of little sense in return" [or, following Lubac's suggested alternative reading: "given difficult ones in exchange for those of a little sense"] — "Et si aliquis requirit quare post b. Hieronymum hoc ausus fuerim agere, respondeo, quia perspexi b. Hieronymum multa verba quasi levia praeterisse et parvuli sensus (= parvulis sensu?) difficilia reddidisse" (1261-2).

83. "If then I see that you find this first accomplishment satisfactory, let me set my hand to the gospel of John; since Augustine, following the eagle, namely blessed John, who has been likened unto an eagle, goes off to the clouds whenever the evangelist goes beyond them, for which reason a humble expositor sticking close to the earth is needed for those who are little ones in sense, so that they can understand what he has left untouched as being well-known to everyone" — "Si ergo videro quod vobis hoc primum factum placeat, ad evangelium Joannis manum mittam; quia Augustinus, aquilam sequens, id est, b. Joannem, qui aquilae assimilatus[,] est, cum ille ultra nubes, iste prope nubes incedit, propterea parvulis sensu necessarius est humilis et terrae gradiens expositor, ut possint intelligere quod ille quasi omnibus notum relinquit intactum" (1263 A). Nevertheless, the surviving fragments of Christian on St. John have all been taken from Augustine, just as the fragments on Luke came from Bede: J. Lebon, "Notes sur Christian de Stavelot," *RHE*, 9 (1908), 491-6. (But are these fragments authentic? Laistner, *Int. Heritage*, 218.) The Johannine eagle inspired the poets in the train of Sedulius (*Carmen pasc.*, l. 1, v. 358); cf. the poem of the 9th century cited by Neuss (1912), 200:

Sciendo penetras coelum tu mente Joannes.
By knowing you penetrate heaven with your mind, John.

84. "stultiloquium": "I have also treated the context itself in clear language, since there is, so to speak, gibberish in the exposition of one fellow's book, so that it is necessary to look for someone to explain the explanation itself" — "Aperta quoque locutione ipsum contextum digessi, quoniam stultiloquium est in

expositione alicujus libri ita loqui, ut necessarium sit expositorem ipsius expositionis quaerere" (1262 C).

85. *In Luc.*, ep. ad Accam (PL, XCII, 303-8; cf. letter from Accas, 301-4).

86. "The bishop Augustine, flying through the mountain tops like an eagle, not considering what may be happening at the foot of the mountains, has with clear voice described the many spaces of the heavens and the lands as well as the circle of the waters" — "Augustinus episcopus, volans per montium culmina quasi aquila, ea quae in montium radicibus fiunt non considerans, multa caelorum spatia terrarumque situs et aquarum circulum claro sermone pronuntiat" (XCIV, 522 B). Cf. Godfroy of Saint Victor, Easter sermon: "That sublime beholder of God's secrets, who . . . alone deserves to be honored . . . in the figure of a flying eagle, flitting often betwixt heaven and earth, saw in the apocalypse of the Lord things too marvelous to behold both in heaven and on earth" — "Sublimis ille contemplator secretorum Dei, qui . . . solus in figura aquilae volantis . . . meruit honorari, saepius inter medium caeli et terrae volitans, in apocalypsi dominica, miranda nimis tam in caelo quam in terra vidit" (Ph. Delhaye, RTAM, 21, 201). Richard, *In Ap.*, l. 2, c. 2 (CXCVI, 751 C).

87. *The Study*, 43. Miss Smalley does not try to make a precursor out of Christian.

88. So Alcuin, *In Gen.* (PL, C, 557 C).

89. "c'est qu'il a pu consulter un moine, nommé Euphemius, qui sait lire ces auteurs dans leur langue"; "les étymologies qu'il étale avec complaisance montrent ou que ce moine n'était pas très fort"; "ne profitait guère de ses leçons": *Essai sur l'hist. de la Bible dans la Fr. chrét. au moyen âge* (1878), 16.

90. *Op. cit.*, 304: "Il donne . . . des preuves évidentes qu'il était bien peu versé dans la langue grecque."

91. "Christus hebraice dicitur Messias"; "Ieron hebraice munitio dicitur": PL, CVI, 1275 D, 1281 D, etc.

92. "l'outillage philologique": Spicq, *Esquisse*, 47-9. Cf. PL, 122, 203, 325, etc.

93. B. Smalley, *The Study*, 39.

94. "d'être le meilleur exégète du moyen âge": *Litt. latine*, 2, 107.

95. that "pour l'exégèse il n'a pas son rival, en Italie, du VIe au XIIe siècle": *H. de l'Ordre de S. Benoît*, 2, 127.

96. "cujus auctoritate et prudentia non parum sancta Ecclesia roboratur": PL, CLXV, 605 A.

97. "Apocalypsis Joannis tot habet sacramenta, quot verba; parum dixi, et pro merito voluminis laus omnis inferior est; in verbis singulis multiplices latent intelligentiae": cf. *In Matt.*, on the parable of those invited to the feast: "What else is this whole feast but the spiritual understanding of each of the two Testaments?" — "Totum hoc prandium quid aliud est, nisi spiritualis intelligentia utriusque Testamenti?" (CLXV, 251 B).

98. *De sacr. Eccl.* (PL, CLXV, 1095 BC).

99. Spicq, *Esquisse*, 113, etc.; *Pourquoi le moyen âge*, 171.

100. "Tum leo comedit paleas, quando potentes hujus saeculi, qui spiritualis intelligentiae sunt jejuni, ipsa superficie et historia satiantur": *Sp. cas.*, 3. The prologue has been edited by Dom Amelli in 1903.

101. "Cum sint multa et pene innumerabilia in divinis voluminibus quae sponsam Christi Ecclesiam significant": *Sent.*, l. 1 (PL, CLXV, 875 A).

102. "breviter historiis praenotatis"; "satis compendiose allegorias": "From the beginning of the book till just after the making of Noah's ark all things have been continually explained (it had seemed quite necessary), since they seemed to be rather difficult. From then on, however . . . once the histories have briefly been sketched, we have put under them the allegories in a fashion compendious enough. You will also find the blessings of Jacob dealt with with a continuous exposition, since they too seem to involve some difficulty" — "A principio autem libri usque post arcae Noe fabricationem, quoniam difficiliora esse videbantur, pernecessarium visum fuit continue cuncta exposita sunt. Inde vero . . . breviter historiis praenotatis, satis compendiose allegorias subposuimus. Benedictiones quoque Jacob, quoniam et ipsae difficultatis aliquid habere videbantur, continua expositione digestas invenies" (CLXIV, 147-8).

103. "His autem ad litteram dispositis, quid etiam allegorice significent videamus": C. 1 (150 A), etc. (150-550).

104. "profunda Scripturarum mysteria": *In Lev.*, c. 6: "A love of learning God's marvels and investigating the truth somehow overcomes the deep mysteries of the Scriptures and leads to ease of understanding" — "Amor discendi Dei mirabilia et veritatem investigandi, profunda Scripturarum mysteria quodammodo vincit et ad intelligentiae facilitatem perducit" (398 B).

105. Spicq, *Pourquoi le moyen âge,* 171.

106. "non carnalem, sed spiritualem intelligentiam"; "Quot enim puteos Hieronymus, quot Augustinus, quot Ambrosius fodit, ut merito locus ille, in quo isti habitant, Ecclesia vid., Bersabee, id est, puteus satietatis appelletur!": *In Gen.*, c. 26 (CLXIV, 204-5). Thus Godet more rightly said, DTC, 2, 1151: "Without neglecting the literal sense, he prefers to examine and emphasize the mystic and allegorical sense" — "Sans négliger le sens littéral, il recherche de préférence et met en relief le sens mystique et allégorique."

107. "Caetera autem quae sequuntur, non necessarium est cuncta exponere. Summatim igitur breviterque exponentes, ibi tantum, ubi necesse fuerit, allegorias ponamus": *In Gen.*, c. 6 (180 AB); thus the history of the rainbow and the mention of all the animals sheltered in the ark are applied allegorically to the life of the Church.

108. "Quae quidem valde necessaria erant, et Levitae ejus tabernaculi onera cunctamque supellectilem difficile ferre poterant. In his allegoriam quaerere non videtur necessarium. Ibi allegoria necessario quaerenda est, ubi littera aliquid jubet, vel quod inutile sit, vel quod omnino careat ratione": *In Num.*, c. 7 (474 B).

109. *Ib.* (474-5).

110. "nova et spiritualis intelligentia"; "Ego sum finis legis. In me legis littera completa est. *Ecce nova facio omnia*. Spiritualiter intelligantur, quae hactenus ad litteram intelligebantur": *In Jo.*, c. 2 and 7 (CLXV, 462 A, 514 BC). "For as often as we relate and preach what has been done in each age, so often . . . do we fill the urns with water" — "Quoties enim narramus et praedicamus quid in unaquaque aetate factum sit, toties . . . hydrias aqua implemus" (462 C).

111. "homme du cloître"; "il aime la culture intellectuelle du cloître et se meut comme naturellement dans les idées et la formes allégoriques reçues,

admises et comprises de tous à l'époque où il écrivait": X., "S. Bruno de Segni," RB, 15 (1898), 277, 279.

112. C. 15 (CLXIV, 131 B).
113. C. 2 (99-100); c. 15 (129-31).
114. C. 5 (103 AB).
115. Cf. RB, 15, 277. *Sent.*, l. 4, c. 1-3, *de S. Trinitate* (CLXV, 973-84). *Tr. de incarn. Dom.* (1079-84).
116. "se méfier de la dialectique": Ghellinck, *Litt. lat.*, 2, 136.
117. "stulta sapientia haereticorum et philosophorum": *In Ap.*, l. 5, c. 16 (CLXV, 693 A); cf. c. 18 (705 B, 706 C).
118. "pravitas haeretica et philosophica": *In Gen.*, c. 6 (CLXIV, 176 C).
119. "ad dialecticas quaestiones sese convertunt": *In Ap.*, l. 3, c. 9: "Quasi scorpius cauda ferientes" (CLXV, 653 B).
120. H. Silvestre, "Les citations et réminiscences classiques dans l'œuvre de Rupert de Deutz," RHE, 1950, 140-74. He has read Virgil, Horace, Lucian, Boethius, Prudentius, Sallust, Seneca, Trogus Pompeius, Calpurnius, and Flaccus directly; and maybe Chalcidius, Cicero, Claudian, Ovid, Persius, Sedulius, Statius, Symmachus, and Terence, too. He gives second-hand citations from Pliny the Elder, Servius, and Varro.
121. Rh. Haacke, f. 79, 358.
122. *De Sp. sancto*, l. 7, c. 19 (PL, CLXVII, 1782-4).
123. *Ib.*, c. 18: "An outstanding fellow among those [doctors of ours], blessed Jerome . . . , sufficiently educated a long time ago by secular masters . . . pursued the truth . . . of all the books of the old Testament. . . . He translated all the scrolls contained in the canon into Latin and commented on them, and in the translation of the Lord's Scriptures he showed us that we need not go to the fountain of the Hebrews when he is known to have satisfied us with the great clarity of his eloquence" — "Quidam de praecipuis illorum (= nostrorum doctorum) b. Hieronymus . . . , jamdudum a magistris saecularibus sufficienter edoctus . . . omnium librorum veteris Testamenti . . . veritatem consecutus est . . . Cuncta volumina quae in canone continentur, ex veteris T. editione in latinam linguam vertit atque commentatus est, et nobis in translatione Dominicae Scripturae praestitit ut ad Hebraeorum fontem non egeamus accedere, quando nos facundiae suae multa cognoscitur claritate satiasse" (1781-2).
124. As *In Reg.*, l. 1, c. 3 (1062 A); l. 2, c. 19 (1117 D); *In Gen.*, l. 8, c. 5 (495 D); *Div. off.*, l. 5, c. 11 (CLXX, 133 BC; cf. 454 A). *De glorif.*, l. 7, c. 7: "the illustrious blessed Jerome, an expert in the Hebrew tongue" — "vir illustris b. Hieronymus hebraicae linguae peritus etc." (CLXIX, 148-9); etc.
125. *Esquisse*, 114-5. The author made a fine elogy of Rupert, whose work "recalls Scotus Eriugena and anticipates Hugh of Saint Victor in religious inspiration" — "rappelle Scot Erigène et annonce Hugues de SV par l'inspiration religieuse."
126. DTC, 14, 180.
127. "la recherche du sens littéral prédomine": Spicq, 140.
128. *De vict. Verbi*, l. 3, c. 1; l. 4, c. 11 (PL, CLXIX, 1269 D, 1301 C); cf. l. 1, c. 1 (1217 AB); l. 2, c. 18 (1257-8).
129. "la tendance mystique et allégorique en exégèse"; "fortune littéraire":

Art. "Rupert," *Bibliogr. nat. de Belgique,* 20 (1909-10), 434-5. But in them there are merely "private musings" — "rêveries personnelles" (456).

130. "son système allégorique pénètre toute son œuvre": *H. de l'Église en Belg.,* 2 (1940), 189: this precludes crediting it with "a very scientific character" — "un caractère très scientifique": besides, this is not what we would look for in it.

131. *L'essor,* 1, 118-20.

132. "rien n'est critique, tout est mystique; il n'y a pas une phrase de l'Écriture qui ne l'incite à chercher une allégorie" — "la haine de la science": *Hist. de la philos. scolastique,* 1, 319, 317.

133. DTC, 14, 183.

134. *De Sp. sancto,* l. 1, c. 7, on the depth of the immensity of God's love for man, which explains the Incarnation of the Word in the womb of the Virgin, then within the heart of the believer: "Let not the suspicion of an affected likeness extenuate the reality of the truth. For indeed whatever things the holy and veridical Scripture tells us of God's love or the loving God, are both true and constant, so that these carnal affairs of ours from which likenesses are drawn are, as it were, shadows or transitory images for those of constant truth" — "Rem veritatis non extenuet suspicio affectatae similitudinis. Nam revera quaecumque sancta et veridica Scriptura nobis de amore Dei vel amante Deo loquitur, tam vera tamque constantia sunt, ut potius haec nostra carnalia de quibus similitudines ducuntur, illis constantis veritatis quaedam quasi umbrae vel transitoriae imagines sint" (PL, CLXVII, 1577 BC). Cf. Chenu, "Hist. et allégorie au XIIe s.," in *Festgabe Lortz* (1957), 67.

135. In Cant., l. 4: "Rise up, then, north wind! . . . keep doing what you are doing . . . — Come, south wind! Come holy Spirit, to whom the devil is the contrary north wind, blow through my garden, and its spicy aromas will flow" — "Surge, igitur, aquilo! . . . age quod agis . . . — Veni, auster! Veni sancte Spiritus, cui diabolus aquilo contrarius est, perfla hortum meum, et fluent aromata illius . . ." (CLXVIII, 960-1). This is the basic principle of the whole *De Victoria Verbi Dei.*

136. *In Jos.:* "planam tritamque historiae superficiem transilientes" (CLXVII, 1024 A).

137. *In Ex.,* l. 1, c. 1: "In these as well as in other matters . . . we shall pluck the letter while running by, and we shall strive as diligently as we can to present with complete fidelity the mysteries of Christ that have been hidden within" — "In his et in caeteris . . . litteram cursim vellicabimus, et quae instrinsecus condita sunt mysteria Christi . . . diligenter pro posse . . . proferre integra fide conabimur" (567 B). *In Matt.,* l. 12: "fiduciam talem habere tractandi sanctarum Scripturarum sacramenta" (CLXVIII, 1603 D), etc.

138. "jucundo carmine digna": *In Num.,* l. 2, c. 13 (CLXVII, 891 C).

139. *In Gen.,* l. 6, c. 41 (439 D); c. 43: this golden interior is the "most precious mysteries of Christ and the Church" — "pretiosissima Christi et Ecclesiae sacramenta" (442 A).

140. "plenitudinem Scripturarum cum dulcedine et desiderio percipiunt, et absconditos in litterarum profundo thesauros subtilium sententiarum": *In Deut.,* l. 2, c. 16 (990 D).

141. "juxta anagogen"; "juxta altiorem sensum": PL, CLXVII, 641 D, etc.

142. "spiritus intellectus": *In ev.,* c. 2 (1536 BC). *In Gen.,* l. 5, c. 4 (369 C).

143. "sensus judaicus"; "aridus nimis et exiguus": *De vict. Verbi*, l. 11, c. 19 (CLXIX, 1455 A).

144. "quidnam sacramenti latet in illis rebus gestis": *In Gen.*, l. 9, c. 33 (CLXVII, 558 A). *De Trin., ep. ad Cun.* (194-5). Everything is full of "divina ratio," of "mystica ratio" (471 C, 596 D, 612 D, etc.).

145. *In Gen.*, l. 7, c. 4 (449 A).

146. "What would be the point for us to know the number of springs and the number of palms unless some mystery worth knowing were also present under them?" — "Quid erat opus scire nos numerum fontium, numerumque palmarum, nisi et in his quoque scitu dignum subesset mysterium?" (655 B; cf. 658-9, 843 A, 854 AB, 891 C, 1037-9, etc.). *In Cant.*, l. 1 (CLXVIII, 849 B).

147. *In Ex.*, l. 1, c. 28 (CLXVII, 596 CD).

148. *In Gen.*, l. 6, c. 45 (444 D).

149. *In Deut.*, l. 1, c. 28 (946 C).

150. *In Reg.*, l. 2, c. 37, after having listed the names of David's warriors: "In the letter we are looking at strong men; let us search for other strong men in the spirit" — "Fortes istos in littera spectamus, fortes alios in spiritu requiramus" (1139 B).

151. Thus PL, CLXVII, 418 C, 419 B, 422 A, 444-5, 471-2, 509 A, 611 A, 796 A.

152. "Et in historia spiritus habeas intelligentiam, et in tropologia historiae veritatem"; "perfecta caret scientia": *In Ez.*, l. 2, c. 24 (1489 BC).

153. "ecclesiastico more": *In Matt.*, l. 12 (CLXVIII, 1600 B). *In Amos* (356 D). *In Deut.*: "vir ecclesiasticus" (CLXVII, 928 A).

154. *In Is.*, l. 1, c. 2: "Now . . . we are entering the temple of this Scripture, scrutinizing not all the historical nor all the moral points contained in it but, using faith alone, the testimonies of Christ, the temple at which we have what is set forth in this whole work" — "Nunc . . . templum hujus Scripturae ingredimur, non cuncta historica aut cuncta moralia quae in eo continentur sed sola fidei Christi testimonia scrutantes, juxta quod in toto hoc opere propositum habemus" (1273 D); etc.

155. "Quomodo invenient, qui miro modo sine Verbo Dei, quod Christus est, verbum Dei quaerunt?": *In Ap.*, l. 4 (CLXVIII, 363 D).

156. *In Matt.*, l. 7 (1458 A).

157. "Signatum est super nos lumen vultus tui, Domine": *In ps.*, l. 1: "that we might understand the Scriptures when you open up their sense to us" — "ut intelligeremus Scripturas, te sensum nobis aperiente" (CLXVII, 1183 C). *De glorif.*, l. 1, c. 13: "Let us raise our eyes, the eyes of the inner man, the eyes of loving faith and inquiring understanding" — "Levemus oculos nostros, oculos hominis interioris, oculos fidei diligentis et intellectu quaerentis" (CLXIX, 25 C).

158. *In Matt.*, l. 7 (CLXVIII, 1456 AC). *De vict. Verbi*, l. 3, c. 26: "They have sensed the Lord hidden there in figurative deeds and mystical sayings" — "Senserunt Dominum latentem illic in factis figurativis et dictis mysticis" (CLXIX, 1291 A).

159. *In Matt.*, l. 12 (CLXVIII, 1585-7).

160. *In Gen.*, l. 8, c. 39 (CLXVII, 526 B). *In Ap.*, l. 4 (CLXIX, 932-3); etc. See above, vol. 1, ch. 2.1.

161. *De vict. Verbi*, l. 6, c. 24: "We who are now and are striving to contemplate

the mysteries of the eternal kingdom within the things done in time" — "Nos qui nunc sumus et in rebus temporaliter gestis aeterni regni mysteria contemplari studemus" (1354 C).

162. "Nunc sensum allegoricum prosequamur": *In Gen.*, l. 7, c. 6 (CLXVII, 451 B). *In Deut.*, l. 1, c. 15: "per spiritualem intelligentiam" let us look for the "allegoriarum sensus" (935 B). *In Habac.*, l. 1: "as much as we can, let us magnify the majesty of the mystic senses" — "quantum possumus, mysticorum majestatem sensuum magnificemus" (CLXVIII, 589 C).

163. *In Ez.*, c. 2 (CLXVII, 1421 D).

164. *In Jer.*, c. 12: "This was the Babylonian captivity of God's people, a captivity that he had seen with his own eyes" — "Haec erat populi Dei captivitas Babylonica, quam sub oculis suis viderat" (1379 A); c. 82: "These things happened both in bodily and in spiritual fashion to the wretched Jews" — "Haec tam corporaliter quam spiritualiter miseris acciderunt Judaeis" (1414 B).

165. PL, CLXXV, 255 ff.

166. Gerhoh, *In ps.* lxiv, c. 3: "It has been noted by the history that Jeremiah both foretold and saw the captivity of the Jews ... but since these things occurred to them in figure ..." — "Nota est historia, quod Jeremias captivitatem Judaeorum in Babyloniam et praedixit et vidit ... quoniam autem haec in figura contingebant illis ..." (CXCIV, 148 C; cf. 997 C).

167. *Ep.* 30, to Paula, on the mystic sense of the Hebrew alphabet; etc.

168. *In Jer.*, c. 12: "We are related to that alphabet set out in alphabetical order four times as children learning their ABCs, not doubting that under those words is contained a knowledge that has been hidden from the wise and the prudent, so that they should know not even the first elements" — "Ad istum alphabetum quadruplici ordine distinctum, tanquam pueri abecedarii disponamur, sub istis vocibus contineri non dubitantes scientiam quae abscondita est sapientibus et prudentibus, ut nec prima noverint elementa" (CLXVII, 1378-9).

169. "luce clarior": *In ps.*, l. 1 (*ps.* viii; 1184 C). He divides the Psalter into three sections, in which he successively sees celebrated the faith, hope, and charity of the Church (1189-90). *In ps.* lxxvii (1211 A), etc.

170. "mysterium similitudinis Filii Dei peragit": *In Gen.*, l. 8, c. 26 (513 C).

171. "Mysticis depictam figuris contemplemur imaginem regni Christi Filii Dei": *In Reg.*, l. 1, c. 18 (1086 CD).

172. "Christi Domini et Regis in isto quoque praecone ejus speculamur gloriam": *In Dan.*, c. 10 (1511 B). For Isaiah: *In Is.*, l. 1, c. 1 (1271 B).

173. "Quis intendere nesciat in gratiae vel gloriae Christi sacramentum?": *In reg. s. Ben.*, l. 2, c. 6 (CLXX, 503 AB).

174. *In Eccl.*, c. 1 (CLXVIII, 1197 A). The authenticity of this commentary is doubtful (Silvestre, 145). The spirit, at any event, is that of Rupert.

175. *Oritur sol, et occidit, et ad locum suum revertitur: ib.* (1200-1). Origen used to love that biblical expression (Mal. 4:2): *In Jo.*, l. 1, c. 25 (30-1); *In Cant.*, l. 2 (125-30); *C. Cels.*, l. 6, c. 79 (150). Cf. Jerome, followed by the *Gloss in Eccl.*, ii, 11 (PL, CXIII, 1119 D).

176. *De vict. Verbi*, l. 13, c. 20 (CLXIX, 1500-2); l. 8, c. 25: "because of Christ, the one and only sun of justice" — "propter Christum solem justitiae unum et solum"; "the end and final cause of the things that were done at that time is

Christ" — "finis et causa finalis eorum quae tunc facta sunt, Christus est" (1396 BC).

177. *In Num.*, l. 2, c. 22: "Therefore water will flow from his bucket, i.e., the true understanding of the Scriptures will spring from his Christ" — "Fluet igitur aqua de situla ejus, id est vera manabit intelligentia Scripturarum de Christo ejus" (CLXVII, 902 C).

178. *In Matt.*, l. 2 (CLXVIII, 1342 AB).

179. *De vict. Verbi*, l. 4, c. 6: "prefiguring the mysteries and victories of the eternal Saviour with brilliant deeds and mystical victories" — "sacramenta victoriasque Salvatoris aeterni gestis praeclaris et victoriis mysticis praefigurantes" (CLXIX, 1298 A).

180. *In Ex.*, l. 2, c. 28: "And where bright stars occur in this heaven of holy Scripture, all looking back to the source of their own light, namely Christ, the true sun" — "Ubique in hoc sanctae Scripturae caelo lucida occurrunt sidera, omnia in fontem sui luminis, sc. in verum solem Christum respicientia" (CLXVII, 636 C). Cf. *In Jer.*, c. 1 (1363 B).

181. "splendida facies"; "sacramentorum Christi Filii Dei cognitio": *In Ex.*, l. 2, c. 4 (611 D).

182. *In Matt.*, l. 4 (CLXVIII, 1389 C).

183. *In Ez.*, l. 2, c. 28 (CLXVII, 1489 BC); c. 3: "He stands in the door, since truly no one . . . enters into the sacred understanding of the sacred Scripture except through him" — "Stat in porta, quia vere nullus . . . ad sacram sacrae Scripturae intelligentiam nisi per ipsum intrat" (1465 B); c. 7 (1469 A), etc.

184. *In Ez.*, l. 2, c. 1 and 35 (1463 B, 1498 B). *In Sophr.*, l. 1 (CLXVIII, 663 A).

185. *De vict. Verbi*, l. 6, c. 7 (CLXIX, 1342-3). *In Gen.*, l. 8, c. 39 (CLXVII, 526 B).

186. *Div. off.*, l. 10, c. 24 (CLXX, 287 CD). *In Deut.*, l. 2, c. 10: "For the depths of the Scriptures are understood in no other way than through the faith of Christ" — "Nec enim aliter quam per Christi fidem profunda Scripturarum intelliguntur" (CLXVII, 983 A).

187. *In Gen.*, l. 8, c. 22: "All truth is perfected in Christ according to the spiritual sense" — "Juxta spiritalem sensum veritas omnis in Christo perficitur" (509 B).

188. *De glor.*, l. 3, c. 20: "Man was not made because of the angels, but rather even the angels, just as all other things, were made because of a certain man, as the Apostle testifies when he says, 'For it was fitting because of whom all things and through whom all things. . . .'" — "Non homo propter angelos, imo propter hominem quemdam angeli quoque facti sunt, sicut et caetera omnia, testante Apostolo cum dicit: Decebat enim propter quem omnia et per quem omnia" (CLXIX, 72 B).

189. Cf. *De Sp. sancto*, l. 1, c. 31 (CLXVII, 1604 CD), etc.

190. "Sanctus sanctorum"; "Novus homo": *In Ez.*, l. 4, c. 42: "Novus homo, J. C. Filius Dei" (741 C), etc. *In Jer.*, c. 5 (1368 D, 1369 A), etc.

191. *In Reg.*, l. 3, c. 8 (1149 AB).

192. *In Gen.*, l. 7, c. 31: "Whoever . . . desiring to follow Christ inclines to the studies of sacred Scripture" — "Quisquis . . . Christum sequi cupiens sacrae Scripturae studiis incumbit" (476 B). *De Sp. sancto*, l. 2, c. 3 (1607 D).

193. *In Jos.*, c. 22 (1024 A); "And so Gideon coming to battle signals the com-

ing of our Redeemer" — "Gedeon itaque ad praelium veniens, Redemptoris nostri signat adventum" (1038 A). Like Irenaeus (PG, VII, 486), Origen (*In Gen.*, h. 8, SC, 174), and Isidore (*Q. in Gen.*, PL, LXXXIII, 251), in Rupert's eyes too Abraham's readiness to sacrifice Isaac evokes the Eternal Father sacrificing his Son for the salvation of the world: *In Gen.*, l. 6, c. 31-2 (CLXVII, 429-31).

194. *In Ex.*, l. 3, c. 24 (673 D).
195. "schola Christi": *In Dan.*, c. 1 (1499 A).
196. *In Ap.*, l. 1 (CLXIX, 846 D).
197. *In reg. Ben.*, l. 1 (CLXX, 480-3).
198. *In Habac.*, l. 3 (CLXVIII, 629 B).
199. "Christi sensum in Scripturis invenire": *In Gen.*, l. 8, c. 26 (CLXVII, 513 C). *In Zach.*, l. 3 (CLXVIII, 749 D).
200. "fidem Christi et gloriam quaerere regni ejus": *In Ez.*, l. 2, c. 1 (CLXVII, 1463 B).
201. "ad evangelicam Ecclesiam, in qua Christus est": *In Ex.*, l. 4, c. 44 (743 B).
202. *De sua conversione*, c. 4 (CLXX, 812 D). This writing might be just "a plagiarism of Gilbert Crispin's *Disputatio*" — "qu'un démarquage de la *Disputatio* de Gilbert Crispin," under an assumed name: B. Blumenkranz, *Juifs et chrétiens*, 21.
203. Spicq, *Esquisse*, 117; cf. RSPT, 1958, 216-7.
204. "Rudbertus, abbas Tutiensis, homo sanctae recordationis, inter sanctae Scripturae tractatores valde illustris": *Dial. de cler. saec. et reg.* (1131; PL, CXCIV, 1397 C; *L. de lite*, 3, 218). One can see in the edition of Gerhoh's *Opera inedita*, 1 (1955) the numerous passages that come from Rupert. Cf. Honorius, *De lumin. Eccl.* (CLXXII, 232 A).
205. "Aperuit illi sensum Sapientia Dei, ut intelligeret Scripturas": *De claris script. monast. sui*, l. 1, c. 11 (CCI, 21 A); cf. 20-4, an elogy of his wisdom, his prayer, and his depth of thought.
206. "Sola delectatus dulcedine Verbi divini": *De glor.*, ep. (CLXIX, 11-2).
207. Thus PL, CLXVIII, 203 D, 1593 C; CLXIX, 68-9, 827-8, 1233 BC; CLXX, 13-4: "I call upon the holy Spirit, the maker of all the mysteries, that he may open up for me the very same things by the grace by which he ordered these things through the holy Fathers, according to the sense and authority of the Scriptures" — "sacramentorum omnium opificem invoco Spiritum sanctum ut qua per sanctos Patres haec ordinavit, eadem mihi secundum sensum et auctoritatem Scripturarum, aperire dignetur gratia."
208. *Sup. quaedam cap.*, l. 1 (CLXX, 496 B).
209. "sanctas omnes Scripturas, quae solae dicuntur et sunt canonicae": *In Cant.*, l. 4 (CLXVIII, 898 B).
210. This is why the parallel with Andrew of Saint Victor proposed by M. Smalley, *The Study*, 125 and 380, even taking into account the expressed reservations, seems to me rather forced.
211. *In Matt.*, l. 12 (CLXVIII, 1393 C).
212. *De vict.*, l. 6, c. 16 (CLXIX, 1349 B).
213. *De glor.*, l. 9, c. 3: "It is more pleasing and the divine authority itself produces more abundant joy just when any passage of divine Scripture simultaneously gives authority or testimony about an earlier passage of Scripture" — "Tunc melius placet et abundantius laetificat ipsa divina auctoritas, cum divina

quaelibet Scriptura simul auctoritatem sive testimonium habet de aliqua priore Scriptura" (182 D). *In Ap.*, l. 8 (1095 A); etc.

214. Hugh, *In Eccl.*, praef. (PL, CLXXV, 114 C). Angelome, *In Reg.*, l. 3: "Every prophecy of Scripture gives mutual support to the sense as founded by God's one Spirit" — "Omnis Scripturae prophetia sibimet invicem consentanea est utpote uno Dei Spiritu condita" (CXV, 447 A); etc.

215. *In Ex.*, l. 4, c. 44 (CLXVII, 744 B), etc.

216. *In Ex.*, l. 4, c. 9 (753 AB).

217. *In Ap.*, prol. (CLXIX, 826-8). Cf. *Ad Cunonem* (210-2).

218. "Iste scribit quod necessarium non est, sanctorum scripta sufficiunt et superabundant": *Div. off.*, ep. (CLXX, 9-10): "passing by these and other more serious matters with a deaf ear" — "haec et alia multo graviora surda aure praeteriens."

219. He gives an account of it, *In Matt.*, l. 12 (CLXVIII, 1588-1612). There is an account of another vision in Renier de Liège, *De claris script.*, l. 1, c. 11 (CCIV, 22 BC).

220. *In Matt.*, l. 12: "having blessed Jerome as an example" — "in exemplo habens beatum Hieronymum" (CLXVIII, 1588 D). The realism of these dreams inspires Cauchie, col. 432, with another comparison: "this strange Huysmans of the 12th century" — "cet étrange Huysmans du XIIe s."

221. Thus Bernard de Morval, *De Trin. et fide cath.*, prol.: "I have fettered not only the sense but even the words of the Fathers in meter" — "Non modo sensum sed et verba Patrum metro alligavi" (Wilmart, RB, 45, 251). Peter of Cella, *L. de panibus*, letter sent to John of Salisbury: "From the cornfield of the Lord I have gathered what I could in a bundle for new loaves, but I have not composed them out of a new flour of senses; for the sort of novelty that departs from the footsteps of the Fathers, in faith and in morals as well as in the novelties of words and names, I have always regarded as to be condemned" — "De segete Domini, quos potui manipulo legi et novos panes, non tamen ex nova sensuum farina composui; novitatem enim illam quae a Patrum vestigiis exhorbitet tam in fide quam in moribus necnon et in vocum seu nominum novitatibus, semper anathematizandam duxi" (PL, CCII, 927).

222. *Op.* 36, c. 1; *op.* 59, c. 4 (CXLV, 596 CD, 840 AB). Cf. Beatus, *In Ap.*, l. 1, c. 1 (44, 47).

223. *Liber quo ordine* (CLVI, 32 C).

224. Which led them to exploit the same heritage of Greek thought in Christology. Cf. Rupert, *In Cant.*, l. 4: "and the flesh (of Christ) has crossed over into the glory of divinity" — "et caro (Christi) in divinitatis gloriam transivit" (CLXVIII, 904 C). Gerhoh, letter to St. Bernard (tr. J. Leclercq, COCR, 15, 82); etc.

225. Commenting in a very personal manner on Psalm 64, Gerhoh nonetheless says of it: "For in this exposition we intend nothing other than that, by gathering the senses of the Fathers in this rustic little book as in a container — or as it is called, a chamber-pot — we may rouse ourselves to read what we are writing" — "Non enim aliud hac expositione magis intendimus, quam ut Patrum sensus congerendo in hoc opusculo rusticano, velut in cophino, vase ut dicitur stercorario nosmetipsos et ea quae scribimus lecturos excitemus" (PL, CXCIV, 55 CD).

226. Gerhoh, *In psalmos*, P. 2, praef.: "wherever we dig a new well, we cover it, as it is prescribed in the Law, with the strong covering of the opinions of the Fathers" — "Ubicumque novum puteum fodimus, Paternarum sententiarum forti operimento illud, sicut in lege praecipitur, operimus" (CXCIII, 988 C). Cf. Rupert, *In Ap.*, prol. (CLXIX, 827-8).

227. *In ps.* magister ad discipulos: "through the nectar-filled understanding of the Psalms that, with God's favor, we want to apprehend, by sticking to the footsteps of the Fathers and collecting their opinions and not inserting anything into them but what is consonant with their faith and what builds up the faith, hope, and charity of the readers" — "per nectaream psalmorum intelligentiam quam Deo favente apprehendere optamus, Patrum vestigiis inhaerendo atque illorum sententias colligendo, neque his aliquid interserendo nisi quod eorum fidei consonet, quodque legentium fidem, spem et caritatem aedificet" (CXCIII, 623 A).

228. "salva Patrum reverentia": *Apologeticus* (Weichert, 106-7, etc.).

229. "vestigiis Patrum inhaerentes, nil de nobis praesumentes": *De erroribus G. de Conchis* (CLXXX, 334 A). St. Bonaventure will say, *In Hexaem.*, l. 11, c. 4, that he is doing nothing but gleaning in the tracks of his two teachers, Anselm and Augustine (Q., 5, 380-1).

230. The summa "Quoniam homines," prol. (Glorieux, 120).

231. *In Jud.*, praef.: "You may know this, then, that the work I am sending you has been produced not only from the sayings of our ancestors that I have found written in their books, but also from my own labor, to the extent that divine favor has granted us the ability, so that it offers partly the opinions of the Fathers, and partly, where I have thought it necessary, a little bit of our sense, too" — "Hoc ergo scias quia opus quod tibi transmitto non tantum ex majorum dictis quam in eorum libris conscripta reperi, sed ex nostro labore, quantum divina gratia nos posse concessit, editum constat: ita ut partim Patrum sententias, partim etiam et nostri sensus exiguitatem ubi necessarium existimavi, proferat" (PL, CVIII, 1109-10). *In Ez.*, praef.: "But I have at the same time included what divine grace has granted me to investigate from above" — "Quod autem mihi insuper divina gratia investigare concessit, simul interposui"; l. 14, proem. (CX, 497 A, 880-1). H. H. Glunz, *History of the Vulgate in England from Alcuin to Roger Bacon* (1933), 100-1, observes a bit too subtly perhaps that Rabanus Maurus interprets very freely the liberal principles advanced by Augustine and Cassiodorus, so as to favor, in spite of them, the absolute authority of the Fathers in exegesis: whence from the 9th century the "scholastic method" begins to prevail over the "patristic method" in the interpretation of Scripture. The principal agent responsible would be Alcuin, followed by Fredegisius, Rabanus, Claudius of Turin, Angelome, Remigius, etc.

232. *Indic. lumin.*, c. 31 (CXXI, 550 C).

233. *De anima*, l. 3: "These words of the blessed man are hard to understand; though many things might be advanced by the contentious against them, nevertheless one ought to work to understand the mind of so great a man" — "Haec verba beati viri difficilia sunt intellectu; quibus licet multa a contentiosis opponi possint, tamen laborandum est ut tanti viri mens intelligatur etc." (Talbot, 144).

234. "canticum novissimum"; "canticum amoris"; "quo Deus in beatam

Virginem descendit, ita ut Filium ex ea generaret, qui est Christus Jesus, homo verus et Deus super omnia benedictus": *In Cant.*, prol. (PL, CLXVIII, 839-40).

235. "Diximus, secundum Patrum sanctorum sententiam fideique catholicae regulam . . ."; "qui tanquam Arcturi numquam occidentis lucida sidera, stabili fide semper fixi steterunt et lucem fidei fundentes, erroris occasum nescierunt": *In Joel* (205 A). *In Jo.*, l. 3 (CLXIX, 291 BC). Cf. *In Gen.*, l. 7, c. 42 (486 B).

236. "praecedentium Patrum auctoritas": *In Gen.*, l. 7, c. 26: this account "might greatly astonish the studious reader, unless the authority of the earlier Fathers had already disclosed the reasons to him" — "grandem studioso lectori admirationem faceret, nisi jam praecedentium Patrum auctoritas rationes illi aperuisset" (471 C).

237. Cf. R. Wasselynck, *L'influence des Moralia,* 168: "If the name of this pope is never mentioned, the work copies the *Moralia* so slavishly that the author could not have done it at a moment when his adversaries would have had a good chance to emphasize the illogical character of his attitude" — "Si le nom de ce pape n'est jamais mentionné, l'œuvre copie les Moralia avec une telle servitude que l'auteur n'aurait pu le faire à un moment où ses adversaires auraient eu beau jeu de souligner le caractère illogique de son attitude." This is perhaps ill warranted. *Div. off.*, ep. nuncup.: "abridged from the abundance of senses and sayings of blessed Gregory" — "abbreviatum ex abundantia sensuum atque dictorum beati Gregorii" (CLXX, 10). In the *In Matt.*, l. 12, he comments on the first vision of Ezekiel in the manner of Gregory, but stops at the second sense (CLXVIII, 1585-7).

238. The typically Gregorian sentence is notably frequent: "For what [else is indicated] through 'Saul', besides 'bad rulers'?" — "Quid enim per Saul, nisi mali rectores?" (*In Reg.*, l. 2, c. 15; CLXVII, 1114 D; cf. 1098 BC, 1114 B, 584 D, etc.).

239. "tout un arrière-plan archaïque et oriental, dont le contenu est difficile à préciser": Leclercq, *L'amour des lettres,* 91.

240. H. Silvestre has noted his admirer Renier's attachment to the most traditional tendencies: "Renir de S.-Laurent et le déclin des éc. liégeoises du XIIe s.," *Misc. Tornacensia,* 122-3.

241. The more facile genius of Abelard, his more varied gifts, his rowdier reputation, have too much overshadowed Gilbert in the works of historians.

242. The 1100s are also the epoch of the Bayeux Tapestry, the frescoes of Saint Savin, the sculptures of Toulouse and of Molissac, of the heavenly Jerusalem of San Pietro al Monte (Civate), the basilicas of Cluny and Vézelay, and of the first mosaics of Saint Mark. Cf. G. Salet, introd. to *Richard de SV, De Trinitate* (SC, 63, 9): "a moment perhaps unique in the history of theology" — "moment peut-être unique dans l'histoire de la théologie." Edmond Faral, *R. critique,* 34 (1927), 304-5.

243. Cf. *Ap.*, ii.

244. Cf. Greg., *Mor.*, l. 29, c. 31, n. 67-8: "The Pleiades . . . are so called from [the Greek word for] many-ness. . . . The twinking Pleiades, which are also seven" — "Pleiades . . . a pluralitate vocati sunt. . . Micantes Pleiades, quae et septem sunt" (PL, LXXVI, 515 AB); n. 73-4 (518-9). Ambrose, *De fide,* l. 5, c. 16, n. 196 (XVI, 689 A). Isidore, *Etym.*, l. 3, c. 71, cited by Martin of Léon (CCIX, 159 AC); cf. Fontaine, 522-3. Aldhelm (*A. ant.*, 15, 101-2).

245. Other stars also shone in the firmament of that time with great brilliance:

Bernard of Chartres, "the most abundant source of letters in Gaul," William of Conches, the "divine Hildebert," Guigo the Carthusian. With Anselm of Laon, or Peter the Venerable, or Suger, or someone else, it would not be hard to fill out the dozen. Cf. Honorius, *Spec. Eccl.*: "The twelve prophets, too, shone like the Pleiades" — "Duodecim prophetae quoque ut Pleiades micuerunt" (CLXXII, 1081 BC).

246. "viri spirituales, qui sunt luminaria mundi": Alexander Neckam, *De nat. rer.*, l. 1, c. 6, de stellis (37). The epithet was classically used to designate the great theologians: Gozechin, *Ep.* (PL, CXLIII, 903 A). Gerhoh, *De inv. Antich.*, c. 59 (*L. de lite*, 3, 374); etc. Cf. Ghellinck, *Mouvement*, 191; RSR, 1 270. Arno of Reichersberg, *L. de ordine canonicorum*, c. 29, *de illustr. auct.*, elogized Rupert at the same time as Hugh, Bernard, and Norbert (the Cluniac, the canon regular, the Cistercian, the archbishop). He does not, however, make him a star of the heavens, as he does Hugh: "he shone like the morning star" — "tanquam stella matutina effulsit," or Bernard: "great for lighting the heavenly hall" — "magnum caelestis aulae luminare," or Norbert: "brilliant at shedding light upon the churches of God" — "in Ecclesias Dei luminare praeclarum"; of him he says: "the illustrious expositor of almost the whole Old and New Testament, like topaz, adorned it with a golden order" — "totius pene veteris ac novi Testamenti expositor illustris, ordinem illum aureum tanquam topazius perornat" (PL, CXXXVIII, 111 CD). *Id., Apol.* (142-3, 184).

247. Schmitz, *H. de l'ordre bén.*, 2, 121.

248. "in altum fidei vela pandenda sunt . . . .": *De Sp. sanct.*, l. 1, c. 31 (CLXVII, 1603 C).

249. "le témoin par excellence de la théologie monastique traditionnelle": Leclercq, *L'amour des lettres*, 208.

250. *De vic. Verbi*, praef. (CLXIX, 1215-6). *In Ap.*, prol.: "the majesty of the divine senses" — "divinorum sensuum majestatem" (826). *In Cant.*, l. 3 (CLXVIII, 881 C). The expression was traditional: Bede, *In Mc.*, viii (XCII, 218 B).

251. *In Ap.*, prol. (CLXIX, 826). *In Gen.*, l. 7, c. 4: "The true Isaac, namely the Lord Jesus Christ, took up holy Scripture, the mother of us all, according as we are reborn for God, as his wife, i.e., to use in preaching the gospel" — "Verus Isaac, sc. Dominus Jesus Christus, matrem omnium nostrum sanctam Scripturam, secundum quam Deo renascimur, in conjugium suum, id est evangelicae praedicationis usum assumpsit" (CLXVII, 449 A).

252. *In Ex.*, l. 3, c. 24 (673 D).

253. "pudice ambulat, et sub honesto et humili sacramentorum velamine Christi amatoris sui sese obsequio praesentat": *In Gen.*, l. 6, c. 45 (444 B).

254. *In Mich.*, l. 1 (CLXVIII, 455 A). *In Gen.*, l. 8, c. 9: "and he strove to hang on to the fleeting sense of God's word" — "sensumque verbi Dei fugientem tenere contendit" (CLXVII, 498 B). Cf. Origen, *In Cant.*, l. 3 (216). Richard, *De Trin.*, l. 1, c. 1 (Salet, SC, 63, 64).

255. *In Gen.*, l. 7, c. 10-1 (CLXVII, 455-6).

256. *De vict. Verbi*, l. 2, c. 18 (CLXIX, 1257 D).

257. "*Dulcis colluctatio, et omni pace jucundior!*"; "Spiritus enim est Deus, et . . . eum qui luctatur, colluctari oportet in spiritu et veritate. Exemplum laudandae hujus fortitudinis habemus in patre nostro Jacob. . . . Secundum illud exemplum,

vir ille (qui cum eo luctabatur) adhuc sese a colluctante patitur vinci, quoties studiosus et fidelis animus tamdiu versatur circa verbum Dei, donec extorqueat ab illo benedictionem Spiritus sancti, quae est verus et utilis intellectus mysterii, vel Scripturae quam Deus rationabiliter signavit, ut non facile possit apprehendi . . . ."

"Igitur, o domina Dei genitrix Maria, et incorrupta mater Verbi aeterni Dei et hominis Jesu Christi, non meis sed tuis armatus meritis, cum isto viro, sc. cum Verbo Dei cupio luctari, ut de Canticis canticorum opus extorqueam quod non dedeceat vocari de incarnatione Domini": *In Cant.*, prol. (CLXVIII, 837-8). *In Matt.*, l. 7 (1455 AC). The image is already present in Ambrose, *In Luc.*, prol., 6: "these contests of hallowed disputations" — "haec sacratarum disputationum certamina" (Tissot, SC, 45, 43). Cf. H. de Marcy, *De per. civ. Dei*, tr. 17: "Here Jacob wrestled with an angel and after a long struggle with difficulty at last earned the blessing" — "Hic Jacob luctatur cum angelo et post longam luctam vix tandem benedictionem meretur" (PL, CCIV, 390 AB; but it is not a matter specifically of exegesis). A closely related image of the kingdom is of those conquered by the violent: Innocent III, s. 18 (CCXVII, 540 CD). Irimbert, *In Jud.*: "The sons of Judah are besieging Jerusalem, whilst the elect, having been formed to praise God, while still located in the lands, strive to investigate the secrets of the heavenly Jerusalem, and in the same way besiege holy Scripture by force of continual meditation" — "Filii Juda Jerusalem oppugnant dum electi ad laudandum Deum formati, caelestis Jerusalem arcana in terris adhuc positi, investigare laborant, ac proinde sanctam Scripturam continuae meditationis instantia oppugnant" (Pez, 4, 150-1).

258. *In Gen.*, l. 8, c. 9 (CLXVII, 498 BD).

259. *In Cant.*, prol.: "What is it right to wrestle? Obviously to use the fortitude of true and holy humility in prayers and tears" — "Quid est legitime luctari? Nimirum fortitudine uti verae et sanctae humilitatis in precibus et lacrimis" (CLXVIII, 839-40). *In Matt.*, l. 12: "I rejoice . . . that I have wrestled in this way, namely, with prayer and tears; for this was Jacob's struggle, to weep and to pray" — "Gaudeo . . . quia sic luctatus sum, sc. prece et lacrimis; nam haec fuit lucta Jacob, sc. flere et rogare" (1397-8).

260. *lucta pulcherrima*; Greg., *In Ez.*, l. 2, h. 2, n. 12 (PL, LXXVI, 955 BC).

261. See above, vol. 2, ch. 9.4.

262. *Fervor sancti studii: De vict. Verbi*, praef.: "The fever of holy zeal must be great to be pleasing to the Word of God" — "Magnus debet esse fervor sancti studii, ad placendum Verbo Dei" (CLXIX, 1217-8).

263. *In Ex.*, l. 1, c. 9 (CLXVII, 575 D).

264. "decor virgineus": *In Gen.*, l. 6, c. 44 (443 B).

265. *In Gen.*, l. 6, c. 41 (439 D). *In Ex.*, l. 2, c. 35 (643 A). *In Reg.*, l. 1, c. 23 (1092 B). *In Ap.*, l. 1 (CLXIX, 846 D).

266. *In Cant.*, l. 1 (CLXVIII, 853 D). *In Matt.*, l. 11 (1556 D).

267. *In Ez.*, l. 1, c. 6, comparing the respective order of the four faces in Ezekiel and the Apocalypse: "The contention is beautiful, like that of two men racing ahead of each other for honor, while the man of the New Testament keeps the sacred order of the Old and the one of the Old observes the sacrosanct effect and order of the newness of the Gospel" — "Pulchra est contentio quasi duorum

hominum honore se invicem praevenientium, dum et ille de N.T. sacrum servat ordinem Scripturae veteris et hic de V.T. sacrosanctum observat effectum ordinemque evangelicae novitatis" (CLXVII, 1427 C).

268. *In Gen.*, l. 8, c. 19 (500 BC).

269. "Tu animadvertisti quia quae scripsi, vel quae scribo, non sunt sine spiritu Dei": *Annulus*, prol. (CLXX, 559-60).

270. *De luminaribus Eccl.*, l. 3, c. 16: "Illuminated by a vision from the Holy Spirit, Rupert, the abbot of the monastery at Deutz, explained practically the whole of Scripture in an outstanding style" — "Rupertus, Tuitiensis monasterii abbas, a Spiritu sancto per visionem illuminatus, totam pene Scripturam egregio stylo exposuit" (CLXXII, 232 A).

271. *De vict. Verbi*, l. 1, c. 3 (CLXIX, 1219-20).

272. *In Ap.*, l. 12, c. 1: "But why does no one know this name but he who accepts it? Because it is not some alien or extrinsic document but one's own internal experience that brings about knowledge of this name" — "Quare autem hoc nomen nemo scit, nisi qui accipit? Vid. quia nominis hujus scientiam, non alienum extrinsecum documentum, sed proprium intrinsecus efficit experimentum etc." (881 AB).

273. *In Ap.*: "If one asks me whether I presume to do this after all the Church writers have been silent, I reply quickly with all humility: I know that I have been driven to it by divine grace" — "Quod si a me quaeritur an, postquam omnes ecclesiastici scriptores siluerunt, hoc agere praesumo: cum humilitatis satisfactione cito respondeo, quia ad hoc ipsum divina gratia impulsum me esse cognosco etc." (404 GH).

274. *In Matt.*, l. 7: "I have learned by experience, but, fearing this very fact, I confess, etc. And what necessity compels me, who have learned such a thing by experience, to confess it? ... To have said this may be enough, since indeed even if I should have wanted to be silent or to cease from the effort of writing, I am unable to.... To be unable to keep hold of a good and needful word, once conceived, is a glorious thing, like Jeremiah being unable to hold back, when he had said: 'And the word of the Lord is made a reproach to me ...', he added: 'and there came in my heart as a burning fire ... and I was wearied, not being able to bear it'" — "Experimento didici, sed hoc ipsum timens, confiteor etc. Et quae me necessitas cogit istud confiteri, qui tale quid experimento didicerim? ... Hoc dixisse satis sit, quia revera etiam si tacere sive a scribendi studio cessare voluero, non valeo.... Conceptum sermonem bonum et necessarium non posse tenere, gloriosum, quemadmodum Hieremias tenere non valens, cum dixisset: 'Et factus mihi sermo Domini in opprobrium ...', ita subjunxit: 'Et factus est in corde meo quasi ignis exaestuans ... et defeci ferre non sustinens' (Jer. 20)" (CLXVIII. 1453).

275. *De omn. Dei*, c. 23: "When I was absent or even present, they kept saying in mockery that I had come too late to the study of the dialectical art" — "Me absente, me interdum praesente, irridentes dicebant sero me ad studium venisse artis dialecticae" (CLXX, 473 B). He was, as one historian anachronistically would put it, an "autodidact." Cf. the focus of J. Beumer, SJ, "Rupert von Deutz und seine Vermittlungstheologie, *Münchener theol. Zeitschr.*, 1953, 257 ff.

276. Rabanus, *In Matt.*, praef. (PL, CVII, 729-30; cf. CX, 497-8; CXI, 793). Bardy, DTC, 14, 1510-1.

277. "Angustiae mihi sunt undique": cf. Or. and St. Columban, *ep.* 4, n. 4 (Walker, 28). Jean de Fécamp, *Lamentatio* (Leclercq-Bonnes, RB, 54, 55).

278. *Sup. quaed. cap. Reg.*, l. 1 (CLXX, 481 B).

279. *In Matt.*, l. 12; nevertheless at the same time he thinks it worthwhile to say that he did not lack masters: "So let those wise fellows speak out as much as they want, and let them not conceal their fathers to whom alone, they claim, the earth has been given, i.e., the knowledge of the Scriptures and of the liberal arts. I, though I have had a fair number of fathers in the scholarly disciplines myself and have been no mean student in the books of the liberal arts, for my part I profess that a visitation by the Most High is for me better than ten fathers of that sort, under whose rod, having been struck on the lips. . . ." — "Confiteantur ergo sapientes illi quantum volunt, nec abscondant patres suos, quibus solis ut aiunt, data est terra, id est Scripturarum artiumque liberalium scientia. Ego, quamvis et ipse nonnullos in discipulis (disciplinis) scholaribus patres habuerim, et in libris artium liberalium non segniter studiosus exstiterim, hoc profiteor, quia visitatio ab Altissimo melior mihi est quam decem patres ejusmodi, cujus sub virga saepe in labiis percussus etc." (CLXVIII, 1604 A).

280. "Quis est hic?": *Sub quaed. cap.*, l. 1: "I have mentioned as briefly as I could the reasons that instigated the hatred many people bore against this poor fellow, so that they would say while he was speaking: 'Who is this?' intent on looking for some offense in his speech as a pretext to undo him" — "Causas dixi quam breviter potui quae odii multorum seminaria fuerunt pauperi huic, ut eo loquente dicerent: Quis est hic, intenti ad perscrutandum ut, si in locutione sua quidquam offenderet, subverterent eum" (CLXX, 489 C).

281. *In Matt.*, l. 10 (CLXVIII, 1539 AC).

282. *In Matt.*, prol. (1307-8); l. 9 (1521-2). We see how Hauréau had been wrong to deny anything "pathétique" to Rupert (*op. cit.*, 319).

283. Renier, *De claris scr. mon. sui.*, l. 1, c. 11: He "whose eye is not scandalized by cataracts of envy or the bleariness of incompetency" — "cujus oculum vel glaucoma invidiae vel lippitudo imperitiae non scandalizat" will see the wisdom of his writings; his little work on St. Benedict "reports how many assaults of the envious and what sort of annoyances he suffered from calumniators" — "denarrat quantos invidorum assultus, quales passus sit molestias calumniantium" (PL, CCIV, 21 B, 22 D).

284. *In Jo.*, ad Cun.: "They say I'm arrogant and incredibly proud" — "Aiunt me arrogantem et incredibiliter elatum etc." (CLXIX, 203-4). *De omn. Dei*, prol. (CLXX, 455 C); c. 23 (473 B).

285. "flumen diabolicum, flumen haereticae loquacitatis, laqueosum et sophisticis retibus plenum": *In Ap.*, l. 7, c. 12 (CLXIX, 1061 B).

286. *In Ap.*, l. 9, c. 16: "Unclean spirits, i.e., the sects, as it were, of 'wisdom', and magical, poetical, and philosophical 'science'" — "Spiritus immundos, id est sectas quasi sapientiae, et scientiae magicae, poeticae et philosophicae . . ." (1124 B). *In Jo.*, l. 1: "Condemn the things that the sons of night, i.e., the philosophers of this age, are dreaming" — "Ea contemne, quae filii noctis, id est philosophi hujus saeculi somniarunt" (209 C).

287. "fabulosa didacitas": *In Gen.*, l. 8, c. 12 (CLXVII, 501 A). Cf. l. 7, c. 11 (456 A).

288. Cf. PL, CLXX, 660 A. One will also recall his fallings out with St. Norbert. Rupert often speaks of him; it is not, it seems to me, "silly boasting" — "forfanterie naïve" (Ghellinck, *Mouvement*, 127); his tone is not that which a Gerhoh takes, for example.

289. "Desinant igitur vel nunc adversari de paupere isto, qui locutus est, dicere: 'Quis est hic, vel quid opus est eum loqui, cum sancti et antiqui doctores sufficienter locuti sint?' Quod si necdum desinunt, audebo adhuc loqui, et dicere illud Isaianum: Quia post omnes, vel infra omnes terminos terrae, id est, humiles qui recordati sunt nominis Domini, et locuti sunt in nomine Domini, fortasse istum quoque pauperem contingit: 'Domine, in angustia requisierunt te: in tribulatione murmuris doctrina tua eis. Sicut quae concipit, cum appropinquaverit ad partum, dolens clamat in doloribus suis, sic facti sumus a facie tua, Domine. Concepimus, et quasi parturivimus et peperimus' (Isa. 26)."

"Quis, rogo, sapiens est, qui dicat mulieri quae concepit, cum appropinquaverit ad partum: 'Quid clamas, cur non taces, cur non imponis ori tuo silentium?' Forte dicat mihi aliquis: 'Tune es ejusmodi? Quando vel quomodo concepisti? Unde scis quod a facie Domini conceperis, ut illa quae scripsisti quasi parturiens loquereris?' Ad haec, inquam: 'Secretum meum mihi, secretum meum mihi' (Isa. 24). Verum tamen desinant, propter illud quod itidem Isaias dicit: 'Vae qui dicit patri: Quid generas, et mulieri: Quid parturis?' (Isa. 45). Derogat enim patri, qui invidet praegnanti; derogat generanti, qui invidet parturienti. Pater misericordiarum et Deus totius consolationis misericordiam generat, et viduam verbo suo consolatur animam, et tu dicis: 'Quid generas?' Verbum mente conceptum vocem quaerit, et tu dicis: "Mulier, quid parturis?" Defensa est Thamar nurus Judae testimoniis congruis, 'de viro,' inquiens, 'cujus haec sunt concepi: cognosce cujus sit annulus, et armilla, et baculus' (Gen. 38). Cognosce et tu, si vis, utrum necne sit in scriptis meis annulus fidei, baculus spei, armilla caritatis, et dicentem audi animam meam: 'De viro, cujus haec sunt, concepi.' Nam et aliquid recolo in me sensibiliter factum, ut indubitanter dicam, quia 'datum' hoc sive 'donum desursum est, descendens a Patre luminum' (*Jac.*, i)": *Sup. quaed. cap.*, l. 1 (CLXX, 497-8). *In Matt.*, l. 12 (CLXVIII, 1599 A). *De incendio oppidi Tuitii*, c. 15 (CLXX, 348 B). *Div off.*, ep.: "totus eram possessus ab ea quae me tacere non sinebat dilectione Verbi Dei" (9-10). This image of the woman about to give birth, like the one in the Apocalypse, holds a central place in his interpretation of biblical history; it dominates the whole *De vict. Verbi Dei*: cf. l. 9, c. 28 (CLXIX, 1419 CD); l. 7, c. 17 (1368-9). On Rupert, one will want to read the beautiful work by Dom Mariano Magrassi, O.S.B.: *Téologia e storia, nel Pensiero di Ruperto di Deutz* (Roma, 1959).

290. "Tradunt Hebraei"; "Haec est Hebraeorum traditio"; "Hebraei autumant"; "Hoc loco Hebraei exponent"; "Haec juxta traditionem Hebraeorum dicta sunt": thus Julian of Toledo (PL, XCVI, 569 CD), Bede (XCI, 232 B, 262 B), Alcuin (C, 536 B, 544 D, 557 B, 670 A), Paschasius (CXX, 477 C, etc.), Angelome (CXV, 176 C, 180 A, 384 D, 459 B, 535 D, 536 C), Remigius (CXVII, 186 A, 230 D, 233 C, 255 B, 257 A), etc. Cf. Jerome (XXIV, 398 C, etc.).

291. Aug., *In Hept.*, l. 7, q. 8 (PL, XXXIV, 796); *Civ. Dei*, l. 18 (XLI, 559-620). Bede (XCI, 147 A). Bruno of Segni: "For the histories of the Greeks report" — "Narrant enim Graecorum historiae" (*Sp. cas.*, 3, 69), etc. Cf. Rupert (PL, CLXVII, 445 B; CLXIX, 1406 D: Trogus Pompeius), etc.

292. Sigebert de Gembloux, *L. de scr. eccl.*, c. 90: "Bishop Freculph wrote . . . a history from the foundation of the world. . . . He did not neglect to resolve the difficulty of questions as they came up, and by adding secular histories to the divine history, etc." — "Friculphus episcopus scripsit . . . historiam a conditione mundi. . . . Difficultatem etiam intercurrentium quaestionum enodare non neglexit et interponendo divinae historiae saeculares historias etc." (PL, CLX, 568 A). Freculph wrote around 840.

293. *De 42 mansionibus:* "All of which Josephus previously wrote of at length" — "Quae omnia Josephus fuso sermone praescripsit" (XVII, 39 D), etc. Angelome (CXV, 384 D, 411 C, 460 B, 490 D). Alvarus (CXXI, 489-90). Rabanus, *ep.* 19 (praef. in Mach.): "I have woven the work together, then, partly from the divine history, partly from Josephus . . . , and partly from the history of other gentiles, so that since mention is made in the book itself not only of the tribe of Judah and its leaders but also likewise of other tribes, the truth of the sacred history would be obvious from a comparison of the many books and the sense of the narrative might be clearer to the reader" — "Opus ideo partim de divina historia, partim de Josephi . . . traditione, partim vero de aliarum gentium historia contexui, ut quia non tantum gentis Judaeae ac principum ejus sed et aliarum gentium similiter in ipso libro mentio fit, ex multorum librorum conlatione veritas sacrae historiae pateat et sensus narrationis ejus lectori lucidior fiat" (MGH, *Ep.*, 5, 424-5); cf. ep. 18 (423) Walafried Strabo, *De subversione Jerus* (PL, CXIV, 966-9). Abelard. Peter the Venerable, *C. Judaeos;* etc. Again R. Bacon, *Comp. studii philosophiae* (Brewer, 474, 490). Cf. Bede (XCI, 72 B, 76 B, 115 D, 121 B, 178 C); etc.

294. *Inst.*, c. 17 (LXX, 1130 C). Cf. Bardy, "Le souvenir de Josèphe chez les Pères," RHE, 43 (1948), 179-91.

295. *De int. div. Script.*, c. 12 (PL, CXXXI, 1004 A).

296. *De vict. Verbi* (CLXIX, 1361 C, 1409 A, 1413 A, 1424 B, 1435 A, 1448 D, 1464 C).

297. "Credimus post Graecam, multis quam ostendis, regulam
    Te jam doctis traditurum Hebraeorum studia
    Quibus ille Gamalihel doctor legis claruit."

Paul modestly replies:

Graiam nescio loquelam, ignoro Hebraicam;	The Grecian language I know not, am ignorant of Hebrew;
Tres aut quatuor in scolis quas didici syllabas	The three or four syllables I have learned at school
Ex his mihi est ferendus manipulus ad aream . . .	I have to carry like barbells to the playing-field.

Pauli et Petri carmina (*P. lat. m. aevi*, i, 48-9). At this very time Paul was giving Greek lessons to a group of clerics who were to accompany an embassy to Byzantium.

298. "quid inter Hebraeos et nostros codices distet": Bede (see below, section 5, "Criticism in the Middle Ages"). Julian of Toledo (PL, XCVI, 569-81). Wigbode (1105 CD). Sedulius Scotus (CIII, 100 CD). Alvarus (CXXI, 472-92). Raoul Glaber, *Hist.*, ep. ad. Odilon: "Although the [number of] years from the origin of the

world as noted according to the histories of the Hebrews disagrees with the translation by the LXX interpreters, nevertheless we commend it with the greatest certitude, because the thousandth and second year of the incarnate Word is the first of the reign of King Henry of the Saxons" — "Quanquam salus annorum a mundi origine pernotata secundum Hebraeorum historias a Septuaginta interpretum translatione discrepet, illud tamen certissime commendamus, quod annus incarnati Verbi millesimus secundus sit regni Henrici Saxonum regis primus" (CXLII, 614 A). Siger of Gembloux (CLX, 588 B). Honorius, *De im. mundi*, l. 3 (CLXXII, 166 A); etc. Cf. Aug., *Civ. Dei*, l. 15, c. 10 (Bardy, 4, 74-7; and the note 695-7).

299. Sedulius Scotus, *In Rom.*: "What he says, namely, 'let there be a table' etc., is not found written in the Psalm nor in our manuscripts of the Septuagint translators nor in those of the Hebrews" — "Quod dicit, fiat mensa, etc., non habetur scriptum in psalmo neque in nostris Septuaginta interpretum exemplaribus neque in Hebraeorum" (PL, CIII, 102 B).

300. Aside from the Hebrew, Angelome cites the Septuagint, Aquila, Theodotion (CXV, 168 AC, etc.). Wigbode compares the Greek and the Hebrew (XCVI, 1116 C, 1163 BC). The same for Amalarius, *ep.* 5 (CV, 1335 BC), Walifrid Strabo (CXIV, 772 A), etc. Rabanus, *In Ez.*: "A difficult passage involving a great discrepancy between the Hebrew and the LXX, to which many things have been added from Theodotion's edition, so that they might appear to have some sort of coherence" — "Locus difficilis et inter hebraicum et Sept. multum discrepans, quibus pleraque de Theodotionis editione addita sunt ut aliquam habere consequentiam viderentur" (CX, 612 B; cf. 630 D, 636 CD, 676 AB, etc.). Rosenmüller himself here recognized the merit of Angelome: "Angelome's diligence is praiseworthy, for he applied it by comparing the ancient versions with each other" — "Laudanda est Angelomi diligentia, quam adhibuit in comparandis inter se versionibus antiquis" (*H. interpr.*, 5, 148).

301. *Mor.*, l. 20, c. 32, n. 62 (LXXVI, 174 B).

302. Honorius, *Sel. ps. exp.*, dedic.: "We however shall treat the Septuagint translation and where needed we shall take something from the others" — "Nos autem Sept. interpretum translationem tractabimus et ubi opus fuerit de aliis assumemus" (CLXXII, 269-70). For Nahum 1:9, Lupus of Ferrières compares the Latin and the Sept. (L. Levillain, 1, 28-30). In the same way, Aimo, *In Hebr.* (PL, CXVII, 854 C); Bede (XCI, 72 A, 87 B, 120 A, 134 D); etc.

303. Dispute between Amalarius and Jeremiah of Sens on how best to write the name of Jesus: PL, CV, 1334.

304. C. 15 (LXX, 1126-31).

305. Sedulius Scotus, *In Gal.*: "not, as it badly reads in the Latin manuscripts" — "non ut male in latinis codicibus legitur" (CIII, 191 D); *In Eph.*: "to sum up, instaurare stands written in the Latin manuscripts" — "pro recapitulare, in latino codice scriptum est instaurare" (1096 C); *Explanationes praef. Hieron. ad evangelia*, nn. 2 (333-4); etc. See below, section 5.

306. "mendosi codices"; "in Hebraeo non habetur": Angelome, *In Reg.*, l. 2 (CXV, 370 BD, 378 A).

307. "sicut in exemplaribus quae in Hebraeo sunt invenitur": Ps.-Hincmar, *De diversa animae*, c. 8 (CXXV, 946 B).

Notes to Pages 178-79

308. "hebraeus fons"; "veritas hebraea"; "hebraicae veritatis": Greg., *In Ez.*, l. 1, h. 7, n. 23 (LXXVI, 852 BC). Bede, *Hexaem.* (XCI, 33 D; Siger of Gembloux, *De vir. ill.* (MGH, *Scr.*, 6, 272).

309. "veritas hebraica": Alcuin, on Bede: "the Psalter that he collected . . . according to the Hebraic truth" — "psalterium quem ille collegit . . . juxta hebraicam veritatem" (C, 407 B). Bede (XCI, 19 B, 79 AB). Angelome, *In Reg.*, l. 2: "Beware, reader, of many faulty manuscripts . . . but in the older manuscripts and in the Hebrew truth" — "Cave, lector, plerosque mendosos codices . . . in vetustioribus vero codicibus et in hebr. veritate" (CXV, 370 B; cf. 507 B, etc.). Honorius (CLXXII, 166 A). Hugh (*Speculum*, 18, 492); etc.

310. "veritas hebraica per Origenem prodita, per Hieronymum edita, per Augustinum laudata, et per Josephum confirmata": Bede, *ep.* 3 (PL, XCIV, 675 AB); "for if anyone should ever say that the Hebrew books were later falsified by the Jews . . . , let him listen to Origen" — "quod si aliquis dixerit Hebraeos libros postea a Judaeos esse falsatos . . . , audiat Origenem" (671 C). Rabanus, *In Ez.*, praef.: "But I have omitted the Septuagint edition in many places, namely, where I thought it unnecessary to put it down, observing St. Jerome's instruction in this matter" — "Septuaginta vero editionem in plerisque locis omisi, ubi eam vid. ponere non necessarium arbitrabar, praeceptum S. Hieronymi in hoc ipso observans" (CX, 497 B).

311. "The belief in the inspiration (of the LXX) was gradually weakening owing to the views of St. Jerome on the *hebraica veritas*; but these views took a long time to become dominant; they became general only at the beginning of the 7th century" — "La croyence en l'inspiration (des Sept.) est allée s'affaiblissant à cause des vues de S. Jérôme sur l'hebraica veritas; mais celles-ci mirent longtemps à s'imposer; elles ne se sont généralisées qu'à partir du viie s.": Dom Pierre Salmon, *Richesses*, 11. For the Psalms in particular, the *Juxta Hebraeos* of Jerome "moreover had a very specific goal: to furnish the means to respond to the Jews and to give the sense of the Hebrew text with precision. . . . This was not a book intended for prayer or for the liturgy; St. Jerome expressly says as much in his preface" — "avait d'ailleurs un but très spécial: fournir le moyen de répondre aux Juifs et donner avec précision le sens du texte hébreu. . . . Ce n'était pas un livre destiné à la prière, à la liturgie; S. Jérôme le déclare expressément dans la préface" (13, 4).

312. Thus Rabanus, *In Jer.* (PL, CXI, 954-83), etc.

313. "Si quis in hac interpretatione voluerit quid reprehendere, interroget Hebraeos. . . .": S. Berger, *H. de la Vulgate latine dans les premiers s. du m. âge*, 94.

314. "proprietas hebraicae linguae": Abelard, *s.* 3 (CLXXVIII, 396 B). Hervaeus, *In Is.*, l. 6 (CLXXXI, 421 C).

315. "l'application de la dialectique aux problèmes théologiques" . . . "qu'une intention": P. Hadot, AHDLMA, 21 (1955), 6.

316. "Super pectus tuum et ventrem gradieris: nomine etenim pectoris significatur superbia mentis; nomine autem ventris, ut LXX transtulere, significantur desideria carnis. His enim duabus rebus serpit diabolus ad eos quos vult decipere . . .": *L. quaest. sup. Gen.* (PL, XCVI, 1163 C).

[Trans.: de Lubac's reference to a "generous eclecticism of Platonic lineage" alludes to the wild etymologizing in Plato's dialogue *Cratylus*.]

317. *In Luc.*: "So some, violently searching down a Hebrew etymology for a Latin or Greek name, say that Peter is rendered 'untying' or 'unshod' or 'recognizing'; though an exposition of John's Gospel that I recall and the Hebrew language itself (which has no sound for the letter P) attest that this name is not Hebrew. . . . For they, writing the misspelling 'Feter' instead of 'Peter', violently annex a false interpretation for that made-up name" — "Violenter ergo quidam latino vel graeco nomini Hebraeam quaerentes aetymologiam, dicunt Petrum dissolventem, sive discalcientem, vel agnoscentem interpretari; cum et expositio Joannis evangelistae cujus memini, et ipsa lingua Hebraea, quae P litteram omnino non sonat, Hebraeum hoc nomen non esse testetur. . . . Abusivum enim Fetrum pro Petro scribentes, violenter dicto nomini falsam interpretationem subnectunt" (XCII, 397 C). [Trans.: though the main point is readily conceded, the justification for it needs to be qualified: there are also some "p" sounds in Hebrew, e.g., verb conjugations called piel, pual, hithpael, mentioned in Gesenius's *Hebrew Grammar*.]

318. *L. retractationis in Act.*, c. 16 (1025 CD).

319. *In Rom.*: "But we do not much favor the view which others maintain — that Paul in Latin means 'a little' and in Greek 'resting', since the name is not Greek or Latin, but Hebrew, and so to be understood according to its Hebrew meaning" — "Quod autem alii dicunt Paulum dici latine modicum, et graece quietum, nos multum non approbamus, quia hoc nomen non est graecum aut latinum, sed hebraicum, ideoque juxta hebraicum sensum intelligendum" (CLXXXI, 598 C).

320. *In Ap.*, xiii, 18 (CXIV, 734 B).

321. "hebraicae veritatis magis peritus"; "quae omnia conducunt sibique convenient"; "congruit autem utraque interpretatio"; *"Mem* interpretatur *ex ipsis,* ut vult Hieronymus; *viscera,* ut vult Ambrosius. Copulemus utramque interpretationem ei ut dicamus: *ex ipsis visceribus": In ps.* cxviii (CXCIV, 790 B; cf. 797 B, 819 B, 928 B). In this commentary Gerhoh often cites Hebrew words; he observes that such and such words of the Latin are not in the original, compares the Hebrew and the Septuagint, appeals from it constantly to the *hebraica veritas,* namely Jerome's *Psalterium ex Hebraeo,* etc. (1012 D, etc. Van den Eynde *passim*). Cf. Sedulius Scotus on the name Mark in Hebrew and in Greek (CIII, 279 D). The explication of the names comes most often from Jerome, sometimes by way of the *Instructiones* of Eucherius.

322. "libertas Spiritus"; "alicujus causa mysterii": *Sup. 4 ev.* (14-5). He notes, however: "A significant number of writers, as St. Jerome relates, are willing to be seduced by this vice" — "Volunt hoc nonnulli, ut tradit S. Hieronymus, scriptorum vitio fore depravatum."

323. *Q. hebr. in Gen.* (PL, XXIII, 936 AB, etc.).

324. He had written, *Adv. Jov.*, l. 2, c. 38: "Rome signifies either 'force', according to the Greek, or 'sublimity', according to the Hebrew. Keep this title that you are named with: that virtue may make you sublime and pleasure may not cast you to the ground" — "Roma signifie ou bien la force, selon le grec, ou bien la sublimité, selon l'hébreu. Conserve ce titre dont tu te nommes: que la vertu te rende sublime et la volupté ne te jette point à la terre" (tr. P. Antin, 22; PL, XXIII, 357). Cf. an analogous case in Peter Damian, *op.* 47 (CXLV, 710, CD).

325. S. Denis 7, n. 1 (Morin, 32-3), regarding *pascha:* however, Augustine does not want to keep the authentic etymology of this Hebrew word: *In ps.* cxx, n. 6 (CCL, 40, 1791), and especially *In ps.* cxl, n. 25 (2044).

326. *In Gen.*, h. 12, n. 4 (SC, 7, 208-9). Origen gives three possible etymologies for Esau, but without taking them into his own account.

327. Isidore and his disciples know Hebrew. Julian of Toledo entrusts a Jew, Restitutus, with delivering his *De comprobatione aetatis sextae* to Idalius of Barcelona: *ep.* 1 (PL, XCVI, 816-7).

328. The layman Paul Alvarus debates about the Hebrew text with Eleazar; he himself was of Jewish origin; when he says "our Jesus" — "Jesus noster," it seems that they had to understand: Jesus who is of our race (PL, CXXI, 495 CD, 496 AD). He compares Hebrew and Arabic (540 BC). Cf. Solomon Katz, *The Jews in the Visigothic and Frankish Kingdoms of Spain and Gaul* (Cambridge, Mass.: The Mediaeval Academy of America, 1937).

329. *Defl.*, l. 2 (PL, CLVII, 1055 B). Cf. Origen, *In ps.* 1; *In Ez.*, h. 4, n. 8, etc. G. Bardy, "Les traditions juives dans l'œuvre d'Or.," *R. Bibl.*, 34 (1925). Gezon of Tortone: "I think it not inappropriate to utter what . . . I learned from a certain Hebrew informant" — "Non incompetenter edere arbitror illud quod . . . quodam Hebraeo didici referente" (CXXXVII, 393 B); but it is not a question of exegesis: it is the report of a eucharistic miracle.

330. Thus, *ep.* 18, c. 15 (1, 70). Cf. G. Bardy, "S. Jérôme et ses maîtres hébreux," RB, 46 (1934), 145-64.

331. See below, section 5.

332. Abelard's comm. *In Ep. Pauli:* "For the Jew, howsoever poor he be, if he should ever have sons with him, he would send them all off to learn the letters, not, like Christians, for the sake of gain, but to understand the law of God — and not just his sons but his daughters as well" — "Judaeus enim, quantumcumque pauper, etiamsi secum haberet filios, omnes ad litteras mitteret, non propter lucrum sicut christiani, sed propter legem Dei intelligendam, et non solum filios sed et filias" (Landgraf, 2, 433-4).

333. "mediocriter etiam instructus in lingua Hebraeorum": *De nat. rer.*, l. 1, c. 1 (7-11). On the knowledge of Hebrew in the Middle Ages: B. Altaner, "Zur Kenntnis des Hebraischen in Mittelalter," *Bibl. Zeitschr.*, 1933, 288-308.

334. "de lire et de citer l'hébreu à travers le grec d'Origène": P. Peeters, *Recherches d'hist. et de philologie orient.*, 2, 12.

335. "Secundum nostram translationem, hebraicam scilicet veritatem": *In Eccl.* (PL, CLXVIII, 1198).

336. Compare, e.g., Alvarus, *ep.* 18, and Jerome, *In Is.*, l. 13, c. 49 (J. Madoz, *Epistolario de Alv.*, 75-6). Cf. Sigebert of Gembloux, *Ep. de 4 temp.*; the version of Jerome based on the Hebrew is that "which the Church now uses" — "qua modo Ecclesia utitur" (CLX, 816 B).

337. "stridentia anhelantia verba": *ep.* 125, c. 12 (PL, XXII, 1079). *In Dan.*, praef., on the "Chaldaic" = Aramaic (XXVIII, 1191-2).

338. "stridor quidam non latinus interstrepat": *ep.* 29, c. 7 (2, 30).

339. "Omnem sermonis elegantiam et latini eloquii venustatem stridor lectionis hebraicae sordidavit": *In Gal.*, l. 3 (XXVI, 399 C). *Q. Hebr.:* "pro stridulo

Hebraeorum" (XXIII, 980 A). *Ep.* 20, c. 7: "a certain un-Latin hissing broke in" — "stridor quidam non latinus interstrepat" (2, 30).

340. *Oracional visig.,* 206: "O Christ, who hast not been moved by the teeth of your hissing enemies" — "Christe, qui stridentium inimicorum dentibus non es commotus." Guibert of Nogent, *De pign. sanct.,* l. 4, c. 4, n. 2: "To make harsh noises . . . is characteristic of those who are mad or enraged" — "Stridere . . . furentium est" (PL, CLVI, 674 B). Cf. Matt. 8:12. But, *L. moz. sacr.:* "The cherubim and seraphim singing you songs with a voice of eternal praise from the whizzing of their sixfold wings" — "Tibi Cherubim ac Seraphim senarum volatus stridore alarum aeternae laudis voce carmina concinenetes" (523).

341. PL, CXXI, 452 A, 534 C, etc.

342. *De schem. et tropis.* Cf. Curtius, 56.

343. *In Lam.,* l. 2: "Where first the structure of the words (with what great splendor it flashes in Hebrew!) is to be noted, which, once translated into ours throughout the beginnings of the verses, has such copious elegance of expressions" — "Ubi primum notanda est structura verborum, quanto splendore in Hebraeo reniteat, quae translata in nostra per principia versuum, tam diffusam sermonum elegantiam habet" (PL, CXX, 1116 A).

344. *De S. Sp.,* l. 2, c. 17: "Behold! In this Scripture, which is more ancient than all the Greek or Latin orators, they utter argumentation as perfect and unparalleled as possible, the speech is beautiful and sweet, etc." — "Nam ecce quam dicunt perfectissimam atque absolutissimam argumentationem in hac Scriptura, quae utique cunctis rhetoribus Graecis sive Latinis antiquior est, pulchra et suavis oratio etc." (CLXVII, 1622 C); l. 7, c. 13 (1777-8). *De vict. Verbi,* l. 3, c. 4 (CLXIX, 1272-3). Cf. Luther, to Wenceslas Link, 14 June 1528: "My God! What huge and painful effort, to make the Hebrew writers speak in German! They keep resisting, they do not want to abandon their Hebraism and to imitate Germanic barbarism. It is as if a nightingale had been obliged, abandoning her sweet song, to imitate the coo-coo, whose monotone cry she hates" (*Œuvres,* Fr. tr., t. 8, Geneva, 1959, p. 120).

345. *Th. chr.,* l. 2: "What urbanities of diction are there that Hebrew, the mother of languages, has not taught us?" — "Quae sunt urbanitates locutionum, quae mater linguarum Hebraica non docuerit?" (PL, CLXXVIII, 1210 A).

346. John Beleth, *Rat. div. off.,* c. 79 (CCII, 85 B).

347. Isidore, *Etym.,* l. 1, c. 39, n. 11 (LXXXII, 119 A); cf. Jerome (XXVII, 36 A; XXVIII, 1081 B). Marius Victorinus, *Ars grammatica,* l. 1: "Homer, the source and starting-point of the metrical craft" — "Homerum fontem atque originem metricae disciplinae" (H. Keil, *Grammat. latini,* 6, 68). Some think that the Muse of the Greeks is none other than Moses: John of Salisbury combats this opinion, *Enthet.,* iv, 1191-4 (CXCIX, 991 AB).

348. Paschasius, *In ps.* xliv (PL, CXX, 1010 CD); Philip of Harvengt (CCIII, 186 A). Cf. E. Faye, *Speculum,* 23 (1948), 40.

349. Isidore, *Etym.,* l. 1, c. 39, n. 19; l. 6, c. 2, n. 23 (PL, LXXXII, 120 B, 232 BC). On all this: Fontaine, 169-72.

350. Rabanus Maurus, *Cl. inst.,* l. 3, c. 3 (PL, CVII, 380 A).

351. Jerome, *In Soph.,* iii, 14-19 (XXV, 1384 B).

352. Thus Remigius, *In Soph.:* "One should know that *nugas* is a Hebrew

Notes to Page 182

word used among the Latins; hence we can know that Hebrew is the mother of all languages" — "Sciendum *nugas* Hebraeum esse verbum, apud latinos usitatum; unde scire possumus Hebraeam linguam materem esse omnium linguarum" (CXVII, 210 B). Bede, *Hexaem.*, l. 1: "Now Hebrew seems to be the first language for the human race, because it is well known that all the names that we read up to the division of the languages in Genesis, belong to that speech" — "Prima autem lingua fuisse generi humano Hebraea videtur, ex eo quod nomina cuncta quae usque ad divisionem linguarum in Genesi legimus, illius constat esse loquelae" (XCI, 50 D).

353. Quodvultdeus, *De prom.*, P. 1, c. 9, n. 15: "But the mystical caption written by Pilate shows that Hebrew is the first language" — "Primam vero Hebraicam esse linguam, mysticus ille titulus a Pilato conscriptu ostendit" (LI, 741 C).

354. Rupert, *De vict. Verbi*, l. 3, c. 25 (CLXIX, 1289-90); c. 4 (1272-3). These ideas will be maintained right up to the modern age: cf. Lancelot, *Mémoire touchant la vie de M. L'abbé de Saint-Cyran* (1738), 2, 153-4; cited by J. Orcibal, *La genèse d'Esther et d'Athalie* (1950), 107.

355. Bede, *De linguis gentium:* "Until the haughtiness of that tower divided human society into separate sounds of signs, there was one language of all the nations, and it is called Hebrew" — "Prousquam superbia turris illius in diversos signorum sonos humanam divisit societatem, una omnium nationum lingua fuit, quae Hebraea vocatur" (PL, XC, 1179). I was not able to consult A. Borst, *Der Turmbau von Babel, Geschichte der Meinungen über Ursprung und Vielfalt der Sprachen und Völker*, 2 v. (Stuttgart, 1957-8).

356. Hugh, *De vanit. mundi*, l. 3 (PL, CLXXVI, 726 D).

357. Bede, *Hexaem.*, l. 3: "Finally, with the construction of the tower . . . the first speech of the human race remained as the tongue of the whole land within the house of Heber, which the Hebrew names of the following age manifestly prove" — "Denique soli in constructione turris. . . . Labio universae terrae in domo Heber . . . prima humani generis loquela remansit, quod nomina sequentis aevi hominum Hebraea manifeste probant" (XCI, 120 BC; 121 A). Cf. Filaster, *Haer.* 105, n. 4: "Heber signifies holy," just as God willed, "that the Hebrews might be called . . . by a name derived from Heber" — "ut ab Heber . . . Hebraei nomine appellarentur" (CCL, 9, 268).

358. *In Cant. Moys.*, 2: "Once the confusion of tongues had come about, the original tongue remained within the house and family of Heber; whence through Abraham, who himself was called a Hebrew, this people went forth Hebrew: 'the Lord's only portion'" — "Facta namque confutatione linguarum, remansit lingua primitiva in domo et familia Heber, unde per Abraham qui et ipse Hebraeus dictus est, exivit hic populus Hebraeus pars Domini solus" (PL, CXCIV, 1050 C). Ps.-Bede (XCIII, 299 B). Angelome (CXV, 168 A). Hervaeus, *In Phil.* (CLXXXI, 1300 B). Garnier, *s.* 19 (CCV, 696 D). Romuald of Salerno, *Chron.* (Muratori, 7, 12); etc.

359. *Etym.*, l. 9, c. 1, n. 1 (PL, LXXXII, 325 CD).

360. Aimo, *In II Cor.*, xi (117, 654 A). Abelardian comm. *In Phil.*; "'Hebrew' from 'Abraham', as if it were 'Abrahemus', not from 'Heber', as some would have it" — "Hebraeus ab Abraham, quasi Abrahemus, non ab Heber, ut quidam volunt" (Landgraf, 466). *Glossa in Gen.*, x, 21: "Hence it is deservedly asked,

Which is more probable, that the 'Hebrews' are so called as being 'Heber-ews' or as 'Abrah-ews'?" — "Quid ergo probabilius sit, Hebraeos dici tanquam Hebraeos vel tanquam Abraeos, merito quaeritur" (CXIII, 114 B). Cf. Rabanus, *In Ez.*, l. 5, c. 7 (CX, 610 BC). For Bede, *Hexaem.*, l. 3, "Those who think that the tribe of the Hebraeans have been named from Abraham as though it were 'Ebrean' are greatly mistaken, since even Abraham himself is called a Hebraean" — "errant nimium qui gentem Hebraeorum a nomine Abraham esse cognominatam quasi Ebream putant, cum et ipse Abraham Hebraeus appellatur" (XCI, 148 B).

361. *L. quaest. hebr.*, *In Gen.*, x, 24 (XXIII, 955 B).

362. Augustine at first derived "Hebrew" from Abraham: *Q. in Heptat.*, l. 1, q. 29 (XXXIV, 552); in *Retract.*, l. 2, c. 16, he regards Heber as being more probable (Bardy, 478).

363. Natus est homo in mundum, patriarcha nobilis,
Abraham Dei amicus, puer fidelissimus;
Heber aurea de stirpe oriendus exstitit,
A quo caepit Hebraeorum diffamari populus.

From *Versus de Jacob et Joseph* (*P. lat. aevi car.*, 4, 462).

364. *Civ. Dei*, l. 16, c. 3, n. 2 (Bardy, 4, 191); c. 11, n. 1: "The house of Heber, where the language that everyone previously shared still remained, did not fail. . . . Hence since this language remained in his family, when the other tribes had been divided into various languages, this language is not undeservedly thought to have been previously the language common to the human race, and so it was then called Hebrew" — "Non defuit domus Heber, ubi ea quae antea fuit omnium lingua remaneret. . . . Quia ergo in ejus familia remansit haec lingua, divisis per alias linguas, caeteris gentibus, quae lingua prius humano generi non immerito creditur fuisse communis, ideo deinceps Hebraea est nuncupata" (220-4); cf. l. 18, c. 39 (598). Quodvultdeus, *De prom.*, P. 1, c. 9, n. 15 (LI, 741 C). The connection is kept despite the *Ambrosiaster*, q. 108 (Souter, 251-6), the *Quaestiones* of whom were, however, known under the name of Augustine. Claudius, *In Gen.* (L, 942 B).

365. L. 1, c. 4: "Heber, whence the Hebrews" — "Heber unde Hebraei" (MGH, *Scr.*, 20, 333).

366. Thus, Jacques Roulduc, cap., *De Ecclesia ante legem* (1625), p. 2 and pp. 158-68; G. Horn, *Arca Noe* . . . (1666), 69, or Pastor Morin, letter to Huet, 8 May 1679; see also the response of Huet: *Dissertations sur divers sujects composées par M. Huet* . . . gathered by M. l'abbé de Tilladet (The Hague, 1720, t. 1, 195-221); or Father Tournemine, *Mémoires de Trévoux*, Nov. 1705, 1958: "Quelle langue doit passer pour la plus ancienne du monde?" R. Simon, *H. crit. du V.T.*, 484-8; etc.

367. *Instr. ps.*, n. 15: "Since the mystery of God's will and the expectation of the blessed kingdom is preached especially in these three languages, therefore there was that quotation of Pilate, etc." — "Quia his maxime tribus linguis sacramentum voluntatis Dei et beati regni exspectatio praedicatur; ex quo illud Pilati fuit, etc." (13). Cf. Aug., *In Jo.*, tr. 117, n. 4 (PL, XXXV, 1946). Ps.-Bede, *Collect.* (XCIV, 547 D). For Ireland: Robert E. McNally, SJ, "The 'tres linguae sacrae' in Early Irish Bible Exegesis," *Theol. St.*, 19 (1958), 395-403.

368. The fact is attested in the 12th century for Eugene III (1145) and Alexander III (1163). E. Rodocanachi, *Le Saint-Siège et les Juifs* (1891), 139-40.

369. Anselm of Laon, *In Ap.*, c. 9 (PL, CLXII, 1534 C).

370. Avitus, *s.* 11, fr. 2 (MGH, *A. ant.*, 6, 121). Isidore, *Etym.*, l. 9, c. 1, n. 4: "Greek, however, is regarded as superior to the other languages of the nations in point of clarity; for it is more sonorous than Latin and all the [other] languages" — "Graeca autem lingua, inter caeteras gentium clarior habetur; est enim et latina et omnibus linguis sonantior" (PL, LXXXII, 326 D). Bede, *In Luc.* (XCII, 618 A). Ps.-Bede, *In Matt.* (XCII, 124 A). Alcuin, *Div. off.*, c. 9: Latin is "earthier" — "humilior" (CI, 1186 B). Hugh, *De gramm.*: "One surely ought to know that the studies of three tribes have flourished in excellent manner in the cultivation of literature: of the Hebrews, the Greeks, the Latins; but the literature of the Hebrews is thought to be earlier in time.... Three languages are quite set apart ... that are especially excellent in the whole world.... But the Greek language is regarded as clearer than the rest of the tribes" — "Sciendum sane trium gentium studia in litterarum eruditione excellenter floruisse, Hebraeorum, Graecorum, Latinorum; sed Hebraeorum litterae tempore priores existimantur.... Tres linguae sunt sacratiores ... quae toto orbe maxime excellunt.... Graeca autem lingua inter caeteras gentium clarior habetur" (Leclercq, 269-70).

371. *Ysagoge in theol.*: "This is the mother of all languages and in it were handed down the Law and the Prophets, i.e., the first foundations of theology" — "Haec est omnium mater linguarum et in eadem Lex et Prophetae, theologiae sc. prima fundamenta fuerunt tradita" (Landgraf, 128).

372. Honorius, *Gemma*, l. 3, c. 95: "Hebrew is called the mother of all the languages; Greek, their teacher ... ; Latin, their commander ... , and by all these in combination Christ's passion is praised" — "Hebraea mater omnium linguarum, Graeca doctrix ... , Latina imperatrix ... , praedicatur, et ab his omnibus Christi passio collaudatur" (PL, CLXXII, 667 D). *Sacram.*, c. 12: "Hebrew ... is the nobler; Latin, somewhat lower and, as it were, a daughter" — "Hebraea ... nobilior; Latina inferior et quasi filia" (752 B). Abelard. Ps.-Bede (XCIV, 547 D). Cf. S. Cummian, *De controv. pascali*, on the three languages: "and these languages, as Jerome says, Christ consecrated on the placard of his cross" — "quas linguas, ut Hieronymus ait, in crucis suae titulo Christus consecravit" (LXXXVII, 969 C).

373. *In Ex.*, l. 1, c. 9 (CLXVII, 576 A).

374. "expleto Judicio, ipsa remanebit una": Aimo, *In I Cor.*: "Just as before the tower of Babel there was one language, Hebrew, so, as some doctors think" — "Sicut ante turrim Babel una erat lingua Hebraea, sic, ut quidam putant doctores" (CXVII, 583 D). Goscelin, *Lib. confort.*, c. 4, n. 9 (Wilmart, RB, 50, 8). Again for Fabre d'Olivet, the human race will end up by speaking no more than one language, and that one will be Hebrew (cf. Roland de Renéville, *L'expérience poétique*, 38). This privilege will sometimes be disputed; cf. Basnage, *H. de l'Église* ... , 1 (1679), 468: "The apologists for Latin say that it is so excellent and so much devoted to God's service that the saints in glory will only speak it in paradise" — "Les défenseurs de la langue latine disent qu'elle est si excellente, et tellement consacrée au service de Dieu, que les Saints glorifiés la parleront uniquement dans le Paradis."

375. Aug., *Doct. chr.*, l. 2, c. 11, n. 16 (258); reproduced by Isidore, *Etym.*, l. 6, c.

19, n. 20 (PL, LXXXII, 253 C). *In ps.* xxxii, s. 1, n. 8 (CCL, 38, 254). Paschasius, *In Matt.*, l. 12, c. 27 (CXX, 957 BC).

376. In the same way, says Rupert, they did not translate the Greek word *Apocalypsis* "by reason of the excellence of the things involved" — "ob excellentiam rerum"; "because of the worth of the senses" — "ob dignitatem sensuum": *In Ap.*, l. 1, c. 1 (PL, CLXIX, 827 A). Bruno of Würzburg, *In ps.* cxlvii (CXLII, 522 D).

377. Rabanus, *De laud.*, l. 2, c. 22: "They will sing a new song to the Lord, namely 'alleluia', the angelic song" — "Cantabunt Deo canticum novum, alleluia vid., angelicum carmen" (CVII, 287 C); c. 25: "Hence I have tried to take up some of the words of the heavenly odes to praise thee ... and I have inserted the angelic chant, namely 'amen', putting it in the middle of the cross, and completing it with 'alleluia', so that in this way ... I might designate this sacred effigy by means of heavenly song" — "Quapropter tentavi ex caelestibus odis quaedam verba ad laudandum te sumere ... et inserui angelicos cantus, amen vid., in medio crucis collocans, et cum alleluia cornua illius complens, ut sic ... hanc sacram effigiem caelesti carmine signarem" (290 a). Neckham, *De nat. rer.*, c. 15: "Alleluia is being sung in the courtyards of the heavenly Jerusalem" — "in supernae Jerusalem plateis alleluia decantatur" (55). Cf. Aurelianus mon., *De musica*, on the priest who heard the alleluia sung by the angels (MD, *Vet. script.*, 1, 124-5; with allusions to Greg., *Dial.*).

378. Aug., *s.* 362, n. 29: "Our whole activity will be Amen and Alleluia.... We shall always be saying Amen and Alleluiah with a sufficiency that is never enough" — "Tota actio nostra, amen et alleluia erit.... Amen et alleluia semper dicturi sumus ... insatiabili satietate" (PL, XXXIX, 1632-3); *s.* 243, n. 8 (XXXVIII, 1147). *Misc.*, l. 3, tit. 34: "The angels speak Hebrew.... The Hebrew sounds his praises not in Egypt but in heaven" — "Hebraea loquuntur angeli.... Hebraeus non in Aegypto sed in caelo laudes sonat" (CLXXVII, 655 CD).

379. "apud Deum purus intellectus est sine strepitu et diversitate linguarum": Bede, *Hexaem.*, l. 1 (XCI, 17 C) and 3 (123 CD); etc.

380. *Mor.*, l. 30, c. 4, n. 17 (LXXVI, 533 B).

381. "in spe"; "in re": *S.* 255, n. 5; 256, n. 1 and 3 (XXXVIII, 1188, 1190, 1193). *In Jo.*, tr. 41, n. 3 (CCL, 36, 359).

382. Anselm of Laon, *In Ap.*, c. 19 (CLXII, 1568 BC), on Alleluia.

383. Aug., *s.* 362, c. 27, n. 29 (XXXIX, 1633). *S.* 252, n. 9 (38, 1176-7). Cf. *In ps.* cxlviii, n. 1 (CCL, 40, 2165-6).

384. Isidore, *Etym.*, l. 6, c. 3-4 (LXXXII, 235-6).

385. Cf. Gilbert Crispin, *Disput.* (Blum, 57); but 71: "as is held in the Hebrew" — "sicut in Hebraeo habetur."

386. "prophetico magis dono quam officio interpretandi": *Hexaem.*, l. 2 (PL, 91, 79 C). On the value of the Septuagint according to Aug.: G. Bardy, *Cité de Dieu*, 4, 762-5. Cf. Sigebert, *Chron.*, a. 395 (MGH, *Scr.*, 6, 314).

387. Rupert, *In Gen.*, l. 9, c. 16 (CLXVII, 542 BC).

388. Cf. Sedulius Scotus, *In Rom.*, xi: "it is to be known that the apostolic authority never relies on the manuscripts of the Hebrews" — "sciendum quod auctoritas apostolica numquam Hebraeorum exemplaribus fidem facit etc." (CIII, 102 BC; cf. 100 CD). Lanfranc, *In Rom.*: Many of the citations made by Paul seem

to be "in disagreement with the translation of the Hebrew truth that we use, since the authoritative quotations are sometimes from the translation of the Septuagint" — "a translatione veritatis hebraicae qua nos utimur ideo discordare videntur, quia aliquando auctoritates sunt a translatione Septuaginta interpretum" (CL, 109 A). Hervaeus, *In Rom.* (CLXXXI, 609 A).

389. *Q. in Hept.*, l. 7, c. 37: "that among the languages of the nations Greek is so outstanding that they can all be fittingly expressed through it" — "quod in linguis gentium graeca ita excellat, ut per hanc omnes decenter significentur" (XXXIV, 805).

390. *In Is.*: "in comparison to the Hebrew tongue, [we have] the poverty of both the Greek and the Latin language" — "ad comparationem linguae Hebraeae, tam Graeci quam Latini sermonis pauperiem" (XXIV, 407 B). Cf. P. Antin, *Essai sur S. Jérôme*, 150: "The more he went on, the harder he became on the Greek" — "Plus il allait, plus il devenait sévère pour le Grec." The Greeks paid back his severity, too. Cf. *Apol. adv. libros Ruf.*, l. 1, c. 4; l. 3, c. 6 (XXIII, 408 C, 461-2); *ep.* 58, c. 8 (3, 83).

391. "Deo gratias, credo quia aequiparaverit nostra tarditas eorum prioratum!": Cf. Notker, *de Interpr. div. Script.*, c. 12 (PL, CXXXI, 1003 A). John Scotus had to deny that he was neglecting the Latins: *Div. nat.*, l. 4, c. 17 (CXXII, 830 C).

392. Aeneas of Paris, *Adv. Graecos*, praef. (CXXI, 686 A, 689 B).

393. *Insaniunt Graeci cum ratione*: Hugh Métel, *ep.* 1 (314).

394. Guibert of Nogent, *Gesta Dei*, l. 1, c. 2 (PL, CLVI, 686-9); "should the catalogues of all the heresies be scanned, should the books of the ancients written against the heretics be reviewed, I should be surprised if scarcely any be found outside the East and Africa" — "omnium haereseon catalogi perlegantur, libri antiquorum scripti adversus haereticos recenseantur, mirabor si praeter Orientem et Africam vix aliqui subcernentur" (687 AB). Cf. Joachim of Flora, *Sup. 4 ev.*: "While [the Greeks] want to arrogate a teaching authority they do not have, not to the extent that they are in themselves becoming affirmers of the truth but rather provokers of it, which has been ever more often proved through the many heresies they have incurred" — "Dum ipsi (Graeci) volunt sibi vindicare magisterium quod non habent, non quantum in se est assertores veritatis fiunt, sed praecipitatores, quod in multis haeresibus quas incurrerunt saepe saepius probatum est" (221-2). *Concordia*, l. 5, c. 47: The tribe of the Greeks "has been divided from the placenta and it has for the most part erred from the womb and uttered falsities" — Gens Graecorum "divisa est a vulva et secundum majorem sui partem erravit ab utero et locuta est falsa" (f. 89 r).

395. Guibert, *loc. cit.* (PL, CLVI, 687 B).

396. Gerard of Csanad (11th cent.), *In cant. Dan.*: "Italy has not been wont to nourish heresies; at present in certain places it is heard that they abound in the fomentations of heresies, whereas happy Gaul is kept pure of them. Unhappy Greece, never was willing to live without them" — "Italia non consuevit haereses nutrire; ad praesens in quibusdam partibus haeresium fomentis abundare auditur. Gallia vero felix, quae his munda perhibetur. Graecia infelix, sine quibus nunquam vivere voluit" (Morin, RB, 27, 520).

397. Aeneas of Paris, *Adv. Graec.*, praef. (686 A). It is from Asia and from

Greece that one sees always "that the crises of such fallacies arise" — "tantarum fallaciarum oriri discrimina"; from there, history shows, "broods of vipers have sprouted, i.e., a huge number of inventors of perverse opinions . . . and other plagues of scattered heresy, which did not cease at every occurrence to wound and attack catholic minds" — "pullulasse genimina viperarum, id est quamplurimi inventores perversorum dogmatum . . . caeteraeque pestes dilatatae haereseos, quibus non fuit requies omni instantia catholicas dilacerare et oppugnare mentes" (686 CD; cf. 687 AD).

398. *Carmen "Hanc libam"* (PL, CXXII, 1029 A).

399. *Disp. alt. adv. Ab.*, l. 1: "He seems to draw it from a certain Maximus, whom I think to have been a Greek, whom John Scotus also imitated to the point of heresy" — "Id trahere videtur a quodam Maximo, quem puto Graecum fuisse, quem et J. Scotus usque ad haeresim imitatus est" (CLXXX, 288 A).

400. *Ep.* 15, c. 1 (1, 46).

401. "Luget hoc Graecia novis invidiae aculeis lacessita; quam sui quondam incolae jamdudum cum Asianis apibus aspernantur, vestra potius magnanimitate delectati, studiis allecti, liberalitate confisi; dolet, inquam, se olim singulariter mirabilem ac mirabiliter singularem a suis destitui; dolet certe sua illa privilegia (quod nunquam hactenus verita est) ad climata nostra transferri" (in 873; *Poetae lat.*, 3, 429).

402. From Solomon of Constance: Dümmler, 67; cited by Curtius, 567-8. *De int.*, c. 12: "Even the West itself, though late, finally at some time or other did erupt into bud" — "Occidens etiam ipse, licet sero, tandem tamen aliquando in germen erupit . . ." (PL, CXXXI, 1003 A).

403. Godfrey of Viterbo, *Pantheon*, P. 16 and 17 (PL, CXCVIII, 879, 919, 939 A). P. Teilhard de Chardin, SJ, *Lettres de voyage*, 62: "If one wants to understand the Far East, the hour at which one must look at it is not at dawn or at high noon; it is at dusk, when the sun in its glory, carrying away the slough of Asia, rises triumphantly over the sky of Europe." — "L'heure à laquelle, faut regarder l'Extrême-Orient, si on veut le comprendre, ce n'est pas à l'aurore, ni au grand midi; c'est au crépuscule, quand le soleil, emportant dans sa gloire les dépouilles de l'Asie, se lève, en plein triomphe, sur le ciel d'Europe."

404. "translatio studii"; "translatio sapientiae"; "translatio potentiae"; "translatio regni": Cf. A. Van den Baar, "Die kirchliche Lehre der Translatio Imperii romani," *Anal. gregoriana*, 78 (1956). Werner Goez, *Translatio imperii* (1958). Robert E. McNally, *Theol. Studies*, 21 (1960), 103-8. Robert Folz, CCM, 2, 355-7. Eugenio Dupré Theseider, *L'idea imperiale de Roma nella tradizione del Medioevo* (Milan, 1942).

405. Ansel Choquart will say, in the 14th cent.: "It is obvious to anyone that scholarship had been transferred from Rome to Paris through blessed Charles the Great, and this glory of the Romans was transferred to the Gauls at Paris" — "Cuicumque patet quod studium translatum fuit a Roma Parisius per B. Carolum magnum, et haec gloria Romanorum Parisius in Gallos est translata" (Du Boulay, *Hist. Univ. Parisiensis*, 1668, 4, 408). The topic remains alive through the 15th and 16th centuries (Franco Simone, in *Pensée humaniste et tradit. Chrét.*, 1950, 243-53). In 1599 Bellarmine published a treatise "De translatione imperii romani a Graecis ad Francos, adv. Matthiam Flaccium Illyricum" and Maim-

bourg will write an *Hist. de l'hérésie des Iconoclastes et de la translation de l'Empire aux François*. Nicholas of Cusa, *De concordantia cath.*, l. 3, c. 3, appears skeptical (G. Kaller, 1959, 337).

406. "Omnis humana sapientia vel potentia ab oriente ordiens in occidente terminari caepit": *Chron.*, l. 5, prol. (MGH, *Scr.*, 20, 213).

407. "serie rerum ab oriente in occidentem recta linea decurrente": *De arca Noe mor.*, l. 4, c. 9 (PL, CLXXVI, 677-8).

408. *Registr.*, 6, ep. 14: "Now the Roman manuscripts are much truer than the Greek ones, since we have your [words] as devoid of subtleties and so not involving impostures either" — "Romani autem codices multo veriores sunt quam Graeci quia nos vestra sicut non acumina, ita nec imposturas habemus" (1, 393). Cf. 476 and 2, 330.

409. *Vita Hadriani*: "Ne quid Graeca levitas falsum suatim congesserit" (*Lib. pontif.*, 2, 181).

410. "astuta perversitas": *Vita Greg.*, l. 4, c. 75 (PL, LXXV, 225 B).

411. Cf. the account of his legation (CXXXVI, 909-38); n. 3 and 41, portrait of Nicephorus (911 BD, 926 AB). This is a pamphlet that inspires resentment.

412. *Ep.* 3, n. 2 (CXXXVI, 650 A).

413. "de haeresibus Graecorum": Hugh Etherianus (CCII, 292-3, 364-5, etc.).

414. *De cond. G. Porret.*, c. 6 (CLXXXV, 590-1).

415. Notker, *De int.* (CXXXI, 993-1004). Lanfranc, *Adv. Ber.*, c. 22 (CL, 441 A). Anselm, *ep.* 104 (CLIX, 254), etc. Cf. Greg., *Ep.*, 1, 10, 14: "Regarding all the inquiries of the Romans and the Greeks, the Fathers, whose followers we are, have spoken with one Spirit" — "De cunctis inquisitionibus Romanorum atque Graecorum Patres, quorum nos sequaces sumus, uno Spiritu sunt locuti"; "the venerable Fathers whom I love much" — "venerandos Patres quos multum diligo" (2, 249).

416. L. Bréhier, *Le schisme oriental du XIe s.* (1899), 18-9. On the pro-Greek attitude of the emperors Henry III and Otto III: p. 16 and 27.

417. Cf. Fontaine, 851.

418. J.-M. Parent, *Beiträge Baümker*, 1935, 3, 290.

419. "Graeci autem solito more res acutius considerantes expressiusque significantes ": *De div. nat.*, l. 5, c. 55 (PL, CXXII, 955 A).

420. "O verum sagacissimum qui, quod in latinis defecerit, ad graeca nos retrahit, et in romanis sermonibus graecas origines effingit! In latinis dictionibus nobis atticas origines importas!": *De praed.* (CXV, 1305 B, 1313 D).

421. "glossaire de Laon" — "pour la seule lettre A, donne la traduction d'environ douze cent mots (grecs) appartenant à tous les usages": E. Delaruelle, in *H. du cathol. en Fr.*, 1, 196. Cf. H. Silvestre, "Une copie du Xe s. non utilisée du premier glossaire grec-latin Abscida Lucida (fragment)," *Bull. du Cange*, 21 (1951), 159-70.

422. A number of well-read people educated at Canterbury at that time spoke Greek fluently: Duchesne, *L'Egl. au VIe s.*, 623.

423. Since the 6th cent., Hellenism flourished in Ireland. Such Greek as scholars of the 9th cent. knew often came to them from Irish masters. W. Levison, *England and the Continent in the Eighth Century* (2^d ed., 1949). L. Bieler, "The Island of Scholars," RMAL, 8 (1952), 213-34. Laistner, 238-45. See also L. Gougaud,

"L'œuvre des Scotti dans l'Eur. contin." (RHE, 1908, 259-60); *Les chrétientés celtiques* (1911, ch. 8). Cappuyns, *J. Scot Er.* (1933), 21-7, 128-32. Ghellinck, *Lit. lat.*, 1, 29-31, 92-3. Bernard Bischoff, *Il Monachesimo Irlandese nei suoi rapporti col continente*, in *Seltimane di Studio del Centro Italiano di Studi sull'Alto Medioevo*, 4, *Il Monachesimo . . . e la formazione della Civiltà occidentale* (Spoleto, 1957), 123-38, 165-84.

424. It has been supposed that the "Graeci" at the court of Charles the Bald were Irish, but the matter is uncertain, and it seems that the Irish influence at this period has been exaggerated. Fr. Masai, in *Seltimane . . .* , 4, p. 163, 184. Still it pentrated to Auxerre, Laon, Sankt Gall, etc. Cf. Ermneric of Elwangen (†874) to Grimaldus on Ireland, "whence the radiance of such great light has come to us" — "unde nobis tanti luminis jubar advenit" (MGH, *Ep.*, 5, 575).

425. For an earlier period: E. Delaruelle, "La connaiss. du grec en occident du Ve au IXe s.," Soc. toulousaine d'ét. classiques, *Mél.*, 1 (1946), 207-26. For the 7th-10th cent.: Laistner, 239-50. "In memory of Dionysius the Areopagite, in the 9th cent. they were keen on advertising some modest acquaintance with Greek" — "En souvenir de Denys l'Ar., on tenait, au IXe s., à afficher à Saint-Denis une modeste connaissance du grec": Lesne, 5, 268; cf. 4, 208.

426. It has wrongly been inferred from his letter to Solomon of Constance that he did not know Greek. After that he was "morte praeventus"; he had had all the means to learn the language at Sankt Gall; he had copied the Catholic Epistles in Greek: Ekkehard IV, *Casus S. Galli*, c. 46 (160-1). Cf. J. M. Clark, *The Abbey of St. Gall* (1926), 109-12.

427. Ruotgerus, *Vita Brunonis Colon. arch.*, c. 4, 6, 7 (MGH, *Scr.*, 4, 256-7).

428. Egli, *Liber bened.*, p. xxxvi-vii. Cf. Lesne, 5, 413.

429. Jean de Saint-Arnoul, *Via . . .* , n. 116: "He stood head and shoulders above everyone in his own time and almost equaled the ancients; in addition a good deal of instruction in reading Greek had come to him" — "Sui temporis omnes superaret et antiquos pene aequiparet; cui insuper et graecae lectionis multa accesserat instructio" (PL, CXXXVII, 298 B).

430. A dozen toasts in verse, edited by Dümmler; two hexameters are entirely in Greek (Ebert, 3, 381-2). Another anonymous document at the end of the 11th cent. blends its verses with Greek and Hebrew terms: BL, 50; cf. V.-G., 78: variation on the Alleluia ("Prosa sancti Jacobi latinis, graecis et hebraicis verbis," D. Calixto [II] Papa abreviata).

431. Cf. Ozanam, 2, 407.

432. Cf. William of Malmesbury, *De gestis Pont. Angl.*: "A certain Fridegod executed that task with some not so much to be disapproved verses, except that he loves Greek with utter hatred for Latin; he uses so many little Greek words that he fittingly adds to his words the dictum of Plautus: 'No one but a Prophet will be able to read this'" — "Exsecutus est id munus Fridegodus quidam versibus non ita improbandis, nisi quod latinitatem perosus graecitatem amat, graecula verba frequentat, ut merito dictis ejus aptetur illud Plautinum: Hoc quidem praeter Sibyllam leget nemo" (Hamilton, 22; Manitius, 2, 500; from the Life of St. Wilfrid in verse). H. Focillon, *L'An Mil* (1952), 81: "This completely artificial taste for Greek is attested for us by a certain Peter, a subdeacon, who, in 1010, signs his

name in Greek, but warns us frankly that he is ignorant of the language: 'Peter ὑποδιάκονος wrote this, though untutored in the Greek language.'"

433. *Ep.* 9 (PL, CLXXVIII, 335 A). Heloise knew Greek and Hebrew (Gildon, *Hél. et Abélard*, 178).

434. Cf. *ep.* 149 (PL, CXCIX, 143-4); etc. C. Théry, "Documents concernant Jean Sarrazin," AHDLMA, 8, 48-79.

435. "viri sapientes, in utraque lingua periti": G. Théry, "Jean Sarrazin 'traducteur' de Scot Er." (*St. mediaevalia, Mél. J. Martin*, 1948, 363). On John Damascene in the West: Ghellinck, *Mouvement*, 335-45 and 374-415. Ch.-H. Haskings, *Studies in the Hist. of Medieval Science* (1924), c. 8-11: Translations from the Greek. A. Dondaine, AHDLMA, 19 (1953), 79. R. Lechat, "La patristique grecque chez un théol. latin du XIIe s.," *Mél. d'hist. offerts à Ch. Moeller*, 1 (1914; on Hugh Etherien). On the colleges of translators: Ghellinck, *L'essor*, 2, 20-3.

436. *Sent.:* "It is a fault to prostitute Catholic doctrine by weighing it down with the vain din of sounds, and it is a still greater fault to want to give it a festive adornment by planting Greek terms in it with strange resonances that, it would seem, ought to adorn the whole of the Latin text" — "C'est une faute de prostituer la doctrine catholique en la chargeant du vain tintamarre des sonores, et c'est une faute plus grande encore que de vouloir lui donner une parure de fête en y semant des vocables grecs aux résonances étranges qui, paraît-il, doivent orner l'ensemble du texte latin" (tr. E. De Bruyne, 2, 170). Hugh of Fouilloy (PL, CLXXVI, 1131 A).

437. "minus authenticum": *Inter ep. Gerh.,* 16: "But since what you say you have taken from Greece is less authoritative, though the authority of your religion is great, it is as easily rejected as accepted" — "Sed quia minus authenticum est, quod a Graecia vos accepisse dicitis, licet magna sit vestrae religionis auctoritas, eadem facilitate contemnitur quam probatur" (CXCIII, 555 AB).

438. "quosdam vaniloquos graecorum haereticis consentaneos": *In ps.* xxxi (Van den Eynde, 52).

439. Cf. Ghellinck, *Mouvement*, 243. Alain, a Porretanian, loves Greek words: *Regulae*, praef. (PL, CCX, 621 AB); *Anticl.*, prol. (Bossuat, 56), etc.

440. William of Malmsbury, *Gesta regum Angl.*, l. 2, n. 122: "He even composed a book that he entitled *Perì phýseôn merismoû*, or *On the division of nature*, because of the quite useful perplexity involved in solving the necessary questions; provided, however, that he may be pardoned for certain points in which he has wandered off the path of the Latins whilst he kept his eyes sharply focused on the Greeks" — "Composuit etiam librum quem περὶ φύσεων μερισμοῦ, id est De naturae divisione titulavit, propter perplexitatem necessariarum quaestionum solvendam bene utilem; si tamen ignoscatur ei in aliquibus in quibus a Latinorum tramite deviavit dum in Graecos acriter oculos intendit" (Th. D. Hardy, 1840, 190). The 4th ch. of the council is known to have been entitled "De superbia Graecorum contra Latinos" (Mansi, 22, 990). Other facts in Chenu, 275-88; Ghellinck, *L'essor,* 2,15-42; A. Dondaine, AHDLMA, 19 (1953), 79.

441. *In Is.:* "I wonder what the LXX may have meant" — "Miror quid voluerint Septuaginta" (PL, XXIV, 607 A). Compare Aug., *In ps.* lxxxvii, n. 10: "In the Hebrew. . . . But the Septuagint translators, whose authority is so great because of their marvelous consistency that they are not undeservedly believed to

have translated by the aid of the divine Spirit" — "In hebraeo. . . . Verum Septuaginta interpretes, quorum auctoritas tanta est ut non immerito propter mirabilem consonantiam divino Spiritu interpretati esse credantur" (CCL, 39, 1215); and Orig., *In Jer.*, h. 11: "For Scripture is twofold. . . . So it is necessary both to expound what is in use especially in the churches and also not to pass by untouched what is found in the Hebrew manuscripts" — "Duplex quippe Scriptura est. . . . Oportet igitur et id quod in usu est atque in ecclesiis legitur exponere et hoc quod in hebraeis codicibus invenitur intactum non praeterire" (PL, XXV, 664 B). On Jerome's excessive exclusivism: Bardy, *La question des langues* . . . , 264-6.

442. Agobard, *Adv. Fred.*, c. 13: "Paul is, as Jerome . . . writes, more fluent in Hebrew than in Greek" — "Paulus dissertior invenitur in hebraica lingua quam in graeca, sicut Hieronymus . . . scribit" (PL, CIV, 167-8). Agobard had a smattering of these two languages: J. Allen Cabaniss, "Agobard of Lyon," *Speculum*, 26 (1951), 50. Aimo, *In Gal.:* "At the end of all of his epistles the Apostle used to write his name in Hebrew letters" — "In fine omnium epistolarum suarum Apostolus nomen suum hebraeis litteris scribebat" (PL, CXVII, 698 A).

443. PL, CIII, 331-52. Angelome, *In Reg.*, l. 2: "I believe our translation to be true, just as our translator, so expert in the three languages, provides a well-defended example in his preface" — "Nostram interpretationem veram credo, sicut in praefatione noster interpres in tribus linguis peritus galeatum ponit exemplum" (CXV, 348 A). Cf. Wandalbert of Prüm (†ca. 870), *Commendatio martyrologio praemissa* (MGH, *P. Lat.*, 1, 57).

444. In the new Claudian materials consulted by Wilmart, Jerome is the most frequently mentioned: RB, 32, 170. Like Rabanus, Claude used to give his references carefully.

445. "Sicut beatus Hieronymus dicit": PL, CXVII, 28 B, 31 D, 55 A, 69 B, 95 C, etc.

446. "Beato Hieronymo testante": *In ps.* cxviii (LXX, 835 BC).

447. Ps.-Hincmar: "but as Jerome the priest has translated from the Hebrew" — "sicut autem ex hebraeo interpretatus est presbyter Hier." (CXXV, 945 A). Angelome, *In Gen.*, c. 17: "as blessed Jerome manifests" — "B. Hieronymo propalante" (CXV, 180 C). Gerhoh, *In ps.* lxiv, c. 120: "when St. Jerome says these things" — "haec dicente s. Hieronymo" (CXCIV, 79 A); etc.

448. "licet in omnes prophetas laborantissimus et desudantissimus studioso lectori sufficiat Hieronymus": PL, CXXXI, 995 B.

449. "assiduus librorum Hieronymi lector"; "ille sanctus et incomparabilis in divina et humana sapientia, sacer Hieronymus": Epitaph of the Empress Adelaide, l. 1 (in 999; MGH, *Scr.*, 4, 638).

450. Cf. B. B. [Botte]: "Jerome is an excellent philologist, a formidable polemicist and a good writer; but he is not a historian" — "Jérôme est un excellent philologue, un redoutable polémiste et un bon écrivain; mais ce n'est pas un historien" (BTAM, 6, no. 596). Let us note a rather astonishing reflection of P. de Labriolle, "La science et l'ascèse chez S. Jér.," *R. des cours et conf.*, 20 April 1905, 334: "Jerome can be considered to have renewed hagiographic literature by means of his lives of hermits, the success of which was considerable" — "On peut considérer que par ses vies de solitaires, dont le succès fut considérable, Jérôme a renouvelé la littérature hagiographique." H. Leclercq, *S. Jérôme*, 74, says it better:

"Having been conditioned to it by St. Jerome, fiction flourished only too well at the expense of the truth" — "La fiction, acclimatée par S. Jérôme, n'a connu qu'une trop magnifique efflorescence aux dépens de la vérité." At Canterbury too, Nigel of Longchamp will paraphrase [Jerome's] *Life of Paul of Thebes*.

451. "scriptor mirificus"; "totius Ecclesiae simmistes"; "theca sophiae": RMAL, 2, 317-8. V. *supra*, I, ch. IV, ii.

452. "mundi lucerna": *Vita S. Bernardi Tiron.*, prol., c. 1 (PL, CLXXII, 1367 A).

453. "Hieronymus catholicorum magister, cujus scripta per universum mundum quasi divinae lampades rutilant": *De incarn.*, l. 7, c. 26 (L, 256 A).

454. *Dial.*, l. 1, c. 8 (XX, 189 A).

455. *Inst.*, c. 21 (LXX, 1135-6).

456. "per evangelicae frameam dictionis": *L. moz. sacr.*, Mass of St. Jerome (63-4).

457. Hieronyme, intrepres variis doctissime linguis,
    Te Bethlem celebrat, te totus personat orbis,
    Te quoque nostra tuis promet bibliotheca libris:

C. H. Beeson, *Isidorstudien* (1913).

458. "vir beatae memoriae Hieronymus, qui divinas Scripturas de Hebraeo in Latinum eloquium vertit": *De comprob. aet. sextae*, l. 3, c. 25 (PL, XCVI, 581 B).

459. "Hebraea romanis vertens oracula verbis": *De laud. virginum* (LXXXIX, 266 D).

460. Archivum penetrans Hebraeum lampade cordis
    Hieronymus sacros adytos et eburnea templa
    Discipulis reserat, Latio transmittit habenda,
    Judaeumque nemus, quod eatenus invia nostris
    Sepserat, ingressus cordato lumine lustrat:

Bibliothecarum et psalteriorum versus, 6. (*P. lat. aevi car.*, 3, 259-60: an elogy of Jerome in 16 verses.)

461. "ut beato Hieronymo hebraicae linguae peritissimo docente didicimus": L. 2, c. 30 (PL, XCVIII, 1104-5); l. 1, c. 6: "Most blessed Jerome, a man educated in the divine laws and with expertise in many languages" — "Beatissimus H., vir divinis legibus et multarum linguarum peritia eruditus" (1021 A).

462. L. 4, c. 13: "Let him read blessed Jerome" — "Legat beatum H." (1209 A), etc.

463. "clarissimum in sancta Ecclesia divinae Scripturae doctorem": Gisela et Rectruda, *Ad Alb.* (C, 740 A).

464. *Cler. inst.*, l. 2, c. 54 (CVII, 366 D).

465. *Praef. ad Ludov. regem* (CXI, 10 BC).

466. "Medullas et ipsa viscera Scripturae sacrae investigando, Domino inspirante, penetrare promeruit": *De praed. diss. post.* (CXXV, 246 C).

467. Hieronymus mundi celeberrimus extat in orbe . . .
    Testamenta Dei geminaeque consona legis
    Tradidit ac vertit mutans sermone latino.
    Haec quoque Psalmorum gratissima cantica nobis
    Transtulit ac demum rectum correxit ad unguem:

P. lat. m. aevi, 6, 164.

468. M. L. W. Laistner, "The Study of St. Jerome in the Early Middle Ages," in F. X. Murphy, *A Monument to St. Jerome* (1952), 251: "He cites from the commentaries on Isaiah, Ezekiel, Daniel, Joel, Hosea, Matthew, Galatians, Ephesians, and Titus, and the quotidians deal with a wide variety of topics." Cf. *L. de ordine antiph.*, c. 5 (PL CV, 1254 B). With Bede, Jerome is the most cited author after Augustine (Hanssens, 3, 351-2).

469. B. Bischoff, *Studien und Mittel. zur Gesch. des Benedikinerordens*, 5 (1933), 124.

470. Donatum habuit praeceptorem in arte grammatica,
> septiformem spiritum lustrantem et electum vas sibi praeparentem.
Postquam omnem mundanarum capitum litterarum est adeptus
> studium,
sanctorum probatum est consectatus virorum habitum,
> tenens continua quae tibi placent, o vera Sapientia":

P. Gall-Morel, 242.

471. Details in Laistner, *loc. cit.*, 242-5.

472. *S.* 22 (PL, CCXII, 665 A).

473. Laistner, "Antiochene Exegesis in W. Eur. during the M. Ages" (HRT, 40, 1947, 29), not finding a trace of Junilius in Bede, thinks that the reason for it is Bede's attachment to Gregorian allegorism; but Aldhelm, as completely allegorical as he was, had cited the *Instituta* (MGH, A. Ant., 14, 81). Paul Alvarus will do the same, as will John of Salisbury, etc.

474. *The Oldest Mansucript of the Vulgate Gospels* (1931), xix; critiqued by Laistner (1952), 236.

475. "cujus scripta tanta constant auctoritate, ut adversus ea nullus audeat mutire": *In Ap.* (576 GH, 40 G, 406 G).

476. *Indic. lum.* (PL, CXXI, 517 B, 525 C, 535 AB). *Ep.* 4, n. 3 and 13; *ep.* 16, n. 2: "The very abyss and unapproachable ocean of knowledge, Jerome" — "Ipse abyssus scientiae et inadibilis oceanus H." (Madoz, 128, 225, etc.) Alvarus cites Jerome, *ep.* 58, n. 9: "Certain people sprout in a husk" — "Virent quidem in cortice, etc." (128).

477. Cf. Madoz, 68-80.

478. *In laudem b. H.* (*P. lat. aevi car.*, 3, 138-9).

479. *Ep.* 1, he cites Jer., Aug., Ambrose, etc. (PL, CXXI, 411-8).

480. *In Eccl.* (C, 667 D, 670 AB). He largely uses Aug., Jer., Bede, Chrysostom.

481. Totius Hieronymus doctor mirabilis orbis . . .
> Gregorius doctor, pastor, patriarca, sacerdos:

P. lat. med. aevi, 1, 317.

482. "ad aram sanctorum Gregorii et Hieronymi";

Gregorius praesul doctorque Hieronymus almus,
> Ecclesiae ille pater, iste magister erat.
Nostra ferant precibus pariter quodque vota tonanti
> Ut nos conservet semper ubique Deus:

Ib., 310.

483. *De cultu imag.*, l. 1 (PL, CI, 309 C, 310 D).

484. J. Jolivet, *Godescalc d'Orbais*, 19-20.

485. "duo clarissima lumina doctorum, Augustinum et Hieronymum, et post illos Gregorium et Bedam": *De trib. quaest.* (PL, CXIX, 665 B).

486. PL, CXV, 552-3, 197 AB, etc. "Our translator expert in three languages" — "Noster interpres in tribus linguis peritus" (348 A).

487. *In Is.*, l. 2, c. 30 (CXVI, 871 D); the two exegeses are otherwise compatible. *In Zech.*, c. 13 (CXVII, 266 CD); each is allegorical.

488. *De varia*, c. 3: "But even Pope St. Gregory affirms that his translation is more reliable than the rest" — "Sed et S. Gregorius papa, ipsius translationem caeteris asserit esse veraciorem" (CXLII, 1132 D).

489. PL, CXXXIII, 638. They were both monks, which is why they were cited together by the *Altercatio monachi et clerici* (CLXX, 539 A).

490. *L. confort.*, 2 and 3 (Talbot, *St. Ans.*, 37). Of Jerome he says, 59: "we know no one more learned in the Scripture from the original languages" — "nullum eruditiorem in divina pagina a fontibus linguarum novimus" (but this is in regard to texts of Origen).

491. *C. Fel. Urg.*, l. 3, c. 12, 21, 22 (PL, XCIX, 444-5, 454-6).

492. PL, CLXV, 63.

493. Comp. Bernard, *ep.* 161, n. 3 (CLXXXII, 620 CD) and Jerome, *In Is.*, l. 7 (XXIV, 274 CD); cf. *Glossa* (CXIII, 1263 CD). Anselme Dimier, "S. Bernard et S. Jérôme," COCR, 15 (1953), 216-22.

494. *De omn. sanct.*, s. 4 (Tissier, 6, 112-3).

495. *De tabern.* (Leclercq, 60).

496. *Ep.* 283 (PL, CXCIX, 127-30).

497. *In psalm.*, text edited by H. H. Glunz, *Hist. of the Vulgate in England*, 342-5.

498. Reg. of Prüm, *De eccl. disc.*, l. 1, can. 1, after the conc. of Meaux and Burchard (CXXXII, 192 A).

499. "variis linguarum perspicue insignitus loquelis": Paulinus (XCIX, 455 C). "O marvelous translator of Scripture"; a hymn (attested in the 15th cent.: G.-M. Dreves, *Hymni inediti m. aevi*, 4, 1889, 152) addresses him "O wondrous translator of Scripture" — "Mire Scripturae translator."

500. Agobard, *Adv. Fred.*, c. 13 (PL, CIV, 167 C). Cf. Paschasius, *In Matt.*, prol. (CXX, 35 C). Abelard, *Th. chr.*, l. 2 (CLXXVIII, 1210 B).

501. G. Morin, *Miscell. Isidoriana*, 151-63.

502. "En respondi pedestri et peculiari sermone.... Mallem tamen ut, si hoc quod praemisi tribuat Deus, de allegorizandis quaestionibus et mystice intelligendis, et veteris Instrumenti in novi affirmatione exercitatio nostra constaret, ut vere abyssus abyssum in voce cataractarum tuarum invocaret, quia illud praecedit tempore, istud dignitate; hoc enim est pabulum animae christianae; his enim anima pascitur quibus delectatur. . . .": Ep. 44 (Madoz, 195-203). On Braulio and the Bible: C. H. Lynch and P. Galindo, *San Braulio obispo de Zaragoza* (1950), 39-45.

503. *De virg.*, c. 24, 54, 56 (MGH, *A. ant.*, 15, 256, 313, 316). On his knowledge of Greek and Hebrew: Fabricius, *V. Aldhelmi*, c. 1 (*Ald. opera*, Giles, 1844, 357).

504. "vetus translatio"; "veritas hebraica": *Hexaem.* (PL, XCI, 65 A, 76-80, 132

BD, 134 D, etc.). Cf. Dom Pierre Salmon, *Richesses*, 16; *Les "tituli psalmorum" des MSS latins* (1959), 23. Laistner, 161.

505. "venerabilia Patrum scripta"; "nihil aliud quam hoc quod sonat": *Aliquot quaest. liber*, q. 3 (PL, CXIII, 456-7). Bede does not see why it would be more difficult to admit the miracle of Paul at the bottom of the water than that of Peter at the surface, and he draws a spiritual lesson from each of them. We should thank M. Pierre Riché for having drawn our attention to this text.

506. "son grand jugement" — "au nombre des plus habiles critiques": *Critique de la Bibliothèque des auteurs eccl.*, 1 (1730), 280-3.

507. Power, *Biblica* (1924), 197-201, 233-58. Smalley, 43. El. S. Duckett, *Alcuin* (1951), 263. L. Deslisle, *Les Bibles de Théodulphe*. Bibl. de l'Ec. des chartes, 40 (1879). S. Berger, *H. de la Vulgate*, 145-84.

508. G. Morin, "Une révision du psautier sur le texte grec par un anonyme du IXe s.," RB, 10 (1893), 193-7. Cf. H. Pirenne, *Sedulius de Liège* (1882). Sed., on the prefaces of Jerome: PL, CIII, 338 C; 336 D; etc.

509. "une fort belle œuvre" — "complétés par le texte grec transcrit en lettres latines": *H. de la Vulgate*, 130-1.

510. "sens critique le plus aigu": C. Charlier, "Les manuscrits personnels de Fl. de Lyon," *Mél. Podechard* (1945), 71.

511. "valde mihi molesta et gravis extitit multorum codicum perplexa ac mendosa varietas, quae dormitantium librariorum exorta vitio, imperitorum quotidie ignavia alitur, ac propagatur": *Letter to Eldrad* (MGH, *Ep. car. aevi*, 5, 340): "I have also applied the Hebrew and the volume itself to the reading . . . , I have scraped off the mistakes . . . , I have noted what the Hebraic truth wins for itself against them" — "etiam hebraicum et ipsum volumen ad lectionem adhibui . . . , erasi vitia . . . , quid in hos hebraica sibi vindicet veritas adnotavi."

512. A. Lapôtre, *Mél. d'arch. et d'hist.*, 21 (1901), 344. One will also note that Rabanus, following the example of Bede, and on the recommendation of Alcuin, takes care to give his references exactly.

513. "nimia lectoris incuria": L. 3, c. 11 (PL, CVII, 387-8).

514. "Hebraei cujusdam, modernis temporibus in legis scientia non ignobiliter eruditi, opinionem quam ille dixit . . . traditionem Hebraeorum habere, non paucis locis simul cum nota nominis ejus inserui": *ep*. 14: "not as though asserting his authority to anyone but simply putting down what I found written, I leave the testing of it to the judgment of the reader" — "non quasi ingerens alicui auctoritatem ipsius, sed simpliciter ponens, quod scriptum reperi, ejus probationem lectoris judicio derelinquo" (MGH, *Ep.*, 5, 403).

515. Laistner (HTR, 46, 1953, 30) has had the merit of stating it, as Ebert (3, 148) had also done. Cf. S. Katz, *The Jews in the Visigothic and Frankish Kingdoms*, 69-70. Blumenkranz, *Juifs et chrétiens*, 48. R. Simon, *Crit. de la Bibl.*, 1, 295.

516. *In Matt.*, l. 12, c. 27 (PL, CXX, 957 B).

517. "Hebraei cujusdam, modernis temporibus in legis scientia florentis, opiniones plerisque in locis interposui" — "nostrum est citare testes, ipsorum de fide testium judicare": *ep*. 18 (MGH, *Ep.*, 5, 423). Cf. Pietro Galatino, OFM, announcing in 1510 that he was going to correct the biblical text according to the Hebrew: "I have no doubts that many may attack me on this point; but they are chiefly those who do nothing but attack others and censure all that they do not

understand" — "Je ne doute pas que beaucoup ne m'attaquent à ce sujet; mais ce sont ceux-là surtout qui ne font rien, qui attaquent les autres et blâment tout ce qu'ils ignorent." (Cited by A. Humbert, *Origines de la théol. mod.*, 171). Angelome cites the same unknown Jewish writer as Rabanus does, and does so independently.

518. "Nec solummodo christianis, sed et Judaeis in eadem urbe commanentibus erat carissimus, pro eo quod Hebraicam veritatem a caeteris editionibus secernere erat peritus, et in his, quae secundum veritatem hebraicam dicebant, Judaeorum erat consentiens assertionibus": *Gesta abbatum Gemblacensium, continuatio auct. Godeschalco* (PL, CLX, 641 B).

519. *In Jer.*, xxviii, 5: "But the truth and order of the history is kept . . . not with respect to what was, but with respect to what was thought at that time" — "Sed historiae veritas et ordo servatur . . . non juxta id quod erat, sed juxta id quod illo tempore putabatur" (XXIV, 856-7); in v. 10 (955). *In Matt.*, xiv, 9 (XXVI, 987).

520. "Scias vero quod in Scripturis multa non ut sunt in se, sed uti sunt in opinione ponantur": *Trop. in Amos*, v, 22 (CLVI, 435 A). Father Lagrange will say the same thing, *R. bibl.*, 5 (1896), 510: certain stories recall "legends that no one can control"; in that case, if the historian passes along the stories that circulate from his own time to preserve them for future generations, he gives them to them only so that they can be kept" — "des légendes que nul ne peut contrôler"; "dans ce cas, si l'historien transmet les récits qui circulent de son temps pour les conserver aux générations futures, il ne les leur donne que pour ce qu'on les tient." Only Guibert's formulation suffers from less embarrassment.

521. "aptitudes critiques": "Le Traité des Reliques de G. de Nogent et les commencements de la critique histor.," *Études d'hist. du moyen âge dédiées à Gabriel Monod* (1896), 285-306.

522. L. 4 (PL, CLVI, 665-80).

523. "Magna luminaria ideo dicuntur, quia nobis magna videntur: caeterum, luna minima stellarum fertur": *Hex.*, c. 3 (PL, CLXXII, 257 B). Bede, *Hexaem.*, l. 1 (CXI, 23 AB). Cf. Neckham, *De nat. rer.*, l. 1, c. 13: "For the moon does not seem to be counted among the great luminaries; but the historical narrative follows the judgment of sight and popular opinion" — "Luna enim inter magna luminaria . . . non videtur enumeranda; sed visus judicium et vulgarem opinionem sequitur historialis narratio" (49). Cf. Lagrange, *Méthode historique* (1903), 105: "There is no assertion when one sticks to the appearances; one is not really making a judgment" — "Il n'y a pas de proposition quand on s'en tient aux apparences; on ne juge pas au fond, etc." F. Prat, *La Bible et l'histoire* (1904), 20.

524. "ut aliquid enuntietur simpliciter, quod nisi sub alicujusmodi distinctione fidelem non recipit intellectum": *ep.* 284 (PL, CXCIX, 320 B).

525. PL, CLX, 1052-3. Cf. J. Fischer, "Die hebr. Bibelzitate des Scholastikers Odo," *Biblica*, 15 (1934), 50-93.

526. "ex Scripturis divinis per intelligentiam spiritualem capiunt solatium": *In Rom.* (PL, CLXXXI, 797 A).

527. "nudam historiae superficiem"; "intelligere mysteria": *In Is.* (21 A).

528. G. Morin, "Un critique en liturgie au XIIIe s., le traité inédit d'Hervé . . . ," *RB*, 24 (1907), 36-61.

529. In L. d'Achery, *Spicil.*, 3, 461-2: "nor could he be torn away from the search for truth by any obstacle" — "nec quolibet impedimento ab inquisitione veritatis avelli potuit." Cf. B. Hauréau, *H. litt. du Maine*, 6, 108.

530. One might recall the critical concerns of Guigo I, fifth prior general of the Carthusians (†1137), who was Erasmus's precursor in rejecting Jerome's apocryphal letters: *ep.* 1 (PL, CLIII, 593). Cf. Ghellinck, in *Mél. P. Lehmann*, 63-4.

531. Cf. Jean-Berthold Malm, *L'ordre cistercien et son gouvernement des origines au milieu du XIIIe s.* (2e éd., 1951), 69-70. R. Duvernay, "Cîteaux, Vallombreuse et Harding," ASOC, 8 (1952), 490.

532. One will note the analogous concerns of St. Bernard, in the prologue to his correction of the Cistercian antiphonary (PL, CLXXXII, 1121-2).

533. St. Jerome is the one he has in mind.

534. "Non modice de dissonantia historiarum turbati sumus. . . . Unde nos, multum de discordia nostrorum librorum, quos ab uno interprete suscipimus, admirantes, Judaeos quosdam in sua Scriptura peritos adivimus, ac diligentissime lingua Romana inquisivimus de omnibus illis Scripturarum locis, etc. . . . Qui, suos libros plures coram nobis revolventes, et in locis illis ubi eos rogabamus, Hebraicam, sive Chaldaicam scripturam Romanis verbis nostris exponentes, partes vel versus, pro quibus turbabamur, minime repererunt. . . . Quapropter, Hebraicae atque Chaldaicae veritati, et multis libris Latinis, qui illa non habebant, sed per omnia duabus illis linguis concordabant, credentes, omnia illa superflua prorsus abrasimus": *Frater Stephanus* (PL, CLXVI, 1373-6).

535. C. Oursel, "La Bible de S. Et. Harding et le scriptorium de Cîteaux" (*Cîteaux, commentarii cisterc.*, abbatia Westmale, Belgica, 10, 1959, 34-43).

536. *Hist. eccl.*, l. 9, c. 1 (PL, CLXXXVIII, 647 B). Odericus especially marvels at political deeds, and at the crusade.

537. "Zur Methode der biblischen Textkritik im 12 Jahrh.," *Biblica*, 10 (1920), 445-74.

538. Aug., *ep.* 82, c. 1, n. 3 (PL, XXXIII, 277).

539. Jer., *ep.* 71, n. 5, ad Lucinum: "Just as the reliability of the Old [Testament] books is to be tested from the Hebrew scrolls, so does that of the New call for the norm of the Greek language" — "Ut veterum librorum fides de hebraeis voluminibus examinanda est, ita novorum graeci sermonis normam desiderat" (4, 13).

540. Gratian, P. 1, dist. 9, c. 5-6 (Friedberg, 17). Spicq, 84: "The principle of textual criticism had been divulged through two sentences of St. Augustine and St. Jerome that were published . . . in the *Decretum* of Gratian" — "Le principe de la critique textuelle avait été divulgué par deux sentences de S. Aug. et de S. Jérôme, publiées . . . dans le Décret de Gratien." The author rightly observes, however, that the principle could not receive current application in a period when the knowledge of the Greek language was rare.

541. *Decr.*, 4, 74; *Panormia*, 2, 119.

542. L. 2, particularly c. 14, n. 21: "the skill of those who crave to know the divine Scriptures ought first to watch out for books that need to be corrected" — "codicibus emendandis primitus debet invigilare solertia eorum qui Scripturas divinas nosse desiderant" (PL, XXXIV, 46). Cf. Othloh, *De eo quod legitur in psalmis:* "Because if the books are incoherent, they are to be corrected both by the

rule of grammar and by the sense of the reading. For just as such incoherence happens through the lack of expertise or carelessness of scribes, so is it to be corrected by the expertise of masters" — "Quod si dissonant libri, tam grammaticae regula quam lectionis sententia sunt corrigendi. Hujusmodi enim dissonantia sicut imperitia vel incuria scriptorum contigit, ita peritia magistrorum corrigenda erit" (XCIII, 1114 AB). See also *C. Faustum* (above, ch. 1, note 111).

543. J. P. P. Martin, *Introd. à la crit. générale de l'A.T., De l'origine du Pent.*, 1 (Paris, polyc., 1996-7), ciii-iv. J. Van den Gheym, SJ, "Nicolas M. correcteur de la Bible," *R. bibl*, 8 (1899), 289-95. Wilmart. R. Weber, "Deux préfaces au psautier dues à N. Man.," RB, 63 (1953), 3-17. Cf. A. Vaccari, "I tre Salteri di S. Girolamo al Vaglio di Nicolo M.," in *Scritti* . . . , 2 (1958), 53-68.

544. "appositione, diminutione et transpositione"; "corruptissima (faciens) de corruptis": Martin, *loc. cit.*; Weber, 6-7.

545. "I have worked hard to get reliable texts. . . . In this way therefore I have worked . . . to eliminate superfluities, to get deformed passages back into shape, and to put back the things that had been chopped off by the presumptuous as extras" — "Pro veracibus exemplaribus non modicum laboravi. . . . Hoc ergo modo studui . . . superflua reserare, transformata reformare, et ea readdere quae a praesumptoribus tanquam superflua fuerant amputata": Martin, *ib.*

546. "I am content with this advice: that if a number of manuscripts should disagree anywhere, I should rather trust in those — even if they happen to be fewer in number — that agree with the Hebraic texts; thinking their assertions to be true, to which the schoolmistress Truth bears witness. Doing this everywhere, I have never on that account found the Hebraic debaters to be suspect on the ground that their discussion was not necessary for me in something that might manifestly impugn Judaic lack of faith, because of which they are indeed said both to hide the truth and to distort the letter" — "Hac deliberatione contentus sum, ut si alicubi exemplariorum numerositas discordaret, his potius crederem, etiam si forte contingerent pauciora, quae cum bibliothecis hebraicis concordarent; veras eorum assertiones arbitrans, quibus magistra veritas testimonium perhiberet. Quod utique faciens, idcirco dissertores hebraicos suspectos nequaquam habui, quia vid. in aliquo mihi non fuit eorum dissertio necessaria, quod Judaicam manifeste perfidiam impugnaret, cujus nimirum gratia et veritatem occultare et litteram depravare dicuntur." Martin, civ: "I sometimes use a Hebrew speaker according to the mind of Jerome or the other Fathers" — "mente beati Hieronymi vel aliorum Patrum necnon Hebraei quo dissertore utor" (cviii).

547. "propter styli dissonantiam"; "multo esse melius vera rustice quam diserte falsa proferre"; "It is to be known therefore that there are some things in the Latin manuscripts that the Hebrew ones do not contain. . . . I thought I ought to consult Hebrew manuscripts only in the instances in which ours seemed to be obviously excessively inconsistent among themselves" — "Sciendum ergo est esse quaedam in latinis codicibus quae non habent Hebraei. . . . In his tantummodo hebraicos codices mihi censui consulendos, in quibus nostri aperte sibi nimium dissonarent": Martin, civ. "They do us this great disservice who take away or add things by the conjecture of their own judgment, the source of truth having been left behind" — "Ipsi faciunt nobis malum hoc grande, qui fonte

veritatis postposito, ad sui conjecturam arbitrii vel minuunt vel apponunt": Wilmart, 141. Weber, 7, 10.

548. A. Wilmart, "Nicolas Manjacoria, cistercien à Trois-Fontains," RB, 33 (1921), 140: Nicolas "attribue la rédaction du 'lectionnaire de l'église' à S. Jérôme et pense que celui-ci s'est appliqué à faire concorder l'Ancien et le Nouveau Testament; il donne divers exemples du parallélisme des épîtres et des évangiles, mais aussi de la correspondance des stations romaines. De cet arrangement traditionnel de la liturgie il est l'admirateur convaincu" — Nicolas "attributes the redaction of the 'lectionary of the Church' to St. Jerome and thinks that J. had tried to make the Old Testament concord with the New; he gives various examples of the parallelism between the epistles and the gospels, but also of the correspondence of the Roman stations. He is a firm admirer of this traditional arrangement of the liturgy."

549. Art. cited. Cf. J. Van den Gheyn, *loc. cit.*

550. "Opus pietatis est, evangelica verba cunctis erroribus eradicatis expurgare": *Explanationes in praef. S. Hier. ad evangelia*, n. 2 (PL, CIII, 334 A). Cf. *Mémoires de Trévoux*, août 1713, p. 1313: "Les soins des Religieux de Cîteaux pour corriger des manuscrits de la Bible montrent que les règles et l'usage de la critique n'étaient pas inconnus dans le XIe siècle, etc." — "The pains taken by the Religious of Cîteaux to correct manuscripts of the Bible show that the rules and use of textual criticism were not unknown in the 11th century."

551. "d'accord avec la foi orthodoxe": *Hist. de la lutte entre la science et la théol.*, tr. H. de Varigny and G. Adam (1899), 483.

552. "le premier" — "toucha du doigt les fautes de la Vulgate": *Les origines de la Réforme*, 2 (1909), 322.

553. "les Réformateurs du XVIe siècle": "La question juive pendant le premier millénaire chrétien," RHPR, 15 (1935), 333.

554. "Non sunt utiles Ecclesiae novae traductiones Bibliae quae de graeco vel hebraico in latinum fiunt, sed perniciosae . . . , et ideo nullo modo permittendae aut tolerandae, sed per Ecclesiae praelatos omni via ab Ecclesia eliminandae": L. Delisle, *Notice sur le registre des procès-verbaux de la Fac. de th. de Paris* (1899), 56.

555. "dicens quod nolebat illud asserere, sed quasi disputate (disputans?) dixerat, nec vellet in tali dicto persistere": Delisle, *ib.* Cf. Théodore de Bèze, *H. ecclés. des églises réformées au roy. de Fr.* (Anvers, 1580), l. 1, p. 2, regarding some corrections made by Lefèvre following the Greek: "which so displeased the barbarous doctors of the Sorbonne, and particularly two crude beasts, namely, Beda and Quercu, who were then the heads of that Faculty, that they never stopped, nor would they ever have been constrained by conceding their position to him, as was necessary with Erasmus, who, although holding to his own position for a time, recoiled" — "ce qui déplut tellement aux barbares docteurs de Sorbonne, et nommément à deux grosses bêtes, à savoir Beda et Quercu, qui étaient lors les chefs de cette Faculté, que jamais ils ne cessèrent, qu'ils ne l'eussent contraint de leur quitter la place; comme aussi il fallut qu'Érasme s'y étant tenu quelque temps s'en retirât." More moderate, R. Simon will recognize that, if Beda is "too carried away" — "trop emporté" — in this affair, he is nevertheless "not as despicable" — "pas si méprisable" — as some would say: *Critique de la Bibl. des auteurs*

eccl., 1, 597. Under the pseudonym of Romainville, he is more severe (Steinmann, *R. Simon*, 318).

556. "toute la littérature juive doit être rejetée comme nuisible du champ des études sacrées": A. Humbert, *op. cit.*, 166-70; and 204, regarding the medieval "correctoria": "In the course of the 15th century this liberty of revision had gone away, along with certain others" — "Au cours du XVe s., cette liberté de révision s'en était allée avec quelques autres."

557. "Je n'ignore pas que de partout on jettera les hauts cris; cet interprète, que l'on croit à tort être saint Jérôme, jouit d'un crédit inébranlable; la version usitée chez nous est considérée comme sacro-sainte, et beaucoup s'écrient qu'on n'y saurait toucher sans commettre un sacrilège. Pour moi, je tiens comme sacro-saint le récit de Luc, qui, lui, a écrit en grec; quant à notre version, je pourrais aisément montrer qu'en bien des endroits elle s'écarte du texte original, mais nos lecteurs seraient-ils seulement capables d'entendre la vérité?": *Annotations aux Pandectes* (1508), 150; regarding Luke 10. Analogous reflections on the Vulgate of the Book of Wisdom: *De Asse* (1515). Cf. L. Delaruelle, *Guillaume Budé* (1907), 117-8; A. Renaudet, *Préréforme*, 2e éd. (1953), 667.

558. "The Old Testament, which Jerome claims that he translated following the Hebrew, is so corrupt, that if anyone should want to discuss [the matter] and to yield to the Hebrew, i.e., the pristine purity, he would be faulted as the fashioner of a new library; yet . . . I acknowledge that I have presumed this in the case of a book of hymns" — "V. Testamentum, quod se Jeronimus secundum hebraicum asserit transtulisse, adeo corruptum est, ut si quis vellet discutere et hebraicae, id est pristinae reddere puritatis, novae bibliothecae conditor culparetur; quod tamen . . . de libro Imnorum me fateor praesumpsisse" (Vaccari, 56).

559. "Il n'est pas admissible de penser que l'Église catholique ait erré depuis tant de siècles, elle qui s'est toujours servi de ce texte et aujourd'hui encore l'approuve et s'en sert; et il n'est pas vraisemblable que tant de saints Pères, tant d'hommes accomplis se soient trompés. . . .": Louvain, Sept. 1514 (Allen, 2, 14). We know that Leo X accepted the dedication of Erasmus's New Testament and thanked the author with the Brief of 10 July 1515. The confessor of Queen Catherine of England told his penitent that by correcting St. Jerome Erasmus had committed an unforgivable crime (Dom Gasquet, *The Eve of the Reformation*, 178). "The labor of Jerome," wrote Blessed Thomas More, "was opposed long ago by the selfsame movements that today menace the Erasmians, the jealousy and ignorance of the very ones he wanted to help": "Le travail de Jérôme," a écrit le bienheureux Thomas More, "fut jadis contrecarré par ces mêmes gestes qui aujourd'hui menacent les Érasmiens, la jalousie et l'ignorance de ceux-là mêmes à qui il voulait être utile" (H. Bremond, *Le Bx Thomas More*, 1904, 35).

560. Fol. 52-3, 60-3, 77. Cf. Imbart de la Tour, 3, 221-2.

561. D'Argentré, *Collectio judiciorum*, 2, 78. The incident is recounted in A. Lefranc, *Hist. du collège de Fr.* (1893), 144-9.

562. 30 Dec. 1531: H. Laemmer, *Monumenta vaticana historiam eccl. s. XVI illustrantia* (1861), 95. The author of the letter has been identified by Father Tacchi-Venturi. Cf. H. Bernard-Maitre, RAM, 1958, 406-7. At the end of the 17th cent., many will be shocked by the relations of R. Simon with certain Jews: R. de

la Broise, *Bossuet et la Bible* (1891), 370. Again in 1713, Honoré de Sainte-Marie, *Réflexions sur les règles et l'usage de la Critique*, 1, 90: "Si les Protestants, qui préfèrent le texte hébreu aux anciennes versions, estiment beaucoup la nouvelle méthode, et lui donnent de grands éloges, M. Simon ne peut pas se promettre un pareil succès de la part des Catholiques." "If the Protestants, who prefer the Hebrew text to the old versions, have high regard for the new method, and offer it great praise, M. Simon can not look forward to similar success on the part of the Catholics."

563. Nicholas V had already charged the Hebraist Giannozzo Manetti to translate the whole Bible anew: J. Guiraud, *L'Église rom. et les origines de la Renaissance*, 3ᵉ éd. (1904), 248-9. Cf. R. Simon, *H. cr. des versions du N.T.*, 80.

564. Details in M. Bataillon, *Érasme et l'Espagne* (1937), 748. There are more recent examples, such as that of the Canon A. M. Maunoury, *Comm. sur l'Ep. de S. Paul aux Romains* (1878), protesting against Father F.-X. Patrizi in the name of the Vulgate. Cf. St. Lyonnet, RSR, 1956, 71, n. 26, and *In Rom. I–IV*, 2ᵉ éd., 149-55.

565. Sedulius Scotus (PL, CIII, 334 AB).

566. *Consuetudines*, 2, 58: "Nulli liceat abbati nec monacho nec novitio libros facere, nisi forte cuiquam in generali abbatum capitulo concessum fuerit" — "It is not permitted to any abbot, monk, or novice, to produce books, except perhaps for one to whom [this privilege] shall have been granted by the general chapter of abbots."

567. "Monachi qui rhythmos fecerint, ad domos alienas emittantur, non reversuri nisi per capitulum generale": "Let monks who shall have composed 'rhythms', be sent off to other houses, not to return unless [authorized] by the general chapter." "On comprend sans peine," says Hauréau, *Des poèmes latins attribués à S. Bernard* (1890), ii-iii, "qu'il ait paru un jour nécessaire de condamner une si grande licence, après l'avoir trop longtemps tolérée": but "jamais il ne fut défendu, chez les cisterciens, de faire des vers métriques."

568. MD, *Thes. nov. anecd.*, 4 (1717), 1292, *Statuta selecta cap. gen. cist.*, 1198, n. 24: "De monacho Populeti, quia quodam Judaeo litteras hebraicas didicisse dicitur, abbati committitur Claraevallis, ut inquirat et corrigat."

569. Cf. Emm. Aegerter, *Vie de J. de Flore* (1928), 79-80, who wants thereby to explain Joachim's departure from the order. But Father de Ghellinck, *Essor*, 1, 98, seems to see in this incident an indication that scientific affairs had been forbidden in principle in the Cistercian order.

570. *S.* 32: "Ita adolescentia solemus dicere; sed Hebraeus melius nos corrigit: in adolescentula" (PL, CCV, 776 D).

571. "peritissimi Hebraeorum": *S.* 21 (CCII, 657 AD).

572. In *Les intellectuels du moyen âge* (1957), ch. 1, M. Jacque Le Goff opposes the urban professor to the monk, who represents the obscurantism of an age gone by; but to back up his thesis he cites with praise chiefly some monks: Peter the Venerable, Arnaud of Bonneval, Gerhoh of Reichersberg, Anselm, Honorius. Another author, a historian of civilization, thinks that Abelard's teaching was needed so that religion should not be "plus seulement un ensemble de recettes efficaces contre l'hostilité des forces naturelles, ni une effusion sentimentale . . ." — "any more merely a collection of tips useful against the hostility of the forces of nature, or sentimental gush. . . ."

573. "n'a aucune culture véritable": vs. Petrarch, *De vita solitaria*, l. 2, sect. 3, c. 14: "quarum (litterarum) nescio an alius sua aetate copiosior fuerit" (cited by Gilson, AHDLMA, 25, 61). Watkin Williams has shown that Bernard had had intimate familiarity with Ovid, Terence, Virgil, Horace, Persius, Juvenal, Boethius: *St. Bernard, Abbot of Clairvaux* (1935), app. 1. To say nothing of his familiarity with the Bible!

574. Cf. Amatus Van den Bosch, *L'intelligence de la foi chez S. Bernard, Cîteaux in de Nederlanden*, 1957, 108.

575. C. H. Talbot, ed. of the *De anima* of Aelred (1952), 51-2.

576. the "orientale lumen": *Ep. ad fr. de Monte Dei*, 7 (M. M. Davy, 70).

577. "Cum in omnimoda paupertate se deprimant, ditissimam tamen bibliothecam coaggerant: quo enim minus panis hujus copia materialis exuberant, tanto magis illo, qui non perit, sed in aeternum permanet, cibo operose insudant": *De vita sua*, l. 1, c. 11 (PL, CLVI, 854-5).

578. Ghellinck, in *Liber floridus* (*hommage à Paul Lehmann*, 1950), 64.

579. M. A. Fracheboud, "L'influence du Ps.-Denys sur Isaac de l'Et.," COCR, 9 (1947), 328-41; 10 (1948), 19-34. M. Jacquin, "L'influence doctrinale de J. Scot au début du XIIIe s.," RSPT, 4 (1910), 105-7. Fr. Bleimetzrieder, "Isaac de l'Et., sa spéculation théol.," RTAM, 4 (1932), 134-59. Alberic, *Chronica* (MGH, Scr. 26, 915).

580. "infléchissements"; Y. M. J. Congar, "Église et Cité de Dieu chez quelques auteurs cisterciens à l'époque des Croisades, en particulier dans le *De peregrinante civ. Dei* d'Henri d'Albano" (*Mél. E. Gilson*, 1959, 173-202).

581. Isaac on Alcher: PL, CCXI, 1882 AB.

582. s. 6 (CCXII, 530-1).

583. Against excessively well-built monasteries and excessively beautiful churches: s. 23 (676-8). His taste is not always ours: s. 22 (663 D).

584. Adrien Baillet (HLF, 18, 101). COCR, 14, 133. Ghellinck, *Essor*, 1, 221-2, Zumthor, 202.

585. "conjunctio trivialis eloquentiae et quadrivialis sapientiae": *In Cant.*, praef., (PL, CCVI, 17-8). B. Griesser, *Cisterciense Chronik*, 50 (1958), and 51 (1959). Cf. BTAM, 4, no. 1045. Hauréau sees nothing in his work but "un amas confus de divagations mystiques" (2, 1891, 144). Father Spicq more fairly says that this is an interpretation "à la fois rhétorique, allégorique et mystique."

586. "intellectuels des villes"; "La forêt et le désert mystiques";"mirages": Cf. J. Le Goff, *op. cit.*, 28. It is true that the author without taking adequate precautions seems to suggest that everything that belongs to the order of faith and the spiritual life is "mirage." The monks, strangely the Cistercians (to whom he tacks on Peter of Cella), are the object of his contempt; the least mention of a "goliard" amazes him, and the whole genius of a man like St. Bernard for him is merely a dark force. Such judgments can, here or there, appear to coincide with that of historians of Christian thought who are interested in the 12th century only to the extent that it paves the way for the scholasticism of the golden age; but, from that time on, will scholasticism be anything but a stage on the route that leads to the total and anti-Christian emancipation of "nature" and "reason"?

587. "allegoriarum floribus plenum curavi colligere librum" — "I have taken care to gather a book full of the flowers of allegories": *Collectiones*, praef. (PL, CII,

13-4). The work will have the honor of being translated into German by the Lutheran Gaspard Hedion (Labbé, *De scr. eccl.*, 2, 352; Ceillier, 18, 528).

588. A. Souter, *Pelagius's Expositions* (*Texts and Studies*, 9), 1, 333-6. On Smaragdus: Hauréau, *Singularités*, 100-28; Laistner, 308-9; Leclercq, introd. to *Diadème des moines* (1950).

589. Collect. (CII, 15-552); e.g.: 43 A, 55 A, 190 B, 382 A, 391 A, 394 B, 451 A, 479 C.

590. Cf., in the admirable *Via regia*, addressed to Louis the Pious, c. 27 and 30, his protests against the luxury of the palace and his pleas for the abolition of serfdom (CII, 965-6, 967-9).

591. "Not only the historical but also the spiritual understanding" — "Non solam historicam sed et spiritualem intelligentiam" (506 A); etc.

592. *historiae veritas*: Coll., *In Jerem.*, 1 regarding Psalm 2: "de quibus et in psalmo post historiae veritatem tropikos loquitur" (378 D).

593. "la tête du mouvement intellectuel de son époque": G. Kurth, *Origines de la civ. mod.*, 2 (4e éd., 1898), 254; the beautiful portrait of Alcuin, 253-6, is worth reading. Cf. the caricature drawn by H. Fichtenau, *L'empire carolingien* (tr. Barbey-Vaudou, 1958), 102-22: Alcuin was very interested in his cult of wisdom, since, having "crossed the Channel with a single companion, at the end he became the master of twenty thousand men" — "traversé la Manche avec un seul compagnon, il devint à la fin le maître de vingt mille hommes" (110)! He was a drunkard; though a simple deacon, he used to say the Mass, etc.

594. "maxime historiae sunt"; "sed etiam ei historica proprietate invenitur hoc responsum....": *Interr. et resp.* (PL, C, 515-82; 517 A, 541-2, 549 A). Very little allegory in the whole work (however, on the measurements of the ark: 528 BC), which is, truth to tell, more theological than properly historical.

595. *Libri car.*, 1, c. 11, 13, 15 (PL, CXVIII, 1032-3, 1034 D, 1939 B). Cf. Laistner, 239-40.

596. Ep. 27 (C, 183-4). Those who excessively reduce the range of the Carolingian renaissance regard such nicknames as the vanity of barbarians. This is to forget that the fashion had already been widespread much earlier, e.g., in the cultivated and decadent environment of Sidonius Apollinaris; and that in the 16th century, in humanist circles, the learned and virtuous Louise of Bectoz, a cloistered religious of the monastery of Notre Dame and of Saint-Honorat at Tarascon, was known by the name of Sappho (L. Febre, *Or. des Périers*, 1942, 20).

597. *Interr.*, 266: "Ebrietas secundum hebraeam linguam pro satietate ponitur" (C, 556 A), etc.

598. Thus, *In Ap.*, l. 4, c. 9, v. 11 (C, 1141 B).

599. "Pater Hieronymus": *Versus de rer. Eboric. eccl.*, 1540 (*P. lat. aevi car.*, 1, 203).

600. "non sans bonheur": P. Antin, *op. cit.*, 224.

601. PL, C, 544 A, 546 C, 548 A, 552 BC, 560-2, 667 D, 706 A.

602. *L. car.*, 4, c. 11: "apocryphorum naenias"; "ne apocryphorum frivolis rebus ambiguis et necdum deliberatis firmitas valeat exhiberi," etc. (XCVIII, 1204 AC). These are almost the terms of Aldhelm.

603. "tam LXX quam aliorum interpretum et tractatorum incerta et confusa vestigia": Joseph: "For you admonished me that, following in all things merely

the necessary sense and the trail of the Hebraic truth" — "Ita enim mihi praecipiebas, ut in cunctis pernecessarium tantum sensum et hebraicae veritatis tramitem sequens etc." (*P. lat. m. aevi*, 1, 151). Cf. *L. car.*, 3, c. 20: "In circuitu Jerusalem exercitantium, in nullo sanctae legis authenticorum codicum invenitur. Quod ut lucidius comprobetur, ipsa sanctae legis verba, prout in codicibus habentur, per ordinem pondenda sunt" (PL, XCXVIII, 1155 C).

604. "quae ventura sunt in novissimis diebus"; "historiam de divisione terrae promissionis; quae (divisiones) dividendae erant nepotibus illorum; item, allegoriam, de Christo et Ecclesia, in novissimis quid futurum temporibus": PL, C, 558-9. The *Gloss in Gen.*, xlix, will say, according to Alcuin: "In the blessings of Jacob the history is to be retained and the allegory to be explored" — "In benedictionibus Jacob historia tenenda et allegoria investiganda" (CXIII, 178 A).

605. "Sed prius historiae fundamenta ponenda sunt, ut aptius allegoriae culmen priori structurae superponatur": *Int.* 231 *in Gen.* (C, 559 A).

606. the "dulcedo intelligendae sanctae Scripturae": *In Jo.*, l. 3 (803 A).

607. "Licet de Christo grande sit mysterium, tamen secundum litteram significat etc.": *Int.* 231 (559 D). Cf. *In Eccl.*: "Meanwhile, so much for the letter. In terms of the spiritual understanding, however . . ." — "Haec interim juxta litteram. Caeterum per intelligentiam spiritalem . . ." (669 C); "This, meantime, is what was said; but . . ." — "Haec interim dicta sint; caeterum . . ." (686 A); "Though pertaining . . . to the prophecy . . . , nevertheless according to the history . . ." — "Tametsi ad prophetiam . . . pertinentes . . . , tamen secundum historiam . . ." (668 D). This principle of exegesis then-current is worth noting: "Scripture uses commonly-used words understandable to us, so as to fit itself to our smallness, so that we may get to know the unknown things through those that are known" — "Utitur Scriptura usitatis nobis verbis intelligibilibus, ut coaptet se nostrae parvitati, quatenus ex cognitis incognita cognoscamus" (527 A).

608. "une sorte de génie pédagogique et le don de comprendre les besoins de son temps": E. Delaruelle, *Le cathol. en France*, 1, 194. "Pedagogy incarnate" — "La pédagogie faite homme": G. Calmette, *Charlemagne* (1945), 257.

609. "joyeuse ivresse du savoir, extraordinaire confiance en la sagesse éternelle, désire de renouer, par-dessus les siècles de barbarie, les liens de parenté entre le miracle grec et la civilisation chrétienne": E. Amann, in Martin-Fliche, 8, 95.

610. "une grandeur émouvante"; "pour se hausser à nouveau vers les sommets attents par Augustin et par Boèce": P. Hadot, "Marius Victorinus et Alcuin," AHDLMA, 21 (1955), 6.

611.   si quid forte novi librorum vel studiorum
       quod secum ferret, terris reperiret in illis:

De sanctis Euboricae urbis, v. 1546-8 (*P. lat. aevi kar.*, 1, 201-2).

612. Cf. *Dial. de rhetorica et virt.*: "For the love of this world is more laborious than that of Christ" — "Laboriosior est enim amor hujus mundi quam Christi" (PL, CI, 946 AB).

613. *Ep.* 170 (MGH, *Ep.*, 4, 279). Cf. *ep.* 123: "By as much more that one shines with the works of truth and mercy, by so much does he have a greater image of di-

vinity within himself" — "Quanto quisque plus veritatis et misericordiae operibus fulget, tanto majorem habet in se divinitatis imaginem" (180).

614. Others, however, will not be surprised that Jean of Hauville at the end of book 2 of his *Architrenius*, would call Paris: "Attica philosophi" (Wright, *Satirical Poems*, 1, 274). Wanting to flatter Philip Augustus, Guillaume le Breton will say that Paris eclipses Pericleian Athens. The image soon grew stale: cf. P. Damian, *op.* 39, c. 1 (PL, CXLV, 642 D). Already toward 1012 Gerard, the abbot of Seir, is speaking of the school of Bamberg, where the seven arts are being cultivated (Jaffé, 5, 483) as: "in no way inferior to the Stoics, greater than Athens" — "inferior Stoicis nequamquam, major Athenis."

615. "Whose teaching bore such fruit that the the modern Gauls or Franks were made equals with the ancient Romans and Athenians" — "Cujus in tantum doctrina fructificavit, ut moderni Galli sive Franci antiquis Romanis et Atheniensibus aequarentur." Whence arose the legend of the foundation of the University of Paris by Alcuin and Charlemagne, tied to the theme of the "translatio studii": Vincent of Beauvais, *Spec. historiale*, l. 23, c. 173.

616. "inemendati libri": *Capitulary* of 789: "Psalmos, notas, cantus, computum, grammaticam per singula monasteria vel episcopia et libros catholicos bene emendate, quia saepe dum bene aliqui Deum rogare cupiunt, sed per inemendatos libros male, rogant. . . . Si opus est evangelium, psalterium et missale scribere, perfectae aetatis homines scribant cum omni diligentia" (MGH, *Leg., Capitularia regum Franc.*, 1, 60). Cf. the preface to the homiliary of Paul the Deacon (PL, CXV, 1159-60). Charles himself loved to take part in such efforts: Thegan [of Trèves], *Vita Hludovici*, c. 7 (MGH, *Scr.*, 2, 592).

617. Alcuin to Gisla, 19 April 800: "I would perhaps have sent you the exposition of the whole gospel, if the command of our lord the king regarding the emendation of the Old and New Testament had not occupied me" — "Totius forsitan evangelii expositionem direxerim vobis, si me non occupasset domni regis praeceptum in emendatione veteris novique testamenti" (MGH, EP., 4, 322).

618. Cf. Ekkehard of Aura, *Chron. univ.*, on Charlemagne: "He most carefully corrected the study of reading and singing" — "Legendi atque psallendi disciplinam diligentissime emendavit" (PL, CLIV, 853 A), which Agobard and Berno relate to us.

619. Bonifatius Fischer, *Die Alkuin-Bibel* (Aus der Gesch. der Lateinischen Bibel, 1, 1957). Cf. Fr.-L. Ganshof, *La revision de la Bible par Alcuin*, Bibl. d'Hum. et Ren. 9 (1947), 7-20. Arthur Kleinclausz, *Alcuin* (1948), 213-7. E. S. Duckett, *Friend of Charlemagne* (1951), 260-3. Laistner, 205-6. Dom P. Salmon, *Richesses*, 16. J. Gribomont, "L'Église et les versions bibliques," *La Maison-Dieu*, 62 (1960), 58-9. E. K. Rand, *Studies in the Script of Tours* (1929). S. Berger, *H. de la Vulg.*, 185-242.

620. Laistner, HTR, 1937. Angelome uses it also: *In Gen.*, c. 17 (PL, CXV, 180 D).

621. "amendé, interpolé, et, finalment, corrompu": Dom Pierre Salmon, *Richesses*, 17. Cf. R. Simon, *Lettres critiques* (1699), 9-10.

622. "souvent fantaisistes" — "une formule très ancienne" — "élaboré dans sa source hiéronymienne": Spicq, *Esquisse*, 33-5. Fanciful etymologies were not done by Alcuin alone. What seems to be an aggravating circumstance for him turns into a mitigating circumstance for Christian: "his etymologies provoke

laughter, but most come from St. Isidore" — "ses étymologies font sourire, mais beaucoup viennent de S. Isidore" (49).

623. Except for one detail, however. The 281 *Interrogationes et responsiones in Genesim* do not chiefly summarize "le *De Trinitate* de S. Aug."; Alcuin summarizes Augustine in his 28 *Quaestiones de Trinitate ad Fredegisum* (PL, CI, 57 ss.).

Notes to Chapter Four

1. "Il fait de l'histoire le fondement du triple sens": *La Bible au XVIe s.*, 27.
2. "Dicendum prius de arte grammatica, quae est videlicet origo et fundamentum liberalium litterarum": *De artibus*, praef. (PL, LXX, 1151 B). After grammar he will treat "secundo de arte rhetorica . . . , tertio de logica . . . , quarto de mathematica." In the schools, the letter of the alphabet was itself called "fundamentum sapientiae," "the basis of wisdom."
3. *Les origines de la scolastique et H. de SV*, 1 (1895), 225.
4. *Esquisse*, 96.
5. "une vigueur méthodologique consciente": "Les deux âges de l'allégorisme script.," RTAM, 18 (1951), 24.
6. "la nécessité première du *fundamentum*"; "grande opération, non seulement exégétique, mais théologique": M.-D. Chenu, 181-2.
7. On this latter work: H. Weisweiler, *Mél. de Ghellinck* (1951), 2, 570-9.
8. "s'insurge littéralement contre la prétention des allégoristes qui veulent passer à pieds joints sur le sens littéral et ne voir que le sens figuré": P. Mandonnet, *Dante le théologien*, 169.
9. "Cum igitur mystica intelligentia non nisi ex iis quae primo loco littera proponit colligatur, miror qua fronte quidam allegoriarum se doctores jactitant, qui ipsam adhuc primam litterae significationem ignorant": *De scripturis . . .* , c. 5 (PL, CLXXV, 13 AB).
10. "Scio quosdam esse qui statim philosophari volunt, fabulas pseudo-apostolis reliquendas aiunt. Quorum scientia formae asini similis est. Noli hujusmodi imitari": *Did.*, l. 6, c. 3 (CLXXVI, 799 C).
11. "Lege ergo Scripturam, et disce primum diligenter quae corporaliter narrat": *De script.*, c. 5 (CLXXV, 15 A).
12. "une nouvelle période"; "l'étude scientifique": Smalley, *The Study*, 85.
13. *De script.*, c. 5: "So do not glory about your understanding of the Scriptures so long as you do not know the letter. To be ignorant of the letter is to be ignorant of what the letter may signify and what may be signified by the letter. For what is signified by the first, signifies the third. Therefore, since those things that the letter signifies are signs of the spiritual understanding, how can things that have not yet been signified to you be signs to you? So do not leap, lest you fall head over heels. He advances most rightly who advances in order. Therefore strive to acquire knowledge first by reading their signification so that, by later meditating on the basis of things known in outline, you may afterwards gather what you may adduce by way of likeness either for building up the faith or for moral education" — "Noli itaque de intelligentia Scripturarum gloriari, quamdiu litteram ignoras. Litteram autem ignorare est ignorare quid littera significet et

quid significetur a littera. Nam quod significatur a primo, tertium significat. Cum igitur res illae quas littera significat, spiritualis intelligentiae signa sint, quodmodo signa tibi esse possunt, quae necdum tibi significata sunt? Noli ergo saltum facere, ne in praecipitium incidas. Ille rectissime incedit, qui incedit ordinate. Primum igitur illarum significationem stude legendo comparare notitiam, ut ex iis specie cognitis, postmodum meditando colligas quod vel ad fidei aedificationem vel ad instructionem morum per similitudinem adducas" (CLXXC, 13-4). There are analogous warnings in St. Peter Damian, *Op.* 26, c. 5 (CXLV, 603 BC).

14. "Parvis imbutus tentabis grandia tutus": *Did.*, l. 6, c. 3, citing Marbodius, *De ornamentis verborum prol.*, v. 12 (CLXXI, 16897-8; CLXXVI, 789 C). Fr. W. Farrar saw evidence of the "contempt" in which Hugh had held the literal sense: *Hist. of Interpretation* (1886), 295.

15. If the *De scripturis* were prior to the *Didascalicon*, as R. Baron thinks (xlviii), one might conclude that the deviations between times were accentuated, or that Hugh had not immediately perceived all its gravity. But the indications are not strong enough to support this conjecture, and on the other hand, Father Damien Van den Eynde advances serious arguments (though, as far as we can judge them, not decisive ones) in favor of the priority of the *Didascalicon: Essai*, 45-51.

16. *Did.*, l. 6, c. 3-4 (801-4).

17. L. 3, c. 14: it is necessary to have humility to receive the lessons of Scripture from the mouth of the "lectores divinitatis"; an individual cannot, as some pretend, "adequately penetrate the mysteries of truth by his own wits" — "satis proprio ingenio veritatis arcana penetrare" (774 D).

18. "quasi quamdam inconcussae veritatis basim, cui tota fabrica innitatur, fundare": *Did.*, l. 6, c. 4: "but lay open if you can the things that are obscure; if you are not able to reach an understanding of them, pass by, lest whilst you try to presume upon what you are inadequate to attain, you incur the danger of error. Do not hold those things in contempt but rather venerate them, since you have heard what has been written: 'He made darkness his cover'. Because even if you find something contrary to what you have already learned to be held with a faith most firm, it is nevertheless not expedient for you to be changing your opinion daily, unless you first consult those more learned than yourself, and you recognize especially what the universal faith, that can never be wrong, bids to be judged. . . . You see many sliding into various errors, since they do not have the foundation of truth, and changing their opinions almost as often as they read the readings" — "quae vero sunt obscura, resera si potes; quod si ad intellectum eorum penetrare non vales, transi, ne dum praesumere conaris quod non sufficis, periculum erroris incurras. Noli ea contemnere sed potius venerare, quia audisti quod scriptum est: 'Posuit tenebras latibulum suum' (Ps. 17). Quod si etiam aliquid inveneris contrarium illi, quod tu jam firmissima fide tenendum esse didicisti, non tamen expedit tibi quotidie mutare sententiam, nisi prius doctiores te consulueris, et maxime quid fides universalis, quae numquam falsa esse potest, inde jubeat sentiri agnoveris. . . . Vides multos, quia fundamentum veritatis non habent, in errores varios labi et toties fere mutare sententias, quot legerint lectiones etc." (804-5).

19. *In Is.*, l. 5: "For the Pharisee was a literalist, since he used to chase after the bare surface of the letter" — "Litteratus enim Pharisaeus erat, quia solam litterae superficiem sectabatur" (CLXXXI, 318 A).

20. "Judaei litteratores": *ep.* 106, n. 2: "O if once you should taste a little of the juicy part of the fruit from whence Jerusalem is satisfied, how freely you would leave the rinds to be gnawed on by the Jewish litterateurs!" — "O si semel paululum quid de adipe frumenti, unde satiatur Jerusalem, degustares, quam libenter suas crustas rodendas litteratoribus Judaeis relinqueres!" (CLXXXII, 242 A). Cf. Neckam, *De nat rer.*, l. 2, c. 49 (159).

21. "That Scripture itself is for them as a trap and a snare, i.e., that they be caught, since they are merely literalists, who follow the letter that killeth" — "Ipsa Scriptura ista est illis in laquaeum et in captionem, id est, ut capiantur, quia tantum litteratores sunt, litteram vid. sequentes quae occidit" (Landgraf, 160).

22. Smalley, "A Commentary on the Hebraica by Hervaeus of Bourg-Dieu," RTAM, 18 (1951), 29-65.

23. *In ps.* lxx, s. 1, n. 19 (CCL, 39, 956).

24. Gilbert of Hoiland, *In Cant.*, s. 42, n. 5: Judaei "they have stuck to the figures, knowing the literal but not the spiritual sense" — "figuris adhaeserunt, scientes litteraturam, nescientes sensum spiritualem" (PL, CLXXXIV, 223 B).

25. Cf. Aug., *Doct. chr.*, l. 3, c. 29, n. 40: "Let the lettered know that our authors had used ... all the methods of discourse" — "Sciant autem litterati modis omnibus locutionis ... auctores nostros usos fuisse" (3490).

26. "viri litterati et honesti": *ep.* 113 (PL, CCI, 176 B).

27. "vir litteratus admodum et honestus": *Vita S. Martini*, c. 15 (V. G., 246-7).

28. *Vita prima*, l. 3, c. 3: "litteratus apud eruditos" (PL, CLXXXV, 306 D).

29. "litteratiores et meliores viri": *Polycr.*, l. 4, c. 6, quoting the proverb "An uneducated king is like an ass wearing a crown" — "rex illiteratus est quasi asinus coronatus"; at very least "it is necessary that he should deal with the advice of the educated" — "eumdem agi litteratorum consiliis ... necesse est" (CXCIX, 524 D). Regarding this proverb: "at the end of the the 12th cent. cultivated courtesans can tell it to princes by way of flattery" — "à la fin du XIIe s. les courtisans lettrés peuvent le dire aux princes par flatterie" (Ghellinck, *L'essor*, 2, 203). Foulque II of Anjou (†960) was already quoting it when writing to the king of France.

30. "litteratum triplici sermone": Cf. On Jerome, *De Emm.*, l. 1, c. 6 (PL, CXCVI, 612-3).

31. "litterarum peritia": *ep.* 13 (CCII, 415 B).

32. *In Cant.*, s. 36, n. 2: "I am not unaware of how much her scholars have benefited and do benefit the Church, either to refute those who are opposed to her, or to educate the simple" — "Non ignoro quantum Ecclesiae profuerint et prosint litterati sui, sive ad refellendos eos qui ex adverso sunt, sive ad simplices instruendos" (CLXXXIII, 967 D); however, n. 1: "not in knowledge of literature, but in pure conscience and unfeigned faith" — "non in scientia litterarum, sed in conscientia pura et fide non ficta" (967 C).

33. "ars litteratoria": *H. eccl.* (short version), epilogue: "I have dedicated such a compendious and honorable volume not to illiterate princes, by whom grammatical skill is spurned, but fittingly to you" — "tam compendiosum et

honestum volumen non illiteratis principibus, quibus ars litteratoria spretui est, sed vobis merito dedicavi" (CLXIII, 828-9). These terms "ars litteratoria," "litteralis scientia" were current expressions for "grammar": also in Isidore (*Etym.*, l. 1, 3) and in Alcuin.

34. *Hist. cal.*, c. 6 (CLXXVIII, 127 A and C); c. 1: "I was very good at literature": "ingenio exstiti ad litteratoriam disciplinam facilis" (114 A).

35. *Ep.*, l. 4, 21. It is true that Peter adds: "you have traded them in for much better studies": "longe in melius . . . studia commutasti" (CLXXXIX, 347 AC).

36. "bene, idonee, valde, admodum, insigniter, mirabiliter litteratus": Ekkehard jun., *De cas. S. Galli*, c. 9-10 (Gold.-Senck., l. 39, 46). *Peregrinus* (d'Achery, *Spic.*, 2, 575). Renier of Liège (PL, CCIV, 19 C, 20 C). Irimbert, *De vita virg. Admontensium:* "They are indeed very literate and marvelously accomplished in the knowledge of sacred Scripture" — "Valde quippe sunt litteratae et in scientia sacrae Scripturae mirabiliter exercitatate" (CLXXIV, 13-4), etc.

37. *In Cant.*, n. 16: "Not so much in literature as in the power of the Lord and in the justice of him alone" — "Non tam in litteratura quam in potentiis Domini et in justitia ejus solius" (Davy, 46; cf. Ps. 70:15-6). *Spec. fidei:* "Non in litteratura" (PL, CLXXX, 379 A). *Aenigma fidei* (416 C).

38. *"Non litteratus sed spiritualis omnia dijudicat": Did.*, l. 6, c. 4 (CLXXVI, 804 D). Cf. 1 Cor. 2:15. Irenaeus, *Adv. Haer.*, l. 4, c. 33, n. 1 (PG, VII, 1072 AB); etc.

39. "Saecularibus litteris intentus, sacrae Scripturae arcana capere nequit": *Libellus prov.* (PL, CXLVI, 332 A). Cf. Radevin, *Gesta Friderici*, l. 4, c. 14: "not educated at an average or below average level in grammar" — "litterali scientia non mediocriter aut vulgariter instructus" (G. Waitz, MGH, *Rer. g. ad usum schol.*, 250).

40. *Dial. cum Lucif.*, c. 11: "Any of the educated that are ordained today care not how they should drink the pulp of the Scriptures, but how they might caress the ears of the people with flowery declamation" — "Ex litteratis quicumque hodie ordinantur, id habent curae, non quomodo scripturarum medullas ebibant, sed quomodo aures populi declamatorum flosculis mulceant" (XXIII, 166 B).

41. "Erat litterator, et non spiritualis auditor": *In Matt.* (XCII, 42 B).

42. "Quamobrem, sufficiat nobis brevi compendio fidem defendere, quam tenemus; sapientibus autem hujus saeculi, quae sua sunt cedimus. Habeant, qui volunt, litteram occidentem; dummodo, per Dei misericordiam, spiritus a nobis vivificans non recedat": *Op.* 36, *De div. omnip.*, c. 5 (CXLV, 604 B).

43. "super vilem litteraturam spiritualis intelligentiae conspicit ornamentum": *In Ez.*, l. 2, c. 12 (CLXIX, 1473 CD).

44. "Volo te non tam litteraliter quam spiritualiter erudiri": *ep.* 3 (CCIII, 31 D).

45. Gerhoh, *ep.* 18 (CXCIII, 571 B). Neckam, *De nat. rer.*, l. 2, c. 173: "Litteratus est quis, elatus efficitur" (287). Cf. Isidore, *Sent.*, l. 3, c. 13, n. 9: "By as much as the studies of literature grow greater, by so much does the spirit of arrogance bloated with disdain swell with greater boasting" — "Quanto majora fuerint litteraturae studia, tanto animus arrogantiae fastu inflatus majore tumescit jactantia" (LXXXIII, 688 A).

46. John of Salisbury, *Polycr.*, l. 7, c. 9 (CXCIX, 657 AB).

47. On 26 April 1176, Alexander III reminds the "litterati" of Saint-Saulve that they ought to frequent their parish church (Lesne, 5, 517).

48. C. 12 (Wilmart, *An. Praem.*, 9, 231).

49. "litterati et sapientes"; "parvi et humiles": *Praef. in Hom.* (PL, CLXXIV, 386 D).

50. L. 4, c. 8 (CLXXVI, 674 BC). Here one can think of Petrarch speaking of the Averroists, and then of himself: "Erudite ignorance has been laid bare.... My portion, O God,... unlettered virtue" — "Litterata ignorantia patefacta est.... Portio mea, Deus,... virtus illiterata," *De sui ipsius... ignorantia*, c. 2 (Capelli, 29, 30).

51. "Ille rectissime incedit, qui incedit ordinate": *De script.*, c. 5 (CLXXV, 14 A). He is insistent on that maxim: *Did.*, l. 3, c. 14 (CLXXVI, 774 AB).

52. *In ps.* cxviii, prol., 1: "Those who are being prepared for the teaching of reasonable and perfect prudence are at once to be taught by them with the elements of the letters" — "Qui ad doctrinam rationabilis et perfectae prudentiae praeparantur, ab ipsis statim litterarum elementis docendi sunt, etc."; "This psalm... in which, since the knowledge of the truth was to be given out for the education of human ignorance, the order of teaching has been arranged starting each section in alphabetical order" — "Praesentem psalmum... in quo, cum cognitio veritatis ad eruditionem humanae ignorantiae esset edenda, per ipsa litterarum atque elementorum initia doctrinae ordo est distributus" (PL, IX, 500 D, 501 A); *ib.*, s. 2, n. 1 (511 C).

53. "Non ad altiora pervenitur nisi per inferiores gradus ascendatur; nec maceria desuper firma consistit, nisi firmo fundamenti pede subterius fulciatur": *ep.* 6 (CXLII, 724 B). He is arguing on behalf of grammar and secular studies.

54. *Sermo de eo quod legitur in psalmis:* "For we all know that when any fine structure is about to be built, it cannot be constructed until, once pilings and stakes are inserted all over the place for the job, platforms are made on which the workers can stand and through which a path downward and upward may be obtained" — "Scimus enim omnes quod cum quaelibet excellens structura erit aedificanda, non prius in altum potuerit construi, quam palis et sudibus in opus idem undique insertis gradus efficiantur, in quibus et operantes stare possint, et per quos inferius ac superius iter habeatur" (XCIII, 1106 A).

55. "Nisi enim litteram patienter agnoscas, frustra te in studio allegoriae exquirendae vel moralitatis exerceris": *Ad tropologias proem* (CLVI, 339 C).

56. Het. et Be., *Ad Elip.*, l. 1, c. 101: if, in the explication of Scripture, the Spirit is *lux*, to obtain it it is necessary to use the *lucernae* which are the "holy Fathers, i.e., the prophets, apostles, and doctors" — "Patres sancti, id est prophetae, apostoli atque doctores" (CXVI, 956 D). Cf. Jerome, *In Eph.*, prol. (XXVI, 440); *ep.* 53, c. 6-9 (3, 14-23).

57. Godfrey of Admont, *h. dom.* 26: "He is said to taste sacred Scripture by force, who, not in harmony with the holy expositors, tries to explain it not with a sound understanding but temerariously at his own whim" — "Per vim sacram Scripturam sapere dicitur, qui sanctis expositoribus non concordans, non sano intellectu sed pro libitu suo temerarie eam exponere nititur" (CLXXIV, 180 D). Godfrey can be dependent upon Hugh, divers extracts of whose homilies he supplies.

58. C. 17, n. 35: "What is there fuller of temerarious pride than to be unwilling to get to know the books of the divine sacraments from their own inter-

preter?" — "Quid temerariae superbiae plenius quam divinorum sacramentorum libros ab interpretibus suis nolle cognoscere?" (XLII, 91).

59. *Prol.*, n. 4: "Now [as for] those who exult in the divine gift apart from such precepts as I have decided to hand over now, let them boast that they understand and deal with the sacred books . . . their disturbance ought to be reduced as follows" — "Jamvero eorum qui divino munere exsultant et sine talibus praeceptis, qualia nunc tradere institui, se sanctos libros intelligere atque tractare gloriantur, . . . sic est lenienda commotio etc."; n. 5: "Let me learn without pride what can be learned through man . . . , and let us not tempt him whom we have believed" — "quod per hominem discendum est, sine superbia discar . . . , neque tentemus eum cui credidimus"; n. 6: "Let us beware of such extremely proud and dangerous temptations" — "Caveamus tales tentationes superbissimas et periculosissimas . . ." (XXXIV, 17).

60. *In I Reg.*, l. 4, c. 5, n. 13 (LXXIX, 290).

61. "quod sine magistro ad magisterium divinae lectionis accedere praesumpsissem": *Hist. calam.*, c. 8 (CLXXVIII, 140 A). Cf. Hugh, *Did.*, l. 3, c. 14: "that it not be necessary to listen to teachers in these [scriptural matters]" — "ut in eis (Scripturis) magistros audire non oporteat" (CLXXVI, 774 D).

62. "quia acutuli sibi videntur ad intelligendum, et forte promptuli sunt ad loquendum, dedignantur submitti majoribus ad discendum, et impatientes nidi, antequam plumescant, provolant ad disserendum": *Resp. de damnatione Salomonis* (CCIII, 625 B). Cf. *ep.* 2 (17 B).

63. *De script.*, c. 5: "For since the apostle testifies, 'what is carnal comes first; then, what is spiritual', the very Wisdom of God, unless it had first been known corporeally, could never be illuminated by the sharpness of the bleary minded to be contemplated spiritually. So do not look down on the humility in the Word of God, since it is through the humility that you are illuminated for the divinity. All that the Word of God has on the outside seems to you like dust, and so perhaps you crush it under foot since it is dust, and you despise what the letter relates as having been done in bodily and visible fashion. But I bring up this additional point: by that very dust that you trample under foot, he makes the eyes of the blind to see. So read the Scripture, and first learn diligently what it narrates corporeally" — "Teste namque apostolo, 'quod carnale est prius est, deinde quod spirituale' (1 Cor. 15). Et ipsa Dei Sapientia, nisi prius corporaliter cognita fuisset, numquam lippientis mentis acie ad illam spiritualiter contemplandam illuminari potuisset. Noli igitur in verbo Dei despicere humilitatem, quia per humilitatem illuminaris ad divinitatem. Quasi lutum tibi videtur totum hoc quod verbum Dei foris habet, et ideo forte pedibus conculcas quia lutum est, et contemnis quod corporaliter et visibiliter gestum littera narrat. Sed addo: luto isto quod pedibus tuis conculcatur, caeci oculos ad videndum illuminat (John 18). Lege ergo Scripturam, et disce primum diligenter quae corporaliter narrat" (CLXXV, 14-5). Cf. *De sacram.*, l. 2, prol. (CLXXVI, 363-4).

64. *Ad Elip.*, l. 1, c. 97: "without the letter, which is the body, no one can understand" — "sine littera, quae corpus est, nemo intelligere potest" (XCVI, 954 A).

65. *Ib.*, c. 104: "It is as if we should utterly kill our body and not give it its necessities. . . . The soul that kills its own body contrary to nature will now not be

safe" — "Tale est tanquam si corpus nostrum omnino occidamus et non demus ei quae necessaria sunt. . . . Jam non erit anima salva, quae corpus suum occidit contra naturam" (958 A). "The letter is like a man's body; and this letter is the history itself" — "Littera est sicut corpus hominis; quae littera est ipsa historia" (*ib.*). C. 66 (934-5).

66. *Ib.*, c. 105: "There are heretics, the Circumcellions by name, who kill themselves for love of the martyrs. Such too are those doctors who seek to completely strip the soul of the letter from its body" — "Sunt haeretici, nomine Circumcelliones, qui amore martyrum semetipsos interficiunt. Tales sunt et illi doctores qui omnino animam litterae a corpore nudare quaerunt" (958 C). C. 109: "One cannot arrive at the spirit except through the history, which is the body of the letter, just like the body of a man" — "Non potest venire ad spiritum nisi per historiam, quae est corpus litterae, tanquam corpus hominis" (962 B).

67. *Ib.*, c. 110-6 (962-8); etc. See above, vol. 2, ch. 8.4; the text quoted from Claudius of Turin reproduces Origen, *In Lev.*, h. 1, n. 1.

68. Cf. Stephen of Tournai, *ep.* 159: "Let Augustine's moderation be enough for you" — "Sufficiat tibi mediocritas Augustini" (PL, CCXII, 449 A).

69. *Dial.*, l. 2, c. 36 (LXVI, 200 C). *Did.*, l. 3, c. 3 (CLXXVI, 768 C).

70. *Ep.* 48 (CCII, 473 C); etc.

71. "modus congruus": *Did.*, l. 3, c. 3 (CLXXVI, 718 C); c. 5 (769 CD).

72. "Virtus, si modum non habet, in vitium vertitur": *Did.*, l. 3, c. 8 (771 BC). *Exp. in reg. S. Aug.*, c. 9 (909 BC).

73. Father Roger Baron has shown this well, *op. cit.*, 5, etc.

74. Again, *Did.*, l. 6, c. 4: "That food of yours is solid and unless it be chewed it cannot be swallowed. So it is necessary for you to use such moderation that, while you may have been subtle in inquiry, you do not find yourself temerarious in presumption, recalling what the Psalmist says: 'He hath bent his bow and made it ready. And in it he hath prepared the instruments of death'" — "Solidus est cibus iste et nisi masticetur, transglutiri non potest. Tali ergo te moderamine uti oportet, ut dum inquirendo subtilis fueris, in praesumendo temerarius non inveniaris, recolens quod ait Psalmista: arcum suum tetendit et paravit illum, et in eo paravit vasa mortis (Ps. 7)" (CLXXVI, 802 B).

75. "christiano philosopho lectio exhortatio debet esse, non occupatio": *Did.*, l. 5, c. 7 (795 A).

76. "non philosophatur, sed negociatur": *Ib.:* "It is necessary, however, that he who should have entered upon this path should learn in the books he has read to be called forth not only by the style of utterance but by striving for the virtues" — "Oportet autem ut qui hanc ingressus fuerit viam, in libris quos legerit, discat non solum colore dictaminis sed virtutum aemulatione provocari, etc." (794-5).

77. *Ib.:* "I remember a story once related to me about a man of rather good character who so burned with love of the Scriptures" — "Relatum mihi aliquando memini de quodam satis probabilis vitae viro, qui tanto sanctarum Scripturarum amore flagrabat etc." (795 AC).

78. Ch. Trochon, *Essai sur l'hist. de la Bible dans la France chrét.* (1878), 32. The allusion to Andrew will be found in Herbert of Bosham speaking about the "modern men of letters" — "litteratores moderni," "our rabbis" — "rabbini

nostri," and "our judaizers" — "nostri judaizantes": Smalley, RTAM, 18, 29-65. See below, ch. 5.1.

79. "discretionis moderatione uti"; "Finally, imprudently filled with zeal for wisdom, he began, once the simpler Scriptures had been spurned, to tear into whatever was deep and obscure and vehemently to insist on picking out the riddles of the prophets and the mystical understandings of the sacraments; but the human mind, not bearing up so great a burden" — "Caepit tandem sapientiam zelatus imprudenter, spretis simplicioribus scripturis, profunda quaeque et obscura rimari atque aenigmatibus prophetarum enodandis et mysticis sacramentorum intellectibus vehementer insistere; sed mens humana tantum non sustinens pondus, etc." (795 B).

80. Cf. the indications given by R. Baron, introd., xxxv.

81. "tumultuosa vita saeculi abstractus"; "ad quemdam tranquillitatis portum": *Hist. calam.*, c. 8 (PL, CLXXVIII, 136 C); c. 15: "from the billowing of this storm I ran back as it were to a port of tranquility" — "de aestu hujus tempestatis quasi ad quemdam tranquillitatis portum recurrerem" (179 A). It is a question of the abbey of the Paraclete, where he had hoped to flee the storm from the abbey of Saint Gildas. Cf. c. 10: "Where . . . in hiding, I was truly able to chant to the Lord: 'behold I have gone off in flight, and I have remained in solitude'" — "Ubi . . . latitans, illud vere Domino poteram decantare: ecce elongavi fugiens, et mansi in solitudine" (159 A; cf. 162 A).

82. "entre la fin de 1132 et l'année 1134": E. Gilson, *Héloïse et Abélard*, 14.

83. "jeune ambitieux de génie": Gilson, 37.

84. *Hist. calam.*, c. 5: "since I used to think that I was the only philosopher left in the world" — "cum jam me solum in mundo superesse philosophum aestimarem" (PL, CLXXVIII, 126 B).

85. *Hist. cal.*, c. 8 (136 C and 139 A).

86. Letter to Heloise (PL, CLXXXIX, 350 C).

87. *Hist. cal.*, c. 8 (CLXXVIII, 140 A); c. 3: "I am utterly amazed that literate people do not find it enough to understand the expositions of the saints to rely just on their writings themselves or maybe the glosses: they do not need any other teacher" — "me vehementer mirari, quod his qui litterati sunt, ad expositiones sanctorum intelligendas ipsa eorum scripta vel glossae non sufficiant, ut alio sc. non egeant magistro" (124 B).

88. Letter to Abelard (CLXXVIII, 369 B). "The extent and the depth of the impression caused by this outrage (the mutilation of Abelard) is attested by the letter of F. de D." — "L'étendue et la profondeur de l'impression produite par cet attentat (la mutilation d'Abélard) est attestée par la lettre de Foulques de Deuil" (Gilson, 84, note), also prior to the *Hist. cal.* (371-6). Abelard speaks openly of his "impurity of life" — "immunditia vitae," his "luxuria," as well as his "superbia": *H. cal.*, c. 5 (126 BC).

89. "miseratione divina tandem per revelationem admonitus"; "a nobis admonitus, magis autem a Deo ut credimus inspiratus": To Peter the Venerable.

90. *Did.*, l. 6, c. 3 (PL, CLXXVI, 799 C). Following 2 Cor. 11:13, Abelard speaks of "pseudoapostoli"; *In Rom.*, l. 5, c. 16 (CLXXVIII, 975 C).

91. R. Baron, 137, has noted the constant care in Hugh to avoid the dangers that have arisen from Abelard's thought.

92. *Did.*, l. 3, c. 14: "He enters most fitly who enters in orderly fashion. While some want to make a great leap, they fall head over heels" — "Aptissime incedit, qui incedit ordinate. Quidam dum magnum saltum facere volunt, praecipitium incidunt" (CLXXVI, 774 AB). Comp. *De script.*, c. 5 (CLXXV, 14 A). "Hugh does not keep himself from transferring whole passages of which he was the author from one work to another" — "Hugues ne se privait pas de transporter d'une œuvre à l'autre des passages entiers dont il était l'auteur": Baron, xxxv. Examples in D. Van den Eynde, *Essai*. Peter Damian did so as well: Leclercq, *S. Pierre Damien*, 160.

93. *Les œuvres de Hugues de SV* (1886), 97-8.

94. *Les origines de la théologie moderne*, I (1911), 48.

95. "Quand tu commenceras à connaître quelque chose, ne méprise pas les autres. Cette arrogance se remarque chez certain maîtres, qui considèrent leur propre science avec trop de satisfaction et qui, persuadés qu'ils sont quelque chose, pensent que tels ne sont pas, tels ne peuvent être d'autres maîtres qu'ils ne connaissent pas. De ce vicieux ferment viennent de surgir ces colporteurs de sornettes, qui, glorieux on ne sait de quoi, taxent les anciens Pères de puérile bonhomie et croient que la sagesse, créée avec eux, ne doit pas leur survivre. Le style des Écritures, disent-ils, est tellement simple, qu'ils n'ont pas besoin de maîtres pour leur enseigner à les comprendre; il suffit à chacun de sa propre intelligence pour pénétrer les arcanes de la vérité": *Did.*, l. 3, c. 14 (CLXXVI, 774 CD). Cf. Abelard above, note 87.

96. Cf. *Hist. cal.*, c. 10: "a sincere intention and love for our faith . . . forced me to write" — "sincera intentio amorque fidei nostrae . . . me ad scribendum compulerant" (CLXXVIII, 153 A).

97. "ad plenum sacrae paginae intellectum"; "novis allegoriis studendis et novis instructionibus morum meditandis": *Ep. anonymi ad Hugonem amicum suum de modo et ordine legendi sacram Scr.* (PL, CCXIII, 715 A).

98. "Hi sunt qui evanescunt in cogitationibus suis; qui imagines cordis sui in paginis sacrae Scripturae depingunt; qui litteram renitentem suis adinventionibus accommodant, et intellectum Scripturae usque ad sanguinem emungunt": *S.* 2 (CXCVIII, 1755 D).

99. "Sicut enim alibi aqua mutatur in vinum, per quod significatur mutatio populi in melius, ita hic mutatur in sanguinem, per quem caro accipitur, quia spiritualia carnaliter sentient": *In ps.* LXXVII, 49 (CXCI, 737 CD).

100. "laborat emungendo sanguinem ex quibusdam Scripturarum auctoritatibus": *Hexaem.* (CXCIX, 1522 AB).

101. *Ep.* 44 (395); *ep.* 5: "You recall that it is written 'he who squeezes strongly etc.'; for he who fits a sober sense to sacred Scripture, offers a sweet drink; but he who rummages beyond measure, falls into a carnal sense" — "Recolis scriptum esse: qui fortiter premit etc.; qui enim sacrae Scripturae sobrium sensum accommodat, dulcem potum propinat; qui vero ultra modum rimatur, in carnalem sensum praecipitatur" (334) (in 1140). With Absalon, *s.* 7 (PL, CCXI, 50 B), the symbolism will be different.

102. "Incipit (Job) narrare subtilius bona quae fecit, quae ex magna parte juxta solius historiae textum tenenda sunt, ne si plus quam necesse est investigentur, a verborum ejus uberibus sanguis pro lacte respondeat, juxta illud

Salomonis: Qui ubera vehementer emulget, elicit sanguinem. Sic enim sacrae Scripturae serie partim, prout ratio exigit, intellectus litterae solus tenendus, partim candor allegoriae requirendus est. Sicut in facto Jacob mystice figuratur, qui, virgas positurus ante oculos ovium . . . , ex parte decorticavit eas, detractisque corticibus . . . candor apparuit; quae vero integrae erant, virides permanserunt . . . (Gen. 30). Sic, inquam, dum plerumque intellectum litterae figimus, quasi corticem subtrahimus, et dum plerumque intellectum litterae sequimur, quasi corticem reservamus . . .": *In Job* (CLXVIII, 1103 BC). Regarding the peeled branches, again see Garnier, s. 36 (CCV, 802 D), etc. The image of the squeezed udders is found in Peter Lombard and Maurice of Sully (CLXXI, 368 BC, 636 C) without the pejorative prolongation.

103. "Licet ille altius ea voluerit extollere, allegorizare, quam fides catholica permittit; quia 'qui fortius premit ubera', teste Scriptura, 'non elicit lac, sed sanguinem'": *In Matt.*, l. 8, c. 18 (120, 630 AB).

104. "Ubera fortiter premimus, cum verba sacri eloquii subtili intellectu pensamus; qua pressione dum lac quaerimus, butyrum invenimus, quia dum nutriri vel tenui intellectu quaerimus, ubertate internae pinguedinis ungemur; quod nec nimis nec semper agendum est, ne dum lac quaeritur ab uberibus, sanguis sequatur; quia dum verba sacri eloquii plus quam debent discutiuntur, in carnalem intellectum cadunt. . . . Carnale efficitur hoc quod ex nimia spiritus discussione sentitur": *Sup. Par. Sal.*, l. 3 (XCI, 1027 D). One will reproach Alcuin, *In Ap.*, l. 4 in viii, 8: "The water-turned-into-blood is carnal wisdom" — "Aqua in sanguinem versa, sapientia carnalis est," with the citation of 2 Cor. 3:6: "The letter killeth" — "Littera occidit" and of Ps. 50:16: "Deliver me from blood" — "Libera me de sanguinibus" (C, 1137 D).

105. "'Mel invenisti, comede quod sufficit tibi etc.' Dulcedinem invenisti caelestis intellectus, quae spiritualium patrum officio, quasi prudentissimarum apum tibi labore ministrata est. Vide ergo ne in ea plus sapere appetas quam oportet sapere, ne dum summa intelligere ultra vires quaeris, etiam quae bene intellexeris amittas."

"'Sicut mel qui multum comedit etc.' Dulcedo enim mellis si plus quam necesse est sumitur, unde delectatur os, inde vita comedentis necatur. Dulcis quodque est requisitio majestatis; sed qui plus hanc scrutari appetit quam humanitatis agnitio permittit, ipsa hunc ejus gloria premit, quia velut mel sumptum immoderate, perscrutantis sensum, dum non capitur, rumpit. Non hoc autem solum quisque sapiens attendere debet, ne altiora te quaerat, et ne fortiora scrutatus sit, verum etiam ne ea quae recte atque utiliter scire potuit, immoderatis sermonibus sibimet minus utilia reddat": L. 3 (XCI, 1013 CD, 1015 BC). Cf. Prov. 25:16 and 27.

106. "Erit igitur divinarum Scripturarum solertissimus indagator, qui primo totas legerit notasque habuerit, et si nondum intellectu, jam tamen lectione. . . . Cujus operis et laboris prima observatio est, ut diximus, nosse istos libros, etsi nondum ad intellectum, legendo tamen vel mandare memoriae, vel omnino incognitos non habere. Deinde . . .": L. 3, c. 6 (CVII, 383 A); c. 7 (384 B).

107. "diligentiam investigationis"; "sobrium intellectum": *In Paral.*, l. 1: "If the prudent reader furnish diligence in his investigation, he would easily be able to come upon a sober understanding" — "Prudens lector si diligentiam

investigationis adhibuerit, facile sobrium intellectum invenire poterit" (CIX, 287 B).

108. "sobrium lectorem": *In Deut.*, l. 4, c. 1: "Hence it behooves a sober reader to preserve the truth of Scripture at the historical level" — "Unde sobrium lectorem decet ut in historia servet Scripturae veritatem" (CVIII, 967-8).

109. *In Prov. Sal.*, l. 3, c. 30 (CXI, 779 AB).

110. *Ib.* (763 A, 764-5).

111. "Qui fortiter premit ubera ad eliciendum lac, exprimit butyrum; qui vehementer emungit, elicit sanguinem"; "Mel invenisti, comede quod sufficit tibi, ne forte satiatus evomas illud"; "Qui mel multum comedit, non est ei bonum; qui scrutator est majestatis, opprimetur a gloria": *Mutatis mutandis,* one will be able to compare the thought of the Taoist Chuang Tsu: "To know how to stop before the incomprehensible is the supreme Wisdom. Those who do not know how to stop at that limit, Heaven will rout, crushing them": "Savoir s'arrêter devant l'incompréhensible est la suprême Sagesse. Ceux qui ne savent pas s'arrêter à cette limit, le Ciel les dispersera en les écrasant" (Tchouang tsou, trans. René Brémond, 1955, p. 177; 23 D). Cf. Garnier, s. 11, who comments on the text with expressions borrowed from Bernard and from Hugh (CCV, 638 BC).

112. "Altiora te ne quaesieris, et fortiora te ne scrutatus fueris": Cf. Anastasius the Librarian, *ep.* 1: "cogitante ... secundum illud Sal., mel invenisti etc., et alibi: altiora te etc." (MGH, *Ep.*, 7, 396).

113. "Attamen numquid scrutari Scripturas, idem est quod scrutatorem esse majestatis?": *De gloria Trin.*, l. 9, c. 1 (PL, CLXIX, 180-1). Cf. Aug., *In ps.* cviii, n. 23: "He commanded one to scrutinize the Scriptures, which offer testimony about him, not just to skim over the surface" — "Scrutari jussit Scripturas, quae testimonium perhibent de illo, non superficie pertransiri" (CCL, 40, 1597); *In ps.* cv, n. 36 (1561). Julian of Toledo, *De compr. aet. sextae*, l. 1, n. 3 (PL, XCVI, 541 D). *L. carolin.*, 3, c. 6, citing the example of Daniel, "a most holy man and a scrutinizer of God's mysteries" — "virum sanctissimum et arcanorum Dei scrutatorem" (XCVIII, 1125 D). Gerhoh, *De aedificio Dei,* ad Chononem, ep. Ratisp.: "For you, a most sensitive scrutinizer of the holy Scriptures" — "Tibi, delicatissimo sanctarum Scripturarum scrutatori" (*L. de lite,* 3, 139); etc.

114. "Non autem mel comedere, sed multum comedere vetat, quia non omnimodo majestatem Dei scrutari prohibemur ... , sed a tentandis his quae mensuram nostram excedunt revocamur": *In Cant.*, l. 4 (PL, XCI, 1142-3).

115. "etsi ex causis fidei et circa fidem ipsam varie moveantur forte tanti mysterii scrutatores magis temerarii at curiosi magis quam necesse": *Lib. melorum* (*Opera,* Giles, 2, 143).

116. "ne simus nimii scrutatores majestatis"; "non scrutando nimium majestatem Dei": *Matt.,* l. 3 (PL, CLXVIII, 1365 D). Ps.-Hugh, *In Rom.,* q. 288: "lest, through excessive investigation, one" — "ne quis per investigationem nimiam" (CLXXV, 503 A).

117. "reges profunda putei rimantes et verbi Dei arcana ac mystica perscrutantes": *In Num.,* h. 12, n. 2 (101).

118. "Errare eos fecit, eo quod vidissent arcam Domini; eo quod indigne, non dilectionis studio, sed praesumptionis et curiositatis vitio ausi fuissent in Scripturis scrutari secreta divinitatis; et facti sunt haeresiarchae, judicante Deo

superbos ad conspectum divinitatis et veritatis non admitti": *In Reg.*, l. 1, c. 16 (*II Reg.*, xviii, PL, CLXVII, 1084-5); *In Gen.*, l. 2: "it is permissible to inquire soberly, i.e., to marvel" — "sobrie quaerere, id est mirari licet" (265 B). *In Ex.*, l. 2, he opposes "curiositas" to "sapientia" (617 C).

119. "De tertio melle, quod est spiritalis intelligentia Scripturarum, Salomon dicit: . . . 'Comede quod sufficit, ne forte satiatus evomas illud'; comede, inquit, quod sufficit, id est, *ad aedificationem, non ad curiositatem* arcana perscruteris; sicut enim alibi dicit Salomon: 'Qui scrutator est majestatis, opprimetur a gloria'": *S.* 7 (CCXI, 51 D). Cf. Ch. Hauret: the Bible "admits into its intimacy neither the curious nor the snob" — "n'admet dans son intimité ni le curieux ni le snob" (*La table ronde*, Nov. 1956, 140).

120. 1 Cor. 2:10-12.

121. *In Matt.*, l. 4, c. 11, n. 3: "Where he beautifully contrasted to the wise and the prudent not the unwise and foolish, but the little ones, i.e., the humble, so as to prove that he condemned bloatedness, not acuity; since this is the key about which he says elsewhere 'You have taken the key of knowledge' (Luke 11), i.e., the humility of the faith of Christ, you who could have arrived at a recognition of his divinity, have preferred, spurning it, to cast it aside" — "Ubi pulchre sapientibus et prudentibus non insipientes et hebetes, sed parvulos id est humiles opposuit, ut probaret se tumorem damnasse, non acumen; quia haec est clavis de qua alibi dicit: Tulistis clavem scientiae (Luke 11), id est humilitatem fidei Christi, qui ad divinitatis ejus agnitionem pervenire poteratis, spernentes, abjicere maluistis" (PL, CVII, 915). William of Saint Thierry, *Aenigma fidei:* "non scrutator majestatis . . . sed pauper spiritu etc." (CLXXX, 427 AB).

122. "irruptor"; "effractor": *C. quaedam cap. err. Ab.*, c. 5, n. 11 (CLXXXII, 1062 CD). *De consid.*, l. 5, c. 3, n. 6: "If faith has any hesitation, it is weak; again, if the understanding tries to break into things assigned to faith, it is thought a burglar, a scrutinizer of majesty; many have thought their own opinion to be understanding, and they were wrong" — "Fides, si habet haesitationem, infirma est; item intellectus, si signata fidei tentet irrumpere, reputatur effractor, scrutator majestatis; multi suam opinionem intellectum putaverunt et erraverunt" (790 D). *In Cant.*, s. 62, n. 4: "Would any other of the mortals presume by his own efforts to involve himself in this horrific scrutiny of the divine majesty, and break into the terrible mysteries as an importunate contemplator? For I think that the scrutinizers of the majesty are spoken of as house-breakers, to wit, not as those who are taken up into it [by God] but who stampede in [on their own]" — "Quisnam alter praesumat mortalium huic se divinae majestatis horrendo scrutinio propriis intricare conatibus, et importunus contemplator pavenda irrumpere in arcana? Scrutatores proinde majestatis, tanquam irruptores dici reor, non qui sc. rapiuntur in eam sed qui irruunt" (CLXXXIII, 1078 A). Luther will take up the theme again, directed to theologians whose doctrine displeased him; to Scultetus, Bishop of Brandenburg, 13 Feb. 1518: "There is not a single thing hidden in God's highest majesty or in his sacred humanity that they have not sullied through their silly remarks" — "Il n'y a pas une seule chose caché dans la suprême majesté de Dieu ou dans sa sainte humanité, qu'ils n'aient souillée par leurs propos frivoles." *Œuvres*, French trans., 8 (1959), 26.

123. "Non pigeat scrutari adhuc secreta . . . , si forte in his aliquid lateat

spirituale, quod venire ad medium possit!": *In Cant., s.* 86, n. 4 (CLXXXIII, 1196 D); *s.* 80, n. 2 (1167 A). In the wake of E. Gilson, A. Renaudet cites these words of Bernard on several occasions. He rightly sees in them a "glorious definition where mysticism and humanism are reconciled and grounded" — "définition glorieuse, où mystique et humanisme se réconcilient et se fondent"; but he does not quite recognize the exact import of the term "majestas," nor that of the term "capacitas"; he translates: "sublime creature that bears 'a majesty in potency' or 'an element of majesty in it'" — "créature sublime qui porte en puissance une majesté" ou "en elle un élément de majesté." "Autour d'une définition de l'humanisme" (1945), in *Hum. et Renaissance* (1950), 46; *Dante humaniste* (1952), 66 and 371; etc.

124. "cujus immensitatem humani sensus capacitas non valet terminare": *L. moz. sacr.* (17). Cf. Garnier, *s.* 2: "since whatever can be subject to the conscience of the weak is within the consciousness of weakness" — "quoniam intra conscientiam infirmitatis est, quidquid infirmi conscientiae subdi potest" (PL, CCV, 570 C).

125. "ne verearis illud quod Scriptura minatur scrutatoribus majestatis; tantum affer purum et simplicem oculum": *In Cant., s.* 62, n. 4 (PL, CLXXXIII, 1077 C).

126. "labyrinthus divinae revelationis": *Aenigma fidei* (CLXXX, 426 D).

127. Paulinus of Aquilaea, *C. Fel. Urg.*, l. 1, c. 11: "for it is written: '[seek not] things higher than yourself' . . . and again it is written of the more unrestrainedly rash: 'he who strongly squeezes'" — "scriptum est enim: altiora te . . . et de effrenatius praecipiti rursus scriptum est: qui fortiter premit" (XCIX, 362 C). Augustine, *In Jo.,* tr. 53, n. 7 (CCL, 36, 455). Hesychius, *In Lev.*, l. 2 (PG, XCIII, 850 CD); etc. Petrarch will again quote the warning of Ecclesiasticus in addressing the Averroists; *De sui ipsius . . . ignorantia,* c. 4 (L. M. Capelli, 42 and 44).

128. "de Deo indecenter incauta disputare locutione": Aug., *In Jo.,* tr. 53, n. 7 (CCL, 36, 455). Hesychius, *loc. cit.*, etc.

129. Ps.-Isidore, *Test. div. Scr.,* c. 23 (7th cent.): "Do not seek things too high for you and do not scrutinize things stronger than you, but always think those that the Lord has instructed you, and you will not be curious for more of it; for suspicion of those things seduces many and will engage their sense in vanity" — "Altiora te ne quaesieris et fortiora te ne perscruteris, sed quae praecepit tibi Dominus, illa cogita semper, et in pluribus ejus non eris curiosus; multos enim seducit suspicio eorum et in vanitate detinebit sensum illorum" (De Bruyne, RB, 45, 137). Again, Innocent III, *s.* 21 (CCXVII, 404 D).

130. Thus too, Salonius of Geneva, *In Prov.:* "and the sense is: do not raise the eyes of your mind to scrutinize the hidden points of divinity and the secrets of the heavenly mysteries, which you cannot penetrate and are not able to understand, since they are open only to eagles, i.e., they have been made manifest only to the citizens of heaven" — "Et est sensus: ne erigas oculos mentis tuae ad perscrutanda divinitatis arcana et mysteriorum caelestium secreta, quae penetrare non potes nec intelligere vales, quoniam solis aquilis patent, id est supernis tantum manifestata sunt civibus" (CLXXII, 324 C).

131. "Vultum suum propheta pallio operuit, quia in ipsa subtilissima contemplatione veritatis, quanta ignorantia homo tegatur, agnoscit. Vultui

namque pallium superducere est, ne altiora mens quaerere audeat, hanc considerationem propriae infirmitatis velare, et nequaquam intelligentiae oculos ultra se praecipitanter aperiat, sed ad hoc quod apprehendere non valet, reverenter claudat": *In Reg.*, l. 3, c. 19 (CXV, 484 AB). Cf. Rabanus (CIX, 212 AB).

132. *In Cant.*, s. 8, n. 6: "You, too, as you cautiously plant your foot on the secret senses, always remember what the wise man warns: 'Things too high', says he. . . . Walk on them in the spirit and not according to your own sense. The Spirit's teaching does not sharpen curiosity but ignites charity. Fittingly then the betrothed, whom the inquiring soul loves, does not entrust herself to the senses of her own flesh, does not acquiesce in the vain rationalizations of human curiosity, but asks for a kiss, i.e., calls upon the Holy Spirit, through whom she receives at once both the taste of knowledge and the spice of grace" — "Vos quoque, ut caute in arcanis sensibus pedem figatis, mementote semper quod sapiens admonet: Altiora, inquit. . . . In spiritu ambulate in illis et non in sensu proprio. Doctrina Spiritus non curiositatem acuit, sed caritatem accendit. Merito proinde sponsa, quem diligit anima sua inquirens, non se suae carnis sensibus credit, non curiositatis humanae inanibus ratiociniis acquiescit, sed petit osculum, id est Spiritum sanctum invocat, per quem accipiat simul et scientiae gustum et gratiae condimentum" (CLXXXIII, 812-3).

133. "curiosa cupiditas": Heterius and Beata, *Ad Elip.*, l. 2, c. 28 (XCVI, 993 C).

134. "salubris curiositas": An expression of Walafrid Strabo, *De exordiis* (MGH, *Capt.*, 475).

135. "quaedam vis mentis curiosa et sagax, nitens obscura investigare et perplexa evolvere": *In Eccl.*, h. 1 (PL, CLXXV, 117 A).

136. "pia curiositas": *In Cant.*, s. 62, n. 3, regarding Paul (CLXXXIII, 1076 D). William of Saint-Thierry, *Med. orat.*, 3: "so that he may comprehend with pious and sober understanding that [he] does not comprehend the majesty of the divine incomprehensibility" — "ut pio et sobrio intellectu comprehendat non comprehendere majestatem divinae incomprehensibilitatis" (CLXXX, 214 CD).

137. *In Cant.*, s. 37, n. 2: "But still I am not saying that the science of literature is to be contemned or neglected" — "Non tamen dico contemnendam aut negligendam scientiam litterarum" (CLXXXIII, 971 C). It is well known that several interpreters have taken the first name of Rabelais's Bernard Lardon (*The Fourth Book of Pantagruel*) to designate the dull-witted lack of curiosity of the character.

138. "turpis curiositas": *In Cant.*, s. 36, n. 3 (968 D).

139. Cf. E. de Bruyne, 2, 138-9, quoting Peter the Cantor: "in superfluousness, in curiosity, and in sumptuousness of buildings" — "in superfluitate, curiositate et sumptuositate aedificiorum" (CCV, 255 B). Alexander Neckam, *De nat. rer.*, c. 172: "o curiositas! o vanitas! o vana curiositas! o curiosa vanitas!" (282); c. 173: "vanitas curiositatis" (307); c. 174: "o inutilis curiositas!" (311); c. 192: (351).

140. Hugh Metel, *ep.* 28: "Beware, brother, beware of a superstitious understanding. . . . Beware of the stupid and incompetent questions that provoke most fights. Be not curious regarding most of God's works" — "Cave, frater, cave superstitiosam intelligentiam. . . . Cave stultas quaestiones et ineptas, quae plurimas suscitant contentiones. Ne sis curiosus circa plurima Dei opera . . ." (368).

141. *Op.* 36, c. 5 (PL, CXLV, 603 C).

142. "ut ex multis litteris efficiantur insani": *S.* 15 (CCXII, 603 AB).

143. *C. vanam curiositatem* (9 Nov. 1402). Bernard, *s.* 3 *in Pent.* (CLXXXIII, 331 CD), censures it in certain ascetics, whom he puts back to back with the sensuals, and to whom he opposes the "viri prudentiores."

144. "vana et curiosa cupiditas, nomine cognitionis et scientiae palliate": *Conf.*, l. 10, c. 35, n. 55 (281), *Enchir.*, c. 3, n. 9 (116), *Doct. chr.*, l. 2, c. 42, n. 63 (336). Cf. H. Blumenberg, "Curiositas und Veritas: zur Ideengeschichte von Augustinus, *Conf.*, x, 35" (Third International Conference on Patristic Studies, Oxford, 1959). That bent of Augustinism is emphasized in the modern epoch, particularly in Jansenism. Cf. the reflections of Tillemont regarding Origen, *Mémoires . . .* , 3 (2e éd., 1701), 593-4.

145. "sollicitudo curiositatis"; "voluptas carnis"; "aestus ambitionis": *In Ev.*, h. 36, n. 11 (PL, LXXVI, 1273 A). Cf. Adam Scot, *De quadr. ex. cellae,* c. 7 and 10 (CLIII, 813 A, 819 A). Gerhoh, *In ps.* xxxv (Van den Eynde, 431-2).

146. "vanitas curiositatis vel cupiditatis"; "appetitus vanitatis"; "desiderium veritatis"; "O pessima occupatio! o distentio perniciosa! quo trahis animum? Quantum promittis, et quantum tollis! Promittis homini totum quod ipse non est, et tollis totum quod ipse est": *Miscell.,* l. 1, tit. 126 (CLXXVII, 548 A). *In Eccl.*, h. 1 (CLXXV, 119 AB); h. 4 (151-2); h. 6 (157-8); h. 9 (170 B). Cf. Absalon, *s.* 44 and 49 (CCXI, 253-5, 277 D).

147. Aug., *Civ. Dei,* l. 4, c. 34 (XLI, 140)

148. *Orat.* 31 (PG, XXXVI, 136-8, 160, 164).

149. Aug., *s.* Caill. 2, n. 11 (Morin, *Misc. Agost.,* 1, 256). *De Trin.*, l. 14, c. 1, n. 3 (PL, XLII, 1037).

150. "quaesivi curiose": *C. ep. Manichaei,* c. 3 (XLII, 174).

151. "eviscerantur arcana Dei": *ep.* 188, n. 1 (CLXXXII, 353 A).

152. "anima curiosa Dei": Bernard, *In Cant.*, s. 33, n. 1 (PL, CLXXXIII, 951 C).

153. Hugh, *De sacramentis,* l. 2, P. 14, c. 9: "As long as he lives, he is always seeking. . . . I fail to see how being familiar with everything is to seek the truth" — "Quamdiu vivitur, semper quaeritur. . . . Nescio quo pacto familiare omnibus est veritatem quaerere" (CLXXVI, 570-1).

154. Fragment published by Hauréau, *Not. et extraits*, I (1890), 116.

155. "Ultra vires quaerendo, perdes intellecta": Peter the Cantor will also bring up Proverbs 25 and Ecclesiasticus 3 and will quote the *Gloss: Verbum abbrev.* (CCV, 34 A). Cf. *Summa sent.* (CLXXVI, 69 B, 132 B).

156. "Seek nothing more than the divine Scriptures preach; do not crave to know what is not permitted" — "Nihil amplius perquiras quam divinae Scripturae praedicant, scire ne cupias quae non licet" (after Gregory; Leclercq-Bonnes, *Jean de Fécamp,* 809, note 3).

157. *In ps.* xxxviii: "It does not belong to our frailty to crack open the secrets of the heavens" — "Non enim est fragilitatis nostrae caelorum secreta discutere" (CXCIII, 1417 A).

158. xxiii, 5. Salonius, above, note 130. Honorius, *Q. et resp. in Prov.*: "Raise not your eyes to riches that you cannot have, since, like eagles, they will make themselves wings and fly off into the heavens" — "Ne erigas oculos tuos ad opes quas habere non potes, quia facient sibi pennas quasi aquilae et volabunt in

caelum." "Those riches are the hidden things of the godhead and the secrets of the celestial mysteries, which you cannot penetrate and are unable to understand, since they are clear only to the eagles, i.e., they are manifest only to the citizens of heaven" — "Opes istae arcana sunt divinitatis, et secreta caelestium mysteriorum; et est sensus: Ne erigas oculos mentis tuae ad perscrutanda divinitatis arcana et mysteriorum caelestium secreta, quae penetrare non potes, nec intelligere vales, quoniam solis aquilis patent, id est supernis tantum manifesta sunt civibus."

159. Cf. Auguste Valensin, *Ulysse ou les limites de la raison (Regards*, 3, *Dante)*.

160. "c'est être téméraire de vouloir découvrir les fins que Dieu s'est données dans la construction du monde": *Principes,* first part, art. 28. Malebranche is indignant about it: *Méditations chrét.,* xi, 1, 2 (Gouhier, 205).

161. "haute métaphysique théologique": Martial Guéroult, *Malebranche,* 2 (1959), 7-8.

162. Cf. Acts 19:19: those "who had followed curious arts" — "qui fuerant curiosa sectati" (= who were given to magic). In *Conf.,* l. 10, c. 35, n. 55, Aug. notes this bond between curiosity and magic: "Hence too, if anything is sought through the magical arts with the same end of perverted knowledge" — "Hinc etiam, si quid eodem perversae scientiae fine per artes magicas quaeritur"; he adds: "Hence God is tempted even in religion itself" — "Hinc etiam in ipsa religione Deus tentatur" — but without directly envisioning a temptation from the devil in that chapter.

163. "altitudo cordis": Cf. Origen, *In Jer.,* h. 16, n. 9 (140-1; PG, XIII, 449-50); *In Ez.,* h. 9, n. 5 (414-5); etc.

164. Cf. Paul Ricœur, *Finitude et culpabilité,* 2 (1960), 238.

165. Rupert, *In Matt.,* l. 3: "This was the first elevation of our heart, that men should want to be as gods, and this was the sin of Adam" — "Haec prima fuit altitudo cordis nostri, ut vellent esse homines sicut dii, et hoc est Adae peccatum" (PL, CLXVIII, 1366 B). *In Jo.,* l. 9: "How many excessive scrutinizers involving themselves in these and other such tiny questions, have been crushed by the glory of Majesty, and have rolled about, as though sated by much honey, like the Manichaeans for example" — "His atque hujusmodi quaestiunculis nimii scrutatores semetipsos implicantes, quam plurimi a gloria majestatis oppressi sunt, et tanquam multo melle satiati semetipsos commoverunt ut v.g. Manichaei" (CLXIX, 575 AB; cf. 573-4). This theme is utilized by the pamphleteer of the *Liber de unitate Ecclesiae conservanda,* c. 42: "They imitate the depths of Satan. . . . Wishing to build a tower of their impiety against God . . . , to penetrate with illicit curiosity into the heights of heaven itself" — "Satanae altitudinem imitantur. . . . Adversus Deum impietatis suae turrim aedificavere . . . , curiositate volentes non licita in ipsius caeli alta penetrare" (*L. de lite,* 2, 274).

166. Cf. Leo, *s.* 29, c. 1 (XLIV, 226 C); *s.* 69, c. 1 (376 A), etc.

167. "animus cupidus"; "per curiositatem delectatur scire latentia": Isidore, *De Haeresibus* (Vega, 26).

168. Aug., *Conf.,* loc. cit.

169. Cf. H. Cornélis and A. Léonard, *La gnose éternelle* (1959).

170. "quos haeretici rationis et scientiae fallaci pollicatione decipiunt": Aug.,

De musica, 1. 6, c. 17, n. 58 (Thonnard, 476). Cf. *L. moz. sacr.*, on the "obstinate curiosity of the Chaldaeans" — "Chaldaeorum cervicosa curiositas" (89).

171. *In Gen.*, l. 3 (PL, L, 1002 AB). In Remigius, *h.* 4, the application is different (CXXXI, 888 D).

172. "Omnes haeretici, dum in sacro eloquio plus secreta Dei student perscrutari quam capiunt, fame sua steriles fiunt. Neque enim ea quaerunt ex quibus semetipsos ad humilitatem erudiant . . . , sed ea solummodo quae eos doctos atque loquaces demonstrent . . . cum semetipsos miseri nesciant. . . . Ultra se quippe sunt quae perscrutantur, dumque ad hoc tendunt quod comprehendere nequeunt, ea cognoscere negligunt ex quibus erudiri potuerant": *Mor.*, 1. 20, c. 8, n. 18 (LXXVI, 147-8); l. 23, c. 17, n. 31: "For swell-headedness is a hindrance to attaining the truth, since, while it is puffing up, it beclouds the mind" — "Obstaculum namque veritatis est tumor mentis, quia dum inflat obnubilat" (269 C).

173. "non plus sapere quam oportet, sapere, sed sapere ad sobrietatem" [Rom. 12:3]. "Hinc Salomon ait: 'prudentiae tuae pone modum.' Hinc rursum dicit: 'Mel invenisti, comede quod sufficit tibi, ne forte satiatus, evomas illud.' Dulcedinem quippe spiritualis intelligentiae qui ultra quam capit comedere appetit, etiam quod comederat evomit, quia dum summa intelligere ultra vires quaerit, etiam quae bene intellexerat amittit. Hinc rursum dicit: 'Sicut qui mel multum comedit, non est ei bonum, sic qui perscrutator est majestatis opprimetur a gloria.' Gloria quippe invisibilis conditoris, quae moderate inquisita hos erigit, ultra vires perscrutata premit": *Mor.* (148 AB); l. 14, c. 28, n. 32: "Sicut mel etc."

174. *Mor.*, l. 18, c. 13, n. 20: "since indeed they are trying to bend . . . the thoughts of sacred Scripture to a depraved understanding" — "quippe qui Scripturae sacrae sententias . . . ad intellectum pravum conantur inflectere" (LXXVI, 48 CD). See above, ch. 2.1.

175. "Dum in sacri verbi pabulo plus quaerunt sentire quam capiunt, semper a veritatis cognitione jejunant; et praedicamenta doctrinae quae student ad quaestionem quaerere, habere non valent ad refectionem": *Ib.*, n. 21 (49 AB). Cf. Ps.-Isidore, *L. de variis q.*, c. 50 (147-8).

176. "Solent quidam, scripta sacri eloquii legentes, cum sublimiores ejus sententias penetrant, minora mandata quae infirmioribus data sunt tumenti sensu despicere, et ea velle in alium intellectum permutare. Qui, si recte in eo alta intelligerent, mandata quoque minima despectui non haberent, quia divina praecepta sic in quibusdam loquuntur magnis, ut tamen in quibusdam congruant parvulis, qui per incrementa intelligentiae quasi quibusdam passibus mentis crescant, atque ad majora intelligenda perveniant": *In Ez.*, l. 1, h. 10, a. 1 (LXXVI, 886 C).

177. *De script.*, c. 5 (CLXXV, 14 A).

178. "sublimius": Migne: "subtilius."

179. "Sed jam qui in ostio speluncae consistit et verba Dei in aure cordis percipit, necesse est ut faciem velet, quia dum per supernam gratiam ad altiora intelligenda ducimur, quanto sublimius levamur, tanto semper per humilitatem nosmetipsos in intellectu nostro premere debemus, ne conemur plus sapere quam oportet sapere, sed sapere ad sobrietatem; ne dum nimis invisibilia discutimus,

aberremus; ne in illa natura incorporea corporei luminis aliquid quaeramus": *In Ez.*, l. 2, h. 1, n. 18 (LXXVI, 948 AB).

180. See above, the first several pages of 4.2.

181. "Intellectus sacri eloquii inter textum et mysterium tanta est libratione pensandus, ut utriusque partis lance moderata, nunc neque nimiae discussionis pondus deprimat, neque rursus torpor incuriae vacuum relinquat. Multae quippe ejus sententiae tanta allegoriarum conceptione sunt gravidae, ut quisquis eas ad solam tenere historiam nititur, earum notitia per suam incuriam privetur. Nonnullae vero ita exterioribus praeceptis inserviunt, ut is qui eas subtilius penetrare desiderat, intus quidem nihil inveniat, sed hoc sibi etiam quod foris loquuntur abscondat": *Mor.*, l. 21, c. 1, n. 1 (LXXVI, 187 B).

182. N. 3: "For some frequently fall into a carnal understanding while they are trying to crack open the words of sacred speech more than they ought.... Hence it is necessary for us to scrutinize the works of blessed Job ... according to the weight of their history, lest if the mind should investigate them spiritually more than is necessary, blood should meet us from the udders of its speech instead of milk" — "Plerumque etenim quidam, dum verba sacri eloquii plus quam debent discutient, in carnalem intellectum cadunt.... Unde necesse est ut beati Job opera ... juxta pondus historiae perscrutemur, ne si haec animus plus quam necesse est spiritaliter investiget, a verborum ejus uberibus sanguis nobis pro lacte respondeat" (188-9).

183. *Ep. anon.*: "The whole sequence of the Bible ought first to be scrutinized thoroughly and gone through according to the history three or four times" — "Universa autem sacrae paginae series secundum historiam primo, ter aut quater perscrutanda et pertranseunda" (CCXIII, 715 A).

184. *The Study*, 95: "Hugh is criticizing the Gregorian tradition with its sublime disregard for the letter of Scripture."

185. "Legisse me novi in his libris latissimam et inextricabilem tropologiam.... Quod si quando voluerint altius quippiam sapere, et nimio labore sudantes de Scripturis sanctis mysticum aliquid invenire: nihilominus fruges non afferant doctrinae, sed vepribus compleantur et spinis, quae oriuntur in manibus ebrii": L. 3, c. 8 (PL, XXIV, 113-4).

186. The Origen of Rufinus also knows the other verb, "perscrutari"; but he employs it for the spiritual sense, following 1 Cor. 2:10: *In Gen.*, h. 12, n. 1 (1097); *In Num.*, h. 12, n. 2 (99).

187. "Observet diligentius qui legit litteras divinas, et non ut libet Scripturae verba pertranseat": *In Num.*, h. 11, n. 7 (89).

188. To him also one goes back for the closely related image, not of milk but of water changed into blood: *In Ex.*, h. 4, n. 6 and 8 (178 and 180). But the application of the first plague of Egypt made here by Origen, has been reversed in the sequel. For him, the change of water into blood was the effect of the cross of Christ; the water of error and of lubricity was finally found "converted" to the blood of the two Testaments. On the contrary, the later tradition brings the sense of the second image into alignment with that of the first. Garnier, s. 15: "The first plague, water turned into blood. Now to turn water into blood is to change spiritual into carnal doctrine. Those who change the glory of the incorruptible God into the likeness of corruptible man have turned water into blood" — "Prima plaga, aqua

Notes to Pages 236-37

in sanguinem versa. Aquam autem in sanguinem vertere, est doctrinam spiritualem in carnalem mutare. Aquam in sanguinem verterunt, qui commutarunt gloriam incorruptibilis Dei in similitudinem corruptibilis hominis" (PL, CCV, 670 AB). The evolution takes place in stages. Beatus, *In Ap.*, l. 2, c. 2 (157) is less far from Origen.

189. *In Matt.*, 1.8, c. 18, on the parable of the talents: "There is such a lot of difficulty in the matters that are being proposed, that Origen confesses . . . that no one can understand the text of this parable clearly and . . . he says as much: 'I truly confess that no one can explain this but Christ alone, who secretly resolved all things for his disciples . . . , or perhaps one whom he wanted to illuminate with light of his knowledge. . . . For this is the work of the wisdom of God, let me say, to discuss all these things" — "Talia tantaque difficultas est in his rebus quae proponuntur, ut confiteatur Origenes . . . neminem hujus parabolae textum ad liquidum intelligere posse et . . . ait ita: 'Vere confiteor neminem hanc exponere posse, nisi solum Christum, qui discipulis suis omnia secrete solvit . . . , aut forte eum quem voluerit illuminare lumine scientiae suae. . . . Est enim sapientiae Dei hoc opus, ut ita dicam, ea omnia disserere.' Quapropter perpendat fidelis animus, quanta difficultas in his esse possit, ubi magister Ecclesiae illius temporis tam divina sensit et eximia. Licet etc." (PL, CXX, 629-30). Cf. Or., *In Matt.*, t. 14, c. 6 (287); t. 14, c. 30-1 (440-5).

190. *The Study*, 230. On the contrary, see R. Loewe, *St. patr.*, 1, 504: "the deep-seated contrast between the literal and the three spiritual senses that became traditional in the Church, particularly as the heritage of Gregory."

191. "Nunc demum a principio rursus ingrediamur cum historica demonstratione; situmque prosequamur spiritualis intelligentiae": *In Ex.*, l. 4, c. 9 (PL, CLXVII, 708 D). Or Gerhoh, *In ps.* xxxiii: "It is permissible to repeat that [title of the psalm] more extensively, expounding it a second time, first according to the historical sense, then according to the mystical sense" — "Libet, iterata expositione latius illum (titulum psalmi) replicare, primo secundum sensum historicum, deinde secundum sensum mysticum" (V. den Eynde, 154).

192. "quod lex non tantum historice, sed etiam spiritualiter sentienda sit": L. 5, c. 4 (CLXXVI, 791 D).

193. "dum historicae veritatis et spiritalis sensus non consideratur differentia": *De haeres.* (Vega, 26).

194. "Prius enim paulatim historiam continuando hic tangere decrevimus; ut postmodum quid mystice contineat, indagando propalemus. Jam enim quod secundum historiam ista significent inculcavimus. Caeterum, quantum ad altiorem intelligentiam pertinet. . . . Ecce historiam tetigimus; sed quid spiritaliter significet, breviter indagemus": *In Reg.*, l. 2 (PL, CXV, 371 D, 372 D). Again: "Since . . . we have divulged the history, we then go on in summary fashion to touch on what it signifies allegorically" — "Quia historiam . . . propalavimus, deinceps compendioso sermone strictim tangere aggredimur quid allegorice significet" (348 A).

195. "Quantum ad simplicem historiam pertinet . . . Quantum ad typicos pertinet intellectus": *In Reg.*, l. 3 (398 B). Cf. Rabanus, *In Ez.*, l. 18: "Meanwhile let it be enough to have gathered this sense and to have heard this according to the letter and the truth of the Hebrew. Let us now turn back to the spiritual under-

standing" — "Haec interim juxta litteram et juxta hebraicam veritatem et sensisse et audisse sufficiat. Nunc revertamur ad intelligentiam spiritualem" (following Jerome; CX, 1028 A). Alcuin (C, 669 C). Bruno of Segni (CLXV, 590 AB); etc.

196. "Librum beati Job ... quo modo juxta litteram intelligendus, qualiter ad Christi et Ecclesiae sacramenta referendus, quo sensu unicuique fidelium sit aptandus, per trifarias intelligendi species miranda ratione perdocuit": *Vita s. Greg.*, l. 1, c. 17 (LXXV, 491 B); a eulogy taken up again by Bede, *H. eccl.*, c. 1 (492 D).

197. C. 61, n. 3.

198. *The Study*, 95; cf. 41, where the spiritual sense is a "subjective" sense. Compare Hugh, *In Thren.* (CLXXV, 296-7) and Paschasius (CXX, 1132).

199. "quantum ad litteram spectat"; "secundum allegoriae sensum"; "secundum intellectum moralem": *In Thren.*, 1 (CLXXV, 255 D, 257 B, 258 A), etc. This has been shown by Ford Lewis Battles, "Hugo of Saint Victor as a Moral Allegorist," *Church History*, 18 (1949), 231-2.

200. "Prophetia praecedens istud canticum diligenter inspecta, et non solum historialiter, sed etiam spiritaliter intellecta, pandit materiam et sensum totius cantici hujus": *In Cant. Is.* (PL, CXCIV, 997 C).

201. *Ib.* (998 C).

202. "magnificentius vero impleta sunt in Christo": *In Cant. Ez.* (1006 D).

203. *In ps.* ix (CXCIII, 758 D, 759 B). Bernard is concerned about analogous distinctions. S. Grill, S.O.C., *Bernhard von Cl. als Exeget* (1953); cf. BTAM, 7, 82-3.

204. PL, CLXXVI, 617-80. L. 1, c. 3: "Those who desire more carefully to investigate the truth of these things that are related about Noah's ark according to the letter ought to inquire chiefly about two points, namely, the shape and the quantity of the ark. As to the shape, Origen speaks as follows . . ." — "Qui studiosius indagare cupiunt earum rerum veritatem, quae de arca Noe secundum litteram referuntur, duo praecipue inquirere debent, vid. formam et quantitatem arcae. Et de forma quidem sic dicit Origines . . ." (627).

205. "cui sententiae . . . plura refragari videntur"; "First off, that this shape does not seem suitable to float" — "Primum, quod haec forma ad natandum non videtur esse idonea" (627 A).

206. *De arca myst.*, c. 1 (CLXXVI, 681 AC). V. *infra*, p. 324.

207. *The Study*, 96-7.

208. It does not seem, however, that Hugh proposes an unheard of solution here. In his brief Notes on Genesis, he said without taking sides: "There are various opinions about the composition of the ark, whether it was broad at the bottom and rose ever narrower toward the top, or whether the sides rose evenly at the top, or even more further apart than at the bottom and had been pointed only on the roof" — "De compositione arcae, utrum in imo lata fuerit et semper usque ad summum surgens stringeretur magis ac magis, an parietes surrexerint aequaliter in summo, vel etiam plus quam in imo a se distantes, et in tecto tantum fuerit cacuminata, diversae sunt opiniones" (CLXXV, 46-7).

209. *De arca morali*, l. 1, c. 3 (PL, CLXXVI, 627 A).

210. *In Gen.*, h. 2, n. 1-2 (SC, 7, 90-6). *C. Cels.*, l. 4, c. 41 (1, 314-5).

211. *Civ. Dei*, 1, 15, c. 26-7 (PL, XLI, 472-6). Cf. *C. Faust.*, l. 12, c. 16 (XLII, 263).

212. L. 1, c. 5-6; 7th cent. (XXXV, 2156-7).

213. See above, vol. 2, ch. 7. Bede, *Hexaem.*, l. 2 (XCI, 91-2). Claudius, *In Gen.*:

"But if we think that Origen rather elegantly added . . ." — "Si autem cogitemus quod Origenes non ineleganter astruxit . . ." (L, 927 B). Freculph, *Chronicon,* t. 1, l. 1, c. 21: "There were some who thought it impossible, etc. Those who do not attend [to the fact that] Moses had been educated in every Egyptian science, etc." — "Fuerunt nonnulli impossibile putantes etc. Qui non attendunt Moysen in omni Aegyptiaca eruditum sapientia etc." (CVI, 930 BD). *Lib. de numeris,* 8, 1 (R. E. McNally, 127-32). Angelome, *In Gen.:* "On this matter, read Origen arguing against Apelles" — "Lege Origenem super hac re contra Apellem disputantem" (CXV, 158 A); etc.

214. *In Gen.,* vi (CXIII, 106-8).

215. *De arca mor.,* l. 1, c. 3: "But the doctors solve this question using the following argument" — "Quam quaestionem doctores hac ratione solvunt" (CLXXVI, 628 A).

216. *Ib.:* "There are others who say that there were only three mansions in the ark etc." — Sunt alii qui dicunt in arca non fuisse nisi tres mansiones etc." (629 C). On these two interpretations: Angelome (CXV, 156-7).

217. *Ib.:* "You will find many other things in these triangles and squares pertaining to the subtlety of the geometric discipline, but we turn them down owing to distaste" for that sort of thing — "In trigonis his et tetragonis multa alia invenies ad subtilitatem geometricae disciplinae pertinentia, quae omnia nos propter fastidium declinamus" (629 C).

218. L. 1, c. 2: "But we have undertaken to speak specifically about the ark of wisdom, and so we shall run through the exposition of the other three briefly, so that we may later be able to spend our time more freely in explaining this point" — "Nos tamen specialiter de arca sapientiae loqui suscepimus, et idcirco reliquarum trium expositionem breviter transcurremus, ut in explanatione hujus postmodum liberius morari valeamus" (626 D).

219. For example, John Buteo, or Matthew Hostus (in *Critic. sacr.,* t. 8, Londini, 1660, col. 83-112). Or Jean Le Pelletier, *Dissertation sur l'Arche de Noé* (Ropuen, 1700). Just one ark for so many animals, and with just one window: the author asks himself how could this be enough; then he bethinks himself that "without doing violence to Scripture" — "sans faire violence à l'Écriture" — one can suppose that there was a window a cubit high at a higher level, running all around the ship. The *Mémoires de Trévoux* of May to June 1701, p. 11, approve this ingenious solution.

220. L. 1, c. 3: "The author does not say how tall the walls themselves were, but nevertheless we can conjecture how big" — "Cujus autem altitudinis fuerint parietes ipsi, hoc auctoritas non dicit, sed tamen quantum conjicimus" (627 B).

221. L. 1, c. 3 and 4 (629 CD, 631 CD).

222. "per meritum ascendimus, sed per praesentiam contemplationis ad ipsum (Deum) non inclinimur": C. 4 (631). *De van. mundi,* l. 2 (717 A). Those who favored the pyramidical shape saw the Church in it, rising from the very large base of the Law of the Patriarchs, through Moses, the Prophets and the Gospel, right up to the summit, which is Christ: thus, Beatus, *In Ap.,* l. 2, c. 3 (227-8); cf. l. 2, prol. (134). Angelome (CXV, 156 CD).

223. *In Num.,* h. 21, n. 2 (201).

224. *Ib.* (633 BC).

225. "Primum ad mysticam arcae Noe descriptionem in planitie ubi arcam depingere volo, medium centrum quaero, et ibi fixo puncto parvam quadraturam aequilateram ad similitudinem illius cubiti in quo consummata est arca, ei circumduco. Itemque illi quadraturae aliam paulo majorem circumscribo. . . . In interiori quadratura crucem pingo. . . . Deinde spatia illa, quae in superficie quadraturae inter quatuor angulos crucis et quadraturae remanent, colore vestio, duo superiora flammeo, et duo inferiora sapphirino. . . . Deinde spatium limbi circumquaque purpureo et viridi colore induo, exterius purpureo, et interius viridi, et in medio crucis aureae, quam feceram, agnum anniculum stantem pingo, etc.": *De arca myst.*, c. 1 (CLXXVI, 681 AC).

226. "In ipsa fronte arcae facio parvam quadraturam, ad figurandas quatuor partes mundi": C. 4-11 (686-98).

227. C. 7: "To signify the history we have put the color green; for the tropology, yellow; for the allegory, blue" — "Nos ad significandam historiam viridem colorem posuimus, ad tropologiam croceum, ad allegoriam caeruleum" (695 B). C. 5, the three colors "viridis, croceus, purpureus" distinguish the laws (690-1), etc.

228. *De van. mundi*, l. 1, on a group of schoolboys: "they are drawing figures of various types and diverse colors on pieces of parchment with a learned hand guiding their pen" — "figuras variis modis et diversis coloribus in membranis docta manu calamum ducente designant" (CLXXVI, 709 D).

229. C. 1: "The ark was three hundred cubits long . . . ; but to get a more fitting form in the picture I have shortened the length almost fourfold" — "Arca trecentos cubitos in longitudine habuit . . . ; ego tamen propter competentiorem formam in pictura usque ad quadruplam fere longitudinem breviavi" (682 BC).

230. C. 13, *De sex mansiunculis arcae ad litteram:* "Scripture does not tell the number of these receptacles. But . . . following the example of the six cities that were established as refuges for homicide . . . we have put down six cabins in the ark in this manner" — "Horum receptaculorum numerum Scriptura non dicit. Nos tamen ad similitudinem sex civitatum quae homicidii in refugium deputatae sunt . . . sex mansiunculas in arca disposuimus hoc modo" (699 A).

231. Cf. the imaginative descriptions of the *De van. mundi*, l. 1: "Climb up and look with me and I shall show you great marvels" — "Ascende, et aspice mecum, et ostendam tibi mirabilia magna" (703 BC).

232. *Did.*, l. 7, c. 12 (820-1).

233. C. 1: "And what else does the picture show you than if it were to say . . ." — "Et pictura quid tibi ostendit aliud, quam si diceret . . ." (692 A).

234. *In Hier. cael.*, l. 10 (CLXXV, 1137 C).

235. *In Eccl.*, h. 19 (141 CD).

236. "De quibus gradibus et picturis atque colorum varietatibus, hoc lectori summopere sciendum est, quod in illo visibili Moysi tabernaculo, omnino quidem non fuerit": *Ep.*, c. 10 (CXCVIII, 634 AB).

237. Compare with Ambrose, *De Noe et arca*.

238. Baron, xviii and xx.

239. "De arca (or: triplici arca) Noe pro arca sapientiae cum arca ecclesiae et arca matris gratiae": *De arca mor.*, l. 1, c. 2 (CLXXVI, 262 BD). However, Hugh mentions his plan to pause especially at the moral ark (*ib.*).

Notes to Pages 243-44

240. "De hac, et ad hanc, et propter hanc omnis Scriptura facta est. Propter hanc Verbum caro factum est, Deus humilis, homo sublimis. Si hanc ergo habes, totum habes; si totum habes nihil est amplius, quod exspectes, et requiescit cor tuum.

"Hujus vero spiritualis aedificii exemplar tibi dabo arcam Noe, quam foris videbit oculus tuus, ut ad ejus similitudinem intus fabricetur animus tuus. Videbis ibi colores quosdam, formas et figuras, quae delectent visum. Sed scire debes, ideo haec posita esse, ut in eis discas sapientiam, disciplinam atque virtutem quae exornent animum tuum. Et quia haec arca Ecclesiam significat, Ecclesia autem corpus Christi est, ut evidentius exemplar tibi fiat, totam personam Christi, id est caput cum membris, in forma visibili depinxi, etc.": *De arca mor.*, l. 1, c. 2 (622 BC). There are four arks that correspond to each other: "e quibus duae visibiles . . . , duae autem invisibiles. . . . Prima est in re, secunda in fide, tertia in cognitione, quarta in virtute. Primam vocemus arcam Noe, secundam arcam Ecclesiae, tertiam arcam sapientiae, quartam arcam matris gratiae. . . . Nos tamen specialiter de arca sapientiae loqui suscepimus, etc." (626 BD). Hugh exploits the image of the ark again in the *De vanitate mundi* (719-20). Garnier, s. 40, will distinguish in the same way a multiple ark of the covenant (but its subdivisions will be different: CCV, 827 AB).

241. "Quae est ergo haec arca, de qua tam multa dicuntur, et in qua tam multiplices viae scientiarum continentur? Numquid putas est labyrinthus? Non labyrinthus, nec labor intus, sed requies intus. Unde hoc scio? Quia ille in ea habitat, qui dicebat: 'Venite ad me, omnes qui laboratis et onerati estis, et ego reficiam vos, et invenietis requiem animabus vestris.' . . . Qualis ergo est haec arca? . . . Similis est apothecae omnium deliciarum varietate refertae. Nihil in ea quaesieris quod non invenias, et cum inveneris unum, multa tibi patefacta videbis. Ibi universa opera restaurationis nostrae a principio mundi usque ad finem plenissime continentur. . . . Ibi quid credere, quid agere, quid sperare debeamus ostenditur. Ibi forma vitae hominis et summa perfectionis continetur. . . . Ibi quoddam universitatis corpus effingitur, et concordia singulorum explicatur. . . . Ibi praeteritis praesentia non succedunt, etc.": L. 4, c. 9 (CLXXVI, 679-80). Cf. the gloss on the *Poetic Art* of Evrard the German: "'laborinth', as if holding labor in it" — "laborintus, quasi laborem habens intus" (Faral, 38). Agobard: "lest . . . a labyrinth of error be woven from the Scripture of truth" — "ne . . . de Scriptura veritatis labyrinthus texatur erroris" (PL, CIV, 331 C). Rathier of Verona, *Praeloquia:* "Labyrinthus Scripturarum" (CXXXVI, 339 B). *Life* of Lietbert of Cambrai (Lesne, 5, 585).

242. L. 1, c. 2 (624 BC).

243. Smalley, *The Study*, 88. Nor does it seem any more correct to say that, contrary to the Alexandrian terminology, which confused under the same name 'history' both the facts themselves and the literal sense, or the content and its commentary (on that point, see above, vol. 2, ch. 10.5), Hugh distinguishes them, if only to return to current usage by way of concession later on. The text cited here means something quite different. It says that one can call the primary sense of all the books of the Bible by the name 'history' whether these books be properly historical or not. Miss Smalley writes: "He says that 'history' means either *historical events* or the primary meanings of the words"; Hugh wrote: "But if we use the

meaning of this word ['history'] in a broader sense, that is no problem, e.g., so that we say not only is an *account of deeds accomplished* a 'history', but so also is the main point of any account that is expressed using the normal sense of the words" — "Si tamen hujus vocabuli (historiae) significatione longius utimur, nullum est inconveniens, ut sc. 'historiam' esse dicamus, non tantum *rerum gestarum narrationem,* sed illam primam significationem cujuslibet narrationis, quae secundum proprietatem verborum exprimitur" (CLXXVI, 801 A). The emphasis is ours.

244. "relèvent de l'allégorie plus que de la philologie": AHDLMA, 14, 266.

245. Smalley, 89: "Hugh effected a differentiation between the three senses, which enormously increased the dignity of the historical sense. Instead of contrasting the lowly foundation of the 'letter' with the higher spiritual senses, he groups together the letter and allegory, which pertain to knowledge and contrasts them with tropology! The importance of the letter is constantly stressed."

246. The recommendation of G. Bardy, *La théologie de l'Église,* 2, 162, note 4, is still timely: "One must protect himself from opposing, as is too often done, allegory to history": "Il faut se garder d'opposer, comme on l'a fait trop souvent, l'allégorie à l'histoire."

247. "Magna[e] sunt in Scripturis sacris spiritualium sensuum profunditates": *De sacram.,* l. 2, prol. (CLXXVI, 363-4).

248. "Multa in his omnibus latent sacramenta": *Ib.,* l. 2, p. 5, c. 3 (441 A); cf. c. 1: "And so we are setting down first the form of this mystery that is exhibited in the dedication of a Church, so that we may then search out the mystical understanding of the faith that is formed within it" — "Hujus itaque sacramenti quod in dedicatione Ecclesiae exhibetur, formam primum proponimus, ut deinde mysticam intelligentiam fidei quae in illo formatur exquiramus" (439 C).

249. "Per quam multa sunt alia quae . . . mystica dici potuerunt": L. 1, c. 1 (203 D); "I think that a great mystery is deposited here" — "Ego puto magnum hic aliquod sacramentum commendari" (195 C); "There are great mysteries in all this" — "Magna sunt in his omnibus sacramenta" (202 A).

250. "avec une particulière ferveur": "Une ecclésiol. médiévale," *Irenikon,* 22 (1949), 122.

251. "Hugo of Saint-Victor as a Moral Allegorist," *Church History,* 18 (1949), 220; 223, note: "Hugo draws freely upon the allegorical traditions which Gregory had helped to form, and leans far more on the mystical senses than upon the literal meaning of Scripture."

252. "prédilection exagérée pour l'allégorie": *L'essor,* 1, 219.

253. "indiscretionis stultitia": *In Ex.,* l. 1 (PL, CX, 510-1).

254. "Maximam hanc in Scripturis divinis difficultatem invenio: quod, ubi magna quaedam et sublimia nonnunquam requirere nos causa circumstans cogit, ibi nihil praeter solitum et quod dictu non difficile sit, praetendere littera videatur. Neque enim hoc ego tam laboriosum existimo, ut animus legentis ad ea quae nova et miranda proponuntur, quamlibet sint fortia, et verborum figuris obumbrata, comprehendere valeat, quam ut ea quae modica et humilia primo ingressu reperit, ad sublimem intelligentiam promoveat."

"Ecce enim Canticum Mariae, quod tam celebri et assidua, imo quotidiana recitatione sancta per orbem frequentat Ecclesia, quis ignoret maxima spiritualis intelligentiae mysteria continere? . . . Quis dubitet beatam Mariam, recens Spiritus sancti in se supervenientis tanta plenitudine et gratia repletam, non potuisse parvum aliquid, et quod supra terrenarum mentium capacitatem non esset, in laudem Salvatoris sui proferre? . . ."

"Et tamen ipsam ejus cantici seriem, textumque percurrentes, quaedam prima facie narrationis eo modo proposita invenimus, ut amplius his nihil in eo quaerendum videatur: cum tamen, licet haec ipsa et vera sint, tantis mysteriis tantisque sacramentis an forte sufficiant, dubitari possit. Unde, magis pertimesco in ejus expositione ne vel aliena inducam aliqua, vel propria praetermittam; et sic, vel negligentiae, vel temeritatis reatu astrictus pro gratia apud vos offensae periculum incurram . . .": *Expl. in Cant. B. M.*, prol. (CLXXV, 413-8). Some doubts have been raised about the authenticity of this *Explanatio;* but Ph. Delhaye (ET, 7), R. Baron (p. xxviii), Father H. Weisweiler (*Scholastik*, 20-4, 1949), and Father Damien Van den Eynde (1960) regard it as certain.

255. *La Bible au XVIe s.*

256. *La vie et les œuvres de Guiard de Laon*, 165.

257. *Die patristische und scholastische Philosophie* (1928), 267-9; cited by Smalley, 86, note 4. In his chapter on the mystical numbers, *De scripturis*, c. 15, Hugh scarcely mentions the "quaternarius" or tetrad (PL, CLXXV, 22-3).

258. *De arca Noe morali*, passim, etc.

259. These are extracts of his biblical commentaries. Cf. O. Lottin, RTAM, 25 (1958), 280.

260. *Did.*, l. 3, c. 8 and 11; l. 5, c. 10; l. 2, c. 13 (PL, CLXXVI, 771 C, 772 C, 798, 756 B). *In Eccl.*, 4, 1 (CLXXV, 166 D, 118 B); etc.

261. L. 1, tit. 10: *De trinitate universitatis* (CLXXV, 483 CD). L. 2, c. 73: *Abscondenda quomodo sint eloquia Domini* [*How the words of the Lord are to be hidden*] (629-30). The *De contemplatione* which is strictly dependent upon Hugh is practically a cascade woven from these triads.

262. *Hom.*, 1 (CLXXV, 118-22). An analogous procedure, *In Hier.*, l. 1, c. 1 (927-8).

263. "allegoria subdividitur in simplicem allegoriam et anagogen": *De script.*, c. 3 (CLXXV, 12 B). In Lawrence's *Reportatio:* "Simple allegory is one thing, what is called anagogy is something else" — "Alia simplex allegoria, alia est quae dicitur anagoge"; the explication given next with examples is however not entirely the common explication (O. Lottin, RTAM, 25, 276). See above, vol. 1, ch. 1; and Robert of Melun (Ch. II, t. I, 140).

264. "Super haec ante omnia divinum illud est ad quod ducit divina Scriptura sive in allegoria sive in tropologia": *De sacram.*, prol., c. 6 (CLXXVI, 185 D). Cf. Lasic, 368-9: when anagogy is not treated separately, it is for Hugh "a higher part or end both of allegory and of tropology" — "quaedam superior pars vel finis tam allegoriae quam tropologiae." Gerard of Bologna, *Summa*, q. 11, a. 1, gives two explications of texts from Hugh (Paul de Booght, *Les sources de la doctrine*, 429).

265. H. Weisweiler, *Mél. de Ghellinck* (1951), 335-80.

266. Above, vol. 1, ch. 2.2. There is perhaps an equivalent of anagogy *In Joel:* "There are three kinds of doctrine: contemplative, allegorical, moral" — "Tria sunt genera doctrinae, contemplativum, allegoricum, morale" (CLXXV, 368 D);

or, 359 D, it seems that "anagoge" designates the whole of the spiritual senses, subdivided into "tropologia" and "allegoria": "This passage is very difficult from an anagogical standpoint" — "Locus hic juxta anagogen difficillimus est." But this commentary ought to be restored to Richard.

267. C. 17: "That part [of the intellectual life], however, that is involved in the investigation of the divine utterances, seems fourfold: one part is the history, one allegory, another tropology, another anagoge" — "Illa vero pars (intellectualis vitae) quae in divinorum eloquiorum inquisitione versatur, quadrimoda videtur: alia pars est historia, quaedam allegoria, alia tropologia, alia anagoge" (Hauréau, 196). "Science pertains to earthly things, wisdom to the divine, intelligence to both; or else science pertains to the history, wisdom to anagogy or allegory, and intelligence to tropology" — "Scientia pertinet ad terrena, sapientia ad divina, ad utraque intelligentia; vel scientia pertinet ad historiam, sapientia ad anagogen vel allegoriam, intelligentia ad tropologiam" (Baron, 58). Cf. D. Lasic, OFN: "Hugo de SV auctor operis 'De contemplatione et ejus speciebus,'" *Antonianum*, 18 (1953), 377-88.

268. *Supra*, introduction. In a manuscript cited by Dom Lottin (RTAM, 25, 275), the classic division of the four "regulae": history, allegory, tropology and anagogy is found next to a text attributed to Hugh.

269. PL, CLXXV, 51 BC. Smalley, 100: "Which of Hugh's contemporaries could have commented on the Melchizedek episode without explaining it as a 'type' of the Eucharist?"

270. "per istam historicam narrationem ad altiorum rerum intelligentiam provehimur"; "scilicet, veritas rerum gestarum et forma verborum": *Notulae in Gen.*, c. 3 (33 A).

271. *Notulae in Jud.* (87 A).

272. "universam divinarum Scripturarum seriem . . . exponendo, profunditatis ejus arcana in lucem evocare": *De sacram.*, l. 1, P. 1, init. (CLXXVI, 187 A).

273. *In cael. Hier.*, l. 9: "signifying the future, when either Melchizedek himself will later convert some of the gentiles to God on his own, or else Christ, of whom he was the type, led forth not only some of Israel but also all the gentiles . . . from the shadows of faithlessness" — "futurum significans, quando vel ipse Melchisedech postea per se ex gentibus ad Deum convertit, vel Christus, cujus ille typus erat, non solum ex Israel sed etiam ex omnibus gentibus . . . de tenebris infidelitatis eduxit" (CLXXV, 1095 D).

274. "fundamentum bonum"; "super-aedificare": *De trib. max. circumst. gestorum:* "So there are three features on which knowledge of the deeds done chiefly depends: i.e., the persons . . . , the places, . . . and the times. . . . Whoever remembers these three will find that he has a good foundation, upon which through reading he will later build whatever he will easily and quickly grasp and long retain" — "Tria igitur sunt in quibus praecipue cognitio pendet rerum gestarum: id est, personae . . . , loca . . . et tempora. . . . Haec tria quisquis memoriter animo tenuerit, inveniet se fundamentum habere bonum, cui quicquid per lectionem postea superaedificaverit, sine difficultate et cito capiet et diu retinebit" (W. M. Green, *Speculum*, 18, 491).

275. "Primum quidem fundamentum ponitur, dehinc fabrica super-aedificatur, ad ultimum . . . domus superducto colore vestitur": *Didasc.*, l. 6, c. 2

Notes to Page 249

(176, 799 B); c. 3: "Do not hold these tiny things in contempt. Those who despise the tiny details keep failing a bit at a time. If you had looked down upon learning the alphabet at the start, you would not now have so great a reputation among literary men" — "Noli contemnere minima haec. Paulatim deficiunt, qui minima contemnunt. Si primo alphabetum discere contempsisses, nunc inter grammaticos tantum nomen non haberes" (799 C).

276. *In Jo.*, l. 1, c. 18, commenting on Heb. 5:12 (20).

277. "lac primae eruditionis": *In Cant.*, l. 6 (PL, XCI, 1197 C).

278. "Ordine incede: per umbram venitur ad corpus; figuram disce, et invenies veritatem": Here note this remark: "I am not saying this now so that you should struggle at untangling the figures of the Old Testament before you go on to drink of the things flowing forth from the Gospel. Rather . . ." — "Nec hoc nunc dico, ut prius Veteris Testamenti figuras labores evolvere, et mystica ejus dicta scruteris, quam ad Evangelii fluenta potenda accedas. Sed. . . ." An important remark. For the Christian, the New Testament, the Gospel, is always first. But as to the Old Testament, it is no less necessary to know the history in itself, to see subsequently from it the spiritual signification which matches it with the New and permits a deepening of a knowledge of the New Testament itself.

279. "Sicut vides, quod omnis aedificatio fundamento carens stabilis esse non potest, sic est etiam in doctrina. Fundamentum autem et principium doctrinae sacrae historia est, de qua quasi mel de favo veritas allegoriae exprimitur. Aedificaturus ergo primum fundamentum historiae pone; deinde, per significationem typicam in arcem fidei fabricam mentis erige: ad extremum ergo per moralitatis gratiam quasi pulcherrimo superducto colore aedificium pinge. Habes in historia quo Dei facta mireris; in allegoria, quo ejus sacramenta credas; in moralitate, quo perfectionem ipsius imiteris": *Did.*, l. 6, c. 3 (CLXXVI, 801 CD). In the same way, the *Ep. anon.* (*loc. cit.*): after the care devoted to the history, "the careful mind . . . undauntedly turns both to the allegorical and the moral reading" — "diligens animus . . . intrepide tam ad allegoricam quam ad moralem lectionem se convertat. . . ."

280. See notably, vol. 2, ch. 7 above, the texts of Gregory and Guibert of Nogent. Again, *Ep. missoria*, c. 4: "and whilst he is laboriously striving to find some other esoteric [meaning] in those [words], he loses track of what he could attain on the surface without any difficulty" — "cumque laboriose invenire in eis (verbis) aliud intrinsecus appetit, hoc quod foris sine difficultate assequi poterat amittit" (SC, 32, 120).

281. L. 5, c. 2: "So too the quite pleasing honey in the comb. And whatever he seeks with greater effort is found through even greater desire" — "Sic et mel in favo gratius. Et quidquid majori exercitio quaeritur, majori etiam desiderio invenitur" (CLXXVI, 790 B). It is substantially a question of the same thing: the mystery hidden within the history; but the application is a bit different. Hugh here explains that if the mystery is contained within the history, it is not signified by all the details of that history; he again uses a comparison derived from Augustine to the same effect (see below, vol. 4, ch. 7). In the same sense, *De script.*, c. 4 (CLXXV, 12-3) and c. 5: "Read Scripture, then, and first learn diligently what it reports in bodily manner; for if you impress upon your studious mind the form of these things according to the sequence of the report put forth,

you will later suck in the sweetness of the spiritual understanding like [honey] from the comb, by meditating" — "Lege ergo Scripturam, et disce primum diligenter quae corporaliter narrat; si enim formam horum secundum seriem narrationis propositae studioso animo impresseris, quasi ex favo quodam postmodum meditando spiritualis intelligentiae dulcedinem fuges (= suges)" (15 A).

282. *In Is.*, h. 2, n. 2 (252).

283. "'Littera occidit, spiritus autem vivificat' (2 Cor. 3): quia nimirum oportet divinum lectorem (= divinorum lectorem?) spiritualis intelligentiae veritate esse solidatum, ut eum litterarum apices, quae et perverse nonnunquam intelligi possunt, ad quaelibet diverticula non inclinent. Quare antiquus ille populus, qui legem vitae acceperat, reprobatus est; nisi quia sic solam litteram occidentem secutus est, ut spiritum vivificantem non haberet? Haec vero non ideo ut quibuslibet ad voluntatem suam interpretandi Scripturas occasionem praebeam; sed ut ostendam eum qui solam sequitur litteram, diu sine errore non posse incedere": *Did.*, l. 6, c. 4 (CLXXVI, 804 CD).

284. "super fundamentum historiae spiritale aedificium extruere": Jerome, *In Is.*, l. 6, init. (XXIV, 205 C); l. 5, init. (153-4), etc. *Ep.*, 129, c. 6: "the truth of the history, which is the foundation of the spiritual understanding" — historiae veritatem, quae fundamentum est intelligentiae spiritalis" (Hilberg, 173).

285. Here we recognize his turn of mind and his detailed didacticism. For another example, cf. the explication of the three phases of the fire that symbolize the three phases of contemplation: *In Eccl.*, l. 1 (PL, CLXXV, 117-8).

286. "rotae animalia sequuntur, non animalia rotas"; "rotae hae animalia sequuntur, et sequuntur spiritum"; "Divina eloquia cum legente crescent": *Did.*, l. 6, c. 4 (CLXXVI, 802-4; 804 BC).

287. Greg., *In Ez.*, l. 1, c. 7, n. 8 (LXXVI, 843 CD); n. 9 (844 BC); etc. Compare, e.g., Guerric of Igny, *De adv. Dom.*, s. 4 (CLXXXV, 22 D).

288. *Did.*, l. 4, c. 14, with regard to Rufinus: "since blessed Jerome cited him in some matters regarding freedom of choice, we ought to accept those things that Jerome did in the same sense, too" — "quoniam b. Hieronymus in aliquibus eum de libertate arbitrii notavit, illa sentire debemus quae et Hieronymus" (CLXXVI, 787 A).

289. "doctor doctorum": *ep.* 143 (CXCIX, 126 C).

290. Thus, *Did.*, l. 4, c. 5: "The eighth is [the translation] of Jerome, which is deservedly preferred to the rest, for it is both verbally more accurate and clearer in making out the sense" — "Octava est (interpretatio) Hieronymi, quae merito caeteris antefertur, nam et verborum tenacior est, et perspicuitate sententiae clarior" (CLXXVI, 881 B). Isidore, and Rabanus, *Cler. inst.*, l. 2, c. 54 (CVII, 366 D).

291. "per universam latinitatem": *De scr.*, c. 9: "Jerome came by ... translating the language from Hebrew to Latin; and since his translation was found more to harmonize with the Hebraic truth, for that reason the Church of Christ decided that ... this [version] alone ahead of all the rest was to be read through the whole Latin world and to be held as authoritative" — "Hieronymus accessit ... de Hebraeo in Latinum transferens sermonem; cujus translatio, quia hebraicae veritati concordare magis probata est, idcirco Ecclesia Christi per universam latinitatem prae ceteris omnibus ... hanc solam legendam et in auctoritate

habendam constituit" (CLXXV, 17-8). If Hugh is fascinated by the "veritas hebraica" of Jerome, this does not constitute a distinctive feature: see above, ch. 3.4.

292. *Did.*, l. 4, c. 14: "Yet Augustine has surpassed the studies of all these by his wit or his knowledge. For he wrote so many things that one would scarcely be able [working] day and night just to copy down his books let alone to read them carefully" — "Horum tamen omnium studia Augustinus ingenio vel scientia sua vicit. Nam tanta scripsit ut diebus ac noctibus non solum scribere libros ejus quisquam, sed ne legere quidem accurate valeat" (CLXXVI, 786 D).

293. *Did.*, l. 5, ch. 6: "The education of morals rather looks back to the tropology. All divine Scripture is related to this end" — "Institutio morum ad tropologiam magis respicit. Omnis divina Scriptura refertur ad hunc finem" (794 B).

294. "institutio morum"; L. 5, c. 7: "Amongst the writings of blessed Gregory I hold [some] singularly to be embraced, [ones] that, since they have seemed to be sweeter than the rest and full of the love of eternal life, I do not want to pass over in silence" — "Inter quae beatissimi Gregorii singulariter scripta amplexanda existimo, quae quia mihi prae caeteris dulcia, et aeternae vitae amore plena visa sunt, nolo silentio praeterire" (794 D). *De van. mundi,* l. 4 (739 A). Father Chenu seems to minimize this testimony a bit when he says, 261, note 2, that Hugh takes "the traditional eulogy as his own" — "à son compte l'éloge traditionnel."

295. "Jusque dans le détail . . . sur les sens de l'Écriture découle en droite ligne des *Moralia* . . . avec le *Didascalicon*, avec le *De scripturis,* la méthode grégorienne devient bel et bien . . . l'herméneutique médiévale": *L'influence des Moralia,* 190-4 and 201-2.

296. *Spic. sol.,* 3 (1855), xxiii.

297. "Les deux âges de l'allégorisme," RTAM, 18 (1951), 25-6: for Rabanus, the "ponderous disciple of Bede" — "pesant disciple de Bède" — "the sciences of nature are becoming the preparatory field of study of Scripture, the foundation of typology, and not the history of the kingdom of God recorded in the sacred account" — "les sciences de la nature deviennent le champ préparatoire de l'étude de l'Écriture, fondement de la typologie, et non pas l'histoire du royaume de Dieu enregistrée dans le récit sacré." Still I do not see any such opposition in Rabanus.

298. *De triplici intelligentia sacrae Scr.* (PL, CLXXV, 11-2).

299. *Did.*, l. 2 (CLXXVI, 751-66). *De scr.,* c. 13: "The seven liberal arts subserve this science [of Scripture]. The trivium looks to the signification of words; the quadrivium, to the signification of things. Grammar, etc. Physical [science] teaches the inner natures of things; mathematics, the exterior shapes and numbers" — "Septem liberales artes huic scientiae (Scripturae) subserviunt. Trivium ad significationem vocum, quadrivium ad rerum significationem respicit. Grammatica etc. Physica interiores rerum naturas, mathematica exteriores figuras et numeros docet" (CLXXV, 20 C; history and geography, 25-8). Cf. *De sacram.,* prol.: "How all the arts subserve divine wisdom. . . . So allegory is contained under the sense concerned with the signification of things in reference to mystical things that have been done, and tropology is contained under the sense concerned with the significance of mystical things that are yet to be done; and arithmetic, music, geometry, and physics serve these two" — "Quomodo omnes artes

subserviunt divinae sapientiae.... Sub eo igitur sensu qui est in significatione rerum ad facta mystica continetur allegoria, et sub eo sensu qui est in significatione ad facienda mystica continetur tropologia; et his duobus famulantur arithmetica, musica, geometria, astronomia et physica" (CLXXVI, 185 CD).

300. Rabanus, PL, CVII, 755-6; CIX, 1127-8. Hugh: *De Scripturis,* c. 16-7 (CLXXV, 23-8). To tell the truth, Hugh scarcely envisages a symbolic geography: "The places signify, whence the Lord wanted certain affairs to be conducted in certain determinate places, owing to a signification" — "Loca significant, unde Dominus in certis et determinatis locis certa negotia geri voluit, propter significationem"; in the same way, "the times signify" — "tempora significant," "it signifies a gesture" — "gestum significat" (23 BD), as "the numbers signify" — "numeri significant" (22 A). One can hardly sum up a page like this by saying, with Miss Smalley, 87: that for "the literal historical sense ... [h]istorical and geographical aids to study will therefore be needed" — "Pour l'histoire, il faut étudier spécialment l'histoire et la géographie." Still, the *Didasc.,* l. 6, c. 3, *De historia,* does recommend inquiring "where the deed was done" — "ubi gestum sit" (CLXXVI, 799 B).

301. The *Cler. inst.* also depends on Gregory's *Cura pastoralis.*

302. "rerum naturas"; "verborum proprietates"; "mysticam significationem": *Ad Ludov. regem* (PL, CXI, 9 BC): "so that the diligent reader should find in this book both the proper character of the nature according to the history and also the spiritual signification according to the mystical sense laid down together" — "ut lector diligens in hoc opere et naturae proprietatem juxta historiam et spiritualem significationem juxta mysticum sensum simul posita inveniret" (10 A).

303. Leclercq, *L'amour des lettres,* 151: "The historical writings of Otto of Freising are domininated by grand theological objectives: the mystery of the epiphany, ... the sense of eschatology, the evocation of the heavenly Jerusalem and of the last judgment, the whole vocabulary of the martyrology holds a great place in it" — "Les écrits historiques d'Otton de Freising sont dominés par de grandes vues théologiques: le mystère de l'Épiphanie, ... le sens de l'eschatologie, l'évocation de la Jérusalem céleste et du Judgement dernier, tout le vocabulaire du martyrologe y occupent une grande place." Cf. the translation of Otto by Ch. Christ. Mierow (New York, 1928).

304. an "una et continua et perpetua locutio": *De div.,* s. 5, n. 1 (PL, CLXXXIII, 554 C).

305. Abelard, *De inst. inclusarum,* n. 32: "Whilst you were singing the psalms, did it not sometimes come about that you were illuminated by the brilliance of the spiritual senses?" — "Lorsque tu psalmodiais, que de fois n'est-il pas venu t'illuminer de la clarté des sens spirituels?" (Talbot, 212; cited by Amédée Hallier, *Un éducateur monastique,* Aelred de Rivaulx [1959]).

306. "symbolisme exemplariste dont les racines s'enfoncent simultanément dans le génie du platonisme grec et dans une authentique tradition biblique": Myrrha Lot-Borodine, *Nicolas Cabasilas* [1959]), 13.

307. L. 3 (*in Cant.,* ii, 9; 208-10).

308. Cf. René Roques, *Connaissance de Dieu et théologie symbolique d'après l'*In Hierarchiam cael. S. Dionysii *de Hugues de SV, in Recherches philos.* 3-4, *De la connaissance de Dieu,* especially 219 and 223-4. In a very Augustinian spirit, Hugh

rejects the "theophanies" of John Scotus: *In Hier.*, l. 2 (CLXXV, 954-5); cf. John Scot. (CXXII, 141 AB).

309. On the "cosmos symbolique du XIIe s." according to Honorius' *Clavis Physicae:* M.-Th. d'Alverny, AHDLMA, 20 (1953), 31-81.

310. Ch. Singer, *From Magic to Science* (1928), ch. 6, has called attention to Hildegarde's dependency with regard to Bernardus Sylvestris and a certain number of parallels with the *De arca mystica* (236-7).

311. *The Medieval Mind*, 2 (1911), 75. Cf. F. L. Battles, "Hugh of Saint-Victor as a Moral Allegorist," *Church History,* 18 (1949), 220-40, on the Neoplatonic tradition that he is connected with.

312. Let us also add that he, along with many others, cultivates the symbolism of names and numbers: *De amore sponsi* (CLXXVI, 990-4: Sin and Hermon); *De script.,* c. 15 (CLXXV, 22-3).

313. *Les deux âges,* 29. Cf. *Th. au XIIe s.,* 198-9 and 347.

314. An expression of G. Raynaud de Lage, regarding Alan of Lille and the Porretainians: *Alain de Lille* (1951), 70.

315. "c'est par une réaction vigoureuse en faveur de l'*historia* et de son irremplaçable valeur que se caractérise la vocation d'Hugues": M.-D. Chenu, *Conscience de l'histoire,* 113-8.

316. *Théologie au XIIe siècle,* 40: "milieu augustinien résistant."

317. The *De mundi universitate* of Bernardus Silvestris dates from around 1150. William of Conches, author of the *Glossses* on the *Timaeus,* died about 1154. Adelard's *Quaestiones naturales* would be a bit earlier (between 1130 and 1140?).

318. Chenu, 93-100: "désexistentialiser en quelque sorte les faits majeurs de la *dispensatio,* sous prétexte d'assurer, à travers le temps, l'unité de la foi et du salut."

319. The theory of the man from Chartres was laid out by John of Salisbury, *Metal.,* l. 3, c. 2 (Webb, 123-7), who here decides against his master. Regarding the same tendency in the *Anticlaudianus* of Alan of Lille, see Vincenzo Cilento (1957); but it is no doubt necessary to take account of the poetic character of the work.

320. *Sent.,* l. 1, d. 41, c. 7 (PL, CXCII, 635 C); cf. l. 3, c. 25, c. 1 (809 AB); l. 4, d. 1, c. 2 and 5 (639 D, 640 C); on each occasion, Augustine is cited. It is this lack of consistency on the part of the Lombard that permits Father Chenu, 93, to range him among the partisans of the absolute immutability of the faith across the ages, though Father Congar avers, *Le sens de l'économie salutaire, Festgabe Lortz* (1957), 100: "For Hugh, the 'sacraments' of the Old Testament drew a salvific value from their figurative aim; for the Lombard all the ceremonial works of the Law had no more than an assurance value and could not purify the conscience even if they were acccomplished with charity and devotion" — "Pour Hugues, les 'sacrements' de l'A.T. tiraient de leur visée figurative une valeur salutaire; pour le Lombard toutes les opera legis cérémonielles n'avaient qu'une valeur d'assurance et ne pouvaient purifier la conscience, même si elles étaient accomplies avec charité et dévotion." There is not a formal contradiction to be sure between these two positions of Lombard; they do indicate, however, two hard to reconcile orientations; an intermediate position is held in l. 3, d. 1, where faith and knowledge are distinguished.

321. Texts in Chenu, *Les deux âges*, 26; and *Girum caeli* (Leclercq, AHDLMA, 13, 217).

322. *Did.*, l. 5, c. 4 (PL, CLXXVI, 791-2).

323. "Hujus religionis sectandae caput est historia et dispensatio temporalis divinae providentiae, pro salute generis humani in aeternam vitam reformandi et reparandi": c. 7, n. 13 (42); c. 26, n. 48 (90). The Augustinian perspective is more or less modified by the very ones who maintain it or renew it; no one escapes from his own time. For Henry of Marcy (and Otto of Freising), cf. Yves M. J. Congar, "Église et Cité de Dieu chez quelques auteurs cisterciens à l'époque des Croisades," *Mélanges offerts à Etienne Gilson* (1959), 173-202.

324. "ordo rerum": *De util. cred.*, c. 3, n. 9 (228).

325. "ordinata series": *De fide rerum*, c. 5, n. 8 (332).

326. "ordo historiae": *In Num.*, h. 3, n. 3; h. 5, n. 1; h. 9, n. 5 (16, 26, 60). Cf. Rufinus, *De bened.*, l. 2: "let the order of the history be preserved fittingly here, too" — "etiam hic competenter historiae ordo servetur" (PL, XXI, 1319 A).

327. "historialis narrandi ordo"; "consequentia historialis intelligentiae": *In Reg.*, h. 2, n. 19 (PG, XII, 1014 B). *De princ.*, l. 4, c. 2, n. 5 and 9 (314, 322).

328. Likewise, Rabanus (PL, CVIII, 802 D, 811 C). Agobard: "Scripture searches into the ordered account of the things done" — "in illam ordinatam narrationem gestorum Scriptura exsequitur" (CIV, 101 B); etc.

329. "le trait caractéristique d'une histoire par opposition à la connexion logique des disciplines théoriques": Chenu, *Conscience de l'histoire*, 111.

330. *De div. quaest. 83*, q. 61, n. 7; qu. 66, n. 3 (Beckaert, 204-6, 240; cf. 740). *Ench.*, c. 118-9 (PL, 40, 287-8). *In Gal.*, n. 46 (35, 2138). Cf. H. Rondet, RSR (1939); *La nouv. Eve* (1955-6), 31. This formula about the four ages does not, as is sometimes said, come from the classical formula about the four ages of gold, silver, bronze, and iron, nor from the visions of the Book of Daniel; it reckons only three historical steps.

331. Berengard, *In Ap.* (PL, XVII, 861 AB). Sedulius Scotus, *In Rom.* (103, 41 D). Godfrey of Admont (CLXXIV, 63 C, 104 D, 234 D). Irimbert, *In Ruth* (Pez, 4, 460). *Altercatio* (J. Châtillon, RTAM, 23, 53). John Belethus, *Rat.*, c. 55 (PL, CCII, 60-1). Sicard of Cremona, *Mitrale*, l. 5 (CCXIII, 191); etc.

332. "ante legem, sub lege, sub gratia, in pace": *De sacram.*, l. 1, P. 11, c. 1 (CLXXVI, 343 B). *De sacr. legis nat. et scr.* (37-8). Cf. St. Thomas, 2a 2ae, q. 1, a. 7; q. 174, a. 6.

333. *Civ. Dei*, l. 22, c. 30, n. 5 (PL, XLI, 804); *C. Faust.*, l. 12, c. 8 (XLII, 257); *De Trin.*, l. 4, c. 7 (XLII, 892; concordance with the system of the four states); *De cat. rud.*, c. 22, n. 39 (117); *In Hept.*, l. 7, q. 49, n. 26 (XXXIV, 821); *Gen. Man.*, l. 1, c. 23, n. 15 (XXXIV, 190-3); *In Jo.*, tr. 9, n. 6; tr. 15, n. 9 (CCL, 36, 93, 153-4); *In ps.* xcii, n. 1 (39, 1291); *s.* 259, n. 2 (PL, XXXVIII, 1197-8).

334. Cassiodorus, *In ps.* xcii (PL, LXX, 661 BC). Isidore, *Q. Gen.*, c. 2 (LXXXIII, 213 AB); *Etym.*, l. 5, c. 38, n. 5 (LXXII, 223 BC). Beatus, *In Ap.* (327-31). Julian of Toledo, *De comput. aet. sextae* (XCVI, 581-4). Adon de Vienne, *Chron. de sex aet. mundi* (XCVIII, 23-138). Bede, *Hexaem.* (XCI, 36, 8). *In Marc.* (XCII, 217 B, 293 B); *ep.* 3 (CXIV, 670); h. 14 (CCL, 98-101). Ps.-Bede, (XCIII, 219-20). Freculph, *Chron.*, t. 2, l. 1, c. 2 (CVI, 1118 B). Rupert, *In Gen.* (CLXVII, 324); *In Jer.* (1363-5). Hervaeus, *In I Cor.* (CLXXXI, 913-4). Alselm of Havelberg, *Dial.*, l. 1, c. 3 (CLXXXVIII, 1145-6).

Adam Scotus, *De trip. tab.*, P. 2, c. 87 (CXCVIII, 324); Gerhoh, *Op. ined.*, 1, 102-3; etc. Richard gives the two divisions at once: *L. except.*, P. 1, l. 4, c. 1 (Châtillon, 129). The Ps.-Bede gives the two divisions at once: *L. except.*, P. 1, l. 4, c. 1 (Châtillon, 129). The Ps.-Bede, *In Jo.*, combines them ingeniously (XCII, 784-8 D). Cf. O. Rousseau, "Les Pères de l'Église et la théologie du temps" (Maison-Dieu, 30, 41-4). A. C. De Veer, "Les six ages" (*Bibl. August.*, 11, 552-4). Th. Camelot, (*ib.*, 15, 582-3).

335. "ad similitudinem aetatis hominis"; "non secundum aequalia spatia temporum, sed secundum communes innovationes rerum": *De script.*, c. 17 (PL, CLXXV, 24 BD). *De arca myst.*, c. 4 (CLXXVI, 687-8). Cf. *Except.* (CLXXVII, 215 C). Julian of Toledo, *De compr. aet. sextae*, l. 3, c. 3 (XCVI, 571 AB).

336. *Did.*, l. 6, c. 4 (CLXXVI, 803 AB).

337. Thus *De sacr.*, l. 1, P. 11, c. 6 (CLXXVI, 345 CD).

338. *De vera rel.*, c. 28, n. 51: "showing forth [to the human race] what each age was asking for" — "exhibens (generi humano) quod aetas illa poscebat" (96); c. 7, n. 13 (43). *De fide rer.*, c. 3, n. 5 (321). *Doct. chr.*, l. 3, c. 12, n. 19: "Hence one ought to pay diligent attention to what befits times, places, and persons, lest we condemn shameful practices at random" — "Quid igitur locis et temporibus personisque conveniat, diligenter attendendum est, ne temere flagitia reprehendamus" (364); c. 18, n. 26 (374); c. 22, n. 32 (382). *De div. q. 83*, q. 49 and 53 (Beckaert, 130, 142); etc. Already, for example, Ambrose, *De Abraham*, l. 1, c. 4, n. 23: "Let us first consider that Abraham existed before the law of Moses and before the Gospel" — "Consideremus primum quia Abraham ante legem Moysis et ante Evangelium fuit" (PL, XIV, 429 B).

339. Cf. Chenu, 38, 66, 209.

340. "dialectique curieuse"; "d'une foi qui, en quête d'éternel, valorise le temps, et d'une raison qui, liée au temps et au lieu, cède à l'éternisme de l'abstraction": Chenu, "Situation humaine, corporalité et temporalité," in *L'homme et son destin d'après les penseurs du moyen âge* (1960), 28.

341. "non erant christiani"; "non erat Christus": Agobard, *C. Fredig.*, c. 16 (PL, CIV, 169-70).

342. Thus, the letters exchanged between two Swiss scholars, Hugh and Burkard, a bit later in the course of the century: Fr. Stegmüller, "Conflictus helvetica de Limbo Patrum," *Mél. J. de Ghellinck*, 2, 727-44.

343. Father Damien Van den Eynde has made a comparative study of the texts and shown the detailed refinements successively advanced by Hugh: *Essai*, 130-42.

344. "une considération non légère"; "tam multae sunt existimationes et opiniones hominum, et tam diversa fide de recta fide disputatur": L. 1, P. 10, c. 6 (PL, CLXXVI, 335 B).

345. "ad varietatem locutionis": Abelard, *In Rom.* (CLXXVIII, 838-9). Aug., *De sp. et litt.*, c. 29, n. 50 (XLIV, 231). Cf. Rom. 3:30.

346. "sacramenta sunt mutata, non fides"; "Exspectabat (Israel) a Deo, secundum vetus Testamentum, ignorans ibi esse signa futurorum; exspectabat, ergo, a Deo praesentis vitae felicitatem, et in hac terra quaerebat quod suis Deus in caelo servabat": S. 19, n. 3-4 (XXXVIII, 133-4). *De pecc. meritis*, l. 2, c. 29, n. 47: "So there is one faith . . . , but the signs used by this one faith have varied through

various times for the sake of fittingly communicating its meaning" — "Una ergo fides est . . . , sed hujus unius fidei, pro significationis opportunitate, per varia tempora sacramenta variata sunt" (XLIV, 179).

347. See above, vol. 2, ch. 8.4.

348. *In ps.* lxxvii, n. 2: "For they were not without the faith itself. . . . But doubtless . . ." — "Non enim sine ipsa fide fuerunt. . . . Sed utique . . ." (CCL, 39, 1067).

349. *Adv. Jud.*, c. 3, n. 4 (PL, XLII, 53).

350. Cf. Aug., *In ps.* xc, s. 2, n. 1 (CCL, 39, 1266); *Retract.*, l. 1, c. 13, n. 3 (Bardy, 342). It also seems that in antiquity the desire to give value to the Old Testament in the controversy with the pagans made it necessary to stress the knowledge of the "ancient Fathers." One was always compelled to unite the idea of the antiquity of the revelation with that of its progressive economy. Cf. Tert., *Adv. Jud.*, c. 2 (H. Hoppe, 254-8).

351. *Ep.* 187, c. 11, n. 34 (PL, XXXIII, 845); *ep.* 177, n. 12 (769); *ep.* 190, c. 2, n. 6 (858-9). *In Jo.*, tr. 45, n. 9 (CCL, 36, 392). Cf. 2 Cor. 4:13.

352. *In ps.* lxxii, n. 3: "Hence they were merely praising God, not yet understanding what God was presignifying and promising in those figures" — "hinc solum laudabant Deum, nondum intelligentes quid in illis figuris praesignaret et promitteret Deus" (CCL, 39, 988).

353. "nam non solum sacramenta diversa sunt, verum etiam promissa; ibi videntur temporalia proponi, quibus spiritale praemium occulte significetur": *In Hept.*, l. 4, c. 33, n. 1 (PL, XXXIV, 732).

354. *C. Jul. op. Imp.*, l. 1, c. 88: "doubtless seeing that all the saints, separated from the condition of slaves even before the Old Testament and in the time of the Old Testament, were freed by the selfsame grace of Christ" — "procul dubio etiam ante V.T. et tempore veteris T., omnes sanctos a servorum conditione separatos, eadem liberatos Christi gratia videntes" (XLV, 1107); c. 124: "and he freed the ancient righteous ones with the same grace against which you have declared war; though they had for a time used different signs; since they used to believe what we believe about Christ" — "et ipsos antiquos justos eadem gratia liberavit, cui vos bellum indixistis; quamvis diversis usi fuerint pro tempore sacramentis; quoniam quod de Christo credimus, hoc credebant" (1127).

355. "tunc occulta erat fides, quae postea revelata est": *C. Faust.*, l. 6, c. 9 (XLII, 237); l. 19, c. 14 (356). *In ps.* lxxvii, n. 2 (CCL, 39, 1067).

356. *Doct. chr.*, l. 3, c. 6, n. 10 (352); cf. *De vera rel.*, c. 17 (66-8).

357. "Utique sacramentum regni caelorum velabatur in veteri Testamento, quod plenitudine temporum revelaretur in novo": *In ps.* lxxvii, n. 2 (CCL, 39, 1067). *In ps.* lxxii, n. 1: "Just as Christ himself, about to be born according to the flesh, had been at root hidden in the seed of the patriarchs . . . , so too the New Testament itself, which was in Christ, had been hidden in those earlier times" — "Quemadmodum Christus ipse secundum carnem nasciturus in radice erat occultus in semine patriarcharum . . . , sic etiam ipsum N.T., quod in Christo erat, prioribus illis temporibus occultum erat" (986). *C. Faust.*, l. 22, c. 76: "But when the fullness of time came, that the New Testament, which used to be veiled in the figures of the Old, should be revealed" — "Ubi autem venit plenitudo temporis,

ut N.T. revelaretur, quod figuris veteris velabatur" (PL, XLII, 448). Cf. Louis Villette, *Foi et sacrament, I, du Nouveau Testament à S. Aug.* (1959), 254-64.

358. "scientiae gloriam, sed occultam": *In Ez.*, h. 12, n. 3 (264), etc. *In Num.*, h. 12, n. 2: the prophets "have located the sense, i.e., the buried and submerged prophecy about Christ, in the depths of the letter" — "sensum et prophetiam de Christo defossam et demersam in profundo litterae collocarunt" (90). *In Jo.*, l. 6, c. 5 (112). *In Cant.*, l. 1 (94); l. 2 (161-2); etc. Cf. Huet, *Origeniana* (PG, XVII, 797-9).

359. *In Jos.*, h. 3, n. 2: "We believe that it was already done and fulfilled, whereas they only believed that it was to be" — "Nos factum jam credimus et impletum, illi tantummodo, futurum credebant," etc. (A. Jaubert, SC, 71, 130-6). *In Rom.*, l. 4, n. 7: "What he believed would be is believed by us to have happened" — "Quod ille futurum credidit a nobis creditur factum" (PG, XIV, 985 B). *In Cant.*, l. 2 (163-4). *In Matt.* (702-3). Cf. Irenaeus, *Adv. Haer.*, l. 4, 7 (PG, VII, 990-3).

360. *In Jo.*, l. 6, c. 4: "Before the bodily coming of the Christ, the saints possessed something more than the mass of the believers, they comprehended the mysteries of the divinity" (on John 5:17; 110); l. 19, c. 5 (304). *In Jer.*, h. 5, n. 8, on the veil of Moses (38); etc. Cf. *In Jo.*, l. 6, c. 1: "Solomon saw God in a dream and received wisdom in a dream; the waking state was reserved for him who said 'There is a greater than Solomon here'" (107). *In Luc.*, h. 14 (101; difference between the ass of Balaam and the doves of the Gospel), etc. There are, however, many and various nuances from one text to the other, according to the point of view taken.

361. *Adv. Haer.*, l. 4, c. 7, n. 2 (PG, VII, 991 B).

362. "in figura occultum": *In Jo.*, tr. 43, n. 16: "But I do not doubt that Father Abraham knew the whole matter" — "Sed ego non dubito patrem Abraham totum scisse" (CCL, 36, 380). *C. adv. Legis*, l. 2, c. 7, n. 27: "Indeed not all among that people failed to understand Christ hidden amidst the shadows of the Old Testament; for Moses himself and the other prophets — who foretold him to posterity — did not fail to understand these things" — "Nec sane omnes in illo populo non intelligebant Christum per illas umbras Testamenti veteris figuratum; neque enim haec ipse Moyses et caeteri prophetae non intelligebant, qui eum posteris praenuntiabant" (PL, XLII, 653).

363. S. 14 May (Morin, *Misc. Agost.*, 293).

364. "justi spirituales"; "littera jubens"; "spiritus juvans": *C. adv. Legis*, l. 1, c. 17, n. 35 (PL, XLII, 623).

365. "Etsi pro temporis dispensatione veteris Testamenti ministrabant figuris, ad novum tamen Testamentum, quamvis nondum revelatum, per gratiam Dei pertinebant": *Ib.*, l. 2, c. 8, n. 31 (656). *In Ps.* (CCL, 40, 2010).

366. John 8:56. This text, writes Father Daniélou, "is hard to explain without a certain knowledge that Abraham had had when he was alive about the mystery of the Christ to come" — "peut difficilement s'expliquer en dehors d'une certaine connaissance qu'Abraham a eue de son vivant du mystère du Christ à venir": *Abraham dans la tradition chr., Cahiers sioniens*, 1951, 172. Cf. E. Hoskyns, *The Fourth Gospel* (1947), 347-8. Irenaeus, *Adv. Haer.*, l. 4, c. 21, n. 1; c. 11, n. 1; c. 7, n. 1 (PG, 7, 1043-4, 1001 C, 990-1): "The joy of Abraham descends into Simeon to make the joy of Simeon, and the joy of Simeon in turn climbs back to Abraham: it is the self-

same joy; the joy of the one is at the root of the joy of the other: Simeon has desired the Christ and Abraham has brought him."

367. "non ex manifestatione praesentium, sed ex revelatione futurorum": *De Trin.*, 1. 2, c. 11 (Mellet-Camelot, 232-6). *Civ. Dei*, 1. 16, c. 29 (Bardy-Combès, 4, 265-8). *In ps.* lxxii, n. 1: "For we dare not set the faithful of our own time ahead of God's friends through whom those things have been prophesied to us, since God entrusted us with the fact that he is the God of Abraham, the God of Isaac, and the God of Jacob in such wise that he says that this is his name for ever" — "Non enim audemus fideles temporis nostri praeferre amicis Dei per quos nobis ista prophetata sunt, cum Deum Abraham et Deum Isaac et Deum Jacob ita se Deus esse commendet, ut hoc dicat suum nomen in aeternum" (PL, XXXIII, 845; cf. Ex. 3:15).

368. "congruenter"; "congruis temporibus": *C. Faust.*, 1. 6, c. 7: "certain prefigurations befitting the time" — "quasdam praefigurationes tempori congruentes" (PL, XCII, 233); l. 10, c. 3 (344); l. 22, c. 23, on those who compare the life of the prophets to that of the apostles "not being able to distinguish the custom of the time in which the promise was kept veiled from the custom of the time in which the promise would be revealed" — nec valentes discernere consuetudinem temporis illius quo promissio velabatur, a consuetudine temporis illius, quo promissio revelatur" (417); c. 47 (428); l. 32, c. 8 (501). *Ep.* 138, c. 1, n. 5: on the history which unfolds "like a great song of an ineffable Musician" — "velut magnum carmen cujusdam ineffabilis modulatoris" — God knows "what should be fittingly applied to each time" — "quid cuique tempori accommodate adhibeatur" (XXXIII, 527). *Adv. Jud.*, c. 3, n. 4: "so that all of the signs of things should befit their times" — "ut rerum signa suis quaeque temporibus conveniant" (XLII, 53).

369. "consuetudo"; "Haec gratia in Testamento veteri velata latitabat, quae in Christi Evangelio revelata est, dispensatione temporum ordinatissima, sicut Deus novit cuncta disponere": *De sp. et litt.*, c. 15, n. 27 (PL, XLIV, 217). Other details in J. Plagnieux, "Le chrétien en face de la Loi d'après le *De sp. et littera* de S. Aug." (*Theologie in Geschichte und Gegenwart, Mél. Michael Schmaus*, 1957, 725-54): for Augustine, the Gospel marks something absolutely novel, though prepared for and even forever acting in advance (745).

370. Regarding the culture of Augustine, see the particulars in H. I. Marrou, *S. Aug. et la fin de la culture antique* (1938), 235, 467. Cf. Y. M. J. Congar, *Le mystère du Temple* (1958), app. 3, 310-42. Chenu, in *L'homme et son destin* (1960), 34-5. Gilson, *Le Thomisme*, 4th ed. (1942), 191: the greatness of Augustine is that "d'un théologien que sa philosophie, partout en retard sur sa théologie, n'empêche pas un instant d'avancer" — "of a theologian, in that though his philosophy is always slower than his theology it never ceases to advance."

371. "eadem fides": Peter Cellensis, *s.* 12: "The holy patriarchs ... were justified by the same faith by which we both believe and are saved" — "Sancti Patres ... justificabantur eadem fide qua et nos credimus et salvamur" (PL, CCII, 670 D), etc. Cf. Leo, *s.* 30, c. 7: "All the saints who have preceded the times of our Savior have been justified through this faith and made into a body through this sacrament of Christ" — "Omnes sancti qui Salvatoris nostri tempora praecesserunt,

per hanc fidem justificati et per hoc sacramentum Christi sunt corpus effecti" (LIV, 234 B); s. 66, c. 1: "an undivided faith" — "indiscreta fides" (365 B).

372. "idem spiritus": Bernard, *De laud. V. M.*, s. 2, n. 11: "The spirit of the prophets was undoubtedly one, and, various people with unvarying spirit both foresaw and foretold the same thing, albeit in various ways" — Unus nimirum fuit spiritus prophetarum et licet diversis modis, signis et temporibus, eamdem rem diversi non diverso spiritu et praeviderunt et praedixerunt" (CLXXXIII, 66 C); but here it is a question of the prophets. *Gloss in III Reg.*, vii, 17, according to Bede: "The Fathers of each of the two Testaments through the grace of the one seven-formed Spirit accepted to be chosen" — "Patres utriusque Testamenti per gratiam unius Spiritus septiformis ut essent electi acceperunt" (CXIII, 593 D).

373. "idem amor Trinitatis": Cf. Rabanus, *In Ez.*, l. 14, on the elect of the two Testaments: "They have all been kindled from the love of the Trinity" — "omnes ex amore Trinitatis accensi sunt" (CX, 901 C). Helinand, s. 16 (CCXII, 611-2).

374. Peter Chrysologus, s. 110: "thus they both arrive at salvation by the one path of faith" — "sic uno itinere fidei utrique perveniunt ad salutem" (LII, 503 B); s. 150 (601-2). Cassiodorus, *In ps.* lxxviii: "For they who have shone with the brightness of the Lord's grace are not to be thought by Christians to be aliens" — "Neque enim christianis alieni credendi sunt qui gratiae dominicae claritate fulserunt" (LXX, 573 B). Aimo, *In Cant.*, c. 7: "For none of the just of the heaven was able to enter except through Christ" — "Nullus enim justorum caelorum intrare valuit nisi per Christum" (CXVII, 350 A). From a slightly different point of view, Leo, s. 23, c. 4: "This sign of great piety ... was so powerful even in its significations, that those who believed that it had been promised were no less adept than those who received it as given" — "Hoc magnae pietatis sacramentum ... tam potens etiam in suis significationibus fuit, ut non minus adepti sunt qui illud credidere promissum, quam qui suscipere donatum" (LIV, 202 C); s. 52, c. 1 (314 BC); s. 64, c. 2 (353 B).

375. Gregory, *In Ez.*, l. 2, h. 3, n. 16 (LXXVI, 966 CD). Rabanus, *In Ez.*, l. 16, c. 40: "There is a unity of faith in the heart of all the saints; both the fathers of the Old Testament and the preachers of the New Testament have professed that the Trinity is one God" — "Unitas est fidei in corde omnium sanctorum; unum Deum esse Trinitatem et Patres Testamenti veteris et praedicatores professi sunt T. novi" (CX, 954 CD). Anselm of Havelberg, *Dial.*, l. 1, c. 2 (CLXXXVIII, 1144 C). Aelred, *S. ined.*, 3: "For the place in which you are standing is holy. That holy place was the society of the elect of the Old Testament, who, along with those who belong to the New, constitute the one bride of Christ" — "Locus enim in quo stas sanctus est. Locus iste sanctus, societas erat electorum veteris T., qui cum illis qui ad novum pertinent, una est sponsa Christi" (Talbot, 43). A fine page from Bede on the unity of the Church across diversities of origin and situation: *In Cant.*, l. 5 (PL, CXI, 1182 CD). Martin de Leon, s. 30 and 34 (CCVIII, 1095 C, 1100 B, 1346 D). Cf. Alan of Lille, *De sex alis:* "The Church that began at the beginning of the world and will last unto the end of the age" — "Ecclesia quae incepit a primordio mundi et usque ad finem saeculi durabit" (CCX, 2728); etc.

376. "una est enim Ecclesia in praecedentibus et in sequentibus Patribus" — "Ecclesia, quae incepit a primordio mundi et usque ad finem saeculi durabit": Aimon, *In Cant.*, c. 8 (CXVII, 351 A). Godfrey of Admont: "though the times may

have been various, though the signs may have been various, nevertheless in the presence of God the Church was and is one in the simplicity of the faith" — "licet diversa tempora, licet diversa fuerint sacramenta, una tamen apud Deum erat et est in fidei simplicitate Ecclesia."

377. *Secunda secundae*, q. 1, a. 2: "This is to be held as firm: that the faith of the moderns and the ancients is one; otherwise there would not be one Church" — "Hoc pro firmo est tenendum, unam esse fidem modernorum et antiquorum; alias non esset una Ecclesia"; *Prima secundae*, q. 106, a. 1, ad 3m; a. 3, ad 2m; q. 107, a. 1, ad 2m and 3m. *Tertia*, qu. 8, a. 3, ad 3m. Cf. Congar, *Myst. du Temple*, 97.

378. *In ps.* IX: "The daughter of Zion is the Church of the New Testament, which, having been nourished on the paps of the earlier Church, is like her in faith, as a daughter to her mother" — "Filia Sion, Testamenti novi est Ecclesia, quae, nutrita uberibus prioris Ecclesiae, similis illi est in fide, velut filia matri suae" (PL, CXCIII, 763 A).

379. "quod illi praedixerunt futurum, nos jam credimus factum": Aimon, *h.* 1 de temp. (118, 17 B); cf. Acts, xv, 11. The misunderstanding is manifest. Cf. Aug., *ep.* 190, c. 2, n. 6: "what we believe has happened they believed was to come" — "hoc illi crediderunt futurum, quod nos credimus factum" (XXXIII, 858).

380. "una fides, una exspectatio vel spes": Rupert, *In Ez.*, l. 2, c. 15 (CLXVII, 1477-8).

381. Bede, *Sup. Act. Ap.*: "Though the signs diverge depending upon the times, nevertheless one and the same faith harmonizes through them all" — "Etsi sacramenta pro temporum ratione discrepent, fides tamen una eademque concordat" (XCII, 953A); *In Cant.*, l. 2: "disparate signs depending on the times" — "sacramenta pro temporum ratione disparia" (XCI, 1083 D). Hincmar, *De praed. diss. post.*, c. 32: "sacramenta disparia," "we most clearly know what belonged to them through the mystery veiled within the figure" — "manifestissime cognoscimus quae illis in figura velato mysterio . . . contigerunt" (CXXV, 309 C, 311 D); *De una deit.*: "changed depending on the times" — "pro temporum ratione mutavit" (614 D). Peter Cellensis, *s.* 59 (CCII, 820 B); *De tab. Moysi*: "the earlier fathers believed in Christ with the selfsame faith as do the people of recent grace, albeit with a different way of celebrating the sacraments" — "eadem fide patres priores in Christo crediderunt, et novae gratiae populi, licet diversa celebratione sacramentorum" (Leclercq, 153; see above, note 56); etc. Cf. Leo, *s.* 23, c. 3: "mysteries varied depending on the times, though the faith by which we live was never diverse in any age" — "mysteria pro temporum ratione variata, cum fides qua vivimus nulla fuerit aetate diversa" (LIV, 202 A).

382. Cassiodorus, *In ps.* xcii (LXX, 661 BC). Berengaud, *In Ap.* (XVI, 809 B, 812 AB, 856 D, 861 AB, 922-4). John Scotus, *In Jo.*, fr. 2 (122, 337 AD). Adam Scotus, *De trip. tab.* (CXCVIII, 691-2). Richard, *Nonnullae alleg.* (CXCVI, 199 B); etc.

383. "modus dicendi variatur, et res antiqua ipso modo dicendi renovatur": Lethbert of Saint Ruf, *In ps.*, XLV, n. 12 (XXI, 831 BC).

384. Thus Martin of Leon, *In Ap.*, vi, 9 (CCIX, 337-8); etc.

385. 'connaissance': Anselm of Havelberg, *Dial.*, l. 1, c. 4: "though most of them did not have so much knowledge of the faith as to . . ." — "licet plerique illorum non tantam notitiam fidei haberent ut . . ." (CLXXXVIII, 1146 D). Werner of Saint Blaise takes up the classic formula again to apply it to the opposite situa-

tion: "Awareness of the faith is one thing, faith another. . . . Now awareness of faith can exist without any faith, but faith cannot exist without any awareness" — "Aliud cognitio fidei, aliud fides. . . . Potest autem cognitio fidei esse sine omni fide, fides autem sine omni cognitione esse non potest" (CLVII, 1180 BC). Cf. Garnier, s. 12 (CCV, 654 A). Luke of Mont Cornillon, *Moralitates in Cantica* (CCIII, 508 B).

386. 'science': Rupert, *In Ex.*, l. 2, c. 4: "through the same faith, but not through the same knowledge of the faith" — "per eamdem fidem, non per eamdem fidei scientiam" (CLXVII, 611 C; 612 AC); l. 4, c. 23: "On the one hand, the Hebrews, experts in the Law — not so much of God as by their spirit and wit — and ignorant of heavenly things. . . . We, on the other hand, who both believe the aforementioned heavenly things and now partly know them with science" — "Hebraei quidem, non tam Dei quam suo spiritu vel ingenio legisperiti et caelestia nescientes. . . . Nos autem qui praedicta caelestia et fide credimus et scientia jam ex parte novimus" (722 BC).

387. Rabanus, *In Ez.*, l. 20 (CX, 1001 BC; after Origen; cf. Heb. 11).

388. Honorius, *In Ps. sel.* (CLXXII, 290 B). Anselm of Havelberg, *Ep. apol.*: "Blessed the eyes . . . : clearly teaching that they see with faces now unveiled what used to occur to them within a figure" — "Beati oculi . . . : manifeste docens ea quae illis in figura contingebant, istos revelata jam facie videre" (CLXXXVIII, 1131 C); etc.

389. Hervaeus, *In II Cor.* (CLXXXI, 1026 D); etc. Richard gives this thought a concise and picturesque turn of phrase, *In Ap.*: "There seems to be a big difference between promise and delivery; for he heard a lion in the promise and sees a lamb in the delivery" — "Magna differentia videtur inter promissionem et exhibitionem, nam leonem audivit in promissione, agnum videt in exhibitione" (CXCVI, 756 D).

390. "nos atque illi non minime discernimur": Rupert, *In Matt.*, l. 10 (CLXCVIII, 1549 B).

391. Bede, *In Marc.* (XCII, 158 D); *In Lev.*: "The inner spiritual sense that was clear only to a few is being hidden" — "Intrinsecus occultatur spiritualis sensus, qui paucis omnino patuit" (XCI, 333 D). In *De templo Sal.*, c. 5, these "only a few" — "pauci omnino" become "very many Fathers" — "Patres perplures" (746 D). Walafrid Strabo, *In ps.* lxxi: "Christ was in David and in Abraham, but hidden, as the fruit is in the root, but is not apparent; a few prophets, however, knew Christ and the New Testament, in hidden fashion, and announced that it was to be revealed" — "Christus in David et in Abraham, sed occultus; ut fructus est in radice sed non apparet; noverunt autem pauci prophetae et Christum et novum T., sc. in occulto, et pronuntiaverunt revelandum" (CXIII, 956 A). Raoul de Flaix, *In Lev.*: "Some of them knew that these were figures, and some did not" — "Quidam eorum figuras has esse sciebant, quidam nesciebant" (MBVP, 17, 186 C); etc.

392. Hervaeus, *In Is.*, l. 1 (PL, CLXXXI, 105-6). Already in Hilary, *In ps.*, ii, n. 2: "these elders . . . having acquired spiritual science of hidden types of knowledge as handed down by Moses" — "hi seniores . . . spiritalem secundum Moysi traditionem occultarum cognitionum scientiam adepti" (38-9); etc.

393. "pauci": Leo, *s.* 24, c. 1: "to do which was at that time beneficial to few

believers" — "quod tunc paucis credentibus profuit faciendum" (PL, LIV, 204 AB); s. 76, a. 3 (405-6).

394. "pauci omnino"; "paucissimi"; "rari et obscuri"; "paucissimi perfecti"; "nulli, vel admodum pauci": Peter Lombard, *In ps.* lxxii (CXCI, 669 B). Helinand, s. 3 and 16 (CCXII, 503 B, 612 A). Absalon, *s.* 25 and 37 (CCXI, 149 D, 215 CD). Cf. Joachim of Flora, *Psalt.*, f. 239 v.

395. Gozechin, *Ep. ad Valcherum*, c. 20: "But once the night of the Old Testament had passed, in whose firmament the aforementioned Fathers shone like the brightest stars" — "Transacta autem veteris T. nocte, in cujus firmamento memorati Patres velut clarissimae lucebant stellae" (CXLIII, 896 C; cf. AB). Greg., *Mor.*, l. 29, c. 31, n. 68-71 (LXXVI, 515-7).

396. "futurorum praescii": *De var. q.*, c. 33, n. 1 (99).

397. John of Salisbury, *Polycr.*, l. 3, c. 9: "the faith of the saints of the Old and the New Testament is distinguished in that the latter are rejoicing in things already fulfilled for them, and the former were waiting for and desiring these things to be fulfilled" — "Sanctorum quippe veteris et novi T., in eo distinguitur fides, quod isti jam sibi gaudent impleta, quae illi exspectabant et desiderabant implenda" (PL, CCI, 492 D); l. 4, c. 11: "The Law was speaking to a carnal people" — "Lex carnali populo loquebatur"; it accordingly promised temporal goods, etc. (533 AB).

398. Bede, *Hexaem.*, l. 4 (XCI, 190 B). Text cited by Landgraf, "Die Gnadesökonomie des Alt. Bundes nach der Lehre der Frühschol.," Z. F. k. Th., 57, 226: "At that time there were some who belonged to the New Testament, just as now there are some who belong to the Old" — "Tunc temporis erant aliqui qui pertinebant ad N.T., sicut nunc sunt aliqui qui pertinent ad vetus." On this distinction in Aug.: J. Wang Tch'ang-tche, SJ, *S. Aug. et les vertues des païens* (1938), 83-94 and 171-3.

399. Hervaeus, *In Gal.*: "who served God not with fear of punishment but with love of justice, and having more faith about Christ, they already belonged to the grace of the New Testament and lived in the freedom of sons" — "qui non timore paenae sed amore justitiae Deo serviebant et pluram habentes de Christo fidem, jam ad novi T. gratiam pertinebant et in filiorum libertate vivebant" (PL, CLXXXI, 1157 D).

400. "non extra mysterium, sed extra tempus": Greg., *In Ez.*, l. 2, h. 3, n. 16 (LXXVI, 967 A).

401. Abelard's commentary *in Rom.*: "Moses who understood the mysteries that had been wrapped within the Law" — "Moyses qui mysteria quae in lege involuta erant intelligebat" (Landgraf, 146). Bodo of Prufning, *De statu domus Dei*, l. 2 (493 G).

402. "ex parte": Guibert of Nogent, *De pign. sanct.*, l. 4, c. 2 (PL, CLVI, 669 B).

403. Aimon, *In Ap.*, l. 2 (CXVII, 1003 B).

404. "ad plenum": Martin of Leon, *In Ap.*, v, 4 (CCIX, 330 B).

405. S. 3 (CCXII, 506 BC).

406. "Nec tamen omnia Moyses novit in eis, quae novit in eis Spiritus sanctus ipsum qui docuit": *Tr. in Hexaem.*, ep. to Arnoul of Liseux (Fr. Lacombe, 235). For our authors, the "ancient Fathers" could therefore not know the Christian facts or

the Christian truths in advance, like Aeneas reading the future exploits of his people on the shield of Vulcan (*Aeneid*, 8, 729-30):

> Through the shield of Vulcan, his parent's gift,
> he marvels at such things, and, though not knowing them in their reality,
> he rejoices in their image.
> Talia per clipeum Volcani, dona parentis,
> Miratur, rerumque ignarus imagine gaudet.

407. Godfrey of Admont, *H. in Scr.*, 12 (CLXXIV, 1112 A).

408. A distinction of Origen's, taken up again by Absalon, s. 37 (CCXI, 217 C).

409. *Adv. Fred.*, c. 22: "The religion of the Christians is not something new or recently arisen, but, coming down from the very origin of the world, with the selfsame Christ as teacher and retailer" — "Non novella vel nuper exorta est christianorum religio, sed ab ipsa mundi origine descendens, eodem Christo doctore et institore" (which is again from Augustine), etc. (CIV, 174 A); c. 21: "There is absolutely no other difference between them and us except that the signs of salvation that were performed through the Mediator for their sake and for ours save us in their pastness and saved them in their futurity" — "Nihil omnino differt aliud inter illos et nos, nisi quia sacramenta salutis, quae per mediatorem operata sunt propter nos et propter illos, nos salvant praeterita, illos futura, etc." (CLXXIII, C).

410. *Ib.*, c. 21: "and they in mere awareness and figures of things to come, we also in public profession, with the promises and announcement of things past along with the meaning of the tangible signs" — "et illi in sola conscientia et figuris futurorum, nos etiam in publica professione, votis et annuntiatione praeteritarum rerum cum significatione tractabilium sacramentorum" (173 C).

411. "Columnae hujus mysteria novimus quae in nocte, id est nondum revelata lumine gratiae, ignis erat, et exiguum, id est perpaucis in prophetalem gratiam lucebat.... (Hodie) totus fons ignis verus Sol et fons luminis totus cum nube suae carnis venit; quamvis sit sol in nube, clarius tamen lucet quam dudum ignis in nocte": *In Ez.*, l. 2, c. 29 (CLXVII, 637 AB).

412. *In Ez.*, l. 2, h. 3, n. 7 and 16 (LXXVI, 961-2, 966-7).

413. *S. de Act. Ap.* (CCIX, 166-8).

414. "Eo tempore, invalescente fama verbi Dei, modicum farinae habuit vidua, id est plebs judaica, parumque olei; fit tamen inde subcinericius panis parvulus, id est parva quaedam notitia de Christo": *S. ined.*, 17 (Talbot, 120). The image was applied by Rupert, *In Abdiam*, to the Gentiles: "that is, the Gentile race was able to have a bit of knowledge through nature" — "id est modicum scientiae per naturam habere poterat gentilitas" (CLXVIII, 399 BC).

415. *In ps.* xxxv and xxxvi (Van den Eynde, 439-41, 536-7).

416. "quodammodo parcus, ne dicam avarus": *S*. 35 and 37 (PL, CCXI, 205 A, 215 CD).

417. *S*. 3 (CCV, 587-8).

418. "(Ante incarnationem Verbi) prophetia verbis infantium similis erat quorum verba intelligi non possunt, sed postquam maturiores fuerint, tunc verba ipsorum intelliguntur; et sic ante incarnatum Dei Filium prophetia ignota fuit, nec intelligebatur; in Christo autem aperiebatur, quia Ipse radix ramorum om-

nium bonorum existit": PL, CXCVII, 978 B: "For the root brings forth the first bit of stem, and the stem the bud, then the bud brings forth the branches, the branches blossoms, and the blossoms fruit; and even so too the root betokens Adam, the stem the patriarchs, the branches the wise, whereas the blossoms betoken the precepts of the Law and the fruit the incarnate Son of God" — "Radix enim primum granum profert, et granum germen, deinde germen ramos, rami vero flores, et flores fructum: et sic etiam et radix Adam ostendit, gramen patriarchas, germen prophetas, rami sapientes, flores vero legalia praecepta, fructus autem Filium Dei incarnatum."

419. Rupert, *In Num.*, l. 1, c. 37 (CLXVII, 874 C).

420. It came from Cyrian, Ambrose, Jerome, Augustine, Prosper, Primasius (LXVIII, 850 A), Caesarius of Arles (Ps.-Augustine, s. 28: XXXIX, 1800), the *Altercatio Evagrii* (v. 440; Bratke, 30). Already in Hippolytus, *Blessing of Isaac*, 18 (PO, 27, 83), Christ on the cross is compared to a cluster of grapes. Cf. Gregory of Nyssa, *Life of Moses*, 2, 270 (SC, 1 bis, 118).

421. Bede, *Q. sup. Num.* (PL, XCIII, 401 B); *In Num.* (XCI, 364 D). Rabanus, *In Num.* (CVIII, 668 CD). Martine of Leon, s. 32 (CCVIII, 1219-20); *s. in ramis* (836).

422. Gregory of Elvira, *In Cant.*, h. 3; *Tract. Or.*, 11: "who were to leave Christ behind owing to their incredulity" — "qui post se Christum propter incredulitatem relicturus erat."

423. Arno of Reichersberg, *Ep. apol.* (PL, CLXXXVIII, 1131 AB). Bernard, *In Cant.*, s. 44, n. 3 (CLXXXIII, 997 A), speaks only of two choirs: "the chorus of the prophets going on ahead and that of the apostles following behind" — "chorum propheticum praecedentem et subsequentem apostolicum." Franco, *De gratia Dei*, l. 10, unites the symbol of the grape-cluster with that of the cornerstone uniting the two high walls: thus it is more an issue of Christians coming from Judaism and paganism (CLXVI, 778).

424. "propheticus et apostolicus ordo": Honorius, *Spec. Eccl.*, dom. in palmis (CLXXII, 922 B).

425. Agobard, *Adv. Fr.*, c. 21, compares the two bearers with the two groups of children (CIV, 173 C). Aimo expounds the latter symbol, *H. de temp.*, 1 (CXVIII, 17 AB). The same goes for Paschasius, *In Matt.*, l. 9, c. 21: "But they all say one thing . . . , they were all crying out together with a harmonious voice" — "Omnes tamen unum dicunt . . . , omnes simul clamabant consona voce" (CXX, 704 C).

426. "Botrus quippe vecti impositus, Dominus est in cruce exaltatus. . . . Portant autem botrum in vecte duo viri, per quem populo ubertatem terrae repromissionis astruant, quia praedicatores utriusque Testamenti, qui gloriam patriae caelestis Domino revelante didicerunt, idem passionis illius arcanum populis intimare non cessant. . . . Quod autem duo portantes botrum similiter quidem eum portare sed non similiter valebant intueri, hoc nimirum significabat quod Salvator ipse ait: 'Beati oculi qui vident quae vos videtis', etc. Unde hic dicitur, quia Dominus, consummatis incarnationis suae sacramentis, aperuit discipulis sensum ut intelligerent Scripturas": Bede, *h.* 15, *in asc.* (CCL, 122, 704 C).

427. *In Ap.*, l. 5 (509 F).

428. Illa falanga botrum portans de rure gigantum;
Non videt hunc primus portatque videndo secundus;

Dat cui Judeus tergum, qui est tempore primus,
Gentilis populus faciem postrema secutus . . .

L. 6, v. 173-6 (A. Swoboda).

429. *Coll. in V.T.:* "but the one in front, because he was carrying, did not gaze; the one who followed, got a glimpse" — "sed praecessor, quod portabat non aspiciebat; qui sequebatur, intuebatur"; "the one who preceded did not see with his eyes what he was carrying on his shoulders" — "qui praecedebat, quod humeris portabat oculis non videbat" (PL, CXLV, 1036 D, 1037 AC).

430. "sub sigillis": *In Num.,* l. 1, c. 37 (CLXVII, 875 AC). Cf. *In Ex.,* l. 2, c. 4 (611 C); everything that we know of Christ was for the ancient Jews "sub sigillis" (612 AC). *In Lev.,* l. 1, c. 39: "Moses . . . did receive the clarity of the spirit from the Lord, but he brought the obscurity of the letter to the people, until there should come those who believed God the Son in God the Father, and, having been illuminated with this faith, they saw the law of the spirit within the law of the letter" — "Moyses . . . a Domino claritatem spiritus accepit, ad populum autem obscuritatem litterae protulit, donec venirent qui crederent Deum Filium in Deo Patre, et hac fide illuminati, viderent legem spiritus in lege litterae" (786-7).

431. "Legebant, sed non intelligebant, et qui optimi erant, qui propheticis oculis videbant, eis dicebatur ne propalerent": *In Matt.,* l. 10 (CLXVII, 1549 AC).

432. *L. except.,* P. 2, l. 2, c. 2: "thus the wedge-formation of prophets that precedes Christ does not see Christ on the cross" — "sic Christum praecedens prophetarum cuneus, Christum non vidit in cruce . . ." (Châtillon, 251). *In Ap.,* l. 2, c. 2: "Though the ancients preceded them in time, they are nevertheless far posterior to them in dignity" — "Etsi antiqui eos praecesserunt tempore, eis tamen longe sunt posteriores dignitate" (PL, CXCVI, 733 D).

433. *Ep. apol.:* "The earlier Fathers . . . were called Seers. They went ahead, and, bearing the precious grape-cluster behind their backs on the carrying-pole of the Old Testament, although they did not see much, nevertheless knew about it in figure and in faith" — "Patres priores . . . Videntes appellati. Illi praecedebant, et in vecte veteris T. pretiosum botrum post dorsum gestantes, quamvis non viderent multa, tamen de ipso figuraliter et cognoverunt fideliter" (CLXXXVIII, 1131 B).

434. *In Ez.,* l. 2, h. 5, n. 2 (CXXVI, 985-6). Cf. *Mor.,* l. 11, c. 20, n. 31: the prophet knew the object of his prophecy (LXXV, 968-9). But also l. 2, c. 36, n. 59 (SC, 32, 224).

435. "una spes, una fides est praecedentium atque sequentium populorum"; "perfectio fidei"; "rudis ille Hebraeorum populus . . . de cognitione sanctae Trinitatis eruditus non est": *In Ez.,* l. 2, h. 4, n. 4, 10, 11 (LXXVI, 976 A, 979-80; a text often cited by St. Thomas); h. 5, n. 2 (986 A); n. 12 (992 B). Cf. Origen, *De princ.,* l. 3, c. 3, n. 1 (256-7); *In Jo.,* 13, 48 (275-6); etc.

436. *In Ez.,* l. 1, h. 6, n. 16: "Through the Law sacred Scripture goes about by signifying the mystery; through the prophets it goes about by prophesying the Lord a bit more openly" — "Scriptura sacra per legem vadit signando mysterium; per prophetas vadit paulo apertius prophetando Dominum" (LXXVI, 836 B).

437. See above, notes 412 and 413.

438. "Per incrementa temporum crevit scientia spiritalium Patrum": *In Ez.,* l.

2, h. 4, n. 12: "For Moses was more educated than Abraham, the prophets more educated than Moses, the apostles more educated than the prophets in the knowledge of the all-powerful God" — "Plus namque Moyses quam Abraham, plus Prophetae quam Moyses, plus Apostoli quam Prophetae in omnipotentis Dei scientia eruditi sunt" (980 B). *Sup. Cant.*, c. 1, n. 2: "For by as much as the Church merited to be enlighted with the grace of a broader vision, by so much did she more broadly increase toward understanding" — "Tanto quippe amplius ad intellectum crevit Ecclesia, quanto et amplioris visionis gratia meruit illustrari" (LXXIX, 479 A).

439. "parvula" vs. "adulta": *Mor.*, l. 19, c. 12, n. 19 (LXXVI, 108 AC). Gregory adds a third period, that of the Church, "as weakened with a certain old age" — "quasi quodam senio debilitata," which no longer has the power to give birth to new children: a short period which will precede the conversion at the end of time.

440. *De sacramentis*, l. 1, P. 10, c. 11 (176, 312-3).

441. *De sacr. legis naturalis et scriptae:* "Erat quippe idem Salvator, eadem fides, eadem gratia: illic venturi, hic exhibiti. Sed quia ipse per quem salus dabatur adhuc longe erat, ejusdem salutis signa obscura esse debuerunt, ut paulatim ejus adventu appropinquante et fides amplius cresceret, et gratia evidentius se manifestaret" (38 B).

442. "Sed, ut ait etiam sanctus Gregorius, secundum incrementa temporum crevit et scientia spiritualium Patrum, et quanto viciniores adventui Salvatoris exstiterunt, tanto mysterium salutis plenius perceperunt. Non est dubium quin his etiam qui praesentes fuerunt, multo amplius contulerit rerum ipsarum exhibitio, atque praesentia exhibentis . . .": *De sacram.*, l. 1, P. 10, c. 6, *An secundum mutationes temporum mutata sit fides* (CLXXVI, 325-40). "Finally, what is a mystery hidden by the ages, and, lest perchance it be thought to be hidden only to the evil, what has been revealed to the saints has become subject to the most recent times" — "Postremo, quod est mysterium a saeculis absconditum, et ne forte putetur solis malis absconditum subjecit novissimis temporibus sanctis revelatum" (338 D). "Only those who have been uniquely illumined for this through the Spirit have come to know it; under grace, however . . ." — "Soli hoc cognoverunt qui per Spiritum singulariter ad hoc illuminati fuerunt; sub gratia autem . . ." (339 CD). P. 11, c. 6: "It is to be known that the order and character of the divine dispensation demanded that just as the coming of the savior approached more and more as time was advancing from the beginning, so the effect of salvation would more and more increase along with knowledge of the truth" — "Sciendum est quod divinae dispensationis ordo et ratio poposcuit, ut sicut ab initio, procurrente tempore, magis ac magis adventus salvatoris appropinquavit, sic semper magis ac magis effectus salutis cresceret et cognitio veritatis etc." (345 CD).

443. *De sacr. legis nat. et scr.:* "Awareness of the faith comes little by little as time advances" — "Paulatim procedente tempore venit agnitio fidei" (CLXXVI, 38 B). *Misc.*, 1, 66: "Faith is one thing, awareness of the faith something else" — "Aliud est fides, aliud cognitio fidei"; 18: "Just as there are three steps through which faith increases, so there are three steps through which awareness of the faith increases" — "Sicut tres sunt gradus per quos fides crescit, ita tres sunt gradus per quos crescit cognitio fidei" (CLXXVII, 506 A, 487 A).

444. "qui praecesserunt, portaverunt quidem, sed non viderunt . . .": *Ib.* (340 CD): "This is how we think what blessed Augustine says is to be understood" — "Sic ergo intelligendum putamus quod dicit b. Aug." (340 CD). In the *De arca myst.*, c. 14, Hugh historically allegorizes, if one can say so, the itinerary of Exodus and Numbers: "the stations through which God's people spiritually travel from the Egypt of natural law through the desert of the written Law to the land of the promise of grace" — "mansiones per quas populus Dei spiritaliter ab Aegypto naturalis legis per desertum scriptae legis tendit ad terram promissionis gratiae" (699 D). Cf. Bernard, *Sup. missus est*, h. 1, n. 3: "in figures and enigmas through the whole journey in the desert right into the land of promise" — "in figuris et aenigmatibus per totum iter in deserto usque in terram promissionis" (CLXXXIII, 58 A).

445. "de cette perception traditionnelle": Chenu, AHDLMA, 21 (1955), 131.

446. "introduit en théologie le sens du temps": an example of an extreme consequence in Herbert Bosham, cited by Congar, 97, in RTAM, 18, 62 (Smalley).

447. *In ps. xcviii*, v. 100: "For frequently the younger understand the divine Scriptures better than their elders. But, just as Jacob . . . Just as Samuel . . . or Daniel. . . . The new people understood better than the older Judaic people" — Frequenter enim Scripturas divinas juniores melius intelligunt senioribus. Sicut Jacob . . . Sicut Samuel . . . vel Daniel . . . Melius utique intellexit populus novus, quam senior ille Judaicus . . ." (PL, LXX, 869 C). See above, note 382.

448. : "Ita enim per intervalla temporum populus Dei ordinatus est, et semper ad meliora commutatus, donec ad plenam perfectionem, etc.": *De var. q.*, c. 3 (Vega-Anspach, 14).

449. "Quanto ipsius veritatis appropinquavit adventus in carne, tanto manifestius revelata sunt sacramenta Patribus": *In Ex.*, l. 1, c. 11 (PL, CVIII, 30 A).

450. "Curabo nunc juxta historiae textum legentibus notificare, quomodo processit in mundo recta eruditio fidei per quosdam gradus et articulos aetatum ac temporum, et quomodo vetus Testamentum evangelicis ministravit principiis, in praefiguratione divinorum sacramentorum, sicut virilem aetatem solet aetas puerilis praecedere": *H. eccl.*, l. 2, prol. (CLXIII, 829-30).

451. "fides"; "fidei scientia"; "fidei vel confessionis scientia": *In Ex.*, l. 2, c. 4 (CLXVII, 611 CD).

452. Cf. Aug., *De vera rel.*, c. 27, n. 50 (94); *Div. quest.*, q. 58, n. 2 (PL, XL, 43).

453. "permissus sibi."

454. *In Jer.*, c. 1 (CLXVII, 1363 AC).

455. *De magna domo sapientiae:* "Look at how the awareness of the heavenly mysteries grew with the advance of time" — "Ecce quomodo per incrementa temporum crevit sacramentorum caelestium notitia" (515 D).

456. "Oportet autem ut, secundum processum temporum, spiritualium gratiarum signa magis ac magis semper evidentia ac declaranda formarentur, ut cum effectu salutis cresceret cognitio veritatis": *Defl.*, l. 2 (PL, CLVII, 1000 C). Werner may be depending on Hugh; cf. Anselm of Havelberg, *Dial.*, l. 1: "Let no one be surprised or complain that God's Church has been distinguished by various laws and observances from the unchangeable God — before the Law, under the Law, and under Grace, since it was necessary that, in accordance with the advance of the times, the signs of spiritual graces would increase, [signs] that would

more and more clarify the truth itself, and thus knowledge of the truth would increase along with the effect of salvation" — "Nemo miretur neque causetur Ecclesiam Dei de invariabili Deo variis legibus et observationibus ante legem et sub lege et sub gratia distinctam, quia oportebat ut secundum processum temporum crescerent signa spiritualium gratiarum, quae magis ac magis ipsam veritatem declararent, et sic cum effectu salutis incrementum acciperet cognitio veritatis" (CLXXXVIII, 1160 A; cf. 1147 CD, 1149 A).

457. "Quanto vicinius accedebat plenitudo temporis, tanto perfectior et, ut ita dicam, rotundior eminebat corona anni hujus benignitatis": S. 1 (CCV, 561 C). Cf. Helinand, s. 16: "the mystery of the Holy Trinity became clear to the world not at once, but partially through the succession of various times" — "Sanctae Trinitatis mysterium non simul, sed per partes et per successiones temporum mundo innotuit, etc." (CCXII, 611 D).

458. II^a II^{ae}, q. 1, a. 7: *Utrum articuli fidei secundum successionem temporum creverint.* Cf. Q. 9, a. 2. A doctrine that is sometimes incorrectly applied to the development of dogma, an application that produces a seriously erroneous meaning.

459. Father H. Weisweiler has shown this in *Scholastik,* 20-4 (1949), 63-4. Cf. Bernard, *Ep. seu tract. de bapt. aliisque quaest.,* c. 3, n. 11-5 (PL, CLXXXII, 1039-41); Hugh (CLXXVI, 336-8). A chapter of the *Didascalicon* (l. 5, c. 10; 798) paraphrases Bernard, *In Cant.,* s. 36, c. 3 (CLXXXIII, 968). Cf. Vernet, DTC, 7, 292. It was concerned with Abelard, probably having to do with his teaching at the Paraclete: D. Van den Eynde, *Essai,* 135.

460. "les prophètes de l'Ancien Testament ont connu le mystère, mais n'ont pu le révéler que sous des symbols; nous, aujourd'hui, nous pénétrons leurs symbols"; "mais dans la mesure où ils connaissaient le mystère, les prophètes étaient, dans le monde ancien, des précurseurs, et leurs prophéties anticipaient; ils étaient des chrétiens avant le temps": *Le Christ dans la théol. de S. Paul* (1951). Cf. Eph. 3:1-19; Col. 1:25-9.

461. Cf. Smalley, *The Study,* 23: "In so far as he was a Neoplatonist, St. Augustine put the spiritual sense above the literal. . . . As an original Christian thinker he gave the 'letter' a concrete chronological reality which it had never had before. The narrative of Scripture is fitted into a philosophy of history based on the Incarnation."

462. Gal. 4:1-4 and 21-31: "As long as the heir is a child. . . . But when the fullness of the time was come. . . . The needy elements, which you desire to serve again. . . . Which things are said by an allegory" — "Quanto tempore haeres parvula est. . . . At ubi venit plenitudo temporis. . . . Egena elementa, quibus rursum servire vultis. . . . Quae sunt per allegoria dicta."

463. Even in a work completely in symbolic figures, like the *Hortus deliciarum,* "the plan follows the development of the religious history of the world, from creation to the second coming" — "le plan suit le développement de l'histoire religieuse du monde, de la création à la parousie": El. And J. G. Rott, *L'hortus deliciarum d'Herrade de Landsberg* (1945, ed. J. Walther, 1952).

Notes to Chapter Five

1. Baron, xxxvi. Cf. the letter of Laurence to Maurice, 12th cent.: "I have dispatched that singularly distinguished professor" — "Illum praecipuum ac singularem doctorem delegi" (B. Bischoff, *Beitr. Bäumker,* 1935, 3, 250); many doubtless did the same at the time. Many have drunk from this "great font... of the waters... of divine things" — "fons divinorum magnus... aquarum" (Epitaph).

2. *The Study,* ch. 4: Andrew of St. Victor.

3. "Septem liberales artes huic scientiae subserviunt": *De script.,* c. 13 (PL, CLXXV, 20 C).

4. Gilson, "Notes sur une frontière contestée," AHDLMA, 25, pp. 60 and 68.

5. Cf. Richard, *Benj. minor,* c. 25: "The differenciation of the sciences, too, will be in accordance with the differentiation of creatures" — "Secundum differentiam creaturarum erit et differentia scientiarum" (PL, CXCVI, 53D).

6. Cassian, *Coll.* 14, c. 10 (SC, 54, 195); c. 9 (194). Ps.-Isidore, *De variis q.,* c. 50, n. 1: "The scriptural science of the holy Scriptures" — "Scriptualis scientia sanctarum Scripturarum" (Vega-Anspach, 145). The "true science of the Scriptures" — "vera Scripturarum scientia" of Cassian corresponds to Evagrius's "theoria," prepared by the "science pertaining to action" — "scientia actualis" (praktikê), i.e., by the "curing of the vices" — "curatio vitiarum," and then by the "perfecting of the virtues" — "perfectio virtutum": Placide Deseille, OCR, "A propos de l'épilogue du ch. 7 de la Règle," COCR, 1959, 293-5.

7. *lumen scientiae, sancti Spiritus eruditio:* Leo, *s.* 66, n. 1 (PL, LIV, 364 D). Cf. Gerhoch, *In ps. xxxv,* commenting on the "sermo scientiae" of 1 Cor. 12:9 (V. Den Eynde, 430).

8. "Implevit eos Dominus spiritu sapientiae et intelligentiae et scientiae omnique doctrina": Philip of Harvengt, *De scientia cler.,* l. 2, c. 23: "If anyone more eagerly wishes to know how certain it is that the science of the Scriptures properly belongs to clerics, he will be able to find it easily if he unrolls the Scriptures" — "Si quis diligentius velit scire quam certum sit, scientiam Scripturarum proprie clericis convenire, revolutis eisdem Scripturis, facile poterit invenire" (citing Ex. 31; CCIII, 693 B); *ep.* 3: to read the Scriptures is to rest, as did John, upon the breast of the Lord, and the "Scripturae scientia spiritualis" renders minds pure and vigorous (31 AB). Elmer of Canterbury, *ep.* 4, n. 15 (Leclercq, *St. Ans.,* 31, 71).

9. *Sup. Cant.,* c. 4 (PL, LXXIX, 513 D).

10. Rupert, *In Ap.,* l. 9 (CLXIX, 1089 A).

11. "scientia universalis quae ad salutem proficit": Richard, *In Ap.,* l. 2, c. 3 (CXCVI, 755 A).

12. Hervaeus, *In I Cor.* (CLXXXI, 817 B; cf. 819 B). Irimbert, *In Jud.:* "whilst the people of the Church, girded with the arms of true knowledge, break up the allegory and the moral sense of Scripture with their interpretation of Genesis" — "dum Ecclesiae populus, verae scientiae armis praecinctus, allegoriam et moralitatem Scripturae Genesis sua interpretatione discutit" (Pez, 4, 152). Ps.-Isidore, *De var. q.,* c. 50, n. 1 (145).

13. "divites in omni scientia, id est litterali, morali et allegorica": Anselm of Laon, *In Matt.,* c. 25 (CLXII, 1462 BC); etc.

14. John of Salisbury, *ep.* 143: "As the Truth itself speaks through its most faithful instrument: Love the knowledge of Scriptures and you will not love the vices of the flesh" — "Ut per fidelissimum organum suum Veritas ipsa eloquitur: ama scientiam Scripturarum, et carnis vitia non amabis" (CXCIX, 130 B).

15. Hervaeus, *In Is.*, l. 1 (CLXXXI, 77 B). Rabanus, *Cl. inst.*, l. 3, c. 2 (CVII, 379 BD).

16. Godfrey of Admont, *h. dom.* 29: "so that they understand the mystery of God's kingdom, which is the hidden, deep knowledge of the Scriptures" — "ut intelligant mysterium regni Dei, quod est latens et profunda scientia Scripturarum" (CLXXIV, 196 B).

17. Irimbert, *In Jud.*: "The true knowledge of holy Scripture shines forth in the unity of the Catholic Church" — "Vera sanctae Scripturae scientia in Ecclesiae catholicae unitate resplendet" (Pez, 4, 309). Anscharius, *Vita S. Willebaldi*, c. 3: "it restored many who were once falling from the faith back to true, Catholic knowledge" — "multos errantes olim a fide, ad veram et catholicam recreavit scientiam" (v. 780; MGH, *Scr.*, 2, 380).

18. Petrus Cellensis, *s.* 12 (PL, CCII, 671 C).

19. Honorius, *In Prov.* (CLXXII, 325-6). Bede, *In Luc.* (XCII, 633 C). Rabanus, *In I Mach.* (CIX, 1165 D). Nigellus de Longchamp (A. Boutemy, 205).

20. *Luc.*, xi, cf. *Ap.* V. Origen, *In Ez.*, h. 14 (PG, XIII, 765-8). Rupert, *In Ap.*, l. 2, c. 2 (PL, CLXIX, 880 A); etc.

21. Hervaeus, *In I Cor.*, 1: "But we of the spirit have the sense of Christ, i.e., we have been made partakers of Christ's knowledge through accepting the holy Spirit" — "Sed nos spiritales sensum Christi habemus, id est participes facti sumus scientiae Christi per acceptionem Spiritus sancti" (CLXXXI, 837 AB); etc.

22. "errantes spiritu": Ps.-Isidore, *De var. q.*, c. 78, n. 3 (219).

23. Honorius, *In Prov.*, XII, 23: "the clever man who hides his knowledge" — "homo versutus qui celat scientiam" (CLXXII, 319 D). Cf. 318 B: "ornamentum scientiae."

24. Richard, *In Ap.*, l. 2, c. 2 (CXCVI, 751-2).

25. "plenitudo scientiae": Adam of Perseigne, *ep.* 8 and 24 (Bouvet, 52-5, 181); *sermo in f. Ben.* (COCR, 4, 1937, 107, 194). Cf. Rabanus, *In I Mach.* (PL, CIX, 1165 D). Angelome, *In Reg.* (CXV, 359-60). Bruno of Würzburg (CXLII, 77 D). Othloh (CXLVI, 32 A, 146 A). Godfrey of Admont, *In Script.*, n. 4 and 6 (CLXXIV, 1074 A, 1083 D). Hervaeus, *In Is.*, l. 5 (CLXXXI, 350 CD). Absalon, *s.* 16 (CCXI, 100 B). Amédée de Lausanne (CLXXXVIII, 1308 A); etc. Cf. Origen, *In Ez.*, h. 1, n. 15 (PG, XIII, 680 C); Jerome, *In Ez.*, l. 12 (PL, XXV, 402 AD); or Gregory (LXXVI, 1191 CD); etc.

26. Anselm of Havelbourg, *Dial.*, l. 2, c. 23 (CLXXXVIII, 1201-2). *Gloss, in Eccli.* (CXIII, 1217 D). Wolberon, *In Cant.*, l. 3, c. 8: "If we consider the moral sense, we shall wish for each faithful soul that voice which, intent upon the sacred Scripture, desires to have knowledge itself, [and] cries out to God with the whole eagerness of its mind in these words: 'O that you were as my brother, nursing at my mother's breasts!'" — "Si moralem sensum consideremus, unicuique fideli animae vocem istam optabimus, quae sacrae Scripturae intenta se ipsam scientiam habere desiderat, tota animi aviditate his verbis ad Deum clamat: Quis mihi det te fratrem meum sugentem ubera matris meae?" (CXCV, 1242 A).

Absalon, s. 11 (CCXI, 68 B); s. 36 (212 A); s. 48 (273-4). Henri de Farne, *Medit. ad crucifixum*, c. 63: "a knowledge of sacred Scripture that is learned from the Holy Spirit and manifested through good works" — "Quaedam scientia sacrae Scripturae, quae Spiritu sancto didiscitur et per bona opera manifestatur" (H. Farner, *St. ans.*, 41, 498).

27. Godfrey of Admont, *h. dom.* 34: "That well is truly the well of Jacob, indeed the well of God almighty, which goes forth ... from him with the knowledge of the Scriptures" — "Fons iste vere fons est Jacob, fons utique Dei omnipotentis, qui ab ipso ... procedit scientia Scripturarum" (PL, CLXXIV, 228 C). Cf. Ps.-Bede, *In Jo.*, c. 2 (XCII, 658 B).

28. Martin of Leon, *In dedic. Ecclesiae, s.* 2 (CCIX, 92 B).

29. "artes naturales": *De sacram.*, prol., c. 6: "it is settled that all the natural arts serve the divine science" — "constat quod omnes artes naturales divinae scientiae famulantur" (CLXXVI, 185 C).

30. "divina scientia"; "Omnes artes deserviunt divinae sapientiae": *De script.*, c. 13 (CLXXV, 20 C). Aelred, *s.* 25: "If [the soul] has knowledge, if she has wisdom, if she has understanding in the Scriptures, she has received all this from her Husband" — "Si habet (anima) scientiam, si habet sapientiam, si intelligentiam in Scripturis, haec omnia a viro suo accepit" (CXCV, 356 D).

31. "le caractère novateur de l'exégèse de Saint-Victor": 202. Cf. P. Calandra, *De historica Andreae Victorini expositione in Ecclesiasten* (Palermo, 1948).

32. *The Study*, 111. On Andrew: J. Chatillon, RMAL, 8 (1952), 252-4.

33. Adam Scotus, *De trip. tab.*: "one no less eloquent than religious" — "quidam non minus disertus quam religiosus" (PL, CXCVIII, 556 A); "that eloquent man" — "ille vir disertus" (645 B); "an extremely expert master among the rest" — "magister vero quidam peritissimus inter alios" (660 A); cf. 635 A and 637 C.

34. B. Smalley, "Andrew of St. Victor, Abbot of Wigmore: A Twelfth Century Hebraist" (RTAM, 10, 1938, 358-73).

35. Cf. Herbert of Bosham: "But all these things ... the Jew and our Judaizers take in the carnal sense, whereas the man of the church takes in the spiritual sense" — "Quae tamen omnia ... Judaeus et nostri judaisantes carnaliter, ecclesiasticus vero spiritualiter accipit" (Smalley, RTAM, 1951, 64); etc. Formulas coming from Origen by way of Jerome.

36. "littera Synagogae": *De Trinitate* (PL, CLXVII, 934 B).

37. "These are the weapons that the Jews hurl against us, calling us corruptors and violent distorters of the sacred letters. It is not necessary for us to reply to them, since others have done this previously (but those who have answered will have seen for themselves whether their response is enough); nor is it useful to do so, lest, if, advancing to undecided combat, we perchance succumb to unequal [i.e., superior] powers, [their] doctors revile not only us but also those the sharpest of whom, if they should meet with them in liveliness of mind, would easily be overcome. And so, once our powers have been measured out, let us, leaving stronger matters to the stronger, pursue the explanation of the literal sense that has been begun." — "Haec sunt quae in nos tela jaciunt Judaei, sacrarum nos litterarum depravatores et violentos distortores appellantes. Quibus ut respondeamus nec opus est, cum alii ante nos hoc fecerunt, sed an

sufficienter responsum sit, ipsi qui responderunt viderint; nec utile, ne si forte anceps certamen imparibus ineuntes viribus succumbamus, non nobis solis sed et illis quorum acutissimi vivacitate ingenii si cum eis congress[i] fuissent, facile superarentur, doctores insultent. Nos itaque, nostris viribus emensis, fortiora fortioribus linquentes, coeptam litteralis sensus explanationem exsequamur." *Objectiones magistri Andreae*, in Richard, *De Emman. prol.* (PL, CXCVI, 603-4).

38. In the introduction to his interesting little work on *Jeanne d'Arc* (1950, 8), Joseph Calmette writes: "The history of Christianity has not changed in any of its smallest details, whether one affirm or deny the divinity of Christ. Hence, the historian, if he is respectful of the objectivity of his science, ought — and because he ought, he can — abstract from all metaphysics as well as all theology alike" — "L'histoire du christianisme n'est changée dans aucun de ses plus minimes détails, soit qu'on affirme, soit qu'on nie la divinité du Christ. L'historien donc, s'il est respectueux de l'objectivité de sa science, doit — et parce qu'il le doit, il le peut — faire abstraction, en pareil cas, de toute métaphysique aussi bien que de toute théologie." But several lines later (p. 9) he also says: "In history, the great rule is to understand" — "La grande règle, en histoire, c'est de comprendre." Does he who affirms the divinity of Christ truly comprehend the history of Christianity completely in the same way as he who denies it, even if they perfectly agree on the inventory of "its most infinitesimal details" — "ses plus infimes détails"?

39. Cf. M. Blondel, *Histoire et dogme*, 2ᵉ partie, "l'historicisme" (*Prémiers écrits*, 2, 1957). Maurice Blondel and August Valensin, *Correspondance*, 1 (1957), 110-31; 113, Blondel to Wehrlé: "We totally disintegrate to complete fragmentation without ever knowing whether we are talking about a mere methodological abstraction or a decisive doctrine" — "On désintègre tout jusqu'à l'effritement complet, sans qu'on sache jamais si c'est d'une abstraction méthodologique ou d'une doctrine définitive qu'on parle." "Methodological problems whose importance and consequences are infinite" — "Problèmes méthodologiques dont l'importance et les conséquences sont infinies," said Blondel again (letter of 6 February 1903): *Au cœur de la crise moderniste, le dossier inédit d'une controverse*, by René Marlé (1960), 75: "the whole question is how to know whether the facts require or exclude a metaphysics and a theology" — "toute la question est de savoir si les faits exigeront ou excluront une métaphysique et une théologie" (76); etc.

40. Calandra, 67-77. Smalley, RTAM, 18 (1951), 29-65.

41. It would be unfitting to explain it, as did the English scholar Bale, by a feeling of envy on the part of the Scotsman Richard toward the Englishman Andrew. Cf. Calandra, 5.

42. "sympathies secrètes entre son œuvre et la philosophie nouvelle": Delhaye, ET, 177.

43. In the *Fons Philosophiae*, however, he does manifest a harsh attitude toward certain contemporary schools.

44. "sagittae potentis acutae": *Microcosmus*, prol: "So take the bow of sacred Scripture and the sharp arrows of the powerful will be given to you, to wit, the judgments of philosophy and theology, crossing unto the hearts of the king's enemies.... According to my capacity I have done what I could, not to kill men but vices, not to ruin souls but to save them" — "Accipe ergo arcum sacrae Scripturae

et dabuntur tibi sagittae potentis acutae, id est sententiae philosophicae et theologicae, transeuntes usque ad corda inimicorum regis. . . . Pro modulo meo operatus sum quod potui, non ad occidendos homines sed vitia, non ad perdendas animas sed salvandas" (30).

45. "qu'une vaste allégorie aux intentions moralisatrices": Delhaye, ET, 276; cf. 62.

46. "triplex gregoriana expositio": L. 3, c. 201 (Delhaye, 222).

47. *Micr.*, l. 3, c. 201 (221). Cf. Delhaye, ET, 199.

48. Strophes 171-2, v. 681-700 (Michaud-Quentin, 59). Cf. Delhaye, ET, 24.

49. *C. quatuor labyrinthos Franciae* (ca. 1177-78), l. 4, c. 4 (Glorieux, AHDLMA, 19, 273). St. Thomas will appear to answer him, *In Boet. de Trin.*, q. 2, a. 3, ad 5m: "Those who make of us philosophical authorities . . . in service of the faith do not mix water with wine but rather change water into wine" — "Illi qui utuntur philosophicis documentis . . . in obsequium fidei, non miscent aquam vino, sed convertunt aquam in vinum."

50. Delhaye, ET, 30-2.

51. "Knowledge falsely so called" — "Falsi nominis scientia"; "they have made a shipwreck of the faith" — "circa fidem naufragaverunt" (Glorieux, 274).

52. "putridae ranarum garrulitates" — "nova ex veteri haeresis": Glorieux, 231.

53. "There are also many other things . . . in their books that are contrary to the Catholic truth" — "Sunt et alia multa . . . in libris istorum contraria catholicae veritati" (MS, cited by Ghellinck, *Mouvement*, 263, note 1). "Those heretics of Lombardy and Poiteau" — "Isti lumbardini sive pictavini haeretici" (Glorieux, 293).

54. "regulae dialecticorum" — "Si eis credis, utrum Deus sit an non Deus . . . , nescis": L. 4, c. 9 (Glorieux, 275): "not a dialectical, but a diabolical art" — "non dialecticam, sed diabolicam artem" (232).

55. In Glorieux's edition: 3 citations from Gregory, 21 from Jerome.

56. the "siliquae porcorum" — the "calix daemoniorum": L. 4, c. 4 and 6 (Glorieux, 273-4). Cf. Jerome, *ep.* 21, to Damasus, c. 13; *ep.* 22, to Eustochius, c. 29 (1, 93, 144).

57. Glorieux, 249, 272, 310, etc. Peter Lombard is "another Origen" — an "alter Origenes": 326.

58. the "princeps dialecticorum": l. 4, c. 7 (274). Cf. Jerome, *In ep. ad Titum* (PL, XXVI, 596 A).

59. *C. quat. labyr.* (P. Glorieux, AHDLMA, 19, 187-335). Cf. P. Glorieux, *Mauvaise action et mauvais travail*, RTAM, 21 (1954), 179-93. R. Baron, RTAM, 22 (1955), 58-9: "He would have had a good hand if he could have extracted any passages warning against reason and science from Hugh's works; but he failed to do precisely that, though Hugh's constant concern was that of putting things in their proper place" — "Il eût eu beau jeu d'extraire de l'œuvre hugonienne des passages mettant en garde contre la raison et la science; mais précisément il eût fallu les extraire, et le souci constant de Hugues fut celui de la mise en place."

60. His editor J. Picard says: "Now our Garnier far excels all abridgers and anthologizers, or at least it is extremely clear to him that epitomes of great works have been put together with this or that intention or taste, so that what tastes

good to your palate tastes bad to mine, and hardly any compendium free from faults is ever brought forth. Over and above this, we have shown that Gregory's other epitomizers attained only one portion of his work, whereas Garnier hit them all" — "Universis autem breviatoribus et anthologis quam longe Garnerus noster antecellat, vel huic potissimum liquet quod magnorum operum epitomata hoc sint ingenio saporeque condita, ut quod tuo sapiat palato, disipiat meo, vixque compendium proferatur alicujus dispendii liberum. Super haec, manifestavimus Gregorii contractores unicum ejus attigere opus, Garnerus omnia" (PL, CXCIII, 21 C). The work was so esteemed in its own day that Nigellus made *Excerptiones* of it: A. Boutemy, *Nigellus de Longchamp*, 1 (1959), 44-5.

61. As to the procedure of the "distinctio" itself, it has justly been said that it was as old as the study of the Bible. H. Dumont, COCR, 1957, 120-1. Cf. HE, 309-11.

62. Cf. Fourier Bonnard, 1, 119. Delhaye, ET, 219-25.

63. Like that of St. Augustine, it always involved a sermon. G. Dumaige, ed. of Richard of Saint Victor, *Les quatre degrés de la violente charité* (1955), 105-6; he also notes the profound influence of Gregorian mysticism upon Richard.

64. "le plus magique artisan verbal qui ait fait résonner le psaltérion latin" — "se nourrissent de la même sève doctrinale, mystique et symbolique": Ghellinck, *L'essor*, 2, 295-8. H. O. Taylor, *The Medieval Mind*, 2, 67, note. On the "spiritual objectivity" which characterizes the poetry of Adam: Chr. Mohrmann, *Le latin médiéval*, CCM, 1 (1958), 292-3. Cf. J. Chatillon, RMAL, 8 (1952), 247-50. F. Wellner, *Adam von Sankt-Viktor, Sämtliche Sequenzen*, 2 (1955). Let us also call attention to Achard, author of a *de Trinitate, de unitate et pluralitate creaturarum* (RTAM, 21, 1954); J. Ribaillier, ed. of the *De Trinitate* of Richard (1958), introd., 27-33; J. Chatillon, *loc. cit.*, 250-2, and *Mél. Cavallera* (1948), 317-37.

65. See below, section 5, "Explosion of the Three Disciplines."

66. S. 28 (PL, CCXI, 164-5). S. 43 (250 A). Cf. s. 33 (198 CD); s. 45 (258 D).

67. S. 4 (CCXI, 36-7). Cf. *Aeneid*, 1. 6, 136-48; *Iliad*, 8, 17-27.

68. S. 49 (282 D).

69. S. 4 (37 BD). S. 30 (179-80).

70. S. 30 (180 CD).

71. S. 30: "Consequently let us see that by the golden cups that are on the candelabra are to be understood the learned men capable of receiving God's word, who, in discussing the Scriptures with others, are held to offer the drink of life" — "Consequenter videamus, quoniam per scyphos aureos qui sunt in candelabro, viri literati capaces verbi Dei, qui aliis Scripturas disserendo potum vitae propinare tenentur, intelligendi sunt" (180 B).

72. S. 6 (47 A). Cf. S. 25, on those who "entirely surrender themselves to the study of secular philosophy, the life-giving knowledge of Christ having been cast aside" — "abjecta vitali scientia Christi, toto studio saeculari philosophiae se tradiderunt" (151 D).

73. S. 7 (52 BC).

74. S. 25 (149 C).

75. S. 7 (52 D); s. 15 (93-4). [Trans.: cf. the remark addressed to Solon in *Timaeus* 22.]

76. S. 31 (183 C).

77. S. 19: "Sacred Scripture informs man's will both through knowledge of the truth and through the love of virtue" — "Sacra siquidem Scriptura voluntatem hominis informat, tum per cognitionem veritatis, tum per amorem virtutis" (114 C). S. 14: "The investigators of sacred Scripture walk along a well-lit path, reading the book of God's law inside and out: inside through knowing the truth, outside through practicing good action. For those who read the book of God's law inside and not outside, i.e., who talk and do not act, ought to be called brooders rather than investigators of Sacred Scripture" — "Via lucida gradiuntur sacrae Scripturae investigatores, legentes librum Dei legis intus et foris: intus per cognitionem veritatis, foris per exercitium boni operis. Qui enim legunt librum legis Dei intus et non foris, hoc est, qui dicunt et non faciunt, magis incubatores sacrae Scripturae quam investigatores debent appellari" (88 CD, 89 A); etc. Cf. S. 7 (50 B).

78. "le mysticisme allégorique à une pensée profonde" — "à santé intellectuelle si manifeste" — "instruits" — "ponderées" — "travers" — "goût abusif": L'essor, 219, 295; Litt. lat., 1, 54.

79. S. 19 (114 D); s. 27 (158 D); s. 28 (164 A, 166 B).

80. S. 46 (263 D); s. 29 (177 B). On the four senses: s. 39 (227 AB).

81. See above, ch. 3.5. Absalon loves trinary and quaternary divisions; for him they are a constant developmental device. In this manner he explains the three or four sorts of shadow, honey, music, water, paradise, bread, clothing, heaven, marriage, banquets, exile, enemies, wisdom, contemplation, obedience, and inspirations of the Spirit. In this procedure he sometimes borrows from real poems: thus *sermon 6*, for Christmas, on the threefold silence and the threefold word (43-8).

82. "dans le sillage des Victorins": *Théol. au XIIe s.*, 192.

83. On his formation at Paris and at Chartres: R. L. Poole, *Engl. Hist. Rev.*, 35 (1950), 321-42.

84. "curiales nugae": *Metal.*, prol.: "since by my Lord's command ... concern for the whole of Britain falls to me, as far as the affairs of the church are concerned" — "cum ex mandato domini mei ... sollicitudo totius Britanniae, quoad causas ecclesiasticas mihi incumbat"; "the yammering at court used to impede study" — "curiales nugae studium excludebant" (c. 1; Webb, 3); l. 3, c. 1: "ten times harder than climbing the passes of the Alps" — "Alpium juga transcendi decies." *Polyc.*, tit.: "on the nonsense of the courtly and the footsteps of the philosophers" — "seu de nugis curialium et vestigiis philosophorum"; prol.: "it partially contained the nonsense at court" — "nugas pro parte continet curiales"; c. 3: "for it wears one down to have been subjected to nonsense for almost a dozen years" — "jam enim annis fere duodecim nugatum esse taedet" (Webb, 1, 13 and 14). Cf. Aug., *Conf.*, l. 1, c. 9, n. 15 (1, 14).

85. *Polycr.*, prol.: "who kept me so long in courtly blatherings and still keeps me subject to slavery" — "qui me in curialibus nugis tamdiu tenuit et tenet adhuc obnoxium servituti"; l. 1, c. 1: "amidst hypocritical lies" — "per exteriora mendacia" (W., 14 and 18).

86. *Pol.*, l. 5, c. 10: "For who is there whose virtue the flatteries of court will not drive away?" — "Quis est enim cui virtutem non excutiant curialium nugae?"; "the triflings of the courtly" — "curialium ineptias" (W., 1, 329). L. 7,

prol.: "Rare indeed is he who is up to preserving his character in philosophical and courtly duties, since he will ever more frequently face the latter quite aghast" — "Rarus est admodum qui philosophicis et curialibus officiis sufficiat morem gerere, cum haec os sibi plerumque constet plurimum adversari" (2, 91). John's fall from favor with the king [Henry II] would date from 1156, not from 1159, and one would understand the tone of the *Polycraticus* better from that time: G. Constable, "The Alleged Disgrace of J. of S. in 1159," *Engl. Hist. Rev.*, 69 (1954). Cf. BTAM, 8, no. 1943.

87. *Ep.* 196: "Of great Aristippus, who was wont to use every situation with equanimity and to be philosophical in the midst of much nonsense, pleasant to all, severe to none" — "Magni Aristippi, qui omni conditione temporis aequanimiter utebatur et in ipsis philosophabatur nugis, jucundus omnibus, nulli gravis" (PL, CXCIX, 216 A).

88. "esprit léger, agréable et sceptique": *La Renaissance*, introd. (H. de Fr., nouv. éd., 9, 1876, 48).

89. "viva ratio": *Met.*, prol. (825 B); l. 1, c. 24 (855 D). *Enthet.*, v. 1145-64 (990 BC). Knowing how to doubt: *Pol.* (W., 1, 18-19). On the Academici: *Pol.*, l. 7, c. 1-3 (W., 2, 93-101).

90. *Enthet.*, v. 11-22 (965 B).

91. *Ep.* 161: "So since the figure of this world is passing like a shadow, and it is vanishing like smoke in the movement of a whirlwind in the sight of the philosophers" — "Cum ergo figura hujus mundi pertranseat velut umbra, et momento turbinis ut fumus evanescat in conspectu philosophantium" (152 CD).

92. "Non satis homo est, quem aliena non movent"; "Patet indignum esse tanto magistro discipulum, qui veritati non congaudet et adversus publicae salutis hostes non excandescit": *Pol.*, l. 3, prol. (1, 170-1).

93. *Pol.*, l. 7, c. 21 and 23 (2, 191-3, 204-210).

94. *Ep.* 168: "I regard no one as wise who opposes a peace that can be confected in the Lord and does not immediately threaten to detract from one's honor" [Trans.: paraphrasing the temporal metaphor, literally "before a winter day" (*himerinus*, "wintry")]. "Neminem tamen arbitror sapientem qui dissuadeat pacem, quae fieri potest in Domino et ante himerinum diem honestati non derogat" (159 B).

95. *Ep.* 245 (287-8).

96. To him he preaches moderation, modesty, humility, mercy: *ep.* 175, 182, 220, 232, 237 (167-9, 181 D, 246 AB, 261 B, 267-8). Cf. *ep.* 138: that Thomas should trust more in prayer and spiritual practises than to "laws civil and canon" — "leges et canones" (117-8).

97. Ph. Delhaye, "Le Bien suprême d'après le *Polycraticus* de Jean de S.," RTAM, 20 (1953), 219. He maintains, however, that the way to *beatitudo* is the moral path: cf. W. Kleincke (1937; BTAM, 4, no. 1023).

98. *Med. Humanism in the Life and Writings of John of Sal.* (1950), 23-6.

99. "Ubi Spiritus Dei, ibi libertas": *Pol.*, l. 4, prol. (1, 234). *Ep.* 197 (216 D); *ep.* 225 (231 D).

100. *Ep.* 138 (117-8).

101. *Pol.*, l. 6, c. 24: "For, as was said by many, the Roman Church, which is the mother of all the churches, presents herself to the others not so much to be a

mother as a step-mother. There are standing within her scribes and Pharisees setting unbearable burdens on the shoulders of men without lifting a finger to help. They lord it over the clergy and do not provide an example for the flock. . . . They batter their churches. . . . They provide justice not so much in truth as for a price. . . . The palaces of the priests are splendid, yet in their hands the Church of Christ is made dirty. They pillage the provinces as if they intend to accumulate the treasures of Croesus" — "Sicut enim dicebatur a multis, Romana Ecclesia, quae mater omnium ecclesiarum est, se non tam matrem exhibet aliis quam novercam. Sedent in ea Scribae et Pharisaei, ponentes onera importabilia in humeris hominum, quae digito non contingunt. Dominatur in clero, nec forma fiunt gregi. . . . Concutiunt ecclesias. . . . Justitiam non tam veritati quam pretio reddunt. . . . Palatia splendent sacerdotum, et in manibus eorum Christi sordidatur Ecclesia. Provinciarum diripiunt spolia, ac si thesauros Cresi studeant reparare etc." (2, 67-8). These matters were addressed to his friend Pope Adrian IV; he will bemoan his death: *Metal.*, l. 4, c. 42 (217).

102. *Pol.*, l. 5, c. 16: "if" that office "were fulfilled with as much care as it is sometimes sought with so much ambition" — "si tanta impleretur (officium) sollicitudine quanta interdum petitur ambitione" (1, 354); l. 8, c. 17: "But priests ought not be upset with me, even if I say that tyrants can be found among them" — "Mihi vero indignari non debent sacerdotes, si et in eis fateor inveniri posse tyrannos" (2, 349). *Ib.*, he calls him as witness: "I call to the defense blessed Gregory, who used to say only true and tactful things, and who pursued them rather rigorously" — "illum qui non nisi vera loquebatur et dulcia, in patrocinium advoco b. Gregorium, qui acerbius ista persequitur" (357).

103. *Pol.*, l. 3, c. 5 (1, 180-4).

104. "assistere veritati pium est, et Romano pontifici devotissime famulari": *Pol.*, l. 8, c. 23 (2, 405).

105. "Cui deest gratia Ecclesiae, tota creatrix Trinitas adversatur": *ep.* 64 (49 D).

106. "Hanc (obedientiam) Christus edicto promulgavit et exemplo, factus obediens usque ad mortem, docens quibus finibus virtus obedientiae deceat limitari. Obediendum enim est non modo usque ad jacturam temporalium et corporis cruciatus, sed usque ad exitum mortis": *ep.* 207 (231 D).

107. Some parallel passages have also been found: *Pol.*, l. 4, c. 3 and l. 6, c. 9: cf. Bernard, *De cons.*, l. 4, c. 3 and *ep.* 256 (Webb, *Pol.*, v. 2, 22, note 16). The two perspectives are, however, not identical.

108. *Met.*, l. 2, c. 17: "to show off their knowledge they educate their hearers in such wise as not to be understood by them" — "ad ostentationem scientiae suae sic suos instituunt auditores ut non intelligantur ab eis" (91). Cf. Cassian, *Coll.* 14, c. 9 (SC, 54, 194).

109. "jettent au vent les feuilles des paroles sans mûrir le fruit des sens": *Met.*, l. 1, c. 3: "Sine fructu sensuum, herborum folia in ventum continue profert" (9); l. 2, c. 7: *Nugidici ventilatores!* (73). *Enthet.*, v. 119-20 (967 D); v. 333 (972 B):

Nugifluus verbum sine tempore fundit ineptus.
The incompetent trifler spills an untimely word.

110. Godfrey's judgment confirms that of John: Lesne, 5, 213.

111. *Ep.* 6 (PL, CCVII, 17-9; v. 1155). Cf. Abelard, *Th. Chr.*, l. 3: "the impudence" that "the life and garrulity of the students of" dialectic develop — "impudentiam scholarium ejus (dialecticae) vita et garrulitas" (CLXXIII, 1215 D).

112. Both groups disdain to study the authors, be they classical writers or Fathers of the Church. But it is difficult to compare two groups each of which is ill-identified. Furthermore, certain criticisms become part of the common vocabulary, applied sometimes to quite distinct adversaries. Cf. Anselm of Laon, letter to the Abbot of S. Laurent de Liège: "certain men very much puffed up by the name of science, though not knowing the sense of the Fathers, languish, as the Apostle says, about questions and fights over words" — "quidam maxime inflati nomine scientiae, sensus Patrum ignorantes, languent, ut ait Apostulus, circa quaestiones et pugnas verborum" (CLXII, 1587 A). One historian believed that he could relate these "quidam" of John's Cornificians and their counterparts criticised by Peter of Blois; indeed, it was Rupert that was in question! As for Hauréau, blinded by his own anti-mystical attitude, he made the Cornifician out to be "un mystique et peut-être un victorin": *H. de la phil. scol.*, 1, 517.

113. Paré, 191-4. Cf. H. Liebschütz, *op. cit.*, app. 4: "The Personality of Cornificius."

114. "et quidquid Latinis Graecia capta dedit": *Enthet.*, v. 112 (967 D).

115. *Met.*, prol.: "I have undertaken a defense of logic" — "logicae suscepi patrocinium" etc. (3).

116. *Met.*, l. 2, c. 7 (72); c. 6 (68). Cf. *Enthet.*, v. 116-7 (967 D).

117. L. 1, c. 1: "Which has given birth to so many outstanding cities, has reconciled and allied so many kingdoms" — "Quae tot egregias genuit urbes, tot conciliavit et federavit regna, etc." (7).

118. *Ep.* 284: "It is the common loss of practically all scholars not that there is a lack of those who profess the obligation to speak, but that there is a lack of those who actually teach it" — "Omnium fere scholarium jactura communis est, non quia desint qui dicendi profiteantur officium, sed quia desunt qui doceant etc." (3129 D). Paré, 135: "There was never so vigorous a criticism of what is today contemptuously called 'scholastic' method, as that by this scholastic of the 12th century; never was the sentiment about the formative value of the modest 'explication of a text' so solidly met with and proclaimed" — "Jamais plus vigoureuse critique ne fut faite de la méthode dite aujourd'hui, par mépris, 'scolastique', que par ce scolastique du XIIe siècle; jamais sentiment de la valeur formatrice de la modeste explication d'un texte ne fut si solidement éprouvé et proclamé."

119. *Met.*, l. 1, c. 24: "But though other disciplines too contribute to literature, this one by singular privilege is said to produce a literate man. . . . Hence it is probable that he who holds grammar in contempt is not only not a man of letters, but ought not even to be so called" — "Licet autem et aliae disciplinae ad litteraturam proficiant, haec privilegio singulari facere dicitur litteratum. . . . Unde probabile est quod contemptor grammaticae non modo litterator non est, sed nec litteratus dici debet" (58).

120. Ghellinck, *L'essor*, 1, 14; 2, 317-21. The same fact seen from the other way around: J.-M. Parent, "Un nouveau témoin de la théol. dionysienne au XIIe siècle," *Beiträge Bauemker*, 1935, 290.

121. Scholastic Latin was "at first completely saturated with technical and

foreign components" — "d'abord tout saturé d'éléments techniques et étrangers"; but it "achieved a clearer, even a nobler, form in the Latin of St. Thomas Aquinas who, perhaps thanks to his Italian origin, turned this drab and technical language of the schools into a more lively and 'human' Latin" — "trouvera une forme plus claire, plus noble aussi, dans le latin de S. Thomas d'Aquin qui, grâce peut-être à son origine italienne, modifie cette langue terne et technique des écoles en un latin plus vivant et plus 'humain.'" Chr. Mohrmann, "Le latin médiéval," CCM, 1 (1958), 283.

122. "sine qua quicquid insulsum et insipidum est, et plane erroneum, et bonis moribus displiciens": *Met.*, l. 2, c. 6 (69).

123. "stimulus quaestionum"; "avide des sept voies": Bernard, *ep.* 361 (PL, CLXXXII, 562 BD). Cf. Webb, *John of Sal.* (1932), 14. J. Milor and H. E. Butler, *The Letters of J. of S.* 1 (1955), xix, xxiv.

124. "optime litterati et admodum eloquentes, sed dissimilibus studiis": C. 8-12 (M. Chibnall, 15-26). Position analogous to that of Otto, *Gesta Friderici*, l. 1, c. 47, 50, 57 (MGH, Scr., 20, 376-7, 379, 384).

125. *Ep.* 96-6 (87 C, 89 A).

126. "Graecus interpres et grammaticus": John could not have failed to know these two dialogues, translated by Aristippus in 1154 and 1156. Abbé Raymond Marcel, "Le Platonisme de Pétrarque à Léon l'Hébreu," Ass. G. Budé, congrès de Tours-Poitiers, 1953-4, 293. Cf. R. Klibansky, *Corpus platonicum medii aevi*, 1-2 (1940; Kordenter-Labowsky and Minio-Paluello). E. Franceschini, *Richerche e studi su Aristotele nel Medioevo latino* (Milan, 1956).

127. *Ep.* 211 (235 C; in 1167). *Met.*, l. 2, c. 10 (81); etc.

128. "quisquis logicum profitetur ridiculus est": *Met.*, l. 2, c. 2-5 (58-62); c. 16: all the masters in dialectic "give way to Aristotle" — "Aristoteli cedunt" (873 BC). Nevertheless, "it is a bit surprising to see John of Salisbury greet the appearance of these books [of Aristotle] as a rebirth, since Gerbert was already using the *Topics* translated by Cicero and commented on by Boethius" — "on s'étonne un peu de voir Jean de S. saluer l'apparition de ces livres (d'Aristote) comme une renaissance, car déjà Gerbert utilisait les Topiques traduits par Cicéron et commentés par Boèce": R. Marcel, *Marsile Ficin*, 40. L. 4, c. 2 (916 D); c. 24, against the disciples of Robert of Melun who denigrate Aristotle (930 CD); c. 27: he is often mistaken, but he excels in logic (931-4).

129. "mira suavitas dicendi": *Pol.*, l. 7, c. 6: "Now though he be regarded as a troubler of names and verbs, he so prevailed not only in subtlety, which is well-known to all, but also in the marvelous sweetness of expression, that he seems to have been deservedly put next to Plato" — "Licet autem nominum et verborum turbator habeatur, non modo subtilitate, quae cunctis celebris est, sed mira suavitate dicendi evaluit adeo quidem ut Platoni merito proximus fuisse videatur" (2, 113).

130. Magnus Aristoteles sermonum possidet artes
　　Et de virtutum culmine nomen habet:

Enthet., v. 821-2 (983 A); cf. v. 671-2 (979 D). [Trans.: Gk. *ariston* means "best," and *telos* means "end," "limit," or "goal."]

131. *Pol.*, l. 7, c. 7 (2, 115-6).

132. "l'évolution qui, au XIIIe siècle, proclamera l'autonomie des formes de la nature, des méthodes de l'esprit, des lois de la société": Chenu, 86; cf. 50.

133. Curtius, 97. Zumthor, 181. Petrarch's reproach against the Averroists, analogous to his reproaches against the Cornificians: *De sui ipsius et multorum ignorantia*, c. 2 (Capelli, 21) and *Rer. Gen.*, passim.

134. *Pol.*, l. 7, c. 11: "If the love of God is being extinguished, the name of philosophy is vanishing!": "Si amor Dei exstinguitur, philosophiae nomen evanescit!" (2, 135).

135. *Met.*, prol.: "Having reckoned that all things that are read just as [those that] are written are useless, except to the extent that they contribute some assistance to life, I have consciously included a few points about morals; for any profession of philosophizing that does not open itself to the cultivation of virtue and the advancement of life is useless and false" — "De moribus vero nonnulla scienter inserui; ratus omnia quae leguntur ut scribuntur, inutilia esse, nisi quatenus afferunt aliquod adminiculum vitae; est enim qualibet professio philosophandi inutilis et falsa, quae seipsam in cultu virtutis et vitae exhibitione non aperit" (825 B). *Ep.* 197: "Nor is there anything that does a philosopher more credit than proclaiming the truth, cultivating justice, not taking the world too seriously, and, when necessary, loving poverty" — "Nec est quod magis philosophum deceat quam professio veritatis, justitiae cultus, contemptus mundi, et paupertatis cum necesse est amor" (216-7).

136. *Pol.*, l. 4, c. 3: "A dead man rising ... refuted Aristotle's subtleties and the snares of all the philosophers" — "Astutias Aristotelis . . . omniumque philosophorum tendiculas resurgens mortuus refutabat" (1, 243). Cf. l. 8, c. 24, for introducing allusions to Virgil and Homer: "If using the words of gentiles is allowed to a Christian, who believes that ingenuity is divine for the elect alone and pleasing to God through indwelling grace, even though I believe that neither the words nor the meanings of the gentiles need to be fled from, so long as their errors are avoided" — "Si verbis gentilium uti licet christiano, qui solis electis divinum et Deo placens per inhabitantem gratiam esse credit ingenium, etsi nec verba nec sensus credam gentilium fugiendos, dummodo vitentur errores etc." (2, 415).

137. *Met.*, l. 2, c. 8 (74).

138. "divinae paginae libri": *Pol.*, l. 7, c. 12: "I might perchance have granted that the books of the divine page, every jot and tittle of which is full of divine sacraments, are to be read with so much seriousness, because the treasury of the Holy Spirit by whose finger [these sacraments] have been written cannot ever be exhausted; for though the surface of the letter is fitted to just one sense, a multiplicity of mysteries lies concealed within" — "Divinae paginae libros, quorum singuli apices divinis pleni sunt sacramentis, tanta gravitate legendos forte concesserim, eo quod thesaurus Spiritus sancti, cujus digito scripta sunt, omnino nequat exhauriri; licet enim ad unum tantummodo sensum accommodata sit superficies litterae, multiplicitas mysteriorum intrinsecus latet, etc." (2, 144; see above, vol. 1, ch. 2.4).

139. *Pol.*, l. 8, c. 1: "Gregory, or rather the Holy Spirit through Gregory, [says] this" — "Haec quidem Gregorius, imo per Gregorium Spiritus sanctus" (2, 230). *Ep.* (118 A, 130 A); etc.

140. "Ecclesiae doctor insignis, vir fere omnium litterarum": *Hist. pont.*, prol. (Chibnall, 1).

141. Aside from Webb, cf. M. Dal Pra, *Giovanni di Sal.* (Milano, 1951); Ghellinck, *L'essor;* J. Leclercq, *St. ans.*, 20, 9. One can also read, though out-dated in certain points, the biography of M. Demiduid (1873).

142. B. Smalley, "The School of Andrew of SV," RTAM, 11 (1939), 145-67.

143. A. Boutemy, *Nigellus de Longchamp*, 61-3.

144. One will soon supplement it by the borrowings in the Parisian Bible and collections of legends. Many editions between 1473 and 1526.

145. At that time didactic works, even in poetry, enjoyed great success; e.g., the *Anticlaudianus* of Alan of Lille.

146. "la décision prise . . . de restaurer l'*historia*, sainte dans sa lettre même"; "curiosité neuve pour les textes scripturaires": Cf. Smalley, *The Study*, c. 5. Chenu, in the *Festgabe Lortz* (1957), 69; *Mél. A. Pelzer* (1947), 162. Peter is, on the other hand, one of those who introduced the deplorable custom of glossing the Gloss: Ghellinck, *Mouvement*, 111.

147. *Hist. scol.*, Incipit (PL, CXCVIII, 1054-5).

148. *Etym.*, l. 1, c. 44 (LXXXII, 123-4): ephemerides, annals, history. It came from Aulus Gellius: Fontaine, 180-5.

149. "consacre et étend dans l'usage courant de l'école et de la prédication la méthode historico-littérale de Saint-Victor": The same goes for Smalley, 259; 214: "The greatest triumph for the Victorine tradition was the success of the *Histories*."

150. "vir facundissimus": Robert of Auxerre (MGH, *Scr.*, 26, 240).

151. See, among others, the sermon edited by Father Martin, RTAM, 1931, 61-4.

152. Sermons "held in school" — "habita in schola"; addressed "to men in the scholasticate" — "ad viros scolasticos"; "to educated men" — "ad litteratos." Cf. Lesne, 5, 549-50.

153. *S.* 10: "Let us also serve up a bit of meal for the mystical understanding, so that the husk and the surface of the letter may be sweetened. So we say that three things are set before us in the surface of the words" — "Apponamus et nos farinulam mysticae intelligentiae, ut dulcoretur cortex et superficies litterae. Dicimus ergo quod in hac superficie verborum tria nobis apponuntur" (PL, CXCVIII, 1749 CD).

154. *S.* 30: "The surface of the letter seems to be dry and bloodless, but it is a deep well (John 4). Let us scrape at it and perhaps we shall find living water sweet to drink" — "Litterae superficies, arida quidem et exsanguis videtur, sed puteus altus est (John 4). Eraderemus ipsum, et fortasse inveniemus aquam vivam et suavem ad bibendum" (1788 D); etc. Cf. Greg., *In ev.*, h. 22, n. 2 (LXXVI, 1174 D). Perhaps the unedited commentary of the Eater on the Gospels (signaled by Hauréau, *Notices et extraits*, I ([1890], 4-6), might contain something to modify these observations somewhat.

155. J. P. Bonnes, RB, 56, compares two unedited sermons, the one by Geoffroy Babion and the other by Peter the Eater, on the same subject, to show the contrast between the two kinds: 209-10. See also Ghellinck, *Mouvement*, 175.

156. Ch. Dumont, COCR, 1957, 120-1. The author shows an analogous contrast between the sermons of Aelred and those of Gilbert Foliot, who, from the

middle of the century, uses the procedure of "distinctions": "he is basically a school-worshipper who gets to play hard at being a spiritual" — "c'est au fond un écolâtre qui se fait fort de jouer au spirituel." Bourgain distinguishes two varieties in Peter: his last sermons, at the time of his retreat to Saint Victor, had more meatiness and simplicity (*La chaire chrét. au XIIe s.*, 122, 250).

157. "Sumitur allegoria, quandoque a persona, quandoque a re, quandoque a loco, quandoque a tempore, quandoque a facto": *Hist. scol.* (CXCVIII, 1055 A). But let's not force the contrast. The methods of development are also found in certain monastic sermons; thus Helinand, s. 4 on the epiphany: "Erant autem in istis stella quinque notabilia: tempus, locus, motus, claritas et magnitudo" (CCXII, 514 A).

158. Cf. Richard, *In Ap.*, l. 1, c. 1: "In eo quidem quod dicit: qui legit, designat litteratos sive doctores; in eo autem quod dicit: qui audit, exprimit laicos sive auditores" (CXCVI, 645 A).

159. "magistrorum parisiensium prim[u]s": *Loc. cit.*

160. *In Cant.*, s. 36, n. 3 (CLXXXIII, 1055 A).

161. "viri literati": 29 Oct. 1174, P. Glorieux, MSR, 11, 22-3. Lesne, 5, 428-9, 477. On the criticism of the venal masters of the 11th and 12th centuries: Lesne, 5, 483-92.

162. S. 10: "John Scotus says: This is how Scripture usually speaks to the God-seeing kind of man, not to the one that follows along on foot. The footman is the kind of man who cannot know God through the understanding of the Scriptures, but somehow tracks his footprints through the visible things of this world.... The things just mentioned are put forth not for this kind of human, but for the God-seeing, namely, the one who sees God through an understanding of the Scriptures, e.g., the cloistered scholars and men of letters; these things are put to them so that, leaving aside their surface, they might labor within the correct meaning of those words, so as to know that beneath the childish surface of words one thing is hidden within, whilst another resounds without" — "Dicit J. Scotus: Sic solet Scriptura loqui deivido generi humano, non pedisequo. Pedisequum genus hominum est, qui Deum cognoscere non possunt per intelligentiam Scripturarum, sed vestigia ejus quoquo modo indagant per visibilia hujus mundi.... Huic generi hominum praedicta non proponuntur, sed deivido, qui sc. Deum videt per intelligentiam Scripturarum, ut sunt scholares et litterati claustrales; quae ad hoc illis proponuntur, ut laborent in justa significatione verborum illorum, praetermittentes superficiem eorum, ut ita sciant sub puerili verborum superficie aliud intus latere, aliud exterius sonare" (1749 BC).

163. *S. de inc. Verbi:* "To us . . . , I mean to the men of letters, to whom knowing has been given" — "Ad nos . . . , ad litteratos inquam, quibus datum est nosse etc." (CLXXI, 364 D; cf. D). This "litteratus," however, is a "speculative," as disdainful of the "pale arguments of the sophists" — "pallida sophistarum argumenta" — as he is of the "fictions of the poets" — "figmenta poetarum" (*s. ined* . . . , cf. Lesne, 5, 241).

164. "Beati ergo sunt litterati, quibus praesto est sacra Scriptura, qui paratas habent auctoritates utriusque Testamenti, quibus possint ignea tela inimici exstinguere! Si sic est, utique beati! Sed . . . non omnes litterati habitant 'in adjutorio Altissimi'. Sunt enim quidam qui sacram Scripturam timent, alii etiam

irrident, alii eam destruunt, alii eam contemnunt, alii per eam transeunt, alii habitant in ea. Qui timent eam, pigri sunt; qui irrident, superbi sunt; qui destruunt, haeretici; qui contemnunt, falsi fratres; qui transeunt, hospites; qui habitant in ea, cives": S. 12 (CXCVIII, 1755 A).

165. "Esca vero grandium, spiritualis est et intellectiva. Haec est sacra Scriptura, quae quot documenta, totidem proponit fercula litterato."

"Grandes enim in Ecclesia litteratos dicimus; de quibus Apostolus: 'Vos qui majores estis, instruite hujusmodi' (Gal. 6)": S. 20 (1778 A). [Trans.: the Vulgate reads 'spirituales' instead of 'majores'.]

166. the "claustrales" and the "scholars"; "Domine, doce nos orare"; "Domine, doce nos lectioni vacare, quoniam suavis est sapientia": S. in Epiph. (Hildebert, s. 14; CLXXI, 412-3). Gébouin de Troyes maintains a perfect balance between the "scholares," who devote themselves to the "expositio Scripturarum," and the "claustrales," who devote themselves to prayer: they were the two sets of Augustine's posterity, whom he nourished from his two breasts, offering the "forma doctrinae" to the scholars and the "forma vitae" to those living in the cloister: Leclercq, RSPT, 41, 640.

167. "Beati litterati!"; "Grandes in Ecclesia litterati!"; "litteratura quae est scientia inflans": S. 12 (1755 C).

168. *V. abbr.*, c. 1: "The practice of holy Scripture consists in three components: readings, disputation, and preaching" — "In tribus igitur consistit exercitium sacrae Scripturae: circa lectiones, disputationem et praedicationem" (PL, CCV, 25 A).

169. Lesne, 5, 246. M. Grabmann, 2, 478. Cf. Ludwig Hödl, *Die Geschichte der scholastischen Literatur und der Theologie der Schlösselgewalt*, 1 (1960), 327-41.

170. *V. abbr.*, passim. He has some fine developments on mercy (c. 98-103: 278-86). For Foulques, see Jacques de Vitry, *Hist. occid.*, c. 8.

171. "Simplicitas autem maxime decet theologum, quia sacra Scriptura amica est simplicitati": C. 82-6 (250-9); c. 128 (323-4); c. 3: "Don't disturb and scatter the dust, lest, by its movement, the eye of your mind should become involved and obscured or even blinded" — "Pulverem ne moveas et dispergas, ne eo moto involvatur et obscuretur, imo excaecetur oculus mentis tuae" (29 B).

172. Denifle-Chatelain, *Chartul.*, 46 (46).

173. "somme de théologie pastorale": Chenu, 261.

174. *Summa de sacramentis et animae consiliis* (J.-A. Dugauquier, 1954-7). In it Peter shows himself to be a "moraliste scrupuleux et pieux, qui s'attache à résoudre des cas concrets" (vii). Cf. C. Dumont, NRT, 79 (1979) 1957, 1090: The material in it is explained "much less under the aspect of speculative research than with a view to an immediately practical discussion" — "beaucoup moins sous forme de recherche spéculative qu'en vue d'une discussion immédiatement pratique."

175. *V. abbr.*, c. 1 (CCV, 24-5); c. 2 (26 B).

176. *In Is.*: "you who follow the letter that killeth, not caring for the spiritual understanding nor for beauty and morality, but for an overflow of glossing" — "qui sequimini litteram occidentem, non intellectum curantes spiritalem, nec pulchritudinem et moralitatem, sed glossae superfluitatem" (Smalley, 243).

177. "homines curiosi et inquieti"; "secretorum Dei scrutatores suspiciosi";

"O homo, qui versas quaestiones hujusmodi! Desine sic pulsare altitudinem majestatis Creatoris!": *De vict. Verbi*, l. 2, c. 12 (PL, CLXIX, 1252-3). A complete evaluation is impossible, the work of the Cantor being in large part unedited. On his classical culture, see M. Sanford, "The V. A. of Petrus Cantor," *Trans. and Proc. of the Amer. Philos. Ass.*, 74 (1943), 33-48. He was even a poet, or at least a versifier; he composed a "Legend of Pilate" and a "Phaedra and Hippolytus."

178. "gymnasii parisiensis quondam decus et rector": J. Ph. Bergomas, *Suppl. chron.*, a. 1199 (HLF, 18, 51).

179. *S.* 30: "lettered men capable of receiving God's Word" — "viri litterati capaces verbi Dei" (PL, CCXI, 180 BD). The word is even now becoming obligatory; but Absalon's requirements regarding these men are entirely ecclesiastical and spiritual.

180. *Ep.* 35 (CXCVI, 1627 A).

181. "The men of letters are great, tall trees, men learned in the Lord's discipline, fervent in spirit, practiced in holy Scripture, ready amid mysteries, of subtle mind, resplendent in eloquence, outstanding in catholic doctrine. . . . Such were Jerome, Augustine, and the other doctors" — "Arbores magnae et altae sunt viri litterati, viri in disciplina Domini eruditi, spiritu ferventes, in Scriptura sacra exercitati, in mysteriis expediti, subtili ingenio, fulgentes eloquio, catholica doctrina insignes. . . . Tales fuerunt Hieronymus, Augustinus et caeteri doctores" (Pitra, *Sp. sol.*, 3, 487-8).

182. "*'Their nobles have perished with famine and their multitude were dried up with thirst'* (Isa. 5:13). The *nobles* are the scholars who have the appropriate nature, very sharp reasoning, and a tenacious memory, and so are well able to chew the solid food of holy Scripture, [yet] *perish with famine* when they labor to establish their reputation through laws, decretals, and other lucrative studies; and from this it comes about that the *multitude* of the laity *has dried up* and is drying up with thirst, not having anyone who ministers to it or offers a drink of the simple understanding of holy Scripture" — "Nobiles interierunt fame et multitudo siti exaruit (Isa. 5:13). Nobiles sunt litterati, qui cum habeant proprium ingenium, acutissimam rationem et memoriam tenacem, et ita bene possunt sacrae Scripturae masticare solidum cibum, intereunt fame, cum per leges et decreta et caeteras scientias lucrativas famem sedare laborant; et ex hoc provenit quod multitudo laicorum siti exaruit et exarescit, non habens qui et ei ministret vel propinet simplicis intelligentiae sacrae Scripturae potum" (Smalley, 253).

183. In 1163 he is fulminating against the monks going off to study "worldly laws" and medicine.

184. "They love the decretals of the Councils, not the secrets of the mysteries; they do not recite the Psalms, but ruminate upon decretals" — "Amant decreta conciliorum, non secreta mysteriorum; non Psalmos recitant, sed decreta ruminant" (PL, CCIX, 131).

185. *Paradiso*, 9, 133: "The Gospels and the great Doctors are neglected; the only thing one studies any more is the Decretals, as can be seen in their margins." Maldonado will warn his own students against the same temptation: J.-M. Prat, *Maldonat et l'Univ. de Paris au XVIe s.* (1856), 271.

186. Or "the seven gifts and the seven vices" (R. Baron, MSR, 13, 175): "[God] opens the sense of the Scriptures [for the soul] in such fashion that as it has lived

so also does it imitate holy Scripture. Thus where animals used to tread, there wheels also follow, [namely] the Scriptures, which are whirling rapidly, which can be expounded according to the life of the human being. He who [lives] spiritually, interprets them mystically. So does the wheel always follow the life of the man" — "Aperit (Deus animae) sensum Scripturarum, ut secundum quod vixerit eum et sanctam Scripturam imitetur. Unde quo animalia gradiebantur, illuc et rotae sequuntur, Scripturae quae volubiles sunt, quae secundum vitam hominis exponi possunt. Qui spiritualiter, mystice eas interpretatur. Sic semper vitam hominis rota sequitur." A true spiritual, Langton is the author of the beautiful sequence *Veni sancte Spiritus*. Cf. Marthe Dulong, "Ét. Langton versificateur," *Mél. Mandonnet*, 2 (1930), 183-90.

187. "Those who travel through explaining the letter inadequately do not have *fine twisted linen*, but simply a thread in *the tabernacle's*, i.e., the Church's, *curtain*" [cf. Vulgate Ex. 26:1] — "Illi qui transeunt minus sufficienter exponentes litteram, non habent byssam retortam, imo filum simpliciter in cortina tabernaculi, id est Ecclesiae" (Smalley, *Speculum*, 6, 63).

188. M.-B. de Vaux Saint-Cyr, OP, "Les deux comment. d'Ét. Langton sur Isaïe," RSPT, 39 (1955), 228-36.

189. Cf. Bede, *In Marc.*, l. 1, c. 4 (PL, XCII, 171 D), cited again by Bernard of Monte Cassino, *Speculum monachorum*, P. 3, c. 5: "He who has love of the Word will also be given the sense of understanding what he loves. But he who has not a love of hearing the Word will not enjoy the sweetness of any true wisdom, even if by reason of natural wit or the practice of literature he believes he is an expert" — "Qui amorem habet verbi, dabitur etiam sensus intelligendi quod amat. At qui verbi amorem non habet audiendi, etiam si naturali ingenio vel litterarum sibi callere videtur exercitio, nulla verae sapientiae dulcedine gaudebit" (Walter, 202). Helinand, *s*. 18: "Who now . . . uses his knowledge for salvation? Whom will you find for me even from among those that pursue the knowledge of the divine Scriptures and follow sacred literature? And is there anyone at all among the licentious illiterates who does not have more licentiousness than literacy? Who amongst all the troops of the Church militant fights no more for his own advantage or for gluttony than for the Bridegroom of the Church, Jesus Christ, on whose patrimony he is feeding? Alas! How rarely today do virtue and knowledge come together! I know not with what bond the lusts and letters of this new faction have ever managed to stick together. . . . Yet when has this monster not ruled?" — "Quis jam . . . sua scientia utitur ad salutem? Quem mihi reperies etiam ex divinarum Scripturarum scientiam assecutis, et litteras sanctas sectantibus, qui quemlibet illiteratum et luxuriosum non magis luxuria quam litteratura? Quis ex omnibus stipendariis Ecclesiae militantis non magis suo aut gulae militat, quam sponso Ecclesiae Jesu Christo, de cujus patrimonio victitat? Heu! quam raro hodie coeunt virtus et scientia! Nescio quo vinculo factionis novae libidines et litterae sibi cohaeserunt. . . . Quando tamen hoc prodigium non regnavit?" (PL, CCXII, 633 C); "And they dare publicly to profess a teaching about the sacrosanct mysteries of holy Scriptures, with the words choked out with reddening cheeks, double chin, distended throat, all too prominent abdomen" — "Audent isti de sanctarum Scripturarum sacrosanctis mysteriis, buccis rubentibus, inflatis

faucibus, turgentes gutture, protento aqualiculo, verbis suffocatis doctrinam publice profiteri" (634 A). Richard (Hauréau, *Not. et extraits*, 1, 118); etc.

190. "style négligée"; "mouvement vif": B. Hauréau, 2 (1891), 114.

191. It is known that, elected Archbishop of Canterbury at Rome in December 1206, he could not re-enter England before June 1213. Cf. R. Foreville, *Le jubilé de S. Thomas Becket* (1959), 6-7. On Langton, see L. Hödl, *op. cit.*, 342-64.

192. "mauvaise scolastique biblique": Chenu, *op. cit.*, 262.

193. B. Smalley, *The Study*, 92, 107-8. On Richard: J. Chatillon, RMAL, 8 (1952), 254-64.

194. *In Ez.*, l. 2, h. 1, n. 3 and 5 (PL, LXXVI, 935-8).

195. "secundum figuralem intelligentiam absque aliquo rerum respectu": Ps.-Isidore, *De ord. Creaturarum*, c. 10, n. 6 (LXXXIII, 939 C). Cf. *Sacris er.*, 5, 147-66.

196. *In Ez.*, l. 4, c. 40 (CX, 882-3).

197. Cf. Wilhelm Neuss, *Das Buch Ezechiel in Theologie und Kunst bis zum Ende des XII. Jahrhunderts* (*Beitr. z. Gesch. des Alters Mönchtums und des Benediktineordens*, her. von P. Ildefons Herwegen, 1-2, 1912).

198. We do not yet know what was said on this subject in the "beautiful manuscript of the 12th century" that was seen by Dom Rivet in the library of Chartres, a "book that Hervaeus composed concerning the prophet Ezekiel's last vision" — "liber quem Hervaeus composuit super ultimam visionem Ezechielis prophetae" (cf. PL, CLXXXI, 17-8).

199. *Expl. aliquorum passuum difficilium Apostoli:* "It is not our custom, especially in great and very deep affairs, to presume anything on the basis of our own sense, or to establish or affirm anything as though on our own authority" — "Non est nostri moris, maxime in rebus magnis et multum profundis, aliquid de nostro sensu praesumere, vel quasi auctoritate nostra aliquid statuere vel affirmare" (CXCVI, 668 D).

200. *In Ap.*, prol. 1 (CXCVI, 683 B).

201. *In vis. Ez.*, prol.: "Many find the divine Scriptures to be much sweeter when they can get a suitable meaning in them at the literal level. And then, as it seems to them, the structure of spiritual understanding is more firmly established when the sense is well grounded in historical solidity. . . . The Fathers of old were gladly disposed when passages occurred that could not stand literally. For using these literally absurd passages, they used to compel some people, who accepted holy Scripture but used to mock the allegorical senses, to take refuge at the spiritual sense, since they would not dare to deny [the proposition] that the Holy Spirit has written nothing in vain even in the most fatuous passage of the letter. This is why I think it happened that the Fathers of old silently by-passed an explanation of the literal level in some of the more obscure passages, or even treated them a bit carelessly, though, if they had insisted on a fuller treatment, they could have done it no doubt more perfectly than any of the moderns" — "Multis divinae Scripturae multo amplius dulcescunt, quando congruum in eis aliquem secundum litteram intellectum percipere possunt. Et tunc, ut eis videtur, spiritualis intelligentiae structura firmius statuitur quando in historici sensus solido apte fundatur. . . . Antiqui Patres libenter accipiebant cum in hujusmodi Scripturarum, loca inciderent, quae juxta litteram stare non poterant. Ex his namque quosdam, quae Scripturam sanctam recipiebant, sensus tamen allego-

ricos subsannabant, ex his, inquam, absurdis litterae locis compellebant ad spiritalem intelligentiam confugere, cum negare non auderent Spiritum sanctum in quantalibet fatuitate litterae nihil inaniter scripsisse. Hinc contigisse arbitror, ut litterae expositionem in obscurioribus quibusdam locis antiqui Patres tacite praeterirent, vel paulo negligentius tractarent, qui si plenius insisterent, multo perfectius procul dubio quam aliquis ex modernis id posuissent, etc." (CXCVI, 527 AD). This analysis is not devoid of subtlety.

202. C. 10: "I know that the Fathers negligently pass by certain passages of Scriptures though they could easily penetrate them, when they desired and rejoiced to have found things that could not stand in respect to the letter, so that thereby men might at least be convinced that they ought to accept allegory, which in those days very few had yet been willing to accept even a little. So let it not scandalize anyone if we say something different or in a different way from what he may have found in the glosses. Let no one disdain us for hanging around willing to collect ears of grain. . . . Pay attention, therefore, not to whether I say anything new, but anything true. I scarcely fear to say something diverse [from the usual opinions], provided I say nothing perverse" — "Scio quidem Patres quaedam Scripturarum loca quae facile possent penetrare negligenter tamen praeterire, dum invenisse desiderarent atque gauderent quae juxta litteram stare non possent, ut per hoc saltem convincerentur homines allegoriam recipi debere, quam illis adhuc temporibus admodum pauci vix voluissent recipere. Neminem ergo scandalizet si quid dicimus aliud vel aliter quam in glossis invenerit. Nemo dedignetur nos remanentes spicas velle colligere. . . . Attende ergo non utrum dicam aliquid novum, sed verum. Parum timeo dicere aliquid diversum, dum tamen nihil dicam perservum" (562 AB).

203. *Prol.*: "Now as to the marvelous vision of the heavenly animals that the prophet Ezekiel saw, blessed Gregory explains it according to its mystical understanding. But he does not say how it is able to stand in relation to the letter. Concerning the second vision he says that it cannot stand according to the letter; this is quite true, but with respect to the interpretation that he assigned to it; for if we are willing to discuss the same literal passage he discusses using a different interpretation, perhaps we will be able to extract a suitable understanding from it even with respect to the historical sense. Certainly, as Gregory says in the same exposition of the book of Ezekiel, often something is said obscurely in holy Scripture so that, with God's marvelous dispensation, it may be expounded in many ways" — "Ecce mirabilem illam visionem de caelestibus animalibus, quam propheta Ezechiel vidit, b. Gregorius secundum mysticam intelligentiam exponit. Sed quomodo ad litteram stare valeat, non dicit. De secunda visione dicit, quod juxta litteram stare non possit. Et hoc quidem verum, sed secundum acceptionem quam ipse sibi assignavit; nam si eamdem de qua hoc dicit litteram velimus secundum aliam acceptionem discutere, fortassis etiam juxta historicum sensum ex ipsa poterimus congruum intellectum eruere. Certe, idem in eadem Ezechielis expositione dicit, plerumque in sacro eloquio ideo aliquid obscure dicitur, ut, dispensante mirabiliter Deo, multipliciter exponatur" (527-8).

204. See above, ch. 3.3.
205. Smalley, *The Study*, 107.
206. *In vis. Ez.*, passim (534 ff.); c. 3 (539 CD); c. 4: "we find many of them both

obscurely pronounced and ambiguously expressed" — "multa de eis tam obscure prolata, tam ambigue dicta invenimus" (542 D); c. 6: "I prefer being fastidious for the benefit of the more subtle to being obscure to slower [readers], especially in such an obscure business, where practically everything that is said requires proof" — "Malo esse subtilioribus fastidosus, quam tardioribus obscurus, praesertim in tam obscura re, ubi pene omnia quae dicuntur probatione indigent" (549-50).

207. C. 5: "Here he designates a portico under the name 'port'" — "Hic porticum sub nomine portae designat" (545 D); c. 8: "as . . . we find practically everywhere in other buildings" — "sicut . . . in caeteris aedificiis pene ubique invenimus" (554 D); c. 9: "He seems to have described no such entry at the first port, and only one at the second; but from the description of it both there and here it is shown that there were several" — "Nullum tale vestibulum videtur descripsisse apud portam primam, nec nisi unum apud secundam; ex hujus tamen descriptione ostenditur ibi sicut et hic plura fuisse" (558-9); "it is to be noted that by 'port' he understands a portico and that he describes only the length of the pavement" — "notandum quod porticum per portam intelligit et quod pavimenti solam longitudinem describit" (559 C).

208. C. 3: "If what is here said of some building or other is related to the whole, the truth and authority of the whole description is voided" — "Si ad totum refertur quod hic de quodam nescio quo aedificio dicitur, totius descriptionis veritas et auctoritas evacuatur" (540 D).

209. "Nonne, obsecro, multo rectius multoque convenientius est ad partem referre, quam ad totum referendo totum evacuare? Nonne magis congruum rationique consentaneum videtur esse, credere Scripturam hoc loco cujusdam aedificii mensuras describere, quod juxta seu supra portam erat . . . ? Numquid quia semel Scriptura totum aedificium nominavit, hoc vocabulo deinceps partem designare non potuit, vel non debuit? Nonne totam similiter domum nominavit, et tamen hoc nomen in subsequentibus ad partem referre non timuit, cum dicit: 'et erat interior domus in lateribus domus'? Quid, si hoc ipsum aedificii nomen invenimus ubi ita positum sit, ut omnino ad totum referri non possit?": C. 3 (540-1). Same reasoning, *De Tab.*, tr. 1, 1, 5, regarding the length of the "cloaks made of hair-cloth" — "sagae cilicinae": "For he who says that Eve was made from a rib says the truth; and he who says that Eve was made from a man says the truth no less; nevertheless the whole substance of the man does not disappear, as a rib does, within a production of this type" — "Nam qui dicit Evam ex costa factam, verum dicit; et qui dicit Evam ex viro factam, nihilominus verumdicit; nec tamen tota viri substantia sicut costa in ejusmodi facturam cessit" (216 C). The analogy is rather far-fetched.

210. "Hoc solum debet nobis in hac re fidem facere; quia, si hoc hic aedificii nomen volumus ad totum referre, omnium quae hic dicuntur, convincimur fidem cassare. Puto tamen neminem esse tam improbum, neminem tam posse inveniri protervum, quem in hac parte in tam aperta ratione nobis contraire non pudeat, qui in hac nos sententia reprehendere non erubescat, cum caetera omnia juxta nostram expositionem ad litteram posse stare perspexerit si in tam perspicua veritate sanum intellectum non subsannaverit": C. 3 (541 AB).

211. *In Gen.*, h. 2, n. 1-2 (SC, 7, 90-6).

212. *In Hept.*, l. 1, q. 4: "and Origen resolves this question by means of the geometrical cubit, etc. So if we understand cubits as great as that, there is no question that the ark was of such great capacity that it could contain them all" — "quam quaestionem cubito geometrico solvit Origenes etc. Si ergo tam magna cubita intelligamus, nulla quaestio est, tantae capacitatis arcam fuisse, ut posset illa omnia continere" (PL, XXXV, 549). Cf. *Civ. Dei*, l. 15, c. 27, n. 3 (XLI, 474).

213. *De prom.*, P. 1, c. 9, n. 10: "For the geometric measure which, as is reported, is six times as long as ours" — "Geometrica quippe mensura quae, ut fertur, sexies tantum quam nostra se extendit" (LI, 738 D).

214. *Hexaem.*, l. 2 (XCI, 91-2).

215. See above, vol. 2, ch. 7 and, in this volume, ch. 4.3.

216. "au monde savant"; "uniquement dirigé par le Prophète architecte"; "permet de combler toutes les lacunes que naturellement s'était permises le récit historique de la Bible"; "le Champollion du Temple"; "a su, sous la pression de sa logique, faire rendre aux mystérieuses descriptions d'Ezéchiel un temple magnifique, achevé, complet"; "sans négliger une pierre désignée par la vision prophétique, sans laisser une lacune ou une brèche, relever en entier l'édifice de Salomon." Pp. 1-6, 2-11, 68, etc.

217. "écrivit un roman historique"; "aucune notion de l'art de construire"; "impossible de signaler entre eux aucune différence"; "Serait-il hétérodoxe de supposer timidement que Dieu, par Ezéchiel, ait légèrement amendé et considérablement embelli les plans de Salomon?"; "En quoi les amender? En quoi les embellir? Dieu, n'étant pas sujet aux surprises et n'ayant pas à profiter de l'expérience, avait doué son Temple de tous les accomplissements qu'il lui jugeait convenables"; "à être unique et éternel, il y avait épuisé; je dis bien *épuisé*; la somme des trésors symboliques, liturgiques, utilitaires, qu'il lui convenait d'attribuer à son Temple": Pp. 124, 134, 206-27, 392, 403, etc.

218. "il va jusqu'à se servir des armes de l'ironie"; "complètement dénué du sentiment des arts"; "devis prophétique"; "établir un système de plans achevés et complets"; "fut inspiré comme architecte"; "Il est incontestable que ses plans furent pris sur le mont Moria et adaptés aux convenances locales. Ce ne peut être qu'à cette fin que le Prophète fut transporté à Jérusalem sur une haute montagne"; "des dangers auxquels l'exposait sa périlleuse mission": Pp. 2, 4, 15, 18, 29, 73, etc. For the same view, see Lucien Gautier, *La mission du Prophète Ezéchiel* (1891), ch. 8, on the temple of Ezekiel (pp. 118-44), which is based upon the "magnifique publication de MM. Perrot et Chipiez, *Le Temple de Jérusalem et la maison du Bois-Liban restitués d'après Ez. et le Livre des Rois*," upon Balmer-Rinck (1858), H. Sulley (1888) and various commentaries. "Il suffit de lire attentivement les ch. 40-42 pour comprendre qu'on a devant soi la description soignée et exacte d'un édifice aisément exécutable d'après les mesures indiquées. Des hommes compétents ont prouvé jusqu'à l'évidence que tel était le cas" (119-20). "Le temple d'Ez. aurait pu se dresser dans le pays de Canaan, marquant le début d'une ère nouvelle. . . . Mais Israël a fait défaut" (153). For the earlier discussions, see Cornelius a Lapide, *Commentaria* (Vivès), 12 (1863), 776-80.

219. *La Saint Bible* (de Jérusalem), 1956, p. 1184, note j.

220. "le temple dont Ezéchiel dessine le plan n'est pas un projet d'architecture, sa signification est prophétique"; "temple idéal"; "la réalisation

messianique d'un domaine de pureté, qui sera celui de l'inhabitation de Dieu, dépassant l'existence matérielle d'Israël et les institutions mosaïques": Yves M.-J. Congar, OP, *Le mystère du Temple* (1958), 90 and 95; 100, regarding analogous texts: it is not a question "of a geographical place, but of a spiritual place" — "d'un lieu géographique, mais d'un lieu spirituel." The opinion of A. Parrot, *The Temple of Jerusalem*, is not very plainly discernible: "The great project was not able to be realized and they devoted themselves to more modest achievements" — "Le grand projet était irréalisable et l'on se consacra à des réalisations plus modestes" (50).

221. "eaux qui ruissellent du mur méridional du temple"; "s'apparente à la littérature d'Utopie": A. Gelin, in Robert-Feuillet, *Introd. à la Bible* (1957), 546.

222. Paul Auvray, *Ezéchiel* (1947), 125-32. Richard did not make such distinctions; with a certain plasticity, he "réalisait" the four living things as well as the Temple.

223. J. Knabenbauer, *Commentarius in Ez. proph.* (Cursus Cornely, 1890), 406-526. The author does not, however, seem to find the measurements of the building incoherent.

224. "l'étrange union d'une réalité hallucinante et visionnaire avec un style de géomètre et de juriste"; "comme un édifice réel"; "des plans précis"; "architecture d'abstraction"; "s'élabore dans un monde idéal"; "une sorte de château en Espagne"; "édifice de rêve": Jean Steinmann, *Le prophète Ezéchiel* (1953), 200, 214, 229; 201: "In fact, the very high mountain is imaginary" — "La très haute montagne est déjà imaginaire." See also his *Le Livre de la Consolation d'Israël* (1960), 74: "Utopie grandiose."

225. "sanctae Ecclesiae aedificium, caelestis civitatis aedificium": *In Ez.*, l. 2, h. 1, n. 18 (PL, LXXVI, 948 C); n. 7 (940 C).

226. "la portée réaliste des espérances prophétiques de la Cité céleste"; "quatre vivants célestes": On the analogous vision of the Apocalypse cf. Beatus, *In Ap.*, l. 3, c. 4 (245).

227. "juxta litteram accipi nullatenus potest": *Ib.*, n. 3 (936 C): "according to the meaning of the letter it expresses no historical sense" — "juxta rationem litterae nihil historicum sonat" (937 B).

228. "Hoc mihi dictum sit, ut prudens lector intelligat quam habeam sententiam super explanatione templi Dei in Ezechiel, de quo dictum est: *Nubes et caligo sub pedibus ejus* (Ps. 96:2), et sursum: *Tenebrae latibulum ejus* (Ps. 17:12)": *In Ez.*, l. 12, c. 40: "When I was a boy at Rome" — "Dum essem Romae puer, etc." (XXV, 375 AB).

229. L. 14, c. 45: "I am now, at the end, about to say in reverse order what I had to say at the beginning of the temple of Ezekiel, mindful as I am of the verse" — "Quod in principio templi Ezechielis debui dicere, nunc praepostero ordine in fine dicturus sum illius versiculi memor" (447 D).

230. *Aeneid*, l. 6, v. 27; l. 5, v. 588-91:

Hic labor ille domus, et inextricabilis error . . .
Ut quondam Creta fertur labyrinthus in alta:
Parietibus textum caecis iter, ancipitemque
Mille viis habuisse dolum, qua signa sequendi
Falleret indeprensus et inremeabilis error.

231. "Ignosce, lector, difficultati, et veniam tribue pauperi intelligentiae": L. 12, c. 41 (403 B).

232. *Ib.:* "Human speech cannot explain how an altar in which fire was to be kindled, namely the table of incense, should suffer nothing from the fire" — "Humanus sermo non potest explicare quomodo altaria, in quo ignis succendendus erat, mensa vid. thymiamatis nihil ab igne patiatur" (403 AB).

233. L. 12, c. 40 (383 B, etc.).

234. L. 12, c. 40: "and not yet fully to know spiritually the mysteries of building the temple" — "templi spiritaliter aedificandi necdum plene novere mysteria" (373 A); "of the prophets and apostles who are building the city of God" — "prophetarum atque apostolorum qui aedificant civitatem Dei" (*ib.*). L. 13, c. 43: "That which belongs to Ezekiel and is shown to the house of Israel through Ezekiel is such that he who would glimpse it with his mind would cease from his iniquities" — "Ista autem quae Ezechieli et per Ezechielem domui Israel ostenditur, talis est ut qui eam mente conspexerit, cesset ab iniquitatibus suis" (419 C); cf. 423 B: "he points it out in a hidden manner" — "illud latenter ostendit."

235. *"A quatuor ventis veni, Spiritus!"*; "juxta mysticos intellectus": L. 12, *init.* (369 D); c. 40 (372 A).

236. L. 12 (378 A, 379 A, 385 B, 388 A, 391 C, 401 D).

237. L. 13 (410 AC).

238. "divinantis magis quam explanantis animo": for this commentary on Ez. "is particularly rich in parallel passages" — "est particulièrement riche en passages parallèles" with that of Or., only fragments of which survive for us. Bardy, RB, 46, 156.

239. L. 12, c. 40: "So it is simply to be stated that I want to discuss the temple of blessed Ezekiel, which all ages have passed over in silence, not with temerity but I desire to show my readers the conjecture of my own mind with faith and love of God" — "Simpliciter igitur est fatendum me templum beati Ez. quod saecula cuncta tacuerunt, non temeritate velle disserere, sed fide et timore Dei conjecturam animi mei cupere legentibus demonstrare" (375-6). "We shall have said this briefly with the mind of a diviner rather than an explainer, wishing to silhouette a picture linked to the obscure and almost invisible letter" — "Haec breviter divinantis magis quam explanantis animo dixerimus, volentes juxta litteram obscuram et pene non apparentem adumbrare picturam" (377 C). "Let not these things seem frivolous to the reader, though they be displeasing even to me who am speaking, perceiving myself to be pounding upon a closed door" — "Haec non frivola videantur esse lectori, licet et mihi ipsi qui dico dispiceant, sentiens me clausam pulsare januam" (380 B).

240. "latenter": L. 12, *in fine:* "that all things are full of reason and measure, and that nothing is found in the temple of the Lord that has been constituted without measure and wisdom" — "cuncta rationis plena esse atque mensurae, et nihil in templo Domini reperiri, quod absque mensura et sapientia constitutum sit" (406 A).

241. L. 12, c. 40: "to me as I read the description of the mystic temple" — "mihi legenti descriptionem templi mystici" (375 C).

242. L. 11, *init.:* "I must consider long and hard whether I ought to set my

hands upon a spiritual temple, or openly to confess my ignorance" — "Diu mihi multumque dubitandum, utrum ad spiritale templum debeam mittere manus, an aperte ignorantiam confiteri etc." (325 C). L. 14, c. 48, v. 20: "whence we see that they are all to be understood spiritually" — "ex quo perspicimus omnia intelligenda spiritualiter" (487 A).

243. L. 13, c. 43 (420 BC).

244. L. 12, c. 41 (404 AB): "The wood of the altar, which comes from the wood of paradise, is not burned by the nearby fire, but is rendered all the purer" — "Altaris ligna, quae de lignis paradisi sunt, non cremantur igne vicino, sed puriora redduntur" (403 B).

245. "Nocturnum iter agimus, restat ergo ut hoc palpando carpamus": *In Ez.*, l. 2, praef. (LXXVI, 935 A).

246. Cf. the *Admonitio* of the Maurists (LXXVI, 783-4).

247. *In Ez.*, l. 16-20, c. 40-8 (CX, 879-1084).

248. Cf. Peter the Eater, *H. scol.*, *In Ez.*, c. 6: "And he shows him the description of the city and the temple; about which our authors have kept silence as to the letter" — "Et ostendit ei descriptionem civitatis et templi; super quam ad litteram nostri siluerunt auctores" (CXCVIII, 1446 BC). Peter himself says nothing more about it.

249. An analogous problem is also posed for the vision of the sealed book: granting that the seven seals, each one of which, broken in turn, would, according to certain commentators, permit one to read one seventh of the book — how could they be represented precisely? The comparison between the temple of Solomon and the city of the Apocalypse had been made by Bede, *Ep. ad Accam* (XCI, 718 AB).

250. "Tantae civitatis mirabilem structuram secundum spiritualem intelligentiam elucidandam ingressuri": *In Ap.*, l. 7, prol. (CXCVI, 859 A); l. 1, c. 4: "just as there was a spiritual vision, so there was a spiritual hearing" — "sicut fuit spiritualis visio, sic fuit spiritualis auditio" (704 D). Cf. Guibert of Nogent, *De pign. sanct.*, l. 4, c. 1 (CLVI, 666-7). Amalarius, *De ord. antiph.*, c. 53, n. 11 (Hanssens, 3, 86). Otto of Freising, *Chron.*, l. 8, c. 20 (MGH, *Scr.*, 20, 287-8); c. 26: "For, saying not that a city is being built . . . but rather it is being built as a city. . . . A thing mystical and profound" — "Non enim civitatem . . . sed ut civitatem aedificari dicens. . . . Res mystica et profunda" (292).

251. "in quo Deus residendo regnat"; "arundo per sonum praedicationis et aurea per fulgurem divinae cognitionis"; "quadrata dispositio": *In Ap.*, l. 7, c. 1-7 (859-77).

252. "Quis sani sensus homo haec juxta litteram accipere velit?": *Benj. minor*, c. 18 (13 A). Cf. Beatus, *In Ap.*, l. 12, c. 22: "It can be asked, etc. What was the right point of inquiry, if [John] had seen not a spiritual but a corporeal building?" — "Quaeri potest etc. Quod rectum quaerendum fuerat, si non spirituale sed corporale aedificium vidisset [Joannes]?" (561).

253. J. Steinmann, *op. cit.*, 200: The utopia of Ezekiel is "equally distant from the real temple of Solomon and the heavenly Jerusalem of the Apocalypse, . . . it is not concrete and earthly like what is described in the first Book of Kings; it is not heavenly, as the depiction of the Apocalypse will be" — "à égale distance du temple réel de Salomon et de la Jérusalem céleste de l'Apocalypse, . . . elle n'est pas

concrète et terrestre comme l'objet des descriptions du premier livre des Rois, elle n'est pas céleste comme le sera le tableau de l'Apocalypse."

254. *Paul Claudel interroge l'Apocalypse*, 230-2: "Here one must wonder how far the literalist prejudice can lead even the most conscientious scholars astray.... A house twelve thousand stadia long, wide, and tall? (and surrounded, let's not forget, with a wall of fourteen cubits).... Let's stretch out these two thousand or so kilometers in the shape of a cone (leaving aside the question of length and breadth) like the ancient Babylonian ziggurats: we'll have something like Dante's Purgatory.... But there is this rather awkward river.... Here is how Father Allo represents it: 'Above the crest of the wall (!) rises to infinity the gold and crystal mass of buildings, of streets, right up to the summit where the throne of God and the Lamb probably (!) rests.... The sweetness of life comes and *cheers him up:* there are trees ..., and water as well (why not luminous fountains?). The river starts from the throne, i.e., the summit of the mountain: it is doubtless not to be taken in nature, but can be represented (!). The course of the waters will not be too torrential (for they are not seen falling at the peak, all of it remaining surrounded by trees, from a height of 2,500 kilometers!), if one considers the waters of life falling in a spiral along the sides (providing the cream puff with a garland), then making many meanders along the streets, in the midst of the arbors'. Just look at the asininities into which fascination with the letter can lead a noteworthy scholar. And he is concerned with a book whose Author, the Holy Spirit, tells us on each page that *we must use our intelligence!* Here at least is one recommendation that Father Allo has not taken literally, neither for himself nor for his readers! And generations of seminarians will respectfully brood over this senseless twaddle" — "C'est ici qu'il faut admirer à quel point le préjugé littéraliste peut égarer les savants les plus consciencieux.... Une ville de douze mille stades en longueur, largeur et hauteur? (et entourée, ne l'oublions pas, d'un mur de quatorze coudées).... Ces deux mille et je ne sais combien de kilomètres, étirons-les en forme de cône (sans nous préoccuper de la question longueur et largeur) comme les anciens *Ziqqurat* babyloniens: nous aurons quelque chose qui ressemble au Purgatoire de Dante.... Mais il y a ce fleuve qui est assez embarrassant.... Voici la représentation que s'en fait le Père Allo: 'Par-dessus la crête du mur (!) s'élève jusqu'à l'infini la masse dorée et cristalline des constructions, des rues, jusqu'au sommet où probablement (!) repose le trône de Dieu et de l'Agneau.... La douceur de la vie vient l'*égayer:* il y a les arbres ..., et aussi de l'eau (pourquoi pas des fontaines lumineuses?). Le fleuve part du trône, c'est à dire du sommet de la montagne: cela n'est sans doute pas pris dans la nature, mais peut se représenter (!). Le cours des eaux ne sera pas trop torrentiel (en effet, on ne les voit pas tombant à pic, tout en restant entourées d'arbres, d'une hauteur de 2.500 kilomètres!), si on ne se figure les eaux de la vie coulant en spirale sur les flancs (enguirlandant le mirliton), puis faisant de nombreux méandres avec les rues, au milieu des bosquets.' Voilà à quelles âneries la fascination de la lettre peut conduire un savant remarquable. Et il s'occupe d'un livre dont l'auteur, qui est l'Esprit-Saint, nous dit à chaque page qu'*il faut faire usage de notre intelligence!* Voilà du moins une recommandation que le Père Allo n'a pas prise à la lettre, ni pour lui ni pour ses lecteurs! Et des générations de séminaristes se pencheront avec respect sur ces fariboles insensées!" Claudel is obviously amusing himself,

and his laughter here does not seem "bitter" — "aigre" to me, as it does to Jacques Petit, "Le rire de Paul Claudel," in the *Cahiers P. Cl.*, 2 (1960), 166. His harshest words seem to be the translation from Robert of Crickade (below, ch. 4): "foolish raving" — "stultitia delirantium."

255. Though contesting Gregory's argument from incoherence, it rather seems that Richard would accept what Gregory says after having cited these words from the prophet, "The hand of the Lord has come upon me and has led me thither in the visions of the Lord" — "Facta est super me manus Domini et adduxit me illuc in visionibus Domini"; "And with these words what else is he openly pointing out except that he is saying nothing literal about the city he had seen?" — "Quibus verbis quid aperte indicat, nisi quia nihil de civitate quam viderat juxta litteram dicat?" (PL, LXXVI, 937 C).

256. Thus, *De Tab.*, tr. 1, prol.: "Look how faithfully he discusses the sense of allegory, who nevertheless laid out an ambiguous exposition of the letter. Therefore he who so faithfully is giving testimony of his certitude as to his allegorical exposition, while denying his historical exposition, plainly implies that there would be something within his exposition that does not satisfy even himself" — "Ecce quam fidenter de allegoriae sensu proponit, qui tamen litterae expositionem sub ambiguitate praemisit. Qui igitur certitudinis suae testimonium allegoricae expositioni tam fidenter dat, historicae denegat, patenter innuit, quod in illa sua expositione nec sibi ipsi satisfecerit" (CXCVI, 211 BC).

257. See again *De Tab.*, prol.: "if I should hesitate to present in public a truth well known as if out of regard for them, I am afraid that I am more likely to offend than to propitiate those who are wont to take part in the contemplation of the truth" — "illos quos jam constat summae veritatis contemplationi assistere, timeo magis offendere quam propitios reddere, si cognitam veritatem dubitavero quasi ob reverantiae eorum gratiam in commune proferre, etc." (211-2).

258. Of the work accomplished in his commentaries, "we give thanks not to ourselves but to God, from whose gift, and to all the doctors, from whose fullness we draw what we are drinking" — "nobis gratiam non damus, sed Deo, de cujus dono, et cunctis doctoribus, de quorum plenitudine haurimus quae propinamus": *In Ap.*, primus prol. (683 B). Cf. *De Trinitate*, l. 3, c. 10: "These things are said for the sake of those who try to delimit or determine the height of the divine mysteries according to the measure of their own capacity, not according to the tradition of the sacred Fathers, who persistently have learned and taught through the Holy Spirit" — "Haec propter illos dicta sunt, qui altitudinem divinorum secretorum nituntur definire vel determinare juxta capacitatis suae modum, non juxta traditionem sanctorum Patrum, quos constat didicisse et docuisse per Spiritum sanctum" (G. Salet, SC, 63, 190).

259. "quadrifaria expositio": See for example the "Nonnullae allegoriae" [the heading "Some allegories"] in the appendix to the *Benjamin major:* "The table of proportion is made of wood; it is overlaid with gold; it is surrounded with a curved edge; it is decorated with a jeweled crown. Through the wooden workmanship we understand the historical sense; through the curved edge, the tropological; through the jeweled crown, the allegorical and anagogical" — "Mensa proportionis fabricatur ex ligno, superducitur auro, labio circumdatur, gemina corona decoratur. Per opus ligneum intelligimus sensum historicum; per labium,

tropologicum; per geminam coronam, allegoricum et anagogicum; etc." (CXCVI, 199 CD). It is with reference to Richard that B. Hauréau once impatiently wrote: "One cannot read anything written from that age without constantly having occasion to cry out, 'O Allegory, what do you want of me?'" — "On ne peut lire un écrit quelconque de ce temps-là sans avoir constamment l'occasion de s'écrier: Allégorie, que me veux-tu?" *Notices et extraits,* 1 (1890), 114.

260. L. Massignon, *Études carmélites,* Oct. 1938, 57. Richard, *De gradibus caritatis,* c. 2: "Hence too God in the meanwhile seems to be playing a little joke with the sons of men, by whom whilst he is thought to be held he slips from their hands: having been pursued he allows himself to be caught, and disappearing again he is not seen, until once again, having been called with tears and prayers, he turns back, and so, though the visit is delightful, the change is irksome" — "Unde et quodam jocundo joco interim Deus ludere videtur cum filiis hominum, a quibus dum teneri putatur e manibus labitur, insectatus se comprehendi patitur, et disparens rursum non videtur, donec denuo lacrimis et precibus vocatus revertatur, et ita, licet delectet visitatio, molestat vicissitudo etc." (1198 CD).

261. "Quid enim Scripturam sacram, nisi Rachel cubiculum dicimus, in qua sapientiam divinam sub decenti allegoriarum velamine latitare non dubitemus?": *Benj. minor,* c. 4 (4 A). What could be more ultra-Gregorian, for content as well as for form?

262. "Nulla Scriptura canonica opinioni illi suffragatur; imo et prophetica veritas apud Ezechielem oppido refragatur. . . . Verius ergo et rationabilius dicimus": *De glorif. Trin.,* l. 3, c. 17 (PL, CLXIX, 69 AB).

263. *In Ez.,* l. 2, c. 1 (167, 1463 B).

264. Thus, l. 2, c. 2 (1464 C); c. 30 (1491 C).

265. L. 2, c. 17 (1479 C).

266. L. 2, c. 21: What "the holy of holies is in the temple, God is in Christ" — "Sanctum sanctorum in templo, Deus est in Christo" (1482 C); c. 23: "In this temple of divinity, in this God or man, Christ" — "In hoc divinitatis templo, in hoc Deo vel homine Christo" (1483 D); "The opening at the side of the temple is the wound in the pierced side of our Lord's body, aside from which there is no approach, there is no opening or door by which anyone may enter, so as to be able to stand before God in any order. For out of that side . . . blood and water flowed" — "Ostium lateris templi, vulnus est in latere lanceato Dominici corporis, praeter quod non est aditus, non est ostium vel janua, qua intret quis, ut in quovis ordine coram Deo stare possit. Nam ex illo latere . . . sanguis et aqua profluxit" (1484 C); etc. Cf. Autpert, *In Ap.,* l. 5 (508-13, 530 CE).

267. H. Scol., *Liber Ez.,* c. 6 (PL, CXCVIII, 1446 BC).

268. "dispositiones maecanicas in aedificiis et in dispositione templi imaginarii": *V. abbr.,* c. 2 (CCV, 27-8). As radically opposed as they are in their attitude, Peter the Cantor and Richard might at any event here with some difficulty both together represent the rise of the emerging critique.

269. "stultitia delirantium"; "quod non solum aedificium est, sed etiam civitas": cited by Smalley, *The Study,* 109.

270. Cf. Neuss, *Das Buch Ezechiel,* 138.

271. G. Salet (SC, 63, 26). Cf. *De erud. hominis,* l. 2, 13 (PL, CXCVI, 1311-2).

272. *L'amour des lettres,* 74: "était vigoureuse, agissante. . . . Elle permettait de

se représenter, de se rendre 'présents' les êtres, de les voir, avec tous les détails que les textes rapportent: couleurs et dimensions des choses, vêtements, attitudes, actions des personnages, cadre complexe où ils se meuvent. On aimait à les décrire et, pour ainsi dire, les créer, en donnant un très vif relief aux images et aux sentiments." Amongst the Victorines the reality of the imagination corresponds to the theory; in it "the field of the imagination" ("le champ de l'imagination") is vast; it "covers both the reproduction of sensible images and the mind's own discovery" ("couvre aussi bien la reproduction des images sensibles que l'invention du génie"): Delhaye, ET, 106.

273. Notably those of the *Scivias* (PL, CXCVII).

274. C. 1, init. (CLXXVI, 681 AC). Hugh's constructive imagination again manifests itself in a page like *Miscell.*, l. 1, tit. 75: "That sacred Scripture is the teaching-chair" — "Quod sacra Scriptura sit cathedra" (CLXXVII, 510-1).

275. "Hujus vero spiritualis aedificii exemplar tibi dabo arcam Noe, quam foris videbit oculus tuus, ut ad ejus similitudinem intus fabricetur animus tuus. Videbis ibi colores quosdam, formas et figuras, quae delectent visum. Sed scire debes, ideo haec posita esse, ut in eis discas sapientiam, disciplinam atque virtutem, quae exornent animum tuum. Et quia haec arca Ecclesiam significat, Ecclesia autem corpus Christi est, ut evidentius exemplar tibi fiat, totam personam Christi, id est caput cum membris in forma visibili depinxi, ut cum totum videris, quae deinde de parte dicuntur facilius intelligere possis": L. 1, c. 2 (622 BC).

276. Leclercq, *La spiritualité de P. de Celle*, 60: "Il essaie de se représenter le bâtiment, il calcule les dimensions que lui assigne l'Exode, les vérifie les unes par les autres, essaie d'en trouver la raison immédiate et pratique; il se réfère au commentaire que Bède le Vénérable a déjà proposé de ce texte afin de compléter le sien; il donne l'équivalent en langue vulgaire d'une des pierres précieuses dont parle l'auteur inspiré, afin qu'on saisisse bien à quoi elle correspond. Dans le but de rendre plus claire la description de l'édifice complexe dont les détails risquent de faire perdre de vue l'ensemble, il modifie parfois le plan suivi par l'*Exode* lui-même: il faut que son lecteur ait l'édifice devant les yeux, qu'il puisse le regarder; il veut d'abord qu'on comprenne la lettre et il fait preuve, à cette fin, d'un souci de précision qui est rare dans tous les temps, mais qu'on s'attendrait peut-être à trouver moins que chez tout autre chez un auteur mystique"; cf. 62; 54: "He is a painter; everywhere he sees lively, variegated, harmonious or contrasting forms and colors; and he represents them. Instead of 'suggesting' he would rather 'depict.' Hence the frequency of expressions like 'pingit' (he paints) and 'describit' (he sketches)" — "C'est un peintre; il voit partout des formes et des couleurs, vives, variées, harmonieuses ou contrastantes; et il les représente. Pour 'suggérer,' il veut 'dépeindre' (s. 7, CCII, 655 D). D'où la fréquence d'expressions comme: 'pingit,' 'describit' (695 c, 733 d, 801 c, 860 c)."

277. "Here in summary is to be explained how that tent, which is called the tabernacle, had been stretched out and stretched across; in length . . . , in breadth . . ." — "Hic in summa explanandum quomodo tentorium illud quod dicitur tabernaculum extensum et distensum sese habuerit; in longitudine . . . , in latitudine . . ." (Leclercq, 151).

278. PL, CCII, 1047-84; and *De tab. Moysi* (ms Troyes): Leclercq, *R. Mab.*, 36 (1946), 6-7.

279. *In Ex.*, l. 4 (CLXVII, 697-744).

280. See below, notes 353, 354.

281. *In ded.*, s. 1-2 (Tissier, 6, 123-5).

282. *S.* 7 (CXCV, 247-51); and *S. ined.*, 146. The texts of the Old Testament on the tabernacle and the Mosaic cult, as Dom Leclercq writes, "seem to have had a role within the Benedictine Order similar to that of the Canticle of Canticles in the Cistercian Order": "semblent avoir dans l'Ordre de S. Benoît un rôle semblable à celui du Cantique des cantiques dans l'Ordre de Cîteaux" (*R. Mab.*, 36, 7; cf. Peter of Cella, 33-6). The Cistercians seem, however, not to have totally neglected them.

283. *S.* 40 (PL, CCV, 822-8).

284. *In ded.*, s. 2 (PL, CCIX, 67-94); cf. CCVIII, 329 AD, 1100-26.

285. PL, CCXI, 163-77, 219-40.

286. A. Noyon, *Inventaire des écrits théol. du XIIe s. non insérés dans* ... *Migne* (1912), 4. In the same genre, Hervaeus of Bourg-Dieu completes Gregory's commentary on the temple of Ezekiel (MS Troyes, 417; Leclercq, *R. Mabillon*, 36, 6).

287. *De tripartito tabernaculo. Laboriosum opus!*: P. 3, c. 1, n. 138 (PL, CXCVIII, 743 B). *Ep.*, c. 7: "First, I have shown how that old tabernacle of Moses had in fact been made and arranged, to the extent that I could conjecture and gather from the sayings of the book of Exodus, from whence the first knowledge of this affair has come to us, and from the book of the venerable priest Bede, in which his allegorical exposition on that same tabernacle is contained" — "Primum quomodo vetus illud Moysis tabernaculum in re factum fuerit vel dispositum, in quantum et ex dictis libri Exodi, unde prima ad nos hujus rei emanavit agnitio, et ex libro Venerabilis Bedae presbyteri, in quo allegorica ipsius super idem tabernaculum continetur expositio, conjicere et capere potui, demonstravi" (631 CD); c. 8: "I have diligently and carefully followed the words of the book of Exodus and of the Venerable Bede, the priest, and I am not aware that I have said anything contrary to them in any respect" — "Verba libri Exodi et Ven. Bedae presb. diligenter et sollicite secutus sum, et nihil eis contrarium in aliquo me dixisse conscius sum" (632 C).

288. *Ib.*, c. 8: "But I have set down simply my opinion only when neither the text of the book of Exodus nor that of the Venerable Bede nor of Josephus nor the words of him whom I mentioned before, whose religious life and doctrine I know to have been catholic, have perchance pointed out to me the full truth of what was done" — "Quando vero nec textus libri Exodi nec Bedae Ven. nec Josephi nec illius verba de quo superius tetigi, cujus et vitam religiosam et doctrinam non ignoro fuisse catholicam, plenam mihi forte rei gestae veritatem ostenderunt, tunc demum quod mihi visum est simpliciter posui" (632 CD). Cf. Aelred (CXCV, 711-28). Petit, *Prémontrés*, 176. Richard shows himself to be resolutely critical with regard to Josephus; certain persons, he said, regard him as an authority; "but to me ... it is clearer than light that he has never seen the tabernacle" — "mihi autem ... luce clarius constat quod tabernaculum numquam viderit": *De Tab.*, tr. 1, c. 5 (CXCVI, 214 C).

289. *De trip. tab.*, P. 2, c. 8 (CXCVIII, 697 CD).

290. P. 3, c. 9, n. 155: "But since one and the same thing in sacred Scripture can

be taken in many ways owing to the causes of diverse meanings, provided that it not depart from the unity of the faith, along with that thing we believe that if, owing to that cause that we pointed out earlier, we said the outer house of the tabernacle expresses the body of some saint, we may now also in turn owing to another cause, using another meaning, relate it to the mind of that holy man" — "Quia vero ob causas diversarum significationum una eademque res in sacra Scriptura etiam modis pluribus, dummodo ab unitate fidei non recedatur, potest accipi, non absque re esse credimus, si etiam exteriorem tabernaculi domum, quam paulo ante ob illam quam tunc ostendimus causam sancti cujuslibet corpus exprimere diximus, nunc quoque versa vice ob causam aliam ad ejusdem viri sancti mentem juxta aliam significationem referamus" (760 C).

291. "mediocriter litteralis intelligentiae scientia imbutus": *Vita*, c. 12: "Since that venerable father was but moderately imbued with knowledge of the literal understanding, he was accustomed to have associates who were wise and experienced men gifted with liberal and encyclopedic knowledge, and indeed prudently enough, [so] that he might the more easily borrow from the others around him the literature and science in which he was less accomplished" — "Quia ille venerabilis pater mediocriter litteralis intelligentiae scientia imbutus erat, viros sapientes et gnaros et totius facultatis ingenue scientia praeditos contubernales habere consuevit, et quidem satis prudenter, se [*sic?*] ut litteraturam et scientiam qua minus pollebat . . . facilius eam ab aliis de prope mutuaret" (Wilmart, *An. praem.*, 9, 1933, 227).

292. "in altitudinem Scripturarum": John of Kelso, *Ep.*, c. 2: "And so the builders of holy Church through such occasions [that is, heretics], were not able to block the sects of the depraved in an irremediable way, except, by constantly quoting the divine eloquence against them, they held them back; knowing that though divine Scripture is open to them in the reading, it is completely closed and hidden in the mystery. But after ascending to the height of the Scriptures through vigorous contemplation as if unto the highest, the holy doctors arrived spiritually up to the very majesty of the Trinity, in a way that holy Scripture ought to be understood mystically in each of the two Testaments clearly enough, though it is demonstrated by their expositions not to all but [only] to those who are perfected by the sense" — "Aedificantes itaque sanctam Ecclesiam per hujusmodi occasiones (haereticorum), pravorum sectas irremediabiliter impedire non potuissent, nisi constanter contra eos proferendo divina eloquia, illis restitissent; scientes quod quanquam divina Scriptura in legendo sit eis aperta, in mysterio clausa sit omnino et occulta. Postquam autem sancti doctores in altitudinem Scripturarum quasi in excelsum per contemplationis vigorem ascendentes, usque ad ipsam Trinitatis majestatem spiritualiter pervenerunt, qualiter sancta Scriptura mystice intelligi debeat in utroque Testamento satis lucide, quanquam non omnibus, tamen sensu perfectis, eorum expositionibus demonstratur" (PL, CXCVIII, 625 AB).

293. *Ep. Jo.*, c. 1 (623 D); c. 7 (627 A). *Ep. Adami*, c. 7 (631 D). *De ex. cellae*, c. 18 (CLIII, 832 B). Compare Greg., *Ep. miss.*, c. 2, n. 3 and John (CXCVIII, 628-8). In his letter, John appears to be "nourished on St. Gregory; he has assimilated his methods, he has followed his text very closely, sometimes amplifying it" — "nourri de s. Grégoire; il s'en est assimilé les méthodes, il en suit le texte de très près, en

amplifiant parfois"; Father Petit, edition of Adam's sermons, *Ad viros religiosos*, 21.

294. "quam bonum sit tripliceter omnes Scripturas intelligere": *Ad viros rel.*, s. 11 (Petit, 220).

295. John to Adam, c. 5: "But since a question usually arises for many about the middle of the cut curtain, whereby a double-folding was made to protect the back of the tabernacle, let the discussion about it be extended more widely in this same part of the book; especially about the altar's lattice-work, about which there seems to be such very great difficulty amongst the Latins" — "Sed quoniam de medietate secti sagi, qua duplicatio ad protegenda posteriora tabernaculi fiebat, a nonullis quaestio oriri solet, de ipsa latius disputatio in hac eadem parte libri protendatur; praecipueque de craticula altaris, de [q]ua tam apud Latinos maxima ambiguitas esse videtur" (626 B). About the same time Absalon declares that the knowledge of these and other details might be somewhat useful, if one could draw a spiritual teaching from them: a debatable allegorism, but, in the context of such proposals, a sensible thought, too. Moreover, John of Kelso and Adam Scot would be far from contradicting him.

296. P. 1, c. 1, n. 1: "it is no wonder if we never understand the words of this book fully according to the letter, since many outstanding doctors far above us both in sanctity of life and in sublimity of knowledge are found to have had diverse opinions on the literal understanding of the same words" — "mirum non esse, si praefati libri verba nequaquam nos plene juxta litteram intelligamus, cum nonnulli doctores eximii longe a nobis tam sanctitate vitae quam sublimitate scientiae remoti, diversa super eorumdem verborum intellectu litterali sensisse inveniantur" (635 A). Cf. c. 14, n. 32-4, on a modern who follows Josephus and the Jews rather than Bede regarding the placement of the curtains; Adam seems to throw in his lot with others who think "Bede is to be accepted on this point without any scruple" — "Bedam absque omni scrupulo super hoc esse accipiendum"; moreover, the discussion takes place "provided that the inner spiritual significance be preserved" — "salva illa quae interius latet significatione spirituali" (651-3). Cf. 17, n. 38: "Modern professors explain this difficulty in this way" — "Hanc doctores moderni hoc modo dubitationem exponunt" (657 B). Information taken from Josephus: 637-80. C. 26, n. 76: the description was very difficult, of a thing that no one of our age has ever seen (684 AB). Cf. John of Kelso, c. 5 (626 BC).

297. *Ep. Ad.*, c. 7 (631 A). P. 2, c. 13, n. 130 (723 C); c. 12, n. 106 (711 B), etc.

298. C. 6 (626 CD).

299. P. Courcelle, 356-7 and 376.

300. "le parti adopté: tenir, avant toute transposition allégorique, l'*historiale tabernaculum* . . . , consentir ensuite aux efflorescences d'un symbolisme polyvalent, cosmique, moral, rituel, eschatologique": *Théol. au XIIe s.*, 195.

301. Hugh, *De arca morali*, l. 1, c. 2: "But we have undertaken to speak specifically about the ark of wisdom, and for that reason we have only briefly run over the explanation of the other three, so that we may presently spend our time explaining this one" — "Nos tamen specialiter de arca sapientiae loqui suscepimus, et idcirco reliquarum trium expositionem breviter transcurremus, ut in explanatione hujus postmodum morari valeamus" (PL, CLXXVI, 626 D). The

three arks over which he passes quickly are those of Noah, of the Church, and of the mother of grace (cf. 626 C).

302. "n'a guère d'attrait pour lui": Petit, 68.

303. He leaves far behind him Beatus de Liebana, who said, *In Ap.*, l. 2, prol.: "It would cost me a whole day if I were to have written all that I could by comparing the mysteries of the ark with the Church" — "Dies me deficiet, si omnia arcae sacramenta cum Ecclesia componens edisserem" (134).

304. *De trip. tab.*, P. 2, c. 13: "as Master Hugh says" — "sicut magister Hugo dicit" (CXCVIII, 726 BC).

305. *De trip. tab.*, passim. The same method of explaining how he traces his figures: "pono, dispono, facio, scribo, depingo."

306. *Ep.*, c. 10 (634 B).

307. "Maître Adam est nettement pour les disciplines du passé": Petit, 169.

308. Cf. Urban II to Bruno, who wanted to become a monk, to impose the bishopric of Segni on him; *Vita S. Brunonis*, in the Chronicle of Monte Cassino: "calm and security itself often bring the most pernicious shipwreck even to monks far from the tumult of the world" — "et monachis a saeculi turbine remotis, quies et securitas ipsa perniciosissimum solet inferre naufragium" (PL, CLXIV, 89 BC).

309. Ans., *Ep. apol.*: they believe that it is possible to lead an honorable contemplative life only "to sit idly in cloisters with folded hands and gathered sleeves, to have unnecessary food, to wear superfluous clothing, to sleep idly and without care, to amble about at pleasure from nook to nook on tip-toe, to explore with subtle inquiry the comings and goings of the abbot and the presence or absence of the prior, to investigate with wandering curiosity what is going on outside from chance visitors . . . , and, to sum it up briefly, to abound idly in all things beyond necessity and by abounding to live idly" — "in claustris complosis manibus et concricatis manicis otiose sedere, victum otiosum habere, vestitum otiosum accipere, secure et otiose dormire, de angulo ad angulum suspenso gradu pro libitu ambulare, abscessum et adventum abbatis et absentiam sive praesentiam prioris astuta inquisitione explorare, ea quae foris sunt a supervenientibus vaga curiositate investigare . . . et, ut breviter includam, omnibus super necessitatem otiose abundare et abundando otiose vivere" (CLXXXVIII, 1135 BC).

310. *De quarta vig. noctis*, c. 21: "I have come, Lord Jesus, I have come to your little boat, holy Church, most grievously in peril on this fourth vigil" — "Veni, Domine Jesu, veni ad naviculam tuam sanctam Ecclesiam in hac vigilia quarta gravissime periclitantem" (*L. de lite*, 3, 525).

311. Gilbert, *In Cant.*, s. 38, n. 4 (PL, CLXXXIV, 201 AB).

312. In Otto we detect a feeling for human tragedy as well as an eschatological tension that do not allow us to turn him into an "optimistic" thinker.

313. *De trip. s. Ecclesiae statu*, s. 8, n. 6: "Now is Jerusalem in possession of peace . . . and winning over to the faith those who used to struggle against her. . . . And especially because a great number of kings and earthly princes have been converted to it" — "Jam est Jerusalem in pacis possessione . . . et eos qui contra se luctabantur lucrans ad fidem. . . . Et in eo maxime quod ad eam conversa est numerositas regum et principum terrenorum" (CXCVIII, 144 A). Cf. his admira-

tion of Constantine, *De trip. tab.*, P. 2, c. 13, n. 110 (713-4). Cf. Aimo, *In Cant.* (CXVII, 320 A).

314. "Per patientiam et consolationem Scripturarum spem habeamus": Bede, *Ep. ad Accam* (XCI, 737-8).

315. *De quadripartito exercitio cellae*, c. 5, 9, 31 (CLIII, 810 D, 815 D, 864 C). Adam composed this treatise once he had become a Carthusian.

316. "sub felicissimo contemplationis somno requiescebat": Adam of Eynsham, *Magna vita S. Hugonis Lincoln* (Wilmart, *Mél. Mandonnet*, 2, 148).

317. *De trip. s. Eccl. statu*, s. 8, n. 8: "And after this what else remains for Jerusalem, except to rejoice in the day of the Lord, so that she may go from peace to peace" — "Et quid post haec Jerusalem restat nisi in die Domini exsultare, ut eat de pace ad pacem?" (144-5).

318. Aelred, *s. ined.*, 21, in festo omn. sanct., *De dispositione turmorum filiorum Israel circa tab.* (Talbot, 146-8). Despite the contrast that we have pointed out, Gerhoh shares this opinion to some extent: *In ps. XXXVI* (V. den Eynde, 663-4); but *Epilogus* (720-1).

319. "un terme un peu gros"; "retardataire." Cited by Petit, 116.

320. *De q. ex. cellae*, c. 35 (CLIII, 878 CD).

321. "Quisquis ad sacrae Scripturae" (PL, CXII, 849-51). Cf. A. Wilmart, "Notes sur les plus anciens recueils de Distinctions bibliques," *Mél. Lagrange.*

322. 171. Cf. CXII, 549 A.

323. "Beatus Gregorius, non minus nitide dixit quam profunde sentit": *S.* 8, c. 9 (CXCVIII, 145 A).

324. "verba melliflua": *S.* 28, n. 1 (259 C), etc. *De trip. tab.*, ep., c. 4: "if I might use the honied words of Gregory" — "ut verbis Gregorii mellifluis utar" (629 B); P. 2, c. 14: "as blessed Gregory says" — "sicut ait b. Gregorius" (728 B), etc. *De ex. cellae*, c. 27-8 (CLIII, 849 A, 852 AB, 855 B). Gregory is the author most cited by Adam: Petit, 24.

325. Cf. *In Ap.*, l. 7, prol.: "Now the seventh vision does this . . . , beautifully describing the qualities of variously shaped figures and marvelously drawing the human mind to the desire and sweetness of the highest good. For if one were to attend more diligently and more studiously merely to the beauty of the words in the series of this vision, he would most perfectly discover the wherewithal to rouse himself to desire so great a good, and would wish with all his prayers to become an inhabitant of so beautiful and joyful a city" — "Agit autem haec septima visio . . . , multiformium figurarum qualitatibus pulchre describens et humanum animum ad summi boni appetitum atque dulcedinem mirabiliter trahens. Nam si quis etiam solam verborum pulchritudinem in serie visionis hujus diligentius ac studiosius attenderet, unde semetipsum ad tanti boni concupiscentiam excitaret, perfectissime reperiret et tam pulchrae ac jucundae civitatis habitator fieri votis omnibus exoptaret" (CXCVI, 858-9).

326. Cf. G. Fritz, "Richard de SV," DTC, 13, 2680: "Richard's exegetical work is hardly original at all, indeed there is very little scientific about it, as Kulesza remarks" — "L'œuvre exégétique de R. est fort peu originale, voire même très peu scientifique, comme le remarque Kulesza"; it is "négligeable."

327. "minus caute dicta, minus catholice disputata": *De Emm.*, prol.: "I have encountered . . . a certain treatise of Master Andrew" — "In quemdam magistri

Andreae tractatum . . . incidi" (CXCVI, 601). Andrew was no longer at Saint Victor, but, for the second time, was abbot of Wigmore. The title of the manuscript consulted by Hauréau is worded thus: *Invectio magistri Ricardi superioris S. Victoris Parisiensis contra Andream socium suum, super illud verbum Isaiae: Ecce virgo concipiet et pariet* (*Not. et extraits*, 2, 172). However, Richard is not directly attacking Andrew, but his disciples. Cf. Smalley, 112-5; Calandra, 23-4.

328. He gives the passage from Jerome *in extenso*, *In Is.*, l. 3, c. 7 (603-6). Also l. 1, c. 6 (612-3).

329. "Ecce ubi agnus ambulat, elephans natat, sed non enatat": *De Emm.*, l. 1, c. 1 (605 D).

330. *Ib.*: "Behold: where Christian simplicity finds a level road, it runs along and does not stumble, Judaic faithlessness is overwhelmed, and the devil strangled" — "Ecce ubi christiana simplicitas planam viam invenit, currit, nec offendit, judaica perfidia submergitur, diabolus suffocatur."

331. L. 1, c. 2 (607 C), etc. Richard can recall Jerome, *In Is.*: "These things, too, the Jews and our Judaizers" — "Haec quoque Judaei et nostri Judaizantes"; "the Jews and our people, no, rather our Judaizers" — "Judaei et nostri, imo non nostri Judaizantes"; "some of our people . . . utter in Judaic fashion" — "quidam nostrorum . . . more Judaico pronuntiant," etc. (XXIV, 147 B, 152 B, 187 C, 378 A, etc.); *In Ez.*, l. 11 (XXV, 353 D, 356 A); etc. The expression was routine: Rabanus (CXI, 912 B). Remigius, (CXVII, 207 D). Richard, *In Joel* (CLXXV, 359 B, 367 D). An anonymous fragment (Landgraf, *Biblica*, 37, 408). Gerhoh, *De novitatibus hujus temporis*, c. 5 (*L. de lite*, 3, 293); etc.

332. "sub quadam fatuitate litterae profunditatem tanti mysterii": L. 1, c. 17 (628 C); cf. c. 1 (606 C).

333. "All these are considered by the prophet to be said in a totally puerile and vain sense, unless they are taken as a figure in a spiritual and mystical sense" — "Omnia ergo haec, nisi ad figuram et spirituali atque mystico sensu dicta accipiuntur, puerili omnino sensu et inani dicta esse a propheta considerantur" (Blumenkranz, 59).

334. L. 2, c. 97 (Delhaye, 109).

335. Ed. of 1537, f. 187 (Châtillon, RTAM, 23, 50). The same in an anonymous fragment published by A. M. Landgraf (*Biblica*, 37, 407-8): "Behold a virgin shall conceive. This will be something new and marvelous, which another prophet says. The Jews falsely claim [this means] that a young woman is conceiving. The word 'alma' . . . in Phoenician means a virgin" — "Ecce virgo concipiet. Hoc erit novum et mirabile, quod dicit alius propheta. Judaei mentiuntur, adolescentulam concipere. Sed 'alma' . . . lingua punica virginem sonat, etc."

336. "quod de regibus spiritalis nequitiae in caelestibus intelligi non possit; sed ita sane deprehenditur Scriptura de quibusdam regibus loqui, ut quod dicitur et spiritalibus et carnalibus regibus possit aptari": *De Emm.*, l. 1, c. 17 (629 A): "So why are not the kings of that land, who used to rule in it through teaching faithlessness and depravity up to the times of Christ, proclaimed to be the spirits of error? . . . Many such kings have been taken captive in the passion of Christ" — "Quare ergo spiritus erroris illius terrae reges non dicantur, qui in ea per infidelitatis et pravitatis magisterium usque ad tempora Christi principabantur? . . . Hujusmodi regum multi in passione Christi sunt captivati" (629 C).

337. *In Ez.*, h. 13, n. 1: "Who is that prince of Tyre? Let us go to Daniel, and, uncovering an opportunity for understanding, let us say that it is not bodily princes that are now being asked about. . . . So these are not men, etc." — "Quis est iste princeps Tyri? Veniamus ad Danielem et occasionem intelligentiae reperientes, dicamus non esse principes corporeos de quibus nunc quaeritur. . . . Non sunt ergo hi homines etc." (PG, XIII, 757-8).

338. Cf. Jerome, *In Dan.*, c. 4 (PL, XXV, 513 B, 515 A); *In Ez.*, l. 11 and 13.

339. *De victoria Verbi*, l. 2, c. 3 (CLXIX, 1245-6).

340. *De Emm.*, l. 2, c. 10 (645 AD); c. 19 (653 C). Here again one will compare Origen, *Sel. in Jer.*, XLIX, 17, on the two princes "according to the history of the fourth Book of Kings" — "juxta historiam quarti Regum," the Assyrian and the Babylonian, who are two lions: they are also the Devil and the Antichrist (PG, XIII, 596 CD). Cf. Joachim of Flora, *Adv. Judaeos* (A. Frugoni, 50).

341. L. 2, c. 20 (654 D); c. 31 (664 D).

342. *H. dom.* 15: "The Jews glory at having great knowledge of the holy Prophets according to the letter, but they regard even as nothing our knowledge or awareness, which is according to the spirit" — "Sancti prophetae, quorum multam notitiam se Judaei habere gloriantur secundum litteram, nostram autem notitiam vel scientiam, quae secundum spiritum est, et pro nihilo ducunt" (CLXXIV, 104 B).

343. *Op. ined.*, 1, 301, 308, 336.

344. PL, CXCVI, 523-8. The chronology of Richard's works is difficult to establish. Cf. C. Ottaviano, *Riccardo di S. Vittore* (1933), 446 and 534; Dumeige, 168.

345. "Utinam Judaei, utinam Judaizantes nostri attendant et intelligant, retractent et recogitent hoc signum quale, quam sublime, quam insigne oporteat esse, si in hoc positum est ut possit profugos Israel et dispersos Juda a quatuor plagis terrae colligere": 523 D. It would be too much, however, to lay stress on the "nostri."

346. *De Emm.*, l. 1, c. 7 (6123 C).

347. Smalley, *The Study*, 111.

348. Smalley, 110: "It is not Andrew's consultation with Jews that shocks him but his acceptance of their view when it undermines the whole Christian interpretation of the Old Testament and endangers the faith of simple folk. If Andrew failed to understand the prophecy, he should at least have refrained from raising doubts in the minds of others." In these last remarks credited to Richard, it seems to me that something like a concession is being undertaken that is not on Richard's mind.

349. *De Tab.*, tr. 3, *De concordia temporum regum conregnantium super Judam et super Israel:* "Before I wrote anything about what you asked for, I consulted with the Jews about the scriptures of the Jews, and I learned that their writings have the same sense as ours" — "Antequam de his juxta petitionem tuam aliquid scriberem, per Judaeos Judaeorum scripta consului, et tam eorum scripta quam nostra in unam sententiam concurrere didici" (241 B).

350. Tr. 1, c. 5: "Let Josephus be accepted regarding matters he knows from experience or gathers from the authentic scriptures. Where he holds another view, I confidently prefer Exodus or whatever books I find in the canon" — "Libenter recipiatur Josephus in his quae per experientiam novit, vel ex

authenticis scripturis colligit. Ubi aliter sentit, confidenter et Exodum praefero, vel quoscumque libros in canone reperio" (214 C). See above, note 288.

351. It is posterior to it. *De Tab.*, tr. 1, c. 8, regarding the dimensions given in Ezekiel 40: "In which place we have explained that matter more fully" — "Istud quo loco plenius exposuimus" (218 CD).

352. Cf. the title: *Expositio difficultatum suborientium in expositione tabernaculi foederis* (CXCVI, 211).

353. *Nonnullae allegoriae tabernaculi foederis* (191-202). In it Richard explains that the wood and the gold of the Ark signify the literal and the spiritual sense.

354. PL, CLXXV, 661-3.

355. The Prologue to the *Liber exceptionum*, P. 1, nicely separates the two senses: "the course of the histories" — "cursum historiarum" — and "the sense of the allegories and tropologies aligned with the underlying history" — "sensus allegoriarum et tropologiarum secundum subjacentis lineam historiae dispositarum" (Châtillon, 97). And again, within the second, the *Nonnullae all.*: "For the business of a tropology is far removed from that of an allegory" — "alia est enim conditio tropologiae, et longe alia conditio allegoriae" (200 B).

356. *Exp. diffic.* (211 B).

357. The following remark of L. W. Laistner, *The Intellectual Heritage of the Early Middle Ages* (1957), 101, is worth bearing in mind: "Bede's acquaintance with the writings of Josephus is a matter of considerable complexity."

358. *De Tabernaculo* ..., *De templo Salomonis* (XCI). One will also note that in 1022 Ekkehard of Saint Gall got a briefing on the temple by a Jew who had come from Jerusalem where he had been converted (E. Duemmler, cited by Blumenkranz, *Juifs et chrétiens*, 52).

359. "articuler la théologie en deux pièces: la *lectio historica* et la construction de l'*allegoria*": "Théologie symbolique ... ," *Melanges de Ghellinck* (1951), 520; "Conscience de l'histoire," AHDLMA, 1955, 110.

360. "La tentative du Victorin ne devait pas, du moins dans son dessein original, se fixer et réussir": M.-E. Chenu, *La théologie, est-elle une science?* (1957), 84.

361. "Modus legendi in dividendo constat": *Didasc.*, l. 3, c. 10 (PL, CLXXVI, 772 A).

362. *The Study*, 105: "The programme was both too conservative and too modern. It would have made any kind of academic specialization quite impossible and yet specialization was just what it demanded. Moreover it implied too high a tension between the academic and the religious life. Hugh's ideal exegete was a combination of Paris master and contemplative religious which only exceptional circumstances could produce."

363. "Non idem ordo librorum in historica et allegorica lectione servandus est: historia ordinem temporis sequitur, ad allegoriam magis pertinet ordo cognitionis": *Did.*, l. 5, c. 6 (805 C).

364. "une mise en ordre théologique": see above, vol. 1, ch. 1.1.

365. "spiritualis fabrica"; "tota divinitas"; "ordines": L. 6, c. 4 (803 AB). *De sacram.*, l. 1, prol. (183-4). The *Chronicon* can in a way be paired with the *De sacramentis*: the one is to *historia* what the other is to *allegoria* (cf. Van de Eynde, *Essai*, 90-3).

366. Smalley, 293-4: "At last theologians felt sufficiently sure of themselves

to drop the fiction that all their work was a mere training for the allegorical interpretation."

367. "comme les éléments d'une *œuvre* de la Sagesse divine plutôt que comme le *dessein* en cours de réalisation": Congar, *Le sens de l'économie salutaire*, 74.

368. "disputes d'école"; "de moins en moins à la Bible, pour se porter vers des problèmes d'ordre philosophique": J. Perrier, OP, *Bulletin thomiste*, 6 (1942), 129; c. 1 of C. Spicq, *Pourquoi le moyen âge a-t-il pratiqué l'exégèse allégorique?* For exegesis: *ib.*, 7 (1943-6), 67: J. Leclercq, critical review of Spicq, *Esquisse*.

369. "la scolastique se détachera de l'histoire sainte": Chenu, *Consc. de l'histoire*, 111. TCF. *Th. au XIIe s.*, 196; and 63, note 4: "The scholastic Masters rarely use the great historical texts from the *De civitate Dei* that the monastic writers, on the other hand, meditate upon" — "Les maîtres scolastiques n'utilisent à peu près pas les grandes textes historiques du *De civitate Dei*, que méditent au contraire les écrivains monastiques." Smalley, 243: "Allegory . . . is ceasing to be the learned, intellectual pursuit that it seemed to Hugh."

370. "dimension historique de la revelation"; "sinon attardés, du moins conservateurs": M.-J. Nicolas, OP, in *La nouvelle Eve* (1955-6), 10-1: "Augustine's theology is above all 'historical': in the 12th-13th centuries, it is the Augustinians, if not backward, at least conservative, who represent a thought of a 'historical' bearing" — "La théologie de saint Augustin est avant tout 'historique': aux XII-XIIIe siècles, ce sont les augustiniens sinon attardés, du moins conservateurs qui représentent une pensée d'allure 'historique'." B. Blumenkranz and J. Châtillon, RTAM, 23 (1956), 60: "that historical dimension of revelation and the faith that scholasticism would more and more neglect" — "cette dimension historique de la révélation et de la foi que la scolastique devait négliger davantage." Cf. A.-D. Sertillanges, *Le christianism et les philosophies*, I, 353-4. Petit, 238: "These Augustinians draw from Scripture a feeling for history that the Scholastics of the following epoch will almost no longer have" — "Ces Augustiniens puisent dans l'Écriture un sentiment de l'histoire que les Scolastiques de l'époque suivante n'auront à peu près plus."

371. "sagesse thomiste"; "sens de l'histoire"; "sentiment de l'irréversible devenir historique": J. Maritain, "La sagesse augustinienne," *Rev. de philos.*, 37 (1930), 738: "The feeling of the irreversible historical process, of the movement and development of the world in the sense of time is, in my opinion, one of the most precious jewels of the Augustinian heritage. There is a whole field there, in my view, to reply to Hegel and to win back for Christian wisdom. Goaded by the spirit of Augustine, will not Thomistic wisdom one day enrich itself with these conjectures on the exegesis of history?" — "Le sentiment de l'irréversible devenir historique, du mouvement et du développement du monde dans le sens du temps est, à notre avis, un des plus précieux joyaux de l'héritage augustinien. Tout un domaine est là, selon nous, à reprendre à Hegel et à revendiquer pour la sagesse chrétienne. Stimulée par l'esprit d'Augustin, la sagesse thomiste s'enrichira-t-elle un jour de ces conjectures en matière d'exégèse de l'histoire?"

372. Cajetan and the Carmelites of Salamanca, for example, will neglect to comment on questions such as *Prima Secundae*, qq. 101-2 [on the diversity of laws and the effects of law] and 107-8 [on changing the laws and on the Old Law]:

Congar, *loc. cit.*, 82, note 40. And what's there to say of a Thomism contaminated by the philosophy of the "Enlightenment"?

373. "où l'Écriture sera moins"; "le mémorial sacré de l'Histoire sainte, qu'un arsenal de textes classés selon des catégories purement idéologiques": Congar, 76. Cf. H.-M. Féret, OP, preface to Joseph Comblin, *La Résurrection* (1959), 10-1. And J. Comblin, 35: "In the current teaching, 'sacred history' will be exiled from the catechism, the ultimate disgrace" — "Dans l'enseignement courant, l'histoire sainte sera reléguée en dehors du catéchisme, disgrâce finale." However, on *S. Thomas et l'histoire:* Th.-G. Chifflot, "Approaches d'une théol de l'hist." (1960, 73-104).

374. Perrier, *loc. cit.*, 129: "Overall, it is the lack of historical sense that the whole Middle Ages evinced which arrested the normal development of exegesis": "C'est le manque de sens historique dont, dans son ensemble, a fait preuve tout le moyen âge, qui a arrêté le développement normal de l'exégèse." Cf. Spicq, 143.

375. Again, L. Cognet, *De la dévotion moderne à la spiritualité française* (1958), 10: "The Middle Ages sees theology constituted as a speculative science and separated from spirituality: more and more, people are coming to think of intellectual research as a specialized activity, entirely independent of prayer. In parallel, spirituality contents itself with rather thin speculative and dogmatic foundations, so as to give greater room for emotional and imaginative components. The divorce will go so far that in the epoch of the *Imitation,* people will come to consider intellectual preoccupations as incompatible with prayer" — "Le moyen âge voit la théologie se constituer comme science spéculative et se séparer de la spiritualité: de plus en plus, on en vient à considérer la recherche intellectuelle comme une activité spécialisée, entièrement indépendante de la prière. Parallèment, la spiritualité se contente de bases spéculatives et dogmatiques assez pauvres, pour donner grande place aux éléments affectifs et imaginatifs. Le divorce ira si loin qu'à l'époque de *l'Imitation* on en viendra à considérer les préoccupations intellectuelles comme incompatibles avec la prière."

376. *Viae Sion lugent* (inter op. S. Bonav., 2, Lyon, 1647, 705-6).

377. "un bien gros risque à courir, mais il était dans la nature des choses et selon les lois du progrès de l'esprit": Chenu, *S. Thomas d'Aquin et la théol.* (1959), 33. The following volume will come back to the evolution broadly sketched out here.

378. Very well noted by Miss Mohrmann, "Le latin médiévale," CCM, 1 (1958), 283.

379. *Did.*, l. 3, c. 20: "He to whom the fatherland is sweet is still soft. The one to whom the fatherland alone is everything is brave. But he for whom the whole world is an exile is perfected" — "Delicatus ille est adhuc, cui patria dulcis est. Fortis autem jam, cui omne solum patria est. Perfectus vero, cui mundus totus exsilium est" (PL, CLXXVI, 778 A). Cf. *In Eccl.*, h. 19 (CLXXV, 253 A).

380. *Hist. occidentalis*, c. 24.

381. At 11 February: "He accepted the gift of heavenly wisdom that had been given to him from on high in such excellent fashion that no one in the whole Latin Church can be found comparable to him in wisdom" — "Caelestis sapientiae donum caelitus sibi datum tam excellenter accepit, ut in tota latina ecclesia nullus

ei in sapientia possit comparabilis inveniri" (Fourier Bonnard, 1, 95, note 1; cf. PL, CLXXV, CLXIII).

382. *De vanitate mundi*, l. 1 (CLXXVI, 710 BC; cf. 709 D).

383. "Nescire quidem infirmitatis est; scientiam vero detestari, parvae voluntatis"; "Omnia disce, videbis postea nihil esse superfluum; coarctata scientia jucunda non est": *Did.*, l. 3, c. 8 (770 D); l. 6, c. 3 (800-1).

384. "non moins indemne du désir de systématisation complete"; "des centres scolaires": Chr. Mohrmann, CCM, 1, 277.

385. Hugh Métel, ep. 4 (331).

386. "compris son temps"; "s'est fait un devoir"; "de combattre les tendances nouvelles": E. Delaruelle, in *Hist. du cath. français*, 1, 325.

387. To try to see "tout le matériau susceptible d'entrer dans les constructions futures"; "apparaître"; "recours à la discipline géologique": Cf. J. J. de Santo-Thomas, *R. thomiste*, 1958, 729.

388. F. L. Battles, *loc. cit.*, 238-9, rightly emphasizes the originality of the *De arca morali*, "as the immediate prototype of works such as the *Cloister of the Soul* . . . and a number of others" — "protype immédiat d'ouvrages tels que le *Cloître de l'âme*, etc. . . . , et nombre d'autres."

389. J. Leclercq, in *Richesses,* 225, with regard to Psalms 20-25.

390. PL, CXCVI, 1073-1116. Egypt and the desert are the "region of unlikeness" — "regio dissimilitudinis"; the crossing of the Red Sea and then the Jordan is the "reordering of charity" — "reordinatio caritatis" through which one passes from the world to oneself, and then from oneself to God.

391. "Benjamin adolescentulus in mentis excessu": PL, CXCVI, 1-64.

392. CXCVI, 63-202. The title of the work: *De gratia contemplationis libri quinque occasione accepta ab arca Moysis* . . . Title of the appendix: *Nonnullae allegoriae tabernaculi foederis cum recapitulatione brevissima contentorum in praefato opere.* . . . Hauréau believes that this appendix is an "additon arbitraire," but the reason that he gives seems hardly convincing: "The author has previously declared that he is putting down his pen, not daring to go further" — "L'auteur a précédemment déclaré qu'il dépose la plume, n'osant aller plus loin" (*Not. et extraits,* 1, 110). Not to wish "to go any further" — "aller plus loin" — is not the same as refusing to summarize what one has already said.

393. "Mysticam Moysi arcam libet, si liceat ex inspirationis illius munere qui habet clavem scientiae lucubratiunculae nostrae expositione, vel ad aliquid reserare, et si quid adhuc in hoc arcanorum divinorum secretario scientiarumque reconditorio repositum latet, quod a nostra exiguitate ad aliquorum utilitatem erui possit, non nos pigebit in publicum exponere. . . . Multa quidem de hac materia utiliter jam dicta sunt. . . . Quid juxta allegoricum sensum haec arca mystice designet, vel quomodo Christum significet, a doctoribus fuit jam ante nos dictum. . . . Nec idcirco tamen temeritatis incuriam incurrere nos suspicamur, si aliud in eamdem adhuc materiam moraliter loquamur."

"Per tabernaculum foederis intellige statum perfectionis."
Benj. major, l. 1, c. 1 (63 BC, 191C).

394. "In morte Rachel contemplatio supra rationem ascendit; in introitu Benjamin in Aegyptum contemplatio usque ad imaginationem descendit; in

deosculatione Benjamin et Joseph divinae revelationi humana ratio applaudit": C. 84 (in fine); 64 A.

395. To be sure, for earlier centuries, one could cite more than one theological or spiritual writer whose bond with exegesis is rather loose. In all this it can only be a question of large collections. See above, vol. 1, ch. 1.5.

396. Cf. *De statu int. hom.*, c. 42 (CXCVI, 1150 D).

397. *Benj. minor*, c. 4 (4 A). *In Ap.*, l. 7, c. 10, on the heavenly Jerusalem (888 AB). On the relation of Richard to Hugh in general: G. Dumeige, "R. de SV et l'ideé chrét. de l'amour" (1952), 166. Cf. J. Beumer, SJ, Richard von SV, "Theologe und Mystiker" (*Scholastik*, 31, 1956, 213-38).

398. Cf. J. Châtillon (*Lib. except.*, 71).

399. Was Gregory himself acquainted with Dionysius? One citation "by hearsay" — "par oui-dire" — in the 34th homily on the gospels, n. 12 ("Fertur...," PL, LXXVI, 1254 B) is not a proof of the thesis, on the contrary. Dom R. Gillet thus dismisses the hypothesis (SC, 32, 83-4). Dom A. Ménacer (Vie sp., suppl., 59, 1939, 164-5), however, thinks it likely that Gregory had brought back the writings of Dionysius from Constantinople: for Peter the Deacon wrote to Maximus the Confessor "that all the books of the divine Dionysius were kept in Rome's library" — "que l'on conservait dans la bibliothèque de Rome tous les livres du divin Denys."

400. M. Cappuyns, *Jean Scot Er.*, 341-6, 251-2. G. Théry, "Scot Er. introducteur de Denys," *The New Scholasticism*, 5 (1933), 91-108.

401. *Vita S. Maioli*, l. 3, c. 17 (PL, CXXXVII, 775 A). J. Leclercq, *Spiritualité et culture à Cluny* (1960).

402. Quaere Dionysium, qui dicitur Areopagita:
Ille duos super his desudat scribere libros.

Carmen ad Rob., v. 219-20 (*Hist. des Gaules*, Delisle, 10-84).

403. D'Achery, *Spic.*, 3, 562.

404. *De statu domus Dei* (1152).

405. *De quadr. ex. cellae*, c. 29 (PL, CLIII, 856 AC).

406. "traumatisme spiritual"; "dont les effets, prestigieux et discutables, saisiront les maîtres du XIIIe siècle": "Lecture de la Bible et philosophie," *Mél. E. Gilson* (1959), 169; *Mél. A. Pelzer* (1947), 165. This then was "l'âge d'or de l'influence érigénienne" (Cappuyns, 245).

407. Glorieux, 119.

408. H.-F. Dondaine, RTAM, 17 (1950), 310-1; *Le Corpus dionysien à l'Univ. de Paris au XIIIe s.* (1953). Cf. J.-M. Parent, "Un nouveau témoin de la th. dionysienne au XIIe s.," *Beitr. Baümker*, 3, 289-309.

409. "tonitrua Dionysii": Helinand, s. 18: "which bring more astonishment and wonder than knowledge" — "quae plus stuporis et admirationis quam cognitionis afferunt" (PL, CCXII, 627 D; cf. 630 B, 631 AC, etc.).

410. Dom Edmond Boissard, RTAM, 26 (1959), 214-63. Cf. Butler, *Western Mysticism* (2d ed., 1927), 181-2, 189-91.

411. See particularly *Sermons* 9 and 35 (PL, CCV, 627-33 and 793-8), commenting on the "theophanies" of John Scotus. Cf. M.-A. Fracheboud, *Dict. de spir.*, 3, 329-40. See above, ch. 3.5.

412. Numerous articles between 1932 and 1936. Cf. Gilson, AHDLMA, 26 (1960): "In memoriam R. P. Gabriel Théry, O.P."

413. Théry, AHDLMA, 12, 163-4. Thus, *In Is.* (Théry, *Vie sp.*, suppl., 47, 160).

414. Théry, "Documents concernant Jean Sarrazin," AHDLMA, 18 (1951). The author seems, however, to understimate the ability of the literary men of that age, notably John of Salisbury, to utilize the version of John Scotus.

415. "qu'il y a pleine harmonie entre le premier des théologiens et les livres inspirés": Théry, "Thomas Gallus et les Concordances bibliques (*Beitr. Bäumker*, 1935, 3, 427-46).

416. Pez, *Thes. anecd. nov.*, 2, 1 (1721), 501-690. Cf. J. Châtillon, RMAL, 8 (1952), 268-72. Spicq, 173. Analogous remarks of J. Leclercq, *St. ans.*, 20, 208-9, regarding Gilbert of Stanford's commentary on the Canticle.

417. M.-T. d'Alverny, "Le second commentaire de Thomas Gallus sur le Cant. de cant.," AHDLMA, 13 (1942), 391-402.

418. "de animi deificatione": Thomas Käppeli, OP, "Der literarische Nachlass des sel. Bartholomäus von Vicenza," *Mél. Aug. Pelzer*, 275-301.

419. Robert Grosseteste, commenting on the *Divine Names*, c. 1 (Francis Ruello, AHDLMA, 26, 134-5).

420. *L. moz. sacr.*, Mass of Saints Peter and Paul: "the admirable faith of each of whom ... made the one accept the keys of the heavenly kingdom, and the other to penetrate unto the third heaven ... here, carried away in ecstasy above the remoteness of the clouds, the future doctor of the gentiles drank in the ineffable secrets of the divine words" — "quorum admirabilis singulorum fides ... unum fecit claves regni caelestis accipere, alium usque caelum tertium penetrare: cum ... hic in excessu supra nubium raptus recessum, ineffabilia divinorum secreta verborum futurus gentium doctor hauriret..." (354). Otto of Freising, *Chron.*, l. 8, prol. (MGH, Scr., 20, 278). Cf. Origen, *C. Cels.*, l. 6, c. 6 and 77 (2, 76, 148); *In Jos.*, h. 23, n. 4 (A. Jaubert, SC, 71, 46-8). Greg. (PL, LXXIX, 356 C), etc. Alan of Lille, *Summa* (Glorieux, 139).

421. "Quia revelata facie Domini speculando gloriam doctor gentium fuerat in eamdem imaginem transformatus a claritate in claritatem tanquam a Domini spiritu, idcirco is cui revelata sunt secreta caelestia, Paulus Apostolus, celsitudinem sapientiae sibi caelitus inspiratae in verbo proposito introducit. Et quia illa salutaris doctrina quam descripsit beatus Dionysius Areopagita fuit ab illa revelatione superna, quae fuit Apostolo facta, radicaliter derivata, cum ipse Apostolus fuerit raptus usque ad tertium caelum, idcirco ad introductionem hujus doctrinae convenienter assumitur verbum istud": Commentary on Dionysius, *prol.* (J. Barbet, AHDLMA, 21, 188); "Since, after the sayings of the sacred canon [of Scripture], among the other authorities of the saints, the teaching of blessed Dionysius the Areopagite is at the forefront" — "Quia inter cetera sanctorum documenta post dicta sacri canonis doctrina b. Dionysii Areopagitae est prior etc." (191).

422. Cf. Théry, "S. Antoine de Padoue et Th. Gallus," *Vie sp.*, suppl., 37 (1933), 50-1. Gilson, *Le Thomisme*, 4e éd. (1924), 194.

423. "novum quoddam expositionis genus"; "In hoc opere non multum ego laborandum existimo tropologiis sive mysticis allegoriarum sensibus per totam dumtaxat narrationis ejus seriem perquirendis.... Sciendum est hunc librum

novum quoddam expositionis genus requirere; quia, cum totus ad commovendos affectus cordis humani intendat, saepius in eo quasi colloquendo quam exponendo sermonem formare oportet. Unde necesse est, in iis etiam aliquando, quae plana et aperta videntur, diutius verbis immorari, ut ipsa locutionis inculcatio validius tangat et efficacius penetret cor audientis. Qui aliter hanc Scripturam tractare voluerit, etiamsi commode intelligentiae audientium servit, vim tamen proprietatemque non retinens, minus fortassis proficit ad aedificationem": *In Eccl.*, praef. et h. 1 (PL, CLXXV, 115 A, 1233 AB). Always moderate, Hugh adds in his preface: "Nor do I deny this: that there are many mystical things included in this narrative that call for appropriate explanation" — "Neque hoc tamen nego, multa huic narrationi mystica inserta, quae propriam explanationem exquirant etc." (115 B).

424. "narrationis superficies"; "secundum contemplationis incrementum"; "magis ac magis spiritualia attingit et a visibilibus sustollitur": *In Eccl.*, praef. (115 A); h. 16 (225-6). In the same way the Augustinian pair "fides-intellectus" is here translated by the pair "meditatio-contemplatio"; h. 1: "What meditation seeks, contemplation possesses" — "Id quod meditatio quaerit, contemplatio possidet" (117 B).

425. H. 15 (218 D).

426. H. 2: "I know not how it is that while the words of Ecclesiastes were being read, which testify that all things under the sun are vain, they were rendered sweet in our ears" — "Verba Ecclesiastes, quae cuncta sub sole vana esse testantur, nescio quo pacto, modo cum legerentur, dulcia facta sunt in auribus nostris" (133 B). H. 29 (256 BC).

427. H. 1 (116 D; 124 A).

428. H. 10: "Hebrew is translated as 'transient'. So he has been made a Hebrew to contemplate wisdom.... O how difficult a transition and how it is by a journey of many days for those who have weak steps" — "Hebraeus transiens interpretatur. Hebraeus ergo factus est iste ad contemplandam sapientiam.... O quam difficilis transitus et quam multorum dierum via infirmos gressus habentibus!" (173 A and D; cf. 172-3).

429. "somnia": *Adnotationes in Eccl.* (WA, 20, 9).

430. *In Eccl.*, l. 1: "According to the spiritual understanding . . . our Ecclesiaster is Christ" — "Secundum intelligentiam spiritualem . . . Ecclesiaster noster est Christus"; in ii, 9; iii, 9; vii, 9-10.

431. *In Eccl.* (PL, C, 667 D, 669 C, 698 C).

432. This "beautiful commentary" is his last work; he left it incomplete. Van den Eynde, *Essai*, 108-10.

433. "poème de décrépitude"; "fleur aux pétales de cendre"; "le sens de l'éternité au cœur de l'homme"; "la vérité profonde"; "Misère de l'homme avec Dieu, si ce n'est pas le Dieu de Jésus-Christ": Contemporaries seem to have been able to appreciate it. Though incomplete, Hugh's homiletic commentary spread rapidly. It was in Styria prior to 1150: Ghellinck, *L'essor*, 1, 52.

434. "Summum igitur in vita solamen est studium sapientiae": *Did.*, ll 1, c. 2 (CLXXVI, 742 D).

435. "mystique sans âge": *La vie en Fr. au moyen âge*, 4 (1928), xvii.

436. "O munde immunde, quare sic dileximus te?": L. 1 (CLXXVI, 703 D). Cf. St. Peter Damian, *Vita S. Romualdi*, prol. (CXLIV, 953 A).

437. "Nihil ergo suo tempore abjiciendum, et nihil non suo tempore eligendum; sed sic animus ad usum temporis praeparetur, ut tamen ad mutabilitatem temporis non mutetur": L. 4, in fine (740 C). *In Eccl.*, h. 16 (CLXXV, 225-6).

Notes to Chapter Six

1. Joachim's major works (summary indications):
Conc. = *Concordia novi ac veteris Testamenti* (Venetiis, 1519).
LI = *Liber introductorius in Apocalypsim* (Venetiis, 1527).
IA = *Expositio in Apocalypsin* (Venetiis, 1527).
Ev. = *Tractatus super quatuor evangelia* (ed. E. Buonaiuti, 1930).
Psalt. = *Psalterium decem chordarum* (Venetiis, 1527).
VB = *De vita sancti Benedicti et de officio divino secundum ejus doctrinam* (ed. C. Barsut, Analecta sacra Tarraconesnia, 24, 1951, pp. 10-90).
Lesser works:
AF = *De articulis fidei* (ed. Buonaiuti, 1936).
Ench. = *Enchiridion super Apocalypsin* (Pavia ms, citation in Tondelli, LF, 1).
Works of less certain authenticity:
LF = *Liber Figurarum* (ed. E. Tondelli, 1940).
S. sig. = *Liber de septem sigillis* (ed. M. Reeves and B. Hirsch-Reich, RTAM, 21, 1954, pp. 121-31).

We have not been able to consult the list of corrections proposed for the edited text of *Ev.* and prepared by E. Franceschini, *Aevum*, 9 (1935), 481-92. The *Enchiridion* is doubtless a first draft of what became the *Liber introductorius*. Detailed indications are to be found in Fr. Russo, *Bibliografia Gioachimita* (1954), P. I.

2. "verba mystica": *Conc.*, l. 5, c. 71 (f. 99, 3-4).

3. "stella splendida, sine cujus notitia legere Scripturas magis est palpare in tenebris, quam viam agnoscere veritatis": *Ev.*, 69.

4. "tantorum mysteriorum maria sine difficultate transire": IA, f. 154, 2. LI, f. 26, 3: "These things have been said about the diversity of the mysteries in brief, summary fashion lest anyone think that what seems different is in opposition; since the truth is in no way subject to the mysteries, but rather the mysteries are to the truth; nor ought one to worry about the diversity of paths, so long as the various routes lead to the same city" — "Haec de diversitate mysteriorum summatim et breviter dicta sunt, ne quis putet esse contrarium quod apparet diversum; quia nequaquam veritas mysteriis, sed veritati mysteria subjecta sunt; nec curandum est de diversitate viarum, dummodo diversae viae ad unam perveniant civitatem." Retrojecting the problematic of his own age into the past, M. J. Denis here saw the subordination of authority to reason being affirmed: *De la philosophie d'Or.* (1884), 583.

5. LI, f. 24-5: "These points ... have been compiled ... succinctly ... about the overall propriety of the manifold understanding of the book, though it is difficult completely to discuss word by word the routes of God's ways and to show in

summary how all the allegories turn out, when Scripture bears witness saying: 'Thy ways are in the sea and thy paths in many waters, and they do not know thy tracks' (Psalm 77). For the ways of the sea are not like the ways of the land, so that when you come upon a narrow spot it is not permitted for you to cross over it using another route by a path laid out for everyone; some follow some routes, others take others. But each of the sailors selects his own course, as the spirit of the winds directs them, and if they sometimes do not err in the signs of the whole sky, if it thus turns out well, they reach a single port" — "Haec succincte ... compilata sunt ... de universa proprietate multiformis intelligentiae libri quamvis difficile sit omnino discutere per singula verba itinera viarum Dei et ostendere in summa universos exitus allegoriarum, Scriptura attestante quae dicit: 'In mari viae tuae et semitae tuae in aquis multis, et vestigia tua non cognoscunt' (ps. lxxvi). Non enim ita sunt viae maris sicut viae terrae, ut cum veneris ad locum angustum non liceat tibi aliunde transire et exposita omnibus via; alii alias subsequuntur. Sed unusquisque nautarum eligit viam suam, secundum quod ducit eos spiritus ventorum, et si quandoque non errant in signis caeli omnis, si sic libet, perveniunt ad unum portum."

6. *Praef. in Psalt.:* "And though after the work of the *Concordia*, which we began first, and the exposition of the Apocalypse ... we decided to dedicate this third little work ... to the Holy Spirit" — "Et quamvis post opus Concordiae quod incepimus primo et expositionem Apocalypsis. ... Spiritui sancto ... hoc tertium opusculum dedicare decreverim" (f. 227, 3-4).

7. It is necessary to say as much of LF, as will be shown, below, in section 2.

8. To us the most important difference seems to be that of the LF, Table XI, where the spiritual understanding is called, by way of exception (a unique instance, unless I am mistaken), "intellectus typicus." See also below, note 45.

9. *Psalt.,* f. 265, 4: "But once the twelve understandings have been assigned in the letter of the Old Testament, which can in equal, albeit in higher and more perfect fashion, be assigned again and again in the letter of the New" — "Assignatis autem duodecim intelligentiis in littera veteris Testamenti, quae pari modo in littera novi, immo altiori et nobiliori modo iterum atque iterum assignari possent." *Conc.,* f. 24, 4: "one, manifold, spiritual and mystical understanding proceeds ... in marvelous fashion ... from each [literal level of the two]" — "miro modo ... ex utraque (littera) procedere unum et multiplicem, spiritualem ac mysticum intellectum."

10. "institutiones sanctorum Patrum": *Psalt.,* f. 262, 4: "But the fountainhead itself belongs to the letter, which we say is triple: the Old and New Testament, and what the Fathers have instituted, among whom the mystery of the Church is contained; which again is manifold" — "Est autem fons ipse litterae, quem trinum esse dicimus: vetus ac novum testamentum, et institutiones sanctorum Patrum, inter quos continetur mysterium Ecclesiae; quod et multiplex est."

11. *Ib.:* "From this triple letter proceed the twelve spiritual understandings" — "Ex hac trina littera duodecim intelligentiae spirituales procedunt."

12. *Conc.,* l. 5, c. I (f. 60, 3).

13. *Ev.,* 289.

14. "omnino prope ipsam et secundum ipsam": *Conc.,* l. 5, c. I (f. 60, 4): "Now some think that the historical understanding is the history itself, which is called

the letter. But that is not the case. For the history is one thing and the historical thing something else. Now that which is dissimilar from the letter has been called the historical understanding, as when one woman is taken for another, a child for a child or a man for a man; as when we say to an old man whom we want to urge to advance in virtue: 'Be thou such as Abraham was.'" — "Quidam autem putant historicam intelligentiam esse ipsam historiam, quae vocatur littera. Sed non est ita. Aliud est enim historia, aliud historica res. Dicta est autem historica intelligentia, ista quae dissimilis est a littera, utpote, ubi mulier pro muliere, puer pro puero, et vir accipitur pro viro; ut cum dicimus alicui seni quem volumus exhortari ut proficiat in bono: esto tu qualis fuit Abraham...." *L. intro.,* f. 26, 3: "It is called the historical understanding because it is not far from the history, but is rather quite close to it and in accordance with it" — "Dicta est autem historica intelligentia, eo quod non longe sit ab historia, sed omnino prope ipsam et secundum ipsam gradiatur." *Psalt.,* f. 1, 2: "The historical understanding differs from the history" itself — "Historialis intellectus differt ab historia"; f. 266, 2: "it is first among the twelve [streams] proceeding from the spring of the letter" — "prima est inter duodecim procedentes de fonte litterae."

15. *Psalt.,* f. 262-3: "The first . . . is called historical, because it teaches that something had been instituted according to the example of history: as when an abbot along with twelve monks is sent to found a new monastery, following the example of Christ and the apostles. . . . It also pertains to this understanding to console the pusillanimous by bringing up examples of just men who have suffered similar things" — "Prima . . . dicitur historica, eo quod ad exemplum historiae institutum aliquid esse doceat: ut cum ad aliquod novum monasterium mittitur abbas cum duodecim monachis, Christi et apostolorum. . . . Pertinet etiam ad hanc intelligentiam consolari pusillanimes, propositis exemplis justorum qui similia passi sunt."

16. *Psalt.,* f. 262, 4: "It is called the 'moral', because morals are developed through it" — "Vocatur moralis eo quod per ipsam componantur mores"; tit.: "it treats of the vices and the virtues" — "agit de vitiis et virtutibus."

17. LI, f. 26. *Conc.,* l. 5, c. I (f. 61, 1).

18. "converso quod animale est per allegoriam in spiritale": *Ev.* 311.

19. "fons litterae": LI, f. 26, 2: "The historical understanding is a likeness of a visible thing to one that is invisible, e.g., there is one virgin designated as freewoman, and another paired with her as a slave-girl. The moral understanding is a likeness of a visible thing to one that is invisible with respect to a part, as obtains anywhere: or with respect to a whole, as by the slave-girl one can signify the flesh, which begat in servitude, and by the free-woman one can signify the mind, etc." — "Historica intelligentia est similitudo rei visibilis ad invisibilem, ut est aliqua virgo designata in libera, aliqua conjugata in ancilla. Moralis intelligentia est similitudo rei visibilis ad invisibilem secundum partem ut alicubi: sive secundum totum, ut est in ancilla significari carnem quae genuit in servitute, in libera mentem"; etc.

20. *Psalt.,* f. 262, 4: "Two of them are lower and humbler, and yet through them more plentiful fruit is found within the human race" — "Harum duae inferiores sunt et humiliores, et tamen per eas in humano genere fructus uberior reperitur."

21. "modos sermonum Dei complectitur et discernit": LI, c. 27: "The tropological understanding is the one that pertains to doctrine, e.g., the letter can be signified by the slave-girl, and spiritual understanding by the free-woman. . . . It is called tropological because it embraces the ways of God's speaking out; for [what is called] 'tropos' in Greek is called 'modus' in Latin [meaning 'way' or 'manner']; and 'logos' [in Greek means the same as the Latin word] 'sermo' [namely, 'speech']; so [it is called] 'tropology' because it embraces and discerns the ways of God's speeches" — "Tropologica intelligentia est quae pertinet ad doctrinam, ut est in ancilla significari litteram, in libera intelligentiam spiritalem. . . . Dicta est tropologica quia complectitur modos eloquiorum Dei; tropos enim graece, latine modus; logos, id est sermo; inde tropologia, quia modos sermonum Dei complectitur et discernit" (f. 26, 2-3). *Psalt.*, f. 264, 1: "The tropological understanding is the one in which one is especially concerned with God's turns of speech" — "Tropologica intelligentia est in qua de modis sermonum Dei specialiter agitur."

22. In Joachim's terminology, then, it is tropology that is the doctrinal sense, the one closest to "allegory" in the tradition. André Pézard, *Dante sous la pluie de feu* (1950), 391: "One will note that the prophet departs from his predecessors when he distinguishes the tropological sense from the moral" — "On notera que le prophète s'écarte de ses prédécesseurs lorsqu'il distingue du sens moral le sens tropologique"; the sequel is less justified: "However he was right, given the etymology of the word" — "C'est d'ailleurs lui qui a raison, vu l'étymologie de ce mot."

23. "invisibilia Dei": LI, f. 26, 2-3: "The contemplative understanding is the one that pertains most properly to the gifts of the Holy Spirit: e.g., the active life can be signified by the slave-girl and the contemplative in the free-woman; or again servile fear can be signified by the slave-girl and the grace of the Holy Spirit by the free-woman. . . . It is called contemplative because it makes one contemplate the invisible things of God, in the words of the Apostle: 'when we are contemplating not the things that are seen but those that are unseen'" — "Contemplativa intelligentia est quae pertinet propriissime ad dona Spiritus sancti: ut est in ancilla significari vitam activam, in libera contemplativam sive in ancilla timorem servilem, in libera gratiam Spiritus sancti. . . . Dicta est contemplativa, quia facit contemplari invisibilia Dei, dicente Apostolo: contemplantibus nobis non ea quae videntur sed quae non videntur." *Psalt.*, l. 2: "In the moral understanding is treated the struggle of the bodily vices; in tropology, the struggle against heresies; in the contemplative, the struggle against the spiritual attacks of the Devil" — "In morali intellectu agitur de pugna corporalium vitiorum; in tropologia, de pugna haeresum; in contemplativa, de pugna spiritualium impugnationum diaboli" (f. 270, 3-4).

24. *Ev.*, 288: "The tropological [understanding] is ascribed to the spiritual doctors; the contemplative, to those who have leisure for prayers and psalms . . . ; the anagogical understanding is proper to those who, having laid aside the burden of the flesh, repose in yon happy fatherland" — "Ascribitur . . . tropologica spiritalibus doctoribus, contemplativa vacantibus orationibus et psalmis . . . , anagogicus intellectus illorum est proprius qui, deposito carnis onere, in illa beata patria requiescunt." *Conc.*, l. 5, c. I (f. 612, 1). LI, f. 26, 3: "Anagocial under-

standing is the one that pertains to the fatherland on high, or sometimes to God himself; e.g., the earthly fatherland can be signified by the slave-girl, and the one that is Jerusalem on high, which is our mother, can be signified by the freewoman" — "Anagogica intelligentia est quae pertinet ad supernam patriam, sive aliquando ad ipsum Deum, ut est in ancilla significari terrenam patriam, in libera illam quae sursum est Hierusalem, quae est mater nostra." Anagogy and contemplation are sometimes synonymous: *Conc.*, l. 5, c. 71 (f. 100, 2).

25. *Psalt.*, f. 264, 3-4: "The fifth understanding is the anagogical ... there is no other understanding above it" — "Quinta intelligentia est anagogica ... supra ipsam nulla alia intelligentia." LI, f. 26, 3: "It is called anagogical because it is superior to the others, dealing with God himself or the fatherland on high" — "Dicta est anagogica, eo quod superior caeteris sit, agens de ipso Deo vel de ipsa superna patria." "Just as charity is the end of the law, so is the anagogical understanding the end of the five understandings that have been cited earlier, than which nothing is higher" — "Sicut caritas finis praecepti est, ita anagogica intelligentia (est) finis quinque intelligentiarum quae praescriptae sunt, eo quod ea altior nulla sit" (at the sequel of AF, f. 163; B., CXXXIII).

26. *Conc.*, l. 5, c. 71: "But what [is meant] by 'oil', that liquid which is of such great price and such great power that it swims below as soon as it is put in any vessel of water or of wine, except that understanding which the ancients called 'anagogy', which the higher understanding or contemplation and that which tends upward is singing out" — "Sed quid per oleum, qui tanti liquor pretii est et tantae virtutis, ut etiam in uno aquae seu vini vase ponatur, subnatet: nisi illa intelligentia quam antiqui anagogen vocaverunt, quod sonat superior intellectus sive etiam contemplatio et quae est illa quae superius tendit" (f. 100, 2).

27. IA, P. 4, c. 13: "Since it teaches the works of the Church that were long ago designated in things written down and in the resources of the Fathers; and through this means the pastors of the Church prove that the possession of the Christian faith is true and reliable" — "Quia docet ecclesastica opera, olim in rebus scriptis et patrum opibus designata; ac per hoc probant pastores Ecclesiae veram esse et fidelem possessionem fidei christianae" (f. 162, 2).

28. *Psalt.*, f. 264, 4: "One ought to come to the typic understanding, of which we said there were seven species, which the seven spirits sent from heaven are effecting upon the earth" — "Veniendum est autem ad typicam intelligentiam, cujus esse diximus species septem, quas missi caelitus septem spiritus operantur in terram." *Conc.*, l. 5, c. 2 (f. 61, 1). It is hardly likely that, in *Purg.*, 29, the seven candelabras described by Dante precisely figure as Joachim's "septem species," as E. Buonaiuti thinks, ed. of the AF, p. 88 of the introduction, note.

29. "concordia non secundum totum exigenda est, sed secundum quod clarius et evidentius est; non secundum cursum historiae, sed secundum quid": *Conc.*, l. 4, c. I (f. 42, 2-3).

30. "In prima specie intelligentiae typicae, Abraham significat pontifices Judaeorum, Agar significat israeliticam plebem, Sara tribum Levi. ... In secunda specie Abraham significat episcopos, Agar ecclesiam laicorum, Sara ecclesiam clericorum. In tertia intelligentia, Abraham significat praelatos caenobiorum, Agar ecclesiam conversorum, Sara monachorum. ... In quarta specie, Abraham significat pontifices Judaeorum et episcopos Latinorum, Agar significat

synagogam ut supra, Sara ecclesiam Latinorum. In sexta intelligentia, Abraham significat praelatos secundi et tertii status, Agar ecclesiam laborantium quae praesens est, Sara ecclesiam quiescentium, quae futura est in tertio statu, cum dabitur sabbatismus populo Dei . . .": *Psalt.*, cf. 264-5. *Conc.*, f. 61. [Trans.: De Lubac's excerpt does not include the fifth or seventh items of the seven.]

31. *Conc.*, l. 5, c. 2: "And so the first (typic) understanding pertains to the Father; the second, to the Son; the third, to the Holy Spirit. The fourth species is the one that pertains jointly to the Father and the Son. . . . The fifth pertains jointly to the Father and the Holy Spirit. . . . The sixth species pertains jointly to the Son and the Holy Spirit. . . . But the seventh species pertains jointly to the three Persons." "Primus itaque intellectus (typicus) pertinet ad Patrem, secundus ad Filium, tertius ad Spiritum sanctum. Quarta species est illa quae pertinet simul ad Patrem et Filium. . . . Quinta pertinet simul ad Patrem et Spiritum sanctum. . . . Sexta species pertinet simul ad Filium et Spiritum sanctum. . . . Septima autem species pertinet simul ad tres personas . . ." (f. 61, 1-2). The whole thing [is] mixed with the symbolism of Hagar and Sarah, with applications to the diverse categories in the Church and even with the calculation of the years. As B., *Ev.*, 288, note, says: "Joachim is the most rigorous systematizer of symbolism" — "Giacchino è il più rigoroso sistematore del simbolismo."

32. VB, c. 1-6 (10-20).

33. *Conc.*, l. 2, tr. 1, c. 4: "The understanding that is called concord is like an uninterrupted path that stretches from the wilderness to a city, with various lower spots interposed in which the traveller is in doubt as to which is the right route to take and yet with mountain ridges also interposed from which he can look back and forth and gauge the rightness of the rest of his route from a look at the path already traversed" — "Intelligentia vero quae concordia dicitur, similis est viae continuae quae a deserto porrigitur ad civitatem, interpositis locis humilioribus in quibus viator ambigat iter rectum adire, et nihilominus interpositis jugis montium a quibus possit posteriora et anteriora respicere, et residui itineris rectitudinem ex retroactae viae contemplatione metiri . . ." (f. 8, 1-2). LI, f. 26, 2: "The typic [understanding] is divided into seven species gathered together as in a bundle under one name" — "Typica dividitur in septem species sub ipso uno nomine velut in fasciculo colligatas"; "The seven typic understandings are to be referred to the divers states of the world" — "Septem vero intelligentiae typicae ad diversos mundi status referendae sunt."

34. *Psalt.*, f. 266, 1: "The chords are ten because the understandings that especially pertain to the knowledge of God and to his great works that he has performed and is performing unto the end according to the counsel of his will are ten. For the two lower ones, which proceed from the letter, are known to pertain . . . to the institution of each of them." — "Decem sunt cordae quia decem sunt intelligentiae, quae specialiter pertinent ad notitiam Dei et ad magna opera ejus quae operatus est et operatur usque in finem secundum consilium voluntatis suae. Nam duae inferiores, quae procedunt de littera, ad institutionem uniuscujusque . . . pertinere noscuntur."

35. "plenitudo intelligentiae": *Psalt.*, f. 262, 3: "On the fullness of the understandings that are contained in the numbers three, five, and seven" — "De plenitudine intelligentiarum quae in numero ternario, quinario et septenario

contentur"; etc. LI, c. 27: "For just as the five general understandings that are distinguished by names of their own. . . . the first . . . is called the historic, the second the moral, the third the troplogical, the fourth the contemplative, and the fifth the anagogic" — "Sicut enim quinque intelligentiae generales quae propriis nominibus distinguuntur. . . . Prima . . . dicitur historica, secunda moralis, tertia tropologica, quarta contemplativa, quinta anagogica" (f. 26, 2). One will note that the typic understanding, which is also under question in the same pages, does not figure in the enumeration.

36. *Psalt.*, f. 265-6: "Now there are fifteen steps, since there are fifteen ways in which man speaks in the divine Scripture" — "Quindecim sane gradus sunt, quia quindecim sunt modi quibus loquitur homo in divina Scriptura."

37. *Ib.*

38. "quatuor intelligentiae principales, quae caeteras omnes, continent infra se": *Conc.*, l. 5, c. 2: "namely the historic and moral; the contemplative, under whose name two are contained, the tropological and the anagogical, the first of which is inferior to the contemplative, whilst the second is superior to it; and the typic, which is divided into seven species" — "historica sc. et moralis; contemplativa, sub cujus nomine continentur duae, tropologica et anagogica, quarum prima inferior est contemplativae, secunda superior; et typica, quae dividitur in septem speciebus" (f. 61, 3). *Ib.:* "Four of these seven types of understanding are kept in use, namely the first three and the last" — "Horum septem intellectuum quatuor habentur in usu, tres sc. primi et ultimus" (61, 1). IA, P. 2, c. 6: "So there are four animals, and four faces of the one wheel, since there are four general understandings of holy Scriptures" — "Quatuor ergo animalia sunt, et quatuor facies unius rotae, quia quatuor generales intelligentiae Scripturarum sanctarum" (f. 115, 2); "the first of these is the typic, the second the historical, the third the moral, the fourth contemplative" — "prima harum typica est, secunda historica, tertia moralis, quarta contemplativa."

39. IA, P. 4, c. 13: "The four winds of the heavens are the four special understandings, just as there are also four gospels. For the first is the typic, the second the historic, the third the moral, the fourth the contemplative. Of these the first is especially fitting for pastors, the second for deacons, the third for doctors, the fourth for virgins and hermits," etc. — "Quatuor venti caeli, quatuor sunt intelligentiae speciales, secundum quod et quatuor evangelia. Nam prima est typica, secunda historica, tertia moralis, quarta contemplativa. Harum prima pastoribus specialiter congruit, secunda diaconibus, tertia doctoribus, quarta virginibus et eremitis, etc." (F. 162, 2-3).

40. At first the *Concordia*, l. 5, c. 1, gives another explication of the four living beings: "The four books of the concords that we have hitherto been going through may be taken in species according to the number of the four animals, so that the first, in which histories are simply compiled, is related to the man; the second, in which one deals with the chief and more evident topics of the concords, refers to the ox; the third, in which one deals with the concords of the seven seals, refers to the lion; the fourth, in which one deals with the fullness of the concord, is related to the eagle" — "Quatuor concordiarum libri, quos hucusque digressimus, ita secundum numerum quatuor animalium accipiantur in specie, ut primus, in quo simpliciter compilantur historiae, referatur ad hominem; secundus, in quo agitur

de praecipuis et evidentioribus locis concordiarum, referatur ad vitulum; tertius in quo agitur de concordiis septem signaculorum, referatur ad leonem; quartus, in quo agitur de plenitudine concordiae, referatur ad aquilam" (f. 60, 3).

41. Slight variations in VB, c. 46: in each monastery there are four sorts of monks tending to perfection: "men, oxen, lions, and eagles. Each of them hears his own reading, whether the morality in Matthew, or the historic understanding in Luke, or the typic in Mark, or the anagogic in John" — "homines, vituli, leones et aquilae. Unumquodque autem istorum audit lectionem suam, sive moralitatem in Matthaeo, sive historicum intellectum in Luca, sive typicum in Marco, sive anagogicum in Joanne" (86).

42. IA, c. 6: "And sometimes the historical understanding, which is fitting to the human animals, is designated by the barley, whereas the typic which befits the spiritual is designated by the wheat; just as the moral [is designated] by the wine, and the anagogic or contemplative by the oil" — "Et historicus quandoque intellectus qui animalibus hominibus congruit in ordeo; typicus vero qui spiritualibus designatur in tritico; sicut et moralis in vino, anagogicus vel contemplativus in oleo . . ." (f. 115, 1-2).

43. *Psalt.*, the second page drawing and legend; cf. f. 48. Or: martyrs, confessors, doctors, and virgins (IA, c. 6; f. 114, 4). Or again: contemplatives, pastors, martyrs, doctors = aquila, leo, vitulus, homo (eagle, lion, ox, man) = ascensio, resurrectio, mors, nativitas = intelligentia anagogica, typica, historica, moralis (LF, table XV).

44. *Conc.*, l. 5, c. I: "according to the allegoric understanding, of which there are many species. . . . Now, regarding the typic understanding" — "secundum allegoricum intellectum, cujus multae sunt species. . . . De typica autem intelligentia" (f. 60, 3). Cf. l. 2, tr. I, c. 3: "And this [is the case] with the spiritual understanding, which properly is called allegory" — "Et hoc quidem de spiritali intellectu, quod proprie dicitur allegoria." C. 4: "But the understanding that is called concord" — "Intelligentia vero illa quae concordia dicitur" (f. 8, 1). It is in a moment of distraction that A. Pézard writes that for Joachim "the anagogic sense takes the name *intelligentia typica* in the primary sense" — "le sens anagogique prend nom d'*intelligentia typica* par excellence."

45. However, *Psalt.*, l. 2, f. 270: "De septem intellectibus spiritualibus"; in fact, it is a question of the seven "species of the typic understanding" — "species typici intellectus." There is an analogous exception in LF, table XI.

46. There are even some hints of geographical concord: *Ev.*, 268-9, on Salem and Bologna.

47. "Pour Joachim de Flore," writes A. Pézard, *op. cit.*, 376, "l'*intelligentia typica* est anagogie, et n'est que cela" — "For Joachim of Flora, the *intelligentia typica* is anagogy and nothing but anagogy." It is the other way around. Even the lowest degree of spiritual understanding, of which anagogy constitutes the insurpassable highest degree, is already more "spiritual" than the typic understanding. *Conc.*, l. 5, c. I: "The historical understanding is that by which one person stands for another, not as obtains in concord but in some other fashion, etc." — "Historica intelligentia, illa est qua persona pro persona, non eo modo quo in concordia, sed alio quodam modo etc." Cf. note 9, above. Hence one ought not write: "Le sensus typicus de saint Grégoire et de Joachim de Flore" (*ib.*).

48. Perhaps with one or two exceptions. VB, c. 26: "In the first state the task for children was to apprehend the letter for the instruction of the outer man, and in the second state it was to learn the spiritual understanding for the instruction of the inner man" — "In primo statu labor fuit pueris apprehendere litteram ad instructionem exterioris hominis, et in secundo spiritalem intellectum agnoscere, ad instructionem interioris" (57); but it is only a question of a moral teaching, of the recognition of sin; and the third state, where the "freedom of the Spirit of the Lord" — "Spiritus Domini libertas" reigns, is opposed to the first state.

49. "Quia sunt nonnulli qui hoc ipsum putant esse concordiam quod spiritualem intellectum, qui proprie dicitur allegoria, primo necesse est ut ostendamus quid distet inter concordiam et allegoriam": *Conc.*, l. 2, tr. I, c. I (f. 7, 2); c. 2: "not in the allegoric sense, but as a concord between the two Testaments" — "non pro sensu allegorico, sed pro concordia duorum testamentorum" (7, 3); etc.

Notes to Pages 332-33

50. "secundum spiritum": *Conc.*, l. 5, c. I: "For in those four books there is little dealt with according to the spirit, but a bit more according to the letter, i.e., according to the concord of the letter, namely the letter of the two Testaments" — "Etenim in iis quatuor libris parum agitur secundum spiritum, magis autem secundum litteram, hoc est, secundum concordiam litterae, litterae sc. duorum testamentorum" (f. 60, 3).

51. There is a reasonably faithful summary of the various senses in the apocryphal *Expositio in Hieremiam,* which was very popular, c. I: "Consider, aside from the historical and moral [understandings] the tropologic, contemplative, and anagogic are rolled up under the single cover of allegory.... But it was necessary that after knowledge of the Trinity as if of a threefold understanding grasped under the unity of allegory or essence, and of the other two [historical and moral] signified in Christ, God and man, according to the faith by which we believe God may be understood, comparatively, in a sevenfold manner, another spiritual or typic [understanding] should be supplied, which would proceed over the waters of the Scriptures like the other sevenfold spirit of God and would fill the surface of the earth.... The typic understanding is to be assigned in the three states of the human race" — "Ecce, praeter historicum et moralem, tropologicus et contemplativus et anagogicus sub uno allegoriae cortice involvuntur.... Sed necesse erat ut post notitiam Trinitatis ac si triplicis intelligentiae sub unitate allegoriae vel essentiae comprehensae, aliorumque duorum in Christo Deo et homine signatorum, secundum fidem qua Deum septupliciter credimus relative, alter mysterialis vel typicus largiretur, qui velut alter spiritus Dei septiformis super aquas Scripturarum procederet, et repleret superficietenus orbem terrae.... Typicus intellectus, in tribus humani generis statibus assignandus" (f. 6).

52. "ante legem," "sub lege," "sub evangelio," or "sub littera evangelii," "sub littera novi Testamenti," "sub spirituali intellectu," and finally, "in patria" or "in manifesta visione Dei": LI, c. 5: "all five times together" — "Omnia tempora simul quinque . . ." (f. 5, 3). *Psalt.*, l. 2, c. 259-60: *De differentia quinque temporum* (but all five are terrestrial; the time under the Law is divided in two).

53. LI, c. 5: "We have decided to keep the states of those times properly to use for expounding the Scriptures; in them the works of the undivided Trinity are

brighter and stand out as more manifest by clear sacraments: i.e., at the time of the spiritual understanding" — "Illos tamen illorum temporum status in usum exponendarum Scripturarum proprie tenere decrevimus, in quibus sunt individuae Trinitatis opera lucidiora et manifestiora claris exhibent sacramentis: hoc est sub tempore spiritualis intellectus" (f. 6, 2).

54. "abusive, non proprie tempus dicitur": Ib. (f. 5, 3).

55. the time "ante gratiam," the time "sub gratia," and the time "quod e vicino exspectamus, sub ampliori gratia": Ib.: "Hence wherever mention is made in this book of three states, leaving aside the time that existed before the Law and second the one to come after the end of the world: let us say that the first state existed from Abraham up to the time of the fullness of the peoples; and that the third extends from thence unto the consummation of the age" — "Ubicumque ergo de tribus statibus absolute fit mentio in hoc libro, praetermisso tempore illo quod fuit ante legem, secundo post finem mundi futuro: primum statum esse dicamus ab Abraham usque ad tempus plenitudinis gentium; tertium ex eo usque ad consummationem saeculi" (f. 6, 2). *Psalt.*, l. 2: "sub lege," "gratiae," "amplioris gratiae" (f. 247, 1).

56. *Conc.*, l. 5, c. 84: "In fine, the sacraments of the divine page commend to us ... the three states of the world ... : the first, in which we were under the Law, the second in which we are under grace, the third which we soon expect, under a fuller grace. ... The first ... consisted in knowledge, the second in the possession of wisdom, the third in the fullness of understanding" — "Tres denique mundi status ... divinae nobis paginae sacramenta commendant: primum in quo fuimus sub lege, secundum in quo sumus sub gratia, tertium quod e vicino exspectamus sub ampliori gratia. . . . Primus . . . in scientia fuit, secundus in proprietate sapientiae, tertius in plenitudine intellectus . . ." (f. 112, 2). *Ev.*, 191: "Consequently both the time that preceded grace by means of the letter of the earlier Testament and the time that the letter of the New Testament precedes will be of still greater grace, since he has given us grace upon grace" — "Denique et tempus illud quod gratiae praecessit littera prioris testamenti, et tempus illud quod erit majoris gratiae quoniam gratiam pro gratia dedit nobis, praecedit littera novi testamenti." Wishing to show that Joachim is a lyrical spirit and not a systematic thinker, M. W. Bloomfield, *Traditio*, 13 (1957), 261, writes: "Sometimes he seems to be paralleling only Old Testament history with known Christian history, sometimes he speaks in triples, bringing in a third age" ("Joachim of Flora, a Critical Survey of His Canon, Teaching, Sources, Biography and Influence"). There is no contradiction in that. As we shall see, the third age does not belong simply to a historical concord.

57. "servitus legis"; "a labore passionis": *Psalt.*, l. 2 (f. 247, 1).

58. VB, c. 42 (81).

59. *Ev.*, 24: "Elizabeth's sterility, which comprehends the first state beginning from Abraham, ends in John the Baptist; his birth, however, is at the end of the second state, i.e., in the coming of Elijah" — "Sterilitas Elizabeth, quae comprehendit primum statum incipientem ab Abraham, terminatur in Joanne Baptista; partus vero ejus in fine secundi status, hoc est in adventu Eliae."

60. "in primo erudiuntur parvuli, in secundo instituuntur adolescentes, in tertio initiantur amici": IA, P. 3: "The first heaven is Scripture as it pertains to the

first state; the second, Scripture as it pertains to the second; and the third, spiritual understanding, which pertains to the third. In the first, etc." — "Primum caelum est Scriptura quae pertinet ad primum statum; secundum, Scriptura quae pertinet ad secundum; tertium, intelligentia spiritalis, quae pertinet ad tertium. In primo, etc." (f. 139, 2).

61. "ordo gignentium, ordo praedicantium, ordo contemplativorum": *Psalt.*, f. 253, 4. LF, t. XIX, *Mysterium Ecclesiae.*

62. *Conc.*, l. 5, c. 84: "The first [consists] in slavish service, the second in filial service, the third in freedom.... The first in fear, in faith, in charity. The first [is] of the old, the second of young men, the third of children" — "Primus in servitute servili, secundus in servitute filiali, tertius in libertate.... Primus in timore, in fide, in caritate. Primus senum, secundus juvenum, tertius puerorum" (f. 112, 2). *Ev.*, 89: "This teaching is well given to the younger.... For hence it is that David, though younger than his brothers, was filled with the spirit of prophecy; hence it is that Solomon, also younger, was filled with the spirit of wisdom. Hence too was it said by the apostle younger than the rest, to whom the Lord gave the prerogative of knowledge: 'If it should be revealed to the younger, let the elder keep silent.'" — "Bene juniori data est haec doctrina.... Hinc est enim quod David junior fratribus repletus est spiritu prophetiae; hinc quod Salomon, aeque junior, spiritu sapientiae. Unde et per apostolum, caeteris juniorem, cui data est a Domino praerogativa scientiae, dicitur: si juniori revelatum fuerit, prior taceat (*1 Cor.* 14:30).''

63. *Conc.*, l. 5, c. 84: "The first ... in starlight, the second in the dawn ..., the third in broad daylight. The first offers water, the second wine, the third oil" — "Primus ... in luce siderum, secundus in aurora ..., tertius in perfecto die. Primus protulit aquam, secundus vinum, tertius oleum ..." (f. 112, 3). C. 68: "In the first state the mystery of the kingdom of God was shown as in the darkness of deep night; in the second, it grew clear as in the dawn; in the third it will shine forth as in broad daylight" — "In primo quidem statu tanquam in profundae noctis caligine ostensum est mysterium regni Dei; in secundo claruit ut in aurora; in tertio splendebit quasi in perfecta die" (f. 96, 3).

64. *Ev.*, 155: "Since in the first state of the age the order of laymen is preeminent; in the second, the order of clerics; and in the third, according to what the principles, i.e., the preeminently splendid mysteries, show, the order of the monks must be preeminent, especially from the advent of Elijah, who was the first in Israel to show this spiritual life about which we are speaking" — "Quia in primo statu saeculi claruit ordo laicorum, in secundo ordo clericorum, in tertio secundum quod ostendunt initia, imo et praeclara mysteria, oportet clarere ordinem monachorum, maxime autem ab adventu Eliae, qui primo ostendit in Israël hanc de qua et loquimur vitam spiritalem." *Conc.*, l. 2, tr. I, c. 5: "The first is [the order] of the married, the second that of the clerics, the third that of the monks" — "Primus conjugatorum est, secundus clericorum, tertius monachorum" (f. 8, 3). LI, c. 5 (f. 5, 2). *Psalt.*, l. I (f. 246-7 and 254-5).

65. VB, c. 30 (65).

66. "Si principia et facies evangeliorum subtilius sufficimus perscrutari, videtur proprietate quadam evangelium Matthaei tangere tempus prioris Testamenti; evangelium Lucae ab ortu nascentis Ecclesiae usque ad adventum

Heliae; evangelium Marci ab adventu Heliae ad consummationem saeculi, quando electi Dei rapientur in caelum; evangelium Joannis, saeculum illud beatum, quod nullo unquam claudetur fine": *Ev.*, 144; *id.*, more developed: 6-7.

67. "secundum spiritum": *Conc.*, l. 2, tr. I, c. 5: "The order of the married was started by Adam and began to be fruitful with Abraham. The order of the clerics was begun by Uzziah . . . , but became fruitful through Christ. The order of the monks properly . . . started with blessed Benedict . . . , and its fructification is in the end times" — "Conjugatorum ordo initiatus est ab Adam, fructificare caepit ab Abraham. Clericorum ordo initiatus est ab Ozia . . . , fructificavit autem a Christo. Monachorum ordo secundum propriam formam . . . incepit a beato Benedicto . . . , cujus fructificatio in temporibus finis" (f. 8, 3). LI, c. 5: "The first state, which came to light under the Law and circumcision, was started by Adam. The second, which came to light under the Gospel, was started by Uzziah. The third, to the extent that it can be gathered from the number of generations, [started] in the time of St. Benedict, and its outstanding clarity is to be expected around the end" of the world — "Et primus quidem status, qui claruit sub lege et circumcisione, initiatus est ab Adam. Secundus, qui claruit sub evangelio, initiatus est ab Ozia. Tertius, quantum datur intelligi ex numero generationum, a tempore sancti Benedicti, cujus praecellens claritas exspectanda est circa finem" (f. 5, 2). *Ev.*, 25: "Mary of youthful age designates the monastic religion, the one that Benedict established, which, conceiving of the Holy Spirit, is about to have a Son within her womb, namely the people consisting of the saints, etc." — "Maria aetate juvencula designat monasticam illam religionem, sc. quam sanctus instituit Benedictus, quae, concipiens de Spiritu sancto, habitura est et ipsa Filium in utero suo, populum sc. illum sanctorum etc."

68. "inter secundum et tertium statum constituti sumus": *Conc.*, l. 5, c. 20 (f. 70, 2).

69. IA, P. 4 (f. 170, 1); cf. Apocalypse 7:9; 14:1-4.

70. VB, 15 (35-6); cf. 45 (85).

71. Cf. *S. sig., apertio quinti:* "the germination of the subsequent time is to be attained from the middle of the preceeding one, but its maturation is to be attained in its end-points" — "a medietate praecedentis temporis initiatio sequentis attendenda est, clarificatio vero in limitibus suis" (243).

72. Cf. the table prepared by M. E. Reeves, RTAM, 21, 216; and *Conc.* (*ib.*, 212).

73. *Ev.*, 32: "Since 'church' or 'synagogue' is customarily taken in a broad or in a narrow sense, since it is sometimes taken as the mother only, sometimes as the mother with her sons, and sometimes only as the perfect ones, it may be more carefully considered that in this place where one is dealing with so much perfection, the totality of the people is not understood by the name 'church' as designated in Elizabeth, but only the church of the clerics, which Peter was in charge of from the start and remains such through the succession up till the coming of Elijah. According to this understanding, Mary too does not refer to the universal church, nor generally to the mass of the monastic profession, but to a certain special church of that monastic profession, to which it was given by the Lord to choose and love a celibate life" — "Quis ecclesia vel synagoga largo solet accipi et stricto modo, quia aliquando mater tantum, aliquando accipitur mater cum filiis et aliquando tantummodo cum perfectis: libet diligentius intueri quod in hoc loco

ubi de tanta agitur perfectione, nequaquam universitas populi intelligenda est nomine ecclesiae, designatae in Elizabeth; sed tantum ecclesiae clericorum, cui Petrus praefuit a principio et manet per successionem usque ad adventum Eliae. Secundum quem intellectum, Maria quoque non universalem ecclesiam, sed neque generaliter monasticae turbam professionis, sed quamdam specialem ejusdem monasticae professionis ecclesiam, cui datum est a Domino specialius celibem eligere et diligere vitam" (f. 23-5).

74. "duplex et geminum": *Ev.*, 33: "God willed there to be a twofold Church, namely Eastern and Western, so that, once Peter had been sent as supreme pontiff to the Western Church, he might confirm in it the ecclesiastical or priestly order designated by John [the Baptist], and, once John the Evangelist had been sent as the mirror of chastity to the Eastern Church, he might confirm in it the virginal and chaste religion designated by Mary. Thus just as the master-preaching was at Rome, so the teaching of the monastic and eremitic profession is known to have taken its origin in the Eastern Church" — "Voluit Deus esse duplicem Ecclesiam, orientalem sc. atque occidentalem, ut, misso Petro summo pontifice ad occidentalem ecclesiam, confirmaret in ea ecclesiasticum seu sacerdotalem ordinem quem designat Joannes (Baptista), et misso Joanne evangelista castitatis speculo ad ecclesiam orientalem, confirmaret in ea virginalem et castam religionem, quam designat Maria. Siquidem ut magisterium praedicationis Romae, ita doctrina monasticae atque eremiticae professionis in ecclesia orientali noscitur accepisse exordium." LI, c. 19: "On the active life betokened in Peter and the contemplative life betokened in John" — "De vita activa designata in Petro et de contemplativa designata in Joanne."

75. *Dialogi*, tit. 6, *de Trinitate* (PL, CLVII, 606-13; see the "geometralis figura," 611 BC). Cf. B. Hirsch-Reich, "Die Quelle der Trinitätskreise von J. von Fiore und Dante" (*Sophia*, 22, 1954, 170-8; BTAM, 7, no. 464). Crocco, 138-44. One may also recall the symbol of the wheel and the six circles explained at length by Hildegarde, *L. div. operum simplicis hominis*, 1, vis. 2 (PL, CXCVII, 751-60); but the analogy is remote.

76. [Trans.: it is not entirely clear whether this means, as I take it, 'interlocking' or 'intersecting' circles, or 'concentric' circles. I have not seen the original edition of Joachim's text.] There is a diagram in *Conc.*, f. 121, 4; and LF, the two schemata of Table XI. Cf. IA, f. 36, 4 and 101, 1. Another schema: a tree with three trunks conjoined, each bearing three branches (*Conc.*, f. 14). The three rings also figure in the edition (Cologne, 1577) of the *In Hieremiam*.

77. LI, c. 6: "The assignment of the concord between the two Testaments" — "Assignatio concordiae duorum testamentorum"; c. 7: "On the second assignment of concord" — "De secunda assignatione concordiae" (f. 6-9); etc. *Conc.*, praef.: "From the old and new histories we have estimated the value of putting together that work, in which, once the wheels of Ezekiel have been diligently examined, we clearly show how much is in the concord of each of them; and we have taken care to assign to the concord of the two Testaments what those two cherubim facing each other were wont to designate, seeing that our faith is strengthened by two witnesses" — "Opere pretium aestimavimus ex veteribus et novis historiis opus istud componere, in quo, Ezechielis rotis diligenter inspectis, quanta sit in utriusque concordia luculenter ostendimus; et quae duo

illa cherubim mutuis se vultibus contemplantis designabant, in duorum testamentorum consonantia assignare curavimus; quatenus duobus testibus veritatis nostra fides munitur." Cf. L. 2, tr. I, c. 29 (f. 18, 1-2); I; 5, c. 85 (f. 113, 3). Cf. *In Hier.*, praef. (f. 2).

78. *Conc.*, l. 2, tr. I, c. 2: "We say that concord is properly speaking a likeness of equal proportion between the New and the Old Testament. By 'equal' I mean with respect to number, not worth: namely, when person and person, one order and another, war and war are looked at from the point of view of some sort of equality as they confront each other: e.g., Abraham and Zacharias, Sarah and Elizabeth, Isaac and John the Baptist, and Jesus the man and Jacob, the twelve patriarchs and the apostles of the same number, and any suchlike; each of which, wherever it may occur, is sure to make for a concord of the two Testaments and not for an allegorical sense" — "Concordiam proprie esse dicimus, similitudinem aequae proportionis novi ac veteris testamenti. Aeque dico quoad numerum non quoad dignitatem; cum vid. persona et persona, ordo et ordo, bellum et bellum ex parilitate quadam mutuis se vultibus intuentur: utpote, Abraham et Zacharias, Sara et Elizabeth, Isaac et J. Baptista, et homo Jesus et Jacob, duodecim patriarchae et numeri ejusdem apostoli, et quodlibet simile; quod totum, ubicumque occurrerit, non pro sensu allegorico, sed pro concordia duorum testamentorum facere certum est" (f. 7, 2-3).

79. VB, c. 13-5 (32-6); 15: "What are we to think Scholastica signifies if not a sort of bond of peace, which brings two divers things into association as if by allying and binding them together, just as what the Lord's mother prefigures is shown to have brought into association what were once two peoples?" — "Quid putandum est quod designat Scholastica, nisi quoddam vinculum pacis quod duo diversa, ac si confaederando et ligando consociat, sicut illud quod figurat mater Domini duos quondam populos sociasse monstratur?"

80. *Conc.*, l. 5, c. 85-92 (f. 112-3). LI, c. I: "But the four Gospels were given in exchange for the four (special) histories, not without showing concord and providing a defense for the spiritual understanding" — "Pro quatuor autem historiis (specialibus) quatuor evangelia data sunt, non sine ostensione concordiae et spiritalis munimine intellectus" (f. 3, 1). VB, c. 22 (47-60).

81. Cf. LF, Tables III and IV.

82. "respondentibus per singula veteribus novis": LI, c. 7: "Just as in the time of the sixth seal the old Babylon was struck, so too now will the new one be struck. And just as the Assyrians and Macedonians terrified the Jews then, so too now the Saracens and the false prophets who are to come after them will perform many wicked deeds on the earth and tribulation such as did not ever exist from the beginning" — "Ut autem in tempore sexti signaculi percussa est vetus Babylon, ita et nunc percutietur nova. Et sicut tunc Assyrii et Macedones deterruerunt Judaeos, ita et nunc Sarraceni et qui post eos venturi sunt pseudo-prophetae facient mala multa in terra et talem tribulationem qualis non fuit ab initio" (f. 9, 4). C. 13 (f. 13, 3).

83. "*O mira concordia*": *Conc.*, l. 5, c. 118 (f. 134, 1).

84. "clavis veterum, notitia futurorum, signatorum apertio, detectio secretorum": LI, c. I (f. 3, 2). Cf. LI, Tables III and IV, "Concordia V.T. et Novi," with its exergue: "I saw a book written inside and out, sealed with seven seals,

etc." — "Vidi librum scriptum intus et foris, signatum sigillis septem etc." And: "Behold the conquering Lion of the tribe of Judah opening the book, etc." — "Ecce vicit Leo de tribu Juda aperire librum etc."

85. LI, c. I: the opening of the seven seals under the Old Testament, then under the New (f. 6, 3-4).

86. LF, Table XIV.

87. VB, c. 24 (51-3). The concordance is not entirely the same in the two cases: on the one hand, it is a question rather of seven kings or persecuting chiefs; in the other, seven great collective persecutions.

88. LF, Table VIII.

89. *Ev.*, 279.

90. VB, c. 24 (52).

91. *Conc.*, l. 4, c. 30: "Indeed the tribulation of that generation, which was started under the king of the Turks, looks back by way of concord to that tribulation which was brought about under Nebuchadnezzar the king of the Assyrians and is contained in the story of Judith" — "Profecto tribulatio generationis istius, quae inchoata est sub rege Turcorum, eam respicit per concordiam quae facta est sub Nabuchodonosoro rege Assyriorum et continetur in historia Judith" (f. 55-6).

92. Thus *Ench.*, f. 29: "Oportet enim sub hoc sexto tempore similem Darii Medi regem christianum a partibus occiduis sicut ego puto, consurgere; qui novum Caldaeorum genus, sanctae matris Ecclesiae inimicum, percutiet, et nihilominus novum Cyrum qui regale sacerdotium in excelsum constituet" (Tondelli, 141). On the contrary, for example, Hervaeus, *In Is.*, l. 7: "So just as there will no longer be a flood to destroy the earth, so there will be no general persecution of the saints until the time of the Antichrist, when the world itself will be brought to an end" — "Sicut ergo jam non erit diluvium dissipans terram, sic generalis persecutio sanctorum non erit usque ad tempus Antichristi, quando et mundus terminabitur" (PL, CLXXXI, 501 AB).

93. "novum genus Sarracenorum": VB, c. 24 (53).

94. "ultimus nondum advenit...": LI, c. 7: "Just as Antiochus, the last king at the end of the first state, was more monstrous than the rest, so, at the end of the age which will be next, there will come that seventh king of whom John says 'and the last has not yet come; and he will be worse than all who were before him, like one who will destroy all things more than can be believed'" — "Ut autem in fine primi status ultimus rex Antiochus ... caeteris immanior fuit, ita in fine saeculi, qui erit in proximo, septimus rex ille venturus est, de quo dicit Joannes: et ultimus nondum advenit; et ipse deterior erit omnium qui fuerunt ante se, utpote qui supra quod credi potest universa vastabit" (f. 10, 1). Cf. c. 6 (f. 9, 1).

95. VB, c. 23 (50-1). *Conc.*, l. 5, c. 23 (f. 12, 1).

96. "sola adhuc initialia quae praesto sunt exhibere sufficimus": *Conc.*, l. 5, c. 20 (f. 70, 1-2); c. 118: "but also sermons noted unto the established time" — "sed et sermones signati usque ad tempus statutum" (f. 133, 4).

97. VB, c. 27: "I also cannot say anything certain about the end of those times; but I shall not be silent as to what I think" — "De termino quoque istorum temporum certum quid exprimere nequeo; quod tamen existimem non tacebo" (58); "We do not have certainty about what comes next" — "De sequenti certitudinem non habemus" (60).

98. "Etsi, respectu praeteritorum, jam nunc patet veritas christianis, respectu tamen futurorum abscondita est adhuc perfectio veritatis": *Ev.*, 71.

99. *Ev.*, 71: "If not until now is the truth of the Scriptures to be sought, why is it that Paul in the type of the believers says: 'we know in part, etc.'? If the truth itself is already fully plain which the faithful have sought from the very rise of the Church, why is it that till now, the net of the Gospel having been broken, so many thousands of heretics have eluded the grasp of the men of the Church? Is it not because they err in ignorance of the Scriptures and the power of God?" — "Si idcirco non usque nunc quaerenda est veritas Scripturarum, quid est quod dicit Paulus in typo credentium: ex parte cognoscimus etc.? Si plene jam patet ipsa veritas, quam ab ipso ortu Ecclesiae quaesiere fideles, quid est quod usque ad praesens, rupto rete evangelii, tot millia haereticorum elabuntur de manibus ecclesiasticorum virorum? Nonne ideo quia errant nescientes Scripturas neque virtutem Dei?"

100. LF, Table VII (the 7 concords). Cf. Table VIII: concord of the 7 persecutions.

101. "spirituales intellectus"; "verba historica": *Conc.*, l. 5, c. I: "But since after those four great works of Christ by which in being born, suffering, rising, and ascending into heaven he conformed himself to the four living creatures [of Ezekiel and Apocalypse], he was shown to be divine only in the fifth order of fire, according as spiritual understandings proceed from his historical words, in this fifth one it is necessary for us to deal spiritually with certain more solemn deeds that have occurred, so that on the basis of many testimonies we may show that the laborious ends of things gain peace for the victors after great stuggles and contests" — "Quia vero post quatuor illa magna opera Christi, quibus se nascendo, patiendo, resurgendo, necnon et ascendendo in caelum quatuor animalibus conformavit, nonnisi in quinto ordine ignis est ostensus divinus, secundum quod et de ipsius verbis historicis spirituales prodeunt intellectus, oportet nos in hoc quinto de quibusdam gestis solemnioribus quae occurrerunt spiritualiter agere, ut ex multis testimoniis ostendamus laboriosos rerum fines et post magnos agones et certamina pacem victoribus impertiri" (f. 60, 3). Cf. above, note 40. VB, c. 323: "I have yet to encounter any place in the authentic Scriptures that cannot be spiritually resolved in this third state" — "Nullus mihi adhuc occurrit locus in Scripturis authenticis qui in hoc tertio statu spiritaliter solvi nequeat" (71).

102. "de virtute in virtutem"; "de claritate in claritatem": LI, c. 5 (f. 5, 3).

103. LA, prol.: "The works of those heavenly udders fecundated with doctrines that have through the course of time flowed down to us testify how with weightier efforts there may have been a struggle by Catholic, orthodox men to institute the newly arisen Church with humbler precepts and to nourish her still temporarily lying in the crib of faith with milk to drink" — "Quam propensioribus studiis a viris catholicis et orthodoxis certatum sit, ut noviter exortam Ecclesiam praeceptis humilioribus instituerent et jacentem adhuc pro tempore in cunabulis fidei lactis potu nutrirent: illorum quae per cursum temporum ad nos usque derivata sunt opera caelestium doctrinis uberum fecundata testantur. Talia nempe illos tunc temporis oportebat docere, talia (Spiritu sancto suggerente) describere, qualia lactenti Hebraeorum et parvulae inexpertaeque a cibo solido convenirent; ut non prius ad alta mysteria ruitura conscenderet, quam plenius

erudita in infimis discreet humilibus consentire. Cum vero hanc adultam et aptam matrimonio cernerent, majora illi ostendere sacramenta caeperunt, quibus exercitata diutius solidi ac perfecti cibi experiretur dulcedinem, et, relicto praeceptorum Christi inchoationis sermone, ad perfectionem ferretur" (f. 1, 4). *Ev.*, 57-8. LI, f. 6, 2.

104. "generalia mysteria": IA: "And there were then some in the spirit who could understand the Scripture of the Old Testament spiritually; in like fashion now there will be some in the spirit who may understand the letter of the New Testament with this understanding" — "Et tunc fuerunt quidam in spiritu qui scripturam testamenti veteris spiritaliter intelligerent; et nunc simili modo erunt quidam in spiritu qui intelligant juxta hunc intellectum litteram testamenti novi." *Ev.*, 56-7: "We answer that the general mysteries look not at those features that are specific to a few, but those that belong to many" — "Respondemus generalia mysteria non respicere ea quae specialia sunt aliquibus, sed quae multis."

105. *Conc.*, l. 4, v. 61 (f. 92, 3).

106. *Ev.*, 21: "Though the preachers of the Gospel reading according to the surface of the letter are preferred to the doctors of the Jews preaching the Law of Moses, nevertheless they are far inferior to those who have spiritual wisdom of the Gospel itself and who do not at all walk according to the flesh, etc." — "Etsi praedicatores evangelicae lectionis secundum superficiem litterae praeferuntur doctoribus Judaeorum praedicantibus legem Moysi, longe tamen inferiores sunt ab illis qui et ipsum quoque evangelium spiritaliter sapiunt et qui omnino non ambulant secundum carnem etc." And IA, prol. (above, note 103).

107. "clausa et involuta voluminibus suis": VB, c. 25 (54-5).

108. "doctrina ipsa spiritalis non est circumscriptibilis, ut claudatur uno magno volumine": *Ev.*, 275.

109. *Conc.*, l. 2, tr. 1, c. I: "Hence it remains that we understand our ultimate perfection to be in the third heaven, the heaven of spiritual understanding, which proceeds from each of the two Testaments" — "Restat ergo ut in tertio caelo finem perfectionis nostrae positum intelligamus caelo utique spiritualis intelligentiae, quae de utroque testamento procedit" (f. 6, 4); etc.

110. VB, c. 25 (54-5).

111. *Ev.*, 57: "But it had not been granted to anyone to unfold the cloth that had been untouched upon the head of Jesus" — "Non tamen concessum fuit alicui expandere sudarium quod erat super caput Jesu intactum."

112. *Ev.*, 193: "When the third day, i.e., the time of the third status, shall have arrived, the one that will begin with the arrival of Elijah, there will be marriages in Cana of Galilee, since a new Church of religious people will be wedded to the heavenly Bridegroom owing to the zeal for crossing over that will be in the hearts of the doctors" — "Cum advenerit tertius dies, hoc est tempus tertii status, quod incipiet ab adventu Eliae, fient nuptiae in Cana Galileae, quia in zelo transmigrationis qui erit in cordibus doctorum, conjungetur caelesti sponso nova religiosorum ecclesia."

113. *Ev.*, 146.

114. *Ev.*, 191: "At one time the letter of the Law was changed to wine, and, all the more, once that time shall have come, the water of the Gospel reading will be changed into wine" — "Quondam littera legis conversa est in vinum et multo

fortius cum venerit tempus illud aqua evangelicae lectionis convertetur in vinum"; cf. 191-201. On the contrary, again, Hildegard, *Scivias*, l. 3, vis 11: The Son on "coming . . . changes the water of the Law into the wine of the Gospel" — Filius "veniens, . . . aquam legis in vinum evangelii convertit" (PL, CXCVII, 716 C).

115. *Ev.*, 190: "For what is it to see the heavens opened except to look within the Old and New Testament, which have been closed to animal men, once the door of the letter has been removed?" — "Quid est videre caelum apertum, nisi vetus et novum Testamentum, quae animalibus hominibus clausa sunt, remota janua litterae, interius intueri?"

116. *Conc.*, l. 5, c. 65: "A new religion, which will be completely free and spiritual" — "Nova quaedam religio, quae omnino erit libera et spiritualis" (f. 95, 3).

117. *Ev.*, 271-2: "In John is designated the sublimity of the priestly dignity, which is placed like a light upon a candelabra, so as to shine upon all who are in the house. In Jesus, who appeared despised from the start, is designated the humility of those who for God's sake have learned to study in silence, who to the extent that they are despicable among men, earn a good rank for themselves with God. But since the justice of the latter consists in action, and that of the former in contemplation, as the world approaches its end, what is signified in John comes to be more despicable, and what is signified in Christ more eminent and sublime" — "Designatur in Joanne sublimitas sacerdotalis dignitatis, quae quasi lucerna posita est super candelabrum, ut luceat omnibus qui in domo sunt. In Jesu, qui a principio despectus apparuit, humilitas eorum qui studere Dei causa silentio didicerunt, qui quo apud homines despicabiles sunt, eo apud Deum bonum sibi gradum acquirunt. Quia vero illorum justitia in actione est, istorum in contemplatione; quo mundus iste appropinquat ad finem, eo despicabilius esse incipit quod significatur in Joanne, clarius vero et sublimius quod significatur in Christo."

118. *Ev.*, 52, 271-2. IA, P. I, c. 3: The virgin mother "signifies the Church that knoweth not man, a Church that rests in the silence of the wilderness, where there are no literary studies, nor doctors of a church institution, but charity flowing from a pure heart and unfeigned faith" — "significat ecclesiam quae nescit virum, quae requiescit in silentio eremi, ubi non sunt studia litterarum, non doctores ecclesiasticae institutionis, sed caritas de corde puro et fide non ficta" (f. 83, 1). "What is signified in Elizabeth will be brought to consummation; what is signified in Mary will remain right up to the end" — "Consummabitur quod designatum est in Elizabeth, manebit usque in finem quod designatum est in Maria" (f. 83, 2). *Ev.*, 32-3: "Just as Elizabeth for her part stands for the Church of the firstlings, whose husband was the order of the Apostles, so Mary stands for the chaste and virginal Church, whose husband is an order of spiritual fathers" — "Sicut Elizabeth in hac parte Ecclesiam primitivorum, cujus vir fuit apostolicus ordo, ita Maria designat castam atque virginalem ecclesiam, cujus vir est ordo quidam spiritualium patrum."

119. "in otio et quiete": LI, c. 9 (f. 12, 1).

120. "pii sacerdotes";"pii pastores";"boni claustrales";"boni eremitae": *Ev.*,
121. Cf. LI, c. 19 (f. 17-9); IA, P. 4, c. 14 (f. 170, 1).

121. IA, f. 175, 3-4. VB, c. 15: "he offers full liberty and preserves what he has offered" — "plenam exhibet et servat exhibitam libertatem" (36).

122. *Conc.*, l. 5, c. 117: "Once this burdensome time which is called the sixth age, i.e., from the first coming of the Lord till the fall of the Antichrist, has been finished there will follow a sort of paschal time, which will be regarded as a sabbath, etc." — "Consummato hoc tempore laborioso quod dicitur sexta aetas, hoc est ab adventu primo Domini usque ad ruinam Antichristi, sequitur quasi tempus paschale, quod reputabitur in sabbatum etc." (f. 133, 1).

123. "ubi jam non erit labor et gemitus, sed requies et otium et abundantia pacis": VB, c. 26 (58). LF, Table XIV: "and the whole people will delight in the beauty of peace" — "et delectabitur universus populus in pulchritudine pacis."

124. *De septem sigillis:* "Under this seventh time, which is soon to come, the openings of the seals and the labor of explaining the books of the Old Testament will cease, and a real sabbath will be given to the people of God, and in his days there will be justice and abundance of peace, and the Lord will rule from sea to sea, and his saints will reign with him, until, etc." — "Sub hoc septimo tempore, quod futurum est in proximo, cessabunt apertiores signaculorum et labor exponendorum librorum testamenti veteris, dabiturque revera sabbatismus populo Dei, et erit in diebus illius justitia et abundantia pacis, et dominabitur Dominus a mare usque ad mare, et sancti ejus regnabunt cum eo, usque etc." (Reeves, 245-6).

125. *Conc.*, l. 5, c. 117: "For it will no longer be the time of Leah the workhorse with bleary eyes, but the time of Rachel of beautiful face and dignified demeanor" — "Non enim erit adhuc tempus Liae laboriosae quae est lippis oculis, sed tempus Rachelis venustae faciei et decori aspectus" (f. 132, 4).

126. Cf. LF, Table XI.

127. This is how he gathers all the gifts of the Spirit into three: "fear of the Lord, love of God, love of neighbor" — "timor Domini, amor Dei, amor proximi (*Ev.*, 75).

128. On the revelation of the Trinity in five time periods: *Psalt.*, l. 2, *De differentia quinque temporum* (f. 259-60).

129. *Tres status mundi, propter tres personas divinitatis: Conc.*, l. 5, c. 23. IA, f. 48, 4. LI, f. 5, 3. *Psalt.*, f. 240, 2; 259, 3-4; 279, 1.

130. IA, p. 1, c. 4, v. 1 (f. 95, 3). LI, c. 5: "For just as the letter of the first Testament ... seems to pertain to the Father, and that of the New Testament to pertain to the Son, so does the spiritual understanding, which proceeds from both, pertain to the Holy Spirit" — "Ut enim littera testamenti prioris ... videtur pertinere ad Patrem, littera testamenti novi pertinere ad Filium, ita spiritalis intelligentia quae procedit ex utraque, ad Spiritum sanctum" (f. 5, 2; cf. 5, 3). *Conc.*, l. 2, tr. 1, c. 29 (f. 18, 1-2); l. 5, c. 84 (f. 112, 3); etc. *Ev.*, 21-2: "Holy mother the Church firmly holds that there are two persons of the godhead, of which one is unbegotten, and the other only-begotten; but there is also a third which proceeds from both. For this reason and in this respect the letter of the New Testament is shown to be born from the letter of the first one, and one spiritual understanding to proceed from both" — "Tenet firmiter sancta mater Ecclesia duas esse personas deitatis, quarum una ingenita, altera unigenita est; esse vero et tertiam quae ab utraque procedit. Et ob hoc et secundum hoc de littera prioris testamenti nata esse

ostenditur littera novi, et ex utraque procedere unus spiritalis intellectus." LF, Table XIII. *Psalt.*, f. 259-60.

131. *Conc.*, l. 5, c. 23, in fine: "But since in one and the same reading three allegorical understandings have been assigned that each belong to one of the Persons of the deity, there must also be assigned a fourth understanding which is common to the three states, and belongs to the divine unity. This is so since it grasps the three times that were mentioned above in their series of sevens under a single series of seven, starting from the beginning of times and reaching up to the end" — "Sed quia in una eademque lectione tres allegorici intellectus qui conveniant sigillatim singulis personis deitatis assignati sunt, necesse est ut assignetur et quartus qui sit communis tribus statibus, et divinae conveniat unitati. Utpote quia tria tempora quae supra dicta sunt in septenariis suis sub uno septenario comprehendit, incipiens ab exordio temporum et perveniens usque ad finem" (f. 72, 1).

132. LI, c. 13 (f. 13, 3).

133. *Conc.*, l. 2, tr. 1, c. 2: "... that one spiritual understanding, however, proceeds from each [Testament]. For if we understand aright, there are two signifying [marks, but only] one [object] signified, showing us who believe in the living God that the Father, to whom the Old Testament especially pertains, is one; that the Son of God, to whom the New especially pertains, is one; that the Holy Spirit, who proceeds from both, to whom the mystical understanding that ... proceeds from both pertains, is one" — "unum vero spiritualem intellectum ex utroque (testamentuo) procedere. Sunt enim, si sane sapimus, duo significantia, unum significatum, ostendentia nobis qui credimus in Deum vivum, unum esse patrem ad quem specialiter pertinet vetus testamentum, unum Dei Filium ad quem specialiter pertinet novum, unum Spiritum sanctum qui ab utroque procedit, ad quem pertinet mysticus intellectus, qui ... a duobus procedit" (f. 7, 3). L. 5, c. 2: seven species of typic understanding and seven subdivisions of time periods, just as there are seven affirmations on the mystery of the Trinity (f. 61, 1-2). LI, c. 9: "For if the first state is especially ascribed to the Father, the second to the Son, and the third to the Holy Spirit, then what could be more fitting than that state which pertains to the Holy Spirit should seem to be a sabbath, both in respect to the six ages of the world and in respect to the six times of the second status, so that thereby one and the same Spirit should be understood to proceed from the Father and the Son?" — "Si enim primus status specialiter ascribitur Patri, secundus Filio, tertius Spiritui sancto: quid convenientius esse potuit quam ut status ille qui pertinet ad Spiritum sanctum, et respectu sex aetatum mundi, et respectu sex temporum secundi status, sabbatum esse videatur: ut per hoc unus idemque Spiritus a Patre Filioque procedere intelligatur?" (f. 12, 1). *Ev.*, 182: "There are two Testaments by which they [Andrew and Peter] instruct the little ones in Christ according to the letter, and the spiritual understanding is one" — "Duo sunt testamenta, quibus instruunt illi (Andreas et Petrus) parvulos in Christo secundum litteram, et unus est spiritalis intellectus."

134. "saepe dictum est, et saepe dicendum": IA, p. 1, c. 4, v. I (f. 95, 3).

135. E. Buonaiuti, ed. of AF, xiii and xvi.

136. *Ev.*, 24: "Even if the promise of the Son concerning the bestowal of the Holy Spirit is literally completed after the Lord's resurrection, nevertheless we

can even now also speak according to the fullness that he is about to show once he has been glorified also by the rebellious people of the Jews on their conversion to the Lord by Elijah and his associates, [saying]: 'The Spirit had not been given, since Christ had not yet been glorified'" — "Etsi secundum litteram completa est post resurrectionem Domini promissio illa Filii de donatione Spiritus sancti, secundum tamen illam plenitudinem quam ostensurus est cum fuerit a rebelli quoque Judaeorum populo converso ad Dominum per Eliam et ejus socios glorificatus, etiam nunc dicere possumus: Spiritus non erat datus quia Jesus nondum erat glorificatus." Cf. 143.

137. *Ev.*, 94.

138. *Tempus prope est! Ecce appropinquat hora! Prope est, immo praesens!*: *Conc.*, c. 45 (f. 80, 1) and 47 (f. 81, 2); etc. *Ev.*, 195: "That great Elijah, who is about to come and complete all things, began monastic or eremetical religion itself" — "Magnus ille Helias, qui venturus est ut compleat omnia, ipsam religionem monasticam sive eremiticam inchoavit": IA (f. 57, 3).

139. VB, c. 45: "Spiritus sanctus etc." (85). *Conc.*, l. 4, c. 37.

140. *Conc.*, l. 3, tr. 2, c. 6: "But I say clearly that the time when these things will be is near; the Lord himself knows the day and the hour. As best I can judge, however, according to the fittingness of the concord, if peace is granted from these evils until the year 1200 A.D., then unless they come about suddenly, I suspect that they could come at just about any moment of time" — "Tempus autem quando haec erunt, dico manifeste quod prope est; diem autem et horam, Dominus ipse novit. Quantum tamen secundum coaptationem concordiae existimare queo, si pax conceditur ab his malis usque ad annum 1200 incarnationis Domini, exinde ne subito ista fiant, suspecta mihi sunt omnimodis et tempora et momenta."

141. *Conc.*, l. 4, c. 30: "The forty-first generation in the Church begins in the year 1201 of our Lord's incarnation" — "In Ecclesia vero incipit generatio quadragesima prima anno Domini 1201 incarnationis dominicae" (f. 55, 4), l. 2, tr. 1, c. 16 (f. 12, 2-3). Cf. f. 118.

142. *Ev.*, 25: "In the other respect, however, Mary designates that monastic religion in its youthful period, namely the one that St. Benedict instituted, which, conceiving of the Holy Spirit, she is herself about to have as Son within her womb, namely the people of the saints, to whom, according to Daniel, is to be given power under the whole heaven and who is to reign in the spirit unto the consummation of the age" — "Secundum autem alteram speciem Maria aetate juvencula designat monasticam illam religionem, sc. quam sanctus instituit Benedictus, quae concipiens de Spiritu sancto habitura est et ipsa Filium in utero suo, populum sc. illum sanctorum, cui danda est secundum Daniel potestas sub omni caelo et regnaturus est in spiritu usque ad consummationem saeculi."

143. IA, P. 1, c. 4 (f. 95, 4). *Conc.*, l. 5, c. 20: "We who are set between the second and the third state are permitted to consider that many things of that third state are at hand" — "nos qui inter secundum et tertium statum constituti sumus, multa adesse de tertio illo statu contemplari permittimur" (f. 70, 2); "Since we are set in the earliest time of that status, we are still able to exhibit only the initial stages that are right here" — "quoniam in primo illius tempore status constituti sumus, sola adhuc initialia quae praesto sunt exhibere sufficimus" (70, 1).

144. *S. Sig.:* "But once those oppressions have ended, there will come a blessed time, a time that will be like the Easter solemnity.... That will be the third state, pertaining to the Holy Spirit" — "Consummatis autem pressuris illis, adveniet tempus beatum, tempus quod erit simile solemnitati pascali.... Iste erit tertius status, pertinens ad Spiritum sanctum" (213).

145. "completis hic ejusdem numeri generationibus, apparebit veritas manifesta, procedens de ventre litterae et de domo novi Testamenti, in qua latuit secundum aliquid usque in praesentem diem": *Conc.*, l. 5, c. 73 (f. 101, 2).

146. LI, c. 6: "Once the opening of the sixth [seal] has been accomplished, there will be the holy Sabbath of the Lord of which the Apostle speaks [in] Hebrews 4. The Sabbath remains for the people of God until the Lord comes at the Last Judgment" — "Completa vero apertione sexta, erit sabbatismum Domini sanctum, de quo dicit Apostolus, *Hebr.*, IV. Relinquitur sabbatismum populo Dei, quousque veniat Dominus ad extremum judicium" (f. 6, 4).

147. VB, 6 (20).

148. VB, 26 (58).

149. "Transibit labor doctrinae, et remanebit diligendi libertas!"; "non tam in una persona, quam in aliqua justorum ecclesia": IA, P. 1, c. 4, v. 1 (f. 95, 3-4). *Conc.* (f. 31, 3).

150. Ev., 131: "in hac sexta saeculi labentis aetate, post cujus consummationem etiam ipse fidelis populus transiens per angustam passionis portam, perducendus est ad sabbatum felicitatis suae." LI, c. 9 (f. 12, 1). Cf. Hebrews 4:9.

151. *Gioacchino de Fiore* (1937), 196. This judgment seems to fit badly with what the author says, 194, about "the purely quantitative originality" of Joachim in relation to patristic exegesis.

152. "In the commentary on the Apocalypse as well as in the *Concordia* he accepts and follows the current methods and the various species of interpretation that were in academic use. The spiritual understanding of the Old and New Testaments was not a novelty. Only it never led to the ends to which he took it, since he thought that it ought to signify a profound spiritual transfiguration of the New Testament itself, analogous to that by which the Gospel transfigured the Old" — "Nel commento all'Apocalisse come nei libri della Concordia egli accetta e segue i metodi correnti e le varie specie di interpretazioni che erano in uso nella scuola. L'intelligentia spiritualis dell'A. e del N.T. non era una novità: solo mai fu condotta ai termini ai quali egli la condusse. Poichè egli penso che dovesse significare una profonda trasfigurazione spirituale del Nuovo Testamento stesse, analoga a quella del Vangelo in cui si trasfiguro l'Antico" (1, 149).

153. "Anche il concetto fondamentale della Concordia dei duo Testamenti non è un concetto nuovo: in quanto era tradizionale la idea che l'Antico fosse figura e typo del Nuovo. Giacchino ne extende soltanto, a dismissura, il campo, vedendo fra essi un costante ricorso di figure, di avvenimenti, di cifre. Con che la sua idea d'un concordare tra la storia avanti Cristo e dopo Cristo scende sino ai dettagli e diventa una aritmetica" (1, 150).

154. For example VB, c. 25 (55); *Conc.*, l. 2, tr. 1, c. 16 (f. 12, 3). According to Ch. Guignebert, *Christianisme médiéval et moderne* (1931), 95-6, it is by "the typologic interpretation" that Joachim had calculated the date of 1260. The use of this mod-

ern epithet here is equivocal; Joachim's "typic" understanding is something quite different.

155. Cf. IA, prol.: "Even though there are pressures threatening . . . I think that with rude and unpolished speech I can prove with sure and necessary arguments" — "Imminere pressuras . . . etsi sermone rustico et impolito, certis tamen et necessariis probare me posse arbitror argumentis" (f. 2, 2).

156. This came in the wake of the crisis opened up by the work of Gerard of Borgo San Donnino, *Liber introductorius in evangelium aeternum* (1254). It is Florentius, bishop of Saint-Jean d'Acre, who prepared the extracts of Joachim arrayed under ten headings. On becoming archbishop of Arles in 1262, he personally convened a provincial synod to condemn Joachim. Héfélé-Leclercq, VI, I, 113-5.

157. "rerum fines": L. 5, c. 1: "In those four books, etc. . . . In this fifth book it is necessary for us to treat spiritually of certain more solemn affairs that have occurred, so that on the basis of many testimonies we may show that the laborious ends of things have brought peace to the victors after many struggles and contests" — "In iis quatuor libris etc. . . . Oportet nos in hoc quinto libro de quibusdam gestis solemnioribus quae occurrerunt spiritualiter agere, ut ex multis testimoniis ostendamus laboriosos rerum fines et post magnos agones et certamina pacem victoribus impertiri" (f. 60, 3; Protocol of Anagni: Denifle, 128).

158. Again, the Prototcol of Anagni cites the *Conc.*, l. 2, tr. 1, c. 7: "One ought to know that the letter of the Old Testament was entrusted to the people of the Jews, while the letter of the New Testament was given to the Roman people, but the spiritual understanding that proceeds from both was entrusted to the spiritual men" — "Sciendum quod littera veteris testamenti commissa fuit populo Judaeorum, littera novi testamenti populo Romano, spiritualibus autem viris spiritualis intelligentia, quae ex utraque procedit" (f. 9, 2; Anagni: Denifle, 127).

159. LI, c. 24: "the man Jesus Christ bears the imprint of the Holy Spirit, just as John the Baptist bears that of Christ" — "homo Christus Jesus Spiritus sancti typum gerit, sicut Joannes Baptista Christi" (f. 23, 3). It is a gross understatement to say with Bloomfield, 307: "He was not a Christocentric."

160. Thus the LF, Table XIV, takes the messianic texts of the Old Testament literally to apply them to the 7th age: "But men will beat their swords into plowshares and their spears into pruning-hooks, nation will not rise against nation, nor will they rush further to war" [Isa. 2:4] — "Conflabunt autem homines gladios suos in vomeres et lanceas suas in falcis, non levabit gens contra gentem gladium, nec excitabunt ultra ad proelium."

161. After others, A. Dempf and E. Benz see in Joachim a precursor of the Reform. Cf. Mme. Bignami-Odier, "Travaux récents sur J. de Flore," *Le moyen âge*, 58 (1952), 151-2.

162. *La Renaissance*, introd. H. de France, n. ed., 9 (1876). In Joachim there is no trace of the humanism that is observed among a number of his contemporaries. The same could be said of anti-humanism.

163. Cf. Renan, *Nouv. ét. d'h. rel.*, 221: "The idea that would lead three centuries later to a religious revolution, i.e., the deep dissimilarity between the Church of the Middle Ages and the primitive Church, is already quite complete in him" — "L'idée qui, trois siècles plus tard, amènera une révolution religieuse, je veux

dire la profonde dissemblance de l'Église du moyen âge et de l'Église primitive, est déjà chez lui tout entière."

164. "De ecclesia carnali in proximo reformanda atque in primaevam sui aetatem redigenda": *Expositio magni prophetae abbatis Joachim in Apocalypsim* (Venice, 1527).

165. The word is that of G. Boas, *Essays on Primitivism and Related Ideas in the Middle Ages* (1948). Cf. BTAM, 6, no. 336.

166. *Per singulas aetates mundi multiplicatur scientia: Conc.*, l. 5, c. 66 (f. 96, 3).

167. "moderna religio": "forma ecclesiae primitivae": "singula pro seipsis, non pro aliis sunt sollicita": *Conc.*, l. 5, c. 22 (f. 71, 3). VB, c. 15 (36-8).

168. "qui sunt impinguati et dilatati de substantia crucifixi": "qui scholastica influantur disciplina": *Ev.*, 243-8, 294-6.

169. *Conc.*, l. 5, c. 37: "What then can a world stuck in evil hope for but the revelation of anger and wrath in the heavens?" — "Quid igitur sperare potest mundus positus in maligno, nisi revelationem irae et furoris in caelo?" (f. 75, 3).

170. IA, P. 7: "We said ... that once the six heads in which the dragon fought for six straight days against the faithful had been dashed and overcome, he would fight on to the last in the seventh head ever more desperately than usual" — "Diximus ... quod, obtrusis et superatis sex capitibus in quibus pugnavit draco per sex continua tempora contra fideles, ad extremum pugnaturus sit in septimo capite, desperatius prae solito" (f. 210, 2). LI, c. 15: "Through each one of the five times of the second state a single head of the dragon is fought down, and in the sixth time two are fought at once; so that, not having any of the rest in which to exercise his powers, he is driven back till the end of the age, when, during the time of his tail, he will remain imprisoned without hope of perpetrating malice" — "Per singulum quinque temporum secundi status singulum draconis caput debellatum est, et in sexto tempore duo simul; ita ut non habens de reliquo in quo exerceat vires suas, cogatur usque ad finem saeculi, quando erit tempus caudae ipsius sine spe perpetrandae malitiae incarceratus manere" (f. 15-6). *Conc.*, l. 5, c. 114: From his first fall, "when the Devil saw that he had lost power and had gone from heaven to earth, he went away angry and wrathful, plotting and planning how he might be avenged" — "ubi se vidit diabolus amisisse virtutem et profectum esse de coelo in terram, abiit iratus et furibundus, cogitans et pertractans quomodo se posset ulcisci etc." (f. 130, 3). Cf. Eugène Anitchkof, *J. de Flore et l'idéal courtois* (1931), 237.

171. *Conc.*, l. 1, c. 1 (f. 1, 1).

172. *Conc.*, l. 2, tr. 1, c. 1 (f. 6, 3-4).

173. One naturally recalls Nietzsche's apologue in *Zarathustra*. Cf. Michelet, *op. cit.*, 63-4: Joachim shows the faith "which grows young from age to age; as fruit of maturity, as crown of wisdom, it promises us childhood. What a sublime expression! The sacred heroic childhood of heart: all life begins there anew!" — "qui devient jeune d'âge en âge; pour fruit de la maturité, pour couronne de la sagesse, il nous promet l'enfance. O sublime parole! La sainte enfance héroïque du cœur: c'est par elle, en effet, que toute vie recommence!"

174. LI, c. 8 (f. 10).

175. "non prophetico spiritu, sed conjectura mentis humanae": 4 *Sent.*, d. 43, q. 1, a. 3; d. 44, a. 3, q. 2, ad 3m: "Through his conjectures, Abbot Joachim foretold

some true things about the future, and in some he was deceived" — "Abbas J. per conjecturas de futuro aliqua vera praedixit, et in aliquibus deceptus fuit." Aug., *Civ. Dei*, l. 18, c. 53, n. 1: "they are using human conjectures" — "conjecturis quippe utuntur humanis" (Bardy).

176. "Utrum lex nova sit duratura usque ad finem mundi": *Prima secundae*, q. 106, a. 4 and ad 3m: "Nullus status praesentis vitae potest esse perfectior, quam status novae legis. . . . Non est expectandum quod sit aliquis status futurus, in quo perfectius gratia Spiritus sancti habeatur, quam hactenus habita fuerit, et maxime ab Apostolis. . . . Lex nova non solum est Christi, sed etiam Spiritus sancti. . . ." The whole article should be read. Nonetheless, in his *Hist. de l'abbé Joachim* (1745) abbot Gervaise wrote: "We see no writer who spoke ill of Abbot Joachim before Guy de Perpignan, general of the Carmelite order in the 14th century" — "On ne voit aucun écrivain qui ait mal parlé de l'abbé J. avant Guy de Perpignan, général de l'ordre des Carmes dans le XIVe s." (547).

177. Q. 5, a. 6, ad 9m: "No other perfective state succeeds to the law of the Gospel in the way that the law of the Gospel succeeded the old Law, and the old Law succeeded the law of nature" — "Non enim legi evangelicae alius status succedit, quae ad perfectum adduxit; sicut ipsa successit legi veteri, et lex vetus legi naturae." Cf. Ernst Benz, "Joachim-Studien, 3: Thomas von Aquin und J." (ZKG, 53, 1934, 52-116). E. Buonaiuti, "G. da Fiore, san Bonaventura, san Tommaso" (*Ricerche relig.*, 6, 1930, 289-97).

178. "Post novum testamentum non erit aliud, nec aliquod semen novae legis subtrahi potest: et ideo testamentum aeternum est": *In Hexaem.*, s. 16, n. 2 (Q. 5, 403).

179. "prêcher un évangile du Saint-Esprit, c'était bouleverser complètement l'économie des âges du monde": *L'esprit de la phil. méd.*, 2d ed. (1944), 277.

180. "les organes essentiels de la société chrétienne étaient gravement menacés et sa constitution sapée jusque dans ses fondements": *R. des q. hist.*, 67 (1900), 496.

181. *Op. cit.*, 555: "The abbot Joachim did not make his third state so spiritual in the rule of St. Benedict, but in the possession of the truth without figure, which obtains only in heaven" — "L'abbé J. ne faisait pas consister son troisième état si spirituel dans la règle de S. Benoît, mais dans la possession de la vérité sans figure, ce qui n'est que dans le ciel."

182. "Joachim se contente de comparer l'Ancien et le Nouveau Testaments et ne jette que très timidement les yeux sur l'avenir": *op. cit.*, 273; and 275-6.

183. *Essai sur le mysticisme spéculatif* . . . (1900), 44: "The writings of Joachim himself doubtless contain the seed of that doctrine of the three ages, but nowhere does he give their full development" — "Les écrits de J. lui-même contiennent sans doute le germe de cette théorie des trois âges, mais nulle part il n'en donne le plein développement . . ." (And see the note, referring to Renan.)

184. "L'Évangile éternel de Joachim n'était que le sens spirituel et la pleine intelligence de l'Évangile du Christ": DTC, 8, 1443. For M. Paul Zumthor (*Merlin le Prophète*, 1943, 99) "it is very probable that Joachim never departed from Catholic orthodoxy. But his doctrine, insufficiently settled, in perpetual becoming, offered itself to the most abusive interpretations" — "il est fort probable que J. ne

s'écarta jamais de l'orthodoxie catholique. Mais sa doctrine, insuffisamment fixée, en perpétuel devenir, s'offrait aux interprétations les plus abusives."

185. ASS, May, t. 7 (1688), 29 May, especially 125-43; *Disquisitio hist. de Florensi ordine, prophetiis, doctrine B. Joachimi*, c. 6: "The fictions on the occasion of which the prophetic spirit of Abbot Joachim had been suspected by some are destroyed" — "Destruuntur figmenta quorum occasione suspectus quibusdam fuit abbatis Joachimi propheticus spiritus (137-8); and 143 E: "No one can be surprised that the holy doctor, having less knowledge of Joachim's holiness and suspecting his spirit of many fictions . . . , did not give very much indication . . . of having read the work the *Concordia* by himself . . . , proceeding not, to be sure, from a spirit less good than [the one in which] Joachim did, but from one very much different. But what he himself did not approve in that time in which such things were read with greater danger owing to the depravity of heretics, the highest pontiff of the Church previously did approve of, when no such cause of concern was present; and so he proved that both he himself and his successors should insist that John himself would also finish the exposition of the Apocalypse in the same spirit" — "Nemo mirari potest quod sanctus doctor, minus cognitam habens Joachimi sanctitatem, et suspectum ejusdem spiritum ob plurima figmenta . . . , lectum a se Concordiae opus . . . non valde probaverit . . . , spiritu non quidem minus bono quam Joachim, valde tamen diverso procedens. Sed quod minus probavit ipse eo tempore quo propter haereticorum pravitatem periculosius talia legebantur, id ante, cum talis nulla causa subesset, probavit summus Ecclesiae pontifex; itaque probavit ut tam ipse quam successores eius instarent, quatenus simili spiritu expositionem quoque Apocalypticam idem Joannes perficeret."

186. The order of Flora having been abolished in 1536, the monastery of St. John of Flora was passed on to Cîteaux; whence the apologia for Joachim in 1660 by Gregory of Laude or Lauro, abbot of another Cistercian monastery of Calabria. This writing was nevertheless less fantastic than one might have believed. Cf. C. Braut, OSB, "Las antiguas biografías de Joaquin de Fiore y sus fuentes," *Anal. sacra Tarrac.*, 26 (1953), 195-232.

187. An attempt at it had already been made in 1346, but apparently without success. Cf. ASS, 111B.

188. On Papebroch's notice: E. Buonaiuti, *G. di Fiore*, 127-8. On the *Virtutum B. Joachim Synopsis* (ASS, 93-5; modern title) of Joachim's secretary Lucas Campano who became archbishop of Cosenza: B., *Ev.*, xvi-xviii.

189. "Deus, qui gloriam tuam tribus apostolis in monte Thabor manifestasti, et in eodem loco beato Joachim veritatem Scripturarum manifestasti": "Spiritu dotatus prophetico, decoratus intelligentia, errore procul haeretico, dixit futura ut praesentia": ASS, 90 B. Crocco, 29. In his *Hist. eccles.*, t. 8, dissert. 2 (1734, 335-7), Noël Alexandre treats only of the trinitarian error condemned at the Lateran.

190. Already in 1938 Chr. Huck, *Joachim von Floris und die joachitische Literatur*, defends Joachim's orthodoxy except on the trinitarian matter. Cf. BTAM, 4, no. 1083. On this work: H. Grundmann in *Theol. Literaturzeit.*, 64 (1939), 176-8.

191. *Cronica*, ed. O. Holder-Egger (MGH, *Scr.*, 32, 202, 293, 440-1).

192. Some of these figures, notably the seven-headed dragon, are found in the first pages of the *Exp. in Ap.* published in 1527.

193. "Dispositio novi ordinis pertinens ad tertium statum ad instar supernae

Jerusalem": this "novus ordo" ("nova religio") is to be understood as a genus with divers species.

194. Leone Tondelli, *Il libro delle Figure dell'abate Gioachino da Fiore, I, Introduzione e commento, le sue rivelazioni dantesche* (Torino, 1940; 2d ed., 1953); *II, Teste e 23 tavole* (1940). Cf. Jeanne Bignami-Odier, *Bibl. de l'Ec. des Chartres,* 103 (1942), 249-53; *Le moyen âge,* 1952, 155-6.

195. Tondelli, I, 165: "However, everything here suggests that the often unqualified and hyperbolical sentences of the Abbot should be interpreted carefully. The *third state,* like the other two preceding ones, unfolds in time, in a unanimity not radically transfigured or completely freed from the necessity of strife, though a period of sabbath and of peace can and should be called for. The ideal and the greatness of the expectation inevitably come to be limited as they are converted into concrete reality" — "Comunque tutto ci indice ad interpretare con prudente criterio le frasi sovente assolute ed iperboliche dell'Abate. Il *terzo stato* si svolgerà ne tempo come gli altri due precedenti, in una unanimità non radicalmente trasfigurato o completamente sciolta dalle necessità della lotta, malgrado si possa e debla chiamare un periodo sabbatico e di pace. L'ideale e la grandiosità dell'attesa prendono inevitabilmente dei limiti trasportandosi nella realtà concreta."

196. *Gioacchino da Fiore e le Fondazioni Florensi in Calabria* (1959), 33-4.

197. *Gioacchino da Fiore* (1960), 12 and 49.

198. M. Reeves, "The *Liber Figurarum* of J. of Fiore," *Med. and Renaiss. Studies,* 1 (1950), 58 ss. M. Reeves and B. Hirsch-Reich, "The Figure of J. of F., genuine and spurious collections," *ib.*, 3 (1954), 170-99. M. Reeves and B. Hirsch-Reich, "The Seven Seals in the Writings of J. of F.," RTAM, 21 (1954), 211-31.

199. In the same way, the eagle of the *Psalterion* would get two explanations: the one, by the number five, which is primary, exterior, literal, active; the other, by the number seven, secondary, interior, spiritual, contemplative. Cf. J. Bignami-Odier, *Le moyen âge,* 1952, 158.

200. "pater spiritualis qui praeerit omnibus": LF, Table XII. There are six categories, as in *Conc.,* l. 5, c. 32 (f. 71, 3-4), six "mansiones."

201. Fr. Russo and Fr. Foberti (numerous articles). A. Crocco offers a lively critique to Russo (33). It is true that Foberti, who shares Tondelli's Joachimite zeal, yields to hyper-criticism: for him, Joachim had never attacked Peter Lombard, and the trinitarian writings that are attributed to him had been forged by Cistercians who wanted to do him harm. Cf. Bloomfield, 254. J. Bignami-Odier, *Bibl. de l'Ec. des Chartres,* 203 (1942), 249-53, doubts its authenticity, except for the figures that are also found in the other works.

202. Msgr. Tondelli asserts that the manuscript is very old, that nothing in it shows knowledge of the events of the 13th century, that the order of Cîteaux is evoked in it, and that no trace of later Joachimism is found in it. None of this is conclusive. For Bloomfield, 258, note 35, "a strong argument for the genuineness of the L. F. is that Joachim frequently in his authentic writings refers to, and uses, figures to clarify his argument." He was not the only one, and a disciple could have imitated him. The title itself is ill attested.

203. Cf. Bloomfield, 259-60: the work is of inestimable value; but is it by

Joachim himself or by a disciple working under his direction, or by a "later and less reliable follower"?

204. One would surely have some difficulty in wholeheartedly subscribing to the following lines of M. Reeves and B. Hirsch-Reich, *Med. and Ren. St.*, 3, 198: "The figures that the Abbot created were in a real sense general expositions of his system of thought, not illustrations to his text merely, but independent designs, embodying the multitudinous patterns of his thought in some ways far more adequately than words could do."

205. "oscillante et variée": Bignami-Odier, *Le moyen âge*, 1952, 154.

206. "litteram et spiritum" vs. "vetus testamentum et novum": "Otherwise, however, there would be the same difference between water and fire, letter and spirit, Old Testament and New, and the first and last coming of Christ as there would be between what is meant by John and what is meant by Elijah" — "Alias autem quod differt inter aquam et ignem, inter litteram et spiritum, inter vetus testamentum et novum, inter primum et ultimum Christi adventum, hoc differt inter significatum Joannis et significatum Heliae": in an appendix to the edition of the *De art. fidei* (106).

207. "Quia voluit ostendere Spiritus sanctus quid differret inter legem et gratiam, inter filios carnis et filios adoptionis, inter doctrinam litterae et doctrinam spiritalem, inter vetus quoque testamentum et novum, voluit haec duo designare in Joanne et Christo": Buonaiutti, 273, 58, 277-8.

208. *Ib.*, 58, 277-8.

209. In the same way that under the single common name of Old Testament he includes both the "tempus ante legem" and the "tempus sub lege." Cf. LF, Table XI.

210. *C. Graecorum opposita*, l. 4, c. 1: "that the institutions of observations were diverse, but yet not diverse in faith, though they were disparate in their observance" — "diversas observationum institutiones fuisse, nec tamen fide diversas, licet observantia dispares exstiterint" (PL, CXXI, 306 CD); "but just as the things instituted by our predecessors . . . were not the same for all the churches, so too they in no way divided the unity of the faith" — "instituta vero majorum . . . , sicut non omnibus ecclesiis eadem, sic unitatem fidei nullo modo divisere" (228 C).

211. *De sacramentorum diversitate, ad Walerami querelas responsio*, c. 1 (PL, CLVIII, 552-3).

212. *Dial.*, 1: "How in and of itself God's Church is one, and how it is of many forms with respect to her children, whom she has informed and still does so in various ways and with various laws and institutions, from the blood of Abel the Just right up to the latest of the elect" — "Quomodo Ecclesia Dei sit una in se et secundum se, et quomodo sit multiformis secundum filios suos, quos diversis modis et diversis legibus et institutis informavit et informat, a sanguine Abel justi usque ad novissimum electum" (PL, CLXXXVIII, 1143 D; cf. 1141-2 and 1149).

213. See above, ch. 4.5. This takes away much weight from the remark made on this subject by H. Grundmann, *Neue Forschungen über Joachim von Floris* (1950).

214. *S. sig.*: "up to the hidden end of that time when the devil is to be released from his prison and that most wicked man, the one who is called Gog, is going to

reign" — "usque ad occultum finem ipsius temporis quo solvendus est diabolus de carcere suo et regnaturus est homo pessimus qui vocatur Gog" (246).

215. *In Luc.*, I, 13: "For behold, according as he designates Elijah, the Lord is about to come in majesty to judge the living and the dead" — "Ecce enim, secundum quod designat Helias, venturus est Dominus in majestate judicare vivos et mortuos" (Buon., 107).

216. RTAM, 21, 230.

217. *S. Sig.*: "That tribulation is to come, after which, once Elijah has been sent ahead, the Lord is to come at the Last Judgment, as is contained more clearly than in light in the seventh part of the Apocalypse, with no discrepancy from the old signs" — "Futura est tribulatio ista, post quam, praemisso Helia, venturus est Dominus ad extremum judicium, secundum quod continetur luce clarius in septima parte Ap., in nullo discordans a veteribus signis" (246). Cf. LI, c. 7 (f. 9-10).

218. "cepit transmigrare in spiritu spiritualis Jerusalem"; "multi fidelium coronabuntur martyrio et aedificabitur rursum sancta civitas quae est Ecclesia electorum": RTAM, 21, 344-6.

219. LI, prol.: "I shall speak as best I am able, if not I shall use winks and nods: that the joys of the world have failed, that pressures are threatening, that the kingdom of the heavens is present in the doorways" — "Loquar ego prout potero, sin minus nutibus indicabo: defecisse mundi gaudia, imminere pressuras, caelorumque regnum adesse in januis."

220. LI, c. 5: "Hence the third state will be around the end of the age, no longer under the veil of the letter, but in full freedom of the spirit, when, once the pseudo-gospel of the son of perdition and his prophets has been eliminated and sapped, those who educate the many to justice will be like the brightness of the firmament and like stars in perpetual eternities" — "Tertius ergo status erit circa finem saeculi, jam non sub velamine litterae, sed in plena spiritus libertate, quando, evacuato et substructo pseudo-evangelio filii perditionis et prophetarum ejus, hi qui ad justitiam erudient multos erunt sicut splendor firmamenti et quasi stellae in perpetuas aeternitates" (f. 5, 2).

221. "In the sixth time, whose beginning we are already grasping, it is necessary that the virginal, or even the continent and contemplative, church conceive and have in the womb of her profession that people of saints to whom, according to Daniel, the kingdom is to be given . . . , and her birthing will be at the consummation of the age" — "In sexto tempore, cujus exordia jam tenemus, oportet concipere ecclesiam virginalem, sive etiam continentem atque contemplativam, et habere in utero professionis suae populum illum sanctorum cui dandum est secundum Danielem regnum . . . , eritque partus ejus in consummatione saeculi" (B., 35).

222. "in tempore novissimo"; "dies novisssimus"; "finis mundi"; "ultimus articulus finis"; "tempora saecularia": IA, P. 1, c. 3, v. 9: "but [the order] is to be multiplied and expanded in that third state of the age which is to come at the latest time" — "multiplicandus vero (ordo) et dilatandus in tertio illo statu saeculi, qui in tempore novissimo futurus est" (f. 83, 3).

223. "tempora saecularia": "circa finem": IA, P. 7: The blessed Remigius had destroyed the "opinion of those who think that the times of the age pass away

with the fall of the Antichrist and that only the end of the age exists, in their ignorance that the latest day or the end of the world is not always to be taken as the last moment of the end of the world, but rather as the time of the end, i.e., as the last age of the world" — "opinionem illorum qui putant cum casu ipsius Antichristi transire tempora saecularia, et omnino instare consummationem saeculi, ignorantes quod dies novissimus, seu finis mundi, non sit semper accipiendus pro ultimo articulo finis mundi, sed magis pro tempore finis, hoc est pro ultima aetate mundi" (f. 210, 1). Cf. *Conc.*, l. 5, c. 66: "de ordine quodam circa finem futuro" (f. 96, 1).

224. LI, c. 7 (f. 9, 3). See below, section 3.

225. "Nescio utrum tempora tertii status . . . breviora sint temporibus secundi"; "Quis scit quam breve esse poterit sabbatum ipsum? . . . Consummato praelio, erit pax magna, qualis non fuit a principio saeculi, cujus terminus erit in arbitrio Dei"; "Sermonem breviatum faciet Dominus super terram" [Rom. 9:28, substituting 'sermonem' for 'verbum']: *Conc.*, l. 5, c. 22 (f. 71, 1). IA, P. 7, f. 210, 3 and 4. Cf. Raoul of Coggeshall, summarizing the doctrine of Joachim: "But after the destruction of the Antichrist, he will say that only God knows how many years or days would constitute the fulfillment of the sixth seal, i.e., the resurrection of the dead, and the beginning of the seventh seal, i.e., the eternal glorification of the saints" — "Post Antichristi vero interitum, quot annorum vel dierum fieret expletio sigilli sexti, id est mortuorum resurrectio et septimi sigilli inchoatio, id est sanctorum aeterna glorificatio, soli Deo cognitum esse fatetur" (*H. de Fr.*, 18-76).

226. Thus *Conc.*, l. 2, tr. 1, c. 4: "There was one time . . . , another [time] . . . , and another [time] in which one lived according to the spirit" — "Aliud tempus fuit . . . , aliud . . . , aliud in quo vivitur secundum spiritum" (f. 8, 4).

227. LI, c. 7: "But once those pressures are over, there will come a blessed time, a time which will be like an Easter solemnity. . . . Almost no one or scarcely anyone will dare any more to deny that Christ is the Son of God, when the earth will be full of the knowledge of God as the waters of an overwhelming sea; except, however, for a few tribes that the Devil will produce at the end of the world, whom, as we think, the word of the Lord will not reach. That will be the third state, the one pertaining to the Holy Spirit" — "Consummatis autem pressuris istis, adveniet tempus beatum, tempus quod erit simile solemnitati pascali. . . . Nullus pene aut vix ullus audebit ultra negare Christum esse Filium Dei, quando plena erit terra scientia Domini sicut aquae maris operientis; exceptis dumtaxat quibusdam gentibus quas producturus est diabolus in fine mundi, ad quas, sicut arbitramur, verbum Domini non perveniet. Iste erit tertius status, pertinens ad Spritum sanctum etc." (f. 9, 10). Cf. IA, l. 7 (f. 210, 2).

228. "tempora saecularia": above, note 223.

229. "tempus tertii status": *Ev.*, 193. IA, P. 7 (f. 212, 1), etc.

230. "sexto in tempore"; "in tertio statu nuda erunt mysteria": IA, P. 6 (f. 195, 4). *Conc.*, l. 5, c. 67 (f. 96, 3).

231. "Tria evangelia, tribus statibus congruunt qui in temporibus hujus saeculi peraguntur; quartum vero, illam vitam mysterialiter tangit, quae post tertium statum futura est, in qua nos oportet et scire omnem veritatem, multo

solemnius et gloriosius quam in tertio statu, qui erit in sabbatum, sicut solemnior est sabbato et beatior dominicus dies": VB, c. 23 (50).

232. "Videmus nunc per speculum in aenigmate"; "ex parte cognoscimus" [1 Cor. 13:12]: *Conc.*, l. 5, c. 74 (f. 103, 2). *Ev.:* "the letter of the New Testament precedes ... that time which will be of greater grace ... ; then that time comes ... , as the apostle says: 'when that which is perfect has come' etc." — "tempus illud quod erit majoris gratiae ... praecedit littera novi testamenti ... ; cum venerit tempus illud ... , dicente apostolo: cum venerit quod perfectum est etc." (191); etc.

233. "paulatim pro tempore aenigma scissum est": *Conc.*, l. 2, tr. 1, c. 1 (f. 7, 1); l. 5, c. 73: "The truth will appear manifest, proceeding from the womb of the letter and from the home of the New Testament, in which it lay concealed until the present day; for though the saints may have seen many things through a mirror in a riddle, they did not dare to presume anything against the knowledge of Paul saying 'but when there comes, etc.'" — "Apparebit veritas manifesta, procedens de ventre litterae et de domo novi testamenti, in qua latuit secundum aliquid usque in praesentem diem; licet enim multa viderint sancti per speculum in aenigmate, non sunt ausi praesumere aliquid contra illam Pauli scientiam dicentis: cum autem venerit etc." (f. 101, 2). *Ev.* 73: "Though with respect to the previous ages it is necessary to say to those whom the splendor of his brightness illuminates: 'Night has preceded, but day has approached', nevertheless with respect to the splendor to come, it is necessary to say to us still tangled in the severe darkness of ignorance: 'Now we see through a mirror, etc.'" — "Etsi respectu praecedentium saeculorum dicendum est his quos claritatis ipsius splendor illustrat: nox praecessit, dies autem appropinquavit, respectu tamen futuri splendoris, dicendum est nobis, gravi adhuc ignorantiae involutis caligine: videmus nunc per speculum etc." Just as there are degrees for passing from the second age to the third, likewise there are [degrees] from the knowledge of the third age to that of eternity.

234. The figure is in reality a bit more complicated. For the terminology, see above, section 1 of this chapter.

235. IA, P. 7: "By 'a thousand years' is designated all the time that runs from the resurrection of the Lord up to the end of the world" — "In mille annis designatur omne tempus quod decurrit a resurrectione Domini usque in finem mundi ..."; "The seventh age, in which that great Sabbath is to come, also partially began in that sabbath wherein the Lord rested in the tomb. ... The beginning of the 'thousand years' started with the Lord's resurrection — not that they are to be thought of as a thousand years without qualification, but because the number one-thousand is most perfect, and designates a great plenitude of years" — "aetas septima, in qua magnum illud sabbatum futurum est, et secundum partem incepit ab illo sabbato quo requievit Dominus in sepulcro. ... Inchoatio mille annorum a resurrectione Domini initiata est; non quod mille anni simpliciter existimanda sint, sed quod millenarius numerus perfectissimus est, et magnam plenitudinem designat annorum" (f. 211, 2).

236. "ceux qui vont jouir de la félicité du sabbat ne seront pas de simple mortels": Anitchkof, *op. cit.*, 233.

237. "un chapitre sublime de l'histoire terrestre": Aegerter, I, 210.

238. "Finis venit" [Ezekiel 7:3]: "Finis utique senescentis Ecclesiae clericorum ... neque proinde finis mundi, quia relinquetur adhuc sabbatismus populo Dei": Cologne, 1577. Some have supposed that the basis of the work was authentic or came from some immediate disciple, but that in the 13th century it had suffered interpolation at the hands of the Minors who became attached to it: Anitchkof, 26 and 248. But cf. Manselli (1955), 113.

239. "usque ad finem mundi": *Conc.*, l. 2, tr. 1, c. 4 (f. 8, 4).

240. "tres status totius saeculi": "Haec doctrina tendit finaliter ad subversionem cleri, hoc est Romanae ecclesiae et obedientium ei": H. Denifle, *Archiv f. Lit. u. Kircheng. des M. A.*, 1 (1885), 102, 120. This protocol, thinks Denifle, is the best analysis of Joachim's ideas. The judgement cited here does not essentially result, as Tondelli, I, 146-7, seems to say, from an error of interpretation committed in fact upon certain texts concerning Rome and Babylon. See below, note 248.

241. "extra catholicam ecclesiam non datur donum Spiritus sancti": IA, P. 6, in *Ap.*, XXII, 1 (f. 221, 3). Thus Gebhart brought up nothing useful to explain the case of Joachim when he supposed that in Calabria "strict communion with Rome seemed to be less necessary for the salvation of souls than it was elsewhere" — "la communion étroite avec Rome semblait moins nécessaire qu'ailleurs au salut des âmes"! *L'Italie mystique*, 4th ed. (1904), 63.

242. "Romana Ecclesia, cui datum est universale magisterium, et cujus mandato et licentia scripsi haec ...": IA, P. 6, in *Ap.*, XXII, 15 (f. 224, 1).

243. "Si me articulus dierum istorum de quibus loquimur in carne repererit adhuc manentem, militiam bonam pro fide Christi militare concedat, et una cum Christi confessoribus qui tunc erunt, ad regna caelestia pervenire. Amen! Amen! Amen!": L. 5, c. 119 (f. 135, 4). Cf. IA, *Ep. prologalis:* "And if there is any other [work] I can do for the edification of Christ's faithful and especially of the monks while I am still in the body, I do not hesitate to do it" — "Et si aliud (opus) dum sum in corpore, posse datur ad aedificationem fidelium Christi et maxime monachorum, dare operam non postpono."

244. "quia extra corpus Ecclesiae seponendum est quod Romanae Ecclesiae non adhaeret": *Ev.*, 277, 280. *Ench.*, in Tondelli, I, 145. He conceives the union only as the "return of the Greeks to the unity of the Roman Church" — "reversio Graecorum ad romanae Ecclesiae unitatem": *Ev.*, 300. He did not set the Greek Church above the Roman: Carmelo Ottaviano, ed. of the *L. c. Lombardum* (Joachim's school), 1934, intro., 23-6.

245. His *Concord* is in part directed against them. Cf. Crocco, 37; Fournier, RAH, 67, 482-7.

246. "conçut dans ses rapports fréquents avec l'Église grecque ... et peut-être avec quelque branche de l'Église cathare, une grande aversion contre l'organisation de l'Église latine": *Nouv. ét. d'hist. rel.*, 221.

247. IA, f. 87, 3.

248. "But from many places it is gathered that by 'the kingdom of Babylon' he understands the dominion of the Roman Church" — "Quod autem per regnum Babylonis intelligit dominium romanae ecclesiae, colligitur ex pluribus locis" (Denifle, 119).

249. Thus in *Med. Faith and Fable*, by canon J. A. MacCulloch (1932), 294; or in

Louis Rougier, "La civilisation occident. et le christianisme," *Cahiers du cercle E. Renan*, 26 (1960), 2: "The Cathars, the Vaudois, the Fraticelli, Joachim of Flora, and the Protestants invoke [the Gospel] against the Roman Church" — "Les Cathares, les Vaudois, les Fraticelles, Joachim de Flore, les protestants l'invoquent (l'Évangile) contre l'Église romaine." But B. Rigaux, in a formula that might lead one into error: "Joachim of Flora had already summoned apocalyptic visions in the service of the condemnation of the Church of his time" — "Déjà J. de Flore avait appelé les visions apocalyptiques au service de la condamnation de l'Église de son temps"; *Les Ep. aux Thessal.* (1956), 262.

250. "ecclesia malignantium": *Conc.*, l. 5, c. 118: "That ancient people of the elect which is signified in Sarah, is said in the spirit of Jerusalem, etc. So too the multitude of the reprobate from the beginning of times down to Christ is to be called Babylon. And much the more is the countless multitude of false Christians; and yet each of the two is simultaneously one Babylon" — "Plebs illa electorum antiqua quae significata est in Sara, dicitur in spiritu Hierusalem etc. Sic multitudo reproborum ab initio temporum usque ad Christum dicenda est Babylon. Et multo amplius innumera multitudo falsorum christianorum; et tamen utraque simul una Babylon" (f. 134, 3). IA, P. 6: "the sons of Babylon, who say that they are faithful and are not, but are the synagogue of Satan" — "filii Babylonis, qui dicunt se esse fideles, et non sunt, sed sunt synagoga Satanae" (f. 201, 4).

251. IA, P. 6 (f. 191, 4): "since both the heavenly city and the infernal city have their walls on four sides" — "quia et civitas caelestis a quatuor partibus habet muros suos, et civitas nihilominus infernalis" (*Conc.*, f. 51, 4; 52, 2; 89, 3, etc.). In the tradition coming from Origen, Egypt was in fact more land of exile (and of chastisement) than of sin.

252. *Conc.*, l. 4, c. 17: "One should consider more carefully that in those 'three peoples' should not be understood peoples in the strict sense but rather, so to say, varieties of one and the same people.... Were not some evil men even in Jerusalem, and were there not some good ones in Babylon?" — "Considerari oportet diligentius non esse in iis tribus populis intelligenda proprietas populorum, sed unius ut ita dicam populi varietates.... Nonne et Hierusalem fuere aliqui mali, et in Babylone boni?" (f. 52, 1-2).

253. Cf. Raoul of Coggeshall, *Chronicon anglicanum*, relating the discussion with Adam of Perseigne: Joachim says that the Antichrist is already at Rome, an adolescent; Adam objects that he ought to be born in Babylon; whereupon Joachim says: "You immediately conclude that what is mystically Rome is mystically called Babylon, according to Peter's remark at the end of his epistle ... ; hence the expositor calls Rome 'Babylon' owing to the manifold confusion of its idolatry" — "Statim intulis Romam mystice Babyloniam mystice vocari, juxta illud b. Petri in fine epistolae suae ... ; unde expositor Romam Babyloniam vocat propter multiplicem idolatriae confusionem" (*Historiens de France*, 18, 76). There is no reason in this, however, to take Raoul's whole account literally.

254. IA, p. 6: "universalis Babylon" (f. 192, 4); "multitudo reproborum, quae dicta est Babylon" (f. 193, 1).

255. "meretrix Babylon"; "fornicaria Babylonia": IA, P. 4 (f. 173, 2); P. 5 (f. 191, 3). Cf. *Conc.*, l. 4, c. 19 (f. 53, 2).

256. IA, P. 6, c. 1: "This great [whore] the catholic Fathers said was Rome, not

as the Church of the just, which was in pilgrimage in it, but as the multitude of the reprobate who by their iniquitous deeds, blaspheme and impugn that Church in pilgrimage among them. . . . Hence the location of this infamous whore is not to be sought in some one kingdom or province; but rather, just as the grain of the elect is found spread throughout the whole area of the Christian empire, so too the straws of the reprobate are scattered throughout its breadth. . . . But the kings of the earth were called 'prelates' . . . , some of whom are fornicating with Babylon whenever they think little of or neglect God's mandate so as to please men" — "Hanc magnam (meretricem) dixerunt Patres catholici esse Romam, non quoad Ecclesiam justorum, quae peregrinata est apud eam, sed quoad multitudinem reproborum, qui blasphemant et impugnant operibus iniquis eamdem apud se peregrinantem Ecclesiam. . . . Non ergo in uno regno aut in una provincia quaerendus est locus hujus famosissimae meretricis: sed, sicut per totam aream christiani imperii diffusum est triticum electorum, ita per omnem latitudinem ejus dispersae sunt paleae reproborum. . . . Reges vero terrae dicti sunt Praelati . . . , quorum nonnulli fornicantur cum Babylone, quandoquidem ut placeant hominibus parvipendunt et negligunt mandatum Dei" (f. 194, 2).

257. See, for example, Caesarius, s. 48 (Morin, 1, 210). Bede, *Hexaem.*, l. 3 (PL, XCI, 127 B). Beatus, *In Ap.* (55 and 487). Bruno of Segni, *In Ap.*, l. 5, c. 16: "For just as Jerusalem signifies the Church of the saints, so Babylon signifies the congregation of all the iniquitous" — "Sicut enim Jerusalem sanctorum Ecclesiam, ita Babylon iniquorum omnium congregationem significat" (CLXV, 696 C). Aimo, *h.* 5 (CXXXI, 893 CD). Honorius (CLXXII, 843 D, 893 C, 921 D: Hierusalem = Ecclesia; 1085-8: Jerusalem, city of the humble, Babylon, city of the proud; 1093-8: the kings of the two cities, Christ and the devil). Anselm of Laon, *In Ap.* (CLXII, 1535 B). Godfrey of Admont, *h.* 14 *in Script.* (CLXXIV, 1116 C: Babyloniae rex, diabolus). Hughes, *Miscell.*, l. 1, tit. 48 and 95 (CXVII, 496-7, 525 A). Richard, *In Ap.*, l. 6, c. 9 (CXCVI, 837-8). Absalon (CCXI, 147 A). *De unit. Eccl. cons.*, c. 41 (L. de lite, 2, 273). Gerhoh, *L. de simoniacis* (L. de lite, 3, 272); *De invest. Antich.*, c. 13 (320), c. 74 (395); etc.

258. *Conc.*, l. 5, c. 61: "But Jerusalem has been stormed. . . . The Church of Christ in it has been stormed: for she is the city of the sun, etc." — "Expugnata est autem Hierusalem. . . . Expugnata est in ea Ecclesia Christi: ipsa est enim civitas solis etc." (f. 92, 3); c. 62: "The kingdom of Jerusalem, i.e., of the Church" — "Regnum Hierusalem, hoc est Ecclesiae" (92, 4).

259. Raoul of Coggeshall, *loc. cit.*: "But our successors will be able to judge more certainly what is to be thought over this man's assertion or, rather, opinion. But we are now seeing that the typic kingdom of Babylon is obtaining the greatest hegemony in the world, day by day taking over the lands of the Christians and spreading pernicious error" — "Quid vero super hujus viri assertione vel potius opinione sentiendum sit, successores nostri certius dijudicare poterunt. Nos tamen jam videmus quod typicum Babylonis regnum maximum in orbe obtinet principatum, terras christianorum de die in diem occupando, et erroris perniciem dilatando. . . ." One can foresee that the Saracens, quartermasters of the Antichrist, are on the point of conquering all of Christendom and persecuting all Christians.

260. IA (f. 192, 2).

261. *Conc.,* l. 4, c. 17: up to the 37th generation the kings and emperors ruling the Latin world are called "kings of Egypt"; those who follow are called "kings of Babylon" (f. 52, 1); "So that is the height of the concord of those generations, whereby we read both that in those days the kings of Babylon had fought against Jerusalem, and that in these days the Roman emperors are fighting against the freedom of the Church" — "Summa itaque concordiae istarum generationum illa est qua et ibi reges Babylonis pugnasse legimus contra Hierusalem, et hic romanos imperatores contra libertatem Ecclesiae" (f. 52, 4). Cf. c. 23 (53, 3). LF, Tables XVI and XVII.

262. IA, P. 6, dist. 2 (f. 203, 1-2): "Babylon, the Church reduced to slavery, is reigning, since he is taking over the former as a whole and is killing the latter lest she bear fruit" — "Regnat Babylon, ancillata Ecclesia, quia illam totam occupat et hanc ne fructum proferat necat." *Ib.*: "When that old Babylon was being persecuted by the Persians [reading 'a Persis' instead of the printed text 'aspersis'] and the Jews freed by King Cyrus were ascending from Babylon, etc." — "Cum Babylon illa vetus percuteretur a Persis (for the printed reading: aspersis) et Judaei liberati per Cyrum regem ascenderunt de Babylon etc."; "Nor does the new Babylon permit us to sing alleluia" — "Nec nos nova Babylon cantare patitur alleluia" (f. 204-5). P. 5: "Their powers are being weakened by the just judgment of the all-powerful God, so that, when their armies fail, there may not be anyone left to stand against the kings and tyrants who ... are to come to strike down the kingdom of Babylon herself. ... After the desolation of the Roman Empire, etc." — "Justo omnipotentis Dei judicio debilitantur vires eorum ut, deficientibus exercitibus suis, non sit qui resistat regibus et tyrannis qui ... venturi sunt ad percutiendum regnum ipsius Babylonis. ... Post desolationem romani imperii etc." (f. 190, 3).

263. *Ev.,* 283, 290. *Conc.,* l. 5, c. 57; etc.

264. "religio ipsa monachorum doctrinam Romanorum pontificum diligentissime retinet": *Conc.,* l. 5, c. 61 (f. 93, 1). One does not find in him those harsh criticisms of the Roman curia that others, such as Gerhoh, did not hesitate to formulate.

265. *Ep. prol.:* "As can be seen from the letters of the former Pope Clement (which are still with us), I have put into writing some things at the behest of Pope Lucius and Pope Urban" — "Sicut ex litteris domini pape quondam Clementis (quae apud nos sunt) percipi potest, ex mandato domini papae Lucii et domini papae Urbani visus sum aliqua scriptitasse."

266. The reasons brought forward by Buonaiuti, 130 and 173-6, are not entirely negligible. The letter aims perhaps a bit too well not only at supporting the enterprise and at authorizing Joachim's doctrine, but at accounting for his departure from Corazzo in 1189(?). Ceillier, t. 14, 2 (1863), 829: "Unable to give the care required for the administration of temporal affairs along with his inclination for study and the orders that he had received from Pope Clement III to continue his commentaries on Scripture, [he] abandoned the governance of the monastery at Corazzo with the permission of" the Pope — "Ne pouvant accorder les soins que demandait l'administration des affaires temporelles avec son inclination pour l'étude et les ordres qu'il avait reçuts du pape Clément III, de continuer ses com-

mentaries sur l'Écriture, (il) renonça, avec sa permission, au gouvernement du monastère de Corace."

267. This implied a canonical censure.

268. "Petri Ecclesia est supra petram, extra quam Spiritus sanctus haberi non potest": *Ev.*, 291. *Conc.* (f. 134).

269. Despite Foberti, one cannot doubt that Joachim had written against the Lombard and one cannot lay the condemnation of 1215 entirely to the account of a Cistercian campaign against him. Cf. the adjustment of C. Ottaviano, "Un nuovo documento ritorno alla condamna di G. da Fiore, nel 1215" (*Sophia*, 3, 1935, 476-82), and L. Tondelli, "G. da Fiore e il concilio Lateran II" (*Scuola cattolica*, 71, 1943, 126-31). For the controversy that preceded the council, one can refer to Roger of Wandover, *Flores historiarum* (H. O. Coxe, 2, 1841, 400-2).

270. *Ep. prol.*: "The prefatory letter of Abbot Joachim of Flora begins under protest with his commands to his brethren to present all of his works, both those already and those about to be compiled by him, to the judgment and examination of the Roman Church; just in case he should happen to die before such works be approved by the Church" — "Incipit epistola prologalis D. abbatis J. Florensis omnium opusculorum suorum tam compilatorum quam compilandorum ab eo omniumque judicio ac examini Romanae Ecclesiae praesentandorum sub protestatione mandatis suis fratribus; casu quod accidat eum e vita decedere antequam hujusmodi opuscula ab ecclesia approbarentur." Again at the end of the epistle, Joachim orders his successors to submit all of his writings to the apostolic See. E. Buonaiuti "thinks that the testament of 1200 is apocryphal. But the omission of many works in that list is not a good argument; nothing demonstrates that the little books did not include the De unitate seu essentia Trinitatis; and if the Tractatus super quatuor evangelia are not mentioned in it, is that not just because they belong to 1200-1202?" — "estime apocryphe le Testament de 1200. Mais l'omission de plusieurs ouvrages dans cette liste n'est pas un bon argument; rien ne démontre que les parvi libelli ne comprennent pas le De unitate seu essentia Trinitatis; et si les Tractatus super quatuor evangelia n'y sont pas mentionés, n'est-ce pas simplement parce qu'ils sont de 1200-1202?" D. M. C. In BTAM, 1, no. 1147. Cf. Crocco, 66-8. See above, note 266.

271. Cf. Tondelli, LF I, 123-30.

272. The others were the Dominican, Franciscan, and Cistercian orders (bull on the canonization of St. Dominic).

273. For how the "spirituals" had in fact falsified the thought of Joachim and nevertheless laid claim to him, see E. Benz, "Die Kategorien der religiösen Geschichtsdeutung Joachims," *Zeitschrift f. Kircheng.*, 3 (1931), 110-1. See below, vol. 4, ch. 9.4.

274. Salimbene will be as hard as the theologians of Anagni on the *Introductorius* of San Donnino, which he will say contains "many misrepresentations of the teaching of Abbot Joachim" — "multas falsitates contra doctrinam abbatis Joachim."

275. *Ev.*, 87: "When such a lad had been made manifest in God's Church, who is contemplative, just, wise, and spiritual and who can succeed to the order of bishops; ... in the way Solomon succeeded king David, in the way that John the Evangelist succeeded Peter the Prince of the Apostles, or rather in the way that

Christ himself succeeded to John the Baptist" — "Cum talis puer manifestatus fuerit in Ecclesia Dei, qui sit utique contemplativus, justus, sapiens, spiritalis et qui ita possit succedere episcoporum ordini; . . . quomodo regi David successit Salomon, quomodo Petro principi apostolorum Joannes evangelista, quin potius quomodo ipse Christus Joanni Baptistae."

276. "Petri navicula"; "Ecclesia Christi": VB, c. 24 (51). *Conc.*, l. 2, tr. 1, c. 7 (f. 9, 2).

277. *Loc. cit.*, 266: "The role of the papacy in the new age is somewhat dubious, but probably the Church would continue to be presided over by a purified Bishop of Rome." He refers to *Conc.*, l. 4, 39; l. 5, 65 and 92.

278. "ecclesiae laborantium"; "desudantium in vita activa"; "ecclesiae quiescentium"; "exultantium in vita contemplativa": *Conc.*, l. 5, c. 62 (f. 92, 4-93, 3).

279. "relinquitur sabbatismus populo Dei"; "pacificus et quietus"; "sic, consummato illo ordine qui significatur in Petro et David, remanebit loco ejus ordo ille qui significatus est in Joanne, discipulo quem amabat Jesus, et puero Salomone, qui dictus est amabilis Domini": LF, Table XIX.

280. "Senectus . . . David, hujus secundi status et ordinis ecclesiae militantis in littera evangelii senectutem designat. Mulier Sunamitis, quae juncta est ei et non concepit ex eo, nova religio erit, quae omnino erit libera et spiritalis. . . . Quia vero in servando ordine suo antiquo incipiet Romanus pontifex frigescere propter senectutem, extollentur adhuc aliqui ex iis qui videbuntur esse strenui ad certamen, ut stent in regno ecclesiae . . . ; sed non obtinebunt, quia non erit adhuc necesse regnare ordinem belli in die pacis; sed magis oportebit religiosos transire in illum ordinem qui designatur in Salomone": *Conc.*, l. 5, c. 65 (f. 95, 3-4).

281. "non translatione facta sed renovatione concessa": Table XIX.

282. "Non igitur, quod absit, deficiet ecclesia Petri, quae est thronus Christi . . . , sed commutata in majorem gloriam manebit stabilis in aeternum": L. 5, c. 65 (f. 95, 4). Crocco, 95-6. Russo, 35-6. Tondelli cites the same chapter again (95, 3): "At that point the Roman Pontiff will begin more and better to reign in the Church of God, when he will be regarded as exiled and alienated from his own" — "Tunc magis et melius incipiet regnare Romanus Pontifex in Ecclesia Dei, cum putabitur expulsus et alienatus a suis," which would be rather curious in the situation of the third age; but in reality it is a question of persecutions endured by the popes in the course of the present history of the Church.

283. "Transeunte illa vita quae pertinet at Petrum, consummabitur sexta aetas. . . . Nunc ergo accingendus est Petrus et ducendus quo non vult, ad peragendum quam citius cursum suum, ut transeat quod pertinet ad laboriosam aetatem et relinquatur quod pertinet ad quietam. . . . Audiant hoc, illi qui significantur in Petro!": Table XIX. Would not this rudeness suggest that the text would rather be by a disciple than by Joachim himself?

284. "Num qui talem sibi fructum intuetur succedere, dolere potest, quia desinit esse in se particularis perfectio, ubi succedit universalis? Absit hoc a Petri successione! Absit ut tabescat invidia super perfectione ordinis spiritalis quem videbit esse unum spiritum cum Deo suo!": *Ev.*, 87: "for neither will he be able to be sad over his own dissolution, since he knows he will persist in a better succes-

sion" — "neque enim super dissolutionem suam poterit dolere, cum se in meliori successione permanere cognoscet."

285. *Ev.*, 88: "The spiritual prelates and the church of those who live spiritually, when they see the spiritual order of the just having within itself so manifestly the gift of the Holy Spirit that the Lord promised to his elect, cannot fail to marvel that by the spirit of understanding it had been disclosed even to that ancient order of the Fathers, the order to which the whole Church of God is subject, upon a change of the right hand of the Exalted" — "Spiritales praelati et ecclesia eorum qui spiritaliter vivunt, ubi viderint spiritalem ordinem justorum, habentem in se tam manifeste donum Spiritus sancti quod promisit Dominus electis suis, etiam illi antiquo patrum ordini, cui subjecta est omnis Ecclesiae Dei, intelligentiae spiritu esse compertum, non poterunt non ammirari super mutatione dexterae Excelsi."

286. "in ulnas fidei et dilectionis suae": *Ev.*, 87: "So just as the old man Simeon will pick the boy up in his arms, when Peter's successors (to whom the prerogative of the faith has been given and to discern between the sacred and the profane), seeing that order, which imitates Christ's footsteps, in spiritual power, he will hold him up by the rampart of his authority and confirm him with the words of his testimony, announcing that in him are to be fulfilled the oracles of the prophets, among which is this: 'a kingdom which is beneath the whole heaven will be given to the people of the saints of the Most High'" (Dan. 7:27). — "Quasi ergo in ulnas suscipiet puerum senex Simeon, cum successores Petri quibus data est praerogativa fidei et discernere inter sanctum et profanum, videntes illum ordinem qui imitatur vestigia Christi, in virtute spirituali, sustentabit eum munimine auctoritatis suae et confirmabit verbis testimonii sui, annuntians complenda esse in ipso vaticinia prophetarum, de quibus est illud: regnum quod est subter omne caelum, dabitur populo sanctorum Altissimi." *Ib.*, 86: "That just and God-fearing old man stands for those in charge of the Roman Church, among whom, God granting it, that promise of the Lord, saying 'I have prayed for you that your faith not fail' will remain unto the end. For Peter's succession always aspires to see what it preaches completed, and when it will be given to it to see what it wishes for, namely the gift of the Holy Spirit confirmed within the Christian people . . . , seeing that order when the spiritual Church has given birth, coming to light from the hidden portions of the crib, he will pick him up in the arms of his faith and love and announce that the life-giving Spirit, in which there is the salvation of the world, is in him" — "Senex iste justus et timoratus Romanae praesules designat Ecclesiae, in quibus, donante Deo, manet usque in finem promissio illa Domini dicentis: 'ego rogavi pro te ut non deficiat fides tua'. Semper enim Petri successio affectat videre completum quod praedicat, et cum dabitur ei videre quod optat, ut vid. ita videat confirmatum donum Spiritus sancti in populo christiano . . . , videns illum ordinem quem Ecclesia peperit spiritalis, quasi de abditis praesepii locis venientem ad lucem, accipiet eum in ulnas fidei et dilectionis suae, et pronuntiabit in eo esse illum vivificantem Spiritum, in quo est salus mundi."

287. "tout le monde latin reconnut Joachim pour prophète": *Nouv. ét.*, 221. Papebroch, 90 A.

288. "Dicat quisquis quod sentit: nos tutius judicamus non discutere quam arguere quod nescimus": *Historiens de Fr.*, 18, 253.

289. Ghellinck, *L'essor*, 1, 190. Papebroch, 138-40, refutes certain assertions of the narrator, but not the judgment of Adam.

290. Leclercq, *St. ans.*, 31, 200-1.

291. "ordinis cisterciensis"; "Cisterciensibus minime subjectus": Raoul of Coggeshall, *loc. cit.* Aegerter, 1, 79-80 and 84-5, says that Joachim left the Cistercian order "with the twofold object of escaping difficulties of a material order which retarded his works and difficulties of a disciplinary order which rendered it difficult to publish them," this Order forbidding its members all study of the Scripture! Cf. above, ch. 3.5.

292. Geoffrey, *ib.*: "Multorum etiam habitus noster ei conciliat animos, et quod cisterciensis ordinis cum voluerit monachum sese exhibet et abbatem esse. Nam et olim quidem exstitit, sed annis jam . . ." (the sequel is missing).

293. In the same way one has sometimes exaggerated the role of the powerful hostility of the Cistercians in the condemnation of 1215; e.g., Henry Bett, *Joachim of Flora* (1931), 65; above all Fr. Foberti, *G. da Fiore, nuovi studi critici* . . . (1934), who exaggerates both the power and the decadence of the Order as well. Cf. Crocco, 63-5. On this hostility: Bloomfield, 255. This was the argument of Joachim's apologists in the 16th century. Cf. Noël Alexandre, *loc. cit.*: "Francis Bivarius . . . , in the Apologia on behalf of Lucius Dexter, writes that Abbot Joachim had suffered calumny at the hands of those who could hardly bear the new reform he introduced into the Cistercian order. Gregory of Laud . . . tries to free him from the error using three moves" — "Franciscus Bivarius, cist. . . . , in Apologia pro Lucio Dextro, scribit calumniam passum Joachimum abbatem ab iis qui novam reformationem in ordinem cistercisensem ab eo introductam aegre ferebant. Gregorius de Laude . . . ipsum ab errore purgare pariter conatur triplici momento."

294. "Siquidem Spiritus sanctus . . . , praevidens futuros haereticos qui dicerent Christum ad tempus regnaturum et Ecclesiam desituram in tempore et fidem catholicam et caetera dona gratiae in exterminium itura . . .": L. 2, c. 103 (Delhaye, 114). How can one not recognize Joachim there? Thus Mr. Delhaye does not hesitate to mention him in a note, though he places (ET, 33) the redaction of the *Microcosmus* toward 1185. Mr. Delhaye wants indeed to tell us that that date was calculated by relation to the *Fons philosophiae*, earlier by some years. If the *Fons philosophiae* ought to be taken as later by five or six years, as seems quite likely, the *Microcosmus* could be dated only from around 1190-2, and from then on all other unlikelihood will fall away. Godfrey was still living, having entered Saint Victor, and exercising the duties of sacristan there, in 1194.

295. Cf. A. Pézard, *op. cit.*, 391.

296. *Conc.*, l. 5, c. 119: "Let them know that it is not from proud presumption, or from confidence of some sort of piety that I wanted to attempt these things, or by my own wit that I say that I have found them for the world, but rather because the end time is at hand" — "Sciant non ex praesumptione superba, sed nec alicujus pietatis securitate haec me attentare voluisse, aut meo hoc ingenio, ut ista mundo loquerer invenisse: sed quia tempus praefinitum adest" (f. 135, 2).

297. *Conc.*, praef.: "Non a fructu operis otiosum existimo, ea quae de temporibus extremis superna mihi indigno dispensatio credidit ad cautelam

reserare fidelium, et torpentia somnolentium corda sono vel in sonito excitare; si quo modo ad contemptum mundi novo saltem genere exponendi evigilent."

298. *Psalt.*, praef.: "I myself was anxious for the words of God, and was seeking to arrive at a notion of the truth through the performance of the reading. And though through zeal of reading I burned to hasten toward that truth, taking on wings like an eagle it kept on receding further and further from me. But when, fixed in a fervor quite new, I began to love singing the Psalms for God's sake, many things in the divine Scripture began to be unlocked for me in silence as I was Psalm-singing that I had been unable previously to track down by reading" — "Eram aliquando ego ipse anxius ad verba Dei, et quaerebam per exercitium lectionis ad veritatis notitiam pervenire. Cumque ad eam per legendi studium properare flagrarem, assumens sibi pennas sicut aquilae, longius quam erat recedebat a me. Cum autem, positus in fervore novissimo, caepi Dei causa diligere psalmodiam, multa mihi in Scriptura divina psallenti sub silentio reserari caeperunt, quae antea legendo vestigare nequiveram" (f. 227, 1).

299. *Ev.*, 69 and 77.

300. *Psalt.*, praef.: "I was not entirely inexperienced with the understanding of the holy oil" — "Non omnino eram expers ab intellectu olei sancti" (f. 227, 2).

301. It is quite likely that there was a modest confidence in these words: "Let men learn to hide the grace given them in the time of their childhood and youth, lest they seem prematurely vainglorious with the gift received" — "Discant homines abscondere gratiam sibi datam tempore pueritiae et adolescentiae suae, ne videantur de accepto dono ante tempus inaniter gloriari": *Ev.* (f. 55, 2).

302. *Psalt.*, praef.: "When I entered the oratory and was adoring God almighty before the holy altar, a sort of hesitation about the faith in the Trinity occurred in me. . . . When this happened, I prayed intensely and deeply terrified I was driven to call upon the Holy Spirit, whose sacred solemnity was at hand, that he might deign to show me the sacred mystery of the Trinity, in which all knowledge of the truth has been promised by the Lord. On saying this I began to sing the Psalms, so as to arrive at the number set out. Suddenly the shape of a ten-stringed lyre appeared before my mind, and in it the mystery of the Holy Trinity appeared so clear and open that I was straightaway compelled to cry: 'Who is a god like our God'" — "Cum ingrederer oratorium et adorarem omnipotentem Deum coram sancto altari, accidit in me velut haesitatio quaedam de fide Trinitatis. . . . Quod cum accideret, oravi valde et conterritus vehementer compulsus sum invocare Spiritum sanctum, cujus sacra solemnitas praesens erat, ut ipse mihi dignaretur ostendere sacrum mysterium Trinitatis, in quo nobis promissa est a Domino omnis notitia veritatis. Haec dicens caepi psallere, ut ad propositum numerum pervenirem. Nec mora occurrit animo modo forma psalterii decachordi, et in ipsa tam lucidum et apertum sacrae mysterium Trinitatis, ut protinus compellerer clamare: Quis Deus sicut Deus noster? . . ." (f. 227, 2-3). That was the dawn of Pentecost.

303. Raoul, *Chronicon anglicanum:* "Respondit se neque prophetiam neque conjecturam neque revelationem habere, sed Deus, inquit, qui olim dedit prophetis spiritum prophetiae, mihi dedit spiritum intelligentiae, ut in Dei spiritu omnia mysteria sacrae Scripturae clarissime intelligam" (J. Stevenson, *Rer. brit. script.*, 69, 1875, 68). Cf G. Morin, RB, 47 (1935), 348-55. Cf. Robert of Auxerre,

Chronologia, a. 1186: "de quo ferebant quia, cum prius non plurimum didicisset, divinitus accepit intelligentiae donum, adeo ut facunde diserteque enodaret difficultates quaslibet Scripturarum" (*Hist. de Fr.,* 18, 253). William of Nangis (*ib.,* 20, 742). William of Auvergne (†1249), *De virtutibus:* "Donum intellectus tantae claritatis est et acuminis in quibusdam, ut valde assimiletur spiritui prophetiae; qualem crediderunt nonnulli fuisse in abbate Joachim et ipsement de seipso dixisse dicitur quia non erat ei datus spiritus prophetiae, sed spiritus intelligentiae. Si quis autem inspexerit libros ejus, quos scripsit super Apocalypsin et super Concordiam duorum Testamentorum, mirabitur donum intellectus in eo" (*Opera,* 1674, 1, 152). Is it certain that this was praise? What is the sense of the word "mirabitur"? Would it not be necessary to take the words "crediderunt nonnulli, ipsemet de seipso dixisse dicitur, si quis autem inspexerit" as so many reservations?

304. Tondelli, 1, 7 and 121-2.

305. "Cum librum hunc (Apocalypsim) lectitare cepissem, et adhuc concordiarum sacramenta nescirem, quo illuc impetu a primo ductus sim nescio, Deus scit, unde scio quod nequaquam historiarum peritia ad concordiae notitiam perductus sim; sed sola praeteritorum operum, hoc est testimonii veteris comparatione pulsatus, credens discordare non posse in corpore quod in capite consors inveni; nec otiosum fore in reliquis sanctis quod in patriarchis et apostolis concordare perpendi: dedi operam in hoc ipso, ut quantum Deus mihi concederet, testimoniorum concordiam compilarem; sed an scrupulosis mentibus satisfecerim, nescio": Cod. of Pavia, f. 37 2 (Tondelli, 1, 148). Whence, *Conc.,* l. 3, c. 1: "But we point new things out better if we examine the old ones more carefully" — "Sed melius ostendimus nova, si diligentius vetera perscrutamur" (f. 25, 4).

306. "s'inspirait d'une habitude d'esprit très répandue au moyen âge, celle de voir partout des symboles et des figures, ainsi que d'un principe exégétique universellement accepté, qui faisait de l'Ancien Testament la figure du Nouveau": E. Jordan, DTC, 8, 1432.

307. "L'idée de trois dispensations est naturelle, voire inévitable, sous une forme ou sous une autre, pour toute pensée qui se meut dans le cadre de la religion chrétienne": Henry Bett, *Joachim of Flore* (1931), 52: "in one form or another"! He cites Augustine (ante legem, sub lege, sub gratia) and Ambrose (umbra, imago, veritas).

308. "le penchant des esprits à voir en toutes choses des symboles et l'habitude de rechercher le sens allégorique"; "devaient conférer à la doctrine joachimite un lustre incomparable": R. Foreville, in Fliche-Martin, IX, 360.

309. "Joachim revient à la division traditionnelle": A. Pézard, *Dante sous la pluie de feu,* 391.

310. Smalley, *The Study,* 289.

311. "le dernier fruit"; "devaient être l'aboutissement inévitable de la méthode allégorique"; "la mise au point des règles de la raison et donc de l'exégèse par la théologie du XIIIe siècle"; "préserver l'exégèse chrétienne de verser dans l'hérésie et l'illuminisme": Spicq, *Esquisse,* 103.

312. M. W. Bloomfield, *Traditio* (1957), 270, 271: "The method was common, but Joachim, by pressing it to its uttermost etc."

313. *Ib.,* 270.

314. Anitchkof, *op. cit.*, 50, thus recalling the principle of St. Nilus: the monk is no longer a man, but an angel (or a demon).

315. Smalley, 287.

316. *Joachim de Flore* ... (2d ed., 1867), 59-61. Through a less serious misapprehension a recent historian attributes a work of this name to Joachim himself. Fr. B. Artz, *The Mind of the Middle Ages* (3d ed., 1958), 425: "In his *Eternal Gospel* Joachim declared that the epochs etc." For Joachim, the "eternal gospel" or "evangelium aeternum" is the same thing as the "Gospel of the Kingdom" or the "evangelium regni": *Ev.*, 86.

317. 1884, 356: "l'Évangile éternel dont (Joachim) se disait l'apôtre, mais qu'Origène admettait avant lui."

318. *De la philosophie d'Origène* (1884), 577-9; that Gospel "ne se manifestera pleinement qu'à la consommation des siècles."

319. *Ib.*, 583-4.

320. "Si quid autem superfuerit quod non divina Scriptura decernat, nullam aliam tertiam scripturam debere ad auctoritatem scientiae suscipi; quia haec dies tertia nominatur; sed igni tradamus quod superest, id est, Deo reservemus. Neque enim in praesenti vita Deus scire nos omnia voluit": *In Lev.*, h. 5, n. 9 (PG, XII, 460 C).

321. *In Jo.*, l. 32, c. 1 (425).

322. *Traditio*, 1957, 275: Such an author "denies any connection between the two, possibly to some extent because he is concerned with defending Origen's orthodoxy"; *ib.*: like Joachim, Origen "was an important exegete and theoretically allowed for a further revelation."

323. "Utrum simpliciter accipi debeat Evangelium per Scripturas propheticas a Deo repromissum, an ad distinctionem alterius Evangelii quod aeternum dicit Joannes in Apocalypsi, quod tunc revelandum est cum umbra transierit et veritas venerit, et cum mors absorpta et aeternitas restituta, considerato etiam tu qui legis": *In Rom.*, l. I, c. 4 (PG, XIV, 847 B): "the eternal years of which the Prophet says 'and I had eternal years in mind' will seem to belong to that eternal Gospel" — "cui aeterno Evangelio convenire videbuntur etiam illi aeterni anni de quibus Propheta dicit: et annos aeternos in mente habui (Ps. 76:6)." Origen subsequently compares that Eternal Gospel with the Book of Life from the Apocalypse, as well as with the books under consideration in Daniel and Ezekiel; again he thinks that one can call by the name Eternal Gospel the announcement that the Word made when he appeared to the angels, according to 1 Tim. 3:16 (847-8). Cf. l. 5, c. 1 (1020 BD).

324. "Sed videndum est, ne forte magis illud indicare videatur, quod sicut in Deuteronomio evidentior et manifestior legislatio declaratur, quam in his quae primo scripta sunt: ita et ab eo adventu Salvatoris quem in humilitate complevit, cum formam servi suscepit, clarior ille et gloriosior secundus in gloria Patris ejus indicetur adventus, et in illo forma Deuteronomii compleatur, cum in regno caelorum sancti omnes aeterni illius Evangeliii legibus vivent, et sicut nunc adveniens legem replevit eam quae umbram habet futurorum bonorum, ita et per illum gloriosum adventum implebitur et ad perfectum adducetur hujus adventus umbra": *De pr.*, l. 4, c. 25 (343-4). Starting with that last line, Jerome's translation: "For just as he fulfilled the shadow of the Law through the shadow of the Gospel,

so, since every law is an example and shadow of the heavenly ceremonies, one ought to inquire more diligently whether we rightly understand that the heavenly law, too, and the ceremonies of the supernal cult do not have their fulfillment, but need the truth of the Gospel, which in John's Apocalypse we read [as] the sempiternal Gospel, i.e., in comparison with this Gospel of ours, which is temporal, and [which is] preached in a passing world and a passing age" — "Sicut enim per umbram Evangelii, umbram legis implevit, sic, quia omnis lex exemplum et umbra est caeremoniarum caelestium, diligentius requirendum, utrum recte intelligamus legem quoque caelestem et caeremonias superni cultus plenitudinem non habere, sed indigere Evangelii veritate, quod in Joannis Apocalypsi Evangelium legimus sempiternum, ad comparationem vid. hujus nostri Evangelii, quod temporale est, et in transituro mundo ac saeculo praedicatum" (398 AB). It is difficult to know where exactly to insert this fragment drawn from the Letter *ad Avitum*. In any case, whatever hypothesis be enunciated, and whatever the precise sense to be assigned to it may be, it is clear that it has nothing in common with the theory of Joachim.

325. In X, 43 (222) the perspective is again that of the *De principiis,* and Origen refers to 1 Cor. 13:12 and to 2 Cor. 5:7, according to his usual practice of putting himself by turns at various points of view, depending upon the text he is commenting on or the circumstances that motivate his discussion, without much concern for verbal harmony.

326. "Voici ce qu'il nous est encore nécessaire de savoir: de même que la Loi ancienne contient l'ombre des biens futurs, de ces biens qui sont annoncés en clair par cette Loi lorsqu'elle est elle-même annoncée selon la vérité, ainsi l'Évangile, celui qui est estimé compris par le tout-venant, enseigne l'ombre des mystères du Christ. Au contraire, l'Évangile que Jean appelle éternel, et qui pourrait être dit proprement spirituel, pose ouvertement devant les yeux du cœur, pour ceux qui comprennent, tout ce qui concerne le Fils de Dieu lui-même, soit les mystères qui faisaient l'objet de ses discours, soit les réalités dont ses actions constituaient les figures énigmatiques": *In Jo.,* l. 1, c. 7 (12). *Ib.* (13) and l. 13, c. 17 (241): one can live Christianity and adore God corporeally or pneumatically; properly speaking, there is no opposition of the one to the other, but rather a progress from the one to the other in terms of deepening.

327. *In Jos.,* h. 9, n. 4, the comparison of Deuteronomy is different: there is no question of a distinction within the Gospel, but of the opposition between the unbelieving Jew and the believer: Deuteronomy is the Gospel itself (SC, 71, 250-4).

328. *In Jos.,* h. 3, n. 2 (132); compare h. 8, n. 4 (226).

329. *In Matt.,* 12, 3 (73). *In Matt. ser.,* 138 (284-6). *In Rom.,* l. 4, c. 2 (PG, XIV, 969 A); etc.

330. *In Rom.,* l. 6, c. 3 (PG, XIV, 1061-2). *In Cant. comm.,* l. 3 (182-4). *Entretien avec Héraclide,* c. 27-8 (J. Schérer, SC, 67, 106-8). *In Matt.,* t. 17, n. 19 (639-40); t. 15, n. 23 (417-9); etc. Cf. Greg., *In Ez.,* l. 2, h. 4, n. 14-5 (PL, LXXVI, 981-2).

331. 1 Cor. 13:12, a text that Origen often cites and comments upon. We have seen, above, in section 2 of this chapter, how Joachim wants first to understand this text with reference to the third state.

332. *In ps.* XXXVIII, h. 2, n. 2: "We walk in the image of knowledge and not in knowledge itself . . . , since we contemplate the glory of the Lord when his face

has not yet been unveiled.... Since, in my opinion, the expression is made about those who are better than the ones who used to live according to the shadow of the Law, scripture says 'though a man walk in the image'. This comes more clearly to mind from the words of the apostle Paul ... talking about shadow, image, and truth." — "In imagine scientiae ambulamus et non in ipsa scientia ..., quia nondum revelata facie gloriam Domini speculamur.... Quia, ut arbitror, de melioribus sermo fit quam erant illi qui secundum umbram legis vivebant, propterea scriptum est: quanquam in imagine ambulet homo. Quod clarius ad intellectum veniet ex sermonibus apostoli Pauli ..., umbram dicens et imaginem et veritatem (Heb. 10:1)" (PG, XII, 1401-3 BD). *In Lev.*, h. 10, n. 1: "The Law which used to have the shadow of future goods has given way to the very image of things" — "La loi, qui possédait l'ombre des biens futurs, a cédé la place à l'image même des choses" (441).

333. *In ps.* XXVIII, n. 25 (PL, XIV, 1051 C). *In Luc.* (XV, 1709 B). *De fide resurr.*, c. 109 (XVI, 1347 C). Here Ambrose's vocabulary appears more fixed than that of Origen, which is "still fluid," as we have noted, HE, 220. Despite M. Harl, 148-53, Origen's doctrine on the matter is no less clear and coherent. This classic view will be expressed by St. Thomas, *Summa Theologiae*, I-II, q. 106, a. 4, ad 1m: "Just as the first state is figurative and imperfect in relation to the state of the Gospel, so here [our] state is figurative and imperfect in relation to the state of the [heavenly] fatherland." — "Sicut primus status est figuralis et imperfectus respectu status evangelii, ita hic status est figuralis et imperfectus respectu status patriae."

334. The same duality of perspective is observed in the two theoretical texts on the three senses of Scripture, *Peri Arch.* and *In Lev.* (above, vol. 1, ch. 3.4; t. I, 199). In the second perspective, where it is a question not of the object but of the mode of knowing, the language of the New Testament "is not clearer than that of the Old" — "n'est pas plus clair que celui de l'Ancien" (Harl, 152); indeed revelation has not changed the conditions of our understanding in the flesh nor the laws of its functioning; but it in no way weakens the "historical vision of revelation" in Origen. Cf. *In Jo.*, l. 2, n. 6: "on becoming flesh, the Logos spoke through shadows, figures, and images" — "devenu chair, le Logos a parlé par ombres, figures et images" (60). *In Num.*, h. 27, n. 4 (261).

335. For Paschasius, *In Matt.*, l. 12, c. 28, all the "sancti Evangelii sacramenta," that are preached and taught on earth or openly declared in the heavens are the Eternal Gospel.

336. "Sed quid dicemus, quia illis haec evenerunt, a nobis vero aliena sunt?": *In Lev.*, h. 13, n. 2 (469).

337. "usque ad consummationem saeculi, et usquequo novus dies futuri saeculi et novae legis effulgeat, ardet unicuique nostrum lucerna haec": *Ib.* (470); "lux aeterna," "in futuro saeculo."

338. "qui frequenter in doctrina evanescunt": *Conc.*, l. 5, c. 71: "Their teachers ... who have frequently erred in teaching, e.g., Origen and many others" — "Illorum doctores ... qui frequenter in doctrina erraverunt, sicut Origenes et multi alii" (f. 100, 2-3). There are "dreams" in Origen: but they are not those of Joachim.

339. Ed. of the *c. Lombardum* (1934), 61.

340. "les premiers commentateurs de l'Apocalypse, saint Irénée et saint Justin": *Vie de Joachim de Flore* (1928), 210-1.

341. *The Study*, 292.

342. "Haec omnia Judaei vel sub Zorobabel expleta confirmant, quando facta est magna commotio, et regnum Chaldaeorum in Medos Persasque translatum, vel in praesentia Christi sui quem putant esse venturum. Nos autem, spiritualiter post crucem Domini Salvatoris completa memoramus, et quotidie fieri in his vel maxime qui, ad instar Lazari, peccatorum suorum facciis colligati, ad vocem Domini suscitantur" [Trans.: for 'facciis', understand 'fasciis' from 'fasciae'.]: *In Ez.*, l. 3 (PL, CX, 862 C; cf. 878 C).

343. *In Ap.*, l. 4, c. 14: "For by the Eternal Gospel we understand the preaching of Christ" — "Aeternum enim evangelium, Christi praedicationem intelligimus" (CLXV, 682 C).

344. "pro eo quod nunquam mutabitur, sicut Testamentum vetus est mutatum, sed, ut a Christo datum est, permanebit": *In Gal.* (CLXXXI, 1134 B).

345. "usque in illum aeternitatis diem sancta Scriptura credentium oculis proponitur, in qua Christus semper requiratur et fideliter inveniatur": *In Jud.*, l. 1 (Pez, 4, 161).

346. "cum, misericordia Domini, receperimus pristinam gloriam, imo cum receperimus pactum evangelii sempiternum": Rabanus, *In Ez.*, l. 7, c. 16 (110, 694 B). Ps.-Remigius, *In ps.* CIV: "so that, owing to the precept of the faith, [Jacob] might come to the eternal testament, i.e., the eternal promise" — "ut propter praeceptum fidei (Jacob) ad testamentum aeternum veniret, id est in aeternam promissionem" (CXXXI, 684 B). Alcuin, *In Eccl.*: "Now all things are discerned in a riddle and understood in part, until the perfect knowledge that will be unable to exist in this mortal body should arrive" — "Modo omnia in aenigmate cernuntur et ex parte intelliguntur, donec perfecta veniat scientia, quae in hoc mortali corpore esse non poterit" (C, 673 A). Anselm of Laon, *In Matt.*, c. 27 (CLXII, 1489). Cf. Augustine, *De div. q. ad Simplicianum*, l. 2, praef.: "But though the veil be removed because we shall have crossed over to Christ, nevertheless now we see in a riddle, but then face to face" — "Quamvis autem ex eo quod transierimus ad Christum auferatur velamen, tamen videmus nunc in aenigmate, tunc autem facie ad faciem" (Boutet, 510); etc.

347. "quamvis sancti evangelistae istis doctoribus priores fuerunt, nequaquam tamen minorem eis intelligentiam habuisse credendi sunt, utpote de quibus sacra auctoritas testatur, quod ipse Jesus aperuit eis sensum ut Scripturas intelligerent": *In Ap.*, l. 2, c. 2 (CXCVI, 752 AB). As to Christian life, see Hildegard, *L. div. operum*, P. 3, vis. 10, c. 7: "that those times may fall short of the pristine bravery of the apostolic discipline into a sort of womanish weakness" — "quod tempora ista a pristina apostolicae disciplinae fortitudine quasi in muliebrem debilitatem deficiant" (CXCVII, 1005 AD).

348. *L. moz. sacr.* (81).

349. Garnier, s. 2 (205, 570 D).

350. "Ecce novi et veteris Testamenti nos haec auctoritate probamus; quibus Berengarius tertium addit, quod non minus quam tertium de caelo cecidisse Catonem reprobamus. Eia ergo, post duo Testamenta, tertium hoc; et ideo tertium, quia ab eis alienatur": *Vita S. Wolphelmi*, c. 11 (CLIV, 413 CD).

351. Above, vol. 2, ch. 10.4.

352. "tria tempora mundi: vid., ante legem, in lege et in evangelio": *L. div. op.*, P. I, vis. 2, c. 33 (CXVII, 780 A).

353. "Praecepta Dei, quae sint ante legem, et in lege, et in gratia demonstrabat": ASS, mart. 2, 31 AB.

354. Anitchkof, 72, 151, 184-5, 220.

355. H. Bett, *op. cit.*, 52. [See note 307, above.]

356. "alia domus est in umbra, alia in imagine, alia in veritate": MBVP, 21, 493 CD. Always a bit complicated, Garnier of Rochefort will take up the threefold distinction so as to apply it otherwise: *s.* 12 (PL, CCV, 656 B).

357. Anitchkof, 398-9. Ottaviano, *loc. cit.*, 63, note 4: "and he recalls that Origen already held the theory of three human-divine historical cycles..., which he transmitted through Pseudo-Dionysius to Eriugena" — "et si ricordi che Origene sosteneva già la teoria dei tre cicli storici umano-divini..., che la lui passo attraverso il Pseudo-Dionigi all'Eriugena."

358. "partim lucet clarissima veritatis cognitione, partim obscuratur in symbolis"; "in qua nulla symbola, nulla figurarum obscuritas, sed tota apparebit clarissima veritas": *In Jo.*, fr. 1 (PL, CXXII, 1080 BD).

359. *Spec. Eccl., in adv. Dom.* (CLXXII, 1080 BD).

360. "Inde jam a nativitate Christi usque nunc, et quidquid restat usque in finem mundi, dies tertius gratiae est": *S.* 4, *in nat. Dom.*, c. 13 (CCVIII, 233 A).

361. The same goes for Berengaud commenting on Apoc. 9:15: "they were ready for the hour and the day and the month and the year" — "parati erant in horam et diem et mensem et annum" — and applying it to the four angels about to exterminate the impious of all the ages: "By the 'hour' is designated the time from the beginning of the world to the flood; by the 'day', the time from the flood to the Law; by the 'month', the time under the Law; and by the 'year', the time under grace" — "Per horam quippe tempus ab initio mundi usque ad diluvium, per diem autem tempus a diluvio usque ad legem, per mensem vero tempus sub lege, per annum autem tempus sub gratia designatur" (XVII, 861 AB). There is no fifth term possible in time.

362. "Tres ergo dies sunt invisibilis lucis, quibus interius spiritualis vitae cursus distinguitur. Primus est timor, secundus est veritas, tertius est caritas. Primus dies solem suum habet, potentiam...; secundus..., sapientiam; tertius..., benignitatem. Potentia ad Patrem, sapientia ad Filium, benignitas pertinet ad Spiritum sanctum": *Did.*, l. 7, c. 26 (CLXXVI, 836 AB). It will bear comparison with the three visions described *In Eccl.*, h. 1: "fire with flame and smoke; fire with flame but without smoke; pure fire with neither flame nor smoke"; "ignis cum flamma et fumo; ignis cum flamma sine fumo; ignis purus sine flamma et fumo" (CLXXV, 117-8).

363. "in nobis compleri debent": *ib.:* "Some of our days are the ones we have exteriorly; others, interiorly.... The exterior days ... pass; but the interior days ... can last to eternity.... First one day was a day of fear; the other day came, the day of truth; it approached but did not succeed, since the earlier day did not go away.... And when that [third day, the day of charity] came, it did not drive out the earlier ones. Blessed are those days!" — "Alii sunt dies nostri quos habemus exterius, alii quos interius habemus.... Dies exteriores ... transeunt; dies vero

interiores ... permanere in aeternum possunt. ... Primum unus dies erat dies timoris; venit dies alter, dies veritatis; accessit, non successit, quia prior non discessit. ... Et ille (dies caritatis) cum venit, priores non expulit. Beati dies isti!" (CLXXVI, 836-7). And c. 27: "That those mystical days have been fulfilled previously in the human race, and are to be fulfilled in us, and how" — "Quod dicti dies mystici prius in genere humano completi sint, et in nobis compleri debeant, et quomodo" (837-8).

364. H. Bett, 55-6: "a very close and striking one." Cf. 54-5, agreement with the three "dispensationes" of the *De sacr.*, l. 2, c. 11-2 (CLXXVI, 312-3): nature, law, grace.

365. Bloomfield recognizes it, 279-80; however, he continues to be impressed by the fact that for Hugh there is a history of redemption in it: *ib.*, and 308, note 256.

366. Spicq, *Esquisse*, 103.

367. Ghellinck, *Essor*, 2, 110.

368. Cf. George E. McCracken and Allen Cabaniss, *Early Medieval Theology* (1957), 253: "Herein there seems to be an anticipation of the three ages of Abbot Joachim of Fiore."

369. M. D. Chenu, *S. Thomas d'Aquin et la théologie* (1958), 96: "ambiguïtés possibles." Cf. *Th. au XIIe s.*, 82 and 282.

370. "Est autem tripartitum Trinitatis opus, a conditione mundi usque ad finem ejus. Primum est ab exortu primae lucis usque ad lapsum primi hominis. Secundum, a[b] eodem lapsu primi hominis usque ad passionem secundi hominis, Jesu Christi Filii Dei. Tertium, a resurrectione ejusdem usque ad saeculi consummationem, id est, generalem mortuorum resurrectionem. Et primum quidem Patris, secundum autem Filii, tertium vero Spiritus sancti proprium opus est": *De Trin. et op. ejus*, prol. (PL, CLXVII, 198-9).

371. "Plane inseparabilis Trinitas, unus Deus inseparabiliter operatur": *Ib.* (199 A). St. Thomas will spurn more strictly appropriations of this kind: 1a 2ae, q. 106, a. 4, ad 3m.

372. "Qua die vel hora credit homo in Christum et baptismi ejus percipit sacramentum, emittit Deus Spiritum suum, et creatur, ut, omni vetustate peccati abolita, jam nova secundum animam creatura sit, et praeter hoc facies terrae, id est terrenum corpus ... renovabitur in novissimo die resurrectionis": *De Trin. et op. ejus, De operibus Sp. sancti*, l. 1, c. 1 (1571 BC). This is the "twin-born resurrection of the dead" — "gemina resurrectio mortuorum" (1571 C; 200 A). In his edition of AF, lvii, Buonaiuti opposes the "static" vision of Rupert to the prophetism of Joachim; he considers this "mystico-monastic interpretation" with a certain disdain; at least he has the merit of reacting against a too frequent confusion.

373. There is in St. Bernard a different distinction, but one analogous to our point of view, *De gratia et lib. arb.*, c. 14, n. 49: creatio, reformatio, consummatio (PL, CLXXXII, 1027-8); *In Cant.*, 2, 23, n. 4: "creatio, reconciliatio, reparatio (in fine saeculi)" (CLXXXIII, 886 AC). For the possible influence of Bernard upon Joachim: B. Schott, "Die Gedanken des Abtes J. von Floris," *Z. f. Kircheng.*, 23, 165.

374. *De vict. Verbi*, l. 12, c. 9 (PL, CLXIX, 1470).

375. PL, CLXIX, 1095 A; cf. 203 A, 206 C.

376. "novo saltem genere exponendi": *Conc.*, praef.

NOTES TO PAGE 373

377. *Psalt.*, l. 2: "I have many things to tell you, but you cannot endure [reading 'portare' instead of 'mortare'] them now; but when the Spirit of truth shall have come, he will teach you all the truth [quoting John 16:12-13]. Lest anyone say that all these things have been completed generally on the day of Pentecost, let him hear the Apostle arguing and saying after that day: 'For we know in part and we prophesy in part, but when he shall have come, etc. So that there could be a time in which the Holy Spirit would speak to us more openly, so that we may begin to see the things that hitherto we have seen in a riddle face to face" — "Multa habeo vobis dicere, sed non potestis mortare modo; cum autem venerit ille Spiritus veritatis, docebit vos omnem veritatem. Ne quis in die Pentecostes dicat generaliter esse ista completa, audiat post diem illum disputantem adhuc apostolum ac dicentem: Ex parte enim cognoscimus et ex parte prophetamus, cum autem venerit etc. Opus ergo esse tempus in quo loquatur nobis apertius Spiritus sanctus, ut quae hactenus vidimus in aenigmate, incipiamus videre facie ad faciem" (f. 275, 2-3).

378. IA, P. 5, c. 21: "'And I John saw a city....' That vision and that descent must not be referred to the final hour in which the glory of Jerusalem will be manifest, but to the time of his birth, when through a hidden plan of the will of God she comes down like a daughter for the living and true God, according to the dictum of John.... 'But as many as received him...'" — "Et ego Joannes vidi civitatem.... Non est referenda ista visio et iste descensus ad horam illam ultimam in qua manifesta erit gloria Hierusalem, sed ad tempus nativitatis ipsius, quando per arcanum quoddam consilium voluntatis Dei descendit quasi filia Deo vivo et vero, juxta illud ipsius Joannis.... Quotquot autem receperunt eum..." (f. 217-8).

379. *Psalt.*, l. 2: "For, on being carried off into the third heaven, which signifies the life of the contemplatives, Paul said that he heard the secret words that it is not right for man to speak. But for how long? Was it for eternity? Far be it. It was rather for a definite time. For just as Moses put a veil on his face so that the children of Israel would not look upon him, so too in this passage Paul seems to have put a veil over his face. But just as the former veil was removed in Christ, so too the latter will be in the Holy Spirit. The second heaven is the New Testament, which was established among the apostles. The third heaven is the spiritual understanding, which teaches us to depart from the Egypt of the present age, to cross over through the northern road of the desert which leads to life, and go into the heavenly Jerusalem.... Now, since it is time for the veil to be removed..." — "Raptus enim Paulus in tertium caelum, quod vitam significat contemplantium, audisse se dicit secreta verba quae non licet homini loqui. Sed quousque? Numquid in aeternum? Absit. Sed usque ad tempus praefinitum. Sicut enim Moyses posuit velamen super faciem suam ut non intenderent in eum filii Israel, ita et Paulus in hoc loco velamen super faciem posuisse videtur. Sed sicut velamen illud evacuatum est in Christo, ita et istud in Spiritu sancto. Secundum caelum, testamentum novum, quod conditum est in apostolis. Tertium caelum est spiritualis intellectus, qui docet nos exire de Egypto praesentis saeculi, et transire per arctam viam deserti quae ducit ad vitam, et ire in supernam Hierusalem.... Nunc ergo, quia tempus est ut auferatur velamen..." (f. 253, 3 and 4).

380. "pacata erunt omnia et quieta"; "magnae virtutis est cum felicitate luctari": Pseudo-Anselm (Hervaeus), *h.* 3 (PL, CLVIII, 602 A).

381. "sexta aetas, quae nunc agitur, usquequo mundus iste finiatur"; "aetas summae pacis et quietis, in alia vita"; "requies sanctorum, quae vesperam non habet": Isidore, *Etym.*, l. 5, c. 38 (PL, LXXXII, 223 C). Bede, *Hexaem.*, l. 1 (XCI, 38 C). Ps.-Bede, *De sex dierum creatione* (XCIII, 219 CD); etc. Sometimes, as we know, the time before Christ was also divided into six ages; hence the time of the Church was the seventh, and eternity the eighth (thus Origen, *In Rom.*, l. 2, c. 13; PG, XIV, 907 D). Joachim recalls it, LF, Table XIX, *Mysterium Ecclesiae*. Or again, following Augustine's first way, the seventh age was that of the elect awaiting the resurrection of their bodies, and the eighth that which followed the resurrection. But these variants did not affect the traditional determination of the homogeneous time of the Church.

382. "sabbatum fidelium animarum in paradiso requiescentium": Gerhoh, *In ps.* XXXII (Van den Eynde, 150). Garnier, *s.* 19: "in celebrating the sabbath that has been left to the people of God, when the heavenly Jerusalem receives her citizens" — "in sabbatismo qui relictus est populo Dei, quando cives suos recipit caelestis illa Jerusalem" (PL, CCV, 698 D).

383. So Rupert (PL, CLXVII, 1568 BC); or Gerhoh, *De ord. donorum:* "In the seventh age, which does not succeed the sixth but runs alongside it, as it were, from which Christ . . . released peace upon the blessed souls" — "In septima aetate quae non sextae succedit sed cum ea quasi lateraliter currit, ex quo Christus . . . requiem beatis animabus aperuit, etc." (*Op. in.*, 1, 112-3). Cf. Amalarius, *Lib. officialis,* l. 4, c. 20, n. 5-6 (J. M. Hanssens, 2, 468).

384. So Bede, *De temp. ratione,* 8-10: "For men this age began when the first martyr Abel bodily entered the ground but spiritually entered the sabbath of perpetual rest" — "Haec aetas hominibus tunc caepit quando primus martyr Abel corpore quidem tumulum, spiritu autem sabbatum perpetuae quietis intravit" (W. Jones, 202); *Hexaem.*, l. 1 (XCI, 38 CD).

385. LF, Table XIX: "For Christ Jesus specifically began the sixth age, and once it was newly begun the Holy Spirit soon began the seventh. . . . And from this two orders and two lives have now been instituted in the Church . . . , one [order] in the active [life], the other in the contemplative. . . . Therefore both ages began to be activated at the same time . . . and each order walks together and runs together, following what was said of Peter and John. . . . But behold: those who began together do not pursue their course together, since when Peter died John remained in this life. . . . In the same way, when the life pertaining to Peter passes, the sixth age will be consummated; but the life pertaining to John will be confirmed and the seventh age will exist in its own brightness" — "Specialiter enim Christus Jesus sextam inchoavit aetatem, et ea ipsa noviter inchoata, mox Spiritus sanctus inchoavit septimam. . . . Et ex hoc jam instituti sunt in Ecclesia duo ordines et duae vitae . . . , unus in activa, alius in contemplativa. . . . Igitur utraque aetas sub eodem tempore agi caepit . . . et uterque ordo simul graditur et simul currit, secundum id quod dictum est de Petro et Joanne. . . . Sed ecce qui simul inceperunt, non simul pergerunt cursum suum, quia obeunte Petro mansit in hac vita Joannes. . . . Eodem modo, transeunte illa vita quae pertinet ad Petrum, consummabitur sexta aetas; firmabitur autem vita illa quae pertinet ad Joannem

et erit septima aetas in claritate sua." Cf. *ib.*, Table XVIII: "It is necessary to accept what the holy doctors say — that the two ages, namely the sixth and the seventh, go on together, either because the souls of the just come to rest in heaven once the six times have been completed, or because celebrating the sabbath has been given to the people of God, so that they might rest from the slavery of the Law, once the freedom of the Spirit had been obtained" — "Accipiendum est illud quod dicunt sancti doctores, agi simul duas aetates, sextam sc. et septimam; sive quia completis sex temporibus animae justorum requiescunt in caelis, sive quia datus est sabbatismus populo Dei, ut quiesceret a servitute legis, percepta Spiritus libertate."

386. See, e.g., note 223 above.

387. "Opinio tamen generalis, et eorum maxime qui nesciunt usum Scripturarum, illum tantum diem tenet vocari diem ultimum et diem judicii, in quo separandi sunt boni a malis sicut segregantur agni ab haedis, hoc est in generali illo et ultimo judicio mortuorum, quando sessurus est Filius hominis in sede majestatis suae. . . . Sed tamen discurrendum est quibus modis dicatur dies ultimus et finis mundi; ne totum quod dicitur deberi fieri die ultimo illi diei ultimo adscribatur, quod tenere et credere magni erroris est et non parvi periculi": LF, *Mysterium Ecclesiae*.

388. "secundum quod longe ante nos docuit sanctus Augustinus in libro *de Civitate Dei*"; "ipsum dicendum est finis mundi"; "totum pertinet ad diem judicii": *Ib*.

389. "Quod si tota sexta aetas dicitur finis mundi, quanto magis una generatio sive duae vel tres finis dici possunt, sive primi status, sive secundi, sive tertii!": LI, c. 7 (f. 9, 3).

390. "tertius status"; "dies novissimus"; "finis mundi"; "ultimus articulus finis": IA, P. 7 (f. 210, 1), etc.: "No one who reads those texts, howsoever carelessly, is unaware that, following the custom of the holy Scriptures, a 'day' usually stands for a time-period" — "Scripturarum more sanctarum, diem pro tempore solere poni, nemo qui illas litteras quantumlibet negligenter legerit, nescit."

391. *In ev.*, h. 38, n. 3 (PL, LXXVI, 1283 B).

392. Irenaeus, *Demonstration*, c. 89 (Froidevaux, SC, 62, 157). *Adv. Haer.*, l. 4, praef.: "But now that the latest times are at hand" — "Nunc autem, quoniam novissima sunt tempora" (PG, VII, 975 A); c. 22, n. 1: "But in the latest times, when the fullness of time's liberty has come" — "In novissimis autem temporibus, cum venit plenitudo temporis libertatis" (1046 B).

393. "Sanctis qui in illo tempore futuri sunt, nuda erunt omnia et manifesta. . . . Jam enim videre incipient facie ad faciem ea quae antiqui patres nostri viderunt per speculum in aenigmate; quia jam deleta erit iniquitas in populo Dei et statuta justitia sempiterna; quia jam regnabunt sancti Dei. . . . In tempore quoque illo dicetur veraciter ab electis . . . : 'Haec dies quam fecit Dominus, exultemus et laetemur in ea.' Et quamvis hoc proprie de die vel tempore octavo dictum sit, tamen et de septimo non incongrue dici potest, quia scriptum est: 'Benedixit diei septimae et sanctificavit illum . . .' ": *Conc.*, l. 5, c. 117 (f. 132, 4).

394. *Conc.*, l. 3, c. 6 (f. 41, 4). [Trans.: according to Lewis and Short, "coaptatio" — 'an accurate joining together' — is "a word coined by Augustine

for translating Gr. *harmonia*." Cf. *De Trin.* 4, 2 and *De Civ. Dei*, 22, 24. The phrase *concordia secundum coaptationem* is thus either redundant or means something like 'a harmony to the second degree'.]

395. IA, P. 3: "For just as [we] who, by God's gift, are imbued with the closeness of this light, implant something more manifest; just as the approach has been made plain to us by Christ's action in the history of the earlier Testament at the end of the first state and the beginning of the second, so too, at the end of the second state and the beginning of the third, in the letter of the New Testament and especially of this book [the Apocalypse], when the one whom the Father sends in the name of Christ opens it up, the seven thunders must utter their voices more sublimely, so that the promise of Christ in the Spirit may yet be fulfilled: 'when that Spirit of truth shall have come, he will teach you all truth'" — "Ut enim qui, donante Deo, vicinitate lucis hujus perfundimur, manifestius aliquid inseramus, sicut nobis, in historia Testamenti prioris, in fine primi status et exordio secundi, operante Christo, aditus patuit, ita in fine secundi status et initio tertii, in littera Testamenti novi, et maxime hujus libri (Ap.), aperiente eo quem misit Pater in nomine Christi, oportet septem tonitrua loqui sublimius voces suas, ut compleatur adhuc in Spiritu promissio illa Christi; cum venerit ille Spiritus veritatis, docebit vos omnem veritatem" (f. 139, 2). Cf. *Conc.*, l. 1, c. 1: "so that we may be able to understand what will happen in the last times through what we read has happened to that ancient people" — "ita ut per ipsa quae antiquo illi populo accidisse legimus, quae futura sunt in extremis temporibus intelligere valeamus" (f. 1, 2).

396. "méthode inédite": B. Allo, DB, suppl., 1, 322.

397. Thus Alcuin, *In Ap.*, l. 1: "Sometimes he starts with the coming of the Lord and before he finishes he returns to the beginning . . . repeating in various figures . . . what he had left out" — "Aliquando ab adventu Domini inclinat, et antequam finiat, ad initium redit . . . ea quae dimiserat . . . diversis figuris repetens" (PL, C, 1089 B); l. 4: "He goes back to the beginning of Christ's incarnation and briefly summarizes what he had dealt with there using different figures for the mysteries" — "Ad initium incarnationis Christi redit et ea quae exsecutus fuerat, mutatis aenigmatum figuris, breviter recapitulat" (1128 D); l. 5: "This expression goes back to the beginning of the faith and interweaves, under different figures, the struggles of the Church" — "Haec locutio ad initium fidei recurrit, et conflictus Ecclesiae sub aliis figuris intexit" (1152 A). Thus again Bruno of Segni, *In Ap.*, praef.: "There are . . . seven principal visions, and though their words be diverse, yet their intention seems to be almost the same. For the persecutions of the Church are narrated in them all, except that in the last are described the buildings of the heavenly Jerusalem" — "Septem . . . principales sunt visiones, quarum et si verba diversa, sententia tamen pene eadem esse videtur. In omnibus enim Ecclesiae persecutiones narrantur, praeter quod in ultimo caelestis Jerusalem aedificia describuntur" (CLXV, 605 BC); l. 2, c. 6 (633 C). Cf. Aug., *Civ. Dei*, l. 16, c. 15, n. 1 (4, 239). For the interpretation of the Apocalypse one may consult M.-É. Boismard, in Robert-Feullet, *Introd. à la Bible*, 2 (1959). For the medieval commentaries: W. Kamlach, *Apokalypse und Geschichtstheorie, Die mittelalter. Auslegung der Apokalypse vor Joachim von Fiore* (*Hist. Studien*, 285, Berlin, 1935). Cf. E. Waldstein, *Die eschatologische Ideengruppe* (Leipzig, 1896).

398. Again Bruno of Segni, l. 6, c. 21: "'Just as the bride bedecked....' For she is the one, the bride of that most noble bridegroom, whose praises resound so elegantly and so sweetly in the Canticle of Canticles" — "Sicut sponsam ornatam.... Haec est enim illa, et illius sponsi nobilissimi sponsa, cujus laudes in Canticis canticorum tam eleganter suaviterque resonant" (PL, CKXV, 7176 BC). Cf. Aponius, *In Cant.*, l. 12: "Everything that has been or is being done from the incarnation of our Lord Jesus Christ, was said from the start of the Canticle up to this verse in various mysteries and figures in the person of the Church" — "Omnia quaecumque ab incarnatione Domini nostri Jesu Christi acta sunt vel aguntur, a capite Cantici usque ad hunc versiculum in persona Ecclesiae aenigmatibus dicta sunt vel figuris" (H. Bottino — J. Martini, Rome, 1983, 244); he does not, however, cite a single exterior fact, nor trace any historical schema, nor anything of the like; what has passed since the Incarnation is the sanctification of the Church, baptism, the Eucharist, life in the body of Christ, the exercise of the Christian virtues.

399. The extraordinary success of the illustrations of the commentary of Beatus are well known. "L'iconographie de l'Ap. domine la sculpture romane" — "The iconography of the Apocalypse dominates Roman sculpture" (H. Focillon, *Art d'Occident*, 1938, 162). It already held a great place in Carolingian painting. "L'Apoc. tient à partir du VIIIe s. une place prééminente parmi les livres canoniques; elle constitue à ce titre un élément fondamental de la pensée religieuse occidentale à son origine": "At the beginning of the eighth century the Apocalypse held a preeminent place among the canonical books; in this regard it constitutes a fundamental building-block of Western religious thought at its origin" (Zumthor, 30-1).

400. "sanctae Scripturae pars uberior": Rupert, *In Ap.*, prol. (PL, CLXIX, 826).

401. "Librum illum ... clausum in mysterio sigillis septem aperuit idem Leo de tribu Juda; qui liber totius sanctae Scripturae apertus est, quia intelligentia ejus hominibus revelatur a Christo": Ps.-Ildefonse, *De cogn. bapt.*, c. 19 (XCVI, 120 A).

402. "Haec septem sigilla, Ecclesia habet soluta": *In Ap.*, l. 3, c. 5 (285).

403. "Tunc Agnus librum aperuit, cum opus voluntariae passionis implevit": Alcuin, *In Ap.*, l. 3 (C, 1122 B); cf. l. 5, c. 10: "The open book is the grace of the New Testament made manifest" — "Libellus apertus declarata gratia est Novi Testamenti" (1144 AB), and c. 11: "But [the temple] is said to be 'open', since Christ has already been born, suffered, raised, and elevated" — "Apertum vero dicitur (templum), quia jam natus, passus, suscitatus et elevatus est Christus" (1152 AB).

404. "In quo libro quid aliud quam sacra Scriptura signatur, quam solus Redemptor noster aperuit, qui homo factus moriendo, resurgendo, ascendendo cuncta mysteria quae in eo fuerant clausa patefecit": Hemmo, *De variet. librorum*, l. 3, c. 24 (CXVIII, 945 C).

405. "Neque illi qui in caelo sunt, id est viri ecclesiastici, neque illi qui in terra, id est philosophi et sapientes, neque qui subtus terram, id est maligni spiritus, hunc librum intelligere vel videre potuerunt, donec Christus eum aperuit et discipulis suis sursum dedit ut Scripturas intelligerent.... Leo de tribu Juda ad hoc vicit, ut librum aperiret et solveret septem signacula.... Postquam Scripturas intellexerunt, omnes sancti apostoli et doctores Christo Domino nostro gratias

egerunt, qui eis per Spiritum sanctum intelligendi sensum dedit." "Et septem quidem signacula sic sibi cohaerent, ut qui unum novit, nihil de aliis dubitet; cui igitur unum sigillum aperitur, nullum clauditur, et cui e contra unum clauditur, nullum aperitur. Qui enim Christi nativitatem non credit, nihil de passione, resurrectione et ascensione . . . intelligit, sic et in aliis. Septem ergo sigilla, septem sunt mysteria in quibus fides nostra principaliter continetur": *In Ap.*, l. 2, c. 5 and 6 (CLXV, 630 B, 633 C). *Ib.:* "Liber iste . . . utriusque Testamenti scientia intelligitur" (629 C). Cf. l. 3, c. 10 (658 C, 660 B).

406. *In Ap.*, l. 4, c. 14 (681 C).

407. "Septem quoque ejusdem libri signacula solvit, quando intellectum eloquii sacri fidelium mentibus reseravit; et quidquid de mysteriis suis lex et prophetae sub allegoriis praedicaverant, de his sc. quae per hominem temporaliter gessit, haec de se praedicat, et in se ac per se completa luce clarius indicavit": *De div.* s. 57, De septem signaculis per Christum solutis, n. 2 (CLXXXIII, 681 C).

408. "Antiquae umbra mortis in lucem transiit veritatis, ita vid. quod nunc oculis nostris opus redemptionis nostrae aspicimus, quod tunc occultis et obscuris prophetarum praedicebatur verbis, et praefigurabatur aenigmatibus": *H. dom.* 6 (CLXXIV, 47 C).

409. "Fuit enim liber iste quandoque signatus, quandoque clausus, sed modo apertus est": *S.* 25 (CCXI, 149 C). It was opened at the Cross (150 A).

410. *In Ap.*, l. 3, c. 4 (CLXIX, 909 BD). Cf. *In Reg.*, l. 3, c. 4: "The books were opened when the Holy Spirit was given to men through Christ's passion; through it the mysteries of the Scriptures were opened and made intelligible" — "Libri aperti sunt quando Spiritus sanctus per Christi passionem datus est hominibus; per quem aperta et intelligibilia facta sunt mysteria Scripturarum" (1145 CD).

411. *In Ap.*, l. 4, c. 7 (CLXIX, 969 BC).

412. Apoc. 20:12. Apringius, *In Ap.:* "And another book was opened, the book of life. The Lord Jesus Christ is the book of life and indeed life itself; it will be opened up and shown to every creature when he renders to each according to his works" — "Et alius liber apertus est, qui est vitae. Liber vitae et vita, Dominus Jesus Christus est; tunc aperietur et ostendetur universae creaturae cum reddiderit unicuique secundum opera sua" (Vega, 64); etc. Cf. Dan. 7. Godfrey of Admont, h. 15 *in Script.:* "The books are opened when one humbly manifests the secrets of consciences, i.e., the secrets of their hearts, which can be understood as 'books', to God in prayer and to one's superior and lays them open in confession. 'And another book was opened, the book of life': the hope of everlasting life . . . is fittingly represented by this other 'book'" — "Aperiuntur libri, quando secreta conscientiarum, secreta, inquam, cordis sui, quae per libros intelligi possunt, et Deo in oratione, et praelato humiliter manifestat et aperit in confessione. 'Et alius liber apertus est, qui est vitae': per alium hunc librum . . . spes vitae perennis congrue designatur" (PL, CLXXIV, 1127 D). One could relate this last revelation to that of the mysteries of Christ, the last of these mysteries consisting then in the last judgment and retribution; thus Bruno of Segni (CLXV, 629 B), etc.

413. "aeternae paginae"; "pagina caeli": Absalon, *s.* 43 (CCXI, 250 A), *L. moz. sacr.* (61, 339, 546).

414. "Aperta sunt prata, et apparuerunt herbae virentes": Honorius, *Quaest.*

et resp. in Prov., XXVII, 25 (CLXXII, 327 B): "Per prata, caelestia designantur mysteria, quae ideo prata dicuntur, quia pascua sunt fidelium; haec enim prata, hoc est divina mysteria, diu clausa fuerant sub signis ac figuris legalibus. . . . Aperta quippe sunt prata, quia per gratiam Domini Salvatoris revelata sunt caelestia sacramenta, quando "aperuit discipulis suis sensum, ut intelligerent Scripturas (Luke 24:45)."

415. "Per septem sigilla . . . plenitudo mysteriorum absconditorum designatur, quae latebant ante adventum Domini": *In Ap.*, c. vii, v. 1 (CCIX, 334 B). In the same way the prologue to the Gospels (12th century) published by O. Lottin, t. 5 (1959), 163. On that symbolic character: Apringius (9). Beatus (53). Rupert (PL, CLXVII, 331 BD). Gerhoh, *In ps.* XXXI (10); etc. Cf. Aug., *Civ. Dei*, l. 11, c. 31 (3, 130-2).

416. Autpert, *In Ap.*, praef. (405 CD); etc.

417. "a passione Domini usque ad finem saeculi"; "Filioli, novissima hora est": Aimon, *In Ap.*, l. 6 (PL, CXVII, 1158 A). Autpert (651 G).

418. Honorius, *Spec. Eccl., De paschali die:* "That day was called the day of life and resurrection because with its beginning Christ is foretold to have risen again along with many and with its ending there is no doubt but that the whole race will rise again on this very day" — "Istud autem tempus, dies vitae et resurrectionis appellatur, quo incipiente Christus cum multis resurrexisse praedicatur, quo finiente totum genus hac eadem die resurrecturum non dubitatur" (CLXXII, 929 A).

419. *ib.:* "The mysteries of [Christ] are opened up to his bride the Church through the key of David, are resolved by the Catholic expositors, and in this way are understood by the faithful" — "Cujus (Christi) mysteria per clavem David uxori Ecclesiae quotidie aperiuntur, a catholicis expositoribus solvuntur, et sic a fidelibus intelliguntur" (934 B). Cf. Ps.-Alcuin, below, note 472.

420. Beatus, *In Ap.*, l. 1, c. 1 (77).

421. *omnium mysteriorum secreta patuerunt:* Aug., *In ps.* LXX, s. 2, n. 9 (CCL, 39, 968); etc.

422. For Augustine, cf. Th. E. Mommsen, "St. Augustine and the Christian Idea of Progress," *J. History of Ideas*, 12 (1951), 346-74. When Honorius, *ib., Dom. in palmis*, writes: "Haec omnia (= the facts of the Old Testament) figuraliter praecesserunt et nostra tempora quasi digito demonstraverunt" (PL, CLXXII, 919 C), these "times" are uniquely those of the mystery of Christ; they are "ours" because this mystery is pursued for the whole length of the life of the Church.

423. *Ev.*, 81, 85, 128; cf. 123. Some also have taken his word too literally, IA, P. 4, dist. 7: "sum homo agricola" — "I am a farming man" (f. 175, 2). They have not recognized the allusion to Zech. 13:5.

424. Cf. Raoul of Coggeshall, *Chron. angl.:* "he published an exposition on the seven visions of the Apocalypse, when in a divine rapture, they say, whereas previously he had been almost illiterate" — "quamdam expositionem in septem visiones Apocalypsis edidit, accepta, ut aiunt, divinitus sapientia, cum fere esset prius illiteratus" (*Hist. de Fr.* 18, 76).

425. He seems by preference to cite Jerome. From Augustine, he cites the *City of God* and the *De Trinitate* above all; from Gregory, the *Moralia* and the *Dialogues*. He records, *In Ap.*, P. 5 (f. 181, 2), a terrible account from the *Dialogues*.

426. "Nos autem, per sanctorum Patrum itinera": *Psalt.*, l. 1 (f. 230, 3): "confess that God is one ... and triune according to the explication of those who underwent many labors" — "in quorum explanatione plures sustinuerunt labores, confiteamur Deum unum ... et trinum."

427. Cf. A. Crocco, *Sophia*, 23 (1955), 192-6 and 25 (1957), 218-32, who concludes against any influence of the Greeks or of Gilbert of Porré upon Joachim; his sources would be: chiefly Hilary, Jerome, Bernard, Augustine; no quaternarism (BTAM, 8, 1958, no. 244-5). His patristic culture is entirely Western.

428. *De art. fidei* (4-6); cf. Protocol of Anagni (Denifle, 138-9). Anselm, against the nominalism of Roscelin, *De fide Trin.*, c. 2: "How can he who does not yet understand how many men can be one man in species — how, in yonder hiddenmost and highest nature, can he grasp how it is that many Persons, each one of which is fully God, is but one God?" — "Qui nondum intelligit quomodo plures homines in specie sint unus homo, qualiter in illa secretissima et altissima natura comprehendet quomodo plures personae, quarum singula est perfectus Deus, sint unus Deus?" (PL, CLVII, 265 AB).

429. On the other hand, we know only that he was converted from the "world" to the monastic life at the time of a stay in Constantinople around 1158-9. On the Jews in Calabria in the 12th century: Buonaiuti, *Gioacchino da Fiore*, 114-9; H. Bett, 59-61.

430. *St. ans.*, 31, 201: "A person has arisen from among the Jews, one educated for many years in Judaism, which he seems not yet sufficiently to have vomited up.... And the barbarous name itself confers no mean authority upon the man; for he is called Joachim. We do not recall having heard this of any one in our days: that he should have kept as his baptismal name the one he had previously had in Judaism" — "Ex Judaeis orta persona est, in judaismo, quem necdum satis evomuisse videtur, annis pluribus educata.... Nec mediocrem confert ei auctoritatem ipsum barbarum nomen; dicitur enim Joachim. Quod de nullo diebus nostris meminimus nos audisse, ut in baptismo retinuerit nomen quod in judaismo prius habuerat."

431. Thus M. Bloomfield, 310, note.

432. "But in all these and like cases I leave aside the allegorical understanding, which you find it hard to be able to listen to, so that in 'Elijah' I say John is to be understood; in the 'daughter of Zion', the Church; in the 'people of Israel' the Christian people; and in 'Judah', the professors of the truth. I merely infer what can be proven according to the letter by the authorities of the Scriptures." — "Sed in omnibus his et similibus omitto allegoricum intellectum, quem vos difficile potestis audire, ut in Helia dicam accipiendum Joannem, in filia Sion Ecclesiam, in populo Israel populum christianum, in Juda confessores veritatis. Illud tantum inferam, quod possit probari secundum litteram auctoritatibus Scripturarum" (A. Frugoni, 86). Robert of Melun, *Sent.*, praef., completely recognizing that the spiritual interpretation of the Law was more difficult, reproached the Jews with not forcing themselves to enter into it (Martin, 31). See above, vol. 2, ch. 8.4.

433. *Neue Forschungen über Joachim von Fiore* (1950).

434. See article "Histoire," in *Catholicisme*, fasc. 20, col. 781.

435. *Les manuscrits de la mer Morte*, Fr. tr. (1957), 285.

436. "spiritu vehementi conteres naves Tharsis": Ps. 48:7. Cf. G. Morin, RB, 25

(1908), 91. On the contrary, e.g., Garnier, s. 2: "Naves (Tharsis) sunt cogitationes etc." (PL, CCV, 572 CD).

437. *Comm. on Daniel*, l. 4, c. 16-24 (M. Lefèvre, SC, 14, 293-311). See below, note 476.

438. Cf. N. Cohn, *The Pursuit of the Millennium* (1957). Paul Alphandéry, *Notes sur le messianisme médiéval latin, XI-XIIe s.* (Ec. pr. des hautes ét., sc. rel., 1911-2). Frédéric Macler, *Les Apocalypses apocryphes de Daniel* (1895).

439. Liutprand (10th century), *Legatio constant.*, c. 39. Cf. S. G. Mercati, "E stato trovato il testa greco della Sibilla Tiburtina," *Mél. H. Grégoire*, 1 (1949), 473-81. MGH, *Scr.*, 22, 375-8. PL, XC, 1181-6. Aug. and the sibylline oracles: Bardy, *Cité de Dieu*, 4, 755-9.

440. J. Bignami-Odier and M. G. Levi Della Vida, "Une version latine de l'Apoc. syro-arabe de Serge-Bahira," *Mél d'arch. et d'hist.*, 62 (1950), 125-48. J. Bignami-Odier, *Et. sur Jean de Roquetaillade* (1952), 193.

441. Paul Zumthor, *Merlin le Prophète* (Lausanne, 1943).

442. *Magni divinique prophetae B. Joannis Joachim abbatis . . . Vaticiniorum de apostolicis viis, sive de Romanis pontificibus historica et symbolica explicatio*, by Gregorius of Laude (Naples, 1660); according to the text edited at Cologne in 1570. The author says he was aided by Ferdinand de Stocco, "a prestigious theologian, philosopher, and celebrated mathematician, . . . an accomplished astrologer."

443. Macler, *op. cit.*, 100.

444. Cf. Samuel Krauss, "Un nouveau texte pour l'hist. judéo-byzantine," REJ, 87 (1929), 1-27. Buonaiuti, *G. da Fiore*, 118.

445. Third Lateran Council, under Alexander III (1179), Roger of Wendover, *Flores historiarum* (H. O. Coxe, 2, 1841, 400). Cf. Hardouin, 6, 2, 1678.

446. "Venerant aliquando deglutire Ecclesiam!": VB, c. 24 (52). On Saladin: IA (f. 10, 2).

447. Raoul of Coggeshall: "He seems to assign this fifth persecution not unfittingly to the fifth persecution of the Old Testament, in which the walls of Jerusalem were overturned and the temple burnt and the people captured by Nebuchadnezzar were led off to Babylon." — "Hanc autem persecutionem quintam quintae persecutionis veteris testamenti non incongrue assignare videtur, in qua muri Jerusalem eversi sunt et templum crematum est, et populus in Babylonem a Nebuchodonosor captivus abductus fuit" (*H. de Fr.*, 18, 76).

448. Gerhoh, *In ps.* XXXIII (Van den Eynde, 262-3).

449. He had begun to write previously; but it is only in 1188 that Clement III (if the letter is authentic) formally engaged him to undertake his work, and in 1191 that he left Corazzo. Cf. VB, c. 24: "A new kind of Saracens . . . looked as though it had been killed at one point, namely when in the days of Pope Urban there came to be a great movement of Christians from every part of the western Church going overseas to free holy Jerusalem. Now, however, provoked by our sins, the head that had seemed to have been killed has come back to life" — "Novum genus Saracenorum . . . aliquando visum est quasi occisum, cum vid. in diebus Urbani papae ex omni parte occidentalis Ecclesiae christianorum commotio facta est euntium ultra mare liberare sanctam Jerusalem. Nunc vero,

exigentibus culpis, caput quod apparuerat occisum revixit . . ." (53). Other allusions, IA (f. 134, 1); *Ev.* (244).

450. For an example in Origen himself: *In Jos.,* h. 17, n. 3 (SC, 71, 380; see Mlle. Jaubert's note).

451. *Indic. lumin.,* c. 21 (PL, CXXI, 535-6). See below, note 669.

452. *Dem. ev.,* l. 3, c. 7 (I. A. Heikel, 145-6). Dan. 7:18.

453. *De claustro animae,* l. 2, c. 18 (PL, CLXXVI, 1071-2).

454. ["On the concord of offices" — "under the Law" — "under grace."] Thus c. 88-9: "All this is related to the Christian people who are being ravaged by the Huns or Hungarians, but afterwards, once the enemy has been overcome, they are united in the praise of God by emperors professing the faith" — "Hoc totum ad christianum populum refertur qui ab Hunnis sive ab Hungaris vastatur, sed per fideles imperatores, superatis hostibus, in laudem Dei postmodum coadunatur" (CLXXII, 724 AD). One will also recall the place that Adam Scotus gave to the history of the Church and even to the history of England in his *De tabernaculo* (above, ch. 5.4).

455. "Ita veritas novorum cum typo antiquitatis congruit, ut concessiones pie per Constantinum principem Ecclesiae Dei factae, concessionibus de reaedificatione templi per Cyrum, Artaxercen et Darium factis concinnanter respondeant": P. 3, c. 31 (*L. de lite,* 3, 340).

456. "De statu Ecclesiae temporibus Henrici IV, quomodo temporibus et actis Antiochi congruat": L. 1, c. 16 (322-3), etc.

457. *L. de lite,* 3, 277. *In ps.* XXXIV: concord between primitive Christian history and current history; but it is no longer a question there of the two Testaments (V. den Eynde, 310).

458. "In reaedificatione Jerusalem portae quaedam principales mysticis nominibus appellabantur: quibus ea quae nunc in Ecclesia sunt agenda prophetalibus figuris praesignabantur. Cuncta enim quae illis reaedificationibus terrenae Jerusalem historialiter acciderunt, eorum quae nunc videmus prophetica quaedam signa fuerunt": C. 58; cf. c. 62 (*L. de lite,* 3, 167, 172).

459. PL, CXCIV, 55 CD. On these writings of Gerhoh: E. W. and A. J. Carlyle, *A History of Medieval Political Theory in the West,* 4 (2d. ed., 1932), 342-83. H. Jacobs, "Studien über G. von R.," *Zeitsch. f. Kircheng.,* 50 (1931), 315-77. A vigorous polemicist, Gerhoh is nonetheless a very reasonable theorist.

460. Cf. the editor's preface (PL, CLXV, 603-4).

461. *In Ap.,* l. 7, c. 12 (CLXIX, 1060-1).

462. *Mor.,* l. 23, c. 19, n. 34: "Now if we each seek our cases in the eloquence of Scripture, we find them there, and it is not necessary to seek what each specifically endures to be specifically answered by a divine utterance. For there an answer is given commonly to all regarding what we each experience in a special way." — "In Scripturae quippe ejus eloquio causas nostras singuli si requirimus, invenimus, nec opus est in eo quod specialiter quisque tolerat responderi sibi divina voce specialiter quaerat. Ibi enim omnibus in eo quod specialiter patimur, communiter respondetur" (LXXVI, 271 C).

463. It is in this way again that we want to understand that remark of a disciple of St. Gregory: "L'histoire humaine s'avance au milieu de péripéties d'avance explicitées sous nos pieds par l'Apocalypse." P. Claudel, *Jérémie* (inédit).

464. Rupert, *De vict. Verbi*, l. 10, c. 7: "The Spirit who is present in all of divinely inspired Scripture is also speaking to the Church" — "Spiritus ille qui, in omni Scriptura divinitus inspirata, praesens est et loquitur Ecclesiae" (PL, CLXIX, 1428 A). Rev. 2:7, 11, 17, 29; 3:6, 13, 22.

465. "Dum sua dicit, nostra praedicit, dumque lamenta propria per sermonem indicat, sanctae Ecclesiae causas per intellectum sonat": *Mor.*, l. 20, c. 1 (LXXVI, 135 D). This passage excited the admiration of the Protestant Basnage: *Hist. de l'Eglise depuis J.-C. jusqu'à présent*, 1 (Rotterdam, 1699), 465.

466. Tyconius, *reg.* 4 (F. C. Burkitt, "The Book of Rules of Tyconius": *Texts and St.*, 3, 31-54). Augustine, on the banquet-guest without a nuptial robe of Matt. 22: "That one [fellow] stood for one class" — "Unus ille unum genus erat"; *s.* 90, n. 4; *s.* 95, n. 6 (PL, XXXVIII, 561, 583). Cf. Paul Claudel, *Emmaüs*, 33: "Ce n'est pas la dernière fois que Caïn tuera son frère"; 39: "Ces premières pages de l'Écriture.... On nous présente, contractés en paraboles et paradigmes enchevêtrés, les principes moraux dont toute l'histoire de l'Humanité va être le développement." J. Steinmann, *Le livre de la Consol. d'Israël* (1960), 303: "Chaque individu torturé peut découvrir dans le Livre de Job la réponse existentielle à son destin" — "Every tortured individual can discover the existential answer to his destiny in the Book of Job."

467. "frequenter historia ipsa metaphorice texitur, et sub imagine mulieris vel unius viri, de toto populo praedicatur": *In Hab.*, l. 2, c. 3 (XXV, 1328 C).

468. *In Ap.* (54, 56, 78, 497-8, 503). Cf. Bede, *In Ap.* (PL, XCIII, 131-2); etc.

469. "*Nunc spiritaliter* intelligendum est quod *tunc specialiter* factum erit": *ib.* (416).

470. *In Threnos Jer.*, praef.: "They are deservedly called the 'lamentations of lamentations', since they are general, and thus they reach from genus to species and again the species is related to the genus" — "Istae merito Lamentationes lamentationum vocantur, quia generales sunt, et sic praetendunt genus ad speciem, ut rursus species ad genus refertur etc. *In Matt.*, l. 11, c. 24: "This is to be considered a rule of the Scriptures, since it says this not only of the apostles, but also of his chosen ones, as this general [feature]" — "Quae nimirum Scripturarum regula consideranda est, quia non de apostolis hoc solum dicit, sed de omnibus electis suis, ut hoc generale etc." (CXX, 803 D); l. 12, c. 28 (983 C).

471. "sermo Dei a specie ad genus transit": *In Ap.*, l. 1 (100, 1107 C); cf. 1089 C, 1097 D; l. 5 (1146 D, 1147 C, 1152 D). There is thus a possible return "a genere ad speciem": l. 2 (1104 B); l. 5 (1147 D).

472. Ps.-Alcuin, *In Ap.*, l. 5, c. 10, v. 9: "Though the holy preachers understood Scripture's mysteries about the Lord to have been already revealed in the person of John, nevertheless, since they still needed an explanation of how they pertained to him, they never said of the opened book: 'Take the book and drink it in' but rather: 'devour it'" — "Quamvis sancti praedicatores in Joannis persona jam revelata Scripturarum sacramenta de Domino intelligerent, tamen, quia adhuc qualiter ad eum pertinerent, expositione indigebant, nequaquam de aperto libello dicitur: accipe librum et bibe, sed: devora" (1146 A). Honorius, above, note 418. Gerhoh, *In ps.* XXXIV: "Et nunc rex Antiochus" (335).

473. "usque ad transitum sancti Martini"; "usque ad transitum Clodovei

regis Francorum"; "usque ad primum regni annum Caroli,": L. 2, c. 1 (MGH, Scr., 4, 116-7).

474. After various hesitations, Augustine adopted six earthly ages, at the same time as he repudiated all trace of millenarianism. Cf. G. Folliet, "La typologie du sabbat chez S. Aug.," R. des ét. august., 2 (1956, Mél. Bardy), 371-90. He has generally been followed. If one counted six ages up to Christ, ours was the seventh: Garnier of Rochefort, s. 19 (PL, CCV, 695 D, 598 D). Luke of Mont-Cornillon (CCII, 544 B).

475. Cf. Helinand, s. 5, which compares them to the five books of Moses, to the five fingers on Jacob's hand (CCXII, 522 D). L. moz. sacr. (165-6).

476. Aug., s. 259, n. 2: "Hence a sixth [day] is brought about from the advent of the Lord; we are in the sixth day. . . . But when that sixth day shall have passed, there will come a repose after that agitation" — "Ab adventu ergo Domini sextus agitur, in sexto die sumus. . . . Sextus autem dies iste cum transierit, veniet requies, post illam ventilationem " (XXXVIII, 1198). Ep. 36, c. 10, n. 24: the "spiritual sabbath" is "the eternal and true rest" (XXXIII, 147). Conf., l. 13, c. 35, n. 50: "the peace of the sabbath, a peace without sundown" — "pacem sabbati, pacem sine vespera"; c. 36, n. 51: "the sabbath of eternal life" — "sabbati vitae aeternae" (2, 407); etc. This doctrine, in certain authors of millenarianist tendency, took a precise chronological form: the six ages were six decades of centuries, and just as 5,530 years passed from the creation of the world till the Passion of the Savior, the "first resurrection" would take place 470 years after that; so Julius Hilarianus, Chronologia seu Libellus de mundi duratione (v. 369; PL, XIII, 1104).

477. "Sexta aetas, a Joanne Baptista usque ad adventum Heliae": Herbert of Losinga (G. S., 2, 62-4). Honorius (CLXXII, 156 D, 358 AB); etc.

478. "usquequo mundus iste finiatur": Isidore, Etym., l. 5, c. 38, n. 5 (LXXXII, 223 C). Cf. Theofrid of Corbie (end of 8th century), the abecedarian poem on the six ages "a proptoplasmo usque in novissimo" (Strecker, 449). Aside from the six days of creation, secondary symbols have been alluded to: the six successive husbands of the Samaritan woman (John Scotus: CXXII, 337 AD); the six urns of Cana (Rupert, Hildebert, Werner, etc.).

479. Cf. Origen, In Lev., h. 13, n. 5: "The number six has a certain closeness with this world" — "Habet enim propinquitatem quamdam cum hoc mundo senarius numerus" (475); In Ex., h. 7, n. 5 (SC, 16, 176-7).

480. *"signorum adapertio, generis humani plena redemptio":* Ps.-Hildefonsus (Justinian of Valencia?), De cogn. bapt. (PL, XCVI, 120 A).

481. Julian of Toledo, De compr. aet. sextae (XCVI, 537-86).

482. "Totum Ecclesiae tempus, ad illam continuatam resurrectionis diem referendum": Ps.-Alcuin, In Ap., l. 3 (C, 1115 D). Paschasius, In Matt., l. 5, c. 24: "The delay from the start of the Church's vocation until the end of the age" — "Moram a principio vocationis Ecclesiae usque ad finem saeculi" (CXX, 842 C).

483. "ab adventu Salvatoris usque in finem saeculi": Hervaeus (Ps.-Anselm, h. 3): "In this reading the status of the Church is described in summary fashion from the coming . . . according to the mystical understanding" — "In hac lectione (Matt. 24:22) juxta mysticam intelligentiam summatim describitur Ecclesiae status ab adventu etc." (CLVIII, 597 D).

484. "Ecce nunc tempus acceptabile, ecce nunc dies salutis": 2 Cor. 6:2. Cf. Jerome, *In Dan.*, l. 2 (XXV, 504 B); etc.

485. 1 Cor. 10:11.

486. Albert of St.-Symphorien, *De diversitate temp.*, l. 2, c. 24: "Since often in the Scriptures the finite is put instead of the infinite, 'a thousand generations' is to be taken to mean all generations" — "Quia in Scripturis saepe finitum pro infinito ponitur, mille generationes omnes generationes accipiendae sunt" (*Heinrici ep. ad Wecelinum*, beginning of the 11th century; CXL, 490 C).

487. *In ps. qui inhabitat*, s. 6, n. 7 (CLXXXIII, 199-200). *In Cant.*, s. 33, n. 13-6 (957-9). Cf. CLXXXIV, 1093-4, 1092. See below, note 511. One already found in Greg., *Mor.*, the elements of a distinction into three ages: persecutions, heresies, triumph of the Church.

488. Richard, *In Ap.* (CXCVI, 776 A, 782 A); on the horror of hypocrisy, "a most wicked crime, to be abominated before all others" — "crimen pessimum et prae ceteris abominandum": *Benj. minor*, c. 69 (50 B). Geoffrey of Auxerre, *s. in ps.* XC, n. 5-6 (Leclercq, *Etudes*, 133-4); etc.

489. Gilbert Foliot, *ep.* 287 (Giles, 2, 27-30).

490. Above, note 359. These were the four classic alliances: Adam, Noah, Moses, the Gospel. Cf. Irenaeus, *adv. Haer.*, l. 3, c. 11, n. 8 (PG, 889-90). For Absalom, s. 43, these are the four watches of the night of the Old Testament (PL, CCXI, 245-6).

491. *De quarta vig. noctis* (L. *de lite*, 3, 509-15, 519-22). On this evil and its historical causes: D. Van den Eynde, *L'œuvre littéraire de Gerhoh de R.* (1957), 169. Cf. Gilbert of Hoiland, *In Cant.*, s. 30, attacking Pope Alexander III, whose cause he nevertheless sustains against the antipope Victor IV: "Why are you selling what you yourself condemn?" — "Quid vendis quod ipse condemnas? etc." (PL, CLXXXIV, 159 CD).

492. *Chron.*, praef.: "I shall briefly explain the order of this history. . . . From the vision of Daniel it can be gathered that . . . four principal kingdoms . . . have existed from the beginning of the world and . . . will last in succession till its end . . . up to the end of times according to Methodius's estimation" — "Quo ordine currat haec historia, breviter exponam. . . . Quatuor prinicipalia regna . . . ab exordio mundi fuisse in finemque ejus . . . successive permansura fore, ex visione Danielis percipi potest (5-6) . . . usque in finem temporum juxta Methodium expectandum aestimans" (6). Cf. Jerome, *In Dan.*, c. 2 (PL, XXV, 504 AB). Ps.-Alcuin, *In Ap.*, l. 4 (C, 1129 A); etc.

493. L. 8, c. 1: "The city of Christ — having suffered violent persecution by the city of the world first under faithless tyrants; second, the fraudulent persecution of the heretics; third, the dissembled persecution of the hypocrites — will suffer under Antichrist the last persecution: violent, fraudulent, dissembled and, additionally, most severe of all" — "Civitas Christi primo violentem a civitate mundi sub tyrannis infidelibus, secundo fraudulentam haereticorum, tertio fictam hypocritarum tempore persecutionem passa, ultimam tam violentem fraudulentam fictamque ac omnium gravissimam sub Antichristo passura erit" (A. Hoffmeister, 393).

494. Text published by J. Leclercq, RSPT, 41, 631-7. Garnier, s. 4, develops it as well, but without a historical perspective (PL, CCV, 598 D).

495. Thus Autpert, *In Ap.*, l. 3 (470 A); l. 8 (590 G), etc.

496. *In Ap.* (PL, XVII, 893-930). Autpert, *In Ap.*, l. 4 (487 G).

497. "In primo igitur sigillo, decus Ecclesiae primitivae; in sequentibus tribus, triforme contra eam bellum; in quinto, gloriam sub hoc bello triumphatorum; in sexto, illa quae ventura sunt tempore Antichristi . . . ; in septimo, sumit initium quietis aeternae": *In Ap.*, l. 1, c. 5 (XCIII, 146 D); *ib., ad Eus.* (129-34).

498. Hervaeus, *In Is.*, l. 1 (CLXXXI, 67 B).

499. *In Ap.*, l. 4, c. 6 (CLXIX, 940 AB).

500. *In Cant.*, l. 4, on Apoc. 12: "the ancient serpent" — "serpens antiquus". "Arise, o north wind! . . . Come, wind of the south!" — "Surge, Aquilo! . . . Veni, Auster!" (CLXVIII, 960-1).

501. *In Cant.*, tr. 2: "Twelve times has a war been fought by the bridegroom or by the bride; six before Christ's coming and again six after Christ's coming" — "Duodecies a sponso vel a sponsa est pugnatum; sexies ante Christi adventum et iterum sexies post Christi adventum" (CLXXII, 452-3). The six wars "sub gratia" are: 1. The war begun by Herod and ended by the destruction of idolatry and the call of the Gentiles; 2. The one begun by Nero or Simon Magus and ended under Constantine; 3. The one between the Catholics and the heretics begun by Arius and ended at the Council of Constantinople; 4. "Nunc geritur sub religiosis inter veros et falsos fratres," begun long ago between Judas and Peter, "sed maxime invaluit quando claustralis religio institui caepit, finietur sub Antichristo" ["A war now being waged among the religious between those who are true and those who are false brothers, but which became especially intense when cloistered religion began to be instituted; it will be ended under the Antichrist"]; 5. "Erit sub Antichristo . . . , incipiet a praedicatione Eliae et Enoch et finietur in morte Antichristi" ["It will be under the Antichrist . . . , it will begin with the preaching of Elijah and Enoch and will end with the death of the Antichrist"]; 6. "Inter regem gloriae et regem superbiae. . . . In hoc bello rex Christus, cum universo exercitu angelorum adveniens, hanc Babylonicam civitatem diaboli comburet" ["Between the king of glory and the king of pride. . . . In this war, Christ the King, coming with the whole host of angels, will burn down this Babylon-like city of the devil"].

502. "Septem sigilla quae vidit Joannes . . . septem sunt status Ecclesiae sibi succedentes ab adventu Christi usquedum in novissimo omnia consummabuntur, et Deus erit omnia in omnibus . . .": *Dial.*, l. 1, c. 7 (CLXXXVIII, 1149 B).

503. *Ib.* (1149-60).

504. "multiplices sanctae Ecclesiae ab inchoatione gratiae usque in finem tribulationes, et sequentes beatitudinis retributionis": *In Ap.*, l. 2, prol. (CXCVI, 743 CD).

505. "Quae septem sigillorum apertione distinguuntur, ad sequentis temporis . . . ordinem referuntur. In quibus videlicet sequentibus electorum virtutes et reproborum in electos persecutiones et patientium tribulationes ab exordio nascentis Ecclesiae usque in finem mundi describuntur, et non simul, semel, sed secundum dispositionem et apertionem sigillorum et processum temporum paulatim et succedenter praedicta compleri et occulta manifestari multiformiter ostendunt": *In Ap.*, l. 2, c. 4 (760 D); c. 10 (776 AB).

506. *In Ap.*, l. 5, c. 9 (834-5).

507. "Effusio vero phialarum illationem signat divinae iracundiae in diversitatem hominum. Prima effusio est in terram, id est, Judaeam primum a fide reprobatam.... Secunda in mare, id est, gentiles fidelium occisores. Tertia in flumina et montes, id est haereticos sacrae paginae fluenta corrumpentes. Quarta in solem, id est, Antichristum, qui se dicit illuminare mundum. Quinta in sedem bestiae, id est, principes gentium, in quibus ipse Antichristus principaliter regnando sedebit. Sexta in flumen Euphratem, id est, reprobos baptizatos.... Septima in aerem, id est, daemones": *Ib.* (838 BC).

508. *Enarr. in Ap.* (CLXII, 1501 A).

509. "quam quidem ultimam fore esse putamus, in qua Enoch et Elias venturi sunt": *In Ap.*, l. 2, c. 7 (CLXV, 633-8); l. 3, c. 8 (647-50).

510. "Inspexi, et vidi omnem Ecclesiae fabricam, et quaecumque usque in saeculi consummationem futura erant": L. 2, c. 4 (625 B). *Glossa, In Ap.*, X, 5: "when there will be such desolation in the Church that even preaching will be eliminated" — "cum tanta desolatio erit in Ecclesia, quod etiam praedicatio erit ablata" (114, 729 C); *In* X, 9: "once the persecution was shown that will exist in the time of the Antichrist, and when thereby even preaching was taken away" — "ostensa persecutione quae erit tempore Antichristi, et inde etiam praedicatione substracta" (730 A).

511. "quatuor tentationes generales in Ecclesia et speciales in unaquaque anima": Leclercq, *Etudes*, 134. *In ps. qui inhabitat*, s. 6, n. 7: "A careful investigator will find ... these four temptations even in the general condition of the Church" — "Quatuor has tentationes ... etiam in generali statu Ecclesiae ... diligens considerator inveniet" (PL, CLXXXIII, 199-200).

512. "nomine tenus fideles": Anselm of Laon, *In Matt.*, XXVI (CLXII, 1478 D); *In Ap.* (1539 D, 1559 CD). Anselm of Havelberg (CLXXXVIII, 1154). Richard (CXCVI, 806).

513. *Neh.*, l. 3, c. 35 (XCI, 921 B).

514. *In Ap.* (297-9, 437, etc.).

515. *In Ap.*: the hypocrites are that part of the heresy "quae nunc inter agnos latitat" — "which now lies hidden among the sheep" (C, 1150 C).

516. "Dolens inimicus quod annulatus esset in patientia et perseverantia martyrum, aliunde se convertit et insanabilem plagam, quod est hypocrisis, induxit, quae hodie per omne corpus Ecclesiae serpit. Per pinnaculum, quod est cathedra doctoris, praelatos accipimus, qui quidem suadente diabolo per hypocrisim mittunt se deorsum, dum humiles Christi ministros se in habitu ostendunt, magisque Antichristo serviunt, omnes quae sua sunt quaerunt, omnes avaritiae student et tamen honorati incedentes, ei cui honorem deberent non deferunt": *H. dom.* 25, on the three temptations of Christ (CLXXIV, 170 AB). Hildegard represents the Antichrist as "alas simulationis hypocritarum habens" — "having the hypocrites' wings of dissimulation": *Scivias*, l. 3, vis. 11 (CXCVII, 715 B). Cf. Paschasius, *In Matt.*, l. 5, c. 24: "una fraus antichristorum" — "a deceit of the antichrists" (CXX, 811 C). Helinand, s. 3 (212, 497-8).

517. "spiritualis sapientiae gratiam suis multiformiter distribuit in diversitate et cursu temporis ut eos congreget ad unum statum aeternitatis": *In. Ap.*, l. 2, prol. (CXCVI, 743 A); etc.

518. *Div. off.*, l. 12, c. 24-5 (CLXX, 330-2).

519. *Epit. psalt.*: "The Body of Christ . . . grows into a perfect man in its members, until it rushes into the bedchamber of its bridegroom" — "Corpus Christi . . . in suis membris crescit in virum perfectum, donec occurrat in sponsi sui thalamum" — and the Psalms offer him all the sorts of food he needs at each age (CLXXII, 308-12).

520. *Scivias*, l. 3, c. 11 (CXCVII, 710 C).

521. *Vita S. Martini* by Luke, deacon of Leon, c. 1: "He produced two huge volumes entitled the *Concords*, because in them the authorities of the Old and New Testament come into harmony, and the judgments of the holy Fathers are brought to completion" — "Duo nimiae magnitudinis volumina edidit, quae Concordia nominantur, eo quod in eis concordent auctoritates novi et veteris testamenti, et sanctorum Patrum sententiae complentur." V. G. 55-60; 219-20; cf. 101.

522. *In Ap.*, c. 16 (CCIX, 379-84).

523. *In Ap.*, c. 6 (334-5).

524. "in quo reparatio nostra facta est"; "usque ad diem judicii": *In Ap.*, c. 17 (388 B); cf. c. 16 (383 A).

525. "mysteria Christi et Ecclesiae": *In Ap.*, c. 1: "quia per septem universitas figuratur, vel quia septiformi Spiritu illustratur" (301 C); c. 5 (329 C). Ps.-Alcuin, *In Ap.* (C, 1099 A, 1120 B, 1135 B).

526. "divina dispositio de humani generis reparatione": *In Ap.*, c. 5 (CCIX, 329-30): "to open this book is to redeem the human race" — "hujus libri apertio, humani generis est redemptio."

527. "magna ex parte adimpleta": *In Ap.*, prol. (299 B).

528. "aetates mundi sunt solummodo sex": *In Ap.*, c. 17 (388 A). Cf. c. 5, on the angels: "They bear witness to Christ in the annunciation, nativity, passion, resurrection, and ascension; they have testified to the judgment to come" — "Testimonium perhibent Christo in annuntiatione, nativitate, passione, resurrectione et ascensione, judicem venturum testati sunt" (332 C). The six wings that the living creatures of ch. 4 have are the six laws by which God lifts his Church up to heaven: the natural, Mosaic, prophetic, evangelical, apostolic, and "sexta, quorumcumque ut Augustini, Gregorii, Hieronymi, Ambrosii, Benedicti et Isidori" (328 AB). Cf. Ps.-Alcuin, *In Ap.*, l. 3 (C, 1118 D).

529. *Ep.* 56 (PL, CLXXXII, 162-3). Bernard adds: "I did not think that I ought to believe that for certain" — "Non me illud pro certo credere debere putavi" (162 B).

530. "Angelus Satanae jam mysteria iniquitatis operatur": *Parable* 2 (CLXXXIII, 770A).

531. "Superest jam ut reveletur homo peccati, filius perditionis": *In ps. qui habitat*, s. 6, n. 7 (200 B).

532. "En tempora ista plane faeda. . . . Intestina et insanabilis est plaga Ecclesiae. . . . Superest ut jam de medio fiat daemonium meridianum. . . . Ipse enim est Antichristus": *Ad clerum in conc. Rem.*, n. 5 (184, 1083-4). *Ad pastores congr.*, n. 9-10, it is no longer a question of the Antichrist but of the devil (1092-3).

533. Hora novissima, tempora pessima sunt, vigilemus . . .

Quid modo detinet? En ferus imminet Antichristus . . .
Hoc prope praedicat esse vel indicat Antichristum.

De contemptu mundi, l. 1, v. 1, 1026, 1064 (Hoskier, 1, 35, 36). This "monotonous music," by which Hauréau's ear was "agacée," i.e., "offended," seems to us to be at least perfectly adapted to its end, in the apocalyptic passages of the poem.

534. *Scivias*, l. 3, vis. 11 (PL, CXCVII, 716 C): "Filius perditionis in brevissimo tempore veniet, cum jam dies abscedit, sole in occasum latente, vid. cum novissimum tempus jam cadit et mundus tenorem suum deserit"; a bit earlier, the theme of aging; but a voice from heaven tells her: "Though . . . the world . . . be bowed down for its departure, nevertheless . . ." — "Quamvis . . . mundus . . . ad exitum suum incurvetur, tamen etc." (710 B).

535. Cf. E. Mühlbacher, in Gerhoh, *De inv. Ant.*, ed. F. Scheibelberger (1875), 2, 378-9.

536. Cyprian, *De mortalitate*, c. 25 (G. Hartel, 1, 313): "Mundus ecce nutat et labitur, et ruinam sui non jam senectute rerum sed fine testatur." Hilary, *C. Auxentium*, c. 5 (PL, X, 611 C). Jerome, *In Dan.* c. 2; *In Ez.*, l. 8, proem.: "The world is falling" — "Cadit mundus" (PL, XXV, 504 AB, 231 C).

537. Eucherius, *De contemptu mundi ad Valerianum:* "Postrema mundi aetas referta est malis, tanquam morbis senectus. . . . Urget nos dies ille, jam non noster tantum, sed et saeculi" (L, 722 CD).

538. St. Orientius, bishop of Auch, *Commonitorium*, l. 2:

Lassa senescentem despectant omnia finem
    Et jam postremo volvitur hora die.
Respice quam raptim totum mors presserit orbem.

(LXI, 995 AB). After having cited a few verses of the same poem, in *Le Bel Aujourd'hui* (1958), 332, Julien Green adds that this "is worthy of Horace" — "vaut bien Horace"; already Sigebert of Gembloux had admired the "sweet brevity" — "suave breviloquium" — in Orientius: *De script. eccl.*, 34 (CLX, 555 A).

539. *Reg.*, 3, 29: "In interitum rerum omnium, pensare debemus, nihil fuisse quod amavimus!" (MGH, *Ep.*, 1, 187). It is necesary to read the whole poignant page.

540. "Mundus senescit!"; "Mundi terminus appropinquat!": Marculfe (7th century), etc.

541. *In Matt.*, l. 11, c. 24: "in proximo est ut veniat hoc pejus ultimum malum" (PL, CXX, 803 A).

542. E. Pognon, *L'An Mille* (1947). X. H. Focillon, *L'An Mil* (1952), 50. We are less impressed than the latter author by such a "parole terrible" by an annalist of barbaric times, "dictated by a feeling that will grip people's hearts until the awakening of the West" — "dictée par un sentiment qui étreindra les cœurs jusqu'au réveil de l'Occident," or by some other such "brève et terrible phrase" by a Merovingian writer (16, 25), because we already find these formulas in Christian antiquity.

543. Paschasius, *In Matt.*, l. 11, c. 24: "Sed nondum statim" (CXX, 802 D). Hildegard (above, note 534). Cf. Greg. (below, note 548).

544. Eucher, *De cont. mundi:* "Patres nostri praeterierunt, nos abibimus, posteri sequentur" (L, 717 C).

545. Nicholas I to Charles the Bald (863): "Since . . . the latest perilous times are already imminent, let Your Excellency prudently take care lest perchance something still worse arise from this": "Quoniam . . . periculosa novissima ecce jam imminent tempora, provideat solers vestra sublimitas, ne ex hoc deterius adhuc forte aliquid oriatur" (PL, CXIX, 834 D).

546. Thus this complaint from the Spanish liturgy: "since the day of time is declining toward evening, the state of the world is hastening to its sunset, and our living corruptibly is tending toward its end" — "quia dies temporis declinat ad vesperum, et status mundi properat ad occasum, et vivere corruptibiliter nostrum tendit ad terminum" (*L. moz. sacr.*, 643).

547. PL, L, 722 B, 723 B: "Omnis fucatus splendor intercidit. Vix jam hoc habet mundus, ut fallat . . . Dirigenda est omnis animi intentio in spem futuri." Cf. St. Leo, *s.* 19, c. 1 (LIV, 186 A).

548. *Mor.*, l. 31, c. 27, n. 54: "For behold, since the day of divine judgment is at hand" — "Ecce enim quia divini judicii dies imminet" (LXXVI, 503 D). And in Bede, *H. eccl.*, l. 1, c. 32 (XCV, 73-4); etc. R. Manselli, *La lettura super Ap. di P. G. Olivi* (1955), has noted "the richness of the eschatological tension" in Gregory.

549. *In Ap.*, l. 10: "Velociter autem Dei Filius venturum se dicit, quia omne tempus vitae praesentis, quamvis longis morarum spatiis proteletur, tamen, quia non stat, sed transit, ipso suo cursu demonstrat quia velociter finitur. Propter hunc ejus velocissimum cursum, unius horae spatio a Joanne quantitas ejus definitur, cum per eum dicitur: 'Filii, novissima hora est'" (651 G). Aimon, *In Ap.*, l. 6 (117, 1158 A). Peter Damian, *Ep.*, l. 8, 8 (CXLIV, 476-81). Bernard of Cluny, I, 7: "Behold, that most dutiful, most venerable King is coming" — "Ille piissimus, ille gravissimus ecce venit Rex."

550. *Brevis chronica* (v. 814), in fine: "Si autem quaeratur a me quam longo tempore aut quot annis debeat praesens mortale saeculum perdurare, nescire me fateor, quia non uspiam me legisse reminiscor; et ideo nec de imperitia erubesco, quia lectione non doceor; nec de periculo formido, quia quae non lego nec praesumo, ne transgressor inveniar divini oraculi, qui apostolis de hoc interrogantibus ita respondit: 'De die autem illo et hora nemo scit'" (CIV, 925-6).

551. *In Matt.*, l. 5, c. 24: "Quotidie in vigilantibus operatur (Dominus) diem adventus sui, dum in animabus eorum qui illuminantur a lumine veritatis venit, . . . et cur celaverit diem et horam adventus sui, totum hic concludit, cum ait: 'Vigilate, quia nescitis diem neque horam.' Ac si dicat: Ideo volui vos nescire, ut semper vigiletis, et semper parati sitis, quando Dominus vester venturus est, ne tenebrae noctis vel torpor somni vos subrepat" (CXX, 832 CD). Beatus, *In Ap.* (325). Cf. the celebrated sermon by Newman, *Waiting for Christ* (1840).

552. *Chronica*, l. 2, c. 13; l. 7, c. 9: "Nos enim circa finem ejus positi, id quod de ipso praedictum est experimur, futurumque in proximo quod restat timendo exspectamus . . ." "Et nota quod haec nostra tempora, quae utique novissima creduntur tanquam prioribus sceleribus finem impositura, ac velut mundi terminum ex flagitiorum immunitate minantia, et ex opposito regnum Christi appropinquaturum prudentia, sicut quosdam, ut dixi, sceleratissimos ac mundi amatores avidissimos, sic alios zelo Dei ferventissimos ac caelesti desiderio

plenissimos habent; ut, sicut hos nequitiae spiritus, jam modicum tempus habens et ob hoc amplius ad vitia inflammat, sic istos dulcedo regni caelestis, quasi in januis posita, ad amorem suum magis alliciat." (Hofmeister, 82, 320). Cf. *Gesta Frid.* (Simpson, *ib.*, 9). Perhaps there was an evolution from the one work to the other (P. Brezzi, "Ottone di Frisinga," *Bulletino dell'Ist. storico ital. per il medioevo*, 54, 1939, 259); but this does not explain everything.

553. L. 4, c. 9: "Ita per divinam providentiam videtur esse dispositum, ut quae in principio mundi gererentur, ac deinde in finem, profluente tempore, usque ad occidentem rerum summa descenderet, ut ex ipso agnoscamus appropinquare finem saeculi, quia rerum cursus jam attingit finem mundi. . . . Primus homo in oriente. . . . Item post diluvium principium regnorum et caput mundi in Assyria et Chaldaeis et Medis in partibus orientis fuit. Deinde ad Graecos venit. Postremo circa finem saeculi ad Romanos in occidente, quasi in fine mundi habitantes. Postea summa descendit" (PL, CLXXVI, 677-8).

554. *Hist. de la civilis. fr., moyen âge, XVIe s.*, by G. Duby and R. Maudron (1958), 29 and 75 (G. Duby).

555. But at the same time, "through a decisive change which took place at the beginning of the 12th century in the most advanced circles of northern France, the apocalyptic and biblical inspiration, a contemplation of the divine transcendence, opened upon the Gospel, upon the sense of humanity in relation to God, and thence upon the sense of man and his natural environment" — "par un changement décisif, qui se produit au début du XIIe s. dans les milieux ecclésiastiques les plus évolués de la France du Nord, l'inspiration apocalyptique et biblique, contemplation de la transcendance divine, débouche sur l'Evangile, sur le sens de l'humanité en Dieu, et par là sur le sens de l'homme et de son environement naturel" (*ib.*, 108).

556. *Coll.*, l. 2, c. 35-8 (PL, CXXXIII, 581-6); s. 3 (722 C); *Occupatio*, l. 7 (A. Swoboda). Some have wanted to make of Odo an advance witness of the terrors of the year 1000; in the face of the spiritual miseries of his own epoch, he cried out: "Dangerous times have come, and at its end *the world is being pressed*" — "Tempora periculosa venerunt, et fine suo *mundus urgetur*" (585 C); but rather than urge the literal sense of those last two words, would it not be fitting to recall that Odo is still imitating St. Gregory? [Cf. vol. 2, chs. 9-10.]

557. In 991 (MGH, *Scr.*, 3, 672).

558. Cf. Zumthor, 135: The notion of "pseudo-prophecy" is "much used in the doctrinal pamphlets of the 12th to 13th centuries" — "très employée au XIIe-XIIIe s. dans les pamphlets doctrinaux."

559. Gerhoh, *De quarta vig. noctis* (v. 1167), c. 10, 14, 18 (*L. de lite*, 3, 508, 513, 515, 521); *In ps.* XXXVI (536). Cf. John the Carthusian, *ep.* 1 (PL, CLIII, 901 A); etc.

560. Greg., *Mor.*, l. 29, c. 7, n. 15 (PL, LXXVI, 484 C). Cf. Aug., *Civ. Dei*, l. 20, c. 19, n. 2 (5, 280).

561. Bernard on Anacletus, *ep.* 125, n. 1 (CLXXXII, 270 AB).

562. *L. de var. q.*, c. 79, n. 17 (Vega-Anspach, 227).

563. Hugh Metel, *ep.* 15, to a bishop on the vices of the time: "The times of the Antichrist are already at the door; these are his preambles; the time is approaching" — "Jam tempora imminent Antichristi, isti sunt ejus praeambuli, adpropinquat tempus etc." (347).

564. Beatus, *In Ap.* (108).
565. *Ep. Adsonis ad Gerbergam reginam de ortu et tempore Antichristi* (Ernst Sackur, *Sibyllinische Texte und Forschungen*, 1898, 105-6).
566. "Praecedit jam ante faciem Antichristi parare vias ejus"; "novi ac moderni Antichristi": Gerhoh, *De ord. donorum sancti Sp.* (*L. de lite*, 3, 276); *De aedif. Dei*, c. 69 (174).
567. "In Ecclesia jam multi Antichristi sunt": Beatus, *In Ap.*, l. 2, prol. (92, 108); c. 2 (154).
568. Bernard, *ep.* 336: "Ni fallor, Antichristus est iste, quem fames et sterilitas totius boni et praeit et comitatur" (on Abelard; PL, CLXXXII, 539 CD); *De vita Malachiae*, praef. (1073). Cf. *ep.* 330, on Anacletus and Abelard (535-6).
569. Martin of Leon, *In I Jo.*, citing Isidore, *Etym.*, l. 8, c. 11 (CCIX, 263-4). Cf. Tertullian, *De praescr.*, c. 4, n. 4 (SC, 46, 92). Hilary, *C. Auxentium*, n. 2 (PL, X, 610 C). Alvarus (below, note 669); etc.
570. Ed. M. Edélestant du Méril, *Poésies pop. du m. âge* (1847), 145:

Ut quid quaeris alium tibi praecursorem
Quam illum Britanniae perversum rectorem,
Qui triplici gladio contra jus et morem
Impudenter messuit sacerdotum florem?

571. 1 John 2:22.
572. L. 20, c. 93: "Omnis qui secundum professionis suae normam aut non vivit aut aliter docet, Antichristus est" (PL, CIX, 1052 BC).
573. Paschasius, *In Matt.*, l. 5, c. 24: "Multi pseudo-christi, et antichristi plurimi" (CXX, 812 A). Helinand, *s.* 3 (CCXII, 509 D).
574. H. I. Marrou, in *Lumière et Vie*, 11, 82.
575. *Ep.* 140, c. 8 (PL, XXII, 1172). *In Mich.*, l. 1, c. 4 (XXV, 1186 B). Cf. Gaudentius, *s.* 10 (XX, 916-7). Beatus, *In Ap.* (322-4). Rabanus, *In Deut.*, l. 1, c. 11 (PL, CVIII, 862-3).
576. "decepta vanitas"; "divinatio ficta": *In ps.* LXXXIX, n. 5 (CCL, 39, 1246-7). *Ep.* 199, to Hesychius, *De fine saeculi* (against Jerome; PL, XXXIII, 904-25). *De Gen. c. Manich.*, l. 1, c. 24, n. 42: "The sixth [age] has not been defined by any number of generations" — "Sexta (aetas) nullo generationum numero definita est" (XXXIV, 193). See the Note of G. Coulée, in *Div. Dei* (Bardy, 5, 763-5).
577. *In ps.* XXXVI, *s.* 1, n. 1 (37, 338).
578. *In Matt.*: "Contenta esse debet humana fragilitas, ne id appetat curiosius scire quod plurimum prodesse potest sine dubio etiam nescire" (PL, CXX, 828 B; cf. 805 C).
579. Isidore, *Etym.*, l. 5, c. 39: "Residuum sextae aetatis tempus Deo soli est cognitum" (LXXXII, 228 D).
580. Werner, 2d Sunday of Advent: "Tempora dinumerare non audemus.... Procul dubio latet quando finis erit" (CLVII, 742 CD).
581. Julian of Toledo, *Prog.*, l. 3, c. 1: "Judicii tempus vel diem Dominus nobis esse voluit incognitum" (XCVI, 497 B).
582. Hildegard, *Scivias*, l. 3, vis. 11: "Quod superest tibi, o homo, sciendum non est, sed in secreto Patris est" (CXCVII, 715-6).
583. Apringius, *In Ap.*, XX (57).

584. Greg., *Mor.* (PL, LXXVI, 77 A, 254 A). Alulphus (LXXIX, 1397 B, 1416 AB). Autpert, *In Ap.*, l. 9: "The number one thousand in sacred speech is regarded as perfect since totality is meant by calling something by this term; hence it is written: 'Of the word that he commanded unto a thousand generations'" [1 Ch. 16:15; Ps. 105:8] — "Millenarius numerus in sacro eloquio perfectus accipitur, quia appellatione ejus universitas designatur; unde scriptum est: 'Verbi quod mandavit in mille generationes.'" Autpert adds a confirmation drawn from his conviction that the world would last a little longer: "For though it is by no means to be believed that the world may last unto a hundred generations, what else is enfigured by a thousand generations but the totality of generations?" — "Cum enim nequaquam credendum sit quod ad centum usque generationes mundus extendatur, quid aliud mille generationibus, nisi generationum universitas figuratur?" (619 A). A thousand years = endless duration: Bruno of Segni, *In Ap.*, l. 6, c. 20 (PL, CLXV, 714 B).

585. A "determinatum pro indeterminato": Beatus, *In Ap.* (532, 536; cf. 164).

586. *Arca myst.*, c. 4: "Sexta aetas, quae nunc agitur, nulla annorum serie certa" (PL, CLXXVI, 688 A). Otto of Freising, *Chronicon*, l. 8, c. 2 (MGH, *Scr.*, 20, 279).

587. *In Ap.*: "Hic numerus propter sui perfectionem omne hoc praesens tempus significat a passione Domini usque ad finem saeculi" (CCIX, 400 A); etc. In the same way Daniel's totals are symbolic. How much time will be granted to do penance after the death of the Antichrist? God alone knows (360-1).

588. "Quoniam saepe Spiritus sanctus, ubi ad novissimi temporis finem praecucurrerit, rursus ad eadem tempora redit": Apringius, *In Ap.*, VIII: "Nor is the order of words to be regarded, since . . ." — "Nec aspiciendus est ordo verborum quia etc." (38).

589. "'Et factum est praelium magnum in caelo, etc.' Absit a fidelium cordibus, ut hoc praelium tunc factum credant, quando per superbiam antiquus hostis cum satellibus suis de caelo cecidit. Sed ab initio fidei christianae usque ad finem vitae praesentis fieri sine ulla dubitatione tenendum est."

"Quotidie draco de caelis in terram ruit": Ps.-Alcuin, *In Ap.*, l. 5 (PL, C, 1154 C, 1155-6). Martin of Leon, *in f. S. Mich.*: this great combat in heaven is, in the Church, the combat conducted against Satan by Christ and his saints (CCIX, 41A).

590. Martin of Leon, *In Ap.*, prol., on the visions of John: "He has seen images and within them has understood the truth" — "Imagines vidit et in eis veritatem intellexit" (300 A).

591. "In hac Apocalypsi non facile juxta litteram quippiam sentiendum est": Ps.-Alcuin, *In Ap.*, l. 1 (C, 1094 B); l. 4 (1128 C).

592. Apringius, *In Ap.*, XIII: "The time in which the Apocalypse was published must be understood, since it was at the time of Caesar Domitian" — "Intelligi oportet tempus quo Apocalysis edita est, quoniam erat tempore Caesaris Domitiani etc." (45).

593. Gerhoh, *Libellus de ord. donorum* (*Op. in.*, 1, 161); etc.

594. Aimon, *In Mal.*: "Having followed the doctors we say this of Elijah, though there are many even of our own who believe that he is about to come liter-

ally" — "Haec de Elia diximus, secuti doctores, quanquam multi sint etiam nostrorum qui credunt eum ad litteram esse venturum" (PL, CXVII, 294 CD).

595. Rupert, *De vict. Verbi*, l. 5, c. 15, on Jerome: "he implies that he agrees with the other doctors, who take the sense of Elijah's coming not literally but spiritually" — "doctoribus aliis, qui non secundum litteram sed secundum spiritum de adventu Heliae sentiunt, sese consentire innuit" (CLXIX, 1328-9). Rupert hesitates: *In Mal.*, IV (CLXVIII, 836 BC).

596. Martin of Leon, *In Ap.*, XI, 3: "multi alii praedicatores intelliguntur" (CCIX, 361 B).

597. *Sibylle Tiburtine:* "But the Lord will shorten those days because of the elect, and the Antichrist will be killed by Michael the archangel using the power of the Lord on the Mount of Olives" — "Adbreviabit autem Dominus dies illos propter electos, et occidetur virtute Domini Antichristus a Michaele archangelo in monte Oliveti" (E. Sackur, *op. cit.*, 186). The *Muspilli*, a High German poem of the 11th century, recounts the struggle between Elijah and the Antichrist, following Apoc. 11:3: Elijah kills his adversary, but he is wounded, and his blood, as it flows onto the earth, raises a conflagration there.

598. Martin of Leon, *In Ap.* (PL, CCIX, 360 CD). Cf. Anselm of Laon (CLXII, 1544 D). Greg., *Mor.*, l. 32, c. 15, n. 27 (LXXVI, 652-3); etc.

599. Anselm of Laon, *In Ap.*, IX (CLXII, 1532-3).

600. *Id., In Ap.*, XX (1572 C). Martin of Leon (CCIX, 399 CD, 400 C).

601. "Judicia Domini abyssus multa": Ps.-Alcuin, *In Ap.*, l. 5 (C, 1148 CD).

602. "caritatis expers": Ditmar, *Chronicon.*, a. 1016 (*Hist. des Gaules*, Delisle, 10, 133). On Gog and Magog from Ezekiel to Augustine: G. Bardy, *Civ. Dei*, 5 (1960), 777-8.

603. Jerome, *Q. in Gen.*, X, 2 (PL, XXIII, 450-1). Isidore, *Hist. Goth.*, recap. (MGH, *Chr. min.*, 2, 293-4); *Laus Spaniae* (267). Ekkehart of Aura, *Chr. univ.* (*Scr.*, 6, 120).

604. "Scythicae gentes": Bruno of Segni, *In Ap.*, l. 6, c. 21 (PL, CLXV, 714-5). Cf. A. Runni, *Alexander's Gate, Gog and Magog and the Enclosed Nations*, Mediaeval Academy of America (1932). Paul Meyer, *Al. le Grand dans la litt. fr. du m. âge*, 2 (1886), app. 2 (386-9). Arturo Graf, *Roma nelle memoria e nelle immaginazioni del M. Evo*, 2 (1883), app.

605. "Exsecranda gens! Monstrifera natio! Moribus et lingua barbari et feroces! Gens Ungarorum, omni bellua crudelior!": Berno, *Vita S. Udalr.*, c. 14 (CXLII, 1195 B). *Annalista Saxo*, a. 890 and 934 (MGH, *Scr.*, 6, 587, 598). Ekk., *Chr. univ.*, a. 900, 925 (*ib.*, 173-4, 183). Otto of Freising, *De gestis Friderici*, l. 1, c. 31 (*ib.*, 20, 368-9); etc. Cf. Johannes Duft, *Die Ungarn in Sankt-Gallen*.

606. Remigius, *Ep. ad episc. Vird.* (c. 890): "It is to be said that the opinion which has reached countless people both in your country and in ours is frivolous and contains no truth, since the people hateful to God, namely the Hungarians, is thought to be Gog and Magog. . . . The Jews and certain Judaizers among ourselves reckon Gog and Magog to be the Scythians. . . . Who doubts the whole [Apocalypse] to be mystical? So Gog and Magog are not to be understood corporeally as determinate peoples" — "Dicendum opinionem quae innumeros tam in vestra quam in nostra regione pervasit, frivolem esse et nihil veri habere, quia putatur Deo odibilis gens Hungrorum esse Gog et Magog. . . . Judaei et quidam

nostrorum judaizantes computant Gog et Magog esse Scythias. . . . Quis dubitat (librum A.) totum esse mysticum? Itaque Gog et Magog non gentes aliquae corporaliter intelligendae sunt" (CXXXI, 966-7). [Trans.: taking 'loqualiter' as a variant of 'localiter' and the phrase "non loqualiter, sed mente" as a whole to mean "not in place but in thought."]

607. "Non potest civitas abscondi supra montem posita": Jerome, *De nom. hebr.* (XXIII, 837). Martin of Leon, *In Ap.* (CCIX, 401-2). Bruno of Segni, *loc. cit.* Gerhoh, *In ps.* XXXIV (311). Cf. Alselm of Laon (CLXII, 1574 A). Richard hesitates; the expedition of Gog and Magog could have taken place "even according to the literal understanding" — "etiam secundum intelligentiam litterae" (CXCVI, 655-6).

608. Peter Comestor, *Hist. scol.*, L. Ez., V (CXCVIII, 1145-6). Nevertheless he believes in the legend of Alexander: L. Esth., V (1498 AB). Cf. Amolon, *C. Judaeos*, c. 12-3 (CXVI, 148-9).

609. Cf. Autpert, *In Ap.*, l. 6, on those who want to identify Gog and Magog: "This opinion is human, not divine. . . . So we ask, since the multitude of the reprobate is designated by the name Gog and Mag . . ." — "Haec sententia humana est, non divina. . . . Quaeramus ergo, cum reproborum multitudo Gog et Magog nomine designetur . . ." (623 GH). This provokes a modern historian to rejoin: "By watering down the sentences of the Apocalypse, he does nothing to heighten anxiety over them" — "En diluant les phrases de l'Ap., il ne fait rien pour en accroître l'angoisse": Gabriel Pepe, *Le moyen âge barbare en Italie* (tr. J. Gonnet, 1956), 263.

610. Rupert, *In Ap.*, l. 8: "Some relate that the spot in the sea from whence [the Antichrist] must arise is Babylonia. . . . But since this does not have any solid authority in the authentic Scriptures . . ." — "Tradunt nonnulli quod ille locus maris unde nasci debeat (Antichristus) Babylonia sit. . . . Verum quoniam hoc certam auctoritatem in Scripturis non habeat authenticis . . ." (CLXIX, 1065 AB). Nevertheless see Hugh, *In II Thess.*, q. 7 (CLXXV, 591 B).

611. Rupert, *De vict. Verbi*, l. 13, c. 14: how the Lord will kill the Antichrist "with the breath of his mouth" — "spiritu oris sui" (1496-7).

612. *L. de var. q.*, c. 78, n. 8 and 11 (223-4).

613. Abbo, *Apologet.* (PL, CXXXIX, 471-2). Abbo berated a superstitious preacher. Adson did not even have to combat a contrary opinion believed in his own milieu: Pognon, *L'An Mille*, xiv.

614. Thus again *In Ap.*, l. 6, c. 21: "By Gog and Magog, however, some wanted to understand the Getes or the Messagetes; others say they are the peoples that Alexander the Great shut off by means of the mountains, where now they have multiplied to an infinite multitude. This is what they say. We, however, expound those names etymologically, to the extent that it is consistent with the Faith: Gog is interpreted as 'roof' and Magog as 'from the roof'. And what is the roof, but sinners . . . ? And what is from the roof, but the vices and unclean spirits?" — "Per Gog et Magog quidam Gothos, quidam vero Getas et Messagetas intelligere voluerunt; alii vero dicunt gentes esse quas Alexander magnus montibus conclusit, ubi jam in infinitam multitudinem sunt multiplicatae. Haec illi dixerunt. Nos autem, secundum nominum interpretationem, salva fide, ista exponamus. Gog enim interpretatur tectum, Magog vero de tecto. Sed quid tec-

tum, nisi peccatores . . . ? Quid vero de tecto, nisi eadem vitia spiritusque immundi?" (CLXV, 714-5).

615. Martin of Leon, *In Ap.*, XI, 2 (CCIX, 358-9).

616. Cf. Odo of Cluny, *Coll.* 2, c. 38: "And so it is quite plain that these times have already come and that a malignant enemy is working out the mystery of iniquity; since the whole order of religion or Christianity has been changed, and impiety does not even deign to blush, but, when the multitude of the iniquitous have been strengthened, he seems everywhere to have carried off the chief of the places" — "Haec itaque tempora jam venisse jamque malignum hostem mysterium iniquitatis operari per hoc manifeste patet, quod omnis ordo religionis aut christianitatis immutatus est, nec impietas erubescere saltem dignatur, sed iniquorum multiplicitate roborata caput ubique locorum extulisse videatur" (CXXXIII, 586 AB).

617. *Mor.*, l. 28, c. 7, n. 15 (LXXVI, 484 C). Beatus, *In Ap.* (212).

618. *De inv. Ant.* (L. de lite, 3, 309-20, 338-9). Cf. *In Matt. ser.*, 31 (57).

619. a "curiosus secretorum inquisitor": *Ib.*, "Nemo tamen aestimet me per sermonem vel scripturam territare velle homines, quasi instet dies Domini; siquidem omnis sermo meus sine praejudicio futurorum sit, et novi a quo dictum est 'non esse nostrum nosse tempora vel momenta. . . .' Totus vero sermo noster ad hoc tendit, ut demonstret praeterita Ecclesiae et inimicorum ejus contra eam gesta sufficientia esse ad impletionem Scripturarum de Antichristo loquentium, etiamsi non veniat talis bestia, qualis vulgo aestimatur venturus Antichristus" (307-8).

620. "sobria cogitatio": *Op.* 59, c. 1 (PL, CXLV, 837 BC).

621. "alioquin, scire possent homines illius aevi tempus judicii": Bede, *De temp. rat.*, c. 69 (PL, XC, 574 CD). Alcuin, *De fide Trin.*, l. 3, c. 19: "It is not to be believed that the day of judgment is to follow immediately, so that what the Lord himself said in the Gospel may be fulfilled: 'But of the day . . .'" — "Non continuo dies judicii secuturus esse credendus est, ut adimpleatur quod ipse Dominus in evangelio ait: De die autem etc." (CI, 51 CD). The habitually recognized delay was one of 40 days; thus Adson (1298 A), Rabanus (1298, in the note). Peter Damian, *Op.* 59, c. 3 (839 C).

622. "nihil historialiter sonat": Ps.-Alcuin, *In Ap.*, l. 1: "His very words are thought to teach that he means nothing historical; for in heaven there are no craftsmen who make leather corselets, nor in heaven was a woman able to give birth" — "Quia nihil historicum sonat, ipsius verba docere probantur; neque enim in caelo sunt fabri qui loricas fabricant, nec mulier in caelo parere potuit" (C, 1089 A).

623. "nihil historicum est accipiendum": Aimo, *In Ap.*, praef.: "If the words are examined with subtlety, they are proven to teach that nothing in this revelation is to be taken as historical" — "In hac autem revelatione nihil historicum est accipiendum, quod verba, si subtiliter inspiciuntur, docere probantur" (CXVII, 938 C). Autpert, *In Ap.*, praef.: "Since, then, he is expressing nothing historical on the surface of this revelation" — "Quia igitur nihil in superficie hujus revelationis sonet historicum" (405 G).

624. "nihil historialiter factum narratur": Autpert, *In Ap.*, l. 7: "It remains therefore that he understands nothing in it to be reported as historical fact, but

rather, as in the Canticle of Canticles, mystic sacraments to be covered under a veil of tropic discourse" — "Restat ergo ut intelligat nihil in ea historialiter factum narrari, sed mystica sacramenta, sicut in Canticis canticorum, sub velamine locutionis tropicae contegi" (567 AB).

625. "les traditions et les légendes d'origine juive que saint Jean utilisa pour son dessin"; "qu'un point de départ": Cf. the pertinent remarks of L. Poirier, OFM, in *Sciences eccl.*, 11 (1959), 439, and in *Nouveau Testament* (the Canadian version), 1953, 630, note. And H. Cazelles and P. Grelot, in *Introd. à la Bible* (Robert et Feuillet), 1 (1959), 150.

626. It has been said that Gregory, interpreting Apoc. 12:7, portrayed Michael coming upon earth to offer the Antichrist single combat. He does speak of a combat between Michael and the devil, but he does not pretend to specify its forms. *In ev.*, h. 34, n. 9: "When the ancient enemy will be left to perish under the extreme penalty in all his power at the end of the world, he will be assigned to fight with Michael the Archangel, as is said by John, so that the one who had proudly exalted himself to a likeness of God might learn by being destroyed through Michael, that no one may rise to a likeness of God through pride" — "Ille antiquus hostis . . . , dum in fine mundi in sua virtute relinquetur extremo supplicio periendus, cum Michaele archangelo praeliaturus esse perhibetur, sicut per Joannem dicitur, ut qui se ad Dei similitudinem superbus extulerat, per Michaelem peremptus discat, quia ad Dei similitudinem per superbiam nullus exsurgat" (PL, LXXVI, 1251 AB). It is not necessary to believe, each time that our authors take up the expressions of Scripture, that their imagination takes them literally; however, it sometimes happens that they contradict themselves; thus, for Honorius, compare, in his *Spec. Ecclesiae*, the sermon of the 23rd Sunday and the sermon on St. Michael (CLXXII, 1076 D, 1011 B).

627. M. D. Chenu, "La fin du monde dans la spiritualité médiévale," *Lumière et Vie*, 11 (1953), 108-10.

628. "sub nominum sive imaginum figuris": Rupert, *In Ap.*, l. 1, c. 1: "[John] hinted that the heavenly mysteries are to be sought under the figures of names or images" — "Innuit (Joannes) sub nominum sive imaginum figuris caelestia debere mysteria requiri" (PL, CLXIX, 832 A).

629. Ps.-Alcuin, *In Ap.*, l. 1: "So our Fathers have taught that one should understand three sorts of visions: bodily . . . , spiritual . . . , intellectual . . ." — "Tres itaque visionum modos Patres nostri intelligendos docuerunt: corporalem . . . , spiritalem . . . , intellectualem. . . ." Jerome thinks that, for the Apocalypse, John got the third kind of vision; Augustine assigns him the second, "through the likeness of bodily images" — "per similitudinem rerum corporalium"; "but they will see which of them will have spoken more truly" — "sed ipsi viderint, quis eorum verius dixerit" (C, 1089 AB). Martin of Leon (above, note 590), Garnier, s. 3 (CCV, 583-6); etc. Cf. Aug., *Gen. litt.*, l. 12, c. 7-12 (XXXIV, 459-64).

630. "per puram intelligentiam, omni imaginatione remota": Anselm of Laon, *Enarr. in Ap.*: "He saw those things not in a material fashion, but by an intimation of the divine spirit he shaped together signs that fittingly designated the passions within his intellect" — "Non realiter ista vidit, sed divino sufflamine intimante, convenientia signa passionum designativa in intellectu suo configuravit" (CLXII, 1499 D). Richard, *In Ap.*, l. 1, c. 4 (CXCVI, 704 D); c. 1: the vi-

sions related by John are of the third kind, where "invisible things are pointed out by signs that are like sensible things" — "per signa sensibilibus similia invisibilia demonstrata sunt"; his book is full of "formal likenesses of temporal things" — "formalibus rerum temporalium similitudinibus" (667 B, D).

631. Beatus, *In Ap.*, l. 6, c. 13: "The time when the scriptural Apocalypse was published must be borne in mind, and then one also sees within it that Caesar Domitian existed then" — "Intelligi oportet tempus, quando Scriptura Ap. edita est, tunc et in hoc visum est, quia tunc Caesar Domitianus erat etc." (438).

632. "Templum Domini in caelo, Christus in Ecclesia": Bruno of Segni, *In Ap.*, l. 6, c. 11 (CLXV, 665 C). Richard, *In Ap.*, 4, c. 1: "What is more fitting for us to take 'the temple in heaven' here to mean than the marvelous sacrament of our redemption . . . ? Hence in sacred discourse 'the temple in heaven' is the divine sacrament" — "Quid aptius hic in caelo accipimus per templum, quam redemptionis nostrae mirabile sacramentum . . . ? Templum ergo in caelo est divinum sacramentum in sacro eloquio" (CXCVI, 797-8). Greg., *Mor.*, l. 32, c. 15, n. 25 (LXXVI, 651 AB); etc.

633. "Percussa tertia pars lunae, illi qui haeresi perierunt": Bruno of Segni, *In Ap.*, l. 3, c. 9 (CLXV, 649 CD).

634. "Manus angeli, dispensatio humanae redemptionis": Autpert, *In Ap.*, l. 5 (517 D).

635. "Sonus grandinis, flagellum persecutionis": Richard, *In Ap.*, l. 4, c. 1 (CXCVI, 798 D). Godfrey of Admont, *h. dom.* 8: "'There will be signs in the sun . . . , lift your heads . . .': according to the words of blessed Gregory this means they are bidden to let their hearts rejoice" — "Erunt signa in sole . . . , levate capita vestra . . . : secundum verba b. Gregorii, id est exhilarare corda jubentur" (CLXXIV, 55 C).

636. "Adjuvit terra mulierem: id est, Christus Ecclesiae suae dedit vires patiendi": *Glossa*, in XII, 16 (114, 733 A).

637. "Quod est mare, hoc abyssus, hoc bestia" — "Templum apertum, et tabernaculum, et caelum, hoc totum una Ecclesia": Beatus, *In Ap.* (418, 426, 465, 491).

638. "Haec omnia etiam juxta litteram magnam audientibus timorem incutiunt; sed non propterea figuratae elocutionis violenter ad litteram inflectendae sunt": Ps.-Alcuin, *In Ap.*, l. 4 (C, 1428 C).

639. Gerhoh, *De inv. Ant.*, c. 4 (313-4).

640. "veritate";"signis et figuris"; "coloratis sermonibus inumbratur": Gilbert of Nogent, *De pign. sanct.*, l. 4, c. 1, n. 2 (PL, CLVI, 666 B); c. 2, n. 2 (671 N); c. 8 (679 A). Here Gilbert is theorizing about what is current practice among our exegetes. Cf. Beatus (351).

641. Bruno of Segni, *In Ap.*, l. 1, c. 1: "'Et conversus sum, ut viderem vocem quae loquebatur mecum' (I, 2). Conversus namque ad spiritualem intelligentiam, beatus Joannes vidit et intellexit vocem illam, quae cum eo loquebatur. Convertere ergo et tu, quicumque hanc prophetiam intelligere cupis, ut nihil carnaliter sapias, totus ad spiritualem capiaris" (CLXV, 611 CD). Cf. Richard (CXCVI, 888 AB).

642. Sackur, 104-13. The Antichrist would not come so long as the French

realm, the heir of the Roman Empire, should last. The *De inv. Antichristi* of Gerhoh, for example, seems to me to be different, despite Ghellick, *Lit. lat.*, 2, 31.

643. Thus Martin of Leon, *In Ap.* (PL, CCIX, 359 BC). Cf. Amalarius, *De ord. antiphonarii*, c. 76 (CV, 1313 CD); etc. On the "translatio imperii": above, ch. 3.4.

644. His ego nec metas rerum nec tempora pono:
 Imperium sine fine dedi. . . .

Aeneid, l. 1, v. 278-9.

645. Again in 1720, Dom Calmet will write, *Dissertation sur l'Antéchrist*: the Roman Empire "subsists in the German Empire, whose emperors are the legitimate successors of the ancient Caesars" — "subsiste dans l'Empire Allemagne, dont les empereurs sont les légitimes successeurs des anciens Césars" (*Dissertations*, 1, 766.).

646. "sacerdotium et romana sedes": Cf. Otto of Freising, *Chronicon*, l. 8, c. 2 (MGH, *Scr.*, 20, 279).

647. *Ep.* 123, c. 16: "He who was holding back is coming from the midst, and do we not understand that the Antichrist is approaching?" — "Qui tenebat, de medio fit, et non intelligimus Antichristum appropinquare?" (PL, XXII, 1057). Cf. *ep.* 121, c. 11 (1037).

648. Beatus, *In Ap.* (116, 408); etc.

649. Cf. Tertullian, *Apol.*, c. 32, n. 1 (Waltzing-Severyns, 72); *De res. carnis*, c. 24 (PL, II, 829-30). On the nature of the obstacle, Augustine showed himself reserved; however, "it is not absurdly believed to be said of the Roman Empire itself" — "non absurde de ipso romano imperio creditur dictum": *Civ. Dei*, l. 20, c. 19, n. 3 (5, 282). Cf. Ambrosiaster, *In II Thess.* (PL, XVII, 456).

650. So Dempf, Grundmann, and on Gerhoh, H. H. Jacobs, *Zeitschr. f. Kircheng.*, 3 (1931), 315-88. Contr: Carmelo Ottaviano, ed. of the *L. c. Lombardum*, intr., 48-9.

651. "As an exegete," writes Bloomfield, *loc. cit.*, 270, "Joachim, especially on the Apocalypse, is an important figure in reorienting the interpretation of the Bible away from the Tyconian-Augustinian moral view to an historical, concrete view." It is difficult to comprehend how, on the very same page, he could write regarding the "method of allegory": "Joachim carried it to its final fruition."

652. IA, p. 1, c. 4: "And on that day the truth will be killed . . . but having been killed, it will live again, it will gloriously rise again; we cannot know this now; but those who are, as it were, to see it, will know" — "Et occidetur veritas in die illo . . . occisa vero, iterum vivet, iterum gloriose resurget; quod nos quidem modo scire non possumus; scient autem illi qui ut visuri sunt" (F. 95, 3).

653. LF, Table XIV: "Here is the seventh king, who is properly called the Antichrist" — "Hic est septimus rex, qui proprie dicitur Antichristus." Cf. IA, P. 6, on Apoc. 17:9-11: "If that beast were to have eight heads, it wouldn't say 'is the eighth and is of the seven,' but merely 'is the eighth.' For 'the eighth' would be expressed within 'the eighth head,' in which case it would be quite superfluous. But, since the seventh head of the beast will die and rise again, and even some of the rest of the errors of the other heads will appear at the same time, the worst congregation will indeed be 'the eighth' both according to time and succession, but nevertheless it will be 'of the seven,' since within it will be the collection of all

the errors that have been exhibited in the seven heads, during the reign of the seventh king, who will be the fountainhead of wickedness and the vessel of error, in whom the fullness of iniquity and the source of injustice will rest" — "Si haberet ista bestia octo capita, non diceretur: 'Ipsa octava est, et de septem est', sed tantum 'octava est'. Diceretur enim octava in octavo capite, in quo tantummodo superesset. Sed, quia septimum caput bestiae morietur et resurget, et etiam de reliquiis errorum aliorum capitum apparebunt simul, erit quidem congregatio illa pessima octava et pro tempore et successione, sed tamen de septem erit, quia in ipsa erit collectio omnium errorum qui in septem capitibus ostensi sunt, regnante illo rege septimo qui erit fons malitiae et vas erroris in quo requiescet plenitudo iniquitatis et origo nequitiae" (F. 196, 4).

654. Ev., 166: "At the end of the sixth age . . . the devil will be more viciously savage against them [the Christians], and finally, at the bidding of Christ the King, he will for a time lose the power to persecute the Church but yet at the end of the times he will return to the south" — "Diabolus . . . in fine hujus aetatis sextae atrocius seviturus est contra eos (christianos), et tandem, jubente rege Christo, amittet ad tempus potestatem persequendi Ecclesiam, qui tamen in fine temporum revertetur ad austrum."

655. "sabbatum requietionis": *Conc.*, l. 3, c. 7: "Just as Christ has suffered on the sixth day, so, in the sixth time-period does suffering come first, so that a sabbath of rest may follow" — "Sicut sexto die passus est Christus, ita sexto tempore praeit passio, ut sequatur sabbatum requietionis" (f. 42, 1).

656. LF, xiv: "But after the fall of this Antichrist there will be justice and an abundance of peace on earth, etc. Moreover the Jews and many peoples devoid of the faith will be converted to the Lord, and the whole people will be delighted at the beauty of peace, since the heads of the great dragon will have been crushed; and the dragon himself will have been imprisoned in a pit, i.e., amid the remnants of the peoples who will be at the uttermost limits of the earth" — "Post ruinam autem hujus Antichristi erit justitia in terra et abundantia pacis etc. Judaei quoque et multae gentes infideles convertentur ad Dominum, et delectabitur universus populus in pulchritudine pacis, quia contrita erunt capita draconis magni; et draco ipse erit incarceratus in abysso; hoc est, in reliquiis gentium qui erunt in extremis finibus terrae."

657. IA, P. 4: "Yet some of the doctors call the eleventh king the Antichrist, just as they do him who is called Gog; and yet this seems to me true, since the dragon is one, but the heads many; and the wickedness that he cannot achieve in one Antichrist, he will achieve in another" — "Nonnulli tamen doctorum, illum regem undecimum nominant Antichristum, sicut et illum qui vocatur Gog quod mihi tamen ideo verum videtur, quia unus est draco; sed multa capita, et malitiam quam non complet in uno Antichristo, complebit in alio" (f. 168, 2). LF, xiv: "though there is another similar and no less in malice, signified in 'the tail'" — "quamvis sit alius similis nec minor eo in malitia, designatus in cauda"; "Satan will be released from his prison again to persecute God's elect, since there will still be another Antichrist left, who has been signified in 'the dragon's tail'" — "Solvetur iterum Satanas de carcere suo ad persequendos electos Dei, quia adhuc residuus erit ille Antichristus alius qui designatus est in cauda draconis."

658. LF, xiv: "'And he shall go forth and seduce the nations which will be

upon the four corners of the earth, and he shall lead them into battle, the number of whom shall be as the sand of the sea, and they will encompass the camp of the saints and the beloved city' [Cf. Rev. 20:7-8]. That battle shall be in the last moment and in the tail of the dragon, since the heads will already have been crushed" — "Exibit et seducet gentes quae erunt super quatuor angulos terrae, e[t] adducet eos in prelium, quorum erit numerus sicut arena maris, et circumdabunt castra sanctorum et civitatem dilectam. Erit autem prelium istud veluti in extremo articulo et in cauda draconis, quia capita jam contrita erunt." *Ib.*: "He who is signified in the seventh head will come hidden, like John the Baptist, who was not known to be Elijah. He who is signified in the tail will come out in the open, just as Elijah is to come out in the open" — "Ille qui designatus est in capite septimo veniet occultus, sicut J. Baptista, qui nesciebatur esse Elias. Ille qui designatus est in cauda, veniet manifestus, sicut venturus est manifeste Elias."

659. *Ib.*: "Furthermore, [as for] the prince of the army of Gog, who shall be the ultimate Antichrist, God shall judge him and his army with fire and brimstone poured down from heaven. And the devil ... shall be sent into a pool of fire burning with brimstone, where both the beast and the false prophet ..." — "Porro princeps exercitus Gog, qui erit ultimus Antichristus, hunc et exercitum ejus judicabit Deus igne et sulphure superfuso de caelo. Et diabolus ... mittetur in stagnum ignis argentis sulphure, ubi et bestia et pseudo-propheta. ..." The same schema is given in Table XIX, where the two "judgments" correspond to Easter and to Pentecost.

660. Cf., in contrast, the *Chronicon* of Otto of Freising, l. 8, c. 5-19: from the return of Enoch and Elijah at the first judgment, everything passes very quickly (MGH, *Scr.*, 20, 279-87).

661. *Chronica magistri Rogeri de Hoveden* (W. Stubbs, *Rerum brit. Script.*, 51, 3 vol., 1868, 9-70).

662. Roger of Hoveden: "Melsemutus"; other forms: Muthselmutus, Meselmotus, Masimuth, Massamuti. It is about Masmudi. (Cf. LF, xiv.)

663. "qui proprie dicitur Antichristus"; "ultimus et maximus Antichristus": IA, P. 4: "he is to be called the greatest Antichrist" — "ipse dicendus est maximus Antichristus" (f. 168, 2).

664. *De vict. Verbi*, l. 8, c. 23 (PL, CLXIX, 1393-4). After Egypt come the wicked kings, over whom Elijah triumphs; Nebuchadnezzar vanquished by Daniel; Haman vanquished by Mordechai and Esther; the Greeks vanquished by the Maccabees.

665. *Ib.*, l. 12, c. 15: "That the dragon rose up against Christ seven times through impious men, and on the seventh was apprehended" — "Draconem septies per impios homines contra Christum insurrexisse, et septimo comprehensum fuisse" (1474-5). See also l. 4, c. 1 (1293-4), the concordism between the 7 heads of the Dragon and the 4 Beasts of Daniel.

666. One will compare Alvarus, *Ind. lum.*, c. 35 (CXXI, 555-6) and Joachim, IA, P. 4, dist. 4: "But the faithlessness of the Saracens, once begun so many years ago, persists in evil, and to the extent of its powers does not cease to attack the Christian name everywhere" — "Sarracenorum vero ex tot annis semel inchoata perfidia, perseverat in malo, et ubique christianum nomen impugnare pro viribus non desistit, etc." (f. 164, 4–165, 1). Already Bede, *Hexaem.*, l. 4 (PL, 91, 159 B).

Paschasius, *In Matt.* (CXX, 804 BD, 807 D). Cf. C. M. Sage, *Paul Albar of Cordoba, Studies on His Life and Writings* (Washington, 1943).

667. *Ind. lum.*, c. 22: "Nos vero, hoc Dei soli intelligentiae relinquimus" (CXXI, 536 D).

668. "Et hoc, in omnibus operibus prophetiae, ut opinor, debet intelligi, et sub varia repetitionis specie totius temporis causas uno prophetiae libro signare." "Ita uno sermonis textu unum indicat, ut alium non dimittat; ita priorem sermo ferit propheticus, ut novissimum intactum divinus non relinquat spiritus": *Ib.* (537 A, 538 A): "for knowledge shall be manifold, while the many will have opined many things, not in error but in discussion, and the causes of the divers time-periods will have been revealed in one speech. Hence I too opine one and the same thing often repeated very many times by means of the lofty signification of the figures and by the multiple induction of problems" — "multiplex namque erit scientia, dum multi non errantes, sed discutientes opinaverint multa, et diversorum temporum causae uno fuerint revelatae sermone. Unde et opinor sublimaria significatione figurarum, et multiplici inductione problematum, unam eamdemque rem saepissime multoties repetitam etc." (537 A).

669. "Quia adversus Christum humilitatis magistrum erectus est, et contra illius lenissima et jucunda praecepta, contumacia, verbere et gladio usus est, recte Antichristus vocatus est, qui christianae religionis apertissimus infamator et subtilissimus eversor inventus est": *Ib.*, c. 33 (552 CD).

670. *In Ap.*, XVII, 15 (CCII, 389 BC).

671. This "kind of understanding" (537 B) therefore consists more in an application of the Scripture, an application in which there always enters a certain "personal factor"; from whence arise formulas like this: "nor will it err from the path of truth if prophecy ... be expounded to them in the same way" — "nec a tramite veritatis errabitur, si prophetia ... in eos itidem exponatur"; "this is more befitting the wisdom of God and the Catholic dogma that we serve" — "hoc magis congruit sapientiae Dei et catholico cui servimus dogmati" (537 B); "and not disagreeing in the prefiguration of things, I have transplanted the whole image of the Antichrist into this [beast]" — "nec in rerum praefiguratione discordans, Antichristi totam in hanc (bestiam) imaginem transplantavi" (551 D).

672. IA, P. 6 (f. 215, 2).

673. This schema will be found again in Bonaventure, *In Hexaem.*, coll. 16 (Q., 5, 403-8). St. Thomas will resist it: Yves M.-J. Congar, *Le sens de l'économie salutaire*, 110-1.

674. "in ultima aetate sumus": Hervaeus, *In I Cor.* (PL, CLXXXI, 913 D); etc. When the author of the *Miracula S. Apri* (Adson?) writes, c. 7: "For us who now stand almost at the end of the age" — "Nobis autem jam pene in fine saeculi constitutis" (ASS, sept., 5, 71 A), his formula has a different, simply temporal significance. The same for Gerhoh, *In ps.* X (PL, CXCIII, 791 A); etc.

675. On the sense of these words of Paul: B. Allo, *Prem. Ep. aux Cor.* (1934), 234-5.

676. Martin of Leon, *In I Petr.*: "there is therefore one Church, one part of which went before the coming of Christ, and the other follows" — "una est igitur Ecclesia, cujus pars praecessit adventum Christi, pars sequitur" (PL, CCIX, 221 B); etc.

677. *De oper. Sp. S.*, l. 1, c. 31: "In those cases we were climbing from fear to wisdom; here, however, we are descending from wisdom to fear, possessing at the end of the age what we always fear howsoever perfect we be" — "In illis a timore ad sapientiam ascendebamus; hic autem a sapientia ad timorem descendimus, habentes in fine saeculi quod semper timeamus, quamlibet perfecti simus" (167, 1604 C); l. 9: "he who does not quiver in fear is wise" — "qui non trepidat in timore, iste sapiens est" (1805 C). Dom P. Séjourné, DTC, 14, 183, seems to force the meaning of this schema a bit, by hardening it so as to attribute a pessimistic aim to it; it is in any case far from Joachimite messianism.

678. Thus in the *Prologus Julii Flori de Historiis sive de aetatibus saeculi*, put at the head of the *Chronicle of Saint Maxentius* (from the creation till the year 1141) (Labbé, *Nova Biblioth. manuscr.*, 2, 190); the 14th and last "shows how the world falls short and to what extent we have arrived at worthlessness, so that now there is nothing more except for us to come willy-nilly to the end of the world and the judgment of the Lord" — "monstrat qualiter deficit mundus et in quantum vilitatem venimus, ut nihil jam superest, nisi ut ad finem mundi et judicium Domini, velimus, nolimus, veniamus."

679. "Potuit contingere ut quod tempore Hieronymi latuit incertum, postmodum revelante Spiritu fieret manifestum": *S.* 26, regarding the assumption (PL, CLXXVIII, 543 D).

680. *Dial.*, l. 2, c. 23 (CLXXVIII, 1200-2).

681. At the beginning of the century, Guibert of Nogent was already invoking the authority of Gregory Nazianzen. Cf. Ghellinck, *l'Essor*, 1, 212.

682. "Vetus Testamentum praedicavit manifeste Deum Patrem, Filium autem . . . obscure. Novum Testamentum manifestavit Deum Filium, sed submonstravit et subinduxit deitatem Spiritus sancti. Praedicatur postea Spiritus sanctus, apertiorem nobis tribuens suae deitatis manifestationem": *Dial.*, l. 1, c. 6 (CLXXXVIII, 1147-8). Cf. Van Lee, "Les idées d'Anselm d'Hav. sur le dév. du dogme," *Anal. Praemonstr.*, 14 (1938), 5-35. *Annuaire de l'Univ. de Louvain*, 1936-9, 750-3. Here Joachim is more reserved than Gregory Nazianzen.

683. "Attamen ipse quoque Spiritus sanctus ubique in evangelio Filio comparatur": *Dial.*, l. 1, c. 6 (1148 AB); and 5: "There were two transpositions made . . . which are even called two Testaments, and each of the two was made with the confirmation of an earthquake, because of their magnitude . . . , that from idolatry to the Law . . . , and that from the Law to the Gospel. . . . A third, future earthquake is foretold, when, once they have come to an end and been consummated, there shall be a transition to things that will neither be moved nor disturbed any longer" — "Duae transpositiones factae sunt . . . quae etiam duo testamenta vocantur, et utraque cum attestatione terraemotus, propter ipsarum magnitudinem . . . , ab idolis ad legem . . . , a lege ad evangelium. . . . Tertius vero terraemotus futurus praedicatur, quando, istis finitis et consummatis, ad ea transitus erit, quae neque amplius movebuntur neque concutientur" (1147 BC).

684. "salvo semper sanctae Trinitatis fidei fundamento": *Dial.*, l. 1, c. 6 (1149 AB). One will recall also that Anselm limited his views on the development in that treatise "On the unity of the faith and the multiplicity among the ways of living from the time of Abel to that of the latest among the elect" — "De unitate fidei et multiformitate vivendi a tempore Abel usque ad novissimum electum," which

forms Book I of the *Dialogues:* in it he justified "the many diverse novelties in religion" — "tam diversas religionis novitates" that appeared in the Church "here, there and everywhere through succeeding ages" — "passim ubique per successiones temporum" (1141-2).

685. *Ib.:* "For indeed in this way the faith of the Holy Trinity, having been measured out little by little in accordance with the virtue of believers and as it were distributed piecemeal, and growing into wholeness, has finally been brought to perfection" — "Ita quippe fides sanctae Trinitatis secundum virtutem credentium paulatim mensurata, et quasi particulariter distributa, et in integrum crescens, tandem perfecta est" (1148). C. 13: "Moreover, it was necessary that signs of spiritual graces that were clarifying the truth itself more and more should grow as the times advanced, and in this way knowledge of the truth would increase from one time to another along with the effectiveness of salvation" — "Oportebat autem ut secundum processum temporum crescerent signa spiritualium gratiarum, quae magis ac magis ipsam veritatem declararent, et sic cum effectu salutis incrementum acciperet de tempore in tempus cognitio veritatis" (1160 A). Cf. Kurt Fina, "Anselm von Hav., Untersuch. zur Kircher- und Geistesgesch. des 12. Jahrh.," *Anal. Praem.,* 32 (1956), 33 (1957), 34 (1958); especially 34, 13-41, "Die Geschichtstheologie Anselms v. Hav."

686. *Defl.,* l. 1: "The Sacraments of the old Law would remain for some time, between the baptism and the death of Jesus: For it was necessary that even those things that were to be brought to an end should at any event in no way be cast down suddenly, but should rather be let go of little by little and, as it were, with a certain reverence, so that they might be shown to have been good in their time; and likewise those that were to be initiated should not be made authoritative suddenly, but should be begun with delay and gravity, lest they suddenly be reckoned as things foreign and consequently invasive" — "Oportuit enim ut et illa quae finienda erant, nequaquam subito vel praecipitarentur, sed paulatim et quasi cum quadam reverentia dimitterentur, ut ostenderentur bona fuisse tempore suo; et similiter quae incipienda erant, non subito in auctoritatem assumerentur, sed cum mora et gravitate inchoarentur, ne velut aliena et propter rem aliunde inducta subito putarentur" (PL, CLVII, 760 B).

687. *S.* 16: "After the incarnate Son offered to make himself known to the world . . . , then . . . the world began to have knowledge . . . of two Persons. . . . But it still knew nothing of the Holy Spirit. But after the Holy Spirit appeared to the world in tongues of fire . . . , then he first made known the mystery of the Holy Trinity. . . . Hence, though there are no stages in the Holy Trinity itself, nevertheless it came to human knowledge, if I may say so, through various stages" — "Postquam Filius incarnatus mundo se ipsum cognoscendum praebuit . . . , tunc duarum personarum notitiam . . . mundus habere caepit. . . . Sed de Spiritu sancto nihil adhuc cognovit. Postquam vero Spiritus sanctus in igneis linguis mundo apparuit . . . , tunc primo sanctae Trinitatis mysterium innotuit. . . . Sic ergo sanctae Trinitatis quamvis in se nullos gradus habeat, tamen per quosdam, ut ita dicam, gradus ad humanam pervenit notitiam" (212, 611-2).

688. *Psalt.,* dist. 6 (f. 239, 3-4).

689. "nunc ex parte inchoata in primitiis contemplationis": *In Hier. eccl.,* l. 2, prol. (PL, CXXII, 265-6). *In Jo.,* fr. 1: "the third [hierarchy], namely the heavenly,

already beginning in this life and to be brought to perfection in the other life" — "tertiam, caelestem dico, jam in hac vita inchoantem et in altera vita perficiendam" (300 BC).

690. "toute une évolution religieuse était contenue dans ces vues"; "vision historique": *L'Italie mystique*, 59-61 and 75.

691. *Medieval Faith and Fable* (1932), 291-2.

692. Paul Alphandéry and Alphonse Dupront, *La chrétienté et l'idée de croisade*, 2 (1959), 104, note 2.

693. Thus Ruysbrock and many others. Thus already, among others, St. Peter Damian; Leclercq, *S. Pierre Damien*, 249-52. Cf. Gerhoh, *In ps.* XXXVII (Van den Eynde, 625-6).

694. *De per. civ. Dei*, tr. 15 (PL, CCIV, 379 BD). Cf., tr. 12, the beautiful but somewhat complicated symbol of "the clock of Christ" (344 AB). It is again a variation on a theme from Origen.

695. "Finietur ergo Testamentum novum, quia perficietur; nam cum ipse de quo loquitur visus fuerit, ejusdem Testamenti verba cessabunt. Unde et sanctae Ecclesiae veri luminis diem quasi tempus vernale praestolanti, per sponsi vocem dicitur: "Surge, propera, amica mea." "Quemadmodum implevit legem per mysterium incarnationis et perfectae humanitatis suae, ita Testamenti novi promissa impleturus est per ostensam gloriam claritatis suae." Greg., *In Ez.*, l. 2, h. 4, n. 15 (LXXVI, 981-2). Rabanus, *In Ez.*, l. 14 (CX, 907 A).

696. "Praecepta, alia legalia, alia evangelica, alia monastica.... Prima incipiunt, secunda proficiunt, tertia perficiunt.... Veteribus, vetera servantibus praecepta, terrena bona promittebantur; credentibus vero sub gratia ... aeternorum promissio est facta; religiosis vero, arctiori via gradientibus, merito debetur copiosior benedictio": Dist. 2 (Leclercq, *S. er.*, 10, 336).

697. "Legalia praecepta non prosunt sine evangelicis; evangelica non sunt sine legalibus; utraque autem sine monasticis et esse et prodesse possunt, sed non e converso": *Ib.*

698. "lex naturalis," "circumcisio," "baptismus," "cuculla": E. Benz, "La messianità di S. Benedetto, contributo alla filosofia di G. da Fiore," *Riserche relig.*, 7 (1931), 336-53. Cf. M. D. Cappuyns, BTAM, 1, no. 1033.

699. "Cum testamentum Dei a lege naturali incipiens et per legem Moysi ascendens usque ad legem Christi, quae est consummata, pervenisset, quartum tamen gradum, non quartam legem adjiciens, ipsam legem consummationis quae dicitur lex fidei, lex gratiae, lex spiritus vitae in Christo Jesu, per regulam beati Benedicti confirmari voluit, ut supra ipsam altiorem religionis quaerere gradum nemo indigeret, cum ipsius firmamento omnis consummationis finem reperire posset": Leclercq, *St. Ans.*, 31, 131.

700. the "ordo conjugatorum"; the "ordo praedicatorum" or "clericorum"; the "ordo monachorum": LI, c. 5, *De tribus stat. mundi* (f. 5, 2-3). *Psalt.*, l. 2 (f. 247-55).

701. "ad quinque sanctae Ecclesiae status, quae post Christi adventum ad fidem vocata est"; "Primus status fuit in persecutione martyrum; secundus, in conversione principum; tertius, in multiplicatione christianorum; quartus, in communione caenobitarum; quintus, in singularitate anachoretarum. Et primus quasi ager fuit, secundus ut hortus, tertius velut atrium, quartus sicut domus,

quintus tanquam thalamus": *De trip. tab.*, P. 2, c. 19 (PL, CXCVIII, 738 D, 742 D); c. 18, on the five corresponding steps of the Old Testament from the time of Adam (ager) up to Jesus Christ (thalamus) (738 CD).

702. "nihil aliud est quam confirmatio evangelii": *loc. cit.*, 134. See above, vol. 2, ch. 9.3.

703. *Paradiso*, cantos 10 and 11. Cf. A. Renaudet, *Dante humaniste* (1952), 272.

704. "Nolo existimet aliquis exigendum a me, qui sum homo agricola a juventute mea, quod ab ipsis quoque prophetis exigi ante sua tempora non licebat": IA, P. 4, d. 7 (f. 175, 2).

705. "rusticus et impolitus": IA, prol. (below, note 710).

706. "Vae mihi esse pertimesco, si taceo": *Conc.*, praef.

707. *Conc.*, l. 5, c. 119: "Therefore let them know, and I pray that they should know that I was willing to attempt these things not from proud presumption, nor again from sureness of some sort of piety, or to have discovered by my own talent that I should utter them to the world; but rather, since the time just before the end is at hand, he who is working throughout the various manifold time-periods of the ages and fulfills the mysteries of his secrets how and when he wills has in this work willed to reveal to his faithful ones speeches long signified with necessity rather than curiosity" — "Sciant ergo, et hoc oro ut sciant, non ex praesumptione superba, sed nec alicujus pietatis securitate haec me attentare voluisse, aut meo ingenio ut ista mundo loquerer invenisse; sed quia tempus praefinitum adest, Is qui per diversa saeculorum tempora multiplicia operatur et complet quomodo vult et quando vult, mysteria secretorum suorum voluit in hoc opere necessarie magis quam curiose sermones diu significatos suis fidelibus aperire" (f. 135, 2).

708. See above, note 302. Cf. *Glossa, In Ap.* XXII, 9: "Those who have the grace of interpretation are not to be reckoned alien to the office of prophecy" — "Non sunt a munere prophetiae alieni putandi qui habent gratiam interpretandi" (PL, CXIV, 750 D).

709. "He was neither a mystic nor a psychologist like the Cistercians," as Bloomfield (282) stated very well, but he goes on, perhaps a bit less felicitously, to say: "His thought was centered on the Bible, but his approach was 'scientific' and sober."

710. IA, prol.: "Hence I shall speak as best I can. If not, I shall at least give hints by nodding: That the joys of the world have failed, that oppressions are threatening, that the kingdom of the heavens is present at the gates — albeit with speech rude and crude — I still think I can prove [these facts] with sure and necessary evidence; provided that he should be present who laughs to scorn those who presume upon themselves and who renders the tongues of infants, when it pleases him, able to speak" — "Loquar ergo prout potero. Sin minus nutibus indicabo. Defecisse mundi gaudia, imminere pressuras, caelorum regnum adesse in januis, et si sermone rustico et impolito, certis tamen et necessariis probare me posse arbitror documentis; si tamen affuerit qui praesumentes de se ipsis irridet et linguas infantium, cum sibi placet, facit disertas" (f. 2, 2).

711. *Conc.*, praef.: "I do not think it detracts from the enjoyment of the work to rouse the sluggish hearts of the sleepy with sound or noise" — "Non a fructu operis otiosum existimo . . . torpentia somnolentorum corda, sono vel insonito, excitare."

712. VB, c. 18: "For it is the time for the light to be uncovered" — "Tempus est enim ut detegatur lux" (42). *Conc.*, praef.: "Let him who thinks it worthwhile to read this work recognize how close the kingdom of life is at the gates" — "ut quam prope sit in januis regnum vitae, is qui hoc opus legere dignum ducit, agnoscat"; l. 5, c. 118: "And if some are unwilling to hear, still I ought not be silent, lest I should be saying that I have accepted what ought to be said.... No, the deafer they are, the louder I am compelled to shout, so that they rather than I should blush at the end" — "Et si aliqui audire nolunt, non ideo tamen tacere debeo, ne loquar quod loquendum accepi. Quin potius quo surdiores sunt aliqui, eo altius clamare compellor, ut ipsi potius quam ego erubescant in fine" (f. 135, 1). IA, P. 6, d. 1: "When God wills to change the status of the Church through successive time-periods, so that they may be consummated one after another in accordance with what has been written, years before there proceed so many lightening-flashes of miracles, voices of encouragers, thunderings of spiritual speeches, either so that some of the sleepy or slothful may be roused from the sleep of death, or so that both they and others may understand that the Lord is about to do something new upon the earth" — "Quando vult Deus per successiones temporum mutare statum Ecclesiae, ut alia post alia secundum quod scriptum est consumentur, praecedunt ante annos aliquot fulgura miraculorum, voces exhortantium, tonitrua spiritualium eloquiorum, sive ut somnolenti quique ac desides excitentur a somno mortis, sive ut tam ipsi quam alii intelligant quod novum aliquid facturus sit Dominus super terram" (f. 191-2).

713. Cf. D. M. C. [Cappuyns]. BTAM, 1, no. 573.

714. He died, says his first biographer Luca, "on the Sunday on which [the introit] *'Those thirsting'* is sung" — "in sabbato quo *Sitientes* cantatur." Compare Gerhoh, *ep.* 18 (PL, CXCIII, 571 C).

715. "Peu conceptualisable en expression théologique et assez scabreux en doctrine ecclésiologique"; "dynamisme interne": Expressions of Father Chenu, "The latest reincarnation of oriental theology" — "Le dernier avatar de la théol. orientale," *Mél. A. Pelzer* (1947), 163-4. One finds in Joachim, "the most serious errors annoyingly intermingled with the most brilliant insights" — "dans le même fâcheux mélange, les plus graves erreurs et les plus perspicaces inspirations."

716. "de verbi eloquentia ad intelligentiam spiritualem": *Conc.* (fol. 31, 3).

717. *Ev.* (275): "Hence he who goes through the forests of the Scriptures in this way ... recognizes that God, who is fulfilling every day in the spirit what has been written down in the letter, is truthful" — "Qui igitur sic transit per nemora Scripturarum ... agnoscit Deum esse veracem, qui hoc quotidie complet in spiritu quod in littera scriptum est."

718. Ev. (285-8): "since, always finding ... something new to meditate upon, he leaps from the historical understanding to the moral, from the moral to the tropological, from the tropological to the contemplative, from the contemplative to the anagogical; from the anagogical he is led to the contemplation of him who is so great he cannot be comprehended by man" — "quia semper inveniens ... quid de novo meditetur, de historica intelligentia salit ad moralem, de morali ad tropologicam, de tropologica ad contemplativam, de contemplativa ad anagogicam; de anagogica ad illius perducitur contemplationem, qui quantus sit ab homine comprehendi non potest."

719. IA, on Apoc. 21; cited and commented on by Buonaiuti, ed. of AF, p. lxii.

720. IA, P. 5, d. 7 (f. 175-8). Cf. f. 181, 3: "How great is the power in the mouth of spiritual men for wreaking vengeance" — "Quanta autem virtus sit in ore spiritualium virorum ad faciendam ultionem."

721. "ferocior et ardentior"; "mitior et suavior": on the Holy Spirit in the Church see Seb. Tromp, SJ, *Corpus Christi quod est Ecclesia*, 3. *De Spiritu Christi anima* (Rome, 1960).

722. "ut enim in collectione lignorum parvus ignis efficitur magnus, ita in unitate animarum et cordium, amor in universum crescit": IA (f. 78, 4).

Index of Names

Abbo of Fleury, 403
Abelard, Peter. *See* Peter Abelard
Absalon, 31, 133, 276-77, 287, 303, 378
Achard of Saint Victor, 303
Adalbéron of Laon, 321
Adam of Perseigne, 358, 360
Adam of Petit Pont, 279
Adam of Saint Victor, 67-68, 276
Adam Scotus (Adam Scot), 125, 147, 216, 242, 273, 303-8, 310-11, 321, 323, 416
Adelard of Bath, 254
Adimantius, 100
Adrian IV, Pope, 278
Adson of Montier-en-Der, 403, 407
Aegerter, Emmanuel, 367
Aelred of Rievaulx, 15, 171, 205, 262, 303, 304, 307, 322
Agobard of Lyon, 18, 24-32, 63, 113, 181, 195, 257, 262
Aimon of Auxerre, 16, 162, 192, 260, 289, 377, 403
Alan of Lille, 10, 65-70, 94, 171, 188, 205, 274-75, 322
Alberic of Reims, 285-86
Alberic of Three Fountains, 205
Albert of Saint Symphorien, 113
Albuin, 407
Alcher of Clairvaux, 205
Alcuin, 9, 21, 27, 31, 50, 82, 83, 114, 153, 189, 191, 206, 207-10, 239-40, 325, 377
Aldhelm, 189, 193, 208
Aldric of Sens, 31
Alexander III, Pope, 284, 287
Alexander IV, Pope, 343
Alexander of Villedieu, 10
Alexander the Great, 402-3
Allo, Bernard, 299
Alvarus of Cordoba. *See* Paul Alvarus of Cordoba
Amalarius, 23-25, 30, 113, 130-32, 190
Amatucci, A. G., 54
Ambrose, 11, 20, 33, 41, 74, 118, 124-25, 142, 148, 161, 366, 395
Ambrose Autpert, 9, 17, 59, 106, 120-21, 174, 191, 264, 377, 396, 403
Ambrosiaster, 20
Ampère, J.-J., 156
Anastasius the Librarian, 18, 187
Andradus Modicus, 136
Andrew, archbishop of Bari, 113
Andrew of Saint Victor, 219, 270-73, 282, 288, 308-11
Angelbert, 207
Angelome of Luxeuil, 18, 33, 48, 121, 153, 192, 228, 231-32, 234, 237, 240
Anselm, 3, 104, 120-21, 163, 170, 172, 244, 278, 318, 349, 380
Anselm of Havelberg, 87-89, 91, 187, 252, 255, 306, 349, 389-90, 408, 413

INDEX OF NAMES

Anselm of Laon, 94, 237, 321, 391
Antin, Paul, 36, 76
Apelles, 293
Apringius, 117
Aquila, 16
Aquinas, Thomas. *See* Thomas Aquinas
Aristotle, 71, 275, 276, 280-81, 321, 367
Arnaud of Bonneval, 223, 322
Arnobius, 381
Arno of Reichersberg, 134, 171, 264
Arnoul of Lisieux, 215
Arnoul of Orleans, 398
Artz, B., 41, 53-54
Athanasius, 186
Audouin, the bishop of Limoges, 114
Augustine, 3, 16-21, 23, 25-26, 31-33, 35, 45-46, 59, 61, 77-79, 85, 90-94, 100-105, 108-9, 117-18, 128, 142, 145, 147-48, 155, 158, 161, 163-64, 169-71, 177-78, 182, 184, 198-99, 208, 215, 217, 230, 237, 239, 250, 251, 255-61, 265-67, 273-74, 292, 321, 353, 374, 376-77, 385-87, 405
Ausonius, 55
Avitus, 55, 121

Bacon, Roger, 255, 270
Barbeyrac, Jean, 37, 39, 40, 48, 53-54
Baron, Roger, 4
Baronius, 200
Barth, Karl, 108-9
Bartholomaus of Vicenza, 322
Bartholomew the Englishman, 255
Battles, Ford Lewis, 244
Beatus, 120, 218, 239-40
Beatus of Liebana, 377, 385, 391-92
Bede, Venerable, 9, 14-16, 38, 50, 56, 70, 82, 93-95, 117-18, 120, 133, 148, 158, 162, 178-79, 181, 184, 186, 191-94, 196, 216, 224-25, 228, 232, 235, 239, 246, 249, 253, 264-65, 292, 303-5, 311, 389-91
Benedict, 24, 331, 334-35, 336
Benjamin of Toledo, 180
Benz, E., 415
Berengar of Tours, 2, 163

Berengaud, 99, 377, 388-89
Berger, Samuel, 194-95, 211, 246
Bernard, 15, 24, 31-32, 92, 141, 145, 172, 174, 192, 204, 214-15, 220, 225, 227-29, 252, 267, 274, 279-80, 300, 318, 322, 353, 378, 380, 387-88, 391-92, 394, 418
Bernard of Chartres, 255
Bernard of Cluny, 134, 395
Bernard of Morval, 38
Bernardus Silvestris, 67, 254
Berno of Reichenau, 1-71, 85, 96, 98-99, 102-3, 130, 147, 159, 177, 192, 197, 207, 210, 251
Blaise, 92
Blanchard, P., 6, 148
Bloomfield, M. W., 356, 362, 364-66
Blumenkranz, Bernard, 127, 131, 132
Bodo-Eleazar, 114
Bodo of Prüfning, 266, 321, 369-70
Boeren, C. E., 246
Boethius, 70, 115, 276
Bonaventure, 317, 345, 416
Boniface, St., 10
Boniface I, Pope, 119
Boniface IV, Pope, 120
Bonneval, Arnaud de, 95
Bossuet, Jacques-Bénigne, 112, 164
Bouyer, Louis, 1
Braulio of Saragossa, 193
Brett, H., 371
Brown, R. E., 4
Brücker, Jakob, 39-40, 48, 53-54
Brunet, 3
Bruno of Cologne, 187
Bruno of Segni, 3, 15, 85, 86, 89, 93, 97, 147, 155-63, 172, 177, 192, 367, 377-78, 384, 391, 393, 403-4, 408, 411
Bruno of Würzburg, 133
Bruno the Carthusian, 133
Bruyne, Edgar de, 23
Budé, Guillaume, 201
Buonaiuti, Ernesto, 341-42
Burchard of Worms, 121
Burgundio of Pisa, 18, 187, 204, 280
Burrows, Millar, 381
Buzelin, Jean, 70

Index of Names

Caesarius, Saint, 53
Caesarius of Arles, 50
Candidus of Fulda, 133
Capelle, Bernard, 47
Cassian, 189
Cassiodorus, 8-9, 14-16, 20-21, 32, 45, 50, 79, 85, 93, 118, 177, 188-89, 211, 266, 305, 310-11
Cauchie, Canon A., 87, 89, 164
Celestine III, Pope, 355
Cerfaux, Lucien, 267
Chaminius, 10
Chapman, Paul, 47
Charlemagne, 27, 60, 83, 185, 209-10
Charles the Bald, 113, 136, 185, 189-90
Charles the Young, 383-84
Châtillon, Jean, 1, 244
Chenu, M.-D., 1, 4-5, 64-65, 251-54, 271, 277, 283, 305, 312-13, 321
Chrétien de Troyes, 185
Christian of Stavelot, 3, 147, 155-63, 177, 207, 208, 210
Chromatius of Aquilaea, 117, 125
Chrysostom, John, 18, 33, 51, 204
Cicero, 9, 11, 38, 45, 59, 68, 276, 278, 279
Claudel, Paul, 39, 299
Claude of Turin, 22, 157, 188, 232, 239-40, 292, 396-97
Claudius, abbot of Classe, 47
Clement III, Pope, 355
Clement of Alexandria, 20
Columba, Saint, 51
Columban, Saint, 120
Comestor, Peter, 32, 92-93
Comparetti, D., 42
Congar, Yves, 381
Conrad II, 114
Couturier, Pierre (Petrus Sutor), 202
Crispin, Gilbert, 104-5, 115-16, 309
Crocco, Antonio, 347, 357
Cyprian, Saint, 115, 124, 395
Cyrus, 337, 354, 383

Daillé, Jean, 35
D'Alverny, Mlle. M.-Th., 322
Damasus, Pope Saint, 117

Dante Alighieri, 287, 416-17
Darius, 337, 383
Delacroix, Henri, 346
De la Taille, Maurice, 47
Delhaye, Philippe, 273-74
Denis, Charles, 363
Denys of Saint-Marthe, 47
Descartes, René, 231
Desiderius, bishop of Vienne in Gaul, 48, 52, 54, 55
Diomedes, 10
Dionysius, 253, 255, 280, 316, 319, 321-23
Donatus, 8-11, 13, 57-64, 70, 276
Donatus of Ireland, Saint, 187

Eberhard of Bamberg, 187
Ebert, A., 54
Ecbert, abbot of Huisbourg, 88
Edmer of Canterbury, 48
Ekkehard IV of Sankt Gall, 187
Ekkehard of Aura, 135
Ennodius, 50
Erasmus, 201, 202
Etienne of Tournai, 286
Eucher, Saint, 396
Euclid, 276
Eugene III, 200, 204
Eusebius, 16, 177, 180, 305, 383
Eusebius of Cremona, 134
Eusebius of Emessa, 17, 79, 205
Eutyches, 9
Evagrius the Gaul, 114

Farrar, Frederick W., 52
Faustus of Milevis, 100-105, 110, 145
Felix of Urgel, 32, 83, 100, 125
Fèvre, V., 40
Fleury, 43
Florus of Lyon, 25-27, 82, 195, 198, 199
Foliot, Gilbert, 121, 310
Fontaine, Jacques, 39, 44
Fournier, Paul, 345
Francis of Meyronnes, 323
Franck, Adolphe, 363
Freculph of Lisieux, 240
Fredegesius, 24-25, 257

Fridegod of Canterbury, 187
Fulbert of Chartres, 135

Gaiseric, king of the Vandals in Betica, 125
Garnier de Rochefort, 204-5, 263, 266-67, 303, 322
Garnier of Saint Victor, 251, 275, 277
Gaudemaris, André de, 41
Gautier de Châtillon, 399-400
Gautier of Saint Victor, 274-75, 276
Gebhart, Émile, 414
Gébouin de Troyes, 388
Geoffrey of Auxerre, 215, 358-59, 380-81
Geoffrey of Clairvaux, 186
Geoffrey the Fat, 189
Gerbert, Martin, 30
Gerhoh of Reichersberg, 32, 89-91, 117, 124-25, 166, 169-71, 179, 187-88, 231, 238, 260, 262-63, 306, 310, 383-84, 391, 403-4, 408
Germain, Saint, 335, 336
Gervaise, Abbot, 345
Geyer, B., 246
Ghellinck, Joseph de, 3, 44, 159, 164, 244-45, 277
Gilbert of Hoyland, 306, 322
Gilbert de la Porrée, 120, 172, 198, 280, 318
Gilbert of Stanford, 32
Gillet, Robert, 39, 41
Gilson, Étienne, 345
Glaber, Raoul, 49, 114, 136
Godescalc of Orbais, 10, 83
Godfrey of Admont, 216-17, 310, 378, 392
Godfrey of Saint Victor, 10, 15, 68-69, 247, 273-74, 279, 306, 309, 359
Godscalc, 192
Godschalk, 59, 62
Gontran, king, 136
Goscelin of Saint Bertin, 192
Gourmont, Remy de, 276
Gratian, 52, 121, 198-99, 276, 282
Gregory IX, Pope, 355
Gregory Nazianzen, Saint, 230, 413
Gregory of Nyssa, Saint, 204

Gregory of Tours, 114, 136
Gregory the Great, Saint, 3, 15, 17, 22-23, 29, 32-34, 36-63, 70, 79-80, 83-86, 90-91, 108, 117-21, 128, 133, 138, 147-48, 157-58, 160, 163, 166, 171-72, 174, 178, 183, 185, 191-92, 197, 208, 217-18, 230, 232-36, 237, 246-53, 262, 264-67, 274-75, 278, 281, 283, 288-90, 293-301, 307-8, 311, 321, 375, 385, 395-96, 404-5, 410, 414-15
Gregory VII, Pope, 336
Gribomont, J., 1
Grudmann, H., 381
Gualbert, Saint John, 120, 124
Guénon, René, 231
Guibert of Nogent, 38, 51, 86, 89, 119, 120, 122, 135-36, 170-71, 196, 204-5, 217, 279
Guitmond of Aversa, 9
Guizot, 48
Guyart des Mouslins, 282

Haag, Eugène, 40
Haller, Max, 132, 200
Harding, Saint Stephen, 197-201, 203-4
Hauréau, B., 164, 203, 221-22
Hélin, Maurice, 40
Helinand of Froidmont, 32, 120, 190, 204-5, 229, 261, 322, 413
Heloïse, 187, 215, 220
Hemmo, 377
Henricus Aristippus, 280
Henry II, emperor, 136
Henry III, emperor, 6-7
Henry II Plantagenet, 399
Henry of Marcy, 255, 414
Herbert of Bosham, 16, 192, 214-15, 226, 273
Heribert, Saint, 113
Heribrand of Saint Laurent at Liège, 163
Heric of Auxerre, 185, 187
Hermann the Cripple, 30
Hermann the Jew, 168
Hermenegild, Saint, 120
Hervaeus of Bourg Dieu, 26-27, 93,

Index of Names

179, 192, 197, 200, 214, 321, 368, 373
Heterius, 120, 218
Highet, Gilbert, 40-41, 48
Hilary, Saint, 11, 16, 35-36, 70, 74, 76, 97, 119, 155, 182, 217, 395
Hildegard, Saint, 180, 253, 263, 301-2, 393, 395, 418
Hildenfinger, Paul, 132
Hilduin, Abbot of Saint Denis of Paris, 195
Hincmar of Reims, 10, 17, 33, 83, 120, 190
Hippolytus, Saint, 381-82, 400
Hirsch-Reich, B., 347
Homer, 156, 181
Honorius, 119, 174, 205, 231, 253, 321, 379, 383, 388-89, 391, 393, 408
Honorius III, Pope, 355
Hrodswitha, the religious dramaturgist of Gandersheim, 119
Hugh of Balma, 316
Hugh of Bologna, 38
Hugh of Fleury, 120, 215, 266
Hugh of Fouilloy, 383
Hugh of Pontigny, 31
Hugh of Rouen, 63-64, 261
Hugh of Saint Victor, 2-5, 15, 18, 21, 31-32, 92, 140, 147, 166, 169-70, 185, 205, 211-67, 269-77, 279, 281-88, 302-8, 312-26, 346-47, 370-72, 398, 401
Humbert, Auguste, 221
Humbert, Cardinal, 117
Humbert of Silva Candida, Cardinal, 187
Hutton, W. H., 40

Idatius, 125
Ildefonse of Toledo, Saint, 377
Imbart de la Tour, Pierre, 200
Innocent III, Pope, 22, 95, 120-21, 355
Irenaeus, Saint, 75, 99-100, 258-59, 367
Irimbert of Admont, 92, 368
Isaac of Stella, 172, 205, 322
Isidore of Seville, 10, 14-15, 17, 19, 21-22, 38, 56, 62, 81, 106, 115, 128, 131, 159, 182, 186, 189, 193, 208, 237, 251, 274, 283, 393, 400, 403

Jacques of Vitry, 318
Jean of Avranches, 135
Jean of Salisbury, 119, 251
Jean Sarrazin, 187, 280, 321, 322
Jeremiah, 49, 182
Jerome, Saint, 3, 4, 8, 11, 15-23, 24, 27-29, 32, 34-36, 45, 48, 56, 58, 74-78, 84, 85, 89, 93, 95, 97, 100, 107, 119-20, 125, 147-50, 155, 156, 158-60, 163-64, 166, 169-70, 177-93, 195-96, 198-99, 201, 207-10, 212, 216, 235-36, 250, 275, 281, 286, 296-98, 301, 308, 325, 395, 400, 405, 407, 410, 412
Jerome Alexander, 202
Joachim of Flora, 5, 119, 138, 180, 327-419
John Damascene, Saint, 187, 204, 274
John of Acre, Saint, 352
John of Cornwall, 18
John of Fécamp, 231
John of Garland, 38
John of Gorze, 187
John of Kelso, 304-5
John of Ravenna, 47
John of Salisbury, 15, 58, 71, 94, 119, 125, 187, 192, 196, 215, 221, 277-82
John Scotus, 69, 83, 120-21, 159, 185-88, 205, 284, 301, 321, 323, 370, 414
John the Baptist, Saint, 70, 136, 335, 336, 338-39, 356, 387
John the Deacon, 37, 118, 185, 237
John the Evangelist, Saint, 335, 339, 400, 405-7, 409
John the Faster, 185
John VIII, 18
Jonas of Orléans, 190, 192
Jordan, Émile, 346
Joseph, Saint, 331
Josephus, 177, 293, 304, 305, 310-11, 402
Julian of Toledo, Saint, 9, 35, 189, 256
Julian the Apostate, 46, 48, 135
Junilius, 191

Justin, Saint, 53, 367
Justinian of Valencia, 377
Juvenal, 31

Lactantius, 124, 382
Lagrange, M.-J., 196
Laistner, L. W., 39, 47, 52
Landgraf, Msgr. A. M., 198-99
Langois, Ch.-V., 326
Langton, Stephen, 95, 273, 281-82, 287-88, 303
Laurence in Damaso, Saint, 200
Laurent de Liège, Saint, 417
Leander of Seville, 36-37
Leclercq, Jean, 1, 244, 301, 303
Lefèvre d'Étaples, Jacques, 201, 202
Lefranc, Abel, 196
Leibniz, Gottfried, 281
Leo, Saint, 25-26, 117, 119
Leon the Jew, 116
Lethbert of Saint-Ruf, 260
Liuddo of Laon, 187
Liutprand of Cremona, 120, 185
Long-Beard, William, 127
Lot, Ferdinand, 51
Lothaire of Segni, 21
Louis the Pious, 113
Lucius III, Pope, 355
Luiz of Leon, 202-3
Luke of Leon, 215
Lupus of Ferrières, 9, 38, 192
Luther, Martin, 145, 325

MacCulloch, J. A., 414
Malachy, Saint, 382
Mandonnet, P., 2-3, 234
Manegold of Lautenbach, 15-16, 86, 93, 118-19
Mani, 75, 146
Marbodius, 134-35
Marcellinus, 119
Marcion, 75
Marius Victorinus, 46, 68
Marrou, H.-I., 51
Martianus Capella, 49, 57
Martin of Braga, Saint, 53
Martin of Ireland, 186-87
Martin of Leon, Saint, 32, 115, 117, 124, 192, 215, 262, 287, 303, 379, 393-94, 401, 403, 408, 411
Maurice, emperor, 185
Metel, Hugh, 223, 228
Michaud-Quentin, Pierre, 273-74
Michelet, Jules, 40, 277, 343
Migne, J.-P., 30, 115
Mignon, 212
Mohrmann, Christine, 39, 58
More, Thomas, 187-88, 278
Moreau, E. de, 164
Moses Sephardi (Peter Alphonse), 335

Naaman the Syrian, 87
Nabridius, the old bishop of Narbonne, 113
Nebuchadnezzar, 130, 167, 337, 410
Neckham, Alexander, 31-32, 70-71, 119, 180
Neschites, the Archbishop of Nicomedia, 88
Nestorius, 126
Nicetas, 187
Nicholas, Pope, 383-84
Nicholas of Clairvaux, 21, 287
Nicholas of Maniacoria, 198, 199-201, 203-4, 206
Nigellus of Longchamp, 282
Nilus the Younger, Saint, 112-13, 362
Norberg, Dap, 39
Norbert, Saint, 394-95
Notker the German, 190
Notker the Stammerer, 177, 187, 188
Novimagio, de, 201

Obadiah, 113-14
Odilon of Cluny, 188
Odo of Cambrai, 197, 200
Odo of Canterbury, 415-16
Odo of Cluny, 9, 49, 116, 144, 192, 264, 398
Olier, Mr., 141
Ordericus Vitalis, 198
Origen, 15-17, 20-23, 36, 43-44, 49, 65, 69, 73-80, 84-86, 92, 95, 99, 119, 133, 155, 157-58, 165-66, 172, 174, 178, 180-81, 191, 195, 197, 199, 208, 212,

Index of Names

218, 220, 223, 226, 236, 238-40, 249-50, 253, 258-59, 275, 289, 292-93, 296-97, 300, 309, 318, 321, 362-69, 381-82
Othloh of Saint Emmeran, 23, 125, 190, 215, 217
Ottaviano, M. C., 367
Otto of Freising, 118, 182, 185, 205, 252, 306, 322, 397
Ozanam, Frédéric, 44
Ozias (Uzziah), King, 334-36, 341, 343

Pailloux, Xavier, SJ, 293-95
Papebroch, D., 346, 358
Paré, G., 3
Pascal, Blaise, 325
Paschasius Radbertus, 3, 15, 18, 84, 86, 147-57, 166, 177, 181, 192, 195, 208, 223-24, 232, 236-38, 385, 396-97, 400, 411
Paterius, Saint, 15, 232
Paul, Saint, 16, 31, 35, 44-45, 60, 86, 108, 119, 123, 168, 188, 197, 233, 257, 267, 270, 272, 276, 322-23, 333-34, 351, 400, 407, 411
Paul Alvarus of Cordoba, 17-18, 55-56, 114-15, 122, 126, 171, 181, 191, 207, 290, 383, 409-11
Paulinus of Aquilaea, Saint, 83, 100, 120, 125, 192, 232
Paulinus of Nola, Saint, 55, 76, 116
Paul the Deacon, 9, 45, 177, 187
Péguy, Charles, 157-58, 259-60
Pelagius, 120, 184-85, 206
Peltier, M. Henri, 153
Peter, Saint, 129, 335, 339
Peter Abelard, 2-3, 31, 58, 63, 120, 172, 181, 187, 198, 215, 217, 219-22, 223, 231, 254-55, 257, 273, 279, 310-11, 318, 412
Peter Alphonse (Moses Sephardi), 335
Peter Cellensis, 33, 58, 59, 94, 192, 215, 218, 278, 302-3, 305, 308, 310-11
Peter Damian, Saint, 21, 33, 51-52, 57-58, 61, 63, 96, 114, 116, 170-71, 216, 229, 264, 404-5
Peter Helias, 10
Peter Lombard, 94, 192, 198, 222-23, 232, 255-56, 282, 353, 355
Peter of Blois, 127, 192, 279, 310-11
Peter of Cornwall, 115
Peter of Pisa, 114
Peter of Poitiers, 303
Peter the Cantor, 33, 93, 232, 273, 279, 281-82, 285-86, 301, 307
Peter the Deacon, 45
Peter the Eater, 222, 273, 281-88, 301, 310-11
Peter the grammarian, 177
Peter the Venerable, 89, 215, 220
Petit, François, 307
Petrarch, 204, 281
Philip Augustus, 120
Philip of Harvengt, 31, 33, 216-17, 310-11
Philip the Chancellor, 95
Philo, 20, 99
Pitra, J. B., 251
Plato, 9, 31, 59, 276, 280
Plutarch, 99, 119, 278
Poole, Reginald L., 40, 48
Primasius, 377
Priscian, 9-11, 53, 59, 156
Priscus, 114
Prudentius of Troyes, 83, 120, 121, 135, 186
Psellos, 276
Pseudo-Alcuin, 377, 386, 391-92
Pseudo-Augustine, 114, 115, 126
Pseudo-Bede, 156
Pseudo-Cyprian, 125
Pseudo-Dionysius, 205, 321, 327, 413-14
Pseudo-Isidore, 237, 266

Quintilian, 48, 64
Quodvultdeus, 292

Rabanus Maurus, 3, 9, 17-18, 20-22, 33, 48, 50, 84, 93-94, 98, 118, 120, 122, 152-53, 155, 156, 170-72, 175, 180, 188-89, 195-96, 225, 227-28,

INDEX OF NAMES

231-35, 240, 245, 251-54, 266, 289, 292, 298, 301, 312, 367-68
Raby, F. J. E., 40
Rand, Edward Kenner, 39, 47
Raoul Ardent (Radulfus Ardens), 64, 65, 92, 322
Raoul de Saint Trond, 104
Raoul of Coggeshall, 360
Rathier of Verona, 185
Ratramnus, 349
Raynaud, count of Sens, 114, 135
Reeves, Miss E., 346-50
Regimbald of Eichstädt, 187
Reginald of Canterbury, 188-89
Remigius of Auxerre, 9, 85, 93, 133, 188, 240, 292, 377
Renan, E., 44, 345-46, 353, 358
Renucci, Paul, 52
Reuchlin, John, 201
Richard of Saint Victor, 48, 58, 96, 125, 147, 174, 205, 215, 231, 264, 269-71, 288-303, 307-11, 319-23, 368, 390-93, 408
Rimbaud, A., 231
Robert of Auxerre, 284, 358
Robert of Basevorn, 38
Robert of Crickade, 301, 308
Robert of Melun, 187
Roger, M., 40, 45, 51
Roger of Hoveden, 409
Roques, René, 253
Roscelin, 163, 220
Rosenmüller, J.-G., 40, 48, 156-57
Rousseau, Jean-Jacques, 41
Rousselot, Xavier, 362-64
Rufinus, 15-16, 49, 80, 119, 125, 134, 239, 255
Rupert of Deutz, 3, 16, 21-22, 24, 35, 86-89, 104, 113-15, 147, 163-77, 181, 183, 216, 223-27, 232, 237, 253, 255, 262, 264, 266, 272, 282-83, 287, 300-301, 303, 309, 318, 324-25, 370-72, 378-79, 384, 389, 392-93, 403, 408-9, 412, 417
Russo, Francesco, 347
Ruysbroeck, John, 323

Saladin, 345, 382, 409
Salimbene, 346, 355-56
Salomon of Constance, 9
Salonius of Geneva, 231
Schmidt, Charles, 157
Schmitz, Philibert, 54, 159
Scholastica, Saint, 335, 336
Sedulius Scotus, 9, 56-57, 117, 119, 187-88, 194-95, 200, 206
Seifrid of Tegernsee, 48, 217
Séjourné, Paul, 164
Seneca, 31, 273
Serlon of Savigny, 192, 303
Sicardus of Cremona, 127, 310-11
Sidonius Apollinaris, 55
Sigebert of Gembloux, 30, 187, 196
Siger of Brabant, 416-17
Simon, Richard, 157, 158, 194
Simon of Tournai, 322
Simon the Jew, 115
Smalley, Beryl, 4, 151-52, 158, 235, 236-39, 241, 247-48, 269, 271, 288, 308, 312, 367
Smaragdus of Saint Mihiel, 9, 57, 60, 62, 153, 206-7, 208
Spicq, C., 3, 5-6, 8, 149, 164, 208, 212
Steinmann, Jean, 325
Stephen, Saint, 129
Stephen Harding. *See* Harding, Saint Stephen
Stephen Langton. *See* Langton, Stephen
Sulpicius Severus, 119, 189
Sylvester, Pope, 336
Symmachus, 16, 22
Synesius, 52

Taio of Saragossa, 232
Taylor, H. O., 253
Teilhard de Chardin, Pierre, 141-42
Terence, 11
Tertullian, 58, 65, 99, 115, 118, 205
Theodore of Mopsuestia, 194
Theodore of Tarsus, 194
Theodoric, 45
Theodosius the Younger, 53
Theodotion, 16, 22
Theodulf of Orléans, 9, 83, 194, 198, 210

Index of Names

Theophilus of Antioch, 16
Théry, Gustave, 322
Thierry of Chartres, 10, 279, 280
Thierry of Echternach, 187
Thomas à Kempis, 278
Thomas Aquinas, Saint, 4, 131, 231, 260, 267, 315, 317, 345-46, 416-17
Thomas Becket, 277-78, 399
Thomas of Perseigne, 32
Thomas of Verceil (Thomas Gallus), 276, 319, 322-23
Thomas the Cistercian, 205-6
Thucydides, 99
Thurot, Charles, 47-48
Tondelli, Msgr. Leone, 342, 346-48, 356
Totila, king of the Goths, 119-20
Tremblay, P., 3
Trochon, Charles, 158
Turner, C. H., 191
Tyconius, 32, 120, 237, 255, 376-77, 385-86, 411

Uldaric (Ulrich), bishop of Augsburg, 23
Urban III, Pope, 355, 382

Valla, Lorenzo, 200
Van den Eynde, Damien, 220
Van Dorp, Martin, 202
Vecelin of the diocese of Metz, 113
Verbraken, P., 47
Victorinus of Pettau, 74

Victor of Paris, Saint, 322
Vilgard of Ravenna, 49
Villalpand, 293
Vincent, Hughes, 3
Vincent of Lerins, 118
Virgil, 9, 11, 45, 49, 59, 407
Vitalis, Saint, 369
Vivian, count, 136

Walafrid of Strabo, 187
Waso, the future bishop of Liège, 114
Wasselynck, René, 156, 251
Werner of Saint Blaise, 18, 180, 266, 413
White, A.-D., 200
Wigbode, 179, 188
William Duke of Aquitaine, 135
William of Champeaux, 275
William of Conches, 254, 279
William of Malmesbury, 114
William of Ramsey, 415
William of Saint Thierry, 17, 31, 95, 171, 172, 204, 215, 227-28, 231, 318, 322
William Rufus, king, 114
Williams, A. Lukyn, 131
Wilmart, A., 32, 33, 200, 307
Wolfgang, bishop of Ratisbon, 120
Wolfhelm, Saint, 369

Yvo of Chartres, 121, 198

Zachary, Pope, 336

www.ingramcontent.com/pod-product-compliance
Lightning Source LLC
Chambersburg PA
CBHW031537300426
44111CB00006BA/83